A CONCISE COURSE IN A-LEVEL STATISTICS

With Worked Examples

Third Edition

J CRAWSHAW BSc

Head of Mathematics Department
Clifton High School, Bristol

J CHAMBERS MA

Head of Mathematics Department
Sutton High School GPDST, Surrey

STANLEY THORNES (PUBLISHERS) LTD

First published in 1984
Second Edition 1990
Third Edition 1994 by

Stanley Thornes (Publishers) Ltd
Ellenborough House
Wellington Street
CHELTENHAM GL50 1YW
UK

99 98 97 96 / 10 9 8 7 6 5 4

A catalogue record of this book is available from the British Library

ISBN 0–7487–1757–9

Typeset by Tech-Set, Gateshead, Tyne & Wear.
Printed and bound in Great Britain by The Bath Press

CONTENTS

PREFACE

This text is intended primarily for use by students and teachers of A- or AS-Level Mathematics.

It contains the *Mathematics of Uncertainty* section of the Mathematics Subject Core (1994), together with a very comprehensive coverage of *statistical applications of mathematical modelling.*

Points of theory are presented concisely and illustrated by worked examples, many taken from previous A-Level papers. These are then supported by very carefully graded exercises which serve to consolidate the theory, link it with previous work and build up the confidence of the reader. There are frequent summaries of main points and miscellaneous exercises containing mainly A-level questions.

Throughout the text we have aimed to provide the reader with a mathematical structure and a logical framework within which to work. We have given special attention to topics which, in our experience, cause great difficulty, in particular probability theory and significance testing.

The text covers the main theory required by all the major examining boards and is equally suitable for modular and linear syllabuses (1996). We are very grateful to the following for permission to reproduce questions:

    University of Cambridge Local Examinations Syndicate (C)
    University of London Examinations and Assessment Council (L)
    University of Oxford Local Delegacy of Examinations (O)
    Oxford and Cambridge School Examinations Board (O & C)
      incorporating MEI and SMP
    Northern Examinations and Assessment Board (NEAB)
      (formerly Joint Matriculation Board JMB)
    The Associated Examining Board (AEB)

A-level questions are followed by the initials of the board. Questions from Additional Mathematics papers are indicated by the word Additional and (P) denotes a part-question. We would stress that the examining boards are in no way responsible for any solutions.

We extend thanks to our colleagues and students and especially to our families for all their encouragement and support.

J Crawshaw
J Chambers
1994

1

DESCRIPTIVE STATISTICS

DISCRETE DATA

These are the numbers of children in 30 randomly chosen families:

1	2	4	0	2	3	1	4	2	3	5	2	2	3	2
2	3	1	2	3	2	0	1	1	2	0	3	2	3	3

This is an example of **discrete raw data**.

Discrete data can take only exact values, for example

the number of cars passing a checkpoint in 30 minutes,

the shoe sizes of children in a class,

the number of tomatoes on each plant in a greenhouse.

The data is 'raw' because it has not been ordered in any way.

To illustrate the data more concisely we count the number of times each value occurs and form a **frequency distribution**:

Number of children in family	0	1	2	3	4	5	
Frequency	3	5	11	8	2	1	Total 30

Ungrouped discrete data in the form of a frequency distribution can be represented diagramatically by a **vertical line graph** in which the height of each line represents the frequency. The distinct lines reinforce the discrete nature of the variable.

Vertical line graph to show numbers of children in 30 families

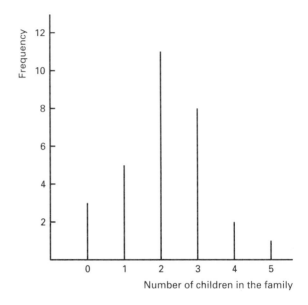

The mode

> The mode is the value that occurs most often.

From the line graph it is easy to see that the mode is 2 children per family.

CONTINUOUS DATA

These are the heights of 20 children in a school. The heights have been measured correct to the nearest cm.

133	136	120	138	133
131	127	141	127	143
130	131	125	144	128
134	135	137	133	129

This is an example of **continuous raw data**.

> Continuous data *cannot take exact values*, but can be given only within a certain range or measured to a certain degree of accuracy.

For example

144 cm (correct to the nearest cm) could have arisen from any value in the interval $143.5 \, \text{cm} \leqslant h < 144.5 \, \text{cm}$.

Other examples of continuous data are

the speeds of vehicles passing a particular point,

the masses of cooking apples from a tree,

the time taken by each of a class of children to perform a task.

To form a frequency distribution for the heights of the 20 children we usually group the information into 'classes' or 'intervals', for example

Height (cm)	(Alternative ways of writing the interval)	
$119.5 \leqslant h < 124.5$	119.5–124.5	120–124
$124.5 \leqslant h < 129.5$	124.5–129.5	125–129
$129.5 \leqslant h < 134.5$	129.5–134.5	130–134
$134.5 \leqslant h < 139.5$	134.5–139.5	135–139
$139.5 \leqslant h < 144.5$	139.5–144.5	140–144

The values $119.5, 124.5, 129.5, \ldots$, are called the **class boundaries.**

The upper class boundary (u.c.b.) of one interval is the lower class boundary (l.c.b.) of the next interval.

Interval width

> **The width of an interval $= $ u.c.b. $-$ l.c.b.**

Therefore the width of the first interval $= 124.5 - 119.5 = 5 \, \text{cm}$.

In fact, in this example, the classes have been chosen so that each has a width of 5 cm.

To group the heights, it helps to use a 'tally' column, entering the numbers in the first row 133, 136, 120, 138, 133, then the second row, and so on.

The final frequency distribution should read:

Height (cm)	Tally	Frequency
$119.5 \leqslant h < 124.5$	I	1
$124.5 \leqslant h < 129.5$	IIII	5
$129.5 \leqslant h < 134.5$	IIII II	7
$134.5 \leqslant h < 139.5$	IIII	4
$139.5 \leqslant h < 144.5$	III	3
		Total 20

However, when the data are presented only in a frequency distribution, then the original information is lost. For example, we do not know the value of the one item in the first interval, only that it lies between 119.5 cm and 124.5 cm.

STEM AND LEAF DIAGRAMS

A very useful way of grouping data into classes whilst retaining the original data is to draw a **stem and leaf diagram**.

These are the marks of 20 children in a geography test:

84	17	38	45	47	53	76	54	75	22
66	65	55	54	51	33	39	19	54	72

We note that the lowest mark is 17 and the highest mark is 84. For stem and leaf diagrams, classes must be of equal width, so it seems sensible to choose classes 10–19, 20–29, 30–39, ..., 80–89 for the data. We can take the 'stem' to represent the tens and the 'leaf' the units, so the first five entries 84, 17, 38, 45, 47 are:

Stem (tens)	Leaf (units)
1	7
2	
3	8
4	5 7
5	
6	
7	
8	4

and the completed diagram is

Stem	Leaf
1	7 9
2	2
3	8 3 9
4	5 7
5	3 4 5 4 1 4
6	6 5
7	6 5 2
8	4

We then arrange the leaves in numerical order and give a key. The final diagram is:

Stem	Leaf
1	7 9
2	2
3	3 8 9
4	5 7
5	1 3 4 4 4 5
6	5 6
7	2 5 6
8	4

Key

$1 \mid 7$ means 17

In the previous example we have written the smaller values at the top of the diagram, but it could be written with the smaller values at the bottom, thus:

Stem	Leaf
8	4
7	2 5 6
6	5 6
5	1 3 4 4 4 5
4	5 7
3	3 8 9
2	2
1	7 9

The stem and leaf diagram gives us a good idea of the shape of the distribution. It is easy to pick out the smallest and the largest values and to see that the mode is 54. It is also obvious that the interval with the most in it, the **modal class**, is 50–59.

Example 1.1   The maximum temperature in °C (measured to the nearest degree) was recorded in Sutton each day during June. The results were as follows:

19	23	19	19	20	12	19	22	22	16
18	16	19	20	17	13	14	12	15	17
16	17	19	22	22	20	19	19	20	20

Draw a stem and leaf diagram.

Solution 1.1   Now the smallest value is 12 and the highest value is 23. If we grouped the data into classes 10–19, 20–29, ... the stem and leaf diagram would give us very little information. The number of classes must be sensible; usually 5 to 10 classes will do. Equal class intervals must be used, so in this instance we could use intervals of 2 °C as follows:

12–13, 14–15, 16–17, 18–19, 20–21, 22–23.

The stem and leaf diagram for the maximum temperature is:

Arranged in order:

Stem	Leaf
1	2 3 2
1	4 5
1	6 6 7 7 6 7
1	9 9 9 9 8 9 9 9 9
2	0 0 0 0 0
2	3 2 2 2 2

Stem	Leaf
1	2 2 3
1	4 5
1	6 6 6 7 7 7
1	8 9 9 9 9 9 9 9
2	0 0 0 0 0
2	2 2 2 2 3

Key 1 | 2 means 12 °C

This shows clearly the shape of the distribution, with the modal class being 18–19 and the mode 19 °C.

NOTE: the stem does not necessarily represent the tens digit, as the following example shows.

Example 1.2 For the data in Example 1.1, draw a stem and leaf diagram using class intervals 12–14, 15–17, 18–20, 21–23.

Solution 1.2 The interval 18–20 cannot be represented by a stem of 1, since the tens digit changes during the interval. For the stem we can use 12, 15, 18, 21. The leaf is then the number that is added to the stem:

Stem	Leaf
12	0 0 1 2
15	0 1 1 1 2 2 2
18	0 1 1 1 1 1 1 1 2 2 2 2 2
21	1 1 1 1 2

> *Key*   15 │ 2 means 17
>   18 │ 0 means 18

NOTE: the key is essential in explaining how the diagram has been formed.

It is important to remember that

> for stem and leaf diagrams,
>   **(a)** class intervals must be equal,
>   **(b)** a key is essential.

For example,

(*i*)

Stem	Leaf
5	1 3
10	2 4 4
15	0 0 1 3 4 4
20	3 3 4
25	1 1

> *Key*   5 │ 1 means 6
>   15 │ 4 means 19

The class intervals are 5–9, 10–14, 15–19, 20–24, 25–29.

The diagram represents the values 6, 8, 12, 14, 14, 15, 15, 16, 18, 19, 19, 23, 23, 24, 26, 26.

(*ii*)

Stem	Leaf
7	0 2 3
11	0 1 1 3 3 3
15	1 2 2 3
19	0 2
23	1

The class intervals are 7–10, 11–14, 15–18, 19–22, 23–26.

The diagram represents the values 7, 9, 10, 11, 12, 12, 14, 14, 14, 16, 17, 17, 18, 19, 21, 24.

Key	15	3 means 18
	7	2 means 9

(*iii*)

Stem	Leaf
16	1 3 3
16	6 8 8 9 9
17	0 0 1 3 3 4
17	5 7 9
18	0

The class intervals are 160–164, 165–169, 170–174, 175–179, 180–184.

The diagram represents the values 161, 163, 163, 166, 168, 168, 169, 169, 170, 170, 171, 173, 173, 174, 175, 177, 179, 180.

Key
16	8 means 168

Example 1.3   The table gives the number of days on which rain fell in 36 consecutive intervals of 30 days. The readings were taken in Bristol during 1990, 1991 and 1992.

21	19	6	12	8	18	9	8	11	17	15	13
16	9	17	18	9	24	17	7	8	17	17	8
7	11	16	17	8	5	13	22	20	16	20	13

Draw stem and leaf diagrams with the following class intervals:

(**a**) 5–9, 10–14, 15–19, 20–24

(**b**) 4–6, 7–9, 10–12, 13–15, 16–18, 19–21, 22–24.

Solution 1.3   (**a**) Using intervals 5–9, 10–14, 15–19, 20–24 the completed stem and leaf diagram is as follows:

Stem	Leaf
0	5 6 7 7 8 8 8 8 8 9 9 9
1	1 1 2 3 3 3
1	5 6 6 6 7 7 7 7 7 7 8 8 9
2	0 0 1 2 4

Key
1	6 means 16

NOTE: this diagram could have been written differently, as follows:

Stem	Leaf
5	0 1 2 2 3 3 3 3 3 4 4 4
10	1 1 2 3 3 3
15	0 1 1 1 2 2 2 2 2 2 3 3 4
20	0 0 1 2 4

> *Key*   15 | 1 means 16
>   5 | 3 means 8

(**b**) Using intervals 4–6, 7–9, 10–12, ... the completed diagram, arranged in order is:

Stem	Leaf
4	1 2
7	0 0 1 1 1 1 1 2 2 2
10	1 1 2
13	0 0 0 2
16	0 0 0 1 1 1 1 1 1 2 2
19	0 1 1 2
22	0 2

> *Key*
>   13 | 2 means 15

Both diagrams show that the mode is 17 rainy days, but the seven intervals used in (**b**) show more clearly the two 'peaks'.

The distribution is approximately **bi-modal**, with modal classes 7–9 and 16–18.

Example 1.4   For the stem and leaf diagram give

(**a**) the value ringed,

(**b**) the width of the class interval containing the ringed value if the diagram represents:

(*i*)   the widths of 30 metal components, with the following key:

> *Key* 1 | 2 means 1.2 cm

(*ii*) the reaction times in 30 experiments, with key:

> *Key* 1 | 2 means 12 hundredths of a second

(*iii*) the attendances at 30 matches, with key:

$$\boxed{Key\ \ 1\ |\ 2\ \text{means}\ 1200\ \text{people}}$$

Stem and leaf diagram:

Stem	Leaf
0	7
0	9
1	0 1
1	2 2
1	4 4 4 5 5
1	6 6 7 7 7
1	8 8 8 8 9 9 ⑨
2	0 0 1 1
2	2 3
2	4

Solution 1.4   (*i*)   (**a**) $1\,|\,9$ means 1.9 cm.

(**b**) The interval is 1.8 cm–1.9 cm. Since width is a continuous variable, and assuming that widths have been measured to the nearest tenth of a cm, then $1.75\,\text{cm} \leqslant \text{width} < 1.95\,\text{cm}$ and the class width is 2 cm.

(*ii*)   (**a**) $1\,|\,9$ means 19 hundredths of a second, or 0.19 seconds.

(**b**) The interval is 0.18 sec–0.19 sec, i.e. $0.175 \leqslant \text{time} < 0.195$, so the class width is 0.02 seconds.

(*iii*)   (**a**) $1\,|\,9$ means 1900 people.

(**b**) The interval is 1800 people–1900 people. Assuming that the number has been given to the nearest hundred, then $1750 \leqslant \text{number} < 1950$, so the class width is 200 people.

Back-to-back stem plots

Stem and leaf diagrams can be used to compare two samples by showing the results together on a back-to-back stem plot.

Example 1.5   Use a stem and leaf diagram to compare the examination marks in French and English for a class of 20 pupils.

French	75 69 58 58 46 44 32 50 53 78
	81 61 61 45 31 44 53 66 47 57
English	52 58 68 77 38 85 43 44 56 65
	65 79 44 71 84 72 63 69 72 79

Solution 1.5   The first four entries for both French and English are entered in a back-to-back stem plot as follows:

	French		English	
		3		
		4		
	8 8	5	2 8	
	9	6	8	
	5	7	7	
		8		

Key (French)

9 | 6 means 69

Key (English)

5 | 2 means 52

The completed diagram is

French		English
1 2	3	8
7 4 5 4 6	4	3 4 4
7 3 3 0 8 8	5	2 8 6
6 1 1 9	6	8 5 5 3 9
8 5	7	7 9 1 2 2 9
1	8	5 4

Key (French)

8 | 5 means 58

Key (English)

6 | 3 means 63

Arranged in order:

French		English
2 1	3	8
7 6 5 4 4	4	3 4 4
8 8 7 3 3 0	5	2 6 8
9 6 1 1	6	3 5 5 8 9
8 5	7	1 2 2 7 9 9
1	8	4 5

From the diagram it is clear that the class had higher marks in English than in French and it therefore appears that they performed better in English. However, this would depend on the standards of marking used in the two examinations.

Exercise 1a

1. Draw stem and leaf diagrams for the following data. What conclusions can you draw from the diagrams? Remember to give a key to each diagram.

    (*a*) The masses, correct to the nearest kg, of 30 men:

    74, 52, 67, 68, 71, 76, 86, 81, 73, 68, 64, 75, 71, 57, 67, 57, 59, 72, 79, 64, 70, 74, 77, 79, 65, 68, 76, 83, 61, 63.

    (Use class intervals 50–54, 55–59, 60–64,...)

    (*b*) The times, correct to the nearest second, taken by 20 boys to swim one length of a pool:

    32, 31, 26, 27, 27, 32, 29, 26, 25, 25, 29, 31, 32, 26, 30, 24, 32, 27, 26, 31.

    (Use class intervals 24–25, 26–27,...)

    (*c*) A group of adults take part in a reaction-timing experiment. Their results are measured to the nearest hundredth of a second.

    0.14, 0.17, 0.21, 0.20, 0.20, 0.22, 0.14, 0.24, 0.26, 0.17, 0.14, 0.17, 0.21, 0.20, 0.22, 0.14, 0.24, 0.26, 0.17, 0.18, 0.17, 0.21, 0.20, 0.23, 0.17, 0.23, 0.21, 0.23, 0.24, 0.23.

    (Use class intervals 0.14–0.15, 0.16–0.17, 0.18–0.19,...)

(*d*) The daily hours of sunshine in London during the month of August:
7.0, 7.6, 12.5, 12.9, 8.3, 9.7, 8.4, 11.1, 7.5, 7.5, 9.8, 10.4, 11.6, 11.3, 7.3, 7.8, 6.5, 6.2, 6.1, 5.6, 5.6, 5.8, 4.8, 4.3, 0.0, 0.6, 0.8, 1.6, 0.2, 2.4, 2.6
(Use class intervals 0.0–0.9, 1.0–1.9, 2.0–2.9,...)
(*e*) 30 girls estimate the length of a line in cm, correct to the nearest mm:
9.2, 7.3, 7.0, 6.5, 5.4, 5.3, 10.1, 8.4, 8.8, 7.1, 7.6, 7.9, 6.7, 9.6, 5.5, 7.4, 7.0, 8.2, 5.5, 7.8, 8.2, 7.5, 6.1, 6.1, 3.9, 6.8, 7.6, 8.1, 8.0, 10.0.(Use class intervals 3.0–3.9, 4.0–4.9,...)

2. Draw back-to-back stem plots for the following data. What conclusions can you draw?
(*a*) The pulse rates of 30 company directors were measured before and after taking exercise.
Before: 110, 93, 81, 75, 73, 73, 48, 53, 69, 69, 66, 111, 105, 93, 90, 50, 57, 64, 90, 111, 91, 70, 70, 51, 79, 93, 105, 51, 66, 93.
After: 117, 81, 77, 108, 130, 69, 77, 84, 84, 86, 95, 125, 96, 104, 104, 137, 143, 70, 80, 131, 145, 106, 130, 109, 137, 75, 104, 75, 97, 80.
(Use class intervals 40–49, 50–59, 60–69,...)
(*b*) The ages of teachers in two schools:
School A: 51, 45, 33, 37, 37, 27, 28, 54, 54, 61, 34, 31, 39, 23, 53, 59, 40, 46, 48, 48, 39, 33, 25, 31, 48, 40, 53, 51, 46, 45, 45, 48, 39, 29, 23, 37.
School B: 59, 56, 40, 43, 46, 38, 29, 52, 54, 34, 23, 41, 42, 52, 50, 58, 60, 45, 45, 56, 59, 49, 44, 36, 38, 25, 56, 36, 42, 47, 50, 54, 59, 47, 58, 57.
(Use class intervals 20–29, 30–39, 40–49,...)

(*c*) 20 boys and 20 girls took part in a reaction-timing experiment. Their results are measured to the nearest hundredth of a second.
Girls: 0.22, 0.21, 0.18, 0.18, 0.16, 0.19, 0.25, 0.22, 0.17, 0.19, 0.16, 0.21, 0.24, 0.22, 0.19, 0.22, 0.25, 0.22, 0.17, 0.22.
Boys: 0.14, 0.20, 0.22, 0.16, 0.19, 0.16, 0.15, 0.23, 0.23, 0.19, 0.16, 0.15, 0.09, 0.23, 0.11, 0.21, 0.22, 0.18, 0.18, 0.16.
(Use class intervals 0.08–0.09, 0.10–0.11, 0.12–0.13,...)

3. Give the value ringed, and the width of the interval it is in, for the stem and leaf diagram given below if the diagram represents
(*a*) the times taken for a journey with key

Key 6	8 means 6.8 hours

(*b*) the masses of components, in g (to 3 d.p.) with key

Key 6	8 means 0.068 g

Stem	Leaf
5	9
6	1 4
6	7 8 9
7	2 3 3 ④
7	5 6 6 6 7 8
8	0 3 4
8	5

FREQUENCY DISTRIBUTIONS — Grouped data

The following frequency distributions show some of the ways that data may be grouped. The information is more concise than the raw data, but the disadvantage is that the original information has been lost.

(i) Frequency distribution to show the lengths of 30 rods
Lengths have been measured to the nearest mm.

Length (mm)	27–31	32–36	37–46	47–51
Frequency	4	11	12	3

The interval '27–31' means $26.5 \, \text{mm} \leqslant \text{length} < 31.5 \, \text{mm}$.

The class boundaries are   26.5, 31.5, 36.5, 46.5, 51.5

The class widths are   5,   5,   10,   5

(ii) Frequency distribution to show the marks in a test of 100 students

Mark	30–39	40–49	50–59	60–69	70–79	80–89
Frequency	10	14	26	20	18	12

This distribution can be interpreted in two ways:

(a) as continuous data
Assuming marks are to the nearest integer, we have the following:

The class boundaries are   29.5, 39.5, 49.5, 59.5, 69.5, 79.5, 89.5
The class widths are   ⁃   10,   10,   10,   10,   10,   10

(b) as discrete data
The class boundaries are   30,   40,   50,   60,   70,   80,   90
The class widths are   10,   10,   10,   10,   10,   10

(iii) Frequency distribution to show the lengths of 50 telephone calls

Length of call (min)	0–	3–	6–	9–	12–	18–
Frequency	9	12	15	10	4	0

The interval '3–' means 3 minutes $\leqslant$ time < 6 minutes, so any time including 3 minutes and up to (but not including) 6 minutes comes into this interval.

The class boundaries are 0,   3,   6,   9,   12,   18
The class widths are   3,   3,   3,   3,   6

(iv) Frequency distribution to show the masses of 40 packages brought to a particular counter at a post office

Mass (g)	–100	–250	–500	–800
Frequency	8	10	16	6

The interval '–250' means $100\,g$ < mass $\leqslant 250\,g$, so any mass over 100 grams up to and including 250 grams comes into this interval.

The class boundaries are 0,   100,   250,   500,   800
The class widths are   100,   150,   250,   300

(v) Frequency distribution to show the speeds of 50 cars passing a checkpoint

Speed (km/h)	20–30	30–40	40–60	60–80	80–100
Frequency	2	7	20	16	5

The class '30–40' means $30\,km/h \leqslant$ speed $< 40\,km/h$.

The class boundaries are 20,   30,   40,   60,   80,   100
The class widths are   10,   10,   20,   20   20

(vi) Frequency distribution to show ages (in completed years) of applicants for a teaching post

Age (years)	21–24	25–28	29–32	33–40	41–52
Frequency	4	2	2	1	1

Since the ages are given in completed years (not to the nearest year) then '21–24' means $21 \leqslant$ age < 25. Someone who is 24 years and 11 months would come into this category. Sometimes this interval is written '21–' and the next is '25–', etc.

The class boundaries are   21,   25,   29,   33,   41,   53
The class widths are   4,   4,   4,   8,   12

HISTOGRAMS

Grouped data can be displayed in a **histogram**.

> In a histogram, rectangles are drawn so that the area of each rectangle is proportional to the frequency.
>
> Area $\propto$ frequency

(a) Histograms with equal class widths

Example 1.6   The lengths of 30 Swiss cheese plant leaves were measured and the information grouped as shown. Measurements were taken correct to the nearest cm. Draw a histogram to illustrate the data.

Length of leaf (cm)	10–14	15–19	20–24	25–29
Frequency	3	8	12	7

Solution 1.6   The class boundaries are 9.5,   14.5,   19.5,   24.5,   29.5
The class widths are   5,   5,   5,   5

Now,   area of rectangle = class width $\times$ height of rectangle

Since the class width is 5 for each interval,

$$\text{area of rectangle} = 5 \times \text{height of rectangle}$$

i.e.   area $\propto$ height of rectangle

So if we make the height of each rectangle the same as the frequency,

$$\text{area} \propto \text{frequency},   \text{as required.}$$

> When all the class intervals are of equal width, the frequency can be used for the height of each rectangle.

Histogram to show the lengths of 30 leaves

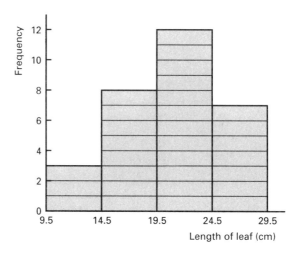

(b) Histograms with unequal class widths

Example 1.7   The frequency distribution gives the masses of 35 objects, measured to the nearest kg. Draw a histogram to illustrate the data.

Mass (kg)	6–8	9–11	12–17	18–20	21–29
Frequency	4	6	10	3	12

Solution 1.7   The class boundaries are 5.5, 8.5, 11.5, 17.5, 20.5, 29.5
The class widths are   3,   3,   6,   3,   9

In this case the class widths are not equal, so the *heights* of the rectangles *must be adjusted* so that the areas of the rectangles are proportional to the frequencies. The best way to do this is to calculate

$$\text{frequency density} = \frac{\text{frequency}}{\text{class width}}$$

We then use 'frequency density' as the height for each rectangle.

Mass (kg)	Class width	Frequency	Frequency density
6–8	3	4	$\frac{4}{3} = 1\frac{1}{3}$
9–11	3	6	$\frac{6}{3} = 2$
12–17	6	10	$\frac{10}{6} = 1\frac{2}{3}$
18–20	3	3	$\frac{3}{3} = 1$
21–29	9	12	$\frac{12}{9} = 1\frac{1}{3}$

Histogram to show the masses of 35 objects

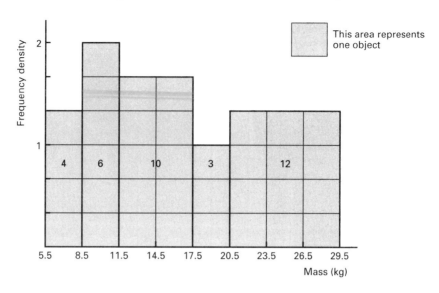

NOTE: it is sometimes helpful to give an area key and to label the blocks with their frequencies.

Example 1.8   The following table gives the distribution of the interest paid to 460 investors in a particular year.

Interest (£)	25–	30–	40–	60–	80–	110–
Frequency	17	55	142	153	93	0

Draw a histogram to illustrate this information.

Solution 1.8   The class boundaries are   25,   30,   40,   60,   80,   110
The class widths are   5,   10,   20,   20,   30

Interest (£)	Class width	Frequency	Frequency density
25–	5	17	$\frac{17}{5} = 3.4$
30–	10	55	$\frac{55}{10} = 5.5$
40–	20	142	$\frac{142}{20} = 7.1$
60–	20	153	$\frac{153}{20} = 7.65$
80–	30	93	$\frac{93}{30} = 3.1$

Histogram to show the interest paid to 460 investors

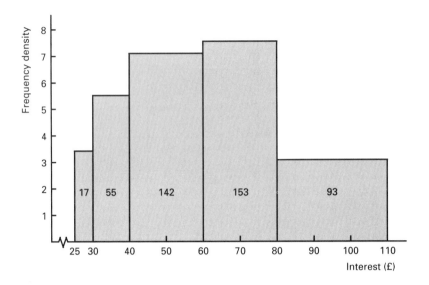

NOTE: sometimes we start the horizontal scale at the lowest class boundary; alternatively a 'broken axis' symbol is used as shown above.

Example 1.9   Sixty Year 9 pupils were asked to record the duration, to the nearest minute, of their next telephone call. The results were as follows.

Time (min)	0–9	10–14	15–19	20–24	25–34
Frequency	13	19	12	7	9

Draw a histogram to represent the data.

Solution 1.9   The class boundaries are   0,   9.5,   14.5,   19.5,   24.5,   34.5
The class widths are   9.5,   5,   5,   5,   10

Time (min)	Class width	Frequency	Frequency density
0–9	9.5	13	$\frac{13}{9.5} = 1.37$
10–14	5	19	$\frac{19}{5} = 3.8$
15–19	5	12	$\frac{12}{5} = 2.4$
20–24	5	7	$\frac{7}{5} = 1.4$
25–34	10	9	$\frac{9}{10} = 0.9$

Histogram to show the times of calls

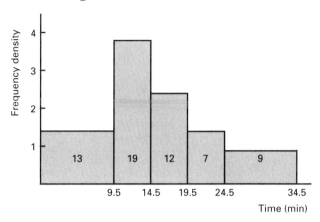

Alternative approach The first interval can be regarded as having a lower class boundary of -0.5, in which case the width of the first interval is 10. Therefore the height of the first rectangle is 1.3 and the histogram looks like this:

Histogram to show the times of calls

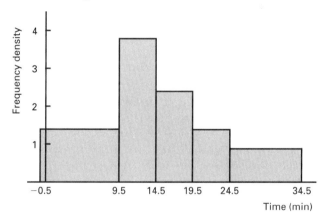

NOTE: 1. frequency = frequency density × class width

2. modal class = interval with greatest frequency density

FREQUENCY POLYGONS — Grouped data

A grouped frequency distribution can be displayed in a **frequency polygon**.

To construct a frequency polygon, plot frequency density against the mid-point of an interval, where

mid-point of an interval $= \frac{1}{2}$(l.c.b. + u.c.b.).

Then join the points with straight lines.

Example 1.10 Draw a frequency polygon to illustrate this frequency distribution, which gives the times taken by 31 competitors to complete a cross-country run.

Time t (min)	$25 \leqslant t < 30$	$30 \leqslant t < 35$	$35 \leqslant t < 40$	$40 \leqslant t < 50$	$50 \leqslant t < 65$
Frequency	4	12	8	4	3

Solution 1.10

Time	Mid-point of interval	Class width	Frequency	Frequency density
$25 \leqslant t < 30$	27.5	5	4	$\frac{4}{5} = 0.8$
$30 \leqslant t < 35$	32.5	5	12	$\frac{12}{5} = 2.4$
$35 \leqslant t < 40$	37.5	5	8	$\frac{8}{5} = 1.3$
$40 \leqslant t < 50$	45	10	4	$\frac{4}{10} = 0.4$
$50 \leqslant t < 65$	57.5	15	3	$\frac{3}{15} = 0.2$

Frequency polygon to show times taken to complete a cross-country run

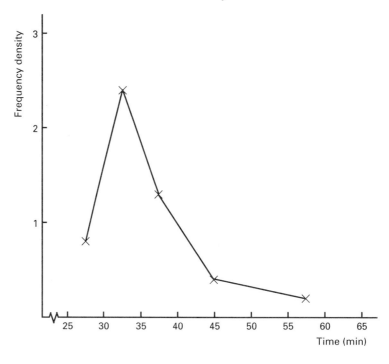

Note that this distribution is skewed with a tail at the right-hand end. We say that it is **positively skewed**.

We can, of course, form a frequency polygon by joining the mid-points of the tops of the rectangles in the histogram. The following diagram shows the frequency polygon for the data of Example 1.7.

Frequency polygon to show the masses of 35 objects

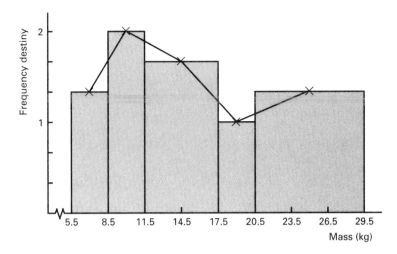

COMPARATIVE FREQUENCY POLYGONS

Frequency polygons are very useful when we wish to compare sets of data.

Example 1.11 Draw frequency polygons to compare the age distributions of the teachers in School A and in School B.

Age	Frequency (School A)	Frequency (School B)
20–	4	0
25–	6	2
30–	11	4
35–	14	7
40–	9	11
45–	5	12
50–	5	11
55–	3	8
60–	0	5
65–	0	0

Solution 1.11 Since the class intervals are of equal width, we can plot the frequency against the mid-point of each interval to form the frequency polygon. For the interval '20–', the lower class boundary is 20 and the upper class boundary is 25, so mid-point $= \frac{1}{2}$(l.c.b. $+$ u.c.b.)

$$= \tfrac{1}{2}(20 + 25)$$
$$= 22.5$$

The other mid-points are 27.5, 32.5, 37.5, ... and so on.

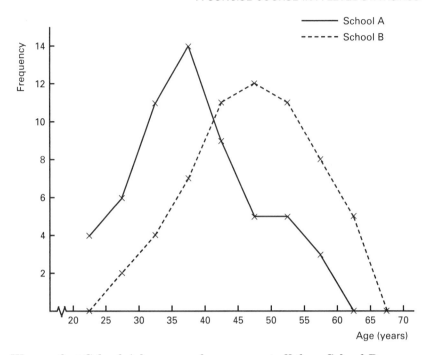

We see that School A has a much younger staff than School B.

FREQUENCY CURVES

If the number of intervals is large, then the frequency polygon will consist of a large number of line segments. The frequency polygon approaches a smooth curve, known as a frequency curve.

Frequency curve

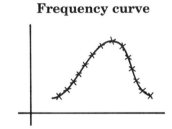

Exercise 1b

1. The masses of 50 apples (measured to the nearest g) were noted and shown in the table.
    Construct a frequency distribution, using equal class intervals of width 5 g, and taking the lower class boundary of the first interval as 84.5 g.
    Draw a histogram to illustrate the data.

86	101	114	118	87	92	93	116
105	102	97	93	101	111	96	117
100	106	118	101	107	96	101	102
104	92	99	107	98	105	113	100
103	108	92	109	95	100	103	110
113	99	106	116	101	105	86	88
108	92						

2. 38 children solved a simple problem and the time taken by each was noted.

Time (seconds)	5–	10–	20–	25–	40–	45–
Frequency	2	12	7	15	2	0

Draw a histogram to illustrate this information.

3. The masses, measured to the nearest kg, of 200 girls were recorded.

Mass (kg)	41–50	51–55	56–60	61–70	71–75
Frequency	21	62	55	50	12

Represent the data by a histogram.

4. On a particular day, the length of stay of each car at a city car park was recorded.

Length of stay (min)	Frequency
$t < 25$	62
$25 \leqslant t < 60$	70
$60 \leqslant t < 80$	88
$80 \leqslant t < 150$	280
$150 \leqslant t < 300$	30

Represent the data by a histogram.

5. In a competition to grow the tallest hollyhock, the heights recorded by 50 competitors were as follows. Heights were measured to the nearest cm.

Height (cm)	Frequency
177–186	12
187–191	8
192–196	8
197–201	9
202–206	7
207–216	6

Draw a histogram and superimpose the frequency polygon.

7. The table shows the duration, in minutes, of 64 telephone calls made from a high street call box in one day.

Length of call (min)	Frequency
0–	3
$1\frac{1}{2}$–	7
3–	22
6–	20
12–	6
15–	6
21–	0

Draw a frequency polygon to illustrate the information.

8. The table shows the ages (in completed years) of women who gave birth to a child at Anytown Maternity Hospital during a particular year.

Age (years)	Number of births
16–	70
20–	470
25–	535
30–	280
35–	118
45–	0

Draw a frequency polygon to illustrate this information. Do not draw a histogram first.

9. The masses (measured to the nearest g) of washers are recorded in the table. Draw a histogram to illustrate the data.

Mass (g)	Frequency
0–2	5
3–5	6
6–11	14
12–14	4
15–17	3

6. This histogram represents the speeds of cars passing a 30 miles per hour sign. Write out the frequency distribution.

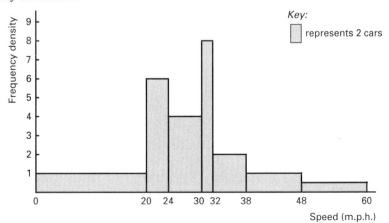

10. 68 smokers were asked to record their consumption of cigarettes each day for several weeks. The table shown is based on the information obtained.

Average number of cigarettes smoked per day	Number of smokers
0–	4
8–	6
12–	12
16–	28
24–	8
28–	6
34–50	4

Illustrate these data by means of a histogram.   (C Additional) P

11. The marks awarded to 136 pupils in an examination are summarised below.

Marks	Frequency
10–29	22
30–39	18
40–49	22
50–59	24
60–64	14
65–69	12
70–84	24

Draw a histogram to illustrate the data. Take the class boundaries to be 10, 30, 40, 50, 60, 65, 70 and 85.

12. Telephone calls arriving at a switchboard are answered by the telephonist. The following table shows the time, to the nearest second, recorded as being taken by the telephonist to answer the calls received during one day.

Time to answer (to nearest second)	Number of calls
10–19	20
20–24	20
25–29	15
30	14
31–34	16
35–39	10
40–59	10

Represent these data by a histogram. Give a reason to justify the use of a histogram to represent these data.   (L)

13. Students were investigating the effects of a growth hormone placed on the growing tip of maize seedlings. The hormone was used in two different concentrations and distilled water was used on one batch of seedlings as a control. After three weeks, the heights of the plants were measured to the nearest cm. The results were as follows:

Control

Height (cm)	Frequency
45	0
46	7
47	11
48	12
49	14
50	14
51	18
52	12
53	8
54	3
55	1
56	0

20% solution

Height (cm)	Frequency
50	0
51	1
52	0
53	2
54	5
55	9
56	17
57	25
58	20
59	12
60	9
61	0

40% solution

Height (cm)	Frequency
54	0
55	2
56	2
57	2
58	7
59	10
60	11
61	18
62	18
63	16
64	9
65	5
66	0

Draw frequency polygons to represent the data and compare the results.

14.

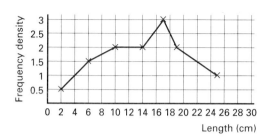

Complete the following frequency distribution, represented by the frequency polygon on the left.

Length (cm)	Frequency
$0 \leqslant x < 4$	2
$4 \leqslant x < 8$	
$8 \leqslant x < 12$	
$12 \leqslant x < 16$	
$16 \leqslant x < 18$	
$18 \leqslant x < 20$	
$20 \leqslant x < 30$	

CIRCULAR DIAGRAMS OR PIE DIAGRAMS

Another useful way of displaying data is to draw a pie diagram, sometimes called a pie chart. As in a histogram, area is proportional to frequency.

Example 1.12   The sales (in thousands of litres) of petrol from four petrol stations A, B, C and D are noted for the first week of March, and are shown in the table:

Petrol station	A	B	C	D
Sales (thousands of litres)	90	140	30	20

Construct a pie diagram to illustrate this information.

Solution 1.12   The total angle of 360° at the centre of a circle is divided according to the sales at each of the stations.

The total sales (thousands of litres) $= 90 + 140 + 30 + 20 = 280$

The angle representing the sales of petrol at station A is given by

$$\left(\frac{90}{280}\right)(360) = 115.7° \quad (1\,\text{d.p.})$$

and so, for each of the petrol stations we have:

Petrol station	Sales (thousands of litres)	Sector angle
A	90	$\left(\frac{90}{280}\right)(360) = 115.7°$
B	140	$\left(\frac{140}{280}\right)(360) = 180°$
C	30	$\left(\frac{30}{280}\right)(360) = 38.6°$
D	20	$\left(\frac{20}{280}\right)(360) = 25.7°$
	280	Total $= 360°$

Pie diagram to show the sales of petrol (in thousands of litres)

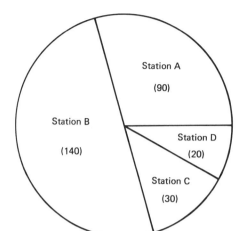

COMPARISON OF DATA USING PIE DIAGRAMS

Pie diagrams are particularly useful when we wish to **compare two or more sets of similar data**.

Suppose that we are given information about the land use (for barley, wheat and woodland) in three parishes. We can draw three pie diagrams to illustrate the land use in each parish. However, if we wish to compare the sets of data we must make the size (or area) of each circle proportional to the total land for each parish. In this example we will refer to the total amount of land as the 'frequency' F.

The area of a circle is πr^2, so we will require, with obvious notation,

$$\pi r_1{}^2 : \pi r_2{}^2 : \pi r_3{}^2 = F_1 : F_2 : F_3$$

so $\qquad\qquad r_1{}^2 : r_2{}^2 : r_3{}^2 = F_1 : F_2 : F_3 \quad$ (cancelling π)

i.e. $\qquad\qquad r_1 : r_2 : r_3 = \sqrt{F_1} : \sqrt{F_2} : \sqrt{F_3} \quad$ (taking square roots)

So the radii of the circles are proportional to the square roots of the frequencies.

We then choose a convenient scale and draw the circles.

Example 1.13 The following agricultural statistics refer to the land use, in hectares, of three parishes. Draw three pie diagrams to compare these data.

Parish	Barley	Wheat	Woodland	Total land, F
Appleford	1830	1640	550	$F_1 = 4020$
Burnford	645	435	120	$F_2 = 1200$
Carnford	320	160	150	$F_3 = 630$

Solution 1.13 Now $F_1 = 4020, F_2 = 1200$ and $F_3 = 630$.

So
$$r_1 : r_2 : r_3 = \sqrt{F_1} : \sqrt{F_2} : \sqrt{F_3}$$
$$= \sqrt{4020} : \sqrt{1200} : \sqrt{630}$$
$$= 63.40 : 34.64 : 25.10$$
$$= 3.17 : 1.732 : 1.255$$

For convenience, we take $r_1 = 3.2\,\text{cm}$, $r_2 = 1.7\,\text{cm}$ and $r_3 = 1.3\,\text{cm}$.

The angles in the pie diagrams are calculated as shown in the table:

Parish	Barley	Wheat	Woodland
Appleford	$\left(\frac{1830}{4020}\right)(360) = 163.9°$	$\left(\frac{1640}{4020}\right)(360) = 146.9°$	$\left(\frac{550}{4020}\right)(360) = 49.2°$
Burnford	$\left(\frac{645}{1200}\right)(360) = 193.5°$	$\left(\frac{435}{1200}\right)(360) = 130.5°$	$\left(\frac{120}{1200}\right)(360) = 36°$
Carnford	$\left(\frac{320}{630}\right)(360) = 182.9°$	$\left(\frac{160}{630}\right)(360) = 91.4°$	$\left(\frac{150}{630}\right)(360) = 85.7°$

Pie diagrams to show land use (in hectares) in three parishes

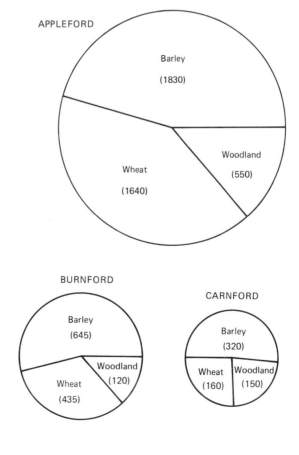

Exercise 1c

1. Construct a pie diagram to illustrate the scores obtained when a die is thrown 120 times.

Number on die	1	2	3	4	5	6
Frequency	22	20	15	25	10	28

2. The results of the voting in an election were as follows:

Mr P	2 045 votes
Mr Q	4 238 votes
Mrs R	8 605 votes
Miss S	12 012 votes

Represent this information on a pie diagram.

3. The pie chart, which is not drawn to scale, shows the distribution of various types of land and water in a certain county. Calculate
   (i)   the area of woodland,
   (ii) the angle of the urban sector,
   (iii) the total area of the county.

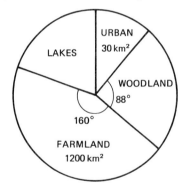

(C Additional) P

4. The table shows the sales, in millions of dollars, of a company in two successive years.

Year	Africa	America	Asia	Europe
1972	8.4	12.2	15.6	23.8
1973	5.5	6.7	13.2	19.6

Draw two pie charts which allow the total annual sales to be compared.   (C Additional)

5. Five companies form a group. The sales of each company during the year ending 5th April, 1988, are shown in the table below.

Company	A	B	C	D	E
Sales (in £1000's)	55	130	20	35	60

Draw a pie chart of radius 5 cm to illustrate this information.

For the year ending 5th April, 1989, the total sales of the group increased by 20%, and this growth was maintained for the year ending 5th April, 1990.
If pie charts were drawn to compare the total sales for each of these years with the total sales for the year ending 5th April, 1988, what would be the radius of each of these pie charts?
If the sales of company *E* for the year ending 5th April, 1990, were again £60 000, what would be the angle of the sector representing them?   (C Additional)

6. Mr Williams worked out how much it had cost him to run his car for each of three consecutive years. The results were as follows:

	Tax and insurance	Maintenance	Petrol
Year 1	£150.00	£72.50	£190.00
Year 2	£187.00	£116.00	£205.00
Year 3	£175.00	£289.90	£253.10

Draw three pie diagrams to compare this information.

7. Shoppers were asked how much they spent last week on various items. Mrs M replied as follows:

	Item *A*	Item *B*	Item *C*
Mrs M	£1.50	£3.50	£3.00

Draw a pie diagram with radius 4 cm to illustrate this information.
A comparison was then made with the pie diagram drawn to illustrate Mrs N's replies, in which the circle representing the total amount had a radius of 5 cm, the sector representing the amount spent on item *A* had an angle of 72° and the amount spent on item *B* was £4.00. Find the amount spent on item *C* by Mrs N and draw a pie diagram to illustrate her expenditure.

8. The following data summarise the expenditure by a county council during a particular year.

Service	Expenditure (£m)
Education	160.2
Highways & Public Transport	35.7
Police	28.9
Social Services	27.9
Other	24.5

These data are to be represented by a pie chart of radius 5 cm. Calculate, to the nearest degree, the angle corresponding to each of the five classifications. (DO NOT DRAW THE PIE CHART.)

The following year the county council spent £305.2 m.

Find the radius of a comparable pie chart which could be used to represent this second set of data. (L)

9. A golf club has 4 categories of membership: men, women, juniors and social members. The pie chart shown, which is not drawn to scale, illustrates the distribution of membership in 1980. Given that there were 147 men and 35 social members, calculate

(i) the number of junior members,

(ii) the angle of the sector representing the social members,

(iii) the number of women.

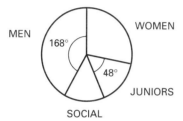

The corresponding pie chart for 1990 indicated that the number of men had increased by 49 although the angle of the corresponding sector remained the same. Calculate the total number of members in 1990.

Given that the radius of the 1980 pie chart was 26 cm, calculate the radius of the 1990 pie chart. (C Additional) P

10. During a particular month a family spends £52.27 on meat, £23.10 on fruit and vegetables, £19.72 on drink, £12.41 on toiletries, £102.68 on groceries and £9.82 on miscellaneous items.

These data are to be represented by a pie chart of radius 5 cm.

(a) Calculate, to the nearest degree, the angle corresponding to each of the above classifications. (DO NOT DRAW THE PIE CHART.)

The following month the family spends 20% more in total.

(b) Find the radius of a comparable pie chart to represent the data on this occasion. (L)

11. Pie charts A, B, C are drawn to compare, over a given period, the total value of the sales of certain items in each of 3 branches of a multiple store. The radii of the charts are 20 cm, 30 cm, 40 cm, respectively.

(i) If the total sales value represented by chart B is £4500, calculate the total sales value represented by each of charts A and C.

(ii) The angle of the sector representing a particular item in chart A is 72°. Calculate the sales value of this item.

(iii) The sales value represented by a sector in chart C is £600. Calculate the angle of the sector.

(iv) One item occupies one quarter of chart A, and the sales value for this item is one half of that for the same item on chart B. Calculate the angle of the sector for this item on chart B. (C Additional)

12. On a certain day, 125 people, each buying one newspaper, were asked which newspaper they had bought. The results of the survey are shown in the table below.

Newspaper	Number bought
The Times	10
The *Telegraph*	25
The *Express*	40
Some other paper	50

Calculate the angles of the sectors of a pie chart of radius 5 cm which would illustrate these data.

The following day a similar survey was carried out and the radius of the pie chart necessary to compare the new set of data with the previous set was 6 cm. Calculate the number of people in the second survey. (C Additional)

13. A householder keeps an annual account of four items of expenditure. The figures for the year 1991 are shown in the table below.

Item	Expenditure (£)
Taxes	x
Travel	1000
Light/Heat	y
Telephone	300

A pie chart was drawn to illustrate these data. Given that the angles of the sectors representing Taxes and Travel were 124° and 80° respectively, calculate

(i) the total expenditure for the year,

(ii) the value of x and of y,

(iii) the angle of each of the remaining sectors.

In 1992, the total expenditure on the same items was £8000. Given that the radius of the pie chart for 1991 was 6 cm, calculate the radius of the pie chart for 1992 in order that the two sets of data may be compared. (C Additional)

THE MEAN, $\bar{x}$

When interpreting data we often look for a 'typical' value. The mode is sometimes used, but a more useful average is the **mean**.

The mean is often denoted by the symbol $\bar{x}$, so if we consider n values $x_1, x_2, x_3, \ldots, x_n$ then

$$\bar{x} = \frac{x_1 + x_2 + \ldots + x_n}{n}$$

$$= \frac{\sum x_i}{n} \qquad \text{for} \quad i = 1, 2, \ldots, n$$

NOTE: the symbol Σ means 'the sum of' and it is read 'sigma'. So Σx_i for $i = 1, 2, \ldots, n$ means 'the sum of the values $x_1, x_2, x_3, \ldots, x_n$', i.e. $x_1 + x_2 + \ldots + x_n$.

Another way of writing this is $\displaystyle\sum_{i=1}^{n} x_i$, so we could also write

$$\bar{x} = \frac{1}{n}\sum_{i=1}^{n} x_i$$

This is very cumbersome and so when the number of terms is obvious, for simplicity we drop the subscript and write

$\bar{x} = \dfrac{1}{n}\Sigma x$ or $\bar{x} = \dfrac{\Sigma x}{n}$.

Example 1.14 Find the mean of the set of numbers   63, 65, 67, 68, 69

Solution 1.14 $n = 5$, $\Sigma x = 63 + 65 + 67 + 68 + 69$

$$= 332$$

Therefore $\bar{x} = \dfrac{\Sigma x}{n}$

$$= \frac{332}{5}$$

$$= 66.4$$

The mean of the set of numbers is 66.4.

Example 1.15 To obtain Grade A, Ben must achieve an average of at least 70 in five tests. If his average mark for the first four tests is 68, what is the lowest mark he can get in his fifth test and still obtain Grade A?

Solution 1.15 The mean for four tests is 68,

i.e.
$$\frac{1}{4}\sum_{i=1}^{4} x_i = 68$$

so
$$\sum_{i=1}^{4} x_i = 272$$

His total mark for the first four tests is 272.

NOTE: the subscript notation is useful in this example, showing that the average is for four tests.

Now for 5 tests, he wants

$$\frac{1}{5}\sum_{i=1}^{5} x_i \geqslant 70$$

i.e.
$$\sum_{i=1}^{5} x_i \geqslant 350$$

His total mark for the five tests must be at least 350. Since his total mark for the first four is 272, his mark for the fifth test must be at least $350 - 272 = 78$.

Therefore, to obtain Grade A, Ben must get at least 78 marks in his fifth test.

FINDING THE MEAN OF A FREQUENCY DISTRIBUTION

(a) Ungrouped data

For a frequency distribution

$$\bar{x} = \frac{\Sigma fx}{\Sigma f}$$

Example 1.16 The 30 members of an orchestra were asked how many instruments each could play. The results are set out in the frequency distribution. Calculate the mean number of instruments played.

Number of instruments, x	1	2	3	4	5
Frequency, f	11	10	5	3	1

Solution 1.16

x	f	fx
1	11	11
2	10	20
3	5	15
4	3	12
5	1	5
	$\Sigma f = 30$	$\Sigma fx = 63$

$$\bar{x} = \frac{\Sigma fx}{\Sigma f}$$

$$= \frac{63}{30}$$

$$= 2.1$$

The mean number of instruments played is 2.1

(b) Grouped data

When the data have been grouped into intervals we do not know the actual values, so we can only *estimate* the mean. We take the mid-point of an interval to represent that interval.

Remember that

> the mid-point of an interval $= \frac{1}{2}$ (l.c.b. + u.c.b.).

Example 1.17   The lengths of 40 bean pods were measured to the nearest cm and grouped as shown. Estimate the mean length, giving the answer to 1 d.p.

Length (cm)	4–8	9–13	14–18	19–23	24–28	29–33
Frequency, f	2	4	7	14	8	5

Solution 1.17   The mid-point of the interval 4–8 is $\frac{1}{2}(3.5 + 8.5) = 6$, so we assume that the two values in that interval are both 6. We find the other mid-points and form a table:

Length (cm)	Mid-point, x	f	fx
4–8	6	2	12
9–13	11	4	44
14–18	16	7	112
19–23	21	14	294
24–28	26	8	208
29–33	31	5	155
		$\Sigma f = 40$	$\Sigma fx = 825$

$$\bar{x} = \frac{\Sigma fx}{\Sigma f}$$

$$= \frac{825}{40}$$

$$= 20.6 \, (1 \, \text{d.p.})$$

Therefore the mean length of the bean pods is 20.6 cm (1 d.p.).

Exercise 1d

1. Find the mean of each of the following sets of numbers.
   (a) 5, 6, 6, 8, 8, 9, 11, 13, 14, 17
   (b) 148, 153, 156, 157, 160
   (c) $44\frac{1}{2}$, $47\frac{1}{2}$, $48\frac{1}{2}$, $51\frac{1}{2}$, $52\frac{1}{2}$, $54\frac{1}{2}$, $55\frac{1}{2}$, $56\frac{1}{2}$
   (d) 1769, 1771, 1772, 1775, 1778, 1781, 1784
   (e) 0.85, 0.88, 0.89, 0.93, 0.94, 0.96

2. If the mean of the following numbers is 17, find the value of c:

   $$12, 18, 21, c, 13$$

3. The mean of 10 numbers is 8. If an eleventh number is now included in the results, the mean becomes 9. What is the value of the eleventh number?

4. The mean of 4 numbers is 5, and the mean of 3 different numbers is 12. What is the mean of the 7 numbers together?

5. The mean of n numbers is 5. If the number 13 is now included with the n numbers, the new mean is 6. Find the value of n.

6. Find the mean for each of the following frequency distributions.

   (i)

x	1	2	3	4	5	6	7
f	4	5	8	10	17	5	1

   (ii)

x	27	28	29	30	31	32
f	30	43	51	49	42	35

   (iii)

x	121	122	123	124	125
f	14	25	32	23	6

   (iv)

Interval	f
5–9	4
10–14	6
15–19	12
20–24	10
25–29	7
30–34	1

   (v)

Interval	f
101–104	13
105–108	18
109–112	21
113–116	12
117–120	6

7. If the mean of the following frequency distribution is 3.66, find the value of a.

x	1	2	3	4	5	6
f	3	9	a	11	8	7

8. A bag contained five balls each bearing one of the numbers 1, 2, 3, 4, 5. A ball was drawn from the bag, its number noted, and then replaced. This was done 50 times in all and the table below shows the resulting frequency distribution.

Number	1	2	3	4	5
Frequency	x	11	y	8	9

   If the mean is 2.7, determine the values of x and y.

9. A sample of 100 boxes of matches was taken and a record made of the number of matches per box. The results were as follows:

Number of matches per box	47	48	49	50	51
Frequency	4	20	35	24	17

   Calculate the mean number of matches per box.

10. The table shows the speeds of 200 vehicles passing a particular point:

Speed (km/h)	30–	40–	50–	60–	70–	80–
Frequency	14	30	52	71	33	0

    Find the mean speed.

11. On a certain day the numbers of books on 40 shelves in a library were noted and grouped as shown. Find the mean number of books on a shelf.

Number of books	Number of shelves
31–35	4
36–40	6
41–45	10
46–50	13
51–55	5
56–60	2

12. The amounts spent by 120 motorists at a petrol station were recorded.

Amount spent, £x	Number of motorists
$x < 5$	12
$5 \leqslant x < 10$	38
$10 \leqslant x < 15$	42
$15 \leqslant x < 20$	20
$20 \leqslant x < 40$	8

(*a*) Draw a histogram to represent the data.
(*b*) Estimate the mean amount spent.

13. The frequency polygons show the heights of pupils in Year 7. Find the mean height for the girls and for the boys.

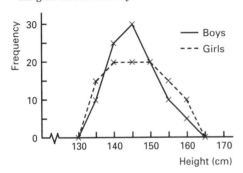

14. The age distribution of the population of a small village is recorded in the table below.

Age (years)	Number of people
0–	54
15–	78
30–	120
50–	88
70–	60
100–	0

Draw, on graph paper, a histogram to represent these data.
Estimate the mean of this distribution.
(C Additional)

15. Find the mean length for the data represented by the stem and leaf diagram.

Stem	Leaf
12	0 0
15	0 1 1
18	1 1 2
21	0 1 1 2 2 2
24	0 0 1 2
27	1 1
30	2

Key 15 | 1 means 16 cm

MEASURES OF DISPERSION

Consider the following sets of numbers

(**a**) 7, 7, 7, 7, 7

(**b**) 5, 6, 7, 8, 9

(**c**) −193, −93, 7, 107, 207

In each case, the mean is 7, but the last set is obviously much more spread out than the other two. We need to have some sort of measure of this spread. There are several types:

The range

The range is based entirely on the extreme values.

$$\text{Range} = \text{highest value} - \text{lowest value}$$

In

(**a**) range $= 7 - 7 = 0$

(**b**) range $= 9 - 5 = 4$

(**c**) range $= 207 - (-193) = 400$

There are also ranges based on particular observations within the data and these **quartile and percentile ranges** are considered on page 64.

The mean deviation from the mean

It is usual to consider how spread out the numbers are either side of the mean. For set (**c**) above

$$-200 \qquad\qquad 200$$

$$-100 \qquad 100$$

| -193 | -93 | 7 | 107 | 207 |

If we consider the **deviations** from the mean we can see that they are

$$-200, \quad -100, \quad 0, \quad 100, \quad 200$$

If we add all these, the sum is zero, which gives us no information about the spread. But if we consider the **modulus** of each of these deviations we have

$$200, \quad 100, \quad 0, \quad 100, \quad 200$$

Since the sum of these deviations is 600, the average deviation is $\frac{600}{5} = 120$.

This average deviation from the mean is one possible measure of the spread and is defined as follows:

The mean deviation from the mean of a set of n numbers, $(x_1, x_2, \ldots, x_n)$, is given by

$$\frac{\Sigma|x_i - \bar{x}|}{n} \quad \text{for} \quad i = 1, 2, \ldots, n$$

where $\bar{x}$ is the mean of the set of numbers.

NOTE ON MODULUS: We write $|x|$ to mean the magnitude or 'modulus' of x. We are interested only in the size of x and we can disregard its sign, so that $|-7| = 7$, $|24| = 24$, $|6 - 10| = 4$, and so on.

For the first set of numbers above, set (**a**)

$$7, \, 7, \, 7, \, 7, \, 7$$

$$\text{mean deviation} = 0$$

For set (**b**)

$$5, \, 6, \, 7, \, 8, \, 9$$

$$\Sigma|x - 7| = |-2| + |-1| + |0| + |1| + |2|$$
$$= 2 + 1 + 0 + 1 + 2$$
$$= 6$$

$$-2 \qquad 2$$
$$-1 \quad 1$$

| 5 | 6 | 7 | 8 | 9 |

$$\text{Therefore mean deviation} = \frac{\Sigma|x - 7|}{5}$$
$$= \frac{6}{5}$$
$$= 1.2$$

For set (**c**)

$$-193, \ -93, \ 7, \ 107, \ 207$$

$$\Sigma |x - 7| = |-200| + |-100| + |0| + |100| + |200|$$

$$= 200 + 100 + 0 + 100 + 200$$

$$= 600$$

Therefore mean deviation $= \dfrac{\Sigma |x - 7|}{5}$

$$= \frac{600}{5}$$

$$= 120$$

NOTE:

> For a frequency distribution
>
> mean deviation from the mean $= \dfrac{\Sigma |f_i(x_i - \bar{x})|}{\Sigma f_i}$ $\qquad i = 1, 2, \ldots, n$

The mean deviation from the mean is not used widely. A much more useful measure of spread is the **standard deviation**.

THE STANDARD DEVIATION, *s*

For each reading, the deviation from the mean, $x - \bar{x}$, is found. This deviation is then squared, $(x - \bar{x})^2$, so that all the values will be *positive*.

The average of these values is then calculated and finally the *positive* square root is taken to give the 'standard deviation'.

> The standard deviation of a set of n numbers, $x_1, x_2, \ldots, x_n$, with mean $\bar{x}$ is given by s, where
>
> $$s = \sqrt{\frac{\Sigma (x_i - \bar{x})^2}{n}} \qquad i = 1, 2, \ldots, n$$

For our three sets of numbers

(**a**) 7, 7, 7, 7, 7
Since $x - 7 = 0$ for every reading, $s = 0$

(**b**) 5, 6, 7, 8, 9

$$\Sigma (x - \bar{x})^2 = (5 - 7)^2 + (6 - 7)^2 + (7 - 7)^2 + (8 - 7)^2 + (9 - 7)^2$$

$$= 4 + 1 + 0 + 1 + 4$$

$$= 10$$

Therefore
$$s = \sqrt{\frac{\Sigma(x - \bar{x})^2}{n}}$$
$$= \sqrt{\frac{10}{5}}$$
$$= \sqrt{2}$$
$$= 1.41 \ (2 \text{ d.p.})$$

(c)
$$-193, \ -93, \ 7, \ 107, \ 207$$
$$\Sigma(x - \bar{x})^2 = (-193 - 7)^2 + (-93 - 7)^2 + (7 - 7)^2$$
$$+ (107 - 7)^2 + (207 - 7)^2$$
$$= 40\,000 + 10\,000 + 0 + 10\,000 + 40\,000$$
$$= 100\,000$$
$$s = \sqrt{\frac{\Sigma(x - \bar{x})^2}{n}}$$
$$= \sqrt{\frac{100\,000}{5}}$$
$$= 141.42 \ (2 \text{ d.p.})$$

IMPORTANT NOTES

(*i*) For most distributions, the bulk of the distribution lies within two standard deviations of the mean, i.e. within the interval $\bar{x} \pm 2s$ or $(\bar{x} - 2s, \bar{x} + 2s)$. This helps to give an idea of the spread of the data.

(*ii*) Remember that the units of standard deviation (sometimes written s.d.) are the same as the units of the original data.

(*iii*) For similar sets of data, it is useful to compare standard deviations.

Example 1.18 Two machines, A and B, are used to pack biscuits. A sample of 10 packets was taken from each machine and the mass of each packet, measured to the nearest gram, was noted. Find the standard deviation of the masses of the packets taken in the sample from each machine. Comment on your answer.

Machine A (mass in g)	196, 198, 198, 199, 200, 200, 201, 201, 202, 205
Machine B (mass in g)	192, 194, 195, 198, 200, 201, 203, 204, 206, 207

Solution 1.18 Machine A $\quad \bar{x} = \dfrac{\Sigma x}{n} = \dfrac{2000}{10} = 200$

Machine B $\quad \bar{x} = \dfrac{\Sigma x}{n} = \dfrac{2000}{10} = 200$

Since the mean mass for each machine is 200 g, we use $x - 200$ for $x - \bar{x}$.

To calculate s, we put the data into a table:

Machine A			Machine B		
x	$x - 200$	$(x - 200)^2$	x	$x - 200$	$(x - 200)^2$
196	-4	16	192	-8	64
198	-2	4	194	-6	36
198	-2	4	195	-5	25
199	-1	1	198	-2	4
200	0	0	200	0	0
200	0	0	201	1	1
201	1	1	203	3	9
201	1	1	204	4	16
202	2	4	206	6	36
205	5	25	207	7	49
		56			240

$$s^2 = \frac{\Sigma(x - 200)^2}{10}$$

$$= 5.6$$

$$s = \sqrt{5.6}$$

$$= 2.37 \quad \text{(2 d.p.)}$$

$$s^2 = \frac{\Sigma(x - 200)^2}{10}$$

$$= 24$$

$$s = \sqrt{24}$$

$$= 4.90 \quad \text{(2 d.p.)}$$

The standard deviation for machine A is 2.37 g and the standard deviation for machine B is 4.90 g, indicating that machine A is more reliable.

Alternative form of the formula for standard deviation

The formula given above is sometimes difficult to use, especially when $\bar{x}$ is not an integer, so an alternative form is often used. This is derived as follows:

$$s^2 = \frac{1}{n} \Sigma(x_i - \bar{x})^2 \qquad i = 1, 2, \ldots, n$$

$$= \frac{1}{n} \Sigma(x_i^2 - 2\bar{x}x_i + \bar{x}^2)$$

$$= \frac{1}{n}(\Sigma x_i^2 - 2\bar{x}\Sigma x_i + \Sigma\bar{x}^2)$$

$$= \frac{\Sigma x_i^2}{n} - 2\bar{x}\frac{\Sigma x_i}{n} + \frac{n\bar{x}^2}{n}$$

$$= \frac{\Sigma x_i^2}{n} - 2\bar{x}(\bar{x}) + \bar{x}^2 \qquad \text{since} \quad \frac{\Sigma x_i}{n} = \bar{x}$$

$$= \frac{\Sigma x_i^2}{n} - \bar{x}^2$$

So we have

$$s = \sqrt{\frac{\Sigma x_i^2}{n} - \bar{x}^2} \qquad i = 1, 2, \ldots, n$$

NOTE: it is useful to remember that $\dfrac{\Sigma x^2}{n} - \bar{x}^2$ can be thought of as 'the mean of the squares minus the square of the mean'.

Example 1.19   Find the mean and the standard deviation of the set of numbers

$$2, \ 3, \ 5, \ 6, \ 8$$

Solution 1.19

$$\bar{x} = \frac{\Sigma x}{n} = \frac{24}{5} = 4.8$$

Standard deviation:

Method 1

using $\quad s = \sqrt{\dfrac{\Sigma (x - \bar{x})^2}{n}}$

x	$x - \bar{x}$	$(x - \bar{x})^2$
2	-2.8	7.84
3	-1.8	3.24
5	0.2	0.04
6	1.2	1.44
8	3.2	10.24
		22.80

$$s^2 = \frac{22.80}{5}$$
$$= 4.56$$
$$s = \sqrt{4.56}$$
$$= 2.14 \quad (2 \text{ d.p.})$$

Method 2

using $\quad s = \sqrt{\dfrac{\Sigma x^2}{n} - \bar{x}^2}$

x	x^2
2	4
3	9
5	25
6	36
8	64
	138

$$s^2 = \frac{138}{5} - (4.8)^2$$
$$= 4.56$$
$$s = \sqrt{4.56}$$
$$= 2.14 \quad (2 \text{ d.p.})$$

Therefore the standard deviation of the set of numbers is 2.14 (2 d.p.).

NOTE: in this case there is far less working involved in Method 2.

THE VARIANCE

Dealing with the square root sign in calculating standard deviation can be very cumbersome, so we often consider the **variance**, where

$$\text{variance} = (\text{standard deviation})^2.$$

The **variance** of the set of numbers is given by s^2, where

$$s^2 = \frac{\Sigma(x_i - \bar{x})^2}{n} \qquad i = 1, 2, \ldots, n$$

The alternative form of the formula is $\quad s^2 = \dfrac{\Sigma x_i^{\,2}}{n} - \bar{x}^2$

So   standard deviation $= \sqrt{\text{variance}}$

In later work we will find that the variance is a very important quantity in its own right.

Exercise 1e

1. Find the mean and the standard deviation of the following sets of numbers. For questions (a), (b) and (c) try using both forms of the formula for the standard deviation. Use whichever you wish for parts (d), (e) and (f). *Do not use the programmed functions on your calculator.*

   (a) 2, 4, 5, 6, 8
   (b) 6, 8, 9, 11
   (c) 11, 14, 17, 23, 29
   (d) 5, 13, 7, 9, 16, 15
   (e) 4.6, 2.7, 3.1, 0.5, 6.2
   (f) 200, 203, 206, 207, 209

2. For the following sets of numbers find
   (i)   the mean deviation from the mean,
   (ii) the standard deviation.
   (a) 6, 10, 14, 18, 22
   (b) 13.8, 13.9, 14, 14.1, 14.2
   (c) 8.9, 7.2, 9.9, 9.8, 6.5
   (d) 0.4, 10.3, 12.7, 5.1, 13.8
   (e) 63.1, 63, 62.9, 62.9, 63
   (f) 5.4, 23.8, 75.9, 86.3, 123.5

3. The mean of the numbers 3, 6, 7, a, 14, is 8. Find the standard deviation of the set of numbers.

4. For a set of 10 numbers $\Sigma x = 290$ and $\Sigma x^2 = 8469$. Find the mean and the variance.

5. For a set of 9 numbers $\Sigma(x - \bar{x})^2 = 234$. Find the standard deviation of the numbers.

6. For a set of 9 numbers $\Sigma(x - \bar{x})^2 = 60$ and $\Sigma x^2 = 285$. Find the mean of the numbers.

7. The numbers a, b, 8, 5, 7 have mean 6 and variance 2. Find the values of a and b, if $a > b$.

8. Find the mean and the standard deviation of the set of integers 1, 2, 3, $\ldots$, 20.

9. Find the mean and the standard deviation of the first n integers.
   You may use

   $$\sum_{r=1}^{n} r = \tfrac{1}{2}n(n+1)$$

   $$\sum_{r=1}^{n} r^2 = \tfrac{1}{6}n(n+1)(2n+1)$$

10. From the information given about each of the following sets of data, work out the missing values in the table:

	n	Σx	Σx^2	$\bar{x}$	s
(a)	63	7623	924 800		
(b)		152.6		10.9	1.7
(c)	52		57 300	33	
(d)	18			57	4

11. Calculate the mean and the standard deviation of the four numbers

    2, 3, 6, 9

    Two numbers, a and b, are to be added to this set of four numbers, such that the mean is increased by 1 and the variance is increased by 2.5. Find a and b.

    (L Additional)

THE USE OF CALCULATORS

If your calculator has SD (standard deviation) mode then it can be used to calculate standard deviations, and you will have access to the following information: $\bar{x}$, s, n, Σx, Σx^2.

The following example has been done using three types of calculator, and you should consult your calculator instructions if yours does not appear to follow one of the patterns.

Example 1.20   Find the mean and standard deviation of the numbers

$$33, \ 28, \ 26, \ 35, \ 38$$

Solution 1.20

	Casio 85/100/115 series	Graphic: Casio 7000 GA
Set SD mode	MODE 3	MODE ×
Clear memories	SHIFT KAC	SHIFT SCI EXE
Input data	33 DATA	33 DT
	28 DATA	28 DT
	26 DATA	26 DT
	35 DATA	35 DT
	38 DATA	38 DT
To obtain		
$\bar{x} = 32$	SHIFT 1	SHIFT 1 EXE
$s = 4.427\ldots$	SHIFT 2	SHIFT 2 EXE
$n = 5$	K out 3	ALPHA 3 EXE
$\Sigma x = 160$	K out 2	ALPHA 2 EXE
$\Sigma x^2 = 5218$	K out 1	ALPHA 1 EXE
To clear SD mode	MODE 0	MODE +

NOTE: $\bar{x}$ and s are found directly, but it is sometimes useful to know Σx and Σx^2.

Therefore the mean is 32 and the standard deviation is 4.43 (2 d.p.)

Exercise 1f

Do Exercise 1e questions 1 and 2(ii) using your calculator in SD mode.

Standard deviation — data in the form of a frequency distribution

If $x_1, x_2, \ldots, x_n$ occur with frequencies $f_1, f_2, \ldots, f_n$ then the standard deviation s is given by:

$$s = \sqrt{\frac{\Sigma f_i(x_i - \bar{x})^2}{\Sigma f_i}} \qquad i = 1, 2, \ldots, n$$

The alternative form of the formula is

$$s = \sqrt{\frac{\Sigma f_i x_i^2}{\Sigma f_i} - \bar{x}^2} \qquad i = 1, 2, \ldots, n$$

For grouped data, the mid-point of an interval is taken to represent the interval.

Example 1.21 The table shows the number of children per family for a group of 20 families. The mean number of children per family is 2.9. Find the standard deviation.

Number of children per family, x	1	2	3	4	5
Frequency, f	3	4	8	2	3

Solution 1.21 **Method 1 — using** $\quad s = \sqrt{\dfrac{\Sigma f(x - \bar{x})^2}{\Sigma f}}$

x	$x - 2.9$	$(x - 2.9)^2$	f	$f(x - 2.9)^2$
1	-1.9	3.61	3	10.83
2	-0.9	0.81	4	3.24
3	0.1	0.01	8	0.08
4	1.1	1.21	2	2.42
5	2.1	4.41	3	13.23
			$\Sigma f = 20$	$\Sigma f(x - \bar{x})^2 = 29.80$

So
$$s^2 = \frac{\Sigma f(x - 2.9)^2}{\Sigma f}$$

$$= \frac{29.80}{20}$$

$$= 1.49$$

$$s = \sqrt{1.49}$$

$$= 1.22 \quad \text{(2 d.p.)}$$

The standard deviation of the number of children per family is 1.22 (2 d.p.).

Method 2 — using $\quad s = \sqrt{\dfrac{\Sigma f x^2}{\Sigma f} - \bar{x}^2}$

x	f	x^2	fx^2
1	3	1	3
2	4	4	16
3	8	9	72
4	2	16	32
5	3	25	75
	$\Sigma f = 20$		$\Sigma fx^2 = 198$

So
$$s^2 = \frac{\Sigma fx^2}{\Sigma f} - (2.9)^2$$
$$= \frac{198}{20} - (2.9)^2$$
$$= 1.49$$
$$s = \sqrt{1.49}$$
$$= 1.22 \quad (2 \text{ d.p.})$$

The standard deviation is 1.22 (2 d.p.), as before.

Method 3 — using the calculator in SD mode.

This time we need to take account of the frequencies, and this is done as follows:

	Casio 85/100/115 series				Graphic: Casio 7000 GA				
Set SD mode	MODE	3			MODE	×			
Clear memories	SHIFT	KAC			SHIFT	SCI	EXE		
Input data	1	×	3	DATA	1	SHIFT	;	3	DT
	2	×	4	DATA	2	SHIFT	;	4	DT
	3	×	8	DATA	3	SHIFT	;	8	DT
	4	×	2	DATA	4	SHIFT	;	2	DT
	5	×	3	DATA	5	SHIFT	;	3	DT
To obtain									
$\bar{x} = 2.9$	SHIFT	1			SHIFT	1	EXE		
$s = 1.220\ldots$	SHIFT	2			SHIFT	2	EXE		
$\Sigma f = 20$	K out	3			ALPHA	3	EXE		
$\Sigma fx = 58$	K out	2			ALPHA	2	EXE		
$\Sigma fx^2 = 198$	K out	1			ALPHA	1	EXE		
To clear SD mode	MODE	0			MODE	+			

Therefore the standard deviation is 1.22 (2 d.p.), as before.

Example 1.22 The lengths of 32 leaves were measured correct to the nearest mm.
Find the mean length and the standard deviation.

Length (mm)	20–22	23–25	26–28	29–31	32–34
Frequency	3	6	12	9	2

Solution 1.22 The mid-points, x, of each interval are considered:

Length (mm)	Mid-point, x	x^2	f	fx	fx^2
20–22	21	441	3	63	1323
23–25	24	576	6	144	3456
26–28	27	729	12	324	8748
29–31	30	900	9	270	8100
32–34	33	1089	2	66	2178
			$\Sigma f = 32$	$\Sigma fx = 867$	$\Sigma fx^2 = 23\,805$

Now
$$\bar{x} = \frac{\Sigma fx}{\Sigma f} = \frac{867}{32} = 27.1 \quad \text{(1 d.p.)}$$

and
$$s^2 = \frac{\Sigma fx^2}{\Sigma f} - \bar{x}^2 = \frac{23\,805}{32} - \left(\frac{867}{32}\right)^2 = 9.835$$

$$s = \sqrt{9.835} = 3.14 \quad \text{(2 d.p.)}$$

The mean length of the leaves is 27.1 mm and the standard
deviation is 3.14 mm (2 d.p.).

Now check this example using your calculator in SD mode.

Exercise 1g

Do questions 1, 2 and 3 without using the calculator
in SD mode, and then check them using SD mode.

1. The score for a round of golf for each of 50
   club members was noted. Find the mean
   score for a round and the standard deviation.

Score, x	Frequency, f
66	2
67	5
68	10
69	12
70	9
71	6
72	4
73	2

2. The scores in an IQ test for 60 candidates are
   shown in the table. Find the mean score and
   the standard deviation.

Score	Frequency
100–106	8
107–113	13
114–120	24
121–127	11
128–134	4

3. Find the mean and the standard deviation for
   each of the following sets of data:

(a)

x	1	2	3	4	5	6
f	2	6	11	15	8	3

(b)

Interval	Frequency
1–3	2
4–6	4
7–9	8
10–12	5
13–15	1

(c)

Interval	Frequency
20–24	1
25–29	6
30–34	10
35–39	2
40–44	1

(d)

x	10	20	30	40	50	60
f	3	9	14	10	6	4

(e)

Interval	Frequency
1–7	4
8–14	5
15–21	10
22–28	6

(f)

x	7	8	9	10	11	12	13
f	1	3	5	7	5	3	1

4. For a particular set of observations $\Sigma f = 20$, $\Sigma fx^2 = 16\,143$, $\Sigma fx = 563$. Find the values of the mean and the standard deviation.

5. For a given frequency distribution $\Sigma f(x - \bar{x})^2 = 182.3$, $\Sigma fx^2 = 1025$, $\Sigma f = 30$. Find Σfx.

6. From the information given about each of the following frequency distributions, work out the missing values in the table:

	Σf	Σfx	Σfx^2	$\Sigma f(x - \bar{x})^2$	$\bar{x}$	s
(a)	20	563	16 143			
(b)		270		160	27	
(c)	50				10	3
(d)	30		1025	182.3		
(e)		240	5100		20	

CALCULATIONS INVOLVING THE MEAN AND THE STANDARD DEVIATION

Example 1.23   For the set of numbers   3, 6, 7, 9, 10   the mean is 7 and the standard deviation is $\sqrt{6}$. If each number in the set is increased by 3, find the new mean and standard deviation. Comment on your answers.

Solution 1.23   The new set of numbers is   6, 9, 10, 12, 13.

$$\text{The mean} = \frac{\Sigma x}{n}$$

$$= \frac{(6 + 9 + 10 + 12 + 13)}{5}$$

$$= 10$$

Now $s^2 = \dfrac{\Sigma(x - \bar{x})^2}{n}$ where $\bar{x} = 10$

x	$(x - \bar{x})$	$(x - \bar{x})^2$
6	−4	16
9	−1	1
10	0	0
12	2	4
13	3	9
	$\Sigma(x - \bar{x})^2 = 30$	

So $s^2 = \dfrac{30}{5}$

$= 6$

and $s = \sqrt{6}$

Therefore, if each member of the set of numbers is increased by 3, then the mean is increased by 3 but the standard deviation remains unaltered.

In general, consider the set of n numbers $x_1, x_2, \ldots, x_n$ with mean $\bar{x}$ and standard deviation s_1.

(i) Increase each number by a constant, c

For the new set of numbers, $y_i = x_i + c$ for $i = 1, 2, \ldots, n$.

$$y_1 = x_1 + c$$

$$y_2 = x_2 + c$$

$$\vdots$$

$$y_n = x_n + c$$

Summing

$$\Sigma y_i = \Sigma x_i + nc$$

and

$$\frac{\Sigma y_i}{n} = \frac{\Sigma x_i}{n} + c$$

So

$$\bar{y} = \bar{x} + c$$

Also

$$s_2{}^2 = \frac{\Sigma (y_i - \bar{y})^2}{n}$$

$$= \frac{\Sigma [x_i + c - (\bar{x} + c)]^2}{n}$$

$$= \frac{\Sigma (x_i - \bar{x})^2}{n} = s_1{}^2$$

$$s_2 = s_1$$

If each number is increased by a constant c,

(a) the mean is increased by c,

(b) the standard deviation remains unaltered.

(ii) Multiply each number by a constant k

For the new set of numbers, $y_i = k x_i$ for $i = 1, 2, \ldots, n$

Summing

$$\Sigma y_i = \Sigma k x_i$$

$$= k \Sigma x_i$$

$$\frac{\Sigma y_i}{n} = k \frac{\Sigma x_i}{n}$$

So

$$\bar{y} = k \bar{x}$$

Also

$$s_2{}^2 = \frac{\Sigma (y_i - \bar{y})^2}{n}$$

$$= \frac{\Sigma (k x_i - k \bar{x})^2}{n}$$

$$= k^2 \frac{\Sigma (x_i - \bar{x})^2}{n} = k^2 s_1{}^2$$

$$s_2 = k s_1$$

> If each number is multiplied by a constant k,
> (a) the mean is multiplied by k,
> (b) the standard deviation is multiplied by k.

Example 1.24 A set of values of a variable x has mean 6 and standard deviation 2. Values of a new variable y are obtained using the formula $y = 4x - 3$. Find the mean and standard deviation of the new set of values.

Solution 1.24 We are given that $\bar{x} = 6$, $s_x = 2$ (using s_x to represent the standard deviation of the x variable).

Now
$$y = 4x - 3$$

Therefore
$$\bar{y} = 4\bar{x} - 3$$
$$= 4(6) - 3$$
$$= 21$$

and
$$s_y = 4s_x$$
$$= 4(2)$$
$$= 8$$

The new mean is 21 and the new standard deviation is 8.

Scaling similar sets of data for comparison

If we wish to compare two sets of data, for example examination marks in two papers, we can 'scale' one of the sets of data so that the two means are the same and the two standard deviations are the same.

Example 1.25 A set of marks (x) has mean 40 and standard deviation 5. The marks are to be scaled to a set (y) so that the mean becomes 50 and the standard deviation becomes 8. If the equation of the transformation is $y = ax + b$, find the values of the constants a and b. Find also the scaled mark which corresponds to a mark of 45 in the original set.

Solution 1.25 If there are n marks, then $y_i = ax_i + b$ for each $i = 1, 2, \ldots, n$.

Now
$$\bar{y} = a\bar{x} + b$$

so
$$50 = a(40) + b \qquad\qquad 40a + b = 50 \quad \text{(i)}$$

Also
$$s_y = a\, s_x$$

so
$$8 = 5a \qquad\qquad\qquad\qquad a = \tfrac{8}{5} \quad \text{(ii)}$$

Substituting for a from (ii) into (i),

$$40\left(\tfrac{8}{5}\right) + b = 50$$

$$b = -14$$

Therefore the equation of the transformation is $y = \tfrac{8}{5}x - 14$.

If $x = 45$, then $y = \tfrac{8}{5}(45) - 14 = 58$.

Therefore a mark of 45 in the original set becomes a mark of 58 when scaled.

Exercise 1h

1. (a) Find the mean and the standard deviation of the set of numbers 4, 6, 9, 3, 5, 6, 9.
   (b) Deduce the mean and the standard deviation of the set of numbers 514, 516, 519, 513, 515, 516, 519.
   (c) Deduce the mean and the standard deviation of the set of numbers 52, 78, 117, 39, 65, 78, 117.

2. (a) Find the mean and the variance of the ordered set of numbers

   $$A = \{1, 2, 3, 4, 5, 6, 7\}.$$

   Hence find the mean and the variance of the following ordered sets

   $$B = \{4, 5, 6, 7, 8, 9, 10\}$$

   $$C = \{10, 20, 30, 40, 50, 60, 70\}$$

   $$D = \{13, 23, 33, 43, 53, 63, 73\}$$

3. It is proposed to convert a set of marks whose mean is 52 and standard deviation is 4 to a set of marks with mean 61 and standard deviation 3. The equation for the transformation necessary to convert the marks is $y = ax + b$. Find
   (i) the values of a and b,
   (ii) the value of the scaled mark which corresponds to a mark of 64 in the original data,
   (iii) the value in the original data if the scaled mark is 79.

4. The marks of 5 students in a mathematics test were 27, 31, 35, 47, 50.
   (i) Calculate the mean mark and the standard deviation.
   (ii) The marks are scaled so that the mean and standard deviation become 50 and 20 respectively. Calculate, to the nearest whole number, the new marks corresponding to the original marks of 31 and 50.   (C Additional)

5. In order to compare the performances of candidates in two schools a test was given. The mean mark at school A was 45, and the mean mark at school B was 31 with a standard deviation of 5. The marks of school A are scaled so that the mean and standard deviation are the same as school B and a mark of 85 at school A becomes 63. Find the values of a and b if the transformation used is $y = ax + b$. Find also the original standard deviation of the marks from school A.

6. Given that the mean and standard deviation of a set of figures are μ and σ respectively, write down the new values of the mean and standard deviation when
   (i) each figure is increased by a constant c,
   (ii) each figure is multiplied by a constant k.
   A group of students sat two examinations, one in algebra and one in biology. In order to compare the results the algebra marks were scaled linearly (that is, a mark of x became a mark of $ax + b$ where a and b are constants) so that the means and standard deviations of the marks in both examinations became the same. The original means and standard deviations are shown in the table.

	Algebra	Biology
Mean mark	48	62
Standard deviation	12	10

   Find a and b.
   The original marks of a particular student are 36 in algebra, 48 in biology. In what sense, if any, has he done better in algebra than in biology?   (C Additional)

7. A linear function $f(x) = ax + b$ transforms

$$X = \{1, 2, 3, 5, 8, 11\}$$

into a set Y, so that $f(5) = 13$ and $f(1) = 5$.
(a) Find f.
(b) Calculate the mean and the variance of X.
(c) Hence calculate the mean and the variance of Y.
An element, k, is added to X forming a set Z. Given that the mean of Z is three greater than the mean of X, find
(d) the value of k,
(e) the variance of Z.   (L Additional)

8. Show that the standard deviation of the integers

$$1, 2, 3, 4, 5, 6, 7$$

is 2.
Using this result find the standard deviation of the numbers
(a) 101, 102, 103, 104, 105, 106, 107.
(b) 100, 200, 300, 400, 500, 600, 700.
(c) 2.01, 3.02, 4.03, 5.04, 6.05, 7.06, 8.07.
(d) Write down seven integers which have mean 5 and standard deviation 6.
                    (L Additional)

9. (a) A set of numbers has a mean of 22 and a standard deviation of 6. If 3 is added to each number of the set, and each resulting number is then doubled, find the mean and standard deviation of the new set.
(b) A group of 20 people played a game. The table below shows the frequency distribution of their scores.

Score	1	2	4	x
Number of people	2	5	7	6

Given that the mean score is 5, find
(i) the value of x,
(ii) the variance of the distribution.
(c) The mean of the marks scored by candidates in an examination is 45. These marks are scaled linearly to give a mean of 50 and a standard deviation of 15. Given that the scaled mark of 80 corresponds to an original mark of 70, calculate
(i) the standard deviation of the original marks,
(ii) the mark which is unchanged by the scaling.
Given that the greatest and least scaled marks are 92 and 2 respectively, calculate the corresponding original marks.
                    (C Additional)

Using a method of 'coding' to find the mean and standard deviation

In general, if the set of numbers $x_1, x_2, \ldots, x_n$ is transformed to the set of numbers $y_1, y_2, \ldots, y_n$ by means of the coding

$$y = \frac{x - a}{b}$$

then

$$x = a + by$$

so

$$\bar{x} = a + b\bar{y}$$

and

$$s_x = b\, s_y$$

This method of coding is particularly useful when the data is in the form of a frequency distribution and the intervals are of equal width.

For data grouped into classes of equal width:

(a) use the mid-point of each interval to represent the class,

(b) choose a central value for a (this is sometimes known as an **assumed mean**),

(c) divide by the class width, b.

Example 1.26 The lengths of 32 leaves were measured correct to the nearest mm. Find the mean length and the standard deviation, using a method of coding.

Length (mm)	20–22	23–25	26–28	29–31	32–34
Frequency	3	6	12	9	2

NOTE: these are the data used in Example 1.22.

Solution 1.26 We note that the class widths are each equal to 3 and a central value is 27. Therefore, we choose the coding $y = \dfrac{x - 27}{3}$ in order to make calculations easier.

If
$$y = \frac{x - 27}{3}$$

then
$$3y = x - 27$$

so
$$x = 3y + 27$$

and
$$\bar{x} = 3\bar{y} + 27$$

$$s_x = 3s_y$$

Length (mm)	Mid-point, x	f	$y = \dfrac{x - 27}{3}$	y^2	fy	fy^2
20–22	21	3	−2	4	−6	12
23–25	24	6	−1	1	−6	6
26–28	27	12	0	0	0	0
29–31	30	9	1	1	9	9
32–34	33	2	2	4	4	8
		$\Sigma f = 32$			$\Sigma fy = 1$	$\Sigma fy^2 = 35$

Now
$$\bar{y} = \frac{\Sigma fy}{\Sigma f}$$
$$= \frac{1}{32}$$

Therefore
$$\bar{x} = 3\bar{y} + 27$$
$$= 3\left(\frac{1}{32}\right) + 27$$
$$= 27.1 \text{ (1 d.p.)}$$

$$s_y{}^2 = \frac{\Sigma fy^2}{\Sigma f} - \bar{y}^2$$
$$= \frac{35}{32} - \left(\frac{1}{32}\right)^2$$
$$= 1.092\ldots$$
$$s_y = 1.045\ldots$$

Therefore
$$s_x = 3(1.045\ldots)$$
$$= 3.14 \text{ (2 d.p.)}$$

The mean length is 27.1 cm (1 d.p.) and the standard deviation is 3.14 cm (2 d.p.).

Example 1.27 Salt is packed in bags which the manufacturer claims contain 25 kg each. Eighty bags are examined and the mass, x kg, of each is found. The results are $\Sigma(x - 25) = 27.2$, $\Sigma(x - 25)^2 = 85.1$. Find the mean and the standard deviation of the masses.

Solution 1.27 We do not know the actual masses and a coding has been used to summarise the results. The coding is $y = x - 25$.

Now $\Sigma y = 27.2$ and $\Sigma y^2 = 85.1$

Therefore
$$\bar{y} = \frac{\Sigma y}{n} \qquad\qquad s_y{}^2 = \frac{\Sigma y^2}{n} - \bar{y}^2$$
$$= \frac{27.2}{80} \qquad\qquad = \frac{85.1}{80} - 0.34^2$$
$$= 0.34 \qquad\qquad = 0.948\,15$$
$$s_y = 0.973\,7\ldots$$

Now if $y = x - 25$, then $x = y + 25$
$$\bar{x} = \bar{y} + 25$$
and $s_x = s_y$

Therefore
$$\bar{x} = 0.34 + 25$$
$$= 25.34$$
and
$$s_x = 0.9737\ldots$$

The mean mass is 25.34 kg and the standard deviation is 0.97 kg (2 d.p.).

Exercise 1i

1. Find the mean and the standard deviation of the following sets of data, using a method of coding:

(a)

x	f
304	1
308	5
312	9
316	4
320	4
324	2

(b)

Interval	f
10–19	3
20–29	7
30–39	12
40–49	18
50–59	12
60–69	6

(c)

x	f
1250	5
1500	19
1750	27
2000	35
2250	24
2500	12
2750	3

(d)

Interval	f
0–	5
5–	10
10–	13
15–	18
20–	12
25–	6
30–	6
35–	0

(e)

x	f
0.1	4
0.4	6
0.7	12
1.0	15
1.3	9
1.6	6
1.9	5
2.2	1

(f)

Interval	f
−200	0
−250	20
−300	33
−350	35
−400	25
−450	14
−600	3

2. The table shows the times taken on 30 consecutive days for a coach to complete one journey on a particular route. Times have been given to the nearest minute. Find the mean time for the journey and the standard deviation, using a method of coding.

Time (min)	Frequency
60–63	1
64–67	3
68–71	12
72–75	10
76–79	4

3. In a practical class students timed how long it took for a sample of their saliva to break down a 2% starch solution. The times, to the nearest second are shown in the table below. Find the mean time, using a method of coding.

Time (seconds)	Frequency
11–20	1
21–30	2
31–40	5
41–50	11
51–60	8
61–70	2
71–90	1

4. Each morning for a month the owner of a smallholding timed how long it took to feed the animals. The results were as shown:

Time (min)	Frequency
−15	0
−20	3
−25	2
−30	6
−35	10
−40	7
−45	2
−50	1

Calculate the mean time taken to feed the animals, using a method of coding.

5. For a particular set of data
$$n = 100, \qquad \Sigma(x - 50) = 123.5,$$
$$\Sigma(x - 50)^2 = 238.4$$
Find the mean and the standard deviation of x.

6. Find the variance of x if
$$\Sigma f(x - 100) = 127, \qquad \Sigma f(x - 100)^2 = 2593,$$
$$\Sigma f = 20$$

Combining sets of numbers

Example 1.28   A set of 12 numbers has mean 4 and standard deviation 2. A second set of 20 numbers has mean 5 and standard deviation 3.

Find the mean and the standard deviation of the combined set of 32 numbers.

Solution 1.28   For the first set of numbers, x,

$$n_1 = 12, \qquad \bar{x} = 4, \qquad s_x = 2$$

Therefore $\Sigma x = n_1 \bar{x} = 12(4) = 48$

and $s_x{}^2 = \dfrac{\Sigma x^2}{n_1} - \bar{x}^2$

so $\Sigma x^2 = n_1(s_x{}^2 + \bar{x}^2)$

$$= 12(2^2 + 4^2)$$

$$= 240$$

For the second set of numbers, y,

$$n_2 = 20, \qquad \bar{y} = 5, \qquad s_y = 3$$

$$\Sigma y = n_2 \bar{y} = 20(5) = 100$$

and $$\Sigma y^2 = n_2(s_y^2 + \bar{y}^2)$$

$$= 20(3^2 + 5^2)$$

$$= 680$$

To find the mean of the combined set of numbers:

$$\text{mean} = \frac{\Sigma x + \Sigma y}{n_1 + n_2} = \frac{48 + 100}{32} = 4.625$$

To find the standard deviation of the combined set of numbers:

$$\Sigma x^2 + \Sigma y^2 = 240 + 680 = 920$$

so $$s^2 = \frac{\Sigma x^2 + \Sigma y^2}{n_1 + n_2} - (\text{mean})^2$$

$$= \frac{920}{32} - (4.625)^2$$

$$= 7.359$$

Therefore the variance of the combined set of numbers is 7.359.

To find the standard deviation:

$$s = \sqrt{\text{variance}}$$

$$= \sqrt{7.359}$$

$$= 2.71 \quad (2 \text{ d.p.})$$

Therefore the mean of the combined set of numbers is 4.625 and the standard deviation is 2.71 (2 d.p.).

NOTE: In general, for a combined set of numbers

$$\text{mean} = \frac{\Sigma x + \Sigma y}{n_1 + n_2}$$

$$\text{variance} = \frac{\Sigma x^2 + \Sigma y^2}{n_1 + n_2} - (\text{mean})^2$$

Remember that

$$\text{standard deviation} = \sqrt{\text{variance}}.$$

Exercise 1j

1. For each of the following sets of data, find the mean and the standard deviation of the combined set.

   (a) $n_1 = 12$, $\bar{x}_1 = 6$, $s_1 = 2$
   $n_2 = 8$, $\bar{x}_2 = 10$, $s_2 = 3$

   (b) $n_1 = 30$, $\bar{x}_1 = 27$, $s_1 = 5.6$
   $n_2 = 40$, $\bar{x}_2 = 33$, $s_2 = 6.4$

   (c) $n_1 = 12$, $\bar{x}_1 = 15$, $s_1 = 2.7$
   $n_2 = 15$, $\bar{x}_2 = 14$, $s_2 = 3.1$
   $n_3 = 13$, $\bar{x}_3 = 12$, $s_3 = 2.4$

2. For a set of 20 numbers $\Sigma x = 300$ and $\Sigma x^2 = 5500$. For a second set of 30 numbers $\Sigma x = 480$ and $\Sigma x^2 = 9600$. Find the mean and the standard deviation of the combined set of 50 numbers.

3. Suppose that the values of a random sample taken from some population are $x_1, x_2, \ldots, x_n$. Prove the formula

$$\sum_{i=1}^{n} (x_i - \bar{x})^2 = \sum_{i=1}^{n} x_i^2 - n\bar{x}^2$$

   Parplan Opinion Polls Ltd conducted a nationwide survey into the attitudes of teenage girls. One of the questions asked was 'What is the ideal age for a girl to have her first baby?' In reply, the sample of 165 girls from the Northern zone gave a mean of 23.4 years and a standard deviation of 1.6 years. Subsequently, the overall sample of 384 girls (Northern plus Southern zones) gave a mean of 24.8 years and a standard deviation of 2.2 years.
   Assuming that no girl was consulted twice, calcualte the mean and standard deviation for the 219 girls from the Southern zone.

(AEB)

4. The manager of a car showroom monitored the numbers of cars sold during two successive five-day periods. During the first five days the numbers of cars sold per day had mean 1.8 and variance 0.56. During the next five days the numbers of cars sold per day had mean 2.8 and variance 1.76. Find the mean and variance of the numbers of cars sold per day during the full ten days.   (JMB)

5. Prior to the start of delicate wage negotiations in a large company, the unions and the management take independent samples of the work force and ask them at what percentage level they believe a settlement should be made. The results are as follows:

Sample	Size	Mean	Standard deviation
'management'	350	12.4%	2.1%
'union'	237	10.7%	1.8%

Assuming that no individual was consulted by both sides, calculate the mean and standard deviation for these 587 workers.

(AEB) P

6. The number of errors, x, on each of 200 pages of typescript was monitored. The results when summarised showed that

$$\Sigma x = 920 \qquad \Sigma x^2 = 5032.$$

(a) Calculate the mean and the standard deviation of the number of errors per page. A further 50 pages was monitored and it was found that the mean was 4.4 errors and the standard deviation was 2.2 errors.
(b) Find the mean and the standard deviation of the number of errors per page for the 250 pages.   (L)

7. The sum of 20 numbers is 320 and the sum of their squares is 5840. Calculate the mean of the 20 numbers and the standard deviation.
(i) Another number is added to these 20 so that the mean is unchanged. Show that the standard deviation is decreased.
(ii) Another set of 10 numbers is such that their sum is 130 and the sum of their squares is 2380. This set is combined with the original 20 numbers. Calculate the mean and the standard deviation of all 30 numbers.

8. In a germination experiment, two hundred rows of seeds, with ten seeds per row, were incubated. The frequency distribution of the number of seeds which germinated per row is shown below.

Number of seeds germinated	Frequency
0	4
1	10
2	16
3	28
4	34
5	44
6	32
7	16
8	10
9	6
10	0

(a) Calculate the mean and the standard deviation of the number of seeds germinating per row.

For another fifty rows an analysis shows that the mean is 4.4 seeds and the standard deviation is 2.2 seeds.

(*b*) Determine the mean and, to 2 decimal places, the standard deviation for the two hundred and fifty rows. (L)

9. An examination is taken by two sets of candidates from the same school. The number of candidates in each set, the mean marks and the variances are shown below.

	Number of candidates	Mean mark	Variance
Set *A*	20	66	9
Set *B*	30	51	39

Calculate the mean mark for all 50 candidates and show that the standard deviation of all 50 marks is 9.

It is suggested that the original marks of the candidates from Set *A* should be linearly scaled so that their scaled marks would have a standard deviation of 9 and a mean mark equal to the mean mark of all 50 candidates.

(i) What effect would this have on an original mark of 60 obtained by a candidate from Set *A*?

(ii) Given that the original marks of the candidates in Set *A* were all integers, explain why no mark would remain unchanged.

(C Additional)

10. The figures in the table below are the ages, to the nearest year, of a random sample of 30 people negotiating a mortgage with a bank.

29	26	31	42	38
45	35	37	38	38
36	39	49	40	32
32	34	27	61	29
33	31	33	52	44
32	30	38	42	33

Copy and complete the following stem and leaf diagram. Use the diagram to identify *two* features of the shape of the distribution.

25	4 1
30	1
35	

Find the mean age of the 30 people. Given that 18 of them are men and that the mean age of the men is 37.72, find the mean age of the 12 women. (MEI)

WEIGHTED MEANS

In some situations it may not be suitable to calculate an ordinary mean. There may be times when we wish to place greater emphasis on some of the values, as illustrated in the following example.

Example 1.29 A candidate obtained the following results in her GCSE mathematics examination:

Paper 1: 72%,   Paper 2: 64%,   Coursework: 73%

The regulations state that the two written papers have equal weighting and count for 80% of the final result, whereas the coursework counts for 20%. What was the candidate's final mark?

Solution 1.29 Now the results are in the following ratio:

$$40\% : 40\% : 20\% = 4 : 4 : 2 = 2 : 2 : 1.$$

For the final result, we have to take this weighting into account:

$$\text{weighted mean} = \frac{2(72) + 2(64) + 1(73)}{2 + 2 + 1}$$

$$= \frac{345}{5}$$

$$= 69$$

Therefore the final mark is 69%.

In general, if $x_1, x_2, \ldots, x_n$ are given weightings $w_1, w_2, \ldots, w_n$ then

$$\text{weighted mean} = \frac{w_1 x_1 + w_2 x_2 + \ldots + w_n x_n}{w_1 + w_2 + \ldots + w_n}$$

$$= \frac{\sum w_i x_i}{\sum w_i} \quad \text{for} \quad i = 1, 2, \ldots, n$$

Exercise 1k

1. Find the weighted mean of the numbers 8 and 12, if they are given the weights 2 and 3 respectively.

2. The final mark allocated to a student is calculated from her mark in each subject.
   (a) The class teacher worked out an ordinary mean.
   (b) The headteacher decided to weight the subjects in proportion to the number of lessons per week, as shown in the table.

Subject	Mark	Number of lessons per week
Mathematics	64%	5
English	52%	4
Science	71%	6
French	75%	3
History	82%	2

Which method gave the higher mark and by how much?

3. The prices of articles A, B and C are £30, £42 and £65. Find the mean price, if the three articles are given weights of 5, 3 and 2 respectively.

4. The weighted mean of the two numbers 30 and 15 is 20. If the weightings are 2 and x respectively, find x.

5. Two students, Jack and Jill, take an examination in French, German and English. The table below shows the marks for each student and the weight to be applied to each subject.

Subject	French	German	English
Marks for Jack	80	72	46
Marks for Jill	64	82	40
Weight	2	x	3

Calculate the value of x for which Jack and Jill have the same weighted mean mark and find the value of this mean.   (C Additional)

INDEX NUMBERS

Sometimes we wish to *compare quantities*, for example the price of a sliced loaf in 1992 and the price in 1994. A very useful way of doing this is to express one quantity as a percentage of the other, in the form of an **index number**.

The simplest example of an index number is a **price relative**, or **price index**.

First of all, a **base year** is chosen. This is the year on which the price changes are based. If we denote the price in the base year as p_0, and the price in the year to be compared as p_1, then

$$\text{price relative (or price index)} = \frac{p_1}{p_0}$$

It is usual to give the price relative as a percentage, but *the percentage sign is always omitted* in the final answer.

Example 1.30   In January 1992, the price of a sliced loaf was 42 p. In January 1994, the price was 63 p. Taking 1992 as the base year, find the price relative.

Solution 1.30

$$\text{Price relative} = \frac{\text{price in 1994}}{\text{price in 1992}}$$

$$= \frac{p_{94}}{p_{92}} \qquad \text{(This is useful notation)}$$

$$= \frac{63}{42}$$

$$= 1.5$$

$$= 150\%$$

But we omit the % sign in the answer, so price relative = 150.

This indicates that the price of a sliced loaf increased by 50% between 1992 and 1994.

Sometimes we calculate the total price of a group of items as a ratio of the total price of the same group of items in the base year, to give the simple aggregate price index.

$$\text{Simple aggregate price index} = \frac{\Sigma p_1}{\Sigma p_0}$$

Example 1.31   The table shows the price, in pence, of flour and eggs in 1980 and 1990.

	1980	1990
Flour (1 kg)	30	54
Eggs (1 dozen)	50	78

Taking 1980 as the base year, find

(**a**) the price index of a kg of flour,

(**b**) the price index of one dozen eggs,

(**c**) the simple aggregate price index for the total cost of one kg of flour and one dozen eggs.

Solution 1.31   (**a**)

$$\text{price index (flour)} = \frac{p_{90}}{p_{80}} = \frac{54}{30} = 1.8 = 180\%$$

Therefore price index (flour) = 180.   (omit % sign)

(**b**)

$$\text{price index (eggs)} = \frac{p_{90}}{p_{80}} = \frac{78}{50} = 1.56 = 156\%$$

Therefore price index (eggs) = 156.   (omit % sign)

(c)   Total cost (1990) $= 54 + 78 = 132$ pence.

Total cost (1980) $= 30 + 50 = 80$ pence.

Aggregate price index $= \frac{132}{80} = 1.65 = 165\%$

Therefore aggregate price index $= 165$.

(omit % sign)

Example 1.32 The 1994 price index for a pair of shoes was 120 taking 1990 as base year. Calculate the 1990 index, referred to 1994 as base.

Solution 1.32   price index $= \dfrac{p_{94}}{p_{90}} = 120\%$ (Remember to use % sign)

$$= 1.2$$

Therefore, referred to 1994 as base,

$$\text{price index} = \frac{p_{90}}{p_{94}} = \frac{1}{1.2} = 0.833\ldots$$

$$= 83.3\%$$

Therefore, price index $= 83.3$.

NOTE: when we are given the number, such as 120, referring to a price index, we must remember that the % sign is understood. We must use 120%, or 1.2, in the calculation.

Example 1.33 The price of an article in 1990 was £30. The index number for the price of this article in 1980 was 160, based on 1970. In 1990 it was 75, based on 1980. Calculate

(a) the index number in 1990, based on 1970,

(b) the prices of the article in 1970 and 1980.

Solution 1.33 (a) $\dfrac{p_{80}}{p_{70}} = 160\% = 1.6$

and $\dfrac{p_{90}}{p_{80}} = 75\% = 0.75$

$\therefore$ $\dfrac{p_{90}}{p_{70}} = \dfrac{p_{90}}{p_{80}} \times \dfrac{p_{80}}{p_{70}}$

$$= 0.75 \times 1.6$$

$$= 1.2$$

$$= 120\%$$

Therefore index number in 1990, based on 1970, is 120.

(b) $$\frac{p_{90}}{p_{70}} = 1.2 \quad \text{and} \quad p_{90} = £30$$

Therefore $$p_{70} = \frac{£30}{1.2} = £25$$

Also $$\frac{p_{90}}{p_{80}} = 0.75, \quad \text{therefore} \quad p_{80} = \frac{£30}{0.75} = £40$$

The prices are 1970: £25   1980: £40   1990: £30.

Example 1.34 In 1987, the prices of A, B and C were $72\,$p, $83\,$p and $95\,$p. Given that the prices in 1993 were $86\,$p, $94\,$p and $x\,$p, and that the simple aggregate price index was 140, find x.

Solution 1.34 Simple aggregate price index $= \dfrac{\Sigma p_1}{\Sigma p_0} = 140\%$

Therefore $$\frac{86 + 94 + x}{72 + 83 + 95} = 1.4$$

$$180 + x = 1.4\,(250)$$

$$x = 170 \quad \text{(pence)}$$

The price of C in 1993 was £1.70.

Weighted price index

For a price index to be realistic, it should take into account the relative importance of the commodities. The method of 'weighting' allows this to be done.

Suppose, for example, we know that in consumer expenditure, food is twice as important as housing, which in turn is twice as important as transport. Then we can give weights 4, 2 and 1 to the three commodities.

In general:

$$\text{weighted price index} = \frac{\Sigma\left(\dfrac{p_1}{p_0}\right)w}{\Sigma w}$$

NOTE: the weighted price index is sometimes referred to as the **composite index**.

Example 1.35 Calculate a weighted price index for the following figures for 1994 based on 1990.

Item	1990 price (£)	1994 price (£)	Weight, w
Food	55	60	4
Housing	48	52	2
Transport	16	20	1

Solution 1.35   Weighted price index $= \dfrac{\Sigma \left(\dfrac{p_{94}}{p_{90}}\right) w}{\Sigma w}$

$$= \frac{\frac{60}{55} \times 4 + \frac{52}{48} \times 2 + \frac{20}{16} \times 1}{7}$$

$$= \frac{7.780\ldots}{7}$$

$$= 1.111\ldots$$

$$= 111\% \quad \text{(nearest integer)}$$

Weighted price index $= 111$ (nearest integer).

Example 1.36 Calculate, to the nearest integer, the weighted price index from the following table of price relatives and weights:

	Price relative	Weight
Food	118	40
Rent	102	8
Clothing	114	12
Fuel	120	10
Miscellaneous	110	30

Solution 1.36 Weighted price index

$$= \frac{118(40) + 102(8) + 114(12) + 120(10) + 110(30)}{40 + 8 + 12 + 10 + 30}$$

$$= \frac{11\,404}{100}$$

$$= 114.04$$

Therefore weighted price index $= 114$ (nearest integer).

Example 1.37 The table below lists seven categories of household expenditure and records the value of the price index in 1988 for each of the first six, taking 1986 as base year. The weights assigned to the seven categories for calculating a weighted index are also given.

Expenditure category	1988 Price index (1986 = 100%)	Weight
Food	106.7	163
Catering	113.4	50
Alcoholic drink	109.4	78
Tobacco	106.6	36
Housing	118.3	160
Fuel and light	101.6	55
Clothing and footwear		72

Source: *Social Trends 1990*

(*i*) The price index for clothing and footwear rose by 1.8% between 1986 and 1987 and by 3.3% between 1987 and 1988. Show that the 1988 price index, based on 1986, is 105.2, correct to one decimal place.

(*ii*) Calculate a weighted price index for these seven categories of expenditure.

(*iii*) A household's weekly expenditure on these seven categories in 1986 was approximately £115. Estimate the weekly expenditure on these categories for a similar household in 1988, giving your answer correct to the nearest £5. (JMB)

Solution 1.37 (*i*)

$$\frac{p_{87}}{p_{86}} = 101.8\% = 1.018$$

and

$$\frac{p_{88}}{p_{87}} = 103.3\% = 1.033$$

∴

$$\frac{p_{88}}{p_{86}} = \frac{p_{88}}{p_{87}} \times \frac{p_{87}}{p_{86}} = 1.033 \times 1.018 = 1.051\,594$$

$$= 105.2\% \ (1 \text{ d.p.})$$

Price index for 1988 based on 1986 is 105.2 (1 d.p.).

(*ii*)

Category	1988 Price index (%)	Weight (w)	Price index $\times w$
Food	106.7	163	17 392.1
Catering	113.4	50	5670
Drink	109.4	78	8533.2
Tobacco	106.6	36	3837.6
Housing	118.3	160	18 928
Fuel	101.6	55	5588
Clothing	105.2	72	7574.4
		$\Sigma w = 614$	67 523.3

$$\text{Weighted price index} = \frac{67\,523.3}{614} = 109.97\ldots$$

$$= 110.0 \ (1 \text{ d.p.})$$

NOTE: the figures in the Price index column are already in percentages, so the weighted price index will be in the correct form.

(*iii*) Weekly expenditure 1988 ≈ 110% of expenditure 1986

$$= 1.10 \times £115$$

$$= £126.50$$

Exercise 1I

1. In 1992 the price index of a commodity, using 1988 as base year, was 112. In 1994, the index using 1992 as base year was 85. What would have been the index in 1994, using 1988 as base year?

2. In 1991, the index number of the value of a commodity was 135 when 1989 was taken as base year. The value of the commodity in 1991 was £54 and in 1990 was £46. Find
(a) the value of the commodity in 1989,
(b) the index number of the value of the commodity in 1990 when 1989 was taken as base year.

3. A breakfast cereal contains constituents A, B, C and D. The costs, in pence per kg, in April and May are shown in the following table.

	A	B	C	D
April	80	105	120	x
May	88	126	150	108

Using April as base month, calculate the price relatives of A, B and C for May. Weights of 6, 4, 3 and 2 are allocated to A, B, C and D respectively. Using April as base month, the composite index number for the cost of the cereal in May is 119. Calculate
(i) the price relative of D for May,
(ii) the value of x.   (C Additional)

4. The cost of servicing a car depends on three items — cost of materials, cost of labour and cost of overheads. The price relatives of these items in 1990, using 1988 as the base year, are shown below, together with the weights attached to them.

	Materials	Labour	Overheads
Price relative	115	110	x
Weight	2	5	3

Given that the cost of servicing a car was £50 in 1988 and £57 in 1990, find the value of x.
(C Additional)

5. The table shows the value of sales of different types of product made by a large Swiss manufacturer over a two-year period.

Product type	Sales (millions of francs)		Index of sales (1982 = 100)
	1982	1984	
Infant foods	24.57	24.67	100
Chocolate	21.85	27.43	
Dairy products	59.21	62.58	106
Refrigerated products	8.18	9.78	120
Drinks	83.01	79.10	
Frozen foods	26.35	33.57	127

(i) Which product has the highest value of sales?
(ii) Calculate the two index numbers not given.   (NEAB)

6. The following table shows the price relatives for various commodities in 1992, with 1990 as base, with their weights. Calculate an index of retail prices, based on these figures, giving your answer to the nearest integer.

Commodity	Price relative	Weight
A	115	20
B	123	25
C	154	10
D	108	15
E	100	30

7. Using the prices in the year 1990 as base, the price relatives in 1992 of four commodities A, B, C and D, used in the manufacture of a certain article, are shown below, together with the weights allocated to them.

Commodity	Price relative	Weight
A	115	4
B	130	2
C	x	3
D	y	1

Given that the weighted mean of the price relatives of A, B and C and of B, C and D are both 112, calculate
(i) the value of x and of y,
(ii) a composite index number for the cost of an article in 1992.
Given that an article cost £141.50 in 1992, find its cost in 1990.

8. Using 1990 as the base year, the price relatives of a commodity in 1991 and 1992 are 115 and 125 respectively. Calculate the price relatives for 1990 and 1992 if 1991 is taken as base year.

9. There are four grades of workers in a certain factory. The table below shows the average weekly wage, in £, of a worker in each grade in 1978 and in 1988; the final column shows the index number for these wages in 1988, taking 1978 as base year.

Grade	1978 Weekly wage (£)	1988 Weekly wage (£)	1988 Index number
1	120	192	160
2	150	285	x
3	y	330	200
4	170	z	250

Find the values of x, y and z.
The number of workers in each grade in 1988 is shown in the table below.

Grade	1	2	3	4
Number of workers	180	165	100	55

Obtain a composite index number for the average weekly wage for the whole factory in 1988, using 1978 as base year.
(C Additional)

10. The price relative of a commodity in 1991, using 1990 as base year, was 105. The price relative of the same commodity in 1992, using 1991 as base year, was 95.
Given that the cost of the commodity in 1990 was £120, find its cost in 1992.

11. Given below are the retail prices, in pence, of dairy products in 1984 and 1986, and the amount of each item purchased weekly by a particular family.

	1984	1986	Amount purchased weekly
Milk (per pint)	20	24	20 pints
Eggs (per dozen)	84	96	$1\frac{2}{3}$ dozen
Butter (per kg)	190	x	$1\frac{1}{2}$ kg
Cheese (per kg)	200	220	$\frac{1}{2}$ kg

Given that the composite index number for expenditure on dairy products in 1986, using 1984 as base year, is 114, calculate the value of x. (C Additional)
(See simple aggregate price index, p. 55)

12. Table 1 below shows price relatives of commodities A, B, C, D for the years 1983, 1984, using the year 1982 as base.
Table 2 below shows the price relatives of the same commodities for the year 1984, using the year 1983 as base.

Table 1

	Price relative	
	1983	1984
A	120	132
B	112	y
C	z	110
D	130	143

Table 2

	Price relative 1984
A	x
B	125
C	88
D	110

Calculate the values of x, y and z.
Weights of 6, 11, 2, 3 are allocated to A, B, C, D respectively. Calculate a composite index number for 1984, using 1983 as base.
(C Additional)

13. The table below gives the index of retail prices in January 1988 (January 1987 = 100) for each of seven categories of leisure goods and services, together with the weight attached to each category.

Category	Index	Weight
Audio-visual equipment	95.3	13
Records and tapes	100.0	5
Toys, photographic and sports goods	102.2	11
Books and newspapers	109.0	16
Gardening products	104.3	5
Television licenses and rentals	99.4	11
Entertainment and other recreation	106.9	18

Source: *Department of Employment Monthly Bulletin of Statistics.*

(i) Calculate a composite index for leisure goods and services in January 1988 based on January 1987.
(ii) Without further calculations, state, with a reason, whether the composite index would increase or decrease if the weight for audio-visual equipment were changed to 23.
(JMB)

14. The cost of producing a box of chocolates depends on the costs of raw materials, production and packaging. The table opposite shows various price relatives and weights of these items.

(i) Find x, y and z to the nearest integer.

(ii) Calculate a composite index number for the cost of producing a box of chocolates in 1991 using 1989 as base year.

(C Additional)

	Raw materials	Production	Packaging
Price relative for 1989 using 1980 as base	179	x	198
Price relative for 1991 using 1980 as base	y	258	216
Price relative for 1991 using 1989 as base	105	120	z
Weight	5	13	2

MEDIAN

So far we have considered two averages or typical values, the mode and the mean. We now consider another average, the **median**.

> For a set of observations arranged in **order of size**, the **median** is the value 50% of the way through the distribution, i.e. the middle value.

For ungrouped data we can find the middle value according to the following rule:

> If there are n observations, arranged in order of size, the middle value is the $\frac{1}{2}(n+1)$th observation.

We find that:

if n is odd, there *is* a middle value and this is the median,

if n is even, there are *two* middle values. If these are c and d, then the median is $\frac{1}{2}(c+d)$.

Example 1.38 Find the median of each of these sets of data:

(a) 7, 7, 2, 3, 4, 2, 7, 9, 31

(b) 36, 41, 27, 32, 29, 38, 39, 43.

Solution 1.38 (a) Arranging the 9 numbers in order of size:

$$2, \ 2, \ 3, \ 4, \ \boxed{7}, \ 7, \ 7, \ 9, \ 31$$

The median is the $\frac{1}{2}(9+1)$th value, i.e. the 5th value.

So median $= 7$.

(**b**) Arranging the 8 numbers in order of size:

$$27, \ 29, \ 32, \ \boxed{36, \ 38}, \ 39, \ 41, \ 43$$

The median is the $\frac{1}{2}(8+1)$th value, i.e. the 4.5th value.

This does not exist, so we consider the 4th and 5th values:

$$\text{median} = \tfrac{1}{2}(36+38)$$
$$= 37$$

So median $= 37.$

QUARTILES

> For n observations, arranged in order of size, the **lower quartile**, Q_1, is the value 25% of the way through the distribution and the **upper quartile**, Q_3, is the value 75% of the way through the distribution.

Now the quartiles, together with the median, sometimes referred to as Q_2, split the distribution into 4 equal parts.

So the quartiles should divide in half the two distributions either side of the median, for example:

(**a**) 3 3 ⑤ 6 8 ⑨ 12 14 ⑲ 20 24 $Q_1 = 5$
        ↑   ↑   ↑ $Q_2 = 9$
   Q_1 (lower Q_2 (median) Q_3 (upper $Q_3 = 19$
     quartile)   quartile)

(**b**) 20 ㉓ 23 ↑ 26 ㉗ 28 $Q_1 = 23$
       ↑ | ↑ $Q_2 = \frac{1}{2}(23+26) = 24.5$
      Q_1 Q_2 Q_3 $Q_3 = 27$

(**c**) 147 150 ↑ 154 158 ↑ 159 162 ↑ 164 165 $Q_1 = \frac{1}{2}(150+154)$
         Q_1 Q_2 Q_3 $= 152$
                                      $Q_2 = \frac{1}{2}(158+159)$
                                        $= 158.5$
                                        $Q_3 = \frac{1}{2}(162+164)$
                                        $= 163$

(**d**) 10 12 ↑ 13 15 ⑲ 19 24 ↑ 26 26 $Q_1 = \frac{1}{2}(12+13)$
         | ↑ | $= 12.5$
        Q_1 Q_2 Q_3 $Q_2 = 19$
                                        $Q_3 = \frac{1}{2}(24+26)$
                                        $= 25$

We prefer to use this method for finding the values of the quartiles for ungrouped data. However, often the following rule is used:

$$Q_1 = \tfrac{1}{4}(n+1)\text{th value}, \quad Q_3 = \tfrac{3}{4}(n+1)\text{th value}.$$

This rule agrees with our method when n is odd, but there is a discrepancy when n is even. However it does not make a great deal of difference which method is used.

INTERQUARTILE RANGE

The interquartile range is a useful measure of spread of a distribution. It is the range of the middle 50% of the values and is found by subtracting the lower quartile from the upper quartile.

> The interquartile range = upper quartile – lower quartile
>
> $$= Q_3 - Q_1$$

The advantage of this range is that it is not affected by extreme values.

SEMI-INTERQUARTILE RANGE

> The semi-interquartile range $= \tfrac{1}{2}(Q_3 - Q_1)$

Example 1.39 Find the semi-interquartile range of the following set of numbers:

2, 3, 3, 9, 6, 6, 12, 11, 8, 2, 3, 5, 7, 5, 4, 4, 5, 12, 9

Solution 1.39 First, arrange the numbers in ascending order:

2, 2, 3, 3, ③, 4, 4, 5, 5, ⑤, 6, 6, 7, 8, ⑨, 9, 11, 12, 12
$$\qquad\quad \uparrow \qquad\qquad\quad \uparrow \qquad\qquad\quad \uparrow$$
$$\qquad\quad Q_1 \qquad\qquad\quad Q_2 \qquad\qquad\quad Q_3$$

Now from the diagram we see that

$$Q_1 = 3 \quad \text{and} \quad Q_3 = 9$$

Therefore   semi-interquartile range $= \tfrac{1}{2}(Q_3 - Q_1)$

$$= \tfrac{1}{2}(9 - 3)$$

$$= 3$$

The semi-interquartile range of the set of numbers is 3.

The median and quartiles can be found from a stem and leaf diagram. The method is illustrated in the following example.

Example 1.40 A reaction time experiment was performed first with 21 girls and then with 24 boys. The results are shown on the stem and leaf diagram.

Reaction times

Girls		Boys
4	2	4
3 3 2 2	2	2 2
1 0 0	2	0 0 0 1 1
9 9 ⑨ 8 8	1	8 8 8
7 7 6	1	6 6 7 7
5 5 5 4 4	1	4 5 5
	1	2 3
	1	0 1 1
	0	9

Key: 6	1 means 16 hundredths of a second	*Key*: 1	8 means 18 hundredths of a second

Find the median and the interquartile range for both sets of reaction times.

Solution 1.40 For the girls:

There are 21 girls, so the median is the $\frac{1}{2}(21 + 1)$th value, i.e. the 11th value. This value has been ringed on the diagram and is obtained by counting up from the bottom, 14, 14, 15, 15,... or counting down from the top, 24, 23, 23, 22,... until the 11th value is reached.

The median is 19 hundredths of a second, or 0.19 seconds.

We find the quartiles by dividing in half the two distributions either side of Q_2.

So Q_1 is the 5.5th value. This is halfway between the 5th and 6th values which are 15 and 16 hundredths of a second. On this stem and leaf diagram, we count from the bottom up, so that

Q_1 is 15.5 hundredths of a second, or 0.155 s.

Q_3 is the 16.5th value. This is halfway between the 16th and 17th values which are 21 and 22 hundredths of a second, so that

Q_3 is 21.5 hundredths of a second, or 0.215 s.

The interquartile range $= Q_3 - Q_1$

$$= 0.215 - 0.155$$

$$= 0.06 \text{ s.}$$

For the boys:

There are 24 boys, so the median is the $\frac{1}{2}(24+1)$th value, i.e. the 12.5th value. This is halfway between the 12th and 13th values which are both 17 hundredths of a second.

So the median reaction time for the boys is 17 hundredths of a second, or 0.17 s.

Q_1 is the 6.5th value. This is halfway between the 6th and 7th values which are 13 and 14 hundredths of a second so that

Q_1 is 13.5 hundredths of a second, or 0.135 s.

Q_3 is the 18.5th value. This is halfway between the 18th and 19th values, which are both 20 hundredths of a second, so that

Q_3 is 20 hundredths of a second, or 0.2 s.

The interquartile range $= Q_3 - Q_1$

$$= 0.2 - 0.135$$

$$= \underline{0.065 \text{ s.}}$$

Summary of results

	Girls	Boys
Median	0.19 s	0.17 s
Interquartile range	0.06 s	0.065 s

These results confirm what the stem and leaf diagram shows, that the girls generally are slower than the boys to react, but that there is more variability in the boys' results.

CUMULATIVE FREQUENCY — ungrouped frequency distributions

To find the median and quartiles of data in the form of an ungrouped frequency distribution, it is useful to find the **cumulative frequency**. This is the total frequency up to a particular item.

Example 1.41 The table shows the number of children in the family for 35 families in a certain area. Find the median number of children per family, and the interquartile range.

Number of children	0	1	2	3	4	5
Frequency	3	5	12	9	4	2

Solution 1.41 The cumulative frequency distribution is formed as follows:

Number of children	0	$\leqslant 1$	$\leqslant 2$	$\leqslant 3$	$\leqslant 4$	$\leqslant 5$
Frequency	3	8	20	29	33	35

$$\nearrow \qquad \uparrow$$
$$3+5 \qquad 3+5+12$$

Since there are 35 values the median is the $\frac{1}{2}(35+1)$th value, i.e. the 18th value. Since there are 8 families with $\leqslant 1$ child and 20 families with $\leqslant 2$ children, the 18th value must be 2.

Therefore the <u>median number of children per family is 2.</u>

Since n is odd:

$$Q_1 = \tfrac{1}{4}(35+1)\text{th value} = \text{9th value} = 2$$

$$Q_3 = \tfrac{3}{4}(35+1)\text{th value} = \text{27th value} = 3.$$

Therefore, interquartile range $= 3 - 2$

$$= \underline{1 \text{ child per family.}}$$

Exercise 1m

1. Find the median of each of the following sets of numbers:
   (a) 4, 6, 18, 25, 9, 16, 22, 5, 20, 4, 8
   (b) 192, 217, 189, 210, 214, 204
   (c) 1267, 1896, 895, 3457, 2164
   (d) 0.7, 0.4, 0.65, 0.78, 0.45, 0.32, 1.9, 0.0078

2. The table shows the scores obtained when a die is thrown 60 times. Find the median score.

Score, x	1	2	3	4	5	6
Frequency, f	12	9	8	13	9	9

3. Find the median and interquartile range of each of the following frequency distributions:

   (a)
x	5	6	7	8	9	10
f	6	11	15	18	6	5

   (b)
x	12	13	14	15	16
f	3	9	11	15	7

   (c)
x	5	9	13	17	21
f	3	7	32	29	16

   (d)
x	2.4	5.4	8.4	11.4	14.4
f	16	31	18	17	6

4. Find (a) the median, (b) the lower quartile Q_1, (c) the upper quartile Q_3, for each of the following sets of data:
   (i) Test marks of 11 students:
   52, 61, 78, 49, 47, 79, 54, 58, 62, 73, 72

   (ii)
Number of peas per pod	Frequency
5	10
6	13
7	18
8	24
9	22
10	19
11	8
12	5

5. The marks scored by 63 pupils in a test are
shown in the frequency distribution.
Calculate (a) the median, (b) the
interquartile range for the set of marks.

Mark	Frequency
0	2
1	2
2	3
3	4
4	6
5	11
6	15
7	10
8	6
9	3
10	1

6. Find the median and interquartile range of
the following distributions:

(a)
Stem	Leaf
1	0 5
2	3 4 4
3	2 8 8
4	1 5 6 6 7
5	2 3 3
6	5 7 8 8
7	2 4
8	0

Key: 5 | 2 means 52

(b)
Stem	Leaf
3	6
3	1 2
2	5 7
2	0 3 4 4
1	6 7 8 8 9 9
1	2 2 3 4
0	5 5
0	1 3 3

Key: 1 | 2 means 1.2

(c)
Stem	Leaf
6	0 2 2
10	1 1 2 3
14	0 2 2 3 3
18	0 2 3 3 3 3 3
22	3 3 3 3
26	0 0 2
30	1 3

Key: 22 | 1 means 23

(d)
Stem	Leaf
16	0 4
21	1 1 3 3
26	0 2 2 4 4
31	1 1 3 3 3 4 4 4
36	0 1 1 2 3
41	2 2 3

Key: 16 | 4 means 20

CUMULATIVE FREQUENCY — grouped frequency distributions

The cumulative frequency is the total frequency up to a particular
upper class boundary.

Example 1.42 Six weeks after planting, the heights of 30 broad bean plants were
measured, correct to the nearest cm. The frequency distribution is
given below. Construct the cumulative frequency table.

Height (cm)	3–5	6–8	9–11	12–14	15–17	18–20
Frequency	1	2	11	10	5	1

Solution 1.42   The upper class boundaries are   5.5, 8.5, 11.5, 14.5, 17.5, 20.5.

The lower boundary of the first class is 2.5.

Cumulative frequency table to show
heights of plants

Height (cm)	Cumulative frequency
<2.5	0
<5.5	1
<8.5	3
<11.5	14
<14.5	24
<17.5	29
<20.5	30

CUMULATIVE FREQUENCY GRAPHS FOR GROUPED DATA

The information in a cumulative frequency table can be shown in a diagram in which the cumulative frequencies are plotted against the **upper class boundaries** and the points are joined as follows:

For a cumulative frequency polygon:

The points are joined with *straight lines*; this ties in with the fact that we draw horizontal lines at the top of the blocks on a histogram. We assume that the readings are evenly distributed throughout an interval.

For a cumulative frequency curve:

The points are joined with a *smooth curve*. In this case we are not assuming an even distribution of readings throughout an interval.

Example 1.43 (a) Draw a cumulative frequency curve for the data in Example 1.42.

(b) (i) Estimate the number of plants that were less than 10 cm tall.

(ii) 10% of plants were of height x cm or more. Find x.

Solution 1.43 (a)   **Cumulative frequency curve to show the heights of 30 broad bean plants**

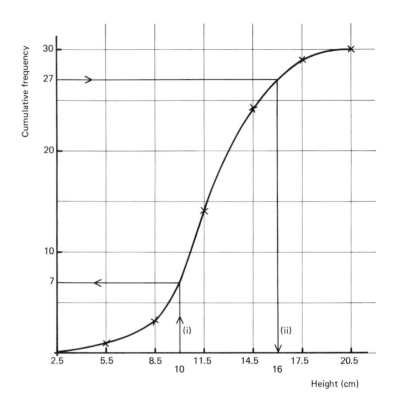

(b)

(i) To find how many plants were less than 10 cm tall, find the height 10 cm on the horizontal axis. Draw a vertical line to meet the curve and then draw a horizontal line to meet the cumulative frequency axis.

From the graph we estimate that 7 plants were less than 10 cm tall.

(ii) 10% of the plants were of height x cm or more, so 90% of the plants were less than x cm tall, i.e. 27 plants were less than x cm tall.

Find 27 on the cumulative frequency axis and draw a horizontal line to meet the curve. Then draw a vertical line to meet the height axis.

From the graph, 27 plants were less than 16 cm tall.

Therefore 10% of the plants were of height 16 cm or more, so the value of x is 16.

Example 1.44 Pupils were asked how long it took them to walk to school on a particular morning. A cumulative frequency distribution was formed:

Time taken (minutes)	Cumulative frequency
<5	28
<10	45
<15	81
<20	143
<25	280
<30	349
<35	374
<40	395
<45	400

(**a**) Draw a cumulative frequency polygon.

(**b**) Estimate how many pupils took less than 18 minutes.

(**c**) Taking equal class intervals of 0–, 5–, 10–, ..., construct a frequency distribution and draw a histogram.

Solution 1.44 (**a**)   **Cumulative frequency polygon to show the times taken to walk to school**

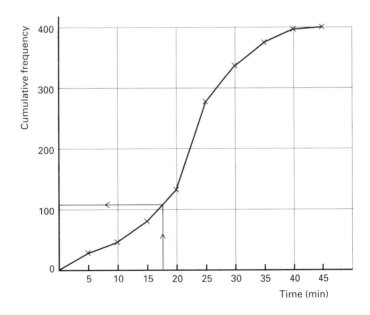

(**b**) From the graph we estimate that 114 pupils took less than 18 minutes.

(c) We form the frequency distribution as follows:

Upper class boundary	Cumulative frequency	Time (min)	Frequency
5	28	0–	28
10	45	5–	45–28 = 17
15	81	10–	81–45 = 36
20	143	15–	143–81 = 62
25	280	20–	280–143 = 137
30	349	25–	349–280 = 69
35	374	30–	374–349 = 25
40	395	35–	395–374 = 21
45	400	40–(45)	400–395 = 5
			Total = 400

Since the class intervals are equal, the frequency can be used for the height of the rectangle.

Histogram to show times taken by 400 pupils to walk to school

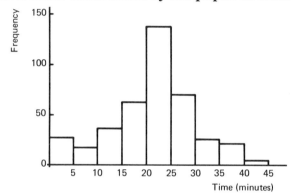

CUMULATIVE PERCENTAGE FREQUENCY DIAGRAMS

These are particularly useful when two or more distributions are to be compared. For example, suppose we have the examination marks of 200 boys and 300 girls.

Mark	Cumulative frequency (boys)	Cumulative frequency (girls)
<10	6	0
<20	22	6
<30	60	12
<40	140	24
<50	172	42
<60	188	75
<70	196	120
<80	198	246
<90	200	294
<100	200	300

We can obtain the cumulative percentage frequencies as follows:

Mark	Boys (total 200)		Girls (total 300)	
	Cumulative frequency	Cumulative % frequency	Cumulative frequency	Cumulative % frequency
<10	6	$\frac{6}{200} = 3\%$	0	$\frac{0}{300} = 0\%$
<20	22	$\frac{22}{200} = 11\%$	6	$\frac{6}{300} = 2\%$
<30	60	$\frac{60}{200} = 30\%$	12	$\frac{12}{300} = 4\%$
<40	140	$\frac{140}{200} = 70\%$	24	$\frac{24}{300} = 8\%$
<50	172	$\frac{172}{200} = 86\%$	42	$\frac{42}{300} = 14\%$
<60	188	$\frac{188}{200} = 94\%$	75	$\frac{75}{300} = 25\%$
<70	196	$\frac{196}{200} = 98\%$	120	$\frac{120}{300} = 40\%$
<80	198	$\frac{198}{200} = 99\%$	246	$\frac{246}{300} = 82\%$
<90	200	$\frac{200}{200} = 100\%$	294	$\frac{294}{300} = 98\%$
<100	200	$\frac{200}{200} = 100\%$	300	$\frac{300}{300} = 100\%$

The cumulative percentage frequency curves are then drawn, as shown on page 74.

Great care must be taken when comparing these curves. A common mistake is to say that the boys have done better than the girls because the boys' graph is above that of the girls. If we calculate the corresponding percentage frequencies and draw the histograms we see that this is not the case.

Boys			
Mark	Cumulative % frequency	Mark	% Frequency
<10	3%	0–	3%
<20	11%	10–	8%
<30	30%	20–	19%
<40	70%	30–	40%
<50	86%	40–	16%
<60	94%	50–	8%
<70	98%	60–	4%
<80	99%	70–	1%
<90	100%	80–	1%
<100	100%	90–	0%
		Total	100%

Cumulative percentage frequency curves

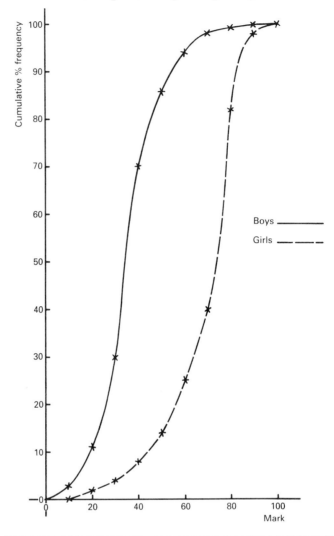

Girls			
Mark	Cumulative % frequency	Mark	% Frequency
< 10	0%	0–	0%
< 20	2%	10–	2%
< 30	4%	20–	2%
< 40	8%	30–	4%
< 50	14%	40–	6%
< 60	25%	50–	11%
< 70	40%	60–	15%
< 80	82%	70–	42%
< 90	98%	80–	16%
< 100	100%	90–	2%
			Total 100%

Boys' results

Girls' results

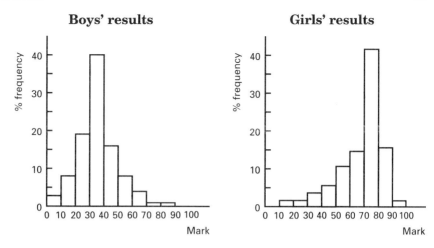

It is easy to see that the girls have done better than the boys. The modal class for the boys' marks is 30–39, whereas the modal class for the girls' marks is 70–79. The type of distribution for the boys' marks is said to be positively skewed and that for the girls' marks is said to be negatively skewed.

Example 1.45 A company wants to make a new tent for young people.

The tent needs to be high enough for children aged 11 to stand up in it.

The company has this graph:

Height of girls and boys aged 11

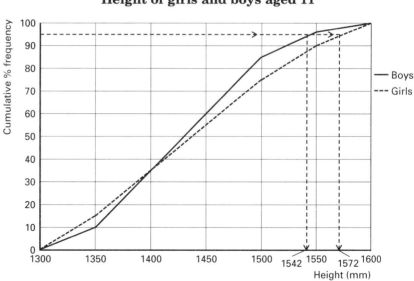

The company wants to be sure that at least 95% of girls and 95% of boys will be able to stand up inside the new tent.

To cut costs, the company wants the height of the tent to be as low as possible. What height must the company make the new tent?

(SCAA)

Solution 1.45 From the graph 95% of boys have heights up to 1542 mm and 95% of girls have heights up to 1572 mm. So in order to allow some headroom, the company should make the tent 1580 mm high.

[It is interesting to note that at the age of 11, the girls are generally taller. You may have thought that because the boys' graph was above the girls', the boys were taller, but this is not the case.]

Example 1.46 The company also has this graph:

Height of girls and boys aged 15

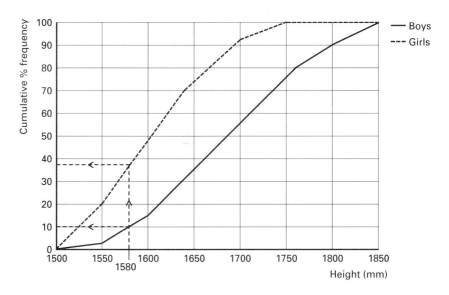

Look at the height that you found for the new tent in Example 1.45.

Lots of 15-year-olds will not be able to stand up in the new tent.

Will a greater percentage of girls or a greater percentage of boys be too tall to stand up in the tent?   (SCAA)

Solution 1.46 From the graph 10% of 15-year-old boys have heights up to 1580 mm and 37% of 15-year-old girls have heights up to 1580 mm. So 90% of boys are too tall for the tent and 63% of girls are too tall for the tent. So a greater percentage of boys will be too tall.

[Again, it is interesting to note that, at the age of 15, the boys are taller, even though you may have thought otherwise from the cumulative percentage frequency graph.]

Drawing frequency polygons from cumulative % frequency curves

The graph below shows the number of hours of paid work done per week in 1990 by women and men employed in the UK. The numbers of hours have been grouped into five-hour intervals.

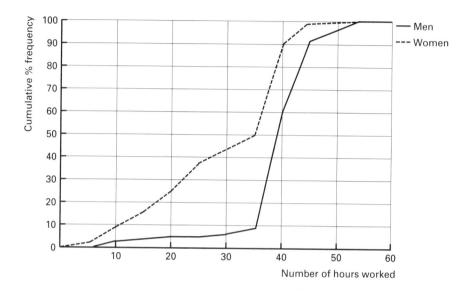

Source: *Social Trends 1992*
(SCAA)

It is interesting to draw the frequency polygons for both distributions in the following way.

Women			
No. of hours (upper class boundary)	Cumulative % frequency	No. hours	% Frequency
<5	2	0–	2
<10	8	5–	6
<15	16	10–	8
<20	25	15–	9
<25	37	20–	12
<30	43	25–	6
<35	50	30–	7
<40	90	35–	40
<45	98	40–	8
<50	99	45–	1
<55	100	50–	1
<60	100	55–	0
			Total 100

Men			
No. of hours (upper class boundary)	Cumulative % frequency	No. hours	% Frequency
<5	0	0–	0
<10	2	5–	2
<15	4	10–	2
<20	5	15–	1
<25	5	20–	0
<30	6	25–	1
<35	8	30–	2
<40	62	35–	54
<45	91	40–	29
<50	97	45–	6
<55	99	50–	2
<60	100	55–	1
			Total 100

The resulting frequency polygons are:

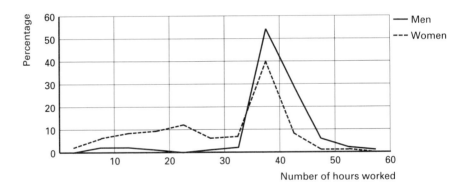

The cumulative percentage frequency graph may have given you the impression that the women work more hours than the men, but the frequency polygons show that this is not the case.

MEDIAN AND QUARTILES — grouped data

When data are grouped into intervals, the original information is lost, so we can only *estimate* the values of the median (Q_2) and the quartiles (Q_1 and Q_3). To do this we make use of the idea of cumulative frequency. Values can be read off the cumulative frequency graph, or cumulative percentage frequency graph as shown:

Cumulative frequency curve

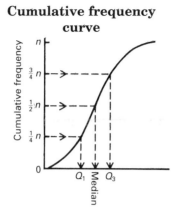

Cumulative % frequency curve

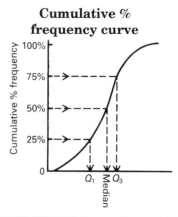

Grouped data	Cumulative frequency curve	Cumulative percentage frequency curve
Lower quartile, Q_1	$\frac{1}{4}n$th reading	25% reading
Median, Q_2	$\frac{1}{2}n$th reading	50% reading
Upper quartile, Q_3	$\frac{3}{4}n$th reading	75% reading

NOTE: (*i*) If, for the median, we use the $\frac{1}{2}(n+1)$th value, as with ungrouped data, then we would not arrive at the same point on the cumulative frequency axis whether we worked down from the top or up from the bottom of the scale. The $\frac{1}{2}n$th value, or 50% value is needed.

(*ii*) If preferred, a cumulative frequency polygon, or cumulative percentage frequency polygon, can be drawn. The values obtained for the median and quartiles will not vary greatly from those obtained from curves.

Example 1.47 The table gives the cumulative distribution of the heights (in cm) of 400 children in a certain school:

Height (cm)	Cumulative frequency
<100	0
<110	27
<120	85
<130	215
<140	320
<150	370
<160	395
<170	400

(**a**) Draw a cumulative frequency curve.

(**b**) Find an estimate of the median.

(**c**) Determine the interquartile range.

(**d**) Determine the 10 to 90 percentile range.

Solution 1.47 For the median, we find the $\frac{1}{2}$(400)th value, i.e. the 200th value. This is shown on the graph.

For the lower quartile, Q_1, we find the 100th value and for the upper quartile, Q_3, the 300th value.

For the 10th percentile (written P_{10}) we find the value which is 10% of the way through the readings, the $\frac{10}{100}$(400)th value, i.e. the 40th value. The 90th percentile is the $\frac{90}{100}$(400)th value, i.e. the 360th value.

(a)   Cumulative frequency curve to show the heights of 400 children

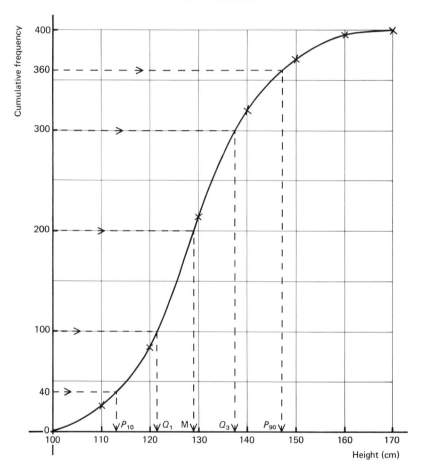

From the curve,

(b) <u>An estimate of the median is 129 cm.</u>

(c) $Q_3 = 137.5\,\text{cm}$, $Q_1 = 121.5\,\text{cm}$.

$$\text{The interquartile range} = Q_3 - Q_1$$
$$= 137.5 - 121.5$$
$$= 16\,\text{cm}$$

<u>The middle half of the readings, that is the interquartile range, has a range of 16 cm.</u>

(**d**) $P_{90} = 147\,\text{cm}, \quad P_{10} = 113\,\text{cm}.$

$$\text{The 10 to 90 percentile range} = P_{90} - P_{10}$$
$$= 147 - 113$$
$$= 34\,\text{cm}$$

Therefore the middle 80% of the readings have a range of 34 cm.

Example 1.48 The masses, measured to the nearest kg, of 50 boys are noted and the distribution formed. Form a cumulative percentage frequency table and draw a cumulative percentage frequency curve. Use it to estimate the median mass and the interquartile range.

Mass (kg)	60–64	65–69	70–74	75–79	80–84	85–89
Frequency	2	6	12	14	10	6

Solution 1.48 The upper class boundaries are 64.5, 69.5, 74.5, 79.5, 84.5, 89.5. The lower class boundary of the first class is 59.5.

Mass (kg)	Frequency	Mass (kg)	Cumulative frequency	Cumulative % frequency
–59	0	<59.5	0	0%
60–64	2	<64.5	2	4%
65–69	6	<69.5	8	16%
70–74	12	<74.5	20	40%
75–79	14	<79.5	34	68%
80–84	10	<84.5	44	88%
85–89	6	<89.5	50	100%

Cumulative % frequency curve to show masses of 50 boys

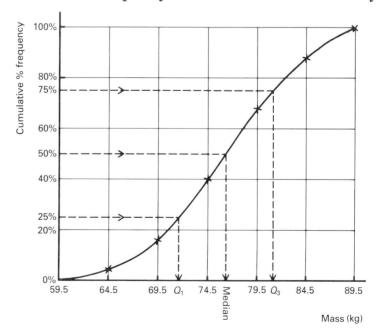

The median is the value of the 50% reading, which we estimate to be 76.3 kg.

The lower quartile, Q_1, is the 25% reading, and the upper quartile, Q_3, is the 75% reading.

From the graph, $Q_1 = 71.5\,\text{kg}$, $Q_3 = 80.5\,\text{kg}$

Therefore interquartile range $= Q_3 - Q_1$

$$= 80.5 - 71.5$$

$$= 9\,\text{kg}$$

The median is 76.3 kg and the interquartile range is 9 kg.

NOTE: it is interesting to note that if the data are represented by a histogram, the median divides the area exactly in half.

Histogram to show the masses of 50 boys

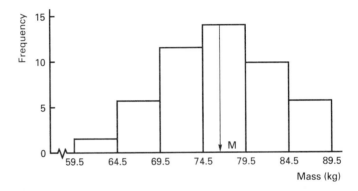

Finding the median of grouped data by linear interpolation

It is possible to estimate the median by calculation, without drawing the cumulative frequency graph. Consider the cumulative frequency data of Example 1.48.

Mass (kg)	Cumulative frequency
<59.5	0
<64.5	2
<69.5	8
<74.5	20
<79.5	34
<84.5	44
<89.5	50

From the cumulative frequency table we note that 20 boys have a mass less than 74.5 kg and 34 boys have a mass less than 79.5 kg. We assume that the masses of the 14 boys in the interval 74.5 kg–79.5 kg are evenly spread, so we divide this interval of 5 kg into 14 equal spaces.

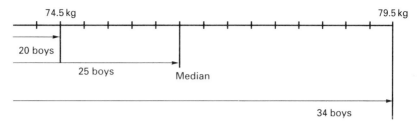

There are 50 boys, so the median value of their masses will be the 25th value, which is shown on the diagram at a position $\frac{5}{14}$ of the way along the interval (of width 5 kg) from 74.5 kg to 79.5 kg.

i.e. estimate of median $= 74.5 + \left(\frac{5}{14}\right)(5)$

$$= 76.3\,\text{kg} \ (1 \text{ d.p.})$$

Therefore we estimate the median to be 76.3 kg (1 d.p.).

NOTE: (*i*) This method uses the same idea as a cumulative frequency polygon since it assumes that values are *evenly spread* through an interval.

(*ii*) A similar method can be employed to find quartiles or percentiles.

Example 1.49   The distribution of the lengths of time of a large number of telephone calls made from an office in a given week was such that the median was 100 seconds and the 80th percentile was 190 seconds. Without drawing the cumulative frequency curve, estimate

(**a**) the upper quartile,

(**b**) the number of calls, out of 500, that lasted less than a minute.

Solution 1.49   (**a**)

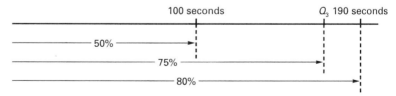

The interval from 100 s to 190 s is of width 90 s and Q_3 is $\frac{25}{30}$ of the way along this interval,

so $Q_3 = 100 + \frac{25}{30}(90) = 175$

The upper quartile is 175 seconds.

(b)

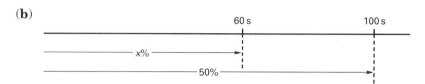

Now $\dfrac{x}{50} = \dfrac{60}{100}$ so $x = 30$

The number of calls $= 30\%$ of 500

$$= 150$$

150 calls lasted less than one minute.

NOTE: we have assumed that the lengths of calls are evenly spread throughout an interval.

Exercise 1n

1. The table below shows the frequency distribution of the masses of 52 women students at a college. Measurements have been recorded to the nearest kg.

Mass (kg)	Frequency
40–44	3
45–49	2
50–54	7
55–59	18
60–64	18
65–69	3
70–74	1

(*a*)   Construct a cumulative frequency table and draw a cumulative frequency curve.
(*b*)   How many students were of mass less than 57 kg?
(*c*)   How many students were of mass greater than 61 kg?
(*d*)   What was the mass exceeded by 20% of the students?
(*e*)   Estimate the median.
(*f*)   Estimate the interquartile range.

2. 50 soil samples were collected in an area of woodland, and the pH value for each sample was found. The cumulative frequency distribution was constructed as shown in the table.

pH value	Cumulative frequency
<4.8	1
<5.2	2
<5.6	5
<6.0	10
<6.4	19
<6.8	38
<7.2	43
<7.6	46
<8.0	49
<8.4	50

(*a*)   Draw a cumulative frequency curve.
(*b*)   What percentage of the samples had a pH value less than 7?
(*c*)   50% of the samples had a pH value greater than x. Find x.
(*d*)   Taking equal class intervals of 4.4–, 4.8–, 5.2–, ..., construct the frequency distribution and draw a histogram. Show the median on the histogram.

3. The cumulative frequency curve has been drawn from information about the amount of time spent by 50 people in a supermarket on a particular day.

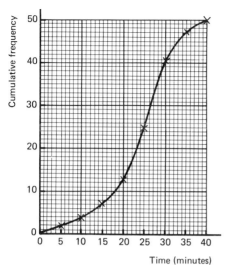

(*a*) Construct the cumulative frequency table, taking boundaries ≤5, ≤10,...
(*b*) How many people spent between 17 and 27 minutes in the supermarket?
(*c*) 60% of the people spent less than or equal to *t* minutes. Find *t*.
(*d*) 60% of the people spent longer than *s* minutes. Find *s*.
(*e*) Estimate the median.
(*f*) Find the semi-interquartile range.

4. Estimate the median of the following frequency distribution
(*a*) by calculation,
(*b*) from a cumulative frequency curve.
The frequency distribution shows the times taken by 55 pupils to do their mathematics homework. Times have been measured to the nearest minute.

Time (min)	Frequency
5–14	5
15–24	7
25–34	19
35–44	17
45–54	7

5. Eggs laid at Hill Farm are weighed and the results grouped as shown:

Mass (g)	Frequency
–50	3
–54	2
–58	5
–62	12
–66	10
–70	6
–74	2

Construct a cumulative frequency table and draw a cumulative frequency curve. Use the curve to estimate the median mass.

6. The table shows the frequency distribution of the speeds of cars passing along a marked stretch of road of length 1 kilometre. Estimate the median speed by linear interpolation.

Speed (km/h)	Frequency
0–	2
20–	8
40–	22
60–	9
80–	2
100–	0

7. The length of life of each of 50 electric light bulbs is noted and the results shown in the table below. Calculate the median length of life and the interquartile range, using linear interpolation. Then draw a cumulative percentage frequency polygon and compare the answers.

Length of life (h)	Frequency
650–	3
670–	7
680–	20
690–	17
700–	3
720–	0

8. Estimate the median diameter of rods produced by a particular machine by drawing a cumulative frequency polygon of the data given in the table.

Diameter (cm)	Frequency
0.49–0.51	12
0.52–0.54	23
0.55–0.57	32
0.58–0.60	18
0.61–0.63	15

9. From the soil of an English garden 100 earthworms were collected. Their lengths were recorded to the nearest millimetre and grouped as shown in the table below.

Length (mm)	Number of worms
95–109	2
110–124	8
125–139	17
140–154	26
155–169	24
170–184	16
185–199	6
200–214	1

Write down the cumulative frequency table and draw a cumulative frequency curve to illustrate this information. Estimate
(i)   the median length of worm,
(ii)   the semi-interquartile range,
(iii) the percentage of worms which are over 180 mm in length.   (C Additional)

10. Every day at 08 28 a train departs from one city and travels to a second city. The times taken for the journey were recorded in minutes over a certain period and were grouped as shown in the table.

Time	Frequency
–80	0
–85	6
–90	12
–95	22
–100	31
–105	15
–110	7
–115	4
–120	2
–125	1
over 125	0

(The interval '–90' indicates all times greater than 85 minutes up to and including 90 minutes.)
From these figures draw a cumulative frequency curve and from this curve estimate
(i)   the median time for the journey,
(ii) the semi-interquartile range,
(iii) the number of trains which arrived at the second city between 10 00 and 10 15.
(C Additional)

11. 30 specimens of sheet steel are tested for tensile strength, measured in $kN\,m^{-2}$. The table below gives the distribution of the measurements.

Tensile strength	Number of specimens
405–415	4
415–425	3
425–435	6
435–445	10
445–455	5
455–465	2

Draw a cumulative frequency diagram of this distribution.
Estimate the median and the 10th and 90th percentiles.   (O&C)

12. The distribution of the times taken when a certain task was performed by each of a large number of people was such that its twentieth percentile was 25 minutes, its fortieth percentile was 50 minutes, its sixtieth percentile was 64 minutes and its eightieth percentile was 74 minutes. Use linear interpolation to estimate (i) the median of the distribution, (ii) the upper quartile of the distribution, (iii) the percentage of persons who performed the task in forty minutes or less.   (JMB)

13. The frequency distribution, given in the table, refers to the heights, in cm, of 50 men, corrected to the nearest 10 cm.

Height (cm)	Frequency
140	1
150	6
160	8
170	21
180	10
190	4

(a)   State the least possible height of the one man whose height is recorded in the table as 140 cm.
(b)   Draw on graph paper a histogram to illustrate the data of the table, drawing five columns, with the first column representing the seven shortest men. Label the axes carefully and explain clearly how frequency has been represented on your histogram.
(c)   Draw a cumulative frequency diagram on graph paper for the data given in the table. From your diagram, estimate the upper and lower quartiles, the median height and the interquartile range.   (L Additional)

14. The following data concern a random sample of 1000 men with heights in the given ranges.

Height (cm)	No. of men	Height (cm)	No. of men
168–	8	180–	130
170–	31	182–	131
172–	84	184–	94
174–	108	186–	64
176–	142	188–	42
178–	141	190–192	25

Draw a cumulative frequency diagram to illustrate these data. Use your diagram to estimate
(a)   the median height,
(b)   the range of heights for men who are between the fortieth and seventieth percentiles,
(c)   the number of men in the sample with heights of at least 183 cm.   (L Additional)

15. The average weekly wages, taken to the nearest £, of 200 factory workers were recorded and are shown in the table below.

Weekly wage (£)	Number of workers
105–124	10
125–144	16
145–164	38
165–184	52
185–204	40
205–224	28
225–244	16

Construct the cumulative frequency table for this distribution and draw the cumulative frequency curve.

Use your curve to estimate
(i)   the median wage,
(ii) the interquartile range of the wages,
(iii) the percentage of workers receiving
more than £190 per week.   (C Additional) P

Draw a histogram to represent this
information.
Estimate the 60th percentile.
(C Additional) P

16. The amounts spent by 140 shoppers at a
supermarket were recorded and are
tabulated below.

Amount spent, £x	Number of shoppers
$x \leqslant 15$	15
$15 < x \leqslant 30$	39
$30 < x \leqslant 40$	40
$40 < x \leqslant 50$	31
$50 < x \leqslant 70$	12
$70 < x \leqslant 100$	3

17. The distribution of the lengths of time of a
large number of telephone calls made by a
company in a given day was such that the
lower quartile was 30 s, the median was 80 s
and the 70th percentile was 160 s. Without
drawing the cumulative frequency curve,
estimate
(i)   the 64th percentile,
(ii) the number of calls, out of a total of 400,
that were timed at less than one minute.
State *briefly* the assumption being made in
these calculations   (C Additional)

18. The figure below shows the cumulative frequency diagram for the distribution of the number of
marks, N, in the range 0 to 99 inclusive, obtained by 120 candidates in an examination. From the
diagram, estimate   (*a*) the median mark,   (*b*) the interquartile range,   (*c*) the number of
candidates who scored more than 59 marks.

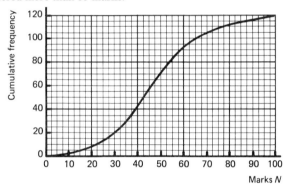

State why the diagram has to be read at $N = 9.5, 19.5, \ldots$ if a grouped frequency table showing how
many candidates are in the class intervals 0–9, 10–19, $\ldots$ is to be found. Draw up such a table and
illustrate it by drawing a histogram. Mark on your diagram the median mark.   (L Additional)

19.   **Frequency polygon to show duration of calls**

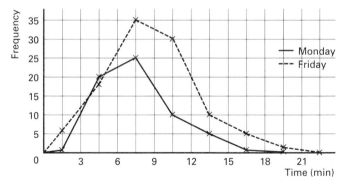

The frequency polygons show the duration in minutes of telephone calls made from a High Street
call box on a Monday and a Friday.
Construct two cumulative percentage frequency polygons on the same grid.
(*a*) What percentage of calls lasted more than 10 min   (i) on Monday   (ii) on Friday?
(*b*) What percentage of calls lasted less than 7 min   (i) on Monday   (ii) on Friday?
(*c*) 80% of calls last up to *a* mins on Monday and up to *b* mins on Friday.   Find *a* and *b*.

SUMMARY — DESCRIPTIVE STATISTICS

Histograms

$$\text{Frequency density} = \frac{\text{frequency}}{\text{class width}}$$

$$\text{Area} \propto \text{frequency}$$

If intervals are of equal width use:

$$\text{height of rectangle} = \text{frequency}$$

If interval widths are not equal use:

$$\text{height of rectangle} = \text{frequency density}$$

Pie charts

$$\text{Area} \propto \text{frequency}$$

To compare sets of data with total frequencies $F_1, F_2, F_3, \ldots$ draw circles with radii in the ratio $\sqrt{F_1} : \sqrt{F_2} : \sqrt{F_3}$ and so on.

Mean, $\bar{x}$

Raw data
$$\bar{x} = \frac{\Sigma x}{n}$$

Frequency distribution
$$\bar{x} = \frac{\Sigma fx}{\Sigma f}$$

For grouped data

Take the mid-point of the interval to represent that interval, where

$$\text{mid-point} = \tfrac{1}{2}(\text{lower class boundary} + \text{upper class boundary})$$

Standard deviation, s

Raw data
$$s = \sqrt{\frac{\Sigma(x - \bar{x})^2}{n}}$$

or
$$s = \sqrt{\frac{\Sigma x^2}{n} - \bar{x}^2}$$

Frequency
distribution
$$s = \sqrt{\frac{\Sigma f(x - \bar{x})^2}{\Sigma f}}$$

or
$$s = \sqrt{\frac{\Sigma fx^2}{\Sigma f} - \bar{x}^2}$$

$$\text{Variance} = (\text{standard deviation})^2$$

Calculations involving mean and standard deviation

Scaling

If $\qquad y = a\,x + b$ where a and b are constants,

then $\qquad \bar{y} = a\,\bar{x} + b$

and $\qquad s_y = a\,s_x$

Coding

If $\qquad\qquad y = \dfrac{x - a}{b}$ then $\quad x = a + b\,y$

$$\bar{x} = a + b\,\bar{y}$$

$$\text{and}\quad s_x = b\,s_y$$

Combining sets of numbers, x and y

$$\text{New mean} = \frac{\Sigma x + \Sigma y}{n_1 + n_2}$$

$$\text{New variance} = \frac{\Sigma x^2 + \Sigma y^2}{n_1 + n_2} - (\text{new mean})^2$$

Weighted means

If $\;x_1, x_2, \ldots, x_n\;$ are given weightings $\;w_1, w_2, \ldots, w_n\;$ then

$$\text{weighted mean} = \frac{\Sigma w_i\, x_i}{\Sigma w_i} \quad \text{for} \quad i = 1, 2, \ldots, n.$$

Index numbers

Price relative (or price index) $= \dfrac{p_1}{p_0}$ (written as a % *without* % sign)

where p_1 is the price in the year to be compared and p_0 is the price in the base year.

$$\text{Simple aggregate price index} = \frac{\Sigma p_1}{\Sigma p_0}$$

$$\text{Weighted price index} = \frac{\Sigma\left(\dfrac{p_1}{p_0}\right) w}{\Sigma w}$$

The weighted price index is also known as the composite index number.

Median, quartiles and percentiles

For n observations arranged in order of size

The median Q_2 is the value 50% of the way through the distribution

The lower quartile, Q_1, is the value 25% of the way through the distribution

The upper quartile, Q_3, is the value 75% of the way through the distribution

The xth percentile, P_x, is the value x% of the way through the distribution.

	Raw data	Data grouped into intervals
Q_2	$\frac{1}{2}(n+1)$th value	$\frac{1}{2}n$th value $= 50\%$ value
Q_1	Divides the distribution either side of the	$\frac{1}{4}n$th value $= 25\%$ value
Q_3	median in half	$\frac{3}{4}n$th value $= 75\%$ value

Ranges

Range = highest value – lowest value

Interquartile range = upper quartile – lower quartile

$$= Q_3 - Q_1$$

Semi-interquartile range $= \frac{1}{2}(Q_3 - Q_1)$

Middle 80% of readings $= P_{90} - P_{10}$

Miscellaneous Exercise 1o

1. (a) Find the median, mean and standard deviation of the set of numbers 3, 5, 12, 1, 6, 3, 12.
(b) A set of digits consists of m zeros and n ones. Find the mean of this set and show that the standard deviation is

$$\frac{\sqrt{(mn)}}{(m+n)}$$ (C Additional)

2. (a) Sketch frequency curves for distributions which have one mode and for which
(i) the mode, median and mean coincide,
(ii) the mode is less than the median,
indicating on each sketch the positions of these measures.

(b) The mean of the set of numbers 3, 1, 7, 2, 1, 1, 7 x, y, where x and y are single digit positive whole numbers, is known to be 4. Show that $x + y = 14$.
Hence, or otherwise, find the mode of this set of numbers when (i) $x = y$, (ii) $x \neq y$.
If the standard deviation is $\frac{1}{3}\sqrt{76}$ find x and y, assuming that $x \leqslant y$. (C Additional)

3. Ten values of a variable x are

8.2, 8.0, 8.1, 8.2, 8.4, 7.9, 8.0, 8.3, 7.8, 8.1

Express each of these values in the form $8 + 0.1y$. Calculate the arithmetic mean and the variance of the ten values of y and hence, or otherwise, deduce the mean and the variance of the ten values of x.

Hence find the mean and the variance of the set of ten numbers

824, 804, 814, 824, 844,
794, 804, 834, 784, 814

A transformation of the form $z = a + bx$, where $b > 0$, is applied to the first set of ten values of x so that the mean is increased by 0.9 and the standard deviation is doubled. Find the values of the constants a and b.

(L Additional)

4. (a) A set of values of a variable X has a mean μ and a standard deviation σ. State the new value of the mean and of the standard deviation when each of the variables is (i) increased by k, (ii) multiplied by p. Values of a new variable Y are obtained by using the formula $Y = 3X + 5$. Find the mean and the standard deviation of the set of values of Y.
(b) It is proposed to convert a set of values of a variable X, whose mean and standard deviation are 20 and 5 respectively, to a set of values of a variable Y whose mean and standard deviation are 42 and 8 respectively. If the conversion formula is $Y = aX + b$, calculate the value of a and of b. (C Additional)

5. Twelve members of a class of children each estimate the height of the top of a church tower. Their estimates, in metres, are

47, 52, 52, 54, 52, 50, 51, 50, 48, 53, 54, 49

(a) Calculate the median of these estimates.
(b) Calculate the mode, m, that is the number which has the highest frequency.
(c) Two extra children join the class and each makes an estimate. The mode for the set of 14 estimates is different from m and unique. Suggest what the two new estimates could be.
(d) Calculate the arithmetic mean, $\bar{x}$, of the original 12 estimates.
(e) One member of the original class of 12 revises his estimate and the new mean for the 12 estimates is $\bar{x} + 0.5$. Find the increase in the estimate of this member.
(f) The teacher of the class makes an estimate of the height of the church tower and when her estimate is taken with the original 12, the mean of all 13 estimates is $\bar{x} + 0.5$. Find the teacher's estimate.
(g) Two extra children, different from those mentioned in (c), join the class and each make an estimate so that the mean of their two estimates and the original 12 estimates is $\bar{x} + 0.5$.
Find the sum of their two estimates.

(L Additional)

6. The following is a set of 109 examination marks ordered for convenience.

6	11	11	12	13	14	16	17	18	20
21	21	23	24	25	25	25	25	26	26
27	27	28	28	28	29	29	29	30	31
31	32	32	32	33	33	34	34	35	36
36	37	37	37	37	38	38	38	39	39
39	39	39	39	39	39	40	40	40	40
40	40	41	41	41	42	42	42	42	43
43	43	44	45	46	46	47	47	47	47
48	50	50	51	51	52	52	52	53	53
54	54	55	57	58	58	59	59	61	62
63	64	66	66	67	70	76	77	82	

(a) Construct a grouped frequency distribution using a class width of 10 and starting with 0–9.
(b) Draw a histogram and comment on the shape of the distribution.
(c) Using the frequency table estimate the mean and standard deviation of the 'marks.
(d) The marks are to be scaled linearly by the relation $Y = a + bX$ where X is the old mark and Y the new mark. The new mean and standard deviation are to be 50 and 10 respectively. Using your estimates in (c) calculate suitable values for a and b.

7. A set of numbers has mean μ and standard deviation σ. A new set of numbers is obtained by subtracting μ from each number and dividing the result by σ. Write down the mean and standard deviation of the new set of numbers.
In an examination in Statistics the mean mark of a group of 120 students was 68 and the standard deviation was 6. In Algebra the mean mark of the group was 62 and the standard deviation was 5. One student scored 76 in Statistics and 70 in Algebra. By scaling the marks for each subject so that each set of marks has the same mean and standard deviation compare the performances of this student in the two subjects. (C Additional)

8. The numbers 4, 6, 12, 4, 10, 12, 3, x, y have a mean of 7 and a mode of 4. Find (i) the values of the two numbers x and y, (ii) the median of this set of nine numbers.
When two additional numbers $7 + n$ and $7 - n$ are included the standard deviation of all eleven numbers is found to be 4. Write down the mean of these eleven numbers and calculate the value of n. (C Additional)

9. The sum of 20 numbers is 320 and the sum of their squares is 5840. Calculate the mean of the 20 numbers and the standard deviation.

(i) Another number is added to these 20 so that the mean is unchanged. Show that the standard deviation is decreased.

(ii) Another set of 10 numbers is such that their sum is 130 and the sum of their squares is 2380. This set is combined with the original 20 numbers. Calculate the mean and standard deviation of all 30 numbers.

(C Additional)

10. A travel agency has two shops, R and S. The number of holidays purchased in a particular week and the mean and standard deviation of the costs of these holidays at each shop are shown in the following table.

	Number of holidays	Mean cost (£)	S.D. (£)
Shop R	32	190.35	10.4
Shop S	24	202.25	15.5

Calculate the mean, and, to the nearest penny, the standard deviation of the costs of all the 56 holidays purchased.   (L)P

11. Three random samples of 50, 30 and 20 bags respectively are taken from the production line of '12 kg bags' of cat litter. The contents of each bag are then weighed. A summary of the results is shown in the table.

Sample	Size	Mean wt. (kg)	S.D. (kg)
1	50	11.8	0.5
2	30	12.1	0.9
3	20	11.7	1.1

Find, in kg to 2 decimal places, the mean weight per bag and the standard deviation for the 100 bags.   (L)P

12. (a) A set of numbers has mean 23 and standard deviation 7. A new set of numbers is obtained by subtracting 23 from each of the original numbers and then dividing the result by 7. Write down the mean and standard deviation of the new set of numbers.

(b) The nine numbers 5, 6, 13, 5, 10, 13, 3, x, y have a mean of 8 and mode of 5. Find
(i)   the values of the two numbers x and y,
(ii) the median of this set of nine numbers,
(iii) the variance of this set of nine numbers.

(c) The table below shows the means and standard deviations of the marks in Mathematics and English obtained by a class of students.

	Mean	Standard deviation
Mathematics	m	12
English	53	s

The marks in each subject were scaled linearly to have a mean of 50 and a standard deviation of 15. The original and the scaled marks of a particular student are shown below.

	Original mark	Scaled mark
Mathematics	40	40
English	61	56

Calculate the value of m and of s.

(C Additional)

13. A manufacturer uses three raw materials, A, B and C, in the production of certain articles. The prices per tonne of these raw materials in the years 1989 and 1991 are shown in the table below.

	A	B	C
1989	£35.50	£53.00	£22.50
1991	£44.00	£60.00	£33.00

Given that the raw materials A, B, C are used, by mass, in the ratio $2:3:4$, calculate a composite index number for the total cost of raw materials in 1991, using 1989 as base year.

Assuming that selling price is directly proportional to the cost of raw materials, what would have been the selling price in 1989 of an article which sold for £37 in 1991? Given also that the increase in selling price from 1989 to 1990 was the same as the increase from 1990 to 1991, calculate the composite index number for the selling price of an article in 1991, using 1990 as base year.

(C Additional)

14. A manufacturer markets a cereal which is a mixture of three different elements A, B and C. The table opposite shows the cost per kg of these elements for the years 1991 and 1992, together with the mass of each expressed as a percentage.

	Cost per kg (p)		
	1991	1992	%
A	50	62.5	x
B	20	22.5	$2x$
C	16	24	y

(i) Calculate price relatives for A, B and C for 1992 using 1991 as base year.
(ii) Given that the composite index number for the cost of the cereal in 1992 is 140, again using 1991 as base year, calculate the value of x and y. (C Additional)

15. The following data was extracted from the *Monthly Digest of Statistics* and relates to the General Index of Retail Prices.

(13 January 1987 = 100)		Index values	
	Weight	May 1988	May 1989
Food and catering	203	105.7	111.5
Alcohol and tobacco	119	105.6	109.9
Housing and household	341	106.6	121.4
Personal expenditure	110	105.3	111.6
Travel and leisure	227	106.7	113.3
All items	1000	106.2	

(a) Explain the meaning of the line '(13 January 1987 = 100)'.
(b) A house was valued at £54,000 in May 1988. A year later, it was decided to revise the value in line with the increase in the appropriate index. Calculate the new value of the house.
(c) Calculate the all items index for May 1989 relative to 13 January 1987.
(d) What does your answer to (c) say about overall prices relative to 13 January 1987?

16. (a) The masses, measured to the nearest kilogram, of 200 girls were recorded and tabulated as shown below.

Mass, kg	Number of girls
46–50	20
51–55	60
56–60	56
61–65	35
66–70	19
71–75	10

Construct the cumulative frequency table for this distribution and draw the cumulative frequency curve.

Use your curve to estimate
(i) the interquartile range,
(ii) the percentage of these girls having a mass greater than 58 kg.
(b) A group of 125 children raised money for a charity by sponsored activities. The amount raised by each child was recorded. These amounts, taken to the nearest £, are grouped in the table below.

Amount raised, £	Number of children
1–5	70
6–10	36
11–15	19

State the smallest possible amount which may have been raised by one child. Without drawing a cumulative frequency curve, estimate the median amount raised. Also estimate the mean amount raised and explain briefly why this is larger than the median. (C Additional)

17. The cumulative frequency table below refers to the lengths, in minutes, of 400 telephone calls made from a certain household during a period of three months.

Length of call in minutes	Number of calls
$\leqslant 1$	20
$\leqslant 2$	67
$\leqslant 2\frac{1}{2}$	118
$\leqslant 3$	177
$\leqslant 5$	315
$\leqslant 10$	400

Construct the corresponding frequency table and draw a histogram to illustrate the data. Use linear interpolation to estimate the median length of call and explain the geometrical significance of a vertical line drawn through the histogram at this value. (C Additional)

18. (a) The yields, to the nearest kilogram, of 140 fruit trees are tabulated below.

Yield (kg)	Number of trees
10–14	4
15–19	8
20–24	13
25–29	28
30–34	39
35–39	30
40–44	11
45–49	7

Construct the cumulative frequency table for this distribution and draw the cumulative frequency curve.

Use your curve to estimate

(i)   the median yield,

(ii) the 80th percentile,

(iii) the number of trees yielding less than 23 kg of fruit.

(b) The masses, to the nearest kilogram, of 60 pigs are tabulated below.

Mass (kg)	Number of pigs
66–75	3
76–85	15
86–95	21
96–105	12
106–115	9

(i)   Find the probability that a pig selected at random will have an actual mass greater then 95.5 kg.

(ii) Without drawing the cumulative frequency curve, estimate the interquartile range.   (C Additional)

19.   (a) The times taken by a group of 150 students to solve a particular problem are given in the cumulative frequency distribution table below.

Time taken (s)	Cumulative frequency
$\leqslant 9.5$	0
$\leqslant 19.5$	4
$\leqslant 29.5$	15
$\leqslant 39.5$	51
$\leqslant 49.5$	111
$\leqslant 59.5$	139
$\leqslant 69.5$	147
$\leqslant 79.5$	150

Without drawing a cumulative frequency diagram, estimate

(i)   the median time,

(ii) the percentage of students solving the problem in under 32 seconds.

(b) The times, correct to the nearest second, for 100 athletes to cover one lap of a running track were recorded and are shown in the table below.

Recorded time (s)	Number of athletes
65–69	0
70–74	8
75–79	20
80–84	25
85–89	31
90–94	10
95–99	6

Draw a cumulative frequency graph and hence determine the interquartile range. To qualify for an athletic meeting, a runner needs to record a lap time of 78 seconds or under. Estimate the number of athletes who qualified and the median time for these qualifiers.   (C Additional)

20.   (a) Sketch the expected frequency curves for each of the following distributions:

(i) the number of light bulbs broken in boxes containing 125 bulbs, assuming that the modal number of breakages is 0,

(ii) the age at marriage of females.

(b) State the assumption that is made in obtaining measures of average and dispersion from grouped frequency tables.

The table below shows the ages, at last birthday, of the employees of a certain firm.

Age (last birthday)	No. of employees
Less than 20	32
20–	35
25–	39
30–	47
40–	45
50 and over	42

Without drawing a cumulative frequency curve, estimate (i) the semi-interquartile range, (ii) the number of employees aged 37 and over.   (C Additional)

21.   Two hundred and fifty Army recruits have the following heights.

Height (cm)	No. of recruits
165–	18
170–	37
175–	60
180–	65
185–	48
190–195	22

Plot the data in the form of a cumulative frequency curve. Use the curve to estimate

(a) the median height,

(b) the lower quartile height.

The tallest 40% of the recruits are to be formed into a special squad. Estimate

(c) the median,

(d) the upper quartile of the heights of the members of this squad.

22.   The following table shows the durations of 40 telephone calls from an office via the office switchboard.

Duration in minutes	Number of calls
$\leqslant 1$	6
1–2	10
2–3	15
3–5	5
5–10	4
$\geqslant 10$	0

Obtain an estimate of the mean and standard deviation of the data. Estimate the median, and the lower and upper quartiles.   (O & C)

23. (*a*) Find, showing your working clearly and not using any pre-programmed function on your calculator, the standard deviation of the following frequency distribution:

x	25	26	27	28
f	2	0	15	11

(*b*) The average height of 20 boys is 160 cm, with a standard deviation of 4 cm. The average height of 30 girls is 155 cm, with a standard deviation of 3.5 cm. Find the standard deviation of the whole group of 50 children.

24. The table below shows the durations of 60 journeys on the same route by a lorry, the variations in journey times being caused by varying traffic conditions.
Calculate, to the nearest minute, estimates of the mean and standard deviation for the duration of the journeys.
When the times for 40 other journeys were taken, it was found that the mean and standard deviation for the times of these 40 journeys were 6 h 24 min and 18 min, respectively. Find, also to the nearest minute, the estimated mean and standard deviation for the duration of all 100 journeys.   (C)

Time of journey in hours	Number of journeys
5.6–5.8	2
5.8–6.0	7
6.0–6.2	16
6.2–6.4	21
6.4–6.6	12
6.6–6.8	2

25. Below are given the number n of hours worked in a week by 64 men.

36.5	15.6	30.8	27.6	33.6	39.4	39.7	39.1
33.0	40.1	21.8	40.6	33.9	36.9	39.1	27.4
29.8	37.0	45.4	42.5	9.6	26.3	36.1	35.2
38.4	28.5	30.5	44.4	38.4	40.6	26.5	38.7
24.4	41.9	52.7	35.7	28.9	38.2	30.4	41.7
43.2	24.5	34.8	37.8	38.0	43.7	40.8	11.7
31.5	37.6	40.1	23.7	31.8	42.0	29.1	41.5
36.3	29.7	37.3	28.4	39.6	22.9	35.2	42.4

(i) Group the numbers into intervals of width 3 hours defined by $9.5 \leqslant n < 12.5$, $12.5 \leqslant n < 15.5, \ldots.$
(ii) Use the grouped data to calculate estimates of the mean and standard deviation of n.
(iii) Estimate the percentage of workmen for whom n is within one standard deviation of the mean.   (MEI)

26. A random sample of 1000 surnames is drawn from a local telephone directory. The distribution of the lengths of the names is as shown in the table below.
Calculate the sample mean and sample standard deviation. Obtain the upper quartile.
Represent graphically the data in the table. Give a reason why the sample of names obtained in this way may not be truly representative of the population of Great Britain.   (JMB)

Number of letters in surname	Frequency
3	13
4	102
5	186
6	237
7	215
8	113
9	83
10	32
11	13
12	6

27. A grouped frequency distribution of the ages of 358 employees in a factory is shown in the table below. Estimate, to the nearest month, the mean and the standard deviation of the ages of these employees.
Graphically, or otherwise, estimate
(*a*) the median and the interquartile range of the ages, each to the nearest month,
(*b*) the percentage, to one decimal place, of the employees who are over 27 years old and under 55 years old.   (L)

Age (last birthday)	Number of employees
16–20	36
21–25	56
26–30	58
31–35	52
36–40	46
41–45	38
46–50	36
51–60	36
61–	0

28. Referring to your projects if possible, give an example of a graphical representation of
(*a*) a discrete frequency distribution,
(*b*) a grouped frequency distribution.
Given the frequency distribution

x	1	2	3	4	5	6	7	8	9
f	1	3	7	9	13	9	5	2	1

find the median and the semi-interquartile range when
(*c*) x is a discrete variable,
(*d*) x is a continuous variable whose values were recorded to the nearest integer.
Calculate also, to 2 decimal places, the mean and the variance of the above distribution.   (L)

29. In a borehole the thickness, in mm, of the 25 strata are shown in the table.

Thickness (mm)	Number of strata
0–	2
20–	5
30–	9
40–	8
50–	1
60–	0

Draw a histogram to illustrate these data.
Construct a cumulative frequency table and draw a cumulative frequency polygon. Hence, or otherwise, estimate the median and the interquartile range for these data.
Find the proportion of the strata that are less than 28 mm thick.   (L)P

30. In a certain industry, the numbers of thousands of employees in 1970 were as shown in the table, by age groups.
Calculate the arithmetic mean, median, variance and standard deviation of the ages of employees in the industry.
Estimate the percentage of the employees whose ages lie within one standard deviation of the arithmetic mean.   (AEB)

Age last birthday	Number of thousands
15–19	66
20–24	65
25–29	56
30–34	50
35–39	42
40–44	37
45–49	35
50–54	30
55–59	24
60–64	22

31. A weather station recorded the number of hours of sunshine each day for 80 days, with the results as shown in the table.
[The grouping symbol 2–3, for example, denotes greater than 2 hours and less than or equal to 3 hours.]
State which is the modal group.
Construct a cumulative frequency table and draw the cumulative frequency curve. Use your curve to estimate (i) the median, (ii) the interquartile range, (iii) the percentage of days for which more than $3\frac{1}{2}$ hours of sunshine were recorded.
                                              (C Additional)

Hours of sunshine	Number of days
0	10
0–1	2
1–2	6
2–3	17
3–4	22
4–5	11
5–6	5
6–7	3
7–8	2
8–12	2
over 12	0

32. 200 candidates sat an examination and the distribution was obtained as shown in the table.
If the limits of class 40–49 are 39.5 to 49.5, what is the mid-interval value of this class?
Calculate the mean of the marks explaining any limitations of your calculation.
Plot a cumulative frequency curve and use it to estimate the upper and lower quartiles. Assuming that your estimates are exact, find values for a and b correct to 2 significant figures, in order that the above marks can be scaled by the equation $y = ax + b$, where y is the new mark, so that the mean becomes 45 and the lower quartile becomes 35.
State, with reason, whether the quartiles of the original marks will scale into the quartiles of the scaled marks.

Marks (x)	Frequency
10–19	10
20–29	18
30–39	20
40–49	30
50–59	49
60–69	46
70–79	20
80–89	5
90–99	2

33. The table opposite gives an analysis by numbers of employees of the size of UK factories of less than 1000 employees manufacturing clothing and footwear. Calculate as accurately as the data allow the mean and the median of this distribution, showing your working.
If 90% of the factories have less than N employees, estimate N.   (O & C)

Number of employees	Number of factories
11–19	1500
20–24	800
25–99	2300
100–199	700
200–499	400
500–999	100
Total	5800

2

SHAPES OF DISTRIBUTIONS

THE SHAPE OF A DISTRIBUTION

If distributions represented by a vertical line graph or a histogram are illustrated using a frequency curve, it is easier to see the general 'shape' of the distribution. For example:

(a)

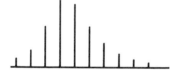

(b)

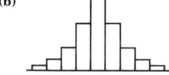

(c)

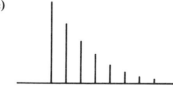
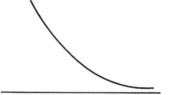

(d)

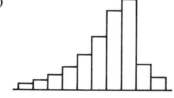
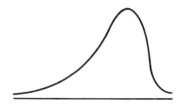

(e)

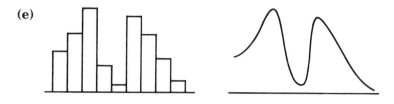

We shall consider some of these general shapes in more detail.

SYMMETRICAL BELL-SHAPED DISTRIBUTIONS

In a symmetrical, bell-shaped distribution, the mean, median and mode coincide.

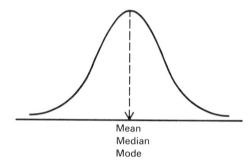

Mean
Median
Mode

This type of distribution is known as 'normal' and an approximately **normal distribution** occurs when measuring quantities such as heights, masses, examination marks.

POSITIVELY SKEWED DISTRIBUTIONS

In this distribution, the long tail indicates the presence of extreme values at the *positive* end of the distribution. This pulls the mean to the right.

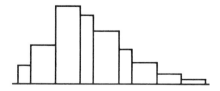

This type of distribution is said to be **positively skewed**.

In a positively skewed distribution, the mean is pulled in a positive direction ($\longrightarrow$). The frequency curve would be:

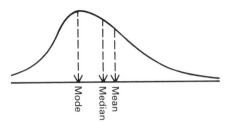

This type of distribution occurs when considering, for example,
   the number of children per family,
   the age at which women marry,
   the distribution of wages in a firm.

NEGATIVELY SKEWED DISTRIBUTIONS

In a negatively skewed distribution, the mean is pulled in a negative direction ($\longleftarrow$). The frequency curve would be:

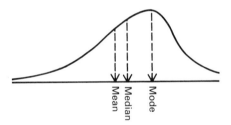

This type of distribution can occur when considering, for example
   reaction times for an experiment,
   daily maximum temperatures for a month in summer.

NOTE: the median generally lies between the mode and the mean, and the following relation is satisfied

$$\text{mean} - \text{mode} \approx 3(\text{mean} - \text{median})$$

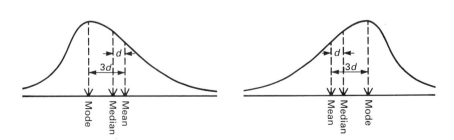

PEARSON'S COEFFICIENT OF SKEWNESS

We need to know two things to describe the 'skewness' of a distribution. One is the direction of the skew, positive or negative, and the other is a measure of the degree of skewness, i.e. how far the distribution is pulled in one direction. One measure of skewness is given by

Pearson's coefficient of skewness

$$\text{Pearson's coefficient of skewness} = \frac{\text{mean} - \text{mode}}{\text{standard deviation}}$$

If mean > mode, the skew is positive.
If mean < mode, the skew is negative.
If mean = mode, the skew is zero and the distribution is symmetrical.

Generally skewness can take any values between 3 and −3.

For example, the measure of skewness for these distributions might be as shown:

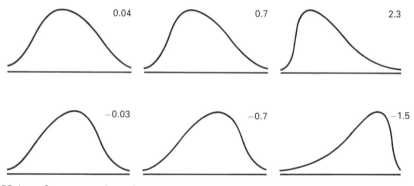

Using the approximation

$$\text{mean} - \text{mode} = 3(\text{mean} - \text{median})$$

the formula for skewness becomes

$$\text{Pearson's coefficient of skewness} = \frac{3\,(\text{mean} - \text{median})}{\text{standard deviation}}$$

Example 2.1   A farmer records the number of eggs he collects from his hens over a 150-day period. The frequency distribution of the eggs collected is shown below.

Number of eggs	15	16	17	18	19	20	21	22	23	24	25
Frequency	1	2	4	6	9	13	18	22	35	30	10

What is the modal number of eggs collected per day?

Calculate

(a) the median number of eggs collected per day,

(b) the mean and standard deviation of the number of eggs collected per day.

Draw a line diagram to illustrate the data and comment on the shape of the diagram.   (AEB)

Solution 2.1   The modal number of eggs is 23.

(a) $n = 150$, so the median is the $\frac{1}{2}(150 + 1)$th value, i.e. the 75.5th value.

Part of the cumulative frequency table indicates:

Number of eggs	...	$\leqslant 21$	$\leqslant 22$	$\leqslant 23$	...
Cumulative frequency	...	53	75	110	...

So the 75th value is 22 and the 76th value is 23. Therefore the 75.5th value is 22.5.

The median is 22.5 eggs.

(b) To find the mean and standard deviation, use

$$\bar{x} = \frac{\sum fx}{\sum f}$$

$$= \frac{3291}{150}$$

$$= 21.94$$

$$s^2 = \frac{\sum fx^2}{\sum f} - \bar{x}^2$$

$$= \frac{72\,917}{150} - (21.94)^2$$

$$= 4.749\ldots$$

$$s = \sqrt{4.749\ldots}$$

$$= 2.179\ldots$$

Therefore the mean is 21.94 and the standard deviation is 2.18 (2 d.p.).

Reminder about use of calculator in SD mode:

	Casio 85/100/115 series	Casio Graphic 7000 GA
Set SD mode	MODE 3	MODE ×
Clear memories	SHIFT KAC	SHIFT SCI EXE
Input data	15 × 1 DATA	15 SHIFT ; 1 DT
	16 × 2 DATA	16 SHIFT ; 2 DT
	... ...	... ...
	25 × 10 DATA	25 SHIFT ; 10 DT
Output:		
$\bar{x}$ = **21.94**	SHIFT 1	SHIFT 1 EXE
s = **2.179**...	SHIFT 2	SHIFT 2 EXE
Clear SD mode	MODE 0	MODE +

Line graph to show number of eggs collected

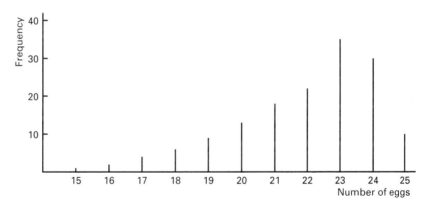

We can see from the line diagram that the distribution is negatively skewed.

From the results obtained above we could calculate the skewness, where

$$\text{skewness} = \frac{\text{mean} - \text{mode}}{\text{standard deviation}}$$

$$= \frac{21.94 - 23}{2.179...}$$

$$= -0.486$$

This also indicates that the distribution is negatively skewed.

Example 2.2   Electric fuses, nominally rated at 30 A, are tested by passing a
gradually increasing electric current through them and recording the
current, x amperes, at which they blow. The results of this test on a
sample of 125 such fuses are shown in the following table.

Current (x A)	Number of fuses
$25 \leqslant x < 28$	6
$28 \leqslant x < 29$	12
$29 \leqslant x < 30$	27
$30 \leqslant x < 31$	30
$31 \leqslant x < 32$	18
$32 \leqslant x < 33$	14
$33 \leqslant x < 34$	9
$34 \leqslant x < 35$	4
$35 \leqslant x < 40$	5

Draw a histogram to represent these data.

For this sample calculate

(i)   the median current,

(ii)   the mean current,

(iii) the standard deviation of current.

A measure of the *skewness* (or asymmetry) of a distribution is given
by

$$\frac{3(\text{mean} - \text{median})}{\text{standard deviation}}$$

Calculate the value of this measure of skewness for the above data.
Explain briefly how this skewness is apparent in the shape of your
histogram.   (L)

Solution 2.2

Current	Class width	Frequency	Frequency density $= \dfrac{\text{frequency}}{\text{class width}}$
$25 \leqslant x < 28$	3	6	2
$28 \leqslant x < 29$	1	12	12
$29 \leqslant x < 30$	1	27	27
$30 \leqslant x < 31$	1	30	30
$31 \leqslant x < 32$	1	18	18
$32 \leqslant x < 33$	1	14	14
$33 \leqslant x < 34$	1	9	9
$34 \leqslant x < 35$	1	4	4
$35 \leqslant x < 40$	5	5	1

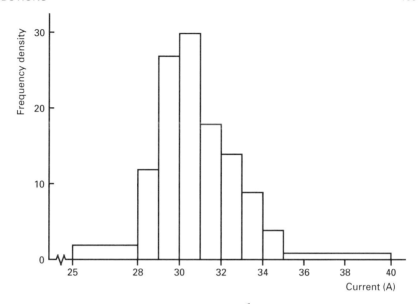

(*i*) For grouped data, the median is the $\frac{1}{2}n$th value, i.e. the 62.5th value, since $n = 125$. We find this by linear interpolation.

Since 45 fuses blew at a current less than 30 A and 75 fuses blew at a current less than 31 A, the median lies in the interval, of width 1 A, from 30 A to 31 A.

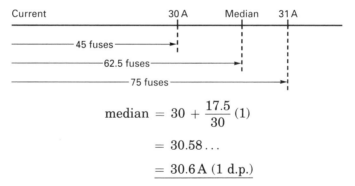

$$\text{median} = 30 + \frac{17.5}{30}\,(1)$$

$$= 30.58\ldots$$

$$= \underline{30.6\,\text{A (1 d.p.)}}$$

Mid-point (x)	f
26.5	6
28.5	12
29.5	27
30.5	30
31.5	18
32.5	14
33.5	9
34.5	4
37.5	5
	$\sum f = 125$

(*ii*) $\quad \bar{x} = \dfrac{\sum fx}{\sum f}$

$\qquad = \dfrac{3861.5}{125}$

$\qquad = 30.892$

(*iii*) $\; s^2 = \dfrac{\sum fx^2}{\sum f} - \bar{x}^2$

$\qquad = \dfrac{119\,905.25}{125} - 30.892^2$

$\qquad = 4.926\ldots$

$\quad\; s = 2.219\ldots$

[Check these on your calculator, using SD mode.]

Therefore the mean is 30.892 A and the standard deviation is 2.22 A (2 d.p.).

Now   skewness $= \dfrac{3(\text{mean} - \text{median})}{\text{standard deviation}}$

$$= \frac{3(30.892 - 30.58\ldots)}{2.219\ldots}$$

$$= 0.42 \text{ (2 d.p.)}$$

Since skewness > 0, the <u>distribution is positively skewed.</u>

If we consider the resulting frequency polygon we can see that the distribution is skewed to the right, i.e. positively skewed.

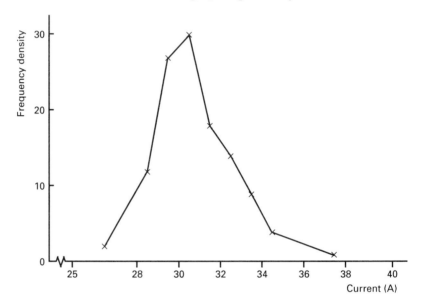

Exercise 2a

1. Calculate Pearson's coefficient of skewness for the following frequency distributions where

    $$\text{skewness} = \frac{\text{mean} - \text{mode}}{\text{standard deviation}}$$

(a)
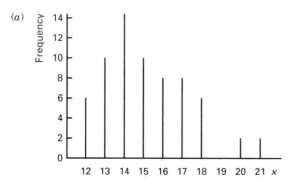

(b)
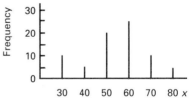

(c)

x	f
60	12
70	14
80	20
90	30
100	15
110	6
120	2

(d)

x	f
15	3
16	5
17	8
18	7
19	4
20	2
21	1
22	1
23	0
24	1

(e)

x	f
20	2
21	1
22	4
23	5
24	7
25	8
26	4
27	1

2. For a skewed distribution, the mean is 16, the median is 20 and the standard deviation is 5. Calculate Pearson's coefficient of skewness and sketch the curve.

3. For a skewed distribution, the mean is 86, the mode is 78 and the variance is 16. Calculate Pearson's coefficient of skewness and sketch the curve.

4. The following table shows the time, to the nearest minute, spent reading during a particular day by a group of school children.

Time	Number of children
10–19	8
20–24	15
25–29	25
30–39	18
40–49	12
50–64	7
65–89	5

(a) Represent these data by a histogram.
(b) Comment on the shape of the distribution. (L)

5. Find Pearson's coefficient of skewness for the distribution represented by this stem and leaf plot, which gives marks in an examination.

Stem	Leaf
1	9
2	2 8
3	3 7
4	5
5	2 5 5 7
6	1 1 6 6 8 8 8
7	3 5 5
8	2 9
9	1

Key 3 | 7 means 37

6. Over a period of four years a bank keeps a weekly record of the number of cheques with errors that are presented for payment. The results for the 200 accounting weeks are as follows.

Number of cheques with errors (x)	Number of weeks (f)
0	5
1	22
2	46
3	38
4	31
5	23
6	16
7	11
8	6
9	2

$$\left(\sum fx = 706 \qquad \sum fx^2 = 3280\right)$$

Construct a suitable pictorial representation of these data.
State the modal value and calculate the median, mean and standard deviation of the number of cheques with errors in a week.

Some textbooks measure the *skewness* (or asymmetry) of a distribution by

$$\frac{3(\text{mean} - \text{median})}{\text{standard deviation}}$$

and others measure it by

$$\frac{(\text{mean} - \text{mode})}{\text{standard deviation}}$$

Calculate and compare the values of these two measures of skewness for the above data. State how this skewness is reflected in the shape of your graph. (AEB)

QUARTILE COEFFICIENT OF SKEWNESS

Another measure of skewness is defined in terms of the quartiles, where Q_1 is the lower quartile, Q_2 is the median and Q_3 is the upper quartile.

$$\text{Quartile coefficient of skewness} = \frac{(Q_3 - Q_2) - (Q_2 - Q_1)}{Q_3 - Q_1}$$

$$= \frac{Q_3 - 2Q_2 + Q_1}{Q_3 - Q_1}$$

Normal distribution

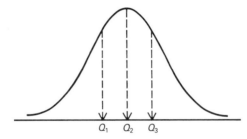

$$Q_3 - Q_2 = Q_2 - Q_1$$
Quartile skewness $= 0$

Positively skewed distribution

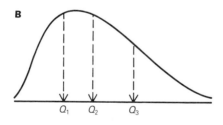

$$Q_3 - Q_2 > Q_2 - Q_1$$
Quartile skewness > 0

Negatively skewed distribution

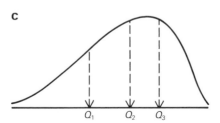

$$Q_3 - Q_2 < Q_2 - Q_1$$
Quartile skewness < 0

Example 2.3 31 students tried to estimate the length of a line. The line was actually 60 mm long. These are their results, in mm.

$$
\begin{array}{ccccccccccc}
61 & 70 & 46 & 44 & 26 & 23 & 30 & 83 & 52 & 44 & 38 \\
37 & 49 & 59 & 58 & 63 & 31 & 29 & 37 & 48 & 76 & 61 \\
46 & 31 & 38 & 41 & 49 & 52 & 56 & 75 & 61 & &
\end{array}
$$

Find the median and the quartiles of this distribution. Use the quartiles to estimate the skewness. Draw a histogram using class intervals 20–, 30–, ..., 80–90.

Solution 2.3 We arrange the results in order. There are 31 results, so the median is the $\frac{1}{2}(31+1)$th value, i.e. the 16th value.

To find the quartiles, since n is odd (see page 64)

$$Q_1 = \tfrac{1}{4}(31+1)\text{th values} = \text{8th value}$$

$$Q_3 = \tfrac{3}{4}(31+1)\text{th values} = \text{24th value}$$

$$
\begin{array}{cccccccccccccc}
23 & 26 & 29 & 30 & 31 & 31 & 37 & \boxed{37} & 38 & 38 & 41 & 44 & 44 & 46 & 46 \\
\boxed{48} & 49 & 49 & 52 & 52 & 56 & 58 & 59 & \boxed{61} & 61 & 61 & 63 & 70 & 75 & 76 & 83
\end{array}
$$

median $Q_2 = 48$, $Q_1 = 37$, $Q_3 = 61$.

Now

$$Q_3 - Q_2 = 61 - 48 = 13$$

$$Q_2 - Q_1 = 48 - 37 = 11$$

Since $Q_3 - Q_2 > Q_2 - Q_1$ the distribution is positively skewed.

$$
\text{Quartile coefficient of skewness} = \frac{(Q_3 - Q_2) - (Q_2 - Q_1)}{Q_3 - Q_1}
$$

$$
= \frac{13 - 11}{61 - 37}
$$

$$
= 0.083\ldots
$$

The frequency distribution is as shown:

Length (mm)	Frequency
20–	3
30–	7
40–	8
50–	5
60–	4
70–	3
80–	1

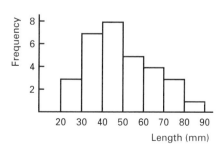

The diagram confirms the positive skew.

Example 2.4   The following table summarises data relating to the lifetimes of a random sample of 200 bulbs taken from the production line of a particular manufacturer.

Lifetime (to nearest hour)	Number of bulbs
700–719	10
720–729	14
730–739	16
740–749	21
750–754	35
755–759	41
760–764	38
765–769	15
770–779	7
780–799	3

(a) By calculation, estimate the median and quartiles of these lifetimes. Give your answers to 1 decimal place.

(b) One method of assessing the skewness of a distribution is to calculate

$$\frac{3(\text{mean} - \text{median})}{\text{standard deviation}}$$

Evaluate this, to 1 decimal place, for the above distribution.

(c) Use the quartiles to assess skewness and state whether or not you feel this result is compatible with your answer to (b).

(d) State, with reason, whether the manufacturer might prefer to use the standard deviation rather than the interquartile range as a measure of spread for the lifetimes of the bulbs from this production line.   (L)

Solution 2.4   (a) For grouped continuous data, where $n = 200$

$$Q_1 \text{ is the } \tfrac{1}{4} n \text{th value, i.e. } 50 \text{th value}$$

$$Q_2 \text{ is the } \tfrac{1}{2} n \text{th value, i.e. } 100 \text{th value}$$

$$Q_3 \text{ is the } \tfrac{3}{4} n \text{th value, i.e. } 150 \text{th value}$$

To give an idea of where these values come in the distribution, we form a cumulative frequency table.

Lifetime (h)	Cumulative frequency
< 719.5	10
< 729.5	24
< 739.5	40
< 749.5	61
< 754.5	96
< 759.5	137
< 764.5	175
< 769.5	190
< 779.5	197
< 799.5	200

So Q_1 lies in the interval 739.5 to 749.5 (a width of 10)

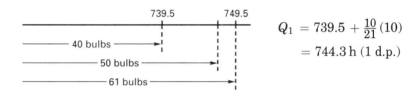

$$Q_1 = 739.5 + \tfrac{10}{21}(10)$$
$$= 744.3\,\text{h (1 d.p.)}$$

Q_2 lies in the interval 754.5 to 759.5 (a width of 5)

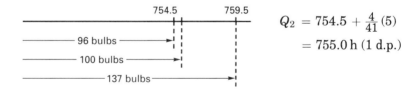

$$Q_2 = 754.5 + \tfrac{4}{41}(5)$$
$$= 755.0\,\text{h (1 d.p.)}$$

Q_3 lies in the interval 759.5 to 764.5 (a width of 5)

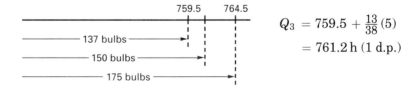

$$Q_3 = 759.5 + \tfrac{13}{38}(5)$$
$$= 761.2\,\text{h (1 d.p.)}$$

Therefore the median is 755.0 h, the lower quartile is 744.3 h
and the upper quartile is 761.2 h.

(b) To calculate the mean and standard deviation:

Lifetime	Mid-point (x)	Frequency (f)
700–719	709.5	10
720–729	724.5	14
730–739	734.5	16
740–749	744.5	21
750–754	752	35
755–759	757	41
760–764	762	38
765–769	767	15
770–779	774.5	7
780–799	789.5	3
		$\sum f = 200$

$$\bar{x} = \frac{\sum fx}{\sum f}$$

$$= 751.1625$$

$$s = \sqrt{\frac{\sum fx^2}{\sum f} - \bar{x}^2}$$

$$= 15.89\ldots$$

Using the calculator in SD mode:

	Casio 85/100/115 series	Casio Graphic 7000 GA
Set SD mode	MODE 3	MODE ×
Clear memories	SHIFT KAC	SHIFT SCI EXE
Input data	709.5 × 10 DATA	709.5 SHIFT ; 10 DT
	724.5 × 14 DATA	724.5 SHIFT ; 14 DT
	... ...	... ...
	789.5 × 3 DATA	789.5 SHIFT ; 3 DT
Output:		
$\bar{x}$ = **751**.1625	SHIFT 1	SHIFT 1 EXE
s = **15**.89...	SHIFT 2	SHIFT 2 EXE
Clear SD mode	MODE 0	MODE +

Therefore the mean is 751.2 h (1 d.p.) and the standard deviation is 15.9 h (1 d.p.).

$$\text{Pearson's coefficient of skewness} = \frac{3(\text{mean} - \text{median})}{\text{standard deviation}}$$

$$= \frac{3(751.1625 - 755.0)}{15.89\ldots}$$

$$= -0.7 \quad (1 \text{ d.p.})$$

So the distribution is negatively skewed.

(**c**) Using the quartiles to assess skewness, where

$$\text{Quartile skewness} = \frac{(Q_3 - Q_2) - (Q_2 - Q_1)}{Q_3 - Q_1}$$

$Q_3 - Q_2 = 761.2 - 755.0 = 6.2 \text{ hours,}$

$Q_2 - Q_1 = 755.0 - 744.3 = 10.7 \text{ hours.}$

Now since $Q_3 - Q_2 < Q_2 - Q_1$, the distribution is negatively skewed, agreeing with the conclusion in (**b**).

(**d**) In general, if a distribution is approximately symmetrical it is better to use the mean for the average and the standard deviation as a measure of spread. If a distribution is skew then it is better to use the median and the interquartile range $(Q_3 - Q_1)$, because these are not affected by the extreme values which are causing the skew.

In this particular case the standard deviation is approximately 16 hours and the interquartile range is $761.2 - 744.3 \approx 17$ hours. For advertising purposes the manufacturer may wish to use the standard deviation as a measure of spread, because it is smaller.

NOTE: for this example it is interesting to draw the histogram to check the direction of the skew.

Lifetime (h)	Class width	Frequency	Frequency density
700–719	20	10	0.5
720–729	10	14	1.4
730–739	10	16	1.6
740–749	10	21	2.1
750–754	5	35	7
755–759	5	41	8.2
760–764	5	38	7.6
765–769	5	15	3
770–779	10	7	0.7
780–799	20	3	0.15

Histogram to show lifetimes of bulbs

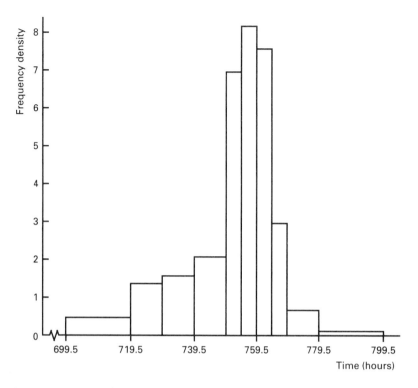

The negative skew can be seen clearly in the histogram.

INTERPRETATION OF THE STANDARD DEVIATION IN THE NORMAL DISTRIBUTION

The standard deviation measures the dispersion of values around the mean. The greater the spread, the larger the standard deviation. For example:

(**a**) Two normal distributions with the same mean, but different standard deviations:

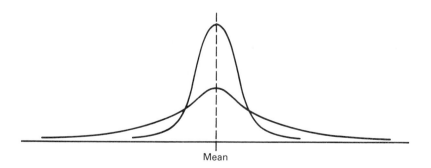

(**b**) Two normal distributions with different means, but the same standard deviation:

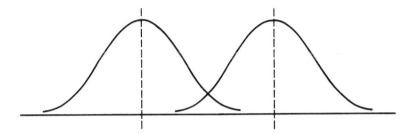

The normal distribution is one of the most important distributions in statistics. It will be considered in detail in Chapter 7, but some useful relationships concerning standard deviation are introduced here.

For a *normal* distribution, approximately 68% of the values lie within one standard deviation either side of the mean.

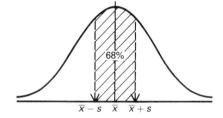

Approximately 95% of the values lie within two standard deviations either side of the mean.

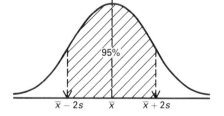

Over 99% of the values (nearly all!) lie within three standard deviations either side of the mean.

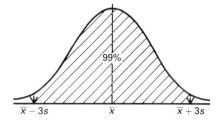

The quartiles are approximately $\frac{2}{3} \times$ standard deviation either side of the mean.

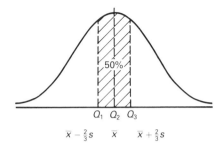

Exercise 2b

1.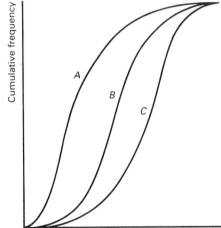

These are the 3 frequency curves associated with the cumulative frequency curves *A, B, C* above. Label each frequency curve with the appropriate letter.

(i)

(ii)

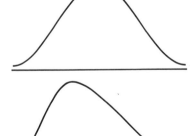

(iii)

2. The following table gives the blood pressure of 60 students.

Blood pressure	Frequency
95–	2
105–	5
110–	6
115–	9
120–	14
125–	3
130–	6
135–	5
140–	4
150–180	6

(*a*) Find
  (i) Pearson's coefficient of skewness
  (ii) the quartile coefficient of skewness
(*b*) Draw the histogram.

3. The following grouped frequency distribution summarises the time, to the nearest minute, spent waiting by a sample of patients in a doctor's surgery.

Waiting time (to nearest minute)	Number of patients
3 or less	6
4–6	15
7–8	27
9	49
10	52
11–12	29
13–15	13
16 or more	9

The mean of the times was 9.63 minutes and the standard deviation was 3.03 minutes.

(a) Using interpolation, estimate the median and semi-interquartile range of these data. For a normal distribution the ratio of the semi-interquartile range to the standard deviation would be approximately 0.67.

(b) Calculate the corresponding value for the above data. Comment on your result.

For a normal distribution, 90% of times would be expected to lie in the interval

(mean $\pm$ 1.645 standard deviations).

(c) Find the theoretical limits for these data.

(d) Using appropriate percentiles, estimate comparable limits. Comment on your result.

(L)

4. Calculate the quartile coefficient of skewness for each of the following distributions:

(a)

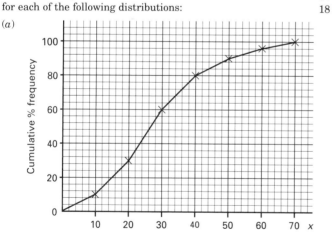

(b)

x	21	22	23	24	25	26	27
f	2	10	14	6	4	2	1

(c)

x	10–	20–	30–	40–	50–
f	6	13	15	20	10

(d)

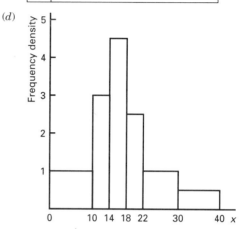

(e)

Stem	Leaf
2	0 0
5	0 1 1
8	1 1 2 2 2
11	0 0 1 2 2 2
14	1 1 2 2
17	0 1
18	1

Key 5 | 1 means 6

BOX AND WHISKER DIAGRAMS

Consider the cumulative percentage frequency curves for girls' and boys' marks given on page 73. We can draw each curve separately and find the median Q_2 and the quartiles Q_1 and Q_3.

We have illustrated these values, together with the range, in a diagram below the axis, called a 'box and whisker' diagram.

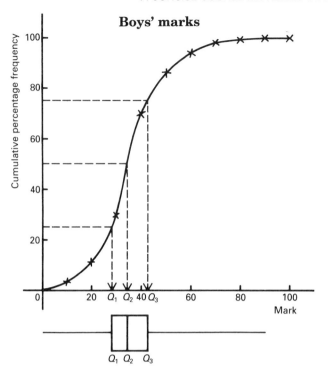

Box and whisker diagram for boys' marks

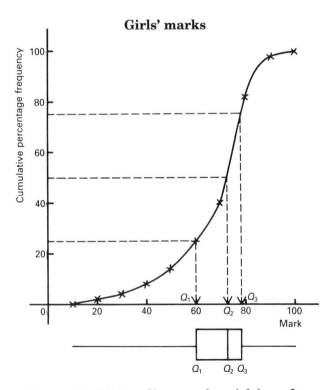

Box and whisker diagram for girls' marks

The box plots can be drawn horizontally, as shown on page 118, or vertically thus:

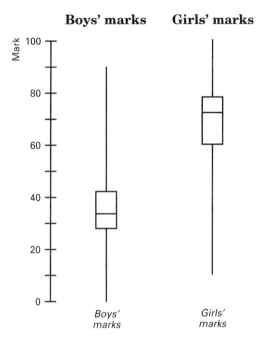

Boys' marks   Girls' marks

The **box and whisker diagram**, or **box plot**, illustrates the dispersion, or spread of the distribution. It uses the highest and lowest values of the data, the quartiles (Q_1 and Q_3) and the median (Q_2). For example, *vertically*:

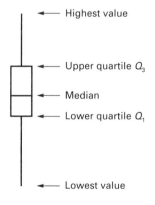

The 'box' extends from Q_1 to Q_3 and so encloses the middle 50% of the data.

The 'whiskers' extend from the box to the highest and lowest values and illustrate the range of the data.

and *horizontally*:

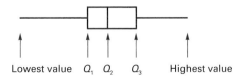

A box plot for a *symmetrical distribution* would look like this:

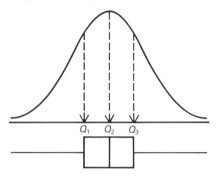

The whiskers are of equal length and the median is in the middle of the box.

For a *positively skewed distribution:*

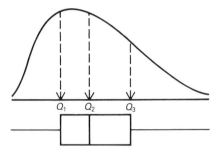

The right hand whisker is longer and the median is nearer to the lower quartile.

For a *negatively skewed distribution:*

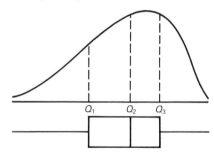

The left hand whisker is longer and the median is nearer to the upper quartile.

Example 2.5   A class of pupils played a computer game which tested how quickly they reacted to a visual instruction to press a particular key. The computer measured their reaction times in tenths of a second and stored a record of the sex and reaction time of each pupil. Finally it displayed the following 'summary statistics' for the whole class.

	Median	Lower quartile	Upper quartile	Min	Max
Girls	10	8	15	6	19
Boys	10	7	13	4	16

(**a**) Draw two box plots suitable for comparing the reaction times of boys and girls.

(**b**) Write a brief comparison of the performance of boys and girls in this game.   (NEAB)

Solution 2.5 (**a**)

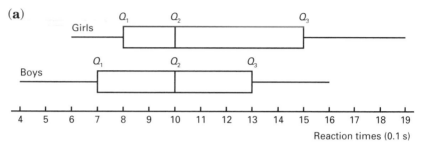

(**b**) The 'typical' (median) reaction time for boys and girls is the same ($10 \times 0.1 = 1$ second). However the times for the boys are more evenly distributed, with a smaller range. There is a bigger spread of times for the girls and their distribution is positively skewed.

Boys generally have the faster reaction time.

Example 2.6 A random sample of 51 people were asked to record the number of miles they travelled by car in a given week. The distances, to the nearest mile, are shown below.

```
67  76  85  42  93  48  93  46  52
72  77  53  41  48  86  78  56  80
70  70  66  62  54  85  60  58  43
58  74  44  52  74  52  82  78  47
66  50  67  87  78  86  94  63  72
63  44  47  57  68  81
```

(**a**) Construct a stem and leaf diagram to represent these data.

(**b**) Find the median and the quartiles of this distribution.

(**c**) Draw a box plot to represent these data.

(**d**) Give one advantage of using
    (*i*) a stem and leaf diagram,
    (*ii*) a box plot,
    to illustrate data such as that given above.   (L)

Solution 2.6 (**a**)

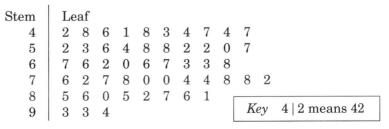

Stem	Leaf
4	2 8 6 1 8 3 4 7 4 7
5	2 3 6 4 8 8 2 2 0 7
6	7 6 2 0 6 7 3 3 8
7	6 2 7 8 0 0 4 4 8 8 2
8	5 6 0 5 2 7 6 1
9	3 3 4

Key 4 | 2 means 42

Arranged in order, we have

Stem	Leaf
4	1 2 3 4 4 6 7 7 8 8
5	0 2 ② 2 3 4 6 7 8 8
6	0 2 3 3 6 ⑥ 7 7 8
7	0 0 2 2 4 4 6 7 8 ⑧ 8
8	0 1 2 5 5 6 6 7
9	3 3 4

Key   4 | 2 means 42

(**b**) The median is the $\frac{1}{2}(n + 1)$th value where $n = 51$.

Therefore $Q_2 = \frac{1}{2}(52)$th value $= 26$th value $= 66$ miles.

Check this for yourself, count from the highest value 94, 93, 93, 87, 86, ..., or from the lowest 41, 42, 43, 44, 44, ...

$$Q_1 = \tfrac{1}{4}(52)\text{th value} = 13\text{th value} = 52 \text{ miles.}$$

$$Q_3 = \tfrac{3}{4}(52)\text{th value} = 39\text{th value} = 78 \text{ miles.}$$

(**c**)

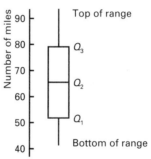

(**d**) (*i*)   The stem and leaf diagram gives a visual impression of the data whilst keeping the details of the original data.

(*ii*)   The box plot gives the immediate impression of an approximately symmetrical distribution, with the middle 50% of the distribution lying between 52 miles and 78 miles.

Example 2.7   A marketing company always buys new cars on 1st August. Before making any purchases on 1st August 1992, they reviewed their fleet of cars. The following table shows the age, x, in years, of the cars in the fleet.

Age (x)	1	2	3	4	5	6	7	8	9	10	11
Number of cars (f)	14	20	16	14	12	8	6	4	3	2	1

Find

(**a**) the mode,

(**b**) the median and quartiles,

(**c**) the mean,

of this distribution.

Draw a box plot to represent these data.

The distribution is positively skewed.

Use your calculations to justify this statement. (L)

Solution 2.7 (a) The mode is 2 years.

(b) For an ungrouped frequency distribution we take the median to be the $\frac{1}{2}(n + 1)$th value, where $n = \sum f = 100$.

Therefore Q_2 is the age of the 50.5th car,
i.e. the average of the ages of the 50th and 51st cars.

We find the quartiles by dividing in half the two distributions either side of Q_2:

$$1\ 2\ 3\ \ldots\ 25\ 26\ \ldots\ 48\ 49\ 50\ 51\ 52\ 53\ \ldots\ 75\ 76\ \ldots\ 99\ 100$$
$$\qquad\qquad\quad \uparrow \qquad\qquad\qquad\qquad\quad \uparrow \qquad\qquad\qquad\quad \uparrow$$
$$\qquad\qquad\quad Q_1 \qquad\qquad\qquad\qquad\quad Q_2 \qquad\qquad\qquad\quad Q_3$$

So Q_1 is the average of the ages of the 25th and 26th cars and Q_3 is the average of the ages of the 75th and 76th cars.

Forming a cumulative frequency table:

x	f	Age	Cumulative frequency
1	14	$\leqslant 1$	14
2	20	$\leqslant 2$	34
3	16	$\leqslant 3$	50
4	14	$\leqslant 4$	64
5	12	$\leqslant 5$	76
6	8	$\leqslant 6$	84
7	6	$\leqslant 7$	90
8	4	$\leqslant 8$	94
9	3	$\leqslant 9$	97
10	2	$\leqslant 10$	99
11	1	$\leqslant 11$	100

The age of both the 25th and 26th cars is 2 years.

Therefore $Q_1 = 2$ years.

The age of the 50th car is 3 years.

The age of the 51st car is 4 years.

Therefore $Q_2 = 3.5$ years.

The age of both the 75th and 76th cars is 5 years.

Therefore $Q_3 = 5$ years.

Therefore the median, Q_2, is 3.5 years, the lower quartile, Q_1 is 2 years and the upper quartile, Q_3 is 5 years.

(c) To find the mean, use the calculator in SD mode or calculate

$$\bar{x} = \frac{\sum fx}{\sum f}$$

$$= \frac{398}{100}$$

$$= 3.98$$

The mean is 3.98 years.

Box plot

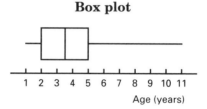

Now
$$\text{mode} = 2 \text{ years}$$
$$\text{median} = 3.5 \text{ years}$$
$$\text{mean} = 3.98 \text{ years}$$

So mode < median < mean, and the distribution is positively skewed.

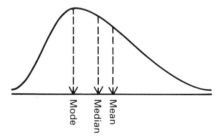

Example 2.8   The times taken by 30 students to solve a mathematical problem were measured to the nearest second. The results were as shown:

Time spent (s)	Frequency
25–29	2
30–34	4
35–39	6
40–44	8
45–49	4
50–54	3
55–59	2
60–64	1

Solution 2.8   For grouped continuous data we take the median to be the $\frac{1}{2}n$ th value, i.e. the 15th value, since $n = 30$.

$$Q_1 = \tfrac{1}{4}n \text{ th value} = 7.5\text{th value.}$$

$$Q_3 = \tfrac{3}{4}n \text{ th value} = 22.5\text{th value.}$$

We form a cumulative frequency distribution and then draw a cumulative frequency polygon.

Time spent	Cumulative frequency
< 24.5	0
< 29.5	2
< 34.5	6
< 39.5	12
< 44.5	20
< 49.5	24
< 54.5	27
< 59.5	29
< 64.5	30

Cumulative frequency polygon to show times taken

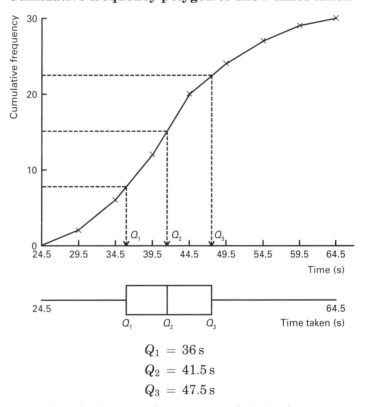

$$Q_1 = 36\,\text{s}$$
$$Q_2 = 41.5\,\text{s}$$
$$Q_3 = 47.5\,\text{s}$$

We assume that the lowest value is 24.5 and the highest is 64.5.

From the box plot the distribution appears to be slightly positively skewed.

Use of box plots to identify 'outliers'

Sometimes an unusually high or low value occurs in a set of data. There may be a good reason for these unusual results, but quite often they occur because an error was made when the data were recorded.

We have already seen (page 116) that for a normal distribution, the quartiles are situated at approximately $\frac{2}{3} \times$ standard deviation either side of the mean, and that nearly all values lie within 3 standard deviations of the mean.

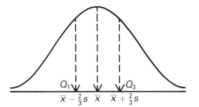
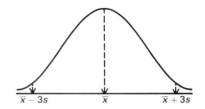

The interquartile range $= Q_3 - Q_1$

$$= \bar{x} + \tfrac{2}{3}s - (\bar{x} - \tfrac{2}{3}s)$$

$$= \tfrac{4}{3}s \qquad \text{where } s \text{ is standard deviation.}$$

Now consider a point lying $1.5 \times (Q_3 - Q_1)$ to the right of Q_3,

i.e. a point lying $1.5 \times \tfrac{4}{3}s = 2s$ to the right of Q_3.

This point would be $2\tfrac{2}{3}s$ to the right of $\bar{x}$.

Now the probability of a point lying to the right of this can be shown to be extremely small. Similarly, the probability of a point lying to the left of $\bar{x} - 2\tfrac{2}{3}s$ is also extremely small.

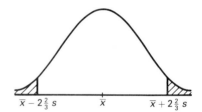

So, as a simple rule, take points lying more than 1.5 times the interquartile range above Q_3 or below Q_1 as 'outliers', and label them clearly as such:

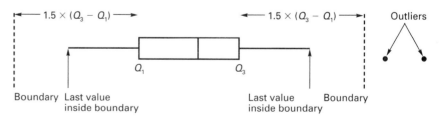

Example 2.9   A class of 31 children recorded the maximum daily temperatures for the month of July with the following results. The median and quartiles are shown on the stem and leaf diagram. Draw the corresponding box plot and use it to identify any outliers.

Temperature in °F

```
9 │ 4
8 │
8 │ 1  1
7 │ 7  7  9  9
7 │ 0  0 (0) 0  2  2  2  3  3  3 (3)
6 │(6) 8  8  8  9  9
6 │ 1  3  4  4  4  4
5 │ 6
```

Key 6 | 8 means 68°F

Solution 2.9

$$Q_1 = \text{8th value} = 66°\text{F}$$

$$Q_2 = \text{16th value} = 70°\text{F}$$

$$Q_3 = \text{24th value} = 73°\text{F}$$

$$Q_3 - Q_1 = 73 - 66 = 7°\text{F}$$

Upper boundary $= Q_3 + 1.5 \times 7° = 73° + 10.5° = 83.5°$

Lower boundary $= Q_1 - 1.5 \times 7° = 66° - 10.5° = 55.5°$

So it would appear that the temperature recorded as 94°F is an outlier. (It was probably recorded wrongly, since it is most unusual to have just one day with extremely high temperatures.) However, the temperature of 56°F is not an outlier.

The whiskers are drawn down to 56°F and up to 81°F and the temperature of 94°F is labelled as an outlier, as shown.

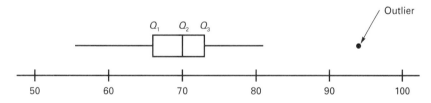

Exercise 2c

1. The table opposite gives the lengths, in minutes, of 50 telephone calls from a school office.

    (a) Draw a cumulative frequency polygon.

    (b) Estimate the median and the quartiles.

    (c) Draw a box plot and comment on the distribution.

Length of call (min)	Number of calls
⩽1	8
1–2	11
2–3	17
3–5	8
5–10	6
⩾10	0

2. Draw cumulative frequency polygons and then construct box and whisker diagrams to represent the following histograms. For each one, calculate $Q_3 - Q_2$ and $Q_2 - Q_1$. What do you notice?

Hint: remember that

$$\text{frequency density} = \frac{\text{frequency}}{\text{class width}}$$

(a)

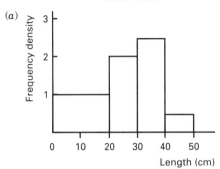

(b)

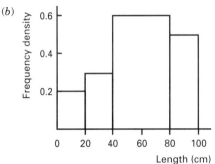

(c)

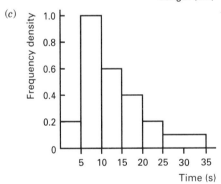

(d)

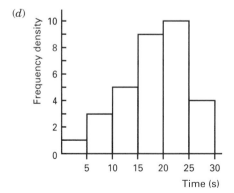

3. The graphs represent the marks of 100 boys and 100 girls in a test. Construct the box plots to represent the distributions, and comment on them.

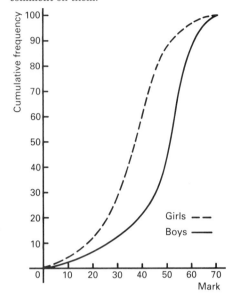

4. Two groups of people took part in a reaction-timing experiment. Their results, to the nearest hundredth of a second, are shown below. Construct box plots to represent the distributions, and comment.

Group 1		Group 2
6 6	2	
5 4 4	2	4 5
3 3 3 3 2 2	2	2 2 2 3 3
1 1 0 0	2	0 0 1
8	1	8 9 9 9 9
7 6 6	1	6 6 7 7
5 4 4	1	4 4
	1	2
	1	
	0	9

Key 4	2 means	*Key* 2	4 means
24 hundredths	24 hundredths
of a second	of a second

5. 21 girls estimated the length of a line, in mm. The results were

51 45 31 43 97 16 18 23 34 35 35
85 62 20 22 51 57 49 22 18 27

Draw the box plot and use it to identify any outliers.

6. 31 people completed a jigsaw in the following times (in minutes). Draw a box plot and use it to identify any outliers.

```
11 53 72 48 48 49 39 87 73 23 120
24 61 36 66 67 86 79 65 47 36 133
78 81 70 75 53 42 42 72 144
```

7. The box plots show the distributions of marks obtained by a class in English and in Mathematics. Comment on the distributions of marks.

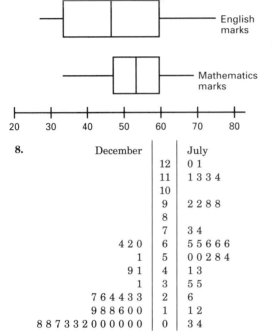

8.

```
        December │    │ July
                 │ 12 │ 0 1
                 │ 11 │ 1 3 3 4
                 │ 10 │
                 │  9 │ 2 2 8 8
                 │  8 │
                 │  7 │ 3 4
           4 2 0 │  6 │ 5 5 6 6 6
               1 │  5 │ 0 0 2 8 4
             9 1 │  4 │ 1 3
               1 │  3 │ 5 5
       7 6 4 4 3 3 │  2 │ 6
       9 8 8 6 0 0 │  1 │ 1 2
 8 8 7 3 3 2 0 0 0 0 0 0 │  0 │ 3 4
```

Key 4 | 6 means	*Key* 6 | 5 means
6.4 hours	6.5 hours

This back-to-back stem plot gives daily hours of sunshine in December and July.
Find the median and quartiles for each month and construct the box plots. Comment on the distributions.

9. These are the times of the postal delivery to my house over four successive weeks.

```
9.01 9.22 9.30 9.19 9.15 9.29
9.45 9.53 9.02 9.05 9.31 9.47
9.17 9.48 9.29 9.09 9.29 9.02
9.10 9.12 9.25 9.10 9.13 9.19
```

(*a*) Draw a stem and leaf diagram.
(*b*) Find the median.
(*c*) Find the quartiles.
(*d*) Draw a box and whisker diagram.

10. Draw box plots to represent the following frequency distributions.

(*a*)

x	f
0	4
1	12
2	6
3	2
4	1

(*b*)

x	f
11	2
12	5
13	13
14	15
15	12
16	6
17	2

(*c*)

x	f
1	3
2	5
3	6
4	6
5	8
6	14
7	12
8	9

SUMMARY — SHAPES OF DISTRIBUTIONS

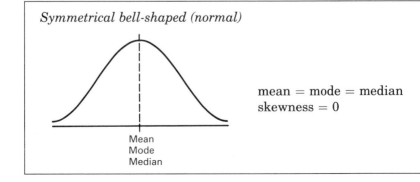

Symmetrical bell-shaped (normal)

Mean
Mode
Median

mean = mode = median
skewness = 0

Positively skewed

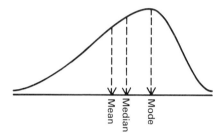

mode < median < mean

skewness > 0

Negatively skewed

mean < median < mode

skewness < 0

Approximate relationship between the three averages

$$\text{mean} - \text{mode} \approx 3\,(\text{mean} - \text{median})$$

Skewness

$$\text{Pearson's coefficient of skewness} = \frac{\text{mean} - \text{mode}}{\text{standard deviation}}$$

$$\approx \frac{3(\text{mean} - \text{median})}{\text{standard deviation}}$$

$$\text{Quartile coefficient of skewness} = \frac{(Q_3 - Q_2) - (Q_2 - Q_1)}{Q_3 - Q_1}$$

Box and whisker diagrams (box plots)

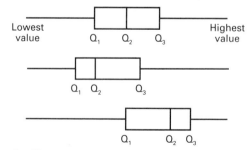

Symmetrical distribution

Positively skewed distribution

Negatively skewed distribution

Outliers

Take points lying more than 1.5 times the interquartile range above Q_3 or below Q_1 as 'outliers'.

Miscellaneous Exercise 2d

1. In 1798 the English scientist Henry Cavendish measured the specific gravity of the earth by careful work with a torsion balance. He obtained the 29 measurements given below.

   4.07 4.88 5.10 5.26 5.27 5.29 5.29 5.30
   5.34 5.34 5.36 5.39 5.42 5.44 5.46 5.47
   5.50 5.53 5.55 5.57 5.58 5.61 5.62 5.63
   5.65 5.75 5.79 5.85 5.86

   The sum of these measurements is 157.17 and the sum of their squares is 855.0227.
   (a) Calculate the mean measurement and the standard deviation of the measurements. Obtain for these data the range, the median and the quartiles.
   Draw a box plot and use it to identify the outlier in Cavendish's data set.
   (b) If the data were analysed without this outlier, calculate the new values of
   (i)   the median
   (ii) the mean
   (iii) the standard deviation.   (NEAB)

2. In an agricultural experiment the gains in mass, in kilograms, of 100 pigs during a certain period were recorded as follows:

Gain in mass (kilograms)	Frequency
5–9	2
10–14	29
15–19	37
20–24	16
25–29	14
30–34	2

   Construct a histogram and a relative cumulative frequency polygon of these data. Obtain (i) the median and the semi-interquartile range, (ii) the mean and the standard deviation.
   Which of these pairs of statistics do you consider more appropriate in this case, and why?   (AEB)

3. The table gives the cumulative frequency distribution of the masses x in kilograms of a group of 200 eighteen-year-old boys.
   Draw a cumulative frequency graph and from this estimate the median.
   Compile a frequency distribution from the data and hence estimate the mean and standard deviation of the sample. State a well known probability distribution which you would expect to fit such data.

x	Number with mass less than x
30	0
35	1
40	4
45	11
50	25
55	47
60	79
65	114
70	146
75	171
80	187
85	195
90	198
95	200

(JMB)

4. The following are the ignition times in seconds (correct to the nearest 100th of a second) of samples of 80 upholstery materials. They are arranged in numerical order by columns.

1.20	2.11	3.10	4.11	5.09	5.92	6.85	8.80
1.38	2.20	3.24	4.19	5.11	5.92	6.90	9.20
1.42	2.32	3.49	4.32	5.12	6.20	7.35	9.45
1.47	2.46	3.62	4.50	5.15	6.25	7.40	9.65
1.52	2.46	3.75	4.54	5.21	6.37	7.41	9.70
1.58	2.50	3.78	4.56	5.33	6.40	7.60	9.79
1.70	2.51	3.81	4.71	5.40	6.43	7.86	10.60
1.76	2.58	3.87	4.72	5.50	6.43	7.95	11.25
1.79	2.65	3.90	4.79	5.62	6.75	8.64	11.75
1.92	2.80	4.04	4.90	5.84	6.77	8.75	12.80

   (a) Group these data into 8 equal classes commencing 1.00–2.49, 2.50–3.99, ... and arrange them in a frequency table.
   (b) Using the frequency table obtain estimates for the mean time and standard deviation.
   (c) Construct a frequency polygon for the distribution and comment on its shape.
   (d) Chebychev's Theorem states that, for any distribution, the proportion of the population that lies outside k standard deviations from the mean is less than $1/k^2$. Verify this for the above distribution when $k = 1.5$.

5. The table overleaf gives the ages in completed years of the 113 persons convicted of shop-lifting in a British town in 1986. Working in years and giving answers correct to 1 place of decimals, calculate

(*a*) the mean age and standard deviation,
(*b*) the coefficient of skewness given by (mean − mode)/standard deviation,
(*c*) the median age.
Which do you consider to be best as a representative average of the distribution — the mean, median or mode? Give reasons for your choice.
Draw a histogram of the data with a class interval of 2 years.

Age	*f*
12	1
13	1
14	5
15	8
16	17
17	19
18	15
19	9
20	8
21	6
22	4
23	3
24	3
25	2
26	2
27	2
28	1
29	1
30–49	6

6. Summarised below are the values of the orders (to the nearest £) taken by a sales representative for a wholesale firm during a particular year.

Value of order (£)	Number of orders
Less than 10	3
10–19	9
20–29	15
30–39	27
40–49	29
50–59	34
60–69	19
70–99	10
100 or more	4

(*a*) Using interpolation, estimate the median and the semi-interquartile range for these data.
(*b*) Explain why the median and semi-interquartile range might be more appropriate summary measures for these data than the mean and standard deviation. (L)

7. A frequency diagram for a set of data is shown below.

(i) Find the median and the mode of the data.
(ii) Given that the mean is 5.95 and the standard deviation is 2.58, explain why the value 15 may be regarded as an outlier.
(iii) Explain how you would treat the outlier if the diagram represents
(*a*) the ages (in completed years) of children at a party,
(*b*) the sums of the scores obtained when throwing a pair of dice.
(iv) Find the median and the mode of the data after the outlier is removed.
(v) *Without doing any calculations* state what effect, if any, removing the outlier would have on the mean and on the standard deviation.
(vi) Does the diagram exhibit positive skewness, negative skewness or no skewness? How is the skewness affected by removing the outlier? (MEI)

8. The table shows the distribution of the lifetimes (measured to the nearest hour) of a sample of batteries.

Lifetime (to nearest hour)	Frequency
690–709	3
710–719	7
720–729	15
730–739	38
740–744	41
745–749	35
750–754	21
755–759	16
760–769	14
770–789	10

(*a*) Draw a histogram to represent the data.
(*b*) Draw a cumulative frequency polygon.
(*c*) Calculate the mean and standard deviation.
(*d*) Estimate the median and the quartiles.
(*e*) Calculate Pearson's coefficient of skewness.
(*f*) Calculate the quartile coefficient of skewness.
(*g*) Draw a box and whisker diagram to illustrate the distribution.

9. Summarised opposite is the distribution of marks obtained by a group of students in a Geography examination.
Explain how the median and quartiles of a distribution can be used when describing the shape of a distribution.
Use interpolation to estimate the median and quartiles of this distribution.
Hence describe its shape.   (L)

Mark range	Frequency
19 or less	2
20–29	14
30–39	21
40–44	34
45–49	39
50–59	42
60–69	13
70–79	9
80–89	4
90 or more	2

3

PROBABILITY

When an event is *absolutely certain* to happen, we say that the probability is 1, and when an event can *never* happen, we say that the probability is 0. For example, the probability that I will obtain a score of 1, 2, 3, 4, 5 or 6 when I throw an ordinary die is 1, whereas the probability that I will obtain an 8 is 0.

Probability is measured on a scale from 0 to 1 and most events therefore have probabilities between these extremes. Here are some examples:

Example	*Probability*
A Obtaining an 8 on a die	0 (absolute impossibility)
B My dog will win an obedience prize at a dog show	Very small, near 0
C The next baby to be born at St Mary's Hospital will be a boy.	Near middle of probability scale
D It will be sunny on 20th August	Quite high
E My dog will wag his tail when he sees me	Very high, near 1
F Obtaining a score of 1, 2, 3, 4, 5 or 6 on the die	1 (absolute certainty)

Illustrating these on a probability scale

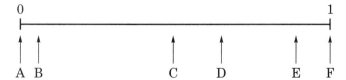

The problem is to decide how to allocate definite numbers to the probabilities. We can do this in several ways, according to the situation being considered.

THE EXPERIMENTAL (OR EMPIRICAL) METHOD OF OBTAINING PROBABILITIES

Suppose we want to find the probability that a shoe will land on its sole when it is thrown in the air. To do this we could collect experimental data by throwing the shoe a number of times and recording after every 100 throws, say, the **relative frequency** of successes, i.e. the number of times the shoe landed on its sole as a proportion of the number of throws. The results might look like this:

Number of times shoe lands on sole	Number of throws	Relative frequency
43	100	$\frac{43}{100} = 0.43$
64	200	$\frac{64}{200} = 0.32$
114	300	$\frac{114}{300} = 0.38$
136	400	$\frac{136}{400} = 0.34$
160	500	$\frac{160}{500} = 0.32$
170	600	$\frac{170}{600} = 0.283\ldots$
203	700	$\frac{203}{700} = 0.29$
252	800	$\frac{252}{800} = 0.315$
274	900	$\frac{274}{900} = 0.304\ldots$
310	1000	$\frac{310}{1000} = 0.31$
336	1100	$\frac{336}{1100} = 0.305\ldots$
355	1200	$\frac{355}{1200} = 0.295\ldots$

These results can be illustrated on a graph:

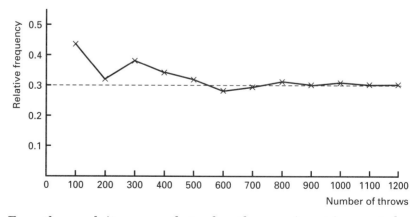

From the graph it appears that, when the experiment is repeated a large number of times, the relative frequency approaches a limiting value which is around 0.3. This is defined as the **experimental probability**.

In general,

if the number of trials is n and the number of times the event occurs is r, then

$$\text{relative frequency} = \frac{r}{n}$$

Denoting the probability of the event A by $P(A)$,

$$\text{Experimental probability, } P(A) = \lim\left(\frac{r}{n}\right)$$

where 'lim' means the limiting value to which $\dfrac{r}{n}$ settles as n increases indefinitely.

Now consider the probability of obtaining a head when an unbiased or fair coin is tossed. If we perform the experiment a large number of times, say 2000, the relative frequency graph might look like this:

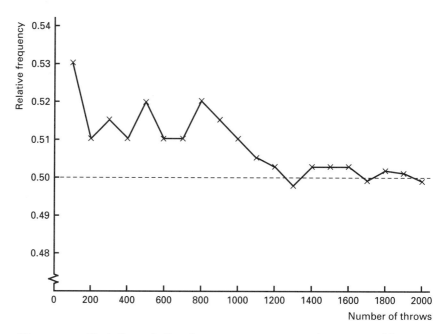

We can see that the relative frequency appears to be approaching a limiting value of 0.5, so

experimental probability of obtaining a head

$$= \lim\left(\frac{\text{number of trials in which a head occurs}}{\text{total number of trials}}\right)$$

$$= \lim\left(\frac{r}{n}\right)$$

$$= 0.5$$

CLASSICAL METHOD OF OBTAINING PROBABILITIES

If you were asked the probability of obtaining a head when a fair coin is tossed, you would probably give the answer $\frac{1}{2}$ without bothering to toss the coin 2000 times. Intuitively you would have used the classical definition of probability, which applies when the outcomes of an experiment are all equally likely. In this case

$$\text{probability} = \frac{\text{number of successful outcomes}}{\text{number of possible outcomes}}$$

When tossing a coin there are two possible and equally likely outcomes (head or tail), of which one is successful (head).

Therefore $P(\text{head}) = \frac{1}{2}$

Similarly, when picking a card from an ordinary pack

$$P(\text{diamond}) = \frac{13}{52} = \frac{1}{4}$$

since there are 52 possible outcomes, of which 13 are successful, i.e. diamonds.

When deriving the mathematical rules for probability it is useful to consider the classical definition of probability.

THE SUBJECTIVE METHOD OF OBTAINING PROBABILITIES

There are occasions when outcomes are not equally likely, and when a good estimate of probability cannot be obtained by the relative frequency method because it is not possible to repeat the experiment a large number of times under similar conditions. For example, we may wish to find the probability that it will snow on Christmas Day next year, or the probability that a particular car will be stolen. In these cases we have to form a **subjective probability**, which might be based on past experience (for example weather records, local crime figures) or on expert opinion or other factors. This method is, of course, open to error — two people faced with the same evidence may give different estimates of the probability. However, sometimes it is the only method available.

Before considering the classical definition of probability in more detail, we define some standard notation.

OUTCOMES

An experiment can result in several possible outcomes. For example:

(**a**) One toss of a coin results in the outcomes (H, T). If the coin is fair, then each outcome is equally likely.

(**b**) Two tosses of a coin result in the outcomes (HH, HT, TH, TT). Again, if the coin is fair, then each outcome is equally likely.

(c) If a machine produces articles, some of which are defective, the outcomes are (defective, not defective). In this case the outcomes should not be equally likely.

(d) If a coin is tossed repeatedly until a head is obtained, the outcomes are (H, TH, TTH, TTTH, TTTTH, ...). These are not equally likely.

(e) The outcomes of a race being run by A and B could be (A wins, B wins, there is a dead heat). These outcomes may not be equally likely.

POSSIBILITY SPACE

Each possible outcome is called a **sample point** and the set of all possible outcomes is the **possibility space** S.

If the possibility space has a finite number of sample points then we denote the number of points in S by $n(S)$.

Consider an event A which is a subset of S, then $n(A) \leqslant n(S)$.

For example, for one throw of an ordinary die the possibility space $S = (1, 2, 3, 4, 5, 6)$ and $n(S) = 6$.

Let A_1 be the event 'the number is even', then $A_1 = (2, 4, 6)$ and $n(A_1) = 3$.

Let A_2 be the event 'the number is less than 3' then $A_2 = (1, 2)$ and $n(A_2) = 2$.

CLASSICAL DEFINITION OF PROBABILITY

If the possibility space S consists of a finite number of *equally likely outcomes*, then the probability of an event A, written $P(A)$, is defined as

$$P(A) = \frac{n(A)}{n(S)}$$

So, in the example above,

$$P(A_1) = \frac{n(A_1)}{n(S)} = \frac{3}{6} = \frac{1}{2}$$

$$P(A_2) = \frac{n(A_2)}{n(S)} = \frac{2}{6} = \frac{1}{3}$$

IMPORTANT RESULTS

Let the number of sample points in the possibility space be n, so that $n(S) = n$.

Let the event A have r sample points, so that $n(A) = r$.

Result 1

$$P(A) = \frac{n(A)}{n(S)}$$

$$= \frac{r}{n}$$

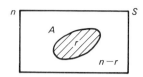

Now, since A is a subset of S

$$0 \leqslant r \leqslant n$$

i.e.

$$0 \leqslant \frac{r}{n} \leqslant 1$$

Hence

$$0 \leqslant P(A) \leqslant 1$$

NOTE: this confirms that the probability of an event A is a number between 0 and 1 inclusive, and

if $P(A) = 0$ then the event cannot possibly occur,

if $P(A) = 1$ then the event is certain to occur.

For example, if a card is drawn *from the clubs suit* of a pack of cards, then

$$P(\text{card is red}) = 0$$

$$P(\text{card is black}) = 1$$

Result 2 Let $\overline{A}$ denote the event 'A does not occur'.

Now

$$P(\overline{A}) = \frac{n(\overline{A})}{n(S)}$$

$$= \frac{n - r}{n}$$

$$= 1 - \frac{r}{n}$$

$$= 1 - P(A)$$

Therefore

$$P(\overline{A}) = 1 - P(A)$$
$$\text{or}\ \ P(A) + P(\overline{A}) = 1$$

NOTE: sometimes $\overline{A}$ is written A^* or A'.

Example 3.1   A card is drawn at random from an ordinary pack of 52 playing cards. Find the probability that the card (**a**) is a seven, (**b**) is not a seven.

Solution 3.1 The possibility space S = (the pack of 52 cards) and $n(S) = 52$.
Let A be the event 'the card is a seven', then $n(A) = 4$.

(a)
$$P(A) = \frac{n(A)}{n(S)}$$
$$= \frac{4}{52}$$
$$= \frac{1}{13}$$

Therefore the probability that the card drawn is a seven is $\frac{1}{13}$.

(b) Let $\overline{A}$ be the event 'the card is not a seven'.
$$P(\overline{A}) = 1 - P(A)$$
$$= 1 - \frac{1}{13}$$
$$= \frac{12}{13}$$

Therefore the probability that the card drawn is not a seven is $\frac{12}{13}$.

Example 3.2 Compare the probabilities of scoring a 4 with one die and a total of 8 with two dice.

Solution 3.2 *With one die*

The possibility space S = (1, 2, 3, 4, 5, 6) and $n(S) = 6$.
Let A be the event 'a 4 occurs', then $n(A) = 1$.

So
$$P(A) = \frac{n(A)}{n(S)}$$
$$= \frac{1}{6}$$

The probability of scoring 4 with one die is $\frac{1}{6}$.

With two dice

The possibility space S has 36 sample points, each of which is equally likely to occur. These can be represented on a diagram as shown. The dots in the first column represent the outcomes (1, 1), (1, 2), (1, 3), (1, 4), (1, 5), (1, 6), . . . , and so on for the other columns.

Let B be the event 'the sum on the two dice is 8'.

The sample points which give a sum of 8 are ringed on the diagram.

We see that $n(B) = 5$.

So $P(B) = \dfrac{n(B)}{n(S)}$

$= \dfrac{5}{36}$

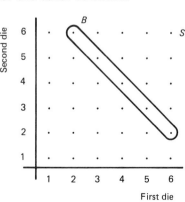

The probability of obtaining a total of 8 with two dice is $\frac{5}{36}$.

It is interesting to note that

$$P(\text{scoring an 8 with two dice}) < P(\text{scoring a 4 with one die})$$

Example 3.3   Two fair coins are tossed. Illustrate the possible outcomes on a possibility space diagram and find the probability that two heads are obtained.

Solution 3.3   Each coin is equally likely to show a head or a tail. The possibility space for the outcomes when two coins are tossed is as shown.

$$n(S) = 4$$

Let A be the event 'two heads are obtained'. From the diagram $n(A) = 1$.

Therefore $P(A) = \dfrac{n(A)}{n(S)}$

               $= \dfrac{1}{4}$

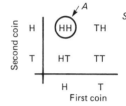

The probability that two heads are obtained when two fair coins are tossed is $\frac{1}{4}$.

Exercise 3a

1. An ordinary die is thrown. Find the probability that the number obtained (a) is a multiple of 3, (b) is less than 7, (c) is a factor of 6.

2. A card is drawn at random from an ordinary pack containing 52 playing cards. Find the probability that the card drawn (a) is the four of spades, (b) is the four of spades or any diamond, (c) is not a picture card (Jack, Queen, King) of any suit.

3. From a set of cards numbered 1 to 20 a card is drawn at random. Find the probability that the number (a) is divisible by 4, (b) is greater than 15, (c) is divisible by 4 and greater than 15.
   If the card is divisible by 4 and it is not replaced, find the probability that (d) the second card drawn is even.

4. A counter is drawn from a box containing 10 red, 15 black, 5 green and 10 yellow counters. Find the probability that the counter is (a) black, (b) not green or yellow, (c) not yellow, (d) red or black or green, (e) not blue.

5. Two ordinary dice are thrown. Find the probability that (a) the sum on the two dice is 3, (b) the sum on the two dice exceeds 9, (c) the two dice show the same number, (d) the numbers on the two dice differ by more than 2, (e) the product of the two numbers is even.

6. The pupils in a class were asked how many brothers and sisters they had. Their answers are shown in the table:

Number of brothers and sisters	0	1	2	3	4	5
Number of pupils	4	12	8	3	2	1

If a child is chosen at random, find the probability that there are three children in his or her family.

7. If
   $\mathscr{E} = \{x : x \text{ is an integer and } 1 \leqslant x \leqslant 20\}$
   $A = \{x : x \text{ is a multiple of 3}\}$
   $B = \{x : x \text{ is a multiple of 4}\}$
   and an integer is picked at random from $\mathscr{E}$, find the probability that (a) it is in A, (b) it is not in B.

8.   A die is in the form of a tetrahedron and its faces are marked 1, 2, 3 and 4. The 'score' is the number on which the die lands. Find the probability that when a tetrahedral die is thrown the score is (*a*) an even number, (*b*) a prime number.
(*NOTE*: 1 is not a prime number.)
If two tetrahedral dice are thrown find the probability that (*c*) the sum of the two scores is 5, (*d*) the difference of the two scores is 1, (*e*) the product of the two scores is a multiple of 4.

9.   An ordinary die and a fair coin are thrown together. Show the possible outcomes on a possibility space diagram and find the probability that (*a*) a head and a 2 are obtained, (*b*) a tail and a 7 are obtained, (*c*) a head and an even number are obtained.

10.   An ordinary die and two coins are thrown together. Show the possible outcomes on a possibility space diagram and find the probability that (*a*) two heads and a number less than 3 are obtained, (*b*) the coins show different faces and a 4 is shown on the die, (*c*) the die shows an odd number and the coins show the same face, (*d*) a 6 and at least one head are obtained.

11.   Two dice are thrown simultaneously. The scores are to be multiplied. Denoting by $P(n)$ the probability that the number n will be obtained, calculate (*a*) $P(9)$, (*b*) $P(4)$,

(*c*) $P(14)$, (*d*) $\sum\limits_{m=15}^{30} P(m)$.

Given that $P(t) = \frac{1}{9}$, find the possible values of t.   (L Additional)

Result 3

> If A and B are any two events of the same experiment such that $P(A) \neq 0$ and $P(B) \neq 0$ then
>
> $$P(A \text{ or } B) = P(A) + P(B) - P(A \text{ and } B)$$

It is important to realise that $P(A \text{ or } B)$ means
$P(A$ occurs or B occurs or both A and B occur).

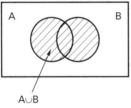

'A or B' can be represented in set notation by $A \cup B$ (read 'A union B') and is illustrated by the shaded area on the Venn diagram.

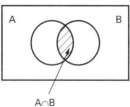

'A and B' is represented by $A \cap B$ (read 'A intersection B') and is illustrated by the shaded area showing the overlap of A and B.

Writing Result 3 in set notation:

$$P(A \cup B) = P(A) + P(B) - P(A \cap B)$$

To illustrate this result let $n(S) = n$ where S is the possibility space, $n(A) = r$, $n(B) = s$, $n(A \cap B) = t$.

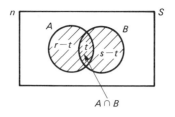

$$P(A \cup B) = \frac{n(A \cup B)}{n(S)}$$

$$= \frac{(r-t)+t+(s-t)}{n}$$

$$= \frac{r+s-t}{n}$$

$$= \frac{r}{n} + \frac{s}{n} - \frac{t}{n}$$

$$= P(A) + P(B) - P(A \cap B)$$

Example 3.4   A coin and a die are thrown together. Draw a possibility space diagram and find the probability of obtaining (**a**) a head, (**b**) a number greater than 4, (**c**) a head and a number greater than 4, (**d**) a head or a number greater than 4.

Solution 3.4   The possibility space S is as shown below.

Let A be the event 'a head is obtained', so $n(A) = 6$.

Let B be the event 'a number greater than 4 is obtained', so $n(B) = 4$.

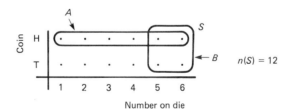

(**a**) $P(A) = \frac{n(A)}{n(S)} = \frac{6}{12} = \frac{1}{2}$

The probability of obtaining a head is $\frac{1}{2}$.

(**b**) $P(B) = \frac{n(B)}{n(S)} = \frac{4}{12} = \frac{1}{3}$

The probability of obtaining a number greater than 4 is $\frac{1}{3}$.

(**c**) P(head and a number greater than 4)

$$= P(A \cap B) = \frac{n(A \cap B)}{n(S)} = \frac{2}{12} = \frac{1}{6}$$

The probability of obtaining a head and a number greater than 4 is $\frac{1}{6}$.

(**d**) P(a head or a number greater than 4)

$$= P(A \cup B) = \frac{n(A \cup B)}{n(S)} = \frac{8}{12} = \frac{2}{3}$$

The probability of obtaining a head or a number greater than 4 is $\frac{2}{3}$.

We now check that this satisfies $P(A \cup B) = P(A) + P(B) - P(A \cap B)$.

$$\text{left hand side} = P(A \cup B) = \frac{2}{3}$$

$$\text{right hand side} = P(A) + P(B) - P(A \cap B)$$

$$= \frac{1}{2} + \frac{1}{3} - \frac{1}{6}$$

$$= \frac{8}{12}$$

$$= \frac{2}{3}$$

Therefore left hand side = right hand side, confirming that $P(A \cup B) = P(A) + P(B) - P(A \cap B)$.

Example 3.5   Events A and B are such that $P(A) = \frac{19}{30}$, $P(B) = \frac{2}{5}$ and $P(A \cup B) = \frac{4}{5}$. Find $P(A \cap B)$.

Solution 3.5   Now $P(A \cup B) = P(A) + P(B) - P(A \cap B)$

so $\frac{4}{5} = \frac{19}{30} + \frac{2}{5} - P(A \cap B)$

$$P(A \cap B) = \frac{19}{30} + \frac{12}{30} - \frac{24}{30}$$

$$= \frac{7}{30}$$

Therefore $P(A \cap B) = \frac{7}{30}$.

Example 3.6   In a group of 20 adults, 4 out of the 7 women and 2 out of the 13 men wear glasses. What is the probability that a person chosen at random from the group is a woman or someone who wears glasses?

Solution 3.6   Let W be the event 'the person chosen is a woman' and G be the event 'the person chosen wears glasses'.

$$P(W) = \tfrac{7}{20}, \quad P(G) = \tfrac{6}{20}, \quad P(W \text{ and } G) = P(W \cap G) = \tfrac{4}{20}$$

$$P(W \text{ or } G) = P(W \cup G) = P(W) + P(G) - P(W \cap G)$$
$$= \tfrac{7}{20} + \tfrac{6}{20} - \tfrac{4}{20}$$
$$= \tfrac{9}{20}$$

Therefore the probability that the person is a woman or someone who wears glasses is $\tfrac{9}{20}$.

MUTUALLY EXCLUSIVE EVENTS

Result 4

> If an event A can occur *or* an event B can occur but *not both* A and B can occur, then the two events A and B are said to be **mutually exclusive**.

In this case, A and B do not overlap, so $P(A \cap B) = 0$.

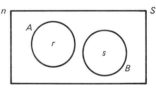

The addition law for mutually exclusive events:

> When A and B are **mutually exclusive**,
> $$P(A \text{ or } B) = P(A \cup B) = P(A) + P(B)$$

This is also referred to as 'the **or** rule'. We must take care to use it only when the two events cannot occur at the same time. For example, if a card is drawn at random from an ordinary pack, then

$$P(\text{king or queen}) = P(\text{king}) + P(\text{queen})$$

The events are mutually exclusive because it is not possible to have a 'king of queens'. However, to find $P(\text{ace or heart})$ it is wrong to use the 'or' rule because the events 'ace' and 'heart' can occur together. Instead we must use Result 3 where

$$P(\text{ace or heart}) = P(\text{ace}) + P(\text{heart}) - P(\text{ace of hearts})$$

Example 3.7   In a race the probability that John wins is 0.3, the probability that Paul wins is 0.2 and the probability that Mark wins is 0.4. Find the probability that (**a**) John or Mark wins, (**b**) neither John nor Paul wins. Assume that there are no dead heats.

Solution 3.7   We assume that only one person can win, so the events are mutually exclusive.

(a) $P(\text{John or Mark wins}) = P(\text{John wins}) + P(\text{Mark wins})$

$$= 0.3 + 0.4$$

$$= 0.7$$

$\underline{P(\text{John or Mark wins}) = 0.7}$

(b) $P(\text{neither John nor Paul wins}) = 1 - P(\text{John or Paul wins})$

$$= 1 - (0.3 + 0.2)$$

$$= 0.5$$

$\underline{P(\text{neither John nor Paul wins}) = 0.5}$

Example 3.8   A card is drawn at random from an ordinary pack of 52 playing cards. Find the probability that the card is (a) a club or a diamond, (b) a club or a king.

Solution 3.8   The possibility space $S = (\text{the pack of 52 cards})$, so $n(S) = 52$.

Let C be the event 'a club is drawn', D be the event 'a diamond is drawn', K be the event 'a king is drawn'.

(a) $$P(\text{club}) = \frac{n(C)}{n(S)} = \frac{13}{52} = \frac{1}{4}$$

$$P(\text{diamond}) = \frac{n(D)}{n(S)} = \frac{13}{52} = \frac{1}{4}$$

Now the events C and D are mutually exclusive since they cannot occur together; a card cannot be both a club and a diamond.

Therefore

$P(\text{club} \cup \text{diamond}) = P(\text{club}) + P(\text{diamond})$

$$= \frac{1}{4} + \frac{1}{4}$$

$$= \frac{1}{2}$$

$\underline{\text{The probability of drawing a club or a diamond is } \frac{1}{2}.}$

(b) $$P(\text{club}) = \frac{13}{52}$$

$$P(\text{king}) = \frac{n(K)}{n(S)} = \frac{4}{52}$$

Now $P(\text{king} \cap \text{club}) = P(\text{king of clubs})$

$$= \frac{1}{52}$$

The events C and K are not mutually exclusive since a card can be both a king and a club.

Therefore

$$P(\text{club} \cup \text{king}) = P(\text{club}) + P(\text{king}) - P(\text{club} \cap \text{king})$$

$$= \frac{13}{52} + \frac{4}{52} - \frac{1}{52}$$

$$= \frac{16}{52}$$

$$= \frac{4}{13}$$

The probability of drawing a club or a king is $\frac{4}{13}$.

In this example we could have noted straight away that the event 'a club or a king is drawn' has 16 sample points:

$$(A_\clubsuit, 2_\clubsuit, 3_\clubsuit, 4_\clubsuit, 5_\clubsuit, 6_\clubsuit, 7_\clubsuit, 8_\clubsuit, 9_\clubsuit, 10_\clubsuit,$$
$$J_\clubsuit, Q_\clubsuit, K_\clubsuit, K_\diamondsuit, K_\spadesuit, K_\heartsuit)$$

and the possibility space has 52 sample points,

so $P(\text{club} \cup \text{king}) = \frac{16}{52} = \frac{4}{13}$ as before.

Exercise 3b

1. An ordinary die is thrown. Find the probability that the number obtained is (a) even, (b) prime, (c) even or prime.

2. In a group of 30 students all study at least one of the subjects physics and biology. 20 attend the physics class and 21 attend the biology class. Find the probability that a student chosen at random studies both physics and biology.

3. From an ordinary pack of 52 playing cards the seven of diamonds has been lost. A card is dealt from the well-shuffled pack. Find the probability that it is (a) a diamond, (b) a queen, (c) a diamond or a queen, (d) a diamond or a seven.

4. For events A and B it is known that $P(A) = \frac{2}{3}$, $P(A \cup B) = \frac{3}{4}$ and $P(A \cap B) = \frac{5}{12}$. Find $P(B)$.

5. In a street containing 20 houses, 3 households do not own a television set; 12 households have a black and white set and 7 households have a colour and a black and white set. Find the probability that a household chosen at random owns a colour television set.

6. For events A and B it is known that $P(A) = P(B)$ and $P(A \cap B) = 0.1$ and $P(A \cup B) = 0.7$. Find $P(A)$.

7. The probability that a boy in class 2 is in the football team is 0.4 and the probability that he is in the chess team is 0.5. If the probability that a boy in the class is in both teams is 0.2, find the probability that a boy chosen at random is in the football or the chess team.

8. Two ordinary dice are thrown. Find the probability that the sum of the scores obtained
(a) is a multiple of 5,
(b) is greater than 9,
(c) is a multiple of 5 or is greater than 9,
(d) is a multiple of 5 and is greater than 9.

9. Given that $P(\overline{A}) = \frac{2}{3}$, $P(B) = \frac{1}{2}$ and $P(A \cap B) = \frac{1}{12}$, find $P(A \cup B)$.

10. Two ordinary dice are thrown. Find the probability that
(a) at least one 6 is thrown,
(b) at least one 3 is thrown,
(c) at least one 6 or at least one 3 is thrown.

EXHAUSTIVE EVENTS

Result 5

> If two events A and B are such that $A \cup B = S$ then
> $P(A \cup B) = 1$ and the events A and B are said to be **exhaustive**.

For example

(i) Let $S = (1, 2, 3, 4, 5, 6, 7, 8, 9, 10)$.

If $A = (1, 2, 3, 4, 5, 6)$ and $B = (5, 6, 7, 8, 9, 10)$ then
$A \cup B = S$ and A and B are exhaustive events.

(ii) Let S be the possibility space when an ordinary die is thrown so
$S = (1, 2, 3, 4, 5, 6)$.

If $A = (2, 4, 6)$ and $B = (1, 3, 5)$ then $A \cup B = S$ and A
and B are exhaustive events.

Example 3.9   Events A and B are such that they are both mutually exclusive and
exhaustive. Find a relationship between A and B. Give an example of
such events.

Solution 3.9   If A and B are mutually exclusive then $P(A \cup B) = P(A) + P(B)$

If A and B are exhaustive then $\qquad P(A \cup B) = 1$

Therefore

$$P(A) + P(B) = 1$$

so $\qquad P(B) = 1 - P(A)$

But $\qquad P(\overline{A}) = 1 - P(A)$

Therefore $\qquad P(B) = P(\overline{A})$

i.e. $\qquad \underline{B = \overline{A}}$

Similarly $\qquad \underline{A = \overline{B}}$

Toss a coin. Let A be the event 'a head is obtained', B be the event 'a
tail is obtained'.

Now A and B are mutually exclusive, since the coin cannot show both
a head and a tail.

A and B are exhaustive since the probability that the outcome is a
head or a tail is 1.

Therefore A and B are both mutually exclusive and exhaustive.

CONDITIONAL PROBABILITY

Result 6

If A and B are two events, where $P(A) \neq 0$ and $P(B) \neq 0$, then the probability of A, *given that B has already occurred* is written $P(A|B)$. We read this as 'the probability of A, given B'.

$$P(A|B) = \frac{P(A \cap B)}{P(B)}$$

Illustrating this by means of the Venn diagram, the possibility space is B, since we know that B has already occurred.

$$P(A|B) = \frac{n(A \cap B)}{n(B)}$$

$$= \frac{t}{s}$$

$$= \frac{t/n}{s/n}$$

$$= \frac{P(A \cap B)}{P(B)}$$

This result is often written

$$P(A \cap B) = P(A|B) \times P(B)$$

NOTE: If A and B are mutually exclusive events then, since

$$P(A \cap B) = 0 \quad \text{and} \quad P(B) \neq 0,$$

it follows that $P(A|B) = 0$.

Example 3.10 Given that a heart is picked at random from a pack of 52 playing cards, find the probability that it is a picture card.

Solution 3.10 We require

$$P(\text{picture card} | \text{heart}) = \frac{P(\text{picture card} \cap \text{heart})}{P(\text{heart})}$$

$$= \frac{3/52}{13/52}$$

$$= \frac{3}{13}$$

The probability that it is a picture card, given that it is a heart, is $\frac{3}{13}$.

Example 3.11 When a die is thrown, an odd number occurs. What is the probability that the number is prime?

Solution 3.11 $$P(\text{prime} \mid \text{odd}) = \frac{P(\text{prime} \cap \text{odd})}{P(\text{odd})}$$

$$= \frac{2/6}{3/6} \quad \text{(The odd prime numbers are 3 and 5)}$$

$$= \frac{2}{3}$$

The probability that the number is prime, given that it is odd, is $\frac{2}{3}$.

Result 7

Since $\quad P(A \mid B) = \dfrac{P(A \cap B)}{P(B)}, \quad P(A \cap B) = P(A \mid B)\,P(B)$

It follows that

$$P(B \mid A) = \frac{P(B \cap A)}{P(A)} \quad \text{and so} \quad P(B \cap A) = P(B \mid A)\,P(A)$$

Since $\qquad\qquad\qquad P(A \cap B) = P(B \cap A),$

$$P(A \mid B)\,P(B) = P(B \mid A)\,P(A)$$

Example 3.12 Two tetrahedral dice, with faces labelled 1, 2, 3 and 4, are thrown and the number on which each lands is noted. The 'score' is the sum of these two numbers. Find the probability that (**a**) the score is even, given that at least one die lands on a 3, (**b**) at least one die lands on a 3, given that the score is even.

Solution 3.12 There are 16 sample points in the possibility space S, as shown in the diagram, so $n(S) = 16$.

Let A be the event 'at least one die lands on a 3' and let B be the event 'the score is even'.

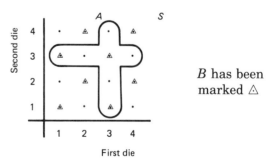

B has been marked $\triangle$

The sample space A is $((1, 3), (2, 3), (3, 3), (4, 3), (3, 1), (3, 2), (3, 4))$, so

$$n(A) = 7 \quad \text{and} \quad P(A) = \frac{n(A)}{n(S)} = \frac{7}{16}$$

Sample space B is $((1, 1), (1, 3), (2, 2), (2, 4), (3, 1), (3, 3), (4, 2), (4, 4))$.

Now $\qquad n(B) = 8 \quad \text{and} \quad P(B) = \dfrac{n(B)}{n(S)} = \dfrac{8}{16}$

There are 3 sample points which are in both A and B, so

$$P(A \cap B) = \frac{n(A \cap B)}{n(S)} = \frac{3}{16}$$

(a) $\quad P(\text{score is even} \,|\, \text{at least one die lands on a 3}) = P(B \,|\, A)$

$$= \frac{P(B \cap A)}{P(A)}$$

$$= \frac{3/16}{7/16}$$

$$= \frac{3}{7}$$

Therefore the probability that the score is even, given that at least one die lands on a 3, is $\frac{3}{7}$.

NOTE: this result could have been obtained directly from the diagram. The possibility space has been reduced to the 7 sample points in A. For 3 of these the event B occurs, so $P(B \,|\, A) = \frac{3}{7}$.

(b) $P(\text{at least one die lands on a 3} \,|\, \text{score is even}) = P(A \,|\, B)$.

Using $\qquad\qquad P(A \,|\, B) \, P(B) = P(B \,|\, A) \, P(A)$

$$P(A \,|\, B) \, \tfrac{8}{16} = \left(\tfrac{3}{7} \right) \left(\tfrac{7}{16} \right)$$

$$P(A \,|\, B) = \tfrac{3}{8}$$

Therefore the probability that at least one die lands on a 3, given that the score is even, is $\frac{3}{8}$.

NOTE: the possibility space has been reduced to the 8 sample points in B. For three of these the event A occurs, so $P(A \,|\, B) = \frac{3}{8}$.

Example 3.13 A bag contains 10 counters, of which 7 are green and 3 are white. A counter is picked at random from the bag and its colour is noted. The counter is not replaced. A second counter is then picked out.

Find the probability that (**a**) the first counter is green, (**b**) the first counter is green and the second counter is white, (**c**) the counters are of different colours.

Solution 3.13 (**a**) Let G_1 be the event 'the first counter is green'.

$$P(G_1) = \tfrac{7}{10} \quad \text{(since there are 10 counters, of which 7 are green)}$$

The probability that the first counter is green is $\frac{7}{10}$.

(**b**) Let W_2 be the event 'the second counter picked is white'. Now

$$P(W_2 \mid G_1) = \tfrac{3}{9} = \tfrac{1}{3} \quad \text{(since there are 9 counters in the bag,}$$
$$\text{of which 3 are white)}$$

We need
$$P(W_2 \cap G_1) = P(W_2 \mid G_1)\, P(G_1)$$
$$= \left(\tfrac{1}{3}\right)\left(\tfrac{7}{10}\right)$$
$$= \tfrac{7}{30}$$

The probability that the first counter is green and the second counter is white is $\tfrac{7}{30}$.

(**c**) With obvious notation, we need $P(W_2 \cap G_1) + P(G_2 \cap W_1)$.

Now $P(W_1) = \tfrac{3}{10}$ and $P(G_2 \mid W_1) = \tfrac{7}{9}$.

Therefore
$$P(G_2 \cap W_1) = P(G_2 \mid W_1)\, P(W_1)$$
$$= \left(\tfrac{7}{9}\right)\left(\tfrac{3}{10}\right)$$
$$= \tfrac{7}{30}$$

So
$$P(W_2 \cap G_1) + P(G_2 \cap W_1) = \tfrac{7}{30} + \tfrac{7}{30}$$
$$= \tfrac{7}{15}$$

Therefore the probability that the counters are different colours is $\tfrac{7}{15}$.

Exercise 3c

1. A card is picked at random from a pack of 20 cards numbered 1, 2, 3, ..., 20. Given that the card shows an even number, find the probability that it is a multiple of 4.

2. If $P(A \mid B) = \tfrac{2}{5}, P(B) = \tfrac{1}{4}, P(A) = \tfrac{1}{3}$, find
(a) $P(B \mid A)$, (b) $P(A \cap B)$.

3. Two digits are chosen at random from a table of random numbers containing the digits 0, 1, 2, ..., 9. Find the probability that (a) the sum of the two numbers is greater than 9, given that the first number is 3, (b) the second number is 2, given that the sum of the two numbers is greater than 7, (c) the first number is 4, given that the difference between the two numbers is 4.

4. A bag contains 4 red counters and 6 black counters. A counter is picked at random from the bag and not replaced. A second counter is then picked. Find the probability that (a) the second counter is red, given that the first counter is red, (b) both counters are red, (c) the counters are of different colours.

5. Two cards are drawn successively from an ordinary pack of 52 playing cards and kept out of the pack. Find the probability that (a) both cards are hearts, (b) the first card is a heart and the second card is a spade, (c) the second card is a diamond, given that the first card is a club.

6. X and Y are two events such that $P(X) = \tfrac{2}{5}$, $P(X \mid Y) = \tfrac{1}{2}$ and $P(Y \mid X) = \tfrac{2}{3}$. Find
(a) $P(X \cap Y)$, (b) $P(Y)$, (c) $P(X \cup Y)$.

7. A box contains two yellow and two black tickets numbered 1 and 2. Two tickets are drawn from the box. Indicate the sample space by listing all possible pairs of results. What is the probability that both tickets drawn will be yellow, (a) if nothing is known about either of them, (b) if one is known to be yellow, (c) if one is known to be yellow ticket numbered 1?

8. A number is picked at random from the digits $1, 2, \ldots, 9$. Given that the number is a multiple of 3, find the probability that the number is (a) even, (b) a multiple of 4.

9. Two tetrahedral dice are thrown; one is red and the other is blue. The number on which each lands is noted, the faces being marked 1, 2, 3 and 4. Find the probability that (a) the sum of the numbers on which the dice land is 6 given that the red die lands on an odd number, (b) the blue die lands on a 2 or a 3, given that the red die lands on a 2.

10. Events A and B are such that $P(A) = \frac{1}{2}$, $P(B) = \frac{1}{5}$ and $P(A \mid B) = 0$. (a) Find $P(A \cup B)$. (b) Are events A and B exhaustive? (Give a reason.)

11. A and B are two events such that $P(A) = \frac{8}{15}$, $P(B) = \frac{2}{3}$ and $P(A \cap B) = \frac{1}{5}$. Are A and B exhaustive events?

12. A and B are exhaustive events and it is known that $P(A \mid B) = \frac{1}{4}$ and $P(B) = \frac{2}{3}$. Find $P(A)$.

13. Give two examples of events which are both mutually exclusive and exhaustive.

14. Two coins are tossed. A is the event 'at least one head is obtained'. Describe an event B such that A and B are exhaustive events.

15. If
$\mathscr{E} = \{(x, y): x \text{ and } y \text{ are positive integers}\}$
$A = \{(x, y): 2 \leqslant x \leqslant 5 \text{ and } 1 \leqslant y \leqslant 4\}$
$B = \{(x, y): x + y = 5\}$
$C = \{(x, y): y = 2\}$
Find the probability that a member of A chosen at random will also be a member of (a) B, (b) C, (c) $B \cap C$, (d) $B \cup C$.

INDEPENDENT EVENTS

Result 8

> If either of the two events A and B can occur without being affected by the other, then the two events are **independent**.

If events A and B are independent,

$$P(A \mid B) = P(A) \quad \text{and} \quad P(B \mid A) = P(B)$$

Now, since $P(A \cap B) = P(A \mid B)\, P(B)$

$$P(A \cap B) = P(A) \times P(B)$$

This is the **multiplication law for independent events** and is sometimes known as 'the **and** rule'

since $P(A \textbf{ and } B) = P(A) \times P(B).$

For example, if a die is thrown and a coin is tossed,

$$P(\text{tail } \textbf{and} \text{ multiple of 3}) = P(\text{tail}) \times P(\text{multiple of 3})$$

Example 3.14   A die is thrown twice. Find the probability of obtaining a 4 on the first throw and an odd number on the second throw.

Solution 3.14   Let A be the event 'a 4 is obtained on the first throw', then $P(A) = \frac{1}{6}$.

Let B be the event 'an odd number is obtained on the second throw'.

Now the result on the second throw is not affected in any way by the result on the first throw. Therefore A and B are independent events and $P(B) = \frac{3}{6} = \frac{1}{2}$.

$$P(A \cap B) = P(A) P(B)$$
$$= \left(\frac{1}{6}\right)\left(\frac{1}{2}\right)$$
$$= \frac{1}{12}$$

The probability that the first throw results in a 4 and the second throw results in an odd number is $\frac{1}{12}$.

NOTE: $P(A \text{ and } B)$ is smaller than either $P(A)$ or $P(B)$.

Example 3.15   A bag contains 5 red counters and 7 black counters. A counter is drawn from the bag, the colour is noted and the counter is replaced. A second counter is then drawn. Find the probability that the first counter is red and the second counter is black.

Solution 3.15   Let R_1 be the event 'the first counter is red'.

Then $P(R_1) = \frac{5}{12}$

Let B_2 be the event 'the second counter is black'.

Since the first counter is replaced before the second draw is made, R_1 and B_2 are independent events.

Now $P(B_2) = \frac{7}{12}$

and $P(R_1 \cap B_2) = P(R_1) P(B_2)$
$$= \left(\frac{5}{12}\right)\left(\frac{7}{12}\right)$$
$$= \frac{35}{144}$$

The probability that the first counter is red and the second counter is black is $\frac{35}{144}$.

Example 3.16   A fair die is thrown twice. Find the probability that (**a**) neither throw results in a 4, (**b**) at least one throw results in a 4.

Solution 3.16   Let A be the event 'the number on the first throw is 4'.

Let B be the event 'the number on the second throw is 4'.

Now $P(A) = \frac{1}{6}$, so $P(\overline{A}) = \frac{5}{6}$ where $\overline{A}$ is the event 'the number on the first throw is not a 4'.

Similarly $P(\overline{B}) = \frac{5}{6}$.

NOTE: $\overline{A}$ and $\overline{B}$ are independent events.

(**a**) $P(\text{neither throw results in a 4}) = P(\overline{A} \cap \overline{B})$

$$= P(\overline{A})\,P(\overline{B})$$

$$= \left(\frac{5}{6}\right)\left(\frac{5}{6}\right)$$

$$= \frac{25}{36}$$

The probability that neither throw results in a 4 is $\frac{25}{36}$.

(**b**) $P(\text{at least one throw results in a 4}) = 1 - P(\text{neither results in a 4})$

$$= 1 - \frac{25}{36}$$

$$= \frac{11}{36}$$

The probability that at least one throw results in a 4 is $\frac{11}{36}$.

Example 3.17   Events A and B are such that $P(A) = \frac{1}{3}$ and $P(A \cap B) = \frac{1}{12}$. If A and B are independent events, find (**a**) $P(B)$, (**b**) $P(A \cup B)$.

Solution 3.17   (**a**)   Since A and B are independent events $P(A \cap B) = P(A)\,P(B)$

so $\frac{1}{12} = \frac{1}{3}\,P(B)$

Hence $P(B) = \frac{1}{4}$

(**b**)   Now $P(A \cup B) = P(A) + P(B) - P(A \cap B)$

so $P(A \cup B) = \frac{1}{3} + \frac{1}{4} - \frac{1}{12}$

$$= \frac{1}{2}$$

Therefore $P(B) = \frac{1}{4}$ and $P(A \cup B) = \frac{1}{2}$.

Example 3.18   Two events A and B are such that $P(A) = \frac{1}{4}$, $P(A\,|\,B) = \frac{1}{2}$ and $P(B\,|\,A) = \frac{2}{3}$.

(**a**) Are A and B independent events? (**b**) Are A and B mutually exclusive events? (**c**) Find $P(A \cap B)$. (**d**) Find $P(B)$.

Solution 3.18 (**a**) If A and B are independent events then $P(A\,|\,B) = P(A)$.

Now $P(A\,|\,B) = \frac{1}{2}$ and $P(A) = \frac{1}{4}$.

Therefore $P(A\,|\,B) \neq P(A)$ and $\underline{A \text{ and } B \text{ are not independent events.}}$

(**b**) If A and B are mutually exclusive events then $P(A\,|\,B) = 0$.

But we are given that $P(A\,|\,B) = \frac{1}{2}$.

$\underline{\text{Therefore } A \text{ and } B \text{ are not mutually exclusive events.}}$

(**c**) Now

$$P(A \cap B) = P(B\,|\,A)\,P(A)$$
$$= \left(\frac{2}{3}\right)\left(\frac{1}{4}\right)$$
$$= \frac{1}{6}$$

$\underline{\text{Therefore } P(A \cap B) = \frac{1}{6}.}$

(**d**) Now

$$P(A\,|\,B)\,P(B) = P(B\,|\,A)\,P(A)$$

so

$$\tfrac{1}{2}\,P(B) = \left(\frac{2}{3}\right)\left(\frac{1}{4}\right)$$

$$\underline{P(B) = \tfrac{1}{3}}$$

Example 3.19 The probability that a certain type of machine will break down in the first month of operation is 0.1. If a firm has two such machines which are installed at the same time, find the probability that, at the end of the first month, just one has broken down.

Solution 3.19 We assume that the performances of the two machines are independent.

Let A be the event 'machine 1 breaks down' and let B be the event 'machine 2 breaks down'.

Then, if just one machine breaks down, either machine 1 breaks down and machine 2 is still working, or machine 2 breaks down and machine 1 is still working. Therefore we require

$$P(A \cap \overline{B}) + P(\overline{A} \cap B) = P(A)\,P(\overline{B}) + P(\overline{A})\,P(B)$$

$$= (0.1)(0.9) + (0.9)(0.1)$$

$$= 0.18$$

NOTE: A and $\overline{B}$ are independent events, as are $\overline{A}$ and B.

$\underline{\text{Therefore the probability that after 1 month just one machine has}}$
$\underline{\text{broken down is 0.18.}}$

Exercise 3d

1. A die is thrown twice. Find the probability of obtaining a number less than 3 on both throws.

2. A card is picked from a pack containing 52 playing cards. It is then replaced and a second card is picked. Find the probability that (a) both cards are the seven of diamonds, (b) the first card is a heart and the second card is a spade, (c) one card is from a black suit and the other is from a red suit, (d) at least one card is a queen.

3. A coin is tossed and a die is thrown. What is the probability of obtaining a head on the coin and an even number on the die?

4. Two men fire at a target. The probability that Alan hits the target is $\frac{1}{2}$ and the probability that Bob does not hit the target is $\frac{1}{3}$. Alan fires at the target first, then Bob fires at the target. Find the probability that (a) both Alan and Bob hit the target, (b) only one hits the target, (c) neither hits the target.

5. The probability that I am late for work is 0.05. Find the probability that, on two consecutive mornings, (a) I am late for work twice, (b) I am late for work once.

6. Events A and B are such that $P(A) = 0.4$ and $P(B) = 0.25$. If A and B are independent events, find (a) $P(A \cap B)$, (b) $P(A \cap \bar{B})$, (c) $P(\bar{A} \cap \bar{B})$.

7. If events A and B are such that they are independent and $P(A) = 0.3, P(B) = 0.5$, find (a) $P(A \cap B)$, (b) $P(A \cup B)$. Are events A and B mutually exclusive?

8. Events A and B are such that $P(A) = \frac{2}{3}$, $P(A|B) = \frac{2}{3}, P(B) = \frac{1}{4}$. Find (a) $P(B|A)$, (b) $P(A \cap B)$.

9. In a group of 120 girls, each is either freckled or blonde or both; 80 are freckled and 60 are blonde. A girl is to be chosen at random from the group. A is the event 'a freckled girl is chosen' and B is the event 'a blonde girl is chosen'. (a) Calculate $P(A \cap B)$. (b) State, giving a reason, if you think A and B are independent events.
(L Additional)

10. A and B are independent events and $P(A) = \frac{1}{3}, P(B) = \frac{3}{4}$. Find the probability that (a) both A and B occur, (b) only one occurs.

11. The probability that I have to wait at the traffic lights on my way to school is 0.25. Find the probability that, on two consecutive mornings, I have to wait on at least one morning.

Result 9

For events A and B, $P(B) = P(B \cap A) + P(B \cap \bar{A})$.

Illustrating this by means of the Venn diagram:

$$P(B) = \frac{s}{n}$$
$$= \frac{t + (s - t)}{n}$$
$$= \frac{t}{n} + \frac{(s - t)}{n}$$
$$= P(B \cap A) + P(B \cap A)$$

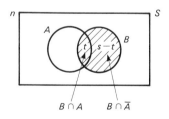

$B \cap A \qquad B \cap \bar{A}$

This result is often written

$$P(B) = P(B|A)\,P(A) + P(B|\bar{A})\,P(\bar{A})$$

Example 3.20   The probability that it will be sunny tomorrow is $\frac{1}{3}$. If it is sunny, the probability that Susan plays tennis is $\frac{4}{5}$. If it is not sunny, the probability that Susan plays tennis is $\frac{2}{5}$. Find the probability that Susan plays tennis tomorrow.

Solution 3.20   Let A be the event 'it is sunny tomorrow' and let B be the event 'Susan plays tennis tomorrow'.

Then $\overline{A}$ is the event 'it is not sunny tomorrow'.

$P(A) = \frac{1}{3}$ and $P(\overline{A}) = \frac{2}{3}$; also $P(B \,|\, A) = \frac{4}{5}$ and $P(B \,|\, \overline{A}) = \frac{2}{5}$.

We require $P(B) = P(B \,|\, A) P(A) + P(B \,|\, \overline{A}) P(\overline{A})$

$$= \left(\frac{4}{5}\right)\left(\frac{1}{3}\right) + \left(\frac{2}{5}\right)\left(\frac{2}{3}\right)$$

$$= \frac{8}{15}$$

Therefore the probability that Susan plays tennis tomorrow is $\frac{8}{15}$.

Example 3.21   If events A and B are independent, show that events $\overline{A}$ and B are independent.

Solution 3.21   Now $P(B) = P(B \cap A) + P(B \cap \overline{A})$

so $P(B \cap \overline{A}) = P(B) - P(B \cap A)$

$$= P(B) - P(B) P(A) \quad \text{since } A \text{ and } B \text{ are independent}$$

$$= P(B)[1 - P(A)]$$

$$= P(B) P(\overline{A})$$

Therefore $P(B \cap \overline{A}) = P(B) P(\overline{A})$ and so $\overline{A}$ and B are independent.

Exercise 3e

1.   A bag contains 6 white counters and 4 blue counters. A counter is drawn, its colour is noted and it is not put back into the bag. A second counter is then drawn. Find the probability that the second counter drawn is blue.

2.   In a restaurant 40% of the customers choose steak for their main course. If a customer chooses steak, the probability that he will choose ice cream to follow is 0.6. If he does not have steak, the probability that he will choose ice cream is 0.3. Find the probability that a customer picked at random will choose (*a*) steak and ice cream, (*b*) ice cream.

3.   Events C and D are such that $P(C) = \frac{4}{7}$, $P(C \cap \overline{D}) = \frac{1}{3}$, $P(C \,|\, D) = \frac{5}{14}$. Find (*a*) $P(C \cap D)$, (*b*) $P(D)$, (*c*) $P(D \,|\, C)$.

4.   Exactly 60% of the members of a form are boys, and 90% of these boys and 75% of the girls each buy one raffle ticket, the rest buying none. Calculate the probability that the winning ticket will be bought by a boy.
                                                                (L Additional)

5. $P(X) = \frac{1}{2}$ and $P(Y) = \frac{1}{4}$. Given that X and Y are mutually exclusive, find (*a*) $P(X \cup Y)$, (*b*) $P(Y \cap \overline{X})$.

6. It is estimated that one-quarter of the drivers on the road between 11 p.m. and midnight have been drinking during the evening. If a driver has not been drinking, the probability that he will have an accident at that time of night is 0.004%; if he has been drinking, the probability of an accident goes up to 0.02%. What is the probability that a car selected at random at that time of night will have an accident? A policeman on the beat at 11.30 p.m. sees a car run into a lamp-post, and jumps to the conclusion that the driver has been drinking. What is the probability that he is right?

(SMP)

EXTENSION OF RESULTS TO MORE THAN TWO EVENTS

Mutually exclusive events

If events A, B and C are mutually exclusive, then

$$P(A \cup B \cup C) = P(A) + P(B) + P(C)$$

This can be extended to any number of mutually exclusive events:

$$P(A_1 \cup A_2 \cup \ldots \cup A_n) = P(A_1) + P(A_2) + \ldots + P(A_n)$$

Example 3.22 Records in a music shop are classed in the following sections: classical, popular, rock, folk and jazz. The respective probabilities that a customer buying a record will choose from each section are 0.3, 0.4, 0.2, 0.05 and 0.05. Find the probability that a person (**a**) will choose a record from the classical or the folk or the jazz sections, (**b**) will not choose a record from the rock or folk or classical sections.

Solution 3.22 A record cannot be classed in more than one section, so the events are mutually exclusive.

(**a**) P(classical or folk or jazz) $= P$(classical) $+ P$(folk) $+ P$(jazz)

$$= 0.3 + 0.05 + 0.05$$

$$= 0.4$$

The probability that the record is classical or folk or jazz is 0.4.

(**b**) P(rock or folk or classical) $= P$(rock) $+ P$(folk) $+ P$(classical)

$$= 0.2 + 0.05 + 0.3$$

$$= 0.55$$

$$P(\text{not rock nor folk nor classical}) = 1 - 0.55$$

$$= 0.45$$

Therefore the probability that the record is not rock nor folk nor classical is 0.45.

Independent events

> If A, B and C are independent events, then
>
> $$P(A \cap B \cap C) = P(A)\,P(B)\,P(C)$$
>
> This result can be extended to n independent events so that
>
> $$P(A_1 \cap A_2 \cap \ldots \cap A_n) = P(A_1)\,P(A_2)\ldots P(A_n)$$

Example 3.23   A die is thrown four times. Find the probability that a 5 is obtained each time.

Solution 3.23   Let 5_1 be the event 'a 5 is obtained on the first throw', 5_2 be the event 'a 5 is obtained on the second throw' and so on.

The events are independent, so

$$P(5_1 \cap 5_2 \cap 5_3 \cap 5_4) = P(5_1)\,P(5_2)\,P(5_3)\,P(5_4)$$
$$= \left(\frac{1}{6}\right)\left(\frac{1}{6}\right)\left(\frac{1}{6}\right)\left(\frac{1}{6}\right)$$
$$= \frac{1}{1296}$$

Therefore the probability that a 5 is obtained each time is $\frac{1}{1296}$.

Example 3.24   Three people in an office decide to enter a marathon race. The respective probabilities that they will complete the marathon are 0.9, 0.7 and 0.6. Find the probability that at least two will complete the marathon. Assume that the performance of each is independent of the performances of the others.

Solution 3.24   Let A be the event 'the first person completes the marathon', then $P(A) = 0.9$.

Let B be the event 'the second person completes the marathon', then $P(B) = 0.7$.

Let C be the event 'the third person completes the marathon', then $P(C) = 0.6$.

$P(\text{all complete the marathon}) = P(A \cap B \cap C)$. We will abbreviate $P(A \cap B \cap C)$ as $P(ABC)$. Then

$$P(\text{all complete the marathon}) = P(ABC)$$
$$= P(A)\,P(B)\,P(C) \quad \text{(independent events)}$$
$$= (0.9)(0.7)(0.6)$$
$$= 0.378$$

P(two out of the three complete the marathon)

$$= P(AB\overline{C}) + P(A\overline{B}C) + P(\overline{A}BC)$$

$$= (0.9)(0.7)(0.4) + (0.9)(0.3)(0.6) + (0.1)(0.7)(0.6)$$

$$= 0.456$$

$$P(\text{at least two complete the marathon}) = 0.378 + 0.456$$

$$= 0.834$$

Therefore the probability that at least two complete the marathon is 0.834.

SUMMARY — PROBABILITY LAWS

Experimental, or empirical, probability

The experimental probability of an event A is the long-term relative frequency of A, so

$$P(A) = \lim \left(\frac{r}{n} \right) \quad \text{as } n \to \infty.$$

Classical probability

For a finite possibility space S, with equally likely outcomes, and a subset A of S,

$$P(A) = \frac{n(A)}{n(S)}$$

$$0 \leqslant P(A) \leqslant 1 \quad \text{and} \quad P(\overline{A}) = 1 - P(A)$$

$$P(A \cup B) = P(A) + P(B) - P(A \cap B)$$

Addition law for mutually exclusive events — the or rule:

If A and B are mutually exclusive, then $P(A \cap B) = 0$

so $P(A \cup B) = P(A) + P(B)$

Exhaustive events

If A and B are exhaustive events, then $P(A \cup B) = 1$

Conditional probability

$$P(A \mid B) = \frac{P(A \cap B)}{P(B)} \qquad P(B \mid A) = \frac{P(B \cap A)}{P(A)}$$

i.e. $P(A \cap B) = P(A \mid B)\,P(B)$ | i.e. $P(B \cap A) = P(B \mid A)\,P(A)$

so that $\qquad P(A \mid B)\,P(B) = P(B \mid A)\,P(A)$

Multiplication law for independent events — the and rule:

If A and B are independent, $P(A \mid B) = P(A)$ and therefore $P(A \cap B) = P(A)\,P(B)$

If A and B are mutually exclusive, $P(A \cap B) = 0$, so that
$P(A \mid B) = 0$.

$P(A) = P(A \cap B) + P(A \cap \overline{B})$

or $P(A) = P(A \mid B) P(B) + P(A \mid \overline{B}) P(\overline{B})$

Miscellaneous Exercise 3f

1. Bag A contains 5 red and 4 white counters.
Bag B contains 6 red and 3 white counters. A
counter is picked at random from bag A and
placed in bag B. A counter is now picked from
bag B. Find the probability that this counter
is white.

2. In a set of 28 dominoes each domino has from
0 to 6 spots at each end. Each domino is
different from every other and the ends are
indistinguishable so that, for example, the
two diagrams in the figure represent the
same domino.

A domino which has no spots at all or the
same number of spots at each end is called a
'double'.
A domino is drawn from the set. Let the
event A be 'The domino is a double', event B
be 'The sum of the spots is 6' and event C be
'The number of spots at each end differ by
more than 3'. On graph paper draw a
diagram to represent the possibility space
with, for example, the point $(1, 2)$
representing the selection of the domino
shown in the figure. On your diagram mark
clearly the set of elements associated with
each of the events A, B and C. Using your
diagram find the probability that (a) both A
and B occur, (b) both A and C occur, (c) both
B and C occur.
State a pair of events which are independent
and also a pair which are mutually exclusive.
Find the probability that A occurs and B does
not occur.   (L Additional)

3. The probability that a person in a particular
evening class is left-handed is $\frac{1}{6}$. From the
class of 15 women and 5 men a person is
chosen at random. Assuming that 'left-
handedness' is independent of the sex of a
person, find the probability that the person
chosen is a man or is left-handed.

4. Two events A and B are such that
$P(A) = 0.2$, $P(A' \cap B) = 0.22$,
$P(A \cap B) = 0.18$.
Evaluate (a) $P(A \cap B')$, (b) $P(A \mid B)$.   (JMB)
(*NOTE*: B' is the event 'B does not occur'.)

5. In a group of 100 people, 40 own a cat, 25
own a dog and 15 own a cat and a dog. Find
the probability that a person chosen at
random (a) owns a dog or a cat, (b) owns a
dog or a cat, but not both, (c) owns a dog,
given that he owns a cat, (d) does not own a
cat, given that he owns a dog.

6. The two events A and B are such that
$P(A) = 0.6$, $P(B) = 0.2$, $P(A \mid B) = 0.1$.
Calculate the probabilities that (i) both of the
events occur, (ii) at least one of the events
occur, (iii) exactly one of the events occurs,
(iv) B occurs, given that A has occurred.
                                        (JMB)

7. Of a group of pupils studying at A-level in
schools in a certain area, 56% are boys and
44% are girls. The probability that a boy of
this group is studying Chemistry is $\frac{1}{5}$ and the
probability that a girl of this group is
studying Chemistry is $\frac{1}{11}$.
(a) Find the probability that a pupil
selected at random from this group is a girl
studying Chemistry.
(b) Find the probability that a pupil
selected at random from this group is not
studying Chemistry.
(c) Find the probability that a Chemistry
pupil selected at random from this group is
male.
(You may leave your answers as fractions in
their lowest terms.)   (O & C)

8. At a fête the vicar has a board in the shape of
a circle, having sectors coloured red and
green, with an arrow which can be spun
above it: you have to try to guess the colour
on which the arrow will come to rest when it
is next spun. It is made so that the results of
successive spins are independent, and

P(the arrow rests on red) $= 0.6$

Find the probability of guessing correctly
(i) if you always guess 'green';
(ii) if you toss a fair coin and guess 'green'
if it comes down 'head' and 'red' otherwise;
(iii) if your guess is always the colour the
arrow is resting on before the spin.   (SMP)

9.   Two soldiers, Alan and Bill, are shooting at a
     target with independent probabilities of $\frac{4}{5}$
     and $\frac{3}{4}$ respectively of hitting the bull with a
     single shot. If they each fire two shots, copy
     and complete the tables which show the
     possible outcomes, together with their
     associated probabilities.

         Alan's two shots at the target

Number of bulls	0	1	2
Probability		$\frac{8}{25}$	

Bill's two shots at the target

Number of bulls	0	1	2
Probability			$\frac{9}{16}$

Calculate the probability that
(a) Alan records two bulls *and* Bill records
two misses,
(b) *either* Alan records two bulls *or* Bill
records two misses with the two events not
occurring simultaneously,
(c) the soldiers record two bulls and two
misses between them.   (L Additional)

10. A die is thrown three times. What is the
     probability of scoring a 2 on just one
     occasion?

11. A coin is tossed four times. Find the
     probability of obtaining less than two heads.

PROBABILITY TREES

A useful way of tackling many probability problems is to draw a
'**probability tree**'. The method is illustrated in the following
examples.

Example 3.25 A bag contains 8 white counters and 3 black counters. Two counters
are drawn, one after the other. Find the probability of drawing one
white and one black counter, in any order, (**a**) if the first counter is
replaced, (**b**) if the first counter is not replaced.

Solution 3.25 (**a**) *With replacement*

Let W_1 be the event 'a white counter is drawn first',

         W_2 be the event 'a white counter is drawn second',

         B_1 be the event 'a black counter is drawn first',

         B_2 be the event 'a black counter is drawn second'.

The results of the first draw and the second draw are shown on the
'tree' overleaf. Since the counter is replaced after the first draw the
events along any one 'branch' of the tree are independent, giving

$$P(W_1 \cap W_2) = P(W_1)\,P(W_2)$$

We multiply terms as we go along the branch.

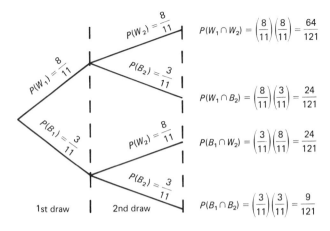

$$P(W_1 \cap W_2) = \left(\frac{8}{11}\right)\left(\frac{8}{11}\right) = \frac{64}{121}$$

$$P(W_1 \cap B_2) = \left(\frac{8}{11}\right)\left(\frac{3}{11}\right) = \frac{24}{121}$$

$$P(B_1 \cap W_2) = \left(\frac{3}{11}\right)\left(\frac{8}{11}\right) = \frac{24}{121}$$

$$P(B_1 \cap B_2) = \left(\frac{3}{11}\right)\left(\frac{3}{11}\right) = \frac{9}{121}$$

NOTE: these events are mutually exclusive, so check that the sum of the probabilities is 1.

P(drawing one white and one black counter)

$$= P(W_1 \cap B_2) + P(B_1 \cap W_2)$$

$$= \frac{24}{121} + \frac{24}{121}$$

$$= \frac{48}{121}$$

The probability of drawing one black and one white counter if the counter is replaced after the first draw is $\frac{48}{121}$.

(b) *Without replacement*   The events along one branch are no longer independent, but we may still multiply as we go along the branch, using the fact

$$P(W_1 \cap W_2) = P(W_1)P(W_2 \mid W_1) \text{ and so on.}$$

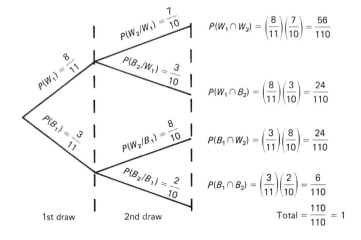

$$P(W_1 \cap W_2) = \left(\frac{8}{11}\right)\left(\frac{7}{10}\right) = \frac{56}{110}$$

$$P(W_1 \cap B_2) = \left(\frac{8}{11}\right)\left(\frac{3}{10}\right) = \frac{24}{110}$$

$$P(B_1 \cap W_2) = \left(\frac{3}{11}\right)\left(\frac{8}{10}\right) = \frac{24}{110}$$

$$P(B_1 \cap B_2) = \left(\frac{3}{11}\right)\left(\frac{2}{10}\right) = \frac{6}{110}$$

$$\text{Total} = \frac{110}{110} = 1$$

P(drawing one white and one black counter)

$$= P(W_1 \cap B_2) + P(B_1 \cap W_2)$$

$$= \frac{24}{110} + \frac{24}{110}$$

$$= \frac{24}{55}$$

The probability of drawing one black and one white counter if the counter is not replaced after the first draw is $\frac{24}{55}$.

NOTE: the diagram can be made simpler if, instead of writing $P(W_2 \mid W_1) = \frac{7}{10}$ on the second branch, we write $P(W_2) = \frac{7}{10}$, since the diagram makes it clear that event W_1 *has already occurred*. The diagram then becomes:

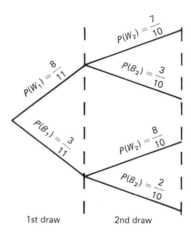

1st draw   2nd draw

Example 3.26 The probability that a golfer hits the ball on to the green if it is windy as he strikes the ball is 0.4, and the corresponding probability if it is not windy as he strikes the ball is 0.7. The probability that the wind will blow as he strikes the ball is 0.3.

Find the probability that (**a**) he hits the ball on to the green, (**b**) it was not windy, given that he does not hit the ball on to the green.

Solution 3.26 Let W be the event 'it is windy', then $P(W) = 0.3$ and $P(\overline{W}) = 0.7$.

Let H be the event 'he hits the ball on to the green'.

Then $P(H \mid W) = 0.4$ and $P(H \mid \overline{W}) = 0.7$.

We can draw a probability tree as follows:

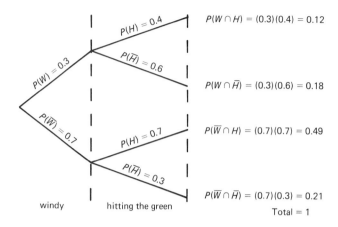

$$P(W \cap H) = (0.3)(0.4) = 0.12$$
$$P(W \cap \overline{H}) = (0.3)(0.6) = 0.18$$
$$P(\overline{W} \cap H) = (0.7)(0.7) = 0.49$$
$$P(\overline{W} \cap \overline{H}) = (0.7)(0.3) = 0.21$$
$$\text{Total} = 1$$

(a)
$$P(H) = P(H \cap W) + P(H \cap \overline{W})$$
$$= 0.12 + 0.49$$
$$= 0.61$$

The probability that he hits the ball on to the green is 0.61.

(b)
$$P(\overline{W} \mid \overline{H}) = \frac{P(\overline{W} \cap \overline{H})}{P(\overline{H})}$$

Now
$$P(\overline{H}) = 1 - P(H)$$
$$= 1 - 0.61$$
$$= 0.39$$

So
$$P(\overline{W} \mid \overline{H}) = \frac{0.21}{0.39}$$
$$= 0.54 \quad \text{(2 d.p.)}$$

The probability that it was not windy, given that he does not hit the ball on to the green, is 0.54 (2 d.p.).

Example 3.27 Events A and B are such that $P(A) = \frac{1}{3}, P(B \mid A) = \frac{1}{4}$ and $P(\overline{B} \mid \overline{A}) = \frac{4}{5}$.

By drawing a tree diagram, or otherwise, find (a) $P(\overline{B} \mid A)$, (b) $P(A \cap B)$, (c) $P(B)$, (d) $P(A \cup B)$.

Solution 3.27   We draw a tree diagram and put on it the information given.

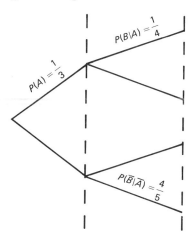

From the diagram, it is obvious that $P(\overline{A}) = \frac{2}{3}$, $P(\overline{B}\,|\,A) = \frac{3}{4}$ and $P(B\,|\,\overline{A}) = \frac{1}{5}$ since the 'total' probability for each set of branches is 1.

The completed tree diagram is

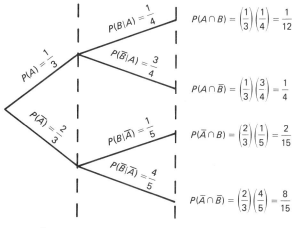

(**a**) $P(\overline{B}\,|\,A) = \frac{3}{4}$

(**b**) $P(A \cap B) = \frac{1}{12}$

(**c**) $P(B) = P(B \cap A) + P(B \cap \overline{A}) = \frac{1}{12} + \frac{2}{15} = \frac{13}{60}$

(**d**) $P(A \cup B) = 1 - P(\overline{A} \cap \overline{B}) = 1 - \frac{8}{15} = \frac{7}{15}$

Example 3.28   A fair coin is tossed three times. What is the probability of obtaining (**a**) exactly two heads, (**b**) at least two heads?

Solution 3.28   We now extend the tree to include three events.

Let H_1 be the event 'a head occurs on the first toss', T_2 be the event 'a tail occurs on the second toss', and so on.

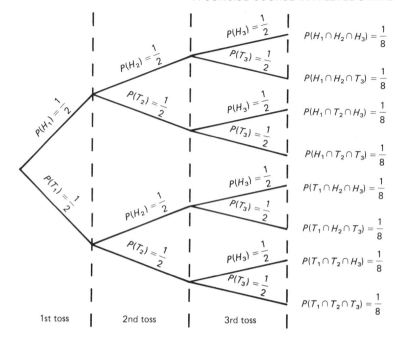

(**a**) $P(\text{exactly two heads}) = P(H_1 \cap H_2 \cap T_3) + P(H_1 \cap T_2 \cap H_3)$
$$+ P(T_1 \cap H_2 \cap H_3)$$

$$= \tfrac{1}{8} + \tfrac{1}{8} + \tfrac{1}{8}$$

$$= \tfrac{3}{8}$$

The probability that exactly two heads are obtained is $\tfrac{3}{8}$.

(**b**) $P(\text{at least two heads}) = P(\text{two heads and a tail})$
$$+ P(\text{three heads})$$

$$= \tfrac{3}{8} + \tfrac{1}{8}$$

$$= \tfrac{1}{2}$$

The probability that at least two heads are obtained is $\tfrac{1}{2}$.

Exercise 3g

1. The probability that a biased die falls showing a 6 is 0.2. This biased die is thrown twice.
    (*a*) Draw a tree diagram showing the possible outcomes and the corresponding probabilities, considering the event 'a six is thrown'.
    (*b*) Find the probability that exactly one six will be obtained.
    An unbiased die is now thrown.
    (*c*) Extend the tree diagram to show the possible outcomes, again with regard to

    whether or not a 6 is thrown.
    (*d*) Find the probability that, in the three throws, exactly one 6 will be obtained.

2. In a class of 24 girls, 7 have black hair.
    (*a*) If 2 girls are chosen at random from the class, find the probability that (i) they both have black hair, (ii) neither has black hair.
    (*b*) If 3 girls are chosen at random, find the probability that more than 1 will have black hair.

3. A coin is biased so that the probability that it lands showing heads is $\frac{2}{3}$. The coin is tossed three times. Find the probability that (a) no heads are obtained, (b) more heads than tails are obtained.

4. A box contains 6 red pens and 3 blue pens.
(a) A pen is selected at random, the colour is noted and the pen is returned to the box. This procedure is performed a second, then a third time. Find the probability of obtaining (i) 3 red pens, (ii) 2 red pens and 1 blue pen, in any order, (iii) more than 1 blue pen.
(b) Repeat (a) but this time find the probabilities if, at each selection, the pen is not returned to the box.

5. In each round of a certain game a player can score 1, 2 or 3 only. Copy and complete the table which shows the scores and two of the respective probabilities of these being scored in a single round.

Score	1	2	3
Probability	$\frac{4}{7}$		$\frac{1}{7}$

Draw a tree diagram to show all the possible total scores and their respective probabilities after a player has completed two rounds. Find the probability that a player has (a) a score of 4 after 2 rounds, (b) an odd number score after 2 rounds. (L Additional)

6. Three bags, A, B and C contain counters as follows:

	Red	Yellow
Bag A	4	3
Bag B	3	6
Bag C	2	4

(a) A counter is taken at random from each of the bags in turn and kept. Draw a tree diagram to show the possible outcomes and find the probability that more red counters than yellow counters are kept.
(b) The counters are now replaced in their original bags. A counter is taken at random from bag A and placed in bag B. Then a counter is taken at random from bag B and placed in bag C. What is the probability that a counter now taken from bag C is yellow?

7. Events X and Y are such that $P(\overline{X}) = \frac{3}{5}$, $P(Y \mid \overline{X}) = \frac{1}{3}$ and $P(\overline{Y} \mid X) = \frac{1}{4}$. By drawing a tree diagram, or otherwise, find (a) $P(Y)$, (b) $P(X \cap Y)$, (c) $P(X \cup Y)$.

8. A mother and her daughter both enter the cake competition at a show. The probability that the mother wins a prize is $\frac{1}{6}$ and the probability that her daughter wins a prize is $\frac{2}{7}$. Assuming that the two events are independent, find the probability that (a) either the mother, or the daughter, but not both, wins a prize, (b) at least one of them wins a prize.

9. A bag contains 7 black and 3 white marbles. Three marbles are chosen at random and in succession, each marble being replaced after it has been taken out of the bag. Draw a tree diagram to show all possible selections.
From your diagram, or otherwise, calculate, to 2 significant figures, the probability of choosing (a) three black marbles, (b) a white marble, a black marble and a white marble in that order, (c) two white marbles and a black marble in any order, (d) at least one black marble.
State an event from this experiment which together with the event described in (d) would be both exhaustive and mutually exclusive. (L Additional)

BAYES' THEOREM

Now we come to an important extension of the result

$$P(A \mid B) = \frac{P(B \mid A)\, P(A)}{P(B)}$$

Suppose $A_1, A_2, \ldots, A_n$ are n mutually exclusive and exhaustive events so that $A_1 \cup A_2 \cup \ldots \cup A_n = S$, the possibility space, and B is an arbitrary event of S. Then for $i = 1, 2, \ldots, n$

$$P(A_i \mid B) = \frac{P(B \mid A_i) \, P(A_i)}{P(B \mid A_1) \, P(A_1) + P(B \mid A_2) \, P(A_2) + \ldots + P(B \mid A_n) \, P(A_n)}$$

This is known as Bayes' theorem and it is useful when we have to 'reverse the conditions' in a problem.

The formula looks very complicated, but in fact it is easy to use if you remember that the denominator is the *total probability of B*.

Example 3.29   Three girls, Aileen, Barbara and Cathy, pack biscuits in a factory. From the batch allotted to them Aileen packs 55%, Barbara 30% and Cathy 15%. The probability that Aileen breaks some biscuits in a packet is 0.7, and the respective probabilities for Barbara and Cathy are 0.2 and 0.1. What is the probability that a packet with broken biscuits found by the checker was packed by Aileen?

Solution 3.29   Let A be the event 'the packet was packed by Aileen', B be the event 'the packet was packed by Barbara', C be the event 'the packet was packed by Cathy', D be the event 'the packet contains broken biscuits'.

We are given $P(A) = 0.55, P(B) = 0.3, P(C) = 0.15$ and $P(D \mid A) = 0.7, P(D \mid B) = 0.2, P(D \mid C) = 0.1$.

We need to find $P(A \mid D)$, so we use Bayes' theorem to 'reverse the conditions':

$$P(A \mid D) = \frac{P(D \mid A) \, P(A)}{P(D)}$$

Now $P(D)$ is the 'total' probability of D, that is the probability that a packet contains broken biscuits. This can be found very easily from the tree diagram. The outcomes resulting in a packet with broken biscuits are shown with an asterisk.

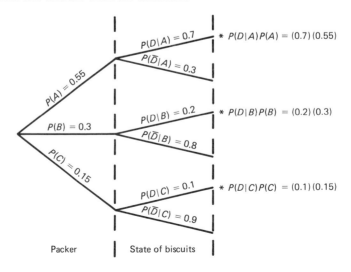

$$P(D) = P(D|A)\,P(A) + P(D|B)\,P(B) + P(D|C)\,P(C)$$

$$= (0.7)(0.55) + (0.2)(0.3) + (0.1)(0.15)$$

$$= 0.46$$

As shown in the tree diagram

$$P(D|A)\,P(A) = (0.7)(0.55)$$

Therefore $$P(A|D) = \frac{(0.7)(0.55)}{0.46}$$

$$= 0.837 \quad (3 \text{ d.p.})$$

The probability that a packet with broken biscuits was packed by Aileen is 0.837 (3 d.p.).

Example 3.30 Three children, Catherine, Michael and David, have equal plots in a circular patch of garden. The boundaries are marked out by pebbles. Catherine has 80 red and 20 white flowers in her patch, Michael has 30 red and 40 white flowers and David has 10 red and 60 white flowers. Their young sister, Mary, wants to pick a flower for her teacher.

(**a**) Find the probability that she picks a red flower if she chooses a flower at random from the garden, ignoring the boundaries.

(**b**) Find the probability that she picks a red flower if she first chooses a plot at random.

(**c**) If she picks a red flower by the method described in (**b**), find the probability that it comes from Michael's plot.

Solution 3.30 (**a**) *If the boundaries are ignored*:

The possibility space S = (flowers in the garden)

and $$n(S) = 100 + 70 + 70 = 240$$

Let R be the event 'a red flower is chosen', then

$$n(R) = 80 + 30 + 10 = 120$$

$$P(R) = \frac{n(R)}{n(S)}$$

$$= \frac{120}{240}$$

$$= \frac{1}{2}$$

The probability that Mary picks a red flower if she ignores the boundaries is $\frac{1}{2}$.

(**b**) *A plot is chosen first*: Each of the three plots is equally likely to be chosen.

Let C be the event 'Catherine's plot is chosen', then $P(C) = \frac{1}{3}$.

With similar notation $P(M) = \frac{1}{3}$ and $P(D) = \frac{1}{3}$.

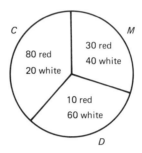

The outcomes resulting in event R are shown with an asterisk on the tree diagram.

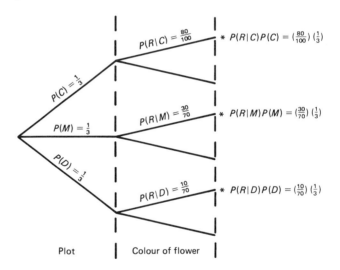

Now $P(R) = P(R \mid C)\, P(C) + P(R \mid M)\, P(M) + P(R \mid D)\, P(D)$

$$= \left(\frac{80}{100}\right)\left(\frac{1}{3}\right) + \left(\frac{30}{70}\right)\left(\frac{1}{3}\right) + \left(\frac{10}{70}\right)\left(\frac{1}{3}\right)$$

$$= \frac{16}{35}$$

The probability that Mary picks a red flower if she chooses a plot at random first is $\frac{16}{35}$.

NOTE: the two different results for part (**a**) and part (**b**) are slightly surprising. In the first case, there is one group of flowers and each flower is equally likely to be chosen. In the second case, even though each plot is equally likely to be chosen, the proportions of red and white flowers within these plots are different.

(**c**) Using Bayes' theorem:

$$P(M\,|\,R) = \frac{P(R\,|\,M)\,P(M)}{P(R)}$$

Now $P(R\,|\,M)\,P(M) = \left(\frac{30}{70}\right)\left(\frac{1}{3}\right) = \frac{1}{7}$ (from tree diagram)

and $P(R) = \frac{16}{35}$ (from part (**b**))

Therefore $P(M\,|\,R) = \dfrac{\frac{1}{7}}{\frac{16}{35}}$

$$= \frac{5}{16}$$

Given that Mary picks a red flower, the probability that it came from Michael's plot is $\frac{5}{16}$.

Exercise 3h

1. In my bookcase there are four shelves and the number of books on each shelf is as shown in the table:

	Hardback	Paperback
Shelf 1	11	8
Shelf 2	8	12
Shelf 3	16	4
Shelf 4	9	3

(a) If I choose a book at random, irrespective of its position in the bookcase, what is the probability that it is a paperback?
(b) I am equally likely to choose any shelf. I choose a shelf at random and then choose a book. (i) What is the probability that it is a hardback? (ii) If the book chosen is a hardback, what is the probability that it is from shelf 3?

2. I travel to work by route A or route B. The probability that I choose route A is $\frac{1}{4}$. The probability that I am late for work if I go via route A is $\frac{2}{3}$ and the corresponding probability if I go via route B is $\frac{1}{3}$.
(a) What is the probability that I am late for work on Monday?
(b) Given that I am late for work, what is the probability that I went via route B?

3. Of the buses leaving the bus station each day, 60% are double deckers and the rest are single deckers; 30% of the double deckers are 'limited stop' buses and 40% of the single

deckers are 'limited stop' buses. Draw a tree diagram to represent this information. Find the probability that a bus leaving the bus station (a) is not a 'limited stop' bus, (b) is a double decker, given that it is a 'limited stop' bus.

4. Susan takes examinations in mathematics, French and history. The probability that she passes mathematics is 0.7 and the corresponding probabilities for French and history are 0.8 and 0.6. Given that her performances in each subject are independent, draw a tree diagram to show the possible outcomes.
Find the probability that Susan (a) fails all three examinations, (b) fails just one examination. Given that Susan fails just one examination, (c) find the probability that she fails history.

5. In an experiment two bags A and B, containing red and green marbles are used. Bag A contains 4 red marbles and 1 green marble and bag B contains 2 red marbles and 7 green marbles. An unbiased coin is tossed. If a head turns up, a marble is drawn at random from bag A while if a tail turns up, a marble is drawn at random from bag B. Calculate the probability that a red marble is drawn in a single trial. Given that a red marble is selected, calculate the probability that when the coin was tossed a head was obtained. (L Additional)

6.

Age group	Percentage
0–16	25
17–25	14
26–64	43
65 and over	18

In a town the percentage of males in particular age groups are as shown in the table above. In a survey it is found that the probability that a male aged 65 or over wearing glasses is 0.8. Similarly if a male is in the age groups 0–16, 17–25 and 26–64 the probabilities of his wearing glasses are 0.2, 0.1 and 0.4 respectively. Given that a particular male is wearing glasses, use Bayes' formula

$$P(A_k \mid B) = \frac{P(A_k)\,P(B \mid A_k)}{\displaystyle\sum_{r=1}^{n} P(A_r)\,P(B \mid A_r)}$$

to calculate the probability that he is 65 or over.
Similarly calculate the probabilities that he is in each of the other age groups and hence state which age group he is most likely to be in.   (L Additional)

7. On a given day a petrol station serves three times as many men as women.
Two types of petrol are available, grade A and grade B. Customers pay by cheque or by cash.
70% of the men and 40% of the women buy grade A petrol.
Of the men buying grade A petrol, 80% pay by cheque, and of the men buying grade B petrol, 60% pay by cheque.
Of the women buying grade A petrol, half pay by cheque and of the women buying grade B petrol, 40% pay by cheque.
Find the probability that (a) a customer buys grade A petrol, (b) a customer pays by cheque, (c) a woman customer pays by cheque, (d) a customer who pays by cheque for grade A petrol is a man.

8. A bag contains 10 counters of which 4 are pink, 3 are green and 3 are yellow. Counters are removed at random, one at a time and without replacement. Find the probability that (a) the first one drawn is green, (b) the first two drawn are both the same colour, (c) the first three drawn are of different colours, (d) the second one drawn is green, given that the first one drawn is pink, (e) the third one drawn is green, given that the first two are the same colour as each other.

9. A and B are two events for which $P(A) = \frac{2}{5}$, $P(\overline{B} \mid A) = \frac{3}{4}$, and $P(B \mid \overline{A}) = \frac{1}{3}$.
(a) Draw a fully labelled tree diagram with A preceding B, that is with A and $\overline{A}$ on the first two branches.
(b) Calculate (i) $P(A \cap B)$, (ii) $P(\overline{A} \cap B)$, (iii) $P(A \cup B)$.
(c) Draw a possibility space diagram to illustrate both the given data and your answers.
(d) Calculate (i) $P(A \mid B)$, (ii) $P(\overline{A} \mid \overline{B})$.
(e) Use your answers to (d) to draw a fully labelled tree diagram with B preceding A.
                                   (L Additional

10.

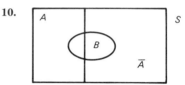

(i) By considering the diagram which represents the sample space S, for $A \cup \overline{A}$, where B is an arbitrary event of S such that $P(B) \neq 0$, show that

$$P(A \mid B) = \frac{P(A)\,P(B \mid A)}{P(A)\,P(B \mid A) + P(\overline{A})\,P(B \mid \overline{A})}$$

(ii) The probabilities that a boy goes to school by bus, bicycle or on foot on a certain day are 0.2, 0.3 and 0.5 respectively. The probabilities of his being late by these methods are 0.6, 0.3 and 0.1 respectively. If he was late on this particular day, using Bayes' theorem or otherwise, calculate the probability that he travelled by bus.   (L Additional)

11. If A_1, A_2 and A_3 are mutually exclusive events whose union is the sample space S of an experiment and B is an arbitrary event of S such that $P(B) \neq 0$, show that

$$P(A_1 \mid B) = \frac{P(A_1)\,P(B \mid A_1)}{\displaystyle\sum_{r=1}^{3} P(A_r)\,P(B \mid A_r)}$$

and write down the results for $P(A_2 \mid B)$ and $P(A_3 \mid B)$.
A factory has three machines 1, 2 and 3, producing a particular type of item. One item is drawn at random from the factory's production. Let B denote the event that the chosen item is defective and let A_k denote the event that the item was produced on machine k where $k = 1, 2$ or 3. Suppose that machines 1, 2 and 3 produce respectively 35%, 45% and 20% of the total production of items and that $P(B \mid A_1) = 0.02$, $P(B \mid A_2) = 0.01, P(B \mid A_3) = 0.03$.
Given that an item chosen at random is defective, find which machine was most likely to have produced it.   (L Additional)

SOME USEFUL METHODS

(a) Problems involving an 'at least' situation

Example 3.31 (**a**) Find the probability of obtaining at least one 6 when 5 dice are thrown.

            (**b**) Find the probability of obtaining at least one 6 when n dice are thrown.

            (**c**) How many dice must be thrown so that the probability of obtaining at least one 6 is at least 0.99?

Solution 3.31 (**a**) In one throw $P(6) = \frac{1}{6}$ and $P(\overline{6}) = \frac{5}{6}$.

When 5 dice are thrown,

$$P(\text{at least one } 6) = 1 - P(\text{no 6s})$$

$$= 1 - P(\overline{6}\,\overline{6}\,\overline{6}\,\overline{6}\,\overline{6})$$

$$= 1 - \left(\tfrac{5}{6}\right)^5$$

$$= 0.598 \quad (3 \text{ d.p.})$$

The probability of obtaining at least one 6 when 5 dice are thrown is 0.598 (3 d.p.).

(**b**) When n dice are thrown, $P(\text{at least one } 6) = 1 - \left(\tfrac{5}{6}\right)^n$.

(**c**) We need to find n such that

$$1 - \left(\tfrac{5}{6}\right)^n \geqslant 0.99$$

i.e.
$$\left(\tfrac{5}{6}\right)^n \leqslant 0.01$$

Taking logs of both sides

$$n \log\left(\tfrac{5}{6}\right) \leqslant \log(0.01)$$

Dividing both sides by $\log\left(\tfrac{5}{6}\right)$ and reversing the inequality sign since $\log\left(\tfrac{5}{6}\right)$ is negative, we have

$$n \geqslant \frac{\log(0.01)}{\log\left(\tfrac{5}{6}\right)}$$

$$n \geqslant 25.3 \quad (1 \text{ d.p.})$$

so   least $n = 26$

Therefore 26 dice must be thrown so that the probability of obtaining at least one 6 is at least 0.99.

(b) Problems involving the use of an infinite geometric progression (G.P.)

Many probability examples involve the use of G.P.s and the following formula is required.

If $S = a + ar + ar^2 + ar^3 + \ldots$ (to infinity),

then

$$S = \frac{a}{1-r} \quad \text{for } |r| < 1 \quad \text{where } a \text{ is the first term,}$$
$$r \text{ is the common ratio}$$

Example 3.32 A, B and C, in that order, throw a tetrahedral die. The first one to throw a 4 wins. The game is continued indefinitely until someone wins. Find the probability that (**a**) A wins, (**b**) B wins, (**c**) C wins.

Solution 3.32 With a tetrahedral die the number 'thrown' is the number on which the die lands. Therefore $P(4 \text{ is thrown}) = \frac{1}{4}$.

(**a**) Let A_1 be the event 'A wins on his first throw', A_2 be the event 'A wins on his second throw', and so on.

Now

$$P(A \text{ wins}) = P(A_1) + P(A_2) + P(A_3) + \ldots \quad \text{(mutually exclusive events)}$$

$$P(A_1) = \tfrac{1}{4} \quad \text{and} \quad P(\overline{A}_1) = \tfrac{3}{4}$$

$$P(A_2) = P(\overline{A}_1 \overline{B}_1 \overline{C}_1 A_2) = \left(\tfrac{3}{4}\right)^3 \left(\tfrac{1}{4}\right)$$

$$P(A_3) = P(\overline{A}_1 \overline{B}_1 \overline{C}_1 \overline{A}_2 \overline{B}_2 \overline{C}_2 A_3) = \left(\tfrac{3}{4}\right)^6 \left(\tfrac{1}{4}\right) \text{ and so on.}$$

Therefore

$$P(A \text{ wins}) = \left(\tfrac{1}{4}\right) + \left(\tfrac{3}{4}\right)^3 \left(\tfrac{1}{4}\right) + \left(\tfrac{3}{4}\right)^6 \left(\tfrac{1}{4}\right) + \ldots$$

$$= \left(\tfrac{1}{4}\right) \left[1 + \left(\tfrac{3}{4}\right)^3 + \left(\tfrac{3}{4}\right)^6 + \ldots\right]$$

$$= \left(\tfrac{1}{4}\right) S \quad \text{where } S \text{ is the sum of an infinite G.P.}$$
$$\text{with} \quad a = 1 \text{ and } r = \left(\tfrac{3}{4}\right)^3$$

$$= \left(\tfrac{1}{4}\right) \left(\frac{1}{1 - \left(\tfrac{3}{4}\right)^3}\right)$$

$$= \left(\tfrac{1}{4}\right) \left(\frac{1}{1 - \tfrac{27}{64}}\right)$$

$$= \tfrac{16}{37}$$

The probability that A wins is $\tfrac{16}{37}$.

(b)
$$P(B \text{ wins}) = P(B_1) + P(B_2) + P(B_3) + \ldots \quad \text{to infinity (mutually exclusive events)}$$

Now $P(B_1) = P(\overline{A}_1 B_1) = \left(\frac{3}{4}\right)\left(\frac{1}{4}\right)$

$$P(B_2) = P(\overline{A}_1 \overline{B}_1 \overline{C}_1 \overline{A}_2 B_2) = \left(\frac{3}{4}\right)^4 \left(\frac{1}{4}\right)$$

$$P(B_3) = P(\overline{A}_1 \overline{B}_1 \overline{C}_1 \overline{A}_2 \overline{B}_2 \overline{C}_2 \overline{A}_3 B_3) = \left(\frac{3}{4}\right)^7 \left(\frac{1}{4}\right) \quad \text{and so on.}$$

So

$$P(B \text{ wins}) = \left(\frac{1}{4}\right)\left(\frac{3}{4}\right) + \left(\frac{1}{4}\right)\left(\frac{3}{4}\right)^4 + \left(\frac{1}{4}\right)\left(\frac{3}{4}\right)^7 + \ldots$$

$$= \left(\frac{1}{4}\right)\left(\frac{3}{4}\right)\left[1 + \left(\frac{3}{4}\right)^3 + \left(\frac{3}{4}\right)^6 + \ldots\right]$$

$$= \left(\frac{3}{16}\right)\left(\frac{1}{1 - \left(\frac{3}{4}\right)^3}\right)$$

$$= \frac{12}{37}$$

Therefore the probability that B wins is $\frac{12}{37}$.

(c)
$$P(C \text{ wins}) = 1 - P(A \text{ wins}) - P(B \text{ wins})$$

$$= 1 - \frac{28}{37}$$

$$= \frac{9}{37}$$

Therefore the probability that C wins is $\frac{9}{37}$.

Exercise 3i

1. A coin is biased so that the probability that it falls showing tails is 0.75.
   (a) Find the probability of obtaining at least one head when the coin is tossed five times.
   (b) How many times must the coin be tossed so that the probability of obtaining at least one head is greater than 0.98?

2. A missile is fired at a target and the probability that the target is hit is 0.7.
   (a) Find how many missiles should be fired so that the probability that the target is hit at least once is greater than 0.995.
   (b) Find how many missiles should be fired so that the probability that the target is not hit is less than 0.001.

3. A die is biased so that the probability of obtaining a 3 is p. When the die is thrown four times the probability that there is at least one 3 is 0.9375. Find the value of p. How many times should the die be thrown so that the probability that there are no threes is less than 0.03?

4. On a safe there are four alarms which are arranged so that any one will sound when someone tries to break into the safe. If the probability that each alarm will function properly is 0.85, find the probability that at least one alarm will sound when someone tries to break into the safe.

5. Two people, A and B, play a game. An ordinary die is thrown and the first person to throw a 4 wins. A and B take it in turns to throw the die, starting with A. Find the probability that B wins.

6. A, B, C and D throw a coin, in turn, starting with A. The first to throw a head wins. The game can continue indefinitely until a head is thrown. However, D objects because the others have their first turn before him. Compare the probability that D wins with the probability that A wins.

7. A box contains five black balls and one white ball. Alan and Bill take turns to draw a ball from the box, starting with Alan. The first boy to draw the white ball wins the game.

Assuming that they do not replace the balls as they draw them out, find the probability that Bill wins the game.

If the game is changed, so that, in the new game, they replace each ball after it has been drawn out, find the probabilities that:

(a) Alan wins at his first attempt;
(b) Alan wins at his second attempt;
(c) Alan wins at his third attempt.

Show that these answers are terms in a Geometric Progression. Hence find the probability that Alan wins the new game.

ARRANGEMENTS

In order to calculate the number of possible outcomes in a possibility space and the number of sample points for an event, the following results are often used.

Result 1

> The number of ways of arranging n unlike objects in a line is $n!$

NOTE: $n! = n(n-1)(n-2)\ldots(3)(2)(1)$.

For example, consider the letters A, B, C, D.

The first letter can be chosen in 4 ways (either A or B or C or D),
the second letter can be chosen in 3 ways,
the third letter can be chosen in 2 ways,
the fourth letter can be chosen in only 1 way.

Therefore the number of ways of arranging the 4 letters is $(4)(3)(2)(1) = 4! = 24$.

On a calculator: $\boxed{4}$ $\boxed{x!}$

The arrangements are

ABCD	ABDC	ACBD	ACDB	ADCB	ADBC
BCDA	BCAD	BDAC	BDCA	BACD	BADC
CDBA	CDAB	CABD	CADB	CBAD	CBDA
DABC	DACB	DBCA	DBAC	DCAB	DCBA

Example 3.33 How many different number plates can be formed if each is to contain the three letters A, C and E followed by the three digits 4, 7 and 8?

Solution 3.33 There are 3! ways of arranging the letters A, C and E, and 3! ways of arranging the digits 4, 7 and 8.

Therefore the total number of different plates $= (3!)(3!)$

$$= 36$$

36 different number plates can be formed.

Result 2

> The number of ways of arranging in a line n objects, of which p are alike, is $\dfrac{n!}{p!}$.

If instead of the letters A, B, C, D we have the letters A, A, A, D then the 24 arrangements listed previously reduce to the following:

$$\text{AAAD} \quad \text{AADA} \quad \text{ADAA} \quad \text{DAAA}$$

So the number of ways of arranging the 4 objects, of which 3 are alike $= \dfrac{4!}{3!} = \dfrac{(4)(3)(2)(1)}{(3)(2)(1)} = 4$.

On a calculator: $\boxed{4}\ \boxed{x!}\ \boxed{\div}\ \boxed{3}\ \boxed{x!}\ \boxed{=}$

The result can be extended as follows:

> The number of ways of arranging in a line n objects of which p of one type are alike, q of a second type are alike, r of a third type are alike, and so on, is $\dfrac{n!}{p!\,q!\,r!\ldots}$

Example 3.34 (a) In how many ways can the letters of the word STATISTICS be arranged?

(b) If the letters of the word MINIMUM are arranged in a line at random, what is the probability that the arrangement begins with MMM?

Solution 3.34 (a) Consider the word STATISTICS.

There are 10 letters and S occurs 3 times,
T occurs 3 times,
I occurs twice.

Therefore

$$\text{number of ways} = \frac{10!}{3!\,3!\,2!}$$

$$= \frac{(10)(9)(8)(7)(6)(5)(4)(3)(2)(1)}{(3)(2)(1)(3)(2)(1)(2)(1)}$$

$$= 50\,400$$

There are 50 400 ways of arranging the letters in the word STATISTICS.

On a calculator: $\boxed{10}\ \boxed{x!}\ \boxed{\div}\ \boxed{3}\ \boxed{x!}\ \boxed{\div}\ \boxed{3}\ \boxed{x!}\ \boxed{\div}\ \boxed{2}\ \boxed{x!}\ \boxed{=}$

(b) Consider the word MINIMUM

The possibility space $S = $ (arrangements of MINIMUM).

Now
$$n(S) = \frac{7!}{3!\,2!}$$
$$= \frac{(7)(6)(5)(4)(3)(2)(1)}{(3)(2)(1)(2)(1)}$$
$$= 420$$

Let E be the event 'the arrangement begins with MMM'.

So we must have MMMxxxx. There is only one way of arranging MMM; then the remaining 4 letters can be arranged in $\dfrac{4!}{2!} = 12$ ways.

Therefore
$$n(E) = 12$$

So
$$P(E) = \frac{n(E)}{n(S)}$$
$$= \frac{12}{420}$$
$$= \frac{1}{35}$$

The probability that the arrangement begins MMM is $\frac{1}{35}$.

Example 3.35 Ten pupils are placed at random in a line. What is the probability that the two youngest pupils are separated?

Solution 3.35 Let the possibility space be S, then $n(S) = 10!$

Let E be the event 'the two youngest pupils are together'.

Now treat these two together as one 'item' and so we have 9 'items' to arrange.

The 9 items can be arranged in 9! ways.

But the two youngest can be arranged in 2! ways ($Y_1 Y_2$ or $Y_2 Y_1$).

Therefore $n(E) = 2!\,9!$

So $P(E) = \dfrac{n(E)}{n(S)}$

$\qquad = \dfrac{2!\,9!}{10!}$

$\qquad = \dfrac{2}{10}$

$\qquad = \dfrac{1}{5}$

On a calculator:

| 2 | $x!$ | $\times$ | 9 | $x!$ | $\div$ | 10 | $x!$ | $=$ |

Now $\overline{E}$ is the event 'the two youngest are not together'.

So
$$P(\overline{E}) = 1 - P(E)$$
$$= 1 - \tfrac{1}{5}$$
$$= \tfrac{4}{5}$$

The probability that the two youngest are separated is $\frac{4}{5}$.

Example 3.36 If a four-digit number is formed from the digits 1, 2, 3 and 5 and repetitions are not allowed, find the probability that the number is divisible by 5.

Solution 3.36 Let S be the possibility space, then $n(S) = 4! = 24$.

Let E be the event 'the number is divisible by 5'.

If the number is divisible by 5 then it must end with the digit 5.

Therefore

$$n(E) = \text{number of ways of arranging the digits 1, 2, 3}$$
$$= 3!$$

So $P(E) = \dfrac{n(E)}{n(S)}$

$$= \dfrac{3!}{24}$$

$$= \dfrac{1}{4}$$

The probability that the number is divisible by 5 is $\frac{1}{4}$.

Result 3

> The number of ways of arranging n unlike objects in a ring when clockwise and anticlockwise arrangements are different is $(n-1)!$

For example, consider 4 people A, B, C and D, who are to be seated at a round table. The following four arrangements are the same, as A always has D on his immediate right and B on his immediate left.

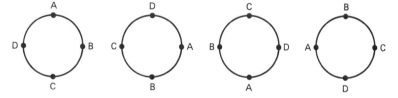

To find the number of different arrangements, we fix A and then consider the number of ways of arranging B, C and D.

Therefore the number of different arrangements of 4 people around the table is 3!

Result 4

> The number of ways of arranging n unlike objects in a ring, when clockwise and anticlockwise arrangements are the same, is $\dfrac{(n-1)!}{2}$.

For example, if A, B, C and D are 4 different coloured beads which are threaded on a ring, then the following two arrangements are the same — the one is the other viewed from the other side.

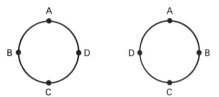

Therefore the number of arrangements of 4 beads on a ring is $\dfrac{3!}{2} = 3$.

Example 3.37 Six bulbs are planted in a ring and two do not grow. What is the probability that the two that do not grow are next to each other?

Solution 3.37 Let S be the possibility space, then $n(S) = 5!$

Let E be the event 'the bulbs that do not grow are next to each other'. Consider the two bulbs that do not grow as one 'item'. They can be arranged in 2! ways. There are now five 'items' to be arranged in a ring and this can be done in 4! ways.

Therefore $\qquad\qquad\qquad n(E) = 2!\,4!$

So $\qquad\qquad\qquad\qquad P(E) = \dfrac{n(E)}{n(S)}$

$$= \dfrac{2!\,4!}{5!}$$

$$= \tfrac{2}{5}$$

The probability that the bulbs that do not grow are next to each other is $\tfrac{2}{5}$.

Example 3.38 One white, one blue, one red and two yellow beads are threaded on a ring to make a bracelet. Find the probability that the red and white beads are next to each other.

Solution 3.38 Let S be the possibility space.

If all the objects are unlike, the number of ways of arranging five beads on a ring is $\dfrac{4!}{2}$, but as there are two yellows

$$n(S) = \dfrac{4!}{(2)(2!)}$$

$$= 6$$

Let E be the event 'the red and the white beads are next to each other'.

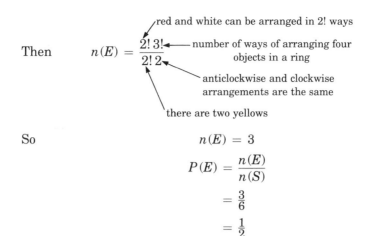

Then $\qquad n(E) = \dfrac{2!\,3!}{2!\,2}$

red and white can be arranged in 2! ways

number of ways of arranging four objects in a ring

anticlockwise and clockwise arrangements are the same

there are two yellows

So $\qquad n(E) = 3$

$$P(E) = \frac{n(E)}{n(S)}$$

$$= \tfrac{3}{6}$$

$$= \tfrac{1}{2}$$

The probability that the red and white beads are next to each other is $\tfrac{1}{2}$.

This result can be shown diagrammatically:

Ways of arranging the beads

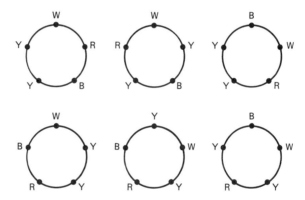

NOTE: in three of the six arrangements the red and white beads are next to each other.

Exercise 3j

1. In how many ways can the letters of the word FACETIOUS be arranged in a line? What is the probability that an arrangement begins with F and ends with S?

2. (a) In how many ways can 7 people sit at a round table?
    (b) What is the probability that a husband and wife sit together?

3. On a shelf there are 4 mathematics books and 8 English books.
    (a) If the books are to be arranged so that the mathematics books are together, in how many ways can this be done?
    (b) What is the probability that all the mathematics books will not be together?

4. If the letters of the word PROBABILITY are arranged at random, find the probability that the two I's are separated.

5. If the letters in the word ABSTEMIOUS are arranged at random, find the probability that the vowels and consonants appear alternately.

6. Nine children play a party game and hold hands in a circle.
(*a*) In how many different ways can this be done?
(*b*) What is the probability that Mary will be holding hands with her friends Natalie and Sarah?

7. (*a*) In how many different ways can the letters in the word ARRANGEMENTS be arranged?
(*b*) Find the probability that an arrangement chosen at random begins with the letters EE.

PERMUTATIONS OF *r* OBJECTS FROM *n* OBJECTS

Consider the number of ways of placing 3 of the letters A, B, C, D, E, F, G in 3 empty spaces.

The first space can be filled in 7 ways. The second space can be filled in 6 ways. The third space can be filled in 5 ways. Therefore there are $(7)(6)(5)$ ways of arranging 3 letters taken from 7 letters. This is the number of permutations of 3 objects taken from 7 and it is written $^7P_3$.

So
$$^7P_3 = (7)(6)(5) = 210$$

Now $(7)(6)(5)$ could be written $\dfrac{(7)(6)(5)(4)(3)(2)(1)}{(4)(3)(2)(1)}$,

i.e.
$$^7P_3 = \frac{7!}{4!} = \frac{7!}{(7-3)!}$$

On a calculator this can be obtained directly: $\boxed{7}$ $\boxed{^nP_r}$ $\boxed{3}$ $\boxed{=}$

NOTE: the order in which the letters are arranged is important — ABC is a different permutation from ACB.

> In general, the number of permutations, or ordered arrangements, of *r* objects taken from *n* unlike objects is written ^nP_r where
> $$^nP_r = \frac{n!}{(n-r)!}$$

NOTE: $^nP_n = \dfrac{n!}{(n-n)!} = \dfrac{n!}{0!}$

But we know that the number of ways of arranging *n* unlike objects is *n*!

So we must *define* 0! to be 1.

i.e.
$$0! = 1$$

Try it on your calculator.

COMBINATIONS OF *r* OBJECTS FROM *n* OBJECTS

When considering the number of combinations of *r* objects from *n* objects, the order in which they are placed is not important.

For example, the one combination ABC gives rise to 3! permutations

ABC, ACB, BCA, BAC, CAB, CBA

So, if the number of combinations of 3 letters from the 7 letters A, B, C, D, E, F, G, is denoted by $^7C_3$ then

$$^7C_3\,(3!) = {}^7P_3$$

$$^7C_3 = \frac{{}^7P_3}{3!}$$

$$= \frac{7!}{3!\,4!}$$

$$= \frac{(7)(6)(5)\,(\cancel{4})\,(\cancel{3})\,(\cancel{2})\,(\cancel{1})}{(3)(2)(1)\,(\cancel{4})\,(\cancel{3})\,(\cancel{2})\,(\cancel{1})}$$

$$= 35$$

On a calculator this can be obtained directly: $\boxed{7}\ \boxed{^nC_r}\ \boxed{3}\ \boxed{=}$

In general, the number of combinations of r objects from n unlike objects is ^nC_r where $^nC_r = \dfrac{n!}{r!(n-r)!}$.

NOTE: ^nC_r is sometimes written $_nC_r$ or $\dbinom{n}{r}$.

Example 3.39   In how many ways can a hand of 4 cards be dealt from an ordinary pack of 52 playing cards?

Solution 3.39   We need to consider combinations, since the order in which the cards are dealt is not important.

Now
$$^{52}C_4 = \frac{52!}{4!\,48!}$$

$$= \frac{(52)(51)(50)(49)\,(\cancel{48})\ldots(\cancel{1})}{(4)(3)(2)(1)\,(\cancel{48})\ldots(\cancel{1})}$$

$$= 270\,725 \text{ ways}$$

On a calculator: $\boxed{52}\ \boxed{^nC_r}\ \boxed{4}\ \boxed{=}$

The number of ways of dealing the hand of 4 cards is 270 725.

Example 3.40   Four letters are chosen at random from the word RANDOMLY. Find the probability that all four letters chosen are consonants.

Solution 3.40   Let S be the possibility space, then

$$n(S) = {}^8C_4$$

$$= \frac{8!}{4!\,4!}$$

$$= 70$$

Let E be the event 'four consonants are chosen'. As there are six consonants

$$n(E) = {}^6C_4$$
$$= \frac{6!}{4!\,2!}$$
$$= 15$$

Now
$$P(E) = \frac{n(E)}{n(S)}$$
$$= \frac{15}{70}$$
$$= \frac{3}{14}$$

The probability that the four letters chosen are consonants is $\frac{3}{14}$.

Example 3.41 A team of 4 is chosen at random from 5 girls and 6 boys.

(a) In how many ways can the team be chosen if (i) there are no restrictions; (ii) there must be more boys than girls?

(b) Find the probability that the team contains only one boy.

Solution 3.41 (a) (i) There are 11 people, from whom 4 are chosen. The order in which they are chosen is not important.

$$\text{Number of ways of choosing the team} = {}^{11}C_4$$
$$= \frac{11!}{4!\,7!}$$
$$= 330$$

If there are no restrictions, the team can be chosen in 330 ways.

(ii) If there are to be more boys than girls, then there must be 3 boys and 1 girl, or 4 boys.

$$\text{Number of ways of choosing 3 boys and 1 girl} = ({}^6C_3)({}^5C_1)$$
$$= \left(\frac{6!}{3!\,3!}\right)\left(\frac{5!}{1!\,4!}\right)$$
$$= 20 \times 5$$
$$= 100$$

On a calculator: $\boxed{6}$ $\boxed{{}^nC_r}$ $\boxed{3}$ $\boxed{=}$ $\boxed{\times}$ $\boxed{5}$ $\boxed{{}^nC_r}$ $\boxed{1}$ $\boxed{=}$

$$\text{Number of ways of choosing 4 boys} = {}^6C_4$$
$$= \frac{6!}{4!\,2!}$$
$$= 15$$

Therefore the number of ways of choosing the team if there are more boys than girls $= 100 + 15 = 115$ ways.

(**b**) The possibility space $S = $ (all possible teams of 4) and $n(S) = 330$.

Let E be the event 'only one boy is chosen'.

Now

$$n(E) = ({}^6C_1)({}^5C_3) \quad \text{(if 1 boy is chosen, then 3 girls must be chosen)}$$

$$= 6 \times 10$$

$$= 60$$

So $\quad P(E) = \dfrac{n(E)}{n(S)}$

$$= \frac{60}{330}$$

$$= \frac{2}{11}$$

The probability that the team contains only one boy is $\frac{2}{11}$.

Example 3.42 Four items are taken at random from a box of 12 items and inspected. The box is rejected if more than 1 item is found to be faulty. If there are 3 faulty items in the box, find the probability that the box is accepted.

Solution 3.42 The box is accepted if (a) there are no faulty items in the sample of 4, or (b) there is one faulty item in the sample of 4.

Let S be the possibility space, then

$$n(S) = {}^{12}C_4$$

$$= 495$$

There are 9 items that are not faulty, so the number of ways of choosing 4 items that are not faulty

$$= {}^9C_4$$

$$= 126$$

The number of ways of choosing 1 faulty item and 3 good items

$$= ({}^3C_1)({}^9C_3)$$

$$= 3 \times 84$$

$$= 252$$

Let E be the event 'the number of faulty items chosen is 0 or 1'.

Then $n(E) = 126 + 252 = 378$

So $P(E) = \dfrac{n(E)}{n(S)}$

$$= \frac{378}{495}$$

$$= 0.76 \quad (2 \text{ d.p.})$$

If the number of faulty items is 0 or 1 then the box is accepted, so the probability that the box is accepted is 0.76 (2 d.p.).

Example 3.43 If a diagonal of a polygon is defined to be a line joining any two non-adjacent vertices, how many diagonals are there in a polygon of (*i*) 5 sides, (*ii*) 6 sides, (*iii*) n sides?

Solution 3.43 (*i*) Number of ways to choose 2 points from 5

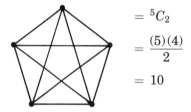

$$= {}^5C_2$$

$$= \frac{(5)(4)}{2}$$

$$= 10$$

So there are 10 possible lines to draw, but as there are 5 sides, 5 of these are joining adjacent vertices.

Therefore the number of diagonals $= 10 - 5 = 5$.

(*ii*) Similarly, for the polygon of 6 sides,

the number of diagonals $= {}^6C_2 - 6$

$$= \frac{(6)(5)}{2} - 6$$

$$= 9$$

The number of diagonals for a polygon with 6 sides is 9.

(*iii*) For a polygon with n sides,

the number of diagonals $= {}^nC_2 - n$

$$= \frac{(n)(n-1)}{2} - n$$

$$= \frac{n^2 - n - 2n}{2}$$

$$= \frac{n(n-3)}{2}$$

The number of diagonals for a polygon with n sides is $\dfrac{n(n-3)}{2}$.

Example 3.44 A certain family consists of Mother, Father and their ten sons.

(a) They are invited to send a group of four representatives to a wedding. Evaluate the number of ways in which the group can be formed, if it must contain (*i*) both parents; (*ii*) one and only one parent; (*iii*) neither parent.

(b) On another occasion, the ten sons decide to play five-a-side football. Evaluate the number of ways in which the teams can be made up. Determine the probability that the two eldest brothers are in the same team.

Solution 3.44 (a) (*i*) If the group contains both parents,

number of ways to choose remaining 2 from $10 = {}^{10}C_2$

$$= 45$$

If the group is to contain both parents, then it can be chosen in 45 ways.

(*ii*) Number of ways to choose one parent $= 2$

Number of ways to choose remaining 3 from $10 = {}^{10}C_3$

$$= 120$$

Therefore number of ways to choose the group of $4 = (2)(120)$

$$= 240$$

If the group is to contain one, and only one parent, then it can be chosen in 240 ways.

(*iii*)   Number of ways to choose 4 from $10 = {}^{10}C_4$

$$= 210$$

If the group is to contain neither parent, then the number of ways in which it can be chosen is 210.

(**b**)   Number of ways to choose 5 from $10 = {}^{10}C_5$

$$= 252$$

When one team has been chosen, the other team is formed automatically. But, since the pairs of teams are interchangeable, e.g. ABCDE versus FGHIJ is the same as FGHIJ versus ABCDE, the total number of ways in which the two teams can be formed is $\frac{1}{2}(252) = 126$.

The two teams can be formed in 126 ways.

If the two eldest are in the same team,

the number of ways in which the
remaining 3 can be chosen $= {}^{8}C_3 = 56$

Let E be the event 'the two eldest are in the same team', then $n(E) = 56$.

If S is the possibility space, then $n(S) = 126$.

$$P(\text{two eldest are in the same team}) = P(E)$$

$$= \frac{n(E)}{n(S)}$$

$$= \frac{56}{126}$$

$$= \frac{4}{9}$$

The probability that the two eldest are in the same team is $\frac{4}{9}$.

Example 3.45 Three letters are selected at random from the word BIOLOGY. Find the probability that the selection (**a**) does not contain the letter O, (**b**) contains both of the letters O.

Solution 3.45 We need to find the total number of selections and, because there are two letters O, we find the number of selections with

(*i*)   0 letter O
(*ii*) 1 letter O
(*iii*) 2 letters O.

(*i*) Number of selections without the letter O

$\qquad\qquad$ = number of ways to choose 3 letters
$\qquad\qquad\quad$ from B, I, L, G, Y

$\qquad\qquad$ = $^5C_3$

$\qquad\qquad$ = 10

(*ii*) Number of selections with 1 letter O

(e.g. $\boxed{\text{O, B, I}}$, $\boxed{\text{O, B, G}}$, and so on)

$\qquad\qquad$ = number of ways to choose 2 letters
$\qquad\qquad\quad$ from B, I, L, G, Y

$\qquad\qquad$ = $^5C_2$

$\qquad\qquad$ = 10

(*iii*) Number of selections with 2 letters O

(e.g. $\boxed{\text{O, O, B}}$, $\boxed{\text{O, O, G}}$, and so on)

$\qquad\qquad$ = number of ways to choose 1 letter
$\qquad\qquad\quad$ from B, I, L, G, Y

$\qquad\qquad$ = 5

Therefore, total number of selections = $10 + 10 + 5 = 25$

(a) P(selection does not contain letter O) $= \frac{10}{25} = \frac{2}{5}$

(b) P(selection contains 2 letters O) $= \frac{5}{25} = \frac{1}{5}$

NOTE: it is easy to write them all out to check:

(i) B, I, L	(ii) O, B, I	(iii) O, O, B
B, I, G	O, B, L	O, O, I
B, I, Y	O, B, G	O, O, L
B, L, G	O, B, Y	O, O, G
B, L, Y	O, I, L	O, O, Y
B, G, Y	O, I, G	5
I, L, G	O, I, Y	
I, L, Y	O, L, G	
I, G, Y	O, L, Y	
L, G, Y	O, G, Y	
10	10	

SUMMARY — ARRANGEMENTS, PERMUTATIONS AND COMBINATIONS

The number of ways of arranging n unlike objects in a line	$n!$
The number of ways of arranging in a line n objects of which p of one type are alike, q of another type are alike, r of a third type are alike, and so on	$\dfrac{n!}{p!\,q!\,r!\ldots}$
The number of ways of arranging n unlike objects in a ring when clockwise and anticlockwise arrangements are different	$(n-1)!$
The number of ways of arranging n unlike objects in a ring when clockwise and anticlockwise arrangements are the same	$\dfrac{(n-1)!}{2}$
The number of permutations of r objects taken from n unlike objects	$^{n}P_{r} = \dfrac{n!}{(n-r)!}$
The number of combinations of r objects taken from n unlike objects	$^{n}C_{r} = \dfrac{n!}{r!\,(n-r)!}$

Exercise 3k

1. From a group of 10 boys and 8 girls, 2 pupils are chosen at random. Find the probability that they are both girls.

2. From a group of 6 men and 8 women, 5 people are chosen at random. Find the probability that there are more men chosen than women.

3. From a bag containing 6 white counters and 8 blue counters, 4 counters are chosen at random. Find the probability that 2 white counters and 2 blue counters are chosen.

4. From a group of 10 people, 4 are to be chosen to serve on a committee.
   (a) In how many different ways can the committee be chosen?
   (b) Among the 10 people there is one married couple. Find the probability that both the husband and the wife will be chosen.
   (c) Find the probability that the 3 youngest people will be chosen.

5. Four persons are chosen at random from a group of ten persons consisting of four men and six women. Three of the women are sisters. Calculate the probabilities that the four persons chosen will: (i) consist of four women, (ii) consist of two women and two men, (iii) include the three sisters.   (JMB)

6. A touring party of 20 cricketers consists of 9 batsmen, 8 bowlers and 3 wicket keepers. A team of 11 players must have at least 5 batsmen, 4 bowlers and 1 wicket keeper. How many different teams can be selected, (a) if all the players are available for selection, (b) if 2 batsmen and 1 bowler are injured and cannot play?

7. Find the number of ways in which 10 different books can be shared between a boy and a girl if each is to receive an even number of books.

8. Four letters are picked from the word BREAKDOWN. What is the probability that there is at least one vowel among the letters?

9. Eight people sit in a minibus: 4 on the sunny side and 4 on the shady side. If 2 people want to sit on opposite sides to each other, another 2 people want to sit on the shady side, in how many ways can this be done?

10. Disco lights are arranged in a vertical line. How many different arrangements can be made from 2 green, 3 blue and 4 red lights (a) if all 9 lights are used, (b) if at least 8 lights are used?

11. A group consisting of 10 boys and 11 girls attends a course for special games coaching.
    (a) When they are introduced, each person hands a card containing his or her photograph, name and address to every other member of the group. State the total number of cards which are exchanged.
    (b) Five boys are selected for basketball and six girls for netball. Find the number of different possible selections for each of these.
    (c) Five particular boys and five particular girls are selected and placed in mixed pairs for tennis. Find the total number of different mixed pairs which can be made using these ten children.
    (d) If 4 children are chosen at random from the whole group find the probability that there is a majority of girls in the 4 selected.
    (L Additional)

12. To enter a cereal competition, competitors have to choose the 8 most important features of a new car, from a possible 12 features, then list the 8 in order of preference. Each cereal packet entry form contains space for 5 entries. A correct entry wins a new car.
    (a) What is the probability that a woman wins a new car if she completes the entry form from one packet?
    (b) How many entry forms would she need to complete, each entry showing different arrangements, if the probability that she wins a car is to be at least 0.8?

13. Three letters are selected at random from the word SCHOOL. Find the probability that the selection (a) does not contain the letter O, (b) contains both the letters O.

14. How many even numbers can be formed with the digits 3, 4, 5, 6, 7 by using some or all of the numbers (repetitions are not allowed)?

15.

Different coloured pegs, each of which is painted in one and only one of the six colours red, white, black, green, blue and yellow, are to be placed in four holes, as shown in the figure, with one peg in each hole. Pegs of the same colour are indistinguishable. Calculate how many different arrangements of pegs placed in the four holes so that they are all occupied can be made from

(a) six pegs, all of different colours,

(b) two red and two white pegs,

(c) two red, one white and one black peg,

(d) twelve pegs, two of each colour.

(L Additional)

16. (a) Calculate how many different numbers altogether can be formed by taking one, two, three and four digits from the digits 9, 8, 3 and 2, repetitions not being allowed.

(b) Calculate how many of the numbers in part (a) are odd and greater than 800.

(c) If one of the numbers in part (a) is chosen at random, calculate the probability that it will be greater than 300.   (L Additional)

17. The positions of nine trees which are to be planted along the sides of a road, five on the north side and four on the south side, are shown in the figure.

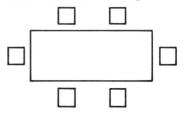

(a) Find the number of ways in which this can be done if the trees are all of different species.

(b) If the trees in (a) are planted at random, find the probability that two particular trees are next to each other on the same side of the road.

(c) If there are 3 cupressus, 4 prunus and 2 magnolias, find the number of different ways in which these could be planted assuming that trees of the same species are identical.

(d) If the trees in (c) are planted at random, find the probability that the 2 magnolias are on the opposite sides of the road.

(L Additional)

18. A committee consisting of 6 persons is to be selected from 5 women and 6 men.

(a) Calculate the number of ways in which the chosen committee will contain exactly two men.

(b) Given that the committee is to contain at least 2 men, show that it can be selected in 456 ways.

(c) Given that these 456 ways are equally likely, calculate the probability that there will be more men than women on the committee.

(d) At a meeting the members of the chosen committee sit at a rectangular table in the fixed seats illustrated in the diagram:

(i) Given that each may sit in any of the six places, calculate the number of different ways they may be seated at the table.

(ii) Given that the committee consists of 3 men and 3 women and that the men and women must sit alternately round the table, calculate in how many different ways they may be seated.   (L Additional)

MISCELLANEOUS WORKED EXAMPLES

Example 3.46 The events A and B are such that $P(A) = \frac{1}{3}$, $P(B) = \frac{2}{5}$ and $P(B \mid \overline{A}) = \frac{11}{20}$. Find

(a) $P(A \cap B)$,

(b) $P(A \cup B)$,

(c) $P(\overline{A} \mid B)$,

(d) $P(A \mid B)$.

State whether A and B are (i) independent, (ii) mutually exclusive.

Solution 3.46 Consider a possibility space S and let $n(S) = n$.

Consider events A and B such that $n(A) = r$ and $n(B) = s$, $n(A \cap B) = t$.

First, draw a Venn diagram, showing this information:

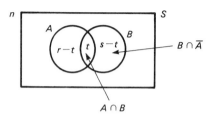

(**a**) Now

$$P(A) = \frac{n(A)}{n(S)} = \frac{r}{n}, \text{ but } P(A) = \frac{1}{3} \text{ so } \frac{r}{n} = \frac{1}{3}$$

$$P(B) = \frac{n(B)}{n(S)} = \frac{s}{n}, \text{ but } P(B) = \frac{2}{5} \text{ so } \frac{s}{n} = \frac{2}{5}$$

Now

$$P(B\,|\,\overline{A}) = \frac{P(B \cap \overline{A})}{P(\overline{A})} = \frac{n(B \cap \overline{A})}{n(\overline{A})} = \frac{s-t}{n-r} = \frac{s/n - t/n}{1 - r/n}$$

But we are given that $P(B\,|\,\overline{A}) = \frac{11}{20}$, therefore

$$\frac{11}{20} = \frac{s/n - t/n}{1 - r/n}$$

$$= \frac{2/5 - t/n}{1 - 1/3}$$

$$\left(\frac{2}{3}\right)\left(\frac{11}{20}\right) = \frac{2}{5} - \frac{t}{n}$$

So

$$\frac{t}{n} = \frac{2}{5} - \frac{11}{30}$$

$$= \frac{1}{30}$$

Now

$$P(A \cap B) = \frac{n(A \cap B)}{n(S)}$$

$$= \frac{t}{n}$$

Therefore $P(A \cap B) = \frac{1}{30}$.

(**b**) $P(A \cup B) = P(A) + P(B) - P(A \cap B)$

So $P(A \cup B) = \frac{1}{3} + \frac{2}{5} - \frac{1}{30}$

$$= \frac{7}{10}$$

Therefore $P(A \cup B) = \frac{7}{10}$.

(c)
$$P(\bar{A}\,|\,B) = \frac{P(\bar{A} \cap B)}{P(B)}$$
$$= \frac{n(\bar{A} \cap B)}{n(B)}$$
$$= \frac{s - t}{s}$$
$$= \frac{s/n - t/n}{s/n}$$
$$= \frac{2/5 - 1/30}{2/5}$$
$$= \frac{11}{12}$$

Therefore $P(\bar{A}\,|\,B) = \frac{11}{12}$.

(d)
$$P(A\,|\,B) = \frac{P(A \cap B)}{P(B)}$$
$$= \frac{1/30}{2/5}$$
$$= \frac{1}{12}$$

Therefore $P(A\,|\,B) = \frac{1}{12}$.

NOTE: $P(A\,|\,B) + P(\bar{A}\,|\,B) = 1.$

(*i*) If two events are independent then $P(A \cap B) = P(A)\,P(B)$.

Now $P(A \cap B) = \frac{1}{30}$ and $P(A)\,P(B) = \left(\frac{1}{3}\right)\left(\frac{2}{5}\right) = \frac{2}{15}$

So $P(A \cap B) \neq P(A)\,P(B)$ and the events A and B are not independent.

(*ii*) If two events are mutually exclusive, then $P(A \cap B) = 0$. Since $P(A \cap B) \neq 0$, A and B are not mutually exclusive.

Example 3.47 Tung-Pong and Ping-Ho play a game of table tennis. The score reaches 20–20. The game continues until one player has scored two more points than the other.

The probability that Tung-Pong wins each point is 0.6. What are the probabilities that:

(a) Tung-Pong wins the game after 2 further points?

(b) Ping-Ho wins the game after 2 further points?

(c) The score is 21–21 after 2 further points?

(d) Tung-Pong wins the game after 3 further points?

(e) Tung-Pong wins the game after 4 further points?

(f) Tung-Pong wins the game after 6 further points?

If the game can continue indefinitely, for each player what is the probability that he will ultimately win?

Solution 3.47 Let W be the event 'Tung wins a point'.

Then $P(W) = 0.6$ and $P(\overline{W}) = 0.4$.

(**a**) $P(\text{Tung wins after 2 further points}) = P(WW)$

$$= (0.6)(0.6)$$

$$= 0.36$$

The probability that Tung wins after 2 further points is 0.36.

(**b**) $P(\text{Ping wins after 2 further points}) = P(\overline{W}\,\overline{W})$

$$= (0.4)(0.4)$$

$$= 0.16$$

The probability that Ping wins after 2 further points is 0.16.

(**c**) $P(\text{score is 21--21 after 2 further points}) = P(W\overline{W}) + P(\overline{W}W)$

$$= 2(0.6)(0.4)$$

$$= 0.48$$

The probability that the score is 21--21 after 2 further points is 0.48.

(**d**) To consider the situation after 3 further points we look first at the situation after 2 further points. Now after 2 further points either Tung has won, or Ping has won, or the score is 21–21. If the score is 21–21 then there is no way that Tung can win after just one more point.

So the probability that Tung wins after 3 further points is 0.

(**e**) After 4 further points, if Tung wins, the sequence of points must be

or $\left.\begin{array}{l}(W\,\overline{W})(W\,W)\\(\overline{W}\,W)(W\,W)\end{array}\right\}$ 2 ways

So

$$P(\text{Tung wins after 4 further points}) = P(W\,\overline{W}\,W\,W) + P(\overline{W}\,W\,W\,W)$$

$$= 2(0.6)^3(0.4)$$

$$= 0.1728$$

The probability that Tung wins after 4 further points is 0.1728.

(**f**) If Tung wins after 6 further points, the sequence must be

$$(W\,\overline{W}) \quad (W\,\overline{W}) \quad (W\,W)$$
$$\uparrow \qquad\quad \uparrow \qquad\quad \uparrow$$
$$(\text{2 ways}) \ (\text{2 ways}) \ (\text{1 way})$$

So $P(\text{Tung wins after 6 further points}) = 4P(W\overline{W}\,W\overline{W}\,W\,W)$

$$= 4(0.6)^4(0.4)^2$$

$$= 0.0829 \quad (3\ \text{S.F.})$$

So the probability that Tung wins after 6 further points is 0.0829 (3 S.F.).

If the game can continue indefinitely,

$$P(\text{Tung wins}) = (0.6)^2 + 2(0.6)^3(0.4) + 4(0.6)^4(0.4)^2 + \ldots$$

$$= (0.6)^2\left(1 + 2(0.6)(0.4) + 4(0.6)^2(0.4)^2 + \ldots\right)$$

$$= (0.6)^2\left(1 + 0.48 + 0.48^2 + \ldots\right)$$

$$= (0.6)^2\left(\frac{1}{1 - 0.48}\right) \quad \begin{array}{l}\text{(sum of an infinite G.P.,}\\ \text{common ratio 0.48)}\end{array}$$

$$= \frac{0.36}{0.52}$$

$$= \frac{9}{13}$$

Therefore

$$P(\text{Ping wins}) = 1 - \frac{9}{13}$$

$$= \frac{4}{13}$$

The probability that Tung wins is $\frac{9}{13}$ and the probability that Ping wins is $\frac{4}{13}$.

Example 3.48 (a) A bag contains 5 red and 4 blue balls. 3 balls are picked out, one at a time, and are not replaced. Find the probability that at least 1 of the 3 balls is blue.

(b) One letter is selected from each of the names: SIMMS, SMITH, THOMPSON. What is the probability that 2, and only 2 are the same?

(c) A candidate attempts a question to which 5 possible answers have been given, one of them correct. For any question, there is a probability of $\frac{1}{3}$ that he knows the correct answer. If he does not know the correct answer he will mark one of the answers at random. He does, in fact, mark the correct answer. What is the probability that he knew the correct answer?

Solution 3.48 (a) Using an obvious notation,

$$P(3\ \text{red balls}) = P(R_1 \cap R_2 \cap R_3)$$

$$= \left(\frac{5}{9}\right)\left(\frac{4}{8}\right)\left(\frac{3}{7}\right) \quad \text{(non-independent events)}$$

$$= \frac{5}{42}$$

So $P(\text{at least one ball is blue}) = 1 - P(\text{3 balls are red})$

$$= 1 - \frac{5}{42}$$

$$= \frac{37}{42}$$

The probability that at least one of the 3 balls is blue is $\frac{37}{42}$.

(b) SIMMS   SMITH   THOMPSON

Let the event S_1 be 'choosing an S from the first name', and so on.

If one letter is selected from each name, then if 2 and only 2 letters are the same the possible outcomes are listed below, with their respective probabilities:

$$P(S_1 S_2 \bar{S}_3) = \left(\tfrac{2}{5}\right)\left(\tfrac{1}{5}\right)\left(\tfrac{7}{8}\right) = 0.07$$

$$P(S_1 \bar{S}_2 S_3) = \left(\tfrac{2}{5}\right)\left(\tfrac{4}{5}\right)\left(\tfrac{1}{8}\right) = 0.04$$

$$P(\bar{S}_1 S_2 S_3) = \left(\tfrac{3}{5}\right)\left(\tfrac{1}{5}\right)\left(\tfrac{1}{8}\right) = 0.015$$

$$P(I_1 I_2 \bar{I}_3) = \left(\tfrac{1}{5}\right)\left(\tfrac{1}{5}\right)(1) = 0.04$$

$$P(M_1 M_2 \bar{M}_3) = \left(\tfrac{2}{5}\right)\left(\tfrac{1}{5}\right)\left(\tfrac{7}{8}\right) = 0.07$$

$$P(M_1 \bar{M}_2 M_3) = \left(\tfrac{2}{5}\right)\left(\tfrac{4}{5}\right)\left(\tfrac{1}{8}\right) = 0.04$$

$$P(\bar{M}_1 M_2 M_3) = \left(\tfrac{3}{5}\right)\left(\tfrac{1}{5}\right)\left(\tfrac{1}{8}\right) = 0.015$$

$$P(\bar{H}_1 H_2 H_3) = (1)\left(\tfrac{1}{5}\right)\left(\tfrac{1}{8}\right) = 0.025$$

$$P(\bar{T}_1 T_2 T_3) = (1)\left(\tfrac{1}{5}\right)\left(\tfrac{1}{8}\right) = 0.025$$

Total   0.340

Therefore $P(\text{2 and only 2 letters are the same}) = 0.34$.

(c) Let K be the event 'he knows the correct answer', then $P(K) = \frac{1}{3}$.

Let M be the event 'he marks the correct answer'.

Now $P(M \,|\, \bar{K}) = \frac{1}{5}$, as he marks an answer at random if he does not know the correct answer.

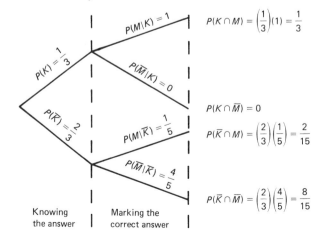

We require $P(K \mid M) = \dfrac{P(K \cap M)}{P(M)}$

Now $\qquad\qquad P(M) = P(M \cap K) + P(M \cap \overline{K})$

$$= \tfrac{1}{3} + \tfrac{2}{15}$$

$$= \tfrac{7}{15}$$

So $\qquad\qquad P(K \mid M) = \dfrac{1/3}{7/15}$

$$= \tfrac{5}{7}$$

The probability that he knew the correct answer, given that he marked the correct answer, is $\tfrac{5}{7}$.

Example 3.49 (**a**) A bag contains a number of counters, alike in shape and size, but x are red and y are green. Counters are to be chosen at random from the bag. Prove that the probability that the second counter chosen will be red is the same, whether the first counter is replaced or not before the second is drawn.

(**b**) A three-figure number, not less than 100, is to be made up using three digits selected at random from the digits 0, 1, 2, 3, 4, 5, 6, 7, 8, 9 *without* using the same digit twice in any number. Show that the total possible number of numbers is 648. Calculate the probabilities: (*i*) that the number is even, (*ii*) that the number is divisible by 5, (*iii*) that the number is greater than 600, (*iv*) that the number is even and greater than 600.
What are the corresponding results for (*i*) and (*ii*) if the same digit may be used two or three times in the same number?

Solution 3.49 (**a**) The bag contains x red counters and y green counters.

When the first counter is replaced

With obvious notation $\qquad P(R_2) = \dfrac{x}{x+y}$

When the first counter is not replaced

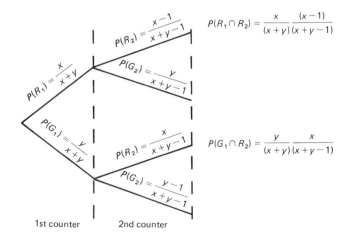

$$P(R_1 \cap R_2) = \frac{x}{(x+y)}\frac{(x-1)}{(x+y-1)}$$

$$P(G_1 \cap R_2) = \frac{y}{(x+y)}\frac{x}{(x+y-1)}$$

1st counter   2nd counter

$$P(R_2) = P(R_2 \cap R_1) + P(R_2 \cap G_1) \quad \text{(mutually exclusive events)}$$

$$= \frac{x}{(x+y)} \frac{(x-1)}{(x+y-1)} + \frac{y}{(x+y)} \frac{x}{(x+y-1)}$$

$$= \frac{x}{(x+y)(x+y-1)}(x-1+y)$$

$$= \frac{x}{x+y}$$

Therefore the probability that the second counter is red is $\dfrac{x}{(x+y)}$

whether or not the first counter is replaced. This is because there is no condition placed on the first counter so that any one of the $x + y$ counters is equally likely to be the second counter.

(**b**)   1st digit can be chosen in 9 ways   (0 not included)
2nd digit can be chosen in 9 ways   (0 included here)
3rd digit can be chosen in 8 ways

So,   total number of ways $= (9)(9)(8)$

$$= 648$$

Therefore the possibility space is 648 equally likely outcomes.

(*i*) *If the number is even*

Either the *3rd digit is 0*	or the *3rd digit is 2, 4, 6 or 8*
3rd digit chosen in 1 way	3rd digit chosen in 4 ways
2nd digit chosen in 9 ways	1st digit chosen in 8 ways (0 excluded)
1st digit chosen in 8 ways	2nd digit chosen in 8 ways
Number of ways $= (1)(9)(8)$	Number of ways $= (4)(8)(8)$
$= 72$	$= 256$

Therefore the number of ways in which the number is even $= 328$.

$$P(\text{number is even}) = \tfrac{328}{648} = \tfrac{41}{81}$$

(*ii*) *If the number is divisible by 5*

Either *the 3rd digit is 0*	or *the 3rd digit is 5*
3rd digit chosen in 1 way	3rd digit chosen in 1 way
1st digit chosen in 9 ways	1st digit chosen in 8 ways (0 excluded)
2nd digit chosen in 8 ways	2nd digit chosen in 8 ways
Number of ways $= (1)(9)(8)$	Number of ways $= (1)(8)(8)$
$= 72$	$= 64$

The number of ways in which the number is divisible by 5 $= 136$.

$$P(\text{number is divisible by 5}) = \tfrac{136}{648} = \tfrac{17}{81}$$

(*iii*) *If the number is greater than 600*

1st digit can be chosen in 4 ways (from 6, 7, 8, 9)
2nd digit can be chosen in 9 ways
3rd digit can be chosen in 8 ways

$$\text{Number of ways} = (4)(9)(8)$$

$$= 288$$

$$P(\text{number is greater than 600}) = \tfrac{288}{648} = \tfrac{4}{9}$$

(*iv*) *If the number is even and greater than 600*

Either *the 1st digit is 6 or 8*	or *the 1st digit is 7 or 9*
1st digit chosen in 2 ways	1st digit chosen in 2 ways
3rd digit chosen in 4 ways	3rd digit chosen in 5 ways
2nd digit chosen in 8 ways	2nd digit chosen in 8 ways
Number of ways $= (2)(4)(8)$	Number of ways $= (2)(5)(8)$
$= 64$	$= 80$

The number of ways in which the number is even and greater than 600 $= 144$.

$$P(\text{number is even and greater than 600}) = \tfrac{144}{648} = \tfrac{2}{9}$$

Now consider the case when the same digit may be used two or three times:

If the number is even

We are concerned with the 3rd digit, which can be chosen in 5 ways. If there was no restriction, this could be chosen in 10 ways.

$$P(\text{number is even}) = \tfrac{5}{10} = \tfrac{1}{2}$$

If the number is divisible by 5

We are concerned with the 3rd digit which can be chosen in 2 ways.

$$P(\text{number is divisible by 5}) = \tfrac{2}{10} = \tfrac{1}{5}$$

Example 3.50 (a) *A* and *B* play a game as follows: an ordinary die is rolled and if a six is obtained then *A* wins and if a one is obtained then *B* wins. If neither a six nor a one is obtained then the die is rolled again until a decision can be made. What is the probability that *A* wins on (*i*) the first roll, (*ii*) the second roll, (*iii*) the *r*th roll? What is the probability that *A* wins?

(**b**) A bag contains 4 red and 3 yellow balls and another bag contains 3 red and 4 yellow. A ball is taken from the first bag and placed in the second, the second bag is shaken and a ball is taken from it and placed in the first bag. If a ball is now taken from the first bag what is the probability that it is red?

(You are advised to draw a tree diagram.)

Solution 3.50 (a) $P(6 \text{ is obtained}) = \frac{1}{6}$ and $P(1 \text{ is obtained}) = \frac{1}{6}$.

(*i*) $P(A \text{ wins on the first roll}) = P(6 \text{ is obtained}) = \frac{1}{6}$

(*ii*) $P(A \text{ wins on the second roll})$

$= P(\text{neither a 6 nor a 1 on the first roll}) \, P(6 \text{ on second roll})$

$= \left(\frac{4}{6}\right)\left(\frac{1}{6}\right)$

$= \frac{1}{9}$

(*iii*) $P(A \text{ wins on the } r\text{th roll})$

$= P(\text{neither a 6 nor a 1 on 1st } r - 1 \text{ rolls}) \, P(6 \text{ on the } r\text{th roll})$

$= \left(\frac{4}{6}\right)^{r-1}\left(\frac{1}{6}\right)$

$= \left(\frac{2}{3}\right)^{r-1}\left(\frac{1}{6}\right)$

These are mutually exclusive events.

So $P(A \text{ wins}) = \frac{1}{6} + \left(\frac{2}{3}\right)\left(\frac{1}{6}\right) + \left(\frac{2}{3}\right)^2\left(\frac{1}{6}\right) + \ldots + \left(\frac{2}{3}\right)^{r-1}\left(\frac{1}{6}\right)$

$+ \ldots \text{to infinity}$

$= \frac{1}{6}\left[1 + \left(\frac{2}{3}\right) + \left(\frac{2}{3}\right)^2 + \ldots\right]$

$= \frac{1}{6} S$

where S is the sum of an infinite G.P. with $a = 1, r = \frac{2}{3}$.

$$P(A \text{ wins}) = \frac{1}{6}\left(\frac{1}{1 - \frac{2}{3}}\right)$$

$$= \frac{1}{6}(3)$$

$$= \frac{1}{2}$$

The probability that A wins is $\frac{1}{2}$.

(b) First we show the possibilities diagrammatically:

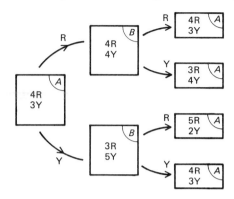

The tree diagram to show the possible outcomes and the probabilities is as follows:

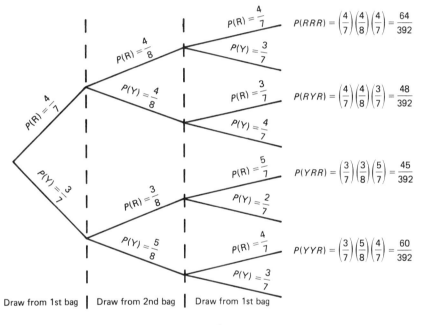

Draw from 1st bag | Draw from 2nd bag | Draw from 1st bag

$$P(\text{red from 1st bag}) = \frac{1}{392}(64 + 48 + 45 + 60)$$

$$= \frac{217}{392}$$

$$= 0.554 \quad (3 \text{ d.p.})$$

The probability that the ball is red is 0.554 (3 d.p.).

Example 3.51 **(a)** A pack of 52 playing cards is cut at random into three piles. Find the probability that the top cards are all (*i*) black, (*ii*) hearts, (*iii*) aces.

After the top cards have been examined and found not to be picture cards, calculate the probability that the three bottom cards are all queens.

(**b**) A bag contains eight black counters and two white ones. Each of two players, A and B, draws one counter in turn, without replacement, until one of them wins by drawing a white counter. A draws first. Calculate his chance of winning.   (AEB)

Solution 3.51 (**a**) The possibility space S = (the pack of 52 cards).

There are 26 black cards in the pack, so with obvious notation,

(*i*) $P(B_1 B_2 B_3) = \left(\frac{26}{52}\right)\left(\frac{25}{51}\right)\left(\frac{24}{50}\right)$ (non-independent events)

$$= \frac{2}{17}$$

The probability that the top cards are all black is $\frac{2}{17}$.

(*ii*) $P(H_1 H_2 H_3) = \left(\frac{13}{52}\right)\left(\frac{12}{51}\right)\left(\frac{11}{50}\right)$ (non-independent events)

$$= \frac{11}{850}$$

The probability that the top cards are all hearts is $\frac{11}{850}$.

(*iii*) $P(A_1 A_2 A_3) = \left(\frac{4}{52}\right)\left(\frac{3}{51}\right)\left(\frac{2}{50}\right)$ (non-independent events)

$$= \frac{1}{5525}$$

The probability that the top cards are all aces is $\frac{1}{5525}$.

If the three top cards have been examined and found not to be picture cards, the possibility space has been reduced by 3 members so that S consists of the 49 remaining cards.

The number of remaining queens = 4.

Therefore $P(Q_1 Q_2 Q_3) = \left(\frac{4}{49}\right)\left(\frac{3}{48}\right)\left(\frac{2}{47}\right) = \frac{1}{4606}$

The probability that the three bottom cards are queens is $\frac{1}{4606}$.

(**b**) Let A_1 be the event 'A wins on the first draw',
         A_2 be the event 'A wins on the second draw', and so on.

Then, with obvious notation for the black and white counters,

$$P(A_1) = P(W) = \frac{2}{10} = \frac{1}{5}$$

$$P(A_2) = P(BBW) = \left(\frac{8}{10}\right)\left(\frac{7}{9}\right)\left(\frac{2}{8}\right) = \frac{7}{45}$$

$$P(A_3) = P(BBBBW) = \left(\frac{8}{10}\right)\left(\frac{7}{9}\right)\left(\frac{6}{8}\right)\left(\frac{5}{7}\right)\left(\frac{2}{6}\right) = \frac{1}{9}$$

$$P(A_4) = P(BBBBBBW)$$

$$= \left(\frac{8}{10}\right)\left(\frac{7}{9}\right)\left(\frac{6}{8}\right)\left(\frac{5}{7}\right)\left(\frac{4}{6}\right)\left(\frac{3}{5}\right)\left(\frac{2}{4}\right) = \frac{1}{15}$$

$$P(A_5) = P(BBBBBBBBW)$$

$$= \left(\frac{8}{10}\right)\left(\frac{7}{9}\right)\left(\frac{6}{8}\right)\left(\frac{5}{7}\right)\left(\frac{4}{6}\right)\left(\frac{3}{5}\right)\left(\frac{2}{4}\right)\left(\frac{1}{3}\right)\left(\frac{2}{2}\right) = \frac{1}{45}$$

$$P(A \text{ wins}) = P(A_1) + P(A_2) + P(A_3) + P(A_4) + P(A_5)$$

$$\text{(mutually exclusive events)}$$

$$= \frac{1}{5} + \frac{7}{45} + \frac{1}{9} + \frac{1}{15} + \frac{1}{45}$$

$$= \frac{5}{9}$$

Therefore the probability that A wins is $\frac{5}{9}$.

Example 3.52 (a) Ruby Welloff, the daughter of a wealthy jeweller, is about to get married. Her father decides that as a wedding present she can select one of two similar boxes. Each box contains three stones. In one box two of the stones are real diamonds, and the other is a worthless imitation; and in the other box one is a real diamond, and the other two are worthless imitations. She has no idea which box is which. If the daughter were to choose randomly between the two boxes, her chance of getting two real diamonds would be $\frac{1}{2}$. Mr Welloff, being a sporting type, allows his daughter to draw one stone from one of the boxes and to examine it to see if it is a real diamond. The daughter decides to take the box that the stone she tested came from if the tested stone is real, and to take the other box otherwise. Now what is the probability that the daughter will get two real diamonds as her wedding present?

(b) A fair die is cast; then n fair coins are tossed, where n is the number shown on the die. What is the probability of exactly two heads?

(c) A fair die is thrown for as long as necessary for a 6 to turn up. Given that 6 does not turn up at the first throw, what is the probability that more than four throws will be necessary?   (AEB)

Solution 3.52 (a) Let A be the event 'she chooses the box with 2 diamonds',

B be the event 'she chooses the box with 1 diamond',

D be the event 'she chooses a diamond from the box'.

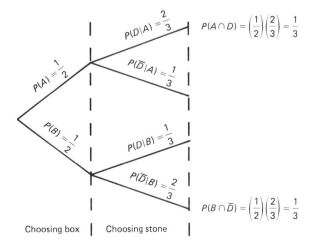

Choosing box | Choosing stone

Now, she takes the box if the tested stone is real, and she takes the other box if the tested stone is worthless.

So the probability of getting 2 real diamonds $= P(A \cap D) + P(B \cap \overline{D})$

$$= \tfrac{1}{3} + \tfrac{1}{3}$$

$$= \tfrac{2}{3}$$

Therefore the probability that she has 2 diamonds for her wedding present is $\tfrac{2}{3}$.

(b)	Number on the die	Number of heads and tails required
(*i*)	2	2H
(*ii*)	3	2H, 1T
(*iii*)	4	2H, 2T
(*iv*)	5	2H, 3T
(*v*)	6	2H, 4T

We will consider first the probability of obtaining the required number of heads and tails for each of the situations:

(*i*) *Two coins are tossed*

The possibility space consists of 2^2 equally likely outcomes.

So $\qquad\qquad\qquad\qquad\qquad P(2\mathrm{H}) = \tfrac{1}{4}$

(*ii*) *Three coins are tossed*

The possibility space consists of 2^3 equally likely outcomes.

Number of ways of arranging H, H, T $= \dfrac{3!}{2!} = 3$

So $\qquad\qquad\qquad\qquad\qquad P(2\mathrm{H},\, 1\mathrm{T}) = \tfrac{3}{8}$

(*iii*) *Four coins are tossed*

The possibility space consists of 2^4 equally likely outcomes.

Number of ways of arranging H, H, T, T $= \dfrac{4!}{2!\,2!} = 6.$

So $\qquad\qquad\qquad\qquad P(2\mathrm{H},\, 2\mathrm{T}) = \tfrac{6}{16} = \tfrac{3}{8}$

(*iv*) *Five coins are tossed*

The possibility space consists of 2^5 equally likely outcomes.

Number of ways of arranging H, H, T, T, T $= \dfrac{5!}{2!\,3!} = 10.$

So $\qquad\qquad\qquad\qquad P(2\mathrm{H},\, 3\mathrm{T}) = \tfrac{10}{32} = \tfrac{5}{16}$

(*v*) *Six coins are tossed*

The possibility space consists of 2^6 equally likely outcomes.

Number of ways of arranging H, H, T, T, T, T $= \dfrac{6!}{2!\,4!} = 15.$

So $\qquad\qquad\qquad\qquad\qquad P(2\mathrm{H}, 4\mathrm{T}) = \frac{15}{64}$

Let $P(n)$ be the probability that n is shown on the die.

$P(\text{exactly 2 heads}) = \frac{1}{4}P(2) + \frac{3}{8}P(3) + \frac{3}{8}P(4) + \frac{5}{16}P(5) + \frac{15}{64}P(6)$

But $\qquad\qquad P(2) = P(3) = P(4) = P(5) = P(6) = \frac{1}{6}$

Therefore

$$P(\text{exactly 2 heads}) = \frac{1}{6}\left(\frac{1}{4} + \frac{3}{8} + \frac{3}{8} + \frac{5}{16} + \frac{15}{64}\right)$$

$$= \frac{33}{128}$$

The probability that exactly two heads are obtained is $\frac{33}{128}$.

(**c**) Let 6_1 be the event 'a 6 is obtained on the first throw' and so on.

We require $\qquad P(\bar{6}_1\,\bar{6}_2\,\bar{6}_3\,\bar{6}_4\,|\,\bar{6}_1) = \dfrac{P(\bar{6}_1\,\bar{6}_2\,\bar{6}_3\,\bar{6}_4 \cap \bar{6}_1)}{P(\bar{6}_1)}$

$$= \dfrac{\left(\frac{5}{6}\right)\left(\frac{5}{6}\right)\left(\frac{5}{6}\right)\left(\frac{5}{6}\right)}{\frac{5}{6}}$$

$$= \left(\frac{5}{6}\right)^3$$

$$= \frac{125}{216}$$

The probability that more than four throws will be necessary is $\frac{125}{216}$.

Example 3.53 (a) When a person needs a minicab, it is hired from one of three firms, X, Y and Z. Of the hirings 40% are from X, 50% are from Y and 10% are from Z. For cabs hired from X, 9% arrive late, the corresponding percentages for cabs hired from firms Y and Z being 6% and 20% respectively. Calculate the probability that the next cab hired
(*i*) will be from X and will not arrive late,
(*ii*) will arrive late.
Given that a call is made for a minicab and that it arrives late, find, to 3 decimal places, the probability that it came from Y.

(**b**) For a certain strain of wallflower, the probability that, when sown, a seed produces a plant with yellow flowers is $\frac{1}{6}$. Find the minimum number of seeds that should be sown in order that the probability of obtaining at least one plant with yellow flowers is greater than 0.98. (L)

Solution 3.53 **(a)**

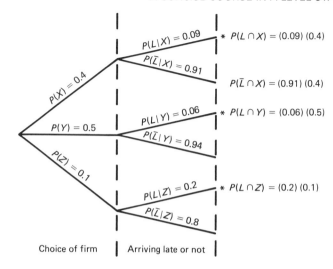

$P(L|X) = 0.09$ * $P(L \cap X) = (0.09)(0.4)$

$P(\overline{L}|X) = 0.91$

$P(\overline{L} \cap X) = (0.91)(0.4)$

$P(X) = 0.4$

$P(Y) = 0.5$

$P(L|Y) = 0.06$ * $P(L \cap Y) = (0.06)(0.5)$

$P(\overline{L}|Y) = 0.94$

$P(Z) = 0.1$

$P(L|Z) = 0.2$ * $P(L \cap Z) = (0.2)(0.1)$

$P(\overline{L}|Z) = 0.8$

Choice of firm | Arriving late or not

(*i*) From the diagram

$$P(\overline{L} \cap X) = P(\overline{L}|X)\,P(X)$$
$$= (0.91)(0.4)$$
$$= 0.364$$

Therefore the probability that the next cab hired will be from X and will not arrive late is 0.364.

(*ii*) $P(L) = P(L \cap X) + P(L \cap Y) + P(L \cap Z)$
$$= P(L|X)\,P(X) + P(L|Y)\,P(Y)$$
$$\qquad + P(L|Z)\,P(Z) \quad \text{(marked with * on diagram)}$$
$$= (0.09)(0.4) + (0.06)(0.5) + (0.2)(0.1)$$
$$= 0.086$$

Therefore the probability that the next cab hired will arrive late is 0.086.

We require $$P(Y|L) = \frac{P(L|Y)\,P(Y)}{P(L)}$$
$$= \frac{(0.06)(0.5)}{0.086}$$
$$= 0.349 \quad (3 \text{ d.p.})$$

Therefore, given that the cab arrives late, the probability that it came from Y is 0.349 (3 d.p.).

(b) When a seed is sown, $P(\text{yellow flower}) = \frac{1}{6}$

When n seeds are sown,

$$P(\text{at least one yellow flower}) = 1 - P(\text{no yellow flowers})$$
$$= 1 - \left(\frac{5}{6}\right)^{n}$$

Now we need

$$P(\text{at least one yellow flower}) > 0.98$$

so
$$1 - \left(\frac{5}{6}\right)^n > 0.98$$

$$\left(\frac{5}{6}\right)^n < 0.02$$

Taking logs of both sides $n \log \left(\frac{5}{6}\right) < \log 0.02$

Dividing both sides by $\log \left(\frac{5}{6}\right)$ and reversing the inequality since $\log \left(\frac{5}{6}\right)$ is negative, we have

$$n > \frac{\log 0.02}{\log \left(\frac{5}{6}\right)}$$

$$n > 21.45\ldots$$

Therefore the minimum number of seeds that should be sown is 22.

Miscellaneous Exercise 3I

1. In a large group of people it is known that 10% have a hot breakfast, 20% have a hot lunch and 25% have a hot breakfast or a hot lunch. Find the probability that a person chosen at random from this group (a) has a hot breakfast and a hot lunch, (b) has a hot lunch, given that the person chosen had a hot breakfast. (L)

2. The probability that a door-to-door salesman convinces a customer to buy is 0.7. Assuming sales are independent find the probability that the salesman makes a sale before reaching the fourth house. (L)

3. Two events A and B are such that

   $P(A) = \frac{8}{15}$, $P(B) = \frac{1}{3}$, $P(A\,|\,B) = \frac{1}{5}$.

   Calculate the probabilities that (i) both events occur, (ii) only one of the two events occurs, (iii) neither event occurs. (JMB)

4. A and B are two independent events such that $P(A) = 0.2$ and $P(B) = 0.15$. Evaluate the following probabilities.
   (a) $P(A\,|\,B)$, (b) $P(A \cap B)$, (c) $P(A \cup B)$. (L)

5. An urn contains 3 red, 4 white and 5 blue discs. Three discs are selected at random from the urn.

Find the probability that (a) all three discs are the same colour, if the selection is with replacement, (b) all three discs are of different colours, if the selection is without replacement. (L)

6. A bag contains 4 red balls, 4 blue balls and 2 green balls. Four balls are drawn at random without replacement from the bag.
   Find (i) the probability that the balls drawn are all of the same colour, (ii) the probability that at least one ball of each colour is drawn. (JMB)

7. In a group of six students, 4 are female and 2 are male. Determine how many committees of 3 members can be formed containing 1 male and 2 females. (L)

8. A golfer observes that, when playing a particular hole at his local course, he hits a straight drive on 80 per cent of the occasions when the weather is not windy but only on 30 per cent of the occasions when the weather is windy. Local records suggest that the weather is windy on 55 per cent of all days.
   (i)   Show that the probability that, on a randomly chosen day, the golfer will hit a straight drive at the hole is 0.525.
   (ii) Given that he fails to hit a straight drive at the hole, calculate the probability that the weather is windy. (JMB)

9. Vehicles approaching a crossroads must go in one of three directions — left, right or straight on. Observations by traffic engineers showed that of vehicles approaching from the north, 45% turn left, 20% turn right and 35% go straight on. Assuming that the driver of each vehicle chooses direction independently, what is the probability that of the next three vehicles approaching from the north
    (i)   all go straight on,
    (ii) all go in the same direction,
    (iii) two turn left and one turns right,
    (iv) all go in different directions,
    (v)   exactly two turn left?
    Given that three consecutive vehicles all go in the same direction, what is the probability that they all turned left?   (AEB 1992)P

10. The results of a traffic survey of the colour and type of car are given in the following table.

	Saloon	Estate
White	68	62
Green	26	32
Black	6	6

    One car is selected at random from this group. Find the probability that the selected car is
    (i)   a green estate car,
    (ii) a saloon car,
    (iii) a white car given that it is not a saloon car.
    Let W and G denote the events that the selected car is White and Green respectively and let S be the event that the car is a Saloon. Show that the event $W \cup G$ is independent of the event S.
    Show, however, that colour and type of car are not independent.   (AEB 1991)P

11. Students in a class were given two statistics problems to solve, the second of which was harder than the first. Within the class $\frac{5}{6}$ of the students got the first one correct and $\frac{7}{12}$ got the second one correct. Of those students who got the first problem correct, $\frac{3}{5}$ got the second one correct. One student was chosen at random from the class.
    Let A be the event that the student got the first problem correct and B be the event that the student got the second one correct.
    (a) Express in words the meaning of $A \cap B$ and of $A \cup B$.
    (b) Find $P(A \cap B)$ and $P(A \cup B)$.
    (c) Given that the student got the second problem right, find the probability that the first problem was solved correctly.
    (d) Given that the student got the second problem wrong, find the probability that the first problem was solved correctly.
    (e) Given that the student got the first problem wrong, find the probability that the student also got the second problem wrong.
                                                    (L)

12. A hospital buys strawberry jam in standard sized tins from suppliers A, B and C. The table below gives information about the contents. Find the probability of a tin selected at random being
    (a) from supplier A, (b) underweight.
    What is the probability of
    (c) a tin from B being both underweight and poor quality,
    (d) an underweight tin from A containing poor quality jam,
    (e) a tin from C being both underweight and poor quality,
    (f) a tin from C which contains poor quality jam being underweight,
    (g) a tin selected at random being both underweight and poor quality,
    (h) a tin being from A given that it is both underweight and of poor quality?
                                                    (AEB 1990)

Supplier	% of hospital requirements supplied	% of tins with underweight contents	% of tins containing poor quality jam	Other information
A	55	3	7	1% are both underweight and poor quality
B	35	5	12	probability of poor quality is independent of probability of being underweight
C	10	6	20	40% of underweight tins contains poor quality jam

13. In a computer game played by a single player, the player has to find, within a fixed time, the path through a maze shown on the computer screen. On the first occasion that a particular player plays the game, the computer shows a simple maze, and the probability that the player succeeds in finding the path in the time allowed is $\frac{3}{4}$. On subsequent occasions, the maze shown depends on the result of the previous game. If the player succeeded on the previous occasion, the next maze is harder, and the probability that the player succeeds is one half of the probability of success on the previous occasion. If the player failed on the previous occasion, a simple maze is shown and the probability of the player succeeding is again $\frac{3}{4}$.

The player plays three games.

(i) Show that the probability that the player succeeds in all three games is $\frac{27}{512}$.

(ii) Find the probability that the player succeeds in exactly one of the games.

(iii) Find the probability that the player does not have two consecutive successes.

(iv) Find the conditional probability that the player has two consecutive successes given that the player has exactly two successes. (C)

14. A book has 60 pages. The letter 'e' is the last letter on 15 of the pages and the letters 's', 't' and 'd' are the last letters on 12, 9 and 6, respectively, of the pages. The last letters on each of the other pages of the book are all different from each other and none is 'e', 's', 't' or 'd'. One page out of the 60 pages is chosen at random and the last letter is observed. This process is carried out two more times. Find

(i) the probability that the letters obtained are 't', 'e', 'e' in that order,

(ii) the probability that the letters obtained are 't', 'e', 'e' in any order,

(iii) the probability that the letters obtained are 't', 'e', 'e' in that order, given that the letters obtained are 't', 'e', 'e' in some order.

A page is chosen at random and then a second different page is chosen at random. Find

(iv) the probability that at least one of the two pages ends with the letter 's',

(v) the probability that the two pages have the same last letter as each other. (C)

15. A bag contains 4 red counters and 6 green counters. Four counters are drawn at random from the bag, without replacement. Calculate the probability that

(i) all the counters drawn are green,

(ii) at least one counter of each colour is drawn,

(iii) at least two green counters are drawn,

(iv) at least two green counters are drawn, given that at least one of each colour is drawn.

State with a reason whether or not the events 'at least two green counters are drawn' and 'at least one counter of each colour is drawn' are independent. (C)

16. [In this question, give your answers in decimal form, correct to three significant figures.]

A choir has 7 sopranos, 6 altos, 3 tenors and 4 basses. The sopranos and altos are women and the tenors and basses are men. At a particular rehearsal, three members of the choir are chosen at random to make the tea.

(i) Find the probability that all three tenors are chosen.

(ii) Find the probability that exactly one bass is chosen.

(iii) Find the conditional probability that two women are chosen, given that exactly one bass is chosen.

(iv) Find the probability that the chosen group contains exactly one tenor or exactly one bass (or both). (C)

17. In a golf tournament, records are kept of the scores of 128 competitors for the 8th hole on the first day of the tournament. The results are summarised in the following table.

Score	3	4	5	6	7
Frequency	21	83	17	5	2

(i) Find the mode, the mean and the variance of the above distribution.

(ii) Two of these competitors are chosen at random.

(*a*) Show that the probability that the sum of their scores for the 8th hole equals 10 is 0.073, correct to three places of decimals.

(*b*) Find, correct to three places of decimals, the conditional probability that the difference in their scores for the 8th hole equals 2, given that the sum of their scores equals 10.

(iii) State whether the above data can be used to predict the expected score for the 8th hole by one particular competitor on the last day of the tournament. Give a reason for your answer. (C)

18. A game is played, by a single player, with a set of ten cards, which are numbered 11, 12, 13, 14, ..., 20 respectively. The cards are placed in a bag, and the player takes one card, chosen at random, from the bag. If the number on this card is prime (i.e. 11, 13, 17 or 19) the player wins the game, and if the number is even the player loses the game. If the number on the card is 15 the player takes a second card, chosen at random from the nine cards remaining in the bag; the player wins the game if the number on this second card is prime and loses the game otherwise. Find the probability that, in a particular game,

(i)   the player wins,

(ii)   only one card is taken from the bag, given that the player loses.

For each of the following possible amendments to the rules, find the probability that the player wins a particular game.

(a)   The player takes two cards, chosen at random, from the bag. The player wins the game if either number (or both) is prime, and loses the game if neither number is prime.

(b)   The player takes cards chosen at random, one by one and with replacement, from the bag, continuing until either a prime number results or an even number results. The player wins if the number on the last card chosen is prime and loses otherwise.   (C)

19.   (a)   Of the households in Edinburgh, 35% have a freezer and 60% have a colour TV set. Given that 25% of the households have both a freezer and a colour TV set, calculate the probability that a household has either a freezer or a colour TV set but not both. State, with your reasons, whether the events of having a freezer and of having a colour TV set are or are not independent.

(b)   State in words the meaning of the symbol $P(B \mid A)$, where A and B are two events.

A shop stocks tinned cat food of two makes, A and B, and two sizes, large and small. Of the stock, 70% is of brand A, 30% is of brand B. Of the tins of brand A, 30% are small size whilst of the tins of brand B, 40% are small size. Using a tree diagram, or otherwise, find the probability that

(i)   a tin chosen at random from the stock will be of small size,

(ii)   a small tin chosen at random from the stock will be of brand A.   (L)

20.   During an epidemic of a certain disease a doctor is consulted by 110 people suffering from symptoms commonly associated with the disease. Of the 110 people, 45 are female of whom 20 actually have the disease and 25 do not. Fifteen males have the disease and the rest do not.

(a)   A person is selected at random. The event that this person is female is denoted by A and the event that this person is suffering from the disease is denoted by B. Evaluate

(i) $P(A)$, (ii) $P(A \cup B)$, (iii) $P(A \cap B)$, (iv) $P(A \mid B)$.

(b)   If three different people are selected at random without replacement, what is the probability of (i) all three having the disease, (ii) exactly one of the three having the disease, (iii) one of the three being a female with the disease, one a male with the disease and one a female without the disease?

(c)   Of people with the disease 96% react positively to a test for diagnosing the disease as do 8% of people without the disease. What is the probability of a person selected at random (i) reacting positively, (ii) having the disease given that he or she reacted positively?   (AEB 1987)

21.   In a simple model of the weather in October, each day is classified as either fine or rainy. The probability that a fine day is followed by a fine day is 0.8. The probability that a rainy day is followed by a fine day is 0.4. The probability that 1 October is fine is 0.75.

(a)   Find the probability that 2 October is fine and the probability that 3 October is fine.

(b)   Find the conditional probability that 3 October is rainy, given that 1 October is fine.

(c)   Find the conditional probability that 1 October is fine, given that 3 October is rainy.   (C)

22.   Two archers A and B shoot alternately at a target until one of them hits the centre of the target and is declared the winner. Independently, A and B have probabilities of $\frac{1}{3}$ and $\frac{1}{4}$, respectively, of hitting the centre of the target on each occasion they shoot.

(a)   Given that A shoots first, find (i) the probability that A wins on his second shot, (ii) the probability that A wins on his third shot, (iii) the probability that A wins.

(b)   Given that the archers toss a fair coin to determine who shoots first, find the probability that A wins.   (JMB)

23.   (a)   Explain in words the meaning of the symbol $P(A \mid B)$ where A and B are two events. State the relationship between A and B when (i) $P(A \mid B) = 0$, (ii) $P(A \mid B) = P(A)$.

When a car owner needs her car serviced she phones one of three garages, A, B, or C. Of her phone calls to them, 30% are to garage A, 10% to B and 60% to C. The percentages of occasions when the garage phoned can take the car in on the day of phoning are 20% for A, 6% for B and 9% for C. Find the probability that the garage phoned will *not* be able to take the car in on the day of phoning.

Given that the car owner phones a garage and the garage can take her car in on that day, find the probability that she phoned garage B.

(b) A shelf contains ten box files of which four are empty and six contain papers. Five files are chosen at random one after another from the shelf. Find, to 3 decimal places, the probability that exactly two of the chosen files will be empty when the files are chosen
(i) with replacement,
(ii) without replacement. (L)

24. Show that, for any two events E and F

$$P(E \cup F) = P(E) + P(F) - P(E \cap F)$$

Express in words the meaning of $P(E \mid F)$. Given that E and F are independent events, express $P(E \cap F)$ in terms of $P(E)$ and $P(F)$, and show that E' and F are also independent. In a college, 60 students are studying one or more of the three subjects Geography, French and English. Of these, 25 are studying Geography, 26 are studying French, 44 are studying English, 10 are studying Geography and French, 15 are studying French and English, and 16 are studying Geography and English. Write down the probability that a student chosen at random from those studying English is also studying French. Determine whether or not the events 'studying Geography' and 'studying French' are independent. A student is chosen at random from all 60 students. Find the probability that the chosen student is studying all three subjects. (L)

25. Explain, by suitably defining events A and B, what is meant by 'the probability of A occurring given that B has occurred'. A local greengrocer sells conventionally grown and organically grown vegetables. Conventionally grown vegetables constitute 80% of his sales; carrots constitute 12% of the conventional sales and 30% of the organic sales. Display this information in an appropriately and accurately labelled tree diagram. One day a customer emerges from the shop and is questioned about her purchases. What is the probability that she bought
(a) conventionally grown carrots,
(b) carrots?
Given that she did buy carrots, what is the probability that they were organically grown? What assumptions have you made in answering this question? (O)

26. Mass-produced glass bricks are inspected for defects. The probability that a brick has air bubbles is 0.002. If a brick has air bubbles the probability that it is also cracked is 0.5 while the probability that a brick free of air bubbles is cracked is 0.005. What is the probability that a brick chosen at random is cracked? The probability that a brick is discoloured is 0.006. Given that discolouration occurs

independently of the other two defects, find the probability that a brick chosen at random has no defects. (O & C)

27. The probabilities of A, B or C winning a game in which all three take part are 0.5, 0.3 and 0.2 respectively. A match is won by a player who first wins two games. Find the probability that A will win a game involving all three players.
When the players are joined by a fourth player, D, the probabilities of A, B or C winning a game, in which all four take part, are reduced to 0.3, 0.2 and 0.1 respectively. A match is played in which all four players take part; again, the first player to win two games wins the match. Find the probabilities that D wins in fewer than (i) four games, (ii) five games, (iii) six games. (JMB)

28. A bag contains 5 red, 4 orange and 3 yellow sweets. One after another 3 children select and eat one sweet each. When the bag contains n sweets, the probability of any one child choosing any particular sweet is $1/n$. What are the probabilities that (a) they all choose red sweets, (b) at least one orange sweet is chosen, (c) each chooses a different colour, (d) all choose the same colour? Answers may be left as fractions in their lowest terms. (O & C)

29. Three men, A, B and C agree to meet at the theatre. The man A cannot remember whether they agreed to meet at the Palace or the Queen's and tosses a coin to decide which theatre to go to. The man B also tosses a coin to decide between the Queen's and the Royalty. The man C tosses a coin to decide whether to go to the Palace or not and in this latter case he tosses again to decide between the Queen's and the Royalty. Find the probability that (a) A and B meet, (b) B and C meet, (c) A, B and C all meet, (d) A, B and C all go to different places, (e) at least two meet. (C)

30. A bag contains red, blue and green counters of equal size and shape. A counter is taken at random from the bag.
The probability that it is red is 1.5 times the probability that it is blue, and the probability that it is blue is twice the probability that it is green. Find the probabilities that the counter is (a) red, (b) blue, (c) green.
A counter is taken at random from the bag, its colour is noted and it is then replaced in the bag. The process continues until at least one of each colour has been seen. Considering the order in which the colours are first seen, find the probabilities that (d) red is seen before green, (e) the order is green, blue and finally red. (O & C)

31. In a game, three cubical dice are thrown by a player who attempts to throw the same number on all three. What is the chance of the player
    (a) throwing the same number on all three?
    (b) throwing the same number on just two?
    If the first throw results in just two dice showing the same number, then the third is thrown again. If no two dice show the same number, then all are thrown again. The player then comes to the end of his turn. What is the chance of the player succeeding in throwing three identical numbers in a complete turn?
    What is the chance that all the numbers are different at the end of a turn?   (O & C)

32. Alec and Bill frequently play each other in a series of games of table tennis. Records of the outcomes of these games indicate that whenever they play a series of games, Alec has the probability 0.6 of winning the first game and that in every subsequent game in the series, Alec's probability of winning the game is 0.7 if he won the preceding game but only 0.5 if he lost the preceding game. A game cannot be drawn. Find the probability that Alec will win the third game in the next series he plays with Bill.   (JMB)

33. 4 girls and 3 boys plan to meet together on the following Saturday. The probability that each boy will be present is $\frac{2}{3}$ independently of the other boys. Find the probability that
    (a) 0, (b) 1, (c) 2, (d) 3 boys will be present.
    The probability that each girl will be present is $\frac{1}{2}$ independently of the other girls and of the boys.
    (e) Find the probability that the number of girls present will equal the number of boys.
    (f) Find the probability that both sexes will be present.
    (g) Afterwards it was reported that the gathering had included at least one boy and at least one girl. What is the probability that there were equal numbers of boys and girls in the light of this additional information?
    (Answers may be left as fractions in their lowest terms.)   (O & C)

34. A sailing competition between two boats, A and B, consists of a series of independent races, the competition being won by the first boat to win three races. Every race is won by either A or B, and their respective probabilities of winning are influenced by the weather. In rough weather the probability that A will win is 0.9; in fine weather the probability that A will win is 0.4. For each race the weather is either rough or fine, the probability of rough weather being 0.2. Show that the probability that A will win the first race is 0.5.
    Given that the first race was won by A, determine the conditional probability that
    (a) the weather for the first race was rough,
    (b) A will win the competition.   (C)

35. Six fuses, of which two are defective and four are good, are to be tested one after another in random order until both defective fuses are identified. Find the probability that the number of fuses that will be tested is
    (a) three,
    (b) four or fewer.   (L)P

36. In this question you may leave the answers as fractions. Your arguments must be carefully explained in both parts.
    (a) A pack of ten cards consists of two marked with the letter A, three with E, four with S and one with T. The pack is well shuffled and six cards are dealt. Find the probability that (i) they form the word ASSETS, the letters appearing in that order; (ii) the letters either form or can be made to form the word ASSETS.
    (b) A manufacturer of tea inserts one of five types of picture card into each packet. Equal numbers of each type are distributed randomly. Estimate the probability that a person buying three packets will have (i) three cards of the same type, (ii) just two the same. If a person buys five packets, estimate the probability of obtaining five different types of card.

37. A census of married couples showed that 50% of the couples had no car, 40% had one car and the remaining 10% had two cars. Three of the married couples are chosen at random.
    (a) Find the probability that one couple has no car, one has one car and one has two cars.
    (b) Find the probability that the three couples have a combined total of three cars.
    The census also showed that both the husband and the wife were in full-time employment in 16% of those couples having no car, in 45% of those having one car and in 60% of those having two cars.
    (c) For a randomly chosen married couple find the probability that both the husband and wife are in full-time employment.
    (d) Given that a randomly chosen married couple is one where both the husband and wife are in full-time employment, find the conditional probability that the couple has no car.   (JMB)

38. Three machines A, B and C produce 25%, 25% and 50% respectively of the output of a factory manufacturing a certain article. A sample of 3 articles is selected at random from the total output. Find the probabilities that (a) they are all from C, (b) at least 2 are from B.

If a second independent sample of 3 articles is selected, find the probability that both samples have the same number of articles produced by A.

Of the articles produced by A, B and C, 1%, 2% and 5% respectively are defective. A single article is selected at random. If D denotes the event 'defective' and C the event 'produced by machine C', find $p(D)$ and $p(C$ and $D)$.

An article is examined and found to be defective. What is the probability that it was produced by C? (SMP)

39. (a) The events A and B are such that $P(A) = 0.6$, $P(B) = 0.25$, $P(A \cup B) = 0.725$. Show that the events A and B are neither mutually exclusive nor independent. Calculate the values of $P(\overline{A} \cup \overline{B})$ and $P(A \mid \overline{B})$.

(b) One red card and two black cards are removed from a pack of cards. From the remainder, three cards are taken at random without replacement. Show that the probability that they are all of the same colour is $\frac{23}{98}$. Assuming that this event occurs, find the probability that a fourth card drawn from the remaining 46 cards will be of the same colour as the previous three.

(L Additional)

40. Events A and B are such that $P(A) = \frac{5}{12}$, $P(A \mid \overline{B}) = \frac{7}{12}$, $P(A \cap B) = \frac{1}{8}$. Find (a) $P(B)$, (b) $P(A \mid B)$, (c) $P(B \mid A)$, (d) $P(A \cup B)$. State whether events A and B are (a) mutually exclusive, (b) independent.

41. The following are three of the classical problems in probability.

(a) Compare the probability of a total of 9 with the probability of a total of 10 when three fair dice are tossed once (Galileo and Duke of Tuscany).

(b) Compare the probability of at least one six in four tosses of a fair die with the probability of at least one double-six in twenty-four tosses of two fair dice (Chevalier de Méré).

(c) Compare the probability of at least one 6 when six dice are tossed with the probability of at least two sixes when 12 dice are tossed (Pepys to Newton).

Solve each of these problems. (AEB)

42. A set consists of 12 observations no two of which are equal. Five of the observations are selected at random. What are the probabilities that

(a) the five observations include the largest and the least among the 12 observations,

(b) the second largest and the second smallest will be included,

(c) the five smallest observations are included,

(d) at least three of the smallest five observations are included? (MEI)

43. In a class of 30 pupils, 12 walk to school, 10 travel by bus, 6 cycle and 2 travel by car. If 4 pupils are picked at random, obtain the probabilities that (a) they all travel by bus, (b) they all travel by the same means.

If 2 are picked at random from the class, find the probability that they travel by different means.

In picking out pupils from the class, find the probability that more than three trials are needed before a pupil who walks to school is selected. (JMB)

44. Four ball-point pen refills are to be drawn at random without replacement from a bag containing ten refills, of which 5 are red, 3 are green and 2 are blue. Find

(a) the probability that both blue refills will be drawn,

(b) the probability that at least one refill of each colour will be drawn. (JMB)

45. At the ninth hole on a certain golf course there is a pond. A golfer hits a grade B ball into the pond. Including the golfer's ball there are then 6 grade C, 10 grade B and 4 grade A balls in the pond. The golfer uses a fishing net and 'catches' four balls. The events X, Y and Z are defined as follows:

X: the catch consists of two grade A balls and two grade C balls

Y: the catch consists of two grade B balls and two other balls

Z: the catch includes the golfer's own ball

Assuming that the catch is a random selection from the balls in the pond, determine

(a) $P(X)$, (b) $P(Y)$, (c) $P(Z)$, (d) $P(Z \mid Y)$.

For each of the pairs X and Y, Y and Z, state, with a brief reason, whether the two events are (i) mutually exclusive, (ii) independent. (C)

46. A committee of 8 members consists of one married couple together with 4 other men and 2 other women. From the committee a working party of 4 persons is to be formed. Find the number of different working parties which can be formed.

Find also the number if the working party
(a)   may not contain *both* the husband and
his wife,
(b)   must contain 2 men and 2 women,
(c)   must contain at least one man and at
least one woman.
The 8 committee members sit round an
octagonal table, their positions being decided
by drawing lots. Find the probability of
(d)   the man sitting next to his wife,
(e)   the man sitting opposite to his wife,
(f)   the 3 women sitting together.   (AEB)

47. In a game of chance, a player's turn starts by
drawing a card at random from a pack of
playing cards. If he draws a black card which is
not an ace, his turn ends. If he draws a black
ace he throws a black die, and if he draws a red
card he throws a red die. After a die has been
thrown, the card that was drawn is replaced in
the pack which is then shuffled and the player
draws again with the same conditions leading
to the throwing of a die. This continues until
the player draws a black card, which is not an
ace, when his turn ends. A player's score in any
turn is the sum of the scores thrown with the
red die plus three times the sum of the scores
thrown with the black die. Calculate the
probability that in a turn a player will score
(a) zero, (b) exactly three.   (L)

48. A company makes a certain type of fan
heater (called an X-heater) at each of its two
factories F_1 and F_2. The factory F_1 produces
one quarter and F_2 three quarters of the total
output. X-heaters are coloured either red or
blue. One third of the X-heaters produced at
F_1 are red and seven-ninths of the X-heaters
produced at F_2 are red.
A customer goes into a shop and selects an
X-heater at random. Show the probability is $\frac{2}{3}$
that when he unpacks it he will find that it is
red.
Two shops A and B stock X-heaters.
Shop A has four and shop B has three. Find
(a)   the probability that neither shop has a
red X-heater;
(b)   the probability that there are at least 3
red X-heaters in shop A;
(c)   the probability that there are the same
number of red X-heaters in each shop;
(d)   the probability that there are two red
X-heaters in each shop, given that all the
X-heaters in shop A come from F_1 and that
all the X-heaters in shop B come from F_2.
(You may leave all your answers as fractions
with powers of 3 as denominators.)   (SMP)

49. (a)   Find the number of ways in which 10
people can be divided into
(i)   two groups consisting of 7 and 3 people,
(ii)   three groups consisting of 4, 3 and 2

people with 1 person rejected.
(b)   Seven coins of which 3 are silver and 4
are copper are in a box. A random selection of
3 coins is made and the coins selected are
placed in a purse (purse A). The remaining
coins are placed in a second purse (purse B).
Find the probabilities associated with each of
the possible numbers of silver coins (ranging
from 0 to 3) in purse A.
On a particular occasion it is known that
purse A has in it 2 silver coins and 1 copper
coin, and that the remaining coins are in
purse B. If one coin is then drawn at random
from a purse selected at random, find the
probability that the coin is silver.   (C)

50. A committee has 22 members, of whom 7
have black hair, do not smoke and do not
wear glasses; 5 have white hair, do not smoke
and do not wear glasses; 4 have white hair,
smoke and wear glasses; 3 have black hair,
smoke and do not wear glasses, 2 have white
hair, do not smoke and wear glasses; 1 has
black hair, smokes and wears glasses.
(a)   One committee member is chosen at
random. Let W be the event that this
member has white hair, G be the event that
this member wears glasses and S the event
that the member smokes. Find (i) $P(W)$,
(ii) $P(W\,|\,S)$, (iii) $P(W\,|\,G)$, (iv) the
probability that this member has either
white hair or glasses (but not both), given
that this member smokes. Are the events W
and S independent? Are the events W and G
independent? Give a reason for each answer.
(b)   Two committee members are chosen at
random. Let W_2 be the event that both have
white hair. Let S_2 be the event that both
smoke. Find (i) $P(W_2)$, (ii) $P(W_2\,|\,S_2)$.   (C)

51. A college has 750 women students and 2250
male students. There is a higher proportion
of male students in engineering, physics and
similar subjects so that 60% of male students
study mathematics and only 30% of women
students study it. If one student studying
mathematics is chosen at random from all
the students studying it, what is the
probability that the student will be a woman?
If three students studying mathematics are
chosen, what is the probability that there will
be at least two men?
25% of all the students study French. The
proportion of male students of mathematics
who also study French is 20% and the proportion of women students of French who also
study mathematics is 20%. There are 500 male
students of French. If four students are selected
what is the probability that at least one is male
and at least one is studying mathematics and
at least one is studying French?   (MEI)

52. (*a*)   In a group of 200 people, each individual is classified as either male or female and according to whether or not he or she wears glasses. The numbers falling into each category are as tabulated.

	Not wearing glasses	Wearing glasses
Male	90	24
Female	66	20

Suppose one of this group is chosen at random. Let A be the event that the person chosen is male and B the event that the person chosen is not wearing glasses.

(i)   Define the events A' and $A \cup B'$.

(ii)   Calculate the probability of occurrence of each of the events in (i).

(iii)   Given that the person chosen is not wearing glasses, calculate the probability that this person is male.

(iv)   Use the available data to determine whether not wearing glasses is independent of sex *within the group*. Give a practical interpretation to your finding.

(*b*)   After advertising for an assistant, a manager decides to interview suitable applicants. The interview of an applicant will take place during the morning or the afternoon with probabilities 0.45 and 0.55 respectively. Each applicant is informed by telephone and in each case a message has to be left. A morning interview is wrongly transmitted to the applicant as an afternoon interview with probability 0.2, and an afternoon interview is wrongly transmitted to the applicant as a morning interview with probability 0.1. Find the probability that an applicant arriving

(i)   for a morning interview is expected for a morning interview,

(ii)   for an afternoon interview is expected for an afternoon interview.   (AEB 1988)

53.   In Camelot it never rains on Friday, Saturday, Sunday or Monday. The probability that it rains on a given Tuesday is $\frac{1}{5}$. For each of the remaining two days, Wednesday and Thursday, the conditional probability that it rains, given that it rained the previous day, is α, and the conditional probability that it rains, given that it did not rain the previous day, is β.

(*a*)   Show that the (unconditional) probability of rain on a given Wednesday is $\frac{1}{5}(\alpha + 4\beta)$, and find the probability of rain on a given Thursday.

(*b*)   If X is the event that, in a randomly chosen week, it rains on Thursday, Y is the event that it rains on Tuesday, and $\overline{Y}$ is the event that it does not rain on Tuesday, show that

$$P(X \mid Y) - P(X \mid \overline{Y}) = (\alpha - \beta)^2$$

(*c*)   Explain the implications of the case $\alpha = \beta$.   (C)

4

PROBABILITY DISTRIBUTIONS I — DISCRETE RANDOM VARIABLES

If we toss a coin twice, the number of heads obtained could be 0, 1 or 2. The probabilities of these occurring are as follows:

P(no heads) $= P(TT) = (0.5)(0.5) = 0.25$

P(one head) $= P(HT) + P(TH) = (0.5)(0.5) + (0.5)(0.5) = 0.5$

P(two heads) $= P(HH) = (0.5)(0.5) = 0.25$

We can show the results in a table, known as a **probability distribution**.

Number of heads	0	1	2
Probability	0.25	0.5	0.25

We now develop some useful notation.

The variable being considered is 'the number of heads obtained in two tosses' and it can be denoted by X. It can only take exact values, 0, 1 and 2 and so is called a **discrete** variable.

The probabilities can be written

$$P(X = 0) = 0.25, \ P(X = 1) = 0.5, \ P(X = 2) = 0.25$$

Sometimes we write $p_0 = 0.25$, $p_1 = 0.5$, $p_2 = 0.25$.

Now if the sum of the probabilities is 1, the variable is said to be **random**.

In this example

$$P(X = 0) + P(X = 1) + P(X = 2) = 0.25 + 0.5 + 0.25 = 1,$$

so X is a discrete random variable.

The probability distribution is often written

x	0	1	2
$P(X = x)$	0.25	0.5	0.25

and the statement 'the sum of the probabilities is 1' is written

$$\sum_{\text{all } x} P(X = x) = 1$$

DISCRETE RANDOM VARIABLE

Let X have the following properties:

(a) it is a discrete variable and can take only values $x_1, x_2, \ldots, x_n$;

(b) the probabilities associated with these values are $p_1, p_2, \ldots, p_n$,

where
$$P(X = x_1) = p_1$$
$$P(X = x_2) = p_2$$
$$\vdots$$
$$P(X = x_n) = p_n.$$

Then X is a discrete random variable if $p_1 + p_2 + \ldots + p_n = 1$.

This can be written

$$\sum p_i = 1, \qquad i = 1, 2, \ldots, n$$

or

$$\sum_{\text{all } x} P(X = x) = 1$$

We usually denote a random variable (r.v.) by a capital letter (X, Y, R, etc.) and the particular value it takes by a small letter (x, y, r, etc.).

Example 4.1   Let X be the discrete variable 'the number of fours obtained when two dice are thrown'. Show that X is a random variable, i.e. that the sum of the probabilities is 1. Illustrate the probability distribution on a diagram.

Solution 4.1   When two dice are thrown, the number of fours obtained is 0, 1 or 2.

Therefore X can take the values 0, 1 and 2 only.

Then, with obvious notation,

$$P(X = 0) = P(\overline{4}\,\overline{4}) = \left(\tfrac{5}{6}\right)\left(\tfrac{5}{6}\right) = \tfrac{25}{36}$$

$$P(X = 1) = P(4\,\overline{4}) + P(\overline{4}\,4) = \left(\tfrac{1}{6}\right)\left(\tfrac{5}{6}\right) + \left(\tfrac{5}{6}\right)\left(\tfrac{1}{6}\right) = \tfrac{10}{36}$$

$$P(X = 2) = P(4\,4) = \left(\tfrac{1}{6}\right)\left(\tfrac{1}{6}\right) = \tfrac{1}{36}$$

Now
$$\sum_{\text{all } x} P(X = x) = \tfrac{25}{36} + \tfrac{10}{36} + \tfrac{1}{36}$$
$$= \tfrac{36}{36}$$
$$= 1$$

Therefore X is a random variable.

The probability distribution is

x	0	1	2
$P(X = x)$	$\tfrac{25}{36}$	$\tfrac{10}{36}$	$\tfrac{1}{36}$

and it can be represented by a vertical line graph:

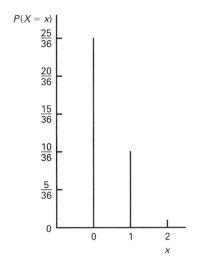

PROBABILITY DENSITY FUNCTION (p.d.f.)

The function that is responsible for allocating probabilities, $P(X = x)$, is known as the **probability density function** (p.d.f.) of X.

Sometimes it can be expressed as a formula, as in the following example.

Example 4.2 Two tetrahedral dice, each with faces labelled 1, 2, 3 and 4 are thrown and the score noted, where the score is the sum of the two numbers on which the dice land. Find the probability density function (p.d.f.) of X, where X is the random variable 'the score when two dice are thrown'.

Solution 4.2 The score for each possible outcome is shown in the table:

Second die					'Score'
4	5	6	7	8	
3	4	5	6	7	
2	3	4	5	6	
1	2	3	4	5	
	1	2	3	4	
		First die			

From the table we can see that X can take the values 2, 3, 4, 5, 6, 7, 8 only.

The probabilities can be found from the table, since each outcome shown is equally likely.

For example, $P(X = 5) = \frac{4}{16}$ since 4 out of the total of 16 outcomes result in a score of 5.

The probability distribution is formed:

x	2	3	4	5	6	7	8
$P(X = x)$	$\frac{1}{16}$	$\frac{2}{16}$	$\frac{3}{16}$	$\frac{4}{16}$	$\frac{3}{16}$	$\frac{2}{16}$	$\frac{1}{16}$

This can be written as a formula, giving the p.d.f. of X as

$$P(X = x) = \frac{x-1}{16} \quad \text{for} \quad x = 2, 3, 4, 5$$

$$P(X = x) = \frac{9-x}{16} \quad \text{for} \quad x = 6, 7, 8$$

NOTE: $\sum_{\text{all } x} P(X = x) = \frac{1}{16}(1 + 2 + 3 + 4 + 3 + 2 + 1) = 1$,

confirming that X is a random variable.

Example 4.3 The p.d.f. of a discrete random variable Y is given by $P(Y = y) = cy^2$, for $y = 0, 1, 2, 3, 4$. Given that c is a constant, find the value of c.

Solution 4.3 The probability distribution of Y is

y	0	1	2	3	4
$P(Y = y)$	0	c	$4c$	$9c$	$16c$

Since Y is a random variable, $\sum_{\text{all } y} P(Y = y) = 1$.

So $$c + 4c + 9c + 16c = 1$$

$$30c = 1$$

$$c = \frac{1}{30}$$

Therefore, since Y is a random variable, $c = \frac{1}{30}$.

Example 4.4 The p.d.f. of the discrete r.v. is given by $P(X = x) = a\left(\frac{3}{4}\right)^x$ for $x = 0, 1, 2, 3, \ldots$. Find the value of the constant, a.

Solution 4.4 Since X is a random variable, $\displaystyle\sum_{\text{all } x} P(X = x) = 1$.

Now $$P(X = 0) = a\left(\frac{3}{4}\right)^0$$

$$P(X = 1) = a\left(\frac{3}{4}\right)^1$$

$$P(X = 2) = a\left(\frac{3}{4}\right)^2$$

$$P(X = 3) = a\left(\frac{3}{4}\right)^3$$

and so on.

So $$\sum_{\text{all } x} P(X = x) = a + a\left(\frac{3}{4}\right) + a\left(\frac{3}{4}\right)^2 + a\left(\frac{3}{4}\right)^3 + \ldots$$

$$= a\left(1 + \frac{3}{4} + \left(\frac{3}{4}\right)^2 + \left(\frac{3}{4}\right)^3 + \ldots\right)$$

$$= a\left(\frac{1}{1 - \frac{3}{4}}\right) \qquad \left(\begin{array}{l}\text{sum of an infinite G.P.} \\ \text{with first term 1 and} \\ \text{common ratio } \frac{3}{4}\end{array}\right)$$

$$= a(4)$$

We have $$4a = 1$$

Therefore $$a = \frac{1}{4}$$

Example 4.5 The discrete random variable W has p.d.f. as shown

w	-3	-2	-1	0	1
$P(W = w)$	0.1	0.25	0.3	0.15	d

Find (**a**) the value of d, (**b**) $P(-3 \leqslant W < 0)$, (**c**) $P(W > -1)$, (**d**) $P(-1 < W < 1)$, (**e**) the mode.

Solution 4.5 (a) Now $\displaystyle\sum_{\text{all } w} P(W = w) = 1$

so
$$0.1 + 0.25 + 0.3 + 0.15 + d = 1$$
$$0.8 + d = 1$$
$$\underline{d = 0.2}$$

(b)
$$P(-3 \leqslant W < 0) = P(W = -3) + P(W = -2) + P(W = -1)$$
$$= 0.1 + 0.25 + 0.3$$
$$= \underline{0.65}$$

(c)
$$P(W > -1) = P(W = 0) + P(W = 1)$$
$$= 0.15 + 0.2$$
$$= \underline{0.35}$$

(d)
$$P(-1 < W < 1) = P(W = 0)$$
$$= \underline{0.15}$$

(e) The value of w that has the highest probability is -1.
Therefore <u>the mode $= -1$</u>.

Exercise 4a

1. The discrete random variable X has p.d.f. as shown

x	1	2	3	4	5
$P(X = x)$	0.2	0.25	0.4	a	0.05

Find (i) the value of a
(ii) $P(1 \leqslant X \leqslant 3)$
(iii) $P(X > 2)$
(iv) $P(2 < X < 5)$
(v) the mode.
Draw a vertical line graph to illustrate the distribution.

2. The probability density function of a discrete random variable X is given by $P(X = x) = kx$ for $x = 12, 13, 14$. Find the value of the constant k.

3. The discrete random variable R has p.d.f. given by $P(R = r) = c(3 - r)$ for $r = 0, 1, 2, 3$. Find the value of the constant c, and draw a vertical line graph to illustrate the distribution.

4. For each of the following random variables write out the probability distributions. Check that the variables are random and for parts (b), (d) and (f) write the formula for the p.d.f.
(a) The number of heads obtained when two fair coins are tossed.
(b) The sum of the scores when two ordinary dice are thrown.
(c) The number of threes obtained when two tetrahedral dice are thrown.
(d) The numerical value of a digit chosen from a set of random number tables.
(e) The number of tails obtained when three fair coins are tossed.
(f) The difference between the numbers when two ordinary dice are thrown.

5. A drawer contains 8 brown socks and 4 blue socks. A sock is taken from the drawer at random, its colour is noted and it is then replaced. This procedure is performed twice more. If X is the r.v. 'the number of brown socks taken', find the probability distribution for X.

6. The r.v. X has p.d.f. $P(X = x) = c\left(\frac{4}{5}\right)^x$ for $x = 0, 1, 2, 3, \ldots$. Find the value of the constant, c.

7. A game consists of throwing tennis balls into a bucket from a given distance. The probability that William will get the tennis ball in the bucket is 0.4. A turn consists of three attempts.
(i) Construct the probability distribution for X, the number of tennis balls that land in the bucket in a turn.
(ii) William wins a prize if, at the end of his turn, there are two or more tennis balls in the bucket. What is the probability that William does not win a prize?

8. A student has a fair coin and two six-sided dice, one of which is white and the other blue. The student tosses the coin and then rolls both dice. Let X be a random variable such that if the coin falls heads, X is the sum of the scores on the two dice, otherwise X is the score on the white die only.
Find the probability function of X in the form of a table of possible values of X and their associated probabilities.
Find $P(3 \leqslant X \leqslant 7)$.
State the assumption you made to enable you to evaluate the probability function.
(AEB 1991)P

EXPECTATION, $E(X)$

Experimental approach

Suppose we throw an unbiased die 120 times and record the results in a **frequency distribution:**

Score, x	1	2	3	4	5	6	
Frequency, f	15	22	23	19	23	18	Total 120

We can calculate the mean score obtained as follows:

$$\bar{x} = \frac{\sum fx}{\sum f} = \frac{15 + 44 + 69 + 76 + 115 + 108}{120} = 3.558 \quad \text{(3 d.p.)}$$

Theoretical approach

The **probability distribution** for the random variable X, where X is 'the number on the die', is as shown:

Score, x	1	2	3	4	5	6
$P(X = x)$	$\frac{1}{6}$	$\frac{1}{6}$	$\frac{1}{6}$	$\frac{1}{6}$	$\frac{1}{6}$	$\frac{1}{6}$

We can obtain a value for the 'expected' mean by multiplying each score by its corresponding probability and summing.

$$\text{Expected mean} = 1\left(\frac{1}{6}\right) + 2\left(\frac{1}{6}\right) + 3\left(\frac{1}{6}\right) + 4\left(\frac{1}{6}\right) + 5\left(\frac{1}{6}\right) + 6\left(\frac{1}{6}\right)$$
$$= \frac{21}{6}$$
$$= 3.5$$

If we have a statistical experiment:

a practical approach results in a frequency distribution and a mean value,

a theoretical approach results in a probability distribution and an expected value, known as the **expectation**.

The expectation of X (or expected value), written $E(X)$, is given by

$$E(X) = \sum_{\text{all } x} xP(X = x)$$

This can also be written

$$E(X) = \sum x_i p_i \qquad i = 1, 2, \ldots, n$$

We often use the symbol μ, pronounced 'mew', for the expectation, so

$$\mu = E(X)$$

Example 4.6   A random variable X has probability density function (p.d.f.) as shown. Find the expectation, $E(X)$.

x	-2	-1	0	1	2
$P(X = x)$	0.3	0.1	0.15	0.4	0.05

Solution 4.6 $E(X) = \displaystyle\sum_{\text{all } x} xP(X = x)$

$$= (-2)(0.3) + (-1)(0.1) + 0(0.15) + 1(0.4) + 2(0.05)$$

$$= -0.2$$

Therefore $E(X) = -0.2$.

NOTE: an important property which some probability distributions possess is that of symmetry. For example,

(**a**) Consider the r.v. with probability distribution:

x	1	2	3	4	5
$P(X = x)$	0.1	0.2	0.4	0.2	0.1

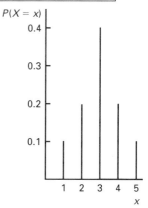

It can be seen from the table or from the vertical line graph that the distribution is symmetrical about the central value $X = 3$, so $E(X) = 3$.

Check: $E(X) = \displaystyle\sum_{\text{all } x} xP(X = x) = 1(0.1) + 2(0.2) + 3(0.4)$

$$+ 4(0.2) + 5(0.1) = 3$$

(**b**) Consider the r.v. with p.d.f. $P(X = x) = 0.1$ for $x = 1, 2, \ldots, 10$.
The probability distribution for X is

x	1	2	3	4	5	6	7	8	9	10
$P(X = x)$	0.1	0.1	0.1	0.1	0.1	0.1	0.1	0.1	0.1	0.1

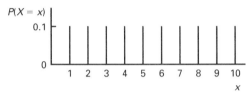

The distribution is symmetrical about the central value mid-way between 5 and 6, so $E(X) = 5.5$.

NOTE: the random variable X with p.d.f. $P(X = x) = k$, for all given values of x, where k is a constant, is said to follow a **uniform distribution**.

Example 4.7   A fruit machine consists of three windows, each of which shows pictures of fruits — lemons or oranges or cherries or plums. The probability that a window shows a particular fruit is as follows:

$P(\text{lemons}) = 0.4, \quad P(\text{oranges}) = 0.1, \quad P(\text{cherries}) = 0.2,$
$P(\text{plums}) = 0.3$

The windows operate independently.

Anyone wanting to play the fruit machine pays 10 p for a turn.

The winning combinations and amounts are as follows:

Oranges in 3 windows	£1.00
Cherries in 3 windows	£0.50
Oranges in 2 windows and cherries in 1 window	£0.80
Lemons in 3 windows	£0.40

Find the expected gain/loss per turn.

Solution 4.7 $P(\text{oranges in 3 windows}) = (0.1)^3 = 0.001$ (independent events)
$P(\text{cherries in 3 windows}) = (0.2)^3 = 0.008$
$P(\text{oranges in 2 and cherries in 1}) = 3(0.1)^2(0.2) = 0.006$
$P(\text{lemons in 3 windows}) = (0.4)^3 = 0.064$

Therefore

$P(\text{combination will not win a prize})$
$$= 1 - (0.001 + 0.008 + 0.006 + 0.064)$$
$$= 0.921$$

Let X be the r.v. 'the amount, in pence, gained per turn'.

Now the amount paid out by the fruit machine could be 100 p, 80 p, 50 p, 40 p or 0 p.

So considering the initial payment of 10 p for a turn, X can take the values 90, 70, 40, 30, -10.

The probability distribution for X is

x	90	70	40	30	-10
$P(X = x)$	0.001	0.006	0.008	0.064	0.921

Now $E(X) = \displaystyle\sum_{\text{all } x} xP(X = x)$

$$= 90(0.001) + 70(0.006) + 40(0.008) + 30(0.064)$$
$$+ (-10)(0.921)$$
$$= -6.46$$

So, the expected *loss* per turn is 6.46 p.

Example 4.8 Three dice are thrown. If a 1 or a 6 turns up, you will be paid 1 p, but if neither a 1 nor a 6 turns up, you will pay 5 p. How much would you expect to gain or lose in 9 games?

You are now given the opportunity to change the rule for payment when a 1 or a 6 appears. To make the game worthwhile to yourself, what is the minimum amount in everyday currency that you would suggest?

Solution 4.8 $P(1 \text{ or } 6 \text{ on die}) = \frac{2}{6} = \frac{1}{3}$.

If three dice are thrown, $P(\text{neither a 1 nor a 6 on all three}) = \left(\frac{2}{3}\right)^3 = \frac{8}{27}$.

So $P(\text{a 1 or a 6 turns up}) = 1 - \frac{8}{27} = \frac{19}{27}$.

Let X be the r.v. 'the number of pence won in a game'. Then X can assume the values -5 and 1 only.

Now $P(X = -5) = P(\text{neither a 1 nor a 6}) = \frac{8}{27}$

$P(X = 1) = P(\text{a 1 or a 6}) = \frac{19}{27}$

The probability distribution for X is

x	-5	1
$P(X = x)$	$\frac{8}{27}$	$\frac{19}{27}$

So

$$E(X) = \sum_{\text{all } x} xP(X = x)$$
$$= (-5)\left(\frac{8}{27}\right) + (1)\left(\frac{19}{27}\right)$$
$$= -\frac{7}{9}$$

Therefore the expected *loss* after one game is $\frac{7}{9}$p,

so, after 9 games, the expected loss is 7 p.

If we change the rule for payment to y pence when a 1 or a 6 turns up then the probability distribution becomes

x	-5	y
$P(X = x)$	$\frac{8}{27}$	$\frac{19}{27}$

We now have
$$E(X) = (-5)\left(\tfrac{8}{27}\right) + (y)\left(\tfrac{19}{27}\right)$$

$$= \frac{-40 + 19y}{27}$$

To make the game worthwhile, we require $E(X) > 0$,

so
$$\frac{-40 + 19y}{27} > 0$$

i.e.
$$-40 + 19y > 0$$

$$19y > 40$$

$$y > 2.105 \ldots$$

Therefore the minimum amount we should be paid, in everyday currency, is 3 p.

Example 4.9   A bag contains 3 red balls and 1 blue ball. A second bag contains 1 red ball and 1 blue ball. A ball is picked out of each bag and is then placed in the other bag. What is the expected number of red balls in the first bag?

Solution 4.9   Assume that the balls are taken from each bag simultaneously.

If a red ball is picked from each bag and placed in the other then the number of red balls in the first bag is now 3, etc.

Let X be the r.v. 'the final number of red balls in the first bag'.

Then X can take the values 2, 3 or 4 only. With obvious notation,

$$P(X = 2) = P(\text{red from first bag and blue from second bag})$$

$$= P(R_1 B_2)$$

$$= \left(\tfrac{3}{4}\right)\left(\tfrac{1}{2}\right)$$

$$= \tfrac{3}{8}$$

$$P(X = 3) = P(R_1 R_2) + P(B_1 B_2)$$

$$= \left(\tfrac{3}{4}\right)\left(\tfrac{1}{2}\right) + \left(\tfrac{1}{4}\right)\left(\tfrac{1}{2}\right)$$

$$= \tfrac{1}{2}$$

$$P(X = 4) = P(B_1R_2)$$

$$= \left(\tfrac{1}{4}\right)\left(\tfrac{1}{2}\right)$$

$$= \tfrac{1}{8}$$

The probability distribution for X is

x	2	3	4
$P(X = x)$	$\frac{3}{8}$	$\frac{1}{2}$	$\frac{1}{8}$

So

$$E(X) = \sum_{\text{all } x} xP(X = x)$$

$$= 2\left(\tfrac{3}{8}\right) + 3\left(\tfrac{1}{2}\right) + 4\left(\tfrac{1}{8}\right)$$

$$= 2\tfrac{3}{4}$$

The expected number of red balls in the first bag after the exchange is $2\tfrac{3}{4}$ balls.

Exercise 4b

1. The probability distribution for the r.v. X is shown in the table:

x	0	1	2	3	4
$P(X = x)$	$\frac{1}{6}$	$\frac{1}{12}$	$\frac{1}{4}$	$\frac{1}{3}$	$\frac{1}{6}$

Find $E(X)$.

2. The r.v. X has p.d.f. $P(X = x)$ for $x = 5, 6, 7, 8, 9$ as defined in the table:

x	5	6	7	8	9
$P(X = x)$	$\frac{3}{11}$	$\frac{2}{11}$	$\frac{1}{11}$	$\frac{2}{11}$	$\frac{3}{11}$

Find μ.

3. The probability distribution of a r.v. X is as shown in the table:

x	1	2	3	4	5
$P(X = x)$	0.1	0.3	y	0.2	0.1

Find (a) the value of y, (b) $E(X)$.

4. Find the expected number of heads when two fair coins are tossed.

5. Find the expected number of ones when three ordinary fair dice are thrown.

6. A bag contains 5 black counters and 6 red counters. Two counters are drawn, one at a time, and not replaced. Let X be the r.v. 'the number of red counters drawn'. Find $E(X)$.

7. An unbiased tetrahedral die has faces marked 1, 2, 3, 4. If the die lands on the face marked 1, the player has to pay 10 p. If it lands on a face marked with a 2 or a 4, the player wins 5 p and if it lands on a 3, the player wins 3 p. Find the expected gain in one throw.

8. A discrete r.v. X can assume values 10 and 20 only. If $E(X) = 16$, write the p.d.f. of X in table form.

9. The discrete r.v. X can assume values 0, 1, 2 and 3 only. Given $P(X \leqslant 2) = 0.9$, $P(X \leqslant 1) = 0.5$ and $E(X) = 1.4$, find (a) $P(X = 1)$, (b) $P(X = 0)$.

10. In a game, a player rolls two balls down an inclined plane so that each ball finally settles in one of five slots and scores the number of points allotted to that slot as shown in the diagram below:

It is possible for both balls to settle in one slot and it may be assumed that each slot is equally likely to accept either ball.
The player's score is the sum of the points scored by each ball.
Draw up a table showing all the possible scores and the probability of each.
If the player pays 10 p for each game and receives back a number of pence equal to his score, calculate the player's expected gain or loss per 50 games.   (C Additional)

11. In a game a player tosses three fair coins. He wins £10 if 3 heads occur, £x if 2 heads occur, £3 if 1 head occurs and £2 if no heads occur. Express in terms of x his expected gain from each game.
Given that he pays £4.50 to play each game, calculate
(a) the value of x for which the game is fair,
(b) his expected gain or loss over 100 games if $x = 4.90$.   (C Additional)

12. A committee of 3 is to be chosen from 4 girls and 7 boys. Find the expected number of girls on the committee, if the members of the committee are chosen at random.

13. The discrete r.v. X has p.d.f. given by $P(X = x) = kx$ for $x = 1, 2, 3, 4, 5$ where k is constant. Find $E(X)$.

14. In an examination a candidate is given the four answers to four questions but is not told which answer applies to which question. He is asked to write down each of the four answers next to its appropriate question.
(a) Calculate in how many different ways he could write down the four answers.
(b) Explain why it is impossible for him to have just three answers in the correct places and show that there are six ways of getting just two answers in the correct places.
(c) If a candidate guesses at random where the four answers are to go and X is the number of correct guesses he makes, draw up the probability distribution for X in tabular form.
(d) Calculate $E(X)$.   (L Additional)

15.

x	0	1	2	3
$P(X = x)$	c	c^2	$c^2 + c$	$3c^2 + 2c$

The above table shows the probability distribution for a random variable X.
Calculate (a) c, (b) $E(X)$.   (L Additional)

16. A box contains 9 discs of which 4 are red, 3 are white and 2 are blue. Three discs are to be drawn at random without replacement from the box. Calculate
(a) the probability that the discs, in the order drawn, will be coloured red, white and blue respectively,
(b) the probability that one disc of each colour will be drawn,
(c) the probability that the third disc drawn will be red,
(d) the probability that no red disc will be drawn,
(e) the most probable number of red discs that will be drawn,
(f) the expected number of red discs that will be drawn, and state the probability that this expected number of red discs will be drawn.   (JMB)

17. A woman has 3 keys on a ring, just one of which opens the front door. As she approaches the front door she selects one key after another at random without replacement. Draw a tree diagram to illustrate the various selections before she finds the correct key. Use this diagram to calculate the expected number of keys that she will use before opening the door.   (L Additional)

18. An urn containing 4 black balls and 8 white balls is used for two experiments. In Experiment 1, two balls are to be drawn at random from the urn, one after the other, without replacement. In Experiment 2, one ball is to be drawn at random from the 12 balls in the urn and replaced before a second ball is drawn at random. Copy and complete the following two tables, which give the probabilities for the different compound events in the two experiments.

		Second ball	
		Black	White
First ball	Black		$\frac{8}{33}$
	White		

Experiment 1

		Second ball	
		Black	White
First ball	Black		
	White	$\frac{2}{9}$	

Experiment 2

For each of the two experiments, calculate the expected number of black balls which will be drawn.

If in Experiment 2, the urn contains b black balls and w white balls, where $b + w = 12$, calculate the expected number of black balls which will be drawn.

(L Additional)

THE EXPECTATION OF ANY FUNCTION OF *X*, *E*[*g*(*X*)]

The definition of expectation can be extended to any function of the random variable such as $10X$, X^2, $(X - 4)$, etc.

In general, if $g(X)$ is any function of the discrete random variable X then

$$E[g(X)] = \sum_{\text{all } x} g(x)P(X = x)$$

For example,
$$E(10X) = \sum 10x\, P(X = x)$$
$$E(X^2) = \sum x^2\, P(X = x)$$
$$E(X - 4) = \sum (x - 4)\, P(X = x)$$

Example 4.10 The random variable X has p.d.f. $P(X = x)$ for $x = 1, 2, 3$.

x	1	2	3
$P(X = x)$	0.1	0.6	0.3

Calculate (**a**) $E(3)$, (**b**) $E(X)$, (**c**) $E(5X)$, (**d**) $E(5X + 3)$,
(**e**) $5E(X) + 3$, (**f**) $E(X^2)$, (**g**) $E(4X^2 - 3)$, (**h**) $4E(X^2) - 3$.

Solution 4.10 We have

x	1	2	3
$5x$	5	10	15
$5x + 3$	8	13	18
x^2	1	4	9
$4x^2 - 3$	1	13	33
$P(X = x)$	0.1	0.6	0.3

Now
$$E[g(X)] = \sum_{\text{all } x} g(x)P(X = x)$$

(**a**)
$$E(3) = \sum_{\text{all } x} 3P(X = x)$$

$$= 3(0.1) + 3(0.6) + 3(0.3)$$

$$= 3$$

$$\underline{E(3) = 3}$$

(**b**)
$$E(X) = \sum_{\text{all } x} xP(X = x)$$

$$= 1(0.1) + 2(0.6) + 3(0.3)$$

$$= 2.2$$

$$\underline{E(X) = 2.2}$$

(**c**)
$$E(5X) = \sum_{\text{all } x} 5xP(X = x)$$

$$= 5(0.1) + 10(0.6) + 15(0.3)$$

$$= 11$$

$$\underline{E(5X) = 11}$$

NOTE: $E(5X) = 5E(X)$

(**d**)
$$E(5X + 3) = \sum_{\text{all } x} (5x + 3)P(X = x)$$

$$= 8(0.1) + 13(0.6) + 18(0.3)$$

$$= 14$$

$$\underline{E(5X + 3) = 14}$$

(**e**)
$$5E(X) + 3 = 5(2.2) + 3$$

$$= 14$$

$$\underline{5E(X) + 3 = 14}$$

NOTE: $E(5X + 3) = E(5X) + E(3) = 5E(X) + 3$

(**f**)
$$E(X^2) = \sum_{\text{all } x} x^2 P(X = x)$$

$$= 1(0.1) + 4(0.6) + 9(0.3)$$

$$= 5.2$$

$$\underline{E(X^2) = 5.2}$$

(**g**)
$$E(4X^2 - 3) = \sum_{\text{all } x} (4x^2 - 3)P(X = x)$$

$$= 1(0.1) + 13(0.6) + 33(0.3)$$

$$= 17.8$$

$$\underline{E(4X^2 - 3) = 17.8}$$

(**h**)
$$4E(X^2) - 3 = 4(5.2) - 3$$

$$= 17.8$$

$$\underline{4E(X^2) - 3 = 17.8}$$

NOTE: $E(4X^2 - 3) = E(4X^2) - E(3) = 4E(X^2) - 3$

In general, the following results hold when X is a discrete random variable.

Result 1 $E(a) = a$, where a is any constant.

Proof:
$$E(a) = \sum_{\text{all } x} aP(X = x)$$

$$= a \sum_{\text{all } x} P(X = x)$$

$$= a \qquad \text{since } \sum_{\text{all } x} P(X = x) = 1$$

Result 2 $E(aX) = aE(X)$, where a is any constant.

Proof:
$$E(aX) = \sum_{\text{all } x} axP(X = x)$$

$$= a \sum_{\text{all } x} xP(X = x)$$

$$= aE(X)$$

Result 3 $E(aX + b) = aE(X) + b$, where a and b are any constants.

Proof:
$$E(aX + b) = \sum_{\text{all } x} (ax + b)P(X = x)$$

$$= \sum_{\text{all } x} axP(X = x) + \sum_{\text{all } x} bP(X = x)$$

$$= aE(X) + b$$

Result 4	$E[f_1(X) + f_2(X)] = E[f_1(X)] + E[f_2(X)]$ where f_1 and f_2 are functions of X.

Proof:
$$E[f_1(X) + f_2(X)] = \sum_{\text{all } x} [f_1(x) + f_2(x)]P(X = x)$$

$$= \sum_{\text{all } x} f_1(x)P(X = x) + \sum_{\text{all } x} f_2(x)P(X = x)$$

$$= E[f_1(X)] + E[f_2(X)]$$

Example 4.11 The discrete random variable X has the probability distribution specified in the following table.

x	-1	0	1	2
$P(X = x)$	0.25	0.10	0.45	0.20

(**a**) Find $P(-1 \leqslant X < 1)$.

(**b**) Find $E(2X + 3)$.   (L)

Solution 4.11 (**a**)
$$P(-1 \leqslant X < 1) = P(X = -1) + P(X = 0)$$
$$= 0.25 + 0.10$$
$$= 0.35$$

Therefore $P(-1 \leqslant X < 1) = 0.35$.

(**b**) $E(2X + 3) = 2E(X) + 3$, so we need to find $E(X)$.

Now
$$E(X) = \sum_{\text{all } x} xP(X = x)$$
$$= (-1)(0.25) + (0)(0.10) + (1)(0.45) + (2)(0.20)$$
$$= 0.6$$

So $E(2X + 3) = 2(0.6) + 3$
$$= 4.2$$

Therefore $E(2X + 3) = 4.2$.

Exercise 4c

1. The discrete r.v. X has p.d.f. $P(X = x)$ for $x = 1, 2, 3$.

x	1	2	3
$P(X = x)$	0.2	0.3	0.5

Find (*a*) $E(X)$, (*b*) $E(X^2)$.

(*c*) Verify that $E(3X - 1) = 3E(X) - 1$.
(*d*) Verify that $E(2X^2 + 4) = 2E(X^2) + 4$.

2. The discrete r.v. X has p.d.f.
$P(X = 0) = 0.05$, $P(X = 1) = 0.45$,
$P(X = 2) = 0.5$.
Find (*a*) $\mu = E(X)$, (*b*) $E(X^2)$,
(*c*) $E(5X^2 + 2X - 3)$.

3. The discrete r.v. X has p.d.f. given by
$P(X = x) = k$ for $x = 1, 2, 3, 4, 5, 6$.
Find   (a) $E(X)$,   (b) $E(X^2)$,   (c) $E(3X + 4)$,
(d) $E(2X^2 + X - 4)$.

4. The discrete r.v. X has p.d.f. given by
$P(X = x) = \dfrac{3x + 1}{22}$ for $x = 0, 1, 2, 3$.

Find   (a) $E(X)$,   (b) $E(X^2)$,   (c) $E(3X - 2)$,
(d) $E(2X^2 + 4X - 3)$.

5. A roulette wheel is divided into 6 sectors of
unequal area, marked with the numbers 1, 2,
3, 4, 5 and 6. The wheel is spun and X is the
r.v. 'the number on which the wheel stops'.
The probability distribution of X is as follows:

x	1	2	3	4	5	6
$P(X = x)$	$\frac{1}{16}$	$\frac{3}{16}$	$\frac{1}{4}$	$\frac{1}{4}$	$\frac{3}{16}$	$\frac{1}{16}$

Calculate   (a) $E(X)$,   (b) $E(X^2)$,
(c) $E(3X - 5)$,   (d) $E(6X^2)$,
(e) $E(6X^2 + 6X - 10)$.

6. The r.v. X has p.d.f. $P(X = x)$ as shown in the
table:

x	-2	-1	0	1	c
$P(X = x)$	0.1	0.1	0.3	0.4	0.1

Find the value of c (a) if $E(X) = 0.3$
(b) if $E(X^2) = 1.8$.

7. The discrete random variable X has
probability function given by

$$p(x) = \begin{cases} \left(\frac{1}{2}\right)^x & x = 1,2,3,4,5, \\ C & x = 6, \\ 0 & \text{otherwise,} \end{cases}$$

where C is a constant.
Determine the value of C and hence the mode
and arithmetic mean of X.   (L)

8. The probability distribution of a discrete
random variable X is given by

$$P(X = r) = kr, \qquad r = 1,2,3,\ldots,n,$$

where k is a constant.
Show that

$$k = \frac{2}{n(n + 1)}$$

and find, in terms of n, the mean of X. (JMB)

VARIANCE, Var (X)

Experimental approach

For a frequency distribution with mean $\bar{x}$, the variance, s^2 is given by

$$s^2 = \frac{\sum f(x - \bar{x})^2}{\sum f}. \quad \text{This can also be written} \quad s^2 = \frac{\sum fx^2}{\sum f} - \bar{x}^2.$$

Theoretical approach

For a discrete random variable X, with $E(X) = \mu$, the variance is
defined as follows:

The variance of X, written Var(X), is given by

$$\text{Var}(X) = E(X - \mu)^2$$

Alternatively, $\text{Var}(X) = E(X - \mu)^2$

$$= E(X^2 - 2\mu X + \mu^2)$$

$$= E(X^2) - 2\mu E(X) + E(\mu^2)$$

$$= E(X^2) - 2\mu^2 + \mu^2$$

$$= E(X^2) - \mu^2$$

So we have $\boxed{\text{Var}(X) = E(X^2) - \mu^2}$

NOTE: $\mu = E(X)$, so $\mu^2 = [E(X)]^2$. We write $[E(X)]^2$ as $E^2(X)$ in a similar way to the notation used in trigonometry where $(\sin A)^2$ is written $\sin^2 A$.

So we have $\boxed{\text{Var}(X) = E(X^2) - E^2(X)}$

Example 4.12 The r.v. X has probability distribution as shown in the table:

x	1	2	3	4	5
$P(X = x)$	0.1	0.3	0.2	0.3	0.1

Find

(**a**) $\mu = E(X)$,

(**b**) $\text{Var}(X)$, using the formula $\text{Var}(X) = E(X - \mu)^2$,

(**c**) $E(X^2)$,

(**d**) $\text{Var}(X)$, using the formula $\text{Var}(X) = E(X^2) - \mu^2$.

Solution 4.12 (**a**) By symmetry, $\mu = E(X) = 3$.

(**b**)
$$E(X - \mu)^2 = E(X - 3)^2$$
$$= \sum_{\text{all } x} (x - 3)^2 P(X = x)$$

x	1	2	3	4	5
$(x - 3)$	-2	-1	0	1	2
$(x - 3)^2$	4	1	0	1	4
$P(X = x)$	0.1	0.3	0.2	0.3	0.1

So $\quad E(X - 3)^2 = 4(0.1) + 1(0.3) + 0(0.2) + 1(0.3) + 4(0.1)$

$$= 1.4$$

Therefore $\underline{\text{Var}(X) = E(X - \mu)^2 = 1.4.}$

(**c**) $\quad E(X^2) = \sum_{\text{all } x} x^2 P(X = x)$

$$= 1(0.1) + 4(0.3) + 9(0.2) + 16(0.3) + 25(0.1)$$

$$= 10.4$$

So $\underline{E(X^2) = 10.4.}$

(**d**) Now
$$\text{Var}(X) = E(X^2) - \mu^2$$
$$= 10.4 - 9$$
$$= 1.4$$

Therefore $\text{Var}(X) = 1.4$, as before.

Example 4.13 Two discs are drawn, without replacement, from a box containing 3 red discs and 4 white discs. The discs are drawn at random. If X is the r.v. 'the number of red discs drawn', find

(**a**) the expected number of red discs
(**b**) the standard deviation of X.

Solution 4.13 X is the r.v. 'the number of red discs drawn'.

Now X can take the values 0, 1, 2 only. We have
$$P(X = 0) = P(W_1 W_2) = \left(\tfrac{4}{7}\right)\left(\tfrac{3}{6}\right) = \tfrac{12}{42} = \tfrac{2}{7}$$
$$P(X = 1) = P(W_1 R_2) + P(R_1 W_2) = \left(\tfrac{4}{7}\right)\left(\tfrac{3}{6}\right) + \left(\tfrac{3}{7}\right)\left(\tfrac{4}{6}\right) = \tfrac{24}{42} = \tfrac{4}{7}$$
$$P(X = 2) = P(R_1 R_2) = \left(\tfrac{3}{7}\right)\left(\tfrac{2}{6}\right) = \tfrac{6}{42} = \tfrac{1}{7}$$

The probability distribution for X is as follows:

x	0	1	2
$P(X = x)$	$\tfrac{2}{7}$	$\tfrac{4}{7}$	$\tfrac{1}{7}$

(**a**) Now
$$E(X) = \sum_{\text{all } x} x P(X = x)$$
$$= 0\left(\tfrac{2}{7}\right) + 1\left(\tfrac{4}{7}\right) + 2\left(\tfrac{1}{7}\right)$$
$$= \tfrac{6}{7}$$

So the expected number of red discs is $\tfrac{6}{7}$.

(**b**) Standard deviation of $X = \sqrt{\text{Var}(X)}$.

Now
$$\text{Var}(X) = E(X^2) - E^2(X)$$

We have
$$E(X^2) = \sum_{\text{all } x} x^2 P(X = x)$$
$$= 0\left(\tfrac{2}{7}\right) + 1\left(\tfrac{4}{7}\right) + 4\left(\tfrac{1}{7}\right)$$
$$= \tfrac{8}{7}$$

So
$$\text{Var}(X) = \tfrac{8}{7} - \left(\tfrac{6}{7}\right)^2$$
$$= \tfrac{20}{49}$$

Therefore the standard deviation of $X = \sqrt{20/49} = 0.639$ (3 d.p.).

The following results are useful

Result 1 $\text{Var}(a) = 0$ where a is any constant.

Proof:
$$\text{Var}(a) = E(a^2) - E^2(a)$$
$$= a^2 - a^2$$
$$= 0$$

NOTE: this is as expected, since a constant does not vary.

Result 2 $\text{Var}(aX) = a^2\text{Var}(X)$ where a is any constant.

Proof:
$$\text{Var}(aX) = E(aX)^2 - E^2(aX)$$
$$= a^2E(X^2) - a^2E^2(X)$$
$$= a^2[E(X^2) - E^2(X)]$$
$$= a^2\text{Var}(X)$$

Result 3 $\text{Var}(aX + b) = a^2\text{Var}(X)$ where a and b are any constants.

Proof:

$$\text{Var}(aX + b) = E(aX + b)^2 - E^2(aX + b)$$
$$= E(a^2X^2 + 2abX + b^2) - [aE(X) + b]^2$$
$$= a^2E(X^2) + 2abE(X) + b^2 - a^2E^2(X) - 2abE(X) - b^2$$
$$= a^2E(X^2) - a^2E^2(X)$$
$$= a^2[E(X^2) - E^2(X)]$$
$$= a^2\text{Var}(X)$$

Example 4.14   The discrete random variable X has probability distribution as shown in the table. Find $\text{Var}(2X + 3)$.

x	10	20	30
$P(X = x)$	0.1	0.6	0.3

Solution 4.14   Now $\text{Var}(2X + 3) = 4\,\text{Var}(X)$ (Result 3)

We will need to find $\text{Var}(X) = E(X^2) - E^2(X)$.

$$E(X) = \sum_{\text{all } x} xP(X = x)$$

$$= 10(0.1) + 20(0.6) + 30(0.3)$$

$$= 22$$

$$E(X^2) = \sum_{\text{all } x} x^2 P(X = x)$$

$$= 100(0.1) + 400(0.6) + 900(0.3)$$

$$= 520$$

$$\text{Var}(X) = E(X^2) - E^2(X)$$

$$= 520 - 22^2$$

$$= 36$$

$$\text{Var}(2X + 3) = 4\,\text{Var}(X)$$

$$= 144$$

Therefore $\underline{\text{Var}(2X + 3) = 144.}$

Exercise 4d

1. Find $\text{Var}(X)$ for each of the following probability distributions:

   (a)
x	-3	-2	0	2	3
$P(X = x)$	0.3	0.3	0.2	0.1	0.1

   (b)
x	1	3	5	7	9
$P(X = x)$	$\frac{1}{6}$	$\frac{1}{4}$	$\frac{1}{6}$	$\frac{1}{4}$	$\frac{1}{6}$

   (c)
x	0	2	5	6
$P(X = x)$	0.11	0.35	0.46	0.08

2. If X is the r.v. 'the number on a biased die', and the p.d.f. of X is as shown,

x	1	2	3	4	5	6
$P(X = x)$	$\frac{1}{6}$	$\frac{1}{6}$	$\frac{1}{5}$	y	$\frac{1}{5}$	$\frac{1}{6}$

   Find   (a) the value of y,   (b) $E(X)$,
   (c) $E(X^2)$,   (d) $\text{Var}(X)$,   (e) $\text{Var}(4X)$.

3. If X is the r.v. 'the sum of the scores on two tetrahedral dice', where the 'score' is the number on which the die lands, find
   (a) $E(X)$,   (b) $\text{Var}(X)$,   (c) $\text{Var}(2X)$,
   (d) $\text{Var}(2X + 3)$.

4. A team of 3 is to be chosen from 4 boys and 5 girls. If X is the r.v. 'the number of girls in the team', find   (a) $E(X)$,   (b) $E(X^2)$,
   (c) $\text{Var}(X)$.

5. Two discs are drawn without replacement from a box containing 3 red and 4 white discs. If X is the r.v. 'the number of white discs drawn', construct a probability distribution table.
   Find   (a) $E(X)$,   (b) $E(X^2)$,   (c) $\text{Var}(X)$,
   (d) $\text{Var}(3X - 4)$.

6. For the following probability distribution find (a) $\mu = E(X)$,   (b) $E(X^2)$,   (c) $E(X - \mu)^2$.
   Verify that

   $$E(X - \mu)^2 = E(X^2) - \mu^2$$

x	-3	-2	1
$P(X = x)$	$\frac{1}{5}$	$\frac{3}{10}$	$\frac{1}{2}$

7. Ten identically shaped discs are in a bag; two of them are black, the rest white. Discs are drawn at random from the bag in turn and not replaced.

Let X be the number of discs drawn up to and including the first black one.

List the values of X and the associated theoretical probabilities.

Calculate the mean value of X and its standard deviation. What is the most likely value of X?

If instead each disc is replaced before the next is drawn, construct a similar list of values and point out the chief differences between the two lists.

8. The discrete r.v. X has p.d.f.

$$P(X = x) = k|x|$$

where x takes the values $-3, -2, -1, 0, 1, 2,$ 3. Find   (a) the value of the constant k, (b) $E(X)$,   (c) $E(X^2)$,   (d) the standard deviation of X.

9. The random variable X takes integer values only and has p.d.f.

$$P(X = x) = kx \qquad x = 1, 2, 3, 4, 5$$
$$P(X = x) = k(10 - x) \qquad x = 6, 7, 8, 9$$

Find   (a) the value of the constant k, (b) $E(X)$,   (c) $\mathrm{Var}(X)$,   (d) $E(2X - 3)$, (e) $\mathrm{Var}(2X - 3)$.

10. (a) In a game a player pays £5 to toss three fair coins. Depending on the number of tails he obtains he receives a sum of money as shown in the table below.

Number of tails	3	2	1	0
Sum received	£10	£6	£3	£1

Calculate the player's expected gain or loss over 12 games.

(b) A variable X has a probability distribution shown in the table below.

Value of X	1	2	5	10
Probability	0.5	0.3	p	q

Given that X can only take the values 1, 2, 5 or 10, and that $E(X) = 2.5$, calculate
(i) the value of p and of q,
(ii) the variance of X.

In a fairground game, a player rolls discs on to a board containing squares, each of which bears one of the numbers 1, 2, 5 or 10. If a disc falls entirely within a square, the player receives the same number of pence as the number in the square; if it does not, the player does not receive anything. The probability that a player will receive money from any given roll is $\frac{1}{4}$. If a player does receive money, the probabilities of receiving 1, 2, 5 or 10 pence are the same as those connected with the values of X above. How many discs should a player be allowed to roll for 5 p, if the game is to be fair?

(C Additional)

11. (a) A man takes part in a game in which he throws two fair dice and scores the sum of the two numbers shown. The rewards for the scores are given in the following table.

Score	12	10	7	5	Any other score
Reward (£)	16	6	3	5	0

Calculate the expected reward for a throw of the two dice.

(b) A bag contains five identical discs, two of which are marked with the letter A and three with the letter B. The discs are randomly drawn, one at a time without replacement, until both discs marked A are obtained. Show that the probability that 3 draws are required is $\frac{2}{10}$.

Given that X denotes the number of draws required to obtain both discs marked A, copy and complete the following table.

Value of X	2	3	4	5
Probability of X		$\frac{2}{10}$		

Evaluate   (i) $E(X)$,   (ii) $E(X^2)$, (iii) the variance of X.   (C Additional)

THE CUMULATIVE DISTRIBUTION FUNCTION

Given a frequency distribution, the corresponding cumulative frequencies are obtained by summing all the frequencies up to a particular value. In the same way, if X is a discrete random variable, the corresponding cumulative probabilities are obtained by summing all the probabilities up to a particular value.

> If X is a discrete random variable with p.d.f. $P(X = x)$ for $x = x_1$, $x_2, \ldots, x_n$, then the cumulative distribution function is given by $F(t)$ where
>
> $$F(t) = P(X \leqslant t)$$
>
> $$= \sum_{x=x_1}^{t} P(X = x) \qquad t = x_1, x_2, \ldots, x_n$$

The cumulative distribution function is sometimes known just as the **distribution function**.

Example 4.15 Find the cumulative distribution function for the r.v. X where X is 'the score on an unbiased die'.

Solution 4.15 The probability distribution for X is shown in the table:

x	1	2	3	4	5	6
$P(X = x)$	$\frac{1}{6}$	$\frac{1}{6}$	$\frac{1}{6}$	$\frac{1}{6}$	$\frac{1}{6}$	$\frac{1}{6}$

$$F(1) = P(X \leqslant 1) = \tfrac{1}{6}$$

$$F(2) = P(X \leqslant 2) = P(X = 1) + P(X = 2) = \tfrac{1}{6} + \tfrac{1}{6} = \tfrac{2}{6}$$

$$F(3) = P(X \leqslant 3) = \tfrac{3}{6}$$

$$F(4) = P(X \leqslant 4) = \tfrac{4}{6}$$

$$F(5) = P(X \leqslant 5) = \tfrac{5}{6}$$

$$F(6) = P(X \leqslant 6) = \tfrac{6}{6}$$

Therefore $F(t) = \frac{t}{6}$ for $t = 1, 2, 3, \ldots, 6$.

Although we work with the variable t, we write the final answer in terms of x, so

$$F(x) = \tfrac{x}{6}, \qquad x = 1, 2, \ldots, 6.$$

NOTE: $F(6) = \frac{6}{6} = 1$, as expected.

Example 4.16 The probability distribution for the r.v. X is shown in the table. Construct the cumulative distribution table.

x	0	1	2	3	4	5	6
$P(X = x)$	0.03	0.04	0.06	0.12	0.4	0.15	0.2

Solution 4.16 Now $$F(t) = \sum_{x=0}^{t} P(X = x) \qquad\qquad t = 0, 1, 2, \ldots, 6$$

So $$F(0) = P(X \leqslant 0) = 0.03$$

$$F(1) = P(X \leqslant 1) = 0.03 + 0.04 = 0.07$$

$$F(2) = P(X \leqslant 2) = 0.03 + 0.04 + 0.06 = 0.13$$

and so on.

The cumulative distribution table is:

x	0	1	2	3	4	5	6
$F(x)$	0.03	0.07	0.13	0.25	0.65	0.8	1

NOTE: it is not possible to write a formula for the cumulative distribution function in this example.

Example 4.17 For a discrete r.v. X the cumulative distribution function $F(x)$ is as shown:

x	1	2	3	4	5
$F(x)$	0.2	0.32	0.67	0.9	1

Find   (a) $P(X = 3)$,   (b) $P(X > 2)$.

Solution 4.17 (a) From the table,

$$F(3) = P(X \leqslant 3) = P(X = 1) + P(X = 2) + P(X = 3) = 0.67$$

$$F(2) = P(X \leqslant 2) = P(X = 1) + P(X = 2) = 0.32$$

Now $$P(X = 3) = F(3) - F(2)$$

Therefore $$P(X = 3) = 0.67 - 0.32$$

$$= 0.35$$

(b) $$P(X > 2) = 1 - P(X \leqslant 2)$$

$$= 1 - F(2)$$

$$= 1 - 0.32$$

$$= 0.68$$

So $P(X = 3) = 0.35$ and $P(X > 2) = 0.68$.

Exercise 4e

1. Construct the cumulative distribution tables for the following discrete random variables:
   (a) the number of sixes obtained when two ordinary dice are thrown,
   (b) the smaller number when two ordinary dice are thrown,
   (c) the number of heads when three fair coins are tossed.

2. The probability distribution for the r.v. Y is shown in the table:

y	0.1	0.2	0.3	0.4	0.5
$P(Y = y)$	0.05	0.25	0.3	0.15	0.25

   Construct the cumulative distribution table.

3. For a discrete r.v. R the cumulative distribution function $F(r)$ is as shown in the table:

r	1	2	3	4
$F(r)$	0.13	0.54	0.75	1

   Find (a) $P(R = 2)$, (b) $P(R > 1)$, (c) $P(R \geqslant 3)$, (d) $P(R < 2)$, (e) $E(R)$.

4. For the discrete r.v. X the cumulative distribution function $F(x)$ is as shown:

x	3	4	5	6	7
$F(x)$	0.01	0.23	0.64	0.86	1

   Construct the probability distribution of X, and find $Var(X)$.

5. For a discrete r.v. X the cumulative distribution function is given by $F(x) = \dfrac{x^2}{9}$ for $x = 1, 2, 3$. Find (a) $F(2)$, (b) $P(X = 2)$. (c) Write out the probability distribution of X. (d) Find $E(2X - 3)$.

6. For a discrete r.v. X the cumulative distribution function is given by $F(x) = kx$, $x = 1, 2, 3$. Find (a) the value of the constant k, (b) $P(X < 3)$, (c) the probability distribution of X, (d) the standard deviation of X.

7. The discrete r.v. X has distribution function $F(x)$ where
   $F(x) = 1 - \left(1 - \frac{1}{4}x\right)^x$ for $x = 1, 2, 3, 4$
   (a) Show that $F(3) = \frac{63}{64}$ and $F(2) = \frac{3}{4}$.
   (b) Obtain the probability distribution of X.
   (c) Find $E(X)$ and $Var(X)$.
   (d) Find $P(X > E(X))$.

TWO INDEPENDENT RANDOM VARIABLES

> If X and Y are any two random variables, then
> $$E(X + Y) = E(X) + E(Y)$$
> If X and Y are *independent* random variables, then
> $$Var(X + Y) = Var(X) + Var(Y)$$

Example 4.18 X is the r.v. 'the score on a tetrahedral die', Y is the r.v. 'the number of heads obtained when two coins are tossed'.

(a) Obtain the probability distributions of X and of Y.

(b) Find $E(X)$ and $E(Y)$.

(c) Find $Var(X)$ and $Var(Y)$.

(d) Obtain the probability distribution for the r.v. $X + Y$.

(e) Find $E(X + Y)$ and $Var(X + Y)$ using the probability distribution for $X + Y$. Comment on your results.

Solution 4.18 (a) The probability distributions are as follows:

x	1	2	3	4
$P(X = x)$	$\frac{1}{4}$	$\frac{1}{4}$	$\frac{1}{4}$	$\frac{1}{4}$

y	0	1	2
$P(Y = y)$	$\frac{1}{4}$	$\frac{1}{2}$	$\frac{1}{4}$

(b) By symmetry, $\underline{E(X) = 2\frac{1}{2}}$ $\underline{E(Y) = 1}$

(c)
$$E(X^2) = \sum_{\text{all } x} x^2 P(X = x)$$
$$= 1\left(\tfrac{1}{4}\right) + 4\left(\tfrac{1}{4}\right)$$
$$+ 9\left(\tfrac{1}{4}\right) + 16\left(\tfrac{1}{4}\right)$$
$$= 7\tfrac{1}{2}$$

$$\text{Var}(X) = E(X^2) - E^2(X)$$
$$= 7\tfrac{1}{2} - 6\tfrac{1}{4}$$
$$= 1\tfrac{1}{4}$$
$$\underline{\text{So Var}(X) = 1\tfrac{1}{4}.}$$

$$E(Y^2) = \sum_{\text{all } y} y^2 P(Y = y)$$
$$= 0\left(\tfrac{1}{4}\right) + 1\left(\tfrac{1}{2}\right)$$
$$+ 4\left(\tfrac{1}{4}\right)$$
$$= 1\tfrac{1}{2}$$

$$\text{Var}(Y) = E(Y^2) - E^2(Y)$$
$$= 1\tfrac{1}{2} - 1$$
$$= \tfrac{1}{2}$$
$$\underline{\text{Var}(Y) = \tfrac{1}{2}.}$$

(d) Consider the r.v. $X + Y$, which can take values 1, 2, 3, 4, 5 and 6.

$$P(X + Y = 1) = P(1 \text{ on die, } 0 \text{ heads}) = \left(\tfrac{1}{4}\right)\left(\tfrac{1}{4}\right) = \tfrac{1}{16}$$

$$P(X + Y = 2) = P(2 \text{ on die, } 0 \text{ heads}) + P(1 \text{ on die, } 1 \text{ head})$$
$$= \left(\tfrac{1}{4}\right)\left(\tfrac{1}{4}\right) + \left(\tfrac{1}{4}\right)\left(\tfrac{1}{2}\right) = \tfrac{3}{16}$$

$$P(X + Y = 3) = P(3 \text{ on die, } 0 \text{ heads}) + P(2 \text{ on die, } 1 \text{ head})$$
$$+ P(1 \text{ on die, } 2 \text{ heads})$$
$$= \left(\tfrac{1}{4}\right)\left(\tfrac{1}{4}\right) + \left(\tfrac{1}{4}\right)\left(\tfrac{1}{2}\right) + \left(\tfrac{1}{4}\right)\left(\tfrac{1}{4}\right) = \tfrac{4}{16}$$

$$P(X + Y = 4) = P(4 \text{ on die, } 0 \text{ heads}) + P(3 \text{ on die, } 1 \text{ head})$$
$$+ P(2 \text{ on die, } 2 \text{ heads})$$
$$= \left(\tfrac{1}{4}\right)\left(\tfrac{1}{4}\right) + \left(\tfrac{1}{4}\right)\left(\tfrac{1}{2}\right) + \left(\tfrac{1}{4}\right)\left(\tfrac{1}{4}\right)$$
$$= \tfrac{4}{16}$$

$$P(X + Y = 5) = P(4 \text{ on die, } 1 \text{ head}) + P(3 \text{ on die, } 2 \text{ heads})$$
$$= \left(\tfrac{1}{4}\right)\left(\tfrac{1}{2}\right) + \left(\tfrac{1}{4}\right)\left(\tfrac{1}{4}\right)$$
$$= \tfrac{3}{16}$$

$$P(X + Y = 6) = P(4 \text{ on die, } 2 \text{ heads})$$
$$= \left(\tfrac{1}{4}\right)\left(\tfrac{1}{4}\right)$$
$$= \tfrac{1}{16}$$

The probability distribution is as follows:

$x + y$	1	2	3	4	5	6
$P(X + Y = x + y)$	$\frac{1}{16}$	$\frac{3}{16}$	$\frac{4}{16}$	$\frac{4}{16}$	$\frac{3}{16}$	$\frac{1}{16}$

(e) By symmetry $\qquad E(X + Y) = 3\frac{1}{2}$

But from (b) $\qquad E(X) + E(Y) = 2\frac{1}{2} + 1 = 3\frac{1}{2}$

Therefore $\qquad \underline{E(X + Y) = E(X) + E(Y)}.$

Now

$$\text{Var}(X + Y) = E[(X + Y)^2] - E^2(X + Y)$$

$$E[(X + Y)^2] = 1\left(\frac{1}{16}\right) + 4\left(\frac{3}{16}\right) + 9\left(\frac{4}{16}\right) + 16\left(\frac{4}{16}\right) + 25\left(\frac{3}{16}\right) + 36\left(\frac{1}{16}\right)$$

$$= \frac{224}{16}$$

$$= 14$$

$$\text{Var}(X + Y) = 14 - \left(3\frac{1}{2}\right)^2$$

$$= 1\frac{3}{4}$$

Therefore $\underline{\text{Var}(X + Y) = 1\frac{3}{4}}.$

Now $\quad \text{Var}(X) + \text{Var}(Y) = 1\frac{1}{4} + 1\frac{1}{2} = 1\frac{3}{4}.$

So $\underline{\text{Var}(X + Y) = \text{Var}(X) + \text{Var}(Y)}.$

In this example, the variables X and Y are independent.

> In general, for random variables X and Y and constants a and b,
>
> $$E(aX + bY) = aE(X) + bE(Y)$$
>
> If X and Y are *independent*, then
>
> $$\text{Var}(aX + bY) = a^2\text{Var}(X) + b^2\text{Var}(Y)$$

Example 4.19 X and Y are independent discrete random variables such that $E(X) = 10$, $\text{Var}(X) = 2$, $E(Y) = 8$, $\text{Var}(Y) = 3$.

Find (a) $E(5X + 4Y)$, (b) $\text{Var}(5X + 4Y)$, (c) $\text{Var}\left(\frac{1}{2}X + Y\right)$.

Solution 4.19 (a) $\qquad\qquad E(5X + 4Y) = 5E(X) + 4E(Y)$

$$= 5(10) + 4(8)$$

$$= \underline{82}.$$

(b) $\qquad\qquad \text{Var}(5X + 4Y) = 25\text{Var}(X) + 16\text{Var}(Y)$

$$= 25(2) + 16(3)$$

$$= \underline{98}.$$

(c)
$$\text{Var}\left(\tfrac{1}{2}X + Y\right) = \tfrac{1}{4}\text{Var}(X) + \text{Var}(Y)$$
$$= \tfrac{1}{4}(2) + 3$$
$$= \underline{3.5.}$$

An important application of the general results occurs when the constant b is negative. For example, if $a = 1$ and $b = -1$,

$$aX + bY = X + (-1)Y = X - Y$$

So
$$E(X - Y) = E(X + (-1)Y)$$
$$= E(X) + (-1)E(Y)$$
$$= E(X) - E(Y)$$

$$\text{Var}(X - Y) = \text{Var}(X + (-1)Y)$$
$$= 1^2\text{Var}(X) + (-1)^2\text{Var}(Y)$$
$$= \text{Var}(X) + \text{Var}(Y)$$

> Remember that, for X and Y *independent,*
> $$E(X - Y) = E(X) - E(Y)$$
> $$\text{Var}(X - Y) = \text{Var}(X) + \text{Var}(Y)$$
> Also note that
> $$E(aX - bY) = aE(X) - bE(Y)$$
> $$\text{Var}(aX - bY) = a^2\text{Var}(X) + b^2\text{Var}(Y)$$

Example 4.20 The random variables X and Y are independent and $E(X) = 2$, $\text{Var}(X) = 0.5$, $E(Y) = 5$, $\text{Var}(Y) = 2$.

Find **(a)** $E(4X - 3Y)$, **(b)** $\text{Var}(4X - 3Y)$.

Solution 4.20 **(a)**
$$E(4X - 3Y) = 4E(X) - 3E(Y)$$
$$= 4(2) - 3(5)$$
$$= \underline{-7.}$$

(b)
$$\text{Var}(4X - 3Y) = 4^2\text{Var}(X) + 3^2\text{Var}(Y)$$
$$= 16\text{Var}(X) + 9\text{Var}(Y)$$
$$= 16(0.5) + 9(2)$$
$$= \underline{26.}$$

Example 4.21 The table gives the joint probability distribution of two random variables X and Y:

	$X = 0$	$X = 1$
$Y = 1$	0.2	0.4
$Y = 2$	0.3	0.1

Calculate (**a**) $E(X)$, (**b**) $E(Y)$, (**c**) $E(X + Y)$.

Solution 4.21 Consider the r.v. X

$$P(X = 0) = P(X = 0)P(Y = 1) + P(X = 0)P(Y = 2)$$

$$= 0.2 + 0.3$$

$$= 0.5$$

$$P(X = 1) = P(X = 1)P(Y = 1) + P(X = 1)P(Y = 2)$$

$$= 0.4 + 0.1$$

$$= 0.5$$

The probability distribution for X is

x	0	1
$P(X = x)$	0.5	0.5

By symmetry $E(X) = \frac{1}{2}$.

Consider the r.v. Y

$$P(Y = 1) = P(Y = 1)P(X = 0) + P(Y = 1)P(X = 1)$$

$$= 0.2 + 0.4$$

$$= 0.6$$

$$P(Y = 2) = P(Y = 2)P(X = 0) + P(Y = 2)P(X = 1)$$

$$= 0.3 + 0.1$$

$$= 0.4$$

The probability distribution for Y is

y	1	2
$P(Y = y)$	0.6	0.4

$$E(Y) = \sum_{\text{all } y} yP(Y = y)$$

$$= 1(0.6) + 2(0.4)$$

$$= 1.4$$

Therefore $E(Y) = 1.4$.

Now $\quad E(X+Y) = E(X) + E(Y)$

$$= 0.5 + 1.4$$

$$= 1.9$$

Therefore $E(X+Y) = 1.9$.

THE DISTRIBUTION OF $X_1 + X_2$

We now consider the distribution of $X_1 + X_2$, where X_1, X_2 are two independent observations *from the same distribution X*.

Now $\qquad\qquad E(X_1 + X_2) = E(X_1) + E(X_2)$

$$= E(X) + E(X)$$

$$= 2E(X)$$

and $\qquad\qquad \text{Var}(X_1 + X_2) = \text{Var}(X_1) + \text{Var}(X_2)$

$$= \text{Var}(X) + \text{Var}(X)$$

$$= 2\text{Var}(X)$$

For the distribution $X_1 + X_2$, where X_1 and X_2 are *independent* observations from the distribution X

$$E(X_1 + X_2) = 2E(X)$$

$$\text{Var}(X_1 + X_2) = 2\text{Var}(X)$$

For n independent observations

$$E(X_1 + X_2 + \ldots + X_n) = nE(X)$$

$$\text{Var}(X_1 + X_2 + \ldots + X_n) = n\text{Var}(X)$$

Example 4.22 The random variable X is such that $E(X) = 2.9$, and the standard deviation of X is 0.7. Its p.d.f. is as shown:

x	2	3	4
$P(X = x)$	0.3	0.5	0.2

Two independent observations are made from X. Construct the probability distribution for $X_1 + X_2$ and find the expectation and variance. Verify that $E(X_1 + X_2) = 2E(X)$ and $\text{Var}(X_1 + X_2) = 2\text{Var}(X)$.

Solution 4.22 Consider the distribution of $X_1 + X_2$. To show the possible outcomes it is useful to draw a probability tree.

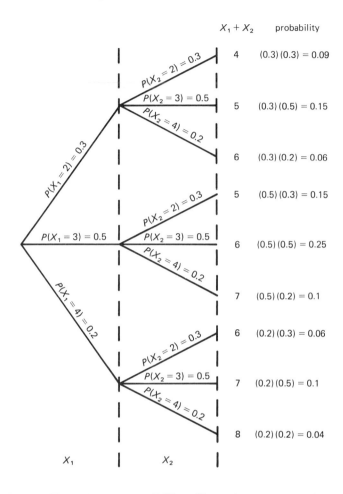

Now $P(X_1 + X_2 = 4) = 0.09$, $P(X_1 + X_2 = 5) = 0.15 + 0.15 = 0.3$, and so on. We see that $X_1 + X_2$ can take values 4, 5, 6, 7, 8 where

$x_1 + x_2$	4	5	6	7	8
$P(X_1 + X_2 = x_1 + x_2)$	0.09	0.3	0.37	0.2	0.04

$$E(X_1 + X_2) = 4(0.09) + 5(0.3) + 6(0.37) + 7(0.2) + 8(0.04)$$

$$= 5.8$$

$$\text{Var}(X_1 + X_2) = 16(0.09) + 25(0.3) + 36(0.37) + 49(0.2)$$

$$+ 64(0.04) - 5.8^2$$

$$= 0.98$$

Therefore $E(X_1 + X_2) = 5.8$ and $\text{Var}(X_1 + X_2) = 0.98$.

Now $\quad E(X_1 + X_2) = 5.8$ $\qquad\qquad\qquad$ $\mathrm{Var}(X_1 + X_2) = 0.98$

and $\qquad\quad 2E(X) = 2(2.9)$ $\qquad\qquad\qquad$ $2\mathrm{Var}(X) = 2(0.7)^2$

$\qquad\qquad\qquad = 5.8$ $\qquad\qquad\qquad\qquad\qquad = 0.98$

Therefore $\qquad\qquad\qquad\qquad\qquad$ Therefore

$\qquad E(X_1 + X_2) = 2E(X).$ $\qquad\qquad \underline{\mathrm{Var}(X_1 + X_2) = 2\mathrm{Var}(X).}$

Example 4.23 Find the expectation and variance of the number of heads obtained when 6 coins are tossed.

Solution 4.23 Let X be the r.v. 'the number of heads when a coin is tossed'. Then X can take the values 0, 1.

x	0	1
$P(X = x)$	0.5	0.5

Now $\qquad\qquad\qquad E(X) = 0.5 \qquad$ (by symmetry)

$\qquad\qquad\qquad E(X^2) = 1(0.5) = 0.5$

so $\qquad\qquad\qquad \mathrm{Var}(X) = E(X^2) - E^2(X)$

$\qquad\qquad\qquad\qquad\qquad = 0.5 - 0.5^2$

$\qquad\qquad\qquad\qquad\qquad = 0.25$

Now consider $\ Y = X_1 + X_2 + \ldots + X_6\ $ where Y is the r.v. 'the number of heads when 6 coins are tossed'.

$E(Y) = 6E(X)$ $\qquad\qquad\qquad$ $\mathrm{Var}(Y) = 6\mathrm{Var}(X)$

$\qquad = 6(0.5)$ $\qquad\qquad\qquad\qquad\qquad = 6(0.25)$

$\qquad = 3$ $\qquad\qquad\qquad\qquad\qquad\qquad = 1.5$

So the expected number of heads is 3, and the variance is 1.5.

Example 4.24 A random variable X has p.d.f. $\ P(X = x) = kx\ $ for $\ x = 1, 2, 3, 4$. Two independent observations of X are made. Let these values be X_1 and X_2.
Find $\quad$ (**a**) $P(X_1 = X_2)$, $\quad$ (**b**) $P(X_1 > X_2)$, $\quad$ (**c**) $P(X_1 = X_2 = 4 \,|\, X_1 = X_2)$.

Solution 4.24

x	1	2	3	4
$P(X = x)$	k	$2k$	$3k$	$4k$

Now $\qquad\qquad\qquad\qquad \displaystyle\sum_{all\ x} P(X = x) = 1$

so $\qquad\qquad\qquad\quad k + 2k + 3k + 4k = 1$

$\qquad\qquad\qquad\qquad\qquad\qquad 10k = 1$

$\qquad\qquad\qquad\qquad\qquad\qquad k = 0.1$

(**a**) $P(X_1 = X_2) = P((X_1 = 1) \cap (X_2 = 1)) + P((X_1 = 2) \cap (X_2 = 2))$
$\qquad\qquad\quad + P((X_1 = 3) \cap (X_2 = 3)) + P((X_1 = 4) \cap (X_2 = 4))$
$\qquad\qquad = (k)(k) + (2k)(2k) + (3k)(3k) + (4k)(4k)$
$\qquad\qquad = k^2 + 4k^2 + 9k^2 + 16k^2$
$\qquad\qquad = 30k^2$
$\qquad\qquad = 30(0.1)^2$
$\qquad\qquad = 0.3$

Therefore $P(X_1 = X_2) = 0.3$.

(**b**) $P(X_1 > X_2) = P((X_1 = 2) \cap (X_2 = 1)) + P((X_1 = 3) \cap (X_2 = 1 \text{ or } 2))$
$\qquad\qquad\quad + P((X_1 = 4) \cap (X_2 = 1, 2 \text{ or } 3))$
$\qquad\qquad = (2k)(k) + (3k)(k + 2k) + 4k(k + 2k + 3k)$
$\qquad\qquad = 2k^2 + 9k^2 + 24k^2$
$\qquad\qquad = 35k^2$
$\qquad\qquad = 35(0.1)^2$
$\qquad\qquad = 0.35$

Therefore $P(X_1 > X_2) = 0.35$.

(**c**) $P((X_1 = X_2 = 4) \,|\, (X_1 = X_2)) = \dfrac{P((X_1 = 4) \cap (X_2 = 4))}{P(X_1 = X_2)}$
$\qquad\qquad\qquad\qquad\qquad\quad = \dfrac{16k^2}{30k^2}$
$\qquad\qquad\qquad\qquad\qquad\quad = \dfrac{8}{15}$

Therefore $P((X_1 = X_2 = 4) \,|\, (X_1 = X_2)) = \dfrac{8}{15}$.

COMPARING THE DISTRIBUTIONS OF $2X$ AND $X_1 + X_2$

Confusion often arises over the different random variables $2X$ and $X_1 + X_2$, where X_1, X_2 are two independent observations of X. We will see from the following example that the distributions of the two random variables are very different.

Example 4.25 When a tetrahedral die is thrown, the number on the face on which it lands, X, has probability distribution:

x	1	2	3	4
$P(X = x)$	0.25	0.25	0.25	0.25

$E(X) = 2.5$ and $Var(X) = 1.25$.

(a) Find the p.d.f. of D, the r.v. 'double the number on which the die lands', where $D = 2X$, and find $E(D)$ and Var(D).

(b) Find the p.d.f. of S, the r.v. 'the sum of the two numbers when the die is thrown twice', where $S = X_1 + X_2$, and find $E(S)$ and Var(S).

Solution 4.25 (a) The probability distribution of D, 'double the number on which the die lands', where $D = 2X$ is as shown:

d	2	4	6	8
$P(D = d)$	0.25	0.25	0.25	0.25

By symmetry, $E(D) = 5$.

$$\text{Var}(D) = E(D^2) - E^2(D)$$
$$= \sum_{\text{all } d} d^2 P(D = d) - 25$$
$$= 0.25(4 + 16 + 36 + 64) - 25$$
$$= 5$$

Therefore $E(D) = 5$ and Var(D) = 5, where $D = 2X$.

NOTE:
$E(2X) = 5$	$\text{Var}(2X) = 5$
$2E(X) = 2(2.5) = 5$	$4\text{Var}(X) = 4(1.25) = 5$
So $E(2X) = 2E(X)$.	So Var($2X$) = 4Var(X).

(b) Consider the r.v. S where S is the sum of the two numbers on which the die lands when it is thrown twice. Therefore $S = X_1 + X_2$.

Now S can take the values 2, 3, 4, 5, 6, 7, 8 and the outcomes (all equally likely) are shown in the diagram:

The probability distribution for S is:

s	2	3	4	5	6	7	8
$P(S = s)$	$\frac{1}{16}$	$\frac{2}{16}$	$\frac{3}{16}$	$\frac{4}{16}$	$\frac{3}{16}$	$\frac{2}{16}$	$\frac{1}{16}$

By symmetry, $E(S) = 5$.

$$\text{Var}(S) = E(S^2) - E^2(S)$$

$$= \sum_{\text{all } s} s^2 P(S = s) - 25$$

$$= \tfrac{1}{16}[4(1) + 9(2) + 16(3) + 25(4) + 36(3) + 49(2) + 64(1)] - 25$$

$$= 2.5$$

Therefore $E(S) = 5$, $\text{Var}(S) = 2.5$, where $S = X_1 + X_2$.

NOTE:

$E(X_1 + X_2) = 5$	$\text{Var}(X_1 + X_2) = 2.5$
$2E(X) = 2(2.5) = 5$	$2\text{Var}(X) = 2(1.25) = 2.5$
So $E(X_1 + X_2) = 2E(X)$.	So $\text{Var}(X_1 + X_2) = 2\text{Var}(X)$.

We can see that the distribution for D, double the number on which the die lands, is very different from the distribution for S, the sum of the numbers on which the die lands when it is thrown twice.

Double the number on one die:

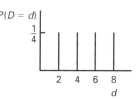

d	2	4	6	8
$P(D = d)$	$\frac{1}{4}$	$\frac{1}{4}$	$\frac{1}{4}$	$\frac{1}{4}$

The sum of the numbers when the die is thrown twice:

s	2	3	4	5	6	7	8
$P(S = s)$	$\frac{1}{16}$	$\frac{2}{16}$	$\frac{3}{16}$	$\frac{4}{16}$	$\frac{3}{16}$	$\frac{2}{16}$	$\frac{1}{16}$

Although the means of the two distributions are the same, the variances are not, with the r.v. 'double the number' having the greater variance.

Summarising, we have

MULTIPLES	SUMS
$E(2X) = 2E(X)$	$E(X_1 + X_2) = 2E(X)$
$\text{Var}(2X) = 4\text{Var}(X)$	$\text{Var}(X_1 + X_2) = 2\text{Var}(X)$
In general	
$E(nX) = nE(X)$	$E(X_1 + X_2 + \ldots + X_n) = nE(X)$
$\text{Var}(nX) = n^2\text{Var}(X)$	$\text{Var}(X_1 + X_2 + \ldots + X_n) = n\text{Var}(X)$

It is important that you understand whether multiples or sums are being considered. Think carefully about this point.

Exercise 4f

1. Independent random variables X and Y have probability distributions as shown in the tables:

x	0	1	2	3
$P(X = x)$	0.3	0.2	0.4	0.1

y	0	1	2
$P(Y = y)$	0.4	0.2	0.4

(a) Find $E(X)$, $E(Y)$, $\text{Var}(X)$, $\text{Var}(Y)$.
(b) Construct the probability distribution for the r.v. $X + Y$.
(c) Verify that $E(X + Y) = E(X) + E(Y)$.
(d) Verify that
$\text{Var}(X + Y) = \text{Var}(X) + \text{Var}(Y)$.
(e) Construct the probability distribution for the r.v. $X - Y$.
(f) Verify that $E(X - Y) = E(X) - E(Y)$.
(g) Verify that
$\text{Var}(X - Y) = \text{Var}(X) + \text{Var}(Y)$.

2. Independent random variables X and Y are such that $E(X) = 4$, $E(Y) = 5$, $\text{Var}(X) = 1$, $\text{Var}(Y) = 2$. Find
(a) $E(4X + 2Y)$, (b) $E(5X - Y)$,
(c) $\text{Var}(3X + 2Y)$, (d) $\text{Var}(5Y - 3X)$,
(e) $\text{Var}(3X - 5Y)$.

	$Y = 0$	$Y = 1$	$Y = 2$
$X = 1$	$\frac{1}{12}$	$\frac{1}{6}$	$\frac{1}{12}$
$X = 2$	$\frac{1}{6}$	$\frac{1}{3}$	$\frac{1}{6}$

The above table gives the joint probability distribution of two random variables X and Y. Calculate (a) $P(Y = 1)$, (b) $P(XY = 2)$, (c) $E(X + Y)$. (L Additional)

4. Independent random variables X and Y are such that $E(X^2) = 14$, $E(Y^2) = 20$, $\text{Var}(X) = 10$, $\text{Var}(Y) = 11$. Find
(a) $E(3X - 2Y)$, (b) $\text{Var}(5X + 2Y)$.

5. Independent random variables X and Y are such that $E(X) = 3$, $E(X^2) = 12$, $E(Y) = 4$, $E(Y^2) = 18$. Find the value of
(a) $E(3X - 2Y)$, (b) $E(2Y - 3X)$,
(c) $E(6X + 4Y)$, (d) $\text{Var}(2X - Y)$,
(e) $\text{Var}(2X + Y)$, (f) $\text{Var}(3Y + 2X)$.

6. Two ordinary dice are thrown, a red and a green die. Let R be the r.v. 'the score on the red die' and let G be the r.v. 'the score on the green die'.
(a) Construct the probability distribution for $R + G$, the r.v. 'the sum of the two scores', and find (i) $E(R + G)$, (ii) $\text{Var}(R + G)$.
(b) Construct the probability distribution for $R - G$ and find (i) $E(R - G)$, (ii) $\text{Var}(R - G)$.
(c) Given that $E(R) = 3.5$ and $\text{Var}(R) = \frac{35}{12}$, comment on your answers.

7. X has probability distribution as shown:

x	0	1	2
$P(X = x)$	0.1	0.6	0.3

(a) Find $E(X)$ and $\text{Var}(X)$.
(b) Find $P(X_1 + X_2 = 4)$ where X_1, X_2 are two independent observations of X.
(c) Find $E(X_1 + X_2)$ and $\text{Var}(X_1 + X_2)$.
(d) Find $P(2X = 4)$.
(e) Find $E(2X)$ and $\text{Var}(2X)$.

8. Rods of length 2 m or 3 m are selected at random with probabilities 0.4 and 0.6 respectively.
(a) Find the expectation and variance of the length of a rod.
(b) Two lengths are now selected at random. Find the expectation and variance of the sum of the two lengths.
(c) Three lengths are now selected at random. Show that the probability distribution of Y, the sum of the three lengths, is:

y	6	7	8	9
$P(Y = y)$	0.064	0.288	0.432	0.216

and find $E(Y)$ and $\text{Var}(Y)$. Comment on your results.

9. Find the variance of the sum of the scores when an ordinary die is thrown 10 times.

10. X has a p.d.f. given by $P(X = x) = kx$, $x = 1, 2, 3, 4$. Find (a) k, (b) $E(X)$,
(c) $\text{Var}(X)$, (d) $P(X_1 + X_2 = 5)$, (e) $E(4X)$,
(f) $\text{Var}(X_1 + X_2 + X_3)$.

SUMMARY — DISCRETE RANDOM VARIABLES

For the discrete random variable X with probability density function $P(X = x)$ for $x = x_1, x_2, \ldots, x_n$,

(1)	$\displaystyle\sum_{\text{all } x} P(X = x) = 1$	
(2)	$\displaystyle F(t) = \sum_{x=x_1}^{t} t\, P(X = x)$	where $F(t)$ is the cumulative distribution function
(3)	$\displaystyle \mu = E(X) = \sum_{\text{all } x} xP(X = x)$	where μ is the expectation of X
(4)	$\mathrm{Var}(X) = E(X^2) - E^2(X)$ $\displaystyle \qquad = \sum_{\text{all } x} x^2 P(X = x) - \mu^2$	

For the random variable X and constants a and b,

$E(a) = a$	$\mathrm{Var}(a) = 0$
$E(aX) = aE(X)$	$\mathrm{Var}(aX) = a^2\mathrm{Var}(X)$
$E(aX + b) = aE(X) + b$	$\mathrm{Var}(aX + b) = a^2\mathrm{Var}(X)$

For any two random variables X and Y and constants a and b,

$E(X + Y) = E(X) + E(Y)$

$E(X - Y) = E(X) - E(Y)$

$E(aX + bY) = aE(X) + bE(Y)$

$E(aX - bY) = aE(X) - bE(Y)$

For independent random variables X and Y and constants a and b,

$\mathrm{Var}(X + Y) = \mathrm{Var}(X) + \mathrm{Var}(Y)$

$\mathrm{Var}(X - Y) = \mathrm{Var}(X) + \mathrm{Var}(Y)$

$\mathrm{Var}(aX + bY) = a^2\mathrm{Var}(X) + b^2\mathrm{Var}(Y)$

$\mathrm{Var}(aX - bY) = a^2\mathrm{Var}(X) + b^2\mathrm{Var}(Y)$

If $X_1, X_2, \ldots, X_n$ are n independent observations of the r.v. X then,

$E(X_1 + X_2 + \ldots + X_n) = nE(X)$

$\mathrm{Var}(X_1 + X_2 + \ldots + X_n) = n\mathrm{Var}(X)$

Miscellaneous Exercise 4g

1. Two tetrahedral dice are thrown and the score is the product of the numbers on which the dice fall. What is the expected score for a throw?

2. A woman removes the labels from three tins of peaches and a tin of baked beans in order to enter a competition and then puts the tins in a cupboard. She discovers that the tins are outwardly identical. Let X be the number of tins she now needs to open in order to have baked beans. List the values that X can take and determine the probabilities for each of these values of X. Calculate the expected value of X.
    Her neighbour has five tins of peaches and two tins of baked beans, again outwardly identical once the labels are removed. This woman removes the labels and puts the tins away. Find the probability that this woman later requires to open at least three tins to have baked beans.

3. On a long train journey, a statistician is invited by a gambler to play a dice game. The game uses two ordinary dice which the statistician is to throw. If the total score is 12, the statistician is paid £6 by the gambler. If the total score is 8, the statistician is paid £3 by the gambler. However if both or either dice show a 1, the statistician pays the gambler £2. Let £X be the amount paid to the statistician by the gambler after the dice are thrown once.
    Determine the probability that (a) $X = 6$, (b) $X = 3$,   (c) $X = -2$.
    Find the expected value of X and show that, if the statistician played the game 100 times, his expected loss would be £2.78, to the nearest penny.
    Find the amount, £a, that the £6 would have to be changed to in order to make the game unbiased.

4. A box contains nine numbered balls. Three balls are numbered 3, four balls are numbered 4 and two balls are numbered 5. Each trial of an experiment consists of drawing two balls without replacement and recording the sum of the numbers on them, which is denoted by X. Show that the probability that $X = 10$ is $\frac{1}{36}$, and find the probabilities of all other possible values of X. Use your results to show that the mean of X is $\frac{70}{9}$, and find the standard deviation of X. Two trials are made. (The two balls in the first trial are replaced in the box before the

    second trial.) Find the probability that the second value of X is greater than or equal to the first value of X.   (MEI)

5. A man stakes £2 to play a game in which he rolls an ordinary (fair) die. If he scores 1 or 2 he wins £3 (plus his stake) and loses his stake if he scores 3, 4 or 5. If he scores a six he may roll the die once again, winning if he scores 1, 2 or 6, losing if he scores 3, 4 or 5. Find   (a) the probability that the man wins the game by rolling   (i) once,   (ii) twice;
    (b) his expected gain,
    (c) the expected number of times he will roll the die.
    If the rules are changed so that the winning scores are 1 and 2 but that every time he scores 6 he may roll the die again, find
    (d) the probability that he wins on his rth roll of the die,
    (e) the probability that he wins the game.

6. A and B each roll a fair die simultaneously. Construct a table for the difference in their scores showing the associated probabilities. Calculate the mean of the distribution. If the difference in scores is 1 or 2, A wins; if it is 3, 4 or 5, B wins and if it is zero, they roll their dice again. The game ends when one of the players has won. Calculate the probability that A wins on (a) the first,   (b) the second, (c) the rth roll. What is the probability that A wins?
    If B stakes £1 what should A stake for the game to be fair?

7. A gambler has 4 packs of cards, each of which is well shuffled and has equal numbers of red, green and blue cards. For each turn he pays £2 and draws a card from each pack. He wins £3 if he gets 2 red cards, £5 if he gets 3 red cards and £10 if he gets 4 red cards.
    (a) What are the probabilities of his drawing 0, 1, 2, 3, 4 red cards?
    (b) What is the expectation of his winnings (to the nearest 10 p)?

8. During winter a family requests 4 bottles of milk every day, and these are left on the door-step. Three of the bottles have silver tops and the fourth has a gold top. A thirsty blue-tit attempts to remove the tops from these bottles. The probability distribution of X, the number of silver tops removed by the blue-tit, is the same each day and is given by

    $$P(X = 0) = \tfrac{5}{15}, \qquad P(X = 1) = \tfrac{6}{15},$$
    $$P(X = 2) = \tfrac{3}{15}, \qquad P(X = 3) = \tfrac{1}{15}$$

The blue-tit finds the gold top particularly attractive, and the probability that this top is removed is $\frac{3}{5}$, independent of the number of silver tops removed. Determine the expectation and variance of

(a) the number of silver tops removed in a day,

(b) the number of gold tops removed in a day,

(c) the total number of tops (silver and gold) removed in 7 days.

Find also the probability distribution of the total number of tops (silver and gold) removed in a day. (C)

9. The probability of there being X unusable matches in a full box of Surelite matches is given by $P(X = 0) = 8k$, $P(X = 1) = 5k$, $P(X = 2) = P(X = 3) = k$, $P(X \geqslant 4) = 0$. Determine the constant k and the expectation and variance of X.

Two full boxes of Surelite matches are chosen at random and the total number Y of unusable matches is determined. Calculate $P(Y > 4)$, and state the values of the expectation and variance of Y. (C)

10. A player throws a die whose faces are numbered 1 to 6 inclusive. If the player obtains a six he throws the die a second time, and in this case his score is the sum of 6 and the second number; otherwise his score is the number obtained. The player has no more than two throws.

Let X be the random variable denoting the player's score. Write down the probability distribution of X, and determine the mean of X.

Show that the probability that the sum of two successive scores is 8 or more is $\frac{17}{36}$.

Determine the probability that the first of two successive scores is 7 or more, given that their sum is 8 or more. (C)

11. The faces of an ordinary die are renumbered so that the faces are 1, 2, 2, 3, 3 and 3. This die and an ordinary, unaltered die are thrown at the same time. The score, X, is the sum of the numbers on the uppermost faces of the two dice. Show that the probability of X being 3 is $\frac{1}{12}$ and of being 4 is $\frac{1}{6}$.

List the values that X can take and determine their respective probabilities. Hence obtain the expected value of X, correct to 3 decimal places.

If the dice are thrown 3 times, determine the probability, correct to 3 significant figures, that none of the three values of X exceeds 3.

12. Alan and his younger brother Bill play a game each day. Alan throws three darts at a dartboard and for each dart that scores a bull (which happens with probability p) Bill gives him a penny, while for each dart which misses the bull (which happens with probability $1 - p$) Alan gives Bill two pence. By considering all possible outcomes for the three throws, or otherwise, find the distribution of the number of pence (positive or negative) that Bill receives each day. Show that, when $p = \frac{1}{3}$, the mean is 3 and the variance 6.

The game takes place on 150 days. What is the mean and standard deviation of Bill's total winnings when $p = \frac{1}{3}$? (O)

13. In a certain field, each puffball which is growing in one year gives rise to a number, X, of new puffballs in the following year. None of the original puffballs is present in the following year. The probability distribution of the random variable X is as follows:

$P(X = 0) = P(X = 2) = 0.3$,

$P(X = 1) = 0.4$.

Find the probability distribution of Y, the number of puffballs resulting from there being two puffballs in the previous year, and show that the variance of Y is 1.2.

Hence, or otherwise, determine the probability distribution of the number, Z, of puffballs present in year 3, given that there was a single puffball present in year 1. Find also the mean and variance of Z. (C)

14. A discrete random variable X can take only the values 0, 1, 2 or 3, and its probability distribution is given by $P(X = 0) = k$, $P(X = 1) = 3k$, $P(X = 2) = 4k$, $P(X = 3) = 5k$, where k is a constant. Find

(a) the value of k,

(b) the mean and variance of X. (JMB)

15. A random variable R takes the integer value r with probability $P(r)$ where

$P(r) = kr^3$, $r = 1, 2, 3, 4$,

$P(r) = 0$, otherwise

Find

(a) the value of k, and display the distribution on graph paper,

(b) the mean and the variance of the distribution,

(c) the mean and the variance of $5R - 3$. (L)P

16. A gambling machine works in the following way. The player inserts a penny into one of five slots, which are coloured Blue, Red, Orange, Yellow and Green corresponding to five coloured light bulbs. The player can choose whichever coloured slot he likes. After the penny has been inserted one of the five bulbs lights up. If the bulb lit up is the same

colour as the slot selected by the player, then the player wins and receives from the machine R pennies, where

$$P(R = 2) = \tfrac{1}{2}, \qquad P(R = 4) = \tfrac{1}{4}$$

$$P(R = 6) = \tfrac{3}{20}, \qquad \text{and}$$

$$P(R = 8) = P(R = 10) = \tfrac{1}{20}$$

If the colour of the bulb lit up and the slot selected are not the same, the player receives nothing from the machine. In either case the player does not get back the penny that he inserted. Assuming that each of the colours is equally likely to light up, and that the machine selects the bulbs at random, determine

(a) the probability that the player receives nothing from the machine,

(b) the expected value of the amount gained by the player from a single try,

(c) the variance of the amount gained by the player from a single try.   (C)

17. Four rods of lengths 1, 2, 3 and 4 units are placed in a bag from which one rod is selected at random. The probability of selecting a rod of length l is kl. Find the value of k.

Show that the expected value of X, the length of the selected rod, is 3 units and find the variance of X.

After a rod has been selected it is not replaced. The probabilities of selection for each of the three rods that remain are in the same ratio as they were before the first selection. A second rod is now selected from the bag. Defining Y to be the length of this rod and writing $P_1 = P(Y = 1 \mid X = 2)$, $P_2 = P(Y = 2 \mid X = 1)$ show that $16P_1 = 9P_2$. Show also that $P(X + Y = 3) = \tfrac{17}{360}$.   (C)

18. A game is played in which a complete throw consists of three fair coins being tossed once each and any which have landed tails being tossed a second time; no coin is tossed more than twice. The score for the complete throw is the total number of heads showing at the end of the throw.

(a) Find the respective probabilities that the score after a complete throw is

(i) 0,   (ii) 1,   (iii) 2,   (iv) 3.

(b) Show that the average score over a large number of complete throws is $\tfrac{9}{4}$.

(You may leave your answers as fractions in their lowest terms.)   (O & C)

19. The random variable X takes values $-2, 0, 2$ with probabilities $\tfrac{1}{4}, \tfrac{1}{2}, \tfrac{1}{4}$ respectively. Find $\text{Var}(X)$ and $E(|X|)$.

The random variable Y is defined by $Y = X_1 + X_2$, where X_1 and X_2 are two independent observations of X. Find the probability distribution of Y. Find $\text{Var}(Y)$ and $E(Y + 3)$.   (C)

20. The discrete random variable X can take only the values 0, 1, 2, 3, 4, 5. The probability distribution of X is given by the following:

$$P(X = 0) = P(X = 1) = P(X = 2) = a$$

$$P(X = 3) = P(X = 4) = P(X = 5) = b$$

$$P(X \geqslant 2) = 3P(X < 2)$$

where a and b are constants.

(i) Determine the values of a and b.

(ii) Show that the expectation of X is $\tfrac{23}{8}$ and determine the variance of X.

(iii) Determine the probability that the sum of two independent observations from this distribution exceeds 7.   (C)

21. A random variable R takes the integer values $1, 2, \ldots, n$ each with probability $1/n$. Find the mean and variance of R.

A pack of 15 cards bearing the numbers 1 to 15 is shuffled. Find the probability that the number on the top card is larger than that on the bottom card, giving reasons for your answer.

If the sum of these two numbers is S, find

(a) the probability that $S \leqslant 4$,

(b) the expected value of S.

(Answers may be left as fractions in their lowest terms.)   (O & C)

22. A discrete random variable X has the distribution function

x	1	2	4	5
$F(x)$	$\tfrac{1}{12}$	$\tfrac{1}{2}$	$\tfrac{5}{6}$	1

(a) Write down the probability distribution of X.

(b) Find the probability distribution of the sum of two independent observations from X and find the mean and variance of the distribution of this sum.

23. A random variable R takes the integer value r with probability $P(r)$ defined by

$$\begin{aligned} P(r) &= kr^2, & r &= 1, 2, 3, \\ P(r) &= k(7 - r)^2, & r &= 4, 5, 6, \\ P(r) &= 0, & &\text{otherwise.} \end{aligned}$$

Find the value of k and the mean and variance of the probability distribution. Exhibit this distribution by a suitable diagram.

Determine the mean and the variance of the variable Y where $Y \equiv 4R - 2$.   (L)P

24. A curiously shaped six-faced die produces a score, X, for which the probability distribution is given in the following table.

r	1	2	3	4	5	6
$P(X = r)$	k	$k/2$	$k/3$	$k/4$	$k/5$	$k/6$

Show that the constant k is $20/49$. Find the mean and variance of X.
The die is thrown twice. Show that the probability of obtaining equal scores is approximately $\frac{1}{4}$. (MEI)

25. A random number generator in a computer game produces values which can be modelled by the discrete random variable X with probability distribution given by

$$P(X = r) = kr! \qquad r = 0, 1, 2, 3, 4,$$

where k is a constant.
(i)   Show that $k = 1/34$ and illustrate the probability distribution with a sketch.
(ii) Find the expectation and variance of X.
Two independent values of X are generated. Let these values be X_1 and X_2.
(iii) Show that $P(X_1 = X_2)$ is a little greater than 0.5.
(iv) Given that $X_1 = X_2$, find the probability that X_1 and X_2 are each equal to 4. (MEI)

26. Write down an expression involving probabilities for $P(B \mid A)$, the probability of event B given that event A occurs.
Alison and Brenda play a tennis match in which the first player to win two sets wins the match. In tennis no set can be drawn. The probability that Alison wins the first set is $\frac{1}{3}$; for sets after the first, the probability that Alison wins the set is $\frac{3}{5}$ if she won the preceding set, but is only $\frac{1}{4}$ if she lost the preceding set.
With the aid of a suitable diagram, or otherwise, determine the probability that
(i)   the match lasts for just two sets,
(ii) Alison wins the match given that it lasts for just two sets,
(iii) Alison wins the match,
(iv) Alison wins the match given that it goes to three sets,
(v) if Alison wins the match, then she does so in two sets.
Calculate the expected number of sets that Alison wins. (JMB)

27. (a) A regular customer at a small clothes shop observes that the number of customers, X, in the shop when she enters has the following probability distribution.

Number of customers, x	0	1	2	3	4
Probability $p(x)$	0.15	0.34	0.27	0.14	0.10

(i) Find the mean and standard deviation of X.
She also observes that the average waiting time, Y, before being served, is as follows.

Number of customers, x	0	1	2	3	4
Average waiting time, v minutes	0	2	6	9	12

(ii) Find her mean waiting time.
(b) The customer decides that, in future, if there are more than two customers waiting when she arrives she will leave immediately and return another day. However when she returns she will wait no matter how long the queue is.
(i)   What is the probability of her leaving immediately on her first visit?
(ii) Given that she leaves immediately, what is the probability of there being more customers in the shop when she returns than on her first visit?
(iii) Find her mean waiting time under these conditions.
(c) The customer now decides that, if there are more than 2 people in the shop she will not wait but will return on another day no matter how many times this occurs. What is the probability that she will have to make more than 3 visits before being served? (AEB 1989)

5

SPECIAL DISCRETE PROBABILITY DISTRIBUTIONS

THE BINOMIAL DISTRIBUTION

Consider an experiment which has two possible outcomes, one which may be termed 'success' and the other 'failure', and perform n independent trials of the experiment. A binomial situation arises when we consider the number of successes occurring. For example

toss a coin six times and consider the number of heads that occur;

throw a die ten times and consider the number of times you obtain a six.

Example 5.1 A coin is biased so that the probability of obtaining a head is $\frac{2}{3}$. The coin is tossed four times. Find the probability of obtaining exactly two heads.

Solution 5.1 We will consider 'obtaining a head' as success.

Now $P(\text{H}) = \frac{2}{3}$ and $P(\overline{\text{H}}) = \frac{1}{3}$.

The probability of obtaining two tails and two heads, in that order, is given by

$$P(\overline{\text{H}}\overline{\text{H}}\text{HH}) = \left(\frac{1}{3}\right)^2 \left(\frac{2}{3}\right)^2 \quad \text{(independent events)}$$

But the result 'two heads and two tails' can be obtained in $\frac{4!}{2!2!}$ ways.

This is the number of ways of choosing the 2 places for the heads from the 4 places, i.e. $^4C_2$ ways. The arrangements are:

$$\overline{\text{H}}\overline{\text{H}}\text{HH} \quad \overline{\text{H}}\text{H}\overline{\text{H}}\text{H} \quad \text{HH}\overline{\text{H}}\overline{\text{H}} \quad \overline{\text{H}}\text{HH}\overline{\text{H}} \quad \text{H}\overline{\text{H}}\overline{\text{H}}\text{H} \quad \text{H}\overline{\text{H}}\text{H}\overline{\text{H}}$$

Therefore

$$P(2 \text{ heads exactly}) = {}^4C_2 \left(\frac{1}{3}\right)^2 \left(\frac{2}{3}\right)^2$$

$$= 6 \left(\frac{1}{3}\right)^2 \left(\frac{2}{3}\right)^2$$

$$= \frac{8}{27}$$

The probability of obtaining exactly two heads when the biased coin is tossed four times is $\frac{8}{27}$.

Example 5.2   An ordinary die is thrown seven times. Find the probability of obtaining exactly three sixes.

Solution 5.2   We will consider 'obtaining a 6' as success.

Now $P(6) = \frac{1}{6}$ and $P(\overline{6}) = \frac{5}{6}$.

$$P(\overline{6}\,\overline{6}\,\overline{6}\,\overline{6}\,666) = \left(\frac{5}{6}\right)^4 \left(\frac{1}{6}\right)^3$$

But the result 'four numbers which are not 6 and three sixes' can be obtained in $\frac{7!}{4!3!}$ ways, i.e. $^7C_3$ ways (the number of ways of choosing the 3 places for the sixes from the 7 places).

So $P(\text{exactly three sixes}) = {}^7C_3 \left(\frac{5}{6}\right)^4 \left(\frac{1}{6}\right)^3$

$$= 0.078 \quad (3 \text{ d.p.})$$

The probability of obtaining exactly three sixes when a die is thrown seven times is 0.078 (3 d.p.).

Example 5.3   The probability that a marksman hits a target is p and the probability that he misses is q, where $q = 1 - p$. Write an expression for the probability that, in 10 shots, he hits the target 6 times.

Solution 5.3   We will consider 'obtaining a hit' as success.

$$P(\text{success}) = p \quad \text{and} \quad P(\text{failure}) = q = 1 - p$$

We require 4 failures and 6 successes, in any order, so

$$P(6 \text{ successes}) = {}^{10}C_6\, q^4\, p^6$$

Therefore the probability that he hits the target exactly six times in ten shots is $^{10}C_6\, q^4\, p^6$.

In general:

> If the probability that an experiment results in a successful outcome is p and the probability that the outcome is a failure is q, where $q = 1 - p$, and if X is the r.v. 'the number of successful outcomes in n independent trials', then the p.d.f. of X is given by
>
> $$P(X = x) = {}^nC_x\, q^{n-x}\, p^x \qquad x = 0, 1, 2, \ldots, n$$

Example 5.4   If p is the probability of success and $q = 1 - p$ is the probability of failure, find the probability of $0, 1, 2, \ldots, 5$ successes in 5 independent trials of the experiment. Comment on your answer.

Solution 5.4   Let X be the r.v. 'the number of successful outcomes'. Then
$P(X = x) = {}^nC_x q^{n-x} p^x$, $x = 0,1,\ldots,5$ and $n = 5$. So

$$P(X = 0) = {}^5C_0 q^5 p^0 = q^5$$

$$P(X = 1) = {}^5C_1 q^4 p^1 = 5q^4 p$$

$$P(X = 2) = {}^5C_2 q^3 p^2 = 10q^3 p^2$$

$$P(X = 3) = {}^5C_3 q^2 p^3 = 10q^2 p^3$$

$$P(X = 4) = {}^5C_4 q^1 p^4 = 5qp^4$$

$$P(X = 5) = {}^5C_5 q^0 p^5 = p^5$$

We note that $q^5, 5q^4 p, \ldots, p^5$ are the terms in the binomial
expansion of $(q+p)^5$ and we have

$$(q+p)^5 = q^5 + 5q^4 p + 10q^3 p^2 + 10q^2 p^3 + 5qp^4 + p^5$$
$$\uparrow \qquad \uparrow \qquad \uparrow \qquad \uparrow \qquad \uparrow \qquad \uparrow \qquad \uparrow$$
$$1 \quad = P(X = 0) + P(X = 1) + P(X = 2) + P(X = 3) + P(X = 4) + P(X = 5)$$

In general:

> The values $P(X = x)$ for $x = 0, 1, \ldots, n$ can be obtained by
> considering the terms in the binomial expansion of $(q + p)^n$, noting
> that $q + p = 1$.
>
> $$(q+p)^n = {}^nC_0 q^n p^0 + {}^nC_1 q^{n-1} p^1 + {}^nC_2 q^{n-2} p^2 + \ldots + {}^nC_r q^{n-r} p^r + \ldots + {}^nC_n q^0 p^n$$
> $$\uparrow \qquad\qquad \uparrow \qquad\qquad \uparrow \qquad\qquad \uparrow \qquad\qquad \uparrow \qquad\qquad \uparrow$$
> $$1 \quad = P(X = 0) + P(X = 1) + P(X = 2) + \ldots + P(X = r) + \ldots + P(X = n)$$

If X is distributed in this way, we write

> $X \sim \text{Bin}(n,p)$ where n is the number of independent trials and p
> is the probability of a successful outcome in one
> trial

n and p are called the **parameters** of the distribution.

So we read the statement $X \sim \text{Bin}(n,p)$ thus: X follows a binomial
distribution with parameters n and p.

Example 5.5   The probability that a person supports Party A is 0.6. Find the
probability that in a randomly selected sample of 8 voters there are
(**a**) exactly 3 who support Party A, (**b**) more than 5 who support
Party A.

Solution 5.5   We will consider 'supporting Party A' as success. Then $p = 0.6$ and
$q = 1 - p = 0.4$. Let X be the r.v. 'the number of Party A supporters'.
Then $X \sim \text{Bin}(n,p)$ with $n = 8$ and $p = 0.6$.

So $X \sim \text{Bin}(8, 0.6)$

and

$$P(X = x) = {}^nC_x q^{n-x} p^x = {}^8C_x (0.4)^{8-x} (0.6)^x, \qquad x = 0, 1, \ldots, 8$$

(**a**) We require

$$P(X = 3) = {}^8C_3 (0.4)^5 (0.6)^3 = 0.124 \quad (3 \text{ d.p.})$$

The probability that there are exactly 3 Party A supporters is 0.124 (3 d.p.).

(**b**) We require

$$\begin{aligned}
P(X > 5) &= P(X = 6) + P(X = 7) + P(X = 8) \\
&= {}^8C_6 (0.4)^2 (0.6)^6 + {}^8C_7 (0.4)(0.6)^7 + {}^8C_8 (0.6)^8 \\
&= 28 (0.4)^2 (0.6)^6 + 8 (0.4)(0.6)^7 + (0.6)^8 \\
&= 0.315 \quad (3 \text{ d.p.})
\end{aligned}$$

The probability that there are more than 5 Party A supporters is 0.315 (3 d.p.).

Example 5.6   A box contains a large number of red and yellow tulip bulbs in the ratio $1:3$. Bulbs are picked at random from the box. How many bulbs must be picked so that the probability that there is at least one red tulip bulb among them is greater than 0.95?

Solution 5.6   Consider 'obtaining a red tulip bulb' as 'success'.

Then $p = P(\text{success}) = \frac{1}{4} = 0.25$ and $q = 0.75$.

Let X be the r.v. 'the number of red tulip bulbs'.

Then $X \sim \text{Bin}(n,p)$ where $p = 0.25$ and n is unknown.

Now $P(X = x) = {}^nC_x q^{n-x} p^x \quad x = 0,1,2,\ldots,n$

We require $P(X \geqslant 1) > 0.95$.

Now $P(X \geqslant 1) = 1 - P(X = 0)$

$$= 1 - (0.75)^n$$

So $1 - (0.75)^n > 0.95$

$$0.05 > (0.75)^n$$

$$\log 0.05 > n \log 0.75 \quad (\text{taking logs to base 10})$$

i.e.

$$n \log 0.75 < \log 0.05$$

$$(-0.125)n < -1.301$$

$$n > \frac{-1.301}{-0.125} \quad \begin{array}{l}(\text{change inequality when dividing} \\ \text{by a negative quantity})\end{array}$$

So $n > 10.4$, and the least value of n is 11.

Therefore at least 11 bulbs must be picked out of the box to ensure that the probability that there is at least one red tulip bulb among them is greater than 0.95.

Exercise 5a

Give answers to 3 S.F. where appropriate.

1. If $X \sim \text{Bin}(6, \frac{1}{3})$, find (a) $P(X = 4)$, (b) $P(X \leqslant 2)$.

2. If $X \sim \text{Bin}(8, 0.4)$, find (a) $P(X = 2)$, (b) $P(X = 0)$, (c) $P(X > 6)$.

3. The probability that a pen drawn at random from a box of pens is defective is 0.1. If a sample of 6 pens is taken, find the probability that it will contain (a) no defective pens, (b) 5 or 6 defective pens, (c) less than 3 defective pens.

4. An unbiased die is thrown 7 times. Find the probability of throwing at least 5 sixes.

5. A fair coin is tossed 6 times. Find the probability of throwing not more than 4 heads.

6. Assuming that a couple are equally likely to produce a girl or a boy, find the probability that in a family of 5 children there will be more boys than girls.

7. The probability that a shopper chooses Soapysuds when buying washing powder is 0.65. Find the probability that in a sample of 8 shoppers, the number who choose Soapysuds is (a) exactly 3, (b) more than 5.

8. A coin is biased so that it is twice as likely to show heads as tails. Find the probability that in five tosses of the coin
    (a) exactly three heads are obtained,
    (b) more than three heads are obtained.

9. The probability that a marksman scores a bull when he shoots at a target is 0.6. Find the probability that in 7 attempts he scores less than 3 bulls. Assume that the outcome of each shot is independent of any other.

10. If the probability that it will rain on any given day in September is 0.3, calculate the probability that in a given week in September, it will rain on
    (a) exactly two days,
    (b) at least two days,
    (c) more than half the days,
    (d) exactly three days that are consecutive.

11. In the mass production of bolts it is found that 5% are defective. Bolts are selected at random and put into packets of 10.
    (i) If a packet is selected at random, find the probability that it will contain
    (a) three defective bolts,
    (b) less than three defective bolts.
    (ii) Two packets are selected at random. Find the probability that there are no defective bolts in either packet.

12. Describe an experiment in which the probabilities involved are the terms of the binomial expansion of $(0.8 + 0.2)^6$. In terms of this experiment describe the event whose probability is given by the fourth term of the expansion, and calculate this probability.

13. (a) A coin is biased so that the probability of obtaining a head is p. The coin is tossed three times. Show the possible outcomes on a tree diagram and compare the probabilities of obtaining 0, 1, 2, 3 heads with the terms in the binomial expansion of $(q + p)^3$ where $q = 1 - p$.
    (b) The coin is now tossed four times. Compare the probabilities $P(X = x)$ for $x = 0, 1, 2, 3, 4$ given in the tree diagram with the binomial expansion of $(q + p)^4$. X is the r.v. 'the number of heads obtained in four tosses'.

14. In a multiple choice test there are 10 questions and for each question there is a choice of 4 answers, only one of which is correct. If a student guesses at each of the answers, find the probability that he gets (a) none correct, (b) more than 7 correct. If he needs to obtain over half marks to pass, and the questions carry equal weight, find the probability that he passes.

15. Of the pupils in a school, 30% travel to school by bus. From a sample of 10 pupils chosen at random, find the probability that (a) only 3 travel by bus, (b) more than 8 travel by bus.

16. If $X \sim \text{Bin}(n, 0.6)$ and $P(X < 1) = 0.0256$, find n.

17. 1% of a box of light bulbs are faulty. What is the largest sample size which can be taken if it is required that the probability that there are no faulty bulbs in the sample is greater than 0.5?

18. If $X \sim \text{Bin}(n, 0.3)$ and $P(X \geqslant 1) > 0.8$, find the least possible value of n.

19. The probability that a target is hit is 0.3. Find the least number of shots which should be fired if the probability that the target is hit at least once is greater than 0.95.

20. State the conditions under which the binomial distribution may be used for the calculation of probabilities.

The probability that a girl chosen at random has a weekend birthday in 1993 is $\frac{2}{7}$. Calculate the probability that, among a group of ten girls chosen at random,
(i) none has a weekend birthday in 1993,
(ii) exactly one has a weekend birthday in 1993.
Among 100 groups of ten girls, how many groups would you expect to contain more than one girl with a weekend birthday in 1993? (C Additional)

EXPECTATION AND VARIANCE

> If the random variable X is such that $X \sim \text{Bin}(n, p)$
>
> then $\qquad E(X) = np$
>
> and $\qquad \text{Var}(X) = npq$ where $q = 1 - p$

A proof of these results is shown in Appendix 2 on page 728.

Example 5.7 If the probability that it will be a fine day is 0.4, find the expected number of fine days in a week, and the standard deviation.

Solution 5.7 Let 'fine day' be 'success'. Then $p = 0.4$ and $q = 0.6$. Let X be the r.v. 'the number of fine days in a week'.

Then $X \sim \text{Bin}(n, p)$ where $n = 7$ and $p = 0.4$.

Now $\qquad E(X) = np = (7)(0.4) = 2.8$

$\qquad \text{Var}(X) = npq = (7)(0.4)(0.6) = 1.68$

Therefore the standard deviation of $X = \sqrt{1.68} = 1.30$ days (2 d.p.).

The expected number of fine days in a week is 2.8 and the standard deviation is 1.30 days (2 d.p.).

Example 5.8 The r.v. X is such that $X \sim \text{Bin}(n, p)$ and $E(X) = 2$, $\text{Var}(X) = \frac{24}{13}$. Find the values of n and p.

Solution 5.8 If $X \sim \text{Bin}(n, p)$ then $E(X) = np$ and $\text{Var}(X) = npq$.

Now

$$E(X) = 2, \quad \text{so} \quad np = 2 \qquad \qquad \text{(i)}$$

$$\text{Var}(X) = \frac{24}{13}, \quad \text{so} \quad npq = \frac{24}{13} \qquad \qquad \text{(ii)}$$

Substituting for np in (ii) we have

$$2q = \frac{24}{13}$$

$$q = \frac{12}{13}$$

Therefore $$p = 1 - q$$

$$= 1 - \frac{12}{13}$$

$$= \frac{1}{13}$$

Now substituting for p in (i) we have

$$n\left(\frac{1}{13}\right) = 2$$

$$n = 26$$

Therefore $n = 26$ and $p = \frac{1}{13}$, so that $X \sim \text{Bin}\left(26, \frac{1}{13}\right)$.

Exercise 5b

1. Of the articles from a certain production line, 10% are defective. If a sample of 25 articles is taken, find the expected number of defective articles and the standard deviation.

2. The probability that an apple, picked at random from a sack, is bad is 0.05. Find the standard deviation of the number of bad apples in a sample of 15 apples.

3. X is a r.v. such that $X \sim \text{Bin}(n, p)$. Given that $E(X) = 2.4$ and $p = 0.3$, find n and the standard deviation of X.

4. In a group of people the expected number who wear glasses is 2 and the variance is 1.6. Find the probability that (a) a person chosen at random from the group wears glasses, (b) 6 people in the group wear glasses.

5. If the r.v. X is such that $X \sim \text{Bin}(10, p)$ where $p < \frac{1}{2}$ and $\text{Var}(X) = 1\frac{7}{8}$, find (a) p, (b) $E(X)$, (c) $P(X = 2)$.

6. A die is biased and the probability, p, of throwing a six is known to be less than $\frac{1}{6}$. An experiment consists of recording the number of sixes in 25 throws of the die. In a large number of experiments the standard deviation of the number of sixes is 1.5. Calculate the value of p and hence determine, to two places of decimals, the probability that exactly three sixes are recorded during a particular experiment.   (C Additional)

7. (i) For each of the experiments described below, state, giving a reason, whether a binomial distribution is appropriate.
Experiment 1. A bag contains black, white and red marbles which are selected at random, one at a time with replacement. The colour of each marble is noted.
Experiment 2. This experiment is a repeat of Experiment 1 except that the bag contains black and white marbles only.
Experiment 3. This experiment is a repeat of Experiment 2 except that marbles are not replaced after selection.
(ii) On average 20% of the bolts produced by a machine in a factory are faulty. Samples of 10 bolts are to be selected at random each day. Each bolt will be selected and replaced in the set of bolts which have been produced on that day.
(a) Calculate, to 2 significant figures, the probability that, in any one sample, two bolts or less will be faulty.
(b) Find the expected value and the variance of the number of bolts in a sample which will not be faulty.   (L Additional)

8. In two binomial distributions the ratio of the number of independent trials is $5:6$, the ratio of the arithmetic means is $2:9$ and the ratio of the variances is $32:45$. For each distribution, find the probability of success.

9. (a) In the mass production of a certain component it is found that 5% are defective. Components are selected at random and packed in boxes of 10. If one box is selected, calculate the probability that there will be
(i) exactly 2 defectives,
(ii) more than 1 defective.
If 2 boxes are selected, calculate the probability that there will be exactly 1 defective among the 20 components.
If 150 boxes are selected, estimate the number of boxes which contain no defectives.
(b) An experiment consists of taking 12 shots at a target and counting the number of hits. When this experiment was repeated a large number of times the mean number of hits was found to be 3. Calculate
(i) the probability of hitting the target with a single shot,

(ii) the standard deviation of the number of hits in an experiment.   (C Additional)

10. (a) On a particular television channel the news occurs at the same time each working day. The probability that a certain man arrives home from work in time to watch the news is 0.4. Calculate the probability that, in any given week of 5 working days, he arrives home in time to watch the news
(i)   on exactly 3 days,
(ii) on at least 3 days,
(iii) on exactly 3 days which are consecutive.
(b) Each day a bakery delivers the same number of loaves to a certain shop which sells, on average, 98% of them. Assuming that the number of loaves sold per day has a binomial distribution with a standard deviation of 7, find the number of loaves the shop would expect to sell per day.   (C Additional)

DIAGRAMMATIC REPRESENTATION OF THE BINOMIAL DISTRIBUTION

Consider $X \sim \text{Bin}(5, p)$ for various values of p. The probability distributions are illustrated on the following page. It is useful to compare, for example, the distributions of $X \sim \text{Bin}(5, 0.1)$ and $X \sim \text{Bin}(5, 0.9)$ and these have been printed side by side to facilitate this.

Consider $X \sim \text{Bin}(5, 0.1)$ and $X \sim \text{Bin}(5, 0.9)$.

Notice that

$$P(X = 0 \,|\, X \sim \text{Bin}(5, 0.1)) = P(X = 5 \,|\, X \sim \text{Bin}(5, 0.9))$$

$$P(X = 1 \,|\, X \sim \text{Bin}(5, 0.1)) = P(X = 4 \,|\, X \sim \text{Bin}(5, 0.9))$$

and so on.

Also, considering $X \sim \text{Bin}(5, 0.2)$ and $X \sim \text{Bin}(5, 0.8)$

$$P(X = 2 \,|\, X \sim \text{Bin}(5, 0.2)) = P(X = 3 \,|\, X \sim \text{Bin}(5, 0.8))$$

In general

$$P(X = r \,|\, X \sim \text{Bin}(n,p)) = P(X = n - r \,|\, X \sim \text{Bin}(n, 1 - p))$$

NOTE: If $p = 0.5$ then the distribution of X, where $X \sim \text{Bin}(n, 0.5)$, is symmetrical.

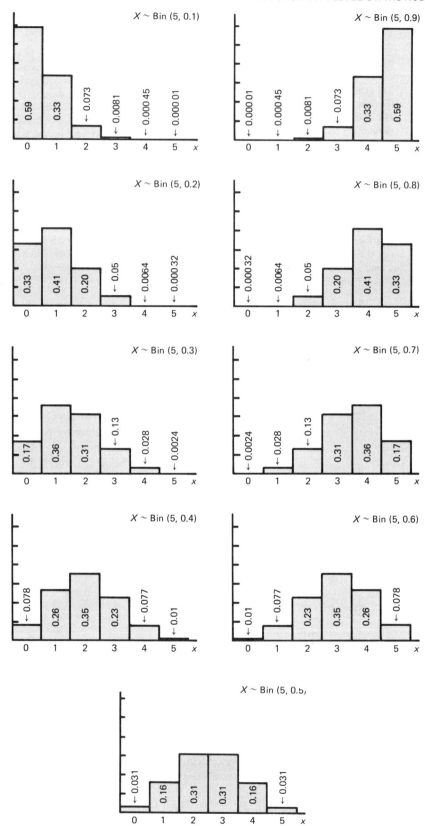

CUMULATIVE BINOMIAL PROBABILITY TABLES

The task of finding binomial probabilities is made much easier if tables are available. These give the cumulative probabilities $F(r) = P(X \leqslant r)$ for the possible values of r. The tables are printed on page 718 and an extract is shown below. In this we are considering $X \sim \text{Bin}(5, 0.3)$.

	$p = 0.3$
$n = 5, \ r = 0$	0.1681
$r = 1$	0.5282
$r = 2$	0.8369
$r = 3$	0.9692
$r = 4$	0.9976
$r = 5$	1.0000

Example 5.9   If $X \sim \text{Bin}(5, 0.3)$ find **(a)** $P(X \leqslant 4)$, **(b)** $P(X = 2)$, **(c)** $P(X < 3)$, **(d)** $P(X > 1)$, **(e)** $P(X \geqslant 3)$.

Solution 5.9   **(a)** $P(X \leqslant 4) = 0.9976$ (directly from the tables)

(b) $P(X = 2) = P(X \leqslant 2) - P(X \leqslant 1)$

$$= 0.8369 - 0.5282$$

$$= 0.3087$$

(c) $P(X < 3) = P(X \leqslant 2)$

$$= 0.8369$$

(d) $P(X > 1) = 1 - P(X \leqslant 1)$

$$= 1 - 0.5282$$

$$= 0.4718$$

(e) $P(X \geqslant 3) = 1 - P(X \leqslant 2)$

$$= 1 - 0.8369$$

$$= 0.1631$$

In the tables values of p are given from 0.1 to 0.5. However we are still able to use them for $p = 0.6, 0.7, 0.8$ and 0.9 by using the fact that

$$P(X = r \mid X \sim \text{Bin}(n, p)) = P(X = n - r \mid X \sim \text{Bin}(n, 1 - p))$$

Consider again the probability distributions for $X \sim \text{Bin}(5, 0.3)$ and $X \sim \text{Bin}(5, 0.7)$.

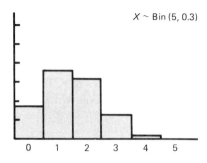
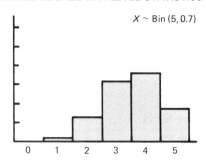

We see that $P(X \leqslant 3 \mid p = 0.3) = P(X \geqslant 2 \mid p = 0.7)$

and $P(X \geqslant 4 \mid p = 0.3) = P(X \leqslant 1 \mid p = 0.7)$

In general

$$P(X \leqslant r \mid X \sim \text{Bin}(n,p)) = P(X \geqslant n - r \mid X \sim \text{Bin}(n, 1 - p))$$

$$P(X \geqslant r \mid X \sim \text{Bin}(n,p)) = P(X \leqslant n - r \mid X \sim \text{Bin}(n, 1 - p))$$

Example 5.10 If $X \sim \text{Bin}(5, 0.7)$ find **(a)** $P(X \geqslant 3)$, **(b)** $P(X \leqslant 4)$,
(**c**) $P(X = 4)$.

Solution 5.10 Using the column headed $p = 0.3$, with $n = 5$:

(**a**) $P(X \geqslant 3 \mid p = 0.7) = P(X \leqslant 2 \mid p = 0.3)$

                        $= 0.8369$

(**b**) $P(X \leqslant 4 \mid p = 0.7) = P(X \geqslant 1 \mid p = 0.3)$

                                    $= 1 - P(X \leqslant 0 \mid p = 0.3)$

                                    $= 1 - 0.1681$

                                    $= 0.8319$

(**c**) $P(X = 4 \mid p = 0.7) = P(X = 1 \mid p = 0.3)$

                                    $= P(X \leqslant 1 \mid p = 0.3) - P(X \leqslant 0 \mid p = 0.3)$

                                    $= 0.5282 - 0.1681$

                                    $= 0.3601$

NOTE: Obviously there are times when it is not advantageous to
use the tables and it is quicker to calculate the probabilities directly.
However they are particularly useful when finding the probability
distribution $P(X = x)$ for all values of x.

Example 5.11 Given $X \sim \text{Bin}(8, 0.2)$ write out the probability distribution of X.

Solution 5.11 Using the cumulative probability tables on page 718 with $n = 8$
and $p = 0.2$, and writing $P(X \leqslant r)$ as $F(r)$,

$$P(X = 0) = F(0) = 0.1678$$

$$P(X = 1) = F(1) - F(0) = 0.5033 - 0.1678 = 0.3355$$

$$P(X = 2) = F(2) - F(1) = 0.7969 - 0.5033 = 0.2936$$

$$P(X = 3) = F(3) - F(2) = 0.9437 - 0.7969 = 0.1468$$

$$P(X = 4) = F(4) - F(3) = 0.9896 - 0.9437 = 0.0459$$

$$P(X = 5) = F(5) - F(4) = 0.9988 - 0.9896 = 0.0092$$

$$P(X = 6) = F(6) - F(5) = 0.9999 - 0.9988 = 0.0011$$

$$P(X = 7) = F(7) - F(6) = 1.0000 - 0.9999 = 0.0001$$

$$P(X = 8) = F(8) - F(7) = 1 \qquad - 1.0000 = 0.0000$$

NOTE: $P(X = 8) = (0.2)^8 = 0.00000256$, but since the tables give
values to 4 d.p. they will give $P(X = 8) = 0.0000$.

Exercise 5c

1. Use cumulative binomial probability tables to
    find the following:
    (a) $X \sim \text{Bin}(6, 0.2)$, find
        (i) $P(X \leqslant 3)$, (ii) $P(X \geqslant 4)$,
        (iii) $P(X = 5)$.
    (b) $X \sim \text{Bin}(10, 0.45)$, find
        (i) $P(X = 6)$, (ii) $P(X \leqslant 3)$,
        (iii) $P(X < 5)$, (iv) $P(X \geqslant 3)$.
    (c) $X \sim \text{Bin}(4, 0.9)$, find
        (i) $P(X \leqslant 1)$, (ii) $P(X < 2)$,
        (iii) $P(X = 3)$.

    (d) $X \sim \text{Bin}(7, 0.75)$, find
        (i) $F(5)$, (ii) $F(3)$, (iii) $P(X \geqslant 4)$,
        (iv) $P(X = 6)$.

2. Given that $X \sim \text{Bin}(6, 0.4)$, write out the
    probability distribution of X.

3. Given that $X \sim \text{Bin}(5, 0.65)$, write out the
    probability distribution of X.

To find the value of *X* that is most likely to occur

The value of X that is most likely to occur is the one with the highest
probability. This value is often called the **mode**. It can be found by
working out all the probabilities, which is very tedious. It is usually
only necessary to consider the probabilities for values of X close to the
mean.

Example 5.12 If $X \sim \text{Bin}(10, 0.45)$, find the most likely value of X.

Solution 5.12 Now $E(X) = (10)(0.45) = 4.5$, so we will try $x = 3, 4, 5, \ldots$

$$P(X = 3) = {}^{10}C_3 (0.55)^7 (0.45)^3 = 0.1664\ldots$$

$$P(X = 4) = {}^{10}C_4 (0.55)^6 (0.45)^4 = \boxed{0.2383\ldots}$$

$$P(X = 5) = {}^{10}C_5 (0.55)^5 (0.45)^5 = 0.2340\ldots$$

$$P(X = 6) = {}^{10}C_6 (0.55)^4 (0.45)^6 = 0.1595\ldots$$

We can see that the value of X with the highest probability is 4, therefore the most likely value, or mode, is 4.

Example 5.13 Of the inhabitants of a certain African village, 80% are known to have a particular eye disorder. If 12 people are waiting to see the nurse, what is the most likely number of them to have the eye disorder?

Solution 5.13 Let X be the r.v. 'the number of people with the eye disorder'. Then $X \sim \text{Bin}(n, p)$ with $n = 12$ and $p = 0.8$.

Therefore $X \sim \text{Bin}(12, 0.8)$

and $P(X = x) = {}^{12}C_x (0.2)^{12-x}(0.8)^x, \quad x = 0, 1, \ldots, 12.$

Now $E(X) = 12(0.8) = 9.6$ so we will try $x = 8, 9, 10, \ldots$

$$P(X = 8) = {}^{12}C_8 (0.2)^4 (0.8)^8 = 0.1328\ldots$$

$$P(X = 9) = {}^{12}C_9 (0.2)^3 (0.8)^9 = 0.2362\ldots$$

$$P(X = 10) = {}^{12}C_{10} (0.2)^2 (0.8)^{10} = \boxed{0.2834\ldots}$$

$$P(X = 11) = {}^{12}C_{11} (0.2)(0.8)^{11} = 0.2061\ldots$$

Therefore the most likely number of people is 10.

Exercise 5d

1. The random variable X is such that $X \sim \text{Bin}(6, 0.25)$. Find the most likely value of X. Verify your answer by drawing a vertical line graph to illustrate the distribution of X.

2. Given that $X \sim \text{Bin}(10, 0.3)$, find
    (a) $E(X)$, (b) the mode.

3. In a bag there are 6 red counters, 8 yellow counters and 6 green counters. A counter is drawn at random from the bag, its colour is noted and it is then replaced. This procedure is carried out ten times in all. Find
    (a) the expected number of red counters drawn,
    (b) the most likely number of green counters drawn,
    (c) the probability that no more than 4 yellow counters are drawn.

4. The random variable X is distributed binomially with mean 2 and variance 1.6. Find (a) the most likely value of X, (b) $P(X < 6)$.

5. The probability that a student is awarded a pass in the mathematics examination is 0.75.

Find the probability that in a group of 10 students more than half pass the mathematics examination.

6. The random variable X is such that $X \sim \text{Bin}(8, 0.4)$. Find (a) the most likely value of X, (b) $P(X \leqslant 4)$, (c) $P(X \geqslant 4)$.

FITTING A THEORETICAL DISTRIBUTION

It is sometimes useful to compare experimental results with a theoretical distribution.

Example 5.14 A biased coin is tossed 4 times and the number of heads is noted. The experiment is performed 500 times in all. The results obtained are shown in the table:

Number of heads	0	1	2	3	4
Frequency	12	50	151	200	87

(**a**) Find the probability of obtaining a head when the coin is tossed.

(**b**) Calculate the theoretical frequencies of 0, 1, 2, 3, 4 heads, using the associated theoretical binomial distribution.

Solution 5.14 (**a**) For the frequency distribution

$$\text{mean, } \bar{x} = \frac{\Sigma fx}{\Sigma f}$$

$$= \frac{(0)(12)+(1)(50)+(2)(151)+(3)(200)+(4)(87)}{500}$$

$$= \frac{1300}{500}$$

$$= 2.6$$

Let X be the r.v. 'the number of heads obtained in 4 tosses'. Then $X \sim \text{Bin}(n, p)$ with $n = 4$. So the mean, $E(X) = np$.

Therefore $\qquad\qquad\qquad\qquad np = 2.6$

$$4p = 2.6$$

So $\qquad\qquad\qquad\qquad\qquad p = 0.65$

Therefore the probability that the coin will show heads is 0.65.

(**b**) $X \sim \text{Bin}(4, 0.65)$. To find the values of $P(X = x)$ for $x = 0, 1, 2, 3, 4$ using $P(X = x) = {}^4C_x (0.35)^{4-x} (0.65)^x$

$$P(X = 0) = (0.35)^4 = 0.015\,006\,25$$

$$P(X = 1) = 4(0.35)^3 (0.65) = 0.111\,475$$

$$P(X = 2) = 6(0.35)^2 (0.65)^2 = 0.310\,537\,5$$

$$P(X = 3) = 4(0.35)(0.65)^3 = 0.384\,475$$

$$P(X = 4) = (0.65)^4 = 0.178\,506\,2$$

To obtain the theoretical distribution, multiply each of the probabilities by the total frequency, 500.

Therefore the theoretical binomial frequencies (rounded to the nearest integer) are as follows:

Number of heads	0	1	2	3	4
Frequency	8	56	155	192	89

NOTE: this compares reasonably well with the original frequency distribution.

A statistical test to compare the two sets of data is illustrated on page 580 (chi-squared test).

Exercise 5e

1. A biased die is thrown 3 times and the number of fours is noted. The procedure is performed 180 times in all and the results are shown in the table.

Number of fours	0	1	2	3
Frequency	50	69	36	25

(a) What is the mean of this distribution?
(b) What is the probability of obtaining a four when the die is thrown?
(c) Calculate the theoretical probabilities of obtaining 0, 1, 2, 3 fours, using the binomial distribution.
(d) Calculate the corresponding theoretical frequencies.

2. In a large batch of items from a production line the probability that an item is faulty is p. 400 samples, each of size 5, are taken and the number of faulty items in each batch is noted. From the frequency distribution below estimate p and work out the expected frequencies of 0, 1, 2, 3, 4, 5 faulty items per batch for a theoretical binomial distribution having the same mean.

Number of faulty items	0	1	2	3	4	5
Frequency	297	90	10	2	1	0

3. In an experiment a certain number of dice are thrown and the number of sixes obtained is recorded. The dice are all biased and the probability of obtaining a six with each individual die is p. In all there were 60 experiments and the results are shown in the table.

Number of sixes obtained in an experiment	0	1	2	3	4	>4
Frequency	19	26	12	2	1	0

Calculate the mean and the standard deviation of these data.
By comparing these answers with those expected for a binomial distribution, estimate (a) the number of dice thrown in each experiment, (b) the value of p.

(C Additional)

4. Fit a theoretical binomial distribution to the following frequency distribution, given $n = 4$:

x	0	1	2	3	4
f	7	20	35	30	8

5. Seeds are planted in rows of six and after 14 days the number of seeds which have germinated in each of the 100 rows is noted. The results are shown in the table:

Number of seeds germinating	0	1	2	3	4	5	6
Number of rows	2	1	2	10	30	35	20

Find the theoretical frequencies of 0, 1, ..., 6 seeds germinating in a row, using the associated theoretical binomial distribution.

6. Derive the mean and variance of the binomial distribution.

Mass production of miniature hearing aids is a particularly difficult process and so the quality of these products is monitored carefully. Samples of size six are selected regularly and tested for correct operation. The number of defectives in each sample is recorded. During one particular week 140 samples are taken and the distribution of the number of defectives per sample is given in the following table.

Number of defectives per sample (x)	0	1	2	3	4	5	6
Number of samples with x defectives (f)	27	36	39	22	10	4	2

Find the frequencies of the number of defectives per sample given by a binomial distribution having the same mean and total as the observed distribution. (AEB)

WORKED EXAMPLES

Example 5.15 70% of the passengers who travel on the 8.17 to London buy the 'Daily Doom' at the bookstall before boarding the train. The train is full and each compartment holds eight passengers.

(**a**) What is the probability that all the passengers in a compartment have bought the 'Daily Doom'?

(**b**) What is the probability that none of the passengers in a compartment has bought the 'Daily Doom'?

(**c**) What is the probability that exactly three of the passengers in a compartment have bought the 'Daily Doom'?

(**d**) What is the most likely number of passengers in a compartment to have bought the 'Daily Doom'?

(**e**) If there are 40 compartments on the train, in how many of them would you expect there to be exactly three copies of the 'Daily Doom'?

(**f**) The train is so full that in each carriage ten people are standing in the corridor. What is the probability that the third passenger I pass in the corridor of a carriage is the first I meet who has bought the 'Daily Doom'?

(**g**) What is the mean number of buyers of the 'Daily Doom' standing in a corridor?

Solution 5.15 Let 'buying the Daily Doom' be termed 'success'. Therefore $p = 0.7$ and $q = 1 - p = 0.3$.

Let X be the r.v. 'the number of passengers who have bought the Daily Doom'. Then $X \sim \text{Bin}(n, p)$ where $n = 8$ and $p = 0.7$, i.e. $X \sim \text{Bin}(8, 0.7)$.

$$P(X = x) = {}^nC_x q^{n-x} p^x \qquad x = 0, 1, \ldots, 8$$
$$= {}^8C_x (0.3)^{8-x} (0.7)^x$$

(**a**)
$$P(X = 8) = (0.7)^8$$
$$= 0.0576 \quad (3 \text{ S.F.})$$

The probability that all the passengers in a compartment have bought the Daily Doom is 0.0576 (3 S.F.).

(**b**) $P(X = 0) = (0.3)^8$

$$= 6.561 \times 10^{-5}$$

The probability that none of the passengers has bought the Daily Doom is 6.561×10^{-5}.

(**c**) $P(X = 3) = {}^8C_3 (0.3)^5 (0.7)^3$

$$= 0.0467 \quad (3 \text{ S.F.})$$

The probability that exactly three passengers have bought the Daily Doom is 0.0467 (3 S.F.).

(**d**) To find the most likely number of people who have bought the Daily Doom consider $E(X)$.

$$E(X) = np = 8(0.7) = 5.6$$

So we consider $x = 4, 5, 6, \ldots$ to find the value with the highest probability.

$$P(X = 4) = {}^8C_4 (0.3)^4 (0.7)^4 = 0.1361\ldots$$

$$P(X = 5) = {}^8C_5 (0.3)^3 (0.7)^5 = 0.2541\ldots$$

$$P(X = 6) = {}^8C_6 (0.3)^2 (0.7)^6 = \boxed{0.2964\ldots}$$

$$P(X = 7) = {}^8C_7 (0.3)(0.7)^7 = 0.1976\ldots$$

So the most likely number of passengers to have bought the Daily Doom is 6.

(**e**) In one compartment $P(X = 3) = 0.0467$. Let Y be the r.v. 'the number of compartments where there are exactly three copies of the Daily Doom'.

Then $Y \sim \text{Bin}(n, p)$ where $n = 40$ and $p = 0.0467$.

So $E(Y) = np$

$$= (40)(0.0467)$$

$$= 1.87 \quad (3 \text{ S.F.})$$

Therefore the expected number of compartments where there are exactly three copies of the Daily Doom on the train of 40 compartments is 1.87 (3 S.F.).

(**f**) $P(\text{third passenger is the first to have a copy}) = P(\overline{D}\overline{D}D)$ where D is the event 'the person has a copy of the Daily Doom' and $P(D) = 0.7$.

Now $P(\overline{D}\overline{D}D) = (0.3)(0.3)(0.7)$ (independent events)

$$= 0.063$$

The probability that the third person is the first to have a copy is 0.063.

(**g**) Let C be the r.v. 'the number of people in the corridor to have bought the Daily Doom'. Then $C \sim \text{Bin}(10, 0.7)$.

$$E(C) = (10)(0.7)$$
$$= 7$$

Therefore the expected number of buyers standing in a corridor is 7.

Example 5.16 (**a**) State in words the meaning of $P(E')$ and of $P(E \mid F)$ for two events E and F.

(**b**) All the letters in a particular office are typed either by Pat, a trainee typist, or by Lyn, who is a fully trained typist. The probability that a letter typed by Pat will contain one or more errors is 0.3. Find the probability that a random sample of 4 letters typed by Pat will include exactly one letter free from error.

(**c**) The probability that a letter typed by Lyn will contain one or more errors is 0.05. Using the tables provided, or otherwise, find, to 3 decimal places, the probability that in a random sample of 20 letters typed by Lyn, not more than 2 letters will contain one or more errors.

(**d**) On any one day, 6% of the letters typed in the office are typed by Pat. One letter is chosen at random from those typed on that day. Show that the probability that it will contain one or more errors is 0.065.

(**e**) Given that each of 2 letters chosen at random from the day's typing contains one or more errors, find, to 4 decimal places, the probability that one was typed by Pat and the other by Lyn. (L)

Solution 5.16 (**a**) $P(E')$ is the probability that event E does not occur. $P(E \mid F)$ is the probability that E occurs, given that F has occurred.

(**b**) $P(\text{Pat's letter contains errors}) = 0.3$.
$P(\text{Pat's letter is free from errors}) = 1 - 0.3 = 0.7$.
Let X be the r.v. 'the number of letters typed by Pat which are free from errors'. Then $X \sim \text{Bin}(4, 0.7)$.

$$P(X = 1) = {}^4C_3 (0.3)^3 (0.7)$$
$$= 0.0756$$

Therefore the probability that a random sample of 4 letters typed by Pat will include exactly one letter free from error is 0.0756.

(**c**) $P(\text{Lyn's letter contains errors}) = 0.05$.
Let Y be the r.v. 'the number of letters typed by Lyn containing errors'. Then $Y \sim \text{Bin}(20, 0.05)$.

$$P(Y \leqslant 2) = P(Y = 0) + P(Y = 1) + P(Y = 2)$$
$$= (0.95)^{20} + 20(0.95)^{19}(0.05) + 190(0.95)^{18}(0.05)^2$$
$$= 0.925 \quad (3 \text{ d.p.})$$

Therefore the probability that a random sample of 20 letters typed by Lyn will contain not more than two with errors is 0.925 (3 d.p.).

NOTE: $P(Y \leqslant 2)$ can be found directly from cumulative binomial probability tables, page 719, with $n = 20$, $p = 0.05$.

$$P(Y \leqslant 2) = 0.925 \quad (3 \text{ d.p.})$$

(**d**) Let E be the event 'a letter contains one or more errors'.

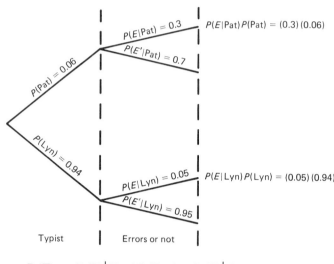

$$P(E) = P(E \mid \text{Pat})P(\text{Pat}) + P(E \mid \text{Lyn})P(\text{Lyn})$$

$$= (0.3)(0.06) + (0.05)(0.94)$$

$$= 0.065$$

Therefore the probability that a letter will contain errors is 0.065, as required.

(**e**) Now
$$P(\text{Pat} \mid E) = \frac{P(E \mid \text{Pat})P(\text{Pat})}{P(E)}$$

$$= \frac{(0.3)(0.06)}{0.065}$$

$$= \frac{18}{65}$$

$$P(\text{Lyn} \mid E) = \frac{P(E \mid \text{Lyn})P(\text{Lyn})}{P(E)}$$

$$= \frac{(0.05)(0.94)}{0.065}$$

$$= \frac{47}{65}$$

$P(1$ typed by Lyn, 1 typed by Pat $\mid 2$ letters contained errors)

$$= 2\left(\frac{18}{65}\right)\left(\frac{47}{65}\right)$$

$$= 0.4005 \quad (4 \text{ d.p.})$$

Therefore the probability that one was typed by Pat and one by Lyn, given that the two letters contained errors, is 0.4005 (4 d.p.).

SUMMARY — BINOMIAL DISTRIBUTION

If $X \sim \text{Bin}(n, p)$ then $P(X = x) = {}^{n}C_{x}\, q^{n-x} p^{x}$,
$x = 0, 1, 2, \ldots, n$, where $q = 1 - p$.

$E(X) = np$

$\text{Var}(X) = npq$

$P(X = r \mid X \sim \text{Bin}(n, p)) = P(X = n - r \mid X \sim \text{Bin}(n, 1 - p))$

$P(X \geqslant r \mid X \sim \text{Bin}(n, p)) = P(X \leqslant n - r \mid X \sim \text{Bin}(n, 1 - p))$

$P(X \leqslant r \mid X \sim \text{Bin}(n, p)) = P(X \geqslant n - r \mid X \sim \text{Bin}(n, 1 - p))$

Miscellaneous Exercise 5f

1. Find the probability of throwing three sixes twice in five throws of six dice.

2. In a large city 1 person in 5 is left-handed.
   (a) Find the probability that in a random sample of 10 people
   (i) exactly 3 will be left-handed,
   (ii) more than half will be left-handed.
   (b) Find the most likely number of left-handed people in a random sample of 12 people.
   (c) Find the mean and the standard deviation of the number of left-handed people in a random sample of 25 people.
   (d) How large must a random sample be if the probability that it contains at least one left-handed person is to be greater than 0.95?

3. A crossword puzzle is published in *The Times* each day of the week, except Sunday. A woman is able to complete, on average, 8 out of 10 of the crossword puzzles.
   (a) Find the expected value and the standard deviation of the number of completed crosswords in a given week.
   (b) Show that the probability that she will complete at least 5 in a given week is 0.655 (to 3 significant figures).
   (c) Given that she completes the puzzle on Monday, find, to three significant figures, the probability that she will complete at least 4 in the rest of the week.
   (d) Find, to three significant figures, the probability that, in a period of four weeks, she completes 4 or less in only one of the four weeks. (C)

4. Samples, each of 8 articles, are taken at random from a large consignment in which 20% of articles are defective. Find the number of defective articles which is most

likely to occur in a single sample, and find the probability of obtaining this number.
If 100 samples of 8 articles are to be examined, calculate the number of samples in which you would expect to find 3 or more defective articles. (C)

5. A small boy plays a game in which he has to guess in which hand his uncle is hiding a toffee. The first time he chooses 'left'. For the next three times he chooses 'same hand as previous time' with probability s, and 'different hand from previous time' with probability d, where $s + d = 1$. Find the probability that he will choose 'left' on the last time.
   By adding together the binomial expansions for $(s + d)^3$ and $(s - d)^3$, deduce that the probability that he chooses 'left' on the last time can be written as $\frac{1}{2}\{1 + (s - d)^3\}$. (SMP)

6. In an inspection scheme a sample of 20 items is selected at random from a large batch and the number of defective items is noted. If this number is more than 2 the batch is rejected; if it is less than 2 the batch is accepted. If the number of defective items is exactly 2, a further sample of 10 items is taken and the batch is rejected if this second sample has any defective items, but otherwise the batch is accepted.
   If the proportion of defective items in a particular batch is 2% evaluate, to two decimal places, the probabilities that
   (a) the batch is accepted as a result of inspection of the first sample,
   (b) a second sample is taken and the batch is accepted as a result of inspection of the second sample,
   (c) the batch is rejected. (C)

7. Thatcher's Pottery produces large batches of coffee mugs decorated with the faces of famous politicians. They are considering adopting one of the following sampling plans for batch inspection.
Method A (single sample plan) Select 10 mugs from the batch at random and accept the batch if there are 2 or less defectives, otherwise reject the batch.
Method B (double sample plan) Select 5 mugs from the batch at random and accept the batch if there are no defectives, reject the batch if there are 2 or more defectives, otherwise select another 5 mugs at random. When the second sample is drawn count the number of defectives in the combined sample of 10 and accept the batch if the number of defectives is 2 or less, otherwise reject the batch.
(a) If the proportion of defectives in a batch is p, find, in terms of p, for each method in turn, the probability that the batch will be accepted.
(b) Evaluate *both* the above probabilities for $p = 0.2$ and $p = 0.5$.
(c) Hence, or otherwise, decide which of these two plans is more appropriate, and why.   (AEB)

8. A trial may have two outcomes, success or failure. If in n such independent trials, the probability p of a success remains constant from trial to trial, write down the probability of r successes in the n trials.
When two friends A and B play chess, the probability that A wins any game is $\frac{2}{5}$, and if A does not win the game, the probabilities then of B winning and of a draw are equal. In the course of an evening they play four games. Calculate the probabilities (a) that A does not win a game, (b) that he wins more than two games.
If it is known that A has won exactly two of these four games, write down the probability distribution of the number of games that B has won.
Calculate the probability that A wins more games than B when four games are played.
                                                                    (JMB)

9. At a certain university in Cambford students attending a first course in statistics are asked by the lecturer, Professor Thomas Bayes, to complete 10 example sheets during the course. At the end of the course each student sits an examination as a result of which she either passes or fails. Assuming that (i) the

number, N, of example sheets completed by any student has a binomial distribution given by

$$P(N = n) = {}^{10}C_n \left(\frac{2}{3}\right)^n \left(\frac{1}{3}\right)^{(10-n)}$$

$$n = 0, 1, \ldots, 10$$

and (ii) the probability of a student passing the examination *given* that she completed n sheets during the course, is $n/10$,
(a) what is the (unconditional) probability that a student passes the examination?
(b) what is the probability that a student selected at random from the examination pass list had in fact completed four example sheets or less?   (AEB)

10. Two random variables X_1 and X_2 have independent binomial probability distributions, where both X_1 and X_2 can only take the values 0, 1 and 2. If $P(X_1 = 2) = p_1{}^2$ and $P(X_2 = 2) = p_2{}^2$, show that $E(X_1 X_2) = 4p_1 p_2$.   (Additional)

11. In an experiment two bags, A and B, contain a very large number of white and black balls. In Bag A, 20% of the balls are white and in Bag B, 70% of the balls are white. Two balls are selected at random from each bag.
(a) Find the expected number of white balls selected from Bag A.
(b) If Z denotes the total number of white balls selected, calculate (i) $P(Z = 2)$, (ii) $E(Z)$.   (L Additional)

12. (a) The probability that a certain type of vacuum tube will shatter during a thermal shock test is 0.15.
What is the probability that if 25 such tubes are tested
(i) 4 or more will shatter,
(ii) between 16 and 20 (inclusive) will survive?
Another type of tube is tested in samples of 30. It is observed that on 40% of occasions all 30 survive the test. What is the probability (assumed constant) of a single tube of this type surviving the test?
(b) A monkey in a cage is rewarded with food if it presses a button when a light flashes. Say, giving a reason, whether or not it is likely that the following variables follow the binomial distribution:
(i) Y is the number of times the light flashes before the monkey is twice successful in obtaining the food.
(ii) Z is the number of times that the monkey obtains the food by the time the light has flashed 20 times.   (AEB)P

THE GEOMETRIC DISTRIBUTION

Consider performing a series of independent trials, each with a constant probability p of success and probability q of failure, where $q = 1 - p$.

Let X be the random variable 'the number of trials *up to and including* the first success'.

Now $P(X = 1) = P(\text{success on the first trial}) = p$

$P(X = 2) = P(\text{failure on first trial, success on second}) = qp$

$P(X = 3) = q^2 p$

$P(X = 4) = q^3 p$

$\qquad \vdots \qquad\qquad \vdots$

$P(X = x) = q^{x-1} p$

A discrete r.v. X having p.d.f. of the form $P(X = x) = q^{x-1} p$, where $0 \leqslant p \leqslant 1$ and $q = 1 - p$, is said to follow a **geometric** distribution, with $x = 1, 2, 3, \ldots$

p is the parameter of the distribution.

If X is defined in this way, we write

$$X \sim \text{Geo}(p)$$

DIAGRAMMATIC REPRESENTATION

Example 5.17 Draw a vertical line graph to illustrate the distribution of X, where $X \sim \text{Geo}(0.3)$ and state the mode.

Solution 5.17 $p = 0.3, q = 0.7$

$$P(X = 1) = p = 0.3$$

$$P(X = 2) = qp = (0.7)(0.3) = 0.21$$

$$P(X = 3) = q^2 p = (0.7)^2 (0.3) = 0.147$$

$$P(X = 4) = q^3 p = (0.7)^3 (0.3) = 0.1029$$

$$P(X = 5) = q^4 p = (0.7)^4 (0.3) = 0.07203$$

$$P(X = 6) = q^5 p = (0.7)^5 (0.3) = 0.050421$$

$$P(X = 7) = q^6 p = (0.7)^6 (0.3) = 0.0352\ldots$$

$$P(X = 8) = q^7 p = (0.7)^7 (0.3) = 0.0259\ldots$$

and so on.

NOTE: we could consider $x = 9, 10, 11, 12, \ldots$, but the probabilities are becoming very small.

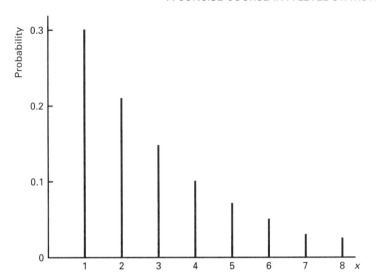

We can see from the diagram that the <u>mode is 1.</u>

NOTE: the mode, or most likely value, in *any* geometric distribution is 1. This is because each successive probability is *smaller* than the one before (because it is multiplied by q which is less than 1) i.e. $p > qp > q^2 p$ etc. The highest probability is p, which occurs when $x = 1$.

The following results are useful:

Result 1   If $X \sim \mathrm{Geo}(p)$ then $P(X > r) = q^r$, where $q = 1 - p$.

Proof: Now $P(X = r) = q^{r-1} p$

$$P(X \leqslant r) = P(\text{success at some trial in the first } r \text{ trials})$$

$$= 1 - P(\text{no success in first } r \text{ trials})$$

$$= 1 - q^r$$

Therefore $P(X > r) = 1 - (1 - q^r)$

$$= q^r$$

Result 2 $P[(X > a + b)\,|\,(X > a)] = P(X > b)$

Proof: $P[(X > a + b)\,|\,(X > a)] = \dfrac{q^{a+b}}{q^a}$

$$= q^b$$

$$= P(X > b)$$

So, for example

$$P[(X > 10)\,|\,(X > 7)] = P(X > 3)$$

$$\text{and} \quad P[(X > 20)\,|\,(X > 15)] = P(X > 5)$$

Example 5.18 A coin is biased so that the probability of obtaining a head is 0.6. If X is the r.v. 'the number of tosses up to and including the first head', find

(a) $P(X \leqslant 4)$,

(b) $P(X > 5)$,

(c) the probability that more than 8 tosses will be required to obtain a head, given that more than 5 tosses are required.

Solution 5.18 $P(X = x) = q^{x-1}p$, $x = 1, 2, 3, \ldots$ with $p = 0.6$ and $q = 0.4$.

(a)
$$P(X > 4) = q^4$$

Therefore
$$P(X \leqslant 4) = 1 - q^4$$
$$= 1 - (0.4)^4$$
$$= 0.9744$$

Therefore $P(X \leqslant 4) = 0.9744$.

(b)
$$P(X > 5) = q^5$$
$$= (0.4)^5$$
$$= 0.010\,24$$

Therefore $P(X > 5) = 0.010\,24$.

(c)
$$P[(X > 8)\,|\,(X > 5)] = P(X > 3)$$
$$= q^3$$
$$= (0.4)^3$$
$$= 0.064$$

The probability that more than 8 tosses will be required given that more than 5 tosses are required is 0.064.

Example 5.19 In a particular board game a player can get out of jail only by obtaining two heads when she tosses two coins.

(a) Find the probability that more than 6 attempts are needed to get out of jail.

(b) What is the smallest value of n if there is to be at least a 90% chance of getting out of jail on or before the nth attempt?

Solution 5.19 $P(2 \text{ heads when 2 coins are tossed}) = \frac{1}{4}$

So $p = P(\text{success}) = \frac{1}{4}$ and $q = \frac{3}{4}$

Let X be the r.v. 'the number of attempts required to get out of jail'.
Then X follows a geometric distribution, $X \sim \text{Geo}\left(\frac{1}{4}\right)$.

(a) $P(X > 6) = q^6$

$$= \left(\frac{3}{4}\right)^6$$

$$= 0.178 \quad (3 \text{ S.F.})$$

The probability that a player needs more than 6 attempts before getting out of jail is 0.178 (3 S.F.).

(b) $P(X > n) = \left(\frac{3}{4}\right)^n$

So $P(X \leqslant n) = 1 - \left(\frac{3}{4}\right)^n$

We require $P(X \leqslant n) \geqslant 0.9$.

So $1 - \left(\frac{3}{4}\right)^n \geqslant 0.9$

$$0.1 \geqslant \left(\frac{3}{4}\right)^n$$

$$\left(\frac{3}{4}\right)^n \leqslant 0.1$$

(Take logs to base 10.)

$$n \log 0.75 \leqslant \log 0.1$$

We want to divide both sides by log 0.75 but since this is negative (check it on your calculator), we must reverse the inequality.

So $n \geqslant \dfrac{\log 0.1}{\log 0.75}$

$$n \geqslant 8.0039$$

Therefore the smallest value of n is 9.

Check: $P(X \leqslant 6) = 1 - \left(\frac{3}{4}\right)^6 = 0.8220 \ldots < 90\%$

$$P(X \leqslant 7) = 1 - \left(\frac{3}{4}\right)^7 = 0.8665 \ldots < 90\%$$

$$P(X \leqslant 8) = 1 - \left(\frac{3}{4}\right)^8 = 0.8998 \ldots < 90\%$$

$$P(X \leqslant 9) = 1 - \left(\frac{3}{4}\right)^9 = 0.9249 \ldots > 90\%$$

So the least value of n is 9.

EXPECTATION AND VARIANCE

> If $X \sim \text{Geo}(p)$, then $E(X) = \dfrac{1}{p}$ and $\text{Var}(X) = \dfrac{q}{p^2}$
> where $q = 1 - p$.

See Appendix 2, page 729 for proof.

Example 5.20 The probability that a marksman hits the bull's eye is 0.4 for each shot, and each shot is independent of all others. Find

  (a) the probability that he hits the bull's eye for the first time on his fourth attempt,

  (b) the mean number of throws needed to hit the bull's eye, and the standard deviation,

  (c) the most likely number of throws until he hits the bull's eye.

Solution 5.20 Let X be the r.v. 'the number of attempts up to and including the first bull's eye'. Now X follows a geometric distribution with $p = 0.4$.

So $P(X = x) = q^{x-1}p$ with $q = 0.6, p = 0.4$.

(a)
$$P(X = 4) = q^3 p$$
$$= (0.6)^3(0.4)$$
$$= 0.0864$$

P(hits bull's eye on fourth attempt) $= 0.0864$.

(b) Now $E(X) = \dfrac{1}{p}$ $\qquad$ $\text{Var}(X) = \dfrac{q}{p^2}$

$\qquad\qquad\qquad = \dfrac{1}{0.4}$ $\qquad\qquad\qquad = \dfrac{0.6}{(0.4)^2}$

$\qquad\qquad\qquad = 2.5$ $\qquad\qquad\qquad = 3.75$

$\qquad\qquad\qquad\qquad\qquad\qquad$ s.d. of $X = \sqrt{3.75}$

$\qquad\qquad\qquad\qquad\qquad\qquad\qquad\qquad = 1.94$ $\quad$ (3 S.F.)

So the mean number of attempts is 2.5 and the standard deviation is 1.94 (3 S.F.).

(c)
$$P(X = 1) = 0.4$$
$$P(X = 2) = 0.6(0.4) = 0.24$$
$$P(X = 3) = 0.6^2(0.4) = 0.144$$

The probabilities are decreasing, and therefore the most likely number of throws is 1.

Example 5.21 Independent identical trials of an experiment are carried out until a success occurs. On average, 10 trials are required. If the probability that a trial is successful is p, find the value of p.

Solution 5.21 Let X be the r.v. 'the number of trials up to and including the first success'.

Then $X \sim \text{Geo}(p)$ and $E(X) = \dfrac{1}{p}$.

So if $E(X) = 10$, then $\dfrac{1}{p} = 10$

$\qquad\qquad\qquad\qquad\qquad p = 0.1$

Example 5.22   Alice runs a stall at a fête, where players throw a die until a four occurs. They have to pay a certain amount per throw and must keep playing until a four is obtained. They then receive £10. How much should Alice charge per throw so that her expected gain, per game, is 50 p?

Solution 5.22   Let X be the r.v. 'the number of throws needed to obtain a four'.

Now $P(\text{four}) = p = \frac{1}{6}, q = \frac{5}{6}$,

so $X \sim \text{Geo}\left(\frac{1}{6}\right)$.

The expected number of throws per game is given by $E(X) = \dfrac{1}{p} = 6$.

If Alice charges £a per throw then she 'expects' to gain (£$6a$ – £10) per game.

If she wishes to gain 50 p per game, then

$$£6a - £10 = £0.50$$

i.e. $$6a = 10.50$$

$$a = 1.75$$

The charge per throw should be £1.75.

Exercise 5g

1. Draw vertical line graphs to illustrate each of the following distributions: (a) $X \sim \text{Geo}(0.4)$, (b) $X \sim \text{Geo}(0.8)$, (c) $X \sim \text{Geo}(0.2)$.

2. If $X \sim \text{Geo}(0.3)$, find (a) $P(X = 4)$, (b) $P(X > 4)$, (c) $P(X \leqslant 2)$, (d) $P((X > 8)\,|\,(X > 3))$.

3. If $X \sim \text{Geo}(0.5)$, find (a) the mode, (b) the mean, (c) the standard deviation of X.

4. A coin is biased so that the probability of obtaining a head is 0.6. Find (a) the expected number of tosses needed to obtain a tail, (b) the most likely number of tosses needed to obtain a tail.

5. During January, the probability that it will rain on any given day is 0.55.
   (a) Find the probability that the first rainy day in January is on the 6th.
   (b) Given that it does not rain on the first 10 days, find the probability that it first rains on 14th January.
   (c) Find the probability that it does not rain before 8th January.

6. (a) When two dice are thrown together a 'double' is obtained when the scores on the two dice are the same. Assuming the two dice to be unbiased, calculate the probabilities that
   (i) in two throws of the two dice, a double will be obtained on the first throw but not on the second throw,
   (ii) in three throws of the two dice, doubles will be obtained on the first two throws but not on the third throw.
   (b) Suppose the two dice are thrown until a double is not obtained. Find the expected number of doubles.   (L Additional)

7. An unbiased coin is tossed repeatedly until a tail appears. Find the expected number of tosses.

8. What is a necessary condition for two events A and B to be described as *statistically independent*?
The Geometric probability distribution arises in circumstances that are decidedly similar to those required for the Binomial distribution. In what way is the random variable for the Geometric different from that for the Binomial?
(*a*) A random variable, X, follows the Geometric distribution with probability $p = 0.3$.
(i)   Write down the probability $P(X = 4)$.
(ii) Carefully explain why $P(X = n)$ is $0.7^{n-1}\,0.3$.
(iii) Describe in words a situation that has probability 0.7^{n-1}.
(*b*) A sixth-former is waiting for a bus to take him to town. He passes the time by counting the number of buses, up to and including one that he wants, that come along his side of the road. If 30% of the buses travelling on that side of the road go to town, what is:
(i)   the most likely count he makes to the arrival of one that will take him to town;
(ii) the probability that he will count at most 4 buses? (O)

9. A darts player practises throwing a dart at the bull's eye on a dart board. Independently for each throw, her probability of hitting the bull's eye is 0.2. Let X be the number of throws she makes, up to and including her first success.
(*a*) Find the probability that she is successful for the first time on her third throw.
(*b*) Write down the distribution of X, and give the name of this distribution.
(*c*) Find the probability that she will have at least 3 failures before her first success.
(*d*) Show that the mean value of X is 5. (You may assume the result

$$\sum_{r=1}^{\infty} rq^{r-1} = \frac{1}{(1-q)^2} \text{ when } |q| < 1.)$$

On another occasion the player throws the dart at the bull's eye until she has 2 successes. Let Y be the number of throws she makes up to and including her second success. Given that $\operatorname{Var}(X) = 20$, determine the mean and the variance of Y, and find the probability that $Y = 4$. (L)

10. A random variable R has probability function $P(R = r)$ defined by

$$P(R = r) = \tfrac{4}{5}\left(\tfrac{1}{5}\right)^{r-1},$$

for $r = 1, 2, 3, \ldots$

$$P(R = r) = 0, \text{ otherwise.}$$

Given that $\displaystyle\sum_{n=1}^{\infty} np^n = \frac{p}{(1-p)^2}$, find $E(R)$.
Given that the variance of R is $\frac{5}{16}$, determine the mean and variance of S where $S = 3R - 2$.
The probability that a telephone box is occupied is $\frac{1}{5}$. Find, to 2 significant figures, the probability that a person wishing to make a phone call will find a telephone box which is not occupied only at the sixth box tried.
Write down the mean number of occupied boxes which will have to be tried before the person finds a box which is not occupied. (L)P

11. (*a*) Describe an experiment you may have carried out which can be modelled by a geometric distribution. State any assumptions you may have made.
(*b*) In many board games it is necessary to 'throw a six with an ordinary die' before a player can start the game. Write down, as a fraction, the probability of a player
(i)   starting on his first attempt,
(ii) not starting until his third attempt,
(iii) requiring more than three attempts before starting.
What is
(iv) the most common number of throws required to obtain a six,
(v)   the mean number of throws required to obtain a six?
Prove that the probability of a player requiring more than n attempts before starting is $\left(\tfrac{5}{6}\right)^n$.
(*c*) What is the smallest value of n if there is to be at least a 95% chance of starting on or before the nth attempt? (O)

12. State conditions which give rise to a geometric distribution whose probability function is $P(X = r) = (1-p)^{r-1}p$, $r = 1, 2, 3, \ldots$, where $0 < p < 1$.
Prove that $P(X \leqslant r) = 1 - (1-p)^r$.
Hence prove that, for any two positive integers s and t,

$$P(X > s + t \mid X > s) = P(X > t)$$

and explain in words the meaning of this result.
During the winter in Glen Shee, the probability that snow will fall on any given day is 0.1. Taking 1st November as the first day of winter and assuming independence from day to day, find, to 2 significant figures, the probability that the first snow of winter will fall in Glen Shee on the last day of November (30th).

Given that no snow has fallen at Glen Shee during the whole of November, a teacher decides not to wait any longer to book a skiing holiday. The teacher decides to book for the earliest date for which the probability that snow will have fallen on or before that date is at least 0.9. Find the date of the booking.   (L)

13. In a sales campaign, a petrol company gives each motorist who buys their petrol a card with a picture of a film star on it. There are 10 different picture cards, one of each of ten different film stars, and any motorist who collects a complete set of all ten pictures gets a free gift. On any occasion when a motorist buys petrol, the card received is equally likely to carry any of the ten pictures in the set.

(a) Find the probability that the first four cards the motorist receives all carry different pictures.

(b) Find the probability that the first four cards received result in the motorist having exactly three different pictures.

(c) Two of the ten film stars in the set are X and Y. Find the probability that the first four cards received result in the motorist having a picture of X or of Y (or both).

(d) At a certain stage the motorist has collected nine of the ten pictures. Find the least value of n such that

P(at most n more cards are needed to complete the set) > 0.99.   (C)

14. A girl fires at a target. The probability of her hitting the bull's eye is p for each shot, and each shot is independent of all others. The random variable X denotes the number of shots previous to that on which the bull's eye is first hit. Show that

$$P(X = x) = q^x p$$

where $q = 1 - p$. Find the mean of X and show that the variance is q/p^2.   (O & C)

THE POISSON DISTRIBUTION

A discrete r.v. X having p.d.f. of the form

$$P(X = x) = e^{-\lambda} \frac{\lambda^x}{x!} \text{ for } x = 0, 1, 2, 3, \ldots \text{ to infinity}$$

where λ can take any positive value, is said to follow the Poisson distribution.

NOTE: λ is the parameter of the distribution.

If X is distributed in this way, then $X \sim \text{Po}(\lambda)$.

Example 5.23 Given that X follows a Poisson distribution with parameter 2, draw a vertical line graph to illustrate the distribution.

Solution 5.23 $X \sim \text{Po}(2)$ so $P(X = x) = e^{-2} \frac{2^x}{x!}$ $x = 0, 1, 2, \ldots$

$$P(X = 0) = e^{-2} \frac{2^0}{0!} = e^{-2} = 0.1353\ldots$$

$$P(X = 1) = e^{-2} \frac{2^1}{1!} = 2e^{-2} = 0.2706\ldots$$

$$P(X = 2) = e^{-2} \frac{2^2}{2!} = 2e^{-2} = 0.2706\ldots$$

$$P(X = 3) = e^{-2} \frac{2^3}{3!} = 0.1804\ldots$$

$$P(X = 4) = e^{-2} \frac{2^4}{4!} = 0.0902\ldots$$

$$P(X = 5) = e^{-2} \frac{2^5}{5!} = 0.0360\ldots$$

$$P(X = 6) = e^{-2} \frac{2^6}{6!} = 0.0120\ldots$$

We could consider $x = 7, 8, 9, \ldots$ but the probabilities are getting very small.

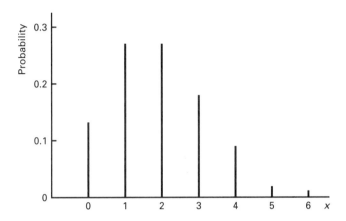

Example 5.24 If $X \sim \mathrm{Po}(3.5)$ find (**a**) $P(X = 0)$, (**b**) $P(X = 4)$, (**c**) $P(X \leqslant 2)$, (**d**) $P(X > 1)$.

Solution 5.24 $X \sim \mathrm{Po}(3.5)$, so $P(X = x) = e^{-3.5} \frac{(3.5)^x}{x!}, \quad x = 0, 1, 2, \ldots$

(**a**) $P(X = 0) = e^{-3.5} \frac{(3.5)^0}{0!}$

$$= e^{-3.5} \qquad \text{since } (3.5)^0 = 1 \quad \text{and } 0! = 1$$

$$= 0.0301\ldots$$

$\underline{P(X = 0) = 0.030 \quad \text{(3 d.p.)}}$

(**b**) $P(X = 4) = e^{-3.5} \frac{(3.5)^4}{4!}$

$$= 0.1888\ldots$$

$\underline{P(X = 4) = 0.189 \quad \text{(3 d.p.)}}$

(**c**) $\qquad P(X \leqslant 2) = P(X = 0) + P(X = 1) + P(X = 2)$

$$= e^{-3.5} + e^{-3.5} \frac{(3.5)^1}{1!} + e^{-3.5} \frac{(3.5)^2}{2!}$$

$$= 0.0301\ldots + 0.1056\ldots + 0.1849\ldots$$

$$= 0.3208\ldots$$

$\underline{P(X \leqslant 2) = 0.321 \quad \text{(3 d.p.)}}$

(d) $$P(X > 1) = 1 - P(X \leqslant 1)$$
$$= 1 - (P(X = 0) + P(X = 1))$$
$$= 1 - (e^{-3.5} + e^{-3.5}(3.5))$$
$$= 1 - 4.5\,e^{-3.5}$$
$$= 0.8641\ldots$$

$P(X > 1) = 0.864 \quad (3 \text{ d.p.})$

EXPECTATION AND VARIANCE

If $X \sim \text{Po}(\lambda)$, then $E(X) = \lambda$

and $\text{Var}(X) = \lambda$

The proof of this result is in Appendix 2 on page 731.

Example 5.25 If $X \sim \text{Po}(2)$, find **(a)** $E(X)$, **(b)** the standard deviation of X.

Solution 5.25 **(a)** If $X \sim \text{Po}(2)$, $\quad\quad E(X) = 2$

(b) $\quad\quad\quad\quad\quad\quad\quad\quad \text{Var}(X) = 2$

so standard deviation of $X = \sqrt{2} = 1.41 \quad (3 \text{ S.F.})$

Example 5.26 The random variable X follows a Poisson distribution with standard deviation 3. Find **(a)** $E(X)$, **(b)** $P(X < 4)$.

Solution 5.26 If $X \sim \text{Po}(\lambda)$ then $\text{Var}(X) = \lambda$.

If the standard deviation is 3, then $\text{Var}(X) = 9$. Therefore $\lambda = 9$.

(a) $\quad\quad\quad\quad\quad\quad\quad\quad\quad E(X) = 9$

(b) $P(X < 4) = P(X = 0) + P(X = 1) + P(X = 2) + P(X = 3)$

$$= e^{-9} + e^{-9}(9) + e^{-9}\frac{(9)^2}{2!} + e^{-9}\frac{(9^3)}{3!}$$

$$= e^{-9}\left(1 + 9 + \frac{9^2}{2!} + \frac{9^3}{3!}\right)$$

$$= 172\,e^{-9}$$

$$= 0.02122\ldots$$

$P(X < 4) = 0.0212 \quad (3 \text{ S.F.})$

Exercise 5h

1. If $X \sim Po(2.5)$, find (a) $P(X = 0)$,
    (b) $P(X = 1)$, (c) $P(X = 2)$, (d) $P(X = 3)$,
    (e) $P(X < 3)$, (f) $P(X \geqslant 4)$, (g) $E(X)$.

2. If $X \sim Po(1.8)$, find (a) $P(X = 6)$,
    (b) $P(X = 8)$, (c) $P(X \leqslant 2)$, (d) $P(X \geqslant 4)$.

3. If $X \sim Po(2.4)$ and $F(X)$ is the cumulative
    distribution, find (a) $F(0)$, (b) $F(1)$,
    (c) $F(2)$, (d) $F(3)$.

4. $X \sim Po(\lambda)$ and $P(X = 0) = 0.2019$. Find
    (a) λ, (b) $P(X \leqslant 4)$, (c) $Var(X)$.

5. Find the first 5 terms of the Poisson
    distribution if (a) $\lambda = 0.5$, (b) $\lambda = 2.8$,
    (c) $\lambda = 3.6$. Draw vertical line graphs to
    illustrate each distribution as far as $x = 5$.

6. If $X \sim Po(\lambda)$ and $E(X^2) = 6$, find (a) λ,
    (b) $P(X = 2)$.

7. The random variable X follows a Poisson
    distribution with standard deviation 2. Find
    $P(X \leqslant 3)$.

USES OF THE POISSON DISTRIBUTION

There are two main practical uses of the Poisson distribution:

(1) when considering the distribution of random events,

(2) as an approximation to the binomial distribution.

We shall now look at these in more detail.

(1) The distribution of random events

If an event is randomly scattered in time (or space) and has mean number of occurrences λ in a given interval of time (or space) and if X is the r.v. 'the number of occurrences in the given interval', then $X \sim Po(\lambda)$.

Examples of events which might follow a Poisson distribution:

The number of

(a) flaws in a given length of material,

(b) car accidents on a particular stretch of road in one day,

(c) accidents in a factory in one week,

(d) telephone calls made to a switchboard in a given minute,

(e) insurance claims made to a company in a given time,

(f) particles emitted by a radioactive source in a given time.

Example 5.27 The mean number of bacteria per millilitre of a liquid is known to be 4. Assuming that the number of bacteria follows a Poisson distribution, find the probability that, in 1 ml of liquid, there will be (a) no bacteria, (b) 4 bacteria, (c) less than 3 bacteria.

Solution 5.27 Let X be the r.v. 'the number of bacteria in 1 ml of liquid'.

Then $X \sim \mathrm{Po}\,(4)$, so that $P(X = x) = \mathrm{e}^{-4} \dfrac{4^x}{x!}$ $x = 0, 1, 2, \ldots$

(**a**) $P(X = 0) = \mathrm{e}^{-4}$

$$= 0.0183 \quad (3 \text{ S.F.})$$

The probability that there will be no bacteria in 1 ml of liquid is 0.0183 (3 S.F.).

(**b**) $P(X = 4) = \mathrm{e}^{-4} \dfrac{4^4}{4!}$

$$= 0.195 \quad (3 \text{ S.F.})$$

The probability that there will be 4 bacteria in 1 ml of liquid is 0.195 (3 S.F.).

(**c**) $P(X < 3) = P(X = 0) + P(X = 1) + P(X = 2)$

$$= \mathrm{e}^{-4} + \mathrm{e}^{-4}\,4 + \mathrm{e}^{-4}\,\dfrac{4^2}{2!}$$

$$= \mathrm{e}^{-4}\,(1 + 4 + 8)$$

$$= \mathrm{e}^{-4}\,(13)$$

$$= 0.238 \quad (3 \text{ S.F.})$$

The probability that there are less than 3 bacteria in 1 ml of liquid is 0.238 (3 S.F.).

UNIT INTERVAL

In Example 5.27 we have considered 1 ml of liquid as the 'unit' interval.

The number of bacteria in 1 ml of liquid follows a Poisson distribution with parameter 4.

It follows that the number of bacteria in 2 ml follows a Poisson distribution with parameter 8, the number in 3 ml follows a Poisson distribution with parameter 12, and so on.

Example 5.28 If the mean number of bacteria per millilitre of a liquid is 4, find the probability that

(**a**) in 3 ml of liquid there will be less than 2 bacteria,

(**b**) in $\frac{1}{2}$ ml of liquid there will be more than 2 bacteria.

Solution 5.28 (**a**) In 1 ml of liquid we 'expect' to find 4 bacteria, so in 3 ml of liquid we 'expect' to find 12 bacteria.

Let Y be the r.v. 'the number of bacteria in 3 ml of liquid'.

So $Y \sim \text{Po}(12)$ and $P(Y = y) = e^{-12} \dfrac{12^y}{y!}$ $y = 0, 1, 2, \ldots$

Now, we require $P(Y < 2) = P(Y = 0) + P(Y = 1)$

$$= e^{-12} + e^{-12}(12)$$

$$= 13\,e^{-12}$$

$$= 7.99 \times 10^{-5} \quad (3 \text{ S.F.})$$

Therefore the probability that there are less than 2 bacteria in $3\,\text{ml}$ of liquid is $7.99 \times 10^{-5}\,(3 \text{ S.F.})$.

(b) In $1\,\text{ml}$ of liquid we 'expect' 4 bacteria, so in $\frac{1}{2}\,\text{ml}$ of liquid we 'expect' 2 bacteria.

Let R be the r.v. 'the number of bacteria in $\frac{1}{2}\,\text{ml}$ of liquid'.

Then $R \sim \text{Po}(2)$ and $P(R = r) = e^{-2} \dfrac{2^r}{r!}$ $r = 0, 1, 2, \ldots$

We require

$$P(R > 2) = 1 - [P(R = 0) + P(R = 1) + P(R = 2)]$$

$$= 1 - \left(e^{-2} + e^{-2}\,2 + e^{-2}\,\dfrac{2^2}{2!}\right)$$

$$= 1 - 5\,e^{-2}$$

$$= 0.323 \quad (3 \text{ S.F.})$$

The probability that there are more than 2 bacteria in $\frac{1}{2}\,\text{ml}$ of liquid is $0.323\,(3 \text{ S.F.})$.

Example 5.29 A book containing 500 pages has 750 misprints.

(a) What is the average number of misprints per page?

(b) Find the probability that page 427 contains (i) no misprints, (ii) exactly 4 misprints, (iii) more than the average number of misprints.

(c) Find the probability that pages 427 and 428 will contain no misprints.

Solution 5.29 (a) Average number per page $= \dfrac{750}{500} = 1.5$

(b) Let X be the r.v. 'the number of misprints per page'. Then, assuming that misprints occur at random, $X \sim \text{Po}(1.5)$

(i) $$P(X = 0) = e^{-1.5}$$

$$= 0.2231\ldots$$

$P(\text{there will be no misprints on page 427}) = 0.223 \quad (3 \text{ d.p.})$.

(ii) $$P(X = 4) = e^{-1.5} \frac{(1.5)^4}{4!}$$

$$= 0.0470\ldots$$

$\underline{P(\text{there will be 4 misprints on page 427}) = 0.047 \quad (3 \text{ d.p.}).}$

(iii) The mean number of misprints per page $= 1.5$

$$P(X > 1.5) = P(X = 2) + P(X = 3) + \ldots$$

$$= 1 - (P(X = 0) + P(X = 1))$$

$$= 1 - (e^{-1.5} + e^{-1.5}(1.5))$$

$$= 1 - 2.5\,e^{-1.5}$$

$$= 0.4421\ldots$$

$\underline{P(\text{page 427 has more than average number of misprints}) = 0.442 \ (3 \text{ d.p.}).}$

(c) On one page we 'expect' 1.5 misprints, so on two pages we 'expect' 3 misprints. Let Y be the r.v. 'the number of misprints on two pages'.

$$Y \sim \text{Po}(3), \text{ so } \quad P(Y = 0) = e^{-3}$$

$$= 0.0497\ldots$$

$\underline{P(\text{pages 427 and 428 contain no misprints}) = 0.050 \quad (3 \text{ d.p.}).}$

Exercise 5i

1. An insurance company receives on average 2 claims per week from a certain factory. Assuming that the number of claims follows a Poisson distribution, find the probability that (a) it receives more than 3 claims in a given week, (b) it receives more than 2 claims in a given fortnight, (c) it receives no claims on a given day, assuming that the factory operates on a 5-day week.

2. Cars arrive at a petrol station at an average rate of 30 per hour. Assuming that the number of cars arriving at the petrol station follows a Poisson distribution, find the probability that
(a) no cars arrive during a particular 5-minute interval,
(b) more than 3 cars arrive during a 5-minute interval,
(c) more than 5 cars arrive in a 15-minute interval,
(d) in a period of half an hour, 10 cars arrive,
(e) less than 3 cars arrive during a 10-minute interval.

3. A sales manager receives 6 telephone calls on average between 9.30 a.m. and 10.30 a.m. on a weekday. Find the probability that
(a) she will receive 2 or more calls between 9.30 and 10.30 on a certain weekday;
(b) she will receive exactly 2 calls between 9.30 and 9.40;
(c) during a normal 5-day working week, there will be exactly 3 days on which she will receive no calls between 9.30 and 9.40.

4. If the number of bacterial colonies on a petri dish follows a Poisson distribution with average number 2.5 per cm^2, find the probability that
(a) in $1\,\text{cm}^2$ there will be no bacterial colonies,
(b) in $1\,\text{cm}^2$ there will be more than 4 bacterial colonies,
(c) in $2\,\text{cm}^2$ there will be less than 4 bacterial colonies,
(d) in $4\,\text{cm}^2$ there will be 6 bacterial colonies.

5. The mean number of flaws per 100 m of material produced on a certain machine at Blanktown Fabrics is 2. If flaws occur randomly, find the probability that (a) in a 200 m length of material there will be more than 3 flaws, (b) in 50 m of material there will be exactly 2 flaws.

6. The number of goals scored in a match by Random Rovers follows a Poisson distribution with mean λ. If the probability that the team scores no goals in a match is 0.301 (3 d.p.) find (a) the value of λ, (b) the probability that the team scores less than 3 goals in a match, (c) the probability that the team scores less than 3 goals in 2 matches.

7. The number of telephone calls made to the school office during a 5-minute interval follows a Poisson distribution with mean 0.5. Find the probability that (a) no calls will be received between 10.05 and 10.10, (b) more than 4 calls will be received during a particular period of 30 minutes.

8. The number of accidents per week in a certain factory follows a Poisson distribution with variance 3.2. Find the probability that (a) no accidents occur in a particular week, (b) more than 4 accidents occur in a particular week, (c) less than 3 accidents occur in a particular fortnight, (d) exactly 7 accidents occur in a particular fortnight.

(2) Using the Poisson distribution as an approximation to the binomial distribution

> A binomial distribution with parameters n and p can be approximated by a Poisson distribution, with parameter $\lambda = np$, if n is large (>50 say) and p is small (<0.1 say). The approximation gets better as $n \to \infty$ and $p \to 0$.

The derivation of this result is given in Appendix 2 on page 733.

Example 5.30 A factory packs bolts in boxes of 500. The probability that a bolt is defective is 0.002. Find the probability that a box contains 2 defective bolts.

Solution 5.30 Let X be the r.v. 'the number of defective bolts in a box'.

This is a binomial situation, with $n = 500, p = 0.002$.

So $\qquad\qquad X \sim \text{Bin}(500, 0.002)$

Method 1 Using the binomial distribution,

$$P(X = x) = {}^nC_x q^{n-x} p^x \quad x = 0, 1, 2, \ldots, n$$

We have $n = 500, p = 0.002$ and $q = 0.998$, so

$$P(X = x) = {}^{500}C_x (0.998)^{500-x} (0.002)^x$$

$$P(X = 2) = {}^{500}C_2 (0.998)^{498} (0.002)^2$$

$$= \frac{(500)(499)}{(2)(1)} (0.998)^{498} (0.002)^2$$

$$= 0.184 \quad (3 \text{ d.p.})$$

Method 2 Since n is large and p is small, we use the Poisson approximation.

The parameter $\lambda = np = 500(0.002) = 1$.

So $X \sim \text{Po}(1)$ and $P(X = x) = \text{e}^{-1} \dfrac{1^x}{x!}$ $x = 0, 1, \ldots$

We require $P(X = 2) = \text{e}^{-1} \dfrac{1^2}{2!} = 0.184$ (3 d.p.)

Therefore the probability that a box contains 2 defective bolts is 0.184 (3 d.p.).

NOTE: the answers agree to 3 d.p. and the calculations were much easier in Method 2.

Example 5.31   Find the probability that at least two double sixes are obtained when two dice are thrown 90 times.

Solution 5.31   Throw two dice, $P(\text{double } 6) = \left(\frac{1}{6}\right)\left(\frac{1}{6}\right) = \frac{1}{36}$.

Let X be the r.v. 'the number of double sixes obtained when two dice are thrown 90 times'. Then $X \sim \text{Bin}\left(90, \frac{1}{36}\right)$ and $np = (90)\left(\frac{1}{36}\right) = 2.5$.

Using the Poisson approximation,

$$X \sim \text{Po}(2.5) \text{ and } P(X = x) = \text{e}^{-2.5} \frac{(2.5)^x}{x!} \quad x = 0, 1, \ldots$$

Now $P(X \geqslant 2) = 1 - [P(X = 0) + P(X = 1)]$

$$= 1 - (\text{e}^{-2.5} + \text{e}^{-2.5}\, 2.5)$$

$$= 1 - \text{e}^{-2.5}\,(3.5)$$

$$= 0.713 \quad (3 \text{ d.p.})$$

The probability that at least two double sixes are obtained when two dice are thrown 90 times is 0.713 (3 d.p.).

Exercise 5j

1.   If $X \sim \text{Bin}(100, 0.03)$, use (a) the binomial distribution, (b) the Poisson distribution to evaluate (i) $P(X = 0)$, (ii) $P(X = 2)$, (iii) $P(X = 4)$.

2.   If $X \sim \text{Bin}(200, 0.006)$, use the Poisson distribution to find   (a) $P(X < 3)$, (b) $P(X > 5)$.

3.   On average one in 200 cars breaks down on a certain stretch of road per day. Find the probability that on a certain day

(a) none of a sample of 250 cars breaks down,

(b) more than 2 of a sample of 300 cars break down.

4. The probability that a particular make of light bulb is faulty is 0.01. The light bulbs are packed in boxes of 100.
    (*a*) Find the probability that in a certain box there are (i) no faulty light bulbs, (ii) 2 faulty light bulbs, (iii) more than 3 faulty light bulbs.
    (*b*) A buyer accepts a consignment of 50 boxes if, when he chooses two boxes at random, he finds that they contain no more than two faulty light bulbs altogether. Find the probability that he accepts the consignment.

5. Eggs are packed in boxes of 500. On average, 0.8% of the eggs are found to be broken when the eggs are unpacked.
    (*a*) Find the probability that in a box of 500 eggs (i) exactly 3 will be broken, (ii) less than 2 will be broken.

(*b*) A hypermarket unpacks 100 boxes of eggs. What is the probability that there will be exactly 4 boxes containing no broken eggs?

6. An aircraft has 116 seats. The airline has found, from long experience, that on average 2.5% of people with tickets for a particular flight do not arrive for that flight. If the airline sells 120 seats for a particular flight determine, using a suitable approximation, the probability that more than 116 people arrive for that flight. Determine also the probability that there are empty seats on the flight. (C)

7. A firm selling electrical components packs them in boxes of 60. On average 2% of the components are faulty. What is the chance of getting more than 2 defective components in a box?

CUMULATIVE POISSON PROBABILITY TABLES

The task of finding Poisson probabilities can be made much easier if tables are available. These give $P(X \leqslant r)$ for given values of λ. The tables are printed on page 720 and an extract is shown below.

	$\lambda = 2.4$
$r = 0$	0.0907
1	0.3084
2	0.5697
3	0.7787
4	0.9041
5	0.9643
6	0.9884
7	0.9967
8	0.9991
9	0.9998
10	1.0000

Example 5.32 If $X \sim \text{Po}(2.4)$ find (**a**) $P(X \leqslant 6)$, (**b**) $P(X \geqslant 3)$, (**c**) $P(X < 8)$, (**d**) $P(X > 7)$, (**e**) $P(X = 4)$.

Solution 5.32 (**a**) $P(X \leqslant 6) = 0.9884$ (directly from the tables)

(**b**) $P(X \geqslant 3) = 1 - P(X \leqslant 2) = 1 - 0.5697 = 0.4303$

(**c**) $P(X < 8) = P(X \leqslant 7) = 0.9967$

(**d**) $P(X > 1) = 1 - P(X \leqslant 1) = 1 - 0.3084 = 0.6916$

(**e**) $P(X = 4) = P(X \leqslant 4) - P(X \leqslant 3) = 0.9041 - 0.7787 = 0.1254$

DIAGRAMMATIC REPRESENTATION OF THE POISSON DISTRIBUTION

The following vertical line graphs show the probability distribution of $X \sim \text{Po}(\lambda)$ for various values of λ. The horizontal axis gives values of x and the vertical axis gives values of $P(X = x)$.

Notice that for small values of λ the distribution is very skew, but it becomes more symmetrical as λ increases.

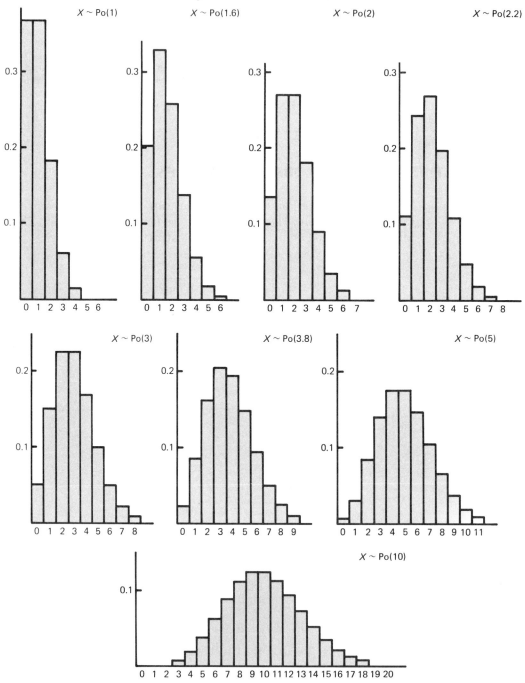

THE MODE OF THE POISSON DISTRIBUTION

The mode is the value which is most likely to occur, that is the one with the highest probability. Consider $X \sim \text{Po}(\lambda)$. From the diagrams, we see that

when $\lambda = 1$, there are two modes, 0 and 1

when $\lambda = 2$, there are two modes, 1 and 2

when $\lambda = 3$, there are two modes, 2 and 3.

In general, if λ is an integer then there are two modes and these occur when $x = \lambda - 1, x = \lambda$.

Notice that

when $\lambda = 1.6$, the mode is 1

when $\lambda = 2.2$, the mode is 2

when $\lambda = 3.8$, the mode is 3.

In general, if λ is not an integer, then the mode m is the integer such that

$$\lambda - 1 < m < \lambda.$$

Exercise 5k

1. Use cumulative Poisson probability tables to find the first six terms of the following Poisson distributions. Verify that the mode m is an integer such that $\lambda - 1 < m < \lambda$.

   (i) $X \sim \text{Po}(1.8)$ (ii) $X \sim \text{Po}(2.6)$
   (iii) $X \sim \text{Po}(4.5)$ (iv) $X \sim \text{Po}(3.8)$.

FITTING A THEORETICAL DISTRIBUTION

As with the binomial distribution it is possible to fit a theoretical Poisson distribution to experimental data.

Example 5.33 I recorded the number of phone calls I received over a period of 150 days:

Number of calls	0	1	2	3	4
Number of days	51	54	36	6	3

(a) Find the average number of calls per day.

(b) Calculate the frequencies of the comparable Poisson distribution.

Solution 5.33   (a)   For the data given

$$\bar{x} = \frac{\Sigma fx}{\Sigma f}$$

$$= \frac{0(51) + 1(54) + 2(36) + 3(6) + 4(3)}{150}$$

$$= 1.04$$

The average number of calls per day is 1.04.

(**b**) We use the mean of 1.04 as the parameter λ of the Poisson distribution.

Let X be the r.v. 'the number of calls per day'.

So $X \sim \text{Po}\,(1.04)$

and $\qquad P(X = x) = \text{e}^{-1.04}\,\frac{(1.04)^x}{x!} \quad x = 0, 1, 2 \ldots$

Now $P(X = 0) = \text{e}^{-1.04} = 0.3534 \ldots$

so when $x = 0$, expected frequency $= 150 \times 0.3534 \ldots$

$$= 53.01 \ldots$$

$$P(X = 1) = 1.04\,\text{e}^{-1.04} = 0.3675 \ldots$$

So when $x = 1$, expected frequency $= 150 \times 0.3675 \ldots$

$$= 55.13 \ldots$$

Similarly, we can find the expected frequencies when $x = 2, 3, 4$. Rounding these to the nearest integer, we have

Number of calls, x	0	1	2	3	4	
Number of days, f	53	55	29	10	3	Total 150

This theoretical Poisson distribution compares reasonably well with the original data. A statistical test to compare the two sets of data, known as a chi-squared test, is illustrated on page 580.

NOTE: the theoretical Poisson distribution gives an expected frequency for x greater than 4, but this is very small so we ignore the error involved.

Exercise 5I

1.   For each of the following sets of data, fit a theoretical Poisson distribution:

(a)

x	0	1	2	3	4
f	45	44	20	8	3

(b)

x	0	1	2	3	4	5
f	110	50	20	12	7	1

2. An inn caters for overnight travellers and during its busy season of 100 days the number of requests each day for rooms has a Poisson distribution with mean 4. The inn has four rooms for hire.

Draw up a table to show the expected frequencies of 0, 1, 2, ..., 12 requests each day for rooms during the 100 days.

Obtain an estimate of the number of requests which will have to be refused during the period. The cost of building an extra room is estimated at £1000 which the owner would pay from capital invested to yield a net $8\frac{1}{2}\%$ per annum. If each room let yields on average £3 net per day, estimate the annual gain or loss of income (excluding the capital outlay) were the owner to have the room built. It may be assumed that during the rest of the year fewer than five rooms are let.

3. A firm investigated the number of employees suffering injuries whilst at work. The results recorded below were obtained for a 52-week period:

Number of employees injured in a week	Number of weeks
0	31
1	17
2	3
3	1
4 or more	0

Give reasons why one might expect this distribution to approximate to a Poisson distribution. Evaluate the mean and variance of the data and explain why this gives further evidence in favour of a Poisson distribution. Using the calculated value of the mean, find the theoretical frequencies of a Poisson distribution for the number of weeks in which 0, 1, 2, 3, 4 or more, employees were injured.

(C)

4. State the conditions under which the binomial distribution approximates to the Poisson distribution. Hence derive the Poisson distribution of mean m and show that its variance is also m.

Tests for defects are carried out in a textile factory on a lot comprising 400 pieces of cloth. The results of the tests are shown in the table below.

Number of faults per piece	Number of pieces
0	92
1	142
2	96
3	46
4	18
5	6
6	0

Show that this is approximately a Poisson distribution and calculate the frequencies on this assumption.

How many pieces from a sample of 1000 pieces may be expected to have 4 or more faults? (AEB)

THE DISTRIBUTION OF TWO INDEPENDENT POISSON VARIABLES

> The sum of two independent Poisson variables with parameters m and n, respectively, is a Poisson variable with parameter $(m + n)$,
>
> i.e. if $X \sim \text{Po}(m)$ and $Y \sim \text{Po}(n)$, then $X + Y \sim \text{Po}(m + n)$

The proof of this result is given in Appendix 2 on page 734.

Example 5.34 Two identical racing cars are being tested on a circuit. For each car, the number of mechanical breakdowns follows a Poisson distribution with a mean of one breakdown in 100 laps.

The first car does 20 laps and the second does 40 laps. What is the probability that there will be (**a**) no breakdowns, (**b**) one breakdown, (**c**) more than two breakdowns altogether? Assume that breakdowns are attended and the cars continue on the circuit.

Solution 5.34   In 100 laps we 'expect' 1 breakdown. So, in 20 laps we 'expect' 0.2 breakdowns and in 40 laps we 'expect' 0.4 breakdowns.

Let X be the r.v. 'the number of breakdowns for the first car'.

Then $X \sim \text{Po}\,(0.2)$

Let Y be the r.v. 'the number of breakdowns for the second car'

Then $Y \sim \text{Po}\,(0.4)$

Let T be the r.v. 'the total number of breakdowns', so $T = X + Y$

$$T \sim \text{Po}\,(0.2 + 0.4)$$

i.e. $T \sim \text{Po}\,(0.6)$

(**a**) $P(T = 0) = e^{-0.6}$

$$= 0.549 \quad (3 \text{ d.p.})$$

Therefore the probability that there are no breakdowns is 0.549 (3 d.p.)

(**b**) $P(T = 1) = e^{-0.6}\,(0.6)$

$$= 0.329 \quad (3 \text{ d.p.})$$

The probability that there will be one breakdown is 0.329 (3 d.p.).

(**c**) $P(T > 2) = 1 - [\,P(T = 0) + P(T = 1) + P(T = 2)\,]$

$$= 1 - \left[e^{-0.6} + e^{-0.6}\,(0.6) + e^{-0.6}\,\frac{(0.6)^2}{2!} \right]$$

$$= 1 - e^{-0.6}\,(1 + 0.6 + 0.18)$$

$$= 1 - e^{-0.6}\,(1.78)$$

$$= 0.023 \quad (3 \text{ d.p.})$$

The probability that there will be more than two breakdowns is 0.023 (3 d.p.).

Example 5.35   The centre pages of the 'Weekly Sentinel' consist of 1 page of film and theatre reviews and 1 page of classified advertisements. The number of misprints in the reviews has a Poisson distribution with mean 2.3 and the number of misprints in the classified section has a Poisson distribution with mean 1.7.

(**a**) Find the probability that, on the centre pages, there will be
(*i*) no misprints, (*ii*) more than 5 misprints.

(**b**) Find the smallest integer n such that the probability that there are more than n misprints on the centre pages is less than 0.1.

Solution 5.35 Let X be the r.v. 'the number of misprints on the review page'.

Then $X \sim \mathrm{Po}\,(2.3)$

Let Y be the r.v. 'the number of misprints on the classified page'.

Then $Y \sim \mathrm{Po}\,(1.7)$

Let T be the r.v. 'the number of misprints on the centre pages'.

Therefore $T = X + Y$ and $T \sim \mathrm{Po}\,(2.3 + 1.7)$

i.e. $T \sim \mathrm{Po}\,(4)$

(**a**) (*i*) $P(T = 0) = \mathrm{e}^{-4} = 0.018\,315\,6 = 0.018$ (3 d.p.)

The probability that there will be no misprints on the centre pages is 0.018 (3 d.p.).

(*ii*) Using cumulative Poisson probability tables, with $\lambda = 4, r = 5$,

$$P(T > 5) = 1 - P(T \leqslant 5)$$
$$= 1 - 0.7851$$
$$= 0.215 \quad (3 \text{ d.p.})$$

The probability that there will be more than 5 misprints on the centre pages is 0.215 (3 d.p.).

(**b**) Now $P(T > 5) = 0.215 > 0.1$

and from tables we find that

$$P(T > 6) = 0.111 > 0.1$$
$$P(T > 7) = 0.051 < 0.1$$

So the smallest integer n, such that the probability that there are more than n misprints on the centre pages is less than 0.1, is 7.

Exercise 5m

1. Telephone calls reach a secretary independently and at random, internal ones at a mean rate of 2 in any 5-minute period, and external ones at a mean rate of 1 in any 5-minute period. Calculate the probability that there will be more than 2 calls in any period of 2 minutes.   (O & C)

2. During a weekday, heavy lorries pass a census point P on a village high street independently and at random times. The mean rate for westward travelling lorries is 2 in any 30-minute period, and for eastward travelling lorries is 3 in any 30-minute period. Find the probability
    (*a*) that there will be no lorries passing P in a given 10-minute period,
    (*b*) that at least one lorry from each direction will pass P in a given 10-minute period,
    (*c*) that there will be exactly 4 lorries passing P in a given 20-minute period.   (O & C)

3. A large number of screwdrivers from a trial production run is inspected. It is found that the cellulose acetate handles are defective on 1% and that the chrome steel blades are defective on $1\frac{1}{2}$% of the screwdrivers, the defects occurring independently.
    (a) What is the probability that a sample of 80 contains more than two defective screwdrivers?
    (b) What is the probability that a sample of 80 contains at least one screwdriver with both a defective handle and a defective blade?
                                                                    (O & C)

4. A restaurant kitchen has 2 food mixers, A and B. The number of times per week that A breaks down has a Poisson distribution with mean 0.4, while independently the number of times that B breaks down in a week has a Poisson distribution with mean 0.1. Find, to 3 decimal places, the probability that in the next 3 weeks
    (a) A will not break down at all,
    (b) each mixer will break down exactly once,
    (c) there will be a total of 2 breakdowns.
                                                                    (L)P

MISCELLANEOUS WORKED EXAMPLES

Example 5.36   Along a stretch of motorway, breakdowns requiring the summoning of the breakdown services occur with a frequency of 2.4 per day, on average. Assuming that the breakdowns occur randomly and that they follow a Poisson distribution, find

(**a**) the probability that there will be exactly 2 breakdowns on a given day,

(**b**) the smallest integer n such that the probability of more than n breakdowns in a day is less than 0.03.

Solution 5.36   (a) Let X be the r.v. 'the number of breakdowns a day requiring the breakdown services'.

Then

$$X \sim \text{Po}\,(2.4) \quad \text{and} \quad P(X = x) = e^{-2.4}\frac{(2.4)^x}{x!} \quad x = 0, 1, 2, \ldots$$

So $$P(X = 2) = e^{-2.4}\frac{(2.4)^2}{2!} = 0.261 \quad (3 \text{ S.F.})$$

The probability that there will be exactly 2 breakdowns on a given day is 0.261 (3 S.F.).

(**b**) We require the least integer n such that $P(X > n) < 0.03$.

Now if $P(X > n) < 0.03$

then $P(X \leqslant n) > 0.97$

From cumulative Poisson probability tables, with $\lambda = 2.4$

$$P(X \leqslant 5) = 0.9643 < 0.97$$

$$P(X \leqslant 6) = 0.9884 > 0.97$$

So the least integer n such that $P(X > n) < 0.03$ is 6.

Example 5.37 The number of white corpuscles on a slide has a Poisson distribution with mean 3.2.

Find the most likely number of white corpuscles on a slide. Calculate correct to 3 d.p. the probability of obtaining this number. If two such slides are prepared, what is the probability, correct to 3 d.p., of obtaining at least two white corpuscles in total on the two slides?

Solution 5.37 Let X be the r.v. 'the number of white corpuscles on a slide'. Then $X \sim \text{Po}(3.2)$.

Now when $\lambda = 3.2$, the mode is 3 (see p.299)

Check: $$P(X = 2) = e^{-3.2}\frac{(3.2)^2}{2!} = 0.2087\ldots$$

$$P(X = 3) = e^{-3.2}\frac{(3.2)^3}{3!} = \boxed{0.2226\ldots}$$

$$P(X = 4) = e^{-3.2}\frac{(3.2)^4}{4!} = 0.1780\ldots$$

Therefore the most likely number of white corpuscles on a slide is 3.

Now $$P(X = 3) = e^{-3.2}\frac{(3.2)^3}{3!}$$

$$= 0.223 \quad (3 \text{ d.p.})$$

The probability of obtaining 3 white corpuscles on a slide is 0.223 (3 d.p.).

Let X_1 be the r.v. 'the number of white corpuscles on the first slide'.

Then $X_1 \sim \text{Po}(3.2)$.

Let X_2 be the r.v. 'the number of white corpuscles on the second slide'.
Then $X_2 \sim \text{Po}(3.2)$.

Let $Y = X_1 + X_2$, then $Y \sim \text{Po}(3.2 + 3.2)$

i.e. $Y \sim \text{Po}(6.4)$

We require $$P(Y \geqslant 2) = 1 - [P(Y = 0) + P(Y = 1)]$$

$$= 1 - (e^{-6.4} + e^{-6.4}\,6.4)$$

$$= 1 - 7.4\,e^{-6.4}$$

$$= 0.988 \quad (3 \text{ d.p.})$$

The probability of obtaining at least two white corpuscles in total on the two slides is 0.988 (3 d.p.).

We now show an alternative approach to the last part:

If two slides are prepared, we require

$$P(\text{total number of white corpuscles} \geqslant 2).$$

Now

$$P(\text{total} \geqslant 2) = 1 - [P(\text{total} = 0) + P(\text{total} = 1)]$$

$$= 1 - [P(X_1 = 0) P(X_2 = 0) + P(X_2 = 0) P(X_1 = 1)$$
$$+ P(X_1 = 1) P(X_2 = 0)]$$

$$= 1 - [(e^{-3.2})(e^{-3.2}) + e^{-3.2}(e^{-3.2} 3.2) + (e^{-3.2} 3.2) e^{-3.2}]$$

$$= 1 - e^{-6.4}(1 + 3.2 + 3.2)$$

$$= 1 - 7.4 \, e^{-6.4}$$

$$= 0.988 \quad \text{as before}$$

Example 5.38   In a large town, one person in 80, on the average, has blood of type X. If 200 blood donors are taken at random, find an approximation to the probability that they include at least five persons having blood of type X.

How many donors must be taken at random in order that the probability of including at least one donor of type X shall be 0.9 or more?   (AEB)

Solution 5.38   Let R be the r.v. 'the number of blood donors of type X'.

Then $R \sim \text{Bin}(n, p)$ where $n = 200$ and $p = P(\text{blood type X}) = \frac{1}{80}$.

Now, as n is large and p is small, we use the Poisson approximation to the binomial distribution.

The parameter $\lambda = np = (200)\left(\frac{1}{80}\right) = 2.5$

The probability that there are at least five donors of type X is

$$P(R \geqslant 5) = 1 - P(R \leqslant 4)$$

$$= 1 - 0.8912 \quad \text{(from tables)}$$

$$= 0.109 \quad \text{(3 d.p.)}$$

The probability that the sample will contain at least five people having blood of type X is 0.109 (3 d.p.).

Suppose n donors are taken, then $\lambda = n\left(\frac{1}{80}\right)$.

So $R \sim \text{Po}\left(\dfrac{n}{80}\right)$.

We require n such that $P(R \geqslant 1) \geqslant 0.9$,

i.e. $1 - P(R = 0) \geqslant 0.9$

$$P(R = 0) \leqslant 0.1$$

Now $P(R = 0) = e^{-n/80}$

So $e^{-n/80} \leqslant 0.1$

$$e^{n/80} \geqslant \frac{1}{0.1}$$

i.e. $e^{n/80} \geqslant 10$

So, taking logs to the base e,

$$\frac{n}{80} \geqslant \ln(10)$$

$$\frac{n}{80} \geqslant 2.30$$

$$n \geqslant (80)(2.30)$$

$$n \geqslant 184.2$$

So we need to take 185 donors in order that the probability of including at least one donor of type X is 0.9 or more.

Check: If $n = 184, \lambda = (184)\left(\frac{1}{80}\right) = 2.3$

So $P(R \geqslant 1) = 1 - e^{-2.3}$

$$= 0.8997 \quad (4 \text{ d.p.})$$

We have $P(R \geqslant 1) < 0.9$ when $n = 184$.

Now consider $n = 185$, then $\lambda = (185)\left(\frac{1}{80}\right) = 2.3125$

$$P(R \geqslant 1) = 1 - e^{-2.3125}$$

$$= 0.901 \quad (3 \text{ d.p.})$$

So $P(R \geqslant 1) > 0.9$ when $n = 185$.

Example 5.39 In the Growmore Market Garden plants are inspected for the presence of the deadly red angus leaf bug. The number of bugs per leaf is known to follow a Poisson distribution with mean one. What is the probability that any one leaf on a given plant will have been attacked (at least one bug is found on it)?

A random sample of twelve plants is taken. For each plant ten leaves are selected at random and inspected for these bugs. If more than eight leaves on any particular plant have been attacked then the plant is destroyed. What is the probability that exactly two of these twelve plants are destroyed?   (AEB)

Solution 5.39 Let X be the r.v. 'the number of bugs per leaf'.

Then $X \sim \mathrm{Po}\,(1)$ and $P(X = x) = \mathrm{e}^{-1} \dfrac{1^x}{x!}$ $\quad x = 0, 1, 2, \ldots$

We require $\qquad P(X \geqslant 1) = 1 - P(X = 0)$

$$= 1 - \mathrm{e}^{-1}$$

$$= 1 - 0.368$$

$$= 0.632 \quad (3 \text{ S.F.})$$

The probability that any one leaf has been attacked is 0.632 (3 S.F.).

Now let Y be the r.v. 'the number of leaves that have been attacked on a plant'.

Then $Y \sim \mathrm{Bin}\,(10, 0.632)$ since $n = 10$, and the probability that a leaf has been attacked is 0.632.

We have

$$P(Y = y) = {}^{10}C_y\,(0.368)^{10-y}\,(0.632)^y \quad y = 0, 1, 2, \ldots, 10$$

We require

$$P(Y > 8) = P(Y = 9) + P(Y = 10)$$

$$= 10\,(0.368)^1\,(0.632)^9 + (0.632)^{10}$$

$$= 0.069 \quad (3 \text{ d.p.})$$

The probability that any one plant is destroyed is 0.069 (3 d.p.).

Now let R be the r.v. 'the number of plants that are destroyed'.

Then $R \sim \mathrm{Bin}\,(12, 0.069)$ since 12 plants are inspected, and the probability that a plant is destroyed is 0.069.

$$P(R = r) = {}^{12}C_r\,(0.931)^{12-r}\,(0.069)^r$$

We require $\quad P(R = 2) = {}^{12}C_2\,(0.931)^{10}\,(0.069)^2$

$$= 0.154 \quad (3 \text{ d.p.}).$$

The probability that exactly two of the twelve plants will be destroyed is 0.154 (3 d.p.).

SUMMARY — BINOMIAL, GEOMETRIC AND POISSON DISTRIBUTIONS

Binomial

If $X \sim \text{Bin}(n,p)$, then $P(X = x) = {}^nC_x q^{n-x} p^x$,
$x = 0, 1, 2, \ldots, n$ where $q = 1 - p$,

so $P(X = 0) = q^n$, $P(X = 1) = {}^nC_1 q^{n-1} p$,
$P(X = 2) = {}^nC_2 q^{n-2} p^2, \ldots, P(X = n) = p^n$.

$E(X) = np$

$\text{Var}(X) = npq$

Geometric

If $X \sim \text{Geo}(p)$, then $P(X = x) = q^{x-1} p$, $x = 1, 2, 3, \ldots$
where $q = 1 - p$,

so $P(X = 1) = p$, $P(X = 2) = qp$, $P(X = 3) = q^2 p, \ldots$

$E(X) = \dfrac{1}{p}$

$\text{Var}(X) = \dfrac{q}{p^2}$

$P(X > r) = q^r$

$P[(X > a + b) \,|\, (X > a)] = P(X > b) = q^b$

Poisson

If $X \sim \text{Po}(\lambda)$, then $P(X = x) = e^{-\lambda} \dfrac{\lambda^x}{x!}$, $x = 0, 1, 2 \ldots$

so $P(X = 0) = e^{-\lambda}$, $P(X = 1) = e^{-\lambda}\lambda$, $P(X = 2) = e^{-\lambda}\dfrac{\lambda^2}{2!}$,

$P(X = 3) = e^{-\lambda}\dfrac{\lambda^3}{3!}, \ldots$

$E(X) = \lambda$

$\text{Var}(X) = \lambda$

If $X \sim \text{Po}(m)$ and $Y \sim \text{Po}(n)$ then $X + Y \sim \text{Po}(m + n)$,
where X and Y are independent.

If $X \sim \text{Bin}(n,p)$, where n is large and p is small, then
$X \sim \text{Po}(np)$ approximately.

Miscellaneous Exercise 5n

1. The random variable X has the binomial distribution B(10, 0.35). Find $P(X \leqslant 4)$. The random variable Y has the Poisson distribution with mean 3.5. Find $P(2 < Y \leqslant 5)$. (L)

2. The number of accidents per week at a certain intersection has a Poisson distribution with parameter 2.5. Find the probability that
   (a) exactly 5 accidents will occur in a week,
   (b) more than 14 accidents will occur in 4 weeks. (L)

3. Fanfold paper for computer printers is made by putting perforations every 30 cm in a continuous roll of paper. A box of fanfold paper contains 2000 sheets. State the length of the continuous roll from which the box of paper is produced.
   The manufacturers claim that faults occur at random and at an average rate of 1 per 240 metres of paper. State an appropriate distribution for the number of faults per box of paper. Find the probability that a box of paper has no faults and also the probability that it has more than 4 faults.
   Two copies of a report which runs to 100 sheets per copy are printed on this sort of paper. Find the probability that there are no faults in either copy of the report and also the probability that just one copy is faulty.
   (MEI)

4. A process for making plate glass produces small bubbles (imperfections) scattered at random in the glass, at an average rate of four small bubbles per $10 \, \text{m}^2$.
   Assuming a Poisson model for the number of small bubbles, determine, to 3 decimal places, the probability that a piece of glass $2.2 \, \text{m} \times 3.0 \, \text{m}$ will contain
   (a) exactly two small bubbles,
   (b) at least one small bubble,
   (c) at most two small bubbles.
   Show that the probability that five pieces of glass, each 2.5 m by 2.0 m, will all be free of small bubbles is e^{-10}.
   Find, to 3 decimal places, the probability that five pieces of glass, each 2.5 m by 2.0 m, will contain a total of at least ten small bubbles.
   (L)P

5. A shop sells a particular make of radio at a rate of 4 per week on average. The number sold in a week has a Poisson distribution.
   (a) Find the probability that the shop sells at least 2 in a week.
   (b) Find the smallest number that can be in stock at the beginning of a week in order to

have at least a 99% chance of being able to meet all demands during that week. (L)

6. Lemons are packed in boxes, each box containing 200. It is found that, on average, 0.45% of the lemons are bad when the boxes are opened. Use the Poisson distribution to find the probabilities of 0, 1, 2, and more than 2 bad lemons in a box.
   A buyer who is considering buying a consignment of several hundred boxes checks the quality of the consignment by having a box opened. If the box opened contains no bad lemons he buys the consignment. If it contains more than 2 bad lemons he refuses to buy, and if it contains 1 or 2 bad lemons he has another box opened and buys the consignment if the second box contains fewer than 2 bad lemons. What is the probability that he buys the consignment?
   Another buyer checks consignments on a different basis. He has one box opened; if that box contains more than 1 bad lemon he asks for another to be opened and does not buy if the second also contains more than 1 bad lemon. What is the probability that he refuses to buy the consignment?

7. Show that, for the Poisson distribution in which the probabilities of 0, 1, 2, ... successes are $e^{-m}, m e^{-m}, \dfrac{m^2 e^{-m}}{2!}, \ldots,$
   the mean number of successes is equal to m. State the variance.
   A manufacturer produces an integrated electronic unit which contains 36 separate pressure sensors. Due to difficulties in manufacture, it happens very often that not all the sensors in a unit are operational. 100 units are tested and the numbers N of pressure sensors which function correctly are distributed according to the table below.

N	Number of units
36	5
35	15
34	22
33	22
32	17
31	11
30	5
29	2
28	1
< 28	0

Calculate the mean number of sensors which are faulty.
The manufacturer only markets those units which have at least 32 of their 36 sensors operational. Estimate, using the Poisson distribution, the percentage of units produced which are not marketed.

(O & C)

8. (a) The probability distribution of a discrete random variable, X, is defined by

$$P(X = x) = \begin{cases} e^{-\lambda} \dfrac{\lambda^x}{x!} & x = 0, 1, 2, \ldots \ (\lambda > 0) \\ 0 & \text{otherwise.} \end{cases}$$

Derive the mean and variance of X.
(b) A shopkeeper hires vacuum cleaners to the general public at £5 per day. The mean daily demand is 2.6.
(i) Calculate the expected daily income from this activity assuming an unlimited number of vacuum cleaners is available. The demand follows a Poisson distribution.
(ii) Find the probability that the demand on a particular day is (a) 0, (b) exactly one, (c) exactly two, (d) three or more.
(iii) If only 3 vacuum cleaners are available for hire calculate the mean of the daily income. A nearby large store is willing to lend vacuum cleaners at short notice to the shopkeeper, so that in practice she will always be able to meet any demand. The store would charge £2 per day for this service regardless of how many, if any, cleaners are actually borrowed. Would you advise the shopkeeper to take up this offer? Explain your answer.   (AEB 1992)

9. Weak spots occur at random in the manufacture of a certain cable at an average rate of 1 per 100 metres.
If X represents the number of weak spots in 100 metres of cable, write down the distribution of X.
Lengths of this cable are wound on to drums. Each drum carries 50 metres of cable.
Find the probability that a drum will have 3 or more weak spots.
A contractor buys five such drums.
Find the probability that two have just one weak spot each and the other three have none.
A special drum of this cable, of length 2 km, is manufactured.
Find the probability that this drum has fewer than 15 weak spots.   (AEB 1991)

10. The number of telephone calls received per minute at the switchboard of a certain office was logged during the period 10 a.m. to noon on a working day. The results were as follows:

Calls per min. (x)	f
0	7
1	18
2	27
3	28
4	20
5	11
6	5
7	3
8	1

f is the number of minutes with x calls per minute.
By consideration of the mean and variance of this distribution show that a possible model is a Poisson distribution.
Using the calculated mean and on the assumption of a Poisson distribution calculate
(a) the probability that two or more calls were received during any one minute,
(b) the probability that no calls were received during any two consecutive minutes.

11. Customers enter an antique shop independently of one another and at random intervals of time at an average rate of four per hour throughout the five days of a week on which the shop is open. The owner has a coffee-break of fifteen minutes each morning; if one or more customers arrive during this period then his coffee goes cold, otherwise he drinks it while it is hot.
Let X be the random variable denoting the number of customers arriving during a Monday coffee-break, and let Y be the random variable denoting the number of days during a week on which the owner's coffee goes cold. Assuming that X has a Poisson distribution, determine (correct to three significant figures) (a) $P(X = 0)$, (b) $P(X \geqslant 2)$, (c) $E(Y)$, (d) $P(Y = 2)$.   (C)

12. A hire company has two electric lawnmowers which it hires out by the day. The number of demands per day for a lawnmower has the form of a Poisson distribution with mean 1.50. In a period of 100 working days, how many times do you expect
(a) neither of the lawnmowers to be used,
(b) some requests for the lawnmowers to have to be refused?
If each lawnmower is to be used an equal amount, on how many days in a period of 100 working days would you expect a particular lawnmower not to be in use?   (MEI)

13. An experimenter marked out ten neighbouring plots of land, all of the same area, and examined them for the occurrence of a certain species of plant. The numbers, f_r, of plots in which r plants were found were as follows:

r	0	1	2	3	4	5
f_r	3	1	1	2	1	2

Calculate the mean number of plants per plot.
Assuming that the plants were scattered randomly with this same mean number of plants per plot, find
(a) the probability of a given plot containing no plants;
(b) the probability of at least three plots being found which contain no plants.
What conclusions, if any, can be drawn from the observed number of plots in which the experimenter found no plants?
(You may assume that $e^{-2.3} \approx 0.1$)   (SMP)

14. Derive the Poisson distribution as the limiting form of the Binomial distribution when n becomes very large and p becomes very small in such a way that np remains constant. Write down the mean and the variance of this distribution.
The mean number of bacteria per millilitre of a liquid is known to be 3. Ten samples of the liquid, chosen at random and each of volume 1 ml, are examined. Assuming the Poisson distribution is applicable, obtain expressions for the probabilities
(a) that each of the ten samples contains at least one bacterium,
(b) that exactly eight of the samples contain at least one bacterium.
If 3 ml of the liquid is examined, show that it is rather improbable that it will contain fewer than 3 or more than 15 bacteria.
(MEI)

15. During each working day in a certain factory a number of accidents occur independently according to a Poisson distribution with mean 0.5.
Calculate the probability that
(a) during any one day there are 2 or more accidents,
(b) during two consecutive days there are exactly three accidents altogether.
Out of 50 consecutive five-day weeks how many would you expect to be accident-free?
Give two further situations where you would expect a Poisson distribution to apply.

16. Prove that for the Poisson distribution in which the probability of r successes is

$$\frac{e^{-m}m^r}{r!} \quad (r \geqslant 0)$$

the expected number of successes is equal to m.
The telephone exchange inside an office building has a number of outside lines of which, on average, 3 are being used at any instant. Assuming that the number of lines in use at any instant follows a Poisson distribution, find
(a) the probability that, at any given instant, not more than 3 lines are in use,
(b) the minimum number of outside lines required if there is to be a probability of more than 0.9 that, at any given instant, at least one of the lines is not being used.   (C)

17. The monthly demand for a certain magazine at a small newsagent's shop has a Poisson distribution with mean 3. The newsagent always orders 4 copies of the magazine for sale each month; any demand for the magazine in excess of 4 is not met.
(a) Calculate the probability that the newsagent will not be able to meet the demand in a given month.
(b) Find the most probable number of magazines *sold* in one month.
(c) Find the expected number of magazines *sold* in one month.
(d) Determine the least number of copies of the magazine that the newsagent should order each month so as to meet the demand with a probability of at least 0.95.   (JMB)

18. A random sample of 500 people born in 1961 is being studied. It can be assumed that birthdays are uniformly distributed throughout the year.
(a) Use the Poisson distribution to find, to 3 decimal places, the probabilities that there are (i) exactly two people, and (ii) no more than two people, with birthdays on 1 January.
(b) Also find, to 3 decimal places, the probability that, if two of the sample are chosen at random, they have birthdays in the same month. (In 1961 there were 7 months with 31 days, 4 months with 30 days and 1 month with 28 days.)   (MEI)

19. Define the Poisson distribution and derive its mean. State the circumstances under which it is appropriate to use the Poisson distribution as an approximation to the binomial distribution.

A lottery has a very large number of tickets, one in every 500 of which entitles the purchaser to a prize. An agent sells 1000 tickets for the lottery. Using the Poisson distribution, find, to three decimal places, the probabilities that the number of prize-winning tickets sold by the agent is (a) less than three, (b) more than five.
Calculate the minimum number of tickets the agent must sell to have a 95% chance of selling at least one prize-winning ticket. (JMB)

20. Define the Poisson distribution and derive its mean and variance.
The number of telephone calls received at a switchboard in any time interval of length T minutes has a Poisson distribution with mean $\frac{1}{2}T$. The operator leaves the switchboard unattended for five minutes. Calculate to three decimal places the probabilities that there are (a) no calls, (b) four or more calls in her absence.
Find to three significant figures the maximum length of time in seconds for which the operator could be absent with a 95% probability of not missing a call. (JMB)

21. Define the Poisson distribution and derive its mean and variance.
In the first year of the life of a certain type of machine, the number of times a maintenance engineer is required has a Poisson distribution with mean four. Find the probability that more than four calls are necessary.
The first call is free of charge and subsequent calls cost £20 each. Find the mean cost of maintenance in the first year. (JMB)

22. The number of oil tankers arriving at a port between successive high tides has a Poisson distribution with mean 2. The depth of the water is such that loaded vessels can enter the dock area only on the high tide. The port has dock space for only three tankers, which are discharged and leave the dock area before the next tide. Only the first three loaded tankers waiting at any high tide go into the dock area; any others must await another high tide.
Starting from an evening high tide after which no ships remain waiting their turn, find (to three decimal places) the probabilities that after the next morning's high tide (a) the three dock berths remain empty, (b) the three berths are all filled.
Find (to two decimal places) the probability that no tankers are left waiting outside the dock area after the following evening's high tide. (JMB)

23. The random variable X has a Poisson distribution with parameter λ.
(a) Prove that $E(X) = \lambda$.
(b) If $P(X = k) = P(X = k+1)$, where k is some integer, show that λ must also be an integer.
(c) If λ is not an integer, show that the mode, m, of the distribution is such that $\lambda - 1 < m < \lambda$.
In the manufacture of commercial carpet, small faults occur at random in the carpet at an average rate of 0.95 per $20\,\text{m}^2$. Find the probability that in a randomly selected $20\,\text{m}^2$ area of this carpet
(d) there are no faults,
(e) there are at most 2 faults.
The ground floor of a new office block has 10 rooms. Each room has an area of $80\,\text{m}^2$ and has been carpeted using the same commercial carpet described above. For any one of these rooms, determine the probability that the carpet in that room
(f) contains at least 2 faults,
(g) contains exactly 3 faults,
(h) contains at most 5 faults.
Find the probability that in exactly half of these 10 rooms the carpets will contain exactly 3 faults. (AEB 1988)

24. A randomly chosen doctor in general practice sees, on average, one case of a broken nose per year and each case is independent of other similar cases.
(a) Regarding a month as a twelfth part of a year,
(i) show that the probability that, between them, three such doctors see no cases of a broken nose in a period of one month is 0.779, correct to three significant figures,
(ii) find the variance of the number of cases seen by three such doctors in a period of six months.
(b) Find the probability that, between them, three such doctors see at least three cases in one year.
(c) Find the probability that, of three such doctors, one sees three cases and the other two see no cases in one year. (C)

25. State, giving your reasons, the distribution which you would expect to be appropriate in describing
(a) the number of heads in 10 throws of a penny,
(b) the number of blemishes per m^2 of sheet metal.
A building has an automatic telephone exchange. The number X of wrong connections in any one day is a Poisson

variable with parameter λ. Find, in terms of λ, the probability that in any one day there will be

(c) exactly 3 wrong connections,

(d) 3 or more wrong connections.

Evaluate, to 3 decimal places, these probabilities when $\lambda = 0.5$. Find, to 3 decimal places, the largest value of λ for the probability of one or more wrong connections in any day to be at most $\frac{1}{6}$.   (L)

6

PROBABILITY DISTRIBUTIONS II — CONTINUOUS RANDOM VARIABLES

A continuous random variable (r.v.) is a theoretical representation of a continuous variable such as height, mass or time. For example, X could be the continuous random variable 'the time taken, in minutes, to perform a given task', Y could be the continuous random variable 'the mass, in g, of a bag of sugar packaged by a particular machine'.

PROBABILITY DENSITY FUNCTION

A continuous random variable X is specified by its probability density function which is written $f(x)$ where $f(x) \geqslant 0$ throughout the range of values for which x is valid. This probability density function (p.d.f.) can be represented by a curve, and the probabilities are given by the area under the curve.

Example 6.1 X is the r.v. 'the delay, in hours, of a flight from Airport A', where

$$f(x) = 0.2 - 0.02x, \qquad 0 \leqslant x \leqslant 10.$$

Find (**a**) the probability that the delay will be less than 4 hours,

(**b**) the probability that the delay will be between 2 and 6 hours.

Solution 6.1   Since $f(x)$ holds for $0 \leqslant x \leqslant 10$, the delay can be between 0 and 10 hours only. We first draw a sketch of $f(x)$:

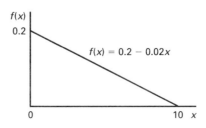

(**a**) We can find the probability that the delay will be less than 4 hours by finding the area under the curve between 0 and 4.

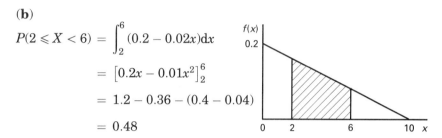

$$P(0 \leqslant X < 4) = \int_0^4 (0.2 - 0.02x)\mathrm{d}x$$

$$= \left[0.2x - 0.01x^2\right]_0^4$$

$$= 0.8 - 0.16$$

$$= 0.64$$

The probability that the delay will be less than 4 hours is 0.64.

(**b**)

$$P(2 \leqslant X < 6) = \int_2^6 (0.2 - 0.02x)\mathrm{d}x$$

$$= \left[0.2x - 0.01x^2\right]_2^6$$

$$= 1.2 - 0.36 - (0.4 - 0.04)$$

$$= 0.48$$

The probability that the delay will be between 2 and 6 hours is 0.48.

NOTE: (1) The total area under the curve gives the total probability, so it must be 1.

Check: $\displaystyle\int_0^{10} (0.2 - 0.02x)\mathrm{d}x = \left[0.2x - 0.01x^2\right]_0^{10}$

$$= 2 - 1$$

$$= 1 \qquad \text{as required.}$$

In this example we could simply find the area of the triangle:

Area $= \frac{1}{2}(10)(0.2) = 1.$

(2) It is not possible to find the probability that the delay is, say, 3 hours.

$$P(X = 3) = \int_3^3 f(x)\mathrm{d}x = 0.$$

We can only find the probability that X lies *within a particular range*.

(3) It is not possible to distinguish between $P(2 \leqslant X \leqslant 6)$, $P(2 < X \leqslant 6)$, $P(2 \leqslant X < 6)$, and $P(2 < X < 6)$, so there is no need to worry about whether the inequality is strict or not.

Example 6.2 X is the continuous random variable 'the mass of a substance, in kg, produced per minute in a particular industrial process', where

$$f(x) = \begin{cases} \frac{1}{36}x(6 - x) & (0 \leqslant x \leqslant 6) \\ 0 & \text{otherwise} \end{cases}$$

Find the probability that the mass is more than 5 kg.

Solution 6.2 X can take values between 0 and 6 only. We sketch $f(x)$, and shade the area required.

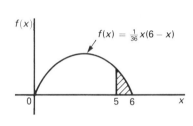

$$P(X > 5) = \int_5^6 \frac{1}{36}\, x(6 - x)\mathrm{d}x$$

$$= \frac{1}{36} \int_5^6 (6x - x^2)\mathrm{d}x$$

$$= \frac{1}{36} \left[3x^2 - \frac{x^3}{3} \right]_5^6$$

$$= 0.074 \quad (3\,\mathrm{d.p.})$$

The probability that the mass is more than 5 kg is 0.074 (3 d.p.).

In general, if X is a continuous r.v. with p.d.f. $f(x)$ valid over the range $a \leqslant x \leqslant b$ then

(*i*)
$$\int_{\text{all } x} f(x)\mathrm{d}x = 1$$

i.e. $\displaystyle\int_a^b f(x)\mathrm{d}x = 1$

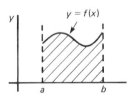

The area under the curve $y = f(x)$ between $x = a$ and $x = b$ is 1.

(*ii*) If $a \leqslant x_1 \leqslant x_2 \leqslant b$ then

$$P(x_1 \leqslant X \leqslant x_2) = \int_{x_1}^{x_2} f(x)\mathrm{d}x$$

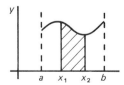

$P(x_1 \leqslant X \leqslant x_2)$ is given by the area under the curve $y = f(x)$ between $x = x_1$ and $x = x_2$.

NOTE: in an experimental approach, the area under the histogram represents frequency. In a theoretical approach, the area under the curve $y = f(x)$ represents probability.

Example 6.3 A continuous random variable has p.d.f. $f(x)$

where $\qquad\qquad f(x) = kx^2, \qquad\qquad 0 \leqslant x \leqslant 4.$

(a) Find the value of the constant k.

(b) Find $P(1 \leqslant X \leqslant 3)$.

Solution 6.3 (a) Since X is a random variable the total probability is 1,

so $\qquad\qquad\qquad\qquad \displaystyle\int_{\text{all }x} f(x)\mathrm{d}x = 1$

i.e. $\qquad\qquad\qquad\qquad \displaystyle\int_0^4 kx^2\,\mathrm{d}x = 1$

$$\left[\frac{kx^3}{3}\right]_0^4 = 1$$

$$64\frac{k}{3} = 1$$

$$k = \tfrac{3}{64}$$

Therefore $f(x) = \frac{3}{64}x^2,\ \ 0 \leqslant x \leqslant 4$

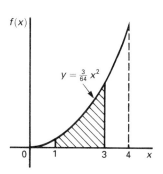

(b) $\displaystyle P(1 \leqslant X \leqslant 3) = \int_1^3 \frac{3}{64}x^2\,\mathrm{d}x$

$$= \frac{3}{64}\left[\frac{x^3}{3}\right]_1^3$$

$$= 0.406\,25$$

Therefore $P(1 \leqslant X \leqslant 3) = 0.406\,25$

Example 6.4 The continuous r.v. X has p.d.f. $f(x)$ where

$$f(x) = \begin{cases} k(x+2)^2 & -2 \leqslant x < 0 \\ 4k & 0 \leqslant x \leqslant 1\tfrac{1}{3} \\ 0 & \text{otherwise} \end{cases}$$

(a) Find the value of the constant k.

(b) Sketch $y = f(x)$.

(c) Find $P(-1 \leqslant X \leqslant 1)$.

(d) Find $P(X > 1)$.

Solution 6.4   (**a**) Since X is a random variable,

$$\int_{\text{all } x} f(x)\mathrm{d}x = 1$$

Therefore $\displaystyle \int_{-2}^{0} k(x+2)^2\mathrm{d}x + \int_{0}^{1\frac{1}{3}} 4k\,\mathrm{d}x = 1$

$$\frac{k}{3}\left[(x+2)^3\right]_{-2}^{0} + 4k\left[x\right]_{0}^{1\frac{1}{3}} = 1$$

$$\frac{k}{3}(8) + 4k\left(\frac{4}{3}\right) = 1$$

$$8k = 1$$

$$\underline{k = \tfrac{1}{8}}$$

(**b**) So the p.d.f. of X is

$$f(x) = \begin{cases} \frac{1}{8}(x+2)^2 & -2 \leqslant x < 0 \\ \frac{1}{2} & 0 \leqslant x \leqslant 1\frac{1}{3} \\ 0 & \text{otherwise} \end{cases}$$

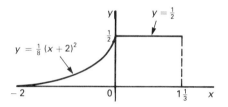

(**c**) We require $P(-1 \leqslant X \leqslant 1)$. This is given by the shaded area in the diagram.

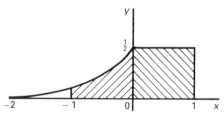

$$P(-1 \leqslant X \leqslant 0) = \int_{-1}^{0} \tfrac{1}{8}(x+2)^2\mathrm{d}x$$

$$= \tfrac{1}{24}\left[(x+2)^3\right]_{-1}^{0}$$

$$= \tfrac{1}{24}(8-1)$$

$$= \tfrac{7}{24}$$

and $P(0 \leqslant X \leqslant 1) = $ area of rectangle

$$= \tfrac{1}{2}$$

Therefore $P(-1 \leqslant X \leqslant 1) = \tfrac{7}{24} + \tfrac{1}{2} = \tfrac{19}{24}$

(**d**) From the diagram,

$P(X > 1) = $ area of rectangle

$$= \frac{1}{3} \times \frac{1}{2}$$

$$= \frac{1}{6}$$

Therefore $P(X > 1) = \frac{1}{6}$

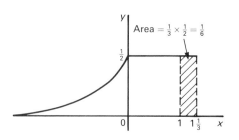

Example 6.5   A continuous r.v. X has p.d.f. $f(x)$ where

$$f(x) = \begin{cases} kx & 0 \leqslant x < 2 \\ k(4 - x) & 2 \leqslant x \leqslant 4 \\ 0 & \text{otherwise} \end{cases}$$

Sketch $y = f(x)$ and find the value of k.

Solution 6.5

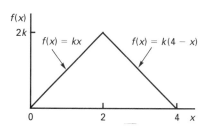

Now $y = kx$ and $y = k(4 - x)$ are both straight lines.

When $x = 0, y = 0$

when $x = 2, y = 2k$

when $x = 4, y = 0$

We can find the area under the graph by finding the area of the triangle.

$$\text{Area} = \frac{1}{2}(4)(2k)$$

$$= 4k$$

Since the total area is 1,

$$4k = 1$$

$$k = 0.25$$

So

$$f(x) = \begin{cases} 0.25\,x & 0 \leqslant x < 2 \\ 1 - 0.25\,x & 2 \leqslant x \leqslant 4 \\ 0 & \text{otherwise} \end{cases}$$

NOTE: in this example it was advantageous to draw a sketch first.

Exercise 6a

1. The continuous r.v. X has p.d.f. $f(x)$ where
    $f(x) = kx^2, 0 \leqslant x \leqslant 2$.
    (a) Find the value of the constant k.
    (b) Sketch $y = f(x)$.
    (c) Find $P(X \geqslant 1)$.
    (d) Find $P(0.5 \leqslant X \leqslant 1.5)$.

2. The continuous r.v. X has p.d.f. $f(x)$ where
    $f(x) = k, -2 \leqslant x \leqslant 3$.
    (a) Sketch $y = f(x)$.
    (b) Find the value of the constant k.
    (c) Find $P(-1.6 \leqslant X \leqslant 2.1)$.

3. The continuous r.v. X has p.d.f. $f(x)$ where
$f(x) = k(4 - x), 1 \leqslant x \leqslant 3$.
(a) Find the value of the constant k.
(b) Sketch $y = f(x)$.
(c) Find $P(1.2 \leqslant X \leqslant 2.4)$.

4. The continuous r.v. X has p.d.f. $f(x)$ where
$f(x) = k(x + 2)^2, 0 \leqslant x \leqslant 2$.
(a) Find the value of the constant k.
(b) Sketch $y = f(x)$.
(c) Find $P(0 \leqslant X \leqslant 1)$ and hence find
$P(X > 1)$.

5. The continuous r.v. X has p.d.f. $f(x)$ where
$f(x) = kx^3, 0 \leqslant x \leqslant c$ and $P\left(X \leqslant \frac{1}{2}\right) = \frac{1}{16}$.
Find the values of the constants c and k and
sketch $y = f(x)$.

6. The continuous r.v. X has p.d.f. $f(x)$ where
$$f(x) = \begin{cases} k & 0 \leqslant x < 2 \\ k(2x - 3) & 2 \leqslant x \leqslant 3 \\ 0 & \text{otherwise} \end{cases}$$
(a) Find the value of the constant k.
(b) Sketch $y = f(x)$.
(c) Find $P(X \leqslant 1)$.
(d) Find $P(X > 2.5)$.
(e) Find $P(1 \leqslant X \leqslant 2.3)$.

7. A continuous r.v. has p.d.f. $f(x)$ where
$f(x) = kx, 0 \leqslant x \leqslant 4$.
(a) Find the value of the constant k.
(b) Sketch $y = f(x)$.
(c) Find $P\left(1 \leqslant X \leqslant 2\frac{1}{2}\right)$.

EXPECTATION

If X is a continuous r.v. with p.d.f. $f(x)$, then the expectation of X is $E(X)$ where

$$E(X) = \int_{\text{all } x} x f(x) \, dx$$

NOTE: $E(X)$ is often denoted by μ and referred to as the mean of X.

Example 6.6   If X is a continuous r.v. with p.d.f. $f(x) = \dfrac{3x^2}{64}, 0 \leqslant x \leqslant 4$, find $E(X)$.

Solution 6.6   Now
$$E(X) = \int_{\text{all } x} x f(x) \, dx$$

$$= \int_0^4 x \left(\frac{3x^2}{64}\right) dx$$

$$= \frac{3}{64} \int_0^4 x^3 \, dx$$

$$= \frac{3}{64} \left[\frac{x^4}{4}\right]_0^4$$

$$= 3$$

Therefore $E(X) = 3$.

Example 6.7 If the continuous r.v. X has p.d.f. $f(x) = \frac{3}{4}(3-x)(x-5)$, $3 \leqslant x \leqslant 5$, find $E(X)$.

Solution 6.7

$$E(X) = \int_{\text{all }x} x f(x) \, dx$$

$$= \int_3^5 \frac{3}{4} x(3-x)(x-5) \, dx$$

$$= \frac{3}{4} \int_3^5 (8x^2 - 15x - x^3) \, dx$$

$$= \frac{3}{4} \left[\frac{8x^3}{3} - \frac{15x^2}{2} - \frac{x^4}{4} \right]_3^5$$

$$= 4$$

Therefore $E(X) = 4$.

NOTE: in this example it would have been advantageous to have drawn a sketch of $y = f(x)$, thus:

From the sketch, we see that there is symmetry about the line $x = 4$.

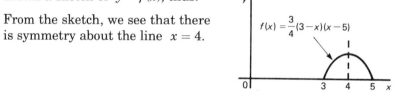

Therefore, by inspection, $E(X) = 4$.

So whenever possible, draw a sketch of $y = f(x)$ and look for symmetry when finding $E(X)$.

Example 6.8 The random variable X has probability density function

$$f(x) = \begin{cases} 3x^k & 0 \leqslant x \leqslant 1, \\ 0 & \text{otherwise,} \end{cases}$$

where k is a positive integer.
Find

(**a**) the value of k,

(**b**) the mean of X,

(**c**) the value, x, such that $P(X \leqslant x) = 0.5$.   (L)

Solution 6.8 (**a**) Since X is a random variable, $\displaystyle\int_{\text{all }x} f(x) \, dx = 1$

Therefore

$$\int_0^1 3x^k \, dx = 1$$

$$3 \left[\frac{x^{k+1}}{(k+1)} \right]_0^1 = 1$$

$$\frac{3}{k+1} = 1$$

$$k + 1 = 3$$

$$\underline{k = 2}$$

Therefore
$$f(x) = \begin{cases} 3x^2 & 0 \leqslant x \leqslant 1 \\ 0 & \text{otherwise} \end{cases}$$

(b)
$$E(X) = \int_0^1 x f(x)\,dx$$

$$= \int_0^1 3x^3\,dx$$

$$= \frac{3}{4}\left[x^4\right]_0^1$$

$$= 0.75$$

Therefore the mean of X is 0.75.

(**c**) Let $P(X \leqslant x_1) = 0.5$

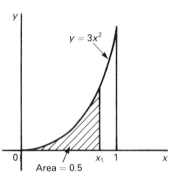

Therefore
$$\int_0^{x_1} 3x^2\,dx = 0.5$$

$$\left[x^3\right]_0^{x_1} = 0.5$$

$$x_1^{\,3} = 0.5$$

$$x_1 = (0.5)^{\frac{1}{3}}$$

$$= 0.794 \quad (3 \text{ d.p.})$$

Therefore, the value of x such that $P(X \leqslant x) = 0.5$, is 0.794 (3 d.p.).

Exercise 6b

For Questions 1–5, find $E(X)$. Don't forget to look for symmetry.

1. The continuous r.v. X has p.d.f. $f(x)$ where $f(x) = \frac{3}{4}(x^2 + 1), 0 \leqslant x \leqslant 1$.

2. The continuous r.v. X has p.d.f. $f(x)$ where $f(x) = \frac{3}{4}x(2 - x), 0 \leqslant x \leqslant 2$.

3. The continuous r.v. X has p.d.f. $f(x)$ where $f(x) = \frac{1}{18}(6 - x), 0 \leqslant x \leqslant 6$.

4. The continuous r.v. X has p.d.f. $f(x)$ where $f(x) = kx^3, 0 \leqslant x \leqslant 2$.

5. The continuous r.v. X has p.d.f. $f(x)$ where

$$f(x) = \begin{cases} \frac{3}{8} & \frac{2}{3} \leqslant x < 2 \\ \frac{3}{32}x(4 - x) & 2 \leqslant x \leqslant 4 \\ 0 & \text{otherwise} \end{cases}$$

6. The continuous r.v. X has p.d.f. $f(x)$ where

$$f(x) = \begin{cases} kx & 0 \leqslant x < 1 \\ k & 1 \leqslant x < 3 \\ k(4 - x) & 3 \leqslant x \leqslant 4 \\ 0 & \text{otherwise} \end{cases}$$

(a) Find k. (b) Calculate $E(X)$.
(c) Now sketch $y = f(x)$.
(d) Check $E(X)$ from the sketch.

7. In a game a wooden block is propelled with a stick across a flat deck. On each attempt the distance, x metres, reached by the block lies between 0 and 10 m, and the variation is modelled by the probability density function

$$\phi(x) = 0.0012x^2(10 - x).$$

Calculate the mean distance reached by the block. (SMP)

8. The continuous random variable X has the probability density function f given by $f(x) = kx, 5 < x < 10, f(x) = 0$ otherwise.
(a) Find the value of k.
(b) Find the expected value of X.
(c) Find the probability that $X > 8$.
The annual income from money invested in a Unit Trust Fund is X per cent of the amount invested, where X has the above distribution. Suppose that you have a sum of money to invest and that you are prepared to leave the money invested over a period of several years. State, with your reasons, whether you would invest in the Unit Trust Fund or in a Money Bond offering a guaranteed annual income of 8 per cent on the money invested. (JMB)

9. The lifetime X in *tens of hours* of a torch battery is a random variable with probability density function

$$f(x) = \begin{cases} \frac{3}{4}\left(1-(x-2)^2\right) & 1 \leqslant x \leqslant 3, \\ 0 & \text{otherwise} \end{cases}$$

Calculate the mean of X.
A torch runs on two batteries, both of which have to be working for the torch to function. If two new batteries are put in the torch, what is the probability that the torch will function for at least 22 hours, on the assumption that the life-times of the batteries are independent? (O & C)

10. A random variable X has a probability density function f given by

$$f(x) = \begin{cases} cx(5 - x) & 0 \leqslant x \leqslant 5 \\ 0 & \text{otherwise} \end{cases}$$

Show that $c = 6/125$ and find the mean of X.
The lifetime X in years of an electric light bulb has this distribution. Given that a lamp standard is fitted with two such new bulbs and that their failures are independent, find the probability that neither bulb fails in the first year and the probability that exactly one bulb fails within two years. (MEI)

11. The mass X kg of a particular substance produced per hour in a chemical process is a continuous random variable whose probability density function is given by
$$f(x) = 3x^2/32 \qquad 0 \leqslant x < 2$$
$$f(x) = 3(6 - x)/32 \qquad 2 \leqslant x \leqslant 6$$
$$f(x) = 0 \qquad \text{otherwise}$$
(a) Find the mean mass produced per hour.
(b) The substance produced is sold at £2 per kg and the total running cost of the process is £1 per hour. Find the expected profit per hour and the probability that in an hour the profit will exceed £7. (JMB)

12. A continuous random variable X has the probability density function f defined by
$$f(x) = \frac{c}{3}x \qquad 0 \leqslant x < 3$$
$$f(x) = c \qquad 3 \leqslant x \leqslant 4$$
$$f(x) = 0 \qquad \text{otherwise}$$
where c is a positive constant. Find
(i) the value of c,
(ii) the mean of X,
(iii) the value, a, for there to be a probability of 0.85 that a randomly observed value of X will exceed a. (JMB)

The expectation of any function of *X*

If $g(x)$ is any function of the continuous r.v. X having p.d.f. $f(x)$, then

$$E[g(X)] = \int_{\text{all } x} g(x)f(x)\,dx$$

In particular

$$E(X^2) = \int_{\text{all } x} x^2 f(x)\,dx$$

As in the case of the discrete r.v. (see p. 233), the following results hold when X is continuous.

Result 1 $$E(a) = a$$

$$E(a) = \int_{\text{all } x} a f(x) \, dx$$

$$= a \int_{\text{all } x} f(x) \, dx$$

$$= a$$

Result 2 $$E(aX) = aE(X)$$

$$E(aX) = \int_{\text{all } x} a x f(x) \, dx$$

$$= a \int_{\text{all } x} x f(x) \, dx$$

$$= aE(X)$$

Result 3 $$E(aX + b) = aE(X) + b$$

Result 4 $$E[(f_1(X) + f_2(X)] = E[f_1(X)] + E[f_2(X)]$$

Example 6.9   The continuous r.v. X has p.d.f. $f(x)$ where $f(x) = \frac{1}{20}(x + 3)$, $0 \leqslant x \leqslant 4$.

(**a**) Find $E(X)$.

(**b**) Find $E(2X + 5)$.

(**c**) Find $E(X^2)$.

(**d**) Find $E(X^2 + 2X - 3)$.

Solution 6.9   Sketch of $y = f(x)$.

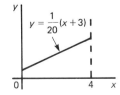

(**a**) We note from the sketch that there is no symmetry.

Now
$$E(X) = \int_{\text{all } x} x f(x) \, dx$$

$$= \int_0^4 \frac{1}{20} x(x+3) \, dx$$

$$= \frac{1}{20} \int_0^4 (x^2 + 3x) \, dx$$

$$= \frac{1}{20} \left[\frac{x^3}{3} + \frac{3x^2}{2} \right]_0^4$$

$$= 2.266\ldots$$

Therefore $E(X) = 2.27 \, (2 \text{ d.p.})$

(**b**)
$$E(2X + 5) = E(2X) + 5 \qquad \text{(Result 3)}$$

$$= 2E(X) + 5 \qquad \text{(Result 2)}$$

$$= 2(2.266\ldots) + 5$$

$$= 9.533\ldots$$

Therefore $E(2X + 5) = 9.53 \, (2 \text{ d.p.})$

(**c**)
$$E(X^2) = \int_{\text{all } x} x^2 f(x) \, dx$$

$$= \frac{1}{20} \int_0^4 x^2(x+3) \, dx$$

$$= \frac{1}{20} \int_0^4 (x^3 + 3x^2) \, dx$$

$$= \frac{1}{20} \left[\frac{x^4}{4} + x^3 \right]_0^4$$

$$= 6.4$$

Therefore $E(X^2) = 6.4$

(**d**)
$$E(X^2 + 2X - 3) = E(X^2) + E(2X) - E(3) \qquad \text{(Result 4)}$$

$$= E(X^2) + 2E(X) - 3 \qquad \text{(Results 1, 2)}$$

$$= 6.4 + 2(2.266\ldots) - 3$$

$$= 7.933\ldots$$

Therefore $E(X^2 + 2X - 3) = 7.93 \, (2 \text{ d.p.})$

Example 6.10 The continuous r.v. X has p.d.f. $f(x)$ where

$$f(x) = \begin{cases} \frac{6}{7}x & 0 \leqslant x \leqslant 1 \\ \frac{6}{7}x(2-x) & 1 \leqslant x \leqslant 2 \\ 0 & \text{otherwise} \end{cases}$$

Find $E(X^2)$.

Solution 6.10
$$E(X^2) = \int_{\text{all } x}^{2} x^2 f(x)\,dx$$

$$= \int_0^1 \frac{6}{7} x^3 dx + \int_1^2 \frac{6}{7} x^3 (2-x)\,dx$$

$$= \frac{6}{7} \int_0^1 x^3\,dx + \frac{6}{7} \int_1^2 (2x^3 - x^4)\,dx$$

$$= \frac{6}{7} \left[\frac{x^4}{4}\right]_0^1 + \frac{6}{7} \left[\frac{x^4}{2} - \frac{x^5}{5}\right]_1^2$$

$$= 1.328\ldots$$

Therefore $E(X^2) = 1.33$ (2 d.p.)

NOTE: $E(X^2)$ is an important value which is needed when calculating the variance of X.

VARIANCE

For a random variable X,

$$\text{Var}(X) = E(X - \mu)^2 \quad \text{where} \quad \mu = E(X)$$

As in the discrete case (see p. 236) the formula can be written:

$$\text{Var}(X) = E(X^2) - E^2(X)$$

$$= E(X^2) - \mu^2$$

If X is a continuous r.v. with p.d.f. $f(x)$, then

$$\text{Var}(X) = \int_{\text{all } x} x^2 f(x)\,dx - \mu^2$$

where $$\mu = E(X) = \int_{\text{all } x} x f(x)\,dx$$

The standard deviation of X is often written as σ, so $\sigma = \sqrt{\text{Var}(X)}$.

As in the case of the discrete r.v. (see p. 238), the following results also hold when X is continuous:

(1) $\text{Var}(a) = 0$

(2) $\text{Var}(aX) = a^2 \text{Var}(X)$

(3) $\text{Var}(aX + b) = a^2 \text{Var}(X)$ where a and b are any constants.

Example 6.11 The continuous r.v. X has p.d.f. $f(x)$ where $f(x) = \frac{1}{8} x$, $0 \leqslant x \leqslant 4$.

Find (**a**) $E(X)$, (**b**) $E(X^2)$, (**c**) $\text{Var}(X)$, (**d**) σ, the standard deviation of X, (**e**) $\text{Var}(3X + 2)$.

Solution 6.11 From the sketch of $y = f(x)$ we note that there is no symmetry.

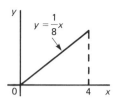

(a)
$$E(X) = \int_{\text{all } x} x f(x) \, dx$$

$$= \int_0^4 \tfrac{1}{8} x^2 \, dx$$

$$= \tfrac{1}{8} \left[\frac{x^3}{3} \right]_0^4$$

$$= 2.666\ldots$$

Therefore $E(X) = 2.67 \,(2 \text{ d.p.})$

(b)
$$E(X^2) = \int_{\text{all } x} x^2 f(x) \, dx$$

$$= \int_0^4 \tfrac{1}{8} x^3 \, dx$$

$$= \tfrac{1}{8} \left[\frac{x^4}{4} \right]_0^4$$

$$= \tfrac{1}{8}(64)$$

$$= 8$$

Therefore $E(X^2) = 8$

(c)
$$\text{Var}(X) = E(X^2) - E^2(X)$$

$$= 8 - (2.666\ldots)^2$$

$$= 0.888\ldots$$

Therefore $\text{Var}(X) = 0.89 \,(2 \text{ d.p.})$

(d)
$$\text{Standard deviation, } \sigma = \sqrt{\text{Var}(X)}$$

$$= \sqrt{0.888\ldots}$$

$$= 0.9428\ldots$$

Therefore $\sigma = 0.94 \,(2 \text{ d.p.})$

(e)
$$\text{Var}(3X + 2) = 9\text{Var}(X)$$

$$= 9(0.888\ldots)$$

$$= 8$$

Therefore $\text{Var}(3X + 2) = 8$

Example 6.12 The continuous r.v. X has p.d.f. $f(x)$ where $f(x) = \frac{3}{4}(1 + x^2), 0 \leqslant x \leqslant 1$.
If $E(X) = \mu$ and $\mathrm{Var}(X) = \sigma^2$, find $P(|X - \mu| < \sigma)$.

Solution 6.12 From the sketch of $y = f(x)$ we see that there is no symmetry.

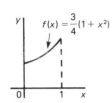

We will need to find $\mu = E(X)$.

Now
$$E(X) = \int_{\text{all } x} x f(x)\, dx$$

$$= \int_0^1 \frac{3}{4} x(1 + x^2)\, dx = \frac{3}{4} \int_0^1 (x + x^3)\, dx$$

$$= \frac{3}{4} \left[\frac{x^2}{2} + \frac{x^4}{4} \right]_0^1$$

$$= 0.5625$$

Therefore $\mu = 0.5625$

To find $\sigma^2 = \mathrm{Var}(X)$, first consider $E(X^2)$.

$$E(X^2) = \int_{\text{all } x} x^2 f(x)\, dx$$

$$= \int_0^1 \frac{3}{4} x^2 (1 + x^2)\, dx$$

$$= \frac{3}{4} \int_0^1 (x^2 + x^4)\, dx$$

$$= \frac{3}{4} \left[\frac{x^3}{3} + \frac{x^5}{5} \right]_0^1$$

$$= 0.4$$

Now
$$\mathrm{Var}(X) = E(X^2) - \mu^2$$

$$= 0.4 - 0.5625^2$$

$$= 0.0835\ldots$$

and
$$\sigma = \sqrt{\mathrm{Var}(X)}$$

$$= 0.289 \ (3 \text{ S.F.})$$

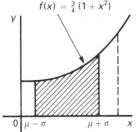

We require

$$P(|X - \mu| < \sigma) = P(-\sigma < X - \mu < \sigma)$$

$$= P(\mu - \sigma < X < \mu + \sigma)$$

$$= P(0.5625 - 0.289 < X < 0.5625 + 0.289)$$

$$= P(0.2735 < X < 0.8515)$$

$$= \int_{0.2735}^{0.8515} \frac{3}{4}(1 + x^2)\,dx$$

$$= \frac{3}{4}\left[x + \frac{x^3}{3}\right]_{0.2735}^{0.8515}$$

$$= \frac{3}{4}\left\{0.8515 + \frac{(0.8515)^3}{3} - \left(0.2735 + \frac{(0.2735)^3}{3}\right)\right\}$$

$$= 0.583 \ (3 \ \text{S.F.})$$

Therefore $P(|X - \mu| < \sigma) = 0.583 \ (3 \ \text{S.F.})$

NOTE: this is the probability that X lies within one standard deviation of the mean.

THE MODE

The mode is the value of X for which $f(x)$ is greatest, in the given range of X. It is usually necessary to draw a sketch of $y = f(x)$ and this will give an idea of the location of the mode.

For some probability density functions it is possible to determine the mode by finding the maximum point on the curve $y = f(x)$ from the relationship $f'(x) = 0$, where $f'(x) = \dfrac{d}{dx} f(x)$.

Example 6.13 The continuous r.v. X has p.d.f. $f(x)$ where $f(x) = \frac{3}{80}(2 + x)(4 - x)$, $0 \leqslant x \leqslant 4$. **(a)** Sketch $y = f(x)$.   **(b)** Find the mode.

Solution 6.13 **(a)** Sketch of $y = f(x)$.

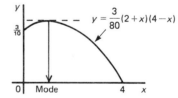

(b) $f(x) = \frac{3}{80}(2 + x)(4 - x) = \frac{3}{80}(8 + 2x - x^2)$

              $f'(x) = \frac{3}{80}(2 - 2x)$

Now $f'(x) = 0$ when $2 - 2x = 0$

                          $x = 1$

To check that this is a maximum, consider $f''(x) = \frac{3}{80}(-2) = -\frac{3}{40}$.

Now $f''(x)$ is negative for all values of x, so there is a maximum at $x = 1$.

The mode is 1.

Example 6.14   A random variable X has a probability density function

$$f(x) = Ax(6-x)^2 \quad 0 \leqslant x \leqslant 6$$

$$= 0 \text{ elsewhere.}$$

Find the value of the constant A.

Calculate the mean, mode, variance and standard deviation of X.

(AEB)

Solution 6.14   Since X is a r.v. $\displaystyle\int_{\text{all } x} f(x)\,dx = 1$

Therefore $\displaystyle 1 = \int_0^6 Ax(6-x)^2\,dx$

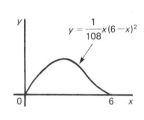

$$= A \int_0^6 (36x - 12x^2 + x^3)\,dx$$

$$= A\left[18x^2 - 4x^3 + \tfrac{1}{4}x^4\right]_0^6$$

$$= 108A$$

So $A = \dfrac{1}{108}$

Therefore $f(x) = \dfrac{1}{108}x(6-x)^2 \quad 0 \leqslant x \leqslant 6$

The mean is $E(X)$ where $E(X) = \displaystyle\int_{\text{all } x} x f(x)\,dx$

$$E(X) = \frac{1}{108}\int_0^6 x^2(6-x)^2\,dx$$

$$= \frac{1}{108}\int_0^6 (36x^2 - 12x^3 + x^4)\,dx$$

$$= \frac{1}{108}\left[12x^3 - 3x^4 + \frac{x^5}{5}\right]_0^6$$

$$= 2.4$$

The mean is 2.4.

To find the mode we consider the maximum point on $y = f(x)$.

$$f(x) = \frac{1}{108}(36x - 12x^2 + x^3)$$

$$f'(x) = \frac{1}{108}(36 - 24x + 3x^2)$$

$$= \frac{3}{108}(6-x)(2-x)$$

$f'(x) = 0$ when $x = 2$ and when $x = 6$

Consider $f''(x) = \dfrac{3}{108}(6x - 24)$.

When $x = 2, f''(x) < 0$ and when $x = 6, f''(x) > 0$.

Therefore $x = 2$ gives a maximum value of $f(x)$, i.e. <u>the mode is 2.</u>

$$\mathrm{Var}(X) = E(X^2) - E^2(X)$$

Now
$$E(X^2) = \int_{\text{all } x} x^2 f(x)\, dx$$

$$= \frac{1}{108} \int_0^6 (36x^3 - 12x^4 + x^5)\, dx$$

$$= \frac{1}{108} \left[9x^4 - \frac{12x^5}{5} + \frac{x^6}{6} \right]_0^6$$

$$= 7.2$$

$$\mathrm{Var}(X) = 7.2 - (2.4)^2$$

$$= 1.44$$

$$\text{Standard deviation of } X = \sqrt{\mathrm{Var}(X)}$$

$$= 1.2$$

Therefore the variance of X is 1.44 and the standard deviation is 1.2.

Example 6.15 The time taken to perform a particular task, t hours, has the probability density function

$$f(t) = \begin{cases} 10ct^2 & 0 \leqslant t < 0.6 \\ 9c(1 - t) & 0.6 \leqslant t \leqslant 1.0 \\ 0 & \text{otherwise.} \end{cases}$$

where c is a constant.

(**a**) Find the value of c and sketch the graph of this distribution.

(**b**) Write down the most likely time.

(**c**) Find the expected time.

(**d**) Determine the probability that the time will be
   (*i*) more than 48 minutes,
   (*ii*) between 24 and 48 minutes.

Solution 6.15 (**a**) Now

$$1 = \int_{\text{all } t} f(t)\, dt$$

$$= 10c \int_0^{0.6} t^2\, dt + 9c \int_{0.6}^{1.0} (1 - t)\, dt$$

$$= \frac{10c}{3} \left[t^3 \right]_0^{0.6} + 9c \left[t - \frac{t^2}{2} \right]_{0.6}^{1.0}$$

$$= 0.72c + 0.72c$$

$$= 1.44c$$

Therefore $\quad c = \dfrac{1}{1.44}$

$\qquad\qquad = \dfrac{100}{144}$

$\qquad\qquad = \dfrac{25}{36}$

We have

$$f(t) = \begin{cases} \dfrac{125}{18}t^2 & 0 \leqslant t < 0.6 \\[2mm] \dfrac{25}{4}(1-t) & 0.6 \leqslant t \leqslant 1.0 \\[2mm] 0 & \text{otherwise} \end{cases}$$

(**b**) $t = 0.6$ gives the maximum value of $f(t)$.

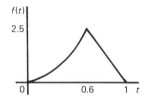

Therefore the mode is 0.6 hours $= 36\,$mins.

The most likely time is 36 minutes.

(**c**) $\qquad\qquad E(t) = \displaystyle\int_{\text{all } t} t f(t)\,\mathrm{d}t$

$$= 10c \int_0^{0.6} t^3 \,\mathrm{d}t + 9c \int_{0.6}^{1.0} (t - t^2)\,\mathrm{d}t$$

$$= \frac{10c}{4}\left[t^4\right]_0^{0.6} + 9c\left[\frac{t^2}{2} - \frac{t^3}{3}\right]_{0.6}^{1.0}$$

$$= 0.225 + 0.366\ldots$$

$$= 0.591\ldots \text{ hours}$$

$$= 35.5 \text{ minutes}$$

The expected time is 35.5 minutes.

(**d**) (*i*) 48 minutes $= 0.8$ hours

$$P(T > 0.8) = 9c \int_{0.8}^{1.0} (1-t)\,\mathrm{d}t$$

$$= 9c\left[t - \frac{t^2}{2}\right]_{0.8}^{1.0}$$

$$= 0.125$$

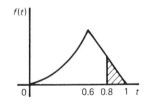

The probability that the time will be more than 48 minutes is 0.125.

(*ii*) 24 minutes $= 0.4$ hours

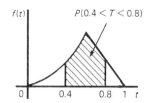

Now

$$P(0.4 < T < 0.8) = 1 - P(T > 0.8) - P(T < 0.4)$$

and

$$P(T < 0.4) = 10c \int_0^{0.4} t^2 \, \mathrm{d}t$$

$$= \frac{10c}{3} [t^3]_0^{0.4}$$

$$= 0.1481 \ldots$$

Therefore

$$P(0.4 < T < 0.8) = 1 - 0.125 - 0.1481 \ldots$$

$$= 0.727 \ (3 \ \text{S.F.})$$

The probability that the time will be between 24 and 48 minutes is 0.727 (3 S.F.).

Exercise 6c

In Questions 1–7 find (*a*) $E(X)$,   (*b*) $E(X^2)$, (*c*) Var(X),   (*d*) the standard deviation of X. It is assumed that the value of the function is zero outside the range(s) stated. Do not forget to look for symmetry when considering $E(X)$.
NOTE: some of these functions were given in Exercise 6a and you may wish to refer to your previous sketches.

1. $f(x) = \frac{3}{8}x^2$ $0 \leqslant x \leqslant 2$

2. $f(x) = \frac{1}{5}$ $-2 \leqslant x \leqslant 3$

3. $f(x) = \frac{1}{4}(4 - x)$ $1 \leqslant x \leqslant 3$

4. $f(x) = \frac{3}{56}(x + 2)^2$ $0 \leqslant x \leqslant 2$

5. $f(x) = 4x^3$ $0 \leqslant x \leqslant 1$

6. $f(x) = \begin{cases} \frac{1}{4} & 0 \leqslant x < 2 \\ \frac{1}{4}(2x - 3) & 2 \leqslant x \leqslant 3 \end{cases}$

7. $f(x) = \begin{cases} \frac{1}{8}(x + 2)^2 & -2 \leqslant x < 0 \\ \frac{1}{2} & 0 \leqslant x \leqslant 1\frac{1}{3} \end{cases}$

8. A continuous r.v. X has p.d.f. $f(x) = kx^2$, $0 \leqslant x \leqslant 4$.
(*a*) Find the value of k, and sketch $y = f(x)$.
(*b*) Find $E(X)$ and Var(X).
(*c*) Find $P(1 < X < 2)$.

9. A continuous r.v. X has p.d.f. $f(x)$ where

$$f(x) = \begin{cases} kx & 0 \leqslant x < 1 \\ k(2 - x) & 1 \leqslant x \leqslant 2 \\ 0 & \text{otherwise} \end{cases}$$

Find (*a*) the value of the constant k,
(*b*) $E(X)$,   (*c*) Var(X),   (*d*) $P\left(\frac{3}{4} \leqslant X \leqslant 1\frac{1}{2}\right)$,
(*e*) the mode.

10. The continuous random variable X has p.d.f. given by $f(x)$ where

$$f(x) = \begin{cases} \frac{1}{27}x^2 & 0 \leqslant x < 3 \\ \frac{1}{3} & 3 \leqslant x \leqslant 5 \\ 0 & \text{otherwise} \end{cases}$$

(*a*) Sketch $y = f(x)$.   (*b*) Find $E(X)$.
(*c*) Find $E(X^2)$.   (*d*) Find the standard deviation σ of X.

11. As an experiment a temporary roundabout is installed at the crossroads. The time, X minutes, which vehicles have to wait before entering the roundabout has probability density function

$$f(x) = \begin{cases} 0.8 - 0.32x & 0 \leqslant x \leqslant 2.5 \\ 0 & \text{otherwise} \end{cases}$$

Find the mean and the standard deviation of X.   (AEB 1992)

12. A continuous random variable X has a probability density function f given by

$$f(x) = \frac{k}{x(4 - x)} \qquad 1 \leqslant x \leqslant 3$$
$$f(x) = 0 \qquad\qquad \text{otherwise}$$

(i) Show that $k = \dfrac{2}{\ln 3}$.

(ii) Calculate the mean and the variance of X.   (JMB)

CUMULATIVE DISTRIBUTION FUNCTION, *F(x)*

When considering a frequency distribution the corresponding cumulative frequencies are obtained by summing all the frequencies up to a particular value.

> In the same way, if X is a continuous random variable with p.d.f. $f(x)$ defined for $a \leqslant x \leqslant b$, then the cumulative distribution function is given by $F(t)$ where
>
> $$F(t) = P(X \leqslant t) = \int_a^t f(x)\,dx$$

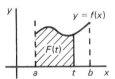

NOTE: (1) $F(b) = \displaystyle\int_a^b f(x)\,dx = 1.$

(2) If $f(x)$ is valid for $-\infty \leqslant x \leqslant \infty$ then

$$F(t) = \int_{-\infty}^t f(x)\,dx,$$

where the interval is taken over all values of $x \leqslant t$.

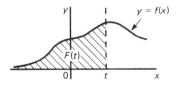

taken over all values of $x \leqslant t$.

(3) The cumulative distribution function is sometimes known just as the **distribution function**.

USING $F(x)$ TO FIND $P(x_1 \leqslant X \leqslant x_2)$

The cumulative distribution function can be used to find $P(x_1 \leqslant X \leqslant x_2)$ as follows:

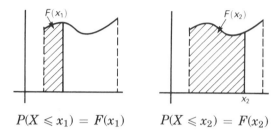

$$P(X \leqslant x_1) = F(x_1) \qquad P(X \leqslant x_2) = F(x_2)$$

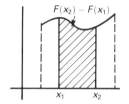

So

$$P(x_1 \leqslant X \leqslant x_2) = F(x_2) - F(x_1)$$

THE MEDIAN

The median splits the area under the curve $y = f(x)$ into two halves. So, if the value of the median is m,

$$\int_a^m f(x)\, dx = 0.5$$

i.e.

$$F(m) = 0.5$$

Example 6.16 If X is a continuous r.v. with p.d.f. $f(x) = \frac{1}{8}x, \; 0 \leqslant x \leqslant 4$,

(**a**) find the cumulative distribution function $F(x)$ and sketch $y = F(x)$,   (**b**) find the median m,   (**c**) find $P(0.3 \leqslant X \leqslant 1.8)$.

Solution 6.16 (**a**) For $0 \leqslant t \leqslant 4$, $F(t) = \int_0^t \frac{1}{8}x\, dx = \left[\frac{x^2}{16}\right]_0^t = \frac{t^2}{16}$

So that

$$F(t) = \frac{t^2}{16}, \qquad 0 \leqslant t \leqslant 4$$

NOTE: (1) $F(4) = \dfrac{4^2}{16} = 1$ as expected, since this gives the total probability.

(2) For $t \geqslant 4$, $F(t) = 1$.

(3) We usually work out the function in terms of t first and then write out the cumulative distribution in terms of x as follows:

$$F(x) = \begin{cases} 0 & x \leqslant 0 \\ \dfrac{x^2}{16} & 0 \leqslant x \leqslant 4 \\ 1 & x \geqslant 4 \end{cases}$$

Sketch of $y = F(x)$

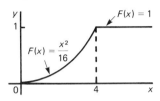

(**b**) For the median m,

$$F(m) = 0.5$$

i.e.

$$\frac{m^2}{16} = 0.5$$

$$m^2 = 8$$

$$m = 2.83 \ (2 \ \text{d.p.})$$

The median $m = 2.83$ (2 d.p.).

NOTE: since $0 < m < 4$, m cannot be negative, so we take the positive square root.

(**c**) $P(0.3 \leqslant X \leqslant 1.8) = F(1.8) - F(0.3)$

Now

$$F(1.8) = \frac{1.8^2}{16}$$

$$= 0.2025$$

and

$$F(0.3) = \frac{0.3^2}{16}$$

$$= 0.005\,625$$

Therefore $P(0.3 \leqslant X \leqslant 1.8) = 0.2025 - 0.005\,625$

$$= 0.196\,875$$

$$= 0.197 \ (3 \ \text{d.p.})$$

So $P(0.3 \leqslant X \leqslant 1.8) = 0.197$ (3 d.p.)

Example 6.17 X is a continuous r.v. with p.d.f. $f(x)$ where

$$f(x) = \begin{cases} \dfrac{x}{3} & 0 \leqslant x \leqslant 2 \\ -\dfrac{2x}{3} + 2 & 2 \leqslant x \leqslant 3 \\ 0 & \text{otherwise} \end{cases}$$

(**a**) Sketch $y = f(x)$.

(**b**) Find the cumulative distribution function $F(x)$.

(**c**) Sketch $y = F(x)$.

(**d**) Find $P(1 \leqslant X \leqslant 2.5)$.

(**e**) Find the median, m.

Solution 6.17 (**a**) Sketch of $y = f(x)$.

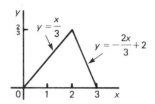

(**b**) Now $F(t) = \displaystyle\int_0^t f(x)\,dx$.

But, as $f(x)$ is given in two parts, we must find $F(x)$ in two stages:

Consider $0 \leqslant t \leqslant 2$

$$F(t) = \int_0^t \frac{x}{3}\,dx$$

$$= \left[\frac{x^2}{6}\right]_0^t$$

$$= \frac{t^2}{6}$$

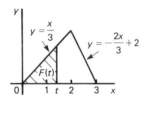

So, for $0 \leqslant x \leqslant 2$, $F(x) = \dfrac{x^2}{6}$

NOTE: $F(2) = \frac{4}{6} = \frac{2}{3}$.

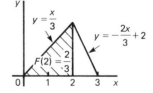

Now, for t in the range $2 \leqslant t \leqslant 3$
we see from the diagram that

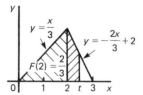

$$F(t) = F(2) + \int_2^t \left(-\frac{2x}{3} + 2\right)dx$$

$$= F(2) + \left[-\frac{x^2}{3} + 2x\right]_2^t$$

$$= \frac{2}{3} + \left\{-\frac{t^2}{3} + 2t - \left(-\frac{4}{3} + 4\right)\right\}$$

$$= -\frac{t^2}{3} + 2t - 2$$

Now check the value of $F(3)$.

$F(3) = -\frac{9}{3} + 6 - 2 = 1,$ as required

For any value of $t \geqslant 3,\ F(t) = 1.$

Writing the answer in terms of x, we have

$$F(x) = \begin{cases} \dfrac{x^2}{6} & 0 \leqslant x \leqslant 2 \\[2mm] -\dfrac{x^2}{3} + 2x - 2 & 2 \leqslant x \leqslant 3 \\[2mm] 1 & x \geqslant 3 \end{cases}$$

(**c**) Sketch of $y = F(x)$.

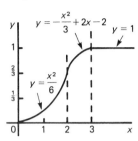

(**d**) $P(1 \leqslant X \leqslant 2.5) = F(2.5) - F(1)$

Since 2.5 is in the interval $2 \leqslant x \leqslant 3$

$$F(2.5) = \frac{x^2}{3} + 2x - 2$$

$$= -\frac{(2.5)^2}{3} + 2(2.5) - 2$$

$$= \frac{11}{12}$$

Since 1 is in the interval $0 \leqslant x \leqslant 2$

$$F(1) = \frac{x^2}{6}$$

$$= \frac{1}{6}$$

Therefore $P(1 \leqslant X \leqslant 2.5\,) = F(2.5) - F(1)$

$$= \frac{11}{12} - \frac{1}{6}$$

$$= 0.75$$

So $P(1 \leqslant X \leqslant 2.5) = 0.75$

(**e**) $F(m) = 0.5,$ where m is the median.

Now $F(2) = \frac{2}{3},$ so the median must lie in the range $0 \leqslant x \leqslant 2.$

Therefore $\qquad\qquad\qquad F(m) = \dfrac{m^2}{6}$

So $\qquad\qquad\qquad\qquad \dfrac{m^2}{6} = 0.5$

$$m^2 = 3$$

$$m = 1.73 \ (2 \text{ d.p.})$$

The median m is 1.73 (2 d.p.).

Example 6.18   A continuous r.v. X takes values in the range $0 \leqslant x \leqslant 1$ and has p.d.f.

$$f(x) = \begin{cases} 3.75x + 0.1 & 0 \leqslant x \leqslant 0.4 \\ 1.6 & 0.4 \leqslant x \leqslant 0.6 \\ 3.85 - 3.75x & 0.6 \leqslant x \leqslant 1 \end{cases}$$

(**a**) Sketch $y = f(x)$ and find the mean μ.

(**b**) Find the cumulative distribution function, $F(x)$ and sketch $y = F(x)$.

(**c**) Find $P(|X - \mu| \leqslant 0.2)$.

Solution 6.18   (**a**) Sketch of $y = f(x)$.

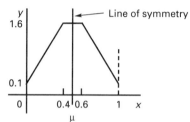

By symmetry, $\mu = E(X) = 0.5$.

(**b**) We must consider $F(x)$ in three stages:

For $0 \leqslant t \leqslant 0.4$

$$F(t) = \int_0^t (3.75x + 0.1)\,dx$$

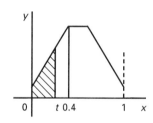

$$= \left[3.75\frac{x^2}{2} + 0.1x \right]_0^t$$

$$= 1.875t^2 + 0.1t$$

Now

$$F(0.4) = (1.875)(0.4)^2 + (0.1)(0.4)$$

$$= 0.34$$

For $0.4 \leqslant t \leqslant 0.6$

$$F(t) = F(0.4) + \int_{0.4}^t 1.6\,dx$$

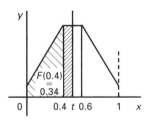

$$= F(0.4) + [1.6x]_{0.4}^t$$

$$= 0.34 + 1.6t - 0.64$$

$$= 1.6t - 0.3$$

Now

$$F(0.6) = (1.6)(0.6) - 0.3$$

$$= 0.66$$

For $0.6 \leqslant x \leqslant 1$

$$F(t) = F(0.6) + \int_{0.6}^{t} (3.85 - 3.75x)\,dx$$

$$= F(0.6) + \left[3.85x - 3.75\frac{x^2}{2} \right]_{0.6}^{t}$$

$$= 0.66 + 3.85t - 1.875t^2 - 2.31 + 0.675$$

$$= 3.85t - 1.875t^2 - 0.975$$

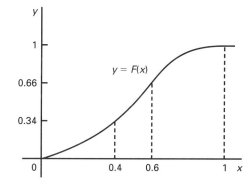

It is useful to check $F(1)$:

$$F(1) = 3.85 - 1.875 - 0.975 = 1 \text{ as required}$$

Writing the answer in terms of x we have:

$$F(x) = \begin{cases} 0 & x \leqslant 0 \\ 1.875x^2 + 0.1x & 0 \leqslant x \leqslant 0.4 \\ 1.6x - 0.3 & 0.4 \leqslant x \leqslant 0.6 \\ 3.85x - 1.875x^2 - 0.975 & 0.6 \leqslant x \leqslant 1 \\ 1 & x \geqslant 1 \end{cases}$$

Sketch of $y = F(x)$.

(d) $P(\,|X - \mu| \leqslant 0.2) = P(-0.2 \leqslant X - \mu \leqslant 0.2)$

$$= P(-0.2 \leqslant X - 0.5 \leqslant 0.2)$$

$$= P(0.3 \leqslant X \leqslant 0.7)$$

$$= F(0.7) - F(0.3)$$

Now 0.7 lies in the range $0.6 \leqslant x \leqslant 1$, so

$$F(0.7) = 3.85x - 1.875x^2 - 0.975$$

$$= (3.85)(0.7) - (1.875)(0.7)^2 - 0.975$$

$$= 0.801\,25$$

0.3 lies in the range $0 \leqslant x \leqslant 0.4$, so

$$F(0.3) = 1.875x^2 + 0.1x$$

$$= (1.875)(0.3)^2 + (0.1)(0.3)$$

$$= 0.198\,75$$

Therefore

$$P(0.3 \leqslant X \leqslant 0.7) = F(0.7) - F(0.3)$$

$$= 0.801\,25 - 0.198\,75$$

$$= 0.6025$$

So $\underline{P(\,|X - \mu|\leqslant 0.2) = 0.6025}$

Exercise 6d

In Questions 1–7, for each of the probability density functions of the continuous r.v. X, find (a) the cumulative distribution function $F(x)$, and for Questions 1, 2, 5 and 7 find also (b) the median, m.
NOTE: These are the functions used in Exercises 6a and 6c.

1. $f(x) = \frac{3}{8}x^2$ $0 \leqslant x \leqslant 2$

2. $f(x) = \frac{1}{5}$ $-2 \leqslant x \leqslant 3$

3. $f(x) = \frac{1}{4}(4 - x)$ $1 \leqslant x \leqslant 3$

4. $f(x) = \frac{3}{56}(x + 2)^2$ $0 \leqslant x \leqslant 2$

5. $f(x) = 4x^3$ $0 \leqslant x \leqslant 1$

6. $f(x) = \begin{cases} \frac{1}{4} & 0 \leqslant x \leqslant 2 \\ \frac{1}{4}(2x - 3) & 2 \leqslant x \leqslant 3 \end{cases}$

7. $f(x) = \begin{cases} \frac{1}{8}(x + 2)^2 & -2 \leqslant x \leqslant 0 \\ \frac{1}{2} & 0 \leqslant x \leqslant 1\frac{1}{3} \end{cases}$

8.   The continuous r.v. X has p.d.f. $f(x) = \frac{1}{3}$, $0 \leqslant x \leqslant 3$. Find (a) $E(X)$, (b) Var(X), (c) $F(x)$ and sketch $y = F(x)$, (d) $P(X \geqslant 1.8)$, (e) $P(1.1 \leqslant X \leqslant 1.7)$.

9. X is the continuous r.v. with p.d.f. $f(x) = kx^2$, $1 \leqslant x \leqslant 2$. Find (a) the constant k and sketch $y = f(x)$, (b) the standard deviation σ, (c) the cumulative distribution function $F(x)$, (d) the median, m.

10.   The continuous r.v. X has continuous p.d.f. $f(x)$ where

$$f(x) = \begin{cases} \dfrac{x}{3} - \dfrac{2}{3} & 2 \leqslant x \leqslant 3 \\ \alpha & 3 \leqslant x \leqslant 5 \\ 2 - \beta x & 5 \leqslant x \leqslant 6 \\ 0 & \text{otherwise} \end{cases}$$

Find (a) α and β, (b) $F(x)$ and sketch $y = F(x)$, (c) $P(2 \leqslant X \leqslant 3.5)$, (d) $P(X \geqslant 5.5)$, (e) $E(X)$, (f) Var(X).

11.   The continuous r.v. X has probability density function given by

$$f(x) = \begin{cases} \dfrac{k}{x} & \text{for } 1 \leqslant x \leqslant 9, \\ 0 & \text{otherwise} \end{cases}$$

where k is a constant. Giving your answers correct to three significant figures where appropriate, find (a) the value of k, and also the median value of X,
(b) the mean and variance of X,
(c) the cumulative distribution function, F, of X, and sketch the graph of $y = F(x)$.   (C)

12.   The continuous r.v. X has probability density function f given by

$$f(x) = \begin{cases} k(4 - x^2) & \text{for } 0 \leqslant x \leqslant 2 \\ 0 & \text{otherwise} \end{cases}$$

where k is a constant. Show that $k = \frac{3}{16}$ and find the values of $E(X)$ and Var(X). Find the cumulative distribution function of X, and verify by calculation that the median value of X is between 0.69 and 0.70. Find also $P(0.69 < X < 0.70)$, giving your answer correct to one significant figure.   (C)

13. A continuous random variable X has probability density function, f, defined by

$$f(x) = \tfrac{1}{4}, \qquad 0 \leqslant x < 1$$

$$f(x) = \frac{x^3}{5}, \qquad 1 \leqslant x \leqslant 2$$

$$f(x) = 0, \qquad \text{otherwise}$$

Obtain the distribution function and hence, or otherwise, find, to 3 decimal places, the median and the interquartile range of the distribution. (L)P

14. Define the probability density function $f(x)$ and the distribution function $F(x)$ of a continuous random variable X.

A factory is supplied with flour at the beginning of each week. The weekly demand, X thousand tonnes, for flour from this factory is a continuous random variable having the probability density function

$$f(x) = k(1-x)^4, \qquad 0 \leqslant x \leqslant 1$$

$$f(x) = 0, \qquad \text{elsewhere}$$

Find
(a) the value of k,
(b) the mean value of X,
(c) the variance of X, to 3 decimal places.
Sketch the probability density function.
Find, to the nearest tonne, the quantity of flour that the factory should have in stock at the beginning of a week in order that there is a probability of 0.98 that the demand in that week will be met. (L)

15. Each batch of a chemical used in drug manufacture is tested for impurities. The percentage of impurity is X, where X is a random variable with probability density function given by

$$f(x) = \begin{cases} kx & 0 < x \leqslant 1 \\ \tfrac{1}{3}k(4-x) & 1 < x \leqslant 4 \\ 0 & \text{otherwise} \end{cases}$$

where k is a constant.
(i) Sketch the graph of $f(x)$.
(ii) Show that $k = \tfrac{1}{2}$.
(iii) Determine, for all x, the distribution function $F(x)$.
In order to purify the chemical it is subjected to one of four possible purification processes, the percentage impurity in the batch determining the actual process used. The process used and its cost, for each level of percentage impurity, is shown in the table.

Percentage impurity x	Process used	Batch cost (£)
$0 < x \leqslant 1$	A	200
$1 < x \leqslant 2$	B	250
$2 < x \leqslant 3$	C	350
$3 < x \leqslant 4$	D	500

(iv) Determine the expected cost per batch of removing the impurities.
(v) Determine the probability that the cost of purifying a batch exceeds the expected cost. (JMB)

16. A continuous random variable X has probability density function f given by

$$f(x) = k(1 + \cos x), \qquad 0 \leqslant x \leqslant \pi$$

$$f(x) = 0, \qquad \text{otherwise}$$

(i) Show that $k = \dfrac{1}{\pi}$.
(ii) Find, to four decimal places, the mean, μ, of the distribution.
[You may use, without proof, the result

$$\int_0^\pi x \cos x \, \mathrm{d}x = -2.]$$

(iii) Find the distribution function of X for all values of x. Hence determine $P(X \leqslant \mu)$ and verify that μ is between the 55th and 56th percentiles. (JMB)

17. The continuous random variable X has probability density function

$$f(x) = \begin{cases} \dfrac{1+x}{6} & 1 \leqslant x \leqslant 3 \\ 0 & \text{otherwise} \end{cases}$$

(a) Sketch the probability density function of X.
(b) Calculate the mean of X.
(c) Specify fully the cumulative distribution function of X.
(d) Find m such that $P(X \leqslant m) = \tfrac{1}{2}$. (L)

18. The continuous random variable X has probability density function f given by

$$f(x) = \begin{cases} k(x+3), & -3 \leqslant x \leqslant 3 \\ 0, & \text{otherwise} \end{cases}$$

where k is a constant.
(i) Show that $k = \dfrac{1}{18}$.
(ii) Find $E(X)$ and $\mathrm{Var}(X)$.
(iii) Find the lower quartile of X, i.e. the value q such that $P(X \leqslant q) = \tfrac{1}{4}$.
(iv) Let $Y = aX + b$, where a and b are constants with $a > 0$. Find the values of a and b for which $E(Y) = 0$ and $\mathrm{Var}(Y) = 1$. (C)

19. A continuous random variable, X, has probability density function given by

$$f(x) = ax - bx^2 \qquad \text{for} \quad 0 \leqslant x \leqslant 2$$

$$= 0 \qquad \text{elsewhere}$$

Observations on X indicate that the mean is 1.
(a) Obtain two simultaneous equations for a and b, show that $a = 1.5$ and find the value of b.

(b) Find the variance of X.

(c) If $F(x)$ is the probability that $X \leqslant x$ find $F(x)$ and verify that $F(2) = 1$.

(d) If two independent observations are made on X what is the probability that at least one of them is less than $\frac{1}{2}$?

20. The random variable X has probability density function given by

$$f(x) = \begin{cases} kx, & 0 \leqslant x \leqslant 1 \\ k, & 1 < x \leqslant 2 \\ 0, & \text{otherwise} \end{cases}$$

where k is a constant.

(i) Show that $k = \frac{2}{3}$.

(ii) Find $E(X)$ and $E(X^2)$.

(iii) Show that the median m of X is 1.25, and find $P\left(|X - m| > \frac{1}{2}\right)$.   (C)

21. The continuous random variable X has probability density function given by

$$f(x) = \begin{cases} \dfrac{k}{(x+1)^4}, & \text{for } x \geqslant 0 \\ 0, & \text{for } x < 0 \end{cases}$$

where k is a constant.

(i) Show that $k = 3$, and find the cumulative distribution function. Find also the value of x such that $P(X \leqslant x) = \frac{7}{8}$.

(ii) Find $E(X + 1)$, and deduce that $E(X) = \frac{1}{2}$.

(iii) By considering $\text{Var}(X + 1)$, or otherwise, find $\text{Var}(X)$.   (C)

22. The amount of vegetables eaten by a family in a week is a random variable W kg. The probability density function is given by

$$f(w) = \begin{cases} \dfrac{20}{5^5} w^3(5 - w) & 0 \leqslant w \leqslant 5 \\ 0 & \text{otherwise} \end{cases}$$

(a) Find the cumulative distribution function of W.

(b) Find, to 3 decimal places, the probability that the family eats between 2 kg and 4 kg of vegetables in one week.

(c) Given that the mean of the distribution is $3\frac{1}{3}$, find, to 3 decimal places, the variance of W.

(d) Find the mode of the distribution.

(e) Verify that the amount, m, of vegetables such that the family is equally likely to eat more or less than m in any week is about 3.431 kg.

(f) Use the information above to comment on the skewness of the distribution.   (L)

23. (a) If $f(x)$ is to be used as a probability density function for a continuous random variable X,

(i) give the *two* conditions that must be satisfied by $f(x)$,

(ii) describe the relationship between $f(x)$ and the distribution function $F(x)$.

(b) The continuous random variable, X, has probability density function defined by

$$f(x) = \begin{cases} kx, & 0 \leqslant x \leqslant 8 \\ 8k, & 8 < x \leqslant 9 \\ 0 & \text{otherwise} \end{cases}$$

where k is a constant.

(i) Sketch the graph of $f(x)$.

(ii) Show that $k = 0.025$.

(iii) Determine, for all x, the distribution function $F(x)$.

(iv) Calculate the probability that an observed value of X exceeds 6.

If three independent observations of X are taken, calculate, correct to 3 decimal places, the probability that

(v) the values of all three observations exceed 6,

(vi) the values of at least two of these three observations exceed 6.   (JMB)

OBTAINING THE p.d.f. FROM THE CUMULATIVE DISTRIBUTION

The probability density function can be obtained from the cumulative distribution as follows:

Now
$$F(t) = \int_a^t f(x)\, \mathrm{d}x \qquad a \leqslant t \leqslant b$$

So
$$f(x) = \frac{\mathrm{d}}{\mathrm{d}x} F(x)$$
$$= F'(x)$$

NOTE: the gradient of the $F(x)$ curve gives the value of $f(x)$.

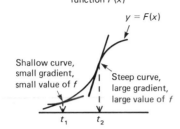

The cumulative distribution function $F(x)$

$y = F(x)$

Shallow curve, small gradient, small value of f

Steep curve, large gradient, large value of f

t_1 t_2

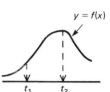

The probability density function $f(x)$

$y = f(x)$

t_1 t_2

Example 6.19 The continuous r.v. X has cumulative distribution function $F(x)$ where

$$F(x) = \begin{cases} 0 & x \leqslant 0 \\ \dfrac{x^3}{27} & 0 \leqslant x \leqslant 3 \\ 1 & x \geqslant 3 \end{cases}$$

Find the p.d.f. of X, $f(x)$, and sketch $y = f(x)$.

Solution 6.19

$$f(x) = \frac{\mathrm{d}}{\mathrm{d}x} F(x)$$

$$= \frac{\mathrm{d}}{\mathrm{d}x} \left(\frac{x^3}{27} \right)$$

$$= \frac{3x^2}{27}$$

$$= \frac{x^2}{9}$$

The p.d.f. for X is $f(x)$ where

$$f(x) = \begin{cases} \dfrac{x^2}{9} & 0 \leqslant x \leqslant 3 \\ 0 & \text{otherwise} \end{cases}$$

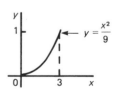

$y = \dfrac{x^2}{9}$

Example 6.20 The continuous r.v. X has cumulative distribution function $F(x)$ where

$$F(x) = \begin{cases} 0 & x < -2 \\ \frac{1}{12}(2 + x) & -2 \leqslant x < 0 \\ \frac{1}{6}(1 + x) & 0 \leqslant x < 4 \\ \frac{1}{12}(6 + x) & 4 \leqslant x < 6 \\ 1 & x \geqslant 6 \end{cases}$$

Find the p.d.f. of X, $f(x)$, and sketch $y = f(x)$.

Solution 6.20   Now $f(x) = \dfrac{d}{dx} F(x)$.

So,   for $-2 \leqslant x < 0$ $f(x) = \dfrac{d}{dx} \dfrac{1}{12}(2+x) = \dfrac{1}{12}$

           for $0 \leqslant x < 4$ $f(x) = \dfrac{d}{dx} \dfrac{1}{6}(1+x) = \dfrac{1}{6}$

           for $4 \leqslant x < 6$ $f(x) = \dfrac{d}{dx} \dfrac{1}{12}(6+x) = \dfrac{1}{12}$

The sketch of $y = f(x)$ is shown:

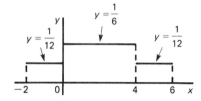

Example 6.21   The cumulative distribution function $F(x)$ for a continuous r.v. X is defined as

$$F(x) = \begin{cases} 0 & x < 0 \\ 2x - 2x^2 & 0 \leqslant x \leqslant 0.25 \\ a + x & 0.25 \leqslant x \leqslant 0.5 \\ b + 2x^2 - x & 0.5 \leqslant x \leqslant 0.75 \\ 1 & x \geqslant 0.75 \end{cases}$$

(**a**) Find a and b and sketch $F(x)$.

(**b**) Find and sketch the p.d.f. $f(x)$.

(**c**) Find the mean μ.

Solution 6.21   (**a**)   Since $F(x) = 1$ for $x \geqslant 0.75$, $F(0.75) = 1$

But for $0.5 \leqslant x \leqslant 0.75$, $F(x) = b + 2x^2 - x$

So $F(0.75) = b + 2(0.75)^2 - 0.75$

                                        $= b + 0.375$

Therefore $b + 0.375 = 1$

                                $\underline{b = 0.625}$

So we have for $0.5 \leqslant x \leqslant 0.75$

                        $F(x) = 0.625 + 2x^2 - x$

Therefore $F(0.5) = 0.625 + 2(0.5)^2 - 0.5$

                                $= 0.625$

But for the range $0.25 \leqslant x \leqslant 0.5$

                        $F(x) = a + x$

                        $F(0.5) = a + 0.5$

                $a + 0.5 = 0.625$

Therefore $\underline{a = 0.125}$

So the cumulative distribution function $F(x)$ is as follows:

$$F(x) = \begin{cases} 0 & x \leqslant 0 \\ 2x - 2x^2 & 0 \leqslant x \leqslant 0.25 \\ 0.125 + x & 0.25 \leqslant x \leqslant 0.5 \\ 0.625 + 2x^2 - x & 0.5 \leqslant x \leqslant 0.75 \\ 1 & x \geqslant 0.75 \end{cases}$$

Sketch of $y = F(x)$.

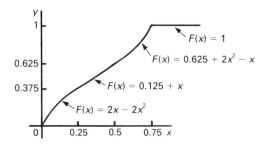

(**b**) $$f(x) = \frac{d}{dx}F(x)$$

Therefore $$f(x) = \begin{cases} 0 & x < 0 \\ 2 - 4x & 0 \leqslant x \leqslant 0.25 \\ 1 & 0.25 \leqslant x \leqslant 0.5 \\ 4x - 1 & 0.5 \leqslant x \leqslant 0.75 \\ 0 & x > 0.75 \end{cases}$$

Sketch of $y = f(x)$.

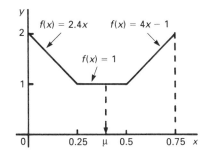

(**c**) By symmetry $\mu = E(X) = 0.375$.

Exercise 6e

1. A continuous random variable X takes values in the interval 0 to 3. It is given that $P(X > x) = a + bx^3$, $0 \leqslant x \leqslant 3$.
(a) Find the values of the constants a and b.

(b) Find the cumulative distribution function $F(x)$.
(c) Find the probability density function $f(x)$.
(d) Show that $E(X) = 2.25$.
(e) Find the standard deviation.

2. The continuous r.v. X has cumulative distribution function $F(x)$ where

$$F(x) = \begin{cases} 0 & x \leqslant 0 \\ \dfrac{2x}{3} & 0 \leqslant x \leqslant 1 \\ \dfrac{x}{3} + k & 1 \leqslant x \leqslant 2 \\ 1 & x \geqslant 2 \end{cases}$$

Find (a) the value of k, (b) the p.d.f. $f(x)$ and sketch it, (c) the mean μ, (d) the standard deviation σ, (e) $P(|X - \mu| \leqslant \sigma)$.

3. The continuous r.v. X has cumulative distribution function $F(x)$ where

$$F(x) = \begin{cases} 0 & x \leqslant 1 \\ \dfrac{(x-1)^2}{12} & 1 \leqslant x \leqslant 3 \\ \dfrac{(14x - x^2 - 25)}{24} & 3 \leqslant x \leqslant 7 \\ 1 & x \geqslant 7 \end{cases}$$

(a) Find and sketch $f(x)$. (b) Find $E(X)$ and Var(X). (c) Find the median m. (d) Find $P(2.8 \leqslant X \leqslant 5.2)$.

4. A random variable X has cumulative (distribution) function $F(x)$ where

$$F(x) = \begin{cases} 0 & x < -1 \\ \alpha x + \alpha & -1 \leqslant x < 0 \\ 2\alpha x + \alpha & 0 \leqslant x < 1 \\ 3\alpha & 1 \leqslant x \end{cases}$$

Determine
(a) the value of α,
(b) the frequency function $f(x)$ of X,
(c) the expected value μ of X,
(d) the standard deviation σ of X,
(e) the probability that $|X - \mu|$ exceeds $\frac{1}{3}$.
                            (C)

5. The length X of an offcut of wooden planking is a random variable which can take any value up to 0.5 m. It is known that the probability of the length being not more than x metres $(0 \leqslant x \leqslant 0.5)$ is equal to kx. Determine
(a) the value of k,
(b) the probability density function of X,
(c) the expected value of X,
(d) the standard deviation of X (correct to 3 significant figures).   (C)

6. A continuous random variable X takes values in the interval 0 to 4. The probability that X takes a value greater than x is equal to $\alpha x^2 + \beta$, $(0 \leqslant x \leqslant 4)$.
(a) Determine the values of α and β.
(b) Determine the probability density function $f(x)$ of X.

(c) Show that the expected value μ of X is $\frac{8}{3}$.
(d) Show that the standard deviation σ of X is $\frac{2}{3}\sqrt{2}$.
(e) Show that the probability that
$$(\mu - \sigma) \leqslant X \leqslant (\mu + \sigma) \text{ is } \tfrac{4}{9}\sqrt{2} \qquad \text{(C)}$$

7. The continuous random variable X has (cumulative) distribution function given by

$$F(x) = \begin{cases} (1+x)/8 & -1 \leqslant x \leqslant 0 \\ (1+3x)/8 & 0 \leqslant x \leqslant 2 \\ (5+x)/8 & 2 \leqslant x \leqslant 3 \end{cases}$$

with $F(x) = 0$ for $x < -1$, and $F(x) = 1$ for $x > 3$.
(a) Sketch the graph of the probability density function $f(x)$.
(b) Determine the expectation of X and the variance of X.
(c) Determine $P(3 \leqslant 2X \leqslant 5)$.   (C)

8. The probability that a randomly chosen flight from Stanston Airport is delayed by more than x hours is $\frac{1}{100}(x - 10)^2$, for $x \in \mathbb{R}$, $0 \leqslant x \leqslant 10$. No flights leave early, and none is delayed for more than 10 hours. The delay, in hours, for a randomly chosen flight is denoted by X.
(i) Find the median, m, of X, correct to three significant figures.
(ii) Find the cumulative distribution function, F, of X and sketch the graph of F.
(iii) Find the probability density function, f, of X and sketch the graph of f.
(iv) Show that $E(X) = \frac{10}{3}$.
A random sample of 2 flights is taken. Find the probability that both flights are delayed by more than m hours, where m is the median of X.   (C)

9. On any day, the amount of time, measured in hours, that Mr Goggle spends watching television is a continuous random variable T, with cumulative distribution function given by

$$F(t) = \begin{cases} 0 & t \leqslant 0 \\ 1 - k(15 - t)^2 & 0 \leqslant t \leqslant 15 \\ 1 & t \geqslant 15 \end{cases}$$

where k is a constant.
(i) Show that $k = \frac{1}{225}$ and find $P(5 \leqslant T \leqslant 10)$.
(ii) Show that, for $0 \leqslant t \leqslant 15$, the probability density function of T is given by
$$f(t) = \frac{2}{15} - \frac{2}{225}t.$$
(iii) Find the median of T.
(iv) Find Var(T).   (C)

SOME SPECIAL CONTINUOUS DISTRIBUTIONS

THE RECTANGULAR OR UNIFORM DISTRIBUTION

A continuous r.v. X having p.d.f. $f(x)$ where

$$f(x) = \frac{1}{b-a} \quad \text{for } a \leqslant x \leqslant b$$

where a and b are constants, is said to follow a **rectangular (or uniform) distribution.**

The parameters of the distribution are a and b.

If X is distributed in this way, we write

$$X \sim R(a,b)$$

Since a and b are constants, $\dfrac{1}{b-a}$ is constant, so the graph of $y = f(x)$ is a straight line parallel to the x-axis.

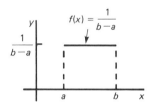

X is a random variable, since

$$\int_{\text{all } x} f(x)\, \mathrm{d}x = \int_a^b \frac{1}{b-a}\, \mathrm{d}x$$

$$= \frac{1}{b-a}\left[x\right]_a^b$$

$$= \frac{b-a}{b-a}$$

$$= 1$$

NOTE: It is easy to see from the diagram that the total area is 1.

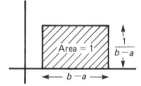

Obviously the graph for $f(x)$ depends on the values for a and b. For example

if $X \sim R(0,4)$

then $f(x) = \frac{1}{4}$ if $0 \leqslant x \leqslant 4$

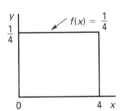

Example 6.22 If $X \sim R(6,9)$ find $P(7.2 \leqslant X \leqslant 8.4)$

Solution 6.22

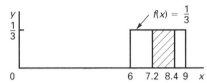

$f(x) = \frac{1}{3}$ if $6 \leqslant x \leqslant 9$

and $P(7.2 \leqslant X \leqslant 8.4) = \frac{1}{3}(8.4 - 7.2)$

$$= 0.4$$

So $\underline{P(7.2 \leqslant X \leqslant 8.4) = 0.4}$

Example 6.23 If $X \sim R\left(0, \frac{\pi}{2}\right)$ find $P\left(\frac{\pi}{3} \leqslant X \leqslant \frac{\pi}{2}\right)$.

Solution 6.23 $f(x) = \frac{2}{\pi}$ if $0 \leqslant x \leqslant \frac{\pi}{2}$.

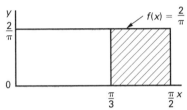

Therefore $P\left(\frac{\pi}{3} \leqslant X \leqslant \frac{\pi}{2}\right) = \frac{2}{\pi}\left(\frac{\pi}{2} - \frac{\pi}{3}\right) = \frac{2}{\pi}\left(\frac{\pi}{6}\right) = \frac{1}{3}$

So $\underline{P\left(\frac{\pi}{3} \leqslant X \leqslant \frac{\pi}{2}\right) = \frac{1}{3}}$

Example 6.24 The lengths of metal rods are measured to the nearest 5 mm. What is the distribution of the random variable E, the rounding error made when measuring?

Solution 6.24 The error is the difference between the true length and the recorded length after rounding to the nearest 5 mm.

Suppose we have recorded a length to be 75 mm, to the nearest 5 mm. Now the true length could have been any length in the interval

$$72.5 \,\text{mm} \leqslant l < 77.5 \,\text{mm}$$

So the error, E, could be anywhere in the interval $-2.5 \leqslant E \leqslant 2.5$.

All points in this interval are equally likely 'stopping places' for E, so E is uniformly distributed in the interval.

We write $\qquad\qquad E \sim \text{R}(-2.5, 2.5)$

Example 6.25 A child spins a 'Spinning Jenny' at a fair. When the wheel stops, the shorter distance of an arrow measured along the circumference from the child is denoted by C. What is the distribution of C?

Solution 6.25 All the points on the circumference are equally likely stopping places for the arrow, so C is uniformly distributed between 0 (when the arrow is next to the child) and πr (when the arrow is diametrically opposite the child).

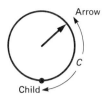

So $C \sim \mathrm{R}(0, \pi r)$

EXPECTATION AND VARIANCE

Example 6.26 The continuous random variable Y has a rectangular distribution

$$f(y) = \begin{cases} \dfrac{1}{\pi} & -\dfrac{\pi}{2} \leqslant y \leqslant \dfrac{\pi}{2} \\ 0 & \text{otherwise} \end{cases}$$

(**a**) Find the mean of Y.

(**b**) Find the variance of Y.   (L)

Solution 6.26 $Y \sim \mathrm{R}\left(-\dfrac{\pi}{2}, \dfrac{\pi}{2}\right)$.

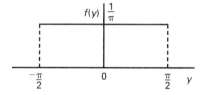

(**a**) By symmetry

   $E(Y) = 0$

Therefore the mean of Y is 0.

(**b**) To find Var(Y) we must first find $E(Y^2)$.

$$E(Y^2) = \int_{\text{all } y} y^2 f(y)\, dy$$

$$= \int_{-\frac{\pi}{2}}^{\frac{\pi}{2}} y^2 \frac{1}{\pi}\, dy$$

$$= \frac{1}{\pi}\left[\frac{y^3}{3}\right]_{-\frac{\pi}{2}}^{\frac{\pi}{2}}$$

$$= \frac{1}{3\pi}\left(\frac{\pi^3}{8} - \left(-\frac{\pi^3}{8}\right)\right)$$

$$= \frac{1}{3\pi}\left(\frac{\pi^3}{4}\right)$$

$$= \frac{\pi^2}{12}$$

$$\text{Var}(Y) = E(Y^2) - E^2(Y)$$

$$= \frac{\pi^2}{12} - 0$$

$$= \frac{\pi^2}{12}$$

Therefore the variance of Y is $\dfrac{\pi^2}{12}$.

It is possible to write the mean and the variance of a rectangular distribution in general formulae:

If $X \sim R(a,b)$ then

$$E(X) = \frac{1}{2}(a+b)$$

$$\text{Var}(X) = \frac{1}{12}(b-a)^2$$

The graph of $y = f(x)$ is as shown, and we see by symmetry that $E(X)$ is half-way between a and b,

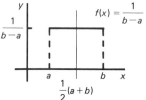

so $E(X) = \frac{1}{2}(a+b)$.

Now $\text{Var}(X) = E(X^2) - E^2(X)$

where $E(X^2) = \displaystyle\int_{\text{all } x} x^2 f(x)\,dx$

$$= \int_a^b x^2 \left(\frac{1}{b-a}\right) dx$$

$$= \frac{1}{b-a}\left[\frac{x^3}{3}\right]_a^b$$

$$= \frac{1}{3(b-a)}(b^3 - a^3)$$

$$= \frac{1}{3(b-a)}(b-a)(b^2 + ab + a^2)$$

$$= \frac{(b^2 + ab + a^2)}{3}$$

So $\text{Var}(X) = E(X^2) - E^2(X)$

$$= \frac{(b^2 + ab + a^2)}{3} - \frac{(a^2 + 2ab + b^2)}{4}$$

$$= \frac{1}{12}\{4(b^2 + ab + a^2) - 3(a^2 + 2ab + b^2)\}$$

$$= \frac{1}{12}(b^2 - 2ab + a^2)$$

$$= \frac{1}{12}(b-a)^2$$

Therefore $E(X) = \frac{1}{2}(a+b)$ and $\text{Var}(X) = \frac{1}{12}(b-a)^2$.

Exercise 6f

1. If the continuous r.v. X is such that $X \sim R(3,6)$ find (a) the p.d.f. of X, (b) $E(X)$, (c) $\text{Var}(X)$, (d) $P(X > 5)$.

2. If the continuous r.v. X has p.d.f. $f(x)$ where $f(x) = k$ and $X \sim R(-5, -2)$ find (a) the value of the constant k, (b) $P(-4.3 < X < -2.8)$, (c) $E(X)$, (d) $\text{Var}(X)$.

3. The continuous r.v. X has p.d.f. $f(x)$ as shown in the diagram:

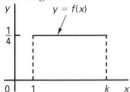

Find (a) the value of k,
(b) $P(2.1 < X < 3.4)$,
(c) $E(X)$,
(d) $\text{Var}(X)$.

4. The random variable X has probability density function given by

$$f(x) = \begin{cases} \dfrac{1}{(b-a)} & a \leqslant x \leqslant b \text{ where } b > a \\ 0 & \text{otherwise} \end{cases}$$

Show that the mean is $(b+a)/2$, and the variance is $(b-a)^2/12$ for this distribution.

Given that the mean equals 1 and the variance equals $4/3$ find
(i) $P(X < 0)$,
(ii) the value of z such that
$$P(X > z + \sigma_x) = \tfrac{1}{4},$$
where σ_x is the standard deviation of X.

(AEB)

5.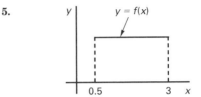

The random variable X has p.d.f. $f(x)$ as shown in the diagram.
If two independent observations of X are made, find the probability that one is less than 1.5 and the other is greater than the mean.

6. The random variable Y has probability density function given by

$$f(y) = \begin{cases} \dfrac{1}{5} & 32 \leqslant y \leqslant 37 \\ 0 & \text{otherwise} \end{cases}$$

Find the probability that Y lies within one standard deviation of the mean.

THE EXPONENTIAL DISTRIBUTION

A continuous r.v. X having p.d.f. $f(x)$ where

$$f(x) = \lambda e^{-\lambda x} \quad \text{for} \quad x \geqslant 0,$$

where λ is a positive constant, is said to follow an **exponential distribution**.

NOTE: this distribution is also known as the negative exponential distribution.

The parameter of the distribution is λ.

The graph of $y = f(x)$ is as shown:

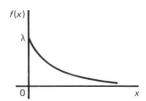

To show that X is the random variable, we need to show that the total area under the curve is 1.

Now
$$\int_{\text{all } x} f(x)\,dx = \int_0^{\infty} \lambda e^{-\lambda x}\,dx$$

$$= -[e^{-\lambda x}]_0^{\infty}$$

$$= -e^{-\infty} + e^0$$

But $e^0 = 1$

and $e^{-\infty} = \dfrac{1}{e^{\infty}} = 0$ (try e^{-100}, e^{-270}, e^{-648}, etc. on your calculator)

So
$$\int_0^{\infty} f(x)\,dx = 0 + 1 = 1$$

Therefore X is a random variable.

The following results are useful:

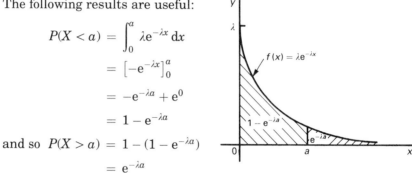

$$P(X < a) = \int_0^a \lambda e^{-\lambda x}\,dx$$

$$= \left[-e^{-\lambda x}\right]_0^a$$

$$= -e^{-\lambda a} + e^0$$

$$= 1 - e^{-\lambda a}$$

and so $P(X > a) = 1 - (1 - e^{-\lambda a})$

$$= e^{-\lambda a}$$

$$P(X < a) = 1 - e^{-\lambda a}$$

$$P(X > a) = e^{-\lambda a}$$

It follows that the cumulative distribution function, $F(x)$ is given by

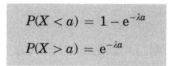

$$F(x) = P(X \leqslant x)$$

$$= 1 - e^{-\lambda x} \quad \text{for} \quad x \geqslant 0$$

Example 6.27 If $f(x) = 5e^{-5x}$ where $x \geqslant 0$, find the median value of x.

Solution 6.27 *NOTE*: it is a good idea to draw this graph accurately, particularly if you are not familiar with the exponential function.

For example, to work out the value of $f(x)$ when $x = 0.1$, key in

| 0.1 | × | 5 | +/− | e^x | × | 5 | = |

This gives the value $3.0326\ldots$

Let the median be m, so

$$F(m) = 0.5$$

Since $F(x) = 1 - e^{-\lambda x}$,

where $\lambda = 5$,

we have $F(m) = 1 - e^{-5m}$

so $1 - e^{-5m} = 0.5$

$$e^{-5m} = 0.5$$

$$\frac{1}{e^{5m}} = \frac{1}{2}$$

Therefore $e^{5m} = 2$

$$5m = \ln 2$$

$$m = \tfrac{1}{5} \ln 2$$

$$\underline{m = 0.139 \text{ (2 d.p.)}}$$

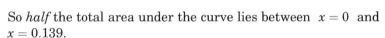

So *half* the total area under the curve lies between $x = 0$ and $x = 0.139$.

Example 6.28 The time, t seconds, between the arrivals of successive vehicles at a particular junction has p.d.f. $f(t) = 0.025\, e^{-0.025t}$, $t \geqslant 0$. A pedestrian, who takes 20 seconds to cross the road, sets off as one vehicle passes. Find the probability that she will complete the crossing before the next vehicle arrives. If she follows the same procedure on the return journey, find the probability that she completes each crossing without a vehicle arriving.

Solution 6.28 For the exponential distribution $f(t) = \lambda e^{-\lambda t}$,

$$P(T > t) = e^{-\lambda t}$$

Now we are given $f(t) = 0.025\, e^{-0.025t}$. This is an exponential distribution with $\lambda = 0.025$.

She will complete the crossing before the next vehicle arrives if $T > 20$.

$$P(T > 20) = e^{-0.025(20)}$$

$$= e^{-0.5}$$

$$= 0.6065\ldots$$

So the probability that she completes the crossing before the next vehicle arrives is 0.607 (3 d.p.)

Now $$P(T_1 > 20) \times P(T_2 > 20) = e^{-0.5} \times e^{-0.5}$$

$$= e^{-1}$$

$$= 0.3670\ldots$$

So the probability that she completes each crossing without a vehicle arriving whilst she is crossing is 0.367 (3 d.p.)

The following result is also useful:

If the continuous r.v. X has p.d.f. $f(x) = \lambda e^{-\lambda x}$, $x \geqslant 0$, then

$$P((X > a + b)\,|\,(X > a)) = P(X > b)$$

Now $$P(X > a) = e^{-\lambda a}$$

and $$P[(X > a + b)\,|\,(X > a)] = \frac{P[(X > a + b) \cap (X > a)]}{P(X > a)}$$

$$= \frac{e^{-\lambda(a+b)}}{e^{-\lambda a}}$$

$$= e^{-\lambda b}$$

$$= P(X > b)$$

So, for example

$$P[(X > 75)\,|\,(X > 30)] = P(X > 45)$$

and $$P[(X > 1200)\,|\,(X > 850)] = P(X > 350)$$

Also $$P[(X > q)\,|\,(X > p)] = P(X > (q - p)) \text{ where } q > p.$$

Example 6.29 The lifetime, in years, of a television tube of a certain make is a random variable T and its probability density function $f(t)$ is given by

$$f(t) = 0.25\,e^{-0.25t} \text{ for } 0 \leqslant t \leqslant \infty$$

If a tube lasts longer than 2 years, find the probability that it will last longer than 5 years.

Solution 6.29 Now $$P[(T > 5)\,|\,(T > 2)] = P(T > 3)$$

$$= e^{-0.25(3)}$$

$$= e^{-0.75}$$

$$= 0.4723\ldots$$

Given that the tube lasts longer than 2 years, the probability that it will last longer than 5 years is 0.472 (3 d.p.).

EXPECTATION AND VARIANCE

> If X has p.d.f. given by $f(x) = \lambda e^{-\lambda x}$, $x \geqslant 0$, then
>
> $$E(X) = \frac{1}{\lambda}$$
>
> $$\text{Var}(X) = \frac{1}{\lambda^2}$$

The proof of this is on page 735 in Appendix 2.

Example 6.30 The lifetime of a particular type of light bulb has a negative exponential distribution with mean lifetime 1000 hours.

(a) Find the probability that a bulb is still working after 1300 hours.

(b) Given that it is still working after 1300 hours, find the probability that it is still working after 1500 hours.

(c) Find the standard deviation of the lifetime of this type of light bulb.

Solution 6.30 Let X be the r.v. 'the lifetime of a light bulb in hours',

Then $\qquad f(x) = \lambda e^{-\lambda x} \quad x \geqslant 0.$

Now $\qquad E(X) = \dfrac{1}{\lambda}$

But $\qquad E(X) = 1000,$ therefore $\dfrac{1}{\lambda} = 1000$

$$\lambda = 0.001$$

So $\qquad f(x) = 0.001 e^{-0.001x}$

(a) $\qquad\qquad P(X > x) = e^{-\lambda x}$ (see p. 354)

$$P(X > 1300) = e^{-0.001(1300)}$$

$$= e^{-1.3}$$

$$= 0.273 \quad \text{(3 S.F.)}$$

The probability that a bulb is still working after 1300 hours is 0.273 (3 S.F.).

(b) $\qquad P[(X > 1500) | (X > 1300)] = P(X > 200)$ (see p. 356)

$$= e^{-0.001(200)}$$

$$= e^{-0.2}$$

$$= 0.819 \quad \text{(3 S.F.)}$$

The probability that the bulb is still working after 1500 hours, given that it is still working after 1300 hours, is 0.819 (3 S.F.).

(c)
$$\text{Var}(X) = \frac{1}{\lambda^2}$$

so
$$\text{standard deviation} = \sqrt{1/\lambda^2}$$

$$= \frac{1}{\lambda}$$

Standard deviation = 1000 hours

NOTE: For the exponential distribution,
standard deviation of X is equal to the mean of X.

Example 6.31 The continuous random variable X has the negative exponential distribution whose probability density function is given by

$$f(x) = \lambda e^{-\lambda x}, \qquad x \geqslant 0$$

$$f(x) = 0, \qquad \text{otherwise}$$

where λ is a positive constant. Obtain expressions, in terms of λ, for

(a) the mean, $E(X)$, of the distribution,

(b) $F(x)$, the (cumulative) distribution function.

Television sets are hired out by a rental company. The time in months, X, between major repairs has the above negative exponential distribution with $\lambda = 0.05$. Find, to 3 significant figures, the probability that a television set hired out by the company will not require a major repair for at least a 2-year period. Find also the median value of X.

The company agrees to replace any set for which the time between major repairs is less than M months. Given that the company does not want to have to replace more than one set in 5, find M.   (L)

Solution 6.31 $f(x) = \lambda e^{-\lambda x}, \; x \geqslant 0$

(a) $E(X) = \dfrac{1}{\lambda}$ (see p. 357)

(b)
$$F(t) = \int_0^t \lambda e^{-\lambda x}\, dx \qquad t \geqslant 0$$

$$= \left[-e^{-\lambda x} \right]_0^t$$

$$= -(e^{-\lambda t} - 1)$$

$$= 1 - e^{-\lambda t}$$

Therefore $F(x) = 1 - e^{-\lambda x}, \; x \geqslant 0$.

Let X be the r.v. 'the time, in months, between major repairs'.

$$f(x) = 0.05e^{-0.05x}$$

$$P(X > 24) = 1 - F(24)$$

$$= e^{-0.05(24)}$$

$$= e^{-1.2}$$

$$= 0.301 \ \ (3 \text{ S.F.})$$

The probability that a television set will not need major repair in a 2-year period is 0.301 (3 S.F.).

Let m be the median value, then

$$F(m) = 0.5$$

So $$1 - e^{-\lambda m} = 0.5$$

$$e^{-\lambda m} = 0.5$$

$$-\lambda m = \ln 0.5$$

$$m = -\frac{1}{0.05} \ln 0.5$$

$$= 13.9 \text{ months} \ \ (3 \text{ S.F.})$$

The median is 13.9 months (3 S.F.).

We require $$P(X < M) \leqslant 0.2$$

Therefore $$1 - e^{-0.05M} \leqslant 0.2$$

$$e^{-0.05M} \geqslant 0.8$$

$$-0.05M \geqslant \ln 0.8$$

$$M \leqslant -\frac{\ln 0.8}{0.05}$$

$$M \leqslant 4.46$$

Since M is an integer, $M = 4$

The company agrees to replace any set for which the time between major repairs is less than 4 months.

> If X has an exponential distribution with mean α, then
>
> $$E(X) = \alpha, \quad \text{so that } X \text{ has p.d.f.} \quad f(x) = \frac{1}{\alpha}e^{-x/\alpha}, \quad x \geqslant 0$$
>
> and $F(x) = 1 - e^{-x/\alpha}$

For example, if $E(X) = 0.6$

then $$f(x) = \frac{1}{0.6}e^{-x/0.6}$$

$$= \frac{5}{3}e^{-5x/3} \qquad x \geqslant 0$$

Example 6.32   A random variable T has exponential distribution with mean α.

Show that $P(t_1 \leqslant T \leqslant t_2) = e^{-t_1/\alpha} - e^{-t_2/\alpha}$.

Solution 6.32   If $E(T) = \alpha$

then
$$f(t) = \frac{1}{\alpha} e^{-t/\alpha}$$

and
$$F(t) = 1 - e^{-t/\alpha}$$

So $P(t_1 \leqslant T \leqslant t_2) = F(t_2) - F(t_1)$

$$= 1 - e^{-t_2/\alpha} - \left(1 - e^{-t_1/\alpha}\right)$$

$$= e^{-t_1/\alpha} - e^{-t_2/\alpha}$$

THE LINK BETWEEN THE EXPONENTIAL DISTRIBUTION AND THE POISSON DISTRIBUTION

The 'waiting times' between successive events in a Poisson distribution can be shown to follow an exponential distribution.

For example, suppose that X is the discrete random variable 'the number of cars arriving at a petrol station in one minute', and suppose that the average number of cars arriving per minute is λ.

Then
$$X \sim \text{Po}(\lambda).$$

We now need to find a probability model for the time in minutes between the arrival of one car and the next. Time is a continuous variable, so we need to find a continuous function for our model.

In one minute we 'expect' λ cars to arrive, so in t minutes we 'expect' λt cars to arrive.

So if Y is 'the number of cars arriving in t minutes' then $Y \sim \text{Po}(\lambda t)$.

So
$$P(Y = 0) = e^{-\lambda t}$$

Therefore $P(\textit{at least one} \text{ car arrives in } t \text{ minutes})$

$$= P(Y \geqslant 1)$$

$$= 1 - P(Y = 0)$$

$$= 1 - e^{-\lambda t}$$

Now let T be the random variable 'the length of time, in minutes, between successive cars'.

Then $P(\text{waiting time} < t) = P(\text{at least one car arrives in } t \text{ minutes})$

$$= 1 - e^{-\lambda t}$$

But $P(\text{waiting time} < t)$ is the same as the distribution function for T.

Therefore $\qquad\qquad\qquad\qquad F(t) = 1 - e^{-\lambda t}$

Differentiating, we get $\qquad f(t) = \lambda e^{-\lambda t}$

Therefore T follows the exponential distribution with parameter λ.

Remember that if T has p.d.f. $f(t) = \lambda e^{-\lambda t}, \ t \geq 0$

then $\qquad\qquad E(T) = \dfrac{1}{\lambda} \ \text{ and } \ \text{Var}(T) = \dfrac{1}{\lambda^2}.$ $\quad$ (see p. 357)

To sum up:

If X is 'the number of cars arriving in one minute'

then $\qquad\qquad\qquad\qquad X \sim \text{Po}(\lambda)$

and if T is 'the time, in minutes, between successive cars'

then $\qquad\qquad$ p.d.f. is $f(t) = \lambda e^{-\lambda t}$ where $E(T) = \dfrac{1}{\lambda}.$

NOTE: the units of time are the same in both distributions.

Example 6.33 Cars arrive at a garage at an average rate of 0.8 per minute. Find the mean and the variance of the waiting times between successive cars.

Solution 6.33 If X is 'the number of cars arriving in one minute', then $X \sim \text{Po}(0.8)$.

Therefore, if T is 'the time, in minutes, between successive cars'

then $\qquad\qquad\qquad\qquad f(t) = 0.8e^{-0.8t}$

and $\qquad\qquad\qquad E(T) = \dfrac{1}{0.8} = 1.25$

$$\text{Var}(T) = \frac{1}{(0.8)^2} = 1.5625$$

So the mean waiting time is 1.25 minutes and the variance is 1.5625 min^2.

Example 6.34 On a busy road, accidents occur at random at the rate of 3 per day. Find the probability that, after a particular accident has occurred, at least one day goes by without another.

Solution 6.34 Let X be 'the number of accidents in *1 day*'

Then $\qquad\qquad\qquad\qquad X \sim \text{Po}(3)$

If T is 'the time *in days* between successive accidents', then $f(t) = 3e^{-3t}$.

P(at least one day goes by without an accident)

$$= P(T > 1)$$

$$= e^{-3}$$

$$= 0.050 \ (3 \ \text{d.p.})$$

(see p. 354)

So there is only a 5% chance that one whole day goes by between successive accidents.

Exercise 6g

1. A continuous r.v. X has p.d.f. $f(x)$ where $f(x) = 5e^{-5x}$, $x \geqslant 0$. Find (a) $P(X > 0.5)$, (b) $E(X)$, (c) $P(X < E(X))$, (d) the standard deviation of X, (e) the median, (f) the mode.

2. The lifetime, in thousands of hours, of Extralight light bulbs follows an exponential distribution with p.d.f. $f(x) = 0.5e^{-0.5x}$
(a) Find the mean lifetime.
(b) A bulb is selected at random. Find the probability that it lasts (i) more than 2500 hours, (ii) less than 1800 hours.
(c) Two light bulbs are selected at random. Find the probability that one lasts more than the mean number of hours and the other lasts for less than the mean number of hours.
(d) A random sample of 6 light bulbs is chosen. Find the probability that exactly 4 will each last more than 2500 hours.

3. A batch of high-power light bulbs is such that the probability that any bulb fails before x hours, when kept on continuously, is $F(x) = 1 - e^{-x/10}$, $x \geqslant 0$. Find
(a) the median time to failure,
(b) the density function of the distribution of the time to failure,
(c) the mean and the variance of the distribution,
(d) the probability that a bulb will fail between five and ten hours.   (O)

4. The lifetime T, in years, of articles produced by a manufacturer can be modelled by the probability density function given by

$$f(t) = ae^{-at}, \quad t \geqslant 0$$

$$f(t) = 0, \qquad t < 0$$

The articles are produced at a unit cost of £10 and sold for £25. Research shows that 50% of those produced fail within the first five years of life. Find the value of a.
After some time in business the manufacturer decides to guarantee free replacement of items which fail during their first year, but at the same time he raises the price so that the increase covers the expected cost of providing the guarantee. What should the new price be?
If two items are purchased what is the probability that just one will be replaced under guarantee?

5. A continuous random variable T has a negative exponential distribution given by

$$f(t) = \lambda e^{-\lambda t} \quad t > 0$$

The life in hours of a type of electric battery can be modelled by the above distribution and when a sample of 800 is tested the mean life is found to be 92.2 h. What is the value of λ based on this figure?
(a) What is the probability that a battery will last for at least 200 h?
(b) If a battery has lasted 200 h what is the probability that it will last for at least a further 100 h?
(c) If two batteries are bought what is the probability that one fails before 200 h and the other after 200 h?

6. The random variable X can take all values between 0 and a inclusive, where $a > 0$. Its probability density function $f(x)$ is zero for $x < 0$ and $x > a$, and, for $0 \leqslant x \leqslant a$, satisfies

$$f(x) = (A/a)\exp(-x/a),$$

where A is a positive constant. Show by integration that $A = 1.582$ to 3 decimal places.

Also use integration to find to 2 decimal places
(i) the probability that X is less than $\frac{1}{2}a$;
(ii) the number λ for which there is a probability $\frac{1}{2}$ that X is less than λa.　(MEI)

7. Explain briefly, from your projects if possible, a real-life situation that can be modelled by an exponential distribution.

An archer shoots arrows at a target. The distance X cm from the centre of the target at which an arrow strikes the target has probability density function, f, defined by

$$f(x) = \tfrac{1}{10}e^{-x/10} \quad x > 0$$

$$f(x) = 0 \qquad \text{otherwise}$$

An arrow scores 8 points if $X \leqslant 2$, 5 points if $2 < X \leqslant 5$, one point if $5 < X \leqslant 15$ and no points otherwise. Find, to 3 decimal places, the expected score when one arrow is shot at the target.　(L)

8. Find the mean of the random variable X which has an exponential distribution with probability density function

$$f(x) = \lambda e^{-\lambda x} \quad \text{for } x \geqslant 0 \text{ where } \lambda > 0$$

$$f(x) = 0 \qquad \text{for } x < 0$$

For people suffering from a mental illness, the time in days from the end of a treatment to the occurrence of renewed symptoms is an exponential random variable with parameter $\lambda > 0$. Find, in terms of λ and t, the probability that neither of two randomly chosen sufferers from the illness will show renewed symptoms for a time t days after a treatment.

Given that two patients have no renewed symptoms for a time t days after a treatment, find, in terms of λ and t, the probability that both will remain free of symptoms for a further t days.

During a routine check at time t days after his treatment, another patient is found to be showing renewed symptoms. Find, in terms of λ, k and t, the probability that the renewed symptoms first showed in this patient less than kt days before the day of the routine check, where $0 \leqslant k \leqslant 1$.　(L)

9. A random variable X has the probability density function f given by

$$f(x) = ce^{-2x} \quad x > 0$$

$$f(x) = 0 \qquad \text{otherwise.}$$

Find the value of c. Find also the mean and the variance of X.

$$\left[\text{You may assume that } \int_0^\infty x^2 e^{-2x} \, dx = \tfrac{1}{4}. \right]$$

Find the distribution function of X. Hence, or otherwise, show that, for positive t and k,

$$P[(X > t + k) \,|\, (X > k)] = P(X > t)$$

Given that X is the lifetime in years of a particular type of indicator lamp that is alight continuously, explain in words the meaning of the above result.

Given that 2 such lamps, A and B, have already been alight for 3 months and 4 months respectively, find the probability that both will still be alight in 3 months' time.　(L)

10. On a stretch of road, breakdowns occur at an average rate of 2 per day, and the number of breakdowns follows a Poisson distribution. Find (a) the mean time between breakdowns, (b) the median time between breakdowns.

11. In any match, the number of goals scored by Rovers follows a Poisson distribution with mean 3 per 90 minutes. Find
(a) the mean and variance of the waiting times between successive goals scored by the team,
(b) the probability that, following a goal by Rovers in the tenth minute, they will not score another goal in the next 35 minutes.

12. Describe the conditions under which it is appropriate to use the exponential distribution, supporting your answer with reference to an experiment you may have carried out.

A major road construction project is underway. In the site supervisor's office, there is an average of two telephone calls every 5 minutes. Stating any assumptions you make, write down the probability that in a period of t minutes there is
(a) no telephone call,
(b) at least one telephone call.
Presenting a carefully reasoned argument, give the cumulative distribution function, $F(t)$, for the length of time between telephone calls. Hence establish that the probability density function, $f(t)$, is

$$f(t) = 0.4e^{-0.4t} \quad t > 0$$

Calculate
(c) the mean time between calls,
(d) the median time between calls.
Given that the supervisor has had no call in the last 3 minutes, what is the probability that she could leave the office for 5 minutes without missing a call?　(O)

SUMMARY — CONTINUOUS RANDOM VARIABLES

For a continuous random variable X,
with p.d.f. $f(x)$ for $a \leqslant x \leqslant b$

$$\int_{\text{all } x} f(x)\, dx = 1$$

$$P(c \leqslant X \leqslant d) = \int_c^d f(x)\, dx \qquad a \leqslant c < d \leqslant b$$

$$E(X) = \int_{\text{all } x} x f(x)\, dx$$

$$\text{Var}(X) = \int_{\text{all } x} x^2 f(x)\, dx - E^2(X)$$

$$F(t) = \int_a^t f(x)\, dx \quad a \leqslant t \leqslant b \qquad \text{where } F(t) \text{ is the cumulative distribution function}$$

$$f(x) = \frac{d}{dx} F(x)$$

The rectangular distribution

If $f(x) = \dfrac{1}{b-a} \quad a \leqslant x \leqslant b$, then $X \sim R(a,b)$

$E(X) = \frac{1}{2}(a+b)$

$\text{Var}(X) = \frac{1}{12}(b-a)^2$

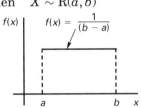

The exponential distribution

If $f(x) = \lambda e^{-\lambda x} \quad x \geqslant 0$

$E(X) = \dfrac{1}{\lambda}$

$\text{Var}(X) = \dfrac{1}{\lambda^2}$

$F(x) = 1 - e^{-\lambda x}$

$P(X > a) = e^{-\lambda a}$

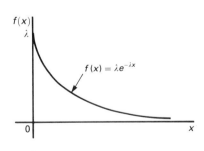

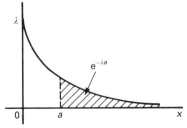

Miscellaneous Exercise 6h

1. (a) A continuous variable X is distributed at random between the values 2 and 3 and has a probability density function of $\dfrac{6}{x^2}$.
Find the median value of X.
(b) A continuous random variable X takes values between 0 and 1, with a probability density function of $Ax(1 - x)^3$. Find the value of A, and the mean and standard deviation of X.

2. A continuous variable X is distributed at random between 2 values, $x = 0$ and $x = 2$, and has a probability density function of $ax^2 + bx$. The mean is 1.25.
(i) Show that $b = \frac{3}{4}$, and find the value of a.
(ii) Find the variance of X.
(iii) Verify that the median value of X is approximately 1.3.
(iv) Find the mode.

3. The random variable X is the distance, in metres, that an inexperienced tight-rope walker has moved along a given tight-rope before falling off. It is given that

$$P(X > x) = 1 - \frac{x^3}{64} \qquad 0 \leqslant x \leqslant 4$$

(a) Show that $E(X) = 3$.
(b) Find the standard deviation, σ, of X.
(c) Show that $P(|X - 3| < \sigma) = \frac{69}{80}\sqrt{\frac{3}{5}}$. (C)

4. The random variable X has a probability density function given by

$$P(x) = \begin{cases} kx(1 - x^2) & (0 \leqslant x \leqslant 1) \\ 0 & \text{elsewhere} \end{cases}$$

k being a constant. Find the value of k and find also the mean and variance of this distribution.
Find the median of the distribution. (O & C)

5. An ironmonger is supplied with paraffin once a week. The weekly demand, X hundred litres, has the probability density function f, where

$$f(x) = c(1 - x)^7 \qquad 0 \leqslant x \leqslant 1$$
$$f(x) = 0 \qquad \text{otherwise}$$

where c is a constant. Find the value of c. Find the mean value of X, and, to the nearest litre, the minimum capacity of his paraffin tank if the probability that it will be exhausted in a given week is not to exceed 0.02. (L)P

6. A continuous random variable X has probability density function $f(x)$ given by $f(x) = 0$ for $x < 0$ and $x > 3$ and between $x = 0$ and $x = 3$ its form is as shown in the graph.

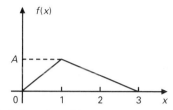

(a) Find the value of A.
(b) Express $f(x)$ algebraically and obtain the mean and variance of X.
(c) Find the median value of X.
A sample X_1, X_2 and X_3 is obtained. What is the probability that at least one is greater than the median value?

7. Determine λ such that

$$f(x) = \begin{cases} 0 & x < 0 \\ \lambda/2 & 0 \leqslant x \leqslant 1 \\ 0 & 1 < x < 2 \\ 3\lambda/2 - 3\lambda(x - 3)^2/4 & 2 \leqslant x \leqslant 4 \\ 0 & x > 4 \end{cases}$$

is a probability density function of the distribution of a random variable X. Sketch the density function and find $E(X)$ and $P(X \leqslant 3.5)$. (MEI)

8. The probability density function of X is given by

$$f(x) = \begin{cases} k(ax - x^2) & 0 \leqslant x \leqslant 2 \\ 0 & x < 0, \quad x > 2 \end{cases}$$

where k and a are positive constants.

Show that $a \geqslant 2$ and that $k = \dfrac{3}{6a - 8}$.

Given that the mean value of X is 1, calculate the values of a and k.
For these values of a and k sketch the graph of the probability density function and find the variance of X. (JMB)

9. A continuous random variable X has probability density function $f(x)$ defined by

$$f(x) = \begin{cases} 12(x^2 - x^3) & 0 \leqslant x \leqslant 1 \\ 0 & \text{otherwise} \end{cases}$$

Find the mean and standard deviation of X; find also its mean deviation about the mean. (O & C)

10. The continuous random variable X has probability density function $f(x)$ defined by

$$f(x) = \begin{cases} \dfrac{c}{x^4} & (x < -1) \\ c(2 - x^2) & (-1 \leqslant x \leqslant 1) \\ \dfrac{c}{x^4} & (x > 1) \end{cases}$$

(a) Show that $c = \frac{1}{4}$.

(b) Sketch the graph of $f(x)$.

(c) Determine the cumulative distribution function $F(x)$.

(d) Determine the expected value of X and the variance of X.   (C)

11. The random variable X takes all values x in the range $0 \leqslant x \leqslant 1$, and has a continuous probability density function $f(x)$ defined by

$$f(x) = kx^{\theta-1}(1-x)^2 \quad (\theta \geqslant 1)$$

(a) Show that $k = \frac{1}{2}\theta(\theta+1)(\theta+2)$.

(b) Find $E(X)$ and $E(X^2)$.

(c) Deduce the variance of X.

(d) For $\theta = \frac{3}{2}$, find the location of the mode and sketch $f(x)$.   (O & C)

12. State the conditions under which the binomial distribution is a suitable model to use in statistical work. Describe briefly how you used, or could have used, a binomial distribution in a project, giving the parameters of your distribution.

A large store sells a certain size of nail either in a small packet at 50 p per packet, or loose at £3 per kg. On any shopping day the number, X, of packets sold is a random variable where $X \sim B(8, 0.6)$, and the weight, Y kg, of nails sold loose is a continuous random variable with probability density function f given by

$$f(y) = \frac{2(y-1)}{25} \qquad 1 \leqslant y \leqslant 6$$

$$f(y) = 0, \qquad\qquad \text{otherwise}$$

Find, to 3 decimal places, the probability that, on any shopping day, the number of packets sold will be

(a) more than one,

(b) seven or fewer.

Find the probability that

(c) the weight of nails sold loose on any shopping day will be between 4 kg and 5 kg,

(d) on any one shopping day the shop will sell exactly 2 packets of nails and less than 2 kg of nails sold loose, giving your answer to 2 significant figures.

(e) Calculate the expected money received on any shopping day from the sale of this size of nail in this store.   (L)

13. A beam of electrons is directed at a solid object. The depth, X, to which any given electron will penetrate the object before colliding with an atom is a random variable whose probability density function is f.

(i) If $f(x) = a - bx$ $(a > 0, b > 0$, $0 \leqslant x \leqslant a/b)$, find b in terms of a. Find $E(X)$ and $Var(X)$ in terms of a.

If $f(x) = a\,e^{-cx}$ $(a > 0, c > 0, x \geqslant 0)$ find c in terms of a. Show that, if a fraction $1/N$ of all electrons penetrates to a depth greater than d, then $d = \dfrac{1}{a}\ln N$.   (C)

14. The number of kilograms of metal extracted from 10 kg of ore from a certain mine is a continuous random variable X with probability density function $f(x)$, where $f(x) = cx(2-x)^2$ if $0 \leqslant x \leqslant 2$ and $f(x) = 0$ otherwise, where c is a constant.

Show that $c = 0.75$, and find the mean and variance of X. The cost of extracting the metal from 10 kg of ore is £$10x$. Find the expected cost of extracting the metal from 10 kg of ore.   (MEI)

15. (a) A discrete random variable R takes integer values between 0 and 4 inclusive with probabilities given by

$$P(R = r) = \begin{cases} \dfrac{r+1}{10} & (r = 0, 1, 2) \\[2mm] \dfrac{9-2r}{10} & (r = 3, 4) \end{cases}$$

Find the expectation and variance of R.

(b) A continuous random variable X takes values in the interval $x \geqslant 0$. The probability density function of X is defined by

$$f(x) = \begin{cases} kx & \text{if } 0 \leqslant x \leqslant 1 \\[2mm] \dfrac{k}{x^4} & \text{if } x > 1 \end{cases}$$

Prove that $k = \frac{6}{5}$ and find the expectation and variance of X.   (C)

16. A continuous random variable X has probability density function defined by

$$f(x) = \begin{cases} 0 & x < 0, \\ kx & 0 \leqslant x \leqslant 2, \\ \dfrac{16k}{x^3} & x > 2. \end{cases}$$

Calculate the value of k. Find the median value and the expectation of X.

Prove that the standard deviation of X is infinite.

Find the value of a such that

$$P(X > x) = 0.005 \qquad (C)$$

17. The distances x, in miles, travelled by customers to the 'Cheep Supermarket' are distributed with density function

$$f(x) = \begin{cases} \frac{1}{5}e^{-x/5} & 0 \leqslant x < \infty \\ 0 & \text{otherwise} \end{cases}$$

Find the proportion of customers travelling less than 1 mile and the proportion travelling more than 15 miles to the supermarket.

The chance that a customer goes twice to the supermarket on one day is $p(x)$ when the customer has to travel x miles each way and the chance of one visit only is $1 - p(x)$, where

$$p(x) = \begin{cases} \frac{1}{4} & 0 \leqslant x < 5 \\ \frac{1}{8} & 5 \leqslant x < \infty \end{cases}$$

Find the expected distance travelled by a customer on one day.   (MEI)

18. A person frequently makes telephone calls to destinations for which each call is charged at the rate of 15 p per minute or part of a minute. The cost of such a call is X pence and its duration, T minutes, has the exponential probability density function

$$f(t) = \alpha\,e^{-\alpha t} \qquad t \geqslant 0$$
$$f(t) = 0 \qquad t < 0$$

Show that

$$P(X = 15r) = e^{-r\alpha}\,(e^{\alpha} - 1) \qquad r = 1, 2, 3, \dots$$

and that the mean cost per call in pence is

$$15/(1 - e^{-\alpha}).$$

$$\left[\text{You may assume that } \sum_{r=1}^{\infty} r x^r = \frac{x}{(1-x)^2}, |x| < 1.\right]$$

When a caller telephones a particular company, there is a probability of $\frac{1}{2}$ that he will be asked to hold the line. When he is asked to hold the line and decides to do so, the total time taken for the call has the above exponential distribution with $\alpha = \frac{1}{6}$; when he is not asked to hold the line the total time for the call has the exponential distribution with $\alpha = \frac{1}{2}$. Calculate the expected cost if he rings the company and is asked to hold the line and he

(a) holds and completes the call,
(b) rings off and then rings later, completing the second call whether he is asked to hold or not.

Assume that a wasted call costs 15 p and take $e^{-1/2} = 0.6065$, $e^{-1/6} = 0.8465$.   (JMB)

19. The continuous random variable X has probability density function given by

$$f(x) = \begin{cases} kx & 0 \leqslant x \leqslant 1, \\ kx^2 & 1 \leqslant x \leqslant 2, \\ 0 & \text{otherwise} \end{cases}$$

(i) Show that $k = \frac{6}{17}$.
(ii) Find the cumulative distribution function of X.
(iii) Find, correct to two decimal places, the median, m, of X.
(iv) Find, correct to two decimal places, $P(|X - m| < 0.75)$.   (C)

20. The continuous random variable X has probability density function given by

$$f(x) = \begin{cases} cx^2 & 0 \leqslant x \leqslant 2 \\ 2c(4 - x) & 2 \leqslant x \leqslant 4 \\ 0 & \text{otherwise} \end{cases}$$

where c is a constant.
(i) Show that $c = 0.15$.
(ii) Find the mean of X.
(iii) Find the lower quartile of X.
(iv) Find the probability that a single observation of X lies between the lower quartile and the mean.
(v) Three independent observations of X are taken. Find the probability that one of the observations is greater than the mean and the other two are less than the median value of X.   (C)

7

THE NORMAL DISTRIBUTION

The normal distribution is the most important continuous distribution in statistics. Many measured quantities in the natural sciences follow a normal distribution, for example heights, masses, ages, random errors, examination results. Under certain circumstances it is a useful approximation to the binomial and Poisson distributions.

PROBABILITY DENSITY FUNCTION OF NORMAL VARIABLE

The normal variable has a very complicated p.d.f. The shape of the curve depends on two parameters, μ and σ^2, where μ is the mean of the distribution and σ^2 is the variance.

> A continuous random variable X having p.d.f. $f(x)$ where
>
> $$f(x) = \frac{1}{\sigma\sqrt{2\pi}}\, e^{-(x-\mu)^2/2\sigma^2} \qquad -\infty < x < \infty$$
>
> is said to have a normal distribution with mean μ and variance σ^2.

If X is distributed in this way we write

$$X \sim \mathrm{N}(\mu, \sigma^2)$$

Main features of the curve of $f(x)$:

(**1**) It is bell-shaped and symmetrical about $x = \mu$.

(**2**) Approximately 95% of the distribution lies within 2 standard deviations of the mean.
This is sometimes known as the '2σ **rule**'.

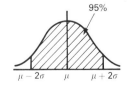

Also approximately 99.8% (nearly all) of the distribution lies within 3 standard deviations of the mean.

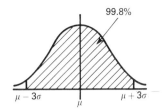

(**3**) The maximum value of $f(x)$ occurs when $x = \mu$ and is given by

$$f(x) = \frac{1}{\sigma\sqrt{2\pi}}.$$

(**4**) There are points of inflexion at $x = \mu - \sigma$ and $x = \mu + \sigma$.

Sketch of $y = f(x)$:

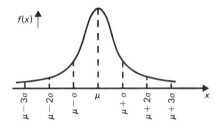

The actual size of the bell-shaped curve depends on the values of μ and σ.

Here are some examples, each drawn to the same scale:

(1) $X \sim N(0, 1)$

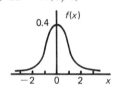

(2) $X \sim N(100, 6.25)$

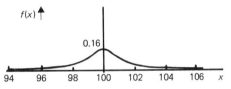

(3) $X \sim N(50, 4)$

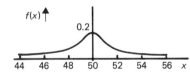

(4) $X \sim N\left(4, \frac{1}{4}\right)$

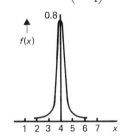

EXPECTATION AND VARIANCE

> If $X \sim N(\mu, \sigma^2)$
>
> then $E(X) = \mu$ and $\mathrm{Var}(X) = \sigma^2$

The proof of this result is given in Appendix 2 on page 736, with a discussion of the mathematical features of the normal variable.

PROBABILITIES

The probability that X lies between a and b is written

$$P(a \leqslant X \leqslant b)$$

and is given by the area under the normal curve between a and b.

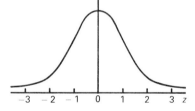

Now the function is very difficult to integrate, so tables are used. In order to use the *same set of tables* for all possible values of μ and σ^2 we perform a process known as **'standardising X'** to obtain the **standard normal variable** which is given the special symbol Z.

We will look first at the standard normal variable and then consider the method of standardising any normal variable.

THE STANDARD NORMAL VARIABLE, Z

The standard normal variable, Z, is the normal variable with mean 0 and variance 1.

So $\boxed{Z \sim \mathrm{N}(0,\,1)}$

We can find the areas under the standard normal curve by referring to **standard normal tables** which give cumulative probabilities.

There is a special symbol for the cumulative probability, $\Phi(z)$, where $\Phi(z) = P(Z < z)$

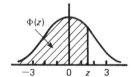

USE OF THE STANDARD NORMAL TABLES USING $\Phi(z)$

The tables are printed on page 722. This is an extract from the first section. We will refer to the highlighted numbers in the following text.

	z	0	1	2	3	4	5	6	7	8	9	1	2	3	4	5	6	7	8	9
																ADD				
	0.0	.5000	.5040	.5080	.5120	.5160	.5199	.5239	.5279	.5319	.5359	4	8	12	16	20	24	28	32	36
(*i*)	0.1	.5398	.5438	.5478	.5517	.5557	.5596	.5636	.5675	.5714	.5753	4	8	12	16	20	24	28	32	36
	0.2	.5793	.5832	.5871	.5910	.5948	.5987	.6026	.6064	.6103	.6141	4	8	12	15	19	23	27	31	35
(*ii*)	0.3	.6179	.6217	.6255	.6293	.6331	.6368	.6406	.6443	.6480	.6517	4	7	11	15	19	22	26	30	34
(*iii*)	0.4	.6554	.6591	.6628	.6664	.6700	.6736	.6772	.6808	.6844	.6879	4	7	11	14	18	22	25	29	32

(*i*) To find $P(Z < 0.16)$ we find row 0.1 and go across to column 6.

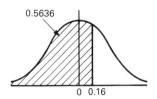

This gives 0.5636, so

$$P(Z < 0.16) = 0.5636$$

This is sometimes written $\Phi(0.16) = 0.5636$.

(*ii*) To find $P(Z < 0.345)$ we find first the value when $z = 0.34$ from row 0.3, column 4. This gives 0.6331. Now for the third decimal place, go to the right-hand section and read the number under 5. This is 19; note the instruction to ADD. This means that 19 is added to the *digits* 6331.

Therefore $\quad\quad\quad\quad P(Z < 0.345) = 0.6350$

$$\begin{array}{r} 6331 \\ + \quad 19 \\ \hline 6350 \end{array}$$

This is sometimes written

$$\Phi(0.345) = 0.6350$$

(*iii*) To find $P(Z < 0.429)$ we need row 0.4, column 2, right-hand section 9.

$$\begin{array}{r} 6628 \\ + \quad 32 \\ \hline 6660 \end{array}$$

So $\quad\quad\quad\quad P(Z < 0.429) = 0.6660$

This is an extract from further down the table:

z	0	1	2	3	4	5	6	7	8	9	1	2	3	4	5	6	7	8	9
														ADD					
3.0	.99865	.99869	.99874	.99878	.99882	.99886	.99889	.99893	.99896	.99900	0	1	1	2	2	2	3	3	4
3.1	$.9^3032$	$.9^3065$	$.9^3096$								3	6	9	13	16	19	22	25	28
(*iv*)				$.9^3126$	$.9^3155$	$.9^3184$	$.9^3211$				3	6	8	11	14	17	20	22	25
								$.9^3238$	$.9^3264$	$.9^3289$	2	5	7	10	12	15	17	20	22
3.2	$.9^3313$	$.9^3336$	$.9^3359$	$.9^3381$	$.9^3402$						2	4	7	9	11	13	15	18	20
						$.9^3423$	$.9^3443$	$.9^3462$	$.9^3481$	$.9^3499$	2	4	6	8	9	11	13	15	17

In row 3.1, for convenience of printing, 0.999 032 has been written $.9^3032$.

(*iv*) To find $P(Z < 3.159)$ we need row 3.1, column 5, right-hand section 9.

$$\begin{array}{r} 999\,184 \\ + \quad 25 \\ \hline 999\,209 \end{array}$$

So $\quad\quad\quad\quad P(Z < 3.159) = 0.999\,209$

Example 7.1   Using the standard normal tables on page 722 find

(**a**) $P(Z < 0.85)$ (**b**) $P(Z > 0.85)$

Solution 7.1   (**a**)

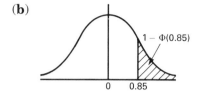

(**b**)

$$P(Z < 0.85) = \Phi(0.85)$$

$$= 0.8023$$

$$P(Z > 0.85) = 1 - \Phi(0.85)$$

$$= 1 - 0.8023$$

$$= 0.1977$$

Notice that the tables start when $z = 0$. For negative values of z we need to use the symmetrical properties of the curve. For example, to find $P(Z < -1)$, consider these diagrams:

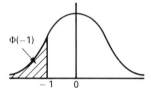 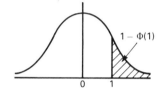

$$P(Z < -1) = P(Z > 1)$$

$$= 1 - \Phi(1)$$

$$= 1 - 0.8413$$

$$= 0.1587$$

In general

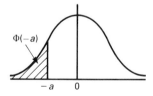 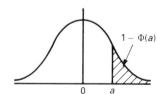

$$P(Z < -a) = 1 - \Phi(a)$$

To find $P(Z > -1)$, consider these diagrams:

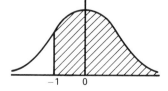 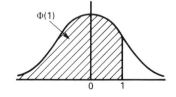

We see that $P(Z > -1) = P(Z < 1)$

$$= \Phi(1)$$

$$= 0.8413$$

In general $\boxed{P(Z > -a) = \Phi(a)}$

Example 7.2   If $Z \sim N(0, 1)$, find from tables   **(a)** $P(Z < 1.377)$,
(b) $P(Z > -1.377)$,   **(c)** $P(Z > 1.377)$,   **(d)** $P(Z < -1.377)$.

Solution 7.2   **(a)**

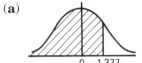

$P(Z < 1.377) = \Phi(1.377)$

$$= 0.9158$$

(b)

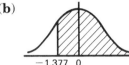

$P(Z > -1.377) = P(Z < 1.377)$

$$= \Phi(1.377)$$

$$= 0.9158$$

(c)

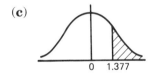

$P(Z > 1.377) = 1 - \Phi(1.377)$

$$= 1 - 0.9158$$

$$= 0.0842$$

(d)

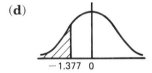

$P(Z < -1.377) = P(Z > 1.377)$

$$= 1 - 0.9158$$

$$= 0.0842$$

NOTE: it is helpful to draw diagrams and to check that your
answers are sensible.

Exercise 7a

1.   If $Z \sim N(0, 1)$, find   *(a)* $P(Z < 0.874)$,
(b) $P(Z > -0.874)$,   *(c)* $P(Z > 0.874)$,
(d) $P(Z < -0.874)$.

(j) $P(Z < 1.63)$,   *(k)* $P(Z > -2.061)$,
(l) $P(Z < -2.875)$.

2.   If $Z \sim N(0, 1)$, find   *(a)* $P(Z > 1.8)$,
(b) $P(Z < -0.65)$,   *(c)* $P(Z > -3.46)$,
(d) $P(Z < 1.36)$,   *(e)* $P(Z > 2.58)$,
(f) $P(Z > -2.37)$,   *(g)* $P(Z < 1.86)$,
(h) $P(Z < -0.725)$,   *(i)* $P(Z > 1.863)$,

3.   If $Z \sim N(0, 1)$, find   *(a)* $P(Z > 1.645)$,
(b) $P(Z < -1.645)$,   *(c)* $P(Z > 1.282)$,
(d) $P(Z > 1.96)$,   *(e)* $P(Z > 2.575)$,
(f) $P(Z > 2.326)$,   *(g)* $P(Z > 2.808)$,
(h) $P(Z < 1.96)$.

Example 7.3   If $Z \sim N(0, 1)$, find   (**a**) $P(0.345 < Z < 1.751)$,
(**b**) $P(-2.696 < Z < 1.865)$,   (**c**) $P(-1.4 < Z < -0.6)$.

Solution 7.3   (**a**) $P(0.345 < Z < 1.751) = \Phi(1.751) - \Phi(0.345)$

$$= 0.9600 - 0.6350$$

$$= 0.3250$$

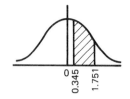

Note $P(a < Z < b) = \Phi(b) - \Phi(a)$

(**b**) $P(-2.696 < Z < 1.865)$

$$= \Phi(1.865) - \Phi(-2.696)$$

$$= \Phi(1.865) - (1 - \Phi(2.696))$$

$$= \Phi(1.865) + \Phi(2.696) - 1$$

$$= 0.9690 + 0.996\,50 - 1$$

$$= 0.9655$$

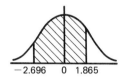

Note $P(-a < Z < b) = \Phi(a) + \Phi(b) - 1$

(**c**) $P(-1.4 < Z < -0.6) = \Phi(-0.6) - \Phi(-1.4)$

$$= \Phi(1.4) - \Phi(0.6)$$

$$= 0.9192 - 0.7257$$

$$= 0.1935$$

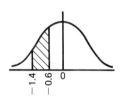

Note $P(-a < Z < -b) = \Phi(a) - \Phi(b)$

Example 7.4   If $Z \sim N(0, 1)$, find   (**a**) $P(|Z| < 1.433)$,   (**b**) $P(|Z| > 1.433)$.

Solution 7.4   (**a**) $P(|Z| < 1.433) = P(-1.433 < Z < 1.433)$

$$= \Phi(1.433) - \Phi(-1.433)$$

$$= \Phi(1.433) - [1 - \Phi(1.433)]$$

$$= 2\Phi(1.433) - 1$$

$$= 2(0.9240) - 1$$

$$= 0.848$$

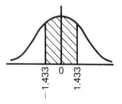

Note $P(|Z| < a) = 2\Phi(a) - 1$

(b) $P(|Z| > 1.433) = \Phi(-1.433) + 1 - \Phi(1.433)$

$$= 1 - \Phi(1.433) + 1 - \Phi(1.433)$$

$$= 2(1 - \Phi(1.433))$$

$$= 2(1 - 0.9240)$$

$$= 0.1520$$

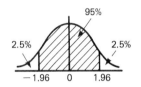

Note

$$P(|Z| > a) = 2(1 - \Phi(a))$$

It is also useful to remember that

$$P(|Z| > a) = 1 - P(|Z| < a)$$

Example 7.5   If $Z \sim \mathrm{N}(0, 1)$, show that   **(a)** $P(-1.96 < Z < 1.96) = 0.95$,
(b) $P(-2.575 < Z < 2.575) = 0.99$.

Solution 7.5   **(a)** $P(-1.96 < Z < 1.96) = 2\Phi(1.96) - 1$

$$= 2(0.975) - 1$$

$$= 0.95$$

Therefore $P(-1.96 < Z < 1.96) = 0.95$.

NOTE: This is an important result:

> The central 95% of the distribution lies between ± 1.96.

(b) $P(-2.575 < Z < 2.575) = 2\Phi(2.575) - 1$

$$= 2(0.995) - 1$$

$$= 0.99$$

Therefore $P(-2.575 < Z < 2.575) = 0.99$.

> The central 99% of the distribution lies between ± 2.575.

Exercise 7b

1.   If $Z \sim \mathrm{N}(0, 1)$, find

(a) $P(0.829 < Z < 1.843)$,

(b) $P(-2.56 < Z < 0.134)$,

(c) $P(-1.762 < Z < -0.246)$,

(d) $P(0 < Z < 1.73)$,

(e) $P(-2.05 < Z < 0)$,

(f) $P(-3.08 < Z < 3.08)$,

(g) $P(1.764 < Z < 2.567)$,

(h) $P(-1.65 < Z < 1.725)$,

(i) $P(-0.98 < Z < -0.16)$,

(j) $P(Z < -1.97 \text{ or } Z > 2.5)$,

(k) $P(|Z| < 1.78)$,

(l) $P(|Z| > 0.754)$,

(m) $P(-1.645 < Z < 1.645)$,

(n) $P(|Z| > 2.326)$.

We now consider how to use the standard normal tables in reverse, that is, to find the z value when we know the probability.

Consider the following extract. The highlighted values are used in the examples.

	z	0	1	2	3	4	5	6	7	8	9	1	2	3	4	5	6	7	8	9
																ADD				
(i)	1.5	.9332	.9345	.9357	.9370	.9382	.9394	.9406	.9418	.9429	.9441	1	2	4	5	6	7	8	10	11
	1.6	.9452	.9463	.9474	.9484	.9495	.9505	.9515	.9525	.9535	.9545	1	2	3	4	5	6	7	8	9
(ii)	1.7	.9554	.9564	.9573	.9582	.9591	.9599	.9608	.9616	.9625	.9633	1	2	3	4	4	5	6	7	8
	1.8	.9641	.9649	.9656	.9664	.9671	.9678	.9686	.9693	.9699	.9706	1	1	2	3	4	4	5	6	6
	1.9	.9713	.9719	.9726	.9732	.9738	.9744	.9750	.9756	.9761	.9767	1	1	2	2	3	4	4	5	5
	2.0	.9772	.9778	.9783	.9788	.9793	.9798	.9803	.9808	.9812	.9817	0	1	1	2	2	3	3	4	4
(iii)	2.1	.9821	.9826	.9830	.9834	.9838	.9842	.9846	.9850	.9854	.9857	0	1	1	2	2	2	3	3	4
	2.2	.9861	.9864	.9868	.9871	.9875	.9878	.9881	.9884	.9887	.9890	0	1	1	1	2	2	2	3	3
	2.3	.9893	.9896	.9898								0	1	1	1	1	2	2	2	2
(iv)					.9901	.99036	.99061	.99086				3	5	8	10	13	15	18	20	23
									.99111	.99134	.99158	2	5	7	9	12	14	16	18	21

(i) To find a if $P(Z < a) = 0.9406$, find 0.9406 in the main body of the table. We see that the z value is 1.56.

Therefore $\underline{P(Z < 1.56) = 0.9406, \text{ so } a = 1.56.}$

(ii) To find a if $P(Z < a) = 0.9579$, look for 0.9579 in the main body of the table. It does not appear, so look for the number below it. This is 0.9573.

To get the digits 9579 we would need to add 6 to 9573. We look at the right-hand section and find 6 under column 7. This means that the z value we require is 1.727.

Therefore $\underline{P(Z < 1.727) = 0.9579, \text{ and so } a = 1.727.}$

(iii) To find a if $\Phi(a) = 0.9832$, we find that $\Phi(2.12) = 0.9830$. When we refer to the end column we have

$$\Phi(2.124) = 0.9830$$

$$\Phi(2.125) = 0.9830$$

$$\Phi(2.126) = 0.9830$$

In the tables, probabilities have been given to 4 decimal places and in this instance it is not possible to distinguish between the z values, so we just decide on one of them, 2.124 say.

Therefore $\underline{\Phi(2.124) = 0.9832, \text{ and so } a = 2.124.}$

(iv) To find a if $P(Z < a) = 0.990\,42$, we see from the tables

$$\Phi(2.342) = 0.990\,41$$

$$\Phi(2.343) = 0.990\,44$$

In this case we choose the value that is closest to our required probability.

Therefore $a = 2.342.$

NOTE: often final answers are given to 2 or 3 significant figures and these discrepancies will not be important.

Example 7.6   If $Z \sim N(0, 1)$, find the value of a if

(**a**) $P(Z < a) = 0.9693$ (**b**) $P(Z > a) = 0.3802$

(**c**) $P(Z > a) = 0.7367$ (**d**) $P(Z < a) = 0.0793$

Solution 7.6   (**a**) $P(Z < a) = 0.9693$

i.e. $\Phi(a) = 0.9693$

From tables $\Phi(1.87) = 0.9693$

Therefore $a = 1.87$

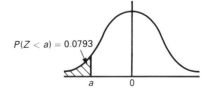

(**b**) $P(Z > a) = 0.3802$

Now $\Phi(a) = 1 - 0.3802$

$= 0.6198$

From tables $\Phi(0.305) = 0.6198$

Therefore $a = 0.305$

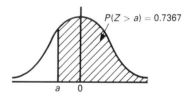

(**c**) $P(Z > a) = 0.7367$

This probability is greater than 0.5, therefore a must be negative.

So $\Phi(-a) = 0.7367$

But $\Phi(0.633) = 0.7367$

Therefore $-a = 0.633$

$a = -0.633$

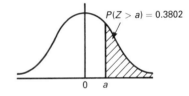

(**d**) $P(Z < a) = 0.0793$

a must be negative

so $\Phi(-a) = 1 - 0.0793$

$= 0.9207$

But $\Phi(1.41) = 0.9207$

Therefore $-a = 1.41$

$a = -1.41$

Example 7.7   If $Z \sim \mathrm{N}(0, 1)$ find a such that $P(\,|\,Z\,|< a) = 0.9$.

Solution 7.7 $P(\,|\,Z\,|< a) = 0.9$,

i.e. $P(-a < Z < a) = 0.9$.

From symmetry

$$2\Phi(a) - 1 \,=\, 0.9$$

$$2\Phi(a) \,=\, 1.9$$

$$\Phi(a) \,=\, 0.95$$

$$\underline{a \,=\, 1.645}$$

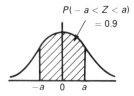

Exercise 7c

1.   If $Z \sim \mathrm{N}(0, 1)$, find a if
     (a) $P(Z < a) = 0.506$,   (b) $P(Z < a) = 0.787$,
     (c) $P(Z < a) = 0.891$,   (d) $P(Z < a) = 0.8297$,
     (e) $P(Z < a) = 0.9738$,
     (f) $P(Z < a) = 0.0003$,
     (g) $P(Z < a) = 0.0296$,   (h) $P(Z < a) = 0.325$.

2.   If $Z \sim \mathrm{N}(0, 1)$, find a if
     (a) $P(Z > a) = 0.001\,22$,
     (b) $P(Z > a) = 0.0100$,
     (c) $P(Z > a) = 0.025$,   (d) $P(Z > a) = 0.198$,
     (e) $P(Z > a) = 0.481$,   (f) $P(Z > a) = 0.692$,
     (g) $P(Z > a) = 0.812$,   (h) $P(Z > a) = 0.9885$.

3.   If $Z \sim \mathrm{N}(0, 1)$, find a if
     (a) $P(\,|\,Z\,|< a) = 0.6372$,
     (b) $P(\,|\,Z\,|> a) = 0.097$,

     (c) $P(\,|\,Z\,|< a) = 0.5$,
     (d) $P(\,|\,Z\,|> a) = 0.0404$.

4.   If $Z \sim \mathrm{N}(0, 1)$, find the upper quartile and
     the lower quartile of the distribution. Find
     also the 70th percentile.

5.   If $Z \sim \mathrm{N}(0, 1)$, find a if $P(\,|\,Z\,|> a)$ takes
     the value   (a) 10%,   (b) 5%,   (c) 4%,
     (d) 2%,   (e) 1%,   (f) 0.5%.

6.   If $Z \sim \mathrm{N}(0, 1)$, find a if $P(\,|\,Z\,|< a)$ takes
     the value   (a) 80%,   (b) 96%,   (c) 97%,
     (d) 99%.

USE OF THE STANDARD NORMAL TABLES FOR ANY NORMAL DISTRIBUTION

We now show how the tables for the standard normal distribution can be adapted for use with *any* normal variable X where $X \sim \mathrm{N}(\mu, \sigma^2)$.

We 'standardise' X by subtracting μ and then dividing by the standard deviation, σ.

This gives the standard normal variable Z.

So

$$Z = \frac{X - \mu}{\sigma} \qquad \text{where } Z \sim \mathrm{N}(0, 1)$$

For example, if $X \sim N(10, 25)$

then $Z = \dfrac{X - 10}{5}$ and using properties of inequalities,

$$P(X > 12) = P\left(\dfrac{X - 10}{5} > \dfrac{12 - 10}{5}\right)$$
$$= P(Z > 0.4)$$

$$P(X < 6) = P\left(\dfrac{X - 10}{5} < \dfrac{6 - 10}{5}\right)$$
$$= P(Z < -0.8)$$

$$P(6 < X < 12) = P\left(\dfrac{6 - 10}{5} < \dfrac{X - 10}{5} < \dfrac{12 - 10}{5}\right)$$
$$= P(-0.8 < Z < 0.4)$$

Example 7.8 The r.v. $X \sim N(300, 25)$. Find **(a)** $P(X > 305)$, **(b)** $P(X < 291)$,
(c) $P(X < 312)$, **(d)** $P(X > 286)$.

Solution 7.8 **(a)** To find $P(X > 305)$, we
standardise X by subtracting the
mean, 300 and dividing by the
standard deviation 5, so that

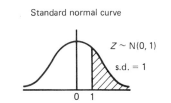

$$Z = \dfrac{X - 300}{5}$$

So $P(X > 305) = P\left(\dfrac{X - 300}{5} > \dfrac{305 - 300}{5}\right)$

$$= P(Z > 1)$$

$$= 1 - \Phi(1)$$

$$= 1 - 0.8413$$

$$= 0.1587$$

Therefore $\underline{P(X > 305) = 0.1587}$.

NOTE: if the two curves had been
drawn to scale, the curve for X
would have been much more spread
out and not as steep as the curve for
Z. However, for convenience of
drawing, we use the same sketch
and write the standardised values
underneath the x values. We use the
abbreviation S.V. for 'standardised
variable'.

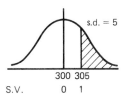

(b) $P(X < 291) = P\left(\dfrac{X - 300}{5} < \dfrac{291 - 300}{5}\right)$

$= P(Z < -1.8)$

$= 1 - \Phi(1.8)$

$= 1 - 0.9641$

$= 0.0359$

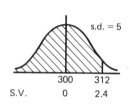

Therefore $P(X < 291) = 0.0359$.

(c) $P(X < 312) = P\left(\dfrac{X - 300}{5} < \dfrac{312 - 300}{5}\right)$

$= P(Z < 2.4)$

$= \Phi(2.4)$

$= 0.9918$

Therefore $P(X < 312) = 0.9918$.

(d) $P(X > 286) = P\left(\dfrac{X - 300}{5} > \dfrac{286 - 300}{5}\right)$

$= P(Z > -2.8)$

$= \Phi(2.8)$

$= 0.997\,44$

Therefore $P(X > 286) = 0.997\,44$.

Example 7.9   The r.v. X is such that $X \sim N(50, 8)$. Find   **(a)** $P(48 < X < 54)$,
(b) $P(52 < X < 55)$,   **(c)** $P(46 < X < 49)$,   **(d)** $P\left(|X - 50| < \sqrt{8}\right)$.

Solution 7.9   Standardise X so that $Z = \dfrac{X - 50}{\sqrt{8}}$.

(a) $P(48 < X < 54) = P\left(\dfrac{48 - 50}{\sqrt{8}} < \dfrac{X - 50}{\sqrt{8}} < \dfrac{54 - 50}{\sqrt{8}}\right)$

$= P(-0.707 < Z < 1.414)$

$= \Phi(1.414) + \Phi(0.707) - 1$

$= 0.9213 + 0.7601 - 1$

$= 0.6814$

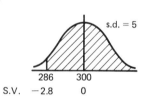

Therefore $P(48 < X < 54) = 0.6814$.

(**b**) $P(52 < X < 55) = P\left(\dfrac{52 - 50}{\sqrt{8}} < \dfrac{X - 50}{\sqrt{8}} < \dfrac{55 - 50}{\sqrt{8}}\right)$

$= P(0.707 < Z < 1.768)$

$= \Phi(1.768) - \Phi(0.707)$

$= 0.9615 - 0.7601$

$= 0.2014$

Therefore $P(52 < X < 55) = 0.2014$.

(**c**) $P(46 < X < 49) = P\left(\dfrac{46 - 50}{\sqrt{8}} < \dfrac{X - 50}{\sqrt{8}} < \dfrac{49 - 50}{\sqrt{8}}\right)$

$= P(-1.414 < Z < -0.354)$

$= \Phi(1.414) - \Phi(0.354)$

$= 0.9213 - 0.6383$

$= 0.283$

Therefore $P(46 < X < 49) = 0.283$.

(**d**) $P\big(|X - 50| < \sqrt{8}\,\big) = P\big(-\sqrt{8} < X - 50 < \sqrt{8}\,\big)$

$= P\left(-1 < \dfrac{X - 50}{\sqrt{8}} < 1\right)$

$= P(-1 < Z < 1)$

$= 2\Phi(1) - 1$

$= 2(0.8413) - 1$

$= 0.6826$

Therefore $P\big(|X - 50| < \sqrt{8}\,\big) = 0.6826$.

Example 7.10   The time taken by a milkman to deliver milk to the High Street is normally distributed with mean 12 minutes and standard deviation 2 minutes. He delivers milk every day. Estimate the number of days during the year when he takes   (**a**) longer than 17 minutes,   (**b**) less than 10 minutes,   (**c**) between 9 and 13 minutes.

Solution 7.10   Let X be the r.v. 'the time taken to deliver the milk to the High Street'. Then $X \sim N(12, 2^2)$.

We standardise X so that $Z = \dfrac{X - 12}{2}$.

(**a**) $P(X > 17) = P\left(\dfrac{X - 12}{2} > \dfrac{17 - 12}{2}\right)$

$= P(Z > 2.5)$

$= 1 - \Phi(2.5)$

$= 1 - 0.993\,79$

$= 0.006\,21$

The number of days when he takes longer than 17 minutes

$= 365(0.006\,21)$

$= 2.27$

≈ 2

Therefore on approximately 2 days in the year he takes longer than 17 minutes.

(**b**) $P(X < 10) = P\left(\dfrac{X - 12}{2} < \dfrac{10 - 12}{2}\right)$

$= P(Z < -1)$

$= 1 - \Phi(1)$

$= 1 - 0.8413$

$= 0.1587$

The number of days when he takes less than 10 minutes

$= 365(0.1587)$

$= 57.9$

≈ 58

Therefore on approximately 58 days in the year he takes less than 10 minutes.

(**c**) $P(9 < X < 13) = P\left(\dfrac{9 - 12}{2} < \dfrac{X - 12}{2} < \dfrac{13 - 12}{2}\right)$

$= P(-1.5 < Z < 0.5)$

$= \Phi(0.5) + \Phi(1.5) - 1$

$= 0.6915 + 0.9332 - 1$

$= 0.6247$

The number of days when he takes between 9 and 13 minutes

$$= 365(0.6247)$$

$$= 228 \text{ days}$$

Therefore on 288 days he takes between 9 and 13 minutes.

NOTE: since X is a continuous variable, we do not need to be concerned whether $9 < X < 13$, $9 \leqslant X < 13$, $9 < X \leqslant 13$, or $9 \leqslant X \leqslant 13$.

Exercise 7d

1. If $X \sim N(300, 25)$, find (a) $P(X > 308)$, (b) $P(X > 311.5)$, (c) $P(X > 294)$, (d) $P(X > 290.5)$, (e) $P(X < 302)$, (f) $P(X < 312)$, (g) $P(X < 299.5)$, (h) $P(X < 293)$.

2. If $X \sim N(50, 20)$, find (a) $P(X > 60.3)$, (b) $P(X < 47.3)$, (c) $P(X > 48.9)$, (d) $P(X > 53.5)$, (e) $P(X < 59.8)$, (f) $P(X < 62.3)$.

3. If $X \sim N(-8, 12)$, find (a) $P(X < -9.8)$, (b) $P(X > 0)$, (c) $P(X < -3.4)$, (d) $P(X > -5.7)$, (e) $P(X < -10.8)$, (f) $P(X > -1.6)$, (g) $P(X > -8.2)$.

4. If $X \sim N(a, a^2)$, find (a) $P(X < 0)$, (b) $P(X > 0)$, (c) $P(X > 0.5a)$, (d) $P(X > 1.5a)$, (e) $P(X < 2.5a)$.

5. If $X \sim N(100, 80)$, find
   (a) $P(85 < X < 112)$,
   (b) $P(105 < X < 115)$,
   (c) $P(85 < X < 92)$,
   (d) $P(|X - 100| < \sqrt{80})$,
   (e) $P(99 < X < 105)$.

6. If $X \sim N(84, 12)$, find (a) $P(80 < X < 89)$, (b) $P(X < 79 \text{ or } X > 92)$, (c) $P(76 < X < 82)$, (d) $P(|X - 84| > 2.9)$, (e) $P(87 < X < 93)$.

7. If $X \sim N(2, 0.3)$, find
   (a) $P(1.8 < X < 2.9)$,
   (b) $P(2.01 < X < 2.8)$,
   (c) $P(|X - 2| < 2\sqrt{0.3})$.

8. Packages from a packing machine have a mass which is normally distributed with mean 200 g and standard deviation 2 g. Find the probability that a package from the machine weighs (a) less than 197 g, (b) more than 200.5 g, (c) between 198.5 g and 199.5 g.

9. The heights of boys at a particular age follow a normal distribution with mean 150.3 cm and standard deviation 5 cm.
   Find the probability that a boy picked at random from this age group has height (a) less than 153 cm, (b) less than 148 cm, (c) more than 158 cm, (d) more than 144 cm, (e) between 147 cm and 149.5 cm, (f) between 150 cm and 158 cm.

10. A random variable X is such that $X \sim N(-5, 9)$. Find the probability that (a) an item chosen at random will have a positive value, (b) out of 10 items chosen at random, just 4 will have a positive value.

11. A certain type of cabbage has a mass which is normally distributed with mean 1 kg and standard deviation 0.15 kg. In a lorry load of 800 of these cabbages, estimate how many will have mass (a) greater than 0.79 kg, (b) less than 1.13 kg, (c) between 0.85 kg and 1.15 kg, (d) between 0.75 kg and 1.29 kg.

De-standardising

Sometimes it is necessary to find a value X which corresponds to the standardised value Z.

Now if $Z = \dfrac{X - \mu}{\sigma}$, then $\boxed{X = \mu + \sigma Z}$

Example 7.11 If $X \sim N(50, 6.8)$, find the value of X which corresponds to a standardised value of (**a**) -1.2, (**b**) 0.6.

Solution 7.11 Now $X = \mu + \sigma Z$, where $\mu = 50$ and $\sigma = \sqrt{6.8}$, so that
$$X = 50 + \sqrt{6.8}Z.$$

(**a**) When $z = -1.2$,
$$x = 50 + \sqrt{6.8}(-1.2)$$
$$= 46.87 \quad (2 \text{ d.p.})$$

(**b**) When $z = 0.6$,
$$x = 50 + \sqrt{6.8}(0.6)$$
$$= 51.56 \quad (2 \text{ d.p.})$$

Exercise 7e

Find the value of X which corresponds to a standardised value of (a) -2.05, (b) 0.86 for each of the following distributions:
(i) $X \sim N(60, 17)$, (ii) $X \sim N(124, 3.2^2)$

(iii) $X \sim N(84.5, 50)$, (iv) $X \sim N(62.3, 38)$
(v) $X \sim N(\mu, \sigma^2)$, (vi) $X \sim N(a, b)$,
(vii) $X \sim N(a, a^2)$, (viii) $X \sim N(49, 49)$.

Example 7.12 If $X \sim N(100, 36)$ and $P(X < a) = 0.8907$, find the value of a.

Solution 7.12 Now
$$P(X < a) = 0.8907$$

so $\quad P\left(Z < \dfrac{\boldsymbol{a - 100}}{\boldsymbol{6}}\right) = 0.8907$

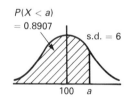

From tables,
$$P(Z < \mathbf{1.23}) = 0.8907$$

Now the quantities in bold type are equal.

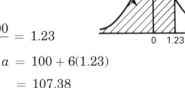

Therefore $\qquad \dfrac{a - 100}{6} = 1.23$
$$a = 100 + 6(1.23)$$
$$= 107.38$$

If $P(X < a) = 0.8907$, $a = 107.38$.

Example 7.13 If $X \sim N(24, 9)$ and $P(X > a) = 0.974$, find the value of a.

Solution 7.13 Since $P(X > a)$ is greater than 0.5, a must be less than the mean 24.

Now $\qquad P(X > a) = 0.974$

Standardising, $P\left(Z > \dfrac{a-24}{3}\right) = 0.974$

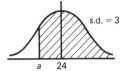

From tables,

$$P(Z > -1.943) = 0.974$$

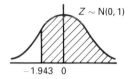

The two quantities in bold type are equal.

Therefore

$$\frac{a-24}{3} = -1.943$$

$$a = 24 - 3(1.943)$$

$$= 18.171$$

If $P(X > a) = 0.974$, then $a = 18.171$.

Example 7.14 If $X \sim N(70, 25)$, find the value of a such that
$P(|X - 70| < a) = 0.8$. Hence find the limits within which the central
80% of the distribution lies.

Solution 7.14 $\qquad\qquad P(|X - 70| < a) = 0.8$

Therefore

$$P(-a < X - 70 < a) = 0.8$$

$$P\left(-\frac{a}{5} < \frac{X-70}{5} < \frac{a}{5}\right) = 0.8$$

$$P\left(-\frac{a}{5} < Z < \frac{a}{5}\right) = 0.8$$

$$P(-0.2a < Z < 0.2a) = 0.8$$

By symmetry $\qquad\qquad 2P(Z < 0.2a) - 1 = 0.8$

$$2P(Z < 0.2a) = 1.8$$

$$P(Z < \mathbf{0.2a}) = 0.9$$

But from tables $\qquad\qquad P(Z < \mathbf{1.282}) = 0.9$

Therefore $\qquad\qquad\qquad 0.2a = 1.282$

$$\underline{a = 6.41}$$

So $\qquad\qquad P(-6.41 < X - 70 < 6.41) = 0.8$

or $\qquad\qquad\qquad P(63.59 < X < 76.41) = 0.8$

The central 80% of the distribution lies between 63.59 and 76.41.

Exercise 7f

1. If $X \sim N(60, 25)$ and if
   (i) $P(X > a) = 0.2324$, find a,
   (ii) $P(X > b) = 0.0702$, find b,
   (iii) $P(X > c) = 0.837$, find c,
   (iv) $P(X > d) = 0.7461$, find d.

2. If $X \sim N(45, 16)$ and if
   (i) $P(X < a) = 0.0317$, find a,
   (ii) $P(X < b) = 0.895$, find b,
   (iii) $P(X < c) = 0.0456$, find c,
   (iv) $P(X < d) = 0.996$, find d.

3. If $X \sim N(80, 36)$, find c such that
   $P(|X - 80| < c) = 0.9$ and hence find the
   limits within which the central 90% of the
   distribution lies.

4. If $X \sim N(400, 64)$, find
   (i) a such that $P(|X - 400| < a) = 0.75$,
   (ii) b such that $P(|X - 400| < b) = 0.98$,
   (iii) c such that $P(|X - 400| < c) = 0.95$,
   (iv) d such that $P(|X - 400| < d) = 0.975$,
   (v) the limits within which the central 95%
   of the distribution lies.

5. The masses of cos lettuces sold at a hypermarket are normally distributed with mean
   mass 600 g and standard deviation 20 g.
   (a) If a lettuce is chosen at random, find the
   probability that its mass lies between 570 g
   and 610 g.
   (b) Find the mass exceeded by 7% of the
   lettuces.
   (c) In one day, 1000 lettuces are sold.
   Estimate how many weigh less than 545 g.

6. The marks of 500 candidates in an
   examination are normally distributed with a
   mean of 45 marks and a standard deviation
   of 20 marks.

   (a) Given that the pass mark is 41, estimate
   the number of candidates who passed the
   examination.
   (b) If 5% of the candidates obtain a
   distinction by scoring x marks or more,
   estimate the value of x.
   (c) Estimate the interquartile range of the
   distribution.   (L Additional)

7. If $X \sim N(k, k^2)$, find
   (i) a such that $P(|X - k| < ak) = 0.9$,
   (ii) b such that $P(|X - k| > bk) = 0.01$,
   (iii) c such that $P(|X - k| > ck) = 0.05$,
   (iv) d such that $P(|X - k| < dk) = 0.995$.

8. Bags of flour packed by a particular machine
   have masses which are normally distributed
   with mean 500 g and standard deviation 20 g.
   2% of the bags are rejected for being
   underweight and 1% of the bags are rejected
   for being overweight. Between what range of
   values should the mass of a bag of flour lie if
   it is to be accepted?

9. A sample of 100 apples is taken from a load.
   The apples have the following distribution of
   sizes

Diameter to nearest cm	6	7	8	9	10
Frequency		11	21	38	17	13

   Determine the mean and standard deviation
   of these diameters.
   Assuming that the distribution is
   approximately normal with this mean and
   this standard deviation find the range of size
   of apples for packing, if 5% are to be rejected
   as too small and 5% are to be rejected as too
   large.   (O & C)

PROBLEMS THAT INVOLVE FINDING THE VALUE OF μ OR σ OR BOTH

Example 7.15 The lengths of certain items follow a normal distribution with mean
μ cm and standard deviation 6 cm. It is known that 4.78% of the items
have a length greater than 82 cm. Find the value of the mean μ.

Solution 7.15 Let X be the r.v. 'the length, in cm,
of an item'.

$X \sim N(\mu, 36)$ and $P(X > 82) = 0.0478$.

Now $P(X > 82) = P\left(Z > \dfrac{82 - \mu}{6}\right)$

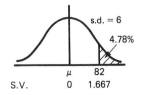

s.d. = 6
4.78%

| | μ | 82 |
| S.V. | 0 | 1.667 |

Therefore $P\left(Z > \dfrac{82 - \mu}{\sigma}\right) = 0.0478$

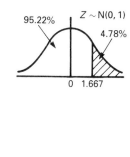

From tables

$$P(Z > \mathbf{1.667}) = 0.0478$$

so $\qquad \dfrac{82 - \mu}{6} = 1.667$

$$82 - \mu = 10.002$$

$$\mu = 72 \quad (2\ \text{S.F.})$$

The mean of the distribution is 72 cm.

Example 7.16 $X \sim \mathrm{N}(100, \sigma^2)$ and $P(X < 106) = 0.8849$. Find the standard deviation, σ.

Solution 7.16 $\qquad\qquad\qquad P(X < 106) = 0.8849$

$$P\left(\dfrac{X - 100}{\sigma} < \dfrac{106 - 100}{\sigma}\right) = 0.8849$$

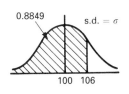

$$P\left(Z < \dfrac{\mathbf{6}}{\sigma}\right) = 0.8849$$

But from tables $\qquad P(Z < \mathbf{1.2}) = 0.8849$

Therefore $\qquad\qquad\qquad \dfrac{6}{\sigma} = 1.2$

 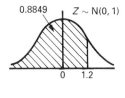

$$\sigma = \dfrac{6}{1.2}$$

$$= 5$$

The standard deviation of the distribution is 5.

Example 7.17 The masses of articles produced in a particular workshop are normally distributed with mean μ and standard deviation σ. 5% of the articles have a mass greater than 85 g and 10% have a mass less than 25 g. Find the values of μ and σ, and find the symmetrical limits, about the mean, within which 75% of the masses lie.

Solution 7.17 Let X be the r.v. 'the mass, in g, of an article'. Then $X \sim \mathrm{N}(\mu, \sigma^2)$ where μ and σ are unknown.

Now 5% have a mass greater than 85 g,

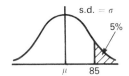

so $\qquad\qquad P(X > 85) = 0.05$

i.e. $P\left(Z > \dfrac{85 - \mu}{\sigma}\right) = 0.05$

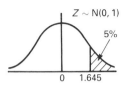

But from tables

$$P(Z > \mathbf{1.645}) = 0.05$$

Therefore $\dfrac{85 - \mu}{\sigma} = 1.645$

$$\underline{85 - \mu = 1.645\sigma} \qquad \text{(i)}$$

Also, 10% have a mass less than 25 g,

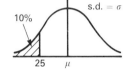

so $P(X < 25) = 0.10$

i.e. $P\left(Z < \dfrac{25 - \mu}{\sigma}\right) = 0.10$

But from tables

$$P(Z < -\mathbf{1.282}) = 0.10$$

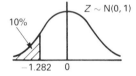

Therefore $\dfrac{25 - \mu}{\sigma} = -1.282$

i.e. $\underline{\mu - 25 = 1.282\sigma} \qquad \text{(ii)}$

Adding (i) and (ii) we have

$$60 = 2.927\sigma$$

$$\sigma = 20.5 \quad \text{(3 S.F.)}$$

Substituting for σ in (ii)

$$\mu = 25 + (1.282)(20.5)$$

$$= 51.3 \quad \text{(3 S.F.)}$$

Therefore the distribution has mean mass 51.3 g and standard
deviation 20.5 g.

Now consider values a and b such that

$$P(a \leqslant X \leqslant b) = 0.75$$

and a and b are symmetrical about the
mean.

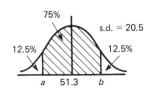

Now $P(X \leqslant b) = 0.875$

i.e. $\quad P\left(Z < \dfrac{b - 51.3}{20.5}\right) = 0.875$

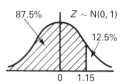

But from tables

$$P(Z < 1.15) = 0.875$$

Therefore $\quad \dfrac{b - 51.3}{20.5} = 1.15$

$$b = 51.3 + (20.5)(1.15) = 74.9 \quad \text{(3 S.F.)}$$

By symmetry $\quad a = 51.3 - (20.5)(1.15) = 27.7 \quad \text{(3 S.F.)}$

Therefore, the central 75% of the distribution lies between the limits 27.7 g and 74.9 g.

Exercise 7g

1. $X \sim N(45, \sigma^2)$ and $P(X > 51) = 0.288$. Find σ.

2. $X \sim N(21, \sigma^2)$ and $P(X < 27) = 0.9332$. Find σ.

3. $X \sim N(\mu, 25)$ and $P(X < 27.5) = 0.3085$. Find μ.

4. $X \sim N(\mu, 12)$ and $P(X > 32) = 0.8438$. Find μ.

5. $X \sim N(\mu, \sigma^2)$ and $P(X > 80) = 0.0113$, $P(X > 30) = 0.9713$. Find μ and σ.

6. $X \sim N(\mu, \sigma^2)$ and $P(X > 102) = 0.42$, $P(X < 97) = 0.25$. Find μ and σ.

7. $X \sim N(\mu, \sigma^2)$ and $P(X < 57.84) = 0.90$, $P(X > 50) = 0.5$. Find μ and σ.

8. $X \sim N(\mu, \sigma^2)$ and $P(X < 35) = 0.2$, $P(35 < X < 45) = 0.65$. Find μ and σ.

9. The marks in an examination were normally distributed with mean μ and standard deviation σ. 10% of the candidates had more than 75 marks and 20% had less than 40 marks. Find the values of μ and σ.

10. The lengths of rods produced in a workshop follow a normal distribution with mean μ and variance 4. 10% of the rods are less than 17.4 cm long. Find the probability that a rod chosen at random will be between 18 and 23 cm long.

11. A man cuts hazel twigs to make bean poles. He says that a stick is 240 cm long. In fact, the length of the stick follows a normal distribution and 10% are of length 250 cm or more while 55% have a length over 240 cm. Find the probability that a stick, picked at random, is less than 235 cm long.

12. The diameters of bolts produced by a particular machine follow a normal distribution with mean 1.34 cm and standard deviation 0.04 cm. A bolt is rejected if its diameter is less than 1.24 cm or more than 1.40 cm. (a) Find the percentage of bolts which are accepted.
The setting of the machine is altered so that the mean diameter changes but the standard deviation remains the same. With the new setting, 3% of the bolts are rejected because they are too large in diameter. (b) Find the new mean diameter of the bolts produced by the machine. (c) Find the percentage of bolts which are rejected because they are too small in diameter.

13. A certain make of car tyre can be safely used for 25 000 km on average before it is replaced. The makers guarantee to pay compensation to anyone whose tyre does not last for 22 000 km. They expect 7.5% of all tyres sold to qualify for compensation. Assuming that the distance, X, travelled before a tyre is replaced has a normal probability distribution, draw a diagram illustrating the facts given above.
Calculate, to 3 significant figures, the standard deviation of X.
Estimate the number of tyres per 1000 which will not have been replaced when they have covered 26 500 km. (L Additional)

14. A cutting machine produces steel rods which must not be more than 100 cm in length. The mean length of a large batch of rods taken from the machine is found to be 99.80 cm and the standard deviation of these lengths is 0.15 cm.

(a) Assuming that the lengths of the rods are normally distributed, calculate, to one decimal place, the percentage of rods which are too long.

(b) The position of the cut can be adjusted without altering the standard deviation of the lengths. Calculate in cm, to 2 decimal places, how small the mean length should be if no more than 2% of the rods are to be rejected for being longer than 100 cm.

(c) If the mean length is maintained at 99.80 cm, calculate, to the nearest tenth of a mm, by how much the standard deviation must be reduced if no more than 4% of the rods are to be rejected for being longer than 100 cm.   (L Additional)

15. The continuous random variable X is normally distributed with mean μ and standard deviation σ. Given that $P(X < 53) = 0.04$ and $P(X < 65) = 0.97$, find the interquartile range of the distribution.

16. Tea is sold in packages marked 750 g. The masses of the packages are normally distributed with mean 760 g, standard deviation σ. What is the maximum value of σ if less than 1% of the packages are underweight?

MISCELLANEOUS WORKED EXAMPLES

Example 7.18   Tests on 2 types of electric light bulb show the following:

Type A, lifetime distributed normally with an average life of 1150 hours and a standard deviation of 30 hours.

Type B, long-life bulb, average lifetime of 1900 hours, with standard deviation of 50 hours.

(a) What percentage of bulbs of type A could be expected to have a life of more than 1200 hours?

(b) What percentage of type B would you expect to last longer than 1800 hours?

(c) What lifetime limits would you estimate would contain the central 80% of the production of type A?

Solution 7.18   (a) Let X be the r.v. 'the length of life in hours of type A bulb'. Then $X \sim N(1150, 30^2)$.

$$P(X > 1200) = P\left(\frac{X - 1150}{30} > \frac{1200 - 1150}{30}\right)$$

$$= P(Z > 1.667)$$

$$= 0.0478$$

Therefore 4.78% of type A bulbs could be expected to have a life of more than 1200 hours.

(**b**) Let Y be the r.v. 'the length of life in hours of type B bulb'.
Then $Y \sim N(1900, 50^2)$.

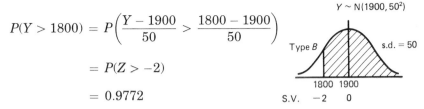

$$P(Y > 1800) = P\left(\frac{Y - 1900}{50} > \frac{1800 - 1900}{50}\right)$$

$$= P(Z > -2)$$

$$= 0.9772$$

Therefore 97.72% of type B bulbs could be expected to have a life of
more than 1800 hours.

(**c**) Now $P(Z < 1.282) = 0.9$
and $P(Z < -1.282) = 0.1$
so the standardised values are ± 1.282.

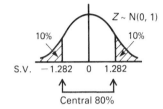

Now $x = \mu + \sigma z$, with $\mu = 1150$ and $\sigma = 30$, $z = \pm 1.282$

So $x_1 = 1150 + 30(-1.282) = 1111.54$

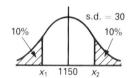

$\quad\quad x_2 = 1150 + 30(1.282) = 1188.46$

The limits are $(1110, 1190)$ (3 S.F.)

Therefore the limits $(1110\,\text{h}, 1190\,\text{h})$ would contain the central 80%
of the production of type A.

Example 7.19 A machine is producing components whose lengths are normally
distributed about a mean of 6.50 cm. An upper tolerance limit of
6.54 cm has been adopted and, when the machine is correctly set, 1
in 20 components is rejected as exceeding this limit. On a certain
day, it is found that 1 in 15 components is rejected for exceeding this
limit.

(**a**) Assuming that the mean has not changed but that the
production has become more variable, estimate the new standard
deviation.

(**b**) Assuming that the standard deviation has not changed but that
the mean has moved, estimate the new mean.

(**c**) If 1000 components are produced in a shift, how many of them
may be expected to have lengths in the range 6.48 to 6.53 cm if
the machine is set as in (**a**)?   (AEB)

Solution 7.19 (**a**) Let X be the r.v. 'the length in cm of a component'.
Then $X \sim N(6.50, \sigma^2)$ where σ is the new standard deviation.

$$P(X > 6.54) = \frac{1}{15} = 0.0667$$

so $P\left(\dfrac{X - 6.50}{\sigma} > \dfrac{6.54 - 6.50}{\sigma}\right) = 0.0667$

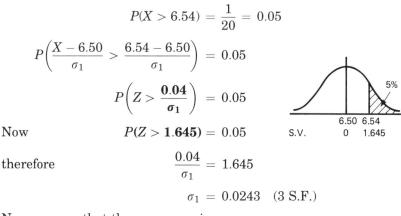

i.e. $P\left(Z > \dfrac{\mathbf{0.04}}{\boldsymbol{\sigma}}\right) = 0.0667$

Now $P(Z > \mathbf{1.501}) = 0.0667$

therefore $\dfrac{0.04}{\sigma} = 1.501$

$\sigma = 0.0266$ (3 S.F.)

The new standard deviation is 0.0266 cm (3 S.F.).

(**b**) Let the original standard deviation be σ_1.
Then $X \sim N(6.50, \sigma_1{}^2)$ originally.

$$P(X > 6.54) = \frac{1}{20} = 0.05$$

$P\left(\dfrac{X - 6.50}{\sigma_1} > \dfrac{6.54 - 6.50}{\sigma_1}\right) = 0.05$

$P\left(Z > \dfrac{\mathbf{0.04}}{\boldsymbol{\sigma_1}}\right) = 0.05$

Now $P(Z > \mathbf{1.645}) = 0.05$

therefore $\dfrac{0.04}{\sigma_1} = 1.645$

$\sigma_1 = 0.0243$ (3 S.F.)

Now suppose that the new mean is μ.

So $X \sim N(\mu, 0.0243^2)$.

$$P(X > 6.54) = 0.0667$$

$P\left(\dfrac{X - \mu}{0.0243} > \dfrac{6.54 - \mu}{0.0243}\right) = 0.0667$

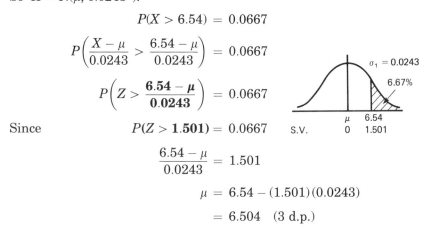

$P\left(Z > \dfrac{\mathbf{6.54 - \mu}}{\mathbf{0.0243}}\right) = 0.0667$

Since $P(Z > \mathbf{1.501}) = 0.0667$

$\dfrac{6.54 - \mu}{0.0243} = 1.501$

$\mu = 6.54 - (1.501)(0.0243)$

$= 6.504$ (3 d.p.)

Therefore the new mean is 6.504 cm (3 d.p.).

(c) If the machine is set as in part (a) then $X \sim N(6.50, 0.0266^2)$.

$$P(6.48 < X < 6.53) = P\left(\frac{6.48 - 6.50}{0.0266} < \frac{X - 6.50}{0.0266} < \frac{6.53 - 6.50}{0.0266}\right)$$

$$= P(-0.752 < Z < 1.128)$$

$$= 0.6442$$

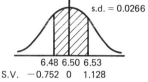

So for 1000 components,

expected number $= 0.6442\,(1000)$

$$= 644 \text{ (approx)}$$

Therefore we expect 644 to have lengths in the range 6.48 to 6.53 cm.

Example 7.20 The speeds of cars passing a certain point on a motorway can be taken to be normally distributed. Observations show that of cars passing the point, 95% are travelling at less than 85 m.p.h. and 10% are travelling at less than 55 m.p.h.

(a) Find the average speed of the cars passing the point.

(b) Find the proportion of cars that travel at more than 70 m.p.h.

(L)

Solution 7.20 Let X be the r.v. 'the speed, in m.p.h. of a car passing a certain point'.

Then $\qquad X \sim N(\mu, \sigma^2)$

(a) Now $P(X < 85) = 0.95$

and $\qquad P(X < 55) = 0.10$

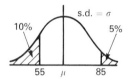

From standard normal tables,

$$P(Z < 1.645) = 0.95$$

and $\qquad\qquad P(Z < -1.282) = 0.10$

Therefore using $Z = \dfrac{X - \mu}{\sigma}$, we have

$$\frac{85 - \mu}{\sigma} = 1.645 \;\Rightarrow\; 85 = \mu + 1.645\sigma \;\text{ (i)}$$

$$\frac{55 - \mu}{\sigma} = -1.282 \;\Rightarrow\; 55 = \mu - 1.282\sigma \;\text{ (ii)}$$

(i) − (ii) $\qquad\qquad\qquad 30 = 2.927\sigma$

$$\sigma = 10.25 \quad \text{(2 d.p.)}$$

Substituting in (i) $\qquad\qquad 85 = \mu + (1.645)(10.25)$

$$\mu = 68.14 \quad \text{(2 d.p.)}$$

Therefore the average speed is 68.14 m.p.h. (2 d.p.).

(b)
$$P(X > 70) = P\left(\frac{X - 68.14}{10.25} > \frac{70 - 68.14}{10.25}\right)$$

$$= P(Z > 0.1815)$$

$$= 1 - 0.5718$$

$$= 0.4282$$

Therefore the proportion of cars that travel at more than 70 m.p.h. is 0.43 (2 d.p.).

Miscellaneous Exercise 7h

1. Batteries for a transistor radio have a mean life under normal usage of 160 hours, with a standard deviation of 30 hours. Assuming that battery life follows a normal distribution,
(a) calculate the percentage of batteries which have a life between 150 hours and 180 hours;
(b) calculate the range, symmetrical about the mean, within which 75% of the battery lives lie;
(c) if a radio takes four of these batteries and requires all of them to be working, calculate the probability that the radio will run for at least 135 hours. (O & C)

2. (a) The life of a certain make of electric light bulb is known to be normally distributed with a mean life of 2000 hours and a standard deviation of 120 hours. Estimate the probability that the life of such a bulb will be
(i) greater than 2150 hours,
(ii) greater than 1910 hours,
(iii) within the range 1850 hours to 2090 hours.
(b) The masses of packets of sugar are normally distributed. In a large consignment of packets of sugar, it is found that 5% of them have a mass greater than 510 g and 2% have a mass greater than 515 g. Estimate the mean and the standard deviation of this distribution. (C)

3. The random variables X_1 and X_2 are both normally distributed such that
$X_1 \sim N(\mu_1, \sigma_1^2)$ and $X_2 \sim N(\mu_2, \sigma_2^2)$.
Given that $\mu_1 < \mu_2$ and $\sigma_1^2 < \sigma_2^2$, sketch both distributions on the same diagram. State the '2σ rule' for a normal random variable. Explain how you used, or could have used, a normal distribution in a project.

The weights of vegetable marrows supplied to retailers by a wholesaler have a normal distribution with mean 1.5 kg and standard deviation 0.6 kg. The wholesaler supplies 3 sizes of marrow:

Size 1, under 0.9 kg,
Size 2, from 0.9 kg to 2.4 kg,
Size 3, over 2.4 kg.

Find, to 3 decimal places, the proportions of marrows in the three sizes. Find, in kg to one decimal place, the weight exceeded on average by 5 marrows in every 200 supplied. The prices of the marrows are 16 p for Size 1, 40 p for Size 2 and 60 p for Size 3. Calculate the expected total cost of 100 marrows chosen at random from those supplied. (L)

4. The random variable X is normally distributed with mean μ and variance σ^2.

Given that $P(X > 58.37) = 0.02$
and $P(X < 40.85) = 0.01$
find μ and σ. (L)

5. A machine is used to fill cans of soup with a nominal volume of 0.450 litres. Suppose that the machine delivers a quantity of soup which is Normally distributed with mean μ litres and standard deviation σ litres. Given that $\mu = 0.457$ and $\sigma = 0.004$, find the probability that a randomly chosen can will contain less than the nominal volume.
It is required by law that no more than 1% of cans contain less than the nominal volume. Find
(i) the least value of μ which will comply with the law if $\sigma = 0.004$,
(ii) the greatest value of σ which will comply with the law if $\mu = 0.457$. (MEI)

6. State the conditions under which the binomial distribution is a suitable model to use in statistical work. Describe briefly how a binomial distribution was used, or could have been used, in one of your projects giving the parameters of your distribution.

It is known that bearings produced at a factory have diameters that are normally distributed with mean 14.2 mm and standard deviation 1.2 mm. Find, to 4 decimal places, the probability that a bearing chosen at random from the production will have a diameter less than 13.9 mm.

Six bearings are to be chosen at random from the production. Find, to 2 significant figures, the probability that at least 5 of these bearings will have diameters between 13.9 mm and 14.6 mm. (L)

7. Describe the principal features of a normal distribution. Draw a sketch of the probability density function of the distribution N(0, 1).

A machine is producing a type of circular gasket. The specifications for the use of these gaskets in the manufacture of a certain make of engine are that the thickness should lie between 5.45 mm and 5.55 mm, and the diameter should lie between 8.45 mm and 8.54 mm. The machine is producing the gaskets so that their thicknesses are N(5.5, 0.0004), that is, normally distributed with mean 5.5 mm and variance $0.0004 \, \text{mm}^2$, and their diameters are independently distributed N(8.54, 0.0025).

Calculate, to one decimal place, the percentage of gaskets produced which will not meet

(a) the specified thickness limits,

(b) the specified diameter limits,

(c) the specifications.

Find, to 3 decimal places, the probability that, if 6 gaskets made by the machine are chosen at random, exactly 5 of them will meet the specifications. (L)

8. A marketing organisation grades onions into 3 sizes: small (diameter less than 60 mm), medium (diameter between 60 mm and 80 mm) and large (diameter greater than 80 mm). A certain grower finds that 61% of his crop falls into the small category and 14% into the large category. Assuming that the distribution of diameters of the onions in his crop is described by a Normal probability function, sketch a graph showing the information given above.

On this basis, calculate the standard deviation and the mean of the diameters of the onions in his crop. (SMP)

9. A machine produces components in batches of 20 000, the lengths of which may be considered to be normally distributed.

At the beginning of production, the machine is set to produce the required mean length of components at 15 mm, and it can then be set to give any one of three standard deviations: 0.06 mm, 0.075 mm, 0.09 mm.

It costs £850, £550 and £100 respectively to set these deviations.

Any length produced must lie in the range 14.82 mm to 15.18 mm, otherwise it is classed as defective and costs the company £1.

Which standard deviation should be used, if the decision is to be made purely on the cost of setting the machine and of the defectives?

10. Six hundred rounds are fired from a gun at a horizontal target 50 m long which extends from 950 m to 1000 m in range from the gun. The trajectories of the rounds all lie in the vertical plane through the gun and the target. It is found that 27 rounds fall short of the target and 69 rounds fall beyond it. Assuming that the range of rounds is normally distributed, find the mean and standard deviation of the range.

Estimate the number of rounds falling within 5 m of the centre of the target. (C)

11. Machine components are mass-produced at a factory. A customer requires that the components should be 5.2 cm long but they will be acceptable if they are within limits 5.195 cm to 5.205 cm. The customer tests the components and finds that 10.75% of those supplied are over-size and 4.95% are under-size. Find the mean and standard deviation of the lengths of the components supplied assuming that they are normally distributed. If three of the components are selected at random what is the probability that one is under-size, one over-size and one satisfactory?

If the standard deviation of the machine producing the components is altered without altering the mean so that 4.95% are over-size, what will be the new standard deviation and what percentage of components will now be under-size?

12. Packets of semolina are nominally 226 g in weight. The actual weights have a Normal distribution with $\mu = 230.00$ g and $\sigma = 1.50$ g. What is the probability that a packet is underweight?

A decision is taken that the probability of an underweight packet should not exceed 0.001.

To change the distribution of weights of the semolina packets to conform to this decision, two methods are considered:
(a) to increase μ, leaving σ unaltered;
(b) to improve the packing machine, thus reducing σ, while leaving μ unaltered.
Find the new values (of μ and of σ respectively) required for each method to succeed, given that, for the standardised Normal distribution,

$$P(Z > 3.0902) = 0.0010$$

(SMP)

13. The acidity of each of 100 random samples of soil from an area of land was measured and the results given in the table below.

Acidity (pH)	No. of samples
4.6–	4
4.8–	6
5.0–	16
5.2–	18
5.4–	22
5.6–	21
5.8–	11
6.0–6.2	2

Assuming that the pH values are determined correct to the nearest tenth of a unit, construct a cumulative frequency curve to illustrate the distribution.
A possible measure of kurtosis (i.e. flatness) is given by

$$k = \frac{Q}{P_{90} - P_{10}}$$

where Q is the semi-interquartile range, P_{90} the 90th percentile and P_{10} the 10th percentile. Estimate the value of k for the above distribution.
Use the standard normal table (p. 372) to estimate the value of k for a Normal distribution. Is the above distribution flatter than a Normal distribution with the same total frequency?

14. Metal bars are manufactured with lengths L_1 which are distributed normally with mean 20 cm and variance 0.01 cm². Calculate $P(L_1 < 20.25 \mid L_1 > 19.85)$, giving the answer correct to 3 decimal places.
The bars are packed lengthwise in boxes whose lengths L_2 are distributed normally with mean 20.2 cm and variance 0.02 cm².
(i) Show that, correct to 3 decimal places, $P(L_1 < 0.99L_2) = 0.495$, and calculate $P(L_1 > 0.98L_2)$ correct to the same degree of accuracy.
(ii) The mean of L_1 is adjusted (without altering its variance) so that $P(L_1 < 0.98L_2) = 0.05$. Find the new mean correct to 3 decimal places and the corresponding value of $P(L_1 < 0.99L_2)$.   (C)

15. The random variable X has a normal distribution with mean μ and standard deviation σ. Find
(i) $P(X - \mu > 2\sigma)$,
(ii) $P(X - \mu > 2\sigma \mid X - \mu > \sigma)$.   (JMB)

THE NORMAL APPROXIMATION TO THE BINOMIAL DISTRIBUTION

Under certain circumstances the normal distribution can be used as an approximation to the binomial distribution. One practical advantage is that calculations are much less tedious to perform.

We will consider some binomial distributions where $n = 5, 12, 20$ and $p = 0.2$ and 0.5. Each probability distribution is illustrated by a vertical line graph, and to make comparisons easier, we have superimposed a frequency curve on each.

(i) $n = 5$

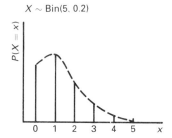

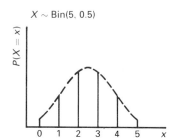

(*ii*) $n = 12$

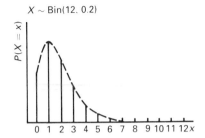

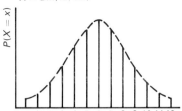

(*iii*) $n = 20$

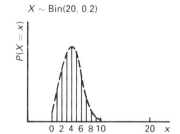

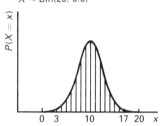

Note that when $p = 0.5$, the distribution is symmetric and as n gets larger it looks more like a normal distribution.

When $p = 0.2$ the distribution is positively skewed for small values of n, but when $n = 20$ it is becoming more symmetrical and bell-shaped.

In general:

If $X \sim \text{Bin}(n, p)$,

then $\mu = E(X) = np$, $\sigma^2 = \text{Var}(X) = npq$ where $q = 1 - p$

> Now, for large n and p close to 0.5,
>
> $X \sim N(np, npq)$ approximately

NOTE: as n gets larger, p can go further from 0.5 in either direction, but the approximation is better for p close to 0.5.

Example 7.21   Find the probability of obtaining between 4 and 7 heads inclusive with 12 tosses of a fair coin,

  (**a**) using the binomial distribution,

  (**b**) using the normal approximation to the binomial distribution.

Solution 7.21   Let X be the r.v. 'the number of heads obtained'.
Let 'success' be 'obtaining a head'.

Then $X \sim \text{Bin}(n, p)$ where $n = 12$ and $p = P(\text{head}) = 0.5$

(**a**) $X \sim \text{Bin}(12, 0.5)$

and $\qquad P(X = x) = {}^{12}C_x(0.5)^{12-x}(0.5)^x$

$$= {}^{12}C_x(0.5)^{12} \quad \text{for} \quad x = 0, 1, 2, \ldots, 12$$

Now $\qquad P(X = 4) = {}^{12}C_4(0.5)^{12} = 0.1208\ldots$

$$P(X = 5) = {}^{12}C_5(0.5)^{12} = 0.1933\ldots$$

$$P(X = 6) = {}^{12}C_6(0.5)^{12} = 0.2255\ldots$$

$$P(X = 7) = {}^{12}C_7(0.5)^{12} = 0.1933\ldots$$

So $\qquad P(4 \leqslant X \leqslant 7) = 0.733 \quad (3 \text{ d.p.})$

Therefore the probability of obtaining between 4 and 7 heads inclusive is 0.733 (3 d.p.).

(**b**) The probability distribution for the number of heads in 12 tosses has been calculated and is shown below. Each vertical line has been replaced by a rectangle to take into account that we intend to use a *continuous* distribution to approximate a discrete variable. The required probability is the sum of the areas of the shaded rectangles. Now this can be approximated by the area under the corresponding normal curve.

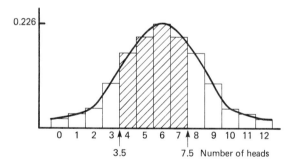

Using the normal approximation

$$X \sim \text{N}(np, npq) \quad \text{where} \quad n = 12 \quad \text{and} \quad p = 0.5$$

So $\qquad X \sim \text{N}(6, 3)$

We make a continuity correction as follows:

For $P(4 \leqslant X \leqslant 7)$ we consider the area from 3.5 to 7.5, thereby including *all* of the rectangles for 4, 5, 6 and 7.

We say that $P(4 \leqslant X \leqslant 7)$ transforms to $P(3.5 < X < 7.5)$, and we write

$$P(4 \leqslant X \leqslant 7) \longrightarrow P(3.5 < X < 7.5)$$

So

$$P(3.5 < X < 7.5) = P\left(\frac{3.5 - 6}{\sqrt{3}} < \frac{X - 6}{\sqrt{3}} < \frac{7.5 - 6}{\sqrt{3}}\right)$$

$$= P(-1.443 < Z < 0.866)$$

$$= 0.732 \quad (3 \text{ d.p.})$$

Therefore the probability of obtaining between 4 and 7 heads inclusive is 0.732 (3 d.p.)

NOTE: this answer compares very well with the answer in part (**a**), and the working is much quicker to perform. Although n is not very large, $p = 0.5$.

CONTINUITY CORRECTIONS

Continuity corrections often cause difficulty so we will look at these in more detail. It will be helpful to refer to the diagram showing the distribution for 12 tosses of the coin.

If we require the probability that there are 3 heads or less, i.e. $P(X \leqslant 3)$, then we consider $P(X < 3.5)$.

So $P(X \leqslant 3)$ transforms to $P(X < 3.5)$,

i.e. $P(X \leqslant 3) \longrightarrow P(X < 3.5)$

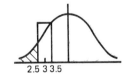

If we require the probability that there are less than 3 heads, i.e. $P(X < 3)$, then we consider $P(X < 2.5)$.

So $P(X < 3) \longrightarrow P(X < 2.5)$

If we require the probability that there are exactly 3 heads, then

$$P(X = 3) \longrightarrow P(2.5 < X < 3.5)$$

Further examples:

$$P(5 \leqslant X \leqslant 8) \longrightarrow P(4.5 < X < 8.5)$$

$$P(5 < X \leqslant 8) \longrightarrow P(5.5 < X < 8.5)$$

$$P(5 \leqslant X < 8) \longrightarrow P(4.5 < X < 7.5)$$

$$P(5 < X < 8) \longrightarrow P(5.5 < X < 7.5)$$

$$P(X < 4) \longrightarrow P(X < 3.5)$$

$$P(X \leqslant 4) \longrightarrow P(X < 4.5)$$

$$P(X \geqslant 4) \longrightarrow P(X > 3.5)$$

$$P(X > 4) \longrightarrow P(X > 4.5)$$

$$P(X = 9) \longrightarrow P(8.5 < X < 9.5)$$

$$P(X = 7) \longrightarrow P(6.5 < X < 7.5)$$

$$P(X \geqslant 0) \longrightarrow P(X > -0.5)$$

$$P(X > 0) \longrightarrow P(X > 0.5)$$

$$P(X = 0) \longrightarrow P(-0.5 < X < 0.5)$$

Exercise 7i

Continuity corrections — write down the transformations for each of the following:
(a) $P(3 \leqslant X \leqslant 9)$, (b) $P(3 < X < 9)$,
(c) $P(10 < X \leqslant 24)$, (d) $P(2 \leqslant X < 8)$,
(e) $P(X > 54)$, (f) $P(X \geqslant 76)$,
(g) $P(45 < X < 67)$, (h) $P(X < 109)$,

(i) $P(X \leqslant 45)$, (j) $P(X = 56)$,
(k) $P(400 < X \leqslant 560)$, (l) $P(X = 67)$,
(m) $P(X > 59)$, (n) $P(X = 100)$,
(o) $P(34 \leqslant X < 43)$, (p) $P(X = 7)$,
(q) $P(X \geqslant 509)$, (r) $P(X < 7)$,
(s) $P(27 \leqslant X < 29)$, (t) $P(X = 53)$.

Example 7.22 It is known that in a sack of mixed grass seeds 35% are ryegrass. Use the normal approximation to the binomial distribution to find the probability that in a sample of 400 seeds there are

(**a**) less than 120 ryegrass seeds,

(**b**) between 120 and 150 ryegrass seeds (inclusive),

(**c**) more than 160 ryegrass seeds.

Solution 7.22 Let X be the r.v. 'the number of ryegrass seeds'.

Let 'success' be 'obtaining a ryegrass seed'.

Then $X \sim \text{Bin}(n, p)$ where $n = 400$ and $p = 0.35$.

Since n is large, we use the normal approximation where

$$X \sim N(np, npq) \quad \text{with} \quad np = (400)(0.35) = 140$$

$$npq = (140)(0.65) = 91$$

so $X \sim N(140, 91)$

(a) $P(X < 120) \longrightarrow P(X < 119.5)$ (continuity correction)

$$P(X < 119.5) = P\left(\frac{X - 140}{\sqrt{91}} < \frac{119.5 - 140}{\sqrt{91}}\right)$$

$$= P(Z < -2.149)$$

$$= 0.0158$$

s.d. $= \sqrt{91}$

119.5 140
S.V. −2.149 0

The probability that there are less than 120 ryegrass seeds is 0.0158.

(b) $P(120 \leqslant X \leqslant 150) \longrightarrow P(119.5 < X < 150.5)$ (continuity correction)

$$P(119.5 < X < 150.5) = P\left(\frac{119.5 - 140}{\sqrt{91}} < \frac{X - 140}{\sqrt{91}} < \frac{150.5 - 140}{\sqrt{91}}\right)$$

$$= P(-2.149 < Z < 1.101)$$

$$= 0.8487$$

s.d. $= \sqrt{91}$

119.5 140 150.5
S.V. −2.149 0 1.101

The probability that there are between 120 and 150 ryegrass seeds is 0.8487.

(c) $P(X > 160) \longrightarrow P(X > 160.5)$ (continuity correction)

$$P(X > 160.5) = P\left(\frac{X - 140}{\sqrt{91}} > \frac{160.5 - 140}{\sqrt{91}}\right)$$

$$= P(Z > 2.149)$$

$$= 0.0158$$

s.d. $= \sqrt{91}$

140 160.5
S.V. 0 2.149

The probability that there are more than 160 ryegrass seeds is 0.0158.

Example 7.23 Show that the probability of obtaining a total of seven when two fair dice are tossed is $\frac{1}{6}$. A pair of fair dice is tossed 100 times and the total observed on each occasion. What is the probability of getting more than 25 sevens? How many tosses would be required in order that the probability of getting at least one seven is 0.9 or more. (AEB)

Solution 7.23 $P(\text{total of 7 when two dice are tossed})$

$$= \frac{6}{36}$$

$$= \frac{1}{6}$$

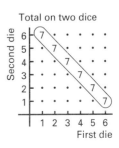

Let X be the r.v. 'the number of sevens when two dice are tossed'.
Let 'success' be 'obtaining a total of 7'.

Then $X \sim \text{Bin}(n, p)$ where $n = 100$ and $p = \frac{1}{6}$, so $X \sim \text{Bin}\left(100, \frac{1}{6}\right)$.

Now p is not that close to 0.5, but since n is very large, we use the normal approximation:

$$X \sim \text{N}(np, npq) \quad \text{with} \quad np = (100)\left(\frac{1}{6}\right) = \frac{50}{3}$$

$$npq = (100)\left(\frac{1}{6}\right)\left(\frac{5}{6}\right) = \frac{125}{9}$$

so $\qquad X \sim \text{N}\left(\frac{50}{3}, \frac{125}{9}\right)$.

The standard deviation is $\qquad \sqrt{125/9} = 3.726\ldots$

$$P(X > 25) \longrightarrow P(X > 25.5) \qquad \text{(continuity correction)}$$

$$P(X > 25.5) = P\left(\frac{X - 50/3}{3.726\ldots} > \frac{25.5 - 50/3}{3.726\ldots}\right)$$

$$= P(Z > 2.370)$$

$$= 0.008\,89$$

The probability of obtaining more than 25 sevens is 0.008 89.

Let the number of tosses required be n.

Then $\qquad\qquad\qquad\qquad X \sim \text{Bin}\left(n, \frac{1}{6}\right)$

Now $\qquad\qquad\qquad\qquad P(X = 0) = \left(\frac{5}{6}\right)^n$

$$P(\text{at least one } 7) = P(X \geqslant 1)$$

$$= 1 - P(X = 0)$$

$$= 1 - \left(\frac{5}{6}\right)^n$$

We need n such that

$$1 - \left(\frac{5}{6}\right)^n \geqslant 0.9$$

i.e. $\qquad\qquad\qquad\qquad \left(\frac{5}{6}\right)^n \leqslant 0.1$

Taking logs to base 10

$$n \log\left(\frac{5}{6}\right) \leqslant \log(0.1)$$

$$n \geqslant \frac{\log(0.1)}{\log(5/6)} \qquad \text{(When dividing by a negative quantity the inequality is reversed.)}$$

$$n \geqslant 12.63$$

The number of tosses required is 13.

Exercise 7j

1. If $X \sim \text{Bin}(200, 0.7)$, use the normal approximation to find (a) $P(X \geqslant 130)$, (b) $P(136 \leqslant X < 148)$, (c) $P(X < 142)$, (d) $P(X > 152)$, (e) $P(141 < X < 146)$.

2. 10% of the chocolates produced in a factory are mis-shapes. In a sample of 1000 chocolates find the probability that the number of mis-shapes is (a) less than 80, (b) between 90 and 115 inclusive, (c) 120 or more.

3. Find the probability of obtaining more than 110 ones in 400 tosses of an unbiased tetrahedral die with faces marked 1, 2, 3 and 4.

4. A coin is biased so that the probability that it will come down heads is double the probability that it will come down tails. The coin is tossed 120 times. Find the probability that there will be (a) between 42 and 51 tails inclusive, (b) 48 tails or fewer, (c) fewer than 34 tails, (d) between 72 and 90 heads inclusive.

5. An experiment consists of tossing two unbiased coins. The outcome is called a success if and only if two heads appear, all other outcomes being called a failure. If the experiment were repeated 27 times, write down the binomial distribution governing this series of experiments in the form $(p + q)^n$, stating the values of p, q and n. Find the expected number of successes and the standard deviation of this distribution. With the normal curve approximation estimate, using tables and giving your answer to 2 decimal places, the probability of obtaining at least 5 successes.
(L Additional)

6. It is estimated that 1/5 of the population of England watched last year's Cup Final on television. If random samples of 100 people are interviewed, calculate the mean and variance of the number of people from these samples who watched the Cup Final on television.
Use normal distribution tables to estimate, to 2 significant figures, the approximate probability of finding, in a random sample of 100 people, more than 30 people who watched the Cup Final on television.
(L Additional)

7. In a series of n independent trials the probability of a 'success' at each trial is p. If R is the random variable denoting the total number of successes, state the probability that $R = r$. State, also, the mean and variance of R.
A certain variety of flower seed is sold in packets containing about 1000 seeds. The packet claims that 40% will bloom white and 60% red. This may be assumed to be accurate.
If five seeds are planted estimate the probability that
(a) exactly three will bloom white;
(b) at least one will bloom white.
If 100 seeds are planted use the normal approximation to estimate the probability of obtaining between 30 and 45 white flowers.

8. A die is biased so that the probability of obtaining a six is 0.25. The die is thrown 200 times. (a) Find the probability of obtaining a six on the die (i) more than 60 times, (ii) less than 45 times, (iii) between 40 and 55 times (inclusive). (b) How many throws would be required if the probability of obtaining at least one six is greater than 0.9?

9. Two hundred fair dice are thrown 1000 times. Use the normal approximation to the binomial distribution to find the number of times you would expect to have the following number of sixes (a) 30, (b) 53, (c) more than 38, (d) less than 28, (e) between 28 and 38 inclusive.

10. A certain tribe is distinguished by the fact that 45% of the males have 6 toes on their right foot. Two explorers discover a group of 200 males from the tribe. Find the probability that the number who have six toes on their right foot is (a) 90, (b) less than 85, (c) between 82 and 91 inclusive, (d) more than 97.

11. Four hundred pupils sit a test which consists of 80 true–false questions. None of the candidates knows any of the answers and so guesses. (a) If the pass mark is 38, how many of the candidates would be expected to pass? (b) What should the new pass mark be if it is decided that only 115 candidates pass?

12. A lorry load of potatoes has, on average, one rotten potato in 6. A greengrocer tests a random sample of 100 potatoes and decides to turn away the lorry if she finds more than 18 rotten potatoes in the sample. Find the probability that she accepts the consignment.

THE NORMAL APPROXIMATION TO THE POISSON DISTRIBUTION

If $X \sim \text{Po}(\lambda)$ then $E(X) = \lambda$

$$\text{Var}(X) = \lambda$$

Now, for *large* λ

$$X \sim \text{N}(\lambda, \lambda) \quad \text{approximately}$$

Generally, we require $\lambda > 20$ for a good approximation.

Example 7.24   A radioactive disintegration gives counts that follow a Poisson distribution with mean count per second of 25. Find the probability that in 1 second the count is between 23 and 27 inclusive,

(**a**) using the Poisson distribution,

(**b**) using the normal approximation to the Poisson distribution.

Solution 7.24   Let X be the r.v. 'the radioactive count in a 1 second interval'. Then $X \sim \text{Po}(25)$.

Now, we need $P(23 \leqslant X \leqslant 27)$,

(**a**) Using the Poisson distribution:

$$P(X = x) = \text{e}^{-25}\frac{25^x}{x!}$$

so $P(X = 23) = \text{e}^{-25}\dfrac{(25)^{23}}{23!} = 0.076\,342$

$$P(X = 24) = \text{e}^{-25}\frac{(25)^{24}}{24!} = 0.079\,522\,9$$

$$P(X = 25) = \text{e}^{-25}\frac{(25)^{25}}{25!} = 0.079\,522\,9$$

$$P(X = 26) = \text{e}^{-25}\frac{(25)^{26}}{26!} = 0.076\,464\,3$$

$$P(X = 27) = \text{e}^{-25}\frac{(25)^{27}}{27!} = 0.070\,800\,3$$

$P(23 \leqslant X \leqslant 27) = 0.383$ (3 d.p.)

Therefore the probability that the count is between 23 and 27 inclusive is 0.383 (3 d.p.).

(**b**) Using the normal approximation, $X \sim N(25, 25)$.

$$P(23 \leqslant X \leqslant 27) \longrightarrow P(22.5 < X < 27.5) \qquad \text{(continuity correction)}$$

$$P(22.5 < X < 27.5) = P\left(\frac{22.5 - 25}{5} < \frac{X - 25}{5} < \frac{27.5 - 25}{5}\right)$$

$$= P(-0.5 < Z < 0.5)$$

$$= 0.383$$

s.d. = 5

22.5 25 27.5
S.V. −0.5 0 0.5

So the probability that the count is between 23 and 27 inclusive is 0.383.

NOTE: this answer compares very well with the answer in part (**a**) and the working is easier.

Exercise 7k

1. If $X \sim \text{Po}(24)$, use the normal approximation to find (a) $P(X \leqslant 25)$, (b) $P(22 \leqslant X \leqslant 26)$, (c) $P(X > 23)$.

2. If $X \sim \text{Po}(35)$, use the normal approximation to find (a) $P(X \leqslant 33)$, (b) $P(33 < X < 37)$, (c) $P(X > 37)$, (d) $P(X = 37)$.

3. If $X \sim \text{Po}(60)$, use the normal approximation to find (a) $P(50 < X \leqslant 58)$, (b) $P(57 \leqslant X < 68)$, (c) $P(X > 52)$, (d) $P(X \geqslant 70)$.

4. The number of calls per hour received by an office switchboard follows a Poisson distribution with parameter 30. Using the normal approximation to the Poisson distribution, find the probability that, in one hour, (a) there are more than 33 calls, (b) there are between 25 and 28 calls (inclusive), (c) there are 34 calls.

5. In a certain factory the number of accidents occurring in a month follows a Poisson distribution with mean 4. Find the probability that there will be at least 40 accidents during one year.

6. The number of bacteria on a plate viewed under a microscope follows a Poisson distribution with parameter 60. Find the probability that there are between 55 and 75 bacteria on a plate.
A plate is rejected if less than 38 bacteria are found. If 2000 such plates are viewed, how many will be rejected?

7. In an experiment with a radioactive substance the number of particles reaching a counter over a given period of time follows a Poisson distribution with mean 22. Find the probability that the number of particles reaching the counter over the given period of time is (a) less than 22, (b) between 25 and 30, (c) 18 or more.

8. The number of accidents on a certain railway line occur at an average rate of one every 2 months. Find the probability that (a) there are 25 or more accidents in 4 years, (b) there are 30 or fewer accidents in 5 years.

9. The number of eggs laid by an insect follows a Poisson distribution with parameter 200. (a) Find the probability that (i) more than 150 eggs are laid, (ii) more than 250 eggs are laid, (iii) between 180 and 240 eggs (inclusive) are laid. (b) If the probability that an egg develops is 0.1, show that the number of survivors follows a Poisson distribution with parameter 20, and find the probability that there are more than 30 survivors.

WHEN TO USE THE DIFFERENT APPROXIMATIONS

	Distribution of X	Restrictions on parameters	Approximation
(1)	$X \sim \text{Bin}(n, p)$	n large (say $n > 50$) p small (say $p < 0.1$)	$X \sim \text{Po}(np)$
(2)	$X \sim \text{Bin}(n, p)$	$n > 10$, p close to $\frac{1}{2}$ or $n > 30$ (say), p moving away from $\frac{1}{2}$	$X \sim \text{N}(np, npq)$
(3)	$X \sim \text{Po}(\lambda)$	$\lambda > 20$ (say)	$X \sim \text{N}(\lambda, \lambda)$

Example 7.25 If $X \sim \text{Bin}(20, 0.4)$, find the probability that $6 \leqslant X \leqslant 10$. Then find the approximations to this probability using (**a**) the normal distribution, (**b**) the Poisson distribution.

Solution 7.25 $X \sim \text{Bin}(n, p)$ where $n = 20$, $p = 0.4$

i.e. $X \sim \text{Bin}(20, 0.4)$

$$P(X = x) = {}^{20}C_x(0.6)^{20-x}(0.4)^x$$

$$P(X = 6) = {}^{20}C_6(0.6)^{14}(0.4)^6 = 0.124\,411\,7$$

$$P(X = 7) = {}^{20}C_7(0.6)^{13}(0.4)^7 = 0.165\,882\,2$$

$$P(X = 8) = {}^{20}C_8(0.6)^{12}(0.4)^8 = 0.179\,705\,7$$

$$P(X = 9) = {}^{20}C_9(0.6)^{11}(0.4)^9 = 0.159\,738\,4$$

$$P(X = 10) = {}^{20}C_{10}(0.6)^{10}(0.4)^{10} = 0.117\,141\,5$$

$$P(6 \leqslant X \leqslant 10) = 0.7469 \quad \text{(4 d.p.)}$$

Using the binomial distribution, $P(6 \leqslant X \leqslant 10) = 0.7469$ (4 d.p.).

(**a**) Using the normal approximation:

$$X \sim \text{N}(np, npq) \qquad \text{where} \qquad np = (20)(0.4) = 8$$

$$npq = (8)(0.6) = 4.8$$

so $\quad X \sim \mathrm{N}(8, 4.8)$

$P(6 \leqslant X \leqslant 10) \longrightarrow P(5.5 < X < 10.5) \qquad$ (continuity correction)

$$P(5.5 < X < 10.5) = P\left(\frac{5.5 - 8}{\sqrt{4.8}} < \frac{X - 8}{\sqrt{4.8}} < \frac{10.5 - 8}{\sqrt{4.8}}\right)$$

$$= P(-1.141 < Z < 1.141)$$

$$= 0.7462$$

s.d. $= \sqrt{4.8}$

5.5   8   10.5

S.V. -1.141 0   1.141

Therefore $P(6 \leqslant X \leqslant 10) = 0.7462$, using the normal approximation.

NOTE: this is a good approximation; p has moved away from $\frac{1}{2}$ but $n = 20$, which is quite large.

(**b**) Using the Poisson approximation:

$$\lambda = np = 8$$

So $\qquad X \sim \mathrm{Po}(8) \qquad$ and $\qquad P(X = x) = \mathrm{e}^{-8}\frac{8^x}{x!}$

$$P(X = 6) = \mathrm{e}^{-8}\frac{8^6}{6!} \qquad (0.122\,138\,2)$$

$$P(X = 7) = \mathrm{e}^{-8}\frac{8^7}{7!} \qquad (0.165\,882\,2)$$

$$P(X = 8) = \mathrm{e}^{-8}\frac{8^8}{8!} \qquad (0.179\,705\,7)$$

$$P(X = 9) = \mathrm{e}^{-8}\frac{8^9}{9!} \qquad (0.159\,738\,4)$$

$$P(X = 10) = \mathrm{e}^{-8}\frac{8^{10}}{10!} \qquad (0.117\,141\,5)$$

$$P(6 \leqslant X \leqslant 10) = 0.6246 \quad \text{(4 d.p.)}$$

So $P(6 \leqslant X \leqslant 10) = 0.6246$ (4 d.p.) using the Poisson approximation.

NOTE: this is a poor approximation since we should have $n > 50$ and $p < \frac{1}{10}$.

Example 7.26   If $X \sim \mathrm{Bin}(100, 0.5)$ find the probability that $X = 4$. Then find the approximations to the probability using (**a**) the normal distribution, (**b**) the Poisson distribution.

Solution 7.26 $\qquad\qquad X \sim \mathrm{Bin}(n, p) \quad$ where $\quad n = 100, \quad p = 0.05$

i.e. $\qquad X \sim \mathrm{Bin}(100, 0.05)$

Now $\qquad P(X = x) = {}^{100}C_x(0.95)^{100-x}(0.05)^x$

so $P(X = 4) = {}^{100}C_4(0.95)^{96}(0.05)^4$

                                        $= 0.1781$ (4 d.p.)

Therefore $P(X = 4) = 0.1781$ (4 d.p.) using the binomial distribution.

(**a**) Using the normal approximation:

$X \sim N(np, npq)$ where $np = (100)(0.05) = 5$

                                        $npq = (5)(0.95) = 4.75$

so $X \sim N(5, 4.75)$

$P(X = 4) \longrightarrow P(3.5 < X < 4.5)$ (continuity correction)

$P(3.5 < X < 4.5)$

$$= P\left(\frac{3.5 - 5}{\sqrt{4.75}} < \frac{X - 5}{\sqrt{4.75}} < \frac{4.5 - 5}{\sqrt{4.75}}\right)$$

$$= P(-0.6882 < Z < -0.2294)$$

$$= 0.1637$$

So $P(X = 4) = 0.1637$ using the normal approximation.

NOTE: this is a fairly good approximation, even though p is small. This is because n is large.

(**b**) Using the Poisson approximation:

$\lambda = np = 5$ $X \sim Po(5)$

$$P(X = x) = e^{-5}\frac{5^x}{x!}$$

so, $P(X = 4) = e^{-5}\dfrac{5^4}{4!} = 0.1755$ (4 d.p.)

So $P(X = 4) = 0.1755$ (4 d.p.) using the Poisson approximation.

NOTE: this is a good approximation, since n is large and p is small; also note that mean $\approx$ variance.

Example 7.27   If $X \sim Po(30)$, find $P(28 \leqslant X \leqslant 32)$. Then find the approximation to this probability using the normal distribution.

Solution 7.27 $X \sim Po(30)$

So $P(X = x) = e^{-30}\dfrac{30^x}{x!}$

and $$P(X = 28) = e^{-30}\frac{8^{28}}{28!} \qquad (0.070\,213\,3)$$

$$P(X = 29) = e^{-30}\frac{30^{29}}{29!} \qquad (0.072\,634\,5)$$

$$P(X = 30) = e^{-30}\frac{30^{30}}{30!} \qquad (0.072\,634\,5)$$

$$P(X = 31) = e^{-30}\frac{30^{31}}{31!} \qquad (0.070\,291\,4)$$

$$P(X = 32) = e^{-30}\frac{30^{32}}{32!} \qquad (0.065\,898\,2)$$

$$\underline{P(28 \leqslant X \leqslant 32) = 0.3517 \quad \text{(4 d.p.)}}$$

Using the normal approximation:

$$X \sim N(30, 30)$$

$$P(28 \leqslant X \leqslant 32) \longrightarrow P(27.5 < X < 32.5) \qquad \begin{array}{l}\text{(continuity}\\ \text{correction)}\end{array}$$

$$P(27.5 < X < 32.5) = P\left(\frac{27.5 - 30}{\sqrt{30}} < \frac{X - 30}{\sqrt{30}} < \frac{32.5 - 30}{\sqrt{30}}\right)$$

$$= P(-0.456 < Z < 0.456)$$

$$= 0.3516$$

s.d. $=\sqrt{30}$

27.5 30 32.5
S.V. -0.456 0 0.456

So $\underline{P(28 \leqslant X \leqslant 32) = 0.3516}$ using the normal approximation.

NOTE: this is a good approximation since $\lambda > 20$.

Exercise 7I

In Questions 1 to 4 calculate the probabilities using the binomial distribution. Then find the approximations to them using

(a) the normal distribution,

(b) the Poisson distribution.

Comment on your answers.

1. $X \sim \text{Bin}\left(15, \frac{1}{2}\right)$, find $P(7 \leqslant X \leqslant 9)$.

2. $X \sim \text{Bin}(60, 0.03)$, find $P(4 \leqslant X \leqslant 6)$.

3. $X \sim \text{Bin}(30, 0.6)$, find $P(X = 17)$.

4. $X \sim \text{Bin}(120, 0.1)$, find $P(X = 8)$.

5. If $X \sim \text{Po}(27)$, (a) find $P(X = 30)$, (b) find an approximation using the normal distribution. Comment on your answer.

6. If $X \sim \text{Po}(12)$, find $P(10 \leqslant X < 12)$. Then find an approximation using the normal distribution. Comment on your answer.

Miscellaneous Exercise 7m

1. A number of different types of fungi are distributed at random in a field. Eighty per cent of these fungi are mushrooms, and the remainder are toadstools. Five per cent of the toadstools are poisonous. A man, who cannot distinguish between mushrooms and toadstools, wanders across the field and picks a total of 100 fungi. Determine, correct to 2 significant figures, using appropriate approximations, the probability that the man has picked
   (a) at least 20 toadstools,
   (b) exactly two poisonous toadstools.   (C)

2. An old car is never garaged at night. On the morning following a wet night, the probability that the car does not start is $\frac{1}{3}$. On the morning following a dry night, this probability is $\frac{1}{25}$. The starting performance of the car each morning is independent of its performance on previous mornings.
   (a) There are 6 consecutive wet nights. Determine the probability that the car does not start on at least 2 of the 6 mornings.
   (b) During a wet autumn there are 32 wet nights. Using a suitable approximation, determine the probability that the car does not start on less than 16 of the 32 mornings.
   (c) During a long summer drought there are 100 dry nights. Using a Poisson approximation, determine the probability that the car does not start on 5 or more of the 100 mornings.
   (Give 3 decimal places in your answers.)   (C)

3. An urn contains 100 balls of which 4 are coloured red and the remainder are coloured white. A ball is drawn at random from the urn, its colour is noted and it is then replaced in the urn.
   Write down (but do not evaluate) an expression for the probability that, in a total of 10 such draws, a red ball is drawn exactly once.
   Determine, correct to two decimal places, making use of a suitable approximation in each case, the probability that
   (a) in a total of 100 such draws, a red ball is drawn on exactly four occasions,
   (b) in a total of 9600 such draws, a red ball is drawn on between 350 and 400 occasions *inclusive*.   (C)

4. Henri de Lade regularly travels from his home in the suburbs to his office in Paris. He always tries to catch the same train, the 08.05 from his local station. He walks to the station from his home in such a way that his arrival times form a normal distribution with mean 08.00 hours and standard deviation 6 minutes.
   (a) Assuming that his train always leaves on time, what is the probability that on any given day Henri misses his train?
   (b) If Henri visits his office in this way 5 days each week and if his arrival times at the station each day are independent, what is the probability that he misses his train once and only once in a given week?
   (c) Henri visits his office 46 weeks every year. Assuming that there are no absences during this time, what is the probability that he misses his train less than 35 times in the year?   (AEB)

5. One fifth of a given population has a minor eye defect. Use the normal distribution as an approximation to the binomial distribution to estimate the probability that the number of people with the defect is:
   (i) more than 20 in a random sample of 100 people,
   (ii) exactly 20 in a random sample of 100 people,
   (iii) more than 200 in a random sample of 1000 people.   (C)

6. A manufacturer of balloons produces 40% long ones and 60% round ones, and 5% of all balloons produced are purple.
   Assuming that packets of balloons contain a random selection from the output, calculate the probability that in a packet containing 20 balloons there are
   (a) equal numbers of long and round ones,
   (b) more long ones than round ones.
   A party pack contains 150 balloons.
   Using a suitable approximation in each case, calculate the probability that the pack contains
   (c) exactly 10 purple balloons,
   (d) between 72 and 78 long balloons inclusive.   (L)

7. The quantity of milk in bottles from a dairy is normally distributed with mean 1.036 pints and standard deviation 0.014 pints.
   Show that the probability of a randomly chosen bottle containing less than a pint is very nearly 0.5%.
   In the rest of this question take the answer of 0.5% to be exact. A crate contains 24 bottles.

Find the probability that
(i)   no bottles contain less than a pint of milk,
(ii) at most 1 bottle contains less than a pint of milk.
A milk float is loaded with 150 crates (3600 bottles) of milk. State the expected number of bottles containing less than a pint of milk.
Give a suitable approximating distribution for the number of bottles containing less than a pint of milk. Use this distribution to find the probability that more than 20 bottles contain less than a pint of milk.   (MEI)

8. During an advertising campaign, the manufacturer of Wolfitt (a dog food) claimed that 60% of dog owners preferred to buy Wolfitt. Assuming that the manufacturer's claim is correct for the population of dog owners, calculate
(a) using the binomial distribution, and
(b) using a normal approximation to the binomial;
the probability that at least 6 of a random sample of 8 dog owners prefer to buy Wolfitt. Comment on the agreement, or disagreement, between your two values. Would the agreement be better or worse if the proportion had been 80% instead of 60%? Continuing to assume that the manufacturer's figure of 60% is correct, use the normal approximation to the binomial to estimate the probability that, of a random sample of 100 dog owners, the number preferring Wolfitt is between 60 and 70 inclusive.   (MEI)

9. On the surface of penny postage stamps there are either one or two phosphor bands. Ninety per cent of penny stamps have two bands and the rest have one band. Of those having one band, 95% have the band in the centre of the stamp and the remainder have the band on the left-hand edge of the stamp.
(a) Determine the probability that in a random sample of ten penny stamps there are exactly eight having two phosphor bands.
(b) Determine, using a normal approximation, the probability that in a random sample of 100 penny stamps there are between five and fifteen stamps (inclusive) having one phosphor band.
(c) Determine, using a Poisson approximation, the probability that in a random sample of 100 stamps there are less than three stamps which have only a single band, this band being on the left-hand edge of the stamp.
(Any expressions evaluated should be clearly exhibited, and answers should be given correct to three significant figures.)   (C)

10. (a) Every year very small numbers of American wading birds lose their way on migration between North and South America and arrive in Great Britain instead, so that in September the proportion of American waders amongst the waders in Great Britain is about one in ten thousand.
At Dunsmere (a bird reserve in Great Britain), one September, there are twenty thousand waders, which may be regarded as a random sample of the waders present in Great Britain. Determine the probability that there are
(i)   no American waders present at Dunsmere,
(ii) more than two American waders present at Dunsmere.
(b) Three-quarters of all the sightings in Great Britain of American waders are made in the autumn. Suppose that in 1980 there were ten sightings of American waders at Dunsmere. Assuming that all sightings are independent of one another, determine the probability that exactly seven of these ten sightings were made in the autumn.   (C)

11. An inter-city telephone exchange has 100 lines and on average 80 are in use at any moment (on a typical business-day morning). Calculate
(a) the probability that all lines are engaged;
(b) the probability that more than 30 lines are free.
We say that a number x of lines is the 'effective minimum level' if the number of lines in use exceeds x for 95% of the time. Find x.
(You may assume that for large n the binomial probability may be approximated by a normal probability with mean np and variance npq.)   (SMP)

12. A telephone exchange serves 2000 subscribers, and at any moment during the busiest period there is a probability of $1/30$ for each subscriber that he will require a line. Assuming that the needs of subscribers are independent, write down an expression for the probability that exactly N lines will be occupied at any moment during the busiest period.
Use the normal distribution to estimate the minimum number of lines that would ensure that the probability that a call cannot be made because all the lines are occupied is less than 0.01.
Investigate whether the total number of lines needed would be reduced if the subscribers were split into two groups of 1000, each with its own set of lines.   (MEI)

13. A population consists of individuals of three types A, B and C occurring in proportions $1:5:14$.
(a) A sample of three individuals is drawn at random from the population.
(i) Determine the probability that all three are of different types.
(ii) Determine the probability that all three are of the same type.
(b) A sample of 40 individuals is drawn at random from the population.
(i) Determine the approximate value of the probability that 4 or more are of type A.
(ii) Determine the approximate value of the probability that exactly 10 are of type B.

(C)

14. In each of n independent trials of an experiment the probability of an event A occurring is 0.05.
(a) When $n = 10$, determine the probability that A occurs exactly once, giving your answer to three decimal places.
(b) When $n = 200$, use a suitable approximate method to determine the probability that A occurs not more than 10 times.

(JMB)

15. A discrete random variable X has the Poisson distribution given by

$$P(X = r) = e^{-a}\frac{a^r}{r!}, \quad r = 0, 1, 2, \ldots$$

Prove that the mean and the variance of X are each equal to a.
When a trainee typist types a document the number of mistakes made on any one page is a Poisson variable with mean 3, independently of the number of mistakes made on any other page. Use tables, or otherwise, to find, to three significant figures,
(a) the probability that the number of mistakes on the first page is less than two,
(b) the probability that the number of mistakes on the first page is more than four.
Find expressions in terms of e for
(c) the probability that the first mistake appears on the second page,
(d) the probability that the first mistake appears on the second page and the second mistake appears on the third page.
Evaluate these expressions, giving your answers to four significant figures.
When the typist types a 48-page document the total number of mistakes made by the typist is a Poisson variable with mean 144. Use a suitable approximate method to find, to three decimal places, the probability that this total number of mistakes is greater than 130.

(JMB)

16. Describe, briefly, the conditions under which the binomial distribution $\text{Bin}(n, p)$ may be approximated by
(a) a normal distribution,
(b) a Poisson distribution,
giving the parameters of each of the approximate distributions.
Among the blood cells of a certain animal species, the proportion of cells which are of type A is 0.37 and the proportion of cells which are of type B is 0.004. Find, to 3 decimal places, the probability that in a random sample of 8 blood cells at least 2 will be of type A.
Find, to 3 decimal places, an approximate value for the probability that
(c) in a random sample of 200 blood cells the combined number of type A and type B cells is 81 or more,
(d) there will be 4 or more cells of type B in a random sample of 300 blood cells.

(L)

17. Manufactured articles are packed in boxes each containing 200 articles, and on average 1.5% of all articles manufactured are defective. A box which contains 4 or more defective articles is substandard. Using a suitable approximation, show that the probability that a randomly chosen box will be substandard is 0.353, correct to three decimal places.
A lorry load consists of 16 boxes, randomly chosen. Find the probability that a lorry load will include at most 2 boxes which are substandard, giving three decimal places in your answer.
A warehouse holds 100 lorry loads. Show that, correct to two decimal places, the probability that exactly one of the lorry loads in the warehouse will include at most 2 substandard boxes is 0.06.

(C)

18. Answer the following question using, in each case, tables of the binomial, Poisson or normal distribution according to which you think is most appropriate. In each example draw attention to any feature which either supports or casts doubt on your choice of distribution.
(a) Cars pass a point on a busy city centre road at an average rate of 7 per five second interval. What is the probability that in a particular five second interval the number of cars passing will be
(i) 7 or less,
(ii) exactly 7?
(b) Weather records show that for a certain airport during the winter months an average of one day in 25 is foggy enough to prevent

landings. What is the probability that in a period of seven winter days landings are prevented on

(i)   2 or more days,

(ii) no days?

(c) The working lives of a particular brand of electric light bulb are distributed with mean 1200 hours and standard deviation 200 hours. What is the probability of

(i)   a bulb lasting more than 1150 hours,

(ii) the mean life of a sample of 64 bulbs exceeding 1150 hours?*   (AEB 1988)

*See 'Distribution of the sample mean', p. 447.

19. Explain briefly the circumstances under which a normal distribution may be used as an approximation to a binomial distribution. Write down the mean and the variance of the normal approximation to the binomial distribution Bin(n, p). Give an example, from your projects if possible, of the use of this approximation stating the parameters of your binomial distribution and of your normal approximation.

In a multiple-choice examination, candidate Jones picks his answer to each question at random from the list of 3 answers provided, of which only one is correct. A candidate answering 18 or more questions correctly passes the examination.

(a) For a paper containing 45 questions, use a normal approximation to find, to 3 decimal places, the probability that Jones passes.

(b) It is required that the probability that Jones passes should be less than 0.005. Use a normal approximation to show that the paper should contain at most 31 questions.   (L)

20. Explain briefly how you used, or could have used, a binomial distribution in a project. State the conditions under which a normal distribution may be used as an approximation to the distribution Bin(n, p) and write down, in terms of n and p, the mean and the variance of this normal approximation.

A large bag of seeds contains three varieties in the ratios $4:2:1$ and their germination rates are 50%, 60% and 80% respectively. Show that the probability that a seed chosen at random from the bag will germinate is $\frac{4}{7}$.

Find, to 3 decimal places, the probability that of 4 seeds chosen at random from the bag, exactly two of them will germinate. Given that 150 seeds are chosen at random from the bag, estimate, to 3 decimal places, the probability that less than 90 of them will germinate.   (L)

21. Describe a project, or an experiment in your course work, which you conducted to demonstrate a Poisson distribution. State the condition under which a normal distribution may be used as an approximation to the Poisson distribution. Write down the mean and the variance of the normal approximation to the Poisson distribution with mean λ.

Tomatoes from a particular nursery are packed in boxes and sent to a market. Assuming that the number of bad tomatoes in a box has a Poisson distribution with mean 0.44, find, to 3 significant figures, the probability of there being

(a) fewer than 2,

(b) more than 2 bad tomatoes in a box when it is opened.

Use a normal approximation to find, to 3 decimal places, the probability that in 50 randomly chosen boxes there will be fewer than 20 bad tomatoes in total.   (L)

22. In the following questions use the binomial, Poisson or normal distribution according to which you think is most appropriate. In each case draw attention to any feature which supports or casts doubt on the suitability of the distribution you have chosen. Indicate, where appropriate, that you are using one distribution as an approximation to another.

(a) The annual income of all employees of a large firm has a mean of £12 500 with a standard deviation of £2200. What is the probability that the mean income of 100 employees selected at random is between £12 000 and £13 000?

(b) A technician looks after a large number of machines on a night shift. She has to make frequent minor adjustments. The necessity for these occurs at random at a constant average rate of 8 per hour. What is the probability that

(i)   in a particular hour she will have to make 5 or fewer adjustments,

(ii) in an eight-hour shift she will have to make 70 or more adjustments?

(c) A number of neighbouring allotment tenants bought a large quantity of courgette seeds which they shared between them. Overall 15% failed to germinate. What is the probability that a tenant who planted 20 seeds would have

(i)   5 or more failing to germinate,

(ii) at least 17 germinating?   (AEB 1992)

23. In Urbania, selection for the Royal Flying Corps (RFC) is by means of an aptitude test based on a week's intensive military training. It is known that the scores of potential recruits on this test follow a normal distribution with mean 45 and standard deviation 10.

(*a*) What is the probability that a randomly chosen recruit will score between 40 and 60?
(*b*) What percentage of the recruits is expected to score more than 30?
(*c*) In a particular year 100 recruits take the test. Assuming that the pass mark is 50, calculate the probability that less than 35 recruits qualify for the RFC.   (AEB)

24. In the manufacture of a particular curtain material small faults occur at random at an average of 0.85 per $10\,\text{m}^2$.
(*a*) Find the probability that in a randomly selected $40\,\text{m}^2$ area of this material there are at most 2 faults.
This curtain material is going to be used in 10 of the rooms of a small block of furnished flats. Each room will require $40\,\text{m}^2$ of the material.
(*b*) Find the probability that for the first room to be furnished the material will contain at least 1 fault.
(*c*) Find the probability that in exactly half of these 10 rooms the material will contain exactly 3 faults.
The hooks on which these curtains are to hang are produced by a company which claims that only 2% of the hooks it produces are defective.
The owner of the block of flats buys 500 of the hooks which have been selected at random from the production.
(*d*) Using a suitable approximation find the probability that this sample contains between 8 and 12 defective hooks, inclusive.   (L)

25. Analysis of the scores in football matches in a local league suggests that the total number of goals scored in a randomly chosen match may be modelled by the Poisson distribution with parameter 2.7. The numbers of goals scored in different matches are independent of one another.
(i)   Find the probability that a match will end with no goals having been scored.
(ii) Find the probability that 4 or more goals will be scored in a match.
One Saturday afternoon, 11 matches are played in the league.
(iii) State the expected number of matches in which no goals are scored.
(iv) Find the probability that there are goals scored in all 11 matches.
(v)   State the distribution for the total number of goals scored in the 11 matches.
Using a suitable approximating distribution, or otherwise, find the probability that more than 30 goals are scored in total.   (MEI)

26. The number of flaws in a length of cloth, $\lambda\,\text{m}$ long, produced on a certain machine has a Poisson distribution with mean 0.04λ.

(i)   Find, to three decimal places, the probability that a $10\,\text{m}$ length of cloth has fewer than 2 flaws.
(ii) Find, to three decimal places, the probability that a $100\,\text{m}$ length of cloth has more than 4 flaws.
(iii) Find, to two decimal places, an approximate value for the probability that a $1000\,\text{m}$ length of cloth has at least 46 flaws.
(iv) Given that the cost of rectifying X flaws in a $1000\,\text{m}$ length of cloth is X^2 pence, find the expected value of this cost.   (JMB)

27. State the conditions under which a binomial distribution may be approximated by a Poisson distribution, and give a reason why this approximation may be useful in practice.
A vending machine will function correctly provided that components *P*, *Q* and *R* do not fail and that at least one of components *S* and *T* does not fail. It is known from past experience that, during normal usage in a 12-hour working day, the probabilities of failure for these five components are as follows.

$$P:0.01 \quad Q:0.02 \quad R:0.01 \quad S:0.10 \quad T:0.05$$

Failures of these components within each machine may be assumed independent.
Show that, correct to three decimal places, the probability that any machine will *not* fail during a particular 12-hour working day is 0.956.
A company has 50 of these machines on its premises. Assuming that different machines fail independently, use a Poisson distribution to estimate the probability that during a given 12-hour working day
(i)   exactly 2 machines fail,
(ii) at most 3 machines fail.
There are 2000 of these machines at various sites in the North of England. Estimate the probability that between 2.5% and 5.0%, inclusive, fail during a particular 12-hour working day.   (JMB)

28. Repeated trials of an experiment are conducted. One condition which must be satisfied in order that a binomial distribution can appropriately model the situation is that the trials be independent. Explain what is meant by *independent trials*.
Give an example of trials that are **not** independent.
State the other conditions needed for a binomial distribution.
It is known that only 95% of petunia seeds of a certain variety produce plants when sown. A nursery grows petunia plants in plastic strips by sowing ten seeds in each strip.

Find the probability, correct to 3 decimal places, that a randomly chosen strip produces
(i) ten plants,
(ii) fewer than nine plants.
The nursery plants 200 strips with petunia seeds. Use a normal approximation to the binomial distribution to find the probability that at least 125 of the strips produce ten plants.
The nursery also plants large trays with petunias by sowing 80 seeds to a tray. Use a Poisson approximation to the binomial distribution to find the probability that a randomly chosen tray produces fewer than 75 plants.   (JMB)

29. (*a*) State the conditions under which a binomial distribution may be approximated by
(i) a normal distribution,
(ii) a Poisson distribution.
(*b*) The magazine 'Readers Review' circulates all of its subscribers with details of its latest book, offering it at a special price. An interested subscriber may buy the book unseen or send for an inspection copy. A subscriber who sends for an inspection copy may keep, and subsequently pay for, the book or may choose to return it.
If 10% of subscribers buy the book unseen and 20% of subscribers send for an inspection copy, with 75% of these deciding to keep the book, show that 25% of subscribers actually buy the book.
A village has five subscribers to the magazine. Determine the probability that of these five subscribers
(i) none buys the book,
(ii) more than three buy the book.
Smalltown has two hundred subscribers to the magazine. Use a suitable approximation to the binomial distribution to estimate the probability that fewer than forty of Smalltown's subscribers buy the book.
All subscribers buying the book *unseen* have their names entered in a prize draw, with 5% of these winning a prize. Find the probability that a subscriber chosen at random wins a prize.

Estimate the probability that at least four of Smalltown's subscribers win a prize.
There are n subscribers to the magazine in Bigborough. If the probability that no Bigborough subscriber wins a prize is less than 0.05, calculate the smallest possible value for n.   (JMB)

30. [In this question give three places of decimals in each answer.]
When a telephone call is made in the country of Japonica, the probability of getting the intended number is 0.95.
(i) Ten independent calls are made. Find the probability of getting eight or more of the intended numbers. Find also the conditional probability of getting all ten intended numbers given that at least eight of the intended numbers are obtained.
(ii) Three hundred independent calls are made. Find the probability of failing to get the intended number on at least ten but not more than twenty of the calls.
(iii) Four hundred independent calls are made. For each call the probability of getting 'number unobtainable' is 0.004. Find the probability of getting 'number unobtainable' fewer than three times.   (C)

31. The life, in years, of a randomly chosen Flashpan car battery is normally distributed with mean 2 and standard deviation 0.4. Show that the probability that a randomly chosen Flashpan battery has a life less than one year is 0.006 21, correct to five places of decimals.
(i) A farmer buys two randomly chosen Flashpan batteries. Find the probability that the batteries each have a life more than one year.
(ii) A wholesaler buys 500 randomly chosen Flashpan batteries. Using a suitable approximation, find the probability that at most three have lives each less than one year.
(iii) A retailer buys 10 randomly chosen Flashpan batteries. Find the probability that at least four have lives each exceeding two years.   (C)

8

RANDOM VARIABLES
AND RANDOM
SAMPLING

We have seen previously that if X and Y are *any* two random variables, continuous or discrete, then

$$E(X + Y) = E(X) + E(Y)$$

$$E(X - Y) = E(X) - E(Y)$$

Also, if X and Y are *independent*, then

$$\text{Var}(X + Y) = \text{Var}(X) + \text{Var}(Y)$$

$$\text{Var}(X - Y) = \text{Var}(X) + \text{Var}(Y)$$

We now consider the application of these results to normal variables.

SUM AND DIFFERENCE OF TWO INDEPENDENT NORMAL VARIABLES

The sum or difference of two independent normal variables is also normally distributed:

> If X and Y are two *independent normal variables* such that
> $$X \sim \text{N}(\mu_1, \sigma_1{}^2) \quad \text{and} \quad Y \sim \text{N}(\mu_2, \sigma_2{}^2)$$
> then $\quad X + Y \sim \text{N}(\mu_1 + \mu_2, \sigma_1{}^2 + \sigma_2{}^2)$
> and $\quad X - Y \sim \text{N}(\mu_1 - \mu_2, \sigma_1{}^2 + \sigma_2{}^2)$

Example 8.1   If $X \sim \text{N}(60, 16)$ and $Y \sim \text{N}(70, 9)$, find   (**a**) $P(X + Y < 140)$, (**b**) $P(120 < X + Y < 135)$,   (**c**) $P(Y - X > 7)$, (**d**) $P(2 < Y - X < 12)$.

Solution 8.1   (**a**) Now $X + Y \sim \text{N}(60 + 70, 16 + 9)$,

i.e. $X + Y \sim \text{N}(130, 25)$

For convenience, let $R = X + Y$,

so $\hspace{4em} R \sim N(130, 25)$

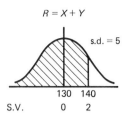

$$P(R < 140) = P\left(\frac{R - 130}{5} < \frac{140 - 130}{5}\right)$$

$$= P(Z < 2)$$

$$= 0.9772$$

Therefore $P(X + Y < 140) = 0.9772$.

(**b**) $P(120 < R < 135) = P\left(\frac{120 - 130}{5} < \frac{R - 130}{5} < \frac{135 - 130}{5}\right)$

$$= P(-2 < Z < 1)$$

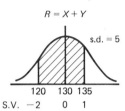

$$= 0.8185$$

Therefore $P(120 < X + Y < 135) = 0.8185$.

(**c**) We need to consider the r.v. $Y - X$.

Now $\hspace{2em} Y - X \sim N(70 - 60, 9 + 16)$

For convenience, let $T = Y - X$.

So $\hspace{4em} T \sim N(10, 25)$

$$P(T > 7) = P\left(\frac{T - 10}{5} > \frac{7 - 10}{5}\right)$$

$$= P(Z > -0.6)$$

$$= 0.7257$$

Therefore $P(Y - X > 7) = 0.7257$.

(**d**) $P(2 < T < 12) = P\left(\frac{2 - 10}{5} < \frac{T - 10}{5} < \frac{12 - 10}{5}\right)$

$$= P(-1.6 < Z < 0.4)$$

$$= 0.6006$$

Therefore $P(2 < Y - X < 12) = 0.6006$.

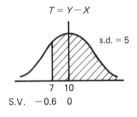

Example 8.2   Each weekday Mr Jones walks to the local library to read the newspapers. The time he takes to walk to and from the library is a normal variable with mean 15 minutes and standard deviation 2 minutes. The time he spends in the library is a normal variable with mean 25 minutes and standard deviation $\sqrt{12}$ minutes. Find the probability that on a particular day   (**a**) Mr Jones is away from the house for more than 45 minutes,   (**b**) Mr Jones spends more time travelling than in the library.

Solution 8.2   Let L be the r.v. 'the time in minutes spent in the library'. Then $L \sim N(25, 12)$.

Let W be the r.v. 'the time in minutes spent walking to and from the library'. Then $W \sim N(15, 4)$.

(**a**) To find the probability that Mr Jones is away from the house for more than 45 minutes we need to consider the distribution of the *total time, T,* spent travelling and at the library.

Let $\qquad\qquad\qquad\qquad T = L + W$

Then $\qquad\qquad\qquad\quad T \sim N(25 + 15, 12 + 4)$

i.e. $\qquad\qquad\qquad\quad T \sim N(40, 16)$

$$P(T > 45) = P\left(\frac{T - 40}{4} > \frac{45 - 40}{4}\right)$$

$$= P(Z > 1.25)$$

$$= 0.1056$$

Therefore the probability that Mr Jones is away from the house for more than 45 minutes is 0.1056.

(**b**) To find the probability that Mr Jones spends more time travelling than in the library we need

$$P(W > L), \quad \text{i.e. } P(W - L > 0)$$

Let $\qquad\qquad\qquad\qquad U = W - L$

Then $\qquad\qquad\qquad\quad U \sim N(15 - 25, 12 + 4)$

i.e. $\qquad\qquad\qquad\quad U \sim N(-10, 16)$

$$P(U > 0) = P\left(\frac{U - (-10)}{4} > \frac{0 - (-10)}{4}\right)$$

$$= P(Z > 2.5)$$

$$= 0.006\,21$$

Therefore the probability that Mr Jones spends more time travelling than in the library is 0.006 21.

Exercise 8a

1. If $X \sim N(100, 49)$ and $Y \sim N(110, 576)$, find
    (a) $P(X + Y > 200)$,
    (b) $P(180 < X + Y < 240)$,
    (c) $P(Y - X < 0)$,
    (d) $P(-20 < Y - X < 50)$.

2. If $X \sim N(75, 5)$ and $Y \sim N(78, 20)$, find
    (a) $P(X + Y > 162)$,
    (b) $P(140 < X + Y < 150)$,
    (c) $P(X + Y < 155)$,   (d) $P(X - Y > 0)$,
    (e) $P(Y - X < 15)$.

3. If $A \sim N(3, 0.05)$ and $B \sim N(2, 0.04)$, find
    (a) $P(A - B > 1.9)$,   (b) $P(A + B < 4.4)$,
    (c) $P(B > A - 0.6)$.

4. If $X \sim N(25, 5)$ and $Y \sim N(30, 4)$, find
    (a) $P(|X + Y - 55| < 5)$,   (b) $P(Y > X)$,
    (c) $P(|Y - X - 5| < 3)$.

5. At a self-service cafeteria a coffee machine is installed which dispenses (a) black coffee in amounts normally distributed with mean 152.5 ml and standard deviation 10 ml,
    (b) white coffee by first releasing a quantity of black coffee normally distributed with mean 122.5 ml and s.d. 7.5 ml and then adding milk normally distributed with mean 30 ml and s.d. 5 ml. Each cup is marked on the inside to a level of 137.5 ml and if this level is not attained the customer receives the drink without charge.
    (i)   What percentage of cups of black coffee will fall short of the 137.5 ml?
    (ii) What is the mean and s.d. of the amount of white coffee dispensed into each cup?
    (iii) What percentage of cups of white coffee will fall short of 137.5 ml?
    (iv) If 10% of cups dispensed are black and the cost per cup for the ingredients is 8 p per cup for both black and white coffee, whilst the customer is charged 20 p per cup, what will be the gross profit on 1000 dispensed cups?
    (v)   What price per cup should the cafeteria charge if the average profit is to be 15 p per cup?

6. Bolts are manufactured which are to fit in holes in steel plates. The diameter of the bolts is normally distributed with mean 2.60 cm and standard deviation 0.03 cm; the diameter of the holes is normally distributed with mean 2.71 cm and standard deviation 0.04 cm.
    (a) Find the probability that a bolt selected at random has a diameter greater than 2.65 cm.
    (b) Find the probability that a hole selected at random has a diameter less than 2.65 cm.
    (c) Prove that, if a bolt and a hole are selected at random, the probability that the bolt will be too large to enter the hole is about 0.0139.
    (d) The random selection of a bolt and a hole described in (c) above is carried out five times. Find the probability that in every case the bolt will be able to enter the hole.   (C)

7. Yuk Ping belongs to an athletics club. In javelin throwing competitions her throws are normally distributed with mean 41.0 m and standard deviation 2.0 m.
    (a) What is the probability of her throwing between 40 m and 46 m?
    (b) What distance will be exceeded by 60% of her throws?
    Gwen belongs to the same club. In competitions 85% of her javelin throws exceed 35 m and 70% exceed 37.5 m. Her throws are normally distributed.
    (c) Find the mean and standard deviation of Gwen's throws, each correct to two significant figures.
    (d) What is the probability that, in a competition in which each athlete takes a single throw, Yuk Ping will beat Gwen?
    (e) The club has to choose one of these two athletes to enter a major competition. In order to qualify for the final rounds it is necessary to achieve a throw of at least 48 m in the preliminary rounds. Which athlete should be chosen and why?   (AEB 1990)

8. A machine produces rubber balls whose diameters are normally distributed with mean 5.50 cm and standard deviation 0.08 cm.
    (a) What proportion of balls will have diameters
    (i) less than 5.60 cm,
    (ii) between 5.34 and 5.44 cm?
    (b) The balls are packed in cylindrical tubes whose internal diameters are normally distributed with mean 5.70 cm and standard deviation 0.12 cm. If a ball, selected at random, is placed in a tube, selected at random, what is the distribution of the clearance? (The clearance is the internal diameter of the tube minus the diameter of the ball.)
    What is the probability that the clearance is between 0.05 and 0.25 cm?

(c) A device may be attached to the machine which automatically removes any balls with diameters greater than a specified value.
(i) What value should be specified so that the largest 16% of balls are removed?
(ii) If the largest 16% are removed find the median diameter of the remaining balls.

(AEB 1992)

9. Ben Wedgewood and Sons in co-operation with the National Enterprise Commission have just developed a sophisticated new microwave oven. The 'in use' lifetimes of two vital components may be considered to be random variables, such that the lifetime of the quality sensitiser, X, is normal with mean 60 hours and standard deviation 5 hours and the lifetime of the overheat warning mechanism, Y, is normal with mean 70 hours and standard deviation 4 hours.
(a) What value of x should be quoted such that $P(X > x) = 0.99$?
(b) The intensive inspection period for the overheat warning mechanism begins at 60 hours and ends at 75 hours. What is the probability of the mechanism failing in this period?
(c) Assuming that X and Y are independent and that $W = Y - X$, what are $E(W)$ and $V(W)$? Further, what is the probability that the overheat warning mechanism lasts longer than the quality sensitiser? (AEB)

10. (a) The random variable X has a normal distribution with mean μ and standard deviation σ. Given that $P(X < 30) = 0.14$ and that $P(X < 60) = 0.79$, calculate the values of μ and σ, giving your answers correct to three significant figures.
(b) The random variable Y has a normal distribution with mean 10 and standard deviation 2. Find the value of the constant a such that

$$P(10 - a < Y < 10 + a) = 0.95.$$

Two independent observations of Y are denoted by Y_1 and Y_2.
Find $P(|Y_1 - Y_2| < 5)$. (C)

EXTENSION TO MORE THAN TWO INDEPENDENT NORMAL VARIABLES

We can extend the results on page 416 as follows:

If $X_1, X_2, \ldots, X_n$ is *any* set of random variables, then

$$E(X_1 + X_2 + \ldots + X_n) = E(X_1) + E(X_2) + \ldots + E(X_n)$$

If the random variables are *independent*, then

$$\text{Var}(X_1 + X_2 + \ldots + X_n) = \text{Var}(X_1) + \text{Var}(X_2) + \ldots + \text{Var}(X_n)$$

Applying these results to independent normal variables:

If $X_1, X_2, \ldots, X_n$ are *n independent normal variables* such that

$$X_1 \sim N\left(\mu_1, \sigma_1^{2}\right),$$

$$X_2 \sim N\left(\mu_2, \sigma_2^{2}\right),$$

$$\vdots \qquad \vdots$$

$$X_n \sim N\left(\mu_n, \sigma_n^{2}\right)$$

then

$$X_1 + X_2 + \ldots + X_n \sim N\left(\mu_1 + \mu_2 + \ldots + \mu_n, \sigma_1^{2} + \sigma_2^{2} + \ldots + \sigma_n^{2}\right)$$

> *NOTE*: In the special case when $X_1, X_2, \ldots, X_n$ are independent observations from the *same* normal distribution so that $X_i \sim N(\mu, \sigma^2)$ for $i = 1, 2, \ldots, n$, then
>
> $$X_1 + X_2 + \ldots + X_n \sim N(n\mu, n\sigma^2).$$

For example, if $X \sim N(10, 4)$ and $X_1, X_2, \ldots, X_8$ are 8 independent observations of X then $X_1 + X_2 + \ldots + X_8 \sim N(80, 32)$.

Example 8.3   If $W \sim N(100, 8)$, $X \sim N(120, 10)$ and $Y \sim N(110, 12)$, find $P(W + X + Y < 320)$.

Solution 8.3   Let $A = W + X + Y$.

Then
$$\begin{aligned} E(A) &= E(W) + E(X) + E(Y) \\ &= 100 + 120 + 110 \\ &= 330 \end{aligned}$$

$$\begin{aligned} \mathrm{Var}(A) &= \mathrm{Var}(W) + \mathrm{Var}(X) + \mathrm{Var}(Y) \\ &= 8 + 10 + 12 \\ &= 30 \end{aligned}$$

So $A \sim N(330, 30)$.

$$\begin{aligned} P(A < 320) &= P\left(\frac{A - 330}{\sqrt{30}} < \frac{320 - 330}{\sqrt{30}}\right) \\ &= P(Z < -1.826) \\ &= 0.0340 \end{aligned}$$

Therefore $P(W + X + Y < 320) = 0.0340$.

Example 8.4   Masses of a particular article are normally distributed with mean 20 g and standard deviation 2 g. If a random sample of 12 such articles is chosen, find the probability that the total mass is less than 230 g.

Solution 8.4   Let X be the r.v. 'the mass, in g, of an article'.

Then
$$X_1 \sim N(20, 4)$$
$$X_2 \sim N(20, 4)$$
$$\vdots \qquad \vdots$$
$$X_{12} \sim N(20, 4)$$

Let $B = X_1 + X_2 + \ldots + X_{12},$

so $\qquad E(B) = E(X_1) + E(X_2) + \ldots + E(X_{12})$

$$= 12E(X)$$

$$= 240$$

and $\qquad \text{Var}(B) = \text{Var}(X_1) + \text{Var}(X_2) + \ldots + \text{Var}(X_{12})$

$$= 12\text{Var}(X)$$

$$= 48$$

We have $\qquad B \sim N(240, 48)$

$$P(B < 230) = P\left(\frac{B - 240}{\sqrt{48}} < \frac{230 - 240}{\sqrt{48}}\right)$$

$$= P(Z < -1.443)$$

$$= 0.0745$$

$B = X_1 + X_2 + \ldots + X_{12}$

s.d. $= \sqrt{48}$

230 240

S.V. -1.443 0

Therefore the probability that the total mass of the articles is less than 230 g is 0.0745.

Example 8.5   If $A \sim N(10, 4)$, $B \sim N(12, 9)$ and $C \sim N(8, 12)$, find

(a) $P(A + B - C < 10)$,   (b) $P(B - C - A > 0)$.

Solution 8.5   Let $Y = A + B - C$.

Then $\qquad\qquad E(Y) = E(A) + E(B) - E(C)$

$$= 10 + 12 - 8$$

$$= 14$$

$$\text{Var}(Y) = \text{Var}(A) + \text{Var}(B) + \text{Var}(C)$$

$$= 4 + 9 + 12$$

$$= 25$$

So $\qquad\qquad\qquad Y \sim N(14, 25)$.

$$P(Y < 10) = P\left(\frac{Y - 14}{5} < \frac{10 - 14}{5}\right)$$

$$= P(Z < -0.8)$$

$$= 0.2119$$

$Y = A + B - C$

s.d. $= 5$

10 14

S.V. -0.8 0

Therefore $P(A + B - C < 10) = 0.2119$.

(**b**) Let $W = B - C - A$.

Then
$$E(W) = E(B) - E(C) - E(A)$$
$$= 12 - 8 - 10$$
$$= -6$$

$$\text{Var}(W) = \text{Var}(B) + \text{Var}(C) + \text{Var}(A)$$
$$= 9 + 12 + 4$$
$$= 25$$

So $W \sim N(-6, 25)$.

$$P(W > 0) = P\left(\frac{W - (-6)}{5} > \frac{0 - (-6)}{5}\right)$$
$$= P(Z > 1.2)$$
$$= 0.1151$$

Therefore $P(B - C - A > 10) = 0.1151$.

Example 8.6 If $A \sim N(10, 4)$, $B \sim N(12, 9)$ and $C \sim N(8, 12)$ find

(**a**) $P[A_1 + A_2 - (B_1 + B_2) + C_1 + C_2 > 20]$ where A_1, A_2 are two independent observations from the population of A, etc.,

(**b**) the probability that three independent observations from the population of A have a sum which is greater than four independent observations from the population of C.

Solution 8.6 (**a**) Let $V = A_1 + A_2 - (B_1 + B_2) + C_1 + C_2$.

Then
$$E(V) = E(A_1) + E(A_2) - E(B_1) - E(B_2) + E(C_1) + E(C_2)$$
$$= 2E(A) - 2E(B) + 2E(C)$$
$$= 20 - 24 + 16$$
$$= 12$$

$$\text{Var}(V) = 2\text{Var}(A) + 2\text{Var}(B) + 2\text{Var}(C)$$
$$= 8 + 18 + 24$$
$$= 50$$

So $V \sim N(12, 50)$

$$P(V > 20) = P\left(\frac{Y - 12}{\sqrt{50}} > \frac{20 - 12}{\sqrt{50}}\right)$$
$$= P(Z > 1.131)$$
$$= 0.1290$$

Therefore $P[A_1 + A_2 - (B_1 + B_2) + C_1 + C_2 > 20] = 0.1290$.

(**b**) Let $U = A_1 + A_2 + A_3 - (C_1 + C_2 + C_3 + C_4)$.

Then $\quad E(U) = 3E(A) - 4E(C)$

$$= 30 - 32$$

$$= -2$$

$$\mathrm{Var}(U) = 3\mathrm{Var}(A) + 4\mathrm{Var}(C)$$

$$= 12 + 48$$

$$= 60$$

So $\quad\quad U \sim \mathrm{N}(-2, 60)$

We need

$$P(A_1 + A_2 + A_3 > C_1 + C_2 + C_3 + C_4)$$

i.e. $\quad P(U > 0) = P\left(\dfrac{U - (-2)}{\sqrt{60}} > \dfrac{0 - (-2)}{\sqrt{60}}\right)$

$$= P(Z > 0.258)$$

$$= 0.3982$$

Therefore the probability that three observations from the population of A have a sum which is greater than four observations from the population of C is 0.3982.

Example 8.7   In a cafeteria, baked beans are served either in ordinary portions or in children's portions. The quantity given for an ordinary portion is a normal variable with mean 90 g and standard deviation 3 g and the quantity given for a children's portion is a normal variable with mean 43 g and standard deviation 2 g. What is the probability that John, who has two children's portions, is given more than his father, who has an ordinary portion?

Solution 8.7   Let C be the r.v. 'the quantity given, in g, in a children's portion'. Then $C \sim \mathrm{N}(43, 4)$.

Let A be the r.v. 'the quantity given, in g, in an ordinary portion'. Then $A \sim \mathrm{N}(90, 9)$.

We need $P(C_1 + C_2 > A)$, i.e. $P(C_1 + C_2 - A > 0)$.

Now let $\quad W = C_1 + C_2 - A$

$$E(W) = E(C_1) + E(C_2) - E(A)$$

$$= 2E(C) - E(A)$$

$$= 86 - 90$$

$$= -4$$

and $\text{Var}(W) = \text{Var}(C_1) + \text{Var}(C_2) + \text{Var}(A)$

$$= 2\text{Var}(C) + \text{Var}(A)$$

$$= 8 + 9$$

$$= 17$$

So $W \sim N(-4, 17)$

Now

$$P(C_1 + C_2 - A > 0) = P(W > 0)$$

$$= P\left(\frac{W - (-4)}{\sqrt{17}} < \frac{(0 - (-4))}{\sqrt{17}}\right)$$

$$= P(Z > 0.970)$$

$$= 0.166$$

$W = C_1 + C_2 - A$

s.d. $= \sqrt{17}$

−4 0

S.V.   0   0.970

Therefore the probability that John has more than his father is 0.166.

Exercise 8b

1. If $A \sim N(50, 6)$, $B \sim N(30, 8)$ and $C \sim N(80, 11)$ find
   (a) $P(A + B + C > 170)$,
   (b) $P(-6 < A + B - C < 10)$,
   (c) $P(A_1 + A_2 - (B + C) < 0)$.

2. A random sample of 20 items is taken from a normal population with mean 15 and variance 5. Find the probability that the sum of the values in the sample is less than 305.

3. Lengths of rod of type A are normally distributed with mean 5 cm and standard deviation 0.5 cm and lengths of rod of type B are normally distributed with mean 10 cm and standard deviation 1 cm. Find the probability that   (a) a length consisting of 2 rods of type A and 4 rods of type B is more than 52 cm long,   (b) a length consisting of 3 rods of type A and 2 rods of type B is between 33 cm and 36 cm long,   (c) a length consisting of 6 rods of type A is longer than a length consisting of 3 rods of type B.

4. If $X \sim N(5, 4)$ and $Y \sim N(6, 9)$, find the probability that a sample consisting of 3 items from the population with r.v. X and 4 items from the population with r.v. Y will have a sum exceeding 50.

5. Chocolate Delight cakes are sold in packets of 6. The mass of each cake is a normal variable with mean 20 g and standard deviation 2 g. The mass of the packing material is a normal variable with mean 30 g and standard deviation 4 g. Find the probability that the total mass of the packet
   (a) exceeds 162 g,
   (b) is less than 137 g,
   (c) lies between 140 g and 153 g.

6. If $X_i \sim N(2, 2)$ and $Y_i \sim N(1.5, 2.2)$
   if $L = \sum_{i=1}^{20} X_i$ and $M = \sum_{i=1}^{26} Y_i$,
   find $P(L > M)$.

7. In a certain village the heights of women follow a normal distribution with mean 164 cm and standard deviation 5 cm and the heights of men are normally distributed with mean 173 cm and standard deviation 6 cm. If a man and woman are picked at random, find the probability that   (a) the woman is taller than the man,   (b) the man is more than 5 cm taller than the woman.

8. The time taken to carry out a standard service on a car of type A is known, to a good approximation, to be a normal variable with mean 1 hour and standard deviation 10 minutes. Assuming that only one car is serviced at a time, find the probability that it will take more than 6.5 hours to service 6 cars.

The time taken to carry out a standard service on a car of type B is a normal variable with mean 1.5 hours and standard deviation 15 minutes. Find the probability that 5 cars of type B can be serviced more quickly than 8 cars of type A.   (C)

9. If $X_i \sim \mathrm{N}(70, 10)$, find

$$P\left(335 < \sum_{i=1}^{5} X_i < 360\right).$$

10. Four runners, A, B, C and D train to run the distances 100 m, 200 m, 500 m and 800 m respectively, in order to take part in a 1600 m relay race. During training their individual times (recorded in seconds) are normally distributed as follows: $A \sim \mathrm{N}(10.8, 0.2^2)$, $B \sim \mathrm{N}(23.7, 0.3^2)$, $C \sim \mathrm{N}(62.8, 0.9^2)$, $D \sim \mathrm{N}(121.2, 2.1^2)$. Find the probability that the runners take less than 3 minutes 35 seconds to run the relay race.

11. Mr Smith has five dogs, two of which are male and three are female. The masses of food they eat in any given week are normally distributed as follows:

	Mean (kg)	Standard deviation (kg)
Male	3.5	0.4
Female	2.5	0.3

Find the probability that the two males eat more than the three females in a particular week.

12. The process of painting the body-work of a mass-produced lorry consists of giving it 1 coat of paint A, 3 coats of paint B and 2 coats of paint C. A record of the quantity of each type of paint used for each coat is kept for each lorry produced over a long period. The following table gives the means and standard deviations of these quantities measured in litres:

	Mean	Standard deviation
The coat of paint A	3.7	0.42
Each coat of paint B	1.3	0.15
Each coat of paint C	1.0	0.12

Assuming independence of the distribution for each coat, calculate the mean and standard deviation for the total quantity of paint used on each lorry.

Assuming that the quantities of paint used for each coat are normally distributed, calculate
(a) the percentage of lorries receiving less than 8.5 litres of paint,
(b) the percentage of lorries receiving more than 10.0 litres of paint.   (C)

13. The means and variances of independent normal variables X and Y are known. State the means and variances of $X \pm Y$ in terms of those of X and Y.

The values of two types of resistors are normally distributed as follows:

Type A: mean: 100 ohms;
standard deviation: 2 ohms
Type B: mean: 50 ohms;
standard deviation: 1.3 ohms

(a) What tolerances would be permitted for type A if only 0.5% were rejected?
(b) 300-ohm resistors are made by connecting together three of the type A resistors, drawn from the total production. What percentage of the 300-ohm resistors may be expected to have resistances greater than 295 ohms?
(c) Pairs of resistors, one of 100 ohms and one of 50 ohms, drawn from the total production for types A and B respectively, are connected together to make 150-ohm resistors. What percentage of the resulting resistors may be expected to have resistances in the range 150 to 151.4 ohms?   (AEB)

14. The time of departure of my train from Temple Meads Station is distributed normally about the scheduled time of 08 25 with a standard deviation of 1 minute. I arrive at Temple Meads Station on another train whose time of arrival is normally distributed about the scheduled time of 08 20 with standard deviation of 1 minute. It takes me 3 minutes to change platforms.
(a) Find the probability that I miss the 08 25 and am late for work.
(b) Find the probability that this happens every day from Monday to Friday in a given week.

15. The mass of a certain grade of apple is normally distributed with mean mass 120 g and standard deviation 10 g.
(a) If an apple of this grade is chosen at random, find the probability that its mass lies between 100.5 g and 124 g.
(b) If four apples of this grade are chosen at random, find the probability that their total mass will exceed 505 g.

16. A, B, C, D are four members of a $4 \times 100\,\text{m}$ freestyle swimming relay team. In a race each member of the team swims a $100\,\text{m}$ leg. The times taken by A, B, C, D to swim their $100\,\text{m}$ legs are independent and normally distributed with means $52.5\,\text{s}$, $52.0\,\text{s}$, $53.5\,\text{s}$, $51.5\,\text{s}$ and standard deviations $0.3\,\text{s}$, $0.6\,\text{s}$, $1.2\,\text{s}$, $0.6\,\text{s}$, respectively.
Calculate the probabilities that in a particular race
(i) A will swim his leg in less than $52.2\,\text{s}$,
(ii) the team will complete the race in less than $3\,\text{min}\ 31.3\,\text{s}$,
(iii) B will swim his leg in a shorter time than D. (JMB)

17. A certain brand of sweet is individually wrapped. Each sweet is machine produced so that its weight is normally distributed with mean $30\,\text{g}$ and standard deviation $3\,\text{g}$. The weight of the individual wrapping is normally distributed with mean $10\,\text{g}$ and standard deviation $2\,\text{g}$. Twelve of these individually wrapped sweets are then packed together and the weight of the packing material is a normal random variable with mean $100\,\text{g}$ and standard deviation $10\,\text{g}$.
Find the probability that

(a) an individual sweet weighs between $28\,\text{g}$ and $32\,\text{g}$,
(b) the total weight of the packet of twelve sweets lies between $552\,\text{g}$ and $600\,\text{g}$.
Similar sweets are machine produced by a different company and 7.5% weigh more than $32\,\text{g}$ and 4.5% weigh less than $28\,\text{g}$. Assuming that the weight of these sweets is normally distributed, find its mean and standard deviation.
Comment on the production capabilities of the machines producing these two types of sweet. (AEB 1991)

18. Foster's Fancy Cakes are sold in packets of 6. The mass of each cake is a normally distributed random variable having mean $25\,\text{g}$ and standard deviation $0.4\,\text{g}$. The mass of the packaging is a normally distributed random variable having mean $20\,\text{g}$ and standard deviation $1\,\text{g}$. Find, to three decimal places, the probabilities that
(i) the mass of a randomly chosen cake is between $24.7\,\text{g}$ and $25.7\,\text{g}$,
(ii) the total mass of a randomly chosen packet is less than $173\,\text{g}$.
State one assumption that you have made in answering (ii). (JMB)

MULTIPLES OF NORMAL VARIABLES

We have shown previously that, for any constant a,

$$E(aX) = aE(X)$$

$$\text{Var}(aX) = a^2\text{Var}(X)$$

Applying these results to normal variables:

> If X is a *normal variable* such that $X \sim \text{N}(\mu, \sigma^2)$ then
>
> $$aX \sim \text{N}(a\mu, a^2\sigma^2)$$
>
> If X and Y are *two independent normal variables* such that $X \sim \text{N}(\mu_1, \sigma_1{}^2)$ and $Y \sim \text{N}(\mu_2, \sigma_2{}^2)$, and a and b are any constants, then
>
> $$aX + bY \sim \text{N}(a\mu_1 + b\mu_2, a^2\sigma_1{}^2 + b^2\sigma_2{}^2)$$
> $$aX - bY \sim \text{N}(a\mu_1 - b\mu_2, a^2\sigma_1{}^2 + b^2\sigma_2{}^2)$$

Example 8.8   If $X \sim \text{N}(50, 25)$ find $P(3X > 160)$.

Solution 8.8   Now $E(3X) = 3E(X) = 150$

$$\text{Var}(3X) = 9\text{Var}(X) = 225$$

So $3X \sim N(150, 225)$

$$P(3X > 160) = P\left(\frac{3X - 150}{15} > \frac{160 - 150}{15}\right)$$

$$= P(Z > 0.667)$$

$$= 0.2523$$

Therefore $P(3X > 160) = 0.2523$.

Example 8.9   If $X \sim N(70, 10)$ and $Y \sim N(50, 8)$, find $P(2X > 3Y)$.

Solution 8.9   We need $P(2X > 3Y)$, i.e. $P(2X - 3Y > 0)$.

Let $A = 2X - 3Y$

then $E(A) = 2E(X) - 3E(Y)$

$$= 140 - 150$$

$$= -10$$

$$\text{Var}(A) = 4\text{Var}(X) + 9\text{Var}(Y)$$

$$= 40 + 72$$

$$= 112$$

So $A \sim N(-10, 112)$

$$P(A > 0) = P\left(\frac{A - (-10)}{\sqrt{112}} > \frac{0 - (-10)}{\sqrt{112}}\right)$$

$$= P(Z > 0.945)$$

$$= 0.1723$$

Therefore $P(2X > 3Y) = 0.1723$.

DISTINGUISHING BETWEEN MULTIPLES AND SUMS OF RANDOM VARIABLES

Care must be taken to distinguish between the r.v. $2X$ and the r.v. $X_1 + X_2$, where X_1 and X_2 are two independent observations of the r.v. X.

If $X \sim N(\mu, \sigma^2)$ then $2X \sim N(2\mu, 4\sigma^2)$ (multiple)

but $X_1 + X_2 \sim N(2\mu, 2\sigma^2)$ (sum)

NOTE: the means of the two distributions are the same, but the variances are different.

Example 8.10 If $X \sim \mathrm{N}(10, 9)$, find (**a**) $P(2X > 23)$, (**b**) $P(X_1 + X_2 > 23)$ where X_1 and X_2 are two independent observations from the population of X.

Solution 8.10 Now $X \sim \mathrm{N}(10, 9)$.

(**a**) Let $V = 2X$, then

$$E(V) = E(2X) \qquad \text{and} \qquad \mathrm{Var}(V) = \mathrm{Var}(2X)$$

$$= 2E(X) \qquad\qquad\qquad\qquad = 4\mathrm{Var}(X)$$

$$= 20 \qquad\qquad\qquad\qquad\qquad = 36$$

So $\qquad\qquad V \sim \mathrm{N}(20, 36)$

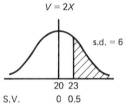

and $\quad P(V > 23) = P\left(\dfrac{V - 20}{6} > \dfrac{23 - 20}{6}\right)$

$$= P(Z > 0.5)$$

$$= 0.3085$$

Therefore $\underline{P(2X > 23) = 0.3085}$.

(**b**) Let $W = X_1 + X_2$, then

$$E(W) = E(X_1) + E(X_2) \qquad \text{and} \qquad \mathrm{Var}(W) = \mathrm{Var}(X_1) + \mathrm{Var}(X_2)$$

$$= 2E(X) \qquad\qquad\qquad\qquad\qquad = 2\mathrm{Var}(X)$$

$$= 20 \qquad\qquad\qquad\qquad\qquad\qquad = 18$$

So $\quad W \sim \mathrm{N}(20, 18)$

and $\quad P(W > 23) = P\left(\dfrac{W - 20}{\sqrt{18}} > \dfrac{23 - 20}{\sqrt{18}}\right)$

$$= P(Z > 0.707)$$

$$= 0.2399$$

Therefore $\underline{P(X_1 + X_2 > 23) = 0.2399}$.

In general, if $X \sim \mathrm{N}\left(\mu, \sigma^2\right)$

then $\qquad\qquad nX \sim \mathrm{N}\left(n\mu, n^2\sigma^2\right) \qquad\qquad$ (multiples)

but $\qquad X_1 + X_2 + \ldots + X_n \sim \mathrm{N}\left(n\mu, n\sigma^2\right) \qquad$ (sums)

The following example illustrates the difference between multiples and sums of random variables.

Example 8.11   A soft drinks manufacturer sells bottles of drinks in two sizes. The amount in each bottle, in ml, is normally distributed as shown in the table:

	Mean (ml)	Variance (ml^2)
Small	252	4
Large	1012	25

(**a**) A bottle of each size is selected at random. Find the probability that the large bottle contains less than four times the amount in the small bottle.

(**b**) One large and four small bottles are selected at random. Find the probability that the amount in the large bottle is less than the total amount in the four small bottles.

Solution 8.11   Let S be the r.v. 'the amount, in ml, in a small bottle'. Then $S \sim N(252, 4)$.

Let L be the r.v. 'the amount, in ml, in a large bottle'. Then $L \sim N(1012, 25)$.

(**a**) We need $P(L < 4S) = P(L - 4S < 0)$.

Now
$$E(L - 4S) = E(L) - E(4S) \quad \text{(multiple of } S\text{)}$$
$$= E(L) - 4E(S)$$
$$= 1012 - 1008$$
$$= 4$$
$$\text{Var}(L - 4S) = \text{Var}(L) + \text{Var}(4S)$$
$$= \text{Var}(L) + 16\text{Var}(S)$$
$$= 25 + 64$$
$$= 89$$

So
$$L - 4S \sim N(4, 89)$$

$$P(L - 4S < 0) = P\left(X < \frac{0-4}{\sqrt{89}}\right)$$

s.d. $= \sqrt{89}$

S.V. -0.424 0

$$= P(Z < -0.424)$$
$$= 0.3358$$

Therefore the probability that the large bottle contains less than four times the amount of a small bottle is 0.3358.

(**b**) We need $P(L < S_1 + S_2 + S_3 + S_4) = P(L - (S_1 + \ldots + S_4) < 0)$.

$$E(L - (S_1 + \ldots + S_4)) = E(L) - E(S_1 + \ldots + S_4) \quad \text{(sum of r.v. } S)$$

$$= E(L) - 4E(S)$$

$$= 1012 - 1008$$

$$= 4$$

$$\text{Var}(L - (S_1 + \ldots + S_4)) = \text{Var}(L) + \text{Var}(S_1 + \ldots + S_4)$$

$$= \text{Var}(L) + 4\text{Var}(S)$$

$$= 25 + 16$$

$$= 41$$

Therefore $\quad L - (S_1 + \ldots + S_4) \sim N(4, 41)$

$$P(L - (S_1 + \ldots + S_4) < 0) = P\left(Z < \frac{0 - 4}{\sqrt{41}}\right)$$

s.d. $= \sqrt{41}$

$$= P(Z < -0.625)$$

0   4

$$= 0.266$$

S.V. -0.625 0

Therefore the probability that the large bottle contains less than the four small bottles is 0.266.

Exercise 8c

1. If $X \sim N(40, 12)$, and $Y \sim N(60, 15)$, find
   (a) $P(2X > 90)$, (b) $P(4Y < 270)$,
   (c) $P(3X - 2Y < 20)$, (d) $P\left[\frac{1}{2}(X + Y) > 55\right]$.

2. If $A \sim N(82, 1.5^2)$, $B \sim N(42, 0.3^2)$ and
   $C \sim N(85, 0.7^2)$, find (a) $P(3A < 250)$,
   (b) $P(6B > 255)$, (c) $P(3A > 6B)$,
   (d) $P(2B + A > 2C)$, (e) $P\left[\frac{1}{2}(A + B) < 64\right]$,
   (f) $P\left[\frac{1}{3}(A + B + C) > 70\right]$.

3. The r.v. X is normally distributed with mean
   μ and variance 6, and the r.v. Y is normally
   distributed with mean 8 and variance σ^2. If
   the r.v. $2X - 3Y$ is normally distributed with
   mean -12 and variance 42, find
   (a) the values of μ and σ^2,
   (b) $P(X > 8)$, (c) $P(Y < 9)$,
   (d) $P(-4 < 3X - 2Y < 7)$.

4. The r.v. X is distributed normally with mean
   25 and standard deviation 4, the r.v. Y is
   distributed normally with mean 30 and
   standard deviation 3, and X and Y are
   independent. Find the probability that a
   single observation from the population of X is
   greater than two-thirds of the value of a
   single observation from the population of Y.

5. If $X \sim N(50, 16)$, and $Y \sim N(40, 9)$, find
   (a) $P(2X + Y > 120)$, (b) $P\left[\frac{1}{2}(X - Y) > 0\right]$,
   (c) $P(100 < 3X - Y < 130)$.

6. If $X \sim N(30, 4)$, find (a) $P(5X > 160)$,
   (b) $P(Y > 160)$, where $Y = X_1 + \ldots + X_5$.

7. The thickness, P cm, of a randomly chosen
   paperback book may be regarded as an
   observation from a normal distribution with
   mean 2.0 and variance 0.730. The thickness,
   H cm, of a randomly chosen hardback book may
   be regarded as an observation from a normal
   distribution with mean 4.9 and variance 1.920.
   (a) Determine the probability that the
   combined thickness of four randomly chosen
   paperbacks is greater than the combined
   thickness of two randomly chosen hardbacks.
   (b) By considering $X = 2P - H$, or
   otherwise, determine the probability that a
   randomly chosen paperback is less than half
   as thick as a randomly chosen hardback.
   (c) Determine the probability that a
   randomly chosen collection of sixteen
   paperbacks and eight hardbacks will have a
   combined thickness of less than 70 cm.
   (Give 3 decimal places in your answers.) (C)

MISCELLANEOUS WORKED EXAMPLES

Example 8.12 (a) A certain liquid drug is marketed in bottles containing a nominal 20 ml of drug. Tests on a large number of bottles indicate that the volume of liquid in each bottle is distributed normally with mean 20.42 ml and s.d. 0.429 ml.
(*i*) Estimate the percentage of bottles which would be expected to contain less than 20 ml of drug.
(*ii*) Find the level to which the mean should be adjusted (without altering the s.d.) so that only 1% of bottles should contain less than 20 ml.

(**b**) If the independent random variables X and Y are normally distributed with means μ_1, μ_2 and variances σ_1^2, σ_2^2 respectively, state what you can about the distribution of $Z = X - Y$.

If the capacity of the bottles in (**a**) is normally distributed with mean 21.77 ml and s.d. 0.210 ml and the liquid with (unadjusted) mean 20.42 ml and s.d. 0.429 ml, estimate what percentage of bottles will overflow during filling.

Solution 8.12 (**a**) Let X be the r.v. 'the volume in ml of liquid in a bottle'

Then
$$X \sim N(20.42, 0.429^2)$$

(*i*) $P(X < 20) = P\left(\dfrac{X - 20.42}{0.429} < \dfrac{20 - 20.42}{0.429}\right)$

$$= P(Z < -0.979)$$

$$= 0.1637$$

Therefore 16.37% of bottles would be expected to contain less than 20 ml of drug.

(*ii*) We need to find μ such that

$$P(X < 20) = 0.01$$

i.e. $P\left(\dfrac{X - \mu}{0.429} < \dfrac{20 - \mu}{0.429}\right) = 0.01$

$$P\left(Z < \dfrac{20 - \mu}{0.429}\right) = 0.01$$

Now $P(Z < -2.326) = 0.01$

so $\dfrac{20 - \mu}{0.429} = -2.326$

$$\mu = 20 + (2.326)(0.429)$$

$$= 21.00$$

The adjusted value of the mean should be 21.00 ml of drug.

(b) $X \sim N(\mu_1, \sigma_1{}^2)$ and $Y \sim N(\mu_2, \sigma_2{}^2)$.

If $Z = X - Y$, then

$$E(Z) = E(X) - E(Y) = \mu_1 - \mu_2$$

$$\text{Var}(Z) = \text{Var}(X) + \text{Var}(Y) = \sigma_1{}^2 + \sigma_2{}^2$$

and $Z \sim N(\mu_1 - \mu_2, \sigma_1{}^2 + \sigma_2{}^2)$.

If X is the r.v. 'the volume in ml of liquid'

then $X \sim N(20.42, 0.429^2)$ as before.

If Y is the r.v. 'the capacity in ml of a bottle',

then $Y \sim N(21.77, 0.210^2)$

and $X - Y \sim N(20.42 - 21.77, \ 0.429^2 + 0.210^2)$

i.e. $X - Y \sim N(-1.35, 0.2281)$

Now, the bottle will overflow if $X > Y$, i.e. if $X - Y > 0$.

$$P(X - Y > 0) = P\left(\frac{X - Y - (-1.35)}{\sqrt{0.2281}} > \frac{0 - (-1.35)}{\sqrt{0.2281}}\right)$$

$$= P(Z > 2.827)$$

$$= 0.002\,35$$

s.d. $= \sqrt{0.2281}$

-1.35 0

S.V.   0   2.827

We estimate that 0.2% of the bottles will overflow during filling.

Example 8.13 The maximum load a lift can carry is 450 kg. The weights of men are normally distributed with mean 60 kg and standard deviation 10 kg. The weights of women are normally distributed with mean 55 kg and standard deviation 5 kg. Find the probability that the lift will be overloaded by 5 men and 2 women, if their weights are independent.

(L)

Solution 8.13 Let M be the r.v. 'the weight, in kg, of a man'.

Then $M \sim N(60, 10^2)$.

Let W be the r.v. 'the weight, in kg, of a woman'.

Then $W \sim N(55, 5^2)$.

Now the lift will be overloaded if

$$M_1 + M_2 + M_3 + M_4 + M_5 + W_1 + W_2 > 450$$

Let $T = M_1 + M_2 + \ldots + M_5 + W_1 + W_2$

$E(T) = 5E(M) + 2E(W)$ $\text{Var}(T) = 5\text{Var}(M) + 2\text{Var}(W)$

$= 300 + 110$ $= 500 + 50$

$= 410$ $= 550$

Therefore $\qquad T \sim \mathrm{N}(410, 550)$

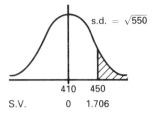

Now $\quad P(T > 450) = P\left(Z > \dfrac{450 - 410}{\sqrt{550}}\right)$

$$= P(Z > 1.706)$$

$$= 0.0441$$

The probability that the lift will be overloaded is 0.0441.

SUMMARY — SUMS, DIFFERENCES AND MULTIPLES OF INDEPENDENT NORMAL VARIABLES

For two independent normal variables such that $X \sim \mathrm{N}\left(\mu_1, \sigma_1{}^2\right)$ and $Y \sim \mathrm{N}\left(\mu_2, \sigma_2{}^2\right)$

$$X + Y \sim \mathrm{N}\left(\mu_1 + \mu_2, \sigma_1{}^2 + \sigma_2{}^2\right)$$
$$X - Y \sim \mathrm{N}\left(\mu_1 - \mu_2, \sigma_1{}^2 + \sigma_2{}^2\right)$$

For n independent normal variables such that $X_i \sim \mathrm{N}\left(\mu_i, \sigma_i{}^2\right)$

$$X_1 + X_2 + \ldots + X_n \sim \mathrm{N}\left(\mu_1 + \mu_2 + \ldots + \mu_n, \sigma_1{}^2 + \sigma_2{}^2 + \ldots + \sigma_n{}^2\right)$$

For n independent observations of the r.v. X where $X \sim \mathrm{N}\left(\mu, \sigma^2\right)$,

$$X_1 + X_2 + \ldots + X_n \sim \mathrm{N}\left(n\mu, n\sigma^2\right)$$

For the normal variable such that $\;X \sim \mathrm{N}\left(\mu, \sigma^2\right),\;$ and for any constant a

$$aX \sim \mathrm{N}\left(a\mu, a^2\sigma^2\right)$$

For two independent normal variables such that $X \sim \mathrm{N}\left(\mu_1, \sigma_1{}^2\right)$ and $Y \sim \mathrm{N}\left(\mu_2, \sigma_2{}^2\right)\;$ and for any constants a and b

$$aX + bY \sim \mathrm{N}\left(a\mu_1 + b\mu_2, a^2\sigma_1{}^2 + b^2\sigma_2{}^2\right)$$
$$aX - bY \sim \mathrm{N}\left(a\mu_1 - b\mu_2, a^2\sigma_1{}^2 + b^2\sigma_2{}^2\right)$$

Miscellaneous Exercise 8d

1. The weights of grade A oranges are normally distributed with mean 200 g and standard deviation 12 g. Determine, correct to 2 significant figures, the probability that
(a) a grade A orange weighs more than 190 g but less than 210 g,
(b) a sample of 4 grade A oranges weighs more than 820 g.

The weights of grade B oranges are normally distributed with mean 175 g and standard deviation 9 g. Determine, correct to 2 significant figures, the probability that
(c) a grade B orange weighs less than a grade A orange,
(d) a sample of 8 grade B oranges weighs more than a sample of 7 grade A oranges.   (C)

2. Prints from two types of film C and D have developing times which can be modelled by normal variables, C with mean 16.18 s and standard deviation 0.11 s and D with mean 15.88 s and standard deviation 0.10 s.
(a) What is the probability that a type C print will take less than 16 s to develop?
(b) A type C print is developed and immediately afterwards a type D print is developed. What is the probability that the total time is greater than 32.5 s?
(c) What is the probability of a type C print taking longer to develop than a type D print?

3. In testing the length of life of electric light bulbs of a particular type, it is found that 12.3% of the bulbs tested fail within 800 hours and that 28.1% are still operating 1100 hours after the start of the test. Assuming that the distribution of the length of life is normal, calculate, to the nearest hour in each case, the mean, μ, and the standard deviation, σ, of the distribution.
A light fitting takes a single bulb of this type. A packet of three bulbs is bought, to be used one after the other in this fitting. State the mean and variance of the total life of the three bulbs in the packet in terms of μ and σ and calculate, to two decimal places, the probability that the total life is more than 3300 hours.
Calculate the probability that all three bulbs have lives in excess of 1100 hours, so that again the total life is more than 3300 hours. Explain why this answer should be different from the previous one.   (JMB)

4. The weight of a large loaf of bread is a normal variable with mean 420 g and standard deviation 30 g. The weight of a small loaf of bread is a normal variable with mean 220 g and standard deviation 10 g.
(a) Find the probability that 5 large loaves weigh more than 10 small loaves.
(b) Find the probability that the total weight of 5 large loaves and 10 small loaves lies between 4.25 kg and 4.4 kg.   (C)

5. The tensile strengths, measured in newtons (N), of a large number of ropes of equal length are independently and normally distributed such that five per cent are under 706 N and five per cent over 1294 N. Four such ropes are randomly selected and joined end-to-end to form a single rope; the strength of the combined rope is equal to the strength of the weakest of the four selected ropes. Derive the probabilities that this combined rope will not break under tensions of 1000 N and 900 N, respectively.
A further four ropes are randomly selected and attached between two rings, the strength

of the arrangement being the sum of the strengths of the four separate ropes. Derive the probabilities that this arrangement will break under tensions of 4000 N and 4200 N, respectively.
Find the smallest number of ropes that should be selected if the probability that at least one of them has a strength greater than 1000 N is to exceed 0.99.   (JMB)

6. The independent random variables X_1 and X_2 are normally distributed with means μ_1, μ_2 and have variances $\sigma_1{}^2$, $\sigma_2{}^2$ respectively. What is the distribution of the random variable $Y = a_1X_1 + a_2X_2$?
Certain components for a revolutionary new sewing machine are assembled by inserting a part of one type (sprotsil) into a part of another type (weavil). Sprotsils have external dimensions which are normally distributed with mean 2.50 cm and standard deviation 0.018 cm. Weavils have internal dimensions which are normally distributed with mean 2.54 cm and standard deviation 0.024 cm. Under suitable pressure, the two types fit together satisfactorily if the dimensions differ by not more than ± 0.035 cm. Show that, if pairs of parts are chosen at random, the difference

$$D = \text{internal dimension of a weavil} \\ - \text{external dimension of a sprotsil}$$

is distributed with mean 0.04 cm and standard deviation 0.030 cm. Hence show that approximately 42.8% of randomly selected pairs will fit together satisfactorily. Now, if it is known that the internal dimension of a given weavil is 2.517 cm, what is the probability that a randomly chosen sprotsil will fit this weavil satisfactorily?   (AEB)

7. The mass of a cheese biscuit has a normal distribution with mean 6 g and standard deviation 0.2 g. Determine the probability that
(a) a collection of twenty-five cheese biscuits has a mass of more than 149 g,
(b) a collection of thirty cheese biscuits has a mass of less than 180 g,
(c) twenty-five times the mass of a cheese biscuit is less than 149 g.
The mass of a ginger biscuit has a normal distribution with mean 10 g and standard deviation 0.3 g. Determine the probability that a collection of seven cheese biscuits has a mass greater than a collection of four ginger biscuits.
(It may be assumed that all the biscuits were sampled at random from their respective populations.)   (C)

8. In a packaging factory, the empty containers for a certain product have a mean weight of 400 g with a standard deviation of 10 g. The mean weight of the contents of a full container is 800 g with a standard deviation of 15 g. Find the expected total weight of 10 full containers and the standard deviation of this weight, assuming that the weights of containers and contents are independent.
Assuming further that these weights are normally distributed random variables, find the proportion of batches of 10 full containers which weigh more than 12.1 kg.
If 1% of the containers are found to be holding weights of product which are less than the guaranteed minimum amount, deduce this minimum weight.   (O & C)

9. Next May, an ornithologist intends to trap one male cuckoo and one female cuckoo. The mass M of the male cuckoo may be regarded as being a normal random variable with mean 116 g and standard deviation 16 g. The mass F of the female cuckoo may be regarded as being independent of M and as being a normal random variable with mean 106 g and standard deviation 12 g. Determine
(a) the probability that the mass of the two birds together will be more than 230 g,
(b) the probability that the mass of the male will be more than the mass of the female.
By considering $X = 9M - 16F$, or otherwise, determine the probability that the mass of the female will be less than nine-sixteenths of that of the male.
Suppose that one of the two trapped birds escapes. Assuming that the remaining bird will be equally likely to be the male or the female, determine the probability that its mass will be more than 118 g.   (C)

10. A train leaves a station punctually at its scheduled time, which is currently 08 08 hours (i.e. 8 minutes past 8 a.m.). A bus is due to arrive at that station at 08 00 hours, but in fact its arrival time is normally distributed about the scheduled time with standard deviation 5 minutes. Transfer from bus to train requires 1 minute. What is the probability that the bus–train connection is made?
It is proposed to change the schedule departure time of the train (it must still be an exact minute, e.g. 08 09 hours, 08 10 hours). What would be the earliest schedule departure time in order that the probability of making the bus–train connection should be at least 99%?

The train travels to a junction station, its journey time being normally distributed with mean 15 minutes and standard deviation 1.6 minutes. A connecting train leaves the junction punctually at 08 29 hours. Transfer between the two trains can be regarded as instantaneous. What is the probability that the two trains will connect with the original train schedule?
Find what departure times (exact minutes) of the train from the first station will result in both connections being made with probability at least 95%. Find also whether it is possible to arrange for this probability to be at least 97.5%.   (MEI)

11. The random variables X_1, X_2, X_3 and X_4 are normal, independent and identically distributed with mean μ and variance σ^2. The random variables Y and Z are defined by

$$Y = 4X_1 \quad \text{and} \quad Z = \sum_{i=1}^{4} X_i.$$

Show that $\text{Var}(Y) = 4\text{Var}(Z)$.
The number of hours per week spent in study by both male and female college students is known to be normally distributed. For male students the mean is 28 hours and the standard deviation 6 hours, with corresponding figures for the female students being 30 hours and 4 hours respectively. If a random sample of 6 male and 2 female students is taken, find the probability that in a given week the mean number of hours spent in study by this sample of students will lie between 25 and 31 hours.
Calculate the probability that the number of hours studied that week by the 2 female students will differ by more than 8 hours.
Two of the students in the sample are twins, one male and the other female. Calculate the probability that in a particular week the female twin works less hours than her brother. Comment briefly on the assumption of independence.   (AEB 1987)

12. A dispenser discharges an amount of soft drink which is normally distributed with standard deviation 20 ml. The mean amount may be set to any required value. If the cups into which it is dispensed have a capacity of 500 ml,
(a) what proportion of cups will overflow if the mean amount is set to 475 ml,
(b) to what value should the mean be set so that only 0.1% of cups will overflow?
A customer requires a double size drink. If the mean is set to 475 ml what is the probability of no overflow occurring if he
(c) uses two 500 ml cups,
(d) makes two discharges into a 1000 ml cup?

If now the capacity of the cups is normally distributed with mean 500 ml and standard deviation 30 ml,

(e) what proportion of cups will overflow if the mean amount discharged is 475 ml,

(f) to what value should the mean be set so that only 0.1% of cups will overflow?

(AEB 1987)

13. The random variables X_1, X_2 and X_3 are independent and normally distributed with means μ_1, μ_2 and μ_3 respectively and common variance σ^2. State precisely the distribution of $X_1 + X_2 - X_3$.

Two types of metal bars, A and B, are produced. The lengths of A bars are distributed normally with mean 20 cm and standard deviation 0.05 cm and the lengths of B bars are distributed normally with mean 30 cm and standard deviation 0.05 cm. An A bar is welded to a B bar with an overlap whose length is normally distributed with mean 5 cm and standard deviation 0.05 cm. The lengths of the welded bars must lie between 44.9 cm and 45.15 cm in order to be acceptable.

(a) Calculate the proportion of welded bars that are unsatisfactory.

(b) If the welded bars cost 40 p each to produce find the price that the manufacturer should charge in order that the expected profit per article should be 50 p.

(c) Before testing the lengths of the welded bars, two are selected at random. What is the probability that their lengths differ by more than 0.1 cm?

14. X and Y are independent normally distributed random variables such that X has mean 32 and variance 25, and Y has mean 43 and variance 96. Find

(a) $P(X > 43)$,

(b) $P(X - Y > 0)$,

(c) $P(2X - Y > 0)$. (JMB)

15. The times taken by two runners A and B to run 400 m races are independent and normally distributed with means 45.0 s and 45.2 s, and standard deviations 0.5 s and 0.8 s respectively. The two runners are to compete in a 400 m race for which there is a track record of 44.5 s.

(a) Calculate, to three decimal places, the probability of runner A breaking the track record.

(b) Show that the probability of runner B breaking the track record is greater than that of runner A.

(c) Calculate, to three decimal places, the probability of runner A beating runner B.

(JMB)

16. Monto sherry is sold in bottles of two sizes — standard and large. For each size, the content, in litres, of a randomly chosen bottle is normally distributed with mean and standard deviation as given in the table.

	Mean	Standard deviation
Standard bottle	0.760	0.008
Large bottle	1.010	0.009

(i) Show that the probability that a randomly chosen standard bottle contains less than 0.750 litres is 0.1056, correct to 4 places of decimals.

(ii) Find the probability that a box of 10 randomly chosen standard bottles contains at least three bottles whose contents are each less than 0.750 litres. Give three significant figures in your answer.

(iii) Find the probability that there is more sherry in four randomly chosen standard bottles than in three randomly chosen large bottles. (C)

17. [In this question give three places of decimals in each answer.]

The mass of tea in 'Supacuppa' teabags has a normal distribution with mean 4.1 g and standard deviation 0.12 g. The mass of tea in 'Bumpacuppa' teabags has a normal distribution with mean 5.2 g and standard deviation 0.15 g.

(i) Find the probability that a randomly chosen Supacuppa teabag contains more than 4.0 g of tea.

(ii) Find the probability that, of two randomly chosen Supacuppa teabags, one contains more than 4.0 g of tea and one contains less than 4.0 g of tea.

(iii) Find the probability that five randomly chosen Supacuppa teabags contain a total of more than 20.8 g of tea.

(iv) Find the probability that the total mass of tea in five randomly chosen Supacuppa teabags is more than the total mass of tea in four randomly chosen Bumpacuppa teabags.

(C)

18. A small bank has two cashiers dealing with customers wanting to withdraw or deposit cash. For each cashier, the time taken to deal with a customer is a random variable having a normal distribution with mean 150 s and standard deviation 45 s.

(i) Find the probability that the time taken for a randomly chosen customer to be dealt with by a cashier is more than 180 s.

(ii) One of the cashiers deals with two customers, one straight after the other.

Assuming that the times for the customers are independent of each other, find the probability that the total time taken by the cashier is less than 200 s.

(iii) At a certain time, one cashier has a queue of 4 customers and the other cashier has a queue of 3 customers, and the cashiers begin to deal with the customers at the front of their queues. Assuming that the cashiers work independently, find the probability that the 4 customers in the first queue will all be dealt with before the 3 customers in the second queue are all dealt with.   (C)

THE SAMPLE MEAN

Let $X_1, X_2, \ldots, X_n$ be a random sample of n independent observations from a population with mean μ and variance σ^2. Consider the sample mean, $\overline{X}$, where

$$\overline{X} = \frac{1}{n}(X_1 + X_2 + \ldots + X_n)$$

$$= \frac{1}{n}\sum X_i \quad \text{for} \quad i = 1, 2, \ldots, n.$$

We now consider the mean and variance of $\overline{X}$:

$$E(\overline{X}) = E\left[\frac{1}{n}(X_1 + X_2 + \ldots + X_n)\right]$$

$$= \frac{1}{n}[E(X_1) + E(X_2) + \ldots + E(X_n)]$$

$$= \frac{1}{n}(n\mu)$$

$$= \mu$$

$$\text{Var}(\overline{X}) = \text{Var}\left[\frac{1}{n}(X_1 + X_2 + \ldots + X_n)\right]$$

$$= \frac{1}{n^2}[\text{Var}(X_1) + \text{Var}(X_2) + \ldots + \text{Var}(X_n)]$$

$$= \frac{1}{n^2}(n\sigma^2)$$

$$= \frac{\sigma^2}{n}$$

Therefore $\qquad E(\overline{X}) = \mu \text{ and } \text{Var}(\overline{X}) = \dfrac{\sigma^2}{n}.$

This is a very important result.

NOTE: we are considering sampling from an infinite population, or from a finite population when sampling is *with replacement*. The observations are independent.

Example 8.14 The discrete r.v. X has probability distribution $P(X = x)$ as shown, with $E(X) = \mu = 0.7$ and $\mathrm{Var}(X) = \sigma^2 = 0.61$.

x	0	1	2
$P(X = x)$	0.5	0.3	0.2

Random samples of size 2 are taken from the distribution. By considering all possible samples, find the probability distribution of $\overline{X}$, the mean of such samples.

Verify that $E(\overline{X}) = \mu$ and $\mathrm{Var}(\overline{X}) = \dfrac{\sigma^2}{2}$.

Solution 8.14

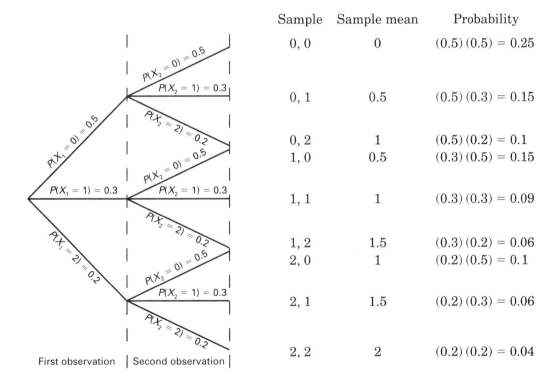

Sample	Sample mean	Probability
0, 0	0	$(0.5)(0.5) = 0.25$
0, 1	0.5	$(0.5)(0.3) = 0.15$
0, 2	1	$(0.5)(0.2) = 0.1$
1, 0	0.5	$(0.3)(0.5) = 0.15$
1, 1	1	$(0.3)(0.3) = 0.09$
1, 2	1.5	$(0.3)(0.2) = 0.06$
2, 0	1	$(0.2)(0.5) = 0.1$
2, 1	1.5	$(0.2)(0.3) = 0.06$
2, 2	2	$(0.2)(0.2) = 0.04$

The probability distribution for $\overline{X}$ is therefore

$\bar{x}$	0	0.5	1	1.5	2
$P(\overline{X} = \bar{x})$	0.25	0.3	0.29	0.12	0.04

We have
$$E(\overline{X}) = 0 + 0.15 + 0.29 + 0.18 + 0.08 = 0.7$$
$$E(\overline{X}^2) = 0 + 0.075 + 0.29 + 0.27 + 0.16 = 0.795$$
$$\mathrm{Var}(\overline{X}) = E(\overline{X}^2) - E^2(\overline{X}) = 0.795 - 0.49 = 0.305$$

Now we are given that $\mu = 0.7 = E(\overline{X})$ and $\sigma^2 = 0.61$,

so $\dfrac{\sigma^2}{2} = 0.305 = \mathrm{Var}(\overline{X})$.

Therefore $\underline{E(\overline{X}) = \mu \ \text{and} \ \mathrm{Var}(\overline{X}) = \dfrac{\sigma^2}{2}}$

Example **8.15** (**a**) For the set of numbers 1, 4, 7 find the mean μ and the variance σ^2.

(**b**) Draw up a frequency distribution of the means of all possible samples of size 3, where sampling is carried out with replacement. Find the mean and variance of this distribution and comment.

Solution **8.15** (**a**) $\mu = 4$ and $\sigma^2 = 6$ (calculator)

(**b**) There are three ways of obtaining a sample containing the numbers 1, 1, 4, i.e. (1, 1, 4), (1, 4, 1), (4, 1, 1) and there are 6 ways of obtaining a sample containing the numbers 1, 4, 7. The frequency distribution of the means of all possible samples of size 3 is shown in the table.

Numbers in sample	Sample mean	Frequency
1, 1, 1	1	1
4, 4, 4	4	1
7, 7, 7	7	1
1, 1, 4	2	3
1, 1, 7	3	3
1, 4, 4	3	3
1, 7, 7	5	3
7, 4, 4	5	3
4, 7, 7	6	3
1, 4, 7	4	6
		27

Now, using a calculator, we find that

$$\text{mean of sample means} = 4$$

and $$\text{variance of sample means} = 2$$

So, when samples of size 3 are taken,

$$\text{mean of sample means} = \text{population mean}$$

$$\text{variance of sample means} = \frac{\text{population variance}}{3}$$

SAMPLING WITHOUT REPLACEMENT

If $X_1, X_2, \ldots, X_n$ is a random sample of size n taken *without replacement* from a finite population of size N with mean μ and variance σ^2, then the sample mean $\overline{X}$ is such that

$$E(\overline{X}) = \mu \quad \text{and} \quad \text{Var}(\overline{X}) = \frac{\sigma^2}{n}\left(\frac{N-n}{N-1}\right).$$

Example 8.16 Find the mean μ and the variance σ^2 of the population 1, 4, 7. Draw up a frequency distribution of the means of all possible samples of size 2, taken without replacement. Find the mean and variance of this distribution and verify that

$$\text{Var}(\overline{X}) = \frac{\sigma^2}{n}\left(\frac{N-n}{N-1}\right)$$

where $\overline{X}$ is the r.v. 'the sample mean', N is the number in the population and n is the sample size.

What happens as $N \to \infty$?

Solution 8.16 $\mu = 4$, $\sigma^2 = 6$ (calculator)

Sample	(1, 4)	(1, 7)	(4, 1)	(4, 7)	(7, 1)	(7, 4)
Mean	2.5	4	2.5	5.5	4	5.5

By calculator, mean $= 4$, variance $= 1.5$.

Now $\dfrac{\sigma^2}{n}\left(\dfrac{N-n}{N-1}\right) = \dfrac{6}{2}\left(\dfrac{3-2}{3-1}\right)$ with $N = 3$, $n = 2$, $\sigma^2 = 6$

$$= 1.5$$

$$= \text{Var}(\overline{X}) \quad \text{as required.}$$

Now, as $N \to \infty$, $\dfrac{N-n}{N-1} \to 1$ and $\text{Var}(\overline{X}) \to \dfrac{\sigma^2}{n}$

(sampling from an infinite population).

Exercise 8e

1. For each of the following distributions,
   (a) find the mean μ and the variance σ^2,
   (b) by taking all possible samples of size 2 verify that $E(\overline{X}) = \mu$ and $\text{Var}(\overline{X}) = \dfrac{\sigma^2}{2}$.

(i)

x	0	1	2
$P(X = x)$	0.6	0.3	0.1

(ii)

x	0	1	2	3
$P(X = x)$	0.2	0.3	0.3	0.2

(iii)

x	-3	2	4
$P(X = x)$	0.4	0.3	0.3

2. The discrete random variable J has the distribution

j	-2	-1	0	1	2
$P(J=j)$	$\frac{1}{12}$	$\frac{1}{4}$	$\frac{1}{3}$	$\frac{1}{4}$	$\frac{1}{12}$

Find the mean, μ, and variance, σ^2, of the distribution.
Random samples of size 2 are taken from the distribution. By considering all possible samples, or otherwise, obtain the probability distribution of the mean of such samples. Give the mean and variance of the distribution of the mean of random samples of size 3 from the original distribution.   (O)

3. Find the mean μ and the variance σ^2 of the population 1, 4, 5, 9. Draw up a frequency distribution of the means of all possible samples of size 2. Find the mean and the variance of the distribution formed and comment on your answers.

4. Find the mean μ and the variance σ^2 of the population 1, 4, 7, 8. Draw up a frequency distribution of the means of all possible samples of size 2, taken *without replacement*. Find the mean and the variance of this distribution and verify that

$$\text{Var}(\overline{X}) = \frac{\sigma^2}{n}\left(\frac{N-n}{N-1}\right)$$

where $\overline{X}$ is the r.v. 'the sample mean', N is the number in the population and n is the sample size.
What happens as $N \to \infty$?

5. Find the mean μ and the variance σ^2 of the five numbers 0, 3, 3, 6, 6. A sample of three of these numbers is to be drawn at random *without* replacement. By making a list of all

such samples, or otherwise, show that the sampling distribution of the sample mean $\overline{X}$ is given by the following table.

$\bar{x}$	2	3	4	5
$P(\overline{X} = \bar{x})$	0.1	0.4	0.3	0.2

Verify that $\overline{X}$ is an unbiased estimator* of μ and calculate the variance. If, instead, the sample is to be taken *with* replacement, state the value of the variance of the sample mean.   (JMB)

*See p. 477 Unbiased estimator.

6. A lecturer sets her students an assignment on sampling. Part of the assignment involves the students sampling from a population which consists of 50 peeled pickling onions kept in a large water-filled bowl. The lecturer knows that the mean and standard deviation of the weight of such onions is 24.5 grammes and 7.7 grammes respectively.
One student randomly selects an onion, finds its weight and then returns it to the bowl. This student repeats the process until he has weighed a total of nine onions. What would you expect to be
(*a*) the mean of the weights of the nine onions,
(*b*) the standard deviation of the mean weight?
Another student adopts a different procedure and she selects nine onions at random without replacing them. What would you expect the standard deviation of the mean weight of the nine onions to be in this case?
For each approach, what is the minimum number of onions that have to be selected if the standard deviation of the sample mean is to be less than 3 grammes?   (O)

THE DISTRIBUTION OF THE SAMPLE MEAN

Consider $X_1, X_2, \ldots, X_n$, a random sample of size n, taken from a population with mean μ and variance σ^2. We know that the sample mean $\overline{X}$, where $\overline{X} = \frac{1}{n}\sum X_i$, has mean μ and variance $\frac{\sigma^2}{n}$. We now consider *how* the sample mean is distributed.

(a) Sampling from a normal population

If the parent population is *normal*, where $X \sim \text{N}(\mu, \sigma^2)$, then the distribution $\overline{X}$ is also *normal*, and we have $\overline{X} \sim \text{N}\left(\mu, \frac{\sigma^2}{n}\right)$.

For example, the diagram shows the distribution of X, where $X \sim \mathrm{N}(\mu, \sigma^2)$, together with the distributions of $\overline{X}$ when $n = 5$ and when $n = 10$.

Each curve is symmetrical about μ, but as n gets larger, the variance gets smaller, so the curve becomes taller and less spread out.

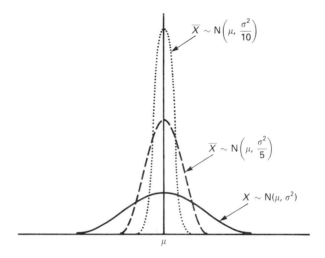

If $X_1, X_2, \ldots, X_n$ is a random sample of size n taken from a *normal* distribution where $X \sim \mathrm{N}(\mu, \sigma^2)$, then the distribution of $\overline{X}$ is also *normal* and

$$\overline{X} \sim \mathrm{N}\left(\mu, \frac{\sigma^2}{n}\right) \quad \text{where} \quad \overline{X} = \frac{1}{n}(X_1 + X_2 + \ldots + X_n).$$

NOTE: The standard deviation of the distribution of $\overline{X}$ is $\sigma/\sqrt{n}$ and is called the **standard error of the mean.**

The distribution of $\overline{X}$ is known as the **sampling distribution of means**.

Example 8.17   A random sample of size 15 is taken from the distribution of X, where $X \sim \mathrm{N}(60, 4^2)$, and the sample mean is calculated. Find the probability that the sample mean is less than 58.

Solution 8.17   We are given that $X \sim \mathrm{N}(60, 4^2)$.

Now $\overline{X} \sim \mathrm{N}\left(\mu, \dfrac{\sigma^2}{n}\right),$ with $\mu = 60$, $\sigma^2 = 16$, $n = 15$

so $\qquad \overline{X} \sim \mathrm{N}\left(60, \frac{16}{15}\right)$

Distribution of $\overline{X}$

$$P(\overline{X} < 58) = P\left(\frac{\overline{X} - 60}{\sqrt{16/15}} < \frac{58 - 60}{\sqrt{16/15}}\right)$$

s.d. $= \sqrt{\dfrac{16}{15}}$

$$= P(Z < -1.936)$$

$$= 0.0264$$

58 60

S.V. -1.936 0

The probability that the mean of the sample is less than 58 is 0.0264.

Example 8.18 The heights of a particular species of plant follow a normal distribution with mean 21 cm and standard deviation $\sqrt{90}$ cm. A random sample of 10 plants is taken and the mean height calculated. Find the probability that this sample mean lies between 18 cm and 27 cm.

Solution 8.18 Let X be the r.v. 'the height in cm of a plant'. Then $X \sim \mathrm{N}(21, 90)$.

Now $n = 10$, so $\overline{X} \sim \mathrm{N}\left(21, \frac{90}{10}\right)$, i.e. $\overline{X} \sim \mathrm{N}(21, 9)$.

$$P(18 < \overline{X} < 27) = P\left(\frac{18 - 21}{3} < \frac{\overline{X} - 21}{3} < \frac{27 - 21}{3}\right)$$

$$= P(-1 < Z < 2)$$

$$= 0.8185$$

Distribution of $\overline{X}$

s.d. $= 3$

18 21   27

S.V. -1 0   2

Therefore the probability that the mean height of the sample lies between 18 cm and 27 cm is 0.8185.

Example 8.19 A large number of random samples of size n is taken from the distribution of X where $X \sim \mathrm{N}(74, 36)$ and the sample mean for each random sample is calculated. If $P(\overline{X} > 72) = 0.854$, estimate the value of n.

Solution 8.19 $X \sim \mathrm{N}(74, 36)$.

Therefore $\qquad \overline{X} \sim \mathrm{N}\left(74, \dfrac{36}{n}\right)$

The standard deviation is $\sqrt{\dfrac{36}{n}} = \dfrac{6}{\sqrt{n}}$

Now $$P(\overline{X} > 72) = P\left(\frac{\overline{X} - 74}{6/\sqrt{n}} > \frac{72 - 74}{6/\sqrt{n}}\right)$$

$$= P\left(Z > \frac{-\sqrt{n}}{3}\right)$$

So $$P\left(Z > \frac{-\sqrt{n}}{3}\right) = 0.854$$

Now $$P(Z > -1.054) = 0.854$$

Therefore $$\frac{\sqrt{n}}{3} = 1.054$$

$$n = 9(1.054)^2$$

$$= 10.0 \quad (3 \text{ S.F.})$$

Samples of size 10 are taken.

Example 8.20   (a) If $X_1, X_2, \ldots, X_n$ is a random sample from $N(\mu, 1)$, state the distribution of the sample mean $\overline{X}$.

  (b) Find the sample size required to ensure that the probability that $\overline{X}$ is within 0.1 of μ is greater than 0.95.

Solution 8.20   (a) $X \sim N(\mu, 1)$, therefore $\overline{X} \sim N\left(\mu, \dfrac{1}{n}\right)$.

  (b) We need to find n such that

$$P(|\overline{X} - \mu| \leqslant 0.1) > 0.95$$

i.e. $$P(-0.1 \leqslant \overline{X} - \mu \leqslant 0.1) > 0.95$$

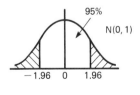

$$P\left(\frac{-0.1}{\sqrt{1/n}} \leqslant \frac{\overline{X} - \mu}{\sqrt{1/n}} \leqslant \frac{0.1}{\sqrt{1/n}}\right) > 0.95$$

$$P(-0.1\sqrt{n} \leqslant Z \leqslant 0.1\sqrt{n}) > 0.95$$

Now $$P(-1.96 \leqslant Z \leqslant 1.96) = 0.95$$

So $$0.1\sqrt{n} > 1.96$$

$$\sqrt{n} > \frac{1.96}{0.1}$$

$$n > 384.16$$

Therefore the smallest sample size required is 385.

Exercise 8f

1. If $X \sim N(200, 80)$ and a random sample of size 5 is taken from the distribution, find the probability that the sample mean
(a) is greater than 207,
(b) lies between 201 and 209.

2. If $X \sim N(200, 100)$ and a random sample of size 10 is taken from the distribution, find the probability that the sample mean lies outside the range 198 to 205.

3. If $X \sim N(50, 12)$ and a random sample of size 12 is taken from the distribution, find the probability that the sample mean
(a) is less than 48.5,   (b) is less than 52.3,
(c) lies between 50.7 and 51.7.

4. At a college, the masses of the male students are distributed approximately normally with mean mass 70 kg and standard deviation 5 kg. Four male students are chosen at random. Find the probability that their mean mass is less than 65 kg.

5. A normal distribution has a mean of 40 and a standard deviation of 4. If 25 items are drawn at random, find the probability that their mean is   (a) 41.4 or more,
(b) between 38.7 and 40.7,   (c) less than 39.5.

6. If a large number of samples, size n are taken from a population which follows a normal distribution with mean 74 and standard deviation 6,   (a) find n if the probability that the sample mean exceeds 75 is 0.282,
(b) find n if the probability that the sample mean is less than 70.4 is 0.001 35.

7. A normal distribution has a mean of 30 and a variance of 5. Find the probability that
(a) the average of 10 observations exceeds 30.5,   (b) the average of 40 observations exceeds 30.5,   (c) the average of 100 observations exceeds 30.5. Find n such that the probability that the average of n observations exceeds 30.5 is less than 1%.

8. The r.v. X is such that $X \sim N(\mu, 4)$. A random sample, size n, is taken from the population. Find the least n such that $P(|\overline{X} - \mu| < 0.5) > 0.95$.

9. $\overline{X}$ is the r.v. 'the sample mean of samples, size 15, taken from N(30, 18)' and $\overline{Y}$ is the r.v. 'the sample mean of samples, size 8, taken from N(20, 16)'. Find the distribution of

(a) $\overline{X} - \overline{Y}$,   (b) $\overline{X} + \overline{Y}$,   (c) $\overline{Y} - \overline{X}$,
(d) $5\overline{X} + 3\overline{Y}$,   (e) $4\overline{X} - 2\overline{Y}$.

10. In a certain country the heights of men are normally distributed with mean 175 cm and standard deviation 5 cm and the heights of women are normally distributed with mean 165 cm and standard deviation 6 cm. Find the probability that the mean height of three women chosen at random is greater than the mean height of four men chosen at random from the population.

11. The continuous random variable X is such that $X \sim N(20, 16)$. If samples of size n are taken and $\overline{X}$ is the random variable 'the mean of the n sample values', find the least value of n such that $P(\overline{X} > 21) \leqslant 0.05$.

12. A random sample X_1, X_2 is drawn from a distribution with mean μ and standard deviation σ. State the mean and standard deviation of the distribution of   (a) $X_1 + X_2$,
(b) $X_1 - X_2$,   (c) $\overline{X}$.
A student's performance is equally good in two subjects. The marks she might be expected to score in each subject may be treated as independent observations drawn from a normal distribution with mean 45 and standard deviation 5. Two procedures might be used to decide whether to give the student an overall pass. One is to demand that she pass separately in each subject, the pass mark being 40; the other is to require that her mean mark in the two subjects exceeds 40. Find the probability that the student will obtain an overall pass by each of these procedures.   (O)

13. In a certain nation, men have heights distributed normally with mean 1.70 m and standard deviation 10 cm. Find the probability that a man chosen randomly has height not less than 1.83 m.
What is the probability that the average height of three men chosen randomly is greater than 1.78 m and the probability that all three will have heights greater than 1.83 m?
For the nation, women have heights distributed normally with mean 1.60 m and standard deviation 7.5 cm. Find the probability that a husband and wife have not more than 5 cm difference in heights and state the assumptions that you have made in the calculation.   (MEI)

14. X_1 and X_2 are random variables such that X_1 is normally distributed with mean 120 and variance 8 and X_2 is normally distributed with mean 150 and variance 22. A random sample of size 20 is taken from the distribution of $3X_1 + 4X_2$. Find the distribution of the sample mean.

15. Random variables X and Y are such that $X \sim N(100, 10)$ and $Y \sim N(120, 20)$. Random samples of size 50 are taken from each distribution. Find the probability that the sample from the distribution of Y will have a mean which is at least 21 more than the mean of the sample from the distribution of X.

16. Every child in a class does an experiment which consists of measuring V, the volume of water displaced by a solid sphere. The children's values of V are distributed approximately normally with mean $27.4\,\text{cm}^3$ and standard deviation $1\,\text{cm}^3$.
(a) Given that the nominal volume V_0 of the sphere is $27.1\,\text{cm}^3$, estimate to 2 decimal places the probability, p, that the value of V of a child chosen at random exceeds $1.05\,V_0$.
(b) The nominal radius r_0 of the sphere, calculated from the formula $r_0 = (3V_0/4\pi)^{\frac{1}{3}}$, is $1.86\,\text{cm}$. Each child calculates a value r for the radius of the sphere, using the formula $r = (3V/4\pi)^{\frac{1}{3}}$. Explain why you would expect the probability that a value of r of a child chosen at random exceeds $1.05\,r_0$ to be different from the value of p you obtained in

(a). Show that, in fact, it is extremely unlikely that any child's value of r exceeds $1.05\,r_0$.
(*Hint*: express $r > 1.05\,r_0$ in terms of V and V_0.)
(c) The measured values of V obtained by a second class of children are also distributed approximately normally with the same mean as the first class, but with a standard deviation of $1.5\,\text{cm}^3$. One child from each class is chosen at random. Estimate to 2 decimal places the probability that the mean of their values of V exceeds $1.05\,V_0$.
(MEI)

17. (a) If X and Y are independent random variables with means μ_x, μ_y and variances $\sigma_x{}^2$, $\sigma_y{}^2$ respectively, show from first principles that the mean and variance of $aX + bY$ are $a\mu_x + b\mu_y$ and $a^2\sigma_x{}^2 + b^2\sigma_y{}^2$ respectively where a and b are constants.
(b) The diameters x of 110 steel rods were measured in centimetres and the results were summarised as follows:

$$\sum x = 36.5, \qquad \sum x^2 = 12.49.$$

Find the mean and standard deviation of these measurements.
Assuming these measurements are a sample from a normal distribution with this mean and this variance, find the probability that the mean diameter of a sample of size 110 is greater than $0.345\,\text{cm}$.
(O & C)

THE DISTRIBUTION OF THE SAMPLE MEAN

(b) From any population, sample size *n* large

We now have a very important result:

The central limit theorem

If $X_1, X_2, \ldots, X_n$ is a random sample of size n from **ANY** distribution with mean μ and variance σ^2 then, *for large n*, the distribution of the sample mean ($\overline{X}$) is *approximately normal* and

$$\overline{X} \sim N\left(\mu, \frac{\sigma^2}{n}\right) \quad \text{where} \quad \overline{X} = \frac{1}{n}(X_1 + X_2 + \ldots + X_n).$$

NOTE: the approximation gets better as n gets larger.

Now if $\overline{X} \sim N\left(\mu, \dfrac{\sigma^2}{n}\right)$ then $n\overline{X} \sim N\left(n\mu, n^2\dfrac{\sigma^2}{n}\right)$ i.e. $n\overline{X} \sim N(n\mu, n\sigma^2)$

But $\qquad\qquad\qquad\qquad n\overline{X} = X_1 + X_2 + \ldots + X_n$

therefore $\qquad\qquad X_1 + X_2 + \ldots + X_n \sim \mathrm{N}(n\mu, n\sigma^2)$

If $X_1, X_2, \ldots, X_n$ is a random sample of size n from **ANY** distribution with mean μ and variance σ^2 then, *for large n*, the distribution of the sum of the random variables is *approximately normal* with mean $n\mu$ and variance $n\sigma^2$.

The definition in this form is also referred to as the **central limit theorem**.

The central limit theorem is a surprising result. The distribution of X can be discrete, for example binomial, Poisson; or continuous, for example rectangular or exponential.

Example 8.21 If a random sample of size 30 is taken from each of the following distributions, find, for each case, the probability that the sample mean exceeds 5.

(a) $X \sim \mathrm{Po}(4.5)$,   (b) $X \sim \mathrm{Bin}(9, 0.5)$,   (c) $X \sim \mathrm{R}(3, 6)$.

Solution 8.21 (a) If $X \sim \mathrm{Po}(4.5)$ then

$$E(X) = \mu = 4.5$$

$$\mathrm{Var}(X) = \sigma^2 = 4.5$$

The sample size is large, so by the central limit theorem

$$\overline{X} \sim \mathrm{N}\left(4.5, \frac{4.5}{30}\right) \quad \text{approximately.}$$

The standard deviation of $\overline{X}$ is $\sqrt{\dfrac{4.5}{30}} = \sqrt{0.15}$.

Now $\qquad P(\overline{X} > 5) = P\left(\dfrac{\overline{X} - 4.5}{\sqrt{0.15}} > \dfrac{5 - 4.5}{\sqrt{0.15}}\right)$

$$= P(Z > 1.291)$$

$$= 0.0983.$$

So, if $X \sim \mathrm{Po}(4.5)$, then $P(\overline{X} > 5) = 0.0983$.

(b) If $X \sim \mathrm{Bin}(9, 0.5)$ then

$$E(X) = \mu = 9(0.5) = 4.5$$

$$\mathrm{Var}(X) = \sigma^2 = 9(0.5)(0.5) = 2.25$$

Now, by the central limit theorem, $\overline{X} \sim \mathrm{N}\left(4.5, \dfrac{2.25}{30}\right)$.

The standard deviation of $\overline{X} = \sqrt{\dfrac{2.25}{30}} = \sqrt{0.075}$.

Now $\quad P(\overline{X} > 5) = P\left(\dfrac{\overline{X} - 4.5}{\sqrt{0.075}} > \dfrac{5 - 4.5}{\sqrt{0.075}}\right)$

$= P(Z > 1.826)$

$= 0.0340$

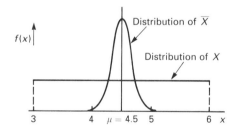

s.d. $= \sqrt{0.075}$

S.V.	4.5	5
	0	1.826

Therefore if $X \sim \text{Bin}(9, 0.5)$ then $P(\overline{X} > 5) = 0.034.$

(c) If $X \sim \text{R}(3, 6)$ then

$$E(X) = \mu = \tfrac{1}{2}(3 + 6) = 4.5$$

$$\text{Var}(X) = \sigma^2 = \dfrac{(6 - 3)^2}{12} = 0.75$$

So $\quad \overline{X} \sim \text{N}\left(4.5, \dfrac{0.75}{30}\right)$ by the central limit theorem

i.e. $\quad \overline{X} \sim \text{N}(4.5, 0.025)$

Now $\quad P(\overline{X} > 5) = P\left(\dfrac{\overline{X} - 4.5}{\sqrt{0.025}} > \dfrac{5 - 4.5}{\sqrt{0.025}}\right)$

$= P(Z > 3.162)$

$= 0.000\,783$

s.d. $= \sqrt{0.025}$

	4.5	5
S.V.	0	3.162

Therefore if $X \sim \text{R}(3, 6)$ then $P(\overline{X} > 5) = 0.000\,783.$

We can illustrate the distributions of X and $\overline{X}$ for part (c) as follows.

We have $\quad X \sim \text{R}(3, 6)$ i.e. $f(x) = \tfrac{1}{3},\ \ 3 \leqslant x \leqslant 6.$

and $\quad \overline{X} \sim \text{N}(4.5, 0.025)$ when $n = 30$

$f(x)$

Distribution of $\overline{X}$

Distribution of X

3 $\qquad$ 4 $\quad \mu = 4.5$ $\ $ 5 $\qquad$ 6 $\ x$

Exercise 8g

1. To find the mean life and the standard deviation of a particular make of fluorescent light bulbs a large number of samples of 100 bulbs are tested. The mean and the standard deviation of the resulting sampling distribution of means were found to be 1580 hours and 120 hours, respectively. Calculate the mean life and the standard deviation of this make of light bulbs.

2. If a large number of samples, size 30, is taken with replacement from the following distribution, find the mean and standard deviation of the sampling distribution of means. Estimate the probability that a sample mean exceeds 4.

x	0	1	2	3	4	5	6
f	3	10	18	27	21	16	5

3. A random sample of size 100 is taken from Bin(20, 0.6). Find the probability that (*a*) $\overline{X}$ is greater than 12.4,   (*b*) $\overline{X}$ is less than 12.2, where $\overline{X}$ is the sample mean.

4. The heights of a new variety of sunflower are normally distributed with mean 2 m and standard deviation 40 cm. 100 samples of 50 flowers each are measured. In how many would you expect the sample mean to be (*a*) greater than 210 cm,   (*b*) between 195 cm and 205 cm,   (*c*) less than 188 cm?

5. A random sample of size 30 is taken from Po(4). Find   (*a*) $P(\overline{X} < 4.5)$,   (*b*) $P(\overline{X} > 3.8)$,   (*c*) $P(3.8 < \overline{X} < 4.5)$.

6. If a large number of samples, of size n, are taken from Po(4.6) and approximately 2.5% of the sample means are less than 4.005, estimate n.

7. If a large number of samples of size n are taken from Po(2.9) and approximately 1% of the sample means are greater than 3.41, estimate n.

8. If a large number of samples of size n are taken from R(2, 30) and approximately 80% of the sample means are less than 17.15, estimate n.

9. If a large number of samples of size n are taken from Bin(20, 0.2) and approximately 90% of the sample means are less than 4.354, estimate n.

10. If a large number of samples of size n is taken from R(2, 6) and approximately 1% of the sample means are less than 2.8, estimate the value of n.

11. To find the mean life and standard deviation of a certain brand of car tyres a large number of random samples of size 50 were tested. The mean and standard error of the sampling distribution obtained were 20 500 km and 250 km respectively. Estimate the mean life and the standard deviation of this brand of car tyre.

12. The standard deviation of the masses of articles in a large population is 4.55 kg. If random samples of size 100 are drawn from the population, find the probability that a sample mean will differ from the true population mean by less than 0.8 kg.

13. The lifetime, X, in hours of an electrical component is modelled by the following probability density function.

$$f(x) = \begin{cases} \dfrac{a}{(x + 10)^2}, & 0 \leqslant x \leqslant 10 \\ 0, & \text{elsewhere} \end{cases}$$

(*a*) Show that $a = 20$ and sketch the graph of $y = f(x)$.
(*b*) Find the mean and variance of X, each correct to three significant figures. (The substitution $u = x + 10$ will help with the integrals.)
(*c*) What is the probability that a random sample of 80 components has a mean life of more than 4 hours?

14. A continuous random variable X has probability density function given by

$$f(x) = \begin{cases} 0, & x < -2, \\ -ax, & -2 \leqslant x \leqslant 0, \\ ax, & 0 \leqslant x \leqslant 2, \\ 0, & 2 < x, \end{cases}$$

where a is a constant. Sketch the graph of f and hence, or otherwise, find the value of a.

Show that $\text{Var}(X) = 2$.

A random sample of 200 independent observations of X is taken. Using a suitable approximation, find the probability that the sample mean exceeds 0.2.   (C)

15. Two red balls and two white balls are placed in a bag. Balls are drawn one by one, at random and without replacement. The random variable X is the number of white balls drawn before the first red ball is drawn.
(i) Show that $P(X = 1) = \frac{1}{3}$, and find the rest of the probability distribution of X.
(ii) Find $E(X)$ and show that $\text{Var}(X) = \frac{5}{9}$.
(iii) The sample mean for 80 independent observations of X is denoted by $\overline{X}$. Using a suitable approximation, find $P(\overline{X} > 0.75)$.   (C)

16. The mass of coffee in a randomly chosen jar sold by a certain company may be taken to have a normal distribution with mean 203 g and standard deviation 2.5 g.
(i) Find the probability that a randomly chosen jar will contain at least 200 g of coffee.
(ii) Find the mass m such that only 3% of jars contain more than m grams of coffee.
(iii) Find the probability that two randomly chosen jars will together contain between 400 g and 405 g of coffee.
(iv) The random variable $\overline{C}$ denotes the mean mass (in grams) of coffee per jar in a random sample of 20 jars. Find the value of a such that
$$P(\,|\overline{C} - 203\,| < a) = 0.95.$$ (C)

17. On the tropical island of Uclesy, weather records have been kept for a long time. On average, there is a hurricane every 50 years. The mid-day temperature, in degrees Celsius, has mean 20 and variance 36. On average, 4 days out of 5 are sunny. Each day's weather is independent of the weather on all preceding days.

(i) Find the probability that there are exactly three hurricanes in a randomly chosen 20-year period. Find also the probability that there are at least three hurricanes in a randomly chosen 20-year period.

(ii) Find the probability that the average mid-day temperature over a randomly chosen period of 62 days lies between 20 and 21.

(iii) Find the probability that there are exactly eight sunny days in a randomly chosen 10-day period.   (C)

18. The random variable X has a Poisson distribution with mean 4. Find $P(X \leqslant 2)$. The random variable $\overline{X}$ is the mean of a random sample of 100 values of X. By using a suitable approximation, find $P(\overline{X} < 3.5)$.   (C)

THE DISTRIBUTION OF THE SAMPLE PROPORTION

Consider a population in which the proportion of 'successes' is p. If a random sample of size n is taken from this population, and X is the random variable 'the number of successes in the sample' then $X \sim \mathrm{Bin}(n, p)$.

Now, for large n, $X \sim \mathrm{N}(np, npq)$, where $q = 1 - p$ (see page 397).

Let P_s be the random variable 'the proportion of successes in the sample', then $P_s = \dfrac{X}{n}$.

$$E(P_s) = E\left(\frac{X}{n}\right) \qquad\qquad \mathrm{Var}(P_s) = \mathrm{Var}\left(\frac{X}{n}\right)$$

$$= \frac{1}{n}E(X) \qquad\qquad\qquad = \frac{1}{n^2}\mathrm{Var}(X)$$

$$= \frac{1}{n}(np) \qquad\qquad\qquad = \frac{1}{n^2}(npq)$$

$$= p \qquad\qquad\qquad\qquad = \frac{pq}{n}$$

Distribution of P_s

Therefore $$P_s \sim \mathrm{N}\left(p, \frac{pq}{n}\right)$$

s.d. $= \sqrt{\dfrac{pq}{n}}$

NOTE: the larger the sample size, the better the approximation.

The distribution of P_s is known as the **sampling distribution of proportions** and the standard deviation of the sampling distribution $\sqrt{pq/n}$ is known as the **standard error of proportion**.

NOTE: when considering the normal approximation to the binomial distribution, a continuity correction of $\pm\frac{1}{2}$ is used.

Now, since $P_s = \dfrac{X}{n}$, we use a continuity correction of $\pm\dfrac{1}{2n}$.

Example 8.22 It is known that 3% of frozen pies arriving at a freezer centre are broken. What is the probability that, on a morning when 500 pies arrive, (**a**) 5% or more will be broken, (**b**) 3% or less will be broken?

Solution 8.22 Let p be the probability that a pie is broken, and let P_s be the r.v. 'the proportion of pies in the sample that are broken'.

Then $P_s \sim N\left(p, \dfrac{pq}{n}\right)$ with $n = 500$, $p = 0.03$, $q = 0.97$

So $P_s \sim N\left(0.03, \dfrac{(0.03)(0.97)}{500}\right)$

i.e. $P_s \sim N(0.03, 0.000\,058\,2)$

The standard deviation is $\sqrt{0.000\,058\,2} = 0.007\,63$ (3 S.F.)

(**a**) $P(P_s \geqslant 0.05) \rightarrow P\left(P_s > 0.05 - \dfrac{1}{(2)(500)}\right)$ (continuity correction)

$= P\left(\dfrac{P_s - 0.03}{0.007\,63} > \dfrac{(0.05 - 1/1000) - 0.03}{0.007\,63}\right)$

$= P(Z > 2.49)$

$= 0.006\,39$

s.d. = 0.007 63

0.03   0.049
S.V.   0   2.49

Therefore the probability that 5% or more will be broken is 0.006 39.

(**b**) $P(P_s \leqslant 0.03) \rightarrow P\left(P_s < 0.03 + \dfrac{1}{(2)(500)}\right)$ (continuity correction)

$= P\left(\dfrac{P_s - 0.03}{0.007\,63} < \dfrac{(0.03 - 1/1000) - 0.03}{0.007\,63}\right)$

$= P(Z < 0.131)$

$= 0.5521$

s.d. = 0.007 63

0.03 0.031
S.V.   0 0.131

Therefore the probability that 3% or less will be broken is 0.5521.

Alternative method

Let X be the random variable 'the number of broken pies in a sample'. Then $X \sim Bin(n, p)$.

Since n is large, using the normal approximation to the binomial, $X \sim N(np, npq)$ with $n = 500$, $p = 0.03$, $q = 0.97$

So $X \sim N(15, 14.55)$

The standard deviation is $\sqrt{14.55} = 3.814$ (4 S.F.)

(**a**) We want the probability that 5% or more are broken, i.e. the probability that 25 or more are broken.

$$P(X \geqslant 25) \rightarrow P(X > 24.5) \qquad \text{(continuity correction)}$$

$$= P\left(\frac{X - 15}{3.814} > \frac{24.5 - 15}{3.814}\right)$$

$$= P(Z > 2.49)$$

$$= 0.006\,39$$

s.d. = 3.814

15 24.5
S.V.   0   2.49

The probability that 5% or more will be broken is 0.006 39, as before.

(**b**) 3% of 500 = 15, so we need

$$P(X \leqslant 15) \rightarrow P(X < 15.5) \qquad \text{(continuity correction)}$$

$$= P\left(\frac{X - 15}{3.814} < \frac{15.5 - 15}{3.814}\right)$$

$$= P(Z < 0.131)$$

$$= 0.5521$$

s.d. = 3.814

15 15.5
S.V.   0 0.131

The probability that 3% or less will be broken is 0.5521, as before.

NOTE: problems of this type may be solved by considering the distribution of the sample proportion, P_s or by using the normal approximation to the binomial distribution. If the continuity corrections are used in both cases, or omitted in both cases, the standardised values will agree exactly.

Exercise 8h

1. 2% of the trees in a plantation are known to have a certain disease. What is the probability that, in a sample of 300 trees (*a*) less than 1%, (*b*) more than 4% are diseased?

2. A fair coin is tossed 150 times. Find the probability that (*a*) less than 40% of the tosses will result in heads, (*b*) between 40% and 50% (inclusive) are heads, (*c*) more than 55% are heads.

3. A fair coin is tossed 300 times. Work through parts (*a*), (*b*), (*c*) as in Question 2. Why are the results different?

4. Mr Hand gained 48% of the votes in the District Council Elections. What is the probability that a poll of (*a*) 100, (*b*) 1000 randomly selected voters would show over 50% in favour of Mr Hand?

5. Three-quarters of the houseowners in a particular area own a colour television set. Find the probability that at least 73 of a random sample of 100 houseowners in the area own a colour television set.

6. A die is biased so that 1 in 5 throws results in a six. Find the probability that, when the die is thrown 300 times, (*a*) more than 70 throws will result in a six, (*b*) at least 70 throws will result in a six, (*c*) less than 57 throws will result in a six.

7. 70% of the strawberry plants of a particular variety produce more than 10 strawberries per plant. Find the probability that the random sample of 50 plants in my garden consist of more than 37 plants which produce more than 10 strawberries per plant.

SUMMARY — THE SAMPLE MEAN AND THE SAMPLE PROPORTION

Distribution of the sample mean $\overline{X}$ **where** $\overline{X} = \dfrac{1}{n} \sum\limits_{i=1}^{n} X_i$

If $X_1, X_2, \ldots, X_n$ is a random sample of size n taken from a *normal* distribution such that $X \sim N(\mu, \sigma^2)$ then

$$\overline{X} \sim N\left(\mu, \frac{\sigma^2}{n}\right)$$

The central limit theorem:

For large n, the result holds for a random sample taken from *any* distribution.

Distribution of the sample proportion P_s.

For large n, $\qquad\qquad P_s \sim N\left(p, \dfrac{pq}{n}\right)$

where p is the proportion of successes in the population,

$q = 1 - p$,

n is the number in the sample.

RANDOM SAMPLING

If we are to select an item *at random* from a population then we must ensure that each item in the population has an *equal chance* of being selected.

To obtain a random sample of n items we repeat n times the procedure for selecting one item. However, each selection must be independent of any other.

Example 8.23 Discuss how to select, at random, a sample of two people from a group of six.

Solution 8.23 Write the name of each person on one of six otherwise identical discs and mix them thoroughly in a hat. Without looking, select a disc, note the name and return it to the hat. Draw again. If the first name reappears, disregard it and repeat the procedure until a different name appears. The sample of two people is then obtained.

An alternative method might be to allocate to each person one of the numbers 1, 2, 3, 4, 5, 6 and then select the people corresponding to the numbers obtained on a die when it is thrown twice, for example (3, 5).

If the population is large then the method of 'drawing out of a hat' is obviously not practical. We can however allocate a number to each item and make the choice by referring to Random Number Tables, shown on page 724. If you have a random number generator

$\boxed{\text{Ran \#}}$ on your calculator you will be able to produce a random

3-digit number every time you press it.

NOTE: most random number tables are computer-generated. These numbers and the numbers produced on your calculator are known as 'pseudo' random numbers. However, they suit our purposes very well indeed.

RANDOM NUMBER TABLES

Random number tables consist of lists of digits 0, 1, 2, ..., 9 which are such that each digit has an *equal chance* of appearing at any stage. Since there are ten digits, each digit has a probability of $\frac{1}{10}$ of occuring.

In random number tables the digits may be listed individually, or grouped in some way. This is solely for convenience of printing. Here are some examples:

List (*a*)	6	8	7	2	5	3	8	1	5	9
	2	5	3	4	7	0	5	4	9	5
	3	2	6	8	7	4	4	7	0	5
List (*b*)	52	74	54	80	68	72	51	96	08	00
	02	52	09	93	60	43	57	42	13	44
List (*c*)	848051	386103	153842							
	242330	580007	479971							

These tables may be used to represent any number, discrete or continuous.

Example 8.24 Using random number tables, select at random a sample of 8 people from a group of 100.

Solution 8.24 Allocate a two-digit number to each person, for example 01 for the first on the list, 02 for the second, ..., to 98, 99, 00 (calling the hundredth person 00, for convenience).

Using list (*a*) above, we might select people corresponding to the following numbers:

68 72 53 81 59 25 34 70

Example 8.25   Choose 8 people from a group of 60.

Solution 8.25   Allocate each person with a number 01 to 60, then disregard any number outside this range. Using list (*a*)

~~68~~   ~~72~~   53   ~~81~~   59   25   34   ~~70~~   54   ~~95~~

32   ~~68~~   ~~74~~   47   05

So the people chosen will correspond to the numbers

53, 59, 25, 34, 54, 32, 47, 05

Example 8.26   Take a random sample of 12 numbers (to 2 d.p.) from the continuous range $0 \leqslant x < 10$.

Solution 8.26   We require the sample values to have 2 d.p. accuracy so we will need to consider groups of 3 digits, inserting the decimal point between the first and second digit. Using list (*b*) on page 455:

5.27, 4.54, 8.06, 8.72, 5.19, 6.08,
0.00, 2.52, 0.99, 3.60, 4.35, 7.42

Example 8.27   Take a random sample of 4 numbers (to 3 d.p.) from the continuous range $0 \leqslant x < 5$.

Solution 8.27   Using list (*c*) on page 455 and disregarding any values out of range, we have

~~8.480~~   ~~5.138~~   ~~6.103~~   1.538   4.224   2.330   ~~5.800~~   0.747

So the numbers chosen are

1.538, 4.224, 2.330, 0.747

SAMPLING FROM GIVEN DISTRIBUTIONS

(a) Frequency distributions

Example 8.28   Take a random sample of size 5 from the following distribution, using the random numbers 364294 588330 923918 400300.

x	1	2	3	4	
f	8	12	14	6	Total 40

Solution 8.28   Consider first the cumulative frequencies and then transfer them to proportional frequencies with a total proportion of 1. Random numbers can then be allocated in accordance with the cumulative proportional frequencies as shown:

x	1	2	3	4
f	8	12	14	6
Cumulative frequency	8	20	34	40
Cumulative proportional frequency	$\frac{8}{40} = 0.20$	$\frac{20}{40} = 0.50$	$\frac{34}{40} = 0.85$	$\frac{40}{40} = 1$
Corresponding random numbers	01 to 20	21 to 50	51 to 85	86 to 99 and 00

Since the proportional frequencies are all given to 2 d.p., we consider 2-digit random numbers. Note that 00 was allocated to the x-value of 4 for convenience.

Random numbers: 36, 42, 94, 58, 83

Sample value: 2,   2,   4,   3,   3

So a random sample of size 5 taken from the distribution gives sample values 2, 2, 3, 3, 4.

(b) Probability distributions

Example 8.29 A discrete random variable X has probability distribution

x	0	1	2	3
$P(X = x)$	0.1	0.2	0.4	0.3

Generate a random sample of size 10 from the distribution, using the random numbers 3, 7, 4, 7, 6, 5, 3, 3, 9, 0.

Solution 8.29 Form the cumulative distribution function $F(x)$ and then allocate random numbers in a convenient way:

x	0	1	2	3
$P(X = x)$	0.1	0.2	0.4	0.3
$F(x)$	0.1	0.3	0.7	1
Corresponding random numbers	1	2, 3	4, 5 6, 7	8, 9, 0

Taking 10 sample values, using the random numbers given, we have

Random number: 3, 7, 4, 7, 6, 5, 3, 3, 9, 0

Sample value: 1, 2, 2, 2, 2, 2, 1, 1, 3, 3

NOTE: we could have decided on a different allocation of the random numbers, for example

x	0	1	2	3
$F(x)$	0.1	0.3	0.7	1
Corresponding random numbers	0	1, 2	3, 4 5, 6	7, 8, 9

In this case, the sample generated would have been

Random number: 3, 7, 4, 7, 6, 5, 3, 3, 9, 0

Sample value: 2, 3, 2, 3, 2, 2, 2, 2, 3, 0

NOTE: when sampling from a given p.d.f. remember that every member of the population must have an equal chance of being selected. In each case, work with the cumulative distribution function $F(x)$. When we know $F(x)$ it is easy to allocate the random numbers.

Example 8.30 Take a random sample of four from a binomial distribution with parameters $n = 4$ and $p = 0.2$, using the random numbers 2811, 5747, 6157, 8988.

Solution 8.30 $X \sim \text{Bin}(4, 0.2)$. Since the given random numbers have 4 digits, we will work to 4 d.p.

$P(X = x)$	Cumulative distribution function, $F(x)$
$P(X = 0) = (0.8)^4 = 0.4096$	$F(0) = 0.4096$
$P(X = 1) = 4(0.8)^3(0.2) = 0.4096$	$F(1) = 0.8192$
$P(X = 2) = 6(0.8)^2(0.2)^2 = 0.1536$	$F(2) = 0.9728$
$P(X = 3) = 4(0.8)(0.2)^3 = 0.0256$	$F(3) = 0.9984$
$P(X = 4) = (0.2)^4 = 0.0016$	$F(4) = 1$ (as expected)

NOTE: we could have used the cumulative binomial probability tables to calculate values of $F(x)$.

Putting these results in table form, together with the corresponding random number allocation, we have:

x	0	1	2	3	4
$F(x)$	0.4096	0.8192	0.9728	0.9984	1
Corresponding random numbers	0001 to 4096	4097 to 8192	8193 to 9728	9729 to 9984	9985 to 9999, and 0000

The given number 2811 is in the range 0001 to 4096 and corresponds to $x = 0$.

Similarly 5747 corresponds to $x = 1$,

　　　　　6157 corresponds to $x = 1$,

and　　　8988 corresponds to $x = 2$.

So the random sample of four is 0, 1, 1, 2.

Example 8.31　Using the random number 8135 take a single random observation from a Poisson distribution with parameter 3.

Solution 8.31　$X \sim Po(3)$

We use the cumulative Poisson probabilities on page 720 with $\lambda = 3$.

Arranging the results in a table, together with the corresponding random number allocation, we have:

x	$F(x)$	Corresponding random numbers
0	0.0498	0001 to 0498
1	0.1991	0499 to 1991
2	0.4232	1992 to 4232
3	0.6472	4233 to 6472
4	0.8153	6473 to 8153
5	0.9161	8154 to 9161
6	0.9665	9162 to 9665
7	0.9881	9666 to 9881
8 or over	1	9882 to 9999 and 0000

The given random number 8135 is in the range 6473 to 8153, so the random observation corresponds to $x = 4$.

Example 8.32 Using the random numbers 723 850, take a random sample of size two from the continuous distribution whose p.d.f. is $f(x)$ where $f(x) = \frac{3}{8}x^2$ $(0 \leqslant x \leqslant 2)$.

Solution 8.32 The cumulative distribution function is given by

$$F(x) = \int_0^x \frac{3}{8}x^2 \,dx$$

$$= \frac{x^3}{8}$$

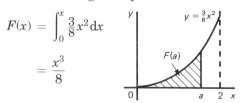

We use the given random numbers in the following way.

Taking the first three random numbers:

if $F(x) = 0.723$, then

$$\frac{x^3}{8} = 0.723$$

and $x = \sqrt[3]{8(0.723)} = 1.80$ (2 d.p.)

Taking the next three random numbers:

if $F(x) = 0.850$, then

$$\frac{x^3}{8} = 0.850$$

and $x = \sqrt[3]{8(0.850)} = 1.89$ (2 d.p.)

So the two random observations are $x = 1.80$ and $x = 1.89$.

Example 8.33 Use the random numbers 382 824 to take a random sample of two from the normal distribution N(30, 4).

Solution 8.33 $X \sim \text{N}(30, 4)$.

The cumulative distribution function is given by $\Phi(z)$ where

$$Z = \frac{X - 30}{2}$$

Now, taking the first three digits of the random number list:

if $\Phi(a) = 0.382$, then

$\qquad P(Z \leqslant a) = 0.382$

and $a = -0.3$

Therefore $\dfrac{x - 30}{2} = -0.3$

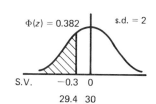

$$x = 30 - 0.6 = 29.4$$

Now take the second three digits:

if $\Phi(a) = 0.824$, then

$a = 0.931$

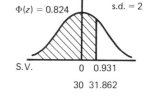

Therefore $\dfrac{x - 30}{2} = 0.931$

$$x = 30 + 1.862 = 31.862 = 31.9 \quad (1 \text{ d.p.})$$

So the two random observations are 29.4 and 31.9.

Exercise 8i

In the following, use the random number tables on page 720 if random numbers have not been given in the question.

1. Select a random sample of size 10 (to 3 d.p.) from the continuous range $3 \leqslant x < 9$.

2. Draw up a random sample of 100 numbers from the discrete integer range 0 to 9. Find the mean and variance of the sample values and compare them with the theoretical mean and variance.

3. The discrete random variable X has probability distribution

x	5	6	7	8	9
$P(X = x)$	0.15	0.2	0.33	0.21	0.11

Simulate a sample of size 12 from the distribution of X. Compare the mean and variance of this sample with $E(X)$ and $\text{Var}(X)$.

4. The discrete random variable X has distribution function $F(x) = \frac{1}{4}(x - 2)$, $x = 3, 4, 5, 6$. Using random number tables, generate 10 observations of X, showing your working clearly.
Describe how you would select a random sample of 30 pupils from a school containing 850 pupils.

5. You wish to select a person at random from a group of 58 people. The following procedure is suggested:
Allocate the numbers 1 to 58 to the people. Choose a line in a table of random numbers and call the first two digits x and y. Let $z = 10x + y$. If $1 \leqslant z \leqslant 58$ then the person who was allocated the number is selected. Otherwise, the person allocated the number $z - 58$ is selected. Comment on this method of selection.

6. Take a random sample of size 6 from the distribution:

x	15	16	17	18	19
f	13	15	12	6	4

7. Take a random sample of size 3 from the distribution:

x	2.3	2.4	2.5	2.6	2.7
f	40	60	90	50	60

8. Take a random sample of size 10 from each of the following probability distributions. In each case, find the sample mean and variance and compare with $E(X)$ and $\text{Var}(X)$.

   (a)

x	1	2	3	4
$P(X = x)$	0.11	0.2	0.45	0.24

   (b)

x	0.1	0.2	0.3
$P(X = x)$	0.175	0.214	0.329

x	0.4	0.5
$P(X = x)$	0.165	0.117

   (c) $P(X = x) = kx$, $x = 0, 1, 2, 3$.

9. Take a random sample of size 5 from the distribution of X where $F(x) = \frac{1}{5}x$, $x = 2, 3, 4, 5$.

10. (a) The discrete r.v. X is such that $X \sim \text{Bin}(3, 0.4)$. Take a random sample of size 5 from this distribution, using the random numbers

   407 315 401 203 972

   (b) Using the random number 6143 take a single random observation from the Poisson distribution with parameter 4.

11. Using the random numbers 267 394 018 take a random sample of size 3 from the normal distribution with mean 35 and variance 9.

12. Using the random numbers 2654 9342, make two random observations from each of the following distributions:
(a) The number of seeds that germinate in a group of 5 selected at random, given that 75% are expected to germinate.
(b) The number of goals in a football match, where the number of goals follows a Poisson distribution with variance 2.4.
(c) The mass of a bag of sugar, where the mass is normally distributed with mean 1010 g and standard deviation 4.5 g.

13. Using the random number 256 construct a random observation of the continuous r.v. X where
(a) $F(x) = \frac{1}{9}x^2$, $0 \leqslant x \leqslant 3$
(b) $F(x) = \frac{4}{15}x^3$, $1 \leqslant x \leqslant 2$

14. Take 20 samples, each of size 2, from the following distribution:

x	1	2	3	4	5
f	10	15	25	35	15

Calculate the mean of each sample and find the mean and variance of the sample means. Find the mean and variance of the original distribution. Comment.

15. The following table gives the frequency distribution of the number of telephone calls per minute received over a period of 2400 minutes at the switchboard of a solicitor's office.

No. of calls	0	1	2	3	4	5
Frequency	592	844	602	269	91	2

(a) Convert the frequencies to probabilities working correct to 4 decimal places. Hence draw up a table of cumulative probabilities.
(b) Using the table of random numbers provided, simulate the number of calls arriving at the switchboard in 30 consecutive minutes. Indicate precisely how your values have been obtained.
(c) Calculate the sample mean number of calls per minute. Given that the mean and standard deviation of the number of calls per minute obtained from the table are 1.345 and 1.087 respectively, calculate the probability of a random sample of 30 giving a mean value of at least that obtained from your sample.

16. The digits 8453276 are obtained from a table of random digits. Use them to obtain a random observation from each of the following distributions:
(a) the number of the winning ticket in a lottery in which there are 500 ticket numbers from 1 to 500 and every ticket has the same chance of being selected.
(b) the number of babies born in a cottage hospital in a week, assuming that on average one baby is born every 3 days and that births are independent (and ignoring the possibility of multiple births),
(c) the time between successive emissions of a particle from a radioactive substance, assuming that the probability density function of this time is $2e^{-2t}(t > 0)$.   (O)

17. You are given the random number 431. Use this number to obtain a sample observation from
(a) a Binomial distribution with $n = 12$ and $p = 0.4$.
(b) a Normal distribution with mean 6.2 and standard deviation 0.1.
You are expected to explain clearly how you obtain the sample observations.   (O)

SAMPLING METHODS

POPULATION

In statistical enquiry we usually need information about a particular group of people or items. This group is known as a **population**. It could be small or large or even infinite. Some examples of populations are:

- pupils in a class,

- people in England who are in full-time employment,

- hospitals in Wales,

– cans of soft drink produced in a factory,

– worms in a garden,

– rational numbers between 0 and 10.

SURVEYS

Information is collected by means of a **survey**. There are two types:

(**a**) a census

(**b**) a sample survey.

(a) A census

If *every member* of the population is surveyed, this is known as a **census**. When the population is small, this could be a straight-forward exercise. For example, it would be easy to find out how each pupil in a class had travelled to school that morning. When populations are large, taking a census can be very time-consuming. The census carried out annually by the Department of Education registers the number of boys and girls in each age group on the roll of every school on the third Thursday in January, and its accuracy relates only to that day. Even more difficult to carry out accurately is the population census taken in Britain every ten years. This attempts to provide details for different age groups for every area of the country.

When populations are very large, or infinite, it is not possible to survey every member. Also, in some circumstances it would not be sensible to carry out a census. For example, to try to establish the length of life of 'Extra-bright' light bulbs, a census would destroy the population!

(b) A sample survey

When a survey covers less than 100% of the population, it is known as a **sample survey**. In many circumstances, taking a sample will be preferable to carrying out a census. Sample data can be obtained relatively cheaply and quickly and if the sample is representative of the population, a sample survey can give an accurate indication of the population characteristic being studied.

SAMPLE DESIGN

Target population

Once the purpose of a survey has been stated precisely, the **target population** must be defined, for example

– all the primary schools in England,

– all the oak trees in Hampshire,

– all the people admitted to St Mary's Hospital last year, suffering from a heart attack.

Sampling units

The **sampling units** must be defined clearly. These are the people or items to be sampled, for example

- the primary school,
- the oak tree,
- the person suffering from a heart attack.

Care must be taken in defining the sampling unit.

In an enquiry about types of washing machine purchased, the correct sampling unit would be the household, rather than the individual, to ensure that individuals from the same household did not report on the same item. If you were trying to estimate the average amount held in accounts at a particular bank, you would need to make sure that only one representative of an account was questioned, so that for example, you did not ask both the husband and the wife who had a joint account. However if your survey concerned opinions about the bank's efficiency, you would require opinions from individuals and could ask both the husband and the wife.

Sampling frame

A **sampling frame** is then compiled. This is an enumeration of the population by sampling units. It could take the form of a list or a map or set of maps. Ideally the sampling frame should be the same as the target population.

For example, if the population constitutes 'the pupils in a school' then the sampling frame would be the school roll, which would give the names of all the pupils. This would be easy to obtain.

A sampling frame for the people eligible to vote is more difficult to form. The electoral register attempts to list all those eligible to vote throughout all the areas in the country, but it is never 100% accurate. Many changes occur during the time that the information is being processed; people move in and out of the area, people die, and some do not return the appropriate forms.

In some instances it is not possible to enumerate all the population, for example 'fish in a reservoir'.

A sampling frame should be as accurate and up-to-date as possible; care must be taken to ensure that it is free from omissions or duplications.

Bias

The purpose of sampling is to gain information about the whole population from a smaller group or sample. We want the sample to be representative of the population so we must try to eliminate any bias in its selection.

Sources of bias include

(**a**) the lack of a good sampling frame:

- using the telephone directory misses all those who do not have a telephone or whose number is ex-directory,
- using the electoral register in a city area misses the more mobile section of the population.

(**b**) the wrong choice of sampling unit;

- choosing an individual rather than a particular group such as 'household' or 'account'.

(**c**) non-response by some of the chosen units:

- it may be difficult to locate the particular unit,
- the co-operation of the respondent may not have been obtained,
- the enquiry may not have been understood, for example a questionnaire may have been badly designed. Questionnaires should be clear, specific, unambiguous and easily understood. Questions should be worded neutrally, especially in opinion surveys, to avoid bias caused by pointing towards a particular response.

(**d**) bias introduced by the person conducting the survey:

- the interviewer may not question someone who does not appear co-operative,
- the interviewer's style of questioning may influence the response.

It should be noted that a sample can only be representative of the population from which it was selected. For example, if we select a sample of teachers from one school, the sample is representative of teachers in *that* school, not of all teachers in all schools.

SAMPLING METHODS

Once a sampling frame has been established we can choose a method of sampling. These fall into two categories: random and non-random. We shall consider a few types of each of these methods:

Random samples: simple, systematic, stratified
Non-random samples: quota, cluster.

RANDOM SAMPLING

When items are selected at random, each member of the population has an *equal chance* of being selected.

Each member of the sampling frame is allocated a number and the sample is selected using random numbers obtained either from random number tables or generated by a computer or calculator. This method was discussed on pages 455–7.

(1) Simple random sampling with or without replacement

Suppose we draw a number from a hat. We have the choice of replacing the number in the hat before drawing again, or of not replacing it.

Sampling where each item may be chosen more than once is called **sampling with replacement**.

Sampling where each item may *not* be chosen more than once is called **sampling without replacement**.

We have seen already (page 438) that if a sample of size n is taken *with replacement* from a population with mean μ and variance σ^2, then

$$E(\overline{X}) = \mu \quad \text{and} \quad \text{Var}(\overline{X}) = \frac{\sigma^2}{n}.$$

Also (page 441) if a sample of size n is taken *without replacement* from a population of size N with mean μ and variance σ^2, then

$$E(\overline{X}) = \mu \quad \text{and} \quad \text{Var}(\overline{X}) = \frac{\sigma^2}{n}\left(\frac{N-n}{N-1}\right)$$

In each case, the expectation of $\overline{X}$ is equal to μ, so if we wish to compare the two methods we look at the variances.

Now $$N - n < N - 1 \quad \text{since} \quad n > 1$$

Therefore $$\frac{N-n}{N-1} < 1$$

and $$\frac{\sigma^2}{n}\left(\frac{N-n}{N-1}\right) < \frac{\sigma^2}{n}$$

So the variance of mean without replacement is smaller than the variance of mean with replacement.

Now variance measures the tendency of a random variable to stray from its expected value or mean. So $\overline{X}$ has a tendency to stay closer to μ when sampling is *without* replacement.

Therefore sampling without replacement is more precise than sampling with replacement.

Example 8.34 Listed below are the numbers of books read during one particular month by each of the 30 children in the class of a teacher.

6	9	10	4	7	5
7	8	3	5	8	9
8	7	1	7	7	6
6	8	3	7	7	4
1	6	8	8	3	2

(a) Calculate the mean and the variance of this population.

(b) Using a table of random numbers, take a random sample of size 6 of the number of books read

(i) without replacement,

(ii) with replacement.

In each case, calculate the sample mean and the standard error of the mean, giving all your answers to 2 decimal places.

(c) State, giving a reason, which of these methods is the better one for estimating the population mean.   (L)P

Solution 8.34 (a) By calculator $\mu = 6$, $\sigma^2 = 5.6$

(b) Allocate two-digit numbers to each child as follows:

6 (01)	9 (02)	10 (03)	4 (04)	7 (05)	5 (06)
7 (07)	8 (08)	3 (09)	5 (10)	8 (11)	9 (12)
8 (13)	7 (14)	1 (15)	7 (16)	7 (17)	6 (18)
6 (19)	8 (20)	3 (21)	7 (22)	7 (23)	4 (24)
1 (25)	6 (26)	8 (27)	8 (28)	3 (29)	2 (30)

Now using part of the table of Random Numbers (page 724) and disregarding numbers over 30 we have

65 ㉓ 68 00	77 82 58 ⑭	⑩ 85 ⑪ 85	57 ⑪ 73 74	45 ㉕ 50 46
⑨ 56 76 51	04 73 94 30	16 74 69 59	04 38 83 98	30 20 87 85
55 99 98 60	01 33 06 93	85 13 23 17	25 51 92 04	52 31 38 70
72 82 45 44	09 53 04 83	03 83 98 41	67 41 01 38	66 83 11 99
04 21 28 72	73 25 02 74	35 81 78 49	52 67 61 40	60 50 47 50

(i) *Without replacement*

The row of random numbers gives

$$23, \quad 14, \quad 10, \quad 11, \quad ⑪, \quad 25, \quad 09$$

$$\uparrow$$

Used before, so we cannot use it again

So the sample of six numbers without replacement is

$$23, \quad 14, \quad 10, \quad 11, \quad 25, \quad 09$$

Referring to the original data, this gives

$$7, \quad 7, \quad 5, \quad 8, \quad 1, \quad 3$$

Using a calculator:

Sample mean = 5.17 (2 d.p.)

Now
$$\text{standard error} = \frac{\sigma}{\sqrt{n}} \sqrt{\frac{N-n}{N-1}}$$

where
$$N = 30, \quad n = 6, \quad \sigma = \sqrt{5.6}$$

so
$$\text{standard error} = \frac{\sqrt{5.6}}{\sqrt{6}} \sqrt{\frac{24}{29}} = 0.88 \quad (2 \text{ d.p.})$$

(ii) *With replacement*

The sample of six numbers with replacement is

$$23, \quad 14, \quad 10, \quad 11, \quad 11, \quad 25$$

This gives

$$7, \quad 7, \quad 5, \quad 8, \quad 8, \quad 1$$

Therefore sample mean = 6,

$$\text{standard error} = \frac{\sigma}{\sqrt{n}} = \sqrt{\frac{5.6}{6}} = 0.97 \ (2 \text{ d.p.})$$

(c) Even though the 'with replacement' method gives the exact value, in this instance, for the population mean, the standard error for the 'without replacement' method is smaller. For a large number of samples chosen in a similar way, the 'without replacement' method would give the more precise estimate for μ.

(2) Systematic sampling

Random sampling from a very large population is cumbersome. An alternative procedure is to list the population in some order, for example alphabetically or in order of completion on a production line, and then choose every kth member from the list after obtaining a random starting point.

For example, if we chose every 10th member on the list, we should form a 10% sample, and if we chose every 20th member we should form a 5% sample. Such a procedure is called **systematic sampling**. Examples of this are to choose every 20th vehicle coming along a road, or every 5th card in an index file.

Example 8.35 Describe how to choose a systematic sample of 30 from a population of 100 items.

Solution 8.35 Now $\frac{100}{30} = 3.\dot{3}$

so every time we select an item we need to move $3.\dot{3}$ places along the list.

A random start between 1 and 3 inclusive is chosen. Let this be 2.

So we would select the 2nd item

Then
$$2 + 3.\dot{3} = 5.\dot{3} \quad \longrightarrow \quad \text{5th item}$$
$$5.\dot{3} + 3.\dot{3} = 8.\dot{6} \quad \longrightarrow \quad \text{9th item}$$
$$8.\dot{6} + 3.\dot{3} = 12 \quad \longrightarrow \quad \text{12th item}$$
$$\ldots$$

and so on until
$$88.\dot{6} + 3.\dot{3} = 92 \quad \longrightarrow \quad \text{92nd item}$$
$$92 + 3.\dot{3} = 95.\dot{3} \quad \longrightarrow \quad \text{95th item}$$
$$95.\dot{3} + 3.\dot{3} = 98.\dot{6} \quad \longrightarrow \quad \text{99th item}$$

giving 30 items in all.

The advantages of systematic sampling are that it is quick to use and it is easy to check for errors. It is much simpler to select every 10th plant in a row than to deal with random numbers. In fact, for large scale sampling, systematic selection is usually used in preference to taking simple random samples.

The disadvantage of this system is that there may be a periodic cycle within the frame itself. For example, say that every 10th item produced by a particular machine is faulty. Systematic sampling of every 5th item, starting at 5, would result in half the items in the sample being faulty, whereas starting at the 2nd item would produce no faulty items in the sample. Of course, if the periodic cycle is recognised then different samples could be taken by varying the starting point and the length of interval between chosen items.

(3) Stratified sampling

This form of sampling is used when the population is split into distinguishable layers or 'strata' which are quite different from each other and which together cover the whole population, for example:

- age groups,
- occupational groups,
- topographical regions.

Separate random samples are then taken from each of the strata and put together to form the sample from the population.

It is usual to have the strata from the population represented proportionately in the sample.

Example 8.36 A certain firm employs 320 drivers, 80 office workers and 40 mechanics. It is required to select a committee of 11 to represent all the employees. Describe how this selection might be made in order to give as close a representation as possible without any bias towards individuals.

Solution 8.36 If we were to take a simple random sample of all 440 employees this would mean that every employee would have an equal chance of being selected. The committee could then easily consist of 11 drivers and would not therefore represent the opinion of all employees.

A stratified random sample will provide a more accurate representation of the population as follows:

Drivers make up $\frac{320}{440}$ of the total.

Therefore,   number of drivers on the committee

$$= \frac{320}{440} \times 11 = 8$$

Similarly,   number of office workers $= \frac{80}{440} \times 11 = 2$

and   number of mechanics $= \frac{40}{440} \times 11 = 1$

The required numbers are 8, 2 and 1.

The people to be included can then be selected from each 'stratum' or group by using simple random sampling or systematic sampling.

In general, the items in each stratum are much more similar to each other than items chosen from the whole population. So if we estimate the mean of each stratum separately and then combine these estimates to give an overall mean, the variance of that mean would be much less than that obtained using a simple random sample. Provided that the population can be split into distinguishable strata, a stratified sample will be more precise than a simple random sample.

Example 8.37 A population consists of the numbers

$$3, \quad 4, \quad 4, \quad 5, \quad 7, \quad 9, \quad 10, \quad 14.$$

(**a**) Calculate the mean and variance of this population.

A random sample of size 4 is taken *with* replacement from this population.

(**b**) Calculate the variance of the sample mean.

A random sample of 4 numbers is taken *without* replacement.

(**c**) Calculate the variance of the sample mean.

$\left(\text{When sampling without replacement from a population of size } N,\right.$
the variance of the sample mean is $\left. \dfrac{N-n}{N-1} \cdot \dfrac{\sigma^2}{n}. \right)$

The numbers are then split into 2 groups as follows:

       Group 1: 3, 4, 4, 5

       Group 2: 7, 9, 10, 14.

(**d**) Calculate the variance of the numbers in each group.

A sample of size 4 is obtained by independently selecting 2 numbers, at random, *without* replacement, from each of the two groups. The population mean is to be estimated by

$$Y = \tfrac{1}{2}(\overline{X}_1 + \overline{X}_2),$$

where $\overline{X}_1$ and $\overline{X}_2$ are the *sample* means of the two groups.

(**e**) Find the variance of Y.

(**f**) State, giving a reason, which of the three samples is likely to give the best estimate of the population mean. (L)

Solution 8.37 Population 3, 4, 4, 5, 7, 9, 10, 14

(**a**) By calculator,

population mean $= 7$, population variance $= 12.5$

(**b**) For a random sample, size 4, taken with replacement, variance of sample mean is given by

$$\text{variance} = \frac{\sigma^2}{n} \quad \text{where} \quad \sigma^2 = 12.5, \quad n = 4$$

i.e. variance $= \dfrac{12.5}{4} = 3.125$

(**c**) For a random sample, size 4, taken without replacement, variance of the sample mean is given by

$$\text{variance} = \frac{\sigma^2}{n}\left(\frac{N-n}{N-1}\right) = \frac{12.5}{4}\left(\frac{8-4}{8-1}\right) = 1.786 \ \ (3 \text{ d.p.})$$

(**d**) Group 1: 3, 4, 4, 5 variance $= 0.5 = \sigma_1^{\,2}$

Group 2: 7, 9, 10, 14 variance $= 6.5 = \sigma_2^{\,2}$

(**e**) We now take a proportionate stratified sample of size 4 by taking a sample of 2 from each stratum (Group 1 and Group 2). Note that the numbers in each group are similar to each other and form two distinguishable strata. Between them, they cover the complete population.

The estimate of the population mean is

$$Y = \tfrac{1}{2}(\overline{X}_1 + \overline{X}_2)$$

Now $\qquad \text{Var}(Y) = \tfrac{1}{4}\text{Var}(\overline{X}_1) + \tfrac{1}{4}\text{Var}(\overline{X}_2)$

Also $\qquad \text{Var}(\overline{X}_1) = \dfrac{\sigma_1^{\,2}}{2}\left(\dfrac{4-2}{4-1}\right) = \dfrac{0.5}{2}\left(\dfrac{2}{3}\right) = 0.1\dot{6}$

$\qquad\qquad \text{Var}(\overline{X}_2) = \dfrac{\sigma_2^{\,2}}{2}\left(\dfrac{4-2}{4-1}\right) = \dfrac{6.5}{2}\left(\dfrac{2}{3}\right) = 2.1\dot{6}$

Therefore variance of stratified estimate is

$$\text{Var}\,(Y) = \tfrac{1}{4}(0.1\dot{6} + 2.1\dot{6}) = \underline{0.583\ (3\ \text{d.p.})}$$

(**f**) The variance of the stratified estimate is much smaller than the random sample variances and so provides the most precise estimate of the population mean.

The next best estimate is the random sample, size 4, taken without replacement; then last of all, the random sample taken with replacement.

NON-RANDOM SAMPLING

(1) Cluster sampling

Sometimes there is a natural subgrouping of the population. These subgroups are called **clusters**. For example, if the population consists of all children in the country attending state primary schools, then the local education authorities form natural clusters.

When a sample survey is carried out on a population which can be broken down into clusters, it is often more convenient to first choose a random sample of clusters and then to sample within each cluster chosen.

Unlike stratified sampling, where the strata are as *different* from each other as possible, each cluster should be as *similar* to other clusters as possible.

One advantage of cluster sampling is that there is no need to have a complete sampling frame of the whole population. In the example given, we would need only a list of pupils in the chosen local education authority. Cluster sampling is usually far less costly than random sampling. For example, consider the fees paid to interviewers and travelling expenses. If interviewers have to visit individuals in a cluster this involves far less travelling and time than visiting individuals in the whole population.

The disadvantage of cluster sampling is that it is non-random. For example, suppose that a town has 7500 primary school children in 250 classes, each with an average size of 30. If we wanted to select a sample of 90 children then we could use simple random sampling. However it would be quicker to use the classes as clusters and to take a sample of 3 clusters. This would give us a sample of 90 children.

The problem is that within each class there will be a certain amount of similarity between the children, such as: similar age; perhaps similar ability group; living in the same area. By selecting one whole class or cluster we are in fact selecting 30 similar children instead of 30 randomly chosen children from throughout the town. Therefore 3 clusters will not give as precise a picture of the whole population as 90 children chosen at random from 7500.

(2) Quota sampling

Quota sampling is very widely used in market research. First the population is divided into groups in terms of age, sex, income level and so on. Then the interviewer is told how many people to interview within each specified group but is given no specific instructions about how to locate them and fulfil the quota. This is the method generally used in street interview surveys commonly carried out in shopping centres. It is quick to use, complications are kept to a minimum and, unlike random sampling, any member of the sample can be replaced by another member with the same characteristics.

If no sampling frame exists, then quota sampling may be the only practical method of obtaining a sample. However, the disadvantage of quota sampling is that it is completely non-random. There is a real possibility of bias in the selection process, with the interviewer selecting those easiest to question, perhaps those who look more co-operative. The location of such surveys in shopping centres automatically excludes a substantial part of the population of an area. Also it is difficult to find out about those who will not co-operate and these are just replaced. High refusal rates by Conservative voters to take part in the surveys is one of the reasons put forward to explain the inaccuracy of the opinion polls for the British General Election in 1992.

Exercise 8j

1. Explain briefly the difference between a census and a sample survey.
Give an example to illustrate the practical use of each method.
A school held an evening disco which was attended by 500 pupils. The disco organisers were keen to assess the success of the evening. Having decided to obtain information from those attending the disco, they were undecided whether to use a census or a sample survey.
Which method would you recommend them to use?
Give one advantage and one disadvantage associated with your recommendation.   (L)

2. A school of 1000 pupils is divided into year groups as follows

Year	Number of pupils
7	150
8	150
9	150
10	150
11	150
12	125
13	125

A survey is to be carried out and a committee representative of the school is to be formed consisting of 40 pupils.
It is decided that stratified sampling should be used.
(a) Calculate the number of pupils chosen from each year group.
(b) Explain how to choose the pupils from Year 7.

3. (a) Explain briefly
(i) why it is often desirable to take samples,
(ii) what you understand by a sampling frame.
(b) State two circumstances when you would consider using
(i) clustering,
(ii) stratification,
when sampling from a population.
(c) Give two advantages and two disadvantages associated with quota sampling.   (L)

4. (i) A television company wishes to estimate the popularity of a particular television series by street interviews. Describe how the method of *quota sampling* might be used for this investigation.

(ii) A meat canning factory supplies a supermarket with cans of meat in three sizes — large, medium and small. The regular consignment is of 300 large cans, 500 medium cans and 400 small cans. Describe how the supermarket could apply the method of *stratified random sampling* to a sample of 60 cans to test the quality of these goods.

5. Write brief notes on
(*a*) simple random sampling,
(*b*) quota sampling.
Your notes should include a description of each method, and an advantage and a disadvantage associated with it.   (L)

6. Listed below are the daily numbers of pupils, *x*, absent from school during a period of 30 consecutive school days.

8	12	11	9	7	6
9	5	10	10	11	7
10	3	9	9	8	9
8	5	10	9	6	9
3	10	8	5	4	10

(*a*) Calculate the mean and variance of this population.

$$\left(\text{Use } \sum x^2 = 2088\right)$$

(*b*) Use the *first row* of the table of random numbers (p. 720) to take a random sample of size 6 *without* replacement.
(*c*) Use the *second row* of the same table to take a random sample of size 6 *with* replacement.
(*d*) For each of your samples, find the sample mean and the standard error of the mean, giving your answers to 2 decimal places.

$\Big($ When sampling without replacement from a population of size N, the variance of the sample mean is $\dfrac{N-n}{N-1} \cdot \dfrac{\sigma^2}{n}$.$\Big)$

(*e*) State, giving a reason, which of these methods is the better one for estimating the population mean.   (L)

7. In a school year group of 140 pupils there are 60 girls and 80 boys. A survey is to be taken to find methods to improve the school's meal services. A sample of 14 members of this group is needed for the survey.
The school decides to use one of the following methods to obtain the names of pupils for the sample:
A: Every 10th name on the year group register is selected for the sample.
B: Each of the 140 names is allocated a different number from 1 to 140 inclusive; the school's computer then picks 14 different random numbers between 1 and 140 inclusive.

(i) State *briefly* one advantage and one disadvantage of each method.
(ii) Explain what is meant by a stratified random sample and describe how method B could be changed to give a stratified random sample.

8. (*a*) Give one advantage and one disadvantage of using
(i) a census,
(ii) a survey.
(*b*) It is decided to take a sample of 100 from a population consisting of 5000 elements. Explain how you would obtain a simple random sample without replacement from this population.   (L)P

9. The 25 members of a City Council were asked to record over a twenty-day period the number of days on which they made a journey by public transport. The results are given below, *c* indicating that the councillor was a car owner.

0c	0c	5c	1c	0c
2c	0c	0c	6c	1c
0c	1c	3c	8c	0c
15	12	9	16	17
11	4	3	9	11

(*a*) Calculate the arithmetic mean and the standard deviation of the population.
(*b*) Explaining fully the procedure you have followed use the extract from a table of random sampling numbers at the end of the question to
(i) take an unrestricted random sample (i.e. allow the same person to be chosen more than once) of size 5 from the population. Calculate the sample mean and state its standard deviation.
(ii) take a simple random sample (i.e. do not allow the same person to be chosen more than once) of size 5 from the population. Calculate the sample mean and state its standard deviation.
(*c*) A councillor suggests that an alternative way of estimating the population mean would be to make up the sample of 5 by taking a simple random sample of size 3 from the car owners and one of size 2 from the rest. Rank the three methods for estimating the mean in order of preference, explaining your choice.

Extract from table of random sampling numbers
70209 23316 32828 00920 61841 64754
94342 91090 94035 02650 36284 91162

(AEB 1987)

10. Write brief notes on
    (*a*) simple random sampling,
    (*b*) stratified sampling,
    (*c*) cluster sampling.
    Your notes should include a definition of the method, how it might be implemented and any advantages or disadvantages associated with it.

11. Explain *briefly* the difference between a *census* and a *sample*, and give **two** reasons why a sample may be preferred to a census. Explain the meaning and purpose of a *sampling frame* in random sampling.
    It is required to obtain the views of the pupils of a school about the school magazine. It is decided to do this by means of a small panel of pupils.
    Describe **briefly** how you would select such a panel using
    (*a*) simple random sampling,
    (*b*) stratified random sampling.
    State, with a reason, which of these two sampling methods you consider to be the more appropriate for this situation.
    (AEB 1991)

12. A research study into the use of hormone replacement therapy for women in the United Kingdom involved a survey of women in three general medical practices in Greater London. The designer of the survey describes his method of obtaining his sample as follows.
    "I obtained the names and addresses of 5025 women aged between 45 and 65 from the practices' age–sex registers. The women were sent a questionnaire that asked whether they had received hormone replacement therapy."

    Source: *British Medical Journal,*
    December 1989

    (i) Suggest *one* advantage and *one* disadvantage of this sampling method.
    (ii) Of the 5025 women contacted, 3238 returned a completed questionnaire, and 330 of these had received hormone replacement therapy. Given that there are approximately 703 000 women in the 45–65 age group living in Greater London, obtain an estimate for the number of 45–65 year old women in Greater London who have received hormone replacement therapy. With reference to the sampling method used, comment on the reliability of this estimate.
    (iii) Suggest an alternative method of obtaining such an estimate.   (JMB)

9

ESTIMATION OF POPULATION PARAMETERS

In order to define a binomial distribution we need to know n and p, and to define a Poisson distribution we need λ.

n, p and λ are known as **parameters**. Here is a summary of some of the distributions encountered so far and their parameters.

Distribution		Parameters
Binomial	$X \sim \text{Bin}(n, p)$	n and p
Poisson	$X \sim \text{Po}(\lambda)$	λ
Geometric	$X \sim \text{Geo}(p)$	p
Rectangular	$X \sim \text{R}(a, b)$	a and b
Normal	$X \sim \text{N}(\mu, \sigma^2)$	μ and σ^2

We now consider what to do when a parameter of a distribution is *unknown*.

Suppose that a population has an unknown parameter, such as the mean, or the variance, or the proportion of 'successes'. We take a random sample (or samples) from the population and make an *estimate* of the unknown parameter from this.

A statistic used to estimate the value of a parameter is called an **estimator** and it is denoted by a capital letter (e.g. U, T, ...). The numerical value taken by the estimator in a particular instance is called an **estimate** and is denoted by a small letter (e.g. u, t, ...).

POINT ESTIMATION — UNBIASED ESTIMATOR

Since we are considering, in the first instance, a general unknown parameter, we use a general symbol, θ say.

> Consider a population with unknown parameter θ.
>
> If U is some statistic derived from a random sample taken from the population, then U is an **unbiased estimator** for θ if
>
> $$E(U) = \theta$$

There are many estimators which could be formed, but the *best (or most efficient) estimator* is the one which is unbiased and has the smallest variance.

Example 9.1   If X_1, X_2, X_3 is a random sample of three independent observations taken from a population with mean μ and variance σ^2, find which of the following estimators for μ are unbiased, and which is the most efficient of these.

$$T_1 = \frac{X_1 + X_2 + X_3}{3}, \quad T_2 = \frac{X_1 + 2X_2}{3}, \quad T_3 = \frac{X_1 + 2X_2 + 3X_3}{3}$$

Solution 9.1   Now $\qquad\qquad E(X_i) = \mu \quad \text{for} \quad i = 1, 2, 3$

So $\qquad\qquad E(T_1) = E\left(\frac{X_1 + X_2 + X_3}{3}\right)$

$$= \tfrac{1}{3}[E(X_1) + E(X_2) + E(X_3)]$$

$$= \tfrac{1}{3}(3\mu)$$

$$= \mu$$

Since $E(T_1) = \mu$, T_1 is an unbiased estimator for μ.

Now $\qquad\qquad E(T_2) = E\left(\frac{X_1 + 2X_2}{3}\right)$

$$= \tfrac{1}{3}[E(X_1) + 2E(X_2)]$$

$$= \tfrac{1}{3}(\mu + 2\mu)$$

$$= \mu$$

Since $E(T_2) = \mu$, T_2 is an unbiased estimator for μ.

Now $\qquad\qquad E(T_3) = E\left(\frac{X_1 + 2X_2 + 3X_3}{3}\right)$

$$= \tfrac{1}{3}[E(X_1) + 2E(X_2) + 3E(X_3)]$$

$$= \tfrac{1}{3}(\mu + 2\mu + 3\mu)$$

$$= 2\mu$$

Since $E(T_3) \neq \mu$, T_3 is not an unbiased estimator for μ.

The more efficient of the two estimators is the one which has the smaller variance.

Now
$$\text{Var}(T_1) = \text{Var}\left(\frac{X_1 + X_2 + X_3}{3}\right)$$

$$= \frac{1}{9}[\text{Var}(X_1) + \text{Var}(X_2) + \text{Var}(X_3)]$$

$$= \frac{3\sigma^2}{9}$$

and
$$\text{Var}(T_2) = \text{Var}\left(\frac{X_1 + 2X_2}{3}\right)$$

$$= \frac{1}{9}[\text{Var}(X_1) + 4\text{Var}(X_2)]$$

$$= \frac{5\sigma^2}{9}$$

Since $\text{Var}(T_1) < \text{Var}(T_2)$, T_1 is a more efficient estimator for μ than T_2.

Exercise 9a

1. If X_1, X_2, X_3 is a random sample taken from a population with mean μ and variance σ^2, find which of the following estimators for μ are unbiased:

    (a) $U_1 = \frac{1}{4}X_1 + \frac{1}{2}X_2 + \frac{1}{4}X_3$

    (b) $U_2 = \frac{1}{3}X_1 + \frac{3}{5}X_2$

    (c) $U_3 = \frac{4}{5}X_1 + \frac{1}{10}X_2 + \frac{1}{10}X_3$

    (d) $U_4 = \frac{1}{6}X_1 + \frac{2}{3}X_2 + \frac{1}{2}X_3$

    (e) $U_5 = \frac{1}{3}(X_1 + X_2 + X_3)$

2. Of the unbiased estimators given in Question 1, which is the most efficient estimator?

3. If $X_1, X_2, \ldots, X_n$ is a random sample taken from a population with mean μ and variance σ^2, show that

    (a) $\frac{1}{n}(X_1 + X_2 + \ldots + X_n)$ is an unbiased and consistent estimator for μ,

    (b) $\dfrac{X_1 + 2X_2 + \ldots + nX_n}{n(n+1)/2}$ is an unbiased and consistent estimator for μ.

MOST EFFICIENT ESTIMATORS FOR POPULATION PARAMETERS

We now consider the most efficient estimators of three important population parameters: the population mean, variance and proportion of 'successes'.

(a) Population mean

From a population with *unknown* mean μ, take a random sample of size n, and consider the sample mean $\overline{X}$, where

$$\overline{X} = \frac{1}{n}\sum X_i \quad \text{for} \quad i = 1, 2, \ldots, n$$

> The most efficient estimator for μ, which we will write as $\hat{\mu}$, is $\overline{X}$, the sample mean.
>
> We write $\qquad \hat{\mu} = \overline{X}$

$\overline{X}$ is unbiased, since $E(\overline{X}) = \mu$.

Note that $\text{Var}(\overline{X}) = \dfrac{\sigma^2}{n} \to 0$ as $n \to \infty$

(b) Population variance

From a population with *unknown* variance σ^2, take a random sample of size n, and consider the sample variance S^2.

> The most efficient estimator for σ^2, which we will write as $\hat{\sigma}^2$, is given by
>
> $$\hat{\sigma}^2 = \frac{nS^2}{n-1}$$

NOTE: this is a surprising result; you might have expected $\hat{\sigma}^2 = S^2$, but this is not the case.

Important note about notation

We are using the notation $\hat{\sigma}^2$ for the estimator of the population variance, and S^2 for the sample variance. However, in some texts, S^2 is used for the estimator of σ^2 and no particular notation is used for the sample variance. To avoid confusion, we will define S^2 as the sample variance each time it is used.

Alternative format for $\hat{\sigma}^2$

Now $S^2 = \dfrac{\sum(X - \overline{X})^2}{n}$, where S^2 is the sample variance,

so $nS^2 = \sum(X - \overline{X})^2$

Therefore
$$\hat{\sigma}^2 = \frac{\sum(X - \overline{X})^2}{n-1}$$

(c) **Population proportion**

From a population in which p, the proportion of 'successes' is *unknown*, take a random sample of size n and consider the proportion of successes in the sample, P_s.

> The most efficient estimator for p, which we will write as $\hat{p}$, is P_s, the proportion of successes in the sample.
>
> We write $\qquad \hat{p} = P_s$

Now P_s is unbiased, since $E(P_s) = p$ (see page 451).

Note that $\quad \text{Var}(P_s) = \dfrac{pq}{n} \to 0 \quad$ as $\quad n \to \infty$

NOTE: when developing the theory we have considered the **estimators** $\overline{X}, S, P_s$ which are **random variables**, so we have used capital letters.

When applying the theory we are often required to find a **numerical value** taken by the estimator, i.e. an **estimate** and in this case we use small letters, $\overline{x}, s, p_s$.

Example 9.2   Obtain the most efficient estimates of the population mean and variance from which the following sample is drawn:

$$19.30, \quad 19.61, \quad 18.27, \quad 18.90, \quad 19.14, \quad 19.90, \quad 18.76, \quad 19.10$$

Solution 9.2   The best estimate of the population mean is $\hat{\mu}$ where $\hat{\mu} = \overline{x}$, the sample mean.

Now $\qquad\qquad\qquad \overline{x} = \dfrac{\sum x}{n} = \dfrac{152.98}{8} = 19.1225$

So $\qquad\qquad\qquad \hat{\mu} = \overline{x}$

$$= 19.1225$$

The best estimate of the population variance is $\hat{\sigma}^2$, where $\hat{\sigma}^2 = \dfrac{ns^2}{(n-1)}$ and s^2 is the sample variance.

Now $\qquad s^2 = \dfrac{\sum x^2}{n} - \overline{x}^2 = \dfrac{2927.1}{8} - \left(\dfrac{152.98}{8}\right)^2 = 0.217\ldots$

So $\qquad\qquad \hat{\sigma}^2 = \dfrac{ns^2}{n-1} = \tfrac{8}{7}s^2 = 0.25 \quad \text{(2 d.p.)}$

The most efficient estimate of the population mean is 19.1225 and of the population variance is 0.25 (2 d.p.)

USE OF CALCULATOR TO FIND $\hat{\sigma}$

We do, in fact, have access to $\hat{\sigma}$ directly when using the calculator in SD mode.

	Casio 85/100/115	**Casio 7000 GA Graphic**
Set SD mode	MODE 3	MODE ×
Clear memries	SHIFT KAC	SHIFT SCI EXE
Input data	19.30 DATA	19.30 DT
	19.61 DATA	19.61 DT
	18.27 DATA	18.27 DT
	19.14 DATA	19.14 DT
	19.90 DATA	19.90 DT
	18.76 DATA	18.76 DT
	19.10 DATA	19.10 DT
To obtain $\bar{x}$	SHIFT 1	SHIFT 1 EXE
$\hat{\sigma}$	SHIFT 3	SHIFT 3 EXE

Now $\hat{\mu} = \bar{x}$

$= 19.12$ (2 d.p.)

and $\hat{\sigma} = 0.5045\ldots$ (written $x\sigma_{n-1}$ on calculator)

So $\hat{\sigma}^2 = 0.25$ (2 d.p.)

Example 9.3 Obtain the best unbiased estimates of the population mean and variance from which the following sample is drawn: $n = 12$, $\bar{x} = 23.5$, $\sum(x - \bar{x})^2 = 48.72$.

Solution 9.3

$$\hat{\mu} = \bar{x}$$

$$= 23.5$$

$$\hat{\sigma}^2 = \frac{\sum(x - \bar{x})^2}{n - 1}$$

$$= \frac{48.72}{11}$$

$$= 4.43 \quad (2 \text{ d.p.})$$

Therefore the best unbiased estimate of the population mean is 23.5, and of the population variance is 4.43.

Example 9.4   A random sample of 50 children from a large school is chosen and the number who are left-handed is noted. It is found that 6 are left-handed. Obtain an unbiased estimate of the proportion of children in the school who are left-handed.

Solution 9.4   From the sample, the proportion of children who are left-handed is p_s where $p_s = \frac{6}{50} = 0.12$.

An unbiased estimate of the proportion of children in the school who are left-handed is 0.12.

Exercise 9b

In Questions 1 to 11, find the best unbiased estimate of the population mean and of the population variance from which each of the following samples is drawn:

1.   46, 48, 51, 50, 45, 53, 50, 48.

2.   35, 42, 38, 55, 70, 69.

3.   1.684, 1.691, 1.687, 1.688, 1.689, 1.688, 1.690, 1.693, 1.685.

4. $\sum x = 120$, $\sum x^2 = 2102$, $n = 8$

5. $\sum x = 120$, $\sum (x - \bar{x})^2 = 302$, $n = 8$.

6. $\sum x = 100$, $\sum x^2 = 1028$, $n = 10$.

7. $n = 34$, $\sum x = 330$, $\sum x^2 = 23\,700$.

8. $n = 27$, $\sum x = 1560$, $\sum (x - \bar{x})^2 = 168\,900$.

9.

Interval	Frequency
1–10	2
11–20	4
21–30	9
31–40	18
41–50	21
51–60	23
61–70	22
71–80	1

10.

Interval	Frequency
0–	3
4–	6
8–	24
12–	10
16–	7
20–	0

11.

x	20	21	22	23	24	25
f	4	14	17	26	20	9

12.   A railway enthusiast simulates train journeys and records the number of minutes, x, to the nearest minute, trains are late according to the schedule being used. A random sample of 50 journeys gave the following times.

17	5	3	10	4	3	10	5	2	14
3	14	5	5	21	9	22	36	14	34
22	4	23	6	8	15	41	23	13	7
6	13	33	8	5	34	26	17	8	43
24	14	23	4	19	5	23	13	12	10

(a) Construct a stem and leaf diagram to represent these data.
(b) Comment on the shape of the distribution produced by your diagram.
(c) Given that $\sum x = 738$ and $\sum x^2 = 16\,526$, calculate to 2 decimal places, unbiased estimates of the mean and the variance of the population from which this sample was drawn.
(d) Explain briefly the effect that grouping of these data would have had on your calculations in (c).   (L)

13.   The concentrations, in mg per litre, of a trace element in 7 randomly chosen samples of water from a spring were:

240.8	237.3	236.7	236.6
234.2	233.9	232.5	

Determine unbiased estimates of the mean and the variance of the concentration of the trace element per litre of water from the spring.   (L)P

14. Using the random numbers on p. 720 take a random sample of size 10 from the following distribution:

x	1	2	3	4	5
f	12	18	28	25	17

Use the sample to obtain unbiased estimates of the population mean and variance. Compare these with the true values.

15. The random variable X has probability distribution

x	10	11	12	13
$P(X = x)$	0.3	0.2	0.4	0.1

Use the random numbers given below to generate a random sample of size 20 from the distribution of X and use it to obtain unbiased estimates of the population mean and variance.

Random numbers: 57048   86526
                   27795   36820

16. A measuring rule was used to measure the length of a rod of stated length 1 m. On 8 successive occasions the following results, in millimetres, were obtained.

   999 1000 999 1002 1001 1000 1002 1001

Calculate unbiased estimates of the mean and, to 2 significant figures, the variance of the errors occurring when this rule is used for measuring a 1 m length.   (L)P

17. Cartons of orange are filled by a machine. A sample of 10 cartons selected at random from the production contained the following quantities of orange (in ml).

   201.2   205.0   209.1   202.3   204.6
   206.4   210.1   201.9   203.7   207.3

Calculate unbiased estimates of the mean and variance of the population from which this sample was taken.   (L)

POOLED ESTIMATORS FROM TWO SAMPLES

Estimates of the population mean, variance, proportion, etc., may be made by 'pooling' values from two samples.

Pooled estimators of population mean and of population variance

From a population with *unknown* mean μ and *unknown* variance σ^2 we take two random samples:

	Sample values		
	Size	Mean	Variance
Sample I	n_1	$\overline{X}_1$	$S_1^{\,2}$
Sample II	n_2	$\overline{X}_2$	$S_2^{\,2}$

Then
$$\hat{\mu} = \frac{n_1\overline{X}_1 + n_2\overline{X}_2}{n_1 + n_2}$$

where $\hat{\mu}$ is an unbiased estimator for the population mean μ.

Also
$$\hat{\sigma}^2 = \frac{n_1 S_1^{\,2} + n_2 S_2^{\,2}}{n_1 + n_2 - 2}$$

where $\hat{\sigma}^2$ is an unbiased estimator for the population variance σ^2 and $S_1^{\,2}$ and $S_2^{\,2}$ are the sample variances.

Since
$$S^2 = \frac{\sum (X - \overline{X})^2}{n}$$

$$n_1 S_1{}^2 = \sum (X_1 - \overline{X}_1)^2 \quad \text{and} \quad n_2 S_2{}^2 = \sum (X_2 - \overline{X}_2)^2$$

So
$$\widehat{\sigma}^2 = \frac{\sum (X_1 - \overline{X}_1)^2 + \sum (X_2 - \overline{X}_2)^2}{n_1 + n_2 - 2}$$

Pooled estimator of population proportion

From a binomial population which has *unknown* proportion p of 'successes', we take two samples:

	Size	Proportion
Sample I	n_1	P_{s_1}
Sample II	n_2	P_{s_2}

Then $\widehat{p}$, an unbiased estimator for the population proportion p, is given by

$$\widehat{p} = \frac{n_1 P_{s_1} + n_2 P_{s_2}}{n_1 + n_2}$$

Example 9.5 Two samples, sizes 40 and 50 respectively, are taken from a population with unknown mean μ and unknown variance σ^2. Using the data from the two samples, obtain unbiased estimates of μ and σ^2.

Sample I

x_1	18	19	20	21	22
f	3	7	15	10	5

Sample II

x_2	18	19	20	21	22	23
f	10	21	8	6	3	2

Solution 9.5 Sample I

$$\overline{x}_1 = \frac{\sum fx}{\sum f} = \frac{807}{40} = 20.175$$

Sample variance

$$s_1{}^2 = \frac{\sum fx^2}{\sum f} - \overline{x}_1{}^2 = \frac{16\,329}{40} - \left(\frac{807}{40}\right)^2 = 1.194$$

Sample II

$$\overline{x}_2 = \frac{\sum fx}{\sum f} = \frac{977}{50} = 19.54$$

Sample variance

$$s_2{}^2 = \frac{\sum fx^2}{\sum f} - \bar{x}_2{}^2 = \frac{19\,177}{50} - \left(\frac{977}{50}\right)^2 = 1.7284$$

An unbiased estimate for μ is $\widehat{\mu}$ where

$$\widehat{\mu} = \frac{n_1\bar{x}_1 + n_2\bar{x}_2}{n_1 + n_2} = \frac{40(20.175) + 50(19.54)}{40 + 50} = 19.82 \quad (2 \text{ d.p.})$$

An unbiased estimate for σ^2 is $\widehat{\sigma}^2$ where

$$\widehat{\sigma}^2 = \frac{n_1 s_1{}^2 + n_2 s_2{}^2}{n_1 + n_2 - 2} = \frac{40(1.194) + 50(1.728)}{40 + 50 - 2} = 1.52 \quad (2 \text{ d.p.})$$

Therefore an unbiased estimate of the population mean is 19.82 (2 d.p.) and an unbiased estimate of the population variance is 1.52 (2 d.p.).

Example 9.6   A count was made of the bacteria in a certain volume of water. Denoting the number of bacteria by $x = 1800 + d$, the results for the first sample were

$$n_1 = 27, \quad \sum d = 162, \quad \sum(d - \bar{d})^2 = 11\,466$$

The results for the second sample, where $y = 1800 + e$, were

$$n_2 = 25, \quad \sum e = 125, \quad \sum(e - \bar{e})^2 = 14\,984$$

Obtain unbiased estimates of the population mean and standard deviation

(**a**) considering the results of the first sample only,

(**b**) considering both samples.

Solution 9.6   (**a**) Sample I: $x = 1800 + d$,

so $$\bar{x} = 1800 + \bar{d} = 1800 + \frac{162}{27} = 1806$$

$$\widehat{\sigma}^2 = \frac{\sum(d - \bar{d})^2}{n_1 - 1} = \frac{11\,466}{26} = 441 = 21^2$$

Therefore, an unbiased estimate of the population mean is 1806 and an unbiased estimate of the population standard deviation is 21.

(**b**) For sample II:

$$\bar{y} = 1800 + \bar{e} = 1800 + \frac{125}{25} = 1805$$

So, for the two samples together,

$$\widehat{\mu} = \frac{n_1\bar{x} + n_2\bar{y}}{n_1 + n_2} = \frac{27(1806) + 25(1805)}{52} = 1805.52 \quad (2 \text{ d.p.})$$

and

$$\widehat{\sigma}^2 = \frac{\sum (d - \overline{d})^2 + \sum (e - \overline{e})^2}{n_1 + n_2 - 2} = \frac{11\,466 + 14\,984}{50} = 529 = 23^2$$

So, on the basis of the two samples, $\widehat{\mu} = 1805.52$ (2 d.p.) and $\widehat{\sigma} = 23$.

Example 9.7 An opinion poll in a certain city indicated that 69 people in a random sample of 120 said that they would vote for Mr Jones, while in a second random sample of 160, 93 said that they would vote for Mr Jones. Find an unbiased estimate of the proportion of people in the city who will vote for Mr Jones.

Solution 9.7 $\qquad n_1 = 120, \quad p_{s_1} = \frac{69}{120}; \quad n_2 = 160, \quad p_{s_2} = \frac{93}{160}$

An unbiased estimate $\widehat{p}$ is given by

$$\widehat{p} = \frac{n_1 p_{s_1} + n_2 p_{s_2}}{n_1 + n_2} = \frac{69 + 93}{120 + 160} = 0.58 \quad (2 \text{ d.p.})$$

So, on the basis of the two samples, it is estimated that approximately 58% of the people in the city will vote for Mr Jones.

Exercise 9c

In each of the following, find unbiased estimates of the population mean and variance, using the data given by the two samples.

1. Sample I   0.68, 0.67, 0.61, 0.78, 0.65
    Sample II 0.64, 0.66, 0.63, 0.69, 0.66, 0.71, 0.64, 0.60

2. Sample I   10.2, 10.1, 10.3, 10.5, 8.9, 9.8
    Sample II 8.7, 10.6, 10.8, 9.6, 9.9, 10.9, 8.4, 8.6, 10.9

3. Sample I

x	1	2	3	4	5
f	2	5	18	12	3

    Sample II

x	1	2	3	4	5	6	7
f	3	6	12	26	17	5	1

4. Sample I $n_1 = 13, \sum x = 109.8,$
                 $\sum x^2 = 1110.7$
    Sample II $n_2 = 15, \sum x = 147.6,$
                 $\sum x^2 = 1529.68$

5. Sample I $n_1 = 23, \sum x = 48,$
                 $\sum x^2 = 333.94$
    Sample II $n_2 = 18, \sum x = 45,$
                 $\sum x^2 = 275$

6. Sample I   5.26, 5.89, 5.64, 5.83, 5.81, 5.28, 5.21, 5.26, 5.74, 5.34
    Sample II 5.31, 5.37, 5.41, 5.45, 5.58, 5.29, 5.36, 5.28

7. Sample I $n_1 = 9, \sum x = 267,$
                 $\sum (x - \overline{x})^2 = 100$
    Sample II $n_2 = 11, \sum x = 336,$
                 $\sum (x - \overline{x})^2 = 114.7$

8. Sample I $n_1 = 15, \sum x = 35.9,$
                 $\sum (x - \overline{x})^2 = 0.269$
    Sample II $n_2 = 20, \sum x = 47.8,$
                 $\sum (x - \overline{x})^2 = 0.638$

In the following questions, find an unbiased estimate of the population proportion, based on the data given by the two samples.

9. $n_1 = 200, p_{s_1} = 0.36; n_2 = 300, p_{s_2} = 0.34.$

10. $n_1 = 50, p_{s_1} = 0.82; n_2 = 80, p_{s_2} = 0.85.$

11. $n_1 = 10, p_{s_1} = 0.6;\ n_2 = 20, p_{s_2} = 0.7.$

12.   A random sample of 600 people from a certain district were questioned and the results indicated that 30% used a particular product. In a second random sample of 300 people, 96 used the product. Find an unbiased estimate of the proportion of people in the district who used the product.

SUMMARY — POINT ESTIMATORS

Population mean	
From one sample	From two samples
$\widehat{\mu} = \overline{X}$	$\widehat{\mu} = \dfrac{n_1\overline{X}_1 + n_2\overline{X}_2}{n_1 + n_2}$
Population variance	
From one sample	From two samples
$\widehat{\sigma}^2 = \dfrac{\sum (X - \overline{X})^2}{n - 1}$ or $\widehat{\sigma}^2 = \dfrac{nS^2}{(n - 1)}$ where S^2 is sample variance	$\widehat{\sigma}^2 = \dfrac{\sum (X_1 - \overline{X}_1)^2 + \sum (X_2 - \overline{X}_2)^2}{n_1 + n_2 - 2}$ or $\widehat{\sigma}^2 = \dfrac{n_1 S_1^{\,2} + n_2 S_2^{\,2}}{n_1 + n_2 - 2}$ where $S_1^{\,2}, S_2^{\,2}$ are sample variances
Population proportion	
From one sample	From two samples
$\widehat{p} = P_s$	$\widehat{p} = \dfrac{n_1 P_{s_1} + n_2 P_{s_2}}{n_1 + n_2}$

INTERVAL ESTIMATION — CONFIDENCE INTERVALS

An **interval estimate** of an unknown population parameter is a random interval constructed so that it has a *given probability of including the parameter*.

Consider a population with unknown parameter θ.

If we can find an interval $(a,\ b)$ such that $P(a < \theta < b) = 0.95$, we say that $(a,\ b)$ is a **95% confidence interval for θ.**

In this case, the probability that the interval includes θ is 0.95. It is *not* the probability that θ lies in the interval.

It is important to realise that θ is **fixed** and the **intervals** themselves vary.

We are saying that if 100 intervals are constructed in the same way, then we expect 95 of them to 'capture' or 'trap' θ. Diagramatically:

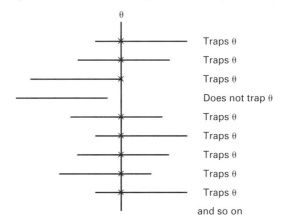

We will consider the confidence intervals for two important parameters, the population mean and the proportion of successes in the population.

THE POPULATION MEAN

(a) Confidence interval for μ, population variance σ^2 known

If X is normally distributed such that $X \sim N(\mu, \sigma^2)$ then, for *any n,*

$$\overline{X} \sim N\left(\mu, \frac{\sigma^2}{n}\right)$$

If X does not follow a normal distribution, and *n is large,* then by the central limit theorem

$$\overline{X} \sim N\left(\mu, \frac{\sigma^2}{n}\right)$$

Standardising, we have $Z = \dfrac{\overline{X} - \mu}{\sigma/\sqrt{n}}$ where $Z \sim N(0, 1)$.

We know that the central 95% of $N(0, 1)$ lies between the values ± 1.96 (see p. 375).

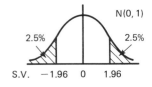

So $\quad P\left(-1.96 \leqslant \dfrac{\overline{X} - \mu}{\sigma/\sqrt{n}} \leqslant 1.96\right) = 0.95$

It is possible to re-arrange this statement to obtain

$$P\left(\overline{X} - 1.96\frac{\sigma}{\sqrt{n}} \leqslant \mu \leqslant \overline{X} + 1.96\frac{\sigma}{\sqrt{n}}\right) = 0.95 \quad \text{(see p. 375).}$$

So we have found an interval such that the probability that the interval includes μ is 0.95. This is called the **95% confidence interval for μ.**

If $\bar{x}$ is the mean of a random sample of size n taken from either

(i) a NORMAL population with *known variance* σ^2,
or
(ii) ANY population with *known variance* σ^2, provided that n is *large*, ($n \geqslant 30$ say),

then a central **95% confidence interval for** μ, is given by

$$\left(\bar{x} - 1.96 \frac{\sigma}{\sqrt{n}}, \bar{x} + 1.96 \frac{\sigma}{\sqrt{n}} \right)$$

This can be written $\bar{x} \pm 1.96 \dfrac{\sigma}{\sqrt{n}}$

NOTE: if a large number of intervals are calculated in the same way, then 95% of them will include, or 'trap', μ, and similarly:

A central 98% confidence interval for μ is given by

$$\left(\bar{x} - 2.326 \frac{\sigma}{\sqrt{n}}, \bar{x} + 2.326 \frac{\sigma}{\sqrt{n}} \right)$$

This can be written

$$\bar{x} \pm 2.326 \frac{\sigma}{\sqrt{n}}$$

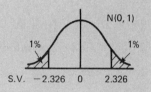

A central 99% confidence interval for μ is given by

$$\left(\bar{x} - 2.575 \frac{\sigma}{\sqrt{n}}, \bar{x} + 2.575 \frac{\sigma}{\sqrt{n}} \right)$$

This can be written

$$\bar{x} \pm 2.575 \frac{\sigma}{\sqrt{n}}$$

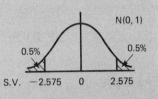

NOTE: often the word 'central' is omitted when considering confidence intervals, but it is assumed, unless otherwise stated, that an interval that is central, or symmetric, about the mean is required. A central 95% confidence interval is sometimes written 95% C.I.

One-sided confidence intervals

A one-sided 95% confidence interval for μ is given by

$$\left(\bar{x} - 1.645 \frac{\sigma}{\sqrt{n}}, \infty \right)$$

since $P\left(\overline{X} - 1.645 \dfrac{\sigma}{\sqrt{n}} \leqslant \mu \leqslant \infty \right) = 0.95$

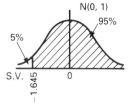

Alternatively $\quad \left(-\infty, \bar{x} + 1.645 \dfrac{\sigma}{\sqrt{n}}\right)$

since $\quad P\left(-\infty \leqslant \mu \leqslant \overline{X} + 1.645 \dfrac{\sigma}{\sqrt{n}}\right) = 0.95$

The format of the one-sided confidence interval depends on the information required in a particular situation.

Example 9.8 After a particularly wet night, 12 worms surfaced on the lawn. Their lengths, measured in cm, were:

$$9.5, \ 9.5, \ 11.2, \ 10.6, \ 9.9, \ 11.1, \ 10.9, \ 9.8, \ 10.1, \ 10.2, \ 10.9, \ 11.0$$

Assuming that this sample came from a normal population with variance 4, calculate a 95% confidence interval for the mean length of all the worms in the garden.

Solution 9.8 $n = 12, \quad \sum x = 124.7.$

So $\qquad\qquad \bar{x} = \dfrac{\sum x}{n} = \dfrac{124.7}{12} = 10.39 \quad \text{(2 d.p.)}$

Now $X \sim N(\mu, \sigma^2)$ with $\sigma = 2$, i.e. $X \sim N(\mu, 2^2)$.

A symmetric, 95% confidence interval for μ, the mean length of the worms is

$$\bar{x} \pm 1.96 \dfrac{\sigma}{\sqrt{n}} = 10.39 \pm (1.96) \dfrac{2}{\sqrt{12}}$$

$$= 10.39 \pm 1.13$$

$$= (9.26, 11.52)$$

The 95% confidence interval for the mean length of the worms in the garden is (9.26 cm, 11.52 cm).

Example 9.9 A plant produces steel sheets whose weights are known to be normally distributed with a standard deviation of 2.4 kg. A random sample of 36 sheets had a mean weight of 31.4 kg. Find 99% confidence limits for the population mean. (L)

Solution 9.9 Let X be the r.v. 'the weight, in kg, of a steel sheet'.

We are given that $X \sim N(\mu, 2.4^2)$

For a random sample, with $n = 36$, $\bar{x} = 31.4$, a 99% confidence interval for the population mean μ is

$$\bar{x} \pm 2.575 \dfrac{\sigma}{\sqrt{n}} = 31.4 \pm (2.575) \dfrac{2.4}{\sqrt{36}}$$

$$= 31.4 \pm 1.03$$

$$= (30.37, 32.43)$$

The 99% confidence limits for μ are (30.37 kg, 32.43 kg).

Example 9.10 On the basis of the results obtained from a random sample of 100 men from a particular district, the 95% confidence interval for the mean height of the men in the district is found to be (177.22 cm, 179.18 cm). Find the value of $\bar{x}$, the mean of the sample, and σ, the standard deviation of the normal population from which the sample is drawn. Calculate the 98% confidence interval for the mean height.

Solution 9.10 The 95% confidence interval is given by

$$\bar{x} \pm 1.96 \frac{\sigma}{\sqrt{n}} = (177.22, 179.18)$$

Hence

$$\bar{x} + 1.96 \frac{\sigma}{10} = 179.18 \qquad\qquad\qquad\text{(i)}$$

$$\bar{x} - 1.96 \frac{\sigma}{10} = 177.22 \qquad\qquad\qquad\text{(ii)}$$

Adding (i) and (ii),

$$2\bar{x} = 356.4$$

$$\bar{x} = 178.2$$

Subtracting (i) and (ii),

$$2(1.96) \frac{\sigma}{10} = 1.96$$

$$\sigma = \frac{10}{2}$$

$$\sigma = 5$$

Therefore the sample mean $\bar{x}$ is 178.2 cm and the population standard deviation σ is 5 cm.

The 98% confidence interval is given by

$$\bar{x} \pm 2.326 \frac{\sigma}{\sqrt{n}} = 178.2 \pm 2.326 \left(\frac{5}{10}\right)$$

$$= 178.2 \pm 1.163$$

$$= (177.037, 179.363)$$

The 98% confidence interval for the mean height of the men in the district is (177.04 cm, 179.36 cm) (2 d.p.).

Example 9.11 The result X of a stress test is known to be a normally distributed random variable with mean μ and standard deviation 1.3. It is required to have a 95% symmetrical confidence interval for μ with total width less than 2. Find the least number of tests that should be carried out to achieve this. (L)P

Solution 9.11 We are given $X \sim N(\mu, 1.3^2)$

95% confidence interval for $\mu = \bar{x} \pm 1.96 \dfrac{\sigma}{\sqrt{n}}$

We see that the width of the confidence interval is $2 \times 1.96 \dfrac{\sigma}{\sqrt{n}}$, with $\sigma = 1.3$

So we need n such that

$$2 \times 1.96 \times \frac{1.3}{\sqrt{n}} < 2$$

i.e.
$$\sqrt{n} > 1.96 \times 1.3$$

$$\sqrt{n} > 2.548$$

$$n > 6.49\ldots$$

Therefore the least number of tests that should be carried out is 7.

(b) Confidence interval for μ, population variance σ^2 unknown, n large

Consider $X \sim N(\mu, \sigma^2)$.

Since σ^2 is *unknown*, it is necessary to use an estimator, $\hat{\sigma}^2$ for it.

Now, $\quad \hat{\sigma}^2 = \dfrac{nS^2}{n-1}$ where S^2 is the sample variance.

> If $\bar{x}$ and s^2 are the mean and variance of a random sample of size n (where *n is large*) from a normal population with *unknown* mean μ and *unknown* variance σ^2, then a central 95% confidence interval for μ is given by
>
> $$\left(\bar{x} - 1.96 \frac{\hat{\sigma}}{\sqrt{n}}, \bar{x} + 1.96 \frac{\hat{\sigma}}{\sqrt{n}}\right) \quad \text{where } \hat{\sigma}^2 = \frac{ns^2}{n-1} = \frac{\sum(x - \bar{x})^2}{n-1}$$
>
> This can be written $\qquad \bar{x} \pm 1.96 \dfrac{\hat{\sigma}}{\sqrt{n}}$

NOTE: $P\left(\overline{X} - 1.96 \dfrac{\hat{\sigma}}{\sqrt{n}} \leqslant \mu \leqslant \overline{X} + 1.96 \dfrac{\hat{\sigma}}{\sqrt{n}}\right) = 0.95.$

Similarly,

> a 99% confidence interval for μ is given by $\bar{x} \pm 2.575 \dfrac{\hat{\sigma}}{\sqrt{n}}$,
>
> a 98% confidence interval for μ is given by $\bar{x} \pm 2.326 \dfrac{\hat{\sigma}}{\sqrt{n}}$.

Example 9.12 A random sample of 120 measurements taken from a normal population gave the following data:

$$n = 120, \qquad \sum x = 1008, \qquad \sum (x - \bar{x})^2 = 172.8$$

Find (**a**) a 97% confidence interval, (**b**) a 99% confidence interval for the population mean μ.

Solution 9.12 Now

$$\bar{x} = \frac{\sum x}{n} = \frac{1008}{120} = 8.4$$

$$\hat{\sigma}^2 = \frac{\sum (x - \bar{x}^2)}{n - 1} = \frac{172.8}{119} = 1.452 \ldots$$

$$\hat{\sigma} = \sqrt{1.452 \ldots} = 1.205 \ldots$$

(**a**) A 97% confidence interval for the population mean is given by

$$\bar{x} \pm 2.17 \, \frac{\hat{\sigma}}{\sqrt{n}} = 8.4 \pm 2.17 \, \frac{1.205}{\sqrt{120}}$$

$$= 8.4 \pm 0.238 \ldots$$

$$= (8.16, 8.64) \quad (2 \text{ d.p.})$$

N(0, 1)

1.5%   1.5%

S.V. -2.17 0   2.17

Therefore a 97% confidence interval for the population mean is (8.16, 8.64).

(**b**) A 99% confidence interval for the population mean is given by

$$\bar{x} \pm 2.575 \, \frac{\hat{\sigma}}{\sqrt{n}} = 8.4 \pm 2.575 \, \frac{1.205}{\sqrt{120}}$$

$$= 8.4 \pm 0.283 \ldots$$

$$= (8.12, 8.68) \quad (2 \text{ d.p.})$$

Therefore a 99% confidence interval for the population mean is (8.12, 8.68).

Example 9.13 A sample of readings from a normal population with unknown mean μ and unknown variance σ^2 gave the following data:

x	17.4	17.5	17.6	17.7	17.8
f	12	16	19	23	10

A second sample of readings taken from the same population gave

$$n_2 = 72, \quad \sum x = 1267.2, \quad \sum x^2 = 22\,536$$

Combine the two samples to give estimates of μ and σ^2, and give the appropriate 90% confidence interval for μ.

Solution 9.13 Let $s_1{}^2$ and $s_2{}^2$ be the sample variances.

Sample I:

$$\bar{x}_1 = \frac{\sum fx}{\sum f} = \frac{1408.3}{80} = 17.604$$

$$s_1{}^2 = \frac{\sum fx^2}{\sum f} - \bar{x}_1{}^2 = \frac{24\,792.63}{80} - \left(\frac{1408.3}{80}\right)^2 = 0.0159 \quad \text{(3 S.F.)}$$

Sample II:

$$\bar{x}_2 = \frac{\sum x}{n_2} = \frac{1267.2}{72} = 17.6$$

$$s_2{}^2 = \frac{\sum x^2}{n_2} - \bar{x}_2{}^2 = \frac{22\,536}{72} - 17.6^2 = 3.24$$

Now, for the combined sample

$$\hat{\mu} = \frac{n_1\bar{x}_1 + n_2\bar{x}_2}{n_1 + n_2} = \frac{80(17.604) + 72(17.6)}{80 + 72} = 17.602 \quad \text{(3 d.p.)}$$

and

$$\hat{\sigma}^2 = \frac{n_1s_1{}^2 + n_2s_2{}^2}{n_1 + n_2 - 2} = \frac{80(0.0159) + 72(3.24)}{80 + 72 - 2} = 1.564 \quad \text{(3 d.p.)}$$

From the two samples, estimates of μ and σ^2 are 17.602 and 1.564 respectively.

A 90% confidence interval for μ based on the combined sample is

$$\bar{x} \pm 1.645\frac{\hat{\sigma}}{\sqrt{n}} \quad \text{where } \bar{x} = 17.602, \ \hat{\sigma} = \sqrt{1.564} = 1.250, \ n = 152$$

90% confidence interval is

$$17.602 \pm 1.645\,\frac{1.250}{\sqrt{152}} = 17.602 \pm 0.167$$

$$= (17.435, 17.769)$$

Therefore a 90% confidence interval for μ based on the two samples is (17.435, 17.769).

Exercise 9d

1. A certain type of tennis ball is known to have a height of bounce which is normally distributed with standard deviation 2 cm. A sample of 60 tennis balls is tested and the mean height of bounce of the sample is 140 cm. Find (a) 95%, (b) 98% confidence intervals for the mean height of bounce of this type of tennis ball.

2. A random sample of 100 is taken from a population. The sample is found to have a mean of 76.0 and standard deviation 12.0. Find (a) 90%, (b) 97%, (c) 99% confidence intervals for the mean of the population.

3. 150 bags of flour of a particular brand are weighed and the mean mass is found to be 748 g with standard deviation 3.6 g. Find (a) 90%, (b) 95%, (c) 98% confidence intervals for the mean mass of bags of flour of this brand.

4. A random sample of 100 readings taken from a normal population gave the following data: $\bar{x} = 82, \sum x^2 = 686\,800$. Find (a) 98%, (b) 99% confidence intervals for the population mean μ.

5. 80 people were asked to measure their pulse rates when they woke up in the morning. The mean was 69 beats and the standard deviation 4 beats. Find (a) 95%, (b) 99% confidence intervals for the population mean.

6. The 95% confidence interval for the mean length of life of a particular brand of light bulb is (1023.3 h, 1101.7 h). This interval is based on results from a random sample of 36 light bulbs. Find the 99% confidence interval for the mean length of life of this brand of light bulb, assuming that the length of life is normally distributed.

7. A random sample of six items taken from a normal population with variance 4.5 cm² gave the following data:

Sample values: 12.9 cm, 13.2 cm, 14.6 cm, 12.6 cm, 11.3 cm, 10.1 cm

Find the 94% confidence interval for the population mean μ.

8. The data is from a random sample of 150 readings taken from a population with mean μ and variance σ^2. Estimate μ and σ^2.

$$n_1 = 150, \quad \sum x_1 = 1623,$$
$$\sum x_1^2 = 17\,814.36$$

A second sample of 100 readings is taken from the same population. For this sample, $n_2 = 100, \sum x_2 = 1119, \sum x_2^2 = 12\,585.61$. Calculate estimates of μ and σ^2 from this second sample. Now combine the two samples to give a further estimate of μ, together with its appropriate 96% confidence interval.

9. A sample of 64 readings from a normal population with mean μ and variance σ^2 gave $n_1 = 64, \sum x = 5452.8, \sum (x - \bar{x})^2 = 973.44$. Estimate μ and σ^2 from this data. A second sample of readings gave:

x	82	83	84	85	86	87
f	6	9	19	27	22	17

Estimate μ and σ^2 for this second sample. Now combine the two samples to give a further estimate of μ, together with the appropriate 97% confidence interval.

10. The age, X, in years at last birthday, of 250 mothers when their first child was born is given in the following table:

x	No. of mothers
18–	14
20–	36
22–	42
24–	57
26–	48
28–	26
30–	17
32–	7
34–	2
36–	0
38–	1

(The notation implies that, for example in row 1, there are 14 mothers for whom the continuous variable X satisfies $18 \leqslant X < 20$.) Calculate, to the nearest 0.1 of a year, estimates of the mean and the standard deviation of X.
If the 250 mothers are a random sample from a large population of mothers, find 95% confidence limits for the mean age, μ, of the total population. (C)

11. The distribution of measurements of thicknesses of a random sample of yarns produced in a textile mill is shown in the following table.

Yarn thickness in microns (mid-interval value)	Frequency
72.5	6
77.5	18
82.5	32
87.5	57
92.5	102
97.5	51
102.5	25
107.5	9

Illustrate these data on a histogram. Estimate to two decimal places the mean and standard deviation of yarn thickness. Hence estimate the standard error of the mean to two decimal places, and use it to determine approximate symmetric 95% confidence limits, giving your answer to one decimal place.   (MEI)

12. The lifetimes of 200 electrical components were recorded to the nearest hour and classified in the frequency tabulation.

Lifetime	Frequency	Lifetime	Frequency
0–	80	600–	4
100–	48	700–	3
200–	30	800–	2
300–	18	900–	0
400–	10	1000–	0
500–	5		

Draw a histogram of the data and estimate the mean and standard deviation of the distribution.
Calculate a symmetric 90% confidence interval for the population means, using a suitable normal approximation for the distribution of the sample mean.   (MEI)

13. A random sample of 250 adult men undergoing a routine medical inspection had their heights (x cm) measured to the nearest centimetre, and the following data were obtained: $\sum x = 43\,205$, $\sum x^2 = 7\,469\,107$. Calculate an unbiased estimate of the population variance. Calculate also a symmetric 99% confidence interval for the population mean.   (C)P

14. The time to failure of a sample of 200 batteries is given in the table below.
(a) Draw a histogram of the data.

(b) Estimate the sample mean and variance of the time to failure by the usual method of considering all observations in a class as being concentrated at the mid-point of that class. Would you expect the actual sample mean to be greater or less than the estimated value? Give a reason for your answer.
(c) Using your calculated values obtain a 95% confidence interval for the population mean.
(d) Estimate the median time to failure of the sample.

Time (hours)	Frequency
0–20	80
20–40	48
40–60	29
60–80	18
80–100	12
100–120	7
120–140	4
140–160	2

15. A machine produces plastic balls for use in an industrial process. It incorporates a device which automatically recycles those balls whose mass is outside certain limits. The mass of the balls produced (measured as a deviation in g from the minimum value) may be regarded as a random variable, X, with probability density function

$$f(x) = \begin{cases} k(2-x) & 0 < x < 2 \\ 0 & \text{otherwise} \end{cases}$$

(a) Show that $k = 0.5$.
(b) Find the mean and the standard deviation of X correct to 3 significant figures.
(c) Find the probability that the mass of a ball is less than the mean. Compare this with the result you would have obtained if X had followed a normal distribution.
(d) The mean of the distribution may change from day to day but the shape and standard deviation do not. A random sample of size 20 yields a sample mean of 0.9. Calculate a 90% confidence interval for the population mean. Explain the relevance of the Central Limit Theorem to your calculations.   (AEB 1988)

16. The lifetime of a shuttlecock is the number of hours of continuous play before it becomes unusable. A random sample of 40 shuttlecocks had a mean lifetime of 4 hours, with standard deviation 1.1 hours. Find the value of c such that $c < \mu < \infty$ is a 95% one-sided confidence interval for μ, the mean lifetime of a shuttlecock.

CONFIDENCE INTERVAL FOR THE PROPORTION OF SUCCESSES IN A POPULATION

If in a random sample of size n $(n \geqslant 30)$ the proportion with a particular property is p_s, the 95% confidence interval for the population proportion p is given by

$$\left(p_s - 1.96\sqrt{p_s q_s/n}, p_s + 1.96\sqrt{p_s q_s/n}\right) \quad \text{where} \quad q_s = 1 - p_s$$

This can be written $\qquad p_s \pm 1.96\sqrt{p_s q_s/n}$

Similarly, a 99% confidence interval for p is $p_s \pm 2.575\sqrt{p_s q_s/n}$

and a 98% confidence interval for p is $p_s \pm 2.326\sqrt{p_s q_s/n}$.

Example 9.14 A manufacturer wants to assess the proportion of defective items in a large batch produced by a particular machine. He tests a random sample of 300 items and finds that 45 are defective. Calculate (**a**) a 95% confidence interval, (**b**) a 98% confidence interval for the proportion of defective items in the complete batch.

Solution 9.14 The proportion of defective items in the sample, $p_s = \frac{45}{300} = 0.15$.

So $q_s = 1 - p_s = 0.85, n = 300$.

The 95% confidence interval for the proportion p of defective items in the complete batch is given by

$$p_s \pm 1.96\sqrt{\frac{p_s q_s}{n}} = 0.15 \pm (1.96)\sqrt{\frac{(0.15)(0.85)}{300}}$$

$$= 0.15 \pm 0.0404$$

$$= (0.1096, 0.1904)$$

The 95% confidence interval is $(0.1096, 0.1904)$.

The 98% confidence interval for p is given by

$$p_s \pm 2.326\sqrt{\frac{p_s q_s}{n}} = 0.15 \pm (2.326)\sqrt{\frac{(0.15)(0.85)}{300}}$$

$$= 0.15 \pm 0.048$$

$$= (0.101, 0.198)$$

The 98% confidence interval is $(0.101, 0.198)$.

Example 9.15 In a survey carried out in Funville, 28 children out of a random sample of 80 said that they bought Bopper comic regularly. Find 95% approximate confidence limits for the true proportion of all children in Funville who buy this comic. A similar survey in

Funville found that 45 children out of a random sample of 100 said that they bought Shooter comic regularly. Find 95% approximate confidence limits for the true proportion of all children in Funville who buy this comic.

On the basis of these surveys, is there any evidence that the sales of Shooter comic are higher than the sales of Bopper comic in Funville? Justify your reply.   (AEB)

Solution 9.15 Let p_B be the true proportion of all children who buy the Bopper.

In the sample of 80,

$$p_s = \tfrac{28}{80} = 0.35 \qquad q_s = 1 - p_s = 0.65.$$

The 95% confidence interval for p_B is

$$p_s \pm 1.96 \sqrt{\frac{p_s q_s}{n}} = 0.35 \pm (1.96) \sqrt{\frac{(0.35)(0.65)}{80}}$$

$$= 0.35 \pm 0.105$$

$$= (0.245, 0.455)$$

The 95% confidence interval for the proportion who buy the Bopper is (0.245, 0.455).

Let p_C be the true proportion of all children who buy the Shooter.

In the sample of 100,

$$p_s = \tfrac{45}{100} = 0.45 \qquad q_s = 0.55.$$

The 95% confidence interval for p_C is

$$p_s \pm 1.96 \sqrt{\frac{p_s q_s}{n}} = 0.45 \pm (1.96) \sqrt{\frac{(0.45)(0.55)}{100}}$$

$$= 0.45 \pm 0.098$$

$$= (0.352, 0.548)$$

The 95% confidence interval for the proportion who buy the Shooter is (0.352, 0.548).

These confidence intervals overlap, so it is possible that $p_B = 0.43$ (say) and $p_C = 0.39$ (say) so that $p_B > p_C$.

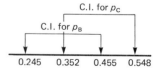

So, on these results there is not sufficient evidence to suggest that the sales of Shooter comic are higher than the sales of Bopper comic.

Example 9.16 A point whose coordinates are (x, y) with respect to rectangular axes is chosen at random where $0 < x < 1$ and $0 < y < 1$. What is the probability that the point lies inside the circle whose equation is $x^2 + y^2 = 1$?

In a computer simulation 1000 such points were generated and 784 of them lay inside the circle. Obtain an estimate for π and give an approximate 90% confidence interval for your estimate. Show that about 290 000 points need to be selected in order to be 90% certain of obtaining a value for π which will be in error by less than 0.005.

Solution 9.16 The point (x, y) is chosen at random, where $0 < x < 1$ and $0 < y < 1$.

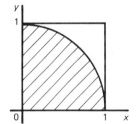

Points thus chosen are spread uniformly over the square with vertices $(0, 0)$, $(1, 0)$, $(1, 1)$, $(0, 1)$.

So the probability that the point lies within the circle $x^2 + y^2 = 1$ is equal to the fraction of the area of the square which lies in the region defined by the inequality $x^2 + y^2 < 1$.

So, $P(\text{point lies within circle}) = \dfrac{\text{area quadrant}}{\text{area square}}$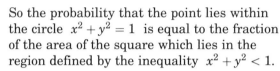

$$= \frac{\pi/4}{1}$$

$$= \pi/4$$

If 1000 points are taken and 784 lie within the circle, then if the true proportion of points lying within the circle is p, an estimate for p is p_s where

$$p_s = \frac{784}{1000}$$

$$= 0.784$$

So an estimate for $\pi/4 = 0.784$ and hence <u>an estimate for π is</u> <u>$(0.784)(4) = 3.136$.</u>

Now, a 90% confidence interval for p is given by

$$p_s \pm 1.645 \sqrt{\frac{p_s q_s}{n}} \quad \text{where} \quad q_s = 1 - p_s$$

$$= 0.784 \pm (1.645) \sqrt{\frac{(0.784)(0.216)}{1000}}$$

$$= 0.784 \pm 0.0214$$

$$= (0.7626, 0.8054)$$

Therefore $P(0.7626 < \pi/4 < 0.8054) = 0.90$

i.e. $P(3.0504 < \pi < 3.2216) = 0.90$

So a 90% confidence interval for π is (3.0504, 3.2216).

If the value for π is to be in error by less than 0.005 then the value for $\pi/4$ must be in error by less than 0.001 25.

When $n = 1000$, the size of the interval was $p_s \pm 0.0214$.

Now we need to find n such that the size of the interval is $p_s \pm 0.001\,25$,

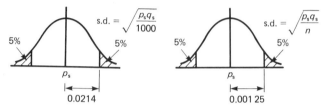

i.e. we require n such that

$$1.645\sqrt{\frac{p_s q_s}{n}} < 0.001\,25$$

so $$\sqrt{n} > \frac{1.645}{0.001\,25}\sqrt{(0.784)(0.216)}$$

$$\sqrt{n} > 541.44$$

$$n > 293\,279$$

So about 290 000 points need to be selected in order to be 90% certain of obtaining a value for π which will be in error by less than 0.005.

Example 9.17   In a sample of 400 shops it was discovered that 136 of them sold carpets at below the list prices which had been recommended by manufacturers.

(**a**) Estimate the percentage of all carpet selling shops selling below list price.

(**b**) Calculate the 95% confidence limits for this estimate, and explain briefly what these mean.

(**c**) What size sample would have to be taken in order to estimate the percentage to within ±2%?

Solution 9.17   From the sample, the proportion of shops selling below list price is p_s where $p_s = \frac{136}{400} = 0.34$.

(**a**) An estimate of the percentage of all carpet selling shops selling below list price is $\hat{p}$ where $\hat{p} = p_s$.

So $\hat{p} = 0.34 = 34\%$.

(**b**) A 95% confidence interval for the true population proportion p is given by

$$p_s \pm 1.96 \sqrt{\frac{p_s q_s}{n}} = 0.34 \pm (1.96) \sqrt{\frac{(0.34)(0.66)}{400}}$$

$$= 0.34 \pm 0.046$$

$$= 34\% \pm 4.6\%$$

The 95% confidence interval is $(34\% \pm 4.6\%) = (29.4\%, 38.6\%)$.

(**c**) In part (**b**) the percentage of shops was estimated to within $\pm 4.6\%$. We now require n such that the percentage of shops is estimated to within $\pm 2\%$ (assuming 95% confidence).

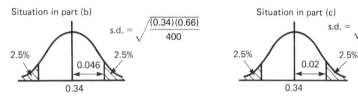

We require n such that

$$p_s \pm 1.96 \sqrt{\frac{p_s q_s}{n}} = p_s \pm 0.02$$

i.e. $$1.96 \sqrt{\frac{(0.34)(0.66)}{n}} = 0.02$$

so $$\sqrt{n} = \frac{1.96}{0.02} \sqrt{(0.34)(0.66)}$$

$$= 46.42$$

$$n = 2155.14$$

So a sample of size 2156 would have to be taken.

Exercise 9e

1. A sample, of size n, is taken from a population in which the proportion of 'successes' is p. From the value of the sample proportion given, calculate the confidence interval indicated for the proportion p.

	n	p_s	% confidence interval
(a)	100	0.42	95%
(b)	70	0.8	97%
(c)	150	0.32	99%
(d)	50	0.66	95%
(e)	150	0.2	90%
(f)	200	0.77	99%
(g)	1000	0.5	95%

2. In a survey carried out in a large city, 170 households out of a random sample of 250 owned at least one pet. Find 95% confidence limits for the proportion of households in the city who own at least one pet.

3. In order to assess the probability of a successful outcome, an experiment is performed 200 times and the number of successful outcomes is found to be 72. Find (*a*) 95%, (*b*) 99% confidence intervals for p, the probability of a successful outcome.

4. In a market research survey 25 people out of a random sample of 100 from a certain area said that they used a particular brand of soap. Find 97% confidence limits for the proportion of people in the area who use this brand of soap.

5. The probability of success in each of a long series of n independent trials is constant and equal to p. Explain how 95% approximate confidence limits for p may be obtained.
In an opinion poll carried out before a local election, 501 people out of a random sample of 925 declare that they will vote for a particular one of two candidates contesting the election. Find 95% confidence limits for the true proportion of all voters in favour of this candidate.
Do you consider there is significant evidence that this candidate will win the election?*
*See p. 530   (AEB)

6. The data in the table below refer to 144 recoveries of a particular type of sea-bird. The distances given are those between the original colonies where the birds were born and the place of recovery.

Distance (miles)	Frequency
1–100	50
101–200	16
201–300	30
301–400	11
401–500	12
501–600	9
601–700	8
701–800	3
801–900	4
901–1000	1

Using an assumed mean of 250.5 obtain the sample mean recovery distance and the sample standard deviation.
Assuming that the recovery distances accurately reflect the dispersal of birds from their original colonies, estimate the proportion of this type of bird at more than 300 miles from the original colony. Give an approximate symmetric 95% confidence interval for this estimate.   (C)

7. A random sample of 600 was chosen from the adults living in a town in order to investigate the number x of days of work lost through illness. Before taking the sample it was decided that certain categories of people would be excluded from the analysis of the number of working days lost although they would not be excluded from the sample. In the sample 180 were found to be from these categories. For the remaining 420 members of the sample $\sum x = 1260$ $\sum x^2 = 46\,000$.

(a) Estimate the mean number of days lost through illness, for the restricted population, and give a 95% confidence interval for the mean.
(b) Estimate the percentage of people in the town who fall into the excluded categories, and give a 99% confidence interval for this percentage.
(c) Give two examples, with reasons, of people who might fall into the excluded categories.   (O)

8. There are n_0 fish in a lake. A random sample of m of these fish is taken. The fish in this sample are tagged and released unharmed back into the lake. After a suitable interval, a second random sample of size n is taken. The random variable R is the number of fish in this second sample that are found to have been tagged. Assuming that the probability that a fish is captured is independent of whether it has been tagged or not, and that n_0 is sufficiently large for a binomial approximation to be used, obtain the expectation of R in terms of m, n and n_0. Suppose that $m = 100$, $n = 4000$ and that the observed value of R is 20. Obtain an approximate symmetric 98% confidence interval for the proportion of fish in the lake which are tagged. Deduce an approximate 98% confidence interval for n_0.   (C)

9. A random sample of 500 fish is taken from a lake, marked, and returned to the lake. After a suitable interval a second sample of 500 is taken, and 25 of these are found to be marked. By considering the proportion of marked fish in the second sample, estimate the number of fish in the lake and, by considering a confidence interval for the proportion of marked fish in the lake, obtain a 95% confidence interval for the number of fish.   (O)

10. In observations of a particular type of event, the probability of a positive result of any one observation is independent of the results of other observations and has the value θ, the same for all observations. In n observations the proportion giving positive results is p. State the mean and standard deviation of the probability distribution of p. Say also how and in what circumstances this probability distribution can be approximated by a normal distribution. Show that, according to this approximation, the probability that p satisfies the inequality

$$|p - \theta| < 1.96 \sqrt{\frac{\theta(1 - \theta)}{n}}$$

is 95%.

In a set of 100 observations of this type, 90 gave a positive result. Obtain an inequality of

the above form, and by squaring both sides of the inequality calculate from the roots of a quadratic equation an approximate 95% symmetric confidence interval for the value of θ for the type of event observed.

(JMB)

SUMMARY — CONFIDENCE INTERVALS

	95% confidence interval	99% confidence interval	
Population mean μ σ^2 *known*	$\bar{x} \pm 1.96 \, \dfrac{\sigma}{\sqrt{n}}$	$\bar{x} \pm 2.575 \, \dfrac{\sigma}{\sqrt{n}}$	n is sample size
σ^2 *unknown,* n *large* s^2 is sample variance	$\bar{x} \pm 1.96 \, \dfrac{\widehat{\sigma}}{\sqrt{n}}$	$\bar{x} \pm 2.575 \, \dfrac{\widehat{\sigma}}{\sqrt{n}}$	n is sample size $\widehat{\sigma}^2 = \dfrac{\sum (x - \bar{x})^2}{n - 1}$ $= \dfrac{ns^2}{n - 1}$
Population proportion p, n *large*	$p_{\text{s}} \pm 1.96 \, \sqrt{\dfrac{p_{\text{s}}q_{\text{s}}}{n}}$	$p_{\text{s}} \pm 2.575 \, \sqrt{\dfrac{p_{\text{s}}q_{\text{s}}}{n}}$	n is sample size. p_{s} is the sample proportion and $q_{\text{s}} = 1 - p_{\text{s}}$

SPECIAL NOTE: As mentioned previously, in some texts the unbiased estimate of the variance is not written as $\widehat{\sigma}^2$, but as s^2, the notation that we have used for the sample variance. Therefore care must be taken to ensure that these formulae are fully understood so that they can be used accurately whichever notation is adopted.

Miscellaneous Exercise 9f

1. (*a*) Before its annual overhaul, the mean operating time of an automatic machine was 103 seconds. After the annual overhaul, the following random sample of operating times (in seconds) was obtained.

| 90 | 97 | 101 | 92 | 101 | 95 | 95 | 98 | 96 | 95 |

Assuming that the time taken to perform the operation is a normally distributed random variable with a known standard deviation of 5 seconds, find 98% confidence limits for the mean operating time after the overhaul.

Comment on the magnitude of these limits relative to the mean operating time before the overhaul.

(*b*) The results of a survey showed that 3600 out of 10 000 families regularly purchased a specific weekly magazine. Find the 95% confidence limits for the proportion of the population buying the magazine.

Estimate the additional number of families to be contacted if the probability that the estimated proportion is in error by more than 0.01 is to be at most 1%. (AEB 1987)

2. From a large pile of industrial diamonds, 20 were put through 6 sieves of different mesh sizes and the number of diamonds passing through each sieve was counted. The table shows the mesh size (mm) and corresponding number of diamonds passing through each sieve.

Mesh size	1	2	4	6	8	12
Number of diamonds	1	2	6	8	14	20

Graphically, or otherwise, estimate the mesh size of the sieve if half the diamonds will pass through it, and the mesh size of the sieve if one quarter of the diamonds will pass through it.
Construct a frequency table showing for each mesh size listed in the table the extra number of diamonds which passed through. Calculate unbiased estimates, in each case to 2 decimal places, of the mean and the variance of the sizes of the diamonds in the original large pile.   (L)

3. Describe briefly the empirical evidence that you acquired for the Central Limit Theorem. The amount, to the nearest mg, of a certain chemical in particles in the atmosphere at a meteorological station was measured each day for 300 days. The results are shown in the table.

Amount of chemical (mg)	12	13	14	15	16
Number of days	5	42	210	31	12

Find the mean daily amount of chemical over the 300 days and estimate, to 2 decimal places, its standard error.
Obtain, to 2 decimal places, approximate 98% confidence limits for the mean daily amount of chemical in the atmosphere.
If daily measurements are taken for a further 300 days, estimate, to 2 decimal places, the probability that the mean of these daily measurements will be less than 14.   (L)

4. A company manufactures bars of soap. In a random sample of 70 bars, 18 were found to be mis-shaped. Calculate an approximate 99% confidence interval for the proportion of mis-shaped bars of soap.
Explain what you understand by a 99% confidence interval by considering
(*a*) intervals in general based on the above method,
(*b*) the interval you have calculated.

The bars of soap are either pink or white in colour and differently shaped according to colour. The masses of both types of soap are known to be normally distributed, the mean mass of the white bars being 176.2 g. The standard deviation for both bars is 6.46 g. A sample of 12 of the pink bars of soap had masses, measured to the nearest gram, as follows.

174	164	182	169	171	187	176
177	168	171	180	175		

Find a 95% confidence interval for the mean mass of pink bars of soap.
Calculate also an interval within which approximately 90% of the masses of the white bars of soap will lie.
The cost of manufacturing a pink bar of soap of mass x g is $(15 + 0.065x)$ p, and it is sold for 32 p. If the company manufactures 9000 bars of pink soap per week, derive a 95% confidence interval for its weekly expected profit from pink bars of soap.   (AEB 1988)

5. Three weeks before an election in a certain constituency an opinion poll was conducted using a random sample of 800 voters selected from the electoral roll. The numbers of persons who said they would vote for parties *A*, *B*, *C* are recorded below; the remainder were categorised as 'Don't know'.

Party *A*	Party *B*	Party *C*	Don't know
264	256	144	136

(i) Calculate an approximate 90 per cent symmetric confidence interval for the proportion of the total electorate in the constituency that will vote for party *A* in the election.
(ii) Give a *very brief* description of how the sample might have been selected, to ensure that it was random.
(iii) In the actual election, 41 per cent of the total electorate voted for party *A*. Give two possible explanations for the fact that this value is not contained within the confidence interval calculated in (i).   (JMB)

6. The random variable X is normally distributed with mean μ and variance σ^2.
(*a*) Write down the distribution of the sample mean $\overline{X}$ of a random sample of size n.
An efficiency expert wishes to determine the mean time taken to drill a fixed number of holes in a metal sheet.
(*b*) Determine how large a random sample is needed so that the expert can be 95% certain that the sample mean time will differ from the true mean time by less than 15 seconds. Assume that it is known from previous studies that $\sigma = 40$ seconds.   (L)

7. In a classroom experiment to estimate the mean height, μ cm, of seventeen-year-old boys, the heights, x cm, of 100 such pupils were obtained. The data were summarised by

$$\sum(x - 170) = 270 \qquad \sum(x - 170)^2 = 7179$$

(i) Find the mean and variance of the data, and use them to find the symmetrical 95% confidence interval for μ.
A larger experiment is planned using the heights of 2000 seventeen-year-old boys.
(ii) What effect will the use of a larger sample have on the width of the confidence interval for μ?

8. If a random sample of n observations is drawn from a normal distribution with mean μ and variance σ^2, specify completely the sampling distribution of $\overline{X}$, the mean of such a sample.
Explain why $\overline{X}$ is an unbiased and consistent estimator of μ.
An experimental physicist needs to estimate the true viscosity, μ Pascal seconds (Pa s), of a light machine oil. Using the same apparatus he takes 12 independent measurements, x Pa s, of the viscosity of the oil, obtaining the values below.

$$
\begin{array}{cccccc}
25.8 & 25.2 & 24.7 & 25.5 & 25.3 & 25.4 \\
25.2 & 25.3 & 25.8 & 25.9 & 25.2 & 24.9
\end{array}
$$

$$(\sum x = 304.2 \qquad \sum x^2 = 7712.9)$$

When using this apparatus, measurements of the oil's viscosity are distributed with mean μ and variance σ^2. Obtain unbiased estimates of μ and σ^2. Hence obtain a symmetric 95% confidence interval for μ. State any distributional assumptions you have made in obtaining your confidence interval.
The physicist explained the meaning of his confidence interval by saying there was a probability of 0.95 that μ lay between the limits of the interval. Explain why this interpretation is wrong and provide a correct explanation of 95% *confidence* as used in this context.
The manufacturer of the oil quotes a viscosity of 25.5 Pa s for the oil. With reference to your confidence interval, state any conclusion you can come to regarding the validity of this figure. (JMB)

9. Packets of baking powder have a nominal weight of 200 g. The distribution of weights is normal and the standard deviation is 7 g. Average quantity system legislation states that, if the nominal weight is 200 g,

(i) the average weight must be at least 200 g,
(ii) not more than 2.5% of packages may weigh less than 191 g,
(iii) not more than 1 in 1000 packages may weigh less than 182 g.
A random sample of 30 packages had the following weights:

218, 207, 214, 189, 211, 206, 203, 217, 183, 186
219, 213, 207, 214, 203, 204, 195, 197, 213, 212
188, 221, 217, 184, 186, 216, 198, 211, 216, 200

(a) Calculate a 95% confidence interval for the mean weight.
(b) Find the proportion of packets in the sample weighing less than 191 g and use your result to calculate an approximate 95% confidence interval for the proportion of all packets weighing less than 191 g.
(c) Assuming that the mean is at the lower limit of the interval calculated in (a), what proportion of packets would weigh less than 182 g?
(d) Discuss the suitability of the packets from the point of view of the average quantity system. A simple adjustment will change the mean weight of future packages. Changing the standard deviation is possible but very expensive. Without carrying out any further calculations, discuss any adjustments you might recommend.
(AEB 1990)

10. (a) The random variable X is such that $X \sim N(\mu, 3.2^2)$. A sample of 12 values of X gave the following data:

$$
\begin{array}{cccccc}
17.6 & 13.4 & 23.7 & 18.6 & 15.3 & 16.4 \\
21.6 & 18.9 & 17.8 & 14.2 & 17.1 & 18.4
\end{array}
$$

(i) Find symmetrical 95% confidence limits for μ.
(ii) Find the value of α such that $-\infty \leqslant \mu \leqslant \alpha$ gives a one-sided 95% confidence interval for μ.
(b) A random sample of size 100 is taken of the variable y with the following results:

$$\sum y = 2856 \qquad \sum y^2 = 81832$$

Find a symmetrical 99% confidence interval for μ, the population mean.
(c) (i) In an opinion poll, 2000 people were interviewed and 527 said that they preferred Brand A washing powder.
Calculate an approximate 95% confidence interval for the population proportion preferring Brand A.
(ii) If the 2% confidence interval, based on a sample of size 500, for the population proportion preferring Brand A is (0.2278, 0.2922), calculate the value of α.

11. A certain brand of beans is sold in tins, the tins being filled and sealed by one of two machines $M1$ or $M2$. From $M1$, the mass of beans in each tin is normally distributed with mean 425 g and standard deviation 25 g and the mass of the tin is normally distributed with mean 90 g and standard deviation 10 g.

(a) Find the probability that the *total* mass of the sealed tin and its beans

(i) exceeds 550 g,

(ii) lies between 466 g and 575 g.

(b) Calculate an interval within which approximately 90% of the masses of the filled tins from $M1$ will lie.

The tins from $M1$ are packed in boxes of 24, the mass of the box being normally distributed with mean 500 g and standard deviation 30 g.

(c) Find the probability that a full box weighs less than 12.75 kg.

A random sample of 10 tins was taken from the production of $M2$ and their total masses (beans and tin), measured to the nearest gram, were as follows

$512, 515, 499, 528, 519, 510, 507, 522, 530, 514.$

(d) Find a 95% confidence interval for the mean mass of tins of beans, produced on $M2$, assuming that the masses of tins of beans from $M2$ are normally distributed with the same standard deviation as $M1$.

After a delivery of 50 boxes to a supermarket, 150 tins were found to be damaged.

(e) Calculate an approximate 99% confidence interval for the proportion of damaged tins a supermarket might expect to receive.

(AEB 1989)

10

SIGNIFICANCE TESTING

NULL AND ALTERNATIVE HYPOTHESES

When making a statistical enquiry, we often put forward a hypothesis concerning a population parameter. For example

the mean height of 15-year-old girls is 1.62 m,

the proportion of left-handed people is 0.05,

the mean number of telephone calls received by a switchboard over a period of 30 minutes is 20.

This hypothesis is called the **null hypothesis** and is denoted by H_0.

In order to test the validity of H_0, we consider observations made from random samples taken from the population and perform a statistical test.

If this test shows that we should reject the null hypothesis, H_0, we do so in favour of an **alternative hypothesis,** denoted by H_1.

There are several types of statistical test and we consider first those involving the *normal distribution*.

The following will be discussed:

Test 1: Testing a mean, based on a sample value.

Test 2: Testing a mean, based on the mean of a random sample of size n.

Test 3: Testing the difference between means, based on the means of two random samples.

Test 4: Testing a proportion, based on the proportion in a random sample, when the sample size is large.

PROCEDURE FOR CARRYING OUT A STATISTICAL TEST

There is a useful standard procedure for performing a test, and to illustrate this we consider Test 1: testing a mean, based on a sample value.

Suppose we have a *normal* population, with *known variance* σ^2, but we do not know the mean μ. We take a value, at random, from the population. Call this value x.

Say, for example, we wish to investigate whether the mean of the population is 25, or whether it is not 25. The hypotheses would be

H_0: $\mu = 25$ (the population mean μ is 25)

H_1: $\mu \neq 25$ (the population mean μ is not 25)

We then assume that H_0 *is* true, so that

$$X \sim N(\mu, \sigma^2) \quad \text{with} \quad \mu = 25$$

i.e. $X \sim N(25, \sigma^2)$

Now we must decide whether it is likely that the sample value has been drawn from this population. We consider whether it is 'close to μ', or whether it is in the tail end of the distribution.

To do this we standardise X. The standardised value Z is known as the **test statistic**.

> Now $Z = \dfrac{X - \mu}{\sigma}$ where Z is distributed as $N(0,1)$
>
> under the null hypothesis that the population mean is μ.

In this example we would use $Z = \dfrac{X - 25}{\sigma}$

We then standardise the sample value x to obtain $z = \dfrac{x - 25}{\sigma}$.

NOTE: we use small letters here because we are now considering specific numerical values of the random variable.

If z is close to zero, i.e. $|z|$ is small, we accept that the sample value could have been taken from a population with mean 25 and we do not reject H_0.

If z is far from zero and is in one of the tail ends of the distribution, i.e. $|z|$ is large, we reject H_0 and conclude that the population mean is not 25.

CRITICAL REGION AND CRITICAL VALUES

We need to select a set of values for z which tells us when to reject H_0. This set of values is known as the **critical region** and it depends on the type and the *level* of the test chosen. The boundaries of the critical region are called the **critical values**.

5% level of significance

Often the critical region is chosen so that the probability that Z falls within it is just 5%. For this we need 2.5% of the area at each end of the distribution.

Now $P(Z < -1.96) = 0.025$ and $P(Z > 1.96) = 0.025$, giving $P(|Z| > 1.96) = 0.05$, so the critical values are ± 1.96.

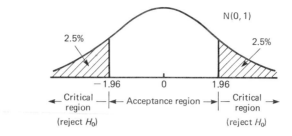

If the test is carried out at the 5% level, we reject H_0 if $z < -1.96$ or if $z > 1.96$, i.e. if $|z| > 1.96$.

If we reject H_0 at this level, we say that 'there is significant evidence, at the 5% level, that the population mean is not μ'.

ONE-TAILED AND TWO-TAILED TESTS

There are two types of test that can be performed, depending on the alternative hypothesis being made. These are (**a**) a two-tailed test, (**b**) a one-tailed test.

(a) Two-tailed test

A two-tailed test looks for *any change* in the parameter. For example, the hypotheses could be

$$H_0: \quad \mu = 25$$

$$H_1: \quad \mu \neq 25$$

The critical region depends on the level of the test. The most usual level chosen is the 5% level, but often a 1% or a 10% level is chosen.

Critical region at 5% level:

$$P(|Z| > 1.96) = 0.05$$

Critical region at 1% level:

$$P(|Z| > 2.575) = 0.01$$

Critical region at 10% level:

$$P(|Z| > 1.645) = 0.1$$

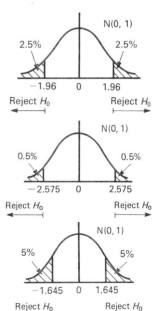

(b) One-tailed test

A one-tailed test looks for a *definite decrease* or a *definite increase* in the parameter. For example, the hypotheses could be:

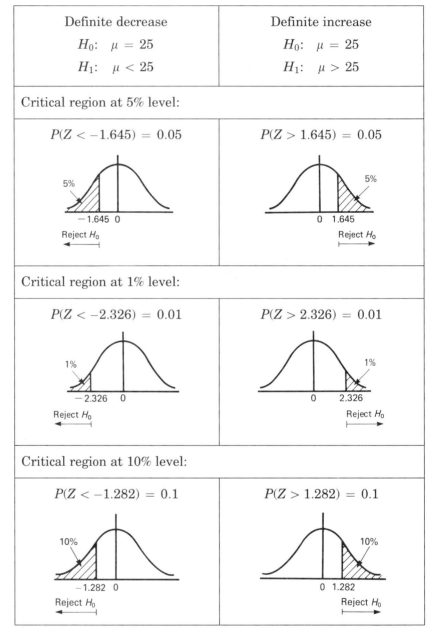

Definite decrease	Definite increase
H_0: $\mu = 25$	H_0: $\mu = 25$
H_1: $\mu < 25$	H_1: $\mu > 25$

Critical region at 5% level:

$P(Z < -1.645) = 0.05$	$P(Z > 1.645) = 0.05$
5% −1.645 0 Reject H_0	5% 0 1.645 Reject H_0

Critical region at 1% level:

$P(Z < -2.326) = 0.01$	$P(Z > 2.326) = 0.01$
1% −2.326 0 Reject H_0	1% 0 2.326 Reject H_0

Critical region at 10% level:

$P(Z < -1.282) = 0.1$	$P(Z > 1.282) = 0.1$
10% −1.282 0 Reject H_0	10% 0 1.282 Reject H_0

If the distribution given by the null hypothesis H_0 *is* true, then the probability that z lies in the region pronounced as 'critical' is 0.05, 0.01, 0.1, ..., depending on the level of the test (5%, 1%, 10%, ...).

But if z lies in the critical region, we reject H_0. Therefore the probability that we reject H_0, when in fact it is true, is determined by the level of the test chosen. For example, if the test is performed at the 5% level, then the probability of wrongly rejecting H_0 is 0.05.

In general, when performing a significance test it is useful to follow a set procedure:

Before any sample readings are considered:

(1) State the null hypothesis, H_0 and the alternative hypothesis H_1.

   If we are looking for a definite increase or a definite decrease in the population parameter, we use a *one-tailed test* and if we are looking for *any* change we use a *two-tailed test*.

(2) Consider the appropriate distribution given by the null hypothesis.

(3) Decide on the level of the test. This fixes the critical values of the test statistic.

(4) Decide on the rejection criteria.

Now consider the sample values.

(5) Calculate the value of the test statistic.

(6) Make a conclusion: If the value of the test statistic lies in the critical region, reject H_0.
   If the value of the test statistic does not lie in the critical region, do not reject H_0.

   If H_0 is rejected at the 5% level, we say that the test value is 'significant'.

   If H_0 is rejected at the 1% level, then the test value is 'highly significant'.

TEST 1: TESTING A MEAN BASED ON A SAMPLE VALUE

Example 10.1   The r.v. X is such that $X \sim N(\mu, 100)$. A value is taken at random from the population and found to be 172. Test, at the 5% level, whether the population mean μ could be 150.

Solution 10.1   We *assume* that μ is 150, and this is the null hypothesis (H_0). The alternative hypothesis (H_1) is that μ is not 150. We write

State H_0 and H_1;
decide whether the
test is one-tailed or
two-tailed

$$H_0: \quad \mu = 150$$

$$H_1: \quad \mu \neq 150 \quad \text{(two-tailed test)}$$

Consider the
distribution given
by H_0

Now *if H_0 is true,* $X \sim N(150, 100)$

Decide on the level
of the test
Decide on rejection
criteria

We will test at the 5% level, and considering the test statistic

$Z = \dfrac{X - \mu}{\sigma}$, we will reject H_0 if $|z| > 1.96$.

Calculate the value
of the test statistic

Now $z = \dfrac{x - \mu}{\sigma}$

$\quad = \dfrac{172 - 150}{10}$

$\quad = 2.2$

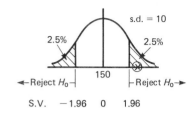

Make conclusion

Since $|z| > 1.96$, we reject H_0 and conclude that there is significant evidence, at the 5% level, to suggest that the population mean is not 150.

NOTE: once z has been calculated, its position can be noted on the diagram thus, $\otimes$, indicating whether it lies in the rejection region or not. In Example 10.1, $z = 2.2$ so $\otimes$ is placed to the right of the standardised value 1.96.

Example 10.2   The r.v. X is such that $X \sim N(\mu, 30)$. A sample value of 54 is obtained. Test, at the 1% level, whether the population mean is less than 65.

Solution 10.2   Although the question asks that we test whether the mean is less than 65, the null hypothesis must state a definite value. So, for the null hypothesis, we assume that the mean is 65, and the alternative hypothesis is that the mean is less than 65.

$$H_0: \quad \mu = 65$$

$$H_1: \quad \mu < 65 \quad \text{(one-tailed test)}$$

Now if H_0 is true, $X \sim N(65, 30)$ and the test statistic is
$Z = \dfrac{X - \mu}{\sigma}$, i.e. $Z = \dfrac{X - 65}{\sqrt{30}}$.

We perform a one-tailed test at the 1% level, and reject H_0 if $z < -2.326$, where

$z = \dfrac{x - \mu}{\sigma}$

$\quad = \dfrac{54 - 65}{\sqrt{30}}$

$\quad = -2.01$

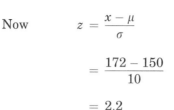

Conclusion: since $z > -2.326$, we do not reject H_0 and we conclude at the 1% level, that the sample value could have been drawn from a population with mean 65.

The following example is a very useful application of Test 1.

Example 10.3 If 100 seeds are planted, and 83 seeds germinate, use the normal approximation to the binomial distribution to test the manufacturer's claim of a 90% germination rate. Use a 5% level of significance.

Solution 10.3 Let X be the r.v. 'the number of seeds that germinate'. Then we have a binomial situation, and $X \sim \text{Bin}(n, p)$ with $n = 100$.

$$H_0: \quad p = 0.9 \quad \text{(the germination rate is 90\%)}$$

$$H_1: \quad p < 0.9 \quad \text{(the germination rate is less than 90\%)}$$

(We have chosen a one-tailed test, since this seems more appropriate to the situation.)

Under H_0, $X \sim \text{Bin}(100, 0.9)$.

Now since n *is large*, we use the normal approximation to the binomial distribution so $X \sim \text{N}(np, npq)$ with

$$np = (100)(0.9) = 90 \quad \text{and} \quad npq = (100)(0.9)(0.1) = 9$$

i.e. $\qquad\qquad\qquad\qquad X \sim \text{N}(90, 9)$

We perform a one-tailed test, at the 5% level, and reject H_0 if $z < -1.645$, where

$$z = \frac{x - np}{\sqrt{npq}}$$

$$= \frac{83 - 90}{3}$$

$$= -2.33$$

Conclusion: since $z < -1.645$ we reject H_0 and <u>conclude that there</u> <u>is significant evidence, at the 5% level, to suggest that the manu-</u><u>facturer's claim is false.</u>

NOTE: when using the normal approximation to the binomial we should use a continuity correction, considering the value 83 to be represented by a rectangle from 82.5 to 83.5. In order to reject H_0 we would want the *whole* of this rectangle to lie in the rejection region. So we use the value 83.5 in the test.

With the continuity correction,

$$z = \frac{83.5 - 90}{3}$$

$$= -2.17$$

and the same conclusion is reached.

Exercise 10a

1. Test the mean in the following normal populations, based on the sample value given. Test at (*a*) the 5% level, (*b*) the 1% level.

	Sample value	Hypotheses	Population variance (σ^2)
(i)	104	H_0: $\mu = 96$, H_1: $\mu \neq 96$	16
(ii)	90	H_0: $\mu = 96$, H_1: $\mu < 96$	16
(iii)	132	H_0: $\mu = 120$, H_1: $\mu > 120$	32
(iv)	106	H_0: $\mu = 120$, H_1: $\mu \neq 120$	32
(v)	22	H_0: $\mu = 18$, H_1: $\mu \neq 18$	1.2
(vi)	16	H_0: $\mu = 18$, H_1: $\mu < 18$,	1.2

2. A coin is tossed 64 times. Test at the 5% level of significance whether the coin is fair, or whether it is biased in favour of showing heads, if (*a*) 38 heads occur, (*b*) 42 heads occur.

3. A manufacturer claims that 8 out of 10 dogs prefer his brand to any other. In a random sample of 120 dogs, it was found that 88 ate that brand. Test at the 5% level whether you would accept the manufacturer's claim.

4. In a survey it was found that 3 out of 10 people supported a particular political party. A month later the party representative claimed that the popularity of the party had increased. Would you accept that the number who supported the party was still 3 out of 10 if a further survey revealed that 38 people in a random sample of 100 supported the party? Test at the 3% level.

5. A gardener sows 150 'Special' cabbage seeds and knows that the germination rate is 75%. (*a*) By using a suitable approximation find the probability that (i) more than 122 seeds germinate, (ii) less than 106 seeds germinate. (*b*) The gardener also sows 120 'Everyday' cabbage seeds and finds that 81 germinate. Test whether the 'Everyday' seeds have a germination rate less than 75%. Test at the 4% level.

TEST 2: TESTING A MEAN, BASED ON A SAMPLE MEAN

Case 1 — Population variance σ^2 known

Instead of taking one sample value, for a more reliable test of the mean we take a random sample of n independent observations and then use the sample mean. We proceed as follows:

Consider the random variable X with known variance σ^2 but unknown mean.

Make the null hypothesis (H_0) that the population mean is μ.

Take a sample of size n and consider the distribution of the sample mean $\overline{X}$.

If H_0 is true, then:

(*i*) if X is normally distributed, $\overline{X} \sim N\left(\mu, \dfrac{\sigma^2}{n}\right)$

(*ii*) if X is *not* normally distributed but n is large, by the Central Limit Theorem,

$$\overline{X} \sim N\left(\mu, \dfrac{\sigma^2}{n}\right)$$

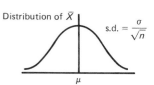

Distribution of $\overline{X}$

s.d. $= \dfrac{\sigma}{\sqrt{n}}$

μ

Reminders: the distribution of $\overline{X}$ is known as the sampling distribution of means; the standard deviation of this distribution ($\sigma/\sqrt{n}$) is known as the standard error of the mean (see p. 443).

Now we want to investigate whether there is a significant difference between the sample mean and the population mean given by the null hypothesis. To do this we need to consider the standard normal variable Z.

Standardising, we have $Z = \dfrac{\overline{X} - \mu}{\sigma/\sqrt{n}}$ where $Z \sim N(0, 1)$.

We use the test statistic $Z = \dfrac{\overline{X} - \mu}{\sigma/\sqrt{n}}$ which is distributed as $N(0, 1)$ under the null hypothesis H_0 that the true population mean is μ.

Example 10.4 The lengths of metal bars produced by a particular machine are normally distributed with mean length 420 cm and standard deviation 12 cm. The machine is serviced, after which a sample of 100 bars gives a mean length of 423 cm. Is there evidence, at the 5% level, of a change in the mean length of the bars produced by the machine, assuming that the standard deviation remains the same?

Solution 10.4 Let X be the r.v. 'the length, in cm, of a metal bar'. Let the population mean be μ and the population variance be σ^2. We know that $\sigma = 12$, so $X \sim N(\mu, 12^2)$.

We are trying to establish whether there has been a change in the mean length of the bars. However the null hypothesis must assume that the mean is still 420.

The alternative hypothesis is that the mean is not 420.

i.e. H_0: $\mu = 420$ cm   (there is no change)

            H_1: $\mu \neq 420$ cm   (there is a change)

Now consider the sampling distribution of means.

$$\overline{X} \sim N\left(\mu, \frac{\sigma^2}{n}\right) \quad \text{with} \quad \sigma^2 = 12^2, \quad n = 100$$

If H_0 is true, $\mu = 420$, so $\overline{X} \sim N\left(420, \dfrac{12^2}{100}\right)$.

The test statistic is

$$Z = \frac{\overline{X} - \mu}{\sigma/\sqrt{n}}$$

i.e.

$$Z = \frac{\overline{X} - 420}{12/\sqrt{100}}$$

$$= \frac{\overline{X} - 420}{1.2}$$

We perform a two-tailed test, at the 5% level, and reject H_0 if $|z| > 1.96$.

We calculate z where

$$z = \frac{\overline{x} - \mu}{\sigma/\sqrt{n}}$$

$$= \frac{423 - 420}{1.2}$$

$$= 2.5$$

Conclusion: since $|z| > 1.96$, we reject H_0 and conclude that there is significant evidence, at the 5% level, of a change in the mean length of the bars produced by the machine.

Example 10.5 Experience has shown that the scores obtained in a particular test are normally distributed with mean score 70 and variance 36. When the test is taken by a random sample of 49 students, the mean score is 68.5. Is there sufficient evidence, at the 3% level, that these students have not performed as well as expected?

Solution 10.5 Let X be the r.v. 'the score of a student'. Let the population mean be μ and the population variance be σ^2, where $\sigma^2 = 36$, so $X \sim N(\mu, 36)$.

We *assume* that μ is 70 and that the students have performed as expected. This is the null hypothesis.

The alternative hypothesis is that the mean is less than 70. We write

$\quad H_0: \quad \mu = 70 \quad$ (the population mean μ is 70)

$\quad H_1: \quad \mu < 70 \quad$ (the population mean is less than 70 and the students have not done as well as expected)

Consider the sampling distribution of means.

$$\overline{X} \sim N\left(\mu, \frac{\sigma^2}{n}\right) \quad \text{with} \quad \sigma^2 = 36, \quad n = 49$$

If H_0 is true, $\mu = 70$, so $\overline{X} \sim N\left(70, \frac{36}{49}\right)$.

The test statistic is

$$Z = \frac{\overline{X} - \mu}{\sigma/\sqrt{n}}$$

i.e. $$Z = \frac{\overline{X} - 70}{6/\sqrt{49}}$$

$$= \frac{\overline{X} - 70}{6/7}$$

We perform a one-tailed test, at the 3% level. The critical value **a** is such that $P(Z < \mathbf{a}) = 0.03$.

From tables $\mathbf{a} = -1.881$.

So, we reject H_0 if $z < -1.881$, where

$$z = \frac{\overline{x} - \mu}{\sigma/\sqrt{n}}$$

$$= \frac{68.5 - 70}{6/7}$$

$$= -1.75$$

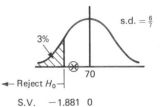

Conclusion: since $z > -1.881$ we do not reject H_0 and we conclude that, at the 3% level, the students have not under-achieved.

Example 10.6   It is claimed that the masses of components produced at a particular workshop are normally distributed with a mean mass of 6 g and a standard deviation of 0.8 g. If this claim is accepted, at the 5% level, on the basis of the mean mass obtained from a random sample of 50 components, between what values must the mean mass of the 50 components in the sample lie?

Solution 10.6   Let X be the r.v. 'the mass, in g, of a component'. Let the population mean be μ and the population variance be σ^2, where $\sigma = 0.8$.

$$H_0: \quad \mu = 6\,\mathrm{g}$$

$$H_1: \quad \mu \neq 6\,\mathrm{g} \quad \text{(two-tailed test)}$$

Consider the sampling distribution of means where

$$\overline{X} \sim \mathrm{N}\!\left(\mu, \frac{\sigma^2}{n}\right) \quad \text{with} \quad \sigma^2 = 0.8^2 \quad \text{and} \quad n = 50$$

Under H_0, $\mu = 6$, so $\overline{X} \sim \mathrm{N}\!\left(6, \frac{0.8^2}{50}\right)$.

The test statistic is

$$Z = \frac{\overline{X} - \mu}{\sigma/\sqrt{n}}$$

i.e. $$Z = \frac{\overline{X} - 6}{0.8/\sqrt{50}}$$

$$= \frac{\overline{X} - 6}{0.113}$$

If the test is performed at the 5% level then H_0 is accepted if $|z| < 1.96$, where

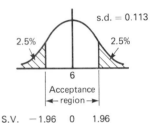

$$z = \frac{\bar{x} - \mu}{\sigma/\sqrt{n}}$$

Now, since H_0 is accepted,

$$-1.96 < z < 1.96$$

i.e. $$-1.96 < \frac{\bar{x} - 6}{0.113} < 1.96$$

$$-1.96(0.113) < \bar{x} - 6 < 1.96(0.113)$$

$$6 - 1.96(0.113) < \bar{x} < 6 + 1.96(0.113)$$

$$5.78 < \bar{x} < 6.22 \quad (\text{2 d.p.})$$

Therefore the mean mass of the 50 components must lie in the interval (5.78 g, 6.22 g).

Example 10.7   Describe, referring to your projects if you wish, the steps used in carrying out a significance test.

Over a long period it has been found that the breaking strengths of cables produced by a factory are normally distributed with mean 6000 Newtons and standard deviation 150 Newtons. Find, to 3 decimal places, the probability that a cable chosen at random from the production will have a breaking strength of more than 6200 Newtons.

A modification is introduced into the production process which only affects the value of the mean breaking strength. Six cables, chosen at random from the modified process, are tested and found to have a mean breaking strength of 5920 Newtons.

(**a**) Test, at the 5% significance level, whether the sample evidence is sufficient to conclude that the mean breaking strength of the cables is actually less than 6000 Newtons.

(**b**) Find, to 3 significant figures, the value C for which we can state with 90% confidence that the mean breaking strength of the cables exceeds C Newtons.   (L)

Solution 10.7   For steps used in carrying out a significance test, see page 511.

Let X be the r.v. 'the breaking strength, in Newtons, of a cable'. Then $X \sim N(6000, 150^2)$.

$$P(X > 6200) = P\left(Z > \frac{6200 - 6000}{150}\right)$$

$$= P(Z > 1.333)$$

$$= 0.091 \quad (3 \text{ d.p.})$$

The probability that a cable chosen at random will have a breaking strength of more than 6200 Newtons is 0.091 (3 d.p.)

A sample of six cables is tested, giving $\bar{x} = 5920$. Let μ be the population mean.

(**a**) H_0: $\mu = 6000$ Newtons

H_1: $\mu < 6000$ Newtons

Consider the sampling distribution of means,

$$\overline{X} \sim N\left(\mu, \frac{\sigma^2}{n}\right) \quad \text{with} \quad \sigma = 150, \quad n = 6$$

Under H_0, $\mu = 6000$, so $\overline{X} \sim N\left(6000, \frac{150^2}{6}\right)$

We perform a one-tailed test, at 5% level and reject H_0 if $z < -1.645$ where

$$z = \frac{\bar{x} - \mu}{\sigma/\sqrt{n}}$$

$$= \frac{5920 - 6000}{150/\sqrt{6}}$$

$$= -1.306$$

Conclusion: since $z > -1.645$ we do not reject H_0 and we conclude that the mean breaking strength is not less than 6000 Newtons.

(**b**) We require a one-sided (not symmetric) confidence interval such that

$$P(C < \mu < \infty) = 0.9$$

This is given by

$$\left(\bar{x} - 1.282\,\frac{\sigma}{\sqrt{n}}, \infty\right)$$

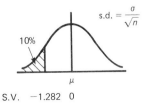

so
$$C = \bar{x} - 1.282\, \frac{\sigma}{\sqrt{n}}$$

$$= 5920 - 1.282\left(\frac{150}{\sqrt{6}}\right)$$

$$= 5840 \quad \text{(3 S.F.)}$$

Therefore we can state, with 90% confidence, that the mean breaking strength of the cables exceeds 5840 Newtons.

Exercise 10b

1. For each of the following, a random sample of size n is taken from a normal distribution with mean μ and variance σ^2.

    The sample mean is $\bar{x}$.
    Test the hypotheses stated, at the level of significance indicated.

	n	$\bar{x}$	σ	Hypotheses	Level of significance
(a)	30	15.2	3	H_0: $\mu = 15.8$, H_1: $\mu \neq 15.8$	5%
(b)	10	27	1.2	H_0: $\mu = 26.3$, H_1: $\mu > 26.3$	5%
(c)	49	125	4.2	H_0: $\mu = 123.5$, H_1: $\mu > 123.5$	1%
(d)	100	4.35	0.18	H_0: $\mu = 4.40$, H_1: $\mu < 4.40$	2%

2. The masses of components produced by a certain machine are normally distributed with mean 15.4 g and standard deviation 2.3 g. The setting on the machine is altered, following which a random sample of 81 components is found to have a mean mass of 15.0 g. Does this provide evidence, at the 5% level, of a reduction in the mean mass of components produced by this machine? Assume that the standard deviation is not altered.

3. A variable with known variance of 32 is thought to have a mean of 55. A random sample of 81 independent observations of the variable gives a mean of 56.2. Is there sufficient evidence that the mean is not 55 (a) at the 10% level, (b) at the 5% level, (c) at the 1% level?

4. A manufacturer claims that his cassettes, advertised as having a playing time of 90 minutes, actually have a mean playing time of 92 minutes, with standard deviation 1.8 minutes. 36 tapes are selected at random and tested. The investigator rejects the manufacturer's claim, at the 5% level, saying that the mean playing time of the tapes is less than 92 minutes. What can be said about the value of the sample mean obtained for this decision to be taken?

5. Mass-produced washers have thicknesses which are normally distributed with mean 3 mm and standard deviation 0.2 mm.
    (a) Find, correct to three decimal places, the probability that the mean thickness of a random sample of 4 washers will lie between 2.9 mm and 3.1 mm.
    (b) During a check on the manufacturing process a random sample of 25 washers is taken from production and the mean thickness $\bar{x}$ mm is calculated. Find the interval in which the value of $\bar{x}$ must lie in order that the hypothesis that the production mean thickness is 3 mm will not be rejected when the significance level is 5 per cent.
    (JMB)

6. Describe briefly how the Central Limit Theorem may be demonstrated.
    The distance driven by a long-distance lorry driver in a week is a normally distributed variable having mean 1130 km and standard deviation 106 km. Find, to 3 decimal places, the probability that in a given week he will drive less than 1000 km. Find, to 3 decimal places the probability that in 20 weeks his average distance driven per week is more than 1200 km.
    New driving regulations are introduced and, in the first 20 weeks after their introduction, he drives a total of 21 900 km. Assuming that

the standard deviation of the weekly distances he drives is unchanged, test, at the 10% level of significance, whether his mean weekly driving distance has been reduced. State clearly your null and alternative hypotheses. (L)

7. A machine packs flour into bags. A random sample of eleven filled bags was taken and the masses of the bags to the nearest 0.1 g were: 1506.8, 1506.6, 1506.7, 1507.2, 1506.9, 1506.8, 1506.6, 1507.0, 1507.5, 1506.3, 1506.4. Obtain the mean and the variance of this sample showing your working clearly. Filled bags are supposed to have a mass of 1506.5 g. Assuming that the mass of a bag has normal distribution with variance $0.16 \, g^2$ test whether the sample provides significant evidence at the 5% level that the machine produces overweight bags. Give the 99% confidence interval for the mass of a filled bag. (C)

8. A sample of size 25 is taken from the distribution of X where $X \sim N(\mu, 4)$. The sample mean $\bar{x}$ is 10.72. At what level test would we reject the null hypothesis that $\mu = 10$ in favour of the alternative hypothesis (a) $\mu > 10$, (b) $\mu \neq 10$?

9. Explain, briefly, the roles of a null hypothesis and a level of significance in a project which you have undertaken.
Records of the diameters of spherical ball bearings produced on a certain machine indicate that the diameters are normally distributed with mean 0.824 cm and standard deviation 0.046 cm. Two hundred samples, each consisting of 100 ball bearings, are chosen. Calculate the expected number of the 200 samples having a mean diameter less than 0.823 cm.
On a certain day it was suspected that the machine was malfunctioning. It may be assumed that if the machine is malfunctioning it will change the mean of the diameters without changing their standard deviation. On that day a random sample of 100 ball bearings had a mean diameter of 0.834 cm. Determine a 98% confidence interval for the mean diameter of the ball bearings being produced that day.
Hence state whether or not you would conclude that the machine is malfunctioning on that day given that the significance level is 2%. (L)

10. X_1 and X_2 are independent random variables with means μ_1 and μ_2, variances σ_1^2 and σ_2^2 respectively. Give the mean and variance of $X_1 - X_2$. If $Y = \lambda X_1$, where λ is a constant, give the mean and variance of Y.

The random variable $\overline{X}_1$ denotes the mean of a random sample of size n_1 from the second of the above distributions. Show how to obtain the mean and variance of the distribution of $\lambda_1 \overline{X}_1 + \lambda_2 \overline{X}_2$ from the results you have stated, λ_1 and λ_2 being constants. The yield of a certain crop per plot of standard area is normally distributed with mean 253.0 kg and variance $67.1 \, kg^2$. A new fertiliser is applied to 10 randomly selected plots, and their mean yield is found to be 257.8 kg. Is there any evidence of significant improvement in the yield? Assume the new fertiliser does not affect the variance of the yields. (O)

11. The masses of loaves from a certain bakery are normally distributed with mean 500 g and standard deviation 20 g.
(a) Determine what percentage of the output would fall below 475 g and what percentage would be above 530 g.
(b) The bakery produces 1000 loaves daily at a cost of 32 p per loaf and can sell all those above 475 g for 80 p each but is not allowed to sell the rest. Calculate the expected daily profit.
(c) A sample of 25 loaves yielded a mean mass of 490 g. Does this provide evidence of a reduced population mean? Use the 5% level of significance and state whether the test is one-tailed or two.

12. Illustrate the role of the null hypothesis with reference, if possible, to one of your projects making sure that you state the alternative hypothesis and the level of significance used. Explain how you decided whether to use a one-tail or a two-tail test.
Research workers measured the body lengths, in mm, of 10 specimens of fish spawn of a certain species off the coast of Eastern Scotland and found these lengths to be

$$12.5 \quad 10.2 \quad 11.1 \quad 9.6 \quad 12.1$$
$$10.7 \quad 11.4 \quad 14.7 \quad 10.4 \quad 9.3$$

Obtain unbiased estimates for the mean and variance of the lengths of all such fish spawn off Eastern Scotland.
Research shows that, for a very large number of specimens of spawn of this species off the coast of Wales, the mean body length is 10.2 mm. Assuming that the variance of the lengths of spawn off Eastern Scotland is 2.56, perform a significance test at the 5% level to decide whether the mean body length of fish spawn off the coast of Eastern Scotland is larger than that of fish spawn off the coast of Wales. (L)

13. Give an example, from your projects if you wish, of the steps used in carrying out a test of significance.

Climbing rope produced by a manufacturer is known to be such that one-metre lengths have breaking strengths that are normally distributed with mean 170.2 kg and standard deviation 10.5 kg. Find, to 3 decimal places, the probability that

(*a*) a one-metre length of rope chosen at random from those produced by the manufacturer will have a breaking strength of 175 kg to the nearest kg.

(*b*) a random sample of 50 one-metre lengths will have a mean breaking strength of more than 172.4 kg.

A new component material is added to the ropes being produced. The manufacturer believes that this will increase the mean breaking strength without changing the standard deviation. A random sample of 50 one-metre lengths of the new rope is found to have a mean breaking strength of 172.4 kg. Perform a significance test at the 5% level to decide whether this result provides sufficient evidence to confirm the manufacturer's belief that the mean breaking strength is increased. State clearly the null and alternative hypotheses which you are using.   (L)

14. (*a*) Write down the mean and the variance of the distribution of the means of all possible samples of size n taken from an infinite population having mean μ and variance σ^2. Describe the form of this distribution of sample means when

(i) n is large,

(ii) the distribution of the population is normal.

Explain briefly how you acquired empirical evidence for the Central Limit Theorem.

(*b*) The standard deviation of all the till receipts of a supermarket during 1984 was £4.25.

(i) Given that the mean of a random sample of 100 of the till receipts is £18.50, obtain an approximate 95% confidence interval for the mean of all the till receipts during 1984.

(ii) Find the size of sample that should be taken so that the management can be 95% confident that the sample mean will not differ from the true mean by more than 50 p.

(iii) The mean of all the till receipts of the supermarket during 1983 was £19.40. Using a 5% significance level, investigate whether the sample in (i) above provides sufficient evidence to conclude that the mean of all the 1984 till receipts is different from that in 1983.   (L)

TEST 2: TESTING A MEAN, BASED ON THE SAMPLE MEAN

Case 2 — Population variance σ^2 unknown, sample size large ($n \geqslant 30$, say)

Again, we have the sampling distribution of means, where

$$\overline{X} \sim N\left(\mu, \frac{\sigma^2}{n}\right)$$

But since σ^2 is unknown, we use an estimator $\widehat{\sigma}^2$ for it,

where
$$\widehat{\sigma}^2 = \frac{\sum(X - \overline{X})^2}{n - 1} = \frac{nS^2}{(n - 1)}$$

Note that S^2 is the sample variance (see page 479).

We use the test statistic $Z = \dfrac{\overline{X} - \mu}{\widehat{\sigma}/\sqrt{n}}$ which, *if n is large*, is distributed as N(0, 1) under the null hypothesis H_0 that the true population mean is μ.

Example 10.8 A normal distribution is thought to have a mean of 50. A random sample of 100 gave a mean of 52.6 and a standard deviation of 14.5. Is there evidence that the population mean has increased? Test (**a**) at the 5% level,   (**b**) at the 1% level.

Solution 10.8 Let the population mean be μ and the population variance be σ^2.

The sample mean $\bar{x}$ is 52.6 and the sample standard deviation s is 14.5.

H_0: $\mu = 50$ (there is no change in the population mean)

H_1: $\mu > 50$ (there is an increase in the population mean)

Consider the sampling distribution of means.

$$\bar{X} \sim N\left(\mu, \frac{\sigma^2}{n}\right) \quad \text{with} \quad n = 100.$$

Now σ^2 is unknown, so we use $\hat{\sigma}^2 = \dfrac{ns^2}{n-1}$

$$\hat{\sigma}^2 = \tfrac{100}{99}(14.5)^2 = 212.3\ldots$$

$$\hat{\sigma} = 14.57\ldots$$

NOTE: since n is large, the sample standard deviation s is approximately equal to $\hat{\sigma}$ and is often used instead. In most calculations it does not affect the outcome of the test.

Now $\bar{X} \sim N\left(\mu, \dfrac{\hat{\sigma}^2}{n}\right)$,   with $\hat{\sigma} = 14.57$, $n = 100$

Under H_0, $\mu = 50$,   so $\bar{X} \sim N\left(50, \dfrac{14.57^2}{100}\right)$

(**a**) We use a one-tailed test at the 5% level and reject H_0 if $z > 1.645$, where

$$z = \frac{\bar{x} - \mu}{\hat{\sigma}/\sqrt{n}}$$

$$= \frac{52.6 - 50}{14.57/\sqrt{100}}$$

$$= 1.784$$

Conclusion: since $z > 1.645$, we reject H_0 and conclude that there is evidence, at the 5% level, that the population mean has increased.

NOTE: using $\hat{\sigma} \approx s$ gives $z = 1.793$ and the same conclusion is reached.

(**b**) We use a one-tailed test at the 1% level and reject H_0 if $z > 2.326$, where

$$z = \frac{\bar{x} - \mu}{\hat{\sigma}/\sqrt{n}}$$

$$= 1.784 \quad \text{(as before)}$$

Conclusion: since $z < 2.326$, we do not reject H_0 and we <u>conclude</u> <u>that there is not sufficient evidence, at the 1% level, that the</u> <u>population mean has increased.</u>

NOTE: the value of the test statistic z is significant at the 5% level, but not at the 1% level, giving some, but not strong, evidence that the mean has increased.

Example 10.9   A manufacturer claims that the average life of her electric light bulbs is 2000 hours. A random sample of 64 bulbs is tested and the life x in hours recorded. The results obtained are as follows:
$\sum x = 127\,808$, $\sum (x - \bar{x})^2 = 9694.6$. Is there sufficient evidence, at the 2% level, that the manufacturer is over-estimating the length of life of her light bulbs? Assume that the distribution of the length of life of light bulbs is normal.

Solution 10.9   *Sample readings*:

$$\sum x = 127\,808, \quad \sum (x - \bar{x})^2 = 9694.6, \quad n = 64$$

$$\bar{x} = \frac{\sum x}{n} = \frac{127\,808}{64} = 1997$$

Significance test: Let X be the r.v. 'the life, in hours, of a light bulb'. Let the population mean be μ and the population variance be σ^2.

Since σ^2 is unknown, we estimate it using $\hat{\sigma}^2 = \dfrac{\sum (x - \bar{x})^2}{n - 1}$

So $\hat{\sigma}^2 = \dfrac{9694.6}{63} = 153.88\ldots, \quad \hat{\sigma} = 12.40\ldots$

H_0: $\mu = 2000$ (the manufacturer is not over-estimating the length of life)

H_1: $\mu < 2000$ (the manufacturer is over-estimating the length of life)

Consider the sampling distribution of means.

$$\bar{X} \sim \text{N}\left(\mu, \frac{\hat{\sigma}^2}{n}\right) \quad \text{with} \quad \hat{\sigma} = 12.4, \quad n = 64.$$

Under H_0 $\mu = 2000$,   so $\bar{X} \sim \text{N}\left(2000, \frac{12.4^2}{64}\right)$

We use a one-tailed test at the 2% level, and reject H_0 if $z < -2.054$, where

$$z = \frac{\bar{x} - \mu}{\hat{\sigma}/\sqrt{n}}$$

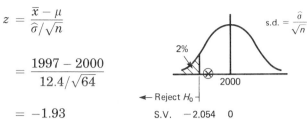

$$= \frac{1997 - 2000}{12.4/\sqrt{64}}$$

$$= -1.93$$

Conclusion: since $z > -2.054$, we do not reject H_0 and we conclude that there is not sufficient evidence, at the 2% level, that the manufacturer is over-estimating the length of life of the light bulbs.

Exercise 10c

1. For each of the following, a random sample of size n is taken from a normal distribution with mean μ and variance σ^2. The sample mean is $\bar{x}$.
Test the hypotheses stated, at the level of significance indicated.

	n	$\bar{x}$	$\sum(x - \bar{x})^2$	Hypotheses	Level of significance
(a)	65	100	842.4	H_0: $\mu = 99.2$, H_1: $\mu \neq 99.2$	5%
(b)	65	100	842.4	H_0: $\mu = 99.2$, H_1: $\mu > 99.2$	5%
(c)	80	85.3	2508.8	H_0: $\mu = 86.2$, H_1: $\mu < 86.2$	10%
(d)	100	6.85	36	H_0: $\mu = 7$, H_1: $\mu \neq 7$	1%

2. A sample of 40 observations from a normal distribution gave $\sum x = 24$ and $\sum x^2 = 596$. Test, at the 5% level, whether the mean of the distribution is zero. Perform a two-tailed test.

3. A random sample of 75 eleven year olds performed a particular task. Denoting the time taken by $(15 + y)$ minutes, the results are summarised as follows: $\sum y = 90$, $\sum (y - \bar{y})^2 = 2025$. Test whether there is sufficient evidence, at the 4% level, to suggest that the mean time to perform the task is greater than 15 minutes.
Determine a symmetric 96% confidence interval for the mean time, based on the sample observations.

4. Explain, briefly, the roles of a null hypothesis, an alternative hypothesis and a level of significance in a statistical test, referring to your projects where possible.
A shopkeeper complains that the average weight of chocolate bars of a certain type that he is buying from a wholesaler is less than the stated value of 8.50 g. The shopkeeper weighed 100 bars from a large delivery and found that their weights had a mean of 8.36 g and a standard deviation of 0.72 g. Using a 5% significance level, determine whether or not the shopkeeper is justified in his complaint. State clearly the null and alternative hypotheses that you are using, and express your conclusion in words. Obtain, to 2 decimal places, the limits of a 98% confidence interval for the mean weight of the chocolate bars in the shopkeeper's delivery. (L)

5. An electronic device is advertised as being able to retain information stored in it 'for 70 to 90 hours' after power has been switched off. In experiments carried out to test this claim, the retention time in hours, X, was measured on 250 occasions, and the data obtained is summarised by $\sum (x - 76) = 683$ and $\sum (x - 76)^2 = 26\,132$. The population mean and variance of X are denoted by μ and σ^2 respectively.
(a) Show that, correct to one decimal place, an unbiased estimate of σ^2 is 97.5.

(b) Test the hypothesis that $\mu = 80$ against the alternative hypothesis that $\mu < 80$, using a 5% significance level.

(c) Calculate a symmetric 95% confidence interval for μ.   (C)

6. At an early stage in analysing the marks scored by the large number of candidates in an examination paper, the Examination Board takes a random sample of 250 candidates and finds that the marks, x, of these candidates give $\sum x = 11\,872$ and $\sum x^2 = 646\,193$. Calculate a 90% confidence interval for the population mean, μ, for this paper.

Using the figures obtained in this sample, the null hypothesis $\mu = 49.5$ is tested against the alternative hypothesis $\mu < 49.5$ at the $x\%$ significance level. Determine the set of values of x for which the null hypothesis is rejected in favour of the alternative hypothesis.

It is subsequently found that the population mean and standard deviation for the paper are 45.292 and 18.761 respectively. Find the probability of a random sample of size 250 giving a sample mean at least as high as the one found in the sample above.   (C)

7. Salt is packed in bags which the manufacturer claims contain 25 kg each, on average. A random sample of 80 bags is examined and the mass, x kg, of the contents of each bag is determined. It is found that $\sum (x - 25) = 27.2$ and $\sum (x - 25)^2 = 85.1$, and that exactly 16 bags each contain less than 24.5 kg.

(i) Find a 90% confidence interval for the population proportion of bags containing less than 24.5 kg.

(ii) Estimate the population mean and variance of the mass of the contents of a bag.

(iii) Test, at the 10% level, whether the manufacturer is understating the average mass of the contents of a bag.   (C)

TEST 3: TESTING THE DIFFERENCE BETWEEN MEANS

Consider two unpaired, independent samples of sizes n_1 and n_2 such that

$$X_1 \sim N(\mu_1, \sigma_1{}^2) \quad \text{and} \quad X_2 \sim N(\mu_2, \sigma_2{}^2)$$

Then

$$\overline{X}_1 - \overline{X}_2 \sim N\left(\mu_1 - \mu_2, \frac{\sigma_1{}^2}{n_1} + \frac{\sigma_2{}^2}{n_2}\right)$$

This distribution is known as the **sampling distribution of the difference between means**.

The following may be used to test whether there is a significant difference between means.

We will consider the case when $\sigma_1{}^2$ *and* $\sigma_2{}^2$ *are known.*

We use the test statistic

$$Z = \frac{\overline{X}_1 - \overline{X}_2 - (\mu_1 - \mu_2)}{\sqrt{\dfrac{\sigma_1{}^2}{n_1} + \dfrac{\sigma_2{}^2}{n_2}}}$$

which is distributed as N(0, 1).

If there is a *known common population variance* such that $\sigma_1{}^2 = \sigma_2{}^2 = \sigma^2$, then

$$\overline{X}_1 - \overline{X}_2 \sim N\left(\mu_1 - \mu_2, \sigma^2\left(\frac{1}{n_1} + \frac{1}{n_2}\right)\right)$$

We use the test statistic

$$Z = \frac{\overline{X}_1 - \overline{X}_2 - (\mu_1 - \mu_2)}{\sigma \sqrt{\dfrac{1}{n_1} + \dfrac{1}{n_2}}} \qquad \text{where} \qquad Z \sim N(0, 1)$$

Example 10.10 A random sample of size 100 is taken from a normal population with variance $\sigma_1^2 = 40$. The sample mean $\overline{x}_1$ is 38.3. Another random sample, of size 80, is taken from a normal population with variance $\sigma_2^2 = 30$. The sample mean $\overline{x}_2$ is 40.1. Test, at the 5% level, whether there is a significant difference in the population means μ_1 and μ_2.

Solution 10.10 Sample 1: $n_1 = 100, \ \overline{x}_1 = 38.3, \ \sigma_1^2 = 40,$

population mean $= \mu_1$

Sample 2: $n_2 = 80, \ \overline{x}_2 = 40.1, \ \sigma_2^2 = 30,$

population mean $= \mu_2$

$H_0: \ \mu_1 = \mu_2$ (there is no difference between the means)

$H_1: \ \mu_1 \neq \mu_2$ (there is a difference)

We consider the sampling distribution of the difference between means

$$\overline{X}_1 - \overline{X}_2 \sim N\left(\mu_1 - \mu_2, \ \frac{\sigma_1^2}{n_1} + \frac{\sigma_2^2}{n_2}\right)$$

Under H_0, $\mu_1 - \mu_2 = 0$, so

$$\overline{X}_1 - \overline{X}_2 \sim N\left(0, \ \frac{40}{100} + \frac{30}{80}\right)$$

i.e. $\overline{X}_1 - \overline{X}_2 \sim N(0, 0.775)$

The test statistic is $\qquad Z = \dfrac{\overline{X}_1 - \overline{X}_2 - 0}{\sqrt{\dfrac{\sigma_1^2}{n_1} + \dfrac{\sigma_2^2}{n_2}}}$

$$= \frac{\overline{X}_1 - \overline{X}_2 - 0}{\sqrt{0.775}}$$

$$= \frac{\overline{X}_1 - \overline{X}_2 - 0}{0.880\ldots}$$

We use a two-tailed test, at the 5% level and reject H_0 if $|z| > 1.96$, where

$$z = \frac{38.3 - 40.1 - 0}{0.880\dots}$$

$$= -2.04$$

s.d. $= \sqrt{\dfrac{\sigma_1{}^2}{n_1} + \dfrac{\sigma_2{}^2}{n_2}} = 0.880$

2.5%   2.5%

$\mu_1 - \mu_2$

←— Reject H_0 —| |—Reject H_0 —→

S.V. -1.96 0   1.96

Conclusion: since $|z| > 1.96$, we reject H_0 and conclude that there is evidence, at the 5% level, of a difference in population means.

Example 10.11 The same test was given to a group of 100 scouts and to a group of 144 guides. The mean score for the scouts was 27.53 and the mean score for the guides was 26.81. Assuming a common population standard deviation of 3.48, test, using a 5% level of significance, whether the scouts' performance in the test was better than that of the guides. Assume that the scores are normally distributed.

Solution 10.11 Let X be the r.v. 'a scout's score'.

Scouts: $\bar{x} = 27.53$, $n_1 = 100$,   population mean $= \mu_1$

Let Y be the r.v. 'a guide's score'.

Guides: $\bar{y} = 26.81$, $n_2 = 144$,   population mean $= \mu_2$

Common population standard deviation $\sigma = 3.48$.

H_0: $\mu_1 = \mu_2$ (there is no difference in the performances)

H_1: $\mu_1 > \mu_2$ (the performance of the scouts was better)

Consider the sampling distribution of the difference between means,

$$\overline{X} - \overline{Y} \sim N\left(\mu_1 - \mu_2,\ \sigma^2\left(\frac{1}{n_1} + \frac{1}{n_2}\right)\right)$$

Now $\sigma^2\left(\dfrac{1}{n_1} + \dfrac{1}{n_2}\right) = 3.48^2\left(\dfrac{1}{100} + \dfrac{1}{144}\right)$

$$= 0.205\,204$$

Under H_0, $\mu_1 - \mu_2 = 0$, so $\overline{X} - \overline{Y} \sim N(0,\ 0.205\,204)$

The test statistic is

$$Z = \frac{\overline{X} - \overline{Y} - 0}{\sigma\sqrt{\dfrac{1}{n_1} + \dfrac{1}{n_2}}}$$

$$= \frac{\overline{X} - \overline{Y} - 0}{\sqrt{0.205\,204}}$$

$$= \frac{\overline{X} - \overline{Y} - 0}{0.452\ldots}$$

We use a one-tailed test, at the 5% level, and reject H_0 if $z > 1.645$, where

$$z = \frac{27.53 - 26.81 - 0}{0.452\ldots}$$

$$= 1.589$$

s.d. $= \sigma\sqrt{\dfrac{1}{n_1} + \dfrac{1}{n_2}} = 0.452\ldots$

5%

$\mu_1 - \mu_2$

— Reject H_0 →

S.V.   0   1.645

Conclusion: since $z < 1.645$, we do not reject H_0 and we conclude that there is not sufficient evidence, at the 5% level, to show that the performance of the scouts in the test was better than that of the guides.

Exercise 10d

1. For each of the following sets of data, perform a test to decide whether there is a significant difference between the means, μ_1 and μ_2, of the normal populations from which the samples are drawn.

	n_1	$\sum x$	σ_1^2	n_2	$\sum y$	σ_2^2	Hypotheses	Level
(a)	100	4250	30	80	3544	35	H_0: $\mu_1 = \mu_2$ H_1: $\mu_1 \neq \mu_2$	5%
(b)	20	95	2.3	25	135	2.5	H_0: $\mu_1 = \mu_2$ H_1: $\mu_1 < \mu_2$	2%
(c)	50	1545	6.5	50	1480	7.1	H_0: $\mu_1 = \mu_2$ H_1: $\mu_1 > \mu_2$	1%

	n_1	$\sum x$	n_2	$\sum y$	Common population standard deviation (σ)	Hypotheses	Level
(d)	50	2480	40	1908	4.5	H_0: $\mu_1 = \mu_2$ H_1: $\mu_1 \neq \mu_2$	2%
(e)	100	12 730	100	12 410	10.9	H_0: $\mu_1 = \mu_2$ H_1: $\mu_1 > \mu_2$	5%
(f)	30	192	45	315	1.25	H_0: $\mu_1 = \mu_2$ H_1: $\mu_1 < \mu_2$	1%
(g)	200	18 470	300	27 663	0.86	H_0: $\mu_1 = \mu_2$ H_1: $\mu_1 \neq \mu_2$	10%

2. The lengths (in millimetres) of nine screws selected at random from a large consignment are found to be 7.99, 8.01, 8.00, 8.02, 8.03, 7.99, 8.00, 8.01, 8.01. Calculate unbiased estimates of the population mean and variance. Assuming a normal distribution with variance 0.0001, test, at the 5% level, the hypothesis that the population mean is 8.00 against the alternative hypothesis that the population mean is not 8.00.

From a second large consignment, sixteen screws are selected at random and their mean length (in millimetres) is found to be 7.992. Assuming a normal distribution with variance 0.0001, test, at the 5% level, the hypothesis that this population has the same mean as the first population, against the alternative hypothesis that this population has a smaller mean than the first population.
(C)

3. An expert golfer wishes to discover whether the average distances travelled by two different brands of golf ball differ significantly. He tests each ball by hitting it with his driver and measuring the distance X (in metres) that it travels. The distribution of X may be assumed to be normal.

His results for a random sample of nine 'Farfly' golf balls were $\bar{x} = 214$ and $\sum (x - \bar{x})^2 = 2048$. Making the assumption that the population variance is equal to the sample variance, obtain a 95% symmetric confidence interval for the mean of X for 'Farfly' golf balls.

His results for a random sample of sixteen 'Gofar' golf balls were $\bar{x} = 224$ and $\sum (x - \bar{x})^2 = 2460$. Assuming that the variance of X is the same for both types of golf ball, obtain a pooled (two-sample) estimate of this variance and, making the assumption that the true variance is equal to

this estimate, test at the 5% level whether his results for 'Gofar' golf balls differ significantly from those for 'Farfly' golf balls.
(C)

4. Mr Smith and Mr Jones are neighbours who work at the same office. Mr Smith drives to work in his old car, and each day records the time (x minutes) his journey takes. After 250 journeys his observations are summarised by $\sum x = 6250$, $\sum x^2 = 158491$. Regarding his observations as constituting a large random sample, give a symmetric 97% confidence interval for his average journey time.

Mr Jones drives to work in his new car, and his average time over a random sample of 50 journeys is found to be 21 minutes. Mr Jones claims that if he leaves home 3 minutes after Mr Smith he will, on average, arrive at work before him. Assuming that Mr Smith and Mr Jones take different routes to work, that their journey times have standard deviation 3 minutes and that the samples may be treated as being large samples, test whether Mr Jones' claim may be accepted at the 2% significance level.
(C)

5. The heights of men can be assumed to be normally distributed with standard deviation 0.11 m.

In 1928 the mean height of men in a certain city was 1.72 m. In a survey in 1978 the mean height of a random sample of 16 men from the same city was 1.77 m. On the hypothesis that the population mean height has not changed, calculate the probability of obtaining a sample mean height greater than that measured.

In another survey in 1978 the mean height of a random sample of 32 men from a second city was 1.73 m. Assuming that the population mean heights are the same in the two cities, calculate the probability that a difference in sample mean heights greater than that measured would be obtained.
(MEI)

TEST 4: TESTING A PROPORTION, SAMPLE SIZE LARGE

We may wish to test whether a random sample of size n, where n is large, with proportion of 'successes' p_s could have been drawn from a population with proportion of 'successes' p.

The sampling distribution of proportions gives

$$P_s \sim N\left(p, \frac{pq}{n}\right)$$ where $q = 1 - p$
and n is large
(see p. 451)

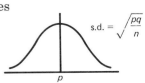

> The test statistic used is
>
> $$Z = \frac{P_s - p}{\sqrt{pq/n}}$$
>
> which is distributed as $N(0, 1)$ under the null hypothesis H_0 that the proportion of 'successes' in the population is p.

Example 10.12 The manufacturer of Chummy Morsels claims that 8 out of 10 dogs choose his product rather than that produced by a rival firm. In a random sample of 200 dogs, 152 chose Chummy Morsels, and the rest chose the rival brand. Comment on the manufacturer's claim.

Solution 10.12 From the sample: $p_s = \frac{152}{200} = 0.76, \quad n = 200$

Let p be the population proportion of dogs who prefer Chummy Morsels and let $q = 1 - p$.

H_0: $p = 0.8$ (80% of dogs prefer Chummy Morsels and the manufacturer's claim is correct)

H_1: $p < 0.8$ (less than 80% of dogs prefer Chummy Morsels and the manufacturer's claim is not correct)

Consider the sampling distribution of proportions,

$$P_s \sim N\left(p, \frac{pq}{n}\right) \quad \text{with} \quad n = 200$$

Under H_0, $p = 0.8$, $q = 0.2$, so $P_s \sim N\left(0.8, \frac{(0.8)(0.2)}{200}\right)$

i.e $P_s \sim N(0.8, 0.0008)$

The test statistic is $Z = \dfrac{P_s - p}{\sqrt{\dfrac{pq}{n}}}$

$$= \frac{P_s - 0.8}{\sqrt{0.0008}}$$

$$= \frac{P_s - 0.8}{0.028\ldots}$$

Use a one-tailed test at the 5% level. We will reject H_0 if $z < -1.645$ where

$$z = \frac{p_s - p}{\sqrt{pq/n}}$$

$$= \frac{0.76 - 0.80}{0.028\ldots}$$

$$= -1.414$$

s.d. $= \sqrt{\dfrac{pq}{n}} = 0.028$

5%

0.8

← Reject H_0

S.V. -1.645 0

Conclusion: since $z > -1.645$, we do not reject H_0 and we conclude that there is not sufficient evidence, at the 5% level, to refute the manufacturer's claim.

NOTE: to obtain the theory for a proportions test we have, in the first instance, approximated from a discrete to a continuous distribution. We should therefore use a **continuity correction** of $\pm \dfrac{1}{2n}$ (see page 451).

This means that instead of the value 0.76 we consider the rectangle from $0.76 - \dfrac{1}{400}$ to $0.76 + \dfrac{1}{400}$, i.e. 0.7575 to 0.7625.

In order to reject H_0 we would want the *whole* of this rectangle to lie in the rejection region. So we would need to consider the right-hand value, $p_s = 0.7625$.

So $\qquad z = \dfrac{0.7625 - 0.80}{0.028}$

$\qquad\qquad = -1.325\ldots$

Therefore we do not reject H_0 and the conclusion is as before.

In practice, if n is large, using the continuity correction makes very little difference to the calculation of z. We need to consider the continuity correction only when the uncorrected value is just inside the rejection region.

NOTE: an alternative approach to this type of problem was introduced in Test 1, on page 513. The method is shown again below.

Alternative Solution 10.12 Let X be the r.v. 'the number of dogs who prefer Chummy Morsels'. Then $X \sim \text{Bin}(n, p)$, with $n = 200$.

$\qquad H_0$: $\quad p = 0.8 \quad$ (80% prefer Chummy Morsels)

$\qquad H_1$: $\quad p < 0.8 \quad$ (less than 80% prefer Chummy Morsels)

Under H_0, $\quad p = 0.8 \quad$ so $\quad X \sim (200, 0.8)$

Now, using the normal approximation to the binomial distribution,

$\qquad X \sim \text{N}(np, npq) \quad$ where $\quad q = 1 - p$

$\qquad$ and $\qquad\qquad\qquad\qquad np = (200)(0.8) = 160$

$\qquad\qquad\qquad\qquad\qquad\qquad npq = (200)(0.8)(0.2) = 32$

So $\qquad X \sim \text{N}(160, 32)$

We use a one-tailed test, at the 5% level and reject H_0 if $z < -1.645$ where

$$z = \frac{x - np}{\sqrt{npq}}$$

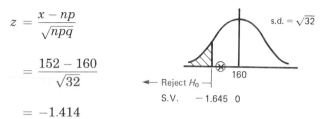

$$= \frac{152 - 160}{\sqrt{32}}$$

$$= -1.414$$

Conclusion: since $z > -1.645$, we do not reject H_0 and we conclude that there is not sufficient evidence at the 5% level to refute the manufacturer's claim.

If the continuity correction is used, the rectangle representing 152 is from 151.5 to 152.5. We consider its right-hand value to check whether the whole of this rectangle would lie in the rejection region.

So $\qquad z = \dfrac{152.5 - 160}{\sqrt{32}}$

$\qquad\qquad = -1.325 \quad$ and the conclusion is the same.

Problems of this type can be tackled by either method. The calculations performed correspond exactly, taking into account whether or not a continuity correction has been used.

Example 10.13 A large college claims that it admits equal numbers of men and women. In a random sample of 500 students at the college there were 267 males. Is there evidence, at the 5% level, that the college population is not evenly divided into males and females?

Solution 10.13 From the sample: $\quad p_s = \frac{267}{500} = 0.534, \quad n = 500$

Let p be the proportion of males in the population and let $q = 1 - p$.

$\quad H_0$: $\quad p = 0.5 \quad$ (there are equal numbers of males and females)

$\quad H_1$: $\quad p \neq 0.5 \quad$ (the college population is not evenly divided into males and females)

Consider the sampling distribution of proportions,

$$P_s \sim N\left(p, \frac{pq}{n}\right) \quad \text{with} \quad n = 500$$

Under H_0, $\quad p = 0.5, \quad q = 0.5, \quad \dfrac{pq}{n} = \dfrac{(0.5)(0.5)}{500} = 0.0005$

so $\quad P_s \sim N(0.5, 0.0005)$

The test statistic is $\quad Z = \dfrac{P_s - p}{\sqrt{pq/n}}$

$$= \dfrac{P_s - 0.5}{\sqrt{0.0005}}$$

$$= \dfrac{P_s - 0.5}{0.022\ldots}$$

We use a two-tailed test, at the 5% level and reject H_0 if $|z| > 1.96$ where, without using the continuity correction,

$$z = \dfrac{p_s - p}{\sqrt{pq/n}}$$

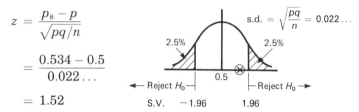

$$= \dfrac{0.534 - 0.5}{0.022\ldots}$$

$$= 1.52$$

Conclusion: since $z < 1.96$, we do not reject H_0 and <u>we conclude</u> <u>that at the 5% level, there is not sufficient evidence to refute the</u> <u>claim that the population is evenly divided into males and females.</u>

NOTE: without using the continuity correction, we found that z was *not* in the rejection region.

Therefore the rectangle representing p_s could not lie wholly in the rejection region, since the value in the middle of it (z as calculated above) did not lie in this region. So in this case it was not necessary to repeat the calculation using the continuity correction.

It is only necessary to use the correction when the uncorrected value for z lies in the rejection region. When you answer examination questions it is wise to mention this fact.

Exercise 10e

1. For each of the following sets of data, carry out a significance test for the hypotheses stated.

	Number in sample	Number of 'successes'	Hypotheses	Level
(a)	50	45	H_0: $p = 0.8$, H_1: $p > 0.8$	5%
(b)	60	42	H_0: $p = 0.55$, H_1: $p \neq 0.55$	2%
(c)	120	21	H_0: $p = 0.25$, H_1: $p \neq 0.25$	5%
(d)	300	213	H_0: $p = 0.65$, H_1: $p \neq 0.65$	1%
(e)	90	56	H_0: $p = 0.76$, H_1: $p < 0.76$	1%

2. A theory predicts that the probability of an event is 0.4. The theory is tested experimentally and in 400 independent trials the event occurred 140 times. Is the number of occurrences significantly less than that predicted by the theory? Test at the 1% level.

3. It is thought that the proportion of defective items produced by a particular machine is 0.1. A random sample of 100 items is inspected and found to contain 15 defective items. Does this provide evidence, at the 5% level, that the machine is producing more defective items than expected?

4. A coin is tossed 100 times and 38 heads are obtained. Is there evidence, at the 2% level, that the coin is biased in favour of tails?

5. A government report states that one-third of teenagers in Great Britain belong to a youth organisation. A survey, conducted among a random sample of 1000 teenagers from a certain city, revealed that 370 belonged to a youth organisation. Does this provide significant evidence, at the 2% level, that the proportion of teenagers who belong to a youth organisation is greater in this city than the national average?

Based on the results of this sample, calculate a 95% confidence interval for the proportion of teenagers in this city who belong to a youth organisation.

6. The probability that an oyster larva will develop in unpolluted water is 0.9, while in polluted water this probability is less than 0.9. Given that 20 oyster larvae are placed in unpolluted water, find the probabilities, each to two decimal places, that the number that will develop is

(a) at least 17,

(b) exactly 17.

An oyster breeder put 20 larvae in a sample of water and observed that only 16 of them developed. Use a 10% significance level to determine whether the breeder would be justified in concluding that the water is polluted. (JMB)

7. A fruit farm grows 'Golden Delicious' apples, and it can be assumed that the distribution of the masses of the apples is described by a normal probability function. The apples are graded by mass (x g) into three grades: 'small' for $x < 80$, 'medium' for $80 < x < 100$, 'large' for $x > 100$. In 1979, 20% of the apples were graded as 'small' and 54% as 'medium'. Estimate, to one decimal place, the mean and standard deviation of the masses of the apples produced on the farm in that year. Estimate also what proportion of the apples had masses exceeding 105 g.

When he begins to harvest his 1980 crop the grower picks out a sample of 100 apples at random and finds that only 9 are 'small'. Find, on the hypothesis that the proportion of 'small' apples in the whole crop is the same as in 1979, the probability of getting 9 or fewer 'small' apples in such a sample. Would he be justified in concluding, on the evidence of this sample, that there has been a reduction (for 1980 as compared with 1979) in the percentage of 'small' apples in the crop as a whole? (SMP)

8. A factory produces large numbers of sweets in a variety of colours. Automatic machines select the sweets at random and pack them in boxes of 20. A random sample of 100 boxes was chosen, the contents of each box

examined and the number of black sweets in each box recorded. The results obtained are summarised in the following table.

No. of black sweets	0	1	2	3	4	5	6 or more
No. of boxes	11	29	27	22	7	4	0

(a) Find an unbiased estimate for the proportion p of sweets produced which are black, and, to three significant figures, an estimate of its standard error.

(b) Using a distributional approximation and a 5 per cent significance level, test the null hypothesis $p = 0.1$ against the alternative hypothesis $p \neq 0.1$. State your conclusion.

(c) Given that $p = 0.1$, use tables to find, to the nearest integer, the expected frequencies corresponding to the observed frequencies tabulated above. (JMB)

9. In a public opinion poll, 1000 randomly chosen electors were asked whether they would vote for the 'Purple Party' at the next election and 357 replied 'Yes'. Find a 95% confidence interval for the proportion p of the population who would answer 'Yes' to the same question.

Twenty similar polls are taken and the 95% confidence interval is determined for each poll. State the expected number of these intervals which will enclose the true value of p.

The leader of the 'Purple Party' believes that the true value of p is 0.4. Test, at the 8% level, whether she is overestimating her support. (C)

10. In an investigation into ownership of calculators, 200 randomly chosen school students were interviewed, and 143 of them owned a calculator. Using the evidence of this sample, test, at the 5% level of significance, the hypothesis that the proportion of school students owning a calculator is 75% against the alternative hypothesis that the proportion is less than 75%. (C)P

11. When a "Thumbnail" drawing pin is dropped on to the floor, the probability that it lands "point up" is p.

(i) A teacher drops a Thumbnail drawing pin 900 times and observes that it lands "point up" 315 times. Test, at the 1% level, the hypothesis that $p = 0.4$ against the alternative $p < 0.4$.

(ii) A student drops a Thumbnail drawing pin 600 times and observes that it lands "point up" 251 times. Using the student's results, find a symmetric 95% confidence interval for p.

As part of a statistics investigation, 1500 students carry out similar experiments and they each calculate (correctly) their own symmetric 95% confidence interval for p. Find the expected number of these intervals that do not contain the true value of p.   (C)

12.   A questionnaire was sent to a large number of people, asking for their opinions about a proposal to alter an examination syllabus. Of the 180 replies received, 134 were in favour of the proposal. Assuming that the people replying were a random sample from the population,
(i)   test, at the 5% level, the hypothesis that the population proportion in favour of the proposal is 0.7 against the alternative that it is more than 0.7,
(ii) find a symmetric 95% confidence interval for the population proportion in favour of the proposal.   (C)

SUMMARY — SIGNIFICANCE TESTING, USING NORMAL DISTRIBUTION

Type of test	Test statistic		
Single sample value	$$Z = \dfrac{X - \mu}{\sigma}$$		
Binomial situation (n large)	$$Z = \dfrac{X - np}{\sqrt{npq}}$$		
Means	σ known	σ unknown, n large	
	$$Z = \dfrac{\overline{X} - \mu}{\sigma/\sqrt{n}}$$	$Z = \dfrac{\overline{X} - \mu}{\hat{\sigma}/\sqrt{n}}$ where $\hat{\sigma}^2 = \dfrac{\sum(X - \overline{X})^2}{n - 1}$ $$= \dfrac{nS^2}{n - 1}$$ (S^2 is sample variance)	
Difference between means	Unequal population variances $\sigma_1{}^2, \sigma_2{}^2$, known		
	$$Z = \dfrac{\overline{X}_1 - \overline{X}_2 - (\mu_1 - \mu_2)}{\sqrt{\dfrac{\sigma_1{}^2}{n_1} + \dfrac{\sigma_2{}^2}{n_2}}}$$		
	Equal population variance σ^2 known		
	$$Z = \dfrac{\overline{X}_1 - \overline{X}_2 - (\mu_1 - \mu_2)}{\sigma\sqrt{\dfrac{1}{n_1} + \dfrac{1}{n_2}}}$$		
Proportions	p known (large n)		
	$$Z = \dfrac{P_s - p}{\sqrt{pq/n}}$$		

Miscellaneous Exercise 10f

1. The random variable X is normally distributed with mean μ and variance σ^2. Write down the distribution of the sample mean $\overline{X}$ of a random sample of size n. Explain what you understand by a 95% confidence interval.
A garage sells both leaded and unleaded petrol. The distribution of the values of sales for each type is normal. During 1990 the standard deviation of individual sales of each type of petrol is £3.25. The mean of the individual sales of leaded petrol during this time is £8.72. A random sample of 100 individual sales of unleaded petrol gave a mean of £9.71. Calculate
(a) an interval within which 90% of the sales of leaded petrol will lie,
(b) a 95% confidence interval for the mean sales of unleaded petrol.
The mean of the sales of unleaded petrol for 1989 was £9.10.
Using a 5% significance level, investigate whether there is sufficient evidence to conclude that the mean of all the 1990 unleaded sales was *greater* than the mean of the 1989 sales.
Find the size of the sample that should be taken so that the garage proprietor can be 95% certain that the sample mean of sales of unleaded petrol during 1990 will differ from the true mean by less than 50 p.   (L)

2. In an investigation into the total distance travelled by cars currently in use, 500 randomly chosen cars were stopped and the distances they had travelled were noted. The sample mean was found to be 50 724 km, and the standard deviation of the distances in the sample was 13 112 km. Calculate a 90% confidence interval for the population mean distance travelled.
In a proposed investigation into standards of safety on the road, it is planned to stop 1000 randomly chosen vehicles and examine them for potentially dangerous defects. The purpose of the investigation is to test the null hypothesis that the proportion of vehicles with potentially dangerous defects on the road is 10%, against the alternative hypothesis that the proportion is more than this. Using a 5% significance level, calculate the least number of vehicles with potentially dangerous defects in the sample which would lead to rejection of the null hypothesis. Explain briefly what could be concluded if the investigation yielded 107 vehicles with potentially dangerous defects.   (C)

3. Explain what you understand by the Central Limit Theorem.
An electrical firm claims that the average lifetime of the bulbs it produces is 800 hours with a standard deviation of 42 hours. To test this claim a random sample of 120 bulbs was taken and these bulbs were found to have an average lifetime of 789 hours. Stating clearly your hypotheses and using a 5% level of significance, test the claim made by the electrical firm.   (L)

4. In a large population of chickens, the distribution of the mass of a chicken has mean μ kg and standard deviation σ kg. A random sample of 100 chickens is taken from the population. The mean mass for the sample is denoted by $\overline{X}$. State the approximate distribution of $\overline{X}$, giving its mean and standard deviation.
The sample values are summarised by $\sum x = 189.1$ and $\sum x^2 = 401.74$, where x kg is the mass of a chicken. Find unbiased estimates of μ and σ^2, and an approximate symmetric 90% confidence interval for μ. Given that, in fact, $\sigma = 0.71$, test, at the 1% level of significance, the null hypothesis $\mu = 1.75$ against the alternative hypothesis $\mu > 1.75$, stating whether you are using a one-tail or a two-tail test and stating your conclusion clearly.   (C)

5. The random variable X is distributed normally with mean μ and variance σ^2. Write down the distribution of the sample mean $\overline{X}$ of a random sample of size n. Records from a dental practice showed that during 1991 the number of minutes per visit spent in the dentist's chair can be taken to be normally distributed with mean 14.5 minutes and standard deviation 2.9 minutes.
(a) Calculate an interval within which 90% of the times spent in the dentist's chair will lie.
In 1992 it was assumed that the standard deviation remained unchanged, and the distribution can be assumed to be normal. A random sample of 16 consultations gave the following times in minutes.

13.2 18.7 14.9 12.1 11.6 17.2 10.6   9.4
14.6 12.9 11.2 13.5 12.9 11.8 14.1 12.5

(b) For 1992, calculate a 95% confidence interval for the mean length of visit to the dentist.
It is suggested by the dental practice that the average number of minutes spent in the dentist's chair has decreased between 1991 and 1992.

(c) Stating clearly your hypotheses and using a 5% significance level, investigate this suggestion and draw an appropriate conclusion.   (L)

6. (a) In a survey concerning ownership of television sets in a certain city, 985 randomly chosen households were investigated. It was found that there was no television set in 77 households, one set in 621 households, and two or more sets in 287 households. Calculate a 95% confidence interval for the proportion of households in the city with at least one television set.

(b) A normal distribution has unknown mean μ and known variance σ^2. A random sample of n observations from the distribution has sample mean $\bar{x}$. The null hypothesis $\mu = \mu_0$ is being tested. Find, in terms of μ_0, σ and n, the set of values of $\bar{x}$ for which $\mu = \mu_0$ is rejected in favour of $\mu \neq \mu_0$ at the 1% level of significance.

Find also, in terms of $\bar{x}$, σ and n, the set of values of μ_0 for which $\mu = \mu_0$ is rejected in favour of $\mu < \mu_0$ at the 5% level of significance.   (C)

7. Explain *briefly* what is meant by the **standard error of the sample mean**.

Over a certain period of time, a random sample of 165 private subscribers connected to telephone exchange A used a total of 87 945 units. It is known that the standard deviation of the number of units used by a private subscriber connected to this exchange during the period is 100.

(i) Calculate a symmetric 95% confidence interval for the mean number of units used by a private subscriber connected to telephone exchange A during the period.

(ii) Calculate an interval within which approximately the central 95% of the number of units used by a private subscriber, connected to telephone exchange A during the period, will lie.

State *in each case* any distributional assumptions which you make.

Over the same period of time, a random sample of 215 private subscribers connected to telephone exchange B used a total of 117 175 units. The standard deviation of the number of units used by a private subscriber at this exchange during the period is also 100. Show that there is no evidence of a difference between the mean number of units used by private subscribers at telephone exchanges A and B.

Provide a symmetric 99% confidence interval for the mean number of units used by private subscribers at these two telephone exchanges.   (JMB)

8. Let p denote the probability of obtaining a head when a certain coin is tossed.
(a) If $p = 0.4$, find the probability of obtaining at least 3 heads in 10 independent tosses of the coin.
(b) If $p = 0.6$, find the probability of obtaining exactly 12 heads in 20 independent tosses of the coin.
(c) Write down an appropriate null hypothesis and an appropriate alternative hypothesis for testing whether the coin is unbiased.

To carry out this test 20 independent tosses of the coin are made and the number of heads that occurs is observed. Given that 15 heads occurred, carry out the test, assuming a 5 per cent significance level. Write down a statement of the conclusion you draw about the value of p for this coin.   (JMB)

9. The lifetime, T, in hours of a certain type of electric lamp is a random variable with distribution

$$f(t) = A e^{-t/1200}, \qquad 0 \leqslant t < \infty$$
$$= 0, \qquad\qquad t < 0$$

Find the value of A and show that the mean and standard deviation of T are both 1200 hours.

To test the reliability of the production a random sample of 40 bulbs was tested and found to have a mean life of 1020 hours. Does this indicate at the 5% level of significance that the batch from which the sample was taken was sub-standard?

10. Blocks of wood used for flooring are cut by machine. Their lengths are normally distributed with mean 230 mm and standard deviation 2 mm, while their widths are normally distributed with mean 80 mm and standard deviation 1.5 mm; the two measurements are independent. Calculate the probabilities
(a) that a block selected at random will lie within the tolerance limits 226.5 mm to 233 mm in length,
(b) that a block selected at random will lie within the tolerance limits 77 mm to 82 mm for width,
(c) that a block selected at random will satisfy both tolerances,
(d) that a block selected at random will be within the tolerance limits for width but not for length.

The setting on the machine which cuts the blocks to length is to be changed so that, while the standard deviation remains unchanged, 95% of the blocks will be no longer than 232.7 mm. Calculate the new mean length.

After this resetting a block is produced that is only 224.6 mm long. Does this suggest that the machine is not correctly set?

11. The length X of a certain component made by a machine is specified by the manufacturer to be 10 cm. X may be considered to be a random variable distributed normally with mean 10 cm and standard deviation 0.05 cm. All components are tested and are acceptable if they lie between 9.95 cm and 10.03 cm. Those less than 9.95 cm are rejected at a loss of 40 p each to the manufacturer; those between 10.03 cm and 10.05 cm can be shortened at a loss of 20 p and those greater than 10.05 cm can be shortened resulting in a loss of 25 p. Calculate the probabilities that if a component is tested the loss $L = 0, 20, 25, 40$ pence and hence calculate the expected value of L.

In order to test the accuracy of the machine a random sample of 25 components is measured and found to have a mean length of 10.014 cm. Is this sufficient evidence at the 5% level of significance to indicate that the mean is greater than 10 cm?

12. A drug company tested a new pain-relieving drug on a random sample of 100 headache sufferers. Of these, 75% said that their headache was relieved by the drug. With the currently marketed drug, 65% of users say that their headache is relieved by it. Test, at the 4% level, whether the new drug will have a greater proportion of satisfied users. Another drug company, wishing to impress the numerate public with its latest drug, states that, as a result of testing a random sample, the 95% confidence interval for the proportion p who find this drug effective is $80\% \pm 3\%$, i.e. $0.77 < p < 0.83$. Use this confidence interval to find the sample size. Find also a 90% confidence interval for p.

(C)

We now consider some tests which do not involve the normal distribution.

Test 5: Testing a proportion, p, of a binomial distribution, when n is small.

Test 6: The Sign Test, which is an application of Test 5.

Test 7: Testing a mean of a Poisson distribution.

TEST 5: TEST FOR PROPORTION, p OF A BINOMIAL DISTRIBUTION, n SMALL

When n is small we *cannot* use the normal approximation where $X \sim \text{Bin}(n, p)$ approximates to $X \sim \text{N}(np, npq)$. However, we can carry out a significance test similar to a test involving the normal distribution.

When dealing with the normal distribution, which is continuous, we consider whether or not a particular *point* lies in the critical region. With the binomial distribution, which is discrete, we must consider whether or not a particular *rectangle* lies in the critical region. We have already met this idea when considering continuity corrections.

Consider $X \sim \text{Bin}(8, p)$. Suppose we wish to test, at the 5% level, on the basis of a sample observation of x, whether p is 0.4 or whether p is greater than 0.4.

Say the sample value obtained is $x = 7$.

We make the hypotheses: H_0: $p = 0.4$

H_1: $p > 0.4$

Then, *if H_0 is true,* $X \sim \text{Bin}(8, 0.4)$

and $P(X = x) = {}^8C_x(0.6)^{8-x}(0.4)^x, \qquad x = 0, 1, \ldots, 8.$

We represent the distribution of X in the following diagram.

Note that we have drawn rectangles instead of vertical lines as this will help to give a better idea of the probabilities, which can be thought of as the areas of the rectangles.

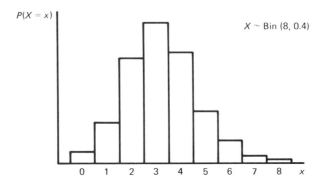

We use a one-tailed test and look at the right-hand tail of the distribution.

We want to draw the boundary line for the critical region so that 5% of the area lies to the right of the boundary.

We find, from tables or calculations, that

$$P(X \geqslant 5) = 0.1737 \quad (> 0.05)$$

$$P(X \geqslant 6) = 0.0498 \quad (< 0.05)$$

So the boundary line must be drawn slightly to the left of the rectangle for $x = 6$.

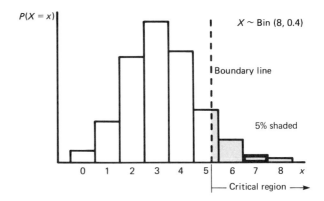

Now we wish to test the value $x = 7$ and will reject H_0 if the rectangle representing $x = 7$ lies *wholly* in the critical region.

From the diagram we see that this is the case, and <u>so we reject H_0 and conclude that $p > 0.4$.</u>

Example 10.14 A coin is tossed 6 times. Test, at the 5% level, whether the coin is biased towards heads if **(a)** 6 heads are obtained, **(b)** 5 heads are obtained.

Solution 10.14 Let X be the r.v. 'the number of heads when the coin is tossed 6 times', and let p be the probability that the coin shows heads.

$$H_0: \quad p = 0.5 \quad \text{(the coin is fair)}$$

$$H_1: \quad p > 0.5 \quad \text{(the coin is biased so that it is more likely to show heads)}$$

Under H_0 $\qquad\qquad\qquad\qquad X \sim \text{Bin}(6, 0.5)$

and $\qquad P(X = x) = {}^6C_x(0.5)^{6-x}(0.5)^x \qquad x = 0, 1, \ldots, 6$

$$= {}^6C_x(0.5)^6$$

From tables or calculations

$$P(X \geqslant 5) = 0.109\,375 \quad (> 0.05)$$

$$P(X = 6) = 0.015\,625 \quad (< 0.05)$$

so the boundary line for the critical region will be drawn as shown in the diagram, to give an area of 5% in the critical region.

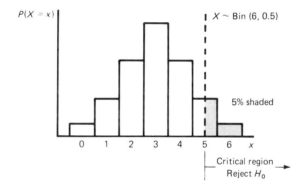

Using a one-tailed test, at the 5% level, we reject H_0 if our observation lies *wholly* in the critical region.

(**a**) 6 heads are obtained:

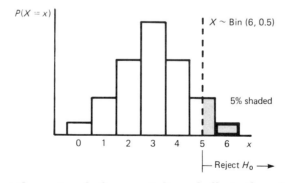

We see that the rectangle for $x = 6$ lies wholly in the critical region, and we conclude that there is evidence, at the 5% level, to suggest that the coin is biased towards heads if 6 heads are obtained in 6 tosses.

(**b**) 5 heads are obtained:

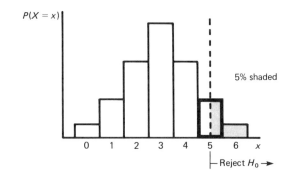

The rectangle for $x = 5$ does not lie wholly in the critical region, so we do not reject H_0 and <u>we conclude that there is no evidence, at the 5% level, to suggest that the coin is biased towards heads if 5 heads are obtained in 6 tosses.</u>

You may find this result surprising.

Example 10.15 The discrete r.v. X is distributed binomially with $n = 10$. If a single observation x is taken from the distribution, test, at the 8% level, the hypothesis that $p = 0.45$ against the alternative hypothesis $p \neq 0.45$ when (**a**) $x = 7$, (**b**) $x = 1$.

Solution 10.15 H_0: $p = 0.45$

H_1: $p \neq 0.45$ (two-tailed test)

Under H_0, $X \sim \text{Bin}(10, 0.45)$

Since the test is two-tailed, we need to consider both tails of the probability distribution and find boundary lines such that 4% of the area is in each tail. Note that it is not necessary to draw the complete probability distribution, since we are interested only in the tails.

(**a**) We test first the single observation $x = 7$. We are interested in the position of the boundary of the critical region in the right-hand tail, and need to know whether the rectangle for $x = 7$ lies wholly to the right of the boundary, i.e. wholly in the critical region.

Now if $x = 7$ does lie wholly in the critical region we would have $P(X \geqslant 7) < 0.04$.

From tables, $P(X \geqslant 7) = 0.102 > 0.04$, so the rectangle for $x = 7$ does not lie wholly in the critical region. We do not reject H_0, and <u>we conclude, at the 8% level, that $p = 0.45$.</u>

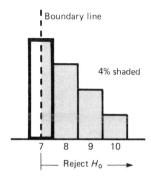

NOTE: from tables we find that $P(X \geqslant 8) = 0.0274$, so the boundary line comes within the rectangle for $x = 7$.

(**b**) We now test the single observation $x = 1$. This time we are interested in the position of the boundary of the critical region in the left-hand tail. Now the rectangle for $x = 1$ will lie wholly in the critical region if $P(X \leqslant 1) < 0.04$.

From tables, $P(X \leqslant 1) = 0.0233 < 0.04$, indicating that the rectangle for $x = 1$ does lie wholly in the critical region. Therefore we reject H_0, and we conclude, at the 8% level, that $p \neq 0.45$.

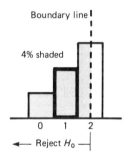

NOTE: from tables we find that $P(X \leqslant 2) = 0.0996$, so the boundary line comes within the rectangle for $x = 2$.

Example 10.16 State the conditions under which the binomial distribution may be used. Illustrate your answer by referring to a specific example, preferably from a project.

Records kept in a hospital show that 3 out of every 10 casualties who come to the casualty department have to wait more than half an hour before receiving medical attention. Find, to 3 decimal places, the probability that of the first 8 casualties who come to that casualty department   (**a**) none,   (**b**) more than two, will have to wait more than half an hour before receiving medical attention. Find also the most probable number of the 8 casualties that will have to wait more than half an hour.

The hospital decided to increase the staff of the department by one member and it was then found that of the next 20 casualties 2 had to wait more than half an hour for medical attention. Test (c) at the 2% level, (d) at the 5% level whether the new staffing has decreased the number of casualties who have to wait more than half an hour for medical attention.   (L)

Solution 10.16 For the first part see page 260.

Let X be the r.v. 'the number of casualties who wait more than half an hour', and let p be the probability that a casualty has to wait more than half an hour.

Then $X \sim \text{Bin}(n, p)$ with $n = 8$, $p = 0.3$

and $P(X = x) = {}^8C_x(0.7)^{8-x}(0.3)^x$ $x = 0, 1, 2, \ldots, 8$

(a) $P(X = 0) = (0.7)^8 = \underline{0.058}$ (3 d.p.)

(b) $P(X > 2) = 1 - P(X \leqslant 2)$

$= 1 - 0.5518$ (from tables)

$= \underline{0.488}$ (3 d.p.)

$P(X = 0) = 0.058$

$P(X = 1) = 8(0.7)^7(0.3) = 0.1977$

$P(X = 2) = 28(0.7)^6(0.3)^2 = \boxed{0.2965}$

$P(X = 3) = 56(0.7)^5(0.3)^3 = 0.2541$

and so on . . .

$P(X = 2) > P(X = 1)$ and $P(X = 2) > P(X = 3)$ and so the most probable number of casualties that will have to wait more than half an hour is 2.

Now let X be the r.v. 'the number of casualties in 20 who wait more than half an hour'.

Then $X \sim \text{Bin}(20, p)$

H_0: $p = 0.3$ (there is no change in the waiting pattern)

H_1: $p < 0.3$ (there is a decrease in the number who wait more than half an hour)

Under H_0, $X \sim \text{Bin}(20, 0.3)$.

(c) To test the significance of $x = 2$, at the 2% level, we perform a one-tailed test, and reject H_0 if $P(X \leqslant 2) < 0.02$ (indicating that the rectangle for $x = 2$ lies wholly in the critical region).

Now, from tables, $P(X \leqslant 2) = 0.0355 > 0.02$, so we do not reject H_0 and we conclude that there is no evidence at the 2% level to suggest a decrease in the number of casualties who wait more than half an hour.

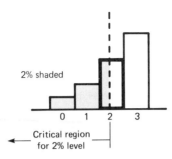

(**d**) At the 5% level, reject H_0 if $P(X \leqslant 2) < 0.05$.

Now $P(X \leqslant 2) = 0.0355 < 0.05$, so we reject H_0 and conclude that there is sufficient evidence, at the 5% level, to suggest a decrease in the number of casualties who wait more than half an hour.

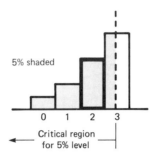

SUMMARY — TESTING A BINOMIAL PROPORTION, *n* SMALL

$X \sim \text{Bin}(n, p)$
Level of test: $\alpha\%$
Test the single value $x = r$

One-tailed test	
H_0: $p = p_0$ H_1: $p > p_0$	Reject H_0 if $P(X \geqslant r) < \dfrac{\alpha}{100}$
H_0: $p = p_0$ H_1: $p < p_0$	Reject H_0 if $P(X \leqslant r) < \dfrac{\alpha}{100}$
Two-tailed test	
H_0: $p = p_0$ H_1: $p \neq p_0$	Reject H_0 if $P(X \leqslant r) < \dfrac{\frac{1}{2}\alpha}{100}$ or if $\qquad P(X \geqslant r) < \dfrac{\frac{1}{2}\alpha}{100}$

Exercise 10g

1. For each of the following, a single observation x is taken from a binomial distribution where $X \sim \text{Bin}(n, p)$. Test the hypotheses at the level of significance stated.

	x	n	Hypotheses	Level of significance
(a)	6	8	H_0: $p = 0.45$, H_1: $p > 0.45$	5%
(b)	1	10	H_0: $p = 0.45$, H_1: $p < 0.45$	5%
(c)	9	15	H_0: $p = 0.35$, H_1: $p > 0.35$	5%
(d)	9	15	H_0: $p = 0.35$, H_1: $p \neq 0.35$	5%
(e)	2	9	H_0: $p = 0.45$, H_1: $p < 0.45$	5%
(f)	16	20	H_0: $p = 0.45$, H_1: $p > 0.45$	1%
(g)	5	7	H_0: $p = 0.4$, H_1: $p > 0.4$	10%
(h)	2	20	H_0: $p = 0.3$, H_1: $p < 0.3$	1%

2. A die is thrown 15 times and it shows a six on twelve occasions. Is the die biased in favour of showing a six? Test at the 1% level.

3. The probability that a certain type of seed germinates is 0.7. The seeds undergo a new treatment, and when a packet of 10 seeds is tested 9 germinate. Is this evidence, at the 5% level, of an increase in the germination rate?

4. In a test of 10 true–false questions a student gets 8 correct. The student claims she was not guessing. Test this claim at the 5% level.

5. Over a long period of time it has been found that in Enrico's restaurant the ratio of non-vegetarian to vegetarian meals ordered is 3 to 1.

   During one particular day at Enrico's restaurant, a random sample of 20 people contained 2 who ordered a vegetarian meal.

   (a) Carry out a significance test to determine whether or not the proportion of vegetarian meals ordered that day is lower than is usual. State clearly your hypotheses and use a 10% significance level.

   In Manuel's restaurant, of a random sample of 100 people ordering meals, 31 ordered vegetarian meals.

   (b) Set up null and alternative hypotheses and, using a suitable approximation, test whether or not the proportion of people eating vegetarian meals at Manuel's is different from that at Enrico's restaurant. Use a 5% level of significance. (L)

TEST 6: THE SIGN TEST

The sign test is an important application of the test for a binomial proportion. It uses the fact that if we take a value at random from *any* distribution, the probability that it is less than the median is 0.5. Similarly the probability that it is greater than the median is 0.5.

In a sign test we make a hypothesis about the *median* of the distribution. No assumption is made about any population parameter, so the test is sometimes referred to as a **'non-parametric test'**.

The procedure is illustrated in the following examples:

Example 10.17 The pupils in class 9A think that the median mark obtained by Year 9 pupils in the mathematics examination was greater than 63. In order to test this, they take a random sample of 10 marks:

$$64 \quad 69 \quad 40 \quad 64 \quad 65 \quad 71 \quad 82 \quad 59 \quad 64 \quad 74$$

Is there evidence, at the 5% level, to suggest that the median mark was greater than 63?

Solution 10.17 The null hypothesis is that the median *was* 63, so

$$H_0: \quad \text{median} = 63$$

$$H_1: \quad \text{median} > 63$$

We consider whether each of the values in the random sample is greater than or less than the value given in the null hypothesis, putting $+$ if it is greater and $-$ if it is less. Since it is equally likely that a sign will be $+$ or $-$ (remember that the probability that a value is greater than the median is 0.5), then the number of $+$ signs will be distributed binomially with $n = 10$, $p = 0.5$.

Similarly the number of $-$ signs is distributed binomially with $n = 10$, $p = 0.5$.

The sample data give the following:

64	69	40	64	65	71	82	59	64	74
$+$	$+$	$-$	$+$	$+$	$+$	$+$	$-$	$+$	$+$

With so many $+$ signs, it seems likely that the median was greater than 63. We will test to see whether it is unusual to get 8 or more $+$ signs.

Let X be the r.v. 'the number of $+$ signs'.

Then, under H_0, $\qquad\qquad X \sim \text{Bin}(10, 0.5)$

and $\qquad\qquad P(X = x) = {}^{10}C_x(0.5)^{10-x}(0.5)^x$

$$= {}^{10}C_x(0.5)^{10}$$

Since there are 8 $+$ signs, we test the observation $x = 8$.

Performing a one-tailed test, at the 5% level, we reject H_0 if $P(X \geqslant 8) < 0.05$, i.e. if the rectangle representing $x = 8$ lies wholly in the critical region.

Now, from tables,

$$P(X \geqslant 8) = 1 - P(X \leqslant 7)$$

$$= 1 - 0.9453$$

$$= 0.0547 > 5\%,$$

so that there is more than a 5% chance of having 8 or more $+$ signs.

Therefore we do not reject H_0 and <u>we conclude that there is not</u> <u>significant evidence, at the 5% level, to suggest that the median</u> <u>mark was greater than 63.</u>

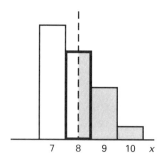

NOTE: if there had been 9 + signs:

$$P(X \geqslant 9) = 1 - P(X \leqslant 8)$$

$$= 1 - 0.9893 = 0.0107 \approx 1\%,$$

so that there is only a 1% chance of having 9 or more + signs and we would have rejected H_0 at the 5% level.

Example 10.18 It is thought that the median of the population from which the following sample is taken is 100. Test, at the 10% level, the following hypotheses:

(**a**) H_0: median $= 100$

        H_1: median < 100

(**b**) H_0: median $= 100$

        H_1: median $\neq 100$

Sample values:

    106 90 95 80 99 119 83 100 88 100 70

Solution 10.18 H_0: median $= 100$

We consider each of the sample values, writing + if it is greater than 100 and − if it is less than 100.

106	90	95	80	99	119	83	100	88	100	70
+	−	−	−	−	+	−	0	−	0	−

The zero values are ignored, so we have 7 − signs and 2 + signs.

This time we will consider the number of − signs.

Let X be the r.v. 'the number of − signs'.

Under H_0, $X \sim \text{Bin}(9, 0.5)$

and $P(X = x) = {}^9C_x(0.5)^9$

Since there are 7 − signs, we test the observation $x = 7$.

(**a**) H_0: median $= 100$

        H_1: median < 100

Performing a one-tailed test, at the 10% level, we reject H_0 if $P(X \geqslant 7) < 0.1$.

Now, from tables

$$P(X \geqslant 7) = 1 - P(X \leqslant 6)$$
$$= 1 - 0.9102$$
$$= 0.0898 < 0.1$$

Therefore we reject H_0 and conclude that the median is less than 100.

(b) H_0: median $= 100$

H_1: median $\neq 100$

This time the test is two-tailed, and we reject H_0, at the 10% level, if $P(X \geqslant 7) < 0.05$.

Now $P(X \geqslant 7) = 0.0898 > 0.05$

Therefore we do not reject H_0 and we conclude that the median could be 100.

TESTING PAIRED SAMPLES USING THE SIGN TEST

Example 10.19 Pupils entered for A-Level first take a 'mock' examination of the same standard. The marks obtained, in both the mock and public examinations, by a random sample of 13 students from a school, are shown below:

Candidate no.	1	2	3	4	5	6	7	8	9	10	11	12	13
Mock mark	40	65	53	79	87	42	80	63	51	82	27	71	29
A-Level mark	45	68	47	75	88	60	77	69	60	88	30	73	35

Test, at the 5% level, whether the candidates did better in the A-Level than in the mock examination.

Solution 10.19 H_0: there is no difference between the marks

H_1: the candidates did better in the A-Level.

In this case we consider the sign of the *difference* between A-Level and mock result

$$+ \quad + \quad - \quad - \quad + \quad + \quad - \quad + \quad + \quad + \quad + \quad + \quad +$$

Let X be the r.v. 'the number of $+$ signs'.

Then, under H_0, $X \sim \text{Bin}(13, 0.5)$

and $P(X = x) = {}^{13}C_x(0.5)^x$

The sample value is $x = 10$, since there are 10 $+$ signs.

We perform a one-tailed test, at the 5% level and reject H_0 if $P(X \geqslant 10) < 0.05$.

Now,

$$P(X \geqslant 10) = P(X = 10) + P(X = 11) + P(X = 12) + P(X = 13)$$
$$= (0.5)^{13}({}^{13}C_{10} + {}^{13}C_{11} + {}^{13}C_{12} + {}^{13}C_{13})$$
$$= 0.046\ldots$$

Since $P(X \geqslant 10) < 0.05$, we reject H_0 and conclude that there is evidence, at the 5% level, that the candidates did better in the A-Level than in the 'mock' examination.

Exercise 10h

1. A machine fills cans of a particular make of soft drink. The quantity of liquid, in ml, in each of a random sample of 14 cans was found to be as follows:

   330.2, 334.5, 332.9, 335.2, 334.0, 332.0, 336.1, 333.7, 335.2, 334.1, 333.1, 334.8, 333.1, 334.9

   Perform a sign test, at the 5% level, to test the hypothesis that the median quantity of liquid in cans produced by the machine is 333 ml against the alternative hypothesis that it is greater than 333 ml.

2. In order to test the hypotheses

   H_0: median = 100

   H_1: median $\neq$ 100

   a random sample of 11 items was taken from the population and the following results were obtained.

   93, 98, 102, 91, 97, 99, 100, 110, 97, 99, 95,

   (a) Is there evidence, at the 10% level, that the median is not 100?
   (b) It was later found that the reading of 100 was incorrect and should have been 94. Does this affect your decision?

3. The ability to withstand pain is known to vary from individual to individual. In a standard test a tiny electric shock is applied to the finger until a tingling sensation is felt. When this test was applied to a random sample of ten adults, the times recorded, in seconds, before they experienced a tingling sensation were

   4.2, 4.5, 3.9, 4.4, 4.1, 4.5, 3.7, 4.8, 4.2, 4.2

   Test, at the 5% level, the hypothesis that the average time before an adult would experience a tingling sensation is 4.0 seconds.

4. The times, in seconds, of a random sample of 12 telephone calls made from an office are shown below.

   112, 178, 416, 172, 203, 530, 72, 315, 70, 824, 227, 35

   Test the hypothesis that the median length of call is 330 seconds, against the alternative hypothesis that it is less than 330 seconds, using an 8% level of significance.

5. Two different German vocabulary tests are given to the same A-Level class of nine students and the marks gained are given in the table below.

Student number	1	2	3	4	5	6	7	8	9
Test 1	72	59	67	37	35	46	86	78	83
Test 2	64	48	46	35	47	45	83	74	74

   Carry out a test of significance, at the 5% level, to assess whether or not the vocabulary tests are of equal difficulty.   (C)P

6. (a) A manufacturer makes a large number of chains of the same type. The breaking strength, in kilograms, of each of a random sample of 12 chains was found. The results, each correct to 4 significant figures, were as follows:

   1294 1310 1297 1312 1341 1315
   1328 1317 1296 1321 1307 1318

Perform a sign test, at the 5% significance level, to test the hypothesis that the average breaking strength is 1300 kg against the alternative that it exceeds 1300 kg.

(b) In order to examine the effect of temperature on the breaking strength of the chains, 10 chains were randomly selected and each was cut in half. One half, chosen at random, was tested at 15°C and the other at 20°C. The results were as follows:

Chain	15°C	20°C
1	1307	1312
2	1324	1320
3	1321	1318
4	1305	1303
5	1306	1298
6	1304	1297
7	1306	1312
8	1321	1310
9	1315	1306
10	1301	1289

Use the sign test to determine whether there is significant evidence at the 5% level that the average breaking strength is less at the higher temperature. (C)P

7. For samples of twelve pairs of items from two populations, let n be the number of + signs obtained using a sign test. Determine the values of n that result in the rejection of the null hypothesis of no difference between the populations, using a symmetric two-tail test at the (nominal) 5% significance level. Calculate the exact tail probability associated with this nominal significance level.

A meteorological station has two rain gauges. Each gauge records, at ten-second intervals, the number of standard sized water droplets that have passed through its funnel in the interval. The numbers obtained during a randomly chosen two-minute period were as follows.

Gauge 1	Gauge 2
21	29
53	75
74	70
91	96
62	77
71	103
51	76
62	55
61	59
27	38
15	14
7	13

Test whether these observations provide significant evidence, at the 5% level, of a difference between the numbers recorded by the gauges, using the sign test. (C)P

8. Explain briefly what is meant by the term 'non-parametric' when referring to tests of significance.

A new golf course is built. The par, i.e. the score in which a professional player could expect to complete the course in good weather, is fixed at 71. A random sample of ten professional players play the course, in good weather, and record the following scores:

Player	1	2	3	4	5	6	7	8	9	10
Score	69	66	70	73	72	68	68	70	70	74

Use a sign test, at the 10% level, to decide whether the par has been fixed correctly. The same players play a second round on another day when the weather is bad. Their scores for the second round are:

Player	1	2	3	4	5	6	7	8	9	10
Score	71	72	72	70	76	70	65	75	73	76

Use a sign test, at the 10% level, to decide whether these figures indicate that professional players' scores are higher in bad weather. (C)

9. An investigator is interested in the effects of alcohol on the accuracy of the throwing of a dart. Eight volunteers each throw a single dart, aiming at the centre of the dart-board. They then each have a pint of beer and throw the dart once more. The distances (in cm) from the centre of the dart-board are recorded in the table below.

Volunteer	1	2	3	4	5	6	7	8
Before beer	5.0	2.4	6.9	0.3	4.1	3.2	2.0	4.2
After beer	3.7	7.6	7.1	5.3	4.7	1.1	2.4	4.9

(i) State explicitly suitable null and alternative hypotheses.
(ii) Using the sign test, determine the set of values of α for which your null hypothesis would be rejected at the α% significance level. (C)P

10. To measure the effectiveness of a drug for asthmatic relief, twelve subjects, all susceptible to asthma, were each randomly administered either the drug or a placebo during two separate asthmatic attacks. After one hour an asthmatic index was obtained on each subject with the following results.

Subject	1	2	3	4	5	6	7	8	9	10	11	12
Drug	28	31	17	18	31	12	33	24	18	25	19	17
Placebo	32	33	23	26	34	17	30	24	19	23	21	24

Using an appropriate non-parametric test, investigate the claim that the drug significantly reduces the asthmatic index. (AEB)

11. In the context of hypothesis testing, explain what is meant by the terms
(i) *null* and *alternative hypotheses,*
(ii) the *significance level* of a test,
(iii) the *critical region* of a test.
An investigation is to be carried out into the theory that high room temperatures cause a reduction in the standard of performance of routine mental tasks. Two sets, A and B, of arithmetic questions are constructed, each consisting of 20 questions. Preliminary tests are carried out to ensure that Set A and Set B are of equal difficulty. A random sample of 14 students is selected to take part in the investigation. Each student is asked to complete both sets of questions within a fixed time limit. One set is to be completed in a room at a temperature of 18°C, and the other in a similar room at a temperature of 30°C. Seven of the students are given Set A in the cooler room and Set B in the warmer room. The sets are reversed for the other seven students. A score out of 20 is recorded for each student on each set of questions.
(iv) Identify the explanatory and response variables in this experiment.
The scores are shown in the following table.

Student	1	2	3	4	5	6	7	8	9	10	11	12	13	14
Score at 18°C	17	15	9	20	16	12	9	13	14	9	12	13	18	10
Score at 30°C	14	15	10	20	15	10	11	13	13	8	12	11	17	12

(v) Carry out a sign test to investigate the hypothesis that temperature has no effect on the standard of performance in arithmetic.
(JMB)

12. In 1988 the Republican candidate for the Presidency of the USA was duly elected President with 54% of the popular vote. The percentage of votes cast in favour of the Republican candidate at each of the elections from 1960 is given in the table:

Year	Percentage voting Republican
1960	50.3
1964	38.9
1968	57.3
1972	62.5
1976	49.9
1980	50.7
1984	58.8
1988	54.0

(a) Locate and write down the median percentage vote.
(b) An opposition politician, a Democrat, put forward the suggestion that the average American voter was as much a Democrat as a Republican. Suggest suitable null and alternative hypotheses (concerning the median percentage vote) to test this claim.
(c) Identify all the occasions where the actual percentage is greater or less than your hypothesised median and assign a + or − appropriately. Use a Binomial sign test to test the Democrat's claim explaining carefully the steps you take and making your conclusions clear. (O)

TEST 7: TESTING A MEAN λ OF A POISSON DISTRIBUTION

Consider $X \sim \text{Po}(\lambda)$. Suppose we wish to test, at the 5% level, whether $\lambda = 8.5$ or whether $\lambda > 8.5$, on the basis of a sample observation. Say this sample value is $x = 14$.

We make the hypotheses: H_0: $\lambda = 8.5$

H_1: $\lambda > 8.5$

We use a one-tailed test and look at the right-hand tail of the distribution.

We want to draw the boundary line for the critical region so that 5% of the area lies to the right of the boundary.

If $X \sim \text{Po}(8.5)$, from tables $P(X \geqslant 14) = 0.0514 > 5\%$ and $P(X \geqslant 15) = 0.0274 < 5\%$, so the boundary line comes within the rectangle for $x = 14$.

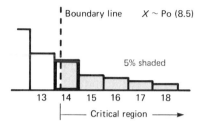

The rectangle representing $x = 14$ does not lie wholly in the critical region and we would not reject the null hypothesis that $\lambda = 8.5$.

Example 10.20 The number of misprints on the front page of the *Daily Informer* is found to have a Poisson distribution with mean 6.5. A new proof-reader is employed and shortly afterwards the front page is found to have 12 misprints. The editor says that the mean number of misprints has increased. Test this claim at the 5% level.

Solution 10.20 Let X be the r.v. 'the number of misprints on the front page'.

Then
$$X \sim \text{Po}(\lambda)$$

$$H_0: \quad \lambda = 6.5 \quad \text{(the mean is unchanged)}$$

$$H_1: \quad \lambda > 6.5 \quad \text{(the mean has increased)}$$

We test at the 5% level and will reject H_0 if $P(X \geqslant 12) < 0.05$, indicating that the rectangle for $x = 12$ lies wholly within the critical region.

Now, from tables or by calculation, we find that $P(X \geqslant 12) = 0.0339 < 0.05$, so we reject H_0 and we conclude that there is evidence, at the 5% level, to suggest that the mean has increased.

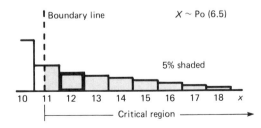

NOTE: since $P(X \geqslant 11) = 0.0668$, the boundary line is drawn within the rectangle for $x = 11$.

Example 10.21 Consider $X \sim \text{Po}(\lambda)$ and H_0: $\lambda = 6.5$. If $x = 2$, test, at the 5% level, (a) H_1: $\lambda \neq 6.5$, (b) H_1: $\lambda < 6.5$.

Solution 10.21 (a)
$$H_0: \quad \lambda = 6.5$$
$$H_1: \quad \lambda \neq 6.5$$

We perform a two-tailed test, at the 5% level, and reject H_0 if $P(X \leqslant 2) < 0.025$, indicating that the rectangle for $x = 2$ lies wholly in the critical region.

We find, from tables or calculation, that $P(X \leqslant 2) = 0.043 > 0.025$, therefore we do not reject H_0 and <u>we conclude that $\lambda = 6.5$.</u>

(b)
$$H_0: \quad \lambda = 6.5$$
$$H_1: \quad \lambda < 6.5$$

We perform a one-tailed test, at the 5% level, and reject H_0 if $P(X \leqslant 2) < 0.05$.

Now, since $P(X \leqslant 2) = 0.043 < 0.05$, we reject H_0 and <u>conclude that the mean is less than 6.5.</u>

Example 10.22 State conditions under which the Poisson distribution is a suitable model to use in statistical work. Describe briefly how a Poisson distribution was used, or could have been used, in a project.

(a) The number, X, of breakdowns per day of the lifts in a large block of flats has a Poisson distribution with mean 0.2. Find, to 3 decimal places, the probability that on a particular day
(i) there will be at least one breakdown,
(ii) there will be at most two breakdowns.

(b) Find, to 3 decimal places, the probability that, during a 20-day period, there will be no lift breakdowns.

(c) The maintenance contract for the lifts is given to a new company. With this company it is found that there are 2 breakdowns over a period of 30 days. Perform a significance test at the 5% level to decide whether or not the number of breakdowns has decreased.

(L)

Solution 10.22 (a) Let X be the r.v. 'the number of breakdowns per day'.

Then
$$X \sim \text{Po}(0.2).$$

(i)
$$P(X \geqslant 1) = 1 - P(X = 0)$$
$$= 1 - e^{-0.2}$$
$$= \underline{0.181} \quad (3 \text{ d.p.})$$

(ii) $$P(X \leqslant 2) = P(X = 0) + P(X = 1) + P(X = 2)$$

$$= e^{-0.2} \left(1 + 0.2 + \tfrac{0.2^2}{2} \right)$$

$$= 1.22 e^{-0.2}$$

$$= \underline{0.999 \quad (3 \text{ d.p.})}$$

(**b**) In 1 day we 'expect' 0.2 breakdowns, so in 20 days we 'expect' $20 \times 0.2 = 4$ breakdowns.

Let Y be the r.v. 'the number of breakdowns in 20 days'.

Then

$$Y \sim \text{Po}(4) \quad \text{and} \quad P(Y = 0) = e^{-4} = 0.018 \quad (3 \text{ d.p.})$$

Therefore the probability that there are no breakdowns is 0.018.

NOTE: we could consider

$$P(\text{no breakdowns in 20 days}) = (P(X = 0))^{20}$$

$$= (e^{-0.2})^{20} = e^{-4} \quad \text{as before.}$$

(**c**) In 30 days we 'expect' $30 \times 0.2 = 6$ breakdowns.

Let B be the r.v. 'the number of breakdowns in 30 days'.

Then $B \sim \text{Po}(\lambda) \quad \text{where} \quad \lambda = 6.$

Now there are 2 breakdowns in 30 days and we wish to test whether there has been a decrease in the average number of breakdowns.

H_0: $\lambda = 6$ (there is no change in the average number of breakdowns)

H_1: $\lambda < 6$ (the average number of breakdowns has decreased)

We perform a one-tailed test, at the 5% level, and will reject H_0 if $P(B \leqslant 2) < 0.05$.

Now, from tables, $P(B \leqslant 2) = 0.062 > 0.05$. Therefore we do not reject H_0 and we conclude that there is no evidence, at the 5% level, to suggest that the average number of breakdowns has decreased.

Example 10.23 In a company, breakdowns occur on a particular machine at an average rate of 3 per month. Assuming that the number of breakdowns follows a Poisson distribution, find, to 3 decimal places, the probability that

(**a**) exactly 2 occur in a particular month,

(**b**) more than 12 occur in a 3-month period,

(**c**) exactly 2 occur in each of 3 successive months.

For this machine, the maintenance contract from the supplier is such that if the number of breakdowns exceeds n during a calendar year, the premium paid for the contract will be refunded.

(**d**) Using a suitable approximation find the smallest value of n so that the probability of having to refund the premium in any year is less than 0.02.

The company replaces the machine with a machine from a different supplier. Over a 3-month period, 3 breakdowns occur.

(**e**) Perform a significance test, at the 5% level, to decide whether or not the average number of breakdowns has decreased. State your conclusion.   (L)

Solution 10.23 (**a**) Let X be the r.v. 'the number of breakdowns in a month'.

Then
$$X \sim \text{Po}(3),$$

so
$$P(X = 2) = e^{-3}\frac{3^2}{2!} = \underline{0.224 \ (3 \text{ d.p.})}$$

(**b**) Let Y be the r.v. 'the number of breakdowns in 3 months'.

Then
$$Y \sim \text{Po}(9),$$

$$P(Y > 12) = 1 - P(Y \leqslant 12) = 1 - 0.8758 = 0.1242 = \underline{0.124 \ (3 \text{ d.p.})}$$
$$\text{(using cumulative probability tables)}$$

(**c**) P(exactly 2 breakdowns in each of 3 successive months)
$$= (0.224)^3$$
$$= \underline{0.011 \ (3 \text{ d.p.})}$$

(**d**) Let A be the r.v. 'the number of breakdowns in 12 months'.

Then
$$A \sim \text{Po}(36)$$

Since λ is large, $A \sim \text{N}(36, 36)$ approximately.

We need to find n such that $P(A > n) < 0.02$.

$P(A > n) \longrightarrow P(A > n + 0.5)$ (continuity correction)

$$= P\left(\frac{A - 36}{6} > \frac{n + 0.5 - 36}{6}\right)$$

$$= P\left(Z > \frac{n - 35.5}{6}\right)$$

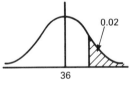

Now $P(Z > 2.055) = 0.02$ S.V.   0   2.055

Therefore
$$\frac{n - 35.5}{6} > 2.055$$

$$n > 47.83$$

The least value of n is 48.

(**e**) Let Y be the r.v. 'the number of breakdowns in 3 months'.

Then
$$Y \sim \text{Po}(\lambda).$$

H_0: $\lambda = 9$

H_1: $\lambda < 9$ (and the average number of breakdowns has decreased)

We use a one-tailed test, at the 5% level, and reject H_0 if
$P(Y \leqslant 3) < 0.05$ (i.e. if the rectangle for $y = 3$ lies wholly within the critical region).

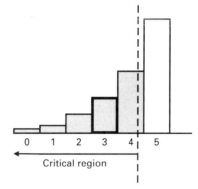

From tables

$$P(Y \leqslant 3) = 0.0212 < 0.05$$

Therefore we reject H_0 and conclude <u>that there is evidence of a</u> <u>decrease in the average number of breakdowns.</u>

NOTE: you should draw the above diagram accurately for yourself and verify the position of the boundary line.

SUMMARY — TESTING A POISSON MEAN

$X \sim \text{Po}(\lambda)$ Level of test: $\alpha\%$ Test the single value $x = r$	
One-tailed test	
H_0: $\lambda = \lambda_0$ H_1: $\lambda > \lambda_0$	Reject H_0 if $P(X \geqslant r) < \dfrac{\alpha}{100}$
H_0: $\lambda = \lambda_0$ H_1: $\lambda < \lambda_0$	Reject H_0 if $P(X \leqslant r) < \dfrac{\alpha}{100}$
Two-tailed test	
H_0: $\lambda = \lambda_0$ H_1: $\lambda \neq \lambda_0$	Reject H_0 if $P(X \geqslant r) < \dfrac{\frac{1}{2}\alpha}{100}$ or if $\qquad P(X \leqslant r) < \dfrac{\frac{1}{2}\alpha}{100}$

Exercise 10i

1. For each of the following a single observation x is taken from a Poisson distribution, where $X \sim \text{Po}(\lambda)$. Test the hypotheses at the level of significance stated.

	x	Hypotheses	Level of significance
(a)	11	H_0: $\lambda = 7$, H_1: $\lambda > 7$	5%
(b)	12	H_0: $\lambda = 7$, H_1: $\lambda \neq 7$	5%
(c)	4	H_0: $\lambda = 10$, H_1: $\lambda < 10$	1%
(d)	18	H_0: $\lambda = 10$, H_1: $\lambda > 10$	5%
(e)	2	H_0: $\lambda = 6.5$, H_1: $\lambda \neq 6.5$	5%
(f)	2	H_0: $\lambda = 6.5$, H_1: $\lambda > 6.5$	5%

2. The number of white corpuscles on a slide has Poisson distribution with mean 3.5. After certain treatment another sample was taken and the number of white corpuscles was found to be 8. Test, at the 5% level, whether the mean has increased.

3. The number of breakdowns in a computer is known to follow a Poisson distribution with a mean of 4.5 per month. A new computer is installed and in the first month there are 2 breakdowns. Test, at the 5% level, the claim that the mean has decreased.

4. The number of telephone calls to an office follows a Poisson distribution with a mean number of 6 per hour on a weekday.
(a) On Monday there were 5 calls between 10.00 and 10.30. Test, at the 5% level, whether the mean has increased.
(b) On Wednesday there were 3 calls between 11.00 and 12.30. Test, at the 5% level, whether the mean has decreased.

5. The number of flaws per 100 m of fabric is known to follow a Poisson distribution with mean 2. A 200 m length of fabric is tested and found to have 7 flaws. Test at the 5% level, whether the mean has increased.

6. Describe, briefly, the experimental evidence which you obtained in order to illustrate the Poisson distribution. State carefully any assumptions which you made.
The number X of emergency telephone calls to a gas board office in t minutes at weekends is known to follow a Poisson distribution with mean $\frac{1}{90}t$. Given that the telephone in that office is unmanned for 10 minutes, calculate, to 2 significant figures, the probability that there will be at least 2 emergency telephone calls to the office during that time.
Find, to the nearest minute, the length of time that the telephone can be left unmanned for there to be a probability of 0.9 that no emergency telephone call is made to the office during the period the telephone is unmanned.
During a week of very cold weather it was found that there had been 10 emergency telephone calls to the office in the first 12 hours of the weekend. Using the tables provided, or otherwise, determine whether the increase in the average number of emergency telephone calls to that office is significant at the 5% level.   (L)

7. Explain briefly, referring to your projects if possible, the role of the null hypothesis and of the alternative hypothesis in a test of significance.
Over a long period, Jane has found that the bus taking her to school arrives late on average 9 times per month. In the month following the start of new summer schedules, Jane finds that her bus arrives late 13 times. Assuming that the number of times the bus is late has a Poisson distribution, test, at the 5% level of significance, whether the new schedules have in fact increased the number of times on which the bus is late. State clearly your null and alternative hypotheses.   (L)P

TYPE I AND TYPE II ERRORS

When conducting a significance test we reach one of four possible conclusions. These are summarised in the table opposite.

	True situation	Our conclusion		
(1)	H_0 is true	Accept H_0	Correct decision	
(2)	H_0 is true	Reject H_0	Wrong decision	Type I error
(3)	H_0 is false	Accept H_0	Wrong decision	Type II error
(4)	H_0 is false	Reject H_0	Correct decision	

We say that

(**a**) a Type I error is made if we reject H_0 when it is true.

(**b**) a Type II error is made if we accept H_0 when it is false.

We write

(**a**) $P(\text{Type I error}) = P(\text{rejecting } H_0 | H_0 \text{ is true})$

(**b**) $P(\text{Type II error}) = P(\text{accepting } H_0 | H_1 \text{ is true})$

NOTE: when considering Type II errors we must state a definite value of the parameter in the alternative hypothesis H_1.

Example 10.24 A box is known to contain either H_0: 10 white counters and 90 black counters or H_1: 50 white counters and 50 black counters. In order to test hypothesis H_0 against hypothesis H_1, four counters are drawn at random from the box, without replacement. If all four counters are black, H_0 is accepted. Otherwise it is rejected.

Find the size of the Type I and Type II errors for this test.   (AEB)

Solution 10.24 H_0:   The bag contains 10 white and 90 black counters

          H_1:   The bag contains 50 white and 50 black counters

H_0 is accepted if all four counters, drawn without replacement, are black.

$P(\text{Type I error}) = P(\text{rejecting } H_0 | H_0 \text{ is true})$

$\qquad\qquad = P(\text{at least 1 white}|\text{there are 10 white and 90 black})$

Now if there are 10 white and 90 black

$$P(\text{drawing 4 black}) = \left(\tfrac{90}{100}\right)\left(\tfrac{89}{99}\right)\left(\tfrac{88}{98}\right)\left(\tfrac{87}{97}\right)$$

$$= 0.652$$

$$P(\text{drawing at least 1 white}) = 1 - 0.652$$

$$= 0.348$$

Therefore $P(\text{Type I error}) = 0.348$.

$P(\text{Type II error}) = P(\text{accepting } H_0 | H_1 \text{ is true})$

$$= P(\text{all 4 are black} | \text{there are 50 white and 50 black})$$

If there are 50 white and 50 black

$$P(\text{drawing 4 black}) = \left(\frac{50}{100}\right)\left(\frac{49}{99}\right)\left(\frac{48}{98}\right)\left(\frac{47}{97}\right)$$

$$= 0.059$$

Therefore $P(\text{Type II error}) = 0.059$.

Example 10.25 A man claims that he can throw a six with a fair die five times out of six on the average. Calculate the probability that he will throw four or more sixes in six throws   (*i*) if his claim is justified   (*ii*) if he can throw a six, on the average, only once in six throws.

To test the claim, he is invited to throw the die six times, his claim being accepted if he throws at least four sixes.

Find the probability that the test will   (**a**) accept the man's claim when hypothesis (*ii*) is true, or   (**b**) reject the claim when it is justified, that is, when hypothesis (*i*) is true.   (AEB)

Solution 10.25 (*i*) If his claim is justified

$$P(\text{throws a six}) = \tfrac{5}{6}$$

So, in six throws, let X be the r.v. 'the number of sixes obtained'.

Then $X \sim \text{Bin}(n, p)$ with $n = 6$, $p = \tfrac{5}{6}$

Now $P(X = x) = {}^6C_x \left(\tfrac{1}{6}\right)^{6-x}\left(\tfrac{5}{6}\right)^x$ $x = 0, 1, \ldots, 6$

$$P(X \geqslant 4) = P(X = 4) + P(X = 5) + P(X = 6)$$

$$= 15\left(\tfrac{1}{6}\right)^2\left(\tfrac{5}{6}\right)^4 + 6\left(\tfrac{1}{6}\right)\left(\tfrac{5}{6}\right)^5 + \left(\tfrac{5}{6}\right)^6$$

$$= \left(\tfrac{5}{6}\right)^4\left(\tfrac{1}{6}\right)^2(15 + 30 + 25)$$

$$= 0.938 \quad (3 \text{ d.p.})$$

Therefore $P(X \geqslant 4) = 0.938$ (3 d.p.)

(*ii*) If $P(\text{throws a six}) = \frac{1}{6}$

Then $\qquad X \sim \text{Bin}(n, p) \quad \text{with} \quad n = 6, \quad p = \frac{1}{6}$

$$P(X = x) = {}^6C_x \left(\frac{5}{6}\right)^{6-x} \left(\frac{1}{6}\right)^x \quad x = 0, 1, 2, \ldots, 6$$

$$P(X \geq 4) = P(X = 4) + P(X = 5) + P(X = 6)$$

$$= 15\left(\frac{5}{6}\right)^2 \left(\frac{1}{6}\right)^4 + 6\left(\frac{5}{6}\right)\left(\frac{1}{6}\right)^5 + \left(\frac{1}{6}\right)^6$$

$$= \left(\frac{1}{6}\right)^6 (375 + 30 + 1)$$

$$= 0.0087 \quad (2 \text{ S.F.})$$

Therefore $P(X \geq 4) = 0.0087$ (2 S.F.)

H_0: the man can throw a six five times out of six

H_1: the man can throw a six, on the average, only once in six throws

H_0 is accepted if the man throws at least four sixes in six throws.

(**a**) $\qquad P(\text{accepting } H_0 | H_1 \text{ is true}) = P\left(X \geq 4 | p = \frac{1}{6}\right)$

$$= 0.0087$$

Therefore the probability of accepting the man's claim, when hypothesis (*ii*) is true $= P(\text{Type II error}) = 0.0087$ (2 S.F.).

(**b**) $\qquad P(\text{rejecting } H_0 | H_0 \text{ is true}) = P\left(X < 4 | p = \frac{5}{6}\right)$

$$= 1 - 0.938$$

$$= 0.062 \quad (3 \text{ d.p.})$$

Therefore the probability of rejecting the man's claim when it is justified (probability of a Type I error) is 0.062 (3 d.p.).

Example 10.26 Dating of archaeological specimens is a difficult task. It is known that specimens emit a certain type of radioactive particle; the number of particles emitted in n minutes has a Poisson distribution with parameter $n\lambda$, where the value of λ depends upon the age of the specimen.

Two hypotheses concerning the age of one particular specimen are put forward:

$\qquad H_A$: specimen is 7000 years old (in which case $\lambda = 1.0$)

$\qquad H_B$: specimen is 15 000 years old (in which case $\lambda = 4.0$)

It is decided to count the number, X, of radioactive particles emitted in n minutes and

$$\text{accept } H_A \text{ (and reject } H_B) \text{ if } X \leqslant 1$$

$$\text{and accept } H_B \text{ (and reject } H_A) \text{ if } X \geqslant 2$$

If $n = 1$ what is (**a**) the probability of rejecting H_A when H_A is in fact true, (**b**) the probability of rejecting H_B when H_B is in fact true?

If the probability of rejecting H_B when H_B is in fact true is to be less than 0.001, show that the minimum number of complete minutes for which counting should be recorded is three. What is the corresponding probability of rejecting H_A when H_A is in fact true? (AEB)

Solution 10.26

$$H_A: \quad \text{specimen is 7000 years old } (\lambda = 1.0)$$

$$H_B: \quad \text{specimen is 15 000 years old } (\lambda = 4.0)$$

Let X be the r.v. 'the number of particles emitted in n minutes'.

Then $X \sim \text{Po}(n\lambda)$.

We accept H_A (and reject H_B) if $X \leqslant 1$
and accept H_B (and reject H_A) if $X \geqslant 2$.

If $n = 1$, then $X \sim \text{Po}(\lambda)$.

(**a**) $P(\text{rejecting } H_A | H_A \text{ is true}) = P(X \geqslant 2 | X \sim \text{Po}(1.0))$

Now, if $X \sim \text{Po}(1.0)$,

$$P(X = x) = e^{-1.0}\frac{(1.0)^x}{x!} \quad x = 0, 1, \ldots$$

So $$\begin{aligned} P(X \geqslant 2) &= 1 - P(X = 0) - P(X = 1) \\ &= 1 - e^{-1} - e^{-1} \\ &= 1 - 2e^{-1} \\ &= 1 - 0.736 \\ &= 0.264 \end{aligned}$$

The probability of rejecting H_A when H_A is true is 0.264 (3 d.p.).

(**b**) $P(\text{rejecting } H_B | H_B \text{ is true}) = P(X \leqslant 1 | X \sim \text{Po}(4.0))$

If $X \sim \text{Po}(4.0)$, then

$$P(X = x) = e^{-4.0}\frac{(4.0)^x}{x!} \quad x = 0, 1, \ldots$$

So $$\begin{aligned} P(X \leqslant 1) &= P(X = 0) + P(X = 1) \\ &= e^{-4} + e^{-4}4 \\ &= 5e^{-4} \\ &= 0.092 \end{aligned}$$

The probability of rejecting H_B when H_B is true is 0.092 (3 d.p.).

Now under H_A: $X \sim \text{Po}((1.0)n)$

under H_B: $X \sim \text{Po}((4.0)n)$

If $P(\text{rejecting } H_B | H_B \text{ is true}) \leqslant 0.001$ then

$P(X \leqslant 1 | X \sim \text{Po}(4n)) \leqslant 0.001$.

If $X \sim \text{Po}(4n)$ then

$$P(X = x) = e^{-4n} \frac{(4n)^x}{x!} \quad x = 0, 1, \ldots$$

We have $P(X \leqslant 1) = P(X = 0) + P(X = 1)$

$$= e^{-4n} + e^{-4n} 4n$$

$$= e^{-4n}(1 + 4n)$$

So, we require to find n such that

$$e^{-4n}(1 + 4n) \leqslant 0.001$$

By, trial,   when $n = 1$ $e^{-4}(5) = 0.092 > 0.001$

when $n = 2$ $e^{-8}(9) = 0.003\,02 > 0.001$

when $n = 3$ $e^{-12}(13) = 0.000\,08 < 0.001$

Therefore, the minimum number of complete minutes is 3.

In this case, when $n = 3$, $X \sim \text{Po}(3\lambda)$.

So $P(\text{rejecting } H_A | H_A \text{ is true}) = P(X \geqslant 2 | X \sim \text{Po}(3(1.0)))$

If $X \sim \text{Po}(3)$ then

$$P(X = x) = e^{-3} \frac{(3)^x}{x!} \quad x = 0, 1, \ldots$$

So $P(X \geqslant 2) = 1 - P(X = 0) - P(X = 1)$

$$= 1 - e^{-3} - e^{-3} 3$$

$$= 1 - 4e^{-3}$$

$$= 0.801 \quad (3 \text{ d.p.})$$

The probability of rejecting H_A when H_A is true is 0.801 (3 d.p.).

Example 10.27 Two hypotheses concerning the probability density function of a random variable X are

$$H_0: \ f(x) = \begin{cases} \frac{1}{4}(x + 1) & 0 < x < 2 \\ 0 & \text{otherwise} \end{cases}$$

$$H_1: \ f(x) = \begin{cases} \frac{1}{4}x^3 & 0 < x < 2 \\ 0 & \text{otherwise} \end{cases}$$

Sketch the p.d.f. in each case.

The following test procedure is decided upon. A single observation of X is made and if X is less than a particular value k, where $0 < k < 2$, then H_0 is accepted, otherwise H_1 is accepted.

(**a**) Find k if $P(\text{Type I error}) = 0.1$.

(**b**) With this value of k, find $P(\text{Type II error})$.

Solution 10.27

Under H_0

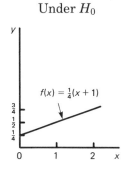

Under H_1

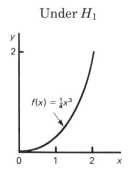

(**a**) If $X < k$, we accept H_0. If $X \geqslant k$, we accept H_1.

We need to find k such that $P(\text{Type I error}) = 0.1$

i.e. $\qquad\qquad P(\text{accept } H_1 | H_0 \text{ is true}) = 0.1$

At this stage it is important to rewrite the statements as follows:

$$P(X \geqslant k \,|\, f(x) = \tfrac{1}{4}(x + 1)) = 0.1$$

Under H_0, $\qquad\qquad P(X \geqslant k) = \int_k^2 \tfrac{1}{4}(x + 1) \, \mathrm{d}x$

So $\qquad\qquad \int_k^2 \tfrac{1}{4}(x + 1) \, \mathrm{d}x = 0.1$

$$\left[\tfrac{1}{2}x^2 + x\right]_k^2 = 0.4$$

$$2 + 2 - \tfrac{1}{2}k^2 - k = 0.4$$

$$k^2 + 2k - 7.2 = 0$$

$$(k + 1)^2 = 8.2$$

$$k + 1 = \pm 2.86$$

Therefore $k = 1.86$ since $0 < k < 2$.

(**b**) Now, when $k = 1.86$

$$P(\text{Type II error}) = P(\text{accept } H_0 | H_1 \text{ is true})$$

$$= P(X < 1.86 | f(x) = \tfrac{1}{4}x^3)$$

$$= \int_0^{1.86} \frac{1}{4}x^3 \, dx$$

$$= \left[\frac{x^4}{16}\right]_0^{1.86}$$

$$= 0.748$$

Therefore, when $k = 1.86$, $P(\text{Type II error}) = 0.748$.

Example 10.28 To test whether a coin is fair, the following decision rule is adopted. Toss the coin 120 times; if the number of heads is between 50 and 70 inclusive, accept the hypothesis that the coin is fair, otherwise reject it.

(**a**) Find the probability of rejecting the hypothesis when it is correct.

(**b**) How should the decision rule be modified if

$$P(\text{Type I error}) < 0.01?$$

(**c**) With the original decision rule, find $P(\text{Type II error})$ if the coin is biased and the probability that a head is obtained is in fact 0.6.

Solution 10.28 Let X be the r.v. 'the number of heads obtained'.

Then $X \sim \text{Bin}(n, p)$ with $n = 120$.

Now, since n is large, $X \sim \text{N}(np, npq)$ approximately, where $q = 1 - p$

$$H_0: \quad \text{the coin is fair} \quad \left(p = \tfrac{1}{2}\right)$$

$$H_1: \quad \text{the coin is biased} \quad \left(p \neq \tfrac{1}{2}\right)$$

Under H_0,

$$np = (120)\left(\tfrac{1}{2}\right) = 60 \quad \text{and} \quad npq = (120)\left(\tfrac{1}{2}\right)\left(\tfrac{1}{2}\right) = 30$$

So $$X \sim \text{N}(60, 30)$$

(a) Under H_0,

$$P(50 \leqslant X \leqslant 70) \rightarrow P(49.5 < X < 70.5) \qquad \text{(continuity correction)}$$

$$= P\left(\frac{49.5 - 60}{\sqrt{30}} < \frac{X - 60}{\sqrt{30}} < \frac{70.5 - 60}{\sqrt{30}}\right)$$

$$= P(-1.917 < Z < 1.917)$$

$$= 0.9446$$

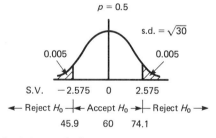

So $\qquad P(\text{accepting } H_0 | H_0 \text{ is true}) = 0.9446$

$P(\text{rejecting } H_0 | H_0 \text{ is true}) = 1 - 0.9446 = 0.0554.$

(b) If $P(\text{Type I error}) < 0.01$ then we need to find a value a such that $\Phi(a) = 0.995$. Now, from tables, $a = 2.575$.

So, if $X \sim N(60, 30)$, then the value of X corresponding to the standardised value of 2.575 is given by

$$60 + 2.575\sqrt{30} = 74.1 \quad \text{(3 S.F.)}$$

The value corresponding to the standardised value of -2.575 is

$$60 - 2.575\sqrt{30} = 45.9 \quad \text{(3 S.F.)}$$

Therefore, the decision rule becomes:

Accept the hypothesis that the coin is fair if the number of heads lies between 46 and 74 inclusive, otherwise reject it.

(c) $\qquad\qquad H_0:$ coin is fair $(p = 0.5)$

$\qquad\qquad H_1:$ coin is biased $(p = 0.6)$

We accept H_0 if the number of heads lies between 50 and 70 inclusive.

Now $\qquad P(\text{Type II error}) = P(\text{accepting } H_0 | H_1 \text{ is true})$

$$= P(49.5 < X < 70.5 | p = 0.6)$$

Now, if $p = 0.6, \qquad np = (120)(0.6) = 72$

$$npq = (120)(0.6)(0.4) = 28.8$$

So $X \sim N(72, 28.8)$.

$$P(49.5 < X < 70.5) = P\left(\frac{49.5 - 72}{\sqrt{28.8}} < \frac{X - 72}{\sqrt{28.8}} < \frac{70.5 - 72}{\sqrt{28.8}}\right)$$

$$= P(-4.193 < Z < -0.2795)$$

$$= 0.390 \quad (3 \text{ S.F.})$$

Therefore, $P(\text{Type II error}) = 0.390$ (3 S.F.).

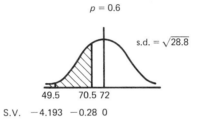

We see that, with the given decision rule, there is a fairly high probability that the coin will be accepted as fair when in fact $p = 0.6$.

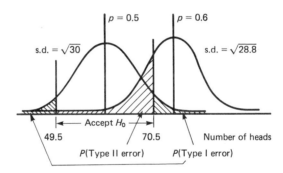

Example 10.29 A sample of size 100 is taken from a normal population with unknown mean μ and known variance 36. An investigator wishes to test the hypotheses $H_0\colon \mu = 65$, $H_1\colon \mu > 65$. He decides on the following criteria:

accept H_0 if the sample mean $\bar{x} \leqslant 66.5$

reject H_0 if $\bar{x} > 66.5$

Find the probability that he makes a Type I error.

If he uses as alternative hypothesis $H_1\colon \mu = 67.9$, find the probability that he makes a Type II error.

On which critical value should he decide for the sample mean if he wants $P(\text{Type I error}) = P(\text{Type II error})$?

Solution 10.29 Under H_0,

$$\overline{X} \sim N\left(\mu, \frac{\sigma^2}{n}\right) \quad \text{with} \quad \mu = 65, \quad \sigma = 6, \quad n = 100$$

He rejects H_0 if $\bar{x} > 66.5$.

Now

$$P(\overline{X} > 66.5) = P\left(\frac{\overline{X} - 65}{6/10} > \frac{66.5 - 65}{6/10}\right)$$

$$= P(Z > 2.5)$$

$$= 0.006\,21$$

Therefore, the probability that he rejects H_0, when in fact H_0 is true (Type I error) is $0.006\,21$.

If H_1: $\mu = 67.9$, then under H_1

$$\overline{X} \sim N\left(67.9, \frac{36}{100}\right)$$

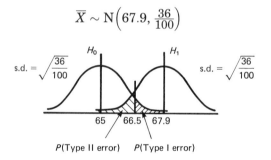

$$P(\text{Type II error}) = P(\text{accept } H_0 | H_1 \text{ is true})$$

$$= P(\overline{X} \leqslant 66.5 \,|\, \mu = 67.9)$$

$$= P\left(\frac{\overline{X} - 67.9}{6/10} \leqslant \frac{66.5 - 67.9}{6/10}\right)$$

$$= P(Z \leqslant -2.333)$$

$$= 0.009\,82$$

Therefore, $P(\text{Type II error}) = 0.009\,82$.

If he wants $P(\text{Type I error}) = P(\text{Type II error})$ then the critical value of $\bar{x}$ should be fixed so that

$$P(\overline{X} > \bar{x} | H_0 \text{ is true}) = P(\overline{X} \leqslant \bar{x} | H_1 \text{ is true})$$

As the variances of the distributions given by H_0 and H_1 are equal, we see, by symmetry, that the value of $\bar{x}$ lies mid-way between 65 and 67.9.

Therefore, he should take as critical value, $\bar{x} = \frac{1}{2}(65 + 67.9) = 66.45$.

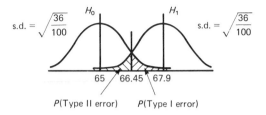

Example 10.30 The ingredients for concrete are mixed together to obtain a mean breaking strength of 2000 Newtons. If the mean breaking strength drops below 1800 Newtons then the composition must be changed. The distribution of the breaking strength is normal with standard deviation 200 Newtons.

Samples are taken in order to investigate the hypotheses:

$$H_0: \quad \mu = 2000 \text{ Newtons}$$

$$H_1: \quad \mu = 1800 \text{ Newtons}$$

How many samples must be tested so that

$$P(\text{Type I error}) = \alpha = 0.05$$

and $$P(\text{Type II error}) = \beta = 0.1?$$

Solution 10.30

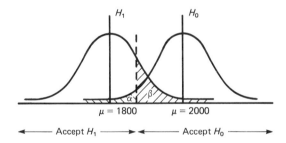

Under H_0, $X \sim N(2000, 200^2)$

So, for a random sample of size n

$$\overline{X} \sim N\left(2000, \frac{200^2}{n}\right)$$

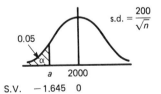

Now a corresponds to a standardised value of -1.645,

i.e. $$a = 2000 - 1.645\left(\frac{200}{\sqrt{n}}\right) \qquad \text{(i)}$$

Under H_1, $X \sim N(1800, 200^2)$

So, for a random sample of size n

$$\overline{X} \sim N\left(1800, \frac{200^2}{n}\right)$$

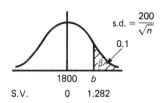

Now b corresponds to a standardised value of 1.282,

i.e. $$b = 1800 + 1.282\left(\frac{200}{\sqrt{n}}\right) \qquad \text{(ii)}$$

Now, if we find a value for n such that $\alpha = 0.05$ and $\beta = 0.1$

then $$a = b$$

Equating (i) and (ii)

$$2000 - 1.645\left(\frac{200}{\sqrt{n}}\right) = 1800 + 1.282\left(\frac{200}{\sqrt{n}}\right)$$

$$200 = \left(\frac{200}{\sqrt{n}}\right)(1.282 + 1.645)$$

$$\sqrt{n} = 2.927$$

$$n = 8.57$$

So the estimated number of samples which needs to be tested is 9.

Exercise 10j

1. Two separate tests are proposed to determine whether a coin is biased or unbiased. These are:
    Test 1 — Toss the coin 4 times, and conclude that it is biased if all 4 tosses give the same result, and unbiased otherwise.
    Test 2 — Toss the coin 7 times, and conclude that it is biased if at least 6 of the tosses give the same result, and unbiased otherwise.
    (a) Suppose that the coin is unbiased. Show that each test has the same probability of giving a wrong conclusion.
    (b) Suppose that the coin is such that the probability of a head in any toss is $\frac{2}{3}$.
    Determine which test is more likely to give the conclusion that the coin is biased.   (MEI)

2. Two alternative hypotheses concerning the probability density function of a random variable are

    H_0: $f(x) = 2x$ $0 < x < 1$
          $= 0$ otherwise

    H_1: $f(x) = 2(1 - x)$ $0 < x < 1$
          $= 0$ otherwise

    Give a sketch of the probability density function for each case.
    The following test procedure is decided upon. A single observation of X is made and if X exceeds a particular value a, where $0 < a < 1$, then H_0 is accepted, otherwise H_1 is accepted. Find the value of a if the probability of accepting H_1 given that H_0 is true is $\frac{1}{9}$. With this value of a, find the probability of accepting H_0 given that H_1 is true.   (C)

3. A manufacturer makes two grades of squash ball — 'slow' and 'fast'. Slow balls have a 'bounce' (measured under standard conditions) which is known to be a normal

variable with mean 10 cm and standard deviation 2 cm. The 'bounce' of fast balls is a normal variable with mean 15 cm and standard deviation 2 cm. A box of balls is unlabelled so that it is not known whether they are all slow or all fast. Devise a test, based on a single observation of the bounce of one ball such that the probability of deciding that the box contains fast balls when in fact it contains slow balls, i.e. the Type I error, is equal to the Type II error.
Devise a test, based on an observation of the mean bounce of a sample of 4 balls from the box such that the Type I error is 0.05 and state the magnitude of the Type II error for this test. (C)

4. Two hypotheses concerning the probability density function of a random variable are

$$H_0: \ f(x) = \begin{cases} 1 & 1 < x < 2 \\ 0 & \text{otherwise} \end{cases}$$

$$H_1: \ f(x) = \begin{cases} 3x^2/7 & 1 < x < 2 \\ 0 & \text{otherwise} \end{cases}$$

Give a sketch of the probability density function for each case.
The following test procedure is decided upon: A single observation of X is made and if X is less than a particular value a, where $1 < a < 2$, then H_0 is accepted; otherwise H_1 is accepted.
Find a such that, when H_0 is true, the test procedure leads, with probability 0.1, to the acceptance of H_1. With this value of a, find the probability that, when H_1 is true, the test procedure leads to the acceptance of H_0. (C)

5. One of two dice is loaded so that there is a probability of 0.2 of throwing a six with it, nothing being known about the other scores. The other die is fair. A person is given one of these dice (which is just as likely to be the fair as the biased one), together with the above information and is asked to discover which die it is. He decides to throw the die 10 times; if there are two or more sixes he will assert that the die is biased, otherwise he will assert that it is fair. Calculate the probability of his asserting that the die is (a) biased when it is, in fact, fair; (b) fair when it is, in fact, biased. What is the probability that his choice will be incorrect? If, instead, he decides to throw the die 240 times and will assert that the die is biased if there are N or more sixes, use the normal approximation to the binomial distribution to estimate N if the probability of his asserting that it is fair when it is biased is to be 0.2.

6. An automated engineering process for manufacturing components includes an automatic screening of the output to reject defective components. The process gives on average 5% of defectives. The probability that the screening stage identifies correctly a defective component is 98% but there is also a probability of 6% that a component which is not defective is rejected at the screening stage. What is the proportion of all components which is rejected and what is the proportion of all components passed from the screening stage that is still defective? (MEI)

7. In order to examine a six-sided die for bias, one face is marked, the die is tossed a pre-determined number of times, and the number of times the marked face is uppermost is recorded.
(a) If this occurred r times in n tosses, explain how you would decide if this provided significant evidence of bias. Do not consider any approximate methods in this part.
(b) Would you consider it likely to be biased if the marked face came up once in 30 tosses?
(c) Would you consider it likely to be biased if the marked face came up 39 times in 180 tosses? (O)

8. Flour is packed in bags. The combined mass, X grams, of a full bag and its contents is a normally distributed random variable with mean μ grams and standard deviation 5 grams. When the packing machine is working correctly $\mu = 136$, but when the packing machine is working incorrectly $\mu = 130$. Show that the probabilities of a randomly chosen bag having a combined mass of less than 131.5 grams when the machine is working (a) correctly, (b) incorrectly, are approximately 0.2 and 0.6 respectively. When X is less than 131.5 the bag is underweight. Using the approximate probability 0.2, determine the probability that, when the machine is working correctly, in a random sample of five bags there are precisely k bags which are underweight, for $k = 3, k = 4$ and $k = 5$.
The machine is presumed to be working incorrectly if the number of underweight bags found in a random sample of five bags is equal to or greater than r.
Determine the minimum value of r which gives a probability less than 0.01 of presuming the machine to be working incorrectly when it is working correctly. (C)

9. One suggested test for deciding whether a coin is fair or not is to toss it four times and call it 'biased' if four heads or four tails are obtained. A second suggested way is to toss it seven times and call it biased if six or seven heads, or six or seven tails, are obtained. Show that both these tests would be equally likely to conclude wrongly that a fair coin was biased. Which of these two suggested tests would be better for correctly judging as biased a coin whose probability of coming down heads was 2/3?
Are any of the above results statistically significant?   (SMP)

10. A fair coin is tossed 100 times. Use a normal approximation to determine the probability of obtaining (a) more than 57 heads,
(b) more than 58 heads.
It is desired to construct a significance test to choose between the following two hypotheses concerning the possible bias of a coin:

H_0: the probability that the coin falls heads is 0.5

H_1: the probability that the coin falls heads is 0.6

The coin is to be tossed 100 times and the number of heads, X, recorded. Construct a significance test based upon the observed value of X such that the probability of accepting H_1 when H_0 is true is as close as possible to 0.05. For this test calculate the probability of accepting H_0 when H_1 is true.   (C)

11. Two alternative hypotheses for the probability density function of a random variable X are given below.

$$H_0:\ f(x) = a + \tfrac{1}{4}x \qquad -1 \leqslant x \leqslant 1$$
$$= 0 \qquad\qquad \text{otherwise}$$
$$H_1:\ f(x) = b - \tfrac{1}{4}x \qquad -1 \leqslant x \leqslant 1$$
$$= 0 \qquad\qquad \text{otherwise}$$

Design a test, based on a single observation of X such that the probability of wrongly accepting H_0 is 0.05.
Design also a test, based on a single observation of X, such that the probability of wrongly accepting H_0 is twice the probability of wrongly accepting H_1.   (C)

12. You are provided with a coin which may be biased. In order to test this you are allowed to toss it 12 times and count the number, r, of heads and to use the value of r to decide. If the coin is really fair you wish to have at least a 95% chance of saying so. For what values of r should you say that the coin is fair?
If you adopt your procedure with a coin which is actually biased two to one in favour of heads, what is the probability that you decide the coin is biased?   (O)

13. Random samples of 400 seeds are taken from a large batch. For this batch the probability of a randomly chosen seed germinating is α. The r.v. X is defined as the number of germinating seeds in a sample. Use an appropriate normal approximation to determine the values of
(a) $P(X \leqslant 340 \,|\, \alpha = 0.9)$
(b) $P(X \geqslant 340 \,|\, \alpha = 0.8)$
The seed assessor knows that the value of α is either 0.8 or 0.9. Suppose that, in fact out of the 400 seeds in a particular sample a total of x germinate. The assessor decides that the value of α is 0.8 if
$Z = P(X \geqslant x \,|\, \alpha = 0.8) - P(X \leqslant x \,|\, \alpha = 0.9)$
is positive. Otherwise he decides that α is 0.9. Determine the assessor's decision for each of the cases $x = 330$, $x = 340$, $x = 350$.   (C)

11

THE χ^2 TEST

χ^2 is pronounced 'kye squared' and is written 'chi-squared'.

The χ^2 test is a significance test that enables us to decide whether it is valid to use a particular distribution, such as binomial, Poisson or normal, as a model so that we can interpret observed data. We can also use the χ^2 test to decide whether two variables are independent.

Here are two examples that we will be considering later in the chapter.

(**a**) A farmer kept a record of the number of heifer cows born during the first five years of breeding of each cow, with the following results:

Number of heifers	0	1	2	3	4	5
Frequency	4	19	41	52	26	8

We may wish to know whether the binomial distribution, with $n = 5$ and $p = 0.5$, is an adequate model for this situation. (See Example 11.18, page 614.)

When performing a χ^2 test we make a hypothesis about the data. In this case we assume that the number of heifers *does* follow a binomial distribution with $n = 5$ and $p = 0.5$. We then work out the expected frequencies (E) given by this hypothesis, and compare these with the observed frequencies (O).

(**b**) Some years ago a Polytechnic decided to require all entrants to a science course to study a non-science subject for one year. In the first year of the scheme entrants were given the choice of studying French or Russian. The number of students of each sex choosing each language is shown in the following table:

	French	Russian
Male	39	16
Female	21	14

Is the choice of language independent of sex? (See Example 11.19, page 618.)

In this case, the null hypothesis (H_0) will be that the choice of language *is* independent of sex.

THE TEST STATISTIC FOR THE χ^2 TEST

We need to compare the observed frequencies (O) with the frequencies expected (E). If we find the value of each of the differences, $O - E$, and then sum them, we find that the total of these differences, $\Sigma(O - E)$ will always be *zero*, since the positive and negative differences will cancel each other out. To overcome this problem we *square each of the differences.*

Also, a difference of 4 arising from an expected frequency of 10 must be shown to be more important than a difference of 4 arising from an expected frequency of 100. (You would be pleased to make a profit of 4 p on an article costing 10 p, but not so pleased to make a profit of 4 p on an article costing £1.)

So we *divide each of the squared differences by E, the expected frequency.* In this way a small difference will be more important when E is small than when E is large.

The test statistic that we use is

$$\sum \frac{(O - E)^2}{E}.$$

Subject to certain conditions, this can be approximated by the χ^2 distribution. We will look briefly at this distribution before considering the test procedure.

THE χ^2 DISTRIBUTION

The χ^2 distribution has a very complicated probability density function. It has one parameter, v (pronounced 'new') and the shape of the distribution is different for different values of v. Here are some examples.

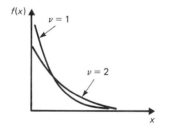
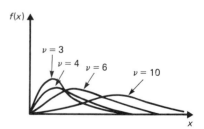

Some features of the χ^2 distribution are:
(*i*)   It is J-shaped for $v = 1$ and $v = 2$.
(*ii*)   It is positively skewed for $v > 2$.
(*iii*)   The larger the value of v, the more symmetric the distribution becomes.
(*iv*)   When v is large, the distribution is approximately normal.

Degrees of freedom

The parameter v is known as the number of degrees of freedom. It is the number of independent variables that are used to calculate χ^2.

Use of χ^2 tables

When performing a χ^2 test we will want to know the **critical value** of χ^2 that gives a certain percentage of the area in the *right-hand tail* of the distribution. For example, if we want 5% of the area in the tail, then we need to find $\chi^2_{5\%}$. For a given value of v, this critical value can be found from tables. For example, consider $v = 9$.

The critical value required is written $\chi^2_{5\%} (9)$.

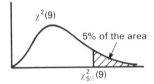

The complete tables are printed on page 725, but an extract is printed below.

α gives the fraction of the area in the right-hand tail, so if we want a 5% level (i.e. 5% of the area in the tail) we look at the column headed 0.050, and for a 1% level, we look at the column headed 0.010.

For $\chi^2_{5\%} (9)$ we find column 0.050 and row $v = 9$.

α / v	0.250	0.100	0.050	0.025	0.010	0.005	0.001
1	1.32330	2.70554	3.84146	5.02389	6.63490	7.87944	10.828
2	2.77259	4.60517	5.99146	7.37776	9.21034	10.5966	13.816
3	4.10834	6.25139	7.81473	9.34840	11.3449	12.8382	16.266
4	5.38527	7.77944	9.48773	11.1433	13.2767	14.8603	18.467
5	6.62568	9.23636	11.0705	12.8325	15.0863	16.7496	20.515
6	7.84080	10.6446	12.5916	14.4494	16.8119	18.5476	22.458
7	9.03715	12.0170	14.0671	16.0128	18.4753	20.2777	24.322
8	10.2189	13.3616	15.5073	17.5345	20.0902	21.9550	26.125
9	11.3888	14.6837	16.9190	19.0228	21.6660	23.5894	27.877
10	12.5489	15.9872	18.3070	20.4832	23.2093	25.1882	29.588
11	13.7007	17.2750	19.6751	21.9200	24.7250	26.7568	31.264

Columns $\chi^2_{5\%}$ (0.050) and $\chi^2_{1\%}$ (0.010) are indicated. $v = 9$ row is indicated.

We find that $\chi^2_{5\%} (9) = 16.9190$

This means that

$$P(\chi^2 > 16.9190) = 0.05$$

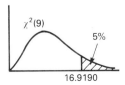

Example 11.1   Use χ^2 tables to find (**a**) $\chi^2_{1\%}(4)$, (**b**) $\chi^2_{10\%}(3)$.

Solution 11.1 (**a**)   For $\chi^2_{1\%}(4)$ we need
row $v = 4$, column 0.010

So $\chi^2_{1\%}(4) = 13.2767$

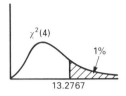

(**b**)   For $\chi^2_{10\%}(3)$ we need
row $v = 3$, column 0.100

So $\chi^2_{10\%}(3) = 6.251\,39$

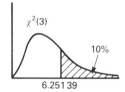

Example 11.2   The random variable X has a χ^2 distribution with two degrees of freedom. Find x such that $P(X > x) = 0.01$.

Solution 11.2   We find x from the tables, since it is the value of $\chi^2_{1\%}(2)$.

Row $v = 2$, column $\alpha = 0.010$
gives $\chi^2_{1\%}(2) = 9.210\,34$

Therefore $x = 9.210\,34$

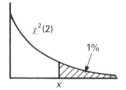

Example 11.3   The random variable Y has a χ^2 distribution with 6 degrees of freedom. Find α such that $P(Y > 14.4494) = \alpha$.

Solution 11.3   For row $v = 6$, the value 14.4494 is found in column $\alpha = 0.025$.

Therefore $P(Y > 14.4494) = 0.025$

or $\chi^2_{2\frac{1}{2}\%}(6) = 14.4494$

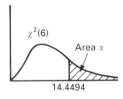

THE χ^2 TEST

Consider the following situation:

By pressing the random number generator $\boxed{\text{Ran }\#}$ on a calculator it is possible to produce a random 3 digit number between 0.000 and 0.999.

For example $\boxed{\text{Ran } \#}$ 0.593 $\boxed{\text{Ran } \#}$ 0.193 $\boxed{\text{Ran } \#}$ 0.132 and so

on. In this case the random digits are   5, 9, 3, 1, 9, 3, 1, 3, 2.

Random number tables consist of lists of the ten digits
0, 1, 2, 3, 4, 5, 6, 7, 8, 9 and are such that each digit has an
equal chance of appearing at any stage. So each digit has a
probability of 0.1 of occurring i.e. $P(X = x) = 0.1$ for
$x = 0, 1, 2, \ldots, 9$. (See uniform distribution, page 226.)

Suppose we want to test whether our $\boxed{\text{Ran } \#}$ generated numbers
are random enough.

Here is a list of 100 digits generated on a calculator

4	9	8	3	3	3	7	1	3	9
9	9	6	1	8	1	3	6	1	6
0	3	7	7	3	3	5	4	7	3
3	8	1	4	2	8	8	6	1	9
4	5	3	4	9	4	3	8	5	5
8	6	6	7	5	9	2	6	3	3
3	8	2	4	8	4	1	9	8	4
1	4	2	2	1	7	0	8	2	5
7	5	8	0	4	7	6	9	1	2
9	7	7	5	3	7	4	0	6	6

Arranged in a frequency table:

Digit	0	1	2	3	4	5	6	7	8	9	
Frequency	4	10	7	16	12	8	10	11	12	10	Total 100

Now if these digits are random, the expected frequency for each one
is given by $100 \times P(X = x)$ for $x = 0, 1, \ldots, 9$

Therefore   expected frequency $= 100 \times 0.1 = 10$

So we add another row to the table:

Digit	0	1	2	3	4	5	6	7	8	9	
Observed frequency (O)	4	10	7	16	12	8	10	11	12	10	Total 100
Expected frequency (E)	10	10	10	10	10	10	10	10	10	10	Total 100

Distribution of 100 random digits generated on a calculator

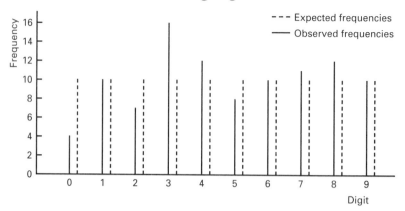

At first glance the observed frequency for 3 seems much too high and the observed frequency for 0 seems much too low. We want to construct a test which compares each observed frequency with the corresponding expected frequency.

We use the test statistic $\sum \dfrac{(O - E)^2}{E}$ which is approximated by the χ^2 distribution.

We write

$$\chi^2 = \sum \frac{(O - E)^2}{E}$$

For each 'cell' of the table we calculate $\dfrac{(O - E)^2}{E}$ and these contributions are summed for all the cells.

Now if, when χ^2 is calculated, it comes to 0, then there is exact agreement between the observed and expected frequencies.

If $\chi^2 > 0$, then O and E do not agree exactly, and the larger the value of χ^2, the greater the discrepancy.

A low value of χ^2 implies a good fit, whereas a high value of χ^2 implies a poor fit.

For our data, using $\chi^2 = \sum \dfrac{(O - E)^2}{E}$

$$\chi^2 = \frac{(4 - 10)^2}{10} + \frac{(10 - 10)^2}{10} + \frac{(7 - 10)^2}{10} + \frac{(16 - 10)^2}{10}$$

$$+ \frac{(12 - 10)^2}{10} + \frac{(8 - 10)^2}{10} + \frac{(10 - 10)^2}{10}$$

$$+ \frac{(11 - 10)^2}{10} + \frac{(12 - 10)^2}{10} + \frac{(10 - 10)^2}{10}$$

$$= 3.6 + 0 + 0.9 + 3.6 + 0.4 + 0.4 + 0 + 0.1 + 0.4 + 0$$

$$= 9.4$$

To decide whether our data give a good fit, we need to consider the appropriate χ^2 distribution. To do this we need the number of degrees of freedom, i.e. the number of independent variables that are used in calculating χ^2. To find this we first count the number of 'cells' in the table and then ask what restrictions we have placed on them.

Now the number of cells is 10 and there is *one* restriction, that the total of the expected frequencies must be 100.

So v = number of independent variables

                         = number of cells – number of restrictions

                         = $10 - 1$

                         = 9.

So we need to consider the χ^2 (9) distribution.

The null hypothesis (H_0) is that the digits are true random digits. The alternative hypothesis (H_1) is that the digits are *not* true random digits.

If there *is* good agreement between the observed and expected frequencies we should have a low value for the χ^2 total.

Our sample of 100 digits gave a total of 9.4. Is this low enough?

Performing a test at the 5% level, we first find $\chi^2_{5\%}$ (9).

On page 575 we found that $\chi^2_{5\%}$ (9) $= 16.919$.

Now we reject H_0 if our value of χ^2 is greater than 16.919.

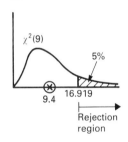

Since $9.4 < 16.919$ we do not reject H_0 and so we accept the digits as true random digits.

NOTE: the symbol $\otimes$ on the diagram represents the value of χ^2 calculated from the data.

PROCEDURE FOR PERFORMING A χ^2 TEST

(**1**) Consider a set of data with observed frequencies (O).

(**2**) Make the null hypothesis (H_0) concerning the distribution followed by the data.

(**3**) Calculate the expected frequencies (E) according to this hypothesis.

(**4**) Work out the number of degrees of freedom v where

           v = number of cells – number of restrictions.

The number of restrictions depends on the null hypothesis and we will consider several cases in the following examples.

(**5**) Decide on the level of the test and the rejection criterion, looking up critical values in the χ^2 tables.

For a test performed at the 5% level:

If $\qquad \chi^2 > \chi^2_{5\%}$

then we consider the discrepancy between observed and expected frequencies to be too large and reject the null hypothesis.

If $\qquad \chi^2 \leqslant \chi^2_{5\%}$

we do not reject the null hypothesis.

(**6**) Calculate $\quad \chi^2 = \sum \dfrac{(O - E)^2}{E}$

(**7**) Make your conclusion.

NOTE:

(**1**) χ^2 is calculated from $\quad \sum \dfrac{(O - E)^2}{E} \quad$ so that very small values of E tend to give a large value of χ^2. It is safe to say that **expected frequencies below 5 should not be used**. To overcome this problem, classes with low expected frequencies are combined to form a class sufficiently large.

(**2**) If $\ v = 1,\ $ it is advisable to use **Yates' continuity correction**. In this case the formula is

$$\chi^2 = \sum_{i=1}^{n} \frac{(\,|\,O_i - E_i\,|\, - 0.5)^2}{E_i}$$

(**3**) When the value of χ^2 is *very small*, it is wise to query the reliability of the observed data and to question whether they have been 'fiddled'.

GOODNESS OF FIT TESTS

We now illustrate the use of the χ^2 test to investigate whether an observed distribution fits a given one, such as a uniform, binomial, Poisson or normal distribution. The test is often referred to as a 'goodness of fit' test.

UNIFORM DISTRIBUTION

When considering the data for the calculator-generated random digits we investigated whether the uniform distribution was an adequate model. Other examples follow.

Example 11.4 The table shows the number of employees absent for a single day during a particular period of time:

Day	Monday	Tuesday	Wednesday	Thursday	Friday	Total
Number of absentees	121	87	87	91	114	500

(a) Find the frequencies expected under the hypothesis that the number of absentees is independent of the day of the week.

(b) Test, at the 5% level, whether the differences in the observed and expected data are significant.

Solution 11.4 H_0: the number of absentees is independent of the day of the week.

NOTE: the alternative hypothesis, H_1 is that the number of absentees is *not* independent of the day of the week. Often we do not state H_1, but take it for granted.

(a) If the number of absentees is independent of the day of the week, then we would expect the total of 500 to be spread uniformly throughout the week, so that the expected number of absentees for any day is 100.

Day	Monday	Tuesday	Wednesday	Thursday	Friday	
Observed number of absentees (O)	121	87	87	91	114	Total 500
Expected number of absentees (E)	100	100	100	100	100	Total 500

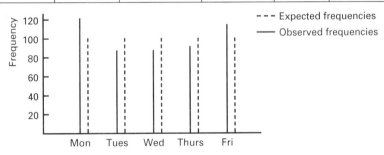

(b) **Degrees of freedom, v**

$$v = \text{number of independent variables}$$
$$= \text{number of cells} - \text{number of restrictions}$$

There are 5 cells, and since the total of the expected frequencies has to be 500, there is one restriction.

Therefore $v = 5 - 1$
$$= 4$$

and we consider a $\chi^2 (4)$ distribution.

We will test at the 5% level and
reject H_0 if $\chi^2 > \chi^2_{5\%}(4)$

From tables $\chi^2_{5\%}(4) = 9.48773$

To calculate χ^2:

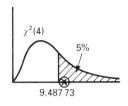

$\chi^2(4)$

5%

9.48773

O	E	$\dfrac{(O-E)^2}{E}$
121	100	4.41
87	100	1.69
87	100	1.69
91	100	0.81
114	100	1.96
$\Sigma O = 500$	$\Sigma E = 500$	10.56

$$\chi^2 = \sum \frac{(O-E)^2}{E}$$

$$= 10.56$$

Since $\chi^2 > 9.48773$, we reject H_0 and <u>conclude that the number</u>
<u>of absentees is not independent of the day of the week.</u>

NOTE: the test does not indicate what the relationship might be
between number of absentees and the day of the week. However, a
look at the observed frequencies suggests a tendency towards a
greater number of absentees on Mondays and Fridays.

Example 11.5 An ordinary die is thrown 120 times and each time the number on
the uppermost face is noted. The results are as follows:

Number on die	1	2	3	4	5	6
Frequency	14	16	24	22	24	20

Is the die fair? Test at the 10% level.

Solution 11.5 H_0: The die is fair.

If the die is fair we would expect each number to occur the same
number of times, i.e. 20.

Number on die	1	2	3	4	5	6	
Observed frequency (O)	14	16	24	22	24	20	Total 120
Expected frequency (E)	20	20	20	20	20	20	Total 120

Since $\Sigma E = 120$, there is one restriction.

Therefore v = number of cells − number of restrictions

$$= 6 - 1$$

$$= 5$$

and we consider the $\chi^2(5)$ distribution.

We will test at the 10% level and
reject H_0 if $\chi^2 > \chi^2_{10\%}$ (5)

i.e. if $\chi^2 > 9.236\,36$

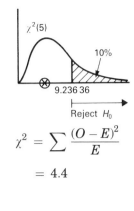

O	E	$\dfrac{(O-E)^2}{E}$
14	20	1.8
16	20	0.8
24	20	0.8
22	20	0.2
24	20	0.8
20	20	0
$\Sigma O = 120$	$\Sigma E = 120$	4.4

$$\chi^2 = \sum \frac{(O-E)^2}{E}$$

$$= 4.4$$

Since $\chi^2 < 9.236\,36$, we do not reject H_0 and we conclude that the die is fair.

DISTRIBUTION IN A GIVEN RATIO

Example 11.6 According to genetic theory the number of colour strains pink, white and blue in a certain flower should appear in the ratio $3:2:5$. For 100 plants, the results were as follows:

Colour	Pink	White	Blue	Total
Number of plants	24	14	62	100

Are the differences between the observed and expected frequencies significant, at the 1% level?

Solution 11.6 H_0: the colours pink, white and blue occur in the ratio $3:2:5$.

Now under H_0 we expect the colours pink, white and blue to appear in the ratio $3:2:5$, so the expected frequencies are

$$\tfrac{3}{10}\,(100): \tfrac{2}{10}\,(100): \tfrac{5}{10}\,(100) = 30:20:50$$

Colour	Pink	White	Blue	
Observed frequency (O)	24	14	62	Total 100
Expected frequency (E)	30	20	50	Total 100

There is one restriction, $\Sigma E = 100$

Therefore v = number of cells – number of restrictions

$$= 3 - 1$$

$$= 2$$

and we consider the χ^2 (2) distribution.

We test at the 1% level and reject H_0
if $\chi^2 > \chi^2_{1\%}$ (2)

i.e. if $\chi^2 > 9.21034$

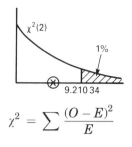

O	E	$\dfrac{(O-E)^2}{E}$
24	30	1.2
14	20	1.8
62	50	2.88
$\Sigma O = 100$	$\Sigma E = 100$	5.88

$$\chi^2 = \sum \frac{(O-E)^2}{E}$$

$$= 5.88$$

Since $\chi^2 < 9.21034$, we do not reject H_0 and we conclude that the differences between the observed and expected frequencies are not significant, at the 1% level.

Exercise 11a

1. A tetrahedral die is thrown 120 times and the number on which it lands is noted.

Number	1	2	3	4	
Frequency	35	32	25	28	Total 120

Test, at the 5% level whether the die is fair.

2. From a list of 500 digits, the occurrence of each digit is noted.

Digit	0	1	2	3	4	5	6	7	8	9
Frequency	40	58	49	53	38	56	61	53	60	32

Test, at the 1% level, whether the sequence is a random sample from a uniform distribution.

3. The outcomes, A, B and C, of a certain experiment are thought to occur in the ratio $1:2:1$. The experiment is performed 200 times and the observed frequencies of A, B and C are 36, 115 and 49 respectively. Is the difference in the observed and expected results significant? Test at the 5% level.

4. According to genetic theory the number of colour strains red, yellow, blue and white in a certain flower should appear in proportions $4:12:5:4$. Observed frequencies of red, yellow, blue and white strains amongst 800 plants were 110, 410, 150, 130 respectively. Are these differences from the expected frequencies significant at the 5% level? If the

number of plants had been 1600 and the observed frequencies 220, 820, 300, 260, would the difference have been significant at the 5% level?   (C Additional)

5. It is thought that each of the 8 outcomes of an experiment is equally likely to occur. When the experiment is performed 400 times, the observed frequencies are 45, 42, 55, 53, 40, 62, 47 and 56. Perform a test at the 1% level to investigate the validity of the theory.

6. In a particular subject students are set multiple choice questions each of which contain 5 alternatives A, B, C, D and E. A teacher suggests that when students do not know the correct answer they are twice as likely to choose one of B, C or D than to choose A or E. For 160 questions where it was known that the student answered without knowing the correct answer, A, B, C, D, E were chosen 23, 45, 36, 43 and 13 times respectively. Is there evidence, at the 5% level, to support the teacher's theory?

7. For a given set of data the observed and expected frequencies are shown:

Result	1	2	3	4	5
Observed frequency	30	31	42	40	57
Expected frequency	38	45	36	36	45

Are the differences between the observed and expected frequencies significant at the 1% level?

8. During the course of one year a tutor marked 111 assignments. The grades he awarded and the comparable national proportions are given in the table:

Grade	A	B	C	D
Number he awarded	86	18	6	1
National proportion	71%	16%	7%	6%

Calculate the expected numbers (to 1 decimal place) based on the national proportions. The χ^2 goodness of fit test requires the summation of terms of the form

$$(O - E)^2/E$$

where O and E are observed and expected frequencies. Suggest reasons why
(a) the difference between O and E is used
(b) this difference is squared, and
(c) the squared difference is divided by E.
Test, at the 5% level, whether there is any difference between the tutor's and the national awarding of grades. State your conclusions clearly.   (O)

9. (i) The random variable X has a normal distribution with mean 16 and variance 0.64. Find x, such that $P(X < x) = 0.025$.
(ii) The random variable Y has a χ^2 distribution with 8 degrees of freedom. Find y, such that $P(Y > y) = 0.05$.   (L)

10. A calibrated instrument is used over a wide range of values. To assess the operator's ability to read the instrument accurately, the final digit in each of 700 readings was noted. The results are tabulated below.

Final digit	Frequency
0	75
1	63
2	50
3	58
4	73
5	95
6	96
7	63
8	46
9	81

Use an approximate χ^2 statistic to test whether there is any evidence of bias in the operator's reading of the instrument. Use a 5% significance level and state your null and alternative hypotheses.   (L)

11. The grades on a statistics examination for a group of students were as follows.

Grade	A	B	C	D	E
Number of students	14	18	32	20	16

Test the hypothesis that the distribution of grades is uniform. Use a 5% level of significance.   (L)

12. In a certain town an investigation was carried out into accidents in the home to children under 12 years of age. The numbers of reported accidents and the ages of the children concerned are summarised in the table.

Group	Age of child (yrs)	No. of accidents
A	0 to <2	42
B	2 to <4	52
C	4 to <6	28
D	6 to <8	20
E	8 to <10	18
F	10 to <12	16

(a) State the modal class.
(b) Calculate, to the nearest month, the mean age and the standard deviation of the distribution of ages.
(c) Draw a cumulative frequency curve, and from it estimate, to the nearest month, the median, and the interquartile range for the ages of all children under 12 years of age concerned in reported accidents in the home. State, giving a reason, whether you consider the mean, the mode or the median best represents the average age for accidents in the home to children under 12 years of age.
(d) An investigator believes that children in the groups A, B, C, D, E, F are likely to have accidents in the home in the ratios $2:2:1:1:1:1$ respectively. Use a χ^2 test at a 5% significance level to decide whether or not this belief is justified.   (L)

BINOMIAL DISTRIBUTION, *p* known

Example 11.7 A game contains 20 pieces, each of which has probability 0.08 of being defective.

(a) Suggest a suitable distribution to model the number of defective pieces in a game.

Let X represent the number of defective pieces in a game.

(**b**) Copy and complete the following probability distribution.

x	0	1	2	3	4	5	6 or more
$P(X = x)$	0.1887			0.1414	0.0523	0.0145	

A random sample of 1000 *games* was checked for defective pieces and the following table produced to summarise the number of defective *pieces* in each game.

Number of defective pieces	0	1	2	3	4	5	6 or more
Number of games	194	344	266	137	46	10	3

(**c**) Use a χ^2 test to test, at the 5% level, whether or not the observed results are consistent with those expected under the model specified in (**a**).   (L)P

Solution 11.7 (**a**) Let X be the r.v. 'the number of defective pieces in 20'.
Then $X \sim \text{Bin}(20, 0.08)$

(**b**) $P(X = 1) = {}^{20}C_1 (0.92)^{19} (0.08) = 0.3282$ (4 d.p.)

$P(X = 2) = {}^{20}C_2 (0.92)^{18} (0.08)^2 = 0.2711$

$P(X \geqslant 6) = 1 - [P(X = 0) + P(X = 1) + \ldots + P(X = 5)]$

$= 1 - 0.9962$

$= 0.0038$

So the probability distribution is:

x	0	1	2	3	4	5	6 or more
$P(X = x)$	0.1887	0.3282	0.2711	0.1414	0.0523	0.0145	0.0038

In 1000 games, the expected frequencies are given by $1000\, P(X = x)$ and the table for observed and expected frequencies is

x	0	1	2	3	4	5	6 or more
O	194	344	266	137	46	10	3
E	188.7	328.2	271.1	141.4	52.3	14.5	3.8

NOTE: the expected frequency for the last cell is *less than 5*, so we combine the last two cells.

The revised table of observed and expected frequencies is:

x	0	1	2	3	4	5 or more	
O	194	344	266	137	46	13	
E	188.7	328.2	271.1	141.4	52.3	18.3	Total 1000

(**c**) We perform a χ^2 test:

H_0: The distribution is binomial with $n = 20, p = 0.08$.

Degrees of freedom:

> Number of cells $= 6$

> Number of restrictions $= 1$ (Expected frequencies total 1000).

Therefore $v = 6 - 1 = 5$ and we consider the χ^2 (5) distribution.

We test at the 5% level and reject H_0 if

$\chi^2 > \chi^2_{5\%}$ (5), i.e. if $\chi^2 > 11.0705$.

O	E	$\dfrac{(O-E)^2}{E}$
194	188.7	0.1488...
344	328.2	0.7606...
266	271.1	0.0959...
137	141.4	0.1369...
46	52.3	0.7588...
13	18.3	1.5349...
		3.4362...

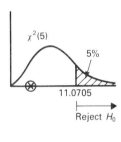

Casio 85/100/115

0	Min

| 194 | $-$ | 188.7 | $=$ | x^2 | $\div$ | 188.7 | M+ |

| 344 | $-$ | 328.2 | $=$ | x^2 | $\div$ | 328.2 | M+ |

$\cdots$ $\cdots$ $\cdots$

| 13 | $-$ | 18.3 | $=$ | x^2 | $\div$ | 18.3 | M+ |

MR	$= 3.4362\ldots$

Therefore $\chi^2 = \sum \dfrac{(O-E)^2}{E} = 3.4362$

Since $\chi^2 < 11.0705$ we do not reject H_0 and we conclude that <u>the observed results are consistent with the binomial model</u>.

BINOMIAL DISTRIBUTION, *p* unknown

Example 11.8   Samples of size 5 are selected regularly from a production line and tested. During one week 500 samples are taken and the number of defective items in each sample is recorded.

Number of defectives, x	0	1	2	3	4	5
Frequency, f	170	180	120	20	8	2

(**a**) Find the frequencies of the number of defectives per sample given by the binomial distribution having the same mean and total as the observed distribution.

(**b**) Test whether the observed distribution follows a binomial pattern.

Solution 11.8 (**a**) To find the mean ($\bar{x}$) of the observed distribution:

$$\bar{x} = \frac{\Sigma f x}{\Sigma f} = \frac{522}{500} = 1.044$$

Let X be the r.v. 'the number of defectives in a sample of 5'.

Then $X \sim \text{Bin}(n, p)$ with $n = 5$.

Now we need $np = 1.044$

$\therefore$ $$p = \frac{1.044}{5} = 0.2088$$

So $X \sim \text{Bin}(5, 0.2088)$.

The expected frequencies can be found by calculating $500\, P(X = x)$ for $x = 0, 1, \ldots, 5$ where $P(X = x) = {}^5C_x\, q^{5-x} p^x$ with $p = 0.2088$, $q = 0.7912$.

These are shown in the table. Frequencies have been rounded to the nearest integer.

Number of defectives	0	1	2	3	4	5
Observed frequency (O)	170	180	120	20	8	2
Expected frequency (E)	155	205	108	28	4	0

(**b**) We perform a χ^2 test:

H_0: The distribution is binomial

NOTE: the expected frequencies for two of the cells are less than 5, so we combine the last three cells to read '3 or more'.

The revised table is:

x	0	1	2	3 or more	
O	170	180	120	30	
E	155	205	108	32	Total 500

Degrees of freedom:

The number of cells $= 4$

Restrictions:

> One restriction is that the total expected frequency is 500. Another restriction is that we have to estimate p from our sample.

Therefore number of restrictions $= 2$.

So $v = 4 - 2 = 2$, and we consider the χ^2 (2) distribution.

We test at the 5% level and reject
H_0 if $\chi^2 > \chi^2_{5\%}(2)$

i.e. if $\chi^2 > 5.991\,46$

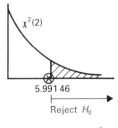

O	E	$\dfrac{(O-E)^2}{E}$
170	155	$1.451\ldots$
180	205	$3.048\ldots$
120	108	$1.333\ldots$
30	32	$0.125\ldots$
$\Sigma O = 500$	$\Sigma E = 500$	$5.9587\ldots$

$$\chi^2 = \sum \frac{(O-E)^2}{E}$$
$$= 5.959$$

Therefore $\chi^2 < 5.991\,46$ (but only just).

So this value of χ^2 is not significant at the 5% level, although it is high and we ought to be suspicious. More samples should be taken and another test should be done, but, on the basis of this sample only, we would not reject H_0 and we conclude that <u>the observed distribution follows a binomial pattern.</u>

Note on accuracy

When calculating expected frequencies it is often necessary to approximate, say to the nearest integer, or to 1 d.p.

If you have memory facilities for retaining several numbers on your calculator then you may prefer to do so, rather than making these approximations. In the above example, if all the figures are retained on the calculator, both for E and in the χ^2 calculation, then the value of χ^2 is $5.9210\ldots$ and in this instance the conclusion reached is the same.

POISSON DISTRIBUTION, λ known

Example 11.9 Analysis of the goals scored per match by a certain football team gave the following results:

No. goals per match (x)	0	1	2	3	4	5	6	7	
No. of matches (f)	14	18	29	18	10	7	3	1	Total 100

Perform a χ^2 goodness of fit test at the 10% level, to determine whether or not the above distribution can be reasonably modelled by a Poisson distribution with mean 2.

Solution 11.9 Let X be the r.v. 'the number of goals scored in a match'.

H_0: $X \sim \text{Po}(2)$ (the distribution is Poisson, with mean 2.)

The expected frequencies are given by

$100\,P(X=x)$ where $P(X=x) = e^{-2}\,\dfrac{2^x}{x!}$.

They have been calculated to 1 d.p. and are shown in the table.

Number of goals	Observed frequency (O)	Expected frequency (E)
0	14	13.5
1	18	27.1
2	29	27.1
3	18	18.0
4	10	9.0
5	7	3.6
6	3	1.2
7 or more	1	0.5
	Total 100	Total 100

The χ^2 test is not valid for expected frequencies less than 5, so we combine the end cells into '5 or more goals'.

The revised table is:

Number of goals	Observed frequency (O)	Expected frequency (E)
0	14	13.5
1	18	27.1
2	29	27.1
3	18	18.0
4	10	9.0
5 or more	11	5.3
	Total 100	Total 100

Degrees of freedom:

Number of cells $= 6$

Number of restrictions $= 1$ (Expected frequencies total 100)

Therefore $v = 6 - 1 = 5$,   and we consider the χ^2 (5) distribution.

Test at the 10% level, and reject H_0

if $\chi^2 > \chi^2_{10\%}$ (5)

i.e. if $\chi^2 > 9.236\,36$

O	E	$\dfrac{(O-E)^2}{E}$
14	13.5	0.018...
18	27.1	3.055...
29	27.1	0.133...
18	18.0	0
10	9.0	0.111...
11	5.3	6.130...
$\Sigma O = 100$	$\Sigma E = 100$	9.448...

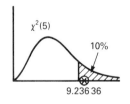

$$\chi^2 = \sum \frac{(O-E)^2}{E}$$

$$= 9.45 \text{ (2 d.p.)}$$

Since $\chi^2 > 9.236\,36$, we reject H_0 and conclude that the distribution cannot be modelled by a Poisson distribution with mean 2.

POISSON DISTRIBUTION, λ unknown

Example 11.10 Can the data in Example 11.9 be reasonably modelled by a Poisson distribution having the same mean as the observed data? Test at the 10% level.

Solution 11.10 For the observed data

$$\bar{x} = \frac{\Sigma fx}{\Sigma f} = \frac{230}{100} = 2.3$$

The null hypothesis, H_0, is that the distribution is Poisson, with the same mean as the observed data, i.e. 2.3.

The expected frequencies are given by $100\,P(X = x)$ where

$$P(X = x) = e^{-2.3}\frac{(2.3)^x}{x!}, \; x = 0, 1, 2, \ldots$$

They have been calculated to 1 d.p.

Number of goals	Observed frequency (O)	Expected frequency (E)
0	14	10.0
1	18	23.1
2	29	26.5
3	18	20.3
4	10	11.7
5	7	5.4
6	3	2.1
7 or more	1	0.9
	Total 100	Total 100

Since the χ^2 test is not valid for expected frequencies less than 5, we combine the end cells into '5 or more goals'.

The revised table is

x	0	1	2	3	4	5 or more	
O	14	18	29	18	10	11	Total 100
E	10.0	23.1	26.5	20.3	11.7	8.4	Total 100

Degrees of freedom:

The number of cells $= 6$

Restrictions:

One restriction is that the total expected frequency is 100.

Another restriction is that we have to estimate the mean of the Poisson model from our sample.

Therefore, the number of restrictions $= 2$.

So $v = 6 - 2 = 4$, and we consider the $\chi^2\,(4)$ distribution.

Test at the 10% level, and reject H_0

if $\chi^2 > \chi^2_{10\%} (4)$

i.e. if $\chi^2 > 7.779\,44$

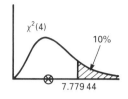

O	E	$\dfrac{(O-E)^2}{E}$
14	10.0	1.6
18	23.1	$1.125\ldots$
29	26.5	$0.235\ldots$
18	20.3	$0.260\ldots$
10	11.7	$0.247\ldots$
11	8.4	$0.804\ldots$
$\Sigma O = 100$	$\Sigma E = 100$	$4.2741\ldots$

$$\chi^2 = \sum \frac{(O-E)^2}{E}$$

$$= 4.274 \ (3 \text{ d.p.})$$

Since $\chi^2 < 7.779\,44$, we do not reject H_0 and <u>we conclude that</u> <u>the distribution can be reasonably modelled by the Poisson</u> <u>distribution having the same mean as the observed data.</u>

NORMAL DISTRIBUTION, mean and variance known

Example 11.11 For a period of six months 100 similar hamsters were given a new type of feedstuff. The gains in mass are recorded in the table below:

Gain in mass (g) x	Observed frequency f
$-\infty < x \leqslant -10$	3
$-10 < x \leqslant -5$	6
$-5 < x \leqslant 0$	9
$0 < x \leqslant 5$	15
$5 < x \leqslant 10$	24
$10 < x \leqslant 15$	16
$15 < x \leqslant 20$	14
$20 < x \leqslant 25$	8
$25 < x \leqslant 30$	3
$30 < x \leqslant \infty$	2

It is thought that these data follow a normal distribution, with mean 10 and variance 100. Use the χ^2 distribution at the 5% level of significance to test this hypothesis.

Describe briefly how you would modify this test if the mean and variance were unknown.   (AEB)

Solution 11.11 Let X be the r.v. 'the gain in mass, in g, of a hamster'.

H_0: The distribution is normal with mean 10 and variance 100, i.e. $X \sim N(10, 100)$.

Assuming this normal distribution, we now need to calculate the
expected frequencies. One way of doing this is to find the expected
cumulative frequencies up to each upper class boundary of
$-10, -5, 0, 5, 10, \ldots$ etc.

$$P(X < -10) = P\left(Z < \frac{-10 - 10}{10}\right)$$

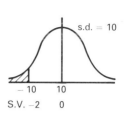

s.d. = 10

-10 10

S.V. -2 0

$$= P(Z < -2)$$

$$= \Phi(-2)$$

$$= 0.0228$$

Expected cumulative frequency $= 100 \times \Phi(-2)$

$$= 100 \times 0.0228$$

$$= \underline{2.28}$$

$$P(X < -5) = P\left(Z < \frac{-5 - 10}{10}\right)$$

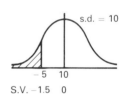

s.d. = 10

-5 10

S.V. -1.5 0

$$= P(Z < -1.5)$$

$$= \Phi(-1.5)$$

$$= 0.0668$$

Expected cumulative frequency $= 100 \times \Phi(-1.5)$

$$= 100 \times 0.0668$$

$$= \underline{6.68}$$

So for the interval $-10 \leqslant x < -5$,

$$\text{expected frequency} = \underline{6.68 - 2.28 - 4.4}$$

$$P(X < 0) = P\left(Z < \frac{0 - 10}{10}\right)$$

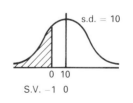

s.d. = 10

0 10

S.V. -1 0

$$= P(Z < -1)$$

$$= \Phi(-1)$$

$$= 0.1587$$

Expected cumulative frequency $= 100 \times \Phi(-1)$

$$= 100 \times 0.1587$$

$$= \underline{15.87}$$

So for the interval $-5 < x \leqslant 0$,

$$\text{expected frequency} = \underline{15.87 - 6.68 = 9.19}$$

We can continue to calculate the expected frequencies for each interval in the same way.

The values needed can be summarised in a table and you may prefer to write out your working in this format.

Interval	Upper class boundary (u.c.b.)	Standardised u.c.b. (z)	$P(Z < z)$ $= \Phi(z)$	Expected cumulative frequency $100 \times \Phi(z)$	Expected frequency
$-\infty < x \leqslant -10$	-10	-2	0.0228	2.28	2.28
$-10 < x \leqslant -5$	-5	-1.5	0.0668	6.68	$6.68 - 2.28 = 4.4$
$-5 < x \leqslant 0$	0	-1	0.1587	15.87	$15.87 - 6.68 = 9.19$
$0 < x \leqslant 5$	5	-0.5	0.3085	30.85	$30.85 - 15.87 = 14.98$
$5 < x \leqslant 10$	10	0	0.5000	50.00	$50.00 - 30.85 = 19.15$
$10 < x \leqslant 15$	15	0.5	0.6915	69.15	$69.15 - 50.00 = 19.15$
$15 < x \leqslant 20$	20	1	0.8413	84.13	$84.13 - 69.15 = 14.98$
$20 < x \leqslant 25$	25	1.5	0.9332	93.32	$93.32 - 84.13 = 9.19$
$25 < x \leqslant 30$	30	2	0.9772	97.72	$97.72 - 93.32 = 4.4$
$30 < x \leqslant \infty$	∞	∞	1	100	$100 - 97.72 = 2.28$
					$\Sigma E = 100$

Interval	Observed frequency (O)	Expected frequency (E)
$-\infty < x \leqslant -10$	3	2.28
$-10 < x \leqslant -5$	6	4.4
$-5 < x \leqslant 0$	9	9.19
$0 < x \leqslant 5$	15	14.98
$5 < x \leqslant 10$	24	19.15
$10 < x \leqslant 15$	16	19.15
$15 < x \leqslant 20$	14	14.98
$20 < x \leqslant 25$	8	9.19
$25 < x \leqslant 30$	3	4.4
$30 < x \leqslant \infty$	2	2.28

Since some of the expected frequencies are less than 5, we must combine the first two and the last two cells. The revised table is as follows:

Interval	Observed frequency (O)	Expected frequency (E)
$-\infty < x \leqslant -5$	9	6.68
$-5 < x \leqslant 0$	9	9.19
$0 < x \leqslant 5$	15	14.98
$5 < x \leqslant 10$	24	19.15
$10 < x \leqslant 15$	16	19.15
$15 < x \leqslant 20$	14	14.98
$20 < x \leqslant 25$	8	9.19
$25 < x \leqslant \infty$	5	6.68
Total 100		Total 100

Degrees of freedom:

The number of cells $= 8$

There is one restriction, the total expected frequency is 100.

Therefore $v = 8 - 1$

                $= 7$

and we consider the χ^2 (7) distribution.

We test at the 5% level and reject H_0 if
$$\chi^2 > \chi^2_{5\%} \, (7)$$

i.e.   if $\chi^2 > 14.0671$

where $\chi^2 = \sum \dfrac{(O-E)^2}{E}$

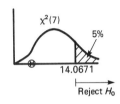

$\chi^2 = 3.197 \; (3 \text{ d.p.})$

O	E	$\dfrac{(O-E)^2}{E}$
9	6.68	0.8057...
9	9.19	0.003 92...
15	14.98	0.000 026 7...
24	19.15	1.2283...
16	19.15	0.5181...
14	14.98	0.0641...
8	9.19	0.1540...
5	6.68	0.4225...
$\Sigma O = 100$	$\Sigma E = 100$	3.1968...

Since $\chi^2 < 14.0671$ we do not reject H_0 and <u>we conclude that the data could follow a normal distribution with mean 10, variance 100</u>.

NORMAL DISTRIBUTION, mean and variance unknown

If the mean and variance are not given for the normal distribution then these have to be *estimated* from the observed data. The expected frequencies are then calculated using these estimates.

This alters the number of degrees of freedom, for if estimates of the mean and the variance are used, then

number of restrictions $= 3$ (total expected frequency is given,
                                    μ is estimated from sample,
                                    σ^2 is estimated from the sample).

In Example 11.11, if μ and σ^2 were not known, then $v = 8 - 3 = 5$, and the χ^2 (5) distribution would be needed.

Example 11.12 A weaving mill sells lengths of cloth with a nominal length of 70 m. The customer measured 100 lengths and obtained the following frequency distribution:

Length (m)	61–67	67–69	69–71	71–73	73–75	75–81
Frequency	1	16	26	19	20	18

Use a χ^2 test at the 5% significance level to show that the normal distribution is not an adequate model for the data.   (AEB 1989)

Solution 11.12 The null hypothesis is that the distribution is normal. However, since we are not given μ or σ^2, the mean and variance of the population, we have to *estimate* them from the sample readings:

Midpoint (x)	64	68	70	72	74	78	
Frequency (f)	1	16	26	19	20	18	Total 100

Now $\widehat{\mu} = \bar{x}$ where $\bar{x}$ is the sample mean

$$\widehat{\sigma}^2 = \frac{n}{n-1}\,s^2 \quad \text{where } s^2 \text{ is the sample variance.}$$

We find these values using a calculator, as follows. Note that we can also find $\widehat{\sigma}^2$ directly on the calculator.

	Casio 85/100/115	**Casio 7000 GA Graphic**
Set SD mode	MODE 3	MODE ×
Clear memories	SHIFT KAC	SHIFT SCI EXE
Input data	64 × 1 DATA	64 SHIFT ; 1 DT
	68 × 16 DATA	68 SHIFT ; 16 DT
	70 × 26 DATA	70 SHIFT ; 26 DT
	72 × 20 DATA	72 SHIFT ; 19 DT
	74 × 20 DATA	74 SHIFT ; 20 DT
	78 × 18 DATA	78 SHIFT ; 18 DT
Output		
$\boxed{\bar{x}}$ = 72.24	SHIFT 1	SHIFT 1 EXE
$s^2 = 11.4624$	SHIFT 2 x^2	SHIFT 2 x^2 EXE
Directly: $\widehat{\sigma}^2 = 11.578...$	SHIFT 3 x^2	SHIFT 3 x^2 EXE
Clear SD mode	MODE 0	MODE +

Therefore $\widehat{\mu} = \bar{x} = 72.24$

$$\widehat{\sigma}^2 = \frac{n}{n-1} s^2 = \frac{100}{99} (11.4624) = 11.578\ldots$$

The best estimates of the mean and variance are 72.24 and 11.578.

H_0: The distribution is normal with mean 72.24 and variance 11.578.

To find the expected frequencies:

(*i*) Standardise each upper class limit z and find $P(Z < z)$ using standard normal tables.

(*ii*) Find the expected cumulative frequencies by multiplying $P(Z < z)$ by the total frequency, in this case 100.

(*iii*) Find the expected frequencies by subtracting the values for the cumulative frequencies as shown in the table:

Length (m)	Upper limit	z	$P(Z < z)$ $= \Phi(z)$	Expected cumulative frequency $100 \times \Phi(z)$	Expected frequency
61–67	67	−1.540	0.0618	6.18	6.18
67–69	69	−0.952	0.1706	17.06	17.06 − 6.18 = 10.88
69–71	71	−0.364	0.3582	35.82	35.82 − 17.06 = 18.76
71–73	73	0.223	0.5883	58.83	58.83 − 35.82 = 23.01
73–75	75	0.811	0.7913	79.13	79.13 − 58.83 = 20.3
75–81	81	2.574	0.994 98	99.498	99.498 − 79.13 = 20.368
over 81	∞	∞	1	100	100 − 99.498 = 0.502

We will consider the final class as 75 and over, with expected frequency $20.368 + 0.502 = 20.87$.

Length	Observed frequency (O)	Expected frequency (E)
61–67	1	6.18
67–69	16	10.88
69–71	26	18.76
71–73	19	23.01
73–75	20	20.3
75 and over	18	20.87
Total 100	Total 100	

Degrees of freedom:

number of cells $= 6$

Restrictions: The total of the expected frequencies must be 100. Also we have estimated μ and σ^2 from our sample, so there are 3 restrictions.

Therefore $v = 6 - 3$

$= 3$ and we must consider the χ^2 (3) distribution.

Test at the 5% level and reject H_0

if $\chi^2 > \chi^2_{5\%}(3)$

i.e.   if $\chi^2 > 7.814\,73$

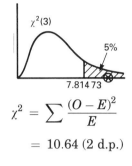

O	E	$\dfrac{(O - E)^2}{E}$
1	6.18	4.34...
16	10.88	2.40...
26	18.76	2.79...
19	23.01	0.69...
20	20.3	0.0044...
18	20.87	0.39...
$\Sigma O = 100$	$\Sigma E = 100$	10.643...

$$\chi^2 = \sum \frac{(O - E)^2}{E}$$

$$= 10.64 \ (2 \text{ d.p.})$$

Since $\chi^2 > 7.814\,73$,   we reject H_0 and conclude that <u>the normal distribution is not an adequate model for the data.</u>

Exercise 11b

1. Perform a χ^2 test to investigate whether the following data is drawn from a binomial distribution with $p = 0.3$.   Use a 5% level of significance.

x	0	1	2	3	4	5
f	12	39	27	15	4	3

2. A six-sided die with faces numbered as usual from 1 to 6 was thrown 5 times and the number of sixes was recorded. The experiment was performed 200 times, with the following results:

x	0	1	2	3	4	5
Frequency	66	82	40	10	2	0

On this evidence, would you consider the die to be biased? Fit a suitable distribution to the data and test and comment on the goodness of fit.   (MEI)

3. Under what circumstances would you expect a variate, X, to have a binomial distribution? What is the mean of X if it has a binomial distribution with parameters n and p? A new fly spray is applied to 50 samples each of 5 flies and the number of living flies counted after one hour. The results were as follows:

Number living	0	1	2	3	4	5
Frequency	7	20	12	9	1	1

Calculate the mean number of living flies per sample and hence an estimate for p, the probability of a fly surviving the spray. Using your estimate calculate the expected frequencies (each correct to one place of decimals) corresponding to a binomial distribution and perform a χ^2 goodness-of-fit test using a 5% significance level.

4. The numbers of cars passing a check-point during 100 intervals each of time 5 minutes, were noted:

Number of cars	Frequency
0	5
1	23
2	23
3	25
4	14
5	10
6 or more	0

Fit a Poisson distribution to these data and test the goodness of fit.

5. Write a short account of the χ^2 test of goodness of fit, giving some indication of its shortcomings.
During the weaving of cloth the thread sometimes breaks. 147 lengths of thread of equal length were observed during weaving and the table records the number of these threads for which the indicated number of breaks occurred.

Number of breaks per thread	0	1	2	3	4	5
Number of threads	48	46	30	12	9	2

Fit a Poisson distribution to the data and examine whether the deviation between theory and experiment is significant.   (MEI)

6. The following data give the heights in cm of 100 male students.

Height (cm)	Frequency
155–160	5
161–166	17
167–172	38
173–178	25
179–184	9
185–190	6

(a) Test, at the 5% level, whether the data follow a normal distribution with mean 173.5 cm and standard deviation 7 cm.
(b) Find the expected frequencies for a normal distribution having the same mean and variance as the data given, and test the goodness of fit, using a 5% level of significance.

7. During observations on a patch of white dead nettles it was noticed that the numbers of flowers visited by bees during 100 5-minute intervals were as follows:

Number of flowers visited/ 5-minute interval	Frequency
0–5	4
6–11	8
12–17	13
18–23	16
24–29	22
30–35	17
36–41	10
42–47	6
48–53	3
54–59	1

(a) Calculate the mean and variance for the data.
(b) Find the expected frequencies for a normal distribution with the same mean and variance.
(c) Test, at the 5% level of significance, how well the observed data fits this normal distribution.

8. Two dice were thrown 216 times, and the number of sixes at each throw were counted. The results were:

No. of sixes	0	1	2	
Frequency	130	76	10	Total 216

Test the hypothesis that the distribution is binomial with the parameter $p = \frac{1}{6}$.
Explain how the test would be modified if the hypothesis to be tested is that the distribution is binomial with the parameter p unknown. (Do not carry out the test.)   (O)

9. The table gives the distribution for the number of heavy rainstorms reported by 330 weather stations in the United States of America over a one-year period.

Number of rainstorms (x)	Number of stations (f) reporting x rainstorms
0	102
1	114
2	74
3	28
4	10
5	2
more than 5	0

(a) Find the expected frequencies of rainstorms given by the Poisson distribution having the same mean and total as the observed distribution.
(b) Use the χ^2 distribution to test the adequacy of the Poisson distribution as a model for these data.   (AEB)

10. A local council has records of the number of children and the number of households in its area. It is therefore known that the average number of children per household is 1.40. It is suggested that the number of children per household can be modelled by the Poisson distribution with parameter 1.40. In order to test this, a random sample of 1000 households is taken, giving the following data.

Number of children	0	1	2	3	4	5+
Number of households	273	361	263	78	21	4

(i) Find the corresponding expected frequencies obtained from the Poisson distribution with parameter 1.40.

(ii) Carry out a χ^2 test, at the 5% level of significance, to determine whether or not the proposed model should be accepted. State clearly the null and alternative hypotheses being tested and the conclusion which is reached.   (MEI)

11. A department store has five doorways, each for entrance and exit. It is claimed that the proportion of shoppers entering or leaving the store is the same for each of the five doorways. The number of customers entering or leaving the store is counted at each doorway for three randomly selected days with the following results.

Doorway	Number of customers
A	601
B	673
C	626
D	618
E	702

Test whether or not these data support the claim.

The same store also records the daily number of sales charged to stolen credit cards. The results for the first four months of 1990 are as follows.

Number of sales	Number of days
0	31
1	39
2	19
3	11
$\geqslant 4$	0

Explain why a Poisson distribution may be appropriate as a model for the daily number of sales charged to stolen credit cards.

Test the hypothesis that the daily number of sales does follow a Poisson distribution.

(JMB)

12. In a European country registration for military service is compulsory for all eighteen-year-old males. All males must report to a barracks where, after an inspection some people, including all those less than 1.6 m tall, are excused service. The heights of a sample of 125 eighteen-year-olds measured at the barracks were as follows:

Height, m	1.2–	1.4–	1.6–	1.8–	2.0–2.2
Frequency	6	34	31	42	12

(a) Use a χ^2 test and a 5% significance level to confirm that the normal distribution is not an adequate model for this data.

(b) Show that, if the second and third classes (1.4– and 1.6–) are combined, the normal distribution does appear to fit the data. Comment on this apparent contradiction in the light of the information at the beginning of the question.   (AEB 1992)

13. A group of students are performing an experiment where 20 drawing pins are dropped randomly on to the floor and the number landing point down is counted. The procedure is then repeated several times. Describe the assumptions you would need to make in order to be satisfied with modelling this situation by a Binomial distribution. The experiment was carried out until the students had 50 observations; their results are given in the table:

Number landing point down	Frequency
3	2
4	2
5	5
6	7
7	17
8	8
9	6
10	1
11	2

(a) Calculate the mean number landing point down. Hence show that an estimate for the probability of a drawing pin landing point down is 0.35.

(b) What are the parameters of the appropriate Binomial distribution for these data? Calculate the probability of exactly 8, and hence write down, accurate to one decimal place, its 'expected frequency'.

(c) Using appropriate tables, find, making your method clear, the expected number of times 5 or fewer pins would land point down.

(d) The chi-squared goodness-of-fit test can be used to judge how well data follow a distribution. Group the above data in the following manner and evaluate the missing expected or observed frequencies:

Number of pins	$\leqslant 5$	6	7	8	$\geqslant 9$
Expected		8.6			11.8
Observed		9	7	17	

Calculate the value of the chi-squared statistic for this data.

(e) How many degrees of freedom does your test have? By referring to your tables carry out the test and make your findings clear. (O)

14. By referring to an experiment you may have carried out, describe the circumstances under which the Poisson distribution would be a suitable model.

(a) The data in the following table are the result of counting radioactive events in five-second intervals:

Number of events	0	1	2	$\geqslant 3$
Number of observations	5	14	13	8

Show that the mean number of events in a five-second interval is 1.7 (taking the group with frequency 8 to have a mean of 3.5).

(b) Write down the probability of 0, 1, 2, $\geqslant 3$ events for a Poisson distribution with mean 1.7. Hence obtain to one decimal place the expected frequencies.

(c) Use the chi-squared goodness of fit test to assess whether it is reasonable to claim that the data come from a Poisson distribution. Make your method clear and conduct your test at the 10% level.

(d) A student conducting a similar experiment found the chi-squared statistic for his results was 0.015. What conclusions do you draw from this value? (O)

15. (a) Every four weeks an electrical goods distributor visits a retailer. At each visit the retailer buys the number of kettle elements needed to make his stock up to 4. The number of customers asking the retailer for such an element in a four-week period has a Poisson distribution with mean 2. Determine the probability that, in a period between visits by the distributor, the retailer
(i) sells exactly two elements,
(ii) sells his complete stock of elements,
(iii) is unable to meet the demand for elements.

(b) During a working day a machine requires occasional adjustments which appear to be randomly distributed throughout the day. A factory foreman records the number of adjustments made to the machine each day for a period of 200 working days, obtaining the data displayed in the table.

Number of adjustments	0	1	2	3	4	5
Number of days	34	78	61	20	5	2

Previous experience has suggested that the daily number of adjustments to this machine follows a Poisson distribution with mean 1.5.
(i) Perform a χ^2 goodness of fit test to decide whether the data in the table can reasonably be considered as conforming to a Poisson distribution with mean 1.5.
(ii) Outline, without detailed calculation, the necessary modifications to your test if the Poisson mean is not assumed to be 1.5.
(iii) The distribution Bin (5, 0.3) is a very good fit to the data in the table. Without further calculation, explain why, despite this good fit, the binomial model is *not* appropriate. (JMB)

USE OF χ^2 TESTS IN CONTINGENCY TABLES

Sometimes situations arise when individuals are classified according to two sets of attributes, for example:

— test scores in a practical and in a theory examination,
— age and voting preference.

We may then wish to investigate whether the attributes are independent, or whether there is evidence of an association between them.

Example 11.13 Two schools enter their pupils for a particular public examination and the results obtained are shown below.

	Credit	Pass	Fail
School A	51	10	19
School B	39	10	21

By using an approximate χ^2 statistic, assess at the 5% level whether or not there is a significant difference between the two schools with respect to the proportions of pupils in the three grades. State your null and alternative hypotheses.   (L)

Solution 11.13 The results can be shown in a table with 2 rows and 3 columns. It is known as a 2×3 (read 2 by 3) **contingency table**. We have introduced the row totals, column totals and the grand total.

	Credit	Pass	Fail	Row totals
School A	51	10	19	80
School B	39	10	21	70
Column totals	90	20	40	Grand total 150

The null hypothesis (H_0) is that there is no difference between the two schools with respect to the proportions of pupils in the three grades, i.e. the proportions are independent of the school.

The alternative hypothesis (H_1) is that there *is* a difference and the proportions are not independent of the school.

To calculate the expected frequencies:

$$P(\text{pupil is from school } A) = \frac{80}{150}$$

$$P(\text{pupil gains a credit}) = \frac{90}{150}$$

Under the null hypothesis, these events are independent, so, using the multiplication law for independent events, $P(A \cap B) = P(A) \times P(B)$

$$P(\text{ pupil is from } A \text{ and gains a credit}) = \left(\frac{80}{150}\right)\left(\frac{90}{150}\right)$$

So the expected number from school A gaining a credit

$$= 150\left(\frac{80}{150}\right)\left(\frac{90}{150}\right) = 48$$

There is a quick way to work this out:

$$\text{Expected frequency} = \frac{(\text{row total}) \times (\text{column total})}{\text{grand total}}$$

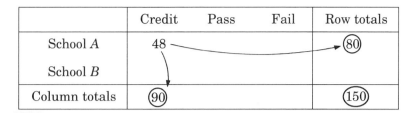

$$\text{Expected frequency} = \frac{(80)(90)}{150} = 48$$

To find out the expected number in School A who pass we need

	Credit	Pass	Fail	Row totals
School A		10.67		⑧⓪
School B				
Column totals		⑳		⑮⓪⓪

$$\text{Expected frequency} = \frac{(80)(20)}{150} = 10.67 \text{ (2 d.p.)}$$

We can then work out all the expected frequencies and check that the row totals and column totals agree with the observed data.

We find that the expected frequencies are

	Credit	Pass	Fail	Row totals
School A	**48**	**10.67**	21.33	80
School B	42	9.33	18.67	70
Column totals	90	20	40	150

Degrees of freedom:

Once the two expected frequencies in bold type have been calculated, the others are known automatically because we know that the row totals and column totals *must* agree with the observed data. So if we expect 48 in School A to obtain a credit, then the expected number in School B is $90 - 48 = 42$.

Since all the other entries are known once *two* values have been found, then the number of independent variables, v, is 2 and we use the χ^2 (2) distribution.

We test at the 5% level and reject H_0 if $\chi^2 > \chi^2_{5\%}$ (2)

i.e. if $\chi^2 > 5.99146$

Observed frequencies

	Credit	Pass	Fail
School A	51	10	19
School B	39	10	21

Expected frequencies

	Credit	Pass	Fail
School A	48	$10\frac{2}{3}$	$21\frac{1}{3}$
School B	42	$9\frac{1}{3}$	$18\frac{2}{3}$

O	E	$\dfrac{(O-E)^2}{E}$
51	48	0.1875
10	10.67	0.0420...
19	21.33	0.2545...
39	42	0.2142...
10	9.33	0.0481...
21	18.67	0.2907...
$\Sigma O = 150$	$\Sigma E = 150$	1.0372...

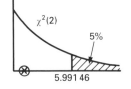

$$\therefore \chi^2 = \sum \frac{(O-E)^2}{E}$$

$$= 1.04 \ (2 \text{ d.p.})$$

Since χ^2 is well below the critical value of 5.991 46 we do not reject H_0 and we conclude that there is not a significant difference between the results of the two schools.

Example 11.14   A survey of 200 families known to be regular television viewers was undertaken. They were asked which of the channels 1, 2, 3 or 4 they watched most during an average week. Their replies are summarised in the table, together with the region in which they lived.

	Channel			
	1	2	3	4
North	29	16	42	23
Central	6	11	26	7
South	15	3	12	10

Is there an association between the channel watched most and the region?

Solution 11.14 H_0: there is no association between the channel watched most and the region, i.e. they are independent.

H_1: there is an association.

Observed data:

	Channel				Row totals
	1	2	3	4	
North	29	16	42	23	110
Central	6	11	26	7	50
South	15	3	12	10	40
Column total	50	30	80	40	Grand total 200

This is a 3×4 contingency table, since there are 3 rows and 4 columns.

Expected data:

Expected number in the *north* who watched *Channel 1*

$$= \frac{(110)(50)}{200}$$

$$= 27.5$$

Expected number in the *north* who watched *Channel 2*

$$= \frac{(110)(30)}{200}$$

$$= 16.5$$

This process is continued for the expected frequencies shown in bold type. The remaining frequencies are found by ensuring that totals and sub-totals agree.

	Channel				Row totals
	1	2	3	4	
North	**27.5**	**16.5**	**44**	22	110
Central	**12.5**	**7.5**	**20**	10	50
South	10	6	16	8	40
Column total	50	30	80	40	Grand total 200

Degrees of freedom:

Once 6 expected frequencies have been found, the others are known automatically (by agreement of totals).

So ν = number of independent variables = 6, and we consider the χ^2 (6) distribution.

We test at the 5% level and reject H_0 if $\chi^2 > \chi^2_{5\%}$ (6),

i.e. if $\chi^2 > 12.5916$

O	E	$\dfrac{(O-E)^2}{E}$
29	27.5	0.0818...
16	16.5	0.0151...
42	44	0.0909...
23	22	0.0454...
6	12.5	3.38
11	7.5	1.633...
26	20	1.8
7	10	0.9
15	10	2.5
3	6	1.5
12	16	1
10	8	0.5
$\Sigma O = 200$	$\Sigma E = 200$	13.4466...

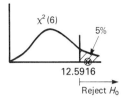

$$\chi^2 = \sum \frac{(O-E)^2}{E}$$

$$= 13.45 \text{ (2 d.p.)}$$

Since $\chi^2 > 12.5916$, we reject H_0 and conclude that <u>there is an association between the channel watched most and the region.</u>

2×2 CONTINGENCY TABLES (2 ROWS AND 2 COLUMNS)

Example 11.15 A driving school examined the results of 100 candidates who were taking their driving test for the first time. They found that out of the 40 men, 28 passed and out of the 60 women, 34 passed. Do these results indicate, at the 5% level of significance, a relationship between the sex of a candidate and the ability to pass first time?

Solution 11.15 The results can be shown in a table, known as a 2×2 (read '2 by 2') contingency table:

		Results of first-time candidates		
		Pass	Fail	Totals
Sex	Male	28	12	40
	Female	34	26	60
	Totals	62	38	100

H_0: there is no relationship between the sex of a candidate and the ability to pass first time; the attributes are independent.

To calculate the expected frequencies:

Expected number who pass and are male $= \dfrac{(40)(62)}{100}$

$$= 24.8$$

We could work through this procedure to give the other expected frequencies, but this is unnecessary, since the other frequencies can be found by using the fact that the sub-totals and totals must agree with those in the observed data.

Expected frequencies:

		Results of first-time candidates		
		Pass	Fail	Totals
Sex	Male	**24.8**	15.2	40
	Female	37.2	22.8	60
	Totals	62	38	100

Degrees of freedom:

number of independent variables $= 1$

(once one expected frequency is known, the others are determined by agreement of totals).

Therefore $v = 1$ and we consider the χ^2 (1) distribution.

We test at the 5% level and reject H_0 if $\chi > \chi^2_{5\%}$ (1),

i.e. if $\chi^2 > 3.841\,46$

O	E	$\dfrac{(O-E)^2}{E}$
28	24.8	0.4129...
12	15.2	0.6736...
34	37.2	0.2752...
26	22.8	0.4491...
$\Sigma O = 100$	$\Sigma E = 100$	1.8109...

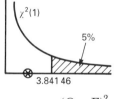

$$\chi^2 = \sum \frac{(O-E)^2}{E}$$

$$= 1.81 \text{ (2 d.p.)}$$

Since $\chi^2 < 3.841\,46$ we do not reject H_0 and we conclude that these results do not indicate a relationship between the sex of a candidate and the ability to pass first time.

NOTE: when $v = 1$ it is advisable to use 'Yates' correction'

In this case $\chi^2 = \sum \dfrac{(|O-E|-0.5)^2}{E}$

O	E	$\dfrac{(\,\lvert O - E \rvert - 0.5)^2}{E}$
28	24.8	0.2939...
12	15.2	0.4796...
34	37.2	0.1959...
26	22.8	0.3197...
$\Sigma O = 100$	$\Sigma E = 100$	1.2892...

$\chi^2 = 1.29$ (3 SF) and the <u>conclusion</u> is as above.

NUMBER OF DEGREES OF FREEDOM (CONTINGENCY TABLES)

Consider the following contingency tables. In each situation, in order to work out all the expected frequencies, we need only find those indicated:

4 by 3

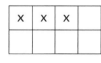

$$v = (4 - 1) \times (3 - 1)$$
$$= (3)(2)$$
$$= 6$$

2 by 4

$$v = (2 - 1) \times (4 - 1)$$
$$= (1)(3)$$
$$= 3$$

2 by 2

$$v = (2 - 1) \times (2 - 1)$$
$$= (1)(1)$$
$$= 1$$

3 by 2

$$v = (3 - 1) \times (2 - 1)$$
$$= (2)(1)$$
$$= 2$$

In general, if there are h rows, then as soon as $h - 1$ expected frequencies in a row have been calculated, the last value in the row is known (agreement of totals). Similarly, if there are k columns, once $k - 1$ expected frequencies in a column have been calculated, the last value in the column is known.

Therefore, number of independent variables $= (h - 1)(k - 1)$.

So, for an $h \times k$ contingency table, $v = (h - 1)(k - 1)$.

Example 11.16 Data are collected in the form of a 4×4 contingency table. To carry out a χ^2 test of significance one of the rows is amalgamated with another row and the resulting value of $\sum \dfrac{(O - E)^2}{E}$ obtained.

Write down the number of degrees of freedom and the critical value of χ^2 appropriate to this test assuming a 5% level of significance. (L)

Solution 11.16

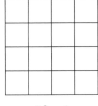

becomes

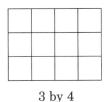

3 by 4

4 by 4

Therefore $v = (3 - 1) \times (4 - 1)$

$\qquad\qquad = (2)(3)$

$\qquad\qquad = 6$

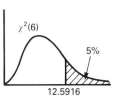

We consider the χ^2 (6) distribution.

From tables $\chi^2_{5\%}$ (6) $= 12.5916$

so the critical value is 12.5916.

Exercise 11c

1. Consider the following contingency tables and for each one, test at the 5% level whether A and B are independent.

(a)

	B_1	B_2	B_3
A_1	16	19	15
A_2	26	14	10

(b)

	B_1	B_2	B_3	B_4
A_1	20	42	28	12
A_2	8	50	24	6
A_3	38	42	94	26

(c)

	B_1	B_2
A_1	20	9
A_2	31	14
A_3	16	12
A_4	23	15

(d)

	B_1	B_2	B_3
A_1	10	26	34
A_2	8	29	43
A_3	27	43	50
A_4	9	14	27

(e)

	B_1	B_2
A_1	43	17
A_2	82	58

(f)

	B_1	B_2
A_1	7	18
A_2	48	47

2. A thousand households are taken at random and divided into three groups *A*, *B* and *C*, according to the total weekly income. The following table shows the numbers in each group having a colour television receiver, a black and white receiver, or no television at all.

	A	*B*	*C*
Colour television	56	51	93
Black and white	118	207	375
None	26	42	32

Calculate the expected frequencies if there is no association between total income and television ownership.
Apply a test to find whether the observed frequencies suggest that there is such an association. (AEB)

3. The following table shows the numbers of students passed and failed by three examiners *A*, *B* and *C*.

	Examiners			
	A	*B*	*C*	Totals
Pass	51	48	58	157
Fail	4	14	7	25
Totals	55	62	65	182

Test the hypothesis that the three examiners fail equal proportions of students by applying χ^2 tests with and without Yates' correction. Comment on the results. (AEB)

4. In an investigation into eye colour and left- or right-handedness the following results were obtained:

		Handedness	
		Left	Right
Eye colour	Blue	15	85
	Brown	20	80

Is there evidence, at the 5% level, of an association between eye colour and left- or right-handedness?

5. An investigation into colourblindness and the sex of a person gave the following results:

		Colourblindness	
		Colourblind	Not colourblind
Sex	Male	36	964
	Female	19	981

Is there evidence, at the 5% level, of an association between the sex of a person and whether or not they are colourblind?

6. The following are data on 150 chickens, divided into two groups according to breed, and into three groups according to yield of eggs:

	Yield		
	High	Medium	Low
Rhode Island Red	46	29	28
Leghorn	27	14	6

Are these data consistent with the hypothesis that the yield is not affected by the type of breed?

7. In a small survey 350 car owners from four districts P, Q, R, S were found to have cars in price ranges A, B, C, D, the frequencies of the prices being as shown in the table.

		P	Q	R	S
Price of car	A	9	10	12	19
	B	13	20	18	29
	C	24	29	12	25
	D	34	41	18	37

Find the expected frequencies on the hypothesis that there is no association between the district and the price of the car. Use the χ^2 distribution to test this hypothesis. (AEB)

8. A research worker studying the ages of adults and the number of credit cards they possess obtained the results shown in the table.

Age / Number of cards possessed	$\leqslant 3$	> 3
< 30	74	20
$\geqslant 30$	50	35

Use the χ^2 statistic and a significance test at the 5% level to decide whether or not there is an association between age and number of credit cards possessed. (L)

9. Students in the Sociology department of a university decided to conduct a survey into the roles of married couples in performing tasks of housework and child care. They designed a questionnaire for this purpose.

They then contacted 240 married couples who were willing to take part in the survey. Each of the participating couples was randomly allocated to one of two groups. In the first group the wife was asked to complete the questionnaire and in the second group the husband was asked to complete it.

Four response categories were available for a question which asked how the work of cleaning the house was shared between husband and wife. The following table shows the numbers of husbands and wives choosing each category.

Response category	Husbands	Wives
Wife does it all	21	30
Wife does most of it	63	58
Shared half and half	28	25
Husband does all or most of it	8	7

Carry out a χ^2 test to investigate whether there is an association between the sex of the respondent and the respondent's view of how the work is shared.

Comment on any differences revealed by this survey between the opinions of husbands and wives about who does the household cleaning.
(JMB)

10. In 1988 the number of new cases of insulin-dependent diabetes in children under the age of 15 years was 1495. The table below breaks down this figure according to age and sex.

Age (yrs)	0–4	5–9	10–14	Total
Boys	205	248	328	781
Girls	182	251	281	714
Total	387	499	609	1495

Perform a suitable test, at the 5% significance level, to determine whether age and sex are independent factors. (C)P

11. When analysing the results of a 3×2 contingency table it was found that

$$\sum_{i=1}^{6} \frac{(O_i - E_i)^2}{E_i} = 2.38.$$

Write down the number of degrees of freedom and the critical value appropriate to these data in order to carry out a χ^2 test of significance at the 5% level. (L)

12. In a college, 3 different groups of students sit the same examination. The results of the examination are classified as Credit, Pass or Fail. In order to test whether or not there is a difference between the groups with respect to

the proportions of students in the three grades the statistic $\sum \frac{(O - E)^2}{E}$ is evaluated and found to be equal to 10.28.
(a) Explain why there are 4 degrees of freedom in this situation.
(b) Using a 5% level of significance, carry out the test and state your conclusions. (L)

13. In an examination 37 out of 47 boys passed and 27 out of 41 girls passed. By considering a suitable 2×2 contingency table, test whether boys and girls differ in their ability in this subject.

14. The results obtained by 200 students in chemistry and biology are shown in the table. Test, at the 5% level, whether the performances in both subjects are related.

		Chemistry	
		Pass	Fail
Biology	Pass	102	45
	Fail	21	32

15. At St. Trinian's College for Young Ladies there are 1000 pupils. Of these 75 have represented the College at both hockey and netball, 10 have represented the College at hockey but do not play netball, 35 have represented the College at netball but do not play hockey, and 100 do not play games at all. In all 100 girls have represented the College at hockey, and 150 at netball. The number who do not play hockey is 200 and the number who do not play netball is 125. Arrange the above data in the form of a 3×3 contingency table, and state how many pupils play both hockey and netball but have not represented the College in either.
Apply the χ^2 test to your 3×3 table, and state the hypothesis which it tests. (AEB)

16. In a 2×2 contingency table, the observed frequencies are as shown:

		A	B	Totals
Group I		a	b	c
Group II		d	e	f
Totals		g	h	k

Show that $\displaystyle\sum_{i=1}^{4} \frac{(O_i - E_i)^2}{E_i} = \frac{k(ae - bd)^2}{cfgh}$

(do not use the continuity correction).

MISCELLANEOUS WORKED EXAMPLES

Example 11.17 A mill weaves cloth in standard lengths. When a length of cloth contains a serious blemish, the damaged section is cut out and the two remaining parts stitched together. This is known as a string. An analysis of the number of strings in 220 lengths of cloth of a particular type revealed the following data.

Number of strings	0	1	2	3	4	5	6	7
Frequency	14	29	57	48	31	41	0	0

(**a**) Test whether the Poisson distribution is an adequate model for the data, using a 5% significance level.

(**b**) On seeing the analysis the manager pointed out that lengths of cloth containing more than 5 strings were unsaleable. If necessary, larger sections of cloth would be removed so that no length contained more than 5 strings. Without this restriction, she estimated that there would be an average of 3 strings per length.

If a Poisson distribution with mean 3 is fitted to the data the expected numbers are as follows:

Number of strings	0	1	2	3	4	5 or more
Expected number	10.96	32.85	49.29	49.29	36.98	40.63

Test whether a Poisson distribution with mean 3 is an adequate model for the data provided all observations of 5 or more are classified together (as is the case in this part). Use a 5% significance level.

(**c**) In the light of your calculations in (**a**) and (**b**) discuss whether it is likely that serious blemishes occur at random at a constant average rate throughout the cloth.   (AEB 1991)

Solution 11.17 Let X be the r.v. 'the number of strings in a length of cloth'.

(**a**) From the observed data

$$\bar{x} = \frac{\sum fx}{\sum f} = \frac{616}{220} = 2.8$$

H_0:   The distribution is Poisson, with the same mean as the observed data

i.e. $X \sim \text{Po}(2.8)$

The expected frequencies are given by

$$220P(X = x) \quad \text{where} \quad P(X = x) = e^{-2.8}\frac{(2.8)^x}{x!}, \quad x = 0, 1, 2, \ldots$$

They have been calculated to 2 d.p.

Number of strings	Observed frequency (O)	Expected frequency (E)
0	14	13.38
1	29	37.46
2	57	52.44
3	48	48.95
4	31	34.26
5	41	19.19
6	0	8.95
7 or more	0	5.37

Degrees of freedom:

The number of cells $= 8$

There are *two* restrictions, the total expected frequency is 220 and we have to estimate the mean of the Poisson model from our sample.

Therefore v = number of cells − number of restrictions

$$= 8 - 2$$

$$= 6$$

We consider the $\chi^2(6)$ distribution.

Test at the 5% level and reject H_0 if $\chi^2 > \chi^2_{5\%}(6)$,

i.e. if $\chi^2 > 12.5916$

O	E	$\dfrac{(O-E)^2}{E}$
14	13.38	0.0287...
29	37.46	1.9106...
57	52.44	0.3965...
48	48.95	0.0184...
31	34.26	0.3102...
41	19.19	24.7877...
0	8.95	8.95
0	5.37	5.37
$\Sigma O = 220$	$\Sigma E = 220$	41.7722...

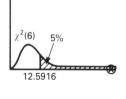

$$\chi^2 = \sum \frac{(O-E)^2}{E}$$

$$= 41.8 \ (1 \text{ d.p.})$$

Since $\chi^2 > 12.5916$, we reject H_0 and conclude that <u>the Poisson distribution with the same mean as the observed data is not an adequate model.</u>

(**b**) H_0: $X \sim \text{Po}(3)$; observations of 5 or more are classed together.

Number of strings	Observed frequency (O)	Expected frequency (E)
0	14	10.96
1	29	32.85
2	57	49.29
3	48	49.29
4	31	36.98
5 or more	41	40.63
	Total 220	Total 220

Degrees of freedom:

number of cells $= 6$

number of restrictions $= 1$ (the total expected frequency is 220)

Therefore $v = 6 - 1 = 5$ and we consider the $\chi^2(5)$ distribution.

We test at the 5% level and reject H_0 if $\chi^2 > \chi^2_{5\%}(5)$,

i.e. if $\chi^2 > 11.0705$

O	E	$\dfrac{(O-E)^2}{E}$
14	10.96	0.843...
29	32.85	0.451...
57	49.29	1.206...
48	49.29	0.033...
31	36.98	0.967...
41	40.63	0.003...
$\Sigma O = 220$	$\Sigma E = 220$	3.504...

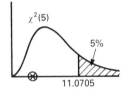

$$\chi^2 = \sum \frac{(O-E)^2}{E}$$

$$= 3.5 \text{ (1 d.p.)}$$

Since $\chi^2 < 11.0705$, we do not reject H_0 and we conclude that, if the observations of 5 or more are classified together, <u>the Poisson distribution with mean 3 is an adequate model.</u>

(**c**) The result in part (**b**) supports the Poisson distribution as an adequate model so it is likely that serious blemishes occur at random at a constant average rate throughout the cloth. It is likely that the model was rejected in part (**a**) because the number of strings was limited to 5 or less.

Example 11.18 (a) A farmer kept a record of the number of heifer calves born to each of his cows during the first five years of breeding of each cow. The results are summarised opposite.

Number of heifers	0	1	2	3	4	5
Number of cows	4	19	41	52	26	8

Test, at the 5% level of significance, whether or not the Binomial distribution with parameters $n = 5$, $p = 0.5$ is an adequate model for these data.

(b) Explain briefly (without doing any further calculations) what changes you would make in your analysis if you were testing whether or not the Binomial distribution with $n = 5$ and unspecified p fitted the data.

(c) The same farmer also kept a record of the time of delivery of each calf and the type of assistance the cow needed. The following table summarises some of his data.

	Day	Night
Unattended	42	58
Farmer assisted	63	117
Veterinary supervised	85	35

Test, at the 5% level of significance, whether there is any association between type of birth and time of day.   (AEB 1990)

Solution 11.18 Let X be the r.v. 'the number of heifer calves born to a cow in the first five years of breeding'.

$$H_0: X \sim \text{Bin}(5, 0.5)$$

The expected frequencies are given by

$$150P(X = x) \quad \text{where} \quad P(X = x) = {}^5C_x(0.5)^{5-x}(0.5)^x$$
$$= {}^5C_x(0.5)^5$$

Number of heifers	0	1	2	3	4	5	
Observed frequency (O)	4	19	41	52	26	8	Total 150
Expected frequency (E)	4.7	23.4	46.9	46.9	23.4	4.7	Total 150

Since the expected frequencies for the first and last cells are less than 5, we must combine them with the next cells. The revised table is:

Number of heifers	0 or 1	2	3	4 or 5	
Observed frequency (O)	23	41	52	34	Total 150
Expected frequency (E)	28.1	46.9	46.9	28.1	Total 150

Degrees of freedom:

The number of cells $= 4$

There is one restriction, that the total expected frequency is 150.

Therefore $v =$ number of cells $-$ number of restrictions

$$= 4 - 1$$

$$= 3$$

and the $\chi^2(3)$ distribution is considered.

We test at the 5% level and reject H_0 if $\chi^2 > \chi^2_{5\%}(3)$,

i.e. if $\chi^2 > 7.814\,73$

O	E	$\dfrac{(O-E)^2}{E}$
23	28.1	0.925...
41	46.9	0.742...
52	46.9	0.554...
34	28.1	1.238...
$\Sigma O = 150$	$\Sigma E = 150$	3.461...

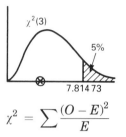

$$\chi^2 = \sum \frac{(O-E)^2}{E}$$

$$= 3.46\ (2\ \text{d.p.})$$

Since $\chi^2 < 7.814\,73$, we do not reject H_0 and we conclude that the binomial distribution with $n = 5$ and $p = 0.5$ is an adequate model for the data.

(**b**) p would be estimated from the mean of the data, where $np = \bar{x}$, with $n = 5$.

Therefore $p = \frac{1}{5}\bar{x}$

In this case, the number of restrictions in calculating χ^2 is 2,

so $v =$ number of cells $- 2$.

The number of cells depends on whether cells need to be combined when the expected frequencies have been calculated.

(**c**) *Observed data:* this is a 3×2 contingency table

	Day	Night	Row totals
Unattended	42	58	100
Farmer assisted	63	117	180
Veterinary supervised	85	35	120
Column totals	190	210	400

H_0: The type of assistance required is independent of the time of delivery.

H_1: There is an association between type of birth and time of day.

Expected frequencies:

Expected number of unattended day deliveries

$$= \frac{\text{(row total)(column total)}}{\text{grand total}}$$

$$= \frac{(100)(190)}{400}$$

$$= 47.5$$

Expected number of farmer assisted day deliveries

$$= \frac{(180)(190)}{400}$$

$$= 85.5$$

It is now possible to work out all the other expected frequencies by making sure that totals agree.

For example,

expected number of veterinary supervised day deliveries

$$= 190 - (47.5 + 85.5)$$

$$= 57$$

expected number of unattended night deliveries

$$= 100 - 47.5$$

$$= 52.5$$

The completed table for the expected frequencies is:

	Day	Night	Row totals
Unattended	47.5	52.5	100
Farmer assisted	85.5	94.5	180
Veterinary supervised	57	63	120
Column totals	190	210	400

Degrees of freedom:

As we have seen, once two expected frequencies have been calculated the others are known by agreement of totals.

Therefore $v = 2$

This agrees with the formula for an $h \times k$ contingency table, where

$$\text{number of degrees of freedom} = (h - 1) \times (k - 1)$$

$$= (3 - 1) \times (2 - 1)$$

$$= (2)(1)$$

$$= 2$$

We consider the $\chi^2(2)$ distribution.

We test at the 5% level and reject H_0 if $\chi^2 > \chi^2_{5\%}(2)$,

i.e. if $\chi^2 > 5.991\,46$

O	E	$\dfrac{(O-E)^2}{E}$
42	47.5	0.636...
63	85.5	5.921...
85	57	13.754...
58	52.5	0.576...
117	94.5	5.357...
35	63	12.444...
$\Sigma O = 400$	$\Sigma E = 400$	38.69...

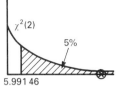

$$\chi^2 = \sum \frac{(O-E)^2}{E}$$

$$= 38.7 \text{ (1 d.p.)}$$

Now χ^2 is very much larger than $5.991\,46$; we reject H_0 and conclude that there is an association between type of birth and time of day.

The biggest contributions to the total for χ^2 come from the veterinary supervised deliveries. It appears that the vet. preferred to deliver in the day time.

Example 11.19 (a) Some years ago a Polytechnic decided to require all entrants to a science course to study a non-science subject for one year. In the first year of the scheme entrants were given the choice of studying French or Russian. The number of students of each sex choosing each language is shown in the following table:

	French	Russian
Male	39	16
Female	21	14

Use a χ^2 test (including Yates' correction) at the 5% significance level to test whether choice of language is independent of sex.

(b) The choice of non-science subjects has now been widened and the current figures are as follows:

	French	Poetry	Russian	Sculpture
Male	2	8	15	10
Female	10	17	21	37

Use a χ^2 test at the 5% significance level to test whether choice of subject is independent of sex. In applying the test you should combine French with another subject. Explain why this is necessary and the reasons for your choice of subject.

(AEB 1992)P

Solution 11.19 (a) *Observed data:*

	French	Russian	Row total
Male	39	16	55
Female	21	14	35
Column total	60	30	Grand total 90

H_0: choice of language is independent of sex
H_1: choice of language is *not* independent of sex.

Expected number of males choosing French $= \dfrac{(55)(60)}{90}$

$$= 36.67 \ (2 \ \text{d.p.})$$

The other expected frequencies are calculated by ensuring that row and column totals agree.

Expected frequencies:

	French	Russian	Row total
Male	**36.67**	18.33	55
Female	23.33	11.67	35
Column total	60	30	90

Degrees of freedom:

$$v = (2-1)(2-1)$$

$$= 1, \ \text{so the } \chi^2(1) \text{ distribution is considered.}$$

We perform a 5% test and reject H_0 if $\chi^2 > \chi^2_{5\%}(1)$,

i.e. if $\chi^2 > 3.841\,46$.

Using Yates' correction

$$\chi^2 = \sum \frac{(|O-E|-0.5)^2}{E}$$

O	E	$\dfrac{(|O-E|-0.5)^2}{E}$
39	36.67	$0.0913\ldots$
16	18.33	$0.1827\ldots$
21	23.33	$0.1435\ldots$
14	11.67	$0.2869\ldots$
$\Sigma O = 90$	$\Sigma E = 90$	$0.7045\ldots$

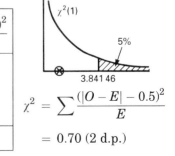

$$\chi^2 = \sum \frac{(|O-E|-0.5)^2}{E}$$

$$= 0.70 \ (2 \ \text{d.p.})$$

Since $\chi^2 < \chi^2_{5\%}(1)$, we do not reject H_0 and we conclude that the choice of language is independent of sex.

(**b**) *Observed frequencies:*

	French	Poetry	Russian	Sculpture	Row totals
Male	2	8	15	10	35
Female	10	17	21	37	85
Column totals	12	25	36	47	120

Expected number of males choosing French $= \dfrac{(35)(12)}{120} = 3.5$

Expected number of males choosing Poetry $= \dfrac{(35)(25)}{120} = 7.29$ (2 d.p.)

Expected number of males choosing Russian $= \dfrac{(35)(36)}{120} = 10.5$

The completed table is now formed, ensuring that totals agree.

	French	Poetry	Russian	Sculpture	Row totals
Male	**3.5**	**7.29**	**10.5**	13.71	35
Female	8.5	17.71	25.5	33.29	85
Column totals	12	25	36	47	120

Now the expected frequency for males choosing French is less than 5, so it will be necessary to combine French with another subject. It seems sensible to combine the two foreign languages, French and Russian, in order to preserve the diversity of subjects. Therefore the amended tables are:

Observed data:

	Foreign language	Poetry	Sculpture
Male	17	8	10
Female	31	17	37

Expected data:

	Foreign language	Poetry	Sculpture
Male	14	7.29	13.71
Female	34	17.71	33.29

Degrees of freedom:

$$v = (2 - 1)(3 - 1)$$
$$= (1)(2)$$
$$= 2$$

So we consider the $\chi^2(2)$ distribution.

We perform a test at the 5% level and reject H_0 if $\chi^2 > \chi^2_{5\%}(2)$,

i.e. if $\chi^2 > 5.99146$

O	E	$\dfrac{(O-E)^2}{E}$
17	14	$0.6428\ldots$
8	7.29	$0.0691\ldots$
10	13.71	$1.0039\ldots$
31	34	$0.2647\ldots$
17	17.71	$0.0284\ldots$
37	33.29	$0.4134\ldots$
$\Sigma O = 120$	$\Sigma E = 120$	$3.4225\ldots$

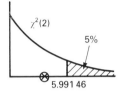

$$\chi^2 = \sum \frac{(O-E)^2}{E}$$

$$= 2.42 \; (3 \text{ SF})$$

Since $\chi^2 < \chi^2_{5\%}(2)$ we do not reject H_0 and we conclude that <u>even</u> <u>with the wider choice of subjects, the choice is still independent of</u> <u>sex</u>.

SUMMARY — χ^2 TEST

$$\chi^2 = \sum \frac{(O-E)^2}{E}$$

For $v = 1$, using Yates' continuity correction,

$$\chi^2 = \sum \frac{(|O-E| - 0.5)^2}{E}$$

Degrees of freedom
  v = number of independent variables used in calculating χ^2

Contingency tables
For an $h \times k$ contingency table,
$$v = (h-1)(k-1)$$

Goodness of fit tests
  v = number of cells − number of restrictions
The number of restrictions depends on the nature of the test, as shown in the following table, where the number of cells is denoted by n.

Distribution	Number of restrictions	Restrictions	Number of degrees of freedom
Uniform distribution and Distribution in a given ratio	1	Total expected frequency is given	$v = n - 1$
Binomial distribution (a) p known	1	Total expected frequency is given	$v = n - 1$
(b) p unknown	2	Total expected frequency is given and p is estimated from the sample	$v = n - 2$
Poisson distribution (a) λ known	1	Total expected frequency is given	$v = n - 1$
(b) λ unknown	2	Total expected frequency is given and λ is estimated from the sample	$v = n - 2$
Normal distribution (a) μ and σ^2 known	1	Total expected frequency is given	$v = n - 1$
(b) μ and σ^2 unknown	3	Total expected frequency is given and μ and σ^2 are estimated from the sample	$v = n - 3$

Miscellaneous Exercise 11d

1. The personnel manager of a large firm is investigating whether there is any association between the length of service of the employees and the type of training they receive from the firm. A random sample of 200 employee records is taken from the last few years and is classified according to these criteria. Length of service is classified as short (meaning less than 1 year), medium (1–3 years) and long (more than 3 years). Type of training is classified as being merely an initial 'induction course', proper initial on-the-job training but little if any more, and regular and continuous training. The data are as follows:

		Length of service		
		Short	Medium	Long
Type of training	Induction course	14	23	13
	Initial on-the-job	12	7	13
	Continuous	28	32	58

Examine at the 5% level of significance whether these data provide evidence of association between length of service and type of training, stating clearly your null and alternative hypotheses.
Discuss your conclusions.   (MEI)

2. A group of students studying A-level statistics was set a paper, to be attempted under examination conditions, containing four questions requiring the use of the χ^2 distribution. The following table shows the type of question and the number of students who obtained good (14 or more out of 20) and bad (fewer than 14 out of 20) marks.

Type of question

	Contingency table	Binomial fit	Normal fit	Poisson fit
Good mark	25	12	12	11
Bad mark	4	11	3	12

(a) Test at the 5% significance level whether the mark obtained (by the students who attempted the question) is associated with the type of question.
(b) Under some circumstances it is necessary to combine classes in order to carry out a test. If it had been necessary to combine the Binomial fit question with another question, which question would you have combined it with and why?
(c) Given that a total of 30 students sat the paper, test, at the 5% significance level whether the number of students attempting a particular question is associated with the type of question.
(d) Compare the difficulty and popularity of the different types of question in the light of your answers to (a) and (c).   (AEB 1990)

3. In the mathematics department of a college, candidates in an examination are graded A, B, C, D or E. Records from previous years show that examiners have awarded a grade A to 15% of candidates, B to 20%, C to 35%, D to 25% and E to 5%. A new syllabus is examined by a new board of examiners who award the grades to 200 candidates as follows:

   A, 33;   B, 37;   C, 81;   D, 36;   E, 13.

(a) Stating clearly your hypotheses and using a 5% level of significance investigate whether or not the new board of examiners awards grades in the same proportions as the previous one.

In addition to being classified by examination grade, these 200 students are classified as male or female and the results summarised in a contingency table. Assuming all expected values are 5 or more, the statistic

$$\sum_{i=1}^{10} \frac{(O_i - E_i)^2}{E_i} \text{ was } 14.27.$$

(b) Stating your hypotheses and using a 1% significance level, investigate whether or not sex and grade are associated.   (L)

4. Describe briefly how the number of degrees of freedom is calculated in a χ^2 goodness of fit test. The following set of grouped data from 100 observations has mean 1.03. The data are thought to come from a normal distribution with known variance 1 but unknown mean. Using an appropriate χ^2-distribution, test this hypothesis at the 1% significance level.

Lower value of grouping interval	Number of Observations
$-\infty$	0
-2.0	1
-1.5	0
-1.0	6
-0.5	10
0.0	12
0.5	15
1.0	23
1.5	16
2.0	13
2.5	3
3.0	1
3.5	0

(C)

5. (a) A market research organisation interviewed a random sample of 120 users of launderettes in London and found that 37 preferred brand X washing powder, 66 preferred brand Y and the remainder preferred brand Z. A similar survey was carried out in Birmingham. In this survey, of 80 people interviewed, 19 preferred brand X, 40 preferred brand Y and the remainder preferred brand Z. Test whether these results provide significant evidence, at the 5% level, of different preferences in the two cities.
(b) A shop that repairs television sets keeps a record of the number of sets brought in for repair each day. The numbers brought in during a random sample of 40 days were as follows.

4 0 0 0 2 1 1 0 0 0   0 1 1 0 3 0 0 0 0 1 0

4 0 0 0 0 0 2 0 1 0   0 0 0 1 1 1 0 2 0 0

Test, at the 5% significance level, the hypothesis that these numbers are observations from a Poisson distribution.   (C)

6. Over a long period of time, a research team monitored the number of car accidents which occurred in a particular county. Each accident was classified as being trivial (minor damage and no personal injuries), serious (damage to vehicles and passengers, but no deaths) or fatal (damage to vehicles and loss of life). The colour of the car which, in the opinion of the research team, caused the accident was also recorded, together with the day of the week on which the accident occurred. The following data were collected.

Colour	Trivial	Serious	Fatal
White	50	25	16
Black	35	39	18
Green	28	23	13
Red	25	17	11
Yellow	17	20	16
Blue	24	33	10

Analyse these data for evidence of association between the colour of the car and the type of accident.

State the condition which sometimes necessitates the amalgamation of rows or columns in contingency tables. Explain why amalgamation might not be appropriate for this table.

The following table summarises the data relating to the day of the week on which the accident occurred.

Day	Number of accidents
Monday	60
Tuesday	54
Wednesday	48
Thursday	53
Friday	53
Saturday	75
Sunday	77

Investigate the hypothesis that these data are a random sample from a uniform distribution.   (AEB)

7. (a) The number of books borrowed from a library during a certain week were 518 on Monday, 431 on Tuesday, 485 on Wednesday, 443 on Thursday and 523 on Friday.
Is there any evidence that the number of books borrowed varies between the five days of the week? Use a 1% level of significance. Interpret fully your conclusions.
(b) Analysis of the rate of turnover of employees by a personnel manager produced the following table showing the length of stay of 200 people who left the company for other employment.

Grade	Length of employment (years)		
	0–2	2–5	>5
Managerial	4	11	6
Skilled	32	28	21
Unskilled	25	23	50

Using a 1% level of significance, analyse this information and state fully the conclusions from your analysis.   (AEB)

8. (a) The number of accidents per day on a stretch of motorway was recorded for 100 days and the following results obtained.

Number of accidents	Frequency
0	44
1	32
2	9
3	10
4	5
5 or more	0

Examine whether or not a Poisson model is suitable to represent the number of accidents per day on this stretch of road. Use a 1% level of significance.
(b) The results of a survey to establish the attitude of individuals to a particular political proposal showed that three-quarters of those interviewed were house owners. Of the 44 interviewed, only 6 of the 35 in favour of the proposal were not house owners.
Does the survey indicate that a person's opinion on the proposal is independent of house ownership? Use a 1% level of significance.   (AEB 1990)

9. It is thought that there is an association between the colour of a person's eyes and the reaction of the person's skin to ultraviolet light. In order to investigate this each of a random sample of 120 people was subjected to a standard dose of ultraviolet light. The degree of their reaction was noted, '−' indicating no reaction, '+' indicating slight reaction and '++' indicating strong reaction. The results are shown in the table below.

		Eye colour		
		Blue	Grey or green	Brown
	−	7	8	18
Reaction	+	29	10	16
	++	21	9	2

(i) Perform an appropriate test at the 5% significance level, stating your null and alternative hypotheses. Find the least value of k given in the mathematical tables for which the null hypothesis can be rejected at the k% significance level.

(ii) Estimate the percentage of people in the population from which the sample was drawn who would not suffer a reaction to ultraviolet light, and calculate an approximate 95% symmetric confidence interval for the percentage. (C)

10. A random variable X has a normal distribution with mean 35 and variance 100. The first table below shows the probability that the value of a single reading, x, lies in some particular interval.
Copy and complete this table.

x	Probability
less than 10	0.0062
10–	
20–	
30–	0.3830
40–	
50–	
60 and above	

The second table shows the frequency distribution of the times, in seconds, required by 200 ten-year-old children to tie both their shoe laces.

Time	Frequency
less than 10	8
10–	11
20–	40
30–	59
40–	66
50–	10
60 and above	6

Perform a χ^2 goodness of fit test to show that there is evidence to suggest that the times taken by ten-year-old children to tie both their shoe laces do not follow a normal distribution with mean 35 seconds and standard deviation 10 seconds.
Given that for these 200 children the mean time is 35.9 seconds and the standard deviation is 12.5 seconds, test H_0: $\mu = 35$ against H_1: $\mu \neq 35$, where μ is the population mean time in seconds.
Explain how the results of the two significance tests can be reconciled. (JMB)

11. The heights (x) of one hundred police officers recruited to a police force in a particular year are summarised in the following table. The mean and standard deviation of the original data are 180 cm and 3 cm respectively.

Height (cm)	Frequency
$x < 175$	2
$175 \leqslant x < 177$	15
$177 \leqslant x < 179$	29
$179 \leqslant x < 181$	25
$181 \leqslant x < 183$	12
$183 \leqslant x < 185$	10
$185 \leqslant x$	7

Fit an appropriate normal distribution to the above data, and test the goodness of fit at the 5% level. (C)

12. A random sample of 100 shoppers were asked by a market research team whether or not they used Sudsey Soap. 58 said yes and 42 said no. In a second random sample of 80 shoppers, 62 said yes and 18 said no. By considering a suitable 2×2 contingency table, test whether these two samples are consistent with each other. (O & C)

13. Two fair dice are thrown 432 times. Find the expected frequencies of the scores 2, 3, 4,...,12.
Two players, A and B are each given two dice and told to throw them 432 times, recording the results. The frequencies reported are given in the table below.
Is there any evidence that either pair of dice is biased? What can be said about B's alleged results? (AEB)

Scores	A's frequency	B's frequency
2	18	14
3	33	22
4	28	34
5	54	51
6	62	58
7	65	73
8	66	63
9	42	45
10	30	38
11	27	25
12	7	9

14. Over a period of 50 weeks the numbers of road accidents reported to a police station are shown in the table below.

No. of accidents	0	1	2	3
No. of weeks	23	13	10	4

Find the mean number of accidents per week. Use this mean, a 5% level of significance, and your table of χ^2 to test the hypothesis that these data are a random sample from a population with a Poisson distribution. (O & C)

15. Smallwoods Ltd. run a weekly football pools competition. One part of this involves a fixed-odds contest where the entrant has to forecast correctly the result of each of five given matches. In the event of a fully correct forecast the entrant is paid out at odds of 100 to 1. During the last two years Miss Fortune has entered this fixed-odds contest 80 times. The table below summarises her results.

Number of matches correctly forecast per entry (x)	Number of entries with x correct forecasts (f)
0	8
1	19
2	25
3	22
4	5
5	1

(a) Find the frequencies of the number of matches correctly forecast per entry given by a binomial distribution having the same mean and total as the observed distribution.
(b) Use the χ^2 distribution and a 10% level of significance to test the adequacy of the binomial distribution as a model for these data.
(c) On the evidence before you, and assuming that the point of entering is to win money, would you advise Miss Fortune to continue with this competition and why?

(AEB)

16. The table summarises the incidence of cerebral tumours in 141 neurosurgical patients.

		Type of tumour		
		Benign	Malignant	Others
Site of tumour	Frontal lobes	23	9	6
	Temporal lobes	21	4	3
	Elsewhere	34	24	17

Find the expected frequencies on the hypothesis that there is no association between the type and site of a tumour. Use the χ^2 distribution to test this hypothesis.

(AEB)

17. Explain how to calculate the degrees of freedom for the χ^2 statistic in
(a) a goodness-of-fit test, (b) a test of no association of the two factors in an $n \times k$ contingency table.
An ecologist collected organisms of a particular species from three beaches and counted the number of females in each sample (the remainder were males).

Beach	1	2	3
No. of females	44	86	110
Total no. in sample	100	200	200

Test if the proportion of females differed significantly between the beaches.
Find the percentage of females at each beach and comment on the results. (O)

18. A factory operates four production lines. Maintenance records show that the daily number of stoppages due to mechanical failure were as shown in the table below (it is possible for a production line to break down more than once on the same day). You may assume that $\Sigma f = 1400$, $\Sigma fx = 1036$.

Number of stoppages, x	0	1	2	3	4	5	6 or more
Number of days, f	728	447	138	48	26	13	0

(a) Use a χ^2 distribution and a 1% significance level to determine whether the Poisson distribution is an adequate model for the data.
(b) The maintenance engineer claims that breakdowns occur at random and that the mean rate has remained constant throughout the period. State, giving a reason, whether your answer to (a) is consistent with this claim.
(c) Of the 1036 breakdowns which occurred 230 were on production line A, 303 on B, 270 on C and 233 on D. Test at the 5% significance level whether these data are consistent with breakdowns occurring at an equal rate on each production line.

(AEB 1988)

19. (a) As part of a statistics project, students observed five private cars passing a college and counted the number which were carrying the driver only, with no passengers. This was repeated 80 times. The results of a particular student were as follows:

Number of cars with driver only	Number of times observed
0	0
1	3
2	12
3	27
4	26
5	12

Use the χ^2 distribution and a 5% significance level to test whether the binomial distribution provides an adequate model for the data.

(b) In a further part of the project the students counted the number of cars passing the college in 130 intervals each of length 5 seconds. The table below shows the results obtained by the same student together with the expected numbers if a Poisson distribution, with the same mean as the observed data, is fitted.

Number of cars passing a point in a 5 second interval	Numbers of intervals observed	Number of intervals expected
0	28	25.85
1	40	41.75
2	32	33.72
3	19	18.16
4	7	7.33
5	3	2.37
6	1	0.64
7 or more	0	0.18

Use the χ^2 distribution and a 5% significance level to test whether the Poisson distribution provides an adequate model for the data.
(c) The teacher suspected that this student had not observed the data but invented them. Explain why the teacher was suspicious and comment on the strength of the evidence supporting her suspicions. (AEB 1987)

20. One formula for the χ^2 statistic is

$$\chi^2 = \sum \frac{(f_o - f_e)^2}{f_e}$$

where f_o is the observed frequency, f_e is the expected frequency and the summation is over the number of groups. Show that the formula may also be written as

$$\chi^2 = \left(\sum \frac{f_o^{\,2}}{f_e} \right) - N$$

where N is the total number of observations.
(a) Ballpoint pens come off a production line and are packed into batches of 100. It is believed that the number of defective pens in each batch follows a Poisson distribution with mean 2.8. 100 batches of pens were examined and the observed frequencies of the number of defective pens in each batch found to be those in the table below. Test whether the suggested Poisson model fits these data.

Number of defective pens	0	1	2	3	4	5	6+
Frequency	5	19	25	20	16	7	8

(b) To find whether there is any association between a person's eye colour and his or her skin's susceptibility to sunburn, a random sample of 180 people was taken and the data in the table below obtained. Test whether there is significant evidence of association.

Eye colour	Susceptibility to sunburn			Total
	High	Medium	Low	
Blue	19	27	4	50
Brown	1	13	16	30
Grey-green	27	48	25	100

(O)

12

REGRESSION AND CORRELATION

SCATTER DIAGRAM

Sometimes we wish to investigate the results of a statistical enquiry or experiment by *comparing two sets of data, x* and *y*, for example:

x	y
The weight at the end of a spring	The length of the spring
Pupil's mark in French	Pupil's mark in German
The diameter of the stem of a plant	The average length of leaf of a plant
The age of a plant	The quantity of fruit produced by a plant

Consider the set of points $(x_1, y_1), (x_2, y_2), \ldots, (x_n, y_n)$. If the values of y are plotted against the values of x, then a **scatter diagram** is obtained. Here are some examples.

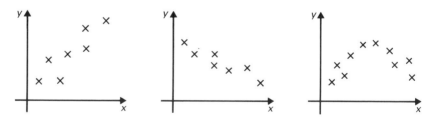

REGRESSION FUNCTION

We then look for a relationship $y = f(x)$, where the function f is to be determined, i.e. *given* the points, we have to 'work backwards' or *'regress'* to the original function f. Hence this function is called the **regression function.**

LINEAR CORRELATION AND REGRESSION LINES

We shall consider only the simplest type of function where $y = f(x)$ is a *straight line*. If all the points in the scatter diagram seem to lie near a straight line, we say that there is **linear correlation** between x and y.

We try to *estimate* fairly accurately the position of this line, and having done so we call it a **regression line**.

(**a**) If y tends to increase as x increases, then there is **positive linear correlation**.

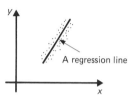

(**b**) If y tends to decrease as x increases, then there is **negative linear correlation**.

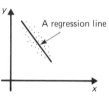

(**c**) If there is no relationship between x and y, then there is **no correlation**.

NOTE: common sense is needed when interpreting scatter diagrams. For example, we might find that, over a period of time in a certain town, there has been an increase in the number of bank robberies and an increase in the number of health food shops. However it would be foolish to look for a relationship between these variables.

DRAWING A REGRESSION LINE 'BY EYE'

(**a**) **If there is very little scatter:**

First calculate the co-ordinates of the point

$(\bar{x}, \bar{y})$ where $\bar{x} = \dfrac{\Sigma x_i}{n}$ and $\bar{y} = \dfrac{\Sigma y_i}{n}$

Then draw a line of good fit, ensuring that it passes through $(\bar{x}, \bar{y})$.

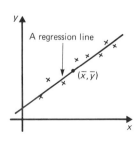

(b) If there is a fair degree of scatter:

In this case we can distinguish *two regression lines*:

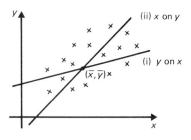

(i) *A line of regression of y on x.* This can be used to estimate y, given a value of x.

(ii) *A line of regression of x on y.* This can be used to estimate x, given a value of y.

Method for drawing these two regression lines by eye

(i) *A line of regression of y on x* — we assume the values of x to be accurate and draw a regression line as follows:
   (a) Find the mean $M(\bar{x}, \bar{y})$ of the distribution.
   (b) Through M draw a line parallel to the y axis. This divides the points into two groups.
   (c) Find the mean M_L of the points on the left.
   (d) Find the mean M_R of the points on the right.
   (e) Draw a line of best fit through M, M_L and M_R.

(ii) *A line of regression of x on y* — we assume the values of y to be accurate and draw a regression line as follows:
   (a) Find the mean $M(\bar{x}, \bar{y})$ of the distribution.
   (b) Through M draw a line parallel to the x axis.
   (c) Find the mean M_A of the points above.
   (d) Find the mean M_B of the points below.
   (e) Draw the line of best fit through M, M_A and M_B.

Example 12.1 The following table gives the test results for 10 children.

Child	A	B	C	D	E	F	G	H	I	J
Arithmetic mark, x	1	8	15	18	23	28	33	39	45	45
English mark, y	3	14	8	20	19	17	36	26	14	29

(a) (i) Draw a scatter diagram, and by finding the means of certain points draw a regression line y on x.
   (ii) Estimate an English mark for a child who missed the English test, but who had 20 in the arithmetic test.

(b) (i) On the scatter diagram draw a regression line x on y.
   (ii) Estimate an arithmetic mark for a child who was absent for the arithmetic test, but who had 30 in the English test.

(c) Would you use one of these lines to estimate an English mark for a child who had 60 in the arithmetic test?

Solution 12.1 (a) (i) $\bar{x} = \dfrac{\Sigma x}{10} = \dfrac{255}{10} = 25.5, \qquad \bar{y} = \dfrac{\Sigma y}{10} = \dfrac{186}{10} = 18.6$

So we plot the point $M(25.5, 18.6)$ and ensure that the line passes through it.

For a regression line y on x, draw a line through M parallel to the y axis.

For the points on the left		For the points on the right	
x	y	x	y
1	3	28	17
8	14	33	36
15	8	39	26
18	20	45	14
23	19	45	29
$\Sigma x = 65 \quad \Sigma y = 64$		$\Sigma x = 190 \quad \Sigma y = 122$	
So $\quad \bar{x}_L = \frac{65}{5} = 13,$		$\bar{x}_R = \frac{190}{5} = 38,$	
$\bar{y}_L = \frac{64}{5} = 12.8$		$\bar{y}_R = \frac{122}{5} = 24.4$	
We plot M_L (13, 12.8)		We plot M_R (38, 24.4)	

Now draw a line of good fit through M, M_L and M_R. This is a regression line y on x (see page 632).

(ii) If a child had 20 in the arithmetic test, <u>since x is given</u>, we use the line y on x to estimate the English mark. From the line, <u>the estimated mark for English is 16.</u>

(**b**) (i) *x on y*: Draw the line through M parallel to the x axis.

For the points above		For the points below	
x	y	x	y
18	20	1	3
23	19	8	14
33	36	15	8
39	26	28	17
45	29	45	14
$\Sigma x = 158 \quad \Sigma y = 130$		$\Sigma x = 97 \quad \Sigma y = 56$	
$\bar{x}_A = \frac{158}{5} = 31.6,$		$\bar{x}_B = \frac{97}{5} = 19.4,$	
$\bar{y}_A = \frac{130}{5} = 26$		$\bar{y}_B = \frac{56}{5} = 11.2$	
We plot M_A (31.6, 26)		We plot M_B (19.4, 11.2)	

Now draw a line of good fit through M, M_A and M_B. This is a regression line x on y.

(ii) If a child had 30 in the English test we use the line x on y, as y is given. From the line, <u>the estimated arithmetic mark is 35.</u>

(**c**) The mark of 60 in the arithmetic test is outside the range of the data. We could use the regression line y on x as drawn on the scatter diagram to give an <u>estimated English mark of 35,</u> but this result should be used with caution. As a general rule, <u>keep within the range of the data.</u>

Scatter diagram to show English and Arithmetic marks for 10 pupils

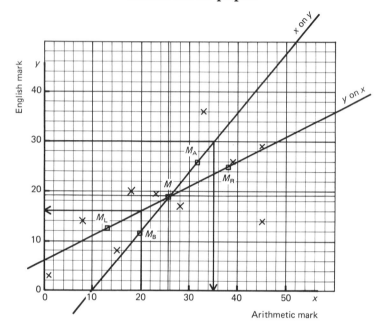

NOTE: it may appear strange to have two regression lines, but it does matter which is considered. Suppose that there is a positive correlation between the height and mass of males. A result of this might be that the average mass of all males of height 1.93 m (6 ft 4 inches) is 85.7 kg ($13\frac{1}{2}$ stone).

So, if you were given a height of 1.93 m you would guess 85.7 kg for the mass.

But, if you were given a mass of 85.7 kg, would you guess 1.93 m for the height? If you would not, then the two regression lines are different.

DEPENDENT AND INDEPENDENT VARIABLES

In a set of data such as:

x	5	10	15	20	25
y	20	21	23	24	23

then it is obvious that the value of x has been *controlled*. In this case x is sometimes called the **explanatory** or **independent** variable and y is called the **response** or **dependent** variable. To estimate the value of y, given the value of x, we would use the regression line of y on x. However it would not be suitable to use the regression line of x on y to estimate x, given a value of y.

Example 12.2 It is suspected that two quantities Q and W are related according to the formula $Q = aW^b$, where a and b are constants. Observations on Q and W were made and the results were as follows:

W	13	16	20	25	32	40	50	60
Q	71	40	50	32	24	31	25	16

Plot a scatter diagram of $\log_{10}Q$ against $\log_{10}W$ and estimate the equation of the regression line of $\log Q$ on $\log W$, using the means of certain points, or otherwise. Use your results to estimate values for a and b.

Solution 12.2

$x = \log_{10}W$	$y = \log_{10}Q$
1.114	1.851
1.204	1.602
1.301	1.699
1.398	1.505
1.505	1.380
1.602	1.491
1.699	1.398
1.778	1.204
$\Sigma x = 11.601$	$\Sigma y = 12.13$

$$\bar{x} = \frac{\Sigma x}{n} = \frac{11.601}{8} = 1.45$$

$$\bar{y} = \frac{\Sigma y}{n} = \frac{12.13}{8} = 1.52$$

We plot $M(\bar{x}, \bar{y})$ and draw a line parallel to the y axis.

For the points on the left:

x	y
1.114	1.851
1.204	1.602
1.301	1.699
1.398	1.505
$\Sigma x = 5.017$	$\Sigma y = 6.657$

$$\bar{x}_L = \frac{5.017}{4} = 1.25$$

$$\bar{y}_L = \frac{6.657}{4} = 1.66$$

We plot M_L (1.25, 1.66)

For the points on the right:

x	y
1.505	1.380
1.602	1.491
1.699	1.398
1.778	1.204
$\Sigma x = 6.584$	$\Sigma y = 5.473$

$$\bar{x}_R = \frac{6.584}{4} = 1.65$$

$$\bar{y}_R = \frac{5.473}{4} = 1.37$$

We plot M_R (1.65, 1.37)

The line of best fit is drawn through M, M_L and M_R, ensuring that the line passes through M. This is a regression line y on x.

Scatter diagram of $\log_{10}Q$ against $\log_{10}W$

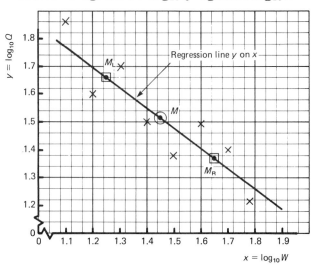

Using these points, we estimate the gradient to be

$$\frac{\bar{y}_L - \bar{y}_R}{\bar{x}_L - \bar{x}_R} = \frac{1.66 - 1.37}{1.25 - 1.65} = -0.73 \ (2 \ \text{d.p.})$$

Now $Q = aW^b$ so, taking logs to the base 10 of both sides,

$$\log_{10}Q = \log_{10}(aW^b)$$
$$= \log_{10}a + \log_{10}W^b$$
$$= \log_{10}a + b\log_{10}W.$$

Taking $\log_{10}Q$ as y and $\log_{10}W$ as x, we have

$$y = \log_{10}a + bx$$

Now b is the gradient of this line, so $b = -0.73$.

To find a, we use the fact that $(\bar{x}, \bar{y})$ lies on the line, where $\bar{x} = 1.45$, $\bar{y} = 1.52$.

Now $$\bar{y} = \log_{10}a + b\bar{x}$$

so $$1.52 = \log_{10}a + (-0.73)(1.45)$$

$$\log_{10}a = 2.5785$$

$$a = 10^{2.5785}$$

$$= 380 \ (2 \ \text{SF})$$

We estimate the values of a and b to be 380 and -0.73 respectively.

Exercise 12a

1. For the following sets of data, draw scatter diagrams and comment on the correlation. Draw regression lines y on x and x on y.

   (a) Use these 11 pairs of data:

x	3	7	9	11	14	14	15	21	22	23	26
y	5	12	5	12	10	17	23	16	10	20	25

   (b) Use these 13 pairs of data:

x	1	5	5	5	6	7.5	7.5
y	85	82	85	89	78	66	77

x	7.5	10	11	12.5	14	14.5
y	81	70	74	65	69	63

   (c) Use these 10 pairs of data:

x	0.6	1	2	2.5	2.8
y	5	10	15	10	2.5

x	3.6	4	4	4	5
y	7.5	2.5	5	15	10

2. Values of two variables x and y obtained from a survey are recorded below.

x	1	2	3	4	5	6	7	8
y	81	73	53	55	43	29	15	3

   Represent these data on a scatter diagram and draw in the line of best fit. Obtain the equation of the line of best fit in the form $y = mx + c$ and estimate the value of y when $x = 5.5$.

3. Four identical money boxes contain different numbers of a particular type of coin and no coins of other types. From the information on the combined weights, which is given in the table below, it is desired to estimate the weight of a box and the mean weight of a coin.

Number of coins in box	x	10	20	30	40
Combined weight of coins and box	y	312	509	682	865

   (a) Plot these data on a scatter diagram, labelling the axes clearly. State whether the data display strong positive, strong negative, or near zero correlation (or otherwise).

   (b) State the co-ordinates of one point through which the line of regression of y upon x must pass.

   (c) Draw on your diagram by eye, this regression line.

   (d) Estimate, from your regression line, (i) the weight of an empty box, (ii) the mean weight of a single coin. (C)

4. The table below gives the rainfall, in cm, for the first nine months of a year at two weather stations. Calculate the mean monthly rainfall over this period at each station and plot the information given in the table on a scatter diagram, drawing a line of best fit.

   Find the equation of this line and use it to predict the rainfall at B in a month when 2.5 cm of rain fell at A. (C Additional)

	A	B
Jan.	5.2	4.6
Feb.	4.8	4.2
Mar.	6.1	5.4
Apr.	5.0	4.4
May	3.2	2.9
June	2.9	2.8
July	4.4	3.9
Aug.	4.0	3.6
Sept.	3.1	3.0

LEAST SQUARES REGRESSION LINES

These are obtained by calculation according to a rule known as 'least squares', rather than just trying to fit the lines 'by eye'.

(a) The least squares regression line y on x

Let the equation of the line be $y = a + bx$.

It is drawn on the scatter diagram which shows the points
$P_i(x_i, y_i)$ where $i = 1, 2, \ldots, n$.

The lengths $P_1Q_1, P_2Q_2, \ldots, P_nQ_n$ are called **residuals**; we
denote them by $m_1, m_2, \ldots, m_n$.

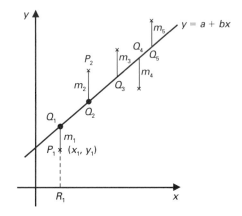

Now the x co-ordinate of Q_1 is x_1. Since Q_1 lies on the line
$y = a + bx$, the y co-ordinate of Q_1 is $a + bx_1$. Therefore
$Q_1R_1 = a + bx_1$.

Now
$$m_1 = Q_1P_1$$
$$= Q_1R_1 - P_1R_1$$
$$= a + bx_1 - y_1$$

So
$$m_1{}^2 = (a + bx_1 - y_1)^2$$

and
$$m_2{}^2 = (a + bx_2 - y_2)^2$$
$$\vdots \qquad\qquad \vdots$$

So
$$\Sigma m_i{}^2 = (a + bx_i - y_i)^2 \qquad i = 1, 2, \ldots, n$$

$\Sigma m_i{}^2$ is the **sum of the squares of the residuals**.

It is possible to find values of a and b such that $\Sigma m_i{}^2$ is a *minimum*.
With these values, the line $y = a + bx$ is known as **the least
squares regression line y on x.**

(b) The least squares regression line x on y

Let the equation of the line be $x = c + dy$.

It is possible to find values of c and d
such that $\Sigma n_i{}^2$ is a minimum. With
these values, the line $x = c + dy$ is
known as the **least squares
regression line x on y.**

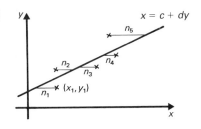

CALCULATING THE EQUATIONS OF THE LEAST SQUARES REGRESSION LINES

There are two main ways of calculating the equations of the regression lines. These are:

(1) using 'normal equations',

(2) using regression coefficients.

The equations can also be found very easily using a calculator, such as Casio 85/100/115 series or Graphics 7000 GA.

(1) Using normal equations

We can find the values of a and b such that Σm_i^2 is a minimum, and the values of c and d such that Σn_i^2 is a minimum, by using the following equations, known as **normal equations**.

Normal equations for y on x:

If the least squares regression line y on x is $y = a + bx$, the values of a and b are found by solving the simultaneous equations

$$\Sigma y = na + b\Sigma x$$

$$\Sigma xy = a\Sigma x + b\Sigma x^2$$

Normal equations for x on y:

If the least squares regression line x on y is $x = c + dy$, the values of c and d are found by solving the simultaneous equations

$$\Sigma x = nc + d\Sigma y$$

$$\Sigma xy = c\Sigma y + d\Sigma y^2$$

NOTE: both regression lines go through $(\bar{x}, \bar{y})$. This can be shown as follows.

y on x:	x on y:
$\Sigma y = na + b\Sigma x$	$\Sigma x = nc + d\Sigma y$
$\dfrac{\Sigma y}{n} = a + b\dfrac{\Sigma x}{n}$	$\dfrac{\Sigma x}{n} = c + d\dfrac{\Sigma y}{n}$
$\bar{y} = a + b\bar{x}$	$\bar{x} = c + d\bar{y}$

Hence the point $(\bar{x}, \bar{y})$ lies on both regression lines.

Example 12.3 Using normal equations, calculate the equations of the least squares regression lines of (**a**) y on x,   (**b**) x on y for the following data. Show the data and the two lines on a scatter diagram.

x	1	2	4	6	7	8	10
y	10	14	12	13	15	12	13

Solution 12.3

x	y	x^2	y^2	xy
1	10	1	100	10
2	14	4	196	28
4	12	16	144	48
6	13	36	169	78
7	15	49	225	105
8	12	64	144	96
10	13	100	169	130
$\Sigma x = 38$	$\Sigma y = 89$	$\Sigma x^2 = 270$	$\Sigma y^2 = 1147$	$\Sigma xy = 495$

For these data $n = 7$.

(**a**) For the least squares regression line y on x, where $y = a + bx$, the normal equations are

$$\Sigma y = na + b\Sigma x$$

$$\Sigma xy = a\Sigma x + b\Sigma x^2$$

Substituting the values found in the table, we have

$$89 = 7a + 38b \qquad \text{(i)}$$

$$495 = 38a + 270b \quad \text{(ii)}$$

We now solve these simultaneous equations:

Multiply (i) by 38 $3382 = 266a + 1444b$ (iii)

Multiply (ii) by 7 $3465 = 266a + 1890b$ (iv)

(iv) − (iii) $83 = 446b$

$$b = \tfrac{83}{446} = 0.186\,09\ldots$$

Substituting for
b in (i) $89 = 7a + 7.071\ldots$

$$7a = 81.92\ldots$$

$$a = 11.704\ldots$$

Taking a and b to 3 SF, we have

$$y = 11.7 + 0.186x$$

(**b**) For the least squares regression line x on y, where $x = c + dy$, the normal equations are

$$\Sigma x = nc + d\Sigma y$$

$$\Sigma xy = c\Sigma y + d\Sigma y^2$$

Therefore $38 = 7c + 89d$ (i)

$$495 = 89c + 1147d \quad \text{(ii)}$$

Multiply (i) by 89 $3382 = 623c + 7921d$ (iii)

Multiply (ii) by 7 $3465 = 623c + 8029d$ (iv)

(iv) − (iii) $83 = 108d$

$$d = \tfrac{83}{108} = 0.7685\ldots$$

Substituting for
d in (i) $38 = 7c + 63.39\ldots$

$$7c = 30.39\ldots$$

$$c = -4.342\ldots$$

Taking c and d to 3 SF, we have

$$x = -4.34 + 0.769y$$

We now plot the scatter diagram. To draw each line we need to work out at least three points on the line.

Now we know that both lines pass through $(\bar{x}, \bar{y})$.

We have $\bar{x} = \dfrac{\Sigma x}{n} = \dfrac{38}{7} = 5.4$ (1 d.p.)

$$\bar{y} = \dfrac{\Sigma y}{n} = \dfrac{89}{7} = 12.7 \quad \text{(1 d.p.)}$$

On the scatter diagram, plot $M(5.4, 12.7)$.

For the line $y = 11.7 + 0.186x$, choose two other x values, say $x = 0$ and $x = 9$.

When $x = 0$, $y = 11.7$

when $x = 9$, $y = 11.7 + 0.186(9) = 13.4$ (1 d.p.)

So we plot (0, 11.7) and (9, 13.4).

For the line $x = -4.34 + 0.769y$:

when $x = 0$ $0 = -4.34 + 0.769y,$

$$0.769y = 4.34$$

$$y = \frac{4.34}{0.769}$$

$$= 5.6 \quad (1 \text{ d.p.})$$

when $x = 9$ $9 = -4.34 + 0.769y,$

$$0.769y = 13.34$$

$$y = \frac{13.34}{0.769}$$

$$= 17.3 \quad (1 \text{ d.p.})$$

So we plot $(0, 5.6)$ and $(9, 17.3)$.

Scatter diagram showing both regression lines

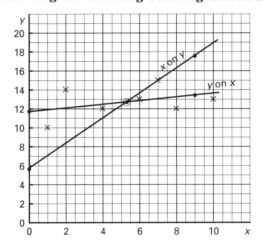

USING A CALCULATOR IN LR MODE

LR (or linear regression) mode enables us to obtain the values of $\bar{x}, \bar{y}$, Σx, Σx^2, Σxy, Σy, Σy^2, directly. We also have access, *without doing any calculations,* to a and b, which are denoted on the calculator by A and B.

The following instructions illustrate the procedures for two particular types of Casio calculators, the *fx* 85/100/115 series and the *fx* 7000 GA graphics calculator.

	Casio 85/100/115	**Casio Graphics 7000 GA**
Set LR mode	MODE 2	MODE ÷
Clear memories	SHIFT KAC	SHIFT SCI EXE
Input data	1 $x_D y_D$ 10 DATA	1 SHIFT , 10 DT
	2 $x_D y_D$ 14 DATA	2 SHIFT , 14 DT
	4 $x_D y_D$ 12 DATA	4 SHIFT , 12 DT
	6 $x_D y_D$ 13 DATA	6 SHIFT , 13 DT
	7 $x_D y_D$ 15 DATA	7 SHIFT , 15 DT
	8 $x_D y_D$ 12 DATA	8 SHIFT , 12 DT
	10 $x_D y_D$ 13 DATA	10 SHIFT , 13 DT

You now have access to:

		Casio 85/100/115	Casio Graphics 7000 GA
A	= 11.704 035 87	SHIFT 7	SHIFT 7 EXE
B	= 0.186 098 654	SHIFT 8	SHIFT 8 EXE
Σx^2	= 270	K_{out} 1	ALPHA 1 EXE
Σx	= 38	K_{out} 2	ALPHA 2 EXE
n	= 7	K_{out} 3	ALPHA 3 EXE
Σy^2	= 1147	K_{out} 4	ALPHA 4 EXE
Σy	= 89	K_{out} 5	ALPHA 5 EXE
Σxy	= 495	K_{out} 6	ALPHA 6 EXE
$\bar{x}$	= 5.428 571 429	SHIFT 1	SHIFT 1 EXE
s_x^2	= 9.102 040 816	SHIFT 2 x^2	SHIFT 2 x^2 EXE
$\bar{y}$	= 12.714 285 71	SHIFT 4	SHIFT 4 EXE
s_y^2	= 2.204 081 634	SHIFT 5 x^2	SHIFT 5 x^2 EXE
To clear LR mode		MODE 0	MODE +

We can see straight away that the equation of the regression line of y on x $(y = A + Bx)$ is

$$y = 11.7 + 0.186x \quad \text{(as before)}.$$

To estimate a value of *y*, given a value of *x*

To estimate y when $x = 9$, say, using $y = A + Bx$, we have $y = A + 9B$, so press

| SHIFT | 7 | + | 9 | × | SHIFT | 8 | = | (or | EXE |)

and this gives $13.378\ldots$

NOTE: this estimated value of y is sometimes written $\widehat{y}$.

Alternatively, on the graphics calculator 7000 GA it is possible to obtain the estimated y value, written $\widehat{y}$, when $x = 9$, as follows:

| 9 | SHIFT | ÷ | EXE |

Using the calculator to find the least squares regression line *x* on *y*

We carry out the procedure as before, but enter the data the other way round, putting for example

| 10 | $x_D y_D$ | 1 | DATA | or | 10 | SHIFT | , | 1 | DT |

| 14 | $x_D y_D$ | 2 | DATA | | 14 | SHIFT | , | 2 | DT | and so on.

| SHIFT | 7 | (| EXE |) gives | A | $= -4.3425\ldots$

| SHIFT | 8 | (| EXE |) gives | B | $= 0.768\,51\ldots$

The regression line x on y has equation

$$x = A + By$$

Therefore $x = -4.34 + 0.769y$ as before.

Example 12.4 For a given set of data it is known that $\bar{x} = 10$ and $\bar{y} = 4$. The gradient of the regression line y on x is 0.6.

Find the equation of this regression line and estimate y when $x = 12$.

Solution 12.4 Let the equation of the regression line of y on x be $y = a + bx$.

Since the gradient is 0.6, we know that $b = 0.6$.

Therefore $y = a + 0.6x$

We know that $(\bar{x}, \bar{y})$ lies on this line,

so $4 = a + 0.6(10)$

$$4 = a + 6$$

$$a = -2.$$

The equation of the regression line of y on x is $y = -2 + 0.6x$.

Now when $x = 12$

$$y = -2 + 0.6(12)$$
$$= 5.2$$

Therefore we estimate that $y = 5.2$ when $x = 12$.

Example 12.5   Find the equation of the regression line of x on y if it goes through $(1, 4)$ and has gradient 2.

Solution 12.5   Let the equation of the regression line x on y be $x = c + dy$.

Since $(1, 4)$ lies on the line,

$$1 = c + 4d \quad \text{(i)}$$

To find the gradient, we must re-arrange the equation, where

$$y = \frac{x - c}{d} \quad \text{or} \quad y = \frac{1}{d}x - \frac{c}{d}$$

Gradient $= \dfrac{1}{d}$,   so $\dfrac{1}{d} = 2$

$$d = 0.5$$

Substituting in (i) $1 = c + 4(0.5)$

$$c = -1$$

The equation of the regression line x on y is $x = -1 + 0.5y$.

Exercise 12b

1. For each of the following sets of data, use the normal equations to find the equation of the least squares regression line of (i) y on x, (ii) x on y.

Check using a calculator in LR mode, if possible. Show the data and the regression lines on a scatter diagram.

(a) Use these 11 pairs of data:

x	3	7	9	11	14	14	15	21	22	23	26
y	5	12	5	12	10	17	23	16	10	20	25

(b) Use these 13 pairs of data:

x	1	5	5	5	6	7.5	7.5
y	85	82	85	89	78	66	77

x	7.5	10	11	12.5	14	14.5
y	81	70	74	65	69	63

In (c), (d) and (e) use the 10 pairs of data:

(c)

x	0.6	1	2	2.5	2.8
y	5	10	15	10	2.5

x	3.6	4	4	4	5
y	7.5	2.5	5	15	10

(d)

x	1	8	15	18	23	28	33	39	45	45
y	3	14	8	20	19	17	36	26	14	28

(e)

x	3	4	5	6	7	8	9	10	11	12
y	9	11	13	15	17	19	21	23	25	27

2. From a set of pairs of observations of the variables x and y, it is found that the regression line of y on x passes through the point $(0, 1.8)$. If the means of the x and y values are 5.0 and 8.3 respectively, find the equation of the regression line of y on x in the form $y = a + bx$. (L)

3. For a set of 20 pairs of observations of the variables x and y, it is known that $\Sigma x = 250$, $\Sigma y = 140$, and that the regression line of y on x passes through $(15, 10)$. Find the equation of the regression line of y on x and use it to estimate y when $x = 10$.

4. The gradient of the regression line x on y is -0.2 and the line passes through $(0, 3)$. If the equation of the line is $x = c + dy$, find the values of c and d and sketch the line on a diagram.

5. For a given set of data

$\Sigma x = 15$, $\Sigma x^2 = 55$, $\Sigma y = 43$, $\Sigma y^2 = 397$,

$\Sigma xy = 145$, $n = 5$

Find the equations of the regression lines of y on x, and of x on y.

6. Following a leak of radioactivity from a nuclear power station an index of exposure to radioactivity was calculated for each of 7 geographical areas close to the power station. In the subsequent 5 years the incidence of death due to cancer (measured in deaths per 100 000 person-years) was recorded. The data were as follows:

Area	Index (x)	Deaths (y)
1	7.6	62
2	23.2	75
3	3.2	51
4	16.6	72
5	5.2	39
6	6.8	43
7	5.0	55

$[\Sigma x = 67.6$, $\Sigma x^2 = 980.08$, $\Sigma y = 397$, $\Sigma y^2 = 23\,649$, $\Sigma xy = 4339.8.]$

(i) Find the estimated regression line of Y on X.

(ii) In another geographical area close to the power station the index of exposure was 6.0. Use the estimated regression line to predict the incidence, in this area, of death

due to cancer (in deaths per 100 000 person-years).

(iii) Estimate the incidence of death due to cancer (in deaths per 100 000 person-years) there would have been if there had been no leak from the power station (i.e. if the index of exposure to radioactivity were zero). (C)

7. Explain, with the aid of diagrams, the difference in the definitions of the least squares regression line of Y on X and the least squares regression line of X on Y. The following table shows the marks (x) obtained in a Christmas examination and the marks (y) obtained in the following summer examination by a group of nine students.

Student	Christmas (x)	Summer (y)
A	57	66
B	35	51
C	56	63
D	57	34
E	66	47
F	79	70
G	81	84
H	84	84
I	52	53

It is given that $\Sigma x = 567$, $\Sigma y = 552$, $\Sigma xy = 36\,261$, $\Sigma x^2 = 37\,777$, $\Sigma y^2 = 36\,112$.

(i) Find the equation of the estimated least squares regression line of Y on X.

(ii) A tenth student obtained a mark of 70 in the Christmas examination but was absent from the summer examination. Estimate the mark that this student would have obtained in the summer examination.

(iii) An eleventh student took only the summer examination and obtained a mark of 55. Estimate the mark that this student would have obtained in the Christmas examination. (C)

8. For a set of 12 observations, $\Sigma x = 43.2$ and $\Sigma y = 56.4$. The regression line y on x goes through $(1.6, 2.5)$ and the regression line x on y goes through $(4, 6.2)$. Find the equations of the two lines.

9. For a set of 10 observations, $\bar{x} = 3.8$, $\bar{y} = 2$. The regression line y on x goes through $(2, 4)$ and the regression line x on y goes through $(1, 3.7)$. Find the equations of the two lines.

COVARIANCE, s_{xy}

For n pairs of data (x_1, y_1), $(x_2, y_2), \ldots, (x_n, y_n)$ the covariance, s_{xy} is given by

$$s_{xy} = \frac{1}{n}\Sigma(x - \bar{x})(y - \bar{y})$$

If x and y are independent, then $s_{xy} = 0$.

NOTE: the formula for covariance is simply an extension of the formula for variance, where

$$s_{xx} = \frac{1}{n}\Sigma(x - \bar{x})(x - \bar{x}) = s_x{}^2$$

$$s_{yy} = \frac{1}{n}\Sigma(y - \bar{y})(y - \bar{y}) = s_y{}^2$$

Alternative forms of the formulae

We know already that

$$s_x{}^2 = \frac{\Sigma x^2}{n} - \bar{x}^2 \quad \text{and} \quad s_y{}^2 = \frac{\Sigma y^2}{n} - \bar{y}^2$$

s_{xy} can also be written in a similar format:

$$s_{xy} = \frac{1}{n}\Sigma(x - \bar{x})(y - \bar{y})$$

$$= \frac{\Sigma xy}{n} - \bar{x}\frac{\Sigma y}{n} - \bar{y}\frac{\Sigma x}{n} + \frac{n\bar{x}\bar{y}}{n}$$

$$= \frac{\Sigma xy}{n} - \bar{x}\bar{y} - \bar{y}\bar{x} + \bar{x}\bar{y}$$

$$= \frac{\Sigma xy}{n} - \bar{x}\bar{y}$$

$$s_{xy} = \frac{\Sigma xy}{n} - \bar{x}\bar{y}$$

The three formulae to remember are:

Covariance of (x, y)	Variance of x	Variance of y
$s_{xy} = \dfrac{\Sigma xy}{n} - \bar{x}\bar{y}$	$s_x{}^2 = \dfrac{\Sigma x^2}{n} - \bar{x}^2$	$s_y{}^2 = \dfrac{\Sigma y^2}{n} - \bar{y}^2$

NOTE: in some texts and formulae booklets you might see the notation

$$S_{xy} = \Sigma(x - \bar{x})(y - \bar{y})$$

The notation we used is

$$s_{xy} = \frac{1}{n} \Sigma(x - \bar{x})(y - \bar{y}) = \frac{S_{xy}}{n}$$

so that $S_{xy} = ns_{xy}$

Similarly $S_{xx} = \Sigma x^2 - n\bar{x}^2 = ns_x^2$

$$S_{yy} = \Sigma y^2 - n\bar{y}^2 = ns_y^2$$

The connection between 'big' S in your formulae booklet and 'little' s in this textbook is

$$S_{xy} = ns_{xy}$$
$$S_{xx} = ns_x^2$$
$$S_{yy} = ns_y^2$$

The 'big' S formulae are useful in calculations where the factor of n cancels, but it should be remembered that they are *not* the formulae for covariance and variance.

REGRESSION COEFFICIENTS

For the least squares regression line y on x, $y = a + bx$

The normal equations are $\Sigma y = na + b\Sigma x$ (i)

$$\Sigma xy = a\Sigma x + b\Sigma x^2 \qquad \text{(ii)}$$

Multiplying (i) by Σx $\Sigma x\Sigma y = na\Sigma x + b(\Sigma x)^2$ (iii)

Multiplying (ii) by n $n\Sigma xy = na\Sigma x + nb\Sigma x^2$ (iv)

(iii) − (iv) $n\Sigma xy - \Sigma x\Sigma y = bn\Sigma x^2 - b(\Sigma x)^2$

$$= b(n\Sigma x^2 - (\Sigma x)^2)$$

Therefore $b = \dfrac{n\Sigma xy - \Sigma x\Sigma y}{n\Sigma x^2 - (\Sigma x)^2}$

Now divide numerator and denominator by n^2

$$b = \frac{\dfrac{\Sigma xy}{n} - \left(\dfrac{\Sigma x}{n}\right)\left(\dfrac{\Sigma y}{n}\right)}{\dfrac{\Sigma x^2}{n} - \left(\dfrac{\Sigma x}{n}\right)^2}$$

$$= \frac{s_{xy}}{s_x^2}$$

b is known as the **coefficient of regression of y on x,** where

$$b = \frac{s_{xy}}{s_x^2}$$

Similarly, for the least squares regression line x on y, $x = c + dy$, it can be shown that

$$d = \frac{s_{xy}}{s_y{}^2} \quad \text{where } d \text{ is the } \textbf{coefficient of regression of } \boldsymbol{x} \textbf{ on } \boldsymbol{y}$$

CALCULATING THE EQUATIONS OF LEAST SQUARES REGRESSION LINES

(2) Using regression coefficients

The equation of the least squares regression line of y on x, $y = a + bx$, has gradient b.

We also know that it passes through $(\bar{x}, \bar{y})$, so we can write the equation in the form

$$y - \bar{y} = b(x - \bar{x}) \quad \text{where} \quad b = \frac{s_{xy}}{s_x{}^2}$$

The equation of the least squares regression line y on x is

$$y - \bar{y} = \frac{s_{xy}}{s_x{}^2}(x - \bar{x})$$

Similarly we can write the equation of the least squares regression line of x on y, $x = c + dy$, in the form

$$x - \bar{x} = d(y - \bar{y}) \quad \text{where} \quad d = \frac{s_{xy}}{s_y{}^2}$$

The equation of the regression line x on y is

$$x - \bar{x} = \frac{s_{xy}}{s_y{}^2}(y - \bar{y})$$

NOTE: using 'big' S notation, $b = \dfrac{\frac{1}{n}S_{xy}}{\frac{1}{n}S_{xx}} = \dfrac{S_{xy}}{S_{xx}}$

and $\qquad\qquad\qquad\qquad d = \dfrac{\frac{1}{n}S_{xy}}{\frac{1}{n}S_{yy}} = \dfrac{S_{xy}}{S_{yy}}$

The equations of the regression lines are:

y on x: $\qquad\qquad\qquad y - \bar{y} = \dfrac{S_{xy}}{S_{xx}}(x - \bar{x})$

x on y: $\qquad\qquad\qquad x - \bar{x} = \dfrac{S_{xy}}{S_{yy}}(y - \bar{y})$

Example 12.6   For the data used in Example 12.3, use the regression coefficient method to find the equations of the two regression lines.

x	1	2	4	6	7	8	10
y	10	14	12	13	15	12	13

Solution 12.6   From the table in Example 12.3 we see that $n = 7$, $\Sigma x = 38$, $\Sigma y = 89$, $\Sigma x^2 = 270$, $\Sigma y^2 = 1147$, $\Sigma xy = 495$.

So $\quad \bar{x} = \frac{38}{7} = 5.4$ (1 d.p.) $\qquad \bar{y} = \frac{89}{7} = 12.7$ (1 d.p.)

Now $\qquad s_{xy} = \dfrac{\Sigma xy}{n} - \bar{x}\bar{y} = \dfrac{495}{7} - \left(\dfrac{38}{7}\right)\left(\dfrac{89}{7}\right) = 1.694$

$\qquad\qquad s_x{}^2 = \dfrac{\Sigma x^2}{n} - \bar{x}^2 = \dfrac{270}{7} - \left(\dfrac{38}{7}\right)^2 = 9.102$

$\qquad\qquad s_y{}^2 = \dfrac{\Sigma y^2}{n} - \bar{y}^2 = \dfrac{1147}{7} - \left(\dfrac{89}{7}\right)^2 = 2.204$

(a) Equation of least squares regression line y on x

$$y - \bar{y} = \frac{s_{xy}}{s_x{}^2}(x - \bar{x})$$

so $\qquad\qquad y - \dfrac{89}{7} = \dfrac{1.694}{9.102}\left(x - \dfrac{38}{7}\right)$

Rearranging, $\qquad\qquad \underline{y = 11.7 + 0.186x}$

(b) Equation of least squares regression line x on y

$$x - \bar{x} = \frac{s_{xy}}{s_y{}^2}(y - \bar{y})$$

so $\qquad\qquad x - \dfrac{38}{7} = \dfrac{1.694}{2.204}\left(y - \dfrac{89}{7}\right)$

Rearranging, $\qquad\qquad \underline{x = -4.34 + 0.769y}$

These agree exactly with the equations obtained by the 'normal equations' method.

Example 12.7   For twelve consecutive months a factory manager recorded the number of items produced by the factory and the total cost of their production. The following table summarises the manager's data.

Number of items (x) thousands	18	36	45	22	69	72	13	33	59	79	10	53
Production cost (y) £1000	37	54	63	42	84	91	33	49	79	98	32	71

(a) Draw a scatter diagram for the data.

(b) Give a reason to support the use of the regression line

$$(y - \bar{y}) = b(x - \bar{x})$$

as a suitable model for the data.

(c) Giving the values of $\bar{x}$, $\bar{y}$ and b to 3 decimal places, obtain the regression equation for y on x in the above form.

(You may use $\Sigma x^2 = 27\,963$, $\Sigma xy = 37\,249$.)

(d) Rewrite the equation in the form

$$y = a + bx$$

giving a to 3 significant figures.

(e) Give a practical interpretation of the values of a and b.

(f) The selling price of each item produced is £1.60. Find the level of output at which total income and estimated total costs are equal. Give a brief interpretation of this value. (L)

Solution 12.7 (a) **Scatter diagram to show the manager's data over twelve consecutive months**

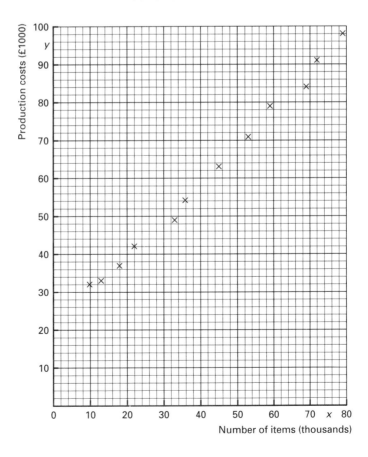

(**b**) The scatter diagram appears to indicate a linear relationship between x and y. It is sensible to consider x as the independent variable and so the regression line y on x, $y - \bar{y} = b(x - \bar{x})$, is a suitable model for the data.

(**c**)
$$\bar{x} = \frac{\Sigma x}{n} = \frac{509}{12} = 42.417 \quad (3 \text{ d.p.})$$

$$\bar{y} = \frac{\Sigma y}{n} = \frac{733}{12} = 61.083 \quad (3 \text{ d.p.})$$

$$s_{xy} = \frac{\Sigma xy}{n} - \bar{x}\,\bar{y}$$

$$= \frac{37\,249}{12} - \left(\frac{509}{12}\right)\left(\frac{733}{12}\right)$$

$$= 513.13\ldots$$

$$s_x{}^2 = \frac{\Sigma x^2}{n} - \bar{x}^2$$

$$= \frac{27\,963}{12} - \left(\frac{509}{12}\right)^2$$

$$= 531.07\ldots$$

$$b = \frac{s_{xy}}{s_x{}^2}$$

$$= 0.966 \quad (3 \text{ d.p.})$$

Equation of regression line y on x:

$$y - \bar{y} = b(x - \bar{x})$$

$$y - 61.083 = 0.966(x - 42.417)$$

(**d**)
$$y - 61.083 = 0.966x - 40.9748\ldots$$

$$y = 0.966x + 20.1$$

$$y = 20.1 + 0.966x$$

so
$$\underline{a = 20.1 \quad (3 \text{ SF}), \qquad b = 0.966 \quad (3 \text{ d.p.})}$$

(**e**) Consider $a \approx 20$ and $b \approx 1$, so $y \approx 20 + x$. This means that the initial costs are £20 000 and since the gradient is approximately 1, costs increase by £1000 for every 1000 items produced.

(**f**) If the selling price for each item is £1.60, the income y, where y is in thousands of pounds, is given by

$$y = 1.6x \quad (\text{where } x \text{ is in thousands})$$

If total costs = total income

$$20.1 + 0.966x = 1.6x$$

$$x = 31.7 \quad (3 \text{ SF})$$

So when the number of items is 31.7 thousand

$$\text{income} = 1.6 \times 31.7$$
$$= 50.7 \ (\text{£}1000)$$
$$\text{costs} = 20.1 + 0.966 \ (31.7)$$
$$= 50.7 \ (\text{£}1000)$$

For income to exceed costs, the least number of items produced should be 32 000 (to nearest thousand).

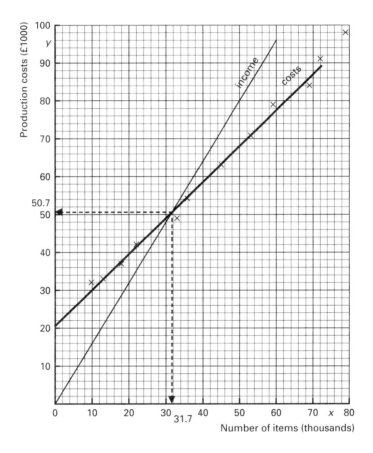

Example 12.8 An electric fire was switched on in a cold room and the temperature of the room was noted at five-minute intervals.

Time, minutes, from switching on fire, x	0	5	10	15	20	25	30	35	40
Temperature, °C, y	0.4	1.5	3.4	5.5	7.7	9.7	11.7	13.5	15.4

You may assume that

$$\Sigma x = 180 \quad \Sigma y = 68.8 \quad \Sigma xy = 1960 \quad \Sigma x^2 = 5100$$

(**a**) Plot the data on a scatter diagram.

(**b**) Calculate the regression line $y = a + bx$ and draw it on your scatter diagram.

(**c**) Predict the temperature 60 minutes from switching on the fire. Why should this prediction be treated with caution?

(**d**) Starting from the equation of the regression line $y = a + bx$, derive the equation of the regression line of

(*i*) y on t where y is temperature in °C (as above) and t is time in hours.

(*ii*) z on x where z is temperature in °K and x is time in minutes (as above).

(A temperature in °C is converted to °K by adding 273, e.g. $10\,°C \rightarrow 283\,°K$)

(**e**) Explain why, in (**b**), the line $y = a + bx$ was calculated rather than $x = a' + b'y$. If, instead of the temperature being measured at five-minute intervals, the time for the room to reach predetermined temperatures (e.g. 1, 4, 7, 10, 13 °C) had been observed, what would the appropriate calculation have been? Explain your answer.   (AEB 1992)

Solution 12.8   Part (**a**) is incorporated in the answer to part (**b**).

(**b**) We could calculate the equation of the regression line using normal equations or the regression coefficient. We show both ways:

(*i*) Using normal equations for the regression line y on x.
Let $y = a + bx$.

$$\Sigma y = na + b\Sigma x \quad \text{gives} \quad 68.8 = 9a + 180b \quad \text{(i)}$$

$$\Sigma xy = a\Sigma x + b\Sigma x^2 \quad \text{gives} \quad 1960 = 180a + 5100b \quad \text{(ii)}$$

Multiply (i) by 20 $1376 = 180a + 3600b$ (iii)

(ii) − (iii) $584 = 1500b$

$$b = 0.389\,33\ldots$$

Substitute in (i) $68.8 = 9a + 70.08$

$$9a = -1.28$$

$$a = -0.1422\ldots$$

So the regression line is $\underline{y = -0.142 + 0.389x}$.

(*ii*) Alternatively, using the regression coefficient $b = \dfrac{s_{xy}}{s_x{}^2}$:

$$\bar{x} = \frac{\Sigma x}{n} = = \frac{180}{9} = 20 \qquad\qquad \bar{y} = \frac{\Sigma y}{n} = = \frac{68.8}{9} = 7.644\ldots$$

$$s_{xy} = \frac{\Sigma xy}{n} - \bar{x}\bar{y} \qquad\qquad s_x{}^2 = \frac{\Sigma x^2}{n} - \bar{x}^2$$

$$= \frac{1960}{9} - (20)(7.644\ldots) \qquad\qquad = \frac{5100}{9} - (20)^2$$

$$= 64.88\ldots \qquad\qquad = 166.66\ldots$$

Therefore

$$b = \frac{s_{xy}}{s_x^{\,2}}$$

$$= \frac{64.88...}{166.66...}$$

$$= 0.3893\ldots$$

so

$$y - \bar{y} = b(x - \bar{x})$$

$$y - 7.644 = 0.3893(x - 20)$$

$$\underline{y = -0.142 + 0.389x} \quad \text{as before.}$$

To plot this line we need to find at least three points on it.

Now we know that the line goes through $(\bar{x}, \bar{y})$

where $\quad \bar{x} = \dfrac{\Sigma x}{n} = \dfrac{180}{9} = 20, \quad \bar{y} = \dfrac{\Sigma y}{n} = \dfrac{68.8}{9} = 7.64\ldots$

i.e. it goes through (20, 7.64). We plot this on the scatter diagram.

We now find two other points, say when $x = 0$ and when $x = 25$.

When $\qquad x = 0, \quad y = -0.142 + 0 = -0.142;$

when $\qquad x = 25, \quad y = -0.142 + 0.389(25) = 9.59,$

so we plot $(0, -0.142)$ and $(25, 9.59)$ on the scatter diagram and draw a line through these three points.

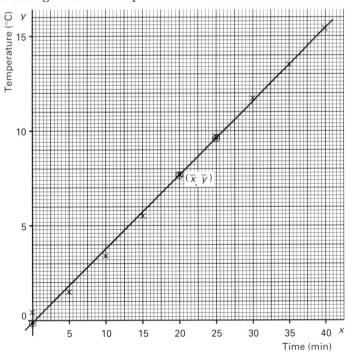

(**c**) Now $\qquad\qquad y = -0.142 + 0.389x$

Therefore when $\qquad x = 60, \quad y = -0.142 + 0.389(60) = 23.2\ldots$

From the regression line we might predict that the temperature will be 23.2 °C sixty minutes from switching on the fire. However the time at 60 minutes is *outside* the range of the data and the resulting temperature is very high. It is obvious that the temperature could not increase indefinitely with time. We must keep within the range of the data.

(**d**) (*i*) $\qquad\qquad\qquad y = -0.142 + 0.389x$

Therefore if t is in hours, $\qquad t = \dfrac{x}{60} \quad\text{or}\quad x = 60t$

Therefore $\qquad\qquad\qquad \underline{y = -0.142 + 23.36t}$

$\qquad$(*ii*) $\qquad\qquad\qquad y = -0.142 + 0.389x$

If z is the temperature in °K, $\quad z = 273 + y \quad\text{or}\quad y = z - 273.$

Therefore $\qquad\qquad z - 273 = -0.142 + 0.389x$

$$\underline{z = 272.86 + 0.389x}$$

(**e**) Since the temperature was noted at five-minute intervals it is obvious that the time has been controlled, so that x is the 'explanatory' or independent variable and y is the 'response' or dependent variable. In this case we would use the regression line y on x to *estimate y, given x.*

If on the other hand the temperature had been the independent variable and the time had been the dependent variable, then we would have used the regression line x on y where $x = a' + b'y$ in order to *estimate x, given y.*

The normal equations needed are

$$\Sigma x = na' + b'\Sigma y$$

$$\Sigma xy = a'\Sigma y + b'\Sigma y^2$$

or alternatively, using the regression coefficient $b' = \dfrac{s_{xy}}{s_y{}^2}$

$$x - \bar{x} = \frac{s_{xy}}{s_y{}^2}(y - \bar{y})$$

Calculator note

If you are using a calculator in LR mode, the procedure is as follows:

	Casio 85/100/115	Casio Graphics 7000 GA
Set LR mode	MODE 2	MODE ÷
Clear memories	SHIFT KAC	SHIFT SCI EXE
Input data	0 $x_D y_D$ 0.4 DATA	0 SHIFT , 0.4 DT
	5 $x_D y_D$ 1.5 DATA	5 SHIFT , 1.5 DT
	⋮ ⋮ ⋮ ⋮	⋮ ⋮ ⋮ ⋮ ⋮
	40 $x_D y_D$ 15.4 DATA	40 SHIFT , 15.4 DT

Output:

A	= $-0.1422\ldots$	SHIFT 7	SHIFT 7 EXE
B	= $0.3893\ldots$	SHIFT 8	SHIFT 8 EXE

If the regression line y on x is $y = A + Bx$, then $\underline{y = -0.142 + 0.389x}$

To work out the value of y when $x = 25$ say, we use $y = A + 25B$

$y = 9.5911\ldots$	SHIFT 7 + 25 ×	SHIFT 7 + 25 ×
	SHIFT 8 =	SHIFT 8 EXE
		or 25 SHIFT ÷ EXE

We can also check the information given in the question and find $\bar{x}$ and $\bar{y}$ directly, as follows:

Σx	= 180	K$_{out}$ 2	ALPHA 2 EXE
Σy	= 68.8	K$_{out}$ 5	ALPHA 5 EXE
Σxy	= 1960	K$_{out}$ 6	ALPHA 6 EXE
Σx^2	= 5100	K$_{out}$ 1	ALPHA 1 EXE
$\bar{x}$	= 20	SHIFT 1	SHIFT 1 EXE
$\bar{y}$	= $7.644\ldots$	SHIFT 4	SHIFT 4 EXE

To clear LR mode	MODE 0	MODE +

Exercise 12c

In the following questions, check your answers using your calculator in LR mode if possible.

1. Calculate (i) the covariance, (ii) the equations of the two least squares regression lines for the following data. Plot the scatter diagrams and draw in the regression lines.

(a)

x	1	2	3	4	4	5	6	8	8	9
y	6	5	7	4	5	4.8	3	1	6	4.6

(b)

x	20	20.2	21.4	21.6	22.8	23.4	24.6
y	5	6	4.9	12	8	13.5	12.5

(c)

x	2	6.5	6.5	11.5	14	16.5
y	5	7.5	4.5	10	12.5	15.5

(d)

x	11	12	12	14	15	16	18	19
y	65	63	64	65	63	62	60	61

2. Calculate the equation of the regression line of y on x for the following distribution:

x	25	30	35	40	45	50
y	78	70	65	58	48	42

Is it possible to calculate from the equation you have just found   (a) an estimate for the value of x when $y = 54$?   (b) an estimate for the value of y when $x = 37$?   In each case, if the answer is 'Yes', calculate the estimate. If the answer is 'No', say why not.

3. The following data show, in convenient units, the yield (y) of a chemical reaction run at various different temperatures (x):

Temperature (x)	Yield (y)
110	2.1
120	4.3
130	3.1
140	3.4
150	2.9
160	5.5
170	3.3

(a) Plot the data. Comment on whether it appears that the usual simple linear regression model is appropriate.
(b) Assuming that such a model is appropriate, estimate the regression line of yield on temperature.
(c) Plot your estimated line on your graph, and indicate clearly on your graph the

distances, the sum of whose squares is minimised by the linear regression procedure.   (MEI)

4. To test the effect of a new drug twelve patients were examined before the drug was administered and given an initial score (I) depending on the severity of various symptoms. After taking the drug they were examined again and given a final score (F). A decrease in score represented an improvement. The scores for the twelve patients are given in the table below.

Patient	Score	
	Initial (I)	Final (F)
1	61	49
2	23	12
3	8	3
4	14	4
5	42	28
6	34	27
7	32	20
8	31	20
9	41	34
10	25	15
11	20	16
12	50	40

Calculate the equation of the line of regression of F on I.
On the average what improvement would you expect for a patient whose initial score was 30?   (MEI)

5. A straight line regression equation is fitted by the least squares method to the n points (x_r, y_r), $r = 1, 2, \ldots, n$. For the regression equation $y = a + bx$, show in a sketch the distances whose sum of squares is minimised, and mark clearly which axis records the dependent variable and which axis records the independent (controlled) variable.
In a chemical reaction it is known that the amount, A grams, of a certain compound produced is a linear function of the temperature $T°$C. Eight trial runs of this reaction are performed, two at each of four different temperatures. The observed values of A are subject to error. The results are shown in the table.

T	10	15	20	25
A	10	15	18	16
	12	12	16	20

Draw a scatter diagram for these data.

Calculate $\bar{A}$ and $\bar{T}$.

Obtain the equation of the regression line of A on T giving the coefficients to 2 decimal places.

Draw this line on your scatter diagram.

Use the regression equation to obtain an estimate of the mean value of A when $T = 20$, and explain why this estimate is preferable to averaging the two observed values of A when $T = 20$.

Estimate the mean increase in A for a one degree increase in temperature.

State any reservations you would have about estimating the mean value of A when $T = 0$.

(L)

6. In an attempt to increase the yield (kg/h) of an industrial process a technician varies the percentage of a certain additive used, while keeping all other conditions as constant as possible. The results are shown below.

Yield, y	% additive, x
127.6	2.5
130.2	3.0
132.7	3.5
133.6	4.0
133.9	4.5
133.8	5.0
133.3	5.5
131.9	6.0

You may assume that $\Sigma x = 34$, $\Sigma y = 1057$, $\Sigma xy = 4504.55$, $\Sigma x^2 = 155$.

(a) Draw a scatter diagram of the data.

(b) Calculate the equation of the regression line of yield on percentage additive and draw it on the scatter diagram.

The technician now varies the temperature (°C) while keeping other conditions as constant as possible and obtains the following results.

Yield, y	Temperature, t
127.6	70
128.7	75
130.4	80
131.2	85
133.6	90

He calculates (correctly) that the regression line is $y = 107.1 + 0.29t$.

(c) Draw a scatter diagram of these data together with the regression line.

(d) The technician reports as follows, 'The regression coefficient of yield on percentage additive is larger than that of yield on temperature, hence the most effective way of

increasing the yield is to make the percentage additive as large as possible, within reason.'

Criticise the report and make your own recommendations on how to achieve the maximum yield. (AEB 1988)

7. In an experiment the temperature of a metal rod was raised from $300\,°\mathrm{K}$. The extensions E mm of the rod at selected temperatures $T\,°\mathrm{K}$ are shown in the table.

T	E
300	0
350	0.38
400	0.80
450	1.22
500	1.60
550	2.00
600	2.42
650	2.80
700	3.18

Draw a scatter diagram of the data and mark on your diagram the point representing the means of T and E.

Find the equation of the regression line of E on T and draw this line on your diagram.

Estimate the extension of the rod at $430\,°\mathrm{K}$.

(L)P

8. A small firm negotiates an annual pay rise with each of its twelve employees. In an attempt to simplify the process it is proposed that each employee should be given a score, x, based on his/her level of responsibility. The annual salary will be £$(a + bx)$ and the annual negotiations will only involve the values of a and b. The following table gives last year's salaries (which were generally accepted as fair) and the proposed scores.

Employee	x	Annual salary (£), y
A	10	5750
B	55	17300
C	46	14750
D	27	8200
E	17	6350
F	12	6150
G	85	18800
H	64	14850
I	36	9900
J	40	11000
K	30	9150
L	37	10400

(You may assume that $\Sigma x = 459$
$\Sigma x^2 = 22\,889$ $\Sigma y = 132\,600$ $\Sigma xy = 6\,094\,750$)

(a) Plot the data on a scatter diagram.
(b) Estimate values that could have been used for a and b last year by fitting the regression line $y = a + bx$ to the data. Draw the line on the scatter diagram.
(c) Comment on whether the suggested method is likely to prove reasonably satisfactory in practice.
(d) Without recalculating the regression line find the appropriate values of a and b if every employee were to receive a rise of (i) £500 a year, (ii) 8%, (iii) 4% plus £300 per year.
(e) Two employees, B and C, had to work away from home for a large part of the year. In the light of this additional information, suggest an improvement to the model.

(AEB 1990)

Units of output (x) (1000's)	Total cost (y) (£1000)
14	35
29	50
55	73
74	93
11	31
23	42
47	65
69	86
18	38
36	54
61	81
79	96

(Use $\Sigma x^2 = 28\,740$; $\Sigma xy = 38\,286$)
(a) Draw a scatter diagram of these data.
(b) Calculate the equation of the regression line of y on x and draw this line on your scatter diagram.
The selling price of each unit of output is £1.60.
(c) Use your graph to estimate the level of output at which the total income and total costs are equal.
(d) Give a brief interpretation of this value.

(AEB 1991)

9. In a certain heathland region there is a large number of alder trees where the ground is marshy but very few where the ground is dry. The number x of alder trees and the ground moisture content y are found in each of 10 equal areas (which have been chosen to cover the range of x in all such areas). The following is a summary of the results of the survey:

$$\Sigma x = 500, \quad \Sigma y = 300, \quad \Sigma x^2 = 27\,818,$$

$$\Sigma xy = 16\,837, \ \Sigma y^2 = 10\,462$$

Find the equation of the regression line of y on x.
Estimate the ground moisture content in an area equal to one of the chosen areas which contains 60 alder trees.   (O & C)

10. For the regression equation $y = a + bx$ the normal equations which give estimates of a and b are

$$\Sigma y = na + b\Sigma x$$

$$\Sigma xy = a\Sigma x + b\Sigma x^2$$

Show that the regression equation can be expressed in the form

$$(y - \bar{y}) = b(x - \bar{x})$$

State the implication this form has for plotting the regression line.
For a period of three years a company monitors the number of units of output produced per quarter and the total cost of producing the units. The table below shows their results.

11. The following data represent the lengths (x) and breadths (y) of 12 cuckoos' eggs measured in millimetres.

x	y
22.3	16.5
23.6	17.1
24.2	17.3
22.6	17.0
22.3	16.8
22.3	16.4
22.1	17.2
23.3	16.8
22.2	16.7
22.2	16.2
21.8	16.6
23.2	16.4

Draw a scatter diagram for the data.
Obtain the least squares regression lines of y on x and plot this on the scatter diagram.

(JMB)

THE PRODUCT-MOMENT CORRELATION COEFFICIENT, r

The product-moment correlation coefficient, r, is a numerical value which indicates the degree of scatter. The value of r lies between -1 and 1.

r is a very useful measure because it is independent of the units of scale of the variables. It is defined as follows:

The product-moment correlation coefficient, r, is given by

$$r = \frac{s_{xy}}{s_x s_y}$$

Diagrammatic representation of the value of *r*

The least squares regression lines of y on x and x on y are:

$$y - \bar{y} = \frac{s_{xy}}{s_x^2}(x - \bar{x}) \quad \text{or} \quad y - \bar{y} = \frac{s_{xy}}{s_x}\frac{(x - \bar{x})}{s_x} \qquad \text{(i)}$$

and $\quad x - \bar{x} = \dfrac{s_{xy}}{s_y^2}(y - \bar{y}) \quad \text{or} \quad x - \bar{x} = \dfrac{s_{xy}}{s_y}\dfrac{(y - \bar{y})}{s_y} \qquad \text{(ii)}$

We 'standardise' these equations as follows:

Dividing (i) by s_y $\qquad \dfrac{y - \bar{y}}{s_y} = \dfrac{s_{xy}}{s_x s_y}\dfrac{(x - \bar{x})}{s_x} \qquad \text{(iii)}$

Dividing (ii) by s_x $\qquad \dfrac{x - \bar{x}}{s_x} = \dfrac{s_{xy}}{s_x s_y}\dfrac{(y - \bar{y})}{s_y} \qquad \text{(iv)}$

Now if we take new axes X and Y, where X is graduated in units of s_x, and Y is graduated in units of s_y, and the origin is $(\bar{x}, \bar{y})$, then

$$Y = \frac{y - \bar{y}}{s_y} \quad \text{and} \quad X = \frac{x - \bar{x}}{s_x}$$

So the regression lines (iii) and (iv) can be written

$$Y = rX \quad \text{and} \quad X = rY, \quad \text{since} \quad r = \frac{s_{xy}}{s_x s_y}$$

With axes X and Y, these represent two lines that pass through the new origin.

For example, the diagram from Example 12.3 would be transformed from Diagram (a) to Diagram (b), with new origin (5.4, 12.7).

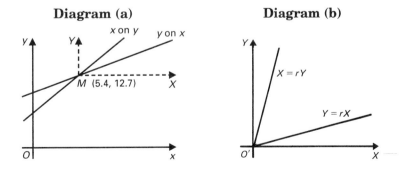

Using the data given in Example 12.3, we find that

$$r = \frac{s_{xy}}{s_x s_y} = \frac{1.694}{\sqrt{9.102}\sqrt{2.204}} = 0.38 \quad \text{(2 SF)}$$

Note that if $Y = rX$ makes an angle θ with the X axis, then
$r = \tan\theta$, so that $X = rY$ makes *the same angle* θ with the Y axis.

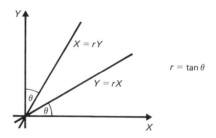

Some examples of regression lines together with the corresponding
lines $Y = rX$ and $X = rY$ are shown below.

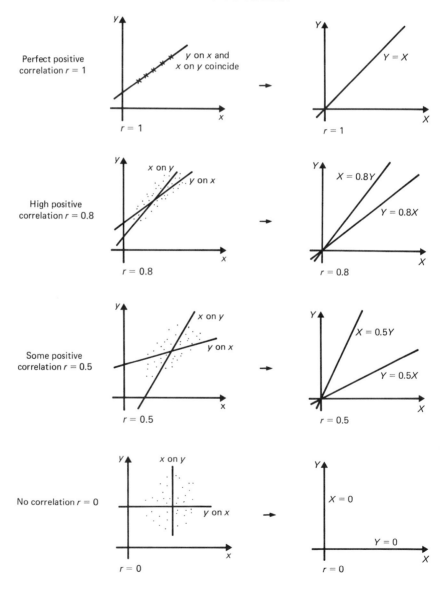

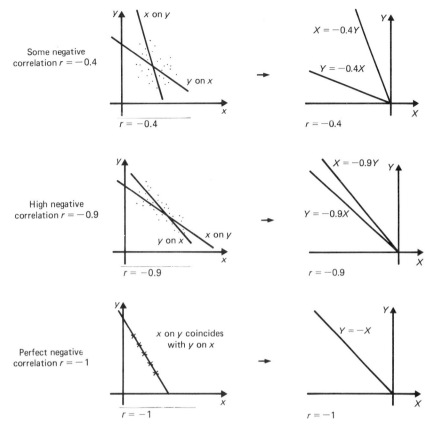

Remember that $-1 \leqslant r \leqslant 1$, and note that the more correlated the variables are, the closer are the two regression lines. In particular:

Linear correlation	Value of r	Regression lines y on x and x on y	
Perfect positive	1	The two lines are identical	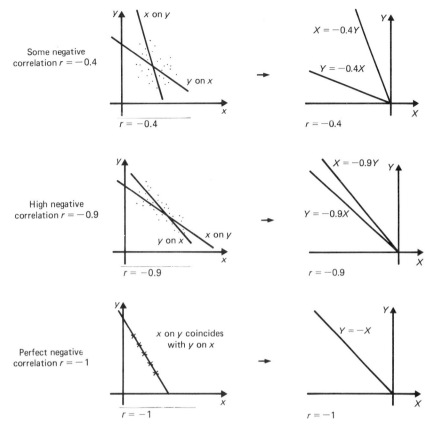
None	0	The two lines are at right angles	
Perfect negative	-1	The two lines are identical	

Example 12.9 The following table shows the marks of 10 candidates in Physics and Mathematics. Find the product-moment correlation coefficient and comment on your value.

Mark in Physics (x)	18	20	30	40	46	54	60	80	88	92
Mark in Mathematics (y)	42	54	60	54	62	68	80	66	80	100

Solution 12.9

x	y	x^2	y^2	xy
18	42	324	1764	756
20	54	400	2916	1080
30	60	900	3600	1800
40	54	1600	2916	2160
46	62	2116	3844	2852
54	68	2916	4624	3672
60	80	3600	6400	4800
80	66	6400	4356	5280
88	80	7744	6400	7040
92	100	8464	10 000	9200
$\Sigma x = 528$	$\Sigma y = 666$	$\Sigma x^2 = 34\,464$	$\Sigma y^2 = 46\,820$	$\Sigma xy = 38\,640$

There are 10 pairs of values, therefore $n = 10$.

$$\bar{x} = \frac{\Sigma x}{n} = \frac{528}{10} = 52.8, \qquad \bar{y} = \frac{\Sigma y}{n} = \frac{666}{10} = 66.6,$$

$$s_{xy} = \frac{\Sigma xy}{n} - \bar{x}\,\bar{y} = \frac{38\,640}{10} - (52.8)(66.6) = 347.52$$

$$s_x^{\,2} = \frac{\Sigma x^2}{n} - \bar{x}^2 = \frac{34\,464}{10} - (52.8)^2 = 658.56$$

$$s_y^{\,2} = \frac{\Sigma y^2}{n} - \bar{y}^2 = \frac{46\,820}{10} - 66.6^2 = 246.44$$

So $\qquad r = \frac{s_{xy}}{s_x s_y} = \frac{(347.52)}{\sqrt{658.56}\sqrt{246.44}} = 0.8626\ldots$

Therefore the product-moment correlation coefficient is 0.86 (2 d.p.), indicating a high positive correlation.

USING A CALCULATOR IN LR MODE

	Casio 85/100/115 series	Casio Graphics 7000 GA
Set LR mode	MODE 2	MODE ÷
Clear memories	SHIFT KAC	SHIFT SCI EXE
Input data	18 $x_D y_D$ 42 DATA	18 SHIFT , 42 DT
	20 $x_D y_D$ 54 DATA	20 SHIFT , 54 DT
	30 $x_D y_D$ 60 DATA	30 SHIFT , 60 DT
	40 $x_D y_D$ 54 DATA	40 SHIFT , 54 DT
	46 $x_D y_D$ 62 DATA	46 SHIFT , 62 DT
	54 $x_D y_D$ 68 DATA	54 SHIFT , 68 DT
	60 $x_D y_D$ 80 DATA	60 SHIFT , 80 DT
	80 $x_D y_D$ 66 DATA	80 SHIFT , 66 DT
	88 $x_D y_D$ 80 DATA	88 SHIFT , 80 DT
	92 $x_D y_D$ 100 DATA	92 SHIFT , 100 DT

Output

$\boxed{r} = \underline{0.8626\ldots}$	SHIFT 9	SHIFT 9 EXE
Clear LR mode	MODE 0	MODE +

NOTE: the value for r should be considered in conjunction with a scatter diagram.

By calculation, the equations of the regression lines are $y = 38.7 + 0.527x$ and $x = -41.1 + 1.41y$.

You can check these on your calculator.

For the data as keyed in above:

Casio 85/100/115		Casio Graphics 7000 GA
SHIFT 7	$A = 38.73\ldots$	SHIFT 7 EXE
SHIFT 8	$B = 0.527\ldots$	SHIFT 8 EXE

This gives the regression line y on x as $\underline{y = 38.7 + 0.527x}$

(Now you check the line x on y. Input the data (y, x).)

The lines have been drawn on the scatter diagram and, as expected since r is high, they are close together. The scatter diagram confirms some positive linear correlation.

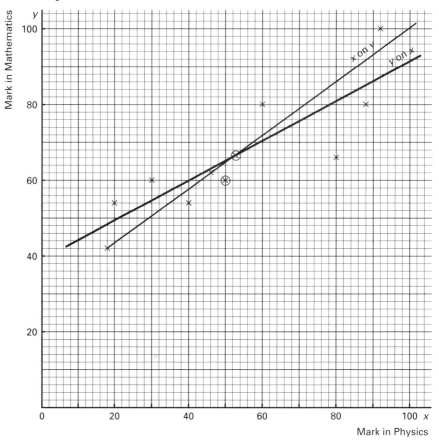

RELATIONSHIP BETWEEN REGRESSION COEFFICIENTS AND *r*

For the regression line y on x

$$y = a + bx \quad \text{where} \quad b = \frac{s_{xy}}{s_x{}^2}$$

and for the regression line x on y

$$x = c + dy \quad \text{where} \quad d = \frac{s_{xy}}{s_y{}^2}.$$

where b and d are the regression coefficients.

Now

$$bd = \frac{s_{xy}}{s_x{}^2} \frac{s_{xy}}{s_y{}^2}$$

$$= \left(\frac{s_{xy}}{s_x s_y}\right)^2$$

$$= r^2$$

Either b and d are both positive or b and d are both negative,

so

$$r^2 = bd \quad \text{and} \quad r = +\sqrt{bd} \quad \text{if } b, d \text{ are positive}$$

$$r = -\sqrt{bd} \quad \text{if } b, d \text{ are negative}$$

Example 12.10 For the data given in Example 12.3:

x	1	2	4	6	7	8	10
y	10	14	12	13	15	12	13

We found that the least squares regression line y on x is $y = 11.7 + 0.186x$ and the least squares regression line x on y is $x = -4.34 + 0.769y$. Using this information find r, the product-moment correlation coefficient.

Solution 12.10 Now

$$y = 11.7 + 0.186x, \quad \text{so} \quad b = 0.186$$

and

$$x = -4.34 + 0.769y, \quad \text{so} \quad d = 0.769$$

Now

$$r^2 = bd$$

and since both b, d are positive

$$r = +\sqrt{bd}$$

$$= \sqrt{(0.186)(0.769)}$$

$$= 0.38 \quad (2 \text{ d.p.})$$

Therefore $r = 0.38$, indicating a low degree of positive correlation. We see from the scatter diagram on page 640 that, as expected, the two regression lines are not close together.

Example 12.11 Show that if $r = \pm 1$, the regression lines of y on x and x on y are identical.

Solution 12.11 The regression line y on x, $y = a + bx$, has gradient b.

The regression line x on y, $x = c + dy$, has gradient $\dfrac{1}{d}$.

Now if

$$r = \pm 1$$

$$r^2 = 1$$

Since $r^2 = bd$,

$$bd = 1$$

so

$$b = \frac{1}{d}$$

Therefore the two lines have the same gradient. Now we know that both lines go through $(\bar{x}, \bar{y})$, so they are identical.

NOTE: if x is the explanatory or independent variable then we use the regression line y *on* x to *estimate* a value of y, *given* a value of x. It is not usually valid to use the regression line x on y. However if $|r| \approx 1$, the lines are *very* close, so the line of x on y could be used in this instance.

Example 12.12 If $r = 0$, show that the two regression lines are at right angles.

Solution 12.12 Now

$$r = \frac{s_{xy}}{s_x s_y}, \quad \text{so if} \quad r = 0, \quad s_{xy} = 0$$

$$b = \frac{s_{xy}}{s_x^2}, \quad \text{therefore} \quad b = 0$$

$$d = \frac{s_{xy}}{s_y^2}, \quad \text{therefore} \quad d = 0$$

The equation of the regression line y on x is

$$y = a + bx, \quad \text{so if} \quad b = 0, \quad y = a$$

The equation of the regression line x on y is

$$x = c + dy, \quad \text{so if} \quad d = 0, \quad x = c$$

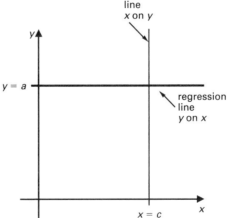

We see that the two regression lines are at right angles.

IMPORTANT NOTE: the product-moment correlation coefficient r is a measure of *linear correlation only*, so it is important to consider it in the light of a scatter diagram. The following example illustrates this point.

Example 12.13 Find the product-moment correlation coefficient for the following sets of data. Then draw a scatter diagram and comment.

(a)

x	−2	−1	0	1	2
y	4	1	0	1	4

(b)

x	1	1	1	2	2	2	3	3	3	9
y	1	2	3	1	2	3	1	2	3	8

Solution 12.13 (a) Using a calculator, we find that $r = 0$, indicating no linear correlation. However this does not necessarily mean that the variables are independent.

In fact the points all lie on the curve $y = x^2$, so there is a *quadratic* relationship in this example.

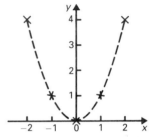

NOTE: $r = 0$ implies *either*

(a) there is no correlation between the variables and they are independent

or

(b) the variables are related in a non-linear way.

(b)

x	1	1	1	2	2	2	3	3	3	9
y	1	2	3	1	2	3	1	2	3	8

Using a calculator we find that $r = 0.86$ (2 d.p.), apparently indicating a high degree of positive correlation.

From the scatter diagram we see that there is *not* a high degree of correlation; the value of r has been distorted by the outlier (9, 8). If (9, 8) is excluded we find that $r = 0$.

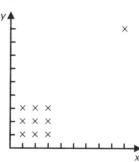

So a high value of r does not necessarily imply a high degree of positive linear correlation.

Example 12.14 Draw a diagram to illustrate the lengths whose sum of squares is minimised in the least squares method for finding the regression line of y on x.

State which is the independent and which is the dependent variable.

State, giving your reason, whether or not the equation of this line can be used to estimate the value of x for a given value of y.

The length (L mm) and width (W mm) of each of 20 individuals of a single species of fossil are measured. A summary of the results is:

$$\Sigma L = 400.20, \quad \Sigma W = 176.00, \quad \Sigma LW = 3700.20,$$

$$\Sigma L^2 = 8151.32, \quad \Sigma W^2 = 1780.52.$$

(**a**) Obtain the product-moment correlation coefficient between the length and the width of these fossils. Without performing a significance test interpret your result.

(**b**) Obtain an equation of the line of regression from which it is possible to estimate the length of a fossil of the same species whose width is known, giving the values of the coefficients to 2 decimal places.

(**c**) From your equation find the average increase or decrease in length per 1 mm increase in width of these fossils.   (L)

Solution 12.14 For the least squares regression line y on x, Σm_i^2 is minimised.

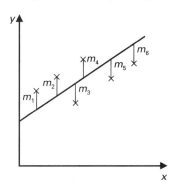

x is the independent variable and y is the dependent variable. Given a value of x we use the line y on x to estimate y.

In general this line should not be used to estimate the value of x for a given value of y, but this is permissible if $r \approx \pm 1$. In this case the two regression lines are very close.

(**a**) $s_{LW} = \dfrac{\Sigma LW}{n} - \overline{L}\,\overline{W}$ $\overline{L} = \dfrac{\Sigma L}{n} = \dfrac{400.20}{20} = 20.01$

$\quad\quad\quad = \dfrac{3700.20}{20} - (20.01)(8.8)$ $\overline{W} = \dfrac{\Sigma W}{n} = \dfrac{176.00}{20} = 8.8$

$\quad\quad\quad = 8.922$

$$s_L{}^2 = \frac{\Sigma L^2}{n} - \overline{L}{}^2$$

$$= \frac{8151.32}{20} - (20.01)^2$$

$$= 7.1659$$

$$s_W{}^2 = \frac{\Sigma W^2}{n} - \overline{W}{}^2$$

$$= \frac{1780.52}{20} - 8.8^2$$

$$= 11.586$$

$$r = \frac{s_{LW}}{s_L s_W}$$

$$= \frac{8.922}{\sqrt{7.1659}\ \sqrt{11.586}}$$

$$= 0.979 \quad (3\ \text{d.p.})$$

There is a high positive correlation between the length and the width of the fossils.

(**b**) Width W is the independent variable. The regression line L on W is given by

$$L - \overline{L} = \frac{s_{WL}}{s_W{}^2}\ (W - \overline{W})$$

$$L - 20.01 = \frac{8.922}{11.586}\ (W - 8.8)$$

$$L - 20.01 = 0.770W - 6.776$$

$$\underline{L = 0.77W + 13.23}$$

(**c**) The gradient of this line gives the increase in length per mm increase in width

Therefore   if W increases by $1\,\text{mm}$, L increases by $0.77\,\text{mm}$ (2 d.p.).

Exercise 12d

1. Calculate the value of the product-moment correlation coefficient for the following. Check using a calculator in LR mode if possible. Comment on your answers.

(a)

x	5	10	15	20	25
y	4.3	5.9	6.9	6.5	8.2

(b)

x	12	14	16	18	20	22
y	100	70	86	49	60	50

(c)

s	1	2	3	4	5	6	7	8
t	12.4	12.8	12.6	13.9	13.4	13.2	14	14.6

(d)

t	27	43	62	89	72
z	48	50	81	75	60

2. For a given set of data $\Sigma x = 680$, $\Sigma y = 996$, $\Sigma x^2 = 20\,154$, $\Sigma y^2 = 34\,670$, $\Sigma xy = 24\,844$, $n = 30$. Find the product-moment correlation coefficient and the equations of the two least squares regression lines.

3. The heights h, in cm, and weights W, in kg, of 10 people are measured. It is found that $\Sigma h = 1710$, $\Sigma W = 760$, $\Sigma h^2 = 293\,162$, $\Sigma hW = 130\,628$ and $\Sigma W^2 = 59\,390$. Calculate the correlation coefficient between the values of h and W.

What is the equation of the regression line of W on h? (O & C)

4. If the equations of the least squares regression lines are

$$y = 0.648x + 2.64 \quad (y \text{ on } x) \quad \text{and}$$

$$x = 0.917y - 1.91 \quad (x \text{ on } y)$$

find the product-moment correlation coefficient for the data.

5. For a given set of data the equations of the least squares regression lines are

$$y = -0.219x + 20.8 \quad (y \text{ on } x) \quad \text{and}$$

$$x = -0.785y + 16.2 \quad (x \text{ on } y)$$

Find the product-moment correlation coefficient for the data.

6. For a given set of data, the regression line y on x is $y = 0.4 + 1.3x$ and x on y is $x = -0.1 + 0.7y$. Find (a) the product-moment correlation coefficient, (b) $\bar{x}$ and $\bar{y}$.

7. The following data relate to the percentage unemployment and percentage change in wages over several years.

% Unemployment (x)	% Change in wages (y)
1.6	5.0
2.2	3.2
2.3	2.7
1.7	2.1
1.6	4.1
2.1	2.7
2.6	2.9
1.7	4.6
1.5	3.5
1.6	4.4

(a) Calculate the product-moment correlation coefficient between x and y.

(Use $\Sigma x = 18.9$, $\Sigma y = 35.2$, $\Sigma x^2 = 37.01$, $\Sigma y^2 = 132.22$, $\Sigma xy = 64.7$)

It has been suggested that low unemployment and a low rate of wage inflation cannot exist together.

(b) Without further calculation use your correlation coefficient to explain briefly whether or not you think the suggestion is justified. (L)

8. In a regression calculation for five pairs of observations one pair of values was lost when the data were filed. For the regression of y on x the equation was calculated as

$$y = 2x - 0.1$$

The four recorded pairs of values are

x	0.1	0.2	0.4	0.3
y	0.1	0.3	0.7	0.4

Find the missing pair of values, using the following data for the four pairs above: $\Sigma x = 1$, $\Sigma x^2 = 0.3$, $\Sigma xy = 0.47$, $\Sigma y = 1.5$. (MEI)

9. The body and heart masses of fourteen 10-month-old male mice are tabulated below:

Body mass (x) (g)	Heart mass (y) (mg)
27	118
30	136
37	156
38	150
32	140
36	155
32	157
32	114
38	144
42	159
36	149
44	170
33	131
38	160

(a) Draw a scatter diagram of these data.

(b) Calculate the equation of the regression line of y on x and draw this line on the scatter diagram.

(c)) Calculate the product-moment coefficient of correlation. (AEB)

10. 12 students were given a prognostic test at the beginning of a course and their scores X_i in the test were compared with their scores Y_i obtained in an examination at the end of the course $(i = 1, 2, \ldots, 12)$. The results were as follows:

X_i	1	2	2	4	5	5	6	7	8	8	9	9
Y_i	3	4	5	5	4	8	6	6	6	7	8	10

Find the equation of the regression line of Y on X and determine the correlation coefficient between X and Y.

11. Ten boys compete in throwing a cricket ball, and the table opposite shows the height of each boy (x cm) to the nearest cm and the distance (y m) to which he can throw the ball.

Find the equations of the regression lines of y on x, and of x on y. No diagram is needed. Calculate also the coefficient of correlation.

Estimate the distance to which a cricket ball can be thrown by a boy 150 cm in height.

Boy	x	y
A	122	41
B	124	38
C	133	52
D	138	56
E	144	29
F	156	54
G	158	59
H	161	61
I	164	63
J	168	67

(AEB)

MINIMUM SUM OF SQUARES OF RESIDUALS

When fitting the least squares regression line of y on x, called $y = a + bx$, values of a and b are found such that the sum of the squares of the residuals (written Σm_i^2) is a minimum. We now consider how to find the value of $\Sigma m_{i(\min)}^2$.

Consider this set of data:

x	2	3	4	5	6
y	5	2	5	3	1

We plot the points P_1 (2, 5), P_2 (3, 2), P_3 (4, 5), P_4 (5, 3) and P_5 (6, 1) on a scatter diagram, and then draw in the least squares regression line of y on x, which we have calculated as $y = 6 - 0.7x$. (You should check this for yourself.)

Now the residuals $P_1 Q_1, P_2 Q_2, \ldots, P_5 Q_5$ are drawn in and the co-ordinates of $Q_1, \ldots, Q_5$ calculated as follows:

for $\quad Q_1, \quad x = 2 \quad$ so $\quad y = 6 - 0.7(2) = 4.6,$

for $\quad Q_2, \quad x = 3 \quad$ so $\quad y = 6 - 0.7(3) = 3.9, \quad$ and so on.

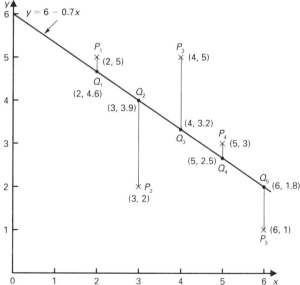

Residuals (m_i)	m_i^2
$P_1Q_1 = m_1 = 0.4$	0.16
$P_2Q_2 = m_2 = 1.9$	3.61
$P_3Q_3 = m_3 = 1.8$	3.24
$P_4Q_4 = m_4 = 0.5$	0.25
$P_5Q_5 = m_5 = 0.8$	0.64
	$\Sigma m_i^2 = 7.9$

So $\quad \underline{\Sigma m_{i(\text{min})}^2 = 7.9}$

NOTE: if we had drawn *any other line* as a regression line of y on x, then Σm_i^2 would have been greater than 7.9.

A formula for $\Sigma m_{i(\text{min})}^2$ can be derived as follows:

The equation of the least squares regression line y on x is

$$y - \bar{y} = \frac{s_{xy}}{s_x^2}(x - \bar{x}).$$

This is drawn on the scatter diagram below. The diagram shows the regression line, together with one general point $P_i(x_i, y_i)$.

The residual P_iQ_i is drawn in, where Q_i has co-ordinates (x_i, y_Q).

Now (x_i, y_Q) lies on the regression line, so

$$y_Q - \bar{y} = \frac{s_{xy}}{s_x^2}(x_i - \bar{x}).$$

Now $\quad m_i = P_iQ_i$

$$= y_i - y_Q$$

$$= y_i - \left[\bar{y} + \frac{s_{xy}}{s_x^2}(x_i - \bar{x})\right]$$

$$\Sigma m_{i(\text{min})}^2 = \Sigma\left[(y_i - \bar{y}) - \frac{s_{xy}}{s_x^2}(x_i - \bar{x})\right]^2$$

$$= \Sigma(y_i - \bar{y})^2 - 2\frac{s_{xy}}{s_x^2}\Sigma(x_i - \bar{x})(y_i - \bar{y}) + \frac{s_{xy}^2}{(s_x^2)^2}\Sigma(x_i - \bar{x})^2$$

$$= ns_y^2 - 2\frac{s_{xy}}{s_x^2}ns_{xy} + \frac{s_{xy}^2}{(s_x^2)^2}ns_x^2$$

$$= ns_y^2 - 2n\frac{s_{xy}^2}{s_x^2} + n\frac{s_{xy}^2}{s_x^2}$$

$$= ns_y^2 - n\frac{s_{xy}^2}{s_x^2}$$

$$= n\left(s_y^2 - \frac{s_{xy}^2}{s_x^2}\right)$$

$$= n(s_y^2 - r^2 s_y^2) \quad \text{since} \quad r = \frac{s_{xy}}{s_x s_y}$$

$$= n(1 - r^2)s_y^2$$

> **For y on x, the minimum sum of squares of residuals is**
>
> $$n(1 - r^2)s_y^2$$

For x on y, it can be shown that

$$\Sigma n_{i(\min)}^2 = n\left(s_x^2 - \frac{s_{xy}^2}{s_y^2}\right)$$

$$= n(s_x^2 - r^2 s_x^2) \quad \text{since} \quad r = \frac{s_{xy}}{s_x s_y}$$

$$= n(1 - r^2)s_x^2$$

> **For x on y, the minimum sum of squares of residuals is**
>
> $$n(1 - r^2)s_x^2$$

> *NOTE*: using 'big' S notation
>
> For y on x, the minimum sum of squares of residuals is
>
> $$\Sigma m_{i(\min)}^2 = S_{yy} - \frac{(S_{xy})^2}{S_{xx}} = S_{yy}(1 - r^2)$$
>
> For x on y, the minimum sum of squares of residuals is
>
> $$\Sigma m_{i(\min)}^2 = S_{xx} - \frac{(S_{xy})^2}{S_{yy}} = S_{xx}(1 - r^2)$$

Using the formula $\Sigma m_{i(\min)}^2 = n(1 - r^2)s_y^2$, and a calculator in LR mode, we now confirm that $\Sigma m_{i(\min)}^2 = 7.9$, for the data given previously:

x	2	3	4	5	6
y	5	2	5	3	1

	Casio 85/100/115	**Casio Graphics 7000 GA**
Set LR mode	MODE 2	MODE ÷
Clear memories	SHIFT KAC	SHIFT SCI EXE
Input data	2 $x_D y_D$ 5 DATA	2 SHIFT , 5 DT
	3 $x_D y_D$ 2 DATA	3 SHIFT , 2 DT
	4 $x_D y_D$ 5 DATA	4 SHIFT , 5 DT
	5 $x_D y_D$ 3 DATA	5 SHIFT , 3 DT
	6 $x_D y_D$ 1 DATA	6 SHIFT , 1 DT
Output		
$\boxed{r}$ $= -0.618\ldots$	SHIFT 9	SHIFT 9 EXE
$s_y^{\,2}$ $= 2.56$	SHIFT 5 x^2	SHIFT 5 x^2 EXE
With $n = 5$	1 − SHIFT 9 x^2 =	5 × (1 − SHIFT 9
$n(1-r^2)s_y^{\,2} = 7.9$	× 5 × SHIFT 5	x^2) × SHIFT 5
	x^2 =	x^2 EXE
	[*NOTE*: the bracket function is not in operation in the LR mode]	
Clear LR mode	MODE 0	MODE +

So the minimum sum of the squares of residuals for y on x is 7.9.

Example 12.15 The moisture content, M, in grams of water per 100 grams of dried solids, of core samples of mud from an estuary was measured at depth D metres. The results are shown in the table:

Depth (D)	0	5	10	15	20	25	30	35
Moisture content (M)	90	82	56	42	30	21	21	18

(**a**) On graph paper, draw a scatter diagram for these data.

(**b**) Obtain, to 3 decimal places, the product-moment correlation coefficient. Without performing a significance test, interpret the meaning of your result.

(**c**) Find the equation of the regression line of M on D, giving the coefficients to 2 decimal places.

(**d**) Find, to 2 decimal places, the minimum sum of squares of the residuals and explain using words and a diagram what this number represents.

(**e**) From your equation estimate, to 2 decimal places, the decrease in M when D increases by 1.   (L)

Solution 12.15 (a)   **Scatter diagram to show moisture content, M, and depth, D.**

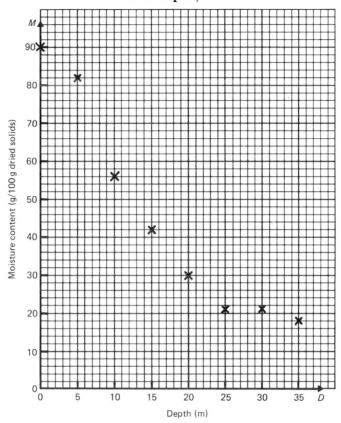

Method 1 — If your calculator does not have LR mode, then make use of the SD mode for some of the calculations.

(b)

D	0	5	10	15	20	25	30	35
M	90	82	56	42	30	21	21	18

$$r = \frac{s_{DM}}{s_D s_M} \qquad \text{where} \qquad s_{DM} = \frac{\Sigma DM}{8} - \overline{D}\,\overline{M}$$

Now ΣDM cannot be found in SD mode, so we calculate

$$\Sigma DM = (0)(90) + (5)(82) + \ldots + (35)(18) = 3985$$

From calculator,

$$\overline{D} = 17.5 \qquad \text{and} \qquad \overline{M} = 45$$

So
$$s_{DM} = \frac{3985}{8} - (17.5)(45)$$

$$= -289.375$$

Also $s_D = 11.456\,439$ and $s_M = 26.528\,287$

Therefore $$r = \frac{-289.375}{(11.45...)(26.52...)}$$

$$= -0.952 \quad (3 \text{ d.p.})$$

This is almost perfect negative correlation.

(c) Equation of least squares regression line M on D is

$$M - \overline{M} = \frac{s_{MD}}{s_D^{\,2}} (D - \overline{D})$$

Therefore $$M - 45 = \frac{-289.375}{(11.45...)^2} (D - 17.5)$$

$$= -2.20(D - 17.5)$$

$$\underline{M = 83.58 - 2.20D}$$

We show the regression line drawn on the scatter diagram. Note that it goes through $(\overline{D}, \overline{M})$ i.e. (17.5, 45) and the intercept on the M axis is 83.58.

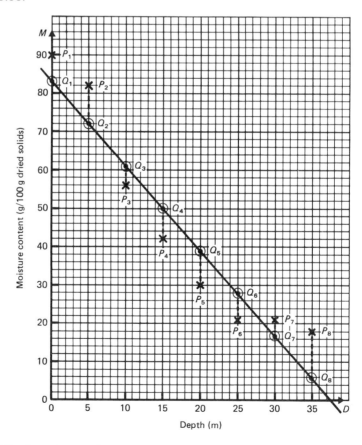

(d) The lengths $P_1 Q_1, P_2 Q_2, \ldots, P_8 Q_8$ are called the residuals. The sum of the squares of the residuals is given by

$$\Sigma m_i^{\,2} = P_1 Q_1^{\,2} + \ldots + P_8 Q_8^{\,2}$$

and the minimum value of this sum is given by

$$\Sigma m_i{}^2{}_{(\min)} = n(1 - r^2)s_M{}^2$$

$$= 8(1 - (-0.952\ldots)^2)(26.5\ldots)^2$$

$$= 525.98 \ \ (2 \ \text{d.p.})$$

(**e**) The gradient of the regression line is -2.20 so that when D increases by 1, M decreases by 2.20.

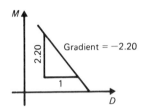

Method 2 — using a calculator in LR mode for parts (**b**), (**c**) and (**d**).

We will use x for depth D and y for moisture content M.

	Casio 85/100/115	Casio Graphics 7000 GA
Set LR mode	MODE　2	MODE　÷
Clear memories	SHIFT　KAC	SHIFT　SCI　EXE
Input data	0　$x_D y_D$　90　DATA	0　SHIFT　,　90　DT
	5　$x_D y_D$　82　DATA	5　SHIFT　,　82　DT
	⋮　⋮　⋮　⋮	⋮　⋮　⋮　⋮　⋮
	35　$x_D y_D$　18　DATA	35　SHIFT　,　18　DT
Output		
r = $-0.9521\ldots$	SHIFT　9	SHIFT　9　EXE
A = $83.583\ldots$	SHIFT　7	SHIFT　7　EXE
B = $-2.204\ldots$	SHIFT　8	SHIFT　8　EXE
$\overline{D}$ = 17.5	SHIFT　1	SHIFT　1　EXE
$\overline{M}$ = 45	SHIFT　4	SHIFT　4　EXE
$s_M{}^2$ = 703.75	SHIFT　5　x^2	SHIFT　5　x^2　EXE
With $n = 8$,	1　−　SHIFT　9　x^2　=	8　×　(　1　−　SHIFT　9
$n(1 - r^2)s_M{}^2 = 525.9$	×　8　×　SHIFT　5	x^2　)　×　SHIFT　5
	x^2　=	x^2　EXE
Clear LR mode	MODE　0	MODE　+

(**b**) The product-moment correlation coefficient, $r = -0.952$ (3 d.p.)
This is almost perfect negative correlation.

(**c**) The least squares regression line M on D is given by

$$M = A + BD$$

so the regression line is $\underline{M = 83.58 - 2.20D}$

(**d**) $\Sigma m_{i(min)}^{2} = n(1 - r^2)s_M^{2}$

$$= \underline{525.98}\ \ (2\ \text{d.p.})$$

Exercise 12e

1. In the table, Y is the mass (in grams) of potassium bromide which will dissolve in 100 grams of water at a temperature of $X°$C.

X	10	20	30	40	50
Y	61	64	70	73	78

Find the equation of the regression line of Y on X.
Find, also, the product-moment correlation coefficient between X and Y, and the minimum sum of the squares of the residuals for Y on X.

2. Referring to your projects if possible, explain clearly the purpose of obtaining a linear regression equation, and describe what use was, or could be, made of this equation.
A large field used for growing potatoes was divided into 6 equal plots, and each plot was treated with a different concentration of a certain fertiliser. At harvest time the yield from each plot was recorded, and the results are given in the table, with potato yield (Y kg m^{-2}) and fertiliser concentration (C g l^{-1}).

Concentration, C	$\frac{1}{2}$	1	2	3	4	6
Yield, Y		10	16	26	36	50	72

Draw a scatter diagram for these data, and mark on your diagram the point representing the mean of the data.
Find the equation of a suitable regression line from which the yield to be expected for a concentration of 5 g l^{-1} can be predicted, and give the value of this expected yield. Sketch the regression line on your scatter diagram. Calculate the sum of squares of the residuals and explain what this value represents with regard to your regression line.
[If required, you may assume in your working that $\Sigma C^2 = 66.25$, $\Sigma CY = 813$, $\Sigma Y^2 = 10\,012$.]   (L)

3. For a given set of data $\Sigma x = 21$, $\Sigma y = 33$, $\Sigma x^2 = 91$, $\Sigma y^2 = 205$, $\Sigma xy = 128$, $n = 6$. Find the product-moment correlation coefficient for the data. Find also the minimum sum of squares of residuals for y on x and for x on y.

4. The weight of a baby boy was recorded each month up to his first birthday. This data, in so far as it is available, is given in the table:

Age in completed months	Weight kg
0	3.16
1	4.21
2	4.83
3	5.41
4	5.86
5	6.34
6	6.79
7	7.62
8	8.15
9	—
10	8.83
11	9.11

(*a*) On graph paper, plot a scattergraph of the data. Calculate and mark on your graph the mean point.
(*b*) Show that the product-moment correlation coefficient for this data is 0.992. Intuitively, do you feel that it is reasonable to use a straight line to fit the data?
(*c*) Calculate the equation of linear regression of weight on age and plot this line on your graph paper. Use the equation to estimate the weight of the baby at nine months.
(*d*) What is meant by the term 'least squares line of best fit'? You may refer freely to the data in this question to illustrate your answer.   (O)

USING A METHOD OF CODING

When the values of x and y are very large or very small we need to avoid exceeding the capacity of the calculator. The least squares calculations can be better done by a change of origin and scaling, that is, using a method of coding.

For the data $(x_1, y_1), (x_2, y_2), \ldots, (x_n, y_n)$ suppose we use the coding

$$X = \frac{x - a}{b} \quad \text{and} \quad Y = \frac{y - c}{d}$$

NOTE: do not confuse the scaling constants b and d used here with the regression coefficients b and d.

Now, rearranging we have

$$x_i = a + bX_i \quad \text{and} \quad y_i = c + dY_i \quad \text{for} \quad i = 1, 2, \ldots, n$$

We have already seen (p. 47) that

$$\bar{x} = a + b\bar{X}, \quad \bar{y} = c + d\bar{Y}$$

and

$$s_x = bs_X, \quad s_y = ds_Y,$$

For the covariance

$$s_{xy} = \frac{\Sigma(x_i - \bar{x})(y_i - \bar{y})}{n}$$

$$= \frac{1}{n}\Sigma[a + bX_i - (a + b\bar{X})][c + dY_i - (c + d\bar{Y})]$$

$$= \frac{1}{n}\Sigma b(X_i - \bar{X})d(Y_i - \bar{Y})$$

So $\quad s_{xy} = bds_{XY}$

For the product-moment correlation coefficient

$$r_{XY} = \frac{s_{XY}}{s_X s_Y}$$

$$= \frac{\frac{1}{bd}s_{xy}}{\frac{1}{b}s_x \times \frac{1}{d}s_y}$$

$$= \frac{s_{xy}}{s_x s_y}$$

$$= r_{xy}$$

So $\quad r_{XY} = r_{xy},$

i.e. the product-moment correlation coefficient remains *unchanged*. This is because r is a measure of the degree of scatter and this is unchanged by a change of origin and scaling.

Example 12.16 For the following data, use a method of coding to find (**a**) the covariance, (**b**) the product-moment correlation coefficient, (**c**) the least squares regression lines y on x and x on y.

x	1000	1012	1009	1007	1010	1015	1010	1011
y	235	240	245	250	255	260	265	270

Solution 12.16 We use the codings

$$X = x - 1000, \qquad Y = \frac{y - 250}{5}$$

So, referring to the results on page 679 with $a = 1000$, $b = 1$, $c = 250$, $d = 5$, we have $s_x = s_X$, $s_y = 5s_Y$ and $s_{xy} = 5s_{XY}$.

X	Y	X^2	Y^2	XY
0	−3	0	9	0
12	−2	144	4	−24
9	−1	81	1	−9
7	0	49	0	0
10	1	100	1	10
15	2	225	4	30
10	3	100	9	30
11	4	121	16	44
$\Sigma X = 74$	$\Sigma Y = 4$	$\Sigma X^2 = 820$	$\Sigma Y^2 = 44$	$\Sigma XY = 81$

(**a**) $\qquad s_{XY} = \dfrac{\Sigma XY}{n} - \overline{X}\,\overline{Y} = \dfrac{81}{8} - \left(\dfrac{74}{8}\right)\left(\dfrac{4}{8}\right) = 5.5$

Therefore $\quad s_{xy} = 5s_{XY}$

$$= 5(5.5)$$

$$= 27.5$$

The covariance s_{xy} is 27.5.

(**b**) Now

$$s_X{}^2 = \frac{\Sigma X^2}{n} - \overline{X}^2 = \frac{820}{8} - \left(\frac{74}{8}\right)^2 = 16.9375$$

$$s_Y{}^2 = \frac{\Sigma Y^2}{n} - \overline{Y}^2 = \frac{44}{8} - \left(\frac{4}{8}\right)^2 = 5.25$$

Therefore

$$r_{XY} = \frac{s_{XY}}{s_X s_Y} = \frac{5.5}{\sqrt{(16.9375)(5.25)}} = 0.58 \qquad \text{(2 d.p.)}$$

So $\qquad r_{xy} = r_{XY} = 0.58 \qquad \text{(2 d.p.)}$

The product--moment correlation coefficient is 0.58 (2 d.p.).

(c) The equation of the least squares regression line Y on X is

$$Y - \overline{Y} = \frac{s_{XY}}{s_X{}^2}(X - \overline{X})$$

i.e. $$Y - \frac{4}{8} = \frac{5.5}{16.9375}\left(X - \frac{74}{8}\right)$$

so $$Y = 0.3247X - 2.5037$$

Now, since $Y = \dfrac{y - 250}{5}$ and $X = x - 1000$, this equation may be written

$$\frac{y - 250}{5} = 0.3247\,(x - 1000) - 2.5037$$

$$y = 1.6235x - 1386.0185$$

Therefore the least squares regression line y on x is $\underline{y = 1.62x - 1386}$

The equation of the least squares regression line X on Y is

$$X - \overline{X} = \frac{s_{XY}}{s_Y{}^2}(Y - \overline{Y})$$

$$X - \frac{74}{8} = \frac{5.5}{5.25}\left(Y - \frac{4}{8}\right)$$

i.e. $$X = 1.048Y + 8.726$$

This equation may be written

$$x - 1000 = 1.048\left(\frac{y - 250}{5}\right) + 8.726$$

$$x = 0.2096y + 956.326$$

Therefore the least squares regression line x on y is $\underline{x = .21y + 956}$

Exercise 12f

In Questions 1–3 use appropriate methods of coding to calculate (a) the covariance, (b) the product–moment correlation coefficient, (c) the least squares lines of regression of y on x and x on y.

1.

x	1701	1722	1717	1718	1703	1701
y	45.1	45.8	45.6	45.3	45.1	45.1

2.

x	981.2	981.3	981.9	981.6	981.5
y	55.6	55.2	54.8	56.1	55.5

3.

x	0.001 57	0.001 56	0.001 49	0.001 65
y	100.4	100.7	100.0	100.4

4. (a) State, with a reason, the effect on the value of the product–moment correlation coefficient between two variables x and y of (i) changing the units of x, (ii) changing the origin of y.

(b) The following data relate to the percentage scores on a physical fitness test, the heights (in centimetres), the weights (in kilograms) and the ages (in years) of ten junior school pupils.

Pupil	Score (s)	Height (h)	Weight (w)	Age (a)
1	58	130	41.8	8
2	60	120	38.6	9
3	59	154	54.1	11
4	72	140	38.6	9
5	62	145	44.9	10
6	54	153	52.4	10
7	81	139	30.2	8
8	62	148	41.4	9
9	86	150	38.4	10
10	94	160	32.1	11

Plot a scatter diagram of weight and score. Given that

$$u = (w - 30)/0.1, \quad v = s - 50,$$

and that

$$\Sigma u = 1125, \quad \Sigma u^2 = 179\,671,$$

$$\Sigma v = 188, \quad \Sigma v^2 = 5226, \quad \Sigma uv = 13\,927,$$

calculate the value of the correlation coefficient, r_{uv}, between u and v. State the value of r_{ws}. Explain how your graph gives an indication that your value is correct. A regression line is to be fitted between s and one of the other three variables in order to predict pupils' scores in the physical fitness test. Given that $r_{hs} = 0.357$ and $r_{as} = 0.188$, which of the three variables would you choose? Give a reason for your choice.   (JMB)

5. The table below gives the average cost per hundredweight of zinc manufactures imported into the UK during each of the years 1873 to 1882.
(a) Plot the data on graph paper, by coding with (year − 1872) as the x variable and (cost − 100) as the y variable.

Year	Cost (p)
1873	147
1874	147
1875	144
1876	140
1877	129
1878	119
1879	112
1880	116
1881	107
1882	109

(b) Given that $\Sigma y = 270$ and $\Sigma xy = 1057$, show that the gradient of the equation of the least squares regression line of y on x is -5.2 (to 2 significant figures). Calculate the equation of this line and plot it on your graph.
(c) Use your equation to predict the cost of zinc manufactures imported in 1883. Comment on your prediction.
(Source: Statistical Abstract for the United Kingdom 1871 to 1885.)   (O)

SUMMARY — REGRESSION AND PRODUCT–MOMENT CORRELATION COEFFICIENT

Least squares regression lines	
y on x Line $y = a + bx$	**x on y** Line $x = c + dy$
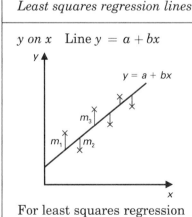	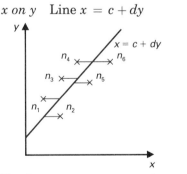
For least squares regression line y on x $\sum m_i^2$ is a minimum	For least squares regression line x on y $\sum n_i^2$ is a minimum

Normal equations	
y on x	*x on y*
$\Sigma y = na + b\,\Sigma x$	$\Sigma x = nc + d\,\Sigma y$
$\Sigma xy = a\,\Sigma x + b\,\Sigma x^2$	$\Sigma xy = c\,\Sigma y + d\,\Sigma y^2$

Covariance method	
y on x	*x on y*
$y - \bar{y} = \dfrac{s_{xy}}{s_x{}^2}\,(x - \bar{x})$	$x - \bar{x} = \dfrac{s_{xy}}{s_y{}^2}\,(y - \bar{y})$

Minimum sum of squares of residuals:	
y on x	*x on y*
$\Sigma m^2_{i_{(\min)}} = n(1 - r^2)s_y{}^2$	$\Sigma n^2_{i_{(\min)}} = n(1 - r^2)s_x{}^2$

Product–moment correlation coefficient, r:

$$r = \frac{s_{xy}}{s_x\,s_y}$$

In terms of the regression coefficients: $r^2 = bd$

where $\quad b = \dfrac{s_{xy}}{s_x{}^2}\quad$ (regression coefficient of y on x)

$\qquad\quad d = \dfrac{s_{xy}}{s_y{}^2}\quad$ (regression coefficient of x on y)

$$s_{xy} = \frac{1}{n}\,\Sigma(x - \bar{x})(y - \bar{y}) = \frac{\Sigma xy}{n} - \bar{x}\bar{y}\quad\text{(covariance)}$$

$$s_x{}^2 = \frac{1}{n}\,\Sigma(x - \bar{x})^2 = \frac{\Sigma x^2}{n} - \bar{x}^2;\quad s_y{}^2 = \frac{1}{n}\,\Sigma(y - \bar{y})^2 = \frac{\Sigma y^2}{n} - \bar{y}^2$$

Using coding:

If $\quad X = \dfrac{x - a}{b}\qquad$ and $\qquad Y = \dfrac{y - c}{d}$

$\qquad s_x = bs_X$

$\qquad s_y = ds_Y$

$\qquad s_{xy} = bds_{XY}$

$r_{xy} = r_{XY} = \dfrac{s_{XY}}{s_X\,s_Y}$

Regression lines:

Y on $X\qquad Y - \overline{Y} = \dfrac{s_{XY}}{s_X{}^2}\,(X - \overline{X})$

X on $Y\qquad X - \overline{X} = \dfrac{s_{XY}}{s_Y{}^2}\,(Y - \overline{Y})$

Miscellaneous Exercise 12g

1. Over a period of time a publishing house
    records the sales, y thousand, of 10 similar
    textbooks, and the amount, £x hundred,
    spent on advertising each book. The following
    table shows the data for the 10 books.

x	y
0.75	2.00
3.90	5.35
1.65	3.00
1.60	2.40
4.40	5.95
3.05	4.50
3.55	4.60
2.65	3.65
0.45	1.30
2.00	3.25

    (a) Find the equation of the regression line
    of y on x, giving the coefficients to 2 decimal
    places.
    (You may use　　$\Sigma x^2 = 73.5450$;
    $\Sigma y^2 = 149.7700$;　$\Sigma xy = 104.1475$)
    (b) Give an interpretation of the coefficients
    in your equation.
    (c) Estimate the number of textbooks sold if
    the publisher spends £375 on advertising.
    For a set of novels, the publisher found the
    sales and advertising to be related by the
    equation

    $$(y - 3.6) = 0.25\,(x - 2.4).$$

    (d) Re-write the equation of the regression
    line in (a) in the form $(y - \bar{y}) = m(x - \bar{x})$ and
    compare the effect of advertising on the sales
    of textbooks and novels.
    (e) For the equation in (a) find, to 2 decimal
    places, the sum of squares of the residuals
    and explain, using words and a diagram, the
    meaning of this number.　　　　　　　(L)

2. Explain, briefly, your understanding of the
    term 'correlation'.
    Describe how you used, or could have used,
    correlation in a project or in classwork.
    Twelve students sat two Biology tests, one
    theoretical and one practical. Their marks
    are shown in the table.
    (a) Draw a scatter diagram to represent
    these data.
    (b) Find, to 3 decimal places, the product–
    moment correlation coefficient.
    (c) Using evidence from (a) and (b) explain
    why a straight line regression model is
    appropriate for these data.
    Another student was absent from the
    practical test but scored 14 marks in the
    theoretical test.

    (d) Find the equation of the appropriate
    regression line and use it to estimate a mark
    in the practical test for this student.　　(L)

Marks in theoretical test (T)	Marks in practical test (P)
5	6
9	8
7	9
11	13
20	20
4	9
6	8
17	17
12	14
10	8
15	17
16	18

3. Given that the gradient of the least squares
    regression line of Y on X is b_1, and the gradient
    of the least squares regression line of X on Y is
    $1/b_2$, prove that $b_1 b_2 = r^2$, where r is the
    linear (product–moment) correlation coefficient.
    Hence show that if $r^2 = 1$ these two
    regression lines are identical.
    The yield of a particular crop on a farm is
    thought to depend principally on the amount
    of rainfall in the growing season. The values
    of the yield Y, in tons per acre, and the
    rainfall X, in centimetres, for seven
    successive years are given in the table below.

x	12.3	13.7	14.5	11.2	13.2	14.1	12.0
y	6.25	8.02	8.42	5.27	7.21	8.71	5.68

    [$\Sigma xy = 654.006$,　$\Sigma x = 91$,　$\Sigma x^2 = 1191.72$,
    $\Sigma y = 49.56$,　$\Sigma y^2 = 362.1628$]
    (i) Find the linear (product–moment)
    correlation coefficient between X and Y.
    (ii) Find the equation of the least squares
    regression line of Y on X and also that of X
    on Y.
    (iii) Given that the rainfall in the growing
    season of a subsequent year was 14.0 cm,
    estimate the yield in that year.
    (iv) Given that the yield in a subsequent year
    was 8.08 tons per acre, estimate the rainfall in
    the growing season of that year.　　　(C)

4. (a) State the quantity which is minimised
    when using the method of least squares. Use
    a sketch to illustrate your answer.
    The heat output of wood is known to vary
    with the percentage moisture content. The
    table opposite shows, in suitable units, the
    data obtained from an experiment carried out
    to assess this variation.

Percentage moisture content (x)	Heat output (y)
50	5.5
8	7.4
34	6.2
22	6.8
45	5.5
15	7.1
74	4.4
82	3.9
60	4.9
30	6.3

(b) Obtain the equation of the regression line for heat output on percentage moisture content, giving the values of the coefficients to 2 decimal places.

(c) Use your equation to estimate the heat output of wood with 40% moisture content. State any reservations you would have about making an estimate from the regression equation of the heat output for a 90% moisture content.

(d) Explain briefly the main implication of your analysis for a person wishing to use wood as a form of heating.

(e) Calculate the sum of squares of the residuals for your line, giving your answer to 2 significant figures. Comment on your result in the light of your answer to (a). (L)

5. (a) Suggest a value for the product–moment correlation coefficient between x and y in **each** of the following cases.

(i)

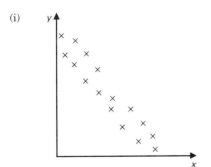

(ii)

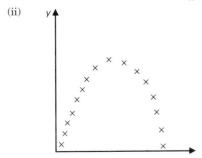

(iii)

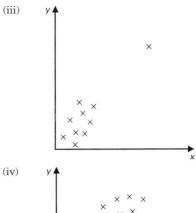

(iv)

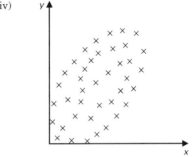

(b) In the machine sewing section of a factory making high fashion clothes, a score is assigned to each finished item on the basis of its quality (the better the quality, the higher the score). Each seamstress's pay is, in part, dependent upon the number of items she finishes. The number of items finished by each of 12 seamstresses on a particular day and their mean quality score are shown.

Seamstress	Number of items finished, x	Mean quality score, y
1	14	7.2
2	13	7.3
3	17	6.9
4	16	7.3
5	17	7.5
6	18	7.6
7	19	6.8
8	32	3.7
9	18	6.5
10	15	7.9
11	15	6.8
12	19	7.1

$\Sigma x = 213$ $\Sigma y = 82.6$ $\Sigma xy = 1414.1$
$\Sigma x^2 = 4043$ $\Sigma y^2 = 581.28$

(i) Calculate the value of the product–moment correlation coefficient between x and y, and interpret your value.

(ii) Plot these data on a scatter diagram. Discuss, briefly, whether or not your interpretation in (i) should now be amended.

(iii) When the results were presented at a Board meeting, the Personnel Manager explained that Seamstress 8 had been experiencing severe financial difficulties at home.

Explain, briefly, the implications of this additional information on your conclusions.

(JMB)

6. The table is a summary of the maximum temperature recorded in Plymouth during each of the seven months from June to December 1986 inclusive.

Month	x	Maximum temp. °C
Jun	1	22.3
Jul	2	20.2
Aug	3	17.9
Sep	4	16.1
Oct	5	16.8
Nov	6	12.6
Dec	7	10.9

(a) Plot a scatter diagram of the data using as x co-ordinates the coding shown in the table and the maximum temperature as the y co-ordinate. Mark the mean point of the data on your graph.

(b) Given that $\Sigma xy = 416.7$, demonstrate that the gradient of the line of regression of y on x is -1.80 (to three significant figures). What is the physical meaning of this gradient?

(c) Calculate the full equation of regression of maximum temperature on month.

(d) Use your equation to predict the maximum temperature in May 1987. The actual maximum temperature was 15.3 °C. Why is your predicted value so different from reality?

(O)

7. State the effect on the product–moment correlation coefficient between two variables x and y of (a) changing the origin for x and (b) changing the units of x.

The following table gives the daily output of the substance creatinine from the body of each of ten nutrition students together with the student's body mass.

Output of creatinine (grams)	Body mass (kilograms)
1.32	55
1.54	48
1.45	55
1.06	53
2.13	74
1.00	44
0.90	49
2.00	68
2.70	78
0.75	51

Draw a scatter diagram for the data. Calculate, correct to two decimal places, the product–moment correlation coefficient. Comment on any relationship which is indicated by the scatter diagram and the correlation coefficient.

(JMB)

8. A purchasing manager of a London-based company, believes that the time in transit of goods sent by road depends upon the distance between the supplier and the company. In an attempt to measure this dependence, twelve packages, sent from different parts of the country, have their transit times (y days) accurately recorded, together with the distance (x miles) of the supplier from the company. The results are summarised as follows:

$\Sigma x = 1800, \qquad \Sigma y = 36.0, \qquad \Sigma xy = 6438.6,$

$\Sigma x^2 = 336\,296, \qquad \Sigma y^2 = 126.34.$

Obtain the least squares straight line regression equation of y on x.

Explain the significance of the regression coefficient.

Predict the transit time of a package sent from a supplier 200 miles away from the company. Give two reasons why you would not use the equation to predict transit time for a package sent from a supplier 1500 miles away.

Calculate the product–moment correlation coefficient between x and y.

Explain why the value you have obtained supports the purchasing manager's attempt to establish a regression equation of y on x.

(AEB 1987)

SPEARMAN'S COEFFICIENT OF RANK CORRELATION r_S

Instead of using the values of the variables x and y, we can rank them in order of size, using the numbers 1, 2, 3, ... , n. A correlation coefficient can then be determined on the basis of these ranks. We will consider **Spearman's coefficient of rank correlation, r_S.**

For each pair of values we calculate

$$d = \text{rank } x - \text{rank } y$$

Then

> Spearman's coefficient of rank correlation, r_S, is given by
>
> $$r_S = 1 - \frac{6\sum d^2}{n(n^2 - 1)}$$

r_S is particularly useful when the actual values of x and y are not known, but the data have been ranked already; for example, order of preference in a competition or position in a class.

Method of ranking

Suppose we have the masses, x (in kg), of five men

$$66, \quad 68, \quad 65, \quad 69, \quad 70$$

Arranged in ascending order of magnitude, these are   65, 66, 68, 69, 70,   so we assign the ranks as follows:

x	66	68	65	69	70
Rank x	2	3	1	4	5

If we have *two or more equal values* we proceed as follows:

x	66	68	65	68	70
Rank x	2	3.5	1	3.5	5

Here, the 3rd and the 4th places represent the same mass (68 kg), so we assign the average rank 3.5 to both these places.

Similarly for the eight values:

x	66	65	66	67	66	64	68	68
Rank x	4	2	4	6	4	1	7.5	7.5

Here the 3rd, 4th and 5th places represent the same mass (66 kg) so we assign the average rank 4 to these places; also the 7th and the 8th places represent the same mass (68 kg) so we assign the average rank 7.5 to both these places.

NOTE: if there are more than just a few equal values, then this method is not appropriate.

Example 12.17 These are the marks obtained by 8 pupils in Mathematics and Physics. Calculate Spearman's coefficient of rank correlation.

Mathematics (x)	67	42	85	51	39	97	81	70
Physics (y)	70	59	71	38	55	62	80	76

Solution 12.17

Rank x	4	2	7	3	1	8	6	5
Rank y	5	3	6	1	2	4	8	7
$|d|$	1	1	1	2	1	4	2	2
d^2	1	1	1	4	1	16	4	4

Now $\Sigma d^2 = 32, \quad n = 8$

So
$$r_S = 1 - \frac{6\,\Sigma d^2}{n\,(n^2 - 1)}$$

$$= 1 - \frac{6(32)}{8(63)}$$

$$= -0.2539\ldots$$

Spearman's coefficient of rank correlation is -0.25 (2 d.p.).

Example 12.18 Two competitors rank the eight photographs in a competition as follows:

Photograph	A	B	C	D	E	F	G	H
1st competitor	2	5	3	6	1	4	7	8
2nd competitor	4	3	2	6	1	8	5	7

Calculate Spearman's coefficient of rank correlation for the data.

Solution 12.18 In this example, the data have already been ranked.

Rank x	2	5	3	6	1	4	7	8	
Rank y	4	3	2	6	1	8	5	7	
$|d|$	2	2	1	0	0	4	2	1	
d^2	4	4	1	0	0	16	4	1	$\Sigma d^2 = 30$

$$r_S = 1 - \frac{6\,\Sigma d^2}{n\,(n^2 - 1)} \quad \text{where} \quad n = 8$$

$$= 1 - \frac{6(30)}{8(64 - 1)}$$

$$= 0.64 \quad \text{(2 d.p.)}$$

Spearman's coefficient of rank correlation for the data is 0.64, indicating some positive correlation between the competitors.

Example 12.19 The marks of 10 pupils in French and German tests are as follows:

French, x	12	8	16	11	7	10	13	17	12	9
German, y	6	5	7	7	4	9	8	13	10	11

Calculate Spearman's coefficient of rank correlation.

Solution 12.19

French mark, x	12	8	16	11	7	10	13	17	12	9	
German mark, y	6	5	7	7	4	9	8	13	10	11	
Rank x	6.5	2	9	5	1	4	8	10	6.5	3	
Rank y	3	2	4.5	4.5	1	7	6	10	8	9	
$|d|$	3.5	0	4.5	0.5	0	3	2	0	1.5	6	
d^2	12.25	0	20.25	0.25	0	9	4	0	2.25	36	$\Sigma d^2 = 84$

$$r_S = 1 - \frac{6 \Sigma d^2}{n(n^2 - 1)} \quad \text{with} \quad n = 10$$

$$= 1 - \frac{6(84)}{10(99)}$$

$$= 0.49 \text{ (2 d.p.)}$$

Spearman's coefficient of rank correlation is 0.49, indicating some positive correlation between the marks in the two tests.

Example 12.20 (**a**) The marks of eight candidates in English and Mathematics are:

Candidate	1	2	3	4	5	6	7	8
English (x)	50	58	35	86	76	43	40	60
Mathematics (y)	65	72	54	82	32	74	40	53

Rank the results and hence find a rank correlation coefficient between the two sets of marks.

(**b**) For the above data, $\bar{x} = 56$, $\bar{y} = 59$, $\Sigma xy = 26\,762$, $\Sigma x^2 = 27\,310$, $\Sigma y^2 = 29\,958$. Calculate the product–moment correlation coefficient, r, and compare your value with r_S found in (**a**).

Solution 12.20 (a)

English (x)	50	58	35	86	76	43	40	60	
Maths (y)	65	72	54	82	32	74	40	53	
Rank x	4	5	1	8	7	3	2	6	
Rank y	5	6	4	8	1	7	2	3	
$|d|$	1	1	3	0	6	4	0	3	
d^2	1	1	9	0	36	16	0	9	$\Sigma d^2 = 72$

$$r_S = 1 - \frac{6\,\Sigma d^2}{n\,(n^2 - 1)}$$

$$= 1 - \frac{6(72)}{8(64 - 1)}$$

$$= 0.17 \ (2 \ \text{d.p.})$$

Spearman's coefficient of rank correlation is 0.17 (2 d.p.).

(b)

$$s_{xy} = \frac{\Sigma xy}{n} - \bar{x}\,\bar{y}$$

$$= \frac{26\,762}{8} - (56)(59)$$

$$= 41.25$$

$$s_x{}^2 = \frac{\Sigma x^2}{n} - \bar{x}^2 \qquad\qquad s_y{}^2 = \frac{\Sigma y^2}{n} - \bar{y}^2$$

$$= \frac{27\,310}{8} - 56^2 \qquad\qquad = \frac{29\,958}{8} - 59^2$$

$$= 277.75 \qquad\qquad\qquad = 263.75$$

Therefore

$$r = \frac{s_{xy}}{s_x\,s_y}$$

$$= \frac{41.25}{\sqrt{277.75}\,\sqrt{263.75}}$$

$$= 0.15 \ (2 \ \text{d.p.})$$

The product--moment correlation coefficient is 0.15 (2 d.p.).

The two values for the correlation coefficient are very close in this example. Both indicate a very low degree of positive correlation.

Example 12.21 Find r_S for the following data. Draw a scatter diagram and comment on your value for r_S.

x	1	2.5	6	7	4.5	3	6.5
y	0.5	1	3.5	6.5	3	2.5	5.5

Solution 12.21

Rank x	1	2	5	7	4	3	6
Rank y	1	2	5	7	4	3	6
$|d|$	0	0	0	0	0	0	0

It is obvious that $\Sigma d^2 = 0$

So
$$r_{\mathrm{S}} = 1 - \frac{6\,\Sigma d^2}{n\,(n^2 - 1)}$$
$$= 1 - 0$$
$$= 1$$

Spearman's coefficient of rank correlation is 1.

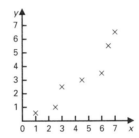

We note that $r_{\mathrm{S}} = 1$ *does not imply* perfect positive correlation.

NOTE: r_{S} will be 1 for any set of values where y increases as x increases and r_{S} will be -1 when y decreases as x increases.

Exercise 12h

1. The table shows the marks awarded to six children in a competition. Calculate a coefficient of rank correlation for the data:

Child	A	B	C	D	E	F
Judge 1	6.8	7.3	8.1	9.8	7.1	9.2
Judge 2	7.8	9.4	7.9	9.6	8.9	6.9

2. The following table shows the marks of eight pupils in biology and chemistry. Rank the results and find the value of Spearman's coefficient of rank correlation.

Biology, x	65	65	70	75	75	80	85	85
Chemistry, y	50	55	58	55	65	58	61	65

3. Mr and Mrs Brown and their son John all drive the family car. Before ordering a new car they decide to list in order their preferences for five optional extras independently. The rank order of their choices is as shown:

Optional extra	Mr Brown	Mrs Brown	John
Heated rear window	1st	2nd	3rd
Anti-rust treatment	2nd	4th	2nd
Headrests	3rd	1st	1st
Inertia-reel seat belts	4th	5th	5th
Radio	5th	3rd	4th

(a) Calculate coefficients of rank correlation between each pair of members of the Brown family.

(b)   A salesman offered to supply three of these extras free with the new car. The family agreed to choose those three which were ranked highest by the two members who agreed most. Which three did they choose, and in what order?   (L Additional)

4.   Two adjudicators at a Music Competition award marks to ten pianists as follows:

	Pianist									
	A	B	C	D	E	F	G	H	I	J
Adjudicator 1	78	66	73	73	84	66	89	84	67	77
Adjudicator 2	81	68	81	75	80	67	85	83	66	78

Calculate a coefficient of rank correlation for these data. Name the method you have used and describe briefly, without proof, the principle on which it is based.

5.   In a skating competition one judge awards the same mark to all 4 competitors. Show that the coefficient of rank correlation (Spearman's) is 0.5, irrespective of the marks awarded to the competitors by the other judge.

6.   Seven army recruits $(A, B, \ldots, G)$ were given two separate aptitude tests. Their orders of merit in each test were

Order of merit	1st	2nd	3rd	4th	5th	6th	7th
1st test	G	F	A	D	B	C	E
2nd test	D	F	E	B	G	C	A

Find Spearman's coefficient of rank correlation between the two orders and comment briefly on the correlation obtained.
(O & C)

7.

Candidate	A	B	C	D	E	F
English	38	62	56	42	59	48
History	64	84	84	60	73	69

The table shows the original marks of six candidates in two examinations. Calculate a coefficient of rank correlation and comment on the value of your result.
The History papers are re-marked and one of the six candidates is awarded five additional marks. Given that the other marks, and the coefficient of rank correlation, are unchanged, state, with reasons, which candidate received the extra marks.   (C Additional)

8.   Sketch two scatter diagrams illustrating the following situations:
(a)   two variables having a large, negative correlation;
(b)   two variables having a small, positive correlation.
The mean rainfall per day and the mean number of hours of sunshine per day observed at a weather station are given below.

Month	Rainfall (mm)	Sunshine (hours)
January	1.26	1.1
February	1.25	2.7
March	0.65	4.5
April	2.10	5.1
May	2.45	5.5
June	2.17	7.6
July	2.84	5.2
August	1.74	5.7
September	2.57	4.8
October	1.65	2.9
November	1.47	2.8
December	1.94	1.8

Calculate, correct to two decimal places, the rank correlation coefficient between rainfall and hours of sunshine.
What is the rank correlation coefficient between rainfall and minutes of sunshine?

9.   In a study of population density in eight suburbs of a town the statistics shown in the table were obtained. The population density is denoted by p, and the distance of the suburb from the centre of the town by d.

Suburb	p (persons/hectare)	d (km)
A	55	0.7
B	11	3.8
C	68	1.7
D	38	2.6
E	46	1.5
F	43	2.6
G	21	3.4
H	25	1.9

(a)   Plot p against d on a scatter diagram.
(b)   Calculate and mark on the diagram the mean of the array.
(c)   Calculate a coefficient of rank correlation between p and d, stating the system of ranking adopted for both quantities.
(d)   State what conclusions can be drawn from your answers to (a) and (c) concerning the general trend of the results.
(e)   Giving a reason for your answer, state which suburb in your opinion fits the general trend least well.   (L Additional)

10. (a) X and Y were judges at a beauty contest in which there were 10 competitors. Their rankings are shown below.

Competitor	X	Y
A	4	6
B	9	10
C	2	5
D	5=	8
E	3	1
F	10	9
G	5=	7
H	7	4
I	8	5
J	1	3

Calculate a coefficient of rank correlation between these two sets of ranks and comment briefly on your result.

(b) Illustrate by means of two scatter diagrams rank correlation coefficients of 0 and -1 between two variables X and Y.

(C Additional)

11 (a) Sketch scatter diagrams which illustrate (i) positive linear correlation, (ii) negative linear correlation, (iii) no correlation, between two variables X and Y.

(b) A doctor asked ten of his patients, who were smokers, how many years they had smoked. In addition, for each patient, he gave a grade between 0 and 100 indicating the extent of their lung damage. The following table shows the results:

Patient	Number of years smoking	Lung damage grade
A	15	30
B	22	50
C	25	55
D	28	30
E	31	57
F	33	35
G	36	60
H	39	72
I	42	70
J	48	75

Calculate a coefficient of rank correlation between the number of years of smoking and the extent of lung damage. Comment on the figure which you obtain. (C Additional)

12. Sketch scatter diagrams for which
(a) the product-moment correlation coefficient is -1,
(b) Spearman's correlation coefficient is $+1$, but the product moment correlation coefficient is *less than* 1.
Five independent observations of the random variables X and Y were:

X	0	1	4	3	2
Y	11	8	5	4	7

Find
(c) the sample product-moment correlation coefficient,
(d) Spearman's correlation coefficient.

(O & C)

13. (a) The following marks were awarded by 2 judges at a music competition:

	Judge 1	Judge 2
Child 1	10	9
Child 2	5	6
Child 3	8	10
Child 4	7	5
Child 5	9	8

Calculate a coefficient of rank correlation.
(b) Determine, by calculation, the equation of the regression line of x on y based on the following information about 8 children:

Child	Arithmetic mark (x)	English mark (y)
1	45	31
2	33	33
3	27	18
4	23	20
5	18	19
6	14	9
7	8	13
8	0	1

14. A company is to replace its fleet of cars. Eight possible models are considered and the transport manager is asked to rank them, from 1 to 8, in order of preference. A saleswoman is asked to use each type of car for a week and grade them according to their suitability for the job (A – very suitable to E – unsuitable). The price is also recorded.

Model	Transport manager's ranking	Saleswoman's grade	Price (£10's)
S	5	B	611
T	1	B+	811
U	7	D−	591
V	2	C	792
W	8	B+	520
X	6	D	573
Y	4	C+	683
Z	3	A−	716

(a) Calculate Spearman's rank correlation coefficient between
(i) price and transport manager's rankings.
(ii) price and saleswoman's grades.

(b) Based on the results of (a) state, giving a reason, whether it would be necessary to use all three different methods of assessing the cars.

(c) A new employee is asked to collect further data and to do some calculations. He produces the following results.

The correlation coefficient between

(i) price and boot capacity is 1.2,

(ii) maximum speed and fuel consumption in miles per gallon is -0.7,

(iii) price and engine capacity is -0.9.

For each of his results say, giving a reason, whether you think it is reasonable.

(d) Suggest two sets of circumstances where Spearman's rank correlation coefficient would be preferred to the product moment correlation coefficient as a measure of association.   (AEB 1988)

SIGNIFICANCE OF SPEARMAN'S RANK CORRELATION COEFFICIENT

METHOD 1 – USING PROBABILITIES OF Σd^2

In order to test the significance of the calculated value of r_S, it is necessary to calculate the probability of obtaining a given value of Σd^2.

We look at the distribution of Σd^2 in the following situation.

These are the rankings of four samples of sparkling wine by two wine-tasters, Enrico and Claude.

Wine	A	B	C	D
Enrico's ranking	1	2	3	4
Claude's ranking	2	1	4	3

If we leave the first row in its natural ranking order, 1, 2, 3, 4, then the second row *could* be ranked in 4! different ways, assuming that there are no equal ranks. These 24 arrangements are shown here, with the corresponding values of Σd^2 and r_S.

	1 2 3 4 1 2 3 4	1 2 3 4 1 2 4 3	1 2 3 4 1 3 4 2	1 2 3 4 1 3 2 4	1 2 3 4 1 4 3 2	1 2 3 4 1 4 2 3
Σd^2	0	2	6	2	8	6
r_S	1	0.8	0.4	0.8	0.2	0.4

	1 2 3 4 2 1 3 4	1 2 3 4 2 1 4 3	1 2 3 4 2 3 1 4	1 2 3 4 2 3 4 1	1 2 3 4 2 4 1 3	1 2 3 4 2 4 3 1
Σd^2	2	4	6	12	10	14
r_S	0.8	0.6	0.4	-0.2	0	-0.4

	1 2 3 4 3 1 2 4	1 2 3 4 3 1 4 2	1 2 3 4 3 2 4 1	1 2 3 4 3 2 1 4	1 2 3 4 3 4 1 2	1 2 3 4 3 4 2 1
Σd^2	6	10	14	8	16	18
r_S	0.4	0	-0.4	0.2	-0.6	-0.8

	1 2 3 4 4 1 2 3	1 2 3 4 4 1 3 2	1 2 3 4 4 2 3 1	1 2 3 4 4 2 1 3	1 2 3 4 4 3 1 2	1 2 3 4 4 3 2 1
Σd^2	12	14	18	14	18	20
r_S	-0.2	-0.4	-0.8	-0.4	-0.8	-1

Arranging Σd^2 and r_S in the form of a frequency distribution:

Σd^2	0	2	4	6	8	10	12	14	16	18	20
$r_S = 1 - \dfrac{6\,\Sigma d^2}{n\,(n^2 - 1)}$	1	0.8	0.6	0.4	0.2	0	-0.2	-0.4	-0.6	-0.8	-1
Frequency	1	3	1	4	2	2	2	4	1	3	1

The distribution is symmetrical about $\Sigma d^2 = 10$.

We illustrate the frequency distribution of both Σd^2 and r_S with a bar chart.

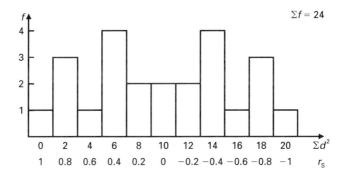

We can now use this bar chart to find probabilities associated with various values of Σd^2.

(**a**)

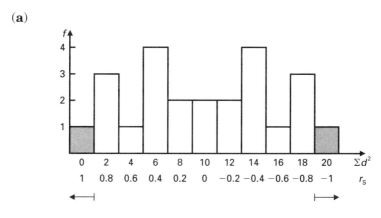

$P(\Sigma d^2 = 0) = P(r_s = 1) = \frac{1}{24} = 0.0417$ $\qquad\qquad$ $P(\Sigma d^2 = 20) = P(r_s = -1) = 0.0417$

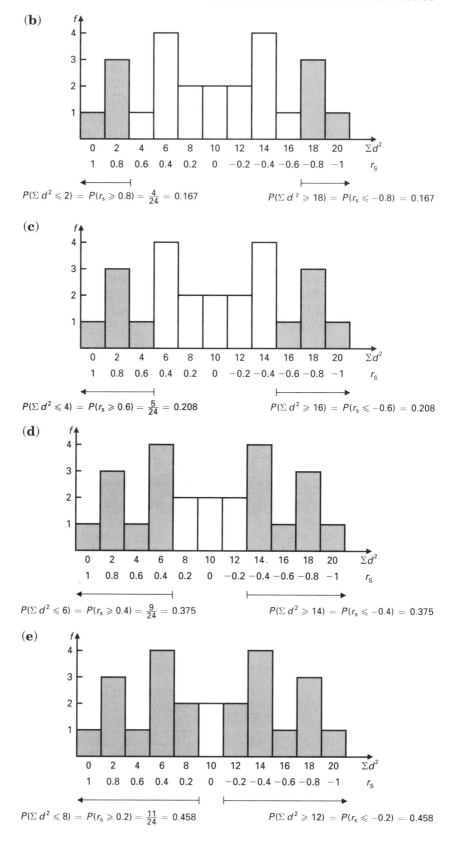

(b)

$P(\Sigma\, d^2 \leqslant 2) = P(r_s \geqslant 0.8) = \frac{4}{24} = 0.167$ $\qquad\qquad$ $P(\Sigma\, d^2 \geqslant 18) = P(r_s \leqslant -0.8) = 0.167$

(c)

$P(\Sigma\, d^2 \leqslant 4) = P(r_s \geqslant 0.6) = \frac{5}{24} = 0.208$ $\qquad\qquad$ $P(\Sigma\, d^2 \geqslant 16) = P(r_s \leqslant -0.6) = 0.208$

(d)

$P(\Sigma\, d^2 \leqslant 6) = P(r_s \geqslant 0.4) = \frac{9}{24} = 0.375$ $\qquad\qquad$ $P(\Sigma\, d^2 \geqslant 14) = P(r_s \leqslant -0.4) = 0.375$

(e)

$P(\Sigma\, d^2 \leqslant 8) = P(r_s \geqslant 0.2) = \frac{11}{24} = 0.458$ $\qquad\qquad$ $P(\Sigma\, d^2 \geqslant 12) = P(r_s \leqslant -0.2) = 0.458$

Putting together the results from all the diagrams we have:

	Probability	
$\Sigma d^2 \leqslant 0, \quad r_S \geqslant 1$	0.0417	$\Sigma d^2 \geqslant 20, \quad r_S \leqslant -1$
$\Sigma d^2 \leqslant 2, \quad r_S \geqslant 0.8$	0.167	$\Sigma d^2 \geqslant 18, \quad r_S \leqslant -0.8$
$\Sigma d^2 \leqslant 4, \quad r_S \geqslant 0.6$	0.208	$\Sigma d^2 \geqslant 16, \quad r_S \leqslant -0.6$
$\Sigma d^2 \leqslant 6, \quad r_S \geqslant 0.4$	0.375	$\Sigma d^2 \geqslant 14, \quad r_S \leqslant -0.4$
$\Sigma d^2 \leqslant 8, \quad r_S \geqslant 0.2$	0.458	$\Sigma d^2 \geqslant 12, \quad r_S \leqslant -0.2$

These results for Σd^2 can also be summarised thus. The highlighted row shows that $P(\Sigma d^2 \leqslant 2) = 0.167$ and $P(\Sigma d^2 \geqslant 18) = 0.167$.

$n = 4$ MAX. $\Sigma d^2 = 20$		
Σd^2		P
$\leqslant$	$\geqslant$	
8	12	.458
6	14	.375
4	16	.208
2	18	.167
0	20	.0417

SIGNIFICANCE TEST FOR r_S, using probabilities of Σd^2

When we test r_S for significance, a suitable null hypothesis is $H_0 : \rho = 0$, where ρ is the true *population* correlation coefficient and $\rho = 0$ indicates that there is no predictable correlation between the rankings. The method is illustrated in the following example.

Example 12.22 For 4 pairs of rankings $\Sigma d^2 = 2$, giving $r_S = 0.8$. Does this indicate a significant positive correlation at the 10% level?

Solution 12.22 $H_0 : \rho = 0$ (there is no correlation)

$H_1 : \rho > 0$ (there is some positive correlation)

Consider the distribution of Σd^2 when $n = 4$. In order to reject H_0 we require the rectangle for Σd^2 to lie *wholly within* a region that gives 10% of the area in the left-hand part of the distribution; i.e. we need $P(\Sigma d^2 \leqslant 2) < 0.1$

However from the table above

$$P(\Sigma d^2 \leqslant 2) = 0.167 > 0.1$$

So we do not reject H_0 and we conclude that there is not significant evidence at the 10% level of a positive correlation.

Referring to the diagram:

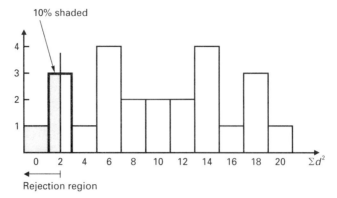

NOTE: We might be surprised at this result, since when $\Sigma d^2 = 2$, $r_S = 0.8$, which is quite high.

USE OF TABLES TO GIVE PROBABILITIES OF Σd^2

Now when $n = 4$ it is fairly easy to work out all the probabilities, as we have just illustrated.

However, when $n = 5$ there are $5! = 120$ different rankings and when $n = 6$ there are 720, so it is very difficult to calculate all the probabilities.

Table A on page 726 in the Appendix gives the probabilities of Σd^2 for values of n from 4 to 10. We use this table in the following examples.

Example 12.23 For 5 pairs of rankings it is found that $\Sigma d^2 = 38$, giving $r_S = -0.9$. Does this provide evidence, at the 5% level, of (**a**) negative correlation, (**b**) a correlation different from zero?

Solution 11.23 (**a**) $H_0 : \rho = 0$ (there is no correlation)

$H_1 : \rho < 0$ (there is some negative correlation)

We consider the table giving values of Σd^2 when $n = 5$, and look for 38. (Table A, page 726)

In the extract printed here, the highlighted row means

$$P(\Sigma d^2 \leqslant 2) = 0.0417$$

and $P(\Sigma d^2 \geqslant 38) = 0.0417$.

Perform a one-tailed test at the 5% level and reject H_0 if $P(\Sigma d^2 \geqslant 38) < 0.05$ i.e. if the rectangle for $\Sigma d^2 = 38$ lies wholly in a region which gives 5% of the area in the right-hand tail.

$n = 5$ MAX. $\Sigma d^2 = 40$		
Σd^2		P
$\leqslant$	$\geqslant$	
18	22	.475
16	24	.392
14	26	.342
12	28	.258
10	30	.225
8	32	.175
6	34	.117
4	36	.0667
2	38	.0417
0	40	.0083

Now from the table $P(\Sigma d^2 \geqslant 38) = 0.0417$, which is less than 0.05.

Although it is not necessary to draw a diagram, the right-hand tail would look like this:

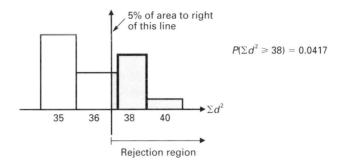

Since $P(\Sigma d^2 \geqslant 38) = 0.0417 < 0.05$ we reject H_0 and conclude that there is significant evidence, at the 5% level, of negative correlation.

(**b**) $H_0 : \rho = 0$ (there is no correlation)

$H_1 : \rho \neq 0$ (there is some correlation different from zero).

This time we use a two-tailed test as we are not asked to consider specifically positive or negative correlation in the alternative hypothesis. Therefore the rejection region contains 2.5% of the area in each of the tails.

In this case we reject H_0 if $P(\Sigma d^2 \geqslant 38) < 0.025$.

Now $P(\Sigma d^2 \geqslant 38) = 0.0417 > 0.025$,   so we do not reject H_0 and we conclude that there is no evidence, at the 5% level, of a correlation different from zero.

Example 12.24 An expert on porcelain is asked to place 7 china bowls in date order of manufacture assigning the rank 1 to the oldest bowl. The actual dates of manufacture and the order given by the expert are shown.

Bowl	A	B	C	D	E	F	G
Date of manufacture	1920	1857	1710	1896	1810	1690	1780
Order given by expert	7	3	4	6	2	1	5

Find, to 3 decimal places, the Spearman rank correlation coefficient between the order of manufacture and the order given by the expert.

Refer to one of the tables of critical values provided to comment on the significance of your result. State clearly the null hypothesis which is being tested.   (L)P

Solution 12.24

	Bowl						
	A	B	C	D	E	F	G
Rank x	7	5	2	6	4	1	3
Rank y	7	3	4	6	2	1	5
$|d|$	0	2	2	0	2	0	2
d^2	0	4	4	0	4	0	4

$\Sigma d^2 = 16,\ n = 7$

Now $\qquad r_S = 1 - \dfrac{6\,\Sigma d^2}{n(n^2-1)}$

$\qquad\qquad = 1 - \dfrac{6(16)}{7(48)}$

$\qquad\qquad = \underline{0.714}\ \text{(3 d.p.)}$

$H_0 : \rho = 0$ (no evidence of correlation)

$H_1 : \rho > 0$ (some positive correlation)

Use a one-tailed test, at the 5% level, and reject H_0 if $P(\Sigma d^2 \leqslant 16) < 0.05$.

In Table A (p. 726) look for $n = 7$.

The highlighted row in the extract printed here means

$\qquad P(\Sigma d^2 \leqslant 16) = 0.0440$

and $P(\Sigma d^2 \geqslant 96) = 0.0440$.

Now since $P(\Sigma d^2 \leqslant 16) = 0.0440 < 0.05$, we reject H_0 and conclude that <u>there is</u> <u>evidence, at the 5% level, of agreement</u> <u>between the order given by the expert and</u> <u>the actual dates of manufacture</u>.

$n = 7$ MAX. $\Sigma d^2 = 112$		
Σd^2		P
$\leqslant$	$\geqslant$	
54	58	.482
52	60	.453
50	62	.420
48	64	.391
46	66	.356
44	68	.331
42	70	.297
40	72	.278
38	74	.249
36	76	.222
34	78	.198
32	80	.177
30	82	.151
28	84	.133
26	86	.118
24	88	.100
22	90	.0833
20	92	.0694
18	94	.0548
16	96	.0440
14	98	.0331
12	100	.0240
10	102	.0171
8	104	.0119
6	106	.0062
4	108	.0034
2	110	.0014

Example 12.25 Applicants for a job with a company are interviewed by two of the personnel staff. After the interviews each applicant is awarded a mark by each of the interviewers. The marks are given below.

	Candidate							
	A	B	C	D	E	F	G	H
Interviewer 1	22	27	24	17	20	22	16	13
Interviewer 2	28	23	25	14	26	17	20	15

(**a**) Calculate, to 2 decimal places, the Spearman rank correlation coefficient between these two sets of marks.

(**b**) Stating your hypotheses and using a 5% level of significance, interpret your result.   (L)

Solution 12.25

	A	B	C	D	E	F	G	H
Rank 1	5.5	8	7	3	4	5.5	2	1
Rank 2	8	5	6	1	7	3	4	2
$|d|$	2.5	3	1	2	3	2.5	2	1
d^2	6.25	9	1	4	9	6.25	4	1

$\Sigma d^2 = 40.5, \ n = 8$

(**a**)
$$r_S = 1 - \frac{6\,\Sigma d^2}{n(n^2 - 1)}$$

$$= 1 - \frac{6(40.5)}{8(63)}$$

$$= 1 - 0.5178\ldots$$

Therefore $r_S = 0.52$ (2 d.p.)

(**b**) $H_0 : \rho = 0$ (no correlation between interviewers)

$H_1 : \rho > 0$ (there is some positive correlation)

Use a one-tailed test, at the 5% level, and reject H_0 if $P(\Sigma d^2 \leqslant 40.5) < 0.05$.

In Table A, (p. 726), look for $n = 8$. This extract is printed here.

The required 'row' value of 40.5 is not printed.

So we use $P(\Sigma d^2 \leqslant 40) = 0.0983$

and $P(\Sigma d^2 \leqslant 42) = 0.108$

to estimate that $P(\Sigma d^2 \leqslant 40.5) \approx 0.10$

Therefore $P(\Sigma d^2 \leqslant 40.5) > 0.05$

So we do not reject H_0 and we conclude that there is no evidence, at the 5% level, of a positive correlation between the interviewers.

$n = 8$ MAX. $\Sigma d^2 = 168$		
Σd^2		P
$\leqslant$	$\geqslant$	
78	90	.441
74	94	.397
68	100	.332
64	104	.291
60	108	.250
56	112	.214
54	114	.195
52	116	.180
48	120	.150
46	122	.134
44	124	.122
42	126	.108
40	128	.0983
38	130	.0855
36	132	.0756
34	134	.0661
32	136	.0575
30	138	.0481
28	140	.0415
24	144	.0288
20	148	.0184
16	152	.0109
14	154	.0077
12	156	.0054
10	158	.0036
6	162	.0011
4	164	.0006

Exercise 12i

In each of the following questions use Table A (p. 726) to test the hypotheses.

	n	Σd^2	Hypotheses	Level of significance
1.	9	212	$H_0 : \rho = 0,\ H_1 : \rho < 0$	1%
2.	8	30	$H_0 : \rho = 0,\ H_1 : \rho > 0$	5%
3.	8	30	$H_0 : \rho = 0,\ H_1 : \rho \neq 0$	5%
4.	10	78	$H_0 : \rho = 0,\ H_1 : \rho > 0$	5%
5.	10	252	$H_0 : \rho = 0,\ H_1 : \rho < 0$	10%
6.	10	274	$H_0 : \rho = 0,\ H_1 : \rho \neq 0$	5%
7.	7	18	$H_0 : \rho = 0,\ H_1 : \rho \neq 0$	10%
8.	7	106	$H_0 : \rho = 0,\ H_1 : \rho < 0$	1%
9.	7	14	$H_0 : \rho = 0,\ H_1 : \rho \neq 0$	5%

Club	Position	Average attendance
A	1	30
B	2	32
C	3	12
D	4	19
E	5	27
F	6	18
G	7	15
H	8	25

Refer to the appropriate table of critical values to comment on the significance of your result, stating clearly the null hypothesis being tested. (L)P

10. The positions in a league of 8 hockey clubs at the end of a season are shown in the table. Shown also are the average attendances (in hundreds) at home matches during that season.

Calculate a coefficient of rank correlation between position in the league and average home attendance.

11. Spearman's rank correlation coefficient between 7 pairs of ranks was calculated to be 0.79, based on $\Sigma d^2 = 12$. Stating your hypotheses and using a 5% level of significance, interpret the result. (L)

NOTE: There are more questions on this section in Exercise 12k.

METHOD 2 – SIGNIFICANCE TEST FOR r_S, USING CRITICAL VALUES

Instead of working with Σd^2 Table B (below and on page 727) gives critical values of r_S.

We reject H_0 if the value for $|r_\mathrm{S}|$ is greater than or equal to the critical value given.

Critical values of Spearman's rank correlation coefficient

n	Significance level (one-tailed test)	
	0.05	0.01
4	1.000	
5	0.900	1.000
6	0.829	0.943
7	0.714	0.893
8	0.643	0.833
9	0.600	0.783
10	0.564	0.746
12	0.506	0.712
14	0.456	0.645
16	0.425	0.601
18	0.399	0.564
20	0.377	0.534
22	0.359	0.508
24	0.343	0.485
26	0.329	0.465
28	0.317	0.448
30	0.306	0.432

Table B

Example 12.26 Using Table B, for $n = 8$ and $r_S = 0.667$, test the following hypotheses:

(a) $H_0 : \rho = 0$, $H_1 : \rho \neq 0$ (10% level of significance)

(b) $H_0 : \rho = 0$, $H_1 : \rho > 0$ (1% level of significance)

Solution 12.26 (a) Using a two-tailed test, at the 10% level, and considering Table B, with $n = 8$, significance level 0.05 (because test is two-tailed), we reject H_0 if $r_S \geqslant 0.643$.

Now $r_S = 0.667$, so we reject H_0 and conclude that <u>there is evidence at the 10% level of a correlation different from zero.</u>

(b) Using a one-tailed test, at the 1% level, and considering Table B, with $n = 8$, significance level 0.01, we reject H_0 if $r_S \geqslant 0.833$.

Now $r_S = 0.667 < 0.833$, so we do not reject H_0 and we conclude that <u>there is no evidence, at the 1% level, of positive correlation.</u>

Example 12.27 For 9 pairs of values, r_S is found to be -0.767. Test, at the 1% level, whether there is evidence of a negative correlation.

Solution 12.27 $H_0 : \rho = 0$ (there is no correlation)

$H_1 : \rho < 0$ (there is negative correlation)

Using Table B, with $n = 9$, significance level 0.01, we reject H_0 if $r_S \leqslant -0.783$.

Now $r_S = -0.767 > -0.783$, so we do not reject H_0 and we conclude that <u>there is no evidence, at the 1% level, of a negative correlation.</u>

Exercise 12j

In each of the following, use Table B to comment on the significance of the value for r_S.

	n	r_S	Hypotheses	Level of significance
1.	7	0.893	$H_0 : \rho = 0$, $H_1 : \rho \neq 0$	2%
2.	14	0.499	$H_0 : \rho = 0$, $H_1 : \rho > 0$	1%
3.	28	0.324	$H_0 : \rho = 0$, $H_1 : \rho \neq 0$	10%
4.	28	0.324	$H_0 : \rho = 0$, $H_1 : \rho > 0$	1%
5.	16	-0.419	$H_0 : \rho = 0$, $H_1 : \rho < 0$	5%
6.	12	-0.689	$H_0 : \rho = 0$, $H_1 : \rho \neq 0$	10%
7.	12	0.689	$H_0 : \rho = 0$, $H_1 : \rho > 0$	1%
8.	10	-0.733	$H_0 : \rho = 0$, $H_1 : \rho > 0$	1%

Exercise 12k

In the following questions, either Table A or Table B may be used.

1. Find r_S and comment on the significance of the result. X and Y have been ranked.

    (a) X 1 2 3 4 5 6
         Y 1 2 3 4 5 6

    (b) X 1 2 3 4 5 6
         Y 6 5 4 3 2 1

    (c) X 1 2 3 4 5 6
         Y 3 5 1 4 6 2

    (d) X 1 2 3 4 5 6
         Y 2 1 3 5 4 6

    (e) X 1 2 3 4 5 6 7 8 9 10
         Y 1 2 3 4 5 6 7 8 9 10

    (f) X 1 2 3 4 5 6 7 8 9 10
         Y 10 9 8 7 6 5 4 3 2 1

    (g) X 1 2 3 4 5 6 7 8 9 10
         Y 3 1 6 4 5 8 10 9 2 7

    (h) X 1 2 3 4 5 6 7 8 9 10
         Y 9 8 10 7 6 5 2 4 3 1

2. Calculate r_S for the following data and comment on the significance of the results.

    (a) (20, 13), (47, 29), (50, 33), (33, 20), (57, 32), (44, 23), (38, 25), (25, 19).

    (b) (4.8, 81), (6.2, 79), (8.4, 86), (4.1, 63), (7.5, 90), (5.1, 87).

3. Explain how you used, or could have used, a correlation coefficient to analyse the results of an experiment. State briefly when it is appropriate to use a rank correlation coefficient rather than a product–moment correlation coefficient.

    Seven rock samples taken from a particular locality were analysed. The percentages, C and M, of two oxides contained in each sample were recorded. The results are shown in the table.

Sample	C	M
1	0.60	1.06
2	0.42	0.72
3	0.51	0.94
4	0.56	1.04
5	0.31	0.84
6	1.04	1.16
7	0.80	1.24

    Given that

    $$\Sigma CM = 4.459 \qquad \Sigma C^2 = 2.9278$$
    $$\Sigma M^2 = 7.196,$$

    find, to 3 decimal places, the product–moment correlation coefficient of the percentages of the two oxides. Calculate also, to 3 decimal places, a rank correlation coefficient.

Using the tables provided state any conclusions which you draw from the value of your rank correlation coefficient. State clearly the null hypothesis being tested. (L)

4. Giving an example from your projects if you wish, describe conditions under which you would use a rank correlation coefficient as a measure of association.

    In a ski-jumping contest each competitor made 2 jumps. The orders of merit for the 10 competitors who completed both jumps are shown in the table.

Ski-jumper	First jump	Second jump
A	2	4
B	9	10
C	7	5
D	4	1
E	10	8
F	8	9
G	6	2
H	5	7
I	1	3
J	3	6

    (a) Calculate, to 2 decimal places, a rank correlation coefficient for the performances of the ski-jumpers in the two jumps.

    (b) Using a 5% level of significance and quoting from the tables of critical values provided, interpret your result. State clearly your null and alternative hypotheses. (L)P

5. (a) Explain briefly, referring to your project work if you wish, the conditions under which you would measure association using a rank correlation coefficient rather than a product moment correlation coefficient.

    At an agricultural show 10 Shetland sheep were ranked by a qualified judge and by a trainee judge. Their rankings are shown in the table.

Qualified judge	Trainee judge
1	1
2	2
3	5
4	6
5	7
6	8
7	10
8	4
9	3
10	9

    Calculate a rank correlation coefficient for these data.

Using one of the tables provided and a 10% significance level, state your conclusions as to whether there is some degree of agreement between the two sets of ranks.

(b) The variables H and T are known to be linearly related. Fifty pairs of experimental observations of the two variables gave the following results:

$$\Sigma H = 83.4, \quad \Sigma T = 402.0, \quad \Sigma HT = 680.2,$$
$$\Sigma H^2 = 384.6, \quad \Sigma T^2 = 3238.2.$$

Obtain the regression equation from which one can estimate H when T has the value 7.8, and give, to 1 decimal place, the value of this estimate. (L)

6. In the table below x is the average weekly household income in £ and y the infant mortality per 1000 live births in 11 regions of the UK in 1985.

Region	x	y
A	170.4	8.4
B	183.2	9.4
C	172.9	10.3
D	187.1	10.5
E	203.2	8.3
F	204.8	9.4
G	208.8	8.5
H	248.0	9.0
I	198.3	9.4
J	187.1	9.8
K	179.1	9.6

It is hypothesised that a high value of x will be associated with a low value of y. Explain why it would not be appropriate to use the product moment correlation coefficient to investigate this. Calculate a rank correlation coefficient and test its significance. It appears that region A is exceptional. What would your findings be if this region were omitted from the analysis?

7. A sample of n pairs (x_i, y_i), $i = 1, 2, \ldots, n$, is drawn from a bivariate population (X, Y) and a rank correlation coefficient, r, calculated.

(a) What range of values is it possible for r to have?

(b) What information about the sample does r indicate?

(c) What can be concluded about the sample points when $r = 1$? Can the same be said about the population from which the sample is drawn? Explain your answer.

The following table gives the average share rate and average mortgage rate calculated on the first day of the months shown for the years 1976 to 1985.

Year	Month	Share %	Mortgage %
1976	Nov	7.8	12.2
1977	Nov	6.0	9.5
1978	Dec	8.0	11.8
1979	Dec	10.5	11.8
1980	Jan	10.5	15.0
1981	Nov	9.8	15.0
1982	Dec	6.2	10.0
1983	Jul	7.2	11.2
1984	Dec	6.8	11.5
1985	Apr	8.2	14.0

Plot a scatter diagram and comment on its implication for r. Indicate on your diagram which point appears to be an outlier (i.e. one that is far from the trend line). Calculate a rank correlation coefficient between share rate and mortgage rate. Comment on the significance of your calculated value of r.

8. (a) On two separate occasions, ranks 1, 2, 3 are assigned at random to three objects A, B, C. Obtain the probability distribution of a coefficient of rank correlation between the pair of rankings.

(b) Five sacks of coal, A, B, C, D and E have different weights, with A being heavier than B, B being heavier than C, and so on. A weight lifter ranks the sacks (heaviest first) in the order A, D, B, E, C. Calculate a coefficient of rank correlation between the weight lifter's ranking and the true ranking of the weights of the sacks. (C)

9. In a random sample of 8 areas, residents were asked to express their approval or disapproval of the services provided by the local authority. A score of 0 represented complete dissatisfaction, and 10 represented complete satisfaction. The table below shows the mean score for each local authority together with the authority's level of community charge.

Authority	Community Charge (£)	Approval rating
A	485	3.0
B	490	4.4
C	378	5.0
D	451	4.6
E	384	4.1
F	352	5.5
G	420	5.8
H	212	6.1

Calculate Spearman's rank correlation coefficient for these data.

Carry out a significance test at the 5% level using the value of the correlation coefficient which you have calculated. State carefully the null and alternative hypotheses under test and the conclusion to be drawn.   (MEI)

10. To test the belief that milder winters are followed by warmer summers, meteorological records are obtained for a random sample of 10 years. For each year the mean temperatures are found for January and July. The data, in degrees Celsius, are given below.

Jan	July
8.3	16.2
7.1	13.1
9.0	16.7
1.8	11.2
3.5	14.9
4.7	15.1
5.8	17.7
6.0	17.3
2.7	12.3
2.1	13.4

(i)   Rank the data and calculate Spearman's rank correlation coefficient.
(ii) Test, at the 2.5% level of significance, the belief that milder winters are followed by warmer summers. State clearly the null and alternative hypotheses under test.
(iii) Would it be more appropriate, less appropriate or equally appropriate to use the product–moment correlation coefficient to analyse these data? Briefly explain why.   (MEI)

11. Explain why it is advisable to plot a scatter diagram before interpreting a correlation coefficient calculated for a sample drawn from a bivariate distribution.

Sketch rough scatter diagrams indicating the following:
(i)   a linear (product–moment) coefficient close to zero but an obvious relation between the variables;
(ii) a non-linear relation between the variables yielding a rank correlation coefficient of +1.
If a sample correlation coefficient has a value close to +1 or to −1, what further information is needed before it can be decided whether a relationship between the variables is indicated?
It is hypothesised that there is a positive correlation between the population of a country and its area. The following table gives a random sample of 13 countries with their area x, in thousand km^2, and population y, in millions.

Country	x	y
1	2.5	0.5
2	28	5
3	30	2
4	72	4
5	98	42
6	121	21
7	128	16
8	176	3
9	239	14
10	313	37
11	407	6
12	435	17
13	538	22

Plot a scatter diagram and comment on its implication for the hypothesis.
Calculate a suitable correlation coefficient and test its significance at the 5% level.   (C)

WORKED EXAMPLE

Example 12.28 A machine-hire company kept records of the age, X months, and the maintenance costs, £Y, of one type of machine. The following table summarises the data for a random sample of 10 of the machines.

Machine	A	B	C	D	E	F	G	H	I	J
Age, x	63	12	34	81	51	14	45	74	24	89
Maintenance cost, y	111	25	41	181	64	21	51	145	43	241

A scatter diagram of the data is shown below.

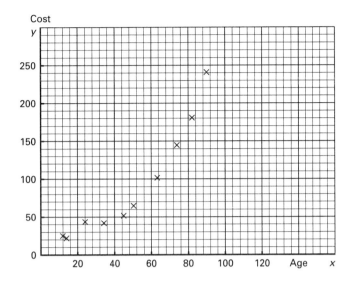

(a) Calculate, to 3 decimal places, the product–moment correlation coefficient.

(You may use $\Sigma x^2 = 30\,625$, $\Sigma y^2 = 135\,481$, $\Sigma xy = 62\,412$.)

(b) Calculate, to 3 decimal places, Spearman's rank correlation coefficient.

(c) It is suggested that it would have been better to have calculated the coefficients above for X and $\ln Y$ instead of X and Y. Without doing any calculations, state any changes you would expect to find in the values of the coefficients.

(d) For a different type of machine similar data were collected. From a large population of such machines a random sample of 10 was taken and the Spearman rank correlation coefficient, based on $\Sigma d^2 = 36$, was 0.782.

Using a 5% level of significance and quoting from the tables of critical values provided, interpret this rank correlation coefficient. Use a two-tailed test and state clearly your null and alternative hypotheses. (L)

Solution 12.28 (a) $\bar{x} = \dfrac{\Sigma x}{n}$ $\bar{y} = \dfrac{\Sigma y}{n}$

$= \dfrac{487}{10}$ $= \dfrac{923}{10}$

$= 48.7$ $= 92.3$

Using the given information

$$s_{xy} = \frac{\sum xy}{n} - \bar{x}\,\bar{y}$$

$$= \frac{62\,412}{10} - (48.7)(92.3)$$

$$= 1746.19$$

$$s_x^2 = \frac{\sum x^2}{n} - \bar{x}^2 \qquad\qquad s_y^2 = \frac{\sum y^2}{n} - \bar{y}^2$$

$$= \frac{30\,625}{10} - (48.7)^2 \qquad\qquad = \frac{135\,481}{10} - (92.3)^2$$

$$= 690.81 \qquad\qquad\qquad = 5028.81$$

$$s_x = 26.283\ldots \qquad\qquad\qquad s_y = 70.914\ldots$$

Now
$$r = \frac{s_{xy}}{s_x\, s_y}$$

$$= \frac{1746.19}{(26.283)\,(70.914)}$$

$$= 0.9368\ldots$$

Therefore
$$r = 0.937 \ \ (3 \text{ d.p.})$$

(b)

Machine	A	B	C	D	E	F	G	H	I	J	
Rank x	7	1	4	9	6	2	5	8	3	10	
Rank y	7	2	3	9	6	1	5	8	4	10	
d^2	0	1	1	0	0	1	0	0	1	0	$\sum d^2 = 4$

$$r_{\mathrm{S}} = 1 - \frac{6\sum d^2}{n(n^2 - 1)}$$

$$= 1 - \frac{6(4)}{10(99)}$$

$$= 0.9757\ldots$$

Therefore
$$r_{\mathrm{S}} = 0.976 \ \ (3 \text{ d.p.})$$

(c) If we calculate $\ln Y$ instead of Y, the values of $\ln Y$ vary from $\ln 21 = 3.044\ldots$ to $\ln 241 = 5.48\ldots$ so that the range is from 3.044 to 5.48 and so the degree of scatter is small and there should be a higher value for r. However the value for r_{S} will remain the same, since the ranks for $\ln Y$ will be the same as the ranks for Y.

NOTE: It is interesting to consider the scatter graphs on one diagram:

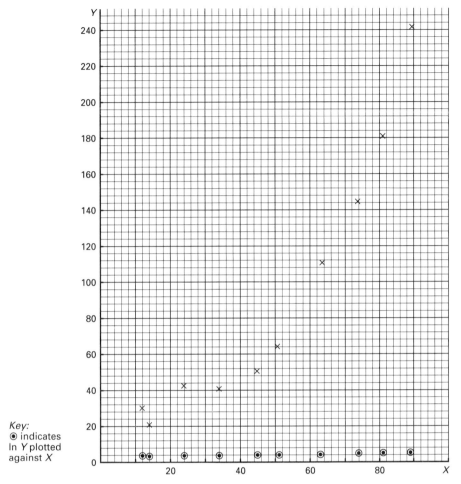

Key:
⊙ indicates
ln Y plotted
against X

Also, you could check that r is higher by using the calculator in LR mode for the data for X and $\ln Y$.

	Casio 85/100/115	**Graphics 7000 GA**
Set LR mode	MODE 2	MODE ÷
Clear memories	SHIFT KAC	SHIFT SCI EXE
Input data	63 $x_D y_D$ 111 ln DATA	63 SHIFT , ln 111 DT
	12 $x_D y_D$ 25 ln DATA	12 SHIFT , ln 25 DT
	⋮ ⋮ ⋮ ⋮ ⋮	⋮ ⋮ ⋮ ⋮ ⋮ ⋮
	89 $x_D y_D$ 241 ln DATA	89 SHIFT , ln 241 DT
Output		
$\boxed{r}$ = 0.986...	SHIFT 9	SHIFT 9 EXE
Clear LR mode	MODE 0	MODE +

The value for r is higher than the value obtained in part (**a**).

(**d**) Given $n = 10$, $\Sigma d^2 = 36$, $r_S = 0.782$,

$H_0 : \rho = 0$ (there is no correlation)

$H_1 : \rho \neq 0$ (there is some correlation different from zero)

Using Σd^2 tables:

We use a two-tailed test, at the 5% level and reject H_0 if
$P(\Sigma d^2 \leqslant 36) < 0.025$.

From Table A (p. 726):

$n = 10$	
Σd^2	P
$\leqslant$ $\geqslant$ 36 294	0.0053

This indicates that $P(\Sigma d^2 \leqslant 36) = 0.0053$.   Since this probability is
less than 0.025 we reject H_0 and conclude that <u>there is evidence, at
the 5% level, of a correlation between the age and the maintenance
cost</u>.

SUMMARY — REGRESSION AND CORRELATION

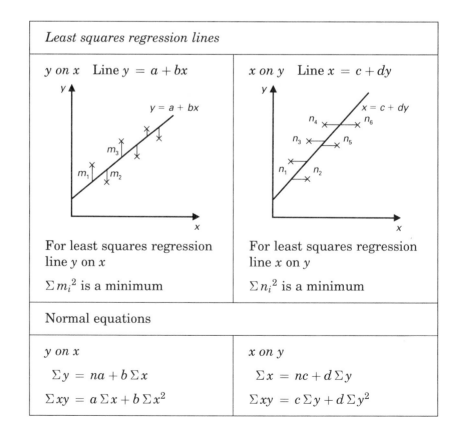

Least squares regression lines	
y on x Line $y = a + bx$	*x on y* Line $x = c + dy$
For least squares regression line y on x $\Sigma m_i{}^2$ is a minimum	For least squares regression line x on y $\Sigma n_i{}^2$ is a minimum
Normal equations	
y on x $\Sigma y = na + b \Sigma x$ $\Sigma xy = a \Sigma x + b \Sigma x^2$	*x on y* $\Sigma x = nc + d \Sigma y$ $\Sigma xy = c \Sigma y + d \Sigma y^2$

Covariance method

y on x	x on y
$y - \bar{y} = \dfrac{s_{xy}}{s_x{}^2}(x - \bar{x})$	$x - \bar{x} = \dfrac{s_{xy}}{s_y{}^2}(y - \bar{y})$

Minimum sum of squares of residuals:

y on x	x on y
$\Sigma m_{i_{(min)}}^2 = n(1 - r^2)s_y{}^2$	$\Sigma n_{i_{(min)}}^2 = n(1 - r^2)s_x{}^2$

Product–moment correlation coefficient, r:

$$r = \frac{s_{xy}}{s_x s_y}$$

In terms of the regression coefficients: $r^2 = bd$

where $b = \dfrac{s_{xy}}{s_x{}^2}$ (regression coefficient of y on x)

$d = \frac{s_{xy}}{s_y{}^2}$ (regression coefficient of x on y)

$$s_{xy} = \frac{1}{n}\Sigma(x - \bar{x})(y - \bar{y}) = \frac{\Sigma xy}{n} - \bar{x}\bar{y} \quad \text{(covariance)}$$

$$s_x{}^2 = \frac{1}{n}\Sigma(x - \bar{x})^2 = \frac{\Sigma x^2}{n} - \bar{x}^2;$$

$$s_y{}^2 = \frac{1}{n}\Sigma(y - \bar{y})^2 = \frac{\Sigma y^2}{n} - \bar{y}^2$$

Using coding:

If $X = \dfrac{x - a}{b}$ and $Y = \dfrac{y - c}{d}$

$s_{xy} = bds_{XY} \qquad s_x = bs_X \qquad s_y = ds_Y$

$r_{xy} = r_{XY} = \dfrac{s_{XY}}{s_X s_Y}$

Regression lines: Y on X $\quad Y - \overline{Y} = \dfrac{s_{XY}}{s_X{}^2}(X - \overline{X})$

X on Y $\quad X - \overline{X} = \dfrac{s_{XY}}{s_Y{}^2}(Y - \overline{Y})$

Spearman's coefficient of rank correlation:

$$r_S = 1 - \frac{6\Sigma d^2}{n(n^2 - 1)}$$

Miscellaneous Exercise 12I

1. The ages, in months, and the weights, in kg, of a random sample of 9 babies are shown below:

Baby	Age, x	Weight, y
A	1	4.4
B	2	5.2
C	2	5.8
D	3	6.4
E	3	6.7
F	3	7.2
G	4	7.6
H	4	7.9
I	5	8.4

(a) Calculate, to 3 decimal places, the product–moment correlation coefficient between weight and age for these babies. Give a brief interpretation of your result.

(b) Find the equation, $y = ax + b$, of the regression line of weight on age for this sample, giving the coefficients a and b to 3 decimal places. Interpret the meaning of your values of a and b.

(c) Use this equation to estimate the mean weight of a baby aged 6 months.
State any reservations you have about this estimate, giving your reasons.

A boy who does not know the weights or ages of these babies is asked to list them, by guesswork, in order of increasing weight. He puts them in the order

A C E B G D I F H.

(d) Obtain, to 3 decimal places, a rank correlation coefficient between the boy's order and the true weight order.

(e) Referring to the tables provided and using a 5% significance level, discuss any conclusions you draw from your result.   (L)

2. An instrument panel is being designed to control a complex industrial process. It will be necessary to use both hands independently to operate the panel. To help with the design it was decided to time a number of operators, each carrying out the same task once with the left hand and once with the right hand.
The times, in seconds, were as follows:

Operator	Left hand, x	Right hand, y
A	49	34
B	58	37
C	63	49
D	42	27
E	27	49
F	55	40
G	39	66
H	33	21
I	72	64
J	66	42
K	50	37

You may assume that $\Sigma x = 554$ $\Sigma x^2 = 29\,902$
$\Sigma y = 466$ $\Sigma y^2 = 21\,682$ $\Sigma xy = 24\,053$

(a) Plot a scatter diagram of the data.

(b) Calculate the product–moment correlation coefficient between the two variables and comment on this value.

(c) Further investigation revealed that two of the operators were left-handed. State, giving a reason, which you think these were. Omitting their two results, calculate Spearman's rank correlation coefficient and comment on this value.

(d) What can you say about the relationship between the times to carry out the task with left and right hands?   (AEB 1992)

3. A teacher recorded the following data which refer to the marks gained by 13 children in an aptitude test and a statistics examination.

Child	Aptitude test, x	Statistics examination, y
A	54	84
B	52	68
C	42	71
D	31	37
E	43	79
F	23	58
G	32	33
H	49	60
I	37	47
J	13	60
K	13	44
L	36	64
M	39	49

(a) Draw a scatter diagram to represent these two sets of marks.

(b) Calculate, to 3 decimal places, the product–moment correlation coefficient between the test mark and the examination mark.

(You may use $\Sigma x^2 = 18\,672$; $\Sigma y^2 = 46\,626$; $\Sigma xy = 28\,234$)

(c) Comment on your result.

(d) The teacher decided that, on the basis of the scatter diagram, children F, J and K performed differently from the rest of the group. Suggest why the teacher might have come to that decision.

(e) The teacher decides to analyse the data ignoring these three children. Calculate, to 3 decimal places, the Spearman rank correlation coefficient between the other ten pairs of observations.

(f) Using a 5% level of significance and quoting from the tables of critical values provided, interpret the rank correlation coefficient. Use a one-tailed test. State clearly the null and alternative hypotheses. (L)

4. (a) State, with a reason in **each** case, *but without doing any calculations*, whether or not

$$y = -4.6 + 1.4x$$

could be the least squares regression line for either of the following data sets.

(i)

x	0.8	1.9	3.6	4.7	6.3
y	12.2	11.0	9.4	8.0	5.7

(ii)

x	3.2	4.1	5.3	7.7	9.4
y	0.1	1.1	2.8	6.4	8.7

(b) As part of a study into the ageing of photographic film, a company's sensitometry laboratory collected the following information on the change in blue balance of a particular type of film at increasing ages from manufacture.

Film age in months, x	Change in blue balance, y
1	17.9
2	20.7
3	30.3
4	36.8
5	45.2
6	52.6
7	63.4
8	66.7
9	66.3
10	70.1
11	80.4
12	85.6

$\Sigma x = 78$ $\Sigma x^2 = 650$ $\Sigma y = 636.0$
$\Sigma xy = 5025.7$

(i) Illustrate these data by a scatter diagram.

(ii) Calculate the equation of the least squares regression line of y on x and draw it on your scatter diagram.

(iii) Three different technicians were involved in the study of the film. A analysed films aged 1, 2, 3 and 4 months, B analysed films aged 5, 6, 7 and 8 months, and C analysed the others. In the light of your analysis, comment on the performance of each technician. (JMB)

5. The data below shows the height above sea level, x metres, and the temperature, $y\,°C$, at 7.00 a.m., on the same day in summer at 9 places in Europe.

Height, x	Temperature, y
1400	6
400	15
280	18
790	10
390	16
590	14
540	13
1250	7
680	13

(a) Plot these data on a scatter diagram.

(b) Calculate the product–moment correlation coefficient between x and y.
(Use $\Sigma x^2 = 5\,639\,200$; $\Sigma y^2 = 1524$; $\Sigma xy = 66\,450$.)

(c) Give an interpretation of your coefficient. On the same day the number of hours of sunshine was recorded and Spearman's rank correlation between hours of sunshine and temperature, based on $\Sigma d^2 = 28$ was 0.767.

(d) Stating clearly your hypotheses and using a 5% two-tailed test, interpret this rank correlation coefficient. (L)

6. A technician monitoring water purity believes that there is a relationship between the hardness of the water and its alkalinity. Over a period of 10 days, she recorded the data in the table:

Alkalinity (mg/l)	Hardness (mg/l)
33.8	51.0
29.1	45.0
22.8	41.3
26.2	46.0
31.8	48.0
31.9	50.0
29.4	46.3
26.1	45.0
28.0	45.3
27.2	43.0

(a)   Plot the data on graph paper with 'Alkalinity' on the horizontal axis. Mark the mean point.

(b)   Given that the product–moment correlation coefficient for these data is 0.913, what conclusion is it reasonable to draw? You are expected to refer to appropriate tables to support your reply.

(c)   The technician decides to calculate the equation for the least squares regression line of **hardness on alkalinity**. Show that this line has gradient 0.821 and find its equation.

(d)   Estimate the hardness of water which has a measured alkalinity of 30 mg/l. Explain *briefly* why the technician would need to do further statistical work to be able to predict the alkalinity of water with a measured hardness of, say, 50 mg/l.

(You are not expected to carry out the work)

(O)

7.   The yield (per hectare) of a crop, c, is believed to depend on the May rainfall, m. For nine region records are kept of the average values of c and m, and these are recorded below.

c	m
8.3	14.7
10.1	10.4
15.2	18.8
6.4	13.1
11.8	14.9
12.2	13.8
13.4	16.8
11.9	11.8
9.9	12.2

($\Sigma c = 99.2$, $\Sigma m = 126.5$, $\Sigma c^2 = 1150.16$, $\Sigma m^2 = 1832.07$, $\Sigma mc = 1427.15$.)

(i)   Find the equation of the appropriate regression line.

(ii)   Find r, the linear (product–moment) correlation coefficient between c and m.

(iii)   In a tenth region the average May rainfall was 14.6. Estimate the average yield of the crop for that region, giving your answer correct to one decimal place.

(iv)   Calculate the value of ρ, Spearman's rank correlation coefficient, for the above data and determine whether it is significantly greater than zero at the 5% level.

(v)   State, with a reason, which of r and ρ you regard as being more appropriate for these data.

(C)

8.   Explain *briefly* the principle of least squares as used to find the equation of a regression line based on a random sample of n pairs of values. Illustrate *on a sketch* the distances whose squares are summed, taking care to distinguish the response and controlled variables.

A car manufacturer, investigating the efficiency of experimental brakes on a new model of car, obtained the following stopping distances, d m, from certain speeds, s km/h.

Speed (km/h)	Stopping distance (m)
20	9.7
25	14.3
30	18.6
35	20.4
40	22.5
45	26.8
50	28.4
55	32.7
60	38.6

$\Sigma s = 360$ $\Sigma s^2 = 15\,900$ $\Sigma d = 212$
$\Sigma sd = 9464$

Plot a scatter diagram of these data.

Calculate the equation of the least squares regression line of d on s and draw this line on your graph.

It is known that the stopping distance is the sum of the thinking distance and the braking distance and that the equation relating thinking distance, h m, to speed, s km/h, is estimated as $h = 0.20s$.

Draw this line on your graph.

Estimate the braking distance of the car when travelling at 56 km/h.

If tyre marks on the road indicate a braking distance of 25 m, estimate the speed of the car.

(JMB)

9.   (a)   What is meant by saying that the (product–moment) correlation coefficient is independent of the scale of measurement?

(b)   Ten architects each produced a design for a new building and two judges, A and B, independently awarded marks, x and y respectively, to the ten designs, as given in the table below.

Design	Judge A (x)	Judge B (y)
1	50	46
2	35	26
3	55	48
4	60	44
5	85	62
6	25	28
7	65	30
8	90	60
9	45	34
10	40	42

It is given that $\Sigma x = 550$, $\Sigma x^2 = 34\,150$, $\Sigma y = 420$, $\Sigma y^2 = 19\,080$, $\Sigma xy = 25\,020$.

Calculate the (product–moment) correlation coefficient between the marks awarded by the two judges.

Calculate also Spearman's rank correlation coefficient for the data and test, at the 1% level, the hypothesis that there is no correlation between the marks awarded by the two judges. Discuss briefly the relative merits of using these two different correlation coefficients with this particular set of data. (C)

10. In an investigation into prediction using the stars and planets, a celebrated astrologist Horace Cope predicted the ages at which thirteen young people would first marry. The complete data, of predicted and actual ages at first marriage, are now available and are summarised below.

Person	Predicted age x (years)	Actual age y (years)
A	24	23
B	30	31
C	28	28
D	36	35
E	20	20
F	22	25
G	31	45
H	28	30
I	21	22
J	29	27
K	40	40
L	25	27
M	27	26

(a) Draw a scatter diagram of these data.
(b) Calculate the equation of the regression line of y on x and draw this line on the scatter diagram.
(c) Comment upon the results obtained, particularly in view of the data for person G. What further action would you suggest?
(AEB)

11. The experimental data below were obtained by measuring the horizontal distance y cm, rolled by an object released from the point P on a plane inclined at $\theta°$ to the horizontal, as shown in the diagram

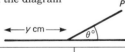

Distance y	Angle θ
44	8.0
132	25.0
152	31.5
87	17.5
104	20.0
91	10.5
142	28.5
76	14.5

$\Sigma y = 828$, $\Sigma y\theta = 18\,147$, $\Sigma\theta = 155.5$, $\Sigma\theta^2 = 3520.25$.

(a) Illustrate the data by a scatter diagram.
(b) Calculate the equation of the regression line of distance on angle and draw this line on the scatter diagram.
(c) It later emerged that one of the points was obtained using a different object.
(i) Suggest which point this was.
(ii) Draw by eye a line of best fit on the scatter diagram ignoring the point apparently obtained with the different object.
(iii) Use the line drawn by eye to estimate the distance the original object would roll if released at an angle of (a) 12°, (b) 40°. Discuss the uncertainty of each of these estimates. (AEB 1987)

12. (a) The 1973 and 1980 catalogue prices (in pence) of five British postage stamps are as follows:

1973 price	50	45	65	25	15
1980 price	500	350	600	500	120

(i) Plot these results on a scatter diagram.
(ii) Write down the coordinates of one point through which the regression line of the 1980 price on the 1973 price must pass.
(iii) Fit, by eye, the regression line of the 1980 price on the 1973 price.
(iv) Denoting the 1980 price by y and the 1973 price by x, write down the equation of your fitted regression line in the form $y = ax + b$, giving the constants a and b to one decimal place. Use this equation to determine the value of y when x has the value 20.
(b) (i) On a certain island there are large numbers of each of two clans, the Fatties and the Thinnies. Two random samples of 50 adult males are taken, one sample from each clan. Each of the clansmen is weighed and measured. For each clan, the value of the correlation coefficient between the heights and weights of the clansmen is found to be near +1. However, for the combined sample of 100 adult males, the value of the correlation coefficient is found to be near −1. Show, by a sketch of the scatter diagram for the combined sample, how this could arise.
(ii) A large sample survey of three-person families is conducted. The value of X, the greatest amount earned by any one member of the family, and the value of Y, the total amount earned by the entire family, are both recorded. Would you expect the value of the correlation coefficient between X and Y to be near +1, near −1 or near 0? Justify your answer. (C)

13. The state of Tempora demands that every household in the country shall have a reliable clock; inspectors are being introduced throughout the country to implement the policy. The Chief Inspector has the following data on the population size of towns, where Inspection Units have been set up, and the number of man-hours spent on inspection.

Population (thousands)	Man-hours (thousands)
3	8
4	11
5	13
9	18
13	24
15	26
18	31
20	32
21	34
22	33

(a) Calculate the regression line for predicting the number of man-hours from the population size (note that the mean value of each variate is a whole number).
(b) Predict the manpower required (in man-hours) for a new Inspection Unit to be installed in a town with a population of 17 000.   (O)

14. Explain clearly what is meant by the statistical term 'correlation'.
Vegboost Industries, a small chemical firm specialising in garden fertilisers, set up an experiment to study the relationship between a new fertiliser compound and the yield from tomato plants. Eight similar plants were selected and treated regularly throughout their life with x grams of fertiliser diluted in a standard volume of water. The yield y, in kilograms, of good tomatoes was measured for each plant. The following table summarises the results.

Plant	Amount of fertiliser x (g)	Yield y (kg)
A	1.2	4.5
B	1.8	5.9
C	3.1	7.0
D	4.9	7.8
E	5.7	7.2
F	7.1	6.8
G	8.6	4.5
H	9.8	2.7

(a) Calculate the product–moment correlation coefficient for these data.
(b) Calculate Spearman's rank correlation coefficient for these data.
(c) Is there any evidence of a relationship between these variables? Justify your answer. (No formal test is required.)   (AEB)

15. Explain briefly what is measured by the product–moment correlation coefficient.
The manager of a large office supervises 15 clerical assistants, each using a word-processor. Because of the pressure of work, the assistants did not all receive the same amount of training in the use of their word-processors. In order to make an assessment of the need for training the manager monitored their work during a given week, recording the number of pieces of work correctly produced without any errors (x_1), the number produced containing errors (x_2), together with the number of days' training received (y). The results are summarised in the table below.

Number correct (x_1)	Number incorrect (x_2)	Number of days' training (y)
35	23	10
26	25	2
33	24	7
22	28	5
40	27	11
31	21	8
22	32	9
20	21	3
24	33	8
23	23	2
30	23	6
22	26	4
30	26	5
26	22	3
23	34	11

(a) Given that $\Sigma x_1^2 = 11\,513$, $\Sigma y^2 = 728$ and $\Sigma x_1 y = 2676$, show that the product–moment correlation coefficient between y and x_1 is 0.491.
(b) Without using a comment of the form 'The correlation between x_1 and y is not very strong', suggest how the manager might have attempted to interpret this value as part of the assessment.
The manager than decided to investigate whether there is any association between the number of days' training and a perceived measure of accuracy based on the difference between x_1 and x_2. Consequently a new variable $z = x_1 - x_2$ was created.

(c)   Plot a scatter diagram of y against z. Explain why the manager should not correlate y and z using the product–moment correlation coefficient.

(d)   Explain why z^2 might be a better variable to correlate with y using the product–moment correlation coefficient. Evaluate the correlation coefficient between y and z^2 and explain why the manager might be pleased with the value obtained. Suggest how this new variable would present the manager with a practical problem.

(AEB 1988)

Student	Sociology (S)	Social Administration (SA)	Quantitative Methods (QM)
1	66	48	44
2	50	46	48
3	44	46	47
4	58	72	64
5	64	68	54
6	26	64	55
7	74	65	59
8	67	42	48
9	36	40	56
10	48	55	48

The following matrix of Spearman rank correlation coefficients was obtained for this sample of ten students.

	S	SA	QM	Total mark
S	1	0.24	−0.01	0.78
SA		1	x	0.77
QM			1	y
Total mark				1

Find the values of x and y.

It has been decided that in future students should only be required to sit two papers. Use these data to decide which two examinations should be used. Give a reason for your choice.   (AEB 1987)

16.   Define a ranking scale and give an example to illustrate your definition. Explain how you would rank values of equal magnitude. At the end of the academic year students on a particular course are given examinations in Sociology (S), Social Administration (SA) and Quantitative Methods (QM). The final grade awarded to each student is based on the total of the marks scored on the three papers. The table shows the marks obtained by a sample of ten students who sat the three papers.

APPENDIX 1

CUMULATIVE BINOMIAL PROBABILITIES

The tabulated value is $P(X \leqslant r)$ where $X \sim \text{Bin}(n,p)$

$p =$		0.05	0.10	0.15	0.20	0.25	0.30	0.35	0.40	0.45	0.50
$n = 2$	$r = 0$	0.9025	0.8100	0.7225	0.6400	0.5625	0.4900	0.4225	0.3600	0.3025	0.2500
	1	0.9975	0.9900	0.9775	0.9600	0.9375	0.9100	0.8775	0.8400	0.7975	0.7500
	2	1.0000	1.0000	1.0000	1.0000	1.0000	1.0000	1.0000	1.0000	1.0000	1.0000
$n = 3$	$r = 0$	0.8574	0.7290	0.6141	0.5120	0.4219	0.3430	0.2746	0.2160	0.1664	0.1250
	1	0.9928	0.9720	0.9393	0.8960	0.8438	0.7840	0.7183	0.6480	0.5748	0.5000
	2	0.9999	0.9990	0.9966	0.9920	0.9844	0.9730	0.9571	0.9360	0.9089	0.8750
	3	1.0000	1.0000	1.0000	1.0000	1.0000	1.0000	1.0000	1.0000	1.0000	1.0000
$n = 4$	$r = 0$	0.8145	0.6561	0.5220	0.4096	0.3164	0.2401	0.1785	0.1296	0.0915	0.0625
	1	0.9860	0.9477	0.8905	0.8192	0.7383	0.6517	0.5630	0.4752	0.3910	0.3125
	2	0.9995	0.9963	0.9880	0.9728	0.9492	0.9163	0.8735	0.8208	0.7585	0.6875
	3	1.0000	0.9999	0.9995	0.9984	0.9961	0.9919	0.9850	0.9744	0.9590	0.9375
	4		1.0000	1.0000	1.0000	1.0000	1.0000	1.0000	1.0000	1.0000	1.0000
$n = 5$	$r = 0$	0.7738	0.5905	0.4437	0.3277	0.2373	0.1681	0.1160	0.0778	0.0503	0.0313
	1	0.9774	0.9185	0.8352	0.7373	0.6328	0.5282	0.4284	0.3370	0.2562	0.1875
	2	0.9988	0.9914	0.9734	0.9421	0.8965	0.8369	0.7648	0.6826	0.5931	0.5000
	3	1.0000	0.9995	0.9978	0.9933	0.9844	0.9692	0.9460	0.9130	0.8688	0.8125
	4		1.0000	0.9999	0.9997	0.9990	0.9976	0.9947	0.9898	0.9815	0.9688
	5			1.0000	1.0000	1.0000	1.0000	1.0000	1.0000	1.0000	1.0000
$n = 6$	$r = 0$	0.7351	0.5314	0.3771	0.2621	0.1780	0.1176	0.0754	0.0467	0.0277	0.0156
	1	0.9672	0.8857	0.7765	0.6554	0.5339	0.4202	0.3191	0.2333	0.1636	0.1094
	2	0.9978	0.9842	0.9527	0.9011	0.8306	0.7443	0.6471	0.5443	0.4415	0.3438
	3	0.9999	0.9987	0.9941	0.9830	0.9624	0.9295	0.8826	0.8208	0.7447	0.6563
	4	1.0000	0.9999	0.9996	0.9984	0.9954	0.9891	0.9777	0.9590	0.9308	0.8906
	5		1.0000	1.0000	0.9999	0.9998	0.9993	0.9982	0.9959	0.9917	0.9844
	6				1.0000	1.0000	1.0000	1.0000	1.0000	1.0000	1.0000
$n = 7$	$r = 0$	0.6983	0.4783	0.3206	0.2097	0.1335	0.0824	0.0490	0.0280	0.0152	0.0078
	1	0.9556	0.8503	0.7166	0.5767	0.4449	0.3294	0.2338	0.1586	0.1024	0.0625
	2	0.9962	0.9743	0.9262	0.8520	0.7564	0.6471	0.5323	0.4199	0.3164	0.2266
	3	0.9998	0.9973	0.9879	0.9667	0.9294	0.8740	0.8002	0.7102	0.6083	0.5000
	4	1.0000	0.9998	0.9988	0.9953	0.9871	0.9712	0.9444	0.9037	0.8471	0.7734
	5		1.0000	0.9999	0.9996	0.9987	0.9962	0.9910	0.9812	0.9643	0.9375
	6			1.0000	1.0000	0.9999	0.9998	0.9994	0.9984	0.9963	0.9922
	7					1.0000	1.0000	1.0000	1.0000	1.0000	1.0000
$n = 8$	$r = 0$	0.6634	0.4305	0.2725	0.1678	0.1001	0.0576	0.0319	0.0168	0.0084	0.0039
	1	0.9428	0.8131	0.6572	0.5033	0.3671	0.2553	0.1691	0.1064	0.0632	0.0352
	2	0.9942	0.9619	0.8948	0.7969	0.6785	0.5518	0.4278	0.3154	0.2201	0.1445
	3	0.9996	0.9950	0.9786	0.9437	0.8862	0.8059	0.7064	0.5941	0.4770	0.3633
	4	1.0000	0.9996	0.9971	0.9896	0.9727	0.9420	0.8939	0.8263	0.7396	0.6367
	5		1.0000	0.9998	0.9988	0.9958	0.9887	0.9747	0.9502	0.9115	0.8555
	6			1.0000	0.9999	0.9996	0.9987	0.9964	0.9915	0.9819	0.9648
	7				1.0000	1.0000	0.9999	0.9998	0.9993	0.9983	0.9961
	8						1.0000	1.0000	1.0000	1.0000	1.0000

CUMULATIVE BINOMIAL PROBABILITIES

The tabulated value is $P(X \leqslant r)$ where $X \sim \text{Bin}(n,p)$

$p =$		0.05	0.10	0.15	0.20	0.25	0.30	0.35	0.40	0.45	0.50
$n = 9$	$r = 0$	0.6302	0.3874	0.2316	0.1342	0.0751	0.0404	0.0207	0.0101	0.0046	0.0020
	1	0.9288	0.7748	0.5995	0.4362	0.3003	0.1960	0.1211	0.0705	0.0385	0.0195
	2	0.9916	0.9470	0.8591	0.7382	0.6007	0.4628	0.3373	0.2318	0.1495	0.0898
	3	0.9994	0.9917	0.9661	0.9144	0.8343	0.7297	0.6089	0.4826	0.3614	0.2539
	4	1.0000	0.9991	0.9944	0.9804	0.9511	0.9012	0.8283	0.7334	0.6214	0.5000
	5		0.9999	0.9994	0.9969	0.9900	0.9747	0.9464	0.9006	0.8342	0.7461
	6		1.0000	1.0000	0.9997	0.9987	0.9957	0.9888	0.9750	0.9502	0.9102
	7				1.0000	0.9999	0.9996	0.9986	0.9962	0.9909	0.9805
	8					1.0000	1.0000	0.9999	0.9997	0.9992	0.9980
	9							1.0000	1.0000	1.0000	1.0000
$n = 10$	$r = 0$	0.5987	0.3487	0.1969	0.1074	0.0563	0.0282	0.0135	0.0060	0.0025	0.0010
	1	0.9139	0.7361	0.5443	0.3758	0.2440	0.1493	0.0860	0.0464	0.0233	0.0107
	2	0.9885	0.9298	0.8202	0.6778	0.5256	0.3828	0.2616	0.1673	0.0996	0.0547
	3	0.9990	0.9872	0.9500	0.8791	0.7759	0.6496	0.5138	0.3823	0.2660	0.1719
	4	0.9999	0.9984	0.9901	0.9672	0.9219	0.8497	0.7515	0.6331	0.5044	0.3770
	5	1.0000	0.9999	0.9986	0.9936	0.9803	0.9527	0.9051	0.8338	0.7384	0.6230
	6		1.0000	0.9999	0.9991	0.9965	0.9894	0.9740	0.9452	0.8980	0.8281
	7			1.0000	0.9999	0.9996	0.9984	0.9952	0.9877	0.9726	0.9453
	8				1.0000	1.0000	0.9999	0.9995	0.9983	0.9955	0.9893
	9						1.0000	1.0000	0.9999	0.9997	0.9990
	10								1.0000	1.0000	1.0000
$n = 15$	$r = 0$	0.4633	0.2059	0.0874	0.0352	0.0134	0.0047	0.0016	0.0005	0.0001	0.0000
	1	0.8290	0.5490	0.3186	0.1671	0.0802	0.0353	0.0142	0.0052	0.0017	0.0005
	2	0.9638	0.8159	0.6042	0.3980	0.2361	0.1268	0.0617	0.0271	0.0107	0.0037
	3	0.9945	0.9444	0.8227	0.6482	0.4613	0.2969	0.1727	0.0905	0.0424	0.0176
	4	0.9994	0.9873	0.9383	0.8358	0.6865	0.5155	0.3519	0.2173	0.1204	0.0592
	5	0.9999	0.9978	0.9832	0.9389	0.8516	0.7216	0.5643	0.4032	0.2608	0.1509
	6	1.0000	0.9997	0.9964	0.9819	0.9434	0.8689	0.7548	0.6098	0.4522	0.3036
	7		1.0000	0.9994	0.9958	0.9827	0.9500	0.8868	0.7869	0.6535	0.5000
	8			0.9999	0.9992	0.9958	0.9848	0.9578	0.9050	0.8182	0.6964
	9			1.0000	0.9999	0.9992	0.9963	0.9876	0.9662	0.9231	0.8491
	10				1.0000	0.9999	0.9993	0.9972	0.9907	0.9745	0.9408
	11					1.0000	0.9999	0.9995	0.9981	0.9937	0.9824
	12						1.0000	0.9999	0.9997	0.9989	0.9963
	13							1.0000	1.0000	0.9999	0.9995
	14									1.0000	1.0000
$n = 20$	$r = 0$	0.3585	0.1216	0.0388	0.0115	0.0032	0.0008	0.0002	0.0000	0.0000	0.0000
	1	0.7358	0.3917	0.1756	0.0692	0.0243	0.0076	0.0021	0.0005	0.0001	0.0000
	2	0.9245	0.6769	0.4049	0.2061	0.0913	0.0355	0.0121	0.0036	0.0009	0.0002
	3	0.9841	0.8670	0.6477	0.4114	0.2252	0.1071	0.0444	0.0160	0.0049	0.0013
	4	0.9974	0.9568	0.8298	0.6296	0.4148	0.2375	0.1182	0.0510	0.0189	0.0059
	5	0.9997	0.9887	0.9327	0.8042	0.6172	0.4164	0.2454	0.1256	0.0553	0.0207
	6	1.0000	0.9976	0.9781	0.9133	0.7858	0.6080	0.4166	0.2500	0.1299	0.0577
	7		0.9996	0.9941	0.9679	0.8982	0.7723	0.6010	0.4159	0.2520	0.1316
	8		0.9999	0.9987	0.9900	0.9591	0.8867	0.7624	0.5956	0.4143	0.2517
	9		1.0000	0.9998	0.9974	0.9861	0.9520	0.8782	0.7553	0.5914	0.4119
	10			1.0000	0.9994	0.9961	0.9829	0.9468	0.8725	0.7507	0.5881
	11				0.9999	0.9991	0.9949	0.9804	0.9435	0.8692	0.7483
	12				1.0000	0.9998	0.9987	0.9940	0.9790	0.9420	0.8684
	13					1.0000	0.9997	0.9985	0.9935	0.9786	0.9423
	14						1.0000	0.9997	0.9984	0.9936	0.9793
	15							1.0000	0.9997	0.9985	0.9941
	16								1.0000	0.9997	0.9987
	17									1.0000	0.9998
	18										1.0000

CUMULATIVE POISSON PROBABILITIES

The tabulated value is $P(X \leqslant r)$ where $X \sim \text{Po}(\lambda)$

$\lambda =$	0.2	0.4	0.5	0.6	0.8	1.0	1.2	1.4	1.5
$r = 0$	0.8187	0.6703	0.6065	0.5488	0.4493	0.3679	0.3012	0.2466	0.2231
1	0.9825	0.9384	0.9098	0.8781	0.8088	0.7358	0.6626	0.5918	0.5578
2	0.9989	0.9921	0.9856	0.9769	0.9526	0.9197	0.8795	0.8335	0.8088
3	0.9999	0.9992	0.9982	0.9966	0.9909	0.9810	0.9662	0.9463	0.9344
4	1.0000	0.9999	0.9998	0.9996	0.9986	0.9963	0.9923	0.9857	0.9814
5		1.0000	1.0000	1.0000	0.9998	0.9994	0.9985	0.9968	0.9955
6					1.0000	0.9999	0.9997	0.9994	0.9991
7						1.0000	1.0000	0.9999	0.9998
8								1.0000	1.0000

$\lambda =$	1.6	1.8	2.0	2.2	2.4	2.5	2.6	2.8	3.0
$r = 0$	0.2019	0.1653	0.1353	0.1108	0.0907	0.0821	0.0743	0.0608	0.0498
1	0.5249	0.4628	0.4060	0.3546	0.3084	0.2873	0.2674	0.2311	0.1991
2	0.7834	0.7306	0.6767	0.6227	0.5697	0.5438	0.5184	0.4695	0.4232
3	0.9212	0.8913	0.8571	0.8194	0.7787	0.7576	0.7360	0.6919	0.6472
4	0.9763	0.9636	0.9473	0.9275	0.9041	0.8912	0.8774	0.8477	0.8153
5	0.9940	0.9896	0.9834	0.9751	0.9643	0.9580	0.9510	0.9349	0.9161
6	0.9987	0.9974	0.9955	0.9925	0.9884	0.9858	0.9828	0.9756	0.9665
7	0.9997	0.9994	0.9989	0.9980	0.9967	0.9958	0.9947	0.9919	0.9881
8	1.0000	0.9999	0.9998	0.9995	0.9991	0.9989	0.9985	0.9976	0.9962
9		1.0000	1.0000	0.9999	0.9998	0.9997	0.9996	0.9993	0.9989
10				1.0000	1.0000	0.9999	0.9999	0.9998	0.9997
11						1.0000	1.0000	1.0000	0.9999
12									1.0000

$\lambda =$	3.2	3.4	3.5	3.6	3.8	4.0	4.5	5.0	5.5
$r = 0$	0.0408	0.0334	0.0302	0.0273	0.0224	0.0183	0.0111	0.0067	0.0041
1	0.1712	0.1468	0.1359	0.1257	0.1074	0.0916	0.0611	0.0404	0.0266
2	0.3799	0.3397	0.3208	0.3027	0.2689	0.2381	0.1736	0.1247	0.0884
3	0.6025	0.5584	0.5366	0.5152	0.4735	0.4335	0.3423	0.2650	0.2017
4	0.7806	0.7442	0.7254	0.7064	0.6678	0.6288	0.5321	0.4405	0.3575
5	0.8946	0.8705	0.8576	0.8441	0.8156	0.7851	0.7029	0.6160	0.5289
6	0.9554	0.9421	0.9347	0.9267	0.9091	0.8893	0.8311	0.7622	0.6860
7	0.9832	0.9769	0.9733	0.9692	0.9599	0.9489	0.9134	0.8666	0.8095
8	0.9943	0.9917	0.9901	0.9883	0.9840	0.9786	0.9597	0.9319	0.8944
9	0.9982	0.9973	0.9967	0.9960	0.9942	0.9919	0.9829	0.9682	0.9462
10	0.9995	0.9992	0.9990	0.9987	0.9981	0.9972	0.9933	0.9863	0.9747
11	0.9999	0.9998	0.9997	0.9996	0.9994	0.9991	0.9976	0.9945	0.9890
12	1.0000	0.9999	0.9999	0.9999	0.9998	0.9997	0.9992	0.9980	0.9955
13		1.0000	1.0000	1.0000	1.0000	0.9999	0.9997	0.9993	0.9983
14						1.0000	0.9999	0.9998	0.9994
15							1.0000	0.9999	0.9998
16								1.0000	0.9999
17									1.0000
18									

CUMULATIVE POISSON PROBABILITIES

The tabulated value is $P(X \leqslant r)$ where $X \sim \text{Po}(\lambda)$

$\lambda =$	6.0	6.5	7.0	7.5	8.0	8.5	9.0	9.5	10.0
$r = 0$	0.0025	0.0015	0.0009	0.0006	0.0003	0.0002	0.0001	0.0001	0.0000
1	0.0174	0.0113	0.0073	0.0047	0.0030	0.0019	0.0012	0.0008	0.0005
2	0.0620	0.0430	0.0296	0.0203	0.0138	0.0093	0.0062	0.0042	0.0028
3	0.1512	0.1118	0.0818	0.0591	0.0424	0.0301	0.0212	0.0149	0.0103
4	0.2851	0.2237	0.1730	0.1321	0.0996	0.0744	0.0550	0.0403	0.0293
5	0.4457	0.3690	0.3007	0.2414	0.1912	0.1496	0.1157	0.0885	0.0671
6	0.6063	0.5265	0.4497	0.3782	0.3134	0.2562	0.2068	0.1649	0.1301
7	0.7440	0.6728	0.5987	0.5246	0.4530	0.3856	0.3239	0.2687	0.2202
8	0.8472	0.7916	0.7291	0.6620	0.5925	0.5231	0.4557	0.3918	0.3328
9	0.9161	0.8774	0.8305	0.7764	0.7166	0.6530	0.5874	0.5218	0.4579
10	0.9574	0.9332	0.9015	0.8622	0.8159	0.7634	0.7060	0.6453	0.5830
11	0.9799	0.9661	0.9467	0.9208	0.8881	0.8487	0.8030	0.7520	0.6968
12	0.9912	0.9840	0.9730	0.9573	0.9362	0.9091	0.8758	0.8364	0.7916
13	0.9964	0.9929	0.9872	0.9784	0.9658	0.9486	0.9261	0.8981	0.8645
14	0.9986	0.9970	0.9943	0.9897	0.9827	0.9726	0.9585	0.9400	0.9165
15	0.9995	0.9988	0.9976	0.9954	0.9918	0.9862	0.9780	0.9665	0.9513
16	0.9998	0.9996	0.9990	0.9980	0.9963	0.9934	0.9889	0.9823	0.9730
17	0.9999	0.9998	0.9996	0.9992	0.9984	0.9970	0.9947	0.9911	0.9857
18	1.0000	0.9999	0.9999	0.9997	0.9993	0.9987	0.9976	0.9957	0.9928
19		1.0000	1.0000	0.9999	0.9997	0.9995	0.9989	0.9980	0.9965
20				1.0000	0.9999	0.9998	0.9996	0.9991	0.9984
21					1.0000	0.9999	0.9998	0.9996	0.9993
22						1.0000	0.9999	0.9999	0.9997
23							1.0000	0.9999	0.9999
24								1.0000	1.0000

THE DISTRIBUTION FUNCTION $\Phi(z)$ OF
THE NORMAL DISTRIBUTION $N(0, 1)$

z	0	1	2	3	4	5	6	7	8	9	1	2	3	4	5	6	7	8	9
															ADD				
0.0	.5000	.5040	.5080	.5120	.5160	.5199	.5239	.5279	.5319	.5359	4	8	12	16	20	24	28	32	36
0.1	.5398	.5438	.5478	.5517	.5557	.5596	.5636	.5675	.5714	.5753	4	8	12	16	20	24	28	32	36
0.2	.5793	.5832	.5871	.5910	.5948	.5987	.6026	.6064	.6103	.6141	4	8	12	15	19	23	27	31	35
0.3	.6179	.6217	.6255	.6293	.6331	.6368	.6406	.6443	.6480	.6517	4	7	11	15	19	22	26	30	34
0.4	.6554	.6591	.6628	.6664	.6700	.6736	.6772	.6808	.6844	.6879	4	7	11	14	18	22	25	29	32
0.5	.6915	.6950	.6985	.7019	.7054	.7088	.7123	.7157	.7190	.7224	3	7	10	14	17	20	24	27	31
0.6	.7257	.7291	.7324	.7357	.7389	.7422	.7454	.7486	.7517	.7549	3	7	10	13	16	19	23	26	29
0.7	.7580	.7611	.7642	.7673	.7704	.7734	.7764	.7794	.7823	.7852	3	6	9	12	15	18	21	24	27
0.8	.7881	.7910	.7939	.7967	.7995	.8023	.8051	.8078	.8106	.8133	3	5	8	11	14	16	19	22	25
0.9	.8159	.8186	.8212	.8238	.8264	.8289	.8315	.8340	.8365	.8389	3	5	8	10	13	15	18	20	23
1.0	.8413	.8438	.8461	.8485	.8508	.8531	.8554	.8577	.8599	.8621	2	5	7	9	12	14	16	19	21
1.1	.8643	.8665	.8686	.8708	.8729	.8749	.8770	.8790	.8810	.8830	2	4	6	8	10	12	14	16	18
1.2	.8849	.8869	.8888	.8907	.8925	.8944	.8962	.8980	.8997	.9015	2	4	6	7	9	11	13	15	17
1.3	.9032	.9049	.9066	.9082	.9099	.9115	.9131	.9147	.9162	.9177	2	3	5	6	8	10	11	13	14
1.4	.9192	.9207	.9222	.9236	.9251	.9265	.9279	.9292	.9306	.9319	1	3	4	6	7	8	10	11	13
1.5	.9332	.9345	.9357	.9370	.9382	.9394	.9406	.9418	.9429	.9441	1	2	4	5	6	7	8	10	11
1.6	.9452	.9463	.9474	.9484	.9495	.9505	.9515	.9525	.9535	.9545	1	2	3	4	5	6	7	8	9
1.7	.9554	.9564	.9573	.9582	.9591	.9599	.9608	.9616	.9625	.9633	1	2	3	4	4	5	6	7	8
1.8	.9641	.9649	.9656	.9664	.9671	.9678	.9686	.9693	.9699	.9706	1	1	2	3	4	4	5	6	6
1.9	.9713	.9719	.9726	.9732	.9738	.9744	.9750	.9756	.9761	.9767	1	1	2	2	3	4	4	5	5
2.0	.9772	.9778	.9783	.9788	.9793	.9798	.9803	.9808	.9812	.9817	0	1	1	2	2	3	3	4	4
2.1	.9821	.9826	.9830	.9834	.9838	.9842	.9846	.9850	.9854	.9857	0	1	1	2	2	2	3	3	4
2.2	.9861	.9864	.9868	.9871	.9875	.9878	.9881	.9884	.9887	.9890	0	1	1	1	2	2	2	3	3
2.3	.9893	.9896	.9898								0	1	1	1	1	2	2	2	2
				.9901	.99036	.99061	.99086				3	5	8	10	13	15	18	20	23
								.99111	.99134	.99158	2	5	7	9	12	14	16	18	21
2.4	.99180	.99202	.99224	.99245	.99266						2	4	6	8	11	13	15	17	19
						.99286	.99305	.99324	.99343	.99361	2	4	6	7	9	11	13	15	17
2.5	.99379	.99396	.99413	.99430	.99446	.99461	.99477	.99492	.99506	.99520	2	3	5	6	8	9	11	12	14
2.6	.99534	.99547	.99560	.99573	.99585	.99598	.99609	.99621	.99632	.99643	1	2	3	5	6	7	8	9	10
2.7	.99653	.99664	.99674	.99683	.99693	.99702	.99711	.99720	.99728	.99736	1	2	3	4	5	6	7	8	9
2.8	.99744	.99752	.99760	.99767	.99774	.99781	.99788	.99795	.99801	.99807	1	1	2	3	4	4	5	6	6
2.9	.99813	.99819	.99825	.99831	.99836	.99841	.99846	.99851	.99856	.99861	0	1	1	2	2	3	3	4	4
3.0	.99865	.99869	.99874	.99878	.99882	.99886	.99889	.99893	.99896	.99900	0	1	1	2	2	2	3	3	4
3.1	.9³032	.9³065	.9³096								3	6	9	13	16	19	22	25	28
				.9³126	.9³155	.9³184	.9³211				3	6	8	11	14	17	20	22	25
								.9³238	.9³264	.9³289	2	5	7	10	12	15	17	20	22
3.2	.9³313	.9³336	.9³359	.9³381	.9³402						2	4	7	9	11	13	15	18	20
						.9³423	.9³443	.9³462	.9³481	.9³499	2	4	6	8	9	11	13	15	17
3.3	.9³517	.9³534	.9³550	.9³566	.9³581						2	3	5	6	8	10	11	13	14
						.9³596	.9³610	.9³624	.9³638	.9³651	1	3	4	5	7	8	9	10	12
3.4	.9³663	.9³675	.9³687	.9³698	.9³709	.9³720	.9³730	.9³740	.9³749	.9³758	1	2	3	4	5	6	7	8	9
3.5	.9³767	.9³776	.9³784	.9³792	.9³800	.9³807	.9³815	.9³822	.9³828	.9³835	1	1	2	3	4	4	5	6	7
3.6	.9³841	.9³847	.9³853	.9³858	.9³864	.9³869	.9³874	.9³879	.9³883	.9³888	0	1	1	2	2	3	3	4	5
3.7	.9³892	.9³896	.9³90	.9⁴04	.9⁴08	.9⁴12	.9⁴15	.9⁴18	.9⁴22	.9⁴250									
3.8	.9⁴28	.9⁴31	.9⁴33	.9⁴36	.9⁴38	.9⁴41	.9⁴43	.9⁴46	.9⁴48	.9⁴500									
3.9	.9⁴52	.9⁴54	.9⁴56	.9⁴58	.9⁴59	.9⁴61	.9⁴63	.9⁴64	.9⁴66	.9⁴670									

For negative values of z use $\Phi(z) = 1 - \Phi(-z)$

UPPER QUANTILES $z_{[P]}$ OF THE NORMAL DISTRIBUTION N(0, 1)

P	Q	z	P	Q	z	P	Q	z	P	Q	z	Q	z
.50	.50	0.000	.85	.15	1.036	.975	.025	1.960	.990	.010	2.326	$.0^34$	3.353
.55	.45	0.126	.86	.14	1.080	.976	.024	1.977	.991	.009	2.366	$.0^33$	3.432
.60	.40	0.253	.87	.13	1.126	.977	.023	1.995	.992	.008	2.409	$.0^32$	3.540
.65	.35	0.385	.88	.12	1.175	.978	.022	2.014	.993	.007	2.457	$.0^31$	3.719
.70	.30	0.524	.89	.11	1.227	.979	.021	2.034	.994	.006	2.512	$.0^45$	3.891
.75	.25	0.674	.90	.10	1.282	.980	.020	2.054	.995	.005	2.576	$.0^41$	4.265
.76	.24	0.706	.91	.09	1.341	.981	.019	2.075	.996	.004	2.652	$.0^55$	4.417
.77	.23	0.739	.92	.08	1.405	.982	.018	2.097	.997	.003	2.748	$.0^51$	4.753
.78	.22	0.772	.93	.07	1.476	.983	.017	2.120	.998	.002	2.878	$.0^65$	4.892
.79	.21	0.806	.94	.06	1.555	.984	.016	2.144	.999	.001	3.090	$.0^61$	5.199
.80	.20	0.842	.950	.050	1.645	.985	.015	2.170	.9991	$.0^39$	3.121	$.0^75$	5.327
.81	.19	0.878	.955	.045	1.695	.986	.014	2.197	.9992	$.0^38$	3.156	$.0^71$	5.612
.82	.18	0.915	.960	.040	1.751	.987	.013	2.226	.9993	$.0^37$	3.195	$.0^85$	5.731
.83	.17	0.954	.965	.035	1.812	.988	.012	2.257	.9994	$.0^36$	3.239	$.0^81$	5.998
.84	.16	0.994	.970	.030	1.881	.989	.011	2.290	.9995	$.0^35$	3.291	$.0^95$	6.109

Reproduced, by permission, from Miller and Powell, *The Cambridge Elementary Mathematical Tables* (Cambridge University Press).

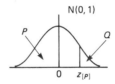

**RANDOM
NUMBERS**

65 23	68 00	77 82	58 14	10 85	11 85	57 11	73 74	45 25	50 46
09 56	76 51	04 73	94 30	16 74	69 59	04 38	83 98	30 20	87 85
55 99	98 60	01 33	06 93	85 13	23 17	25 51	92 04	52 31	38 70
72 82	45 44	09 53	04 83	03 83	98 41	67 41	01 38	66 83	11 99
04 21	28 72	73 25	02 74	35 81	78 49	52 67	61 40	60 50	47 50
87 01	80 59	89 36	41 59	60 27	64 89	47 45	18 21	69 84	76 06
31 62	46 53	84 40	56 31	74 76	52 23	72 95	96 06	56 83	85 22
29 81	57 94	35 91	90 70	94 24	19 35	50 22	23 72	87 34	83 15
39 98	74 22	77 19	12 81	29 42	04 50	62 34	36 81	43 07	97 92
56 14	80 10	76 52	38 54	84 13	99 90	22 55	41 04	72 37	89 33
29 56	62 74	12 67	09 35	89 33	04 28	44 75	01 57	87 45	52 21
93 32	57 38	39 36	87 42	72 55	73 97	98 36	57 41	76 09	11 68
95 69	51 54	43 19	20 49	57 25	90 55	26 20	70 98	43 73	56 45
65 71	32 43	64 67	22 55	65 65	48 86	10 88	20 12	40 18	49.25
90 27	33 43	97 84	20 57	49 91	41 20	17 64	29 60	66 87	55 97
90 29	42 45	61 34	30 13	30 39	21 52	59 28	64 98	08 76	09 27
99 74	06 29	20 55	72 70	11 43	95 82	75 37	90 24	77 43	63 21
87 87	56 91	16 97	51 50	61 36	96 47	76 68	49 11	50 56	51 06
46 24	17 74	97 37	39 03	54 83	34 00	74 61	77 51	43 63	15 67
66 79	81 43	40 92	84 72	88 32	83 24	67 01	41 34	70 19	26 93
36 42	94 58	83 30	92 39	18 40	03 00	12 90	32 37	91 65	48 15
07 66	25 08	99 27	69 48	85 32	16 46	19 31	85 02	86 36	22 96
93 10	05 72	18 26	36 67	68 48	31 69	68 58	93 49	45 86	99 29
49 50	63 99	26 71	47 94	32 71	72 91	34 18	74 06	32 14	40 80
20 75	58 89	39 04	42 73	37 93	11 07	28 77	91 36	60 47	82 62
02 40	62 09	00 71	09 37	80 44	50 37	32 70	20 38	71 86	75 34
59 87	21 38	29 78	72 67	42 83	65 21	54 79	66 42	47 86	31 15
48 08	99 66	43 38	28 13	50 25	47 93	11 15	07 84	28 30	19 07
54 26	86 75	44 15	20 39	20 03	58 54	80 29	62 53	06 97	71 51
35 35	58 45	23 58	63 66	09 62	80 92	14 55	81 41	21 48	87 34
73 84	90 49	01 21	90 29	57 06	68 73	51 10	51 95	63 08	57 99
34 64	78 00	92 59	67 74	58 48	92 09	42 20	40 37	63 80	58 93
68 56	87 47	63 06	24 71	41 98	79 06	07 18	58 29	16 49	67 37
72 47	05 42	88 07	27 55	58 74	82 08	42 28	26 48	25 32	00 31
44 44	96 75	89 57	12 60	42 38	77 36	45 69	21 68	32 70	04 96
28 11	57 47	61 57	89 88	62 18	93 67	57 32	96 72	21 17	13 54
87 22	38 88	91 99	16 08	17 76	27 47	52 14	98 86	35 68	23 85
44 93	14 59	67 40	24 10	11 63	40 47	07 56	14 22	62 74	93 39
81 84	37 25	90 43	56 62	94 58	49 03	84 22	57 22	47 98	86 37
09 75	35 21	04 47	54 08	98 44	08 16	44 86	69 71	20 52	64 94
77 65	05 04	22 18	20 10	81 87	05 69	43 70	96 76	42 05	21 10
19 06	51 61	34 03	61 55	98 58	83 50	01 48	99 85	08 67	15 91
52 91	87 07	19 62	32 28	04 91	42 48	65 24	86 09	87 68	55 51
52 47	25 14	93 91	75 51	49 26	49 41	20 83	30 30	43 22	69 08
52 67	87 40	63 41	91 86	10 47	80 70	56 87	25 86	89 94	21 42
65 25	71 73	78 60	50 62	91 04	95 97	64 16	71 31	32 80	19 61
29 97	56 42	56 90	16 75	74 95	99 26	01 63	25 16	54 18	54 46
15 25	03 68	92 45	53 00	06 29	46 43	46 66	27 12	85 05	22 44
82 08	65 67	64 13	51 14	38 28	24 30	39 62	20 35	23 90	57 36
81 35	03 25	87 24	83 59	04 67	51 52	26 21	69 75	87 28	61 50

Each digit in this table is an independent sample from a population where each of the digits 0 to 9 has a probability of occurrence of 0.1. It should be noted that these digits have been computer generated, and are therefore 'pseudo' random numbers.

THE χ^2 DISTRIBUTION

Table showing $P(X > \chi^2_\alpha(v))$
when v is the number of degrees of freedom.

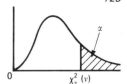

v \ α	0.250	0.100	0.050	0.025	0.010	0.005	0.001
1	1.32330	2.70554	3.84146	5.02389	6.63490	7.87944	10.828
2	2.77259	4.60517	5.99146	7.37776	9.21034	10.5966	13.816
3	4.10834	6.25139	7.81473	9.34840	11.3449	12.8382	16.266
4	5.38527	7.77944	9.48773	11.1433	13.2767	14.8603	18.467
5	6.62568	9.23636	11.0705	12.8325	15.0863	16.7496	20.515
6	7.84080	10.6446	12.5916	14.4494	16.8119	18.5476	22.458
7	9.03715	12.0170	14.0671	16.0128	18.4753	20.2777	24.322
8	10.2189	13.3616	15.5073	17.5345	20.0902	21.9550	26.125
9	11.3888	14.6837	16.9190	19.0228	21.6660	23.5894	27.877
10	12.5489	15.9872	18.3070	20.4832	23.2093	25.1882	29.588
11	13.7007	17.2750	19.6751	21.9200	24.7250	26.7568	31.264
12	14.8454	18.5493	21.0261	23.3367	26.2170	28.2995	32.909
13	15.9839	19.8119	22.3620	24.7356	27.6882	29.8195	34.528
14	17.1169	21.0641	23.6848	26.1189	29.1412	31.3194	36.123
15	18.2451	22.3071	24.9958	27.4884	30.5779	32.8013	37.697
16	19.3689	23.5418	26.2962	28.8454	31.9999	34.2672	39.252
17	20.4887	24.7690	27.5871	30.1910	33.4087	35.7185	40.790
18	21.6049	25.9894	28.8693	31.5264	34.8053	37.1565	42.312
19	22.7178	27.2036	30.1435	32.8523	36.1909	38.5823	43.820
20	23.8277	28.4120	31.4104	34.1696	37.5662	39.9968	45.315
21	24.9348	29.6151	32.6706	35.4789	38.9322	41.4011	46.797
22	26.0393	30.8133	33.9244	36.7807	40.2894	42.7957	48.268
23	27.1413	32.0069	35.1725	38.0756	41.6384	44.1813	49.728
24	28.2412	33.1962	36.4150	39.3641	42.9798	45.5585	51.179
25	29.3389	34.3816	37.6525	40.6465	44.3141	46.9279	52.618
26	30.4346	35.5632	38.8851	41.9232	45.6417	48.2899	54.052
27	31.5284	36.7412	40.1133	43.1945	46.9629	49.6449	55.476
28	32.6205	37.9159	41.3371	44.4608	48.2782	50.9934	56.892
29	33.7109	39.0875	42.5570	45.7223	49.5879	52.3356	58.301
30	34.7997	40.2560	43.7730	46.9792	50.8922	53.6720	59.703
40	45.6160	51.8051	55.7585	59.3417	63.6907	66.7660	73.402
50	56.3336	63.1671	67.5048	71.4202	76.1539	79.4900	86.661
60	66.9815	74.3970	79.0819	83.2977	88.3794	91.9517	99.607
70	77.5767	85.5270	90.5312	95.0232	100.425	104.215	112.317
80	88.1303	96.5782	101.879	106.629	112.329	116.321	124.839
90	98.6499	107.565	113.145	118.136	124.116	128.299	137.208
100	109.141	118.498	124.342	129.561	135.807	140.169	149.449

Reproduced from J. White, A. Yeats and G. Skipworth, *Tables for Statisticians*, 3rd edition (Stanley Thornes (Publishers) Ltd).

TABLE A

Table of probabilities associated with Σd^2 in Spearman's rank correlation coefficient, r_S.
Probability that Σd^2 exceeds, or is less than, certain values, for $4 \leqslant n \leqslant 10$.

n = 4, MAX. $\Sigma d^2 = 20$ Σd^2 ⋁	⋀	P	n = 5, MAX. $\Sigma d^2 = 40$ Σd^2 ⋁	⋀	P	n = 6, MAX. $\Sigma d^2 = 70$ Σd^2 ⋁	⋀	P	n = 7, MAX. $\Sigma d^2 = 112$ Σd^2 ⋁	⋀	P	n = 8, MAX. $\Sigma d^2 = 168$ Σd^2 ⋁	⋀	P	n = 9, MAX. $\Sigma d^2 = 240$ Σd^2 ⋁	⋀	P	n = 10, MAX. $\Sigma d^2 = 330$ Σd^2 ⋁	⋀	P
8	12	.458	18	22	.475	28	42	.357	54	58	.482	78	90	.441	112	128	.440	160	170	.473
6	14	.375	16	24	.392	26	44	.329	52	60	.453	74	94	.397	108	132	.405	154	176	.433
4	16	.208	14	26	.342	24	46	.282	50	62	.420	68	100	.332	104	136	.371	148	182	.393
2	18	.167	12	28	.258	22	48	.249	48	64	.391	64	104	.291	100	140	.339	140	190	.341
0	20	.0417	10	30	.225	20	50	.210	46	66	.356	60	108	.250	96	144	.307	132	198	.292
			8	32	.175	18	52	.178	44	68	.331	56	112	.214	92	148	.276	124	206	.246
			6	34	.117	16	54	.149	42	70	.297	54	114	.195	88	152	.247	116	214	.204
			4	36	.0667	14	56	.121	40	72	.278	52	116	.180	84	156	.218	114	216	.194
			2	38	.0417	12	58	.0875	38	74	.249	48	120	.150	80	160	.193	108	222	.165
			0	40	.0083	10	60	.0681	36	76	.222	46	122	.134	76	164	.168	100	230	.132
						8	62	.0514	34	78	.198	44	124	.122	72	168	.146	92	238	.102
						6	64	.0292	32	80	.177	42	126	.108	68	172	.125	90	240	.0956
						4	66	.0167	30	82	.151	40	128	.0983	64	176	.106	84	246	.0774
						2	68	.0083	28	84	.133	38	130	.0855	62	178	.0969	78	252	.0616
						0	70	.0014	26	86	.118	36	132	.0756	56	184	.0738	74	256	.0524
									24	88	.100	34	134	.0661	50	190	.0540	72	258	.0481
									22	90	.0833	32	136	.0575	48	192	.0484	68	262	.0403
									20	92	.0694	30	138	.0481	40	200	.0294	62	268	.0302
									18	94	.0548	28	140	.0415	34	206	.0184	56	274	.0219
									16	96	.0440	24	144	.0288	28	212	.0107	50	280	.0153
									14	98	.0331	20	148	.0184	26	214	.0086	44	286	.0101
									12	100	.0240	16	152	.0109	22	218	.0054	42	288	.0087
									10	102	.0171	14	154	.0077	20	220	.0041	36	294	.0053
									8	104	.0119	12	156	.0054	16	224	.0023	30	300	.0029
									6	106	.0062	10	158	.0036	14	226	.0015	22	308	.0011
									4	108	.0034	6	162	.0011	12	228	.0010	16	314	.0004
									2	110	.0014	4	164	.0006	10	230	.0007	10	320	.0001

TABLE B

Table of critical values of the Spearman's rank correlation coefficient.

n	Significance level (one-tailed test)	
	0.05	0.01
4	1.000	
5	0.900	1.000
6	0.829	0.943
7	0.714	0.893
8	0.643	0.833
9	0.600	0.783
10	0.564	0.746
12	0.506	0.712
14	0.456	0.645
16	0.425	0.601
18	0.399	0.564
20	0.377	0.534
22	0.359	0.508
24	0.343	0.485
26	0.329	0.465
28	0.317	0.448
30	0.306	0.432

NOTE: Other tables of critical values may differ slightly, depending on the degree of approximation used.

APPENDIX 2

EXPECTATION AND VARIANCE OF THE BINOMIAL DISTRIBUTION

This section follows on from page 265.

> If the random variable X is such that $X \sim \text{Bin}(n, p)$
>
> then $\qquad\qquad E(X) = np$
>
> and $\qquad\qquad \text{Var}(X) = npq$ where $q = 1 - p$

Proof

Now $\qquad P(X = x) = {}^nC_x q^{n-x} p^x \qquad x = 0, 1, 2, \ldots, n$

So X has the probability distribution shown in the table:

x	0	1	2	3	$\ldots$	n
$P(X = x)$	q^n	$nq^{n-1}p$	$\dfrac{n(n-1)}{2!}q^{n-2}p^2$	$\dfrac{n(n-1)(n-2)}{3!}q^{n-3}p^3$	$\ldots$	p^n

$$E(X) = \sum_{\text{all}\,x} xP(X = x)$$

$$= (0)q^n + (1)nq^{n-1}p + \frac{(2)\,n\,(n-1)}{2!}\,q^{n-2}p^2$$

$$+ \frac{(3)\,n\,(n-1)(n-2)}{3!}\,q^{n-3}p^3 + \ldots + np^n$$

$$= np\left[q^{n-1} + (n-1)q^{n-2}p + \frac{(n-1)(n-2)}{2!}\,q^{n-3}p^2 + \ldots + p^{n-1}\right]$$

$$= np[(q + p)^{n-1}]$$

$$= np \quad \text{since} \quad q + p = 1$$

Therefore $\qquad \underline{E(X) = np}$

Now $\qquad \text{Var}(X) = E(X^2) - E^2(X)$

$$E(X^2) = \sum_{\text{all}\,x} x^2 P(X = x)$$

$$= (0)q^n + (1)nq^{n-1}p + \frac{4\,n\,(n-1)}{2!}\,q^{n-2}p^2$$

$$+ \frac{9\,n\,(n-1)(n-2)}{3!}\,q^{n-3}p^3 + \ldots + n^2 p^n$$

$$= np\left[q^{n-1} + 2(n-1)q^{n-2}p + \frac{3(n-1)(n-2)}{2!}\,q^{n-3}p^2 + \ldots + np^{n-1}\right]$$

$$= np\left[q^{n-1} + (n-1)q^{n-2}p + \frac{(n-1)(n-2)}{2!}q^{n-3}p^2 + \ldots + p^{n-1}\right.$$

$$+ (n-1)q^{n-2}p + \frac{2(n-1)(n-2)}{2!}q^{n-3}p^2 + \ldots$$

$$\left. + (n-1)p^{n-1}\right]$$

Now the first row of terms is, as before, the expansion of $(q+p)^{n-1}$.

So $E(X^2) = np\{(q+p)^{n-1}$

$$+ (n-1)p[q^{n-2} + (n-2)q^{n-3}p + \ldots + p^{n-2}]\}$$

$$= np[1 + (n-1)p(q+p)^{n-2}]$$

$$= np[1 + (n-1)p]$$

$$= np(1-p) + n^2p^2$$

Therefore $\text{Var}(X) = np(1-p) + n^2p^2 - (np)^2$

$$= npq \quad \text{where} \quad q = 1 - p$$

Therefore $\underline{\text{Var}(X) = npq}$

THE GEOMETRIC DISTRIBUTION

This section follows on from page 284.

We shall need to use the following formulae relating to Geometric Progressions.

Consider the series

$$1 + r + r^2 + r^3 + r^4 + \ldots$$

The ratio of each term to the previous one is r. This is known as the **common ratio**.

The n th term is given by r^{n-1}.

Suppose that the sum of n terms is S_n.

Then $S_n = 1 + r + r^2 + \ldots + r^{n-1}$

and $rS_n = \quad r + r^2 + \ldots + r^{n-1} + r^n$

Subtracting,

$$S_n - rS_n = 1 - r^n$$

$$S_n(1-r) = 1 - r^n$$

$$S_n = \frac{1 - r^n}{1 - r}$$

Since $|r| < 1$, as n approaches infinity, $r^n \to 0$

i.e.
$$S_\infty = \frac{1}{1-r}$$

or
$$1 + r + r^2 + r^3 + \ldots \to \infty = \frac{1}{1-r}$$

Another useful infinite series is obtained as follows:

$$\frac{1}{1-x} = 1 + x + x^2 + x^3 + \ldots$$

Differentiating with respect to x

$$\frac{1}{(1-x)^2} = 1 + 2x + 3x^2 + \ldots$$

EXPECTATION AND VARIANCE OF THE GEOMETRIC DISTRIBUTION

A discrete r.v. X having p.d.f. of the form $P(X = x) = q^{x-1}p$, where $0 \leqslant p \leqslant 1$ and $q = 1 - p$, is said to follow a **geometric distribution**, with $x = 1, 2, 3, \ldots$

If X is defined in this way, we write

$$X \sim \text{Geo}(p)$$

If $X \sim \text{Geo}(p)$ then $E(X) = \dfrac{1}{p}$ and $\text{Var}(X) = \dfrac{q}{p^2}$ where $q = 1 - p$.

x	1	2	3	4	$\ldots$
$P(X = x)$	p	qp	q^2p	q^3p	$\ldots$

$$E(X) = \sum_{\text{all} x} xP(X = x)$$

$$= p + 2qp + 3q^2p + 4q^3p + \ldots$$

$$= p(1 + 2q + 3q^2 + 4q^3 + \ldots)$$

$$= p(1-q)^{-2} \quad \text{since} \quad (1-q)^{-2} = 1 + 2q + 3q^2 + 4q^3 + \ldots$$

$$= \frac{p}{p^2}$$

$$= \frac{1}{p}$$

$$E(X^2) = \sum_{\text{all } x} x^2 P(X = x)$$

$$= p + 4qp + 9q^2p + 16q^3p + \ldots$$

$$= p(1 + 4q + 9q^2 + 16q^3 + \ldots)$$

$$= p(1 + 2q + 3q^2 + 4q^3 + \ldots + 2q + 6q^2 + 12q^3 + \ldots)$$

$$= p((1 - q)^{-2} + 2q(1 + 3q + 6q^2 + \ldots))$$

$$= p\left(\frac{1}{p^2} + 2q(1 - q)^{-3}\right) \text{ since } (1 - q)^{-3} = 1 + 3q + 6q^2 + \ldots$$

$$= p\left(\frac{1}{p^2} + \frac{2q}{p^3}\right)$$

$$= \frac{1}{p} + \frac{2q}{p^2}$$

$$\text{Var}(X) = E(X^2) - E^2(X)$$

$$= \frac{1}{p} + \frac{2q}{p^2} - \frac{1}{p^2}$$

$$= \frac{p + 2q - 1}{p^2}$$

$$= \frac{q}{p^2} \text{ since } p = 1 - q$$

Therefore $E(X) = \dfrac{1}{p}$ and $\text{Var}(X) = \dfrac{q}{p^2}$.

EXPECTATION AND VARIANCE OF THE POISSON DISTRIBUTION

This section follows on from page 290.

A discrete r.v. X having p.d.f. of the form

$$P(X = x) = e^{-\lambda}\frac{\lambda^x}{x!} \qquad \text{for} \qquad x = 0, 1, 2, 3, \ldots \text{to infinity}$$

where λ can take any positive value, is said to follow the **Poisson distribution**.

If X is distributed in this way, then $X \sim \text{Po}(\lambda)$

If the random variable X is such that $X \sim \text{Po}(\lambda)$,

then $\qquad\qquad E(X) = \lambda$

and $\qquad\qquad \text{Var}(X) = \lambda$

The probability distribution can be written as follows:

x	0	1	2	3	4	...
$P(X = x)$	$e^{-\lambda}$	$e^{-\lambda}\lambda$	$e^{-\lambda}\dfrac{\lambda^2}{2!}$	$e^{-\lambda}\dfrac{\lambda^3}{3!}$	$e^{-\lambda}\dfrac{\lambda^4}{4!}$	...

Now $\qquad E(X) = \displaystyle\sum_{\text{all }x} xP(X = x)$

$$E(X) = \lambda e^{-\lambda}\left(1 + \lambda + \frac{\lambda^2}{2!} + \frac{\lambda^3}{3!} + \dots\right)$$

$$= \lambda e^{-\lambda}(e^{\lambda})$$

$$= \lambda$$

Therefore $E(X) = \lambda$.

$$E(X^2) = \sum_{\text{all }x} x^2 P(X = x)$$

$$= e^{-\lambda}\left(0 + \lambda + \frac{4\lambda^2}{2!} + \frac{9\lambda^3}{3!} + \frac{16\lambda^4}{4!} + \dots\right)$$

$$= \lambda e^{-\lambda}\left(1 + 2\lambda + \frac{3\lambda^2}{2!} + \frac{4\lambda^3}{3!} + \dots\right)$$

$$= \lambda e^{-\lambda}\left(1 + \lambda + \frac{\lambda^2}{2!} + \frac{\lambda^3}{3!} + \dots + \lambda + \frac{2\lambda^2}{2!} + \frac{3\lambda^3}{3!} + \dots\right)$$

$$= \lambda e^{-\lambda}\left[e^{\lambda} + \lambda\left(1 + \lambda + \frac{\lambda^2}{2!} + \dots\right)\right]$$

$$= \lambda e^{-\lambda}(e^{\lambda} + \lambda e^{\lambda})$$

$$= \lambda + \lambda^2$$

So $\qquad\qquad\qquad \text{Var}(X) = E(X^2) - E^2(X)$

$$= \lambda + \lambda^2 - \lambda^2$$

$$= \lambda$$

Therefore $\text{Var}(X) = \lambda$.

USING THE POISSON DISTRIBUTION AS AN APPROXIMATION TO THE BINOMIAL DISTRIBUTION

This section follows on from page 295.

A binomial distribution with parameters n and p can be approximated by a Poisson distribution, with parameter $\lambda = np$, if n is large (> 50 say) and p is small (< 0.1 say). The approximation gets better as $n \to \infty$ and $p \to 0$.

For a binomial distribution $P(X = x)$, $x = 0, 1, \ldots, n$ are given by the terms of the expansion of $(q + p)^n$.

For a Poisson distribution $P(X = x)$, $x = 0, 1, 2, \ldots$, are given by the terms $e^{-\lambda}(1 + \lambda + \frac{\lambda^2}{2!} + \ldots)$.

So we wish to show that

$$(q + p)^n \to e^{-\lambda}\left(1 + \lambda + \frac{\lambda^2}{2!} + \ldots\right) \quad \text{as} \quad n \to \infty$$

We will need the following theory, relating to the binomial theorem.

By the binomial theorem,

$$\left(1 + \frac{x}{n}\right)^n = 1 + n\left(\frac{x}{n}\right) + \frac{n(n-1)}{2!}\frac{x^2}{n^2} + \frac{n(n-1)(n-2)}{3!}\frac{x^3}{n^3} + \ldots$$

$$= 1 + x + \frac{x^2}{2!}\left[\frac{n}{n}\frac{(n-1)}{n}\right] + \frac{x^3}{3!}\left[\frac{n}{n}\frac{(n-1)}{n}\frac{(n-2)}{n}\right] + \ldots$$

$$= 1 + x + \frac{x^2}{2!}\left(1 - \frac{1}{n}\right) + \frac{x^3}{3!}\left(1 - \frac{1}{n}\right)\left(1 - \frac{2}{n}\right) + \ldots$$

Now, as $n \to \infty$, $\left(1 - \frac{1}{n}\right) \to 1$, and

$$\left(1 + \frac{x}{n}\right)^n \to 1 + x + \frac{x^2}{2!} + \frac{x^3}{3!} + \ldots$$

$$= e^x$$

i.e. $$\lim_{n \to \infty}\left(1 + \frac{x}{n}\right)^n = e^x$$

Similarly $$\lim_{n \to \infty}\left(1 - \frac{x}{n}\right)^n = e^{-x} \qquad \textbf{(a)}$$

Now

$$(q + p)^n = q^n + nq^{n-1}p + \frac{n(n-1)}{2!}q^{n-2}p^2 + \frac{n(n-1)(n-2)}{3!}q^{n-3}p^3 + \ldots$$

But $\quad q = 1 - p \quad$ and $\quad p = \dfrac{\lambda}{n} \quad$ so $\quad q = 1 - \dfrac{\lambda}{n}.$ So

$$(q+p)^n = \left(1 - \frac{\lambda}{n}\right)^n + n\left(1 - \frac{\lambda}{n}\right)^{n-1}\left(\frac{\lambda}{n}\right) + \frac{n(n-1)}{2!}\left(1 - \frac{\lambda}{n}\right)^{n-2}\left(\frac{\lambda}{n}\right)^2 + \dots$$

$$= \left(1 - \frac{\lambda}{n}\right)^n \left[1 + \frac{n}{\left(1 - \frac{\lambda}{n}\right)}\left(\frac{\lambda}{n}\right) + \frac{n(n-1)}{2!\left(1 - \frac{\lambda}{n}\right)^2}\left(\frac{\lambda}{n}\right)^2 + \dots\right]$$

$$= \left(1 - \frac{\lambda}{n}\right)^n \left[1 + \frac{\lambda}{\left(1 - \frac{\lambda}{n}\right)} + \frac{\lambda^2\left(1 - \frac{1}{n}\right)}{2!\left(1 - \frac{\lambda}{n}\right)^2} + \dots\right]$$

As $\ n \to \infty\ $ we have $\ \left(1 - \dfrac{\lambda}{n}\right)^n \to \mathrm{e}^{-\lambda}\ $ from (**a**) and $\ \dfrac{\lambda}{n} \to 0.$

$$(q+p)^n \to \mathrm{e}^{-\lambda}\left(1 + \lambda + \frac{\lambda^2}{2!} + \dots\right)\quad \text{as required.}$$

THE DISTRIBUTION OF TWO INDEPENDENT POISSON VARIABLES

This section follows on from page 301.

> The sum of two independent Poisson variables with parameters m and n respectively, is a Poisson variable with parameter $(m + n)$,
>
> i.e.   if $X \sim \mathrm{Po}(m)$ and $Y \sim \mathrm{Po}(n)$, then $X + Y \sim \mathrm{Po}(m + n)$

Proof

$X \sim \mathrm{Po}(m)$ so $P(X = x) = \mathrm{e}^{-m}\dfrac{m^x}{x!}$	$Y \sim \mathrm{Po}(Y)$ so $P(Y = y) = \mathrm{e}^{-n}\dfrac{n^x}{x!}$
$P(X = 0) = \mathrm{e}^{-m}$	$P(Y = 0) = \mathrm{e}^{-n}$
$P(X = 1) = \mathrm{e}^{-m}\, m$	$P(Y = 1) = \mathrm{e}^{-n}\, n$
$P(X = 2) = \mathrm{e}^{-m}\dfrac{m^2}{2!}$	$P(Y = 2) = \mathrm{e}^{-n}\dfrac{n^2}{2!}$
and so on	and so on

Now

$$P(X + Y = 0) = P(X = 0)P(Y = 0)$$
$$= (\mathrm{e}^{-m})(\mathrm{e}^{-n})$$
$$= \mathrm{e}^{-(m + n)}$$

$$P(X + Y = 1) = P(X = 0)P(Y = 1) + P(X = 1)P(Y = 0)$$

$$= (e^{-m})(e^{-n} n) + (e^{-m} m)(e^{-n})$$

$$= e^{-(m+n)} (m + n)$$

$$P(X + Y = 2) = P(X = 0)P(Y = 2) + P(X = 1)P(Y = 1)$$

$$+ P(X = 2)P(Y = 0)$$

$$= (e^{-m}) \left(e^{-n} \frac{n^2}{2!} \right) + (e^{-m} m)(e^{-n} n) + e^{-m} \frac{m^2}{2!} (e^{-n})$$

$$= \frac{e^{-(m+n)}}{2!} (m^2 + 2mn + n^2)$$

$$= e^{-(m+n)} \frac{(m + n)^2}{2!}$$

and so on.

The probability distribution for $X + Y$ is:

$x + y$	0	1	2	...
$P(X + Y = x + y)$	$e^{-(m+n)}$	$e^{-(m+n)} (m + n)$	$e^{-(m+n)} \dfrac{(m + n)^2}{2!}$	...

From the distribution we see that $X + Y \sim \text{Po}(m + n)$, as required.

THE EXPECTATION AND VARIANCE OF THE EXPONENTIAL DISTRIBUTION

This section follows on from page 357.

A continuous r.v. X having p.d.f. $f(x)$ where

$$f(x) = \lambda e^{-\lambda x} \quad \text{for} \quad x \geqslant 0,$$

where λ is a positive constant, is said to follow an exponential distribution.

$$E(X) = \frac{1}{\lambda}$$

$$\text{Var}(X) = \frac{1}{\lambda^2}$$

Proof

$$E(X) = \int_{\text{all } x} x f(x) \, dx$$

$$= \int_0^\infty x(\lambda e^{-\lambda x}) \, dx$$

$$= \left[x(-e^{-\lambda x})\right]_0^\infty - \int_0^\infty (-e^{-\lambda x})\, dx$$

$$= 0 + \int_0^\infty e^{-\lambda x}\, dx \quad (\text{since } \lim_{x \to \infty} x e^{-\lambda x} = 0)$$

$$= -\frac{1}{\lambda}\left[e^{-\lambda x}\right]_0^\infty$$

$$= -\frac{1}{\lambda}(0 - 1)$$

$$= \frac{1}{\lambda}$$

Also $\qquad E(X^2) = \displaystyle\int_{\text{all } x} x^2 f(x)\, dx$

$$= \int_0^\infty x^2(\lambda e^{-\lambda x})\, dx$$

$$= \left[x^2(-e^{-\lambda x})\right]_0^\infty - \int_0^\infty 2x(-e^{-\lambda x})\, dx$$

$$= 0 + 2\int_0^\infty x e^{-\lambda x}\, dx \quad (\text{since } \lim_{x \to \infty} x^2 e^{-\lambda x} = 0)$$

$$= \frac{2}{\lambda^2} \quad \left(\text{since } \int_0^\infty \lambda x e^{-\lambda x}\, dx = \frac{1}{\lambda}\right)$$

$$\text{Var}(X) = E(X^2) - E^2(X)$$

$$= \frac{2}{\lambda^2} - \left(\frac{1}{\lambda}\right)^2$$

$$= \frac{1}{\lambda^2}$$

Therefore $E(X) = \dfrac{1}{\lambda}$ and $\text{Var}(X) = \dfrac{1}{\lambda^2}$.

THE NORMAL DISTRIBUTION

This section follows on from page 369.

A continuous r.v. X having p.d.f. $f(x)$ where

$$f(x) = \frac{1}{\sigma\sqrt{2\pi}}\, e^{-(x-\mu)^2/2\sigma^2} \quad (-\infty < x < \infty)$$

is said to follow a normal distribution.

We write $\qquad X \sim \text{N}(\mu, \sigma^2).$

EXPECTATION AND VARIANCE

If $X \sim N(\mu, \sigma^2)$ then
$$E(X) = \mu$$
$$\text{Var}(X) = \sigma^2$$

In the following, we assume that $\dfrac{1}{\sqrt{2\pi}} \displaystyle\int_{-\infty}^{\infty} e^{-\frac{1}{2}t^2} dt = 1$

Now
$$E(X) = \int_{\text{all } x} x f(x) \, dx$$

$$= \frac{1}{\sigma\sqrt{2\pi}} \int_{-\infty}^{\infty} x e^{-(x-\mu)^2/2\sigma^2} \, dx$$

Now let $t = \dfrac{x - \mu}{\sigma}$ so that $x = t\sigma + \mu$ and $\dfrac{dx}{dt} = \sigma$.

When $x = \infty$, $t = \infty$ and when $x = -\infty$, $t = -\infty$.

So
$$E(X) = \frac{1}{\sigma\sqrt{2\pi}} \int_{-\infty}^{\infty} (\mu + \sigma t) \, e^{-\frac{1}{2}t^2} \, \sigma \, dt$$

$$= \frac{\mu}{\sqrt{2\pi}} \int_{-\infty}^{\infty} e^{-\frac{1}{2}t^2} \, dt + \frac{\sigma}{\sqrt{2\pi}} \int_{-\infty}^{\infty} t \, e^{-\frac{1}{2}t^2} \, dt$$

$$= \mu + \frac{\sigma}{\sqrt{2\pi}} \left[-e^{-\frac{1}{2}t^2} \right]_{-\infty}^{\infty}$$

$$= \mu$$

Therefore $E(X) = \mu$.

$$\text{Var}(X) = \int_{\text{all } x} x^2 f(x) \, dx - \mu^2$$

$$= I - \mu^2 \quad \text{where} \quad I = \frac{1}{\sigma\sqrt{2\pi}} \int_{-\infty}^{\infty} (\mu + \sigma t)^2 \, e^{-\frac{1}{2}t^2} \sigma \, dt$$

$$I = \frac{1}{\sqrt{2\pi}} \left\{ \mu^2 \int_{-\infty}^{\infty} e^{-\frac{1}{2}t^2} \, dt + 2\mu\sigma \int_{-\infty}^{\infty} t \, e^{-\frac{1}{2}t^2} \, dt \right.$$

$$\left. + \sigma^2 \int_{-\infty}^{\infty} t^2 e^{-\frac{1}{2}t^2} \, dt \right\}$$

Now

$$\int_{-\infty}^{\infty} t^2 e^{-\frac{1}{2}t^2} \, dt = \int_{-\infty}^{\infty} t(t e^{-\frac{1}{2}t^2}) \, dt$$

$$= \left[t\left(-e^{-\frac{1}{2}t^2} \right) \right]_{-\infty}^{\infty} - \int_{-\infty}^{\infty} -e^{-\frac{1}{2}t^2} \, dt$$

$$= 0 + \sqrt{2\pi}$$

So
$$I = \frac{1}{\sqrt{2\pi}} \left(\mu^2 \sqrt{2\pi} + 2\mu\sigma \left[-e^{-\frac{1}{2}t^2} \right]_{-\infty}^{\infty} + \sigma^2 \sqrt{2\pi} \right)$$

$$= \mu^2 + \sigma^2 \quad \text{since} \quad e^{-\frac{1}{2}t^2} \to 0 \quad \text{as} \quad t \to \pm\infty$$

$$= \sigma^2$$

So, $\underline{E(X) = \mu}$ and $\underline{\text{Var}(X) = \sigma^2}$.

The following results are also important

Result 1   If $X \sim N(\mu, \sigma^2)$, the maximum value of $f(x)$ occurs when $x = \mu$.

We consider
$$f(x) = \frac{1}{\sigma\sqrt{2\pi}} e^{-(x-\mu)^2/2\sigma^2}$$

$$f'(x) = \frac{1}{\sigma\sqrt{2\pi}} \left\{ -\frac{(x-\mu)}{\sigma^2} \right\} e^{-(x-\mu)^2/2\sigma^2}$$

$$= -\frac{1}{\sigma^3\sqrt{2\pi}} (x-\mu) e^{-(x-\mu)^2/2\sigma^2}$$

So
$$f'(x) = 0 \quad \text{when} \quad x - \mu = 0$$

i.e. when $x = \mu$

Now

$$f''(x) = -\frac{1}{\sigma^3\sqrt{2\pi}} \left\{ -\frac{(x-\mu)^2}{\sigma^2} e^{-(x-\mu)^2/2\sigma^2} + e^{-(x-\mu)^2/2\sigma^2} \right\}$$

$$= -\frac{1}{\sigma^3\sqrt{2\pi}} e^{-(x-\mu)^2/2\sigma^2} \left\{ -\frac{(x-\mu)^2}{\sigma^2} + 1 \right\}$$

When $x = \mu$, $f''(x) < 0$.

There is a maximum value of $f(x)$ when $x = \mu$.

Result 2   If $X \sim N(\mu, \sigma^2)$, then $f(x)$ has points of inflexion at $x = \mu + \sigma$ and $x = \mu - \sigma$.

To show this, consider $f''(x)$.

$$f''(x) = 0 \quad \text{when} \quad (x-\mu)^2 = \sigma^2$$

$$x - \mu = \pm\sigma$$

$$x = \mu + \sigma \quad \text{or} \quad x = \mu - \sigma$$

There are points of inflexion at $x = \mu + \sigma$ and $x = \mu - \sigma$.

NOTE: $f'(x) \neq 0$ at either of these points of inflexion.

NOTE: Sketch of $y = f(x)$.

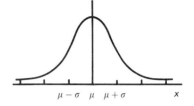

$\mu - \sigma \quad \mu \quad \mu + \sigma \qquad x$

PROBABILITY STATEMENT INVOLVED IN FINDING THE 95% CONFIDENCE INTERVAL FOR μ

This section follows on from page 488.

$$P\left(-1.96 \leqslant \frac{\overline{X} - \mu}{\sigma/\sqrt{n}} \leqslant 1.96\right) = 0.95$$

$$P\left(-1.96 \frac{\sigma}{\sqrt{n}} \leqslant \overline{X} - \mu \leqslant 1.96 \frac{\sigma}{\sqrt{n}}\right) = 0.95$$

Now multiply through by -1, reversing the inequality:

$$P\left(1.96 \frac{\sigma}{\sqrt{n}} \geqslant \mu - \overline{X} \geqslant -1.96 \frac{\sigma}{\sqrt{n}}\right) = 0.95$$

$$P\left(\overline{X} + 1.96 \frac{\sigma}{\sqrt{n}} \geqslant \mu \geqslant \overline{X} - 1.96 \frac{\sigma}{\sqrt{n}}\right) = 0.95$$

Therefore $\quad P\left(\overline{X} - 1.96 \frac{\sigma}{\sqrt{n}} \leqslant \mu \leqslant \overline{X} + 1.96 \frac{\sigma}{\sqrt{n}}\right) = 0.95$

ANSWERS

CHAPTER 1

Exercise 1a (page 10)

NOTE: There are alternative formats.

1. (a)
```
50 | 2
55 | 2 2 4
60 | 1 3 4 4
65 | 0 2 2 3 3 3
70 | 0 1 1 2 3 4 4
75 | 0 1 1 2 4 4
80 | 1 3
85 | 1
```
Key: 85 | 1 means 86

(b)
```
3 | 2 2 2 2
3 | 0 1 1 1
2 | 9 9
2 | 6 6 6 6 7 7 7
2 | 4 5 5
```
Key: 2 | 7 means 27

(c)
```
1 | 4 4 4 4
1 | 7 7 7 7 7 7
1 | 8
2 | 0 0 0 0 1 1 1 1
2 | 2 2 3 3 3 3
2 | 4 4 4
2 | 6 6
```
Key: 2 | 1 means 0.21 seconds

(d)
```
12 | 5 9
11 | 1 3 6
10 | 4
 9 | 7 8
 8 | 3 4
 7 | 0 3 5 5 6 8
 6 | 1 2 5
 5 | 6 6 8
 4 | 3 8
 3 |
 2 | 4 6
 1 | 6
 0 | 0 2 6 8
```
Key: 7 | 3 means 7.3 hours

(e)
```
 3 | 9
 4 |
 5 | 3 4 5 5
 6 | 1 1 5 7 8
 7 | 0 0 1 3 4 5 6 6 8 9
 8 | 0 1 2 2 4 8
 9 | 2 6
10 | 0 1
```
Key: 5 | 3 means 5.3 cm

2. (a)
```
      Before               After
          8 |  4 |
  7 3 1 1 0 |  5 |
  9 9 6 6 4 |  6 | 9
  9 5 3 3 0 0 |  7 | 0 5 5 7 7
            1 |  8 | 0 0 1 4 4 6
3 3 3 3 1 0 0 |  9 | 5 6 7
          5 5 | 10 | 4 4 4 6 8 9
        1 1 0 | 11 | 7
              | 12 | 5
              | 13 | 0 0 1 7 7
              | 14 | 3 5
```
Key: 9 | 7 means 79   Key: 8 | 4 means 84

(b)
```
        School A              School B
        9 8 7 5 3 3 | 2 | 3 5 9
9 9 9 7 7 7 4 3 3 1 1 | 3 | 4 6 6 8 8
8 8 8 8 6 6 5 5 5 0 0 | 4 | 0 1 2 2 3 4 5 5 6 7 7 9
        9 4 4 3 3 1 1 | 5 | 0 0 2 2 4 4 6 6 6 7 8 8 9 9 9
                    1 | 6 | 0
```
Key: 9 | 5 means 59   Key: 5 | 9 means 59

(c)
```
      Boys                   Girls
              | 2 | 4 5 5
    3 3 3 2 2 | 2 | 2 2 2 2 2 2
          1 0 | 2 | 1 1
        9 9 8 8 | 1 | 8 8 9 9 9
        6 6 6 6 | 1 | 6 6 7 7
          5 5 4 | 1 |
              | 1 |
            1 | 1 |
            9 | 0 |
```
Key: 8 | 1 means 0.18 s   Key: 1 | 8 means 0.18 s

3. (a) 7.4 hours [7.0 − 7.4]
   (b) 0.074 g [0.070 g − 0.074 g]

Exercise 1b (page 20)

1. Boundary points 84.5, 89.5, 94.5, 99.5, 104.5, 109.5
Frequencies 4, 6, 7, 13, 10, 5, 5

2. Boundary points 5, 10, 20, 25, 40, 45
Frequency density 0.4, 1.2, 1.4, 1, 0.4

3. Boundary points 40.5, 50.5, 55.5, 60.5, 70.5, 75.5
Frequency density 2.1, 12.4, 11, 5, 2.4

4. Boundary points 0, 25, 60, 80, 150, 300
Frequency density 2.48, 2, 4.4, 4, 0.2

5. Boundary points 176.5, 186.5, 191.5, 196.5, 201.5, 206.5, 216.5
Frequency density 1.2, 1.6, 1.6, 1.8, 1.4, 0.6
Plot polygon at 181.5, 189, 194, 199, 204, 211.5

6. Frequencies 20, 24, 24, 16, 12, 10, 6

7. Plot polygon at $(0.75, 2)$, $(2.25, 2\frac{1}{3})$, $(4.5, 7\frac{1}{3})$, $(9, 3\frac{1}{3})$, $(13.5, 2)$, $(18, 1)$

8. (18, 17.5), (22.5, 94), (27.5, 107), (32.5, 56), (40, 11.8)
9. Boundary points 0, 2.5, 5.5, 11.5, 14.5, 17.5
   Frequency density 2, 2, $2\frac{1}{3}$, $1\frac{1}{3}$, 1
10. Boundary points 0, 8, 12, 16, 24, 28, 34, 50
    Frequency density 0.5, 1.5, 3, 3.5, 2, 1, 0.25
11. Frequency density 1.1, 1.8, 2.2, 2.4, 2.8, 2.4, 1.6
12. Boundary points 9.5, 19.5, 24.5, 29.5, 30.5, 34.5, 39.5, 59.5
    Frequency density 2, 4, 3, 14, 4, 2, 0.5
14. 6, 8, 8, 6, 4, 10

Exercise 1c (page 26)

1. 66°, 60°, 45°, 75°, 30°, 84°
2. 27.4°, 56.7°, 115.1°, 160.8°
3. (i) 660 km² (ii) 4° (iii) 2700 km²
4. Radii in the ratio 7.7 : 6.7
5. 66°, 156°, 24°, 42°, 72°; 5.5 cm, 6 cm; 50°
6. Radii in the ratio 20.3 : 22.5 : 26.8
7. 67.5°, 157.5°, 135°; £6; 72°, 115.2°, 172.8°
8. 208°, 46°, 38°, 36°, 32°; 5.25 cm
9. (i) 42 (ii) 40° (iii) 91; 420, 30.0 cm
10. (a) 86°, 38°, 32°, 20°, 168°, 16° (b) 5.5 cm
11. (i) £2000, £8000 (ii) £400 (iii) 27° (iv) 80°
12. 28.8°, 72°, 115.2°, 144°; 180
13. (i) £4500 (ii) 1550, 1650 (iii) 132°, 24°; 8 cm

Exercise 1d (page 31)

1. (i) 9.7 (ii) 154.8 (iii) 51.375 (iv) $1775\frac{5}{7}$
   (v) 0.908 (3 S.F.)
2. 21
3. 19
4. 8
5. 7
6. (i) 4 (ii) 29.54 (iii) 122.82 (iv) 18.625
   (v) 109.4 (1 d.p.)
7. 12
8. 15, 7
9. 49.3
10. 58.95
11. 45 (2 S.F.)
12. (a) Boundary points 0, 5, 10, 15, 20, 40
       Frequency density 2.4, 7.6, 8.4, 4, 0.4
    (b) £11.92
13. 146.5 cm, 145.5 cm
14. Boundary points 0, 15, 30, 50, 70, 100
    Frequency density 3.6, 5.2, 6, 4.4, 2; 43.35 y
15. 21.4 cm

Exercise 1e (page 38)

1. (a) 5, 2 (b) 8.5, 1.80 (c) 18.8, 6.46
   (d) $10\frac{5}{6}$, 4.10 (e) 3.42, 1.91 (f) 205, 3.16
2. (a) 4.8, 5.66 (b) 0.12, 0.141
   (c) 1.288, 1.38 (d) 4.568, 5.02
   (e) 0.064, 0.0748 (f) 38.704, 43.0
3. 3.74
4. 29, 5.9
5. 5.10
6. 5
7. 6, 4
8. 10.5, 5.77
9. $\frac{1}{2}(n+1)$, $\sqrt{\dfrac{n^2-1}{12}}$
10. (a) 121, 6.19 (b) 14, 1703.8
    (c) 1716, 3.59 (d) 1026, 58 770
11. 5, $\sqrt{7.5}$; 5, 11

Exercise 1f (page 39)

Answers as in Exercise 1e, question 1.

Exercise 1g (page 42)

1. 69.3, 1.7
2. 115.8 (4 S.F.), 7.58
3. (a) $\frac{11}{3}$, 1.23 (b) 7.85, 3.07
   (c) 31, 4.36 (d) 34.1, 13.4
   (e) 16.04, 7.01 (f) 10, 1.44
4. 28.15, 3.84
5. 159
6. (a) 294.55, 28.15, 3.84
   (b) 10, 7450, 4 (c) 500, 5450, 450
   (d) 159, 5.3, 2.47 (e) 12, 300, 5

Exercise 1h (page 46)

1. (a) 6, 2.14 (b) 516, 2.14
   (c) 78, 27.8
2. 4, 4; 7, 4; 40, 400; 43, 400
3. (i) $a = \frac{3}{4}$, $b = 22$ (ii) 70 (iii) 76
4. (i) 38, 8.99 (3 S.F.) (ii) 34, 77
5. $a = 0.8$, $b = -5$; 6.25
6. (i) $\mu + c$, σ (ii) $k\mu$, $k\sigma$; $a = \frac{5}{6}$, $b = 22$
7. (a) $f(x) = 2x + 3$ (b) 5, $12\frac{1}{3}$
   (c) 13, $49\frac{1}{3}$ (d) 26 (e) $64\frac{4}{7}$
8. (a) 2 (b) 200 (c) 2.02
   (d) $-4, -1, 2, 5, 8, 11, 14$
9. (a) 50, 12
   (b) (i) 10 (ii) 11.7
   (c) (i) 12.5 (ii) 20; 80, 5

Exercise 1i (page 49)

1. (a) 313.76, 5.19 (b) 42.6, 13.2
   (c) 1954, 348.4 (d) 17.1, 8.18
   (e) 1.02, 0.507 (f) 321.9, 68.1
2. 71.2, 3.82
3. $46\frac{2}{3}$
4. 31.7
5. 51.235, 0.927
6. 89.3275

Exercise 1j (page 52)

1. (a) 7.6, 3.14 (b) 30.4, 6.76
   (c) 13.65, 3.02
2. 15.6, 7.66
3. 25.9, 1.99
4. 2.3, 1.41
5. 11.7%, 2.2%
6. (a) 4.6, 2 (b) 4.56, 2.04
7. 16, 6; (ii) 15, 7
8. (a) 4.6, 2 (b) 4.56, 2.04
9. 57 (i) It becomes 39
10. (i)

25	1 2 4 4
30	0 1 1 2 2 2 3 3 3 4
35	0 1 2 3 3 3 3 3 4
40	0 2 2 4
45	0 4
50	2
55	
60	1

Key: 45 | 4 means 49

   (ii) 35.59

Exercise 1k (page 54)

1. 10.4
2. Class teacher 1.65%
3. 40.6
4. 4
5. 5, 65.8

Exercise 1l (page 60)

1. 95.2%
2. (a) 40   (b) 115
3. 110, 120, 125; (i) 135 (ii) 80
4. 120
5. (i) Drinks   (ii) 95.3 drinks, 125.5 chocolate
6. 115.35%
7. (i) 96, 124 (ii) 113.2; £125
8. 87, 109
9. $x = 190$, $y = 165$, $z = 425$; 187.8
10. £119.70
11. 203
12. 110, 140, 125; 115.5
13. (i) 103.1
14. 215, 187.95, 109.1; 115

Exercise 1m (page 67)

1. (a) 9   (b) 207   (c) 1896 (d) 0.55
2. 4
3. (a) 7, 2   (b) 14, 3   (c) 17, 4   (d) 5.4, 6
4. (i) (a) 61   (b) 52   (c) 73
    (ii) (a) 8   (b) 7   (c) 10
5. (a) 6   (b) 3 marks
6. (a) 46, 35   (b) 1.8, 1.2
    (c) 20.5, 11.5   (d) 34, 11

Exercise 1n (page 84)

1. (a) u.c.b. 0, 44.5, 49.5, 54.5, 59.5, 64.5, 69.5,
    74.5
    c.f. 0, 3, 5, 12, 30, 48, 51, 52
    (b) 21   (c) 14   (d) 62 kg
    (e) 58.4 kg   (f) 7.2 kg
2. (b) 82%   (c) 6.5
    (d) frequencies 1, 1, 3, 5, 9, 19, 5, 3, 3, 1;
    median = 6.5
3. (a) Cumulative frequencies 2, 4, 7, 13, 25,
    41, 47, 50
    (b) 24   (c) 26   (d) 23
    (e) 25 mins   (f) 4.5 mins
4. 32.7 mins
5. 61.3 g
6. 50.5 km/h
7. 687.5 h, 13.2 h
8. 0.559 cm
9. (i) 153 mm   (ii) 15.3 mm   (iii) 11%
10. (i) 96.6 mins   (ii) 5 mins   (iii) 61
11. 437, 412.5, 453
12. (i) 57   (ii) 71.5   (iii) 32%
13. (a) 135 cm   (c) 176.5, 162, 169.8, 14.5
14. (a) 179.8   (b) 4.5 cm   (c) 290 approx
15. (i) £178   (ii) £44   (iii) $36\frac{1}{2}$%
16. £37.50
17. (i) 136, 160
18. (a) 46   (b) 23   (c) 30
19. Boundary points 0, 3, 6, 9, 12, 15, 18, 21,
    Approximate % cumulative frequencies:
    Monday 0, 2, 34, 74, 90, 98, 100
    Friday 0, 6, 23, 56, 84, 93, 98, 100
    (a) (i) 21%   (ii) 35%
    (b) (i) 47%   (ii) 34%
    (c) (i) 10 mins   (ii) 11.5 mins

Miscellaneous Exercise 1o (page 89)

1. (a) 5, 6, 4.07   (b) $\dfrac{n}{m+n}$
2. (b) (i) 7   (ii) 1; $x = 5$, $y = 9$
3. 1, 3, 8.1, 0.03; 814, 300; $a = -7.2$, $b = 2$
4. (a) (i) $\mu + k$, σ (ii) $p\mu$, $p\sigma$; $3\mu + 5$, 3σ
    (b) $a = 1.6$, $b = 10$
5. (a) 51.5   (b) 52   (c) 50 or 54
    (d) 51   (e) 6   (f) 57.5
    (g) 109

6. Taking mark intervals $0 \leqslant$ mark < 10, etc.
    (c) 40.4, 15.4; $a = 24$ (2 S.F.),
    $b = 0.65$ (2 S.F.)
7. 0, 1; better in algebra
8. (i) 4, 8   (ii) 6; mean = 7, n = ± 6
9. 16, 6   (i) 5.86   (ii) 15, 7
10. £195.45, £14.12
11. 11.87, 0.80
12. (a) 0, 1   (b) (i) 5, 12   (ii) 6   (iii) 14
    (c) 48, 20
13. 130.5, £28.36, 114.2
14. (i) 125, 112.5, 150   (ii) 10, 70
15. (b) Approx. £61 500   (c) 115.1
    (d) Risen 15%
16. (a) (i) 9.5 (ii) 46   (b) 50 p, £4.96, £5.96
17. $3\frac{1}{3}$, cuts area in half
18. (a) (i) 32   (ii) 38   (iii) 21
    (b) (i) 0.35   (ii) 17
19. (a) (i) 43.5 (ii) 16%   (b) 9.3, 22, 75.5
20. (b) Mid-point is representative of interval
    (i) 11   (ii) 101
21. (a) 180.5   (b) 175.5   (c) 187   (d) 189.5
22. 2 min 38 s, 1 min 54 s, 2 min 16 s, 1 min 24 s,
    2 min 56 s
23. (a) 0.785   (b) 4.44
24. 6 h 14 min, 13 min; 6 h 18 min, 16 min
25. (i) 2, 0, 1, 0, 4, 4, 8, 5, 8, 14, 12, 5, 0, 0, 1
    (ii) 34.4 (3 S.F.), 7.88 (3 S.F.)
    (iii) 74%
26. 6.49, 1.71, 7
27. 35 years 1 month, 11 years 3 months
    (a) Approx 33 years 10 months
    (b) Approx 17 years 10 months
    (c) Approx 65.6%
28. (c) 5, 1   (d) 4.88, 1.165; 4.86, 2.84
29. 36.1, 14.9, 0.24
30. 34.9, 32.7, 186.5, 13.7, 61%
31. 3–4; 3.23, 2.15, 41%
32. 44.5, 51.75, 64, 40.5; $a = 0.89$, $b = 1$, yes
33. 86.6, 44.1, $N = 188$

CHAPTER 2

Exercise 2a (page 106)

1. (a) 0.535   (b) -0.392 (c) -0.350
    (d) 0.408   (e) -0.674
2. -2.4
3. 2
4. (a) Frequency density: 0.8, 3, 5, 1.8, 1.2,
    0.47, 0.2
    (b) Positively skewed
5. -0.482
6. 2, 3, 3.53, 1.985; 0.771, 0.801

Exercise 2b (page 116)

1. (i) B   (ii) A   (iii) C
2. (a) (i) $\bar{x} = 127$, median $= 122.9$, $s = 16.54$;
    0.75
    (ii) $Q_1 = 116.1$, $Q_2 = 122.9$, $Q_3 = 135$;
    0.28
3. (a) $Q_1 = 8.54$, $Q_2 = 9.56$, $Q_3 = 10.57$; 1.01
    (b) 0.34
4. (a) $Q_1 = 17$, $Q_2 = 26$, $Q_3 = 38$; 0.143
    (b) $Q_1 = 22$, $Q_2 = 23$, $Q_3 = 24$; 0
    (c) $Q_1 = 27.69$, $Q_2 = 38.67$, $Q_3 = 47$; -0.137
    (d) $Q_1 = 11.9$, $Q_2 = 16.1$, $Q_3 = 20.9$; 0.0668
    (e) $Q_1 = 9$, $Q_2 = 11$, $Q_3 = 15$; 0.333

Exercise 2c (page 127)

1. (a) u.c.b. 0, 1, 2, 3, 5, 10;
    c.f. 0, 8, 19, 36, 44, 50
    (b) $Q_2 = 2.35$, $Q_1 = 1.41$; $Q_3 = 3.38$
    (c) Positively skewed.

2. (a) u.c.b. 0, 20, 30, 40, 50;
c.f. 0, 20, 40, 65, 70;
$Q_1 = 17.5$, $Q_2 = 27.5$, $Q_3 = 35$; 7.5, 10;
negatively skewed
(b) u.c.b. 0, 20, 40, 80, 100;
c.f. 0, 4, 10, 34, 44;
$Q_1 = 41.7$, $Q_2 = 60$, $Q_3 = 78.3$; 18.3, 18.3;
negatively skewed, zero quartile
skewness
(c) u.c.b. 0, 5, 10, 15, 20, 25, 35;
c.f. 0, 1, 6, 9, 11, 12, 13
$Q_1 = 7.25$, $Q_2 = 10.8$, $Q_3 = 16.875$;
6.075, 3.55; positively skewed
(d) u.c.b. 0, 5, 10, 15, 20, 25, 30;
c.f. 0, 5, 20, 45, 90, 140, 160;
$Q_1 = 14$, $Q_2 = 18.9$, $Q_3 = 23$; 4.1, 4.9;
negatively skewed

3. Girls $Q_1 = 28$, $Q_2 = 36$, $Q_3 = 44$, symmetrical
Boys $Q_1 = 43$, $Q_2 = 51$, $Q_3 = 55$,
negatively skewed

4. Group 1: $Q_1 = 0.17$, $Q_2 = 0.21$, $Q_3 = 0.23$;
Range 0.14 to 0.26
Group 2: $Q_1 = 0.16$, $Q_2 = 0.19$, $Q_3 = 0.22$;
Range 0.09 to 0.25

5. $Q_1 = 22$, $Q_2 = 35$, $Q_3 = 51$; 97
6. $Q_1 = 42$, $Q_2 = 65$, $Q_3 = 78$; 133, 144
8. December: $Q_1 = 0.3$, $Q_2 = 1.8$, $Q_3 = 2.7$
July: $Q_1 = 4.1$, $Q_2 = 6.5$, $Q_3 = 9.8$

9. (a)

0	1 2 2 5 9
1	0 0 2 3 5 7 9 9
2	2 5 9 9 9
3	0 1
4	5 7 8
5	3

Key: 2 | 5 means 9.25 a.m.

(b) 9.19 a.m.
(c) 9.10 a.m., $29\frac{1}{2}$ minutes past 9.

10. (a) $Q_1 = 1$, $Q_2 = 1$, $Q_3 = 2$
(b) $Q_1 = 13$, $Q_2 = 14$, $Q_3 = 15$
(c) $Q_1 = 4$, $Q_2 = 6$, $Q_3 = 7$

Miscellaneous Exercise 2d (page 131)

1. (a) 5.42, 0.333; 5.46, 5.295, 5.615, 4.07
(b) (i) 5.465, (ii) 5.47 (iii) 0.218
2. (i) 17, 4 (ii) 17.85, 5.57
3. 63; intervals $30-$, $40-$, ...; frequencies 1, 3, 7,
14, 22, 32, 35, 32, 25, 16, 8, 3, 2; 63.05, 11.3;
normal
4. (b) 5.21, 2.70
5. (a) 20.1, 5.7 (b) 0.46 (c) 18.4
6. (a) £46.74, £12.40; not affected by extreme
values causing the negative skew
7. (i) 6, 5
(ii) more than 3 standard deviations from
the mean
(iv) 5.5, 5 (v) decrease (vi) positive, less.
8. (c) 744.2, 14.9 (d) 744.0, 736.1, 752.1
(e) 0.04 (f) 0.013
9. $Q_1 = 40.7$, $Q_2 = 46.9$, $Q_3 = 55.5$

CHAPTER 3

Exercise 3a (page 141)

1. (a) $\frac{1}{3}$ (b) 1 (c) $\frac{2}{3}$
2. (a) $\frac{1}{52}$ (b) $\frac{7}{26}$ (c) $\frac{10}{13}$
3. (a) $\frac{1}{4}$ (b) $\frac{1}{4}$ (c) $\frac{1}{10}$
(d) $\frac{9}{19}$
4. (a) $\frac{3}{8}$ (b) $\frac{5}{8}$ (c) $\frac{3}{4}$
(d) $\frac{3}{4}$ (e) 1

5. (a) $\frac{1}{18}$ (b) $\frac{1}{6}$ (c) $\frac{1}{6}$
(d) $\frac{1}{3}$ (e) $\frac{3}{4}$
6. $\frac{4}{15}$
7. (a) $\frac{3}{10}$ (b) $\frac{3}{4}$
8. (a) $\frac{1}{2}$ (b) $\frac{1}{2}$ (c) $\frac{1}{4}$
(d) $\frac{3}{8}$ (e) $\frac{1}{2}$
9. (a) $\frac{1}{12}$ (b) 0 (c) $\frac{1}{4}$
10. (a) $\frac{1}{12}$ (b) $\frac{1}{12}$ (c) $\frac{1}{4}$
(d) $\frac{1}{8}$
11. (a) $\frac{1}{36}$ (b) $\frac{1}{12}$ (c) 0
(d) $\frac{1}{3}$; $t = 6$ or 12

Exercise 3b (page 147)

1. (a) $\frac{1}{2}$ (b) $\frac{1}{2}$ (c) $\frac{5}{6}$
2. $\frac{11}{30}$
3. (a) $\frac{4}{17}$ (b) $\frac{4}{51}$ (c) $\frac{5}{17}$
(d) $\frac{5}{17}$
4. $\frac{3}{4}$
5. $\frac{3}{5}$
6. 0.4
7. 0.7
8. (a) $\frac{7}{36}$ (b) $\frac{1}{6}$ (c) $\frac{5}{18}$
(d) $\frac{1}{12}$
9. $\frac{3}{4}$
10. (a) $\frac{11}{36}$ (b) $\frac{11}{36}$ (c) $\frac{5}{9}$

Exercise 3c (page 152)

1. $\frac{1}{2}$
2. (a) $\frac{3}{10}$ (b) $\frac{1}{10}$
3. (a) $\frac{3}{10}$ (b) $\frac{1}{16}$ (c) $\frac{1}{6}$
4. (a) $\frac{1}{3}$ (b) $\frac{2}{15}$ (c) $\frac{8}{15}$
5. (a) $\frac{1}{17}$ (b) $\frac{13}{204}$ (c) $\frac{13}{51}$
6. (a) $\frac{4}{15}$ (b) $\frac{8}{15}$ (c) $\frac{2}{3}$
7. (a) $\frac{1}{6}$ (b) $\frac{1}{5}$ (c) $\frac{1}{3}$
8. (a) $\frac{1}{3}$ (b) 0
9. (a) $\frac{1}{8}$ (b) $\frac{1}{2}$
10. (a) $\frac{7}{10}$ (b) No
11. Yes
12. $\frac{1}{2}$
15. (a) $\frac{3}{16}$ (b) $\frac{1}{4}$ (c) $\frac{1}{16}$
(d) $\frac{3}{8}$

Exercise 3d (page 157)

1. $\frac{1}{9}$
2. (a) $\frac{1}{2704}$ (b) $\frac{1}{16}$ (c) $\frac{1}{2}$
(d) $\frac{25}{169}$
3. $\frac{1}{4}$
4. (a) $\frac{1}{3}$ (b) $\frac{1}{2}$ (c) $\frac{1}{6}$
5. (a) 0.0025 (b) 0.095
6. (a) $\frac{1}{10}$ (b) $\frac{3}{10}$ (c) $\frac{9}{20}$

7. (a) 0.15   (b) 0.65; No

8. (a) $\frac{1}{4}$ (b) $\frac{1}{6}$

9. (a) $\frac{1}{6}$ (b) Not independent

10. (a) $\frac{1}{4}$ (b) $\frac{7}{12}$

11. $\frac{7}{16}$

Exercise 3e (page 158)

1. 0.4

2. (a) 0.24   (b) 0.42

3. (a) $\frac{5}{21}$ (b) $\frac{2}{3}$ (c) $\frac{5}{12}$

4. $\frac{9}{14}$

5. (a) $\frac{3}{4}$ (b) $\frac{1}{4}$

6. 0.008%; 0.625

Miscellaneous Exercise 3f (page 162)

1. $\frac{31}{90}$

2. (a) $\frac{1}{28}$ (b) 0

    (c) $\frac{1}{14}$; A and B, A and C, $\frac{3}{14}$

3. $\frac{3}{8}$

4. (a) 0.02   (b) 0.45

5. (a) 0.5   (b) 0.35   (c) 0.375

    (d) 0.4

6. (i) 0.02   (ii) 0.78   (iii) 0.76

    (iv) $\frac{1}{30}$

7. (a) $\frac{1}{25}$ (b) $\frac{106}{125}$ (c) $\frac{14}{19}$

8. (i) 0.4   (ii) 0.5   (iii) 0.52

9. $\frac{1}{25}, \frac{16}{25}; \frac{1}{16}, \frac{3}{8};$ (a) 0.04

    (b) 0.6225   (c) 0.1825

10. $\frac{25}{72}$

11. $\frac{5}{16}$

Exercise 3g (page 168)

1. (b) $\frac{8}{25}$ (d) $\frac{28}{75}$

2. (a) (i) $\frac{7}{92}$ (ii) $\frac{34}{69}$ (b) $\frac{49}{253}$

3. (a) $\frac{1}{27}$ (b) $\frac{20}{27}$

4. (a) (i) $\frac{8}{27}$ (ii) $\frac{4}{9}$ (iii) $\frac{7}{27}$

    (b) (i) $\frac{5}{21}$ (ii) $\frac{15}{28}$ (iii) $\frac{19}{84}$

5. (a) $\frac{12}{49}$ (b) $\frac{20}{49}$

6. (a) $\frac{23}{63}$ (b) $\frac{65}{98}$

7. (a) $\frac{1}{2}$ (b) $\frac{3}{10}$ (c) $\frac{3}{5}$

8. (a) $\frac{5}{14}$ (b) $\frac{17}{42}$

9. (a) 0.34   (b) 0.063

    (c) 0.19   (d) 0.97; 3 white

Exercise 3h (page 173)

1. (a) $\frac{7}{18}$ (b) (i) $\frac{5}{8}$ (ii) $\frac{8}{25}$

2. (a) $\frac{5}{12}$ (b) $\frac{3}{5}$

3. (a) 0.66   (b) $\frac{9}{17}$

4. (a) 0.024   (b) 0.452

    (c) 0.496 (2 S.F.)

5. $\frac{23}{45}, \frac{18}{23}$

6. $\frac{36}{95}, \frac{5}{38}, \frac{7}{190}, \frac{43}{95}$, 26–64 age group

7. (a) $\frac{5}{8}$ (b) $\frac{133}{200}$ (c) $\frac{11}{25}$

    (d) $\frac{42}{47}$

8. (a) $\frac{3}{10}$ (b) $\frac{4}{15}$ (c) $\frac{3}{10}$

    (d) $\frac{1}{3}$ (e) $\frac{5}{16}$

9. (b) (i) $\frac{1}{10}$ (ii) $\frac{1}{5}$ (iii) $\frac{3}{5}$

    (d) (i) $\frac{1}{3}$ (ii) $\frac{4}{7}$

10. (ii) $\frac{6}{13}$

11. Machine 1

Exercise 3i (page 177)

1. (a) 0.763 (3 S.F.)   (b) 14

2. (a) 5   (b) 6

3. $\frac{1}{2}$, 6

4. 0.999 (3 S.F.)

5. $\frac{5}{11}$

6. 1 : 8

7. $\frac{1}{2}$;   (a) $\frac{1}{6}$ (b) $\frac{25}{216}$

    (c) $\frac{625}{7776}$; $\frac{6}{11}$

Exercise 3j (page 183)

1. 9!; $\frac{1}{72}$

2. (a) 6!   (b) $\frac{1}{3}$

3. (a) 4!9!   (b) $\frac{54}{55}$

4. $\frac{9}{11}$

5. $\frac{1}{126}$

6. (a) 8!   (b) $\frac{1}{28}$

7. (a) $\frac{12!}{(2!)^4}$ (b) $\frac{1}{66}$

Exercise 3k (page 192)

1. $\frac{28}{153}$

2. $\frac{49}{143}$

3. $\frac{60}{143}$

4. (a) 210   (b) $\frac{2}{15}$ (c) $\frac{1}{30}$

5. (i) $\frac{1}{14}$ (ii) $\frac{3}{7}$ (iii) $\frac{1}{30}$

6. (i) 65 268   (ii) 4263

7. 510

8. $\frac{37}{42}$

9. 4608

10. (a) 1260   (b) 2520

11. (a) 420   (b) Boys 252, Girls 462

    (c) 120   (d) $\frac{44}{133}$

12. (a) 2.5×10^{-7} (b) 3 193 344

13. (a) $\frac{2}{7}$ (b) $\frac{2}{7}$

14. 130

15. (a) 360   (b) 6   (d) 12

    (e) 1170

16. (a) 64   (b) 18   (c) $\frac{21}{32}$

17. (a) 9!   (b) $\frac{7}{36}$ (c) 1260

    (d) $\frac{5}{9}$

18. (a) 75   (c) $\frac{181}{456}$

    (d) (i) 6!   (ii) 72

Miscellaneous Exercise 3l (page 209)

1. (a) 0.05   (b) 0.5

2. 0.973

3. (i) $\frac{1}{15}$ (ii) $\frac{11}{15}$ (iii) $\frac{1}{5}$

4. (a) 0.2   (b) 0.03   (c) 0.32

5. (a) $\frac{1}{8}$ (b) $\frac{3}{11}$

6. (i) $\frac{1}{15}$ (ii) $\frac{8}{15}$

7. 12

8. (ii) $\frac{77}{95}$

9. (i) 0.042 875   (ii) 0.142
(iii) 0.1215   (iv) 0.189
(v) 0.334 125, 0.642 (3 d.p.)

10. (i) 0.16   (ii) 0.5   (iii) 0.62

11. (b) $\frac{1}{2}$, $\frac{11}{12}$ (c) $\frac{6}{7}$ (d) $\frac{4}{5}$ (e) $\frac{1}{2}$

12. (a) 0.55   (b) 0.04   (c) 0.006
(d) 0.333   (e) 0.024   (f) 0.12
(g) 0.01   (h) 0.55

13. (ii) $\frac{9}{32}$ (iii) $\frac{83}{128}$ (iv) $\frac{17}{37}$

14. (i) $\frac{3}{320}$ (ii) $\frac{9}{320}$ (iii) $\frac{1}{3}$
(iv) $\frac{108}{295}$ (v) $\frac{89}{295}$

15. (i) $\frac{1}{14}$ (ii) $\frac{97}{105}$ (iii) $\frac{37}{42}$
(iv) $\frac{85}{97}$, not independent

16. (i) 0.000 877   (ii) 0.421
(iii) 0.65   (iv) 0.642

17. (i) 4, 4.09, 0.585   (ii) (b) 0.700

18. (i) $\frac{4}{9}$ (ii) $\frac{9}{10}$ (a) $\frac{2}{3}$ (b) $\frac{4}{9}$

19. (a) 0.45, not   (b) (i) 0.33   (ii) $\frac{7}{11}$

20. (a) (i) $\frac{9}{22}$ (ii) $\frac{6}{11}$ (iii) $\frac{2}{11}$ (iv) $\frac{4}{7}$
(b) (i) 0.0303   (ii) 0.450   (iii) 0.0348
(c) (i) 0.36   (ii) 0.848

21. (a) 0.7, 0.68   (b) 0.28   (c) 0.656 25

22. (a) (i) $\frac{1}{6}$ (ii) $\frac{1}{12}$ (iii) $\frac{2}{3}$ (b) $\frac{7}{12}$

23. (a) 0.88, 0.05   (b) (i) 0.346   (ii) 0.476

24. $\frac{15}{44}$, no, 0.1

25. (a) 0.096   (ii) 0.156; $\frac{5}{13}$

26. 0.005 99, 0.987 (3 S.F.)

27. 0.59; (i) 0.352   (ii) 0.4576   (iii) 0.480 64

28. (a) $\frac{1}{22}$ (b) $\frac{41}{55}$ (c) $\frac{3}{11}$ (d) $\frac{3}{44}$

29. (a) $\frac{1}{4}$ (b) $\frac{1}{4}$ (c) $\frac{1}{16}$ (d) $\frac{1}{4}$ (e) $\frac{3}{4}$

30. (a) $\frac{1}{2}$ (b) $\frac{1}{3}$ (c) $\frac{1}{6}$ (d) $\frac{3}{4}$ (e) $\frac{1}{15}$

31. (a) $\frac{1}{36}$ (b) $\frac{5}{12}$; $\frac{73}{648}$, $\frac{25}{81}$

32. 0.624

33. (a) $\frac{1}{27}$ (b) $\frac{2}{9}$ (c) $\frac{4}{9}$ (d) $\frac{8}{27}$
(e) $\frac{43}{144}$ (f) $\frac{65}{72}$ (g) $\frac{64}{195}$

34. (i) 0.36   (ii) 0.6875

35. (a) $\frac{2}{5}$ (b) $\frac{2}{15}$

36. (a) (i) $\frac{1}{1050}$ (ii) $\frac{4}{35}$
(b) (i) $\frac{1}{25}$ (ii) $\frac{12}{25}$; $\frac{24}{625}$

37. (a) 0.12   (b) 0.184   (c) 0.32
(d) 0.25

38. (a) $\frac{1}{8}$ (b) $\frac{5}{32}$; $P(D) = 0.0325$,
$P(C \cap D) = 0.025$, $P(C \mid D) = \frac{10}{13}$

39. (a) 0.875, $\frac{19}{30}$ (b) $\frac{22}{47}$

40. (a) $\frac{1}{2}$ (b) $\frac{1}{4}$ (c) $\frac{3}{10}$
(d) $\frac{19}{24}$; No, no

41. (a) $\frac{25}{216} : \frac{27}{216}$ (b) 0.5177, 0.4914
(c) 0.6651, 0.6186

42. (a) $\frac{5}{33}$ (b) $\frac{5}{33}$ (c) $\frac{1}{792}$ (d) $\frac{41}{132}$

43. (a) $\frac{2}{261}$ (b) $\frac{16}{609}$, $\frac{308}{435}$, $\frac{204}{1015}$

44. (a) $\frac{2}{15}$ (b) $\frac{1}{2}$

45. (a) $\frac{6}{323}$ (b) $\frac{135}{323}$ (c) $\frac{1}{5}$
(d) $\frac{1}{5}$ (i) Yes, no   (ii) No, yes

46. 70   (a) 55   (b) 30   (c) 65   (d) $\frac{2}{7}$
(e) $\frac{1}{7}$ (f) $\frac{1}{7}$

47. (a) $\frac{6}{13}$ (b) 0.0481 (3 S.F.)

48. (a) $1/3^7$ (b) $16/3^3$
(c) $593/3^7$ (d) $784/3^8$

49. (a) (i) 120   (ii) 12 600
(b) $\frac{4}{35}$, $\frac{18}{35}$, $\frac{12}{35}$, $\frac{1}{35}$; $\frac{11}{24}$

50. (a) (i) $\frac{1}{2}$ (ii) $\frac{1}{2}$ (iii) $\frac{6}{7}$ (iv) $\frac{1}{8}$, No, no
(b) (i) $\frac{5}{21}$ (ii) $\frac{3}{14}$

51. $\frac{1}{7}$, $\frac{324}{343}$, 0.617

52. (a) (ii) 0.43, 0.67   (iii) $\frac{15}{26}$
(b) (i) $\frac{36}{415}$ (ii) $\frac{11}{13}$

53. (a) $\beta + \frac{1}{5}(\alpha - \beta)(\alpha + 4\beta)$

CHAPTER 4

Exercise 4a (page 228)

1. (i) 0.1   (ii) 0.85   (iii) 0.55   (iv) 0.5   (v) 3

2. $\frac{1}{39}$

3. $\frac{1}{6}$

4. (a)

x	0	1	2
$P(X = x)$	$\frac{1}{4}$	$\frac{1}{2}$	$\frac{1}{4}$

(b) $P(X = x) = \dfrac{x - 1}{36}$, $x = 2, \ldots, 7$
$P(X = x) = \dfrac{13 - x}{36}$, $x = 8, \ldots, 12$

(c)

x	0	1	2
$P(X = x)$	$\frac{9}{16}$	$\frac{3}{8}$	$\frac{1}{16}$

(d) $P(X = x) = 0.1$, $x = 0, 1, \ldots, 9$

(e)

x	0	1	2	3
$P(X = x)$	$\frac{1}{8}$	$\frac{3}{8}$	$\frac{3}{8}$	$\frac{1}{8}$

(f) $P(X = 0) = \dfrac{1}{6}$, $P(X = x) = \dfrac{6 - x}{18}$,
$x = 1, 2, \ldots, 5$

5.

x	0	1	2	3
$P(X = x)$	$\frac{1}{27}$	$\frac{2}{9}$	$\frac{4}{9}$	$\frac{8}{27}$

6. $\frac{1}{5}$

7. (i)

x	0	1	2	3
$P(X = x)$	0.216	0.432	0.288	0.064

(ii) 0.648

8.

x	1	2	3	4	5	6
$P(X = x)$	$\frac{6}{72}$	$\frac{7}{72}$	$\frac{8}{72}$	$\frac{9}{72}$	$\frac{10}{72}$	$\frac{11}{72}$

x	7	8	9	10	11	12
$P(X = x)$	$\frac{6}{72}$	$\frac{5}{72}$	$\frac{4}{72}$	$\frac{3}{72}$	$\frac{2}{72}$	$\frac{1}{72}$

$\frac{11}{18}$; Equally likely outcomes

Exercise 4b (page 229)

1. $2\frac{1}{4}$

2. 7

3. (a) 0.3   (b) 2.9

4. 1

5. 0.5

6. $\frac{12}{11}$

7. 0.75 p

8.

x	10	20
$P(X = x)$	0.4	0.6

9. (a) 0.3   (b) 0.2

10.

x	4	6	8	9	11	14
$P(X = x)$	0.16	0.32	0.16	0.16	0.16	0.04

;

loss of £1.20

11. (i) $£\frac{3}{8}(7 + x)$ (a) 5   (b) Loss of £3.75

12. $\frac{12}{11}$

13. $\frac{11}{3}$

14. (a) 24

(c)

x	0	1	2	3	4
$P(X = x)$	$\frac{3}{8}$	$\frac{1}{3}$	$\frac{1}{4}$	0	$\frac{1}{24}$

(d) 1

15. (a) 0.2   (b) 2.08

16. (a) $\frac{1}{21}$ (b) $\frac{2}{7}$ (c) $\frac{4}{9}$

    (d) $\frac{5}{42}$ (e) 1   (f) $\frac{4}{3}$, 0

17. 2

18. $\frac{2}{3}$, $\frac{2}{3}$, $\frac{b}{6}$ or $\frac{2b}{b + w}$

Exercise 4c (page 234)

1. (a) 2.3   (b) 5.9

2. (a) 1.45   (b) 2.45   (c) 12.15

3. (a) 3.5   (b) $15\frac{1}{6}$ (c) 14.5   (d) $29\frac{5}{6}$

4. (a) $\frac{24}{11}$ (b) $\frac{61}{11}$ (c) $\frac{50}{11}$ (d) $16\frac{9}{11}$

5. (a) 3.5   (b) 14   (c) 5.5

    (d) 84   (e) 95

6. (a) 2   (b) 3 or −3

7. $\frac{1}{32}$, 1, $1\frac{31}{32}$

8. $\frac{1}{3}(2n + 1)$

Exercise 4d (page 239)

1. (a) 4.2   (b) $7\frac{1}{3}$ (c) 3.67 (3 S.F.)

2. (a) $\frac{1}{10}$ (b) $3\frac{1}{2}$ (c) $15\frac{7}{30}$

    (d) $2\frac{59}{60}$ (e) $47\frac{11}{15}$

3. (a) 5   (b) 2.5   (c) 10   (d) 10

4. (a) $1\frac{2}{3}$ (b) $3\frac{1}{3}$ (c) $\frac{5}{9}$

5.

x	0	1	2
$P(X = x)$	$\frac{1}{7}$	$\frac{4}{7}$	$\frac{2}{7}$

    (a) $\frac{8}{7}$ (b) $\frac{12}{7}$ (c) $\frac{20}{49}$ (d) $\frac{180}{49}$

6. (a) −0.7   (b) 3.5   (c) 3.01

7. $P(X = x) = \frac{10 - x}{45}$, $x = 1, 2, \ldots, 9$

    $3\frac{2}{3}$, 2.21 (2 d.p.), 1;

    $P(X = x) = \left(\frac{4}{5}\right)^{x-1}\left(\frac{1}{5}\right)$, $x = 1, 2, \ldots$

8. (a) $\frac{1}{12}$ (b) 0   (c) 6

    (d) 2.45 (2 d.p.)

9. (a) 0.04   (b) 5   (c) 4   (d) 7   (e) 16

10. (a) Loss £3

    (b) (i) $p = 0.12$, $q = 0.08$ (ii) 6.45, 8

11. (a) £2   (b) (i) 4   (ii) 17   (iii) 1

Exercise 4e (page 243)

1. (a)

x	0	1	2
$F(x)$	$\frac{25}{36}$	$\frac{35}{36}$	1

(b)

x	1	2	3	4	5	6
$F(x)$	$\frac{11}{36}$	$\frac{5}{9}$	$\frac{3}{4}$	$\frac{8}{9}$	$\frac{35}{36}$	1

(c)

x	0	1	2	3
$F(x)$	$\frac{1}{8}$	$\frac{1}{2}$	$\frac{7}{8}$	1

2.

y	0.1	0.2	0.3	0.4	0.5
$P(Y \leqslant y)$	0.05	0.3	0.6	0.75	1

3. (a) 0.41   (b) 0.87   (c) 0.46

    (d) 0.13   (e) 2.58

4.

x	3	4	5	6	7
$P(X = x)$	0.01	0.22	0.41	0.22	0.14

;

0.9724

5. (a) $\frac{4}{9}$ (b) $\frac{1}{3}$

    (c) $P(X = x) = \dfrac{2x - 1}{9}$, $x = 1, 2, 3$

    (d) $\frac{17}{9}$

6. (a) $\frac{1}{3}$ (b) $\frac{2}{3}$

    (c) $P(X = x) = \frac{1}{3}$, $x = 1, 2, 3$

    (d) 0.816 (3 S.F.)

7. (b)

x	1	2	3	4
$P(X = x)$	$\frac{1}{4}$	$\frac{1}{2}$	$\frac{15}{64}$	$\frac{1}{64}$

    (c) $2\frac{1}{64}$, 0.547 (3 S.F.)   (d) $\frac{1}{4}$

Exercise 4f (page 254)

1. (a) 1.3, 1, 1.01, 0.8

(b)

$x + y$	0	1	2
$P(X + Y = x + y)$	0.12	0.14	0.32

$x + y$	3	4	5
$P(X + Y = x + y)$	0.2	0.18	0.04

(e)

$x - y$	−2	−1	0
$P(X - Y = x - y)$	0.12	0.14	0.32

$x - y$	1	2	3
$P(X - Y = x - y)$	0.2	0.18	0.04

2. (a) 26   (b) 15   (c) 17   (d) 59   (e) 59

3. (a) $\frac{1}{2}$ (b) $\frac{5}{12}$ (c) $2\frac{2}{3}$

4. (a) 0 or 12 or −12   (b) 294

5. (a) 1   (b) −1   (c) 34

    (d) 14   (e) 14   (f) 30

6. (a) (i) 7   (ii) $\frac{35}{6}$ (b) (i) 0   (ii) $\frac{35}{6}$

7. (a) 1.2, 0.36   (b) 0.09   (c) 2.4, 0.72

    (d) 0.3   (e) 2.4, 1.44

8. (a) 2.6, 0.24   (b) 5.2, 0.48   (c) 7.8, 0.72

9. $29\frac{1}{6}$

10. (a) 0.1   (b) 3   (c) 1

    (d) 0.2   (e) 12   (f) 3

Miscellaneous Exercise 4g (page 256)

1. 6.25
2. $2\frac{1}{2}, \frac{10}{21}$
3. (a) $\frac{1}{36}$ (b) $\frac{5}{36}$ (c) $\frac{11}{36}; -\frac{1}{36}, 7$
4.

x	6	7	8	9	10
$P(X=x)$	$\frac{1}{12}$	$\frac{1}{3}$	$\frac{1}{3}$	$\frac{2}{9}$	$\frac{1}{36}$

0.975 (3 S.F.), 0.640 (3 S.F.)
5. (a) (i) $\frac{1}{3}$ (ii) $\frac{1}{12}$ (b) $\pounds\frac{1}{12}$

(c) $1\frac{1}{6}$ (d) $\left(\frac{1}{6}\right)^{r-1}\left(\frac{1}{3}\right)$ (e) $\frac{2}{5}$
6. $\frac{35}{18};$ (a) $\frac{1}{2}$ (b) $\frac{1}{12}$

(c) $\left(\frac{1}{6}\right)^{r-1}\left(\frac{1}{2}\right); \frac{3}{5}, \pounds1.50$
7. (a) $\frac{16}{81}, \frac{32}{81}, \frac{24}{81}, \frac{8}{81}, \frac{1}{81}$ (b) $-50\,\text{p}$
8. (a) $1, \frac{4}{5}$ (b) $\frac{3}{5}, \frac{6}{25}$ (c) 11.2, 7.28

t	0	1	2	3	4
$P(T=t)$	$\frac{2}{15}$	$\frac{9}{25}$	$\frac{8}{25}$	$\frac{11}{75}$	$\frac{1}{25}$

9. $\frac{1}{15}, \frac{2}{3}, \frac{34}{45}, \frac{1}{75}, \frac{4}{3}, \frac{68}{45}$
10. $P(X=x) = \frac{1}{6}, x = 1, 2, 3, 4, 5;$

$P(X=6) = 0, P(X=x) = \frac{1}{36},$

$x = 7, 8, \ldots, 12; 4\frac{1}{12}, \frac{6}{17}$
11.

x	2	3	4	5	6	7	8	9
$P(X=x)$	$\frac{1}{36}$	$\frac{1}{12}$	$\frac{1}{6}$	$\frac{1}{6}$	$\frac{1}{6}$	$\frac{1}{6}$	$\frac{5}{36}$	$\frac{1}{12}$

$5\frac{5}{6}, 0.00137$ (3 S.F.)
12.

x	-3	0
$P(X=x)$	p^3	$3p^2(1-p)$

x	3	6
$P(X=x)$	$3p(1-p)^2$	$(1-p)^3$

$450\,\text{p}, 30\,\text{p}$
13.

y	0	1	2	3	4
$P(Y=y)$	0.09	0.24	0.34	0.24	0.09

z	0	1	2	3	4
$P(Z=z)$	0.447	0.232	0.222	0.072	0.027

1; 1.2
14. (a) $\frac{1}{13}$ (b) $2, \frac{12}{13}$
15. (a) 0.01   (b) 3.54, 0.4684

(c) 14.7, 11.71
16. (a) $\frac{4}{5}$ (b) $-0.24\,\text{p}$

(c) $3.34\,\text{p}^2$ (2 d.p.)
17. 0.1, 1
18. (a) (i) $\frac{1}{64}$ (ii) $\frac{9}{64}$ (iii) $\frac{27}{64}$ (iv) $\frac{27}{64}$
19. 2, 1

y	-4	-2	0	2	4
$P(Y=y)$	$\frac{1}{16}$	$\frac{1}{4}$	$\frac{3}{8}$	$\frac{1}{4}$	$\frac{1}{16}$

; 4, 3
20. (i) $\frac{1}{8}, \frac{5}{24}$ (ii) 2.78 (3 S.F.)

(iii) 0.260 (3 S.F.)
21. $\frac{1}{2}(n+1), \frac{1}{12}(n^2-1), \frac{1}{2};$ (a) $\frac{2}{105}$ (b) 16

22. (a)

x	1	2	4	5
$P(X=x)$	$\frac{1}{12}$	$\frac{5}{12}$	$\frac{1}{3}$	$\frac{1}{6}$

y	2	3	4	5	6	7
$P(Y=y)$	$\frac{1}{144}$	$\frac{5}{72}$	$\frac{25}{144}$	$\frac{1}{18}$	$\frac{11}{36}$	$\frac{5}{36}$

y	8	9	10
$P(Y=y)$	$\frac{1}{9}$	$\frac{1}{9}$	$\frac{1}{36}$

$; 6\frac{1}{6}, \frac{251}{72}$
23. $\frac{1}{28}$, 3.5, 1.25, 12, 20
24. $\frac{120}{49}$, 2.57
25. (ii) 3.5, $\frac{61}{68}$ (iv) $\frac{96}{103}$
26. (i) $\frac{7}{10}$ (ii) $\frac{2}{7}$ (iii) $\frac{1}{3}$ (iv) $\frac{4}{9}$ (v) $\frac{3}{5}; \frac{5}{6}$
27. (a) (i) 1.7, 1.18   (ii) 4.76
   (b) (i) 0.24   (ii) 0.0583
     (iii) 3.44 minutes
   (c) 0.0138

CHAPTER 5

Exercise 5a (page 264)

Answers are given to 3 S.F. where applicable

1. (a) 0.0823   (b) 0.680
2. (a) 0.209   (b) 0.0168   (c) 0.00852
3. (a) 0.531   (b) 0.000055   (c) 0.984
4. 0.00200
5. 0.891
6. 0.5
7. (a) 0.0808   (b) 0.428
8. (a) 0.329   (b) 0.461
9. 0.0963
10. (a) 0.318   (b) 0.671   (c) 0.126
   (d) 0.0324
11. (i) (a) 0.0105   (b) 0.988   (ii) 0.358
14. (a) 0.0563   (b) 0.000416
15. (a) 0.267   (b) 0.000144
16. 4
17. 68
18. 5
19. 9
20. (i) 0.0346   (ii) 0.138; 83

Exercise 5b (page 266)

1. 2.5, 1.5
2. 0.844
3. 8, 1.30
4. (a) 0.2   (b) 0.00551
5. (a) 0.25   (b) 2.5   (c) 0.282
6. 0.1, 0.23 (2 d.p.)
7. (ii) (a) 0.68 (2 S.F.)(b)   8, 1.6
8. $\frac{1}{5}, \frac{3}{4}$
9. (a) (i) 0.0746   (ii) 0.0861; 0.377; 90
   (b) (i) 0.25   (ii) 1.5
10. (a) (i) 0.2304   (ii) 0.31744   (iii) 0.06912
   (b) 2500

Exercise 5c (page 271)

1. (a) (i) 0.9830   (ii) 0.0170   (iii) 0.0015
   (b) (i) 0.1596   (ii) 0.2660   (iii) 0.5044
     (iv) 0.9004
   (c) (i) 0.0037   (ii) 0.0037   (iii) 0.2916
   (d) (i) 0.5551   (ii) 0.0706   (iii) 0.9294
     (iv) 0.3114

2.

x	0	1	2	3
$P(X = x)$	0.0467	0.1866	0.311	0.2765

x	4	5	6
$P(X = x)$	0.1382	0.0369	0.0041

3.

x	0	1	2	3
$P(X = x)$	0.0053	0.0487	0.1812	0.3364

x	4	5
$P(X = x)$	0.3124	0.116

Exercise 5d (page 272)

1. 1
2. (a) 3   (b) 3
3. (a) 3   (b) 3   (c) 0.633
4. (a) 2   (b) 0.994
5. 0.922
6. (a) 3   (b) 0.826   (c) 0.406

Exercise 5e (page 274)

1. (a) 1.2   (b) 0.4
        (c) 0.216, 0.432, 0.288, 0.064
        (d) 39, 78, 52, 11
2. 0.06; 293, 94, 12, 1, 0, 0
3. 1; 0.894   (a) 5   (b) 0.2
4. 5, 22, 37, 28, 8
5. 0, 0, 3, 13, 30, 36, 18
6. 16.5, 42.4, 45.4, 25.9, 8.3, 1.4, 0.1

Miscellaneous Exercise 5f (page 279)

1. 0.0243
2. (a) (i) 0.201   (ii) 0.006 37   (b) 2
        (c) 5, 2   (d) 14
3. (a) 4.8, 0.98 (2 d.p.)   (c) 0.737
        (d) 0.388
4. 1, 0.336, 20
5. $s^3 + 3sd^2$
6. (a) 0.940   (b) 0.0432   (c) 0.0167
7. (a) $(1-p)^8(36p^2 + 8p + 1)$;
            $(1-p)^5 + 5p(1-p)^8(1+4p)$
        (b) 0.678, 0.630, 0.0547, 0.0605
8. $^nC_r(1-p)^{n-r}p^r$ (a) 0.1296

        (b) 0.1792;

x	0	1	2
$P(X = x)$	$\frac{1}{4}$	$\frac{1}{2}$	$\frac{1}{4}$

;
        0.4816
9. (a) $\frac{2}{3}$ (b) 0.0424
11. (a) 0.4   (b) (i) 0.4516   (ii) 1.8
12. (a) (i) 0.529   (ii) 0.316, 0.97
        (b) (i) not binomial, n not constant
            (ii) probably not binomial as p probably
                 changes as monkey learns

Exercise 5g (page 286)

2. (a) 0.1029   (b) 0.2401   (c) 0.51
        (d) 0.168 07
3. (a) 1   (b) 2   (c) 1.414
4. (a) 2.5   (b) 1
5. (a) 0.0101   (b) 0.0501   (c) 0.003 74
6. (a) (i) $\frac{5}{36}$ (ii) $\frac{5}{216}$ (b) $\frac{1}{5}$
7. 2
8. (a) (i) $(0.7)^3(0.3)$ (b) (i) 1   (ii) 0.7599
9. (a) 0.128
        (b) $P(X = r) = (0.8)^{r-1}(0.2)$ Geometric
        (c) 0.512; 10, 40, 0.0768
10. $\frac{5}{4}, \frac{7}{4}, 2\frac{13}{16}, 0.000\,26, \frac{1}{4}$

11. (b) (i) $\frac{1}{6}$ (ii) $\frac{25}{216}$ (iii) $\frac{125}{216}$ (iv) 1 (v) 6
        (c) 17
12. 0.0047, December 22
13. (a) 0.504   (b) 0.432   (c) 0.5904   (d) 44
14. $\frac{q}{p}$

Exercise 5h (page 291)

NOTE: Answers are given to 3 S.F. but *all* the
      numbers are retained in the calculator
      when addition of probabilities is required.

1. (a) 0.0821   (b) 0.205   (c) 0.257
        (d) 0.214   (e) 0.544   (f) 0.242
        (g) 2.5
2. (a) 0.007 81   (b) 0.000 452   (c) 0.731
        (d) 0.109
3. (a) 0.0907   (b) 0.308   (c) 0.570
        (d) 0.779
4. (a) 1.6   (b) 0.976   (c) 1.6
5. (a) 0.607, 0.303, 0.0758, 0.0126, 0.001 58
        (b) 0.0608, 0.170, 0.238, 0.222, 0.156
        (c) 0.0273, 0.0984, 0.177, 0.212, 0.191
6. (a) 2   (b) 0.271
7. 0.433

Exercise 5i (page 294)

1. (a) 0.143   (b) 0.762   (c) 0.670
2. (a) 0.0821   (b) 0.242   (c) 0.759
        (d) 0.0486   (e) 0.125
3. (a) 0.983   (b) 0.184   (c) 0.199
4. (a) 0.0821   (b) 0.109   (c) 0.265
        (d) 0.0631
5. (a) 0.567   (b) 0.184
6. (a) 1.2   (b) 0.879   (c) 0.570
7. (a) 0.607   (b) 0.185
8. (a) 0.0408   (b) 0.219   (c) 0.0463
        (d) 0.145

Exercise 5j (page 296)

1. (i) 0.0476, 0.0498   (ii) 0.225, 0.224
        (iii) 0.171, 0.168
2. (a) 0.879   (b) 0.001 50
3. (a) 0.287   (b) 0.191
4. (a) (i) 0.368   (ii) 0.184   (iii) 0.0190
        (b) 0.677
5. (a) (i) 0.195   (ii) 0.0916   (b) 0.075
6. 0.647, 0.185
7. 0.121

Exercise 5k (page 299)

1. (i) 0.165, 0.298, 0.268, 0.161, 0.0723, 0.0260
        (ii) 0.0743, 0.1931, 0.2510, 0.2176, 0.1414,
             0.0736
        (iii) 0.0111, 0.05, 0.113, 0.169, 0.190, 0.171
        (iv) 0.0224, 0.0850, 0.162, 0.205, 0.194, 0.148

Exercise 5l (page 300)

1. (a) 44, 44, 22, 8, 2   (b) 90, 72, 29, 8, 1, 0
2. 2, 7, 15, 20, 20, 16, 10, 6, 3, 1, 0, 0, 0; 71; 23 (78,
        26 if do not round figures)
3. 0.5, 0.481; 31, 16, 4, 1, 0
4. 95, 137, 98, 47, 17, 5, 1; Approx 58

Exercise 5m (page 303)

1. 0.121
2. (a) 0.189   (b) 0.308   (c) 0.184
3. (a) 0.323   (b) 0.0119
4. (a) 0.301   (b) 0.080   (c) 0.251

Miscellaneous Exercise 5n (page 310)

1. 0.7515, 0.5368
2. (a) 0.067   (b) 0.083
3. 600 m, Po(2.5), 0.0821, 0.109, 0.779, 0.207
4. (a) 0.249 (b) 0.929   (c) 0.508; 0.542
5. (a) 0.908   (b) 9
6. 0.407, 0.366, 0.165, 0.0629; 0.816, 0.0518
7. 3, 18.5%
8. (b) (i) £13
    (ii) (a) 0.0743 (b) 0.193 (c) 0.251
      (d) 0.482
    (iii) £10.70
9. Poisson; 0.0144; 0.2052, 0.109 using normal approximation.
10. (a) 0.788   (b) 0.002 93
11. (a) 0.368   (b) 0.264   (c) 3.16
    (d) 0.199
12. (a) 22   (b) 19; 39
13. (a) 0.100   (b) 0.0702
14. (a) 0.600   (b) 0.0741
15. (a) 0.0902   (b) 0.0613; 4
16. (a) 0.647   (b) 6
17. (a) 0.185   (b) 4   (c) 2.68   (d) 6
18. (a) (i) 0.238   (ii) 0.841   (b) 0.083
19. (a) 0.677   (b) 0.017; 1498
20. (a) 0.082   (b) 0.242; 6.15
21. 0.371, £60.37
22. (a) 0.135   (b) 0.323; 0.81
23. (d) 0.387   (e) 0.929   (f) 0.893
    (g) 0.205   (h) 0.816; 0.0290
24. (a) (ii) 1.5   (b) 0.577   (c) 0.0249
25. (c) $e^{-\lambda}\dfrac{\lambda^3}{6}$ (d) $1 - e^{-\lambda}\left(1 + \lambda + \dfrac{\lambda^2}{2}\right)$;
      0.013, 0.014, 0.182

CHAPTER 6

Exercise 6a (page 320)

1. (a) $\frac{3}{8}$ (c) $\frac{7}{8}$ (d) $\frac{13}{32}$
2. (b) 0.2   (c) 0.74
3. (a) $\frac{1}{4}$ (c) 0.66
4. (a) $\frac{3}{56}$ (c) $\frac{19}{56}, \frac{37}{56}$
5. $c = 1, k = 4$
6. (a) $\frac{1}{4}$ (c) $\frac{1}{4}$ (d) $\frac{5}{16}$ (e) 0.3475
7. (a) $\frac{1}{8}$ (c) 0.328

Exercise 6b (page 323)

1. 0.75
2. 1
3. 2
4. 1.6
5. $2\frac{1}{24}$
6. (a) $\frac{1}{3}$ (b) 2
7. 6 m
8. (a) $\frac{2}{75}$ (b) $\frac{70}{9}$ (c) 0.48; Money bond
9. 2, 0.124 (3 S.F.)
10. 2.5, 0.803 (3 d.p.), 0.456 (3 d.p.)
11. (a) 2.875 kg   (b) £4.75, $\frac{3}{16}$
12. (i) 0.4   (ii) 2.6   (iii) 1.5

Exercise 6c (page 334)

1. (a) $\frac{3}{2}$ (b) $\frac{12}{5}$ (c) $\frac{3}{20}$
    (d) 0.387 (3 S.F.)
2. (a) $\frac{1}{2}$ (b) $\frac{7}{3}$ (c) $\frac{25}{12}$
    (d) 1.44 (3 S.F.)

3. (a) $\frac{11}{6}$ (b) $\frac{11}{3}$ (c) $\frac{11}{36}$
    (d) 0.553 (3 S.F.)
4. (a) $\frac{17}{14}$ (b) $\frac{62}{35}$ (c) $\frac{291}{980}$
    (d) 0.545 (3 S.F.)
5. (a) $\frac{4}{5}$ (b) $\frac{2}{3}$ (c) $\frac{2}{75}$
    (d) 0.163 (3 S.F.)
6. (a) $\frac{43}{24}$ (b) $\frac{97}{24}$ (c) $\frac{479}{576}$
    (d) 0.912 (3 S.F.)
7. (a) $\frac{5}{18}$ (b) $\frac{214}{405}$ (c) $\frac{731}{1620}$
    (d) 0.672 (3 S.F.)
8. (a) $\frac{3}{64}$ (b) 3, $\frac{3}{5}$ (c) $\frac{7}{64}$
9. (a) 1   (b) 1   (c) $\frac{1}{6}$ (d) $\frac{19}{32}$ (e) 1
10. (b) $\frac{41}{12}$ (c) $\frac{571}{45}$ (d) 1.008
11. (a) $\frac{5}{6}$ (b) 0.589
12. (ii) $2, 4 - \dfrac{4}{\ln 3}$

Exercise 6d (page 342)

1. (a) $F(x) = \begin{cases} \frac{x^3}{8} & 0 \leqslant x \leqslant 2 \\ 1 & x \geqslant 2 \end{cases}$
   (b) 1.59 (3 S.F.)

2. (a) $F(x) = \begin{cases} \frac{1}{5}(x+2) & -2 \leqslant x \leqslant 3 \\ 1 & x \geqslant 3 \end{cases}$
   (b) 0.5

3. (a) $F(x) = \begin{cases} \frac{1}{8}(8x - x^2 - 7) & 1 \leqslant x \leqslant 3 \\ 1 & x \geqslant 3 \end{cases}$

4. (a) $F(x) = \begin{cases} \frac{x}{56}(x^2 + 6x + 12) & 0 \leqslant x \leqslant 2 \\ 1 & x \geqslant 2 \end{cases}$

5. (a) $F(x) = \begin{cases} x^4 & 0 \leqslant x \leqslant 1 \\ 1 & x \geqslant 1 \end{cases}$
   (b) 0.841 (3 S.F.)

6. (a) $F(x) = \begin{cases} \frac{x}{4} & 0 \leqslant x \leqslant 2 \\ \frac{1}{4}(x^2 - 3x + 4) & 2 \leqslant x \leqslant 3 \\ 1 & x \geqslant 3 \end{cases}$

7. (a) $F(x) = \begin{cases} \frac{1}{24}(x+2)^3 & -2 \leqslant x \leqslant 0 \\ \frac{1}{3} + \frac{x}{2} & 0 \leqslant x \leqslant \frac{4}{3} \\ 1 & x \geqslant \frac{4}{3} \end{cases}$
   (b) $\frac{1}{3}$
8. (a) 1.5   (b) 0.75
   (c) $F(x) = \begin{cases} \frac{x}{3} & 0 \leqslant x \leqslant 3 \\ 1 & x \geqslant 3 \end{cases}$
   (d) 0.4   (e) 0.2
9. (a) $\frac{3}{7}$ (b) 0.272 (3 S.F.)
   (c) $F(x) = \begin{cases} \frac{1}{7}(x^3 - 1) & 1 \leqslant x \leqslant 2 \\ 1 & x \geqslant 2 \end{cases}$
   (d) 1.65 (3 S.F.)
10. (a) $\frac{1}{3}, \frac{1}{3}$
   (b) $F(x) = \begin{cases} \frac{x^2}{6} - \frac{2x}{3} + \frac{2}{3} & 2 \leqslant x \leqslant 3 \\ \frac{x}{3} - \frac{5}{6} & 3 \leqslant x \leqslant 5 \\ 2x - \frac{x^2}{6} - 5 & 5 \leqslant x \leqslant 6 \\ 1 & x \geqslant 6 \end{cases}$
   (c) $\frac{1}{3}$ (d) $\frac{1}{24}$ (e) 4   (f) $\frac{5}{6}$

11. (a) 0.455, 3 (b) 3.64, 4.95

(c) $F(x) = \begin{cases} \frac{1}{\ln 9} \ln x & 1 \leqslant x \leqslant 9 \\ 1 & x \geqslant 9 \end{cases}$

12. $\frac{3}{4}, \frac{19}{80}$

$F(x) = \begin{cases} \frac{3}{4}x - \frac{1}{16}x^3 & 0 \leqslant x \leqslant 2 \\ 1 & x \geqslant 2 \end{cases}$

0.007

13. $F(x) = \begin{cases} \frac{1}{4}x & 0 \leqslant x \leqslant 1 \\ \frac{1}{5} + \frac{x^4}{20} & 1 \leqslant x \leqslant 2 \\ 1 & x \geqslant 2 \end{cases}$

1.565, 0.821

14. (a) 5 (b) $\frac{1}{6}$ (c) $\frac{5}{252}$; 543 tonnes

15. (iii) $F(x) = \begin{cases} \frac{1}{4}x^2 & 0 \leqslant x \leqslant 1 \\ \frac{2}{3}x - \frac{x^2}{12} - \frac{1}{3} & 1 \leqslant x \leqslant 4 \\ 1 & x \geqslant 4 \end{cases}$

(iv) £283.33 (v) $\frac{1}{3}$

16. (ii) 0.9342

(iii) $F(x) = \begin{cases} \frac{1}{\pi}(x + \sin x) & 0 \leqslant x \leqslant \pi \\ 1 & x \geqslant \pi \end{cases}$

17. (b) $2\frac{1}{9}$

(c) $F(x) = \begin{cases} \frac{1}{6}x + \frac{1}{12}x^2 - \frac{1}{4} & 1 \leqslant x \leqslant 3 \\ 1 & x \geqslant 3 \end{cases}$

(d) 2.16

18. (ii) 1, 2 (iii) 0 (iv) $\frac{1}{\sqrt{2}}, -\frac{1}{\sqrt{2}}$

19. (a) 1.5, 0.75 (b) 0.2

(c) $F(x) = \begin{cases} 0.75x^2 - 0.25x^3 & 0 \leqslant x \leqslant 2 \\ 1 & x \geqslant 2 \end{cases}$

(d) 0.288

20. (ii) $1\frac{2}{9}, \frac{31}{18}$ (iii) $\frac{17}{48}$

21. (i) $F(x) = 1 - \frac{1}{(x+1)^3}$ $x \geqslant 0$; $x = 1$

(ii) 1.5 (iii) 0.75

22. (a) $F(w) = \frac{w^4}{5^5}(25 - 4w)$, $0 \leqslant w \leqslant 5$

(b) 0.650 (c) 0.794 (d) 3.75

(f) Negatively skewed

23. (a) (i) $f(x) \geqslant 0$ for all values of x;

$\int_a^b f(x)\,dx = 1$

(ii) $f(x) = F'(x)$

(b) (iii) $F(x) = \begin{cases} 0 & x < 0 \\ 0.0125x^2 & 0 \leqslant x \leqslant 8 \\ 0.2x - 0.8 & 8 \leqslant x \leqslant 9 \\ 1 & x \geqslant 9 \end{cases}$

(iv) 0.55 (v) 0.166 (vi) 0.575

Exercise 6e (page 347)

1. (a) $1, -\frac{1}{27}$

(b) $F(x) = \begin{cases} \frac{x^3}{27} & 0 \leqslant x \leqslant 3 \\ 1 & x \geqslant 3 \end{cases}$

(c) $f(x) = \frac{x^2}{9}$ $0 \leqslant x \leqslant 3$

(e) 0.581

2. (a) $\frac{1}{3}$ (b) $f(x) = \begin{cases} \frac{2}{3} & 0 \leqslant x < 1 \\ \frac{1}{3} & 1 \leqslant x \leqslant 2 \\ 0 & \text{otherwise} \end{cases}$

(c) $\frac{5}{6}$ (d) $\frac{\sqrt{11}}{6}$ (e) 0.608 (3 S.F.)

3. (a) $f(x) = \begin{cases} \frac{x-1}{6} & 1 \leqslant x \leqslant 3 \\ \frac{7-x}{12} & 3 \leqslant x \leqslant 7 \\ 0 & \text{otherwise} \end{cases}$

(b) $\frac{11}{3}, \frac{14}{9}$ (c) 3.54 (3 S.F.)(d) 0.595

4. (a) $\frac{1}{3}$ (b) $f(x) = \begin{cases} 0 & x < -1 \\ \alpha & -1 \leqslant x < 0 \\ 2\alpha & 0 \leqslant x < 1 \\ 0 & x \geqslant 1 \end{cases}$

(c) $\frac{1}{6}$ (d) 0.553 (e) $\frac{11}{18}$

5. (a) 2 (b) $f(x) = \begin{cases} 2 & 0 \leqslant x \leqslant 0.5 \\ 0 & \text{otherwise} \end{cases}$

(c) 0.25 (d) 0.144

6. (a) $-\frac{1}{16}, 1$ (b) $f(x) = \begin{cases} \frac{x}{8} & 0 \leqslant x \leqslant 2 \\ 0 & \text{otherwise} \end{cases}$

7. $1, \frac{5}{6}, \frac{1}{4}$

8. (i) 2.93

(ii) $F(x) = \begin{cases} 0 & x < 0 \\ 1 - \frac{1}{100}(x - 10)^2 & 0 \leqslant x \leqslant 10 \\ 1 & x \geqslant 10 \end{cases}$

(iii) $f(x) = \begin{cases} \frac{1}{5} - \frac{1}{50}x & 0 \leqslant x \leqslant 10 \\ 0 & \text{otherwise} \end{cases}$

0.25

9. (i) $\frac{1}{3}$ (iii) 4.39 (iv) 12.5

Exercise 6f (page 353)

1. (a) $f(x) = \begin{cases} \frac{1}{3} & 3 \leqslant x \leqslant 6 \\ 0 & \text{otherwise} \end{cases}$

(b) 4.5 (c) 0.75 (d) $\frac{1}{3}$

2. (a) $\frac{1}{3}$ (b) 0.5 (c) -3.5 (d) 0.75

3. (a) 5 (b) 0.325 (c) 3 (d) $\frac{4}{3}$

4. (i) 0.25 (ii) 0.845

5. 0.4

6. 0.577

Exercise 6g (page 362)

1. (a) 0.0821 (b) 0.2 (c) 0.632
   (d) 0.2 (e) 0.139 (f) 0

2. (a) 2000 h (b) (i) 0.287 (ii) 0.593
   (c) 0.465 (d) 0.0515

3. (a) 6.93 (b) $0.1e^{-0.1x}$ (c) 10, 100
   (d) 0.24 (2 S.F.)

4. 0.1386, £26.30, 0.225

5. $a = 92.2, A = 0.0108$
   (a) 0.114 (b) 0.338 (c) 0.202

6. (i) 0.62 (ii) 0.38

7. 2.895

8. $\frac{1}{\lambda}$, $e^{-2\lambda t}$, $e^{-2\lambda t}$, $\frac{1 - e^{-\lambda(1-k)t}}{1 - e^{-\lambda t}}$

9. $2, \frac{1}{2}, \frac{1}{4}, 1 - e^{-2x}, 0.368$

10. (a) Half a day (b) 8 hours

11. (a) 30; 900 (b) 0.311

12. (a) $e^{-0.4t}$ (b) $1 - e^{-0.4t}$ (c) 2.5
   (d) 1.73; 0.135

Exercise 6h (page 365)

1. (a) 2.4   (b) $20, \frac{1}{3}, 0.178$ (3 S.F.)

2. (i) $-\frac{3}{16}$ (ii) $\frac{19}{80}$ (iv) 2

3. (b) $\sqrt{\dfrac{3}{5}}$

4. $4, \frac{8}{15}, \frac{11}{225}, 0.541$ (3 S.F.)

5. $8, \frac{1}{9}, 39$

6. (a) $\frac{2}{3}$ (b) $f(x) = \begin{cases} \dfrac{2x}{3} & 0 \leqslant x \leqslant 1 \\ 1 - \dfrac{x}{3} & 1 \leqslant x \leqslant 3 \\ 0 & \text{otherwise} \end{cases}$

    $\frac{4}{3}, \frac{7}{8}$ (c) 1.27 (3 S.F.), 0.875

7. $\lambda = \frac{1}{3}, 2\frac{7}{12}, \frac{79}{96}$

8. $a = 2, k = \frac{3}{4}, 0.2$

9. 0.6, 0.2, 0.166

10. (c) $F(x) = \begin{cases} -\dfrac{1}{12x^3} & x \leqslant -1 \\ \dfrac{1}{2} + \dfrac{x}{2} - \dfrac{x^3}{12} & -1 \leqslant x \leqslant 1 \\ 1 - \dfrac{1}{12x^3} & x \geqslant 1 \end{cases}$

     (d) $0, \frac{11}{15}$

11. (b) $\dfrac{\theta}{\theta + 3}, \dfrac{\theta(\theta + 1)}{(\theta + 3)(\theta + 4)}$

     (c) $\dfrac{3\theta}{(\theta + 3)^2(\theta + 4)}$ (d) 0.2

12. (a) 0.991   (b) 0.983   (c) 0.28

     (d) 0.0017   (e) £15.40

13. (i) $b = \dfrac{a^2}{2}, \dfrac{2}{3a}, \dfrac{2}{9a^2}$ (ii) $c = a$

14. $\frac{4}{5}, \frac{4}{25}$, £8

15. (a) 2.1, 1.29   (b) $1, \frac{1}{2}$

16. $\frac{1}{4}, 2, \frac{8}{3}, 20$

17. 0.181, 0.0498; 11.6 miles (3 S.F.)

18. (a) 98 p   (b) 83 p

19. (ii) $F(x) = \begin{cases} \dfrac{3}{17}x^2 & 0 \leqslant x \leqslant 1 \\ \dfrac{1}{17}(1 + 2x^3) & 1 \leqslant x \leqslant 2 \\ 1 & x \geqslant 2 \end{cases}$

     (iii) 1.55   (iv) 0.89

20. (ii) 2.2   (iii) 1.71   (iv) 0.264   (v) 0.3645

CHAPTER 7

Exercise 7a (page 373)

1. (a) 0.8089   (b) 0.8089   (c) 0.1911

     (d) 0.1911

2. (a) 0.0359   (b) 0.2578   (c) 0.99973

     (d) 0.9131   (e) 0.00494   (f) 0.99111

     (g) 0.9686   (h) 0.2343   (i) 0.0312

     (j) 0.9484   (k) 0.9803   (l) 0.00201

3. (a) 0.05   (b) 0.05   (c) 0.0999

     (d) 0.025   (e) 0.005   (f) 0.01

     (g) 0.0025   (h) 0.975

Exercise 7b (page 375)

1. (a) 0.1709   (b) 0.54807   (c) 0.3639

     (d) 0.4582   (e) 0.4798   (f) 0.99792

     (g) 0.03368   (h) 0.9082   (i) 0.2729

     (j) 0.03061   (k) 0.925   (l) 0.4508

     (m) 0.9   (n) 0.02

Exercise 7c (page 378)

1. (a) 0.015   (b) 0.796   (c) 1.231/2

     (d) 0.953   (e) 1.94   (f) -3.432

     (g) -1.887 (h) -0.454

2. (a) 3.03   (b) 2.326/7/8/9

     (c) 1.96   (d) 0.849

     (e) 0.047/8   (f) $-0.501/2$

     (g) -0.885 (h) $-2.272/3/4$

3. (a) 0.91   (b) 1.66   (c) 0.674   (d) 2.05

4. 0.674, -0.674, 0.524

5. (a) 1.645   (b) 1.96   (c) 2.054/5

     (d) 2.326   (e) 2.575   (f) 2.808/9

6. (a) 1.282   (b) 2.054/5   (c) 2.17

     (d) 2.575

Exercise 7d (page 383)

1. (a) 0.0548   (b) 0.0107   (c) 0.8849

     (d) 0.9713   (e) 0.6554   (f) 0.9918

     (g) 0.4602   (h) 0.0808

2. (a) 0.0106   (b) 0.273   (c) 0.5971

     (d) 0.2168   (e) 0.9857   (f) 0.99702

3. (a) 0.3015   (b) 0.0105   (c) 0.9079

     (d) 0.2533   (e) 0.2097   (f) 0.0323

     (g) 0.5231

4. (a) 0.1587   (b) 0.8413   (c) 0.6915

     (d) 0.3085   (e) 0.9332

5. (a) 0.8634   (b) 0.2413   (c) 0.1388

     (d) 0.6826   (e) 0.2565

6. (a) 0.8014   (b) 0.085   (c) 0.2714

     (d) 0.4028   (e) 0.18862

7. (a) 0.5923   (b) 0.4208   (c) 0.9544

8. (a) 0.0668   (b) 0.4013   (c) 0.1747

9. (a) 0.7054   (b) 0.3228   (c) 0.0618

     (d) 0.8962   (e) 0.1818   (f) 0.4621

10. (a) 0.0478   (b) 8.17×10^{-4}

11. (a) 735   (b) 646   (c) 546   (d) 740

Exercise 7e (page 384)

(i)	(a) 51.55	(b) 63.55
(ii)	(a) 117.44	(b) 126.752
(iii)	(a) 70.00	(b) 90.58
(iv)	(a) 49.66	(b) 67.60
(v)	(a) $\mu - 2.05\sigma$	(b) $\mu + 0.86\sigma$
(vi)	(a) $a - 2.05\sqrt{b}$	(b) $a + 0.86\sqrt{b}$
(vii)	(a) $-1.05a$	(b) $1.86a$
(viii)	(a) 34.65	(b) 55.02

Exercise 7f (page 386)

1. (i) 63.655   (ii) 67.37   (iii) 55.09

     (iv) 56.69 or 56.695

2. (a) 37.572   (b) 50.012   (c) 38.244

     (d) 55.608

3. $9.87; 70.13 < X < 89.87$

4. (i) 9.2   (ii) 18.608   (iii) 15.68

     (iv) 17.92   (v) (384.32, 415.68)

5. (a) 0.6247   (b) 629.52 g   (c) 3

6. (a) 290   (b) 78   (c) 27

7. (i) 1.645   (ii) 2.575   (iii) 1.96

     (iv) 2.808

8. (458.92, 546.52)

9. 8, 1.158, (6.10, 9.90)

Exercise 7g (page 389)

1. 10.7
2. 4
3. 30
4. 35.5
5. 52.73, 11.96
6. 100.8, 5.71
7. 50, 6.12
8. 39.5, 5.32
9. 53.87, 16.48

10. 0.7725
11. 0.203
12. (a) 92.7% (b) 1.32 (c) 1.7%
13. 2080, 236
14. (a) 9.1% (b) 99.69 (c) 0.4 mm
15. 4.46
16. 4.299

Exercise 7h (page 394)

1. (a) 37.8% (b) (125.5, 194.5)
  (c) 0.405
2. (a) (i) 0.1056 (ii) 0.7734 (iii) 0.6678
  (b) $\mu = 490$ g, $\sigma = 12.2$ g
3. 0.159, 0.775, 0.067, 2.7, £37.56
4. $\mu = 50.154$, $\sigma = 4$
5. 0.0401 (i) 0.4593 (ii) 0.003
6. 0.4013, 0.0031
7. (a) 1.2 (b) 53.6 (c) 54.2; 0.066
8. 24.97, 53.03
9. 0.075
10. 979.27, 17.27, 133
11. 5.2007, 0.003 46; 0.0269; 0.002 61, 1.4%
12. 0.0038, 230.65, 1.29
13. 0.30 (2 d.p.), 0.26 (2 d.p.); steeper
14. 0.993, (i) 0.884 (ii) 20.077, 0.323
15. (i) 0.0228 (ii) 0.144

Exercise 7i (page 400)

(a) $P(2.5 < X < 9.5)$ (b) $P(3.5 < X < 8.5)$
(c) $P(10.5 < X < 24.5)$ (d) $P(1.5 < X < 7.5)$
(e) $P(X > 54.5)$ (f) $P(X > 75.5)$
(g) $P(45.5 < X < 66.5)$ (h) $P(X < 108.5)$
(i) $P(X < 45.5)$ (j) $P(55.5 < X < 56.5)$
(k) $P(400.5 < X < 560.5)$ (l) $P(66.5 < X < 67.5)$
(m) $P(X > 59.5)$ (n) $P(99.5 < X < 100.5)$
(o) $P(33.5 < X < 42.5)$ (p) $P(6.5 < X < 7.5)$
(q) $P(X > 508.5)$ (r) $P(X < 6.5)$
(s) $P(26.5 < X < 28.5)$ (t) $P(52.5 < X < 53.5)$

Exercise 7j (page 403)

1. (a) 0.9474 (b) 0.6325 (c) 0.5914
  (d) 0.0269 (e) 0.2106
2. (a) 0.0154 (b) 0.8145 (c) 0.02
3. 0.1127
4. (a) 0.3729 (b) 0.9501 (c) 0.1039
  (d) 0.929
5. $\frac{1}{4}$, $\frac{3}{4}$, 27; 6.75, 2.25, 0.8413
6. 20, 16, 0.004 36
7. $^nC_r(1-p)^{n-r}p^r$, np, $np(1-p)$
  (a) 0.2304
  (b) 0.922 24; 0.8531 (incl.), 0.7946 (not incl.)
8. (a) (i) 0.0432 (ii) 0.1845 (iii) 0.7723
  (b) at least 9
9. (a) 61.7 (b) 0.075 (c) 163.5
  (d) 134.3 (e) 702.2
10. (a) 0.0566 (b) 0.2171 (c) 0.4708
  (d) 0.1432
11. (a) 285 (b) 43
12. 0.6886

Exercise 7k (page 405)

1. (a) 0.6201 (b) 0.39 (c) 0.5406
2. (a) 0.3998 (b) 0.2004 (c) 0.3361
  (d) 0.0637
3. (a) 0.313 (b) 0.5078 (c) 0.8335
  (d) 0.1101
4. (a) 0.2614 (b) 0.2343 (c) 0.0558
5. 0.8901
6. 0.6887; 4
7. (a) 0.4574 (b) 0.173 (c) 0.8312
8. (a) 0.4594 (b) 0.5363

9. (a) (i) 0.999 767 (ii) 0.000 177
  (iii) 0.924 41
  (b) 0.009 44
10. 86

Exercise 7l (page 409)

1. 0.5455 (a) 0.5462 (b) 0.3983
2. 0.1036 (a) 0.098 812 (b) 0.1061
3. 0.1360 (a) 0.1381 (b) 0.0936
4. 0.063 03 (a) 0.0579 (b) 0.0655
5. (a) 0.061 84 (b) 0.0651
6. 0.2192, 0.2075

Exercise 7m (page 410)

1. (a) 0.55 (b) 0.18
2. (a) 0.649 (b) 0.965 (c) 0.371
3. $^{10}C_1(0.96)^9(0.04)$ (a) 0.20 (b) 0.77
4. (a) 0.2025 (b) 0.410 (c) 0.0238
5. (i) 0.4502 (ii) 0.0996 (iii) 0.484
6. (a) 0.117 (b) 0.1275 (c) 0.0858
  (d) 0.0264
7. (i) 0.887 (ii) 0.994, 18; 0.28
8. (a) 0.3154 (b) 0.3068; worse; 0.5245
9. (a) 0.194 (b) 0.933 (c) 0.986
10. (a) (i) 0.1353 (ii) 0.3233 (b) 0.250
11. (a) 2.04×10^{-10} (b) 0.004 34; $x = 73$
12. $\dfrac{2000!}{(2000-N)!N!}\left(\dfrac{1}{30}\right)^N\left(\dfrac{29}{30}\right)^{2000-N}$;
  86 lines; 2×47 lines > 86; No
13. (a) (i) 0.0525 (ii) 0.358 75
  (b) (i) 0.143 (ii) 0.145
14. (a) 0.315 (b) 0.5644
15. (a) 0.199 (b) 0.353 (c) $e^{-3} - e^{-6}$
  (d) $3e^{-6}(1 - e^{-3})$; 0.047 31, 0.007 066; 0.870
16. 0.859 (c) 0.204 (d) 0.034
17. 0.043
18. (a) (i) 0.5987 (ii) 0.149
  (b) (i) 0.0294 (ii) 0.751
  (c) (i) 0.5987 (ii) 0.9772
19. (a) 0.215
20. 0.360, 0.734
21. (a) 0.927 (b) 0.0102; 0.297
22. (a) 0.977 (Normal)
  (b) (i) Poisson 0.191
    (ii) Normal approx. to Poisson 0.246
  (c) (i) Binomial 0.170 (ii) Binomial 0.648
23. (a) 0.6247 (b) 93.32% (c) 0.7852
24. (a) 0.3397 (b) 0.9666 (c) 0.0366
  (d) 0.5714 (Poisson)
25. (i) 0.0672 (ii) 0.286 (iii) 0.74 (iv) 0.465
  (v) Po(29.7); normal approx. 0.442
26. (i) 0.938 (ii) 0.371 (iii) 0.192 (iv) £16.40
27. n large, p small, $np \approx npq$; easier to calculate
  (i) 0.268
  (ii) 0.819; 0.914 (normal appprox. to binomial)
28. (i) 0.599 (ii) 0.086; 0.25 (2 S.F.), 0.215
29. (i) 0.237
  (ii) 0.0156; 0.0432; 0.005; 0.019;
    598 (binomial), 600 (Poisson approx.)
30. (i) 0.988, 0.606
  (ii) 0.857 (binomial), 0.855 (normal)
  (iii) 0.784 (binomial), 0.783 (Poisson)
31. (i) 0.988 (ii) 0.624 (iii) 0.828

CHAPTER 8

Exercise 8a (page 419)

1. (a) 0.6554 (b) 0.7698 (c) 0.3446
  (d) 0.8301
2. (a) 0.0359 (b) 0.269 64 (c) 0.6554
  (d) 0.2743 (e) 0.9918
3. (a) 0.001 35 (b) 0.0228 (c) 0.0913
4. (a) 0.9044 (b) 0.9522 (c) 0.6826

5. (i)   6.68%   (ii) 152.5 ml, $\sqrt{81.25}$ ml
(iii) 4.8%   (iv) £114   (v) 24 p approx.
6. (a) 0.0478   (b) 0.0668   (d) 0.9324
7. (a) 0.685   (b) 40.5 m
(c) 40 m, 4.9 m   (d) 0.575
(e) Yuk Ping has negligible chance,
Gwen about 0.05; choose Gwen
8. (a) (i) 0.894   (ii) 0.204
(b) $N(0.2, 0.0208)$, 0.487
(c) (i) 5.58   (ii) 5.48
9. (a) 48   (b) 0.8323   (c) 10, 41, 0.9408
10. (a) 47.2, 15.9   (b) 3.92, 0.923

Exercise 8b (page 425)

1. (a) 0.0228   (b) 0.8621   (c) 0.9638
2. 0.6915
3. (a) 0.1728   (b) 0.6127   (c) 0.5
4. 0.0561
5. (a) 0.0289   (b) 0.0200   (c) 0.6252
6. 0.5402
7. (a) 0.1247   (b) 0.6957
8. 0.1103, 0.753
9. 0.9043
10. 0.0651
11. 0.2575
12. 9.6, 0.522;   (a) 0.0177   (b) 0.2218
13. (a) (94.4, 105.6)   (b) 92.55%   (c) 22.14%
14. (a) 0.0787   (b) 3.019×10^{-6}
15. (a) 0.6298   (b) 0.1056
16. (i) 0.1587   (ii) 0.8849   (iii) 0.2779
17. (a) 0.497
(b) 0.854; mean = 30.16 g;
standard deviation = 1.276 g
18. (i) 0.733   (ii) 0.984; independent

Exercise 8c (page 431)

1. (a) 0.0745   (b) 0.9736   (c) 0.9386
(d) 0.0271
2. (a) 0.8131   (b) 0.0478   (c) 0.1078
(d) 0.0306   (e) 0.995 53   (f) 0.2762
3. (a) 6, 2   (b) 0.2074   (c) 0.7601
(d) 0.5143
4. 0.8681
5. (a) 0.990 39   (b) 0.9772   (c) 0.7373
6. (a) 0.1587   (b) 0.0127
7. (a) 0.244   (b) 0.659   (c) 0.409

Miscellaneous Exercise 8d (page 434)

1. (a) 0.60   (b) 0.20   (c) 0.95   (d) 0.5
2. (a) 0.051   (b) 0.001 55   (c) 0.9782
3. 1000, 172.4, 3000, 298.6, 0.16, 0.02
4. (a) 0.0888   (b) 0.6611
5. 0.0625, 0.2574, 0.5, 0.7123, 7
6. $Y \sim N(a_1\mu_1 + a_2\mu_2, a_1{}^2\sigma_1{}^2 + a_2{}^2\sigma_2{}^2)$, 0.84
7. (a) 0.8413   (b) 0.5
(c) 0.4207; 0.9938
8. 12 kg, 57.0 g, 3.97%, 765 g
9. (a) 0.3446
(b) 0.6915; 0.003 29, 0.304
10. 0.9192, 08 13, 0.999 912, 08 10, No
11. 0.8603, 0.1574, 0.3909
12. (a) 0.106   (b) 438.2 ml   (c) 0.800
(d) 0.961   (e) 0.244   (f) 388.6 ml
13. $N(\mu_1 + \mu_2 - \mu_3, 3\sigma^2)$
(a) 0.1657   (b) 108 p   (c) 0.4148
14. (a) 0.0139   (b) 0.1587   (c) 0.9332
15. (a) 0.159   (c) 0.584
16. (ii) 0.0802   (iii) 0.673
17. (i) 0.798   (ii) 0.323   (iii) 0.132   (iv) 0.228
18. (i) 0.252   (ii) 0.0581   (iii) 0.104

Exercise 8e (page 441)

1. (a) (i) 0.5, 0.45   (ii) 1.5, 1.05
(iii) 0.6, 9.24
2. $0, \frac{7}{6}$;

$\bar{x}$	-2	-1.5	-1	-0.5	0
$P(\bar{X} = \bar{x})$	$\frac{1}{144}$	$\frac{6}{144}$	$\frac{17}{144}$	$\frac{30}{144}$	$\frac{36}{144}$

$\bar{x}$	0.5	1	1.5	2
$P(\bar{X} = \bar{x})$	$\frac{30}{144}$	$\frac{17}{144}$	$\frac{6}{144}$	$\frac{1}{144}$

$; 0, \frac{7}{18}$
3. 4.75, 8.1875; 4.75, 4.09 (3 S.F.)
4. 5, 7.5;

Mean	2.5	4	4.5	5.5	6	7.5
f	2	2	2	2	2	2

5; 2.5
5. 0.84, 1.68
6. (a) 24.5   (b) 2.57; 2.35, 7, 6

Exercise 8f (page 446)

1. (a) 0.0401   (b) 0.3891
2. 0.3206
3. (a) 0.0668   (b) 0.9893   (c) 0.1974
4. 0.0228
5. (a) 0.0401   (b) 0.7571   (c) 0.2660
6. (a) 12   (b) 25
7. (a) 0.2399   (b) 0.0787
(c) 0.0127; $n > 108$
8. 62
9. (a) $N(10, 3.2)$ (b) $N(50, 3.2)$
(c) $N(-10, 3.2)$ (d) $N(210, 48)$
(e) $N(80, 27.2)$
10. 0.009 61
11. 44
12. (a) $2\mu, \sqrt{2}\sigma$ (b) $0, \sqrt{2}\sigma$
(c) $\mu, \dfrac{\sigma}{\sqrt{2}}$; 0.7078, 0.9213
13. 0.0968, 0.0828, 0.000 907, 0.2295
14. $N(960, 21.2)$
15. 0.0983
16. (a) 0.1457
(b) Distribution of $V^{1/3}$ different,
prob. $< 10^{-4}$
(c) 0.1210
17. 0.332, 0.0587, 0.009

Exercise 8g (page 449)

1. $1580, 1200^2$
2. 3.21, 0.265 (3 S.F.), 0.001 44
3. (a) 0.034   (b) 0.8194
4. (a) 3.85   (b) 62.34   (c) 1.7
5. (a) 0.9145   (b) 0.7081   (c) 0.6226
6. 50
7. 60
8. 35
9. 42
10. 5
11. 20 500, 1768
12. 0.9212
13. (b) 3.86, 7.82   (c) 0.331
14. 0.25, 0.0228
15. (i) $P(X = 0) = \frac{1}{2}, P(X = 1) = \frac{1}{3}$,
$P(X = 2) = \frac{1}{6}$
(ii) $\frac{2}{3}$
(iii) 0.159
16. (i) 0.885   (ii) 207.7   (iii) 0.344   (iv) 1.096
17. (i) 0.007 15, 0.007 93   (ii) 0.405   (iii) 0.302
18. 0.238, 0.006 21

Exercise 8h (page 453)

1. (a) 0.0745   (b) 0.003 67
2. (a) 0.005 68   (b) 0.527 02   (c) 0.0958
3. (a) 0.000 215   (b) 0.5229   (c) 0.0367
4. (a) 0.3085   (b) 0.0970
5. 0.7181
6. (a) 0.0648   (b) 0.0851   (c) 0.3068
7. 0.22

Exercise 8i (page 461)

Some answers depend on the random numbers used and on the method of allocation. These are possible answers.

10. (a) 1, 1, 1, 0, 3   (b) 4
11. 33.134, 34.193, 28.712
12. (a) 3, 5   (b) 1, 5
    (c) 1007.2, 1016.8
13. 1.52, 1.48
14. 3.3, 1.41
17. (a) 3   (b) 6.1826

Exercise 8j (page 473)

2. (a) 6, 6, 6, 6, 6, 5, 5
4. (ii) Large : medium : small $= 15 : 25 : 24$
6. (a) 8, 5.6
    (d) Without replacement 7.33, 0.88;
    with replacement 7.17, 0.966;
    sampling without replacement has the
    smaller standard error
9. (a) 5.36, 5.53

CHAPTER 9

Exercise 9a (page 478)

1. a, c, e
2. e

Exercise 9b (page 482)

1. 48.875, 6.98 (2 d.p.)
2. 51.5, 241.1
3. 1.69 (2 d.p.), 8×10^{-6} (1 S.F.)
4. 15, 43.14 (2 d.p.)
5. 15, 43.14 (2 d.p.)
6. 10, 3.11 (2 d.p.)
7. 9.71 (2 d.p.), 621.12 (2 d.p.)
8. 57.78 (2 d.p.), 6496.15 (2 d.p.)
9. 46.9, 242.46 (2 d.p.)
10. 10.96, 17.35 (2 d.p.)
11. 22.79 (2 d.p.), 1.81 (2 d.p.)
12. (b) positively skewed
    (c) 14.76, 114.96
    (d) x is estimated using mid-points of each
    interval. Using intervals 0–4, 5–9,
    10–14 etc., results are similar to (c),
    but s.d. is reduced slightly.
13. 236, 7.58
14. 3.17, 1.5611
16. 0.5, 1.428
17. 205.16, 9.223

Exercise 9c (page 486)

1. 0.663, 0.002 21
2. 9.88, 0.796
3. 3.69, 1.33
4. 9.19, 10.0
5. 2.27, 10.2
6. 5.46, 0.0481
7. 30.15, 11.9
8. 2.39, 0.0275
9. 0.348

10. 0.838
11. $\frac{2}{3}$
12. 0.307

Exercise 9d (page 495)

NOTE: $\hat{\sigma}$ has been used when σ is not known.

1. (a) (139.5, 140.5)   (b) (139.4, 140.6)
2. (a) (74.02, 77.98)   (b) (73.38, 78.62)
    (c) (72.89, 79.11)
3. (a) (747.51, 748.49)   (b) (747.42, 748.58)
    (c) (747.31, 748.69)
4. (a) (79.19, 84.81)   (b) (78.89, 85.11)
5. (a) (68.12, 69.88)   (b) (67.84, 70.16)
6. (1011, 1114)
7. (10.82, 14.08)
8. 10.82, 1.70, 11.19, 0.646, 10.968,
    (10.82, 11.12)
9. 85.2, 15.45, 85.01, 2.01, 85.08,
    (84.628, 85.540)
10. 25.3, 3.6, (24.9, 25.8)
11. 91.32, 7.42, 0.43, (90.5, 92.2)
12. 194, 176 (3 S.F.), (173.5, 214.5)
13. 9.71, (172.3, 173.3)
14. (b) 38.1, 1080.39   (c) (33.5, 42.7)   (d) 28.3
15. (b) $\frac{2}{3}$, 0.471   (c) $\frac{5}{9}$ (d) (0.727, 1.073)
16. 3.7 (1 d.p.)

Exercise 9e (page 501)

1. (a) (0.323, 0.517)   (b) (0.696, 0.904)
    (c) (0.222, 0.418)   (d) (0.529, 0.791)
    (e) (0.146, 0.254)   (f) (0.693, 0.847)
    (g) (0.469, 0.531)
2. (0.622, 0.738)
3. (a) (0.293, 0.427)   (b) (0.273, 0.447)
4. (0.156, 0.344)
5. (0.510, 0.574); Yes
6. 267.2 (1 d.p.), 227.9 (1 d.p.), (0.256, 0.410)
7. (a) 3, (2.04, 3.96)   (b) 30%, (25.2, 34.8)
8. $\frac{mn}{n_0}$, (0.002 41, 0.007 59), (13 175, 41 493)
9. 10 000, (7236, 16 181)
10. $\mathrm{Bin}(n\theta, n\theta(1 - \theta))$, n large; (0.826, 0.945)

Miscellaneous Exercise 9f (page 503)

1. (a) (92.32, 99.68)   (b) (0.351, 0.369), 5277
2. 6.6 mm, 3.5 mm

Mesh size	0 to 1	> 1 to 2	> 2 to 4
Additional diamonds	1	1	4

Mesh size	> 4 to 6	> 6 to 8	> 8 to 12
Additional diamonds	2	6	6

    6.30, 9.93
3. 14.01, 0.04, (13.92, 14.10); 0.40
4. (0.123, 0.392), (170.84, 178.16),
    (165.57, 186.83), (£488, £531)
5. (i) (0.303, 0.357)
    (iii) People did not tell the truth; people
    changed their minds at the last minute
6. (a) $\overline{X} \sim N\left(\mu, \dfrac{\sigma^2}{n}\right)$ (b) 28
7. (i) (171.1, 174.3)   (ii) smaller
8. 25.35, 0.13; (25.15, 25.6)
    Assume normal with population variance equal
    to estimate. P(interval traps μ) $= 0.95$. Accept
9. (a) (202.4, 207.4)   (b) 0.2; (0.057, 0.343)
    (c) 0.001 76

10. (a) (i) (15.94, 19.56)   (ii) $\alpha = 19.27$
     (b) (28.14, 28.98)
     (c) (i) (0.244, 0.283)
         (ii) 90
11. (a) (i) 0.097   (ii) 0.953
     (b) (470.7, 559.3)   (c) 0.208
     (d) (498.9, 532.3)   (e) (0.100, 0.150)

CHAPTER 10

Exercise 10a (page 514)

1. (i) $z = 2$ (a) Reject   (b) Accept
    (ii) $z = -1.5$ (a) Accept   (b) Accept
    (iii) $z = 2.12$ (a) Reject   (b) Accept
    (iv) $z = -2.475$ (a) Reject   (b) Accept
    (v) $z = 3.645$ (a) Reject   (b) Reject
    (vi) $z = -1.826$ (a) Reject   (b) Accept

In questions 2–5 the continuity correction has been included.

2. (a) $z = 1.375$, fair   (b) $z = 2.375$, biased
3. $z = -1.712$, reject claim
4. $z = 1.637$, accept
5. (a) (i) 0.0297   (ii) 0.0934
    (b) $z = -1.792$, yes, less than 75%,
    (only just)

Exercise 10b (page 520)

1. (a) $z = -1.095$, accept H_0
    (b) $z = 1.845$, reject
    (c) $z = 2.5$, reject
    (d) $z = -2.778$, reject
2. $z = -1.565$, no
3. $z = 1.909$ (a) Yes   (b) No   (c) No
4. $\bar{x} < 91.51$ min
5. (a) 0.683   (b) $2.9216 < \bar{x} < 3.0784$
6. 0.1101, 0.001 58, reduced
7. $z = 2.487$, yes; 1506.8 ± 0.311
8. (a) $\alpha \geqslant 3.59\%$ (b) $\alpha \geqslant 7.18\%$
9. Approx. 83, (0.823, 0.845), no
10. $\mu_1 - \mu_2$, $\sigma_1{}^2 + \sigma_2{}^2$; $\lambda_1\mu_1 + \lambda_2\mu_2$,
    $\dfrac{\lambda_1{}^2\sigma_1{}^2}{n_1} + \dfrac{\lambda_2{}^2\sigma_2{}^2}{n_2}$ $z = 1.853$, yes at the 5% level
11. (a) 10.6%, 6.7%   (b) £395.20
    (c) $z = -2.5$, one tailed, yes
12. 11.2, 2.54, reject at the 5% level
13. 0.0341, 0.069, do not reject
14. (b) (i) (£$17\frac{2}{3}$, £$19\frac{1}{3}$)   (ii) 279   (iii) Yes

Exercise 10c (page 525)

1. (a) $z = 1.778$, accept
    (b) $z = 1.778$, reject
    (c) $z = -1.428$, reject
    (d) $z = -2.487$, accept
2. $z = 0.971$, accept
3. $z = 1.99$, yes; 16.2 ± 1.24
4. Justified; (8.19, 8.53)
5. (b) Reject H_0 (c) (77.50, 79.96)
6. (45.6, 49.4), $\alpha > 4$, 0.0321
7. (i) (0.126, 0.274),   (ii) 25.34, 0.960
    (iii) $z = 3.10$, yes.

Exercise 10d (page 529)

1. (a) $z = -2.096$, S, reject
    (b) $z = -1.402$, NS, accept
    (c) $z = 2.493$, S, reject
    (d) $z = 1.99$, NS, accept
    (e) $z = 2.076$, S, reject
    (f) $z = -2.036$, NS, accept
    (g) $z = 1.783$, S, reject

2. 8.0067, 0.000 175, $z = 2.00$, S, reject population
    mean is 8.00, $z = 3.52$, S, second population has
    smaller mean than first
3. (204.1, 223.9), 196, $|z| = 1.714$, NS
4. (24.59, 25.41), $|z| = 2.15$, Accept Mr Jones'
    claim
5. 0.0345, 0.1174

Exercise 10e (page 534)

The continuity correction has been considered only when the uncorrected value for z is within the rejection region.

1. (a) without c.c. $z = 1.768$ but with c.c.
        $z = 1.59$, so accept H_0, since whole of
        rectangle not in rejection region
    (b) without c.c. $z = 2.335$ but with c.c.
        $z = 2.205$, so accept H_0
    (c) without c.c. $z = -1.897$, accept
    (d) without c.c. $z = 2.179$, accept
    (e) without c.c. $z = -3.060$, with c.c.
        $z = -2.937$, reject H_0
2. $z = -2.04$ without c.c., accept H_0, no
3. without c.c. $z = 1.667$, with c.c. $z = 1.5$ so
    accept H_0, no
4. without c.c. $z = -2.4$, with c.c. $z = -2.3$, reject
    H_0, yes
5. without c.c. $z = 2.46$, with c.c $z = 2.43$,
    reject H_0, yes
6. (a) 0.87
    (b) 0.19; without c.c. $z = -1.49$, with c.c.
        $z = -1.12$ so accept H_0, not justified
7. 91.3, 13.5; 0.1571; without c.c. 0.003,
    $z = -2.75$; with c.c. 0.004 34, $z = -2.625$;
    yes, justified
8. (a) 0.0985, 0.006 66
    (b) without c.c. $z = -0.224$, do not reject H_0
    (c) 12, 27, 29, 19, 9, 3, 1
9. (0.327, 0.387); 19; without c.c. $z = -2.74$,
    reject H_0, yes
10. without c.c. $z = -1.143$, do not reject
11. (i) without c.c. $z = -3.06$, with c.c.
        $z = -3.03$, reject H_0
    (ii) (0.379, 0.458); 75
12. (i) without c.c. $z = 1.301$, do not reject H_0
    (ii) (0.681, 0.808)

Miscellaneous Exercise 10f (page 537)

1. $\bar{X} \sim N\left(\mu, \dfrac{\sigma^2}{n}\right)$; if $P(a < X < b) = 0.95$, then
    (a, b) is a 95% confidence interval for X
    (a) (£3.37, £14.07)
    (b) (£9.07, £10.35); $z = 1.877$, yes; 163
2. (49 758.4, 51 689.6), 116, do not reject H_0
3. $z = -2.869$, reject claim
4. $\bar{X}$ is approximately normal, mean $= \mu$,
    standard deviation $\frac{\sigma}{10}$ (1.78, 2.00);
    one-tailed, $z = 1.98$, do not reject H_0
5. $\bar{X} \sim N(\mu, \sigma^2/n)$,
    (a) (9.7295, 19.2705)   (b) (11.779, 14.621)
    (c) $z = -1.793$, reject H_0, decrease
6. (a) (0.905, 0.939)
    (b) Reject H_0 if $\bar{x} < \mu_0 - 2.575 \frac{\sigma}{\sqrt{n}}$
        or $\bar{x} > \mu_0 + 2.575 \frac{\sigma}{\sqrt{n}}$;
        Reject H_0 if $\bar{x} < \mu_0 - 1.645 \frac{\sigma}{\sqrt{n}}$
        or $\bar{x} > \mu_0 + 1.645 \frac{\sigma}{\sqrt{n}}$
7. (i) (517.7, 548.3)
    (ii) (337, 729); $z = -1.16$, not significant;
         (513.1, 566.4)

8. (a) 0.833 (b) 0.180
   (c) $H_0: p = 0.5$, $H_1: p \neq 0.5$; $z = 2.236$,
   without c.c., $z = 2.012$ with c.c.;
   Biased, 95% C.I. for p is (0.560, 0.940),
   $p > 0.5$
9. $1/1200$, $z = -0.949$, no
10. (a) 0.8931 (b) 0.8859 (c) 0.7912
    (d) 0.0947; $\mu = 229.41$, $z = 2.405$, yes, not
    correctly set
11. 0.567, 0.1156, 0.1587, 0.1587; 12.6 pence;
    $z = 1.4$, not sufficient evidence, $z = 1.838$,
    sufficient evidence
12. $z = 2.096$ without c.c., $z = 1.99$ with c.c., yes;
    683; (0.775, 0.825)

Exercise 10g (page 546)

1. (a) Accept (b) Reject (c) Reject
   (d) Accept (e) Accept (f) Reject
   (g) Reject (h) Accept
2. Accept
3. No
4. She could have been guessing
5. (a) Evidence that proportion is lower
   (b) No different

Exercise 10h (page 550)

1. Accept H_0
2. (a) Yes, median $\neq 100$
   (b) Yes, now accept median $= 100$
3. Reject H_0
4. Reject H_0
5. Not of equal difficulty
6. (a) Do not reject H_0
   (b) Not significant evidence that breaking
   strength is less
7. $n \leqslant 2$ or $n \geqslant 10$, 3.9%; no
8. Par has been fixed correctly; scores higher in
   bad weather
9. $28.9 < \alpha < 100$
10. Yes, reduces (5% level)
11. (v) Accept hypothesis
12. (a) 52.35
    (b) H_0: median $= 50$, H_1: median > 50
    (c) Accept Democrat's claim

Exercise 10i (page 558)

1. (a) Accept (b) Accept (c) Accept
   (d) Reject (e) Accept (f) Reject
2. Mean has increased
3. Mean has not decreased
4. (a) Not increased (b) Decreased
5. Not increased
6. 0.0057, 9 mins, not significant
7. No

Exercise 10j (page 570)

1. (a) 0.125, 0.125
   (b) 0.2099, 0.2702, Test 2
2. $\frac{1}{3}$, $\frac{4}{9}$
3. Accept as slow if 'bounce' < 12.5, accept as slow
   if 'mean bounce' < 11.64; 0.0004
4. 1.9, 0.837
5. 0.515, 0.376, 0.4455, 43
6. 0.106, 0.02
7. (a) $H_0: p = \frac{1}{6}$, $H_1: p \neq \frac{1}{6}$;
   (b) $z = -1.9595\ldots$, just NS at 5% level, no
   (c) $z = 1.8$, NS, no
8. 0.00032, 0.00672, 0.05792; 4

9. See question 1
10. (a) 0.0668
    (b) 0.0446; if $X > 58$ accept H_1, if $X \leqslant 58$
    accept H_0; 0.380
11. Accept H_0 if $X > 0.817$; accept H_0 if
    $X > -0.255$
12. $3 \leqslant r \leqslant 9$; 0.182
13. (a) 0.000577
    (b) 0.00738; 0.8, 0.8, 0.9

CHAPTER 11

Exercise 11a (page 584)

NOTE: There will be variation in answers,
depending on the degree of approximation
used at various stages in the working.

	χ^2	v	Decision
1.	1.93	3	accept fair
2.	18.16	9	accept
3.	6.19	2	reject H_0, yes
4.	4.95	3	no
	9.90	3	yes
5.	8.24	7	accept
6.	4.15	4	yes
7.	10.68	4	no

8. 78.81, 17.76, 7.77, 6.66; 5.87, $v = 3$, no
   difference
9. (i) 14.432 (ii) 15.5
10. 38.2, $v = 9$, evidence of bias
11. 3, $v = 4$, uniform
12. (a) modal class 2 to < 4
    (b) 4 years 8 months, 3 years 2 months
    (c) 3 years 7 months, 4 years 7 months
    (d) $\chi^2 = 5.72$, $v = 5$, justified

Exercise 11b (page 598)

1. $X \sim \text{Bin}(5, 0.3)$, $E = 17, 36, 31, 13, 3, 0$
   (combine last three classes), $v = 3$, $\chi^2 = 4.49$,
   accept
2. $X \sim \text{Bin}(5, \frac{1}{6})$, $E = 80.5, 80.5, 32, 7$
   (with last three classes combined),
   $v = 3$, $\chi^2 = 8.21$, yes, biased; $\bar{x} = 1$, $p = 0.2$,
   $X \sim \text{Bin}(5, 0.2)$
   $E = 66, 82, 41, 11$ (with last three classes
   combined), $v = 2$, χ^2 is very small, too good a fit,
   query data
3. np, 1.6, 0.32, $E = 7.3, 17.1, 16.1, 7.5, 1.8, 0.2$
   (combine last three classes), $v = 2$, $\chi^2 = 1.79$,
   good fit
4. $\bar{x} = 2.5$, $E = 8, 21, 26, 21, 13, 11$ (combining end
   classes), $v = 4$, $\chi^2 = 2.59$, good
5. $\bar{x} = 1.28$ (2 d.p.), $E = 41, 52, 34, 14, 6$
   (combining end classes), $v = 3$, $\chi^2 = 6.81$, not
   significant
6. (a) $E = 3, 13, 28, 32, 18, 6$ (combine first
   two classes), $v = 4$, $\chi^2 = 11.9$, S, reject
   normal
   (b) $\bar{x} = 171.54$, $s = 7.11$ (2 d.p.), $E = 6, 18$,
   32, 28, 13, 3 (combine last two classes),
   $v = 2$, $\chi^2 = 1.73$, accept normal, good fit
7. $\bar{x} = 25.9$, $s = 11.8$ (1 d.p.), $E = 4, 7, 13, 18, 20$,
   17, 12, 6, 3, 1 (combine first two classes and last
   three classes), $v = 4$, $\chi^2 = 0.95$, very good fit
8. $X \sim \text{Bin}(2, \frac{1}{6})$, $E = 150, 60, 6$, $v = 2$, $\chi^2 = 9.6$,
   reject; use $\bar{x} = 0.444$, $pp = 0.222$, find E, $v = 1$
9. (a) $\bar{x} = 1.2$, $E = 99, 119, 72, 29, 9, 2$
   (combine last two classes),
   (b) $\chi^2 = 0.48$, $v = 3$, very good fit
10. $E = 246.6, 345.2, 241.7, 112.8, 39.5, 14.2$
    $\chi^2 = 32.2$, $v = 5$, not accepted

11. $E = 644$, $\chi^2 = 10.95$, $\nu = 4$, data do not support claim; $\bar{x} = 1.1$, $E = 33.3, 36.6, 20.1, 10$ (combining last two classes) $\chi^2 = 0.48$, $\nu = 2$, accept

12. (a) $\bar{x} = \hat{\mu} = 1.7568$, $\hat{\sigma} = 0.217$ $E = 6.25, 23.1125, 43, 36.2625, 16.375$ $\chi^2 = 10.56$, $\nu = 2$
    (b) $\chi^2 = 2.14$, $\nu = 1$

13. (a) 7   (b) $n = 20$, $p = 0.35$; 0.16135, 8.1
    (c) 12.3
    (d) $E = 12.3, 8.6, 9.2, 8.1, 11.8$; $O = 9, 7, 17, 8, 9$; $\chi^2 = 8.46$
    (e) 3; not good fit at 5% level

14. (b) $E = 7.3, 12.4, 10.6, 9.7$
    (c) $\nu = 2$, $\chi^2 = 1.77$, reasonable
    (d) very low, suspicious

15. (a) (i) 0.271   (ii) 0.0902   (iii) 0.0527
    (b) (i) $E = 44.62, 66.94, 50.2, 25.12, 13.12$ $(X \geqslant 4)$ $\nu = 4$, $\chi^2 = 10.6$; at 5% level, no
        (ii) Use mean from data for λ; $\nu = n - 2$

Exercise 11c (page 609)

NOTE: Minor adjustments need to be made when approximating so that totals agree.

1. (a) $E = 21, 16.5, 12.5, 21, 16.5, 12.5$; $\nu = 2$, $\chi^2 = 4.14$; independent
   (b) $E = 17.3, 35.0, 38.2, 11.5, 14.9, 30.3, 32.9, 9.9, 33.8, 68.7, 74.9, 22.6$; $\nu = 6$, $\chi^2 = 40.1$; not independent
   (c) $E = 18.6, 10.4, 28.9, 16.1, 18, 10, 24.5, 13.5$; $\nu = 3$, $\chi^2 = 1.60$; independent
   (d) $E = 11.8, 24.5, 33.7, 13.5, 28, 38.5, 20.3, 42, 57.7, 8.4, 17.5, 24.1$; $\nu = 6$, $\chi^2 = 7.53$; independent
   (e) $E = 37.5, 22.5, 87.5, 52.5$; $\nu = 1$, $\chi^2 = 2.54$; independent
   (f) $E = 11.5, 13.5, 43.5, 51.5$; $\nu = 1$, $\chi^2 = 3.18$; independent

2. $E = 40, 60, 100, 140, 210, 350, 20, 30, 50$; $\nu = 4$, $\chi^2 = 26.6$; yes

3. $E = 47.4, 53.5, 56.1, 7.6, 8.5, 8.9$; $\nu = 2$ without c.c. $\chi^2 = 6.57$, reject; with c.c. $\chi^2 = 5.13$, accept

4. $E = 17.5, 82.5, 17.5, 82.5$; $\nu = 1$, $\chi^2 = 0.58$, no

5. $E = 27.5, 972.5, 27.5, 972.5$; $\nu = 1$, $\chi^2 = 4.79$, yes

6. $E = 50.1, 29.5, 23.4, 22.9, 13.5, 10.6$; $\nu = 2$, $\chi^2 = 4.00$, yes

7. $E = 11.4, 14.3, 8.6, 15.7, 18.3, 22.9, 13.7, 25.1, 20.6, 25.7, 15.4, 28.3, 29.7, 37.1, 22.3, 40.9$; $\nu = 9$, $\chi^2 = 12.0$, accept

8. $E = 65.1, 28.9, 58.9, 26.1$; $\nu = 1$, $\chi^2 = 7.43$, yes

9. $E = 25.5, 25.5, 60.5, 60.5, 26.5, 26.5, 7.5, 7.5$; $\nu = 3$, $\chi^2 = 2.03$, independent

10. $E = 202.2, 260.7, 318.1, 184.8, 238.3, 290.9$; $\nu = 2$, $\chi^2 = 2.02$; independent

11. $\nu = 2$, $\chi^2 = 5.99$

12. (a) $\nu = (3 - 1)(3 - 1) = 4$;   (b) difference

13. $E = 34.2, 29.8, 12.8, 11.2$; $\nu = 1$, $\chi^2 = 1.24$, no

14. $E = 90.405, 56.595, 35.595, 20.405$; $\nu = 1$, $\chi^2 = 13.3$, related

15. 645; $E = 25, 145, 30, 87.5, 507.5, 105, 12.5, 72.5, 15$; $\nu = 4$, $\chi^2 = 694$, not independent

Miscellaneous Exercise 11d (page 622)

1. $E = 13.5, 15.5, 21, 8.64, 9.92, 13.44, 31.86, 36.58, 49.56$; $\nu = 4$, $\chi^2 = 11.35$, yes

2. (a) $E = 19\frac{1}{3}, 15\frac{1}{3}, 10, 15\frac{1}{3}, 9\frac{2}{3}, 7\frac{2}{3}, 5, 7\frac{2}{3}$; $\nu = 3$, $\chi^2 = 12.03$, mark is associated with type of question
   (b) Poisson, this is the most similar question

(c) $E = 22.5, 22.5, 22.5, 22.5, 7.5, 7.5, 7.5, 7.5$; $\nu = 3$, $\chi^2 = 17.6$, yes it is

(d) Contingency table – popular and well answered; Binomial and Poisson fits – average popularity, relatively badly answered; normal fit – unpopular but well answered by those who attempted it

3. (a) $E = 30, 40, 70, 50, 10$; $\nu = 4$, $\chi^2 = 7.074$; yes, same proportions
   (b) $\nu = 4$, yes there is an association

4. $E = 6.3$ (combine first 4 classes), 8.85, 14.66, 18.99, 19.28, 15.32, 9.52, 7.08 (combine last 3 classes); $\nu = 6$, $\chi^2 = 4.908$, good fit

5. (a) Expected frequencies

	London	Birmingham
X	33.6	22.4
Y	63.6	42.4
Z	22.8	15.2

   $\nu = 2$, $\chi^2 = 4.775$, no difference
   (b) $\bar{x} = 0.65$ $E = 20.88, 13.57, 5.55$, (combining end classes) $\nu = 1$, $\chi^2 = 1.85$, accept hypothesis

6. $E = 38.78, 34.02, 18.2, 39.21, 34.39, 18.4, 27.28, 23.92, 12.8, 22.59, 19.81, 10.6, 22.59, 19.81, 10.6, 28.55, 25.05, 13.4$; $\nu = 10$, $\chi^2 = 16.0$, no association; $E = 60$, $\nu = 6$, $\chi^2 = 13.2$, reject hypothesis

7. (a) $E = 480$, $\nu = 4$, $\chi^2 = 14.8$, yes there is evidence
   (b) $E = 6.405, 6.51, 8.085, 24.705, 25.11, 31.185, 29.89, 30.38, 37.73$; $\nu = 4$, $\chi^2 = 16.9$, length of employment is associated with grade

8. (a) $\bar{x} = 1$, $E = 36.79, 36.79, 18.39, 8.026$ (3 or more); $\nu = 2$, $\chi^2 = 12.9$, not suitable
   (b) $E = 26.25, 6.75, 8.75, 2.25$; $\nu = 1$, $\chi^2 = 3.77$, yes

9. (i) $E = 15.675, 7.425, 9.9, 26.125, 12.375, 16.5, 15.2, 7.2, 9.6$; $\nu = 4$, $\chi^2 = 20.9$, reaction does depend on eye colour; 0.1
   (ii) 0.275, (19.5%, 35.4%)

10. 0.0606, 0.2417, 0.2417, 0.0606, 0.0062. $E = 13.36, 48.34, 76.6, 48.34, 13.36$ (combining first two and last two classes); $\nu = 4$, $\chi^2 = 14.8$; $z = 1.02$, accept H_0

11. $E = 15.87, 21.09, 26.08, 21.09, 15.87$ (combining first two and last two classes); $\nu = 2$, $\chi^2 = 7.1$, does not fit

12. $E = 66.7, 33.3, 53.3, 26.7$; $\nu = 1$, $\chi^2 = 6.81$, no

13. A: $E = 12, 24, 36, 48, 60, 72, 60, 48, 36, 24, 12$; $\nu = 10$, $\chi^2 = 14.5$, not biased
    B: E as in A, $\chi^2 = 2.12$, unbiased, but query whether fiddled

14. $\bar{x} = 0.9$, $E = 21, 18, 11$ (combine last three classes), $\nu = 1$, $\chi^2 = 1.80$, yes, consistent

15. (a) $\bar{x} = 2$, $p = 0.4$, $E = 6, 21, 28, 18, 7$ (combine last two classes)
    (b) $\chi^2 = 2.21$, $\nu = 3$, yes, binomial adequate

16. $E = 21.0, 10.0, 7.0, 15.5, 7.5, 5, 41.5, 19.5, 14$; $\nu = 4$, $\chi^2 = 7.86$, accept hypothesis

17. $E = 48, 52, 96, 104, 96, 104$; $\nu = 2$, $\chi^2 = 6.57$; yes, proportions different; 1: 44%, 2: 42%, 3: 55%, Beach 3 contributed to the high value of χ^2

18. (a) $\bar{x} = 0.74$; combine $\geqslant 4$, $E = 667.96, 494.29, 182.89, 45.11, 9.75$; $\nu = 4$, $\chi^2 = 13.8$, not adequate
    (c) $E = 259$, $\nu = 3$, $\chi^2 = 13.8$, not consistent

19. (a) Combine first 3 classes, $\nu = 2$, $E = 15.24, 25.76, 27.37, 11.63$; $\chi^2 = 0.144$, yes
    (b) Combine $\geqslant 4$, $\nu = 3$, $\chi^2 = 0.404$, $E = 25.85, 41.75, 33.72, 18.16, 10.52$, yes
    (c) Both values of χ^2 are very small – fit too good?

20. (a) $E = 6.081, 17.026, 23.837, 22.248,$
$15.573, 8.721, 6.514; v = 6, \chi^2 = 1.39,$
yes
(b) $E = 13.06, 24.44, 12.5, 7.83, 14.67, 7.5,$
$26.11, 48.89, 25, v = 4, \chi^2 = 24.6,$ yes

CHAPTER 12

NOTE: Answers may vary, depending on the final
approximation used and the number of
figures retained in the calculator during
working.

Exercise 12a (page 635)

1. (a) Positive correlation $(\bar{x}, \bar{y}) = (15, 14.1)$
(b) Negative correlation, $(\bar{x}, \bar{y}) = (8.2, 75.7)$
(c) No correlation, $(\bar{x}, \bar{y}) = (2.95, 8.25)$
2. $y = -10.75x + 93, 34$
3. (a) Strong positive   (b) $(25, 592)$
(d) (i) 130   (ii) 18.5
4. $4.3, 3.87; y = 0.8125x + 0.376; 2.4$

Exercise 12b (page 643)

1. (a) (i) $y = 4.50 + 0.64x$
(ii) $x = 4.42 + 0.75y$
(b) (i) $y = 90.31 - 1.78x$
(ii) $x = 37.80 - 0.39y$
(c) (i) $y = 8.47 - 0.07x$
(ii) $x = 3.01 - 0.007y$
(d) (i) $y = 7.70 + 0.42x$
(ii) $x = 6.26 + 1.04y$
(e) (i) $y = 3 + 2x$
(ii) $x = -1.5 + 0.5y$
2. $y = 1.8 + 1.3x$
3. $y = -8 + 1.2x$
4. $c = 15, d = -5$
5. $y = 3.8 + 1.6x, x = -2.06 + 0.59y$
6. (i) $y = 41.79 + 1.55x$ (ii) 51
(iii) 43, but unwise to extrapolate beyond
range of data
7. (i) $y = 15.83 + 0.72x$ (ii) 66   (iii) 59
8. $y = 0.74 + 1.1x, x = 2.35 + 0.27y$
9. $y = 6.22 - 1.11x, x = 7.09 - 1.65y$

Exercise 12c (page 656)

1. (a) (i) -1.96
(ii) $y = 6.125 - 0.297x,$
$x = 8.51 - 0.757y$
(b) (i) 4.18
(ii) $y = -28.76 + 1.709x,$
$x = 18.92 + 0.348y$
(c) (i) 18.5
(ii) $y = 2.02 + 0.75x,$
$x = -1.37 + 1.19y$
(d) (i) -3.92
(ii) $y = 70.58 - 0.524x,$
$x = 100.8 - 1.37y$
2. $y = 114.4 - 1.45x;$ (a) No, x is controlled
(b) $y = 61$
3. (b) $y = 0.614 + 0.0207x$
4. $F = -6.33 + 0.90I, F = 20.8$
5. $\bar{A} = 14.875, \bar{T} = 17.5, A = 6.3 + 0.49T, 16.1,$
0.49
6. (b) $y = 127.15 + 1.17x$
7. $\bar{T} = 500, \bar{E} = 1.6, E = -2.4 + 0.008T, 1.04$
8. (b) $y = 3710 + 192x$
(c) Appears reasonably satisfactory apart
from B and C who have earned
substantially more than the equation
suggests

(d) (i) $y = 4210 + 192x$
(ii) $y = 4010 + 207x$
(iii) $y = 4160 + 199x$
(e) It would contain a term for employees
who work away from home e.g.
$y = a + bx + c$, where $c \approx £3,000$ for
employees who work away from home
and zero otherwise.
9. $y = -2.59 + 0.65x, 36.5$
10. (b) $y = 20.7 + 0.96x$
(c) 31 000–33 000 units
(d) Break-even point
11. $y = 11.5 + 0.23x$

Exercise 12d (page 669)

1. (a) 0.930, high positive correlation
(b) -0.828, high negative correlation
(c) 0.867, positive correlation
(d) 0.742, positive correlation
2. $0.82; y = 22.36 + 0.48x, x = -24.3 + 1.42y$
3. $0.60, W = -76 + 0.89h$
4. 0.77
5. -0.415
6. 0.954, 2, 3
7. (a) -0.558
(b) How unemployment appears to be linked
to high wage inflation.
8. 0.3, 0.6
9. (b) $y - 145.64 = 2.75(x - 35.36)$ (c) 0.79
10. $Y = 2.9 + 0.56X, 0.79$
11. $y = -25.4 + 0.53x, x = 94.4 + 1.01y;$
$0.73; 53.7$

Exercise 12e (page 678)

1. $Y = 56.3 + 0.43X; 0.995; 1.9$
2. $\bar{C} = 2.75, \bar{Y} = 35; Y = 3.976 + 11.28C; 5.22$
3. $0.616, 14.57, 10.85$
4. (a) $(5.18, 6.39)$ (c) $W = 3.65 + 0.53A; 8.42$

Exercise 12f (page 681)

1. (a) 2.17   (b) 0.895
(c) $y = -2.37 + 0.028x, x = 406.6 + 28.8y$
2. (a) -0.038 (b) -0.359
(c) $y = 677.0 - 0.63x, x = 992.8 - 0.204y$
3. (a) 7.1875×10^{-6} (b) 0.51
(c) $y = 96.9 + 2233x,$
$x = -0.0102 + 0.000116y$
4. (b) -0.762
5. (b) $y = 55.5 - 5.2x$ (c) 98.3 p

Miscellaneous Exercise 12g (page 684)

1. (a) $y = 0.93 + 1.11x$ (c) 5100
(d) $y - 3.6 = 1.11(x - 2.4)$ (e) 0.42
2. (b) 0.935   (d) $P = 2.58 + 0.88T, 15$
3. (i) 0.98
(ii) $y = 1.115x - 7.42, x = 0.862y + 6.89$
(iii) 8.20   (iv) 13.9
4. (b) $y = 7.77 - 0.05x$
(c) 5.77, unwise to extrapolate beyond range
of data
(e) 0.054
5. (b) (i) -0.901 very high negative
correlation
(ii) negative trend, but not high
correlation, outlier (32, 3.7)
(iii) without outlier, $r = -0.312$
6. (a) $(4, 16.7)$
(b) average decrease of $1.80\,°C$ per month
(c) $y = 23.9 - 1.80x$ (d) $23.9\,°C$
7. 0.91, high positive correlation
8. $y = 0.65 + 0.0157x$, 3 days 19 hours, 0.9419

Exercise 12h (page 691)

1.   0.26
2.   0.75
3.   (a) 0.3, 0.5, 0.7
     (b) Mrs Brown and John
          1) Headrests   2) Heated rear window
          3) Anti-rust treatment
4.   0.86
5.   Assume second judge gives no tied ranks
6. -0.036, Very little negative correlation
7.   0.84, E
8.   0.60, Same
9.   (b) (38.375, 2.275)   (c) -0.84
     (d) High negative correlation
10. (a) 0.75, High positive correlation
11. (b) 0.84, High positive correlation
12. (a) Straight line, negative slope
     (b) Monotonically increasing curve
     (c) -0.92 (d) -0.9
13. (a) 0.6   (b) $x = -1.17 + 1.23y$
14. (a) (i) -0.976 (b) -0.292

Exercise 12i (page 702)

1–9: Accept 1, 3, 4, 7, 9
      Reject   2, 5, 6, 8
10. 0.4286; $H_0 : \rho = 0$, do not reject H_0, no evidence
     of positive correlation
11. $H_0 : \rho = 0, H_1 : \rho > 0$; reject H_0, evidence of
     positive correlation

Exercise 12j (page 703)

1–8: Accept 2, 4, 5, 7, 8
      Reject   1, 3, 6

Exercise 12k (page 704)

1.   (a) 1   (b) -1 (c) 0.028
     (d) 0.886   (e) 1   (f) -1
     (g) 0.479   (h) -0.927
2.   (a) 0.952 (significant)
     (b) 0.6 (not significant)
3. $r = 0.825$, $r_s = 0.929$, significant at 1% level
4.   (a) 0.660   (b) significant at 5% level
5.   (a) 0.527, significant
     (b) $H = -11.03 + 1.579T$, 1.3
6. -0.3341, not significant (5%);
     -0.6939, significant $(2\frac{1}{2}\%)$

7.   0.845, significant indicating an association
8.   (a) $P(X = -1) = P(X = 1) = \frac{1}{6}$
          $P(X = -0.5) = P(X = 0.5) = \frac{1}{3}$;
     (b) 0.5
9. $|r_s| = 0.690$, insufficient evidence that
     community charge and approval rating are
     correlated. $H_0 : \rho = 0, H_1 : \rho \neq 0$
10. (i)   0.636
     (ii) $H_0 : \rho = 0, H_1 : \rho > 0$
           Estimate $P(\Sigma d^2 \leqslant 60) \approx 0.025$, accept
           belief (only just)
11. $r_s = 0.555$; significant, there is evidence of
     positive correlation

Exercise 12l (page 712)

1.   (a) 0.972, high positive correlation
     (b) $a = 1.042$, $b = 3.497$; weight at birth is
          3.497 kg and there is an increase of
          1.042 kg per month.
     (c) 9.75 kg, be wary, outside range of data.
     (d) 0.783
     (e) evidence of correlation.
2.   (b) 0.296   (c) E, G; 0.954
3.   (b) 0.535   (c) some positive correlation
     (d) Low mark in x, high mark in y
     (e) 0.794
     (f) evidence of positive correlation
4.   (b) (ii) $y = 12.5 + 6.24x$
5.   (b) -0.975 (c) high negative correlation
     (d) evidence of correlation
6.   (c) $H = 22.57 + 0.821A$ (d) 47.2
7.   (i) $C = 0.607m + 2.48$ (ii) 0.593
     (iii) 11.4   (iv) 0.516, no
8. $d = -2.68 + 0.6565$, 22.9 m, 60 km/h
9.   (b) 0.81; 0.745, reject hypothesis
10. (b) $y = 0.53 + 1.03x$
11. (b) $y = 4.12\theta + 22.3$
     (c) (i)   (10.5, 91)
          (iii) (a) Approx. 64 cm
                (b) Approx. 196 cm
12. (a) (ii) (40, 414)   (iv) 7, 135; 275
     (b) (ii) Near $+1$
13. (a) $y = -2.59 + 0.65x$, 36.5
14. (a) -0.37 (b) -0.26
     (c) Very low linear negative correlation
          0.91, High positive
15. (d) 0.962
16. 0.48, 0.36

INDEX